THIRD EDITION

Making Sense

A Real-World Rhetorical Reader

Cheryl Glenn
Penn State University

with

Jessica Enoch
University of Pittsburgh

BEDFORD/ST. MARTIN'S

Boston ✦ New York

For Bedford/St. Martin's

Senior Developmental Editor: John Elliott
Production Editor: Jessica Skrocki Gould
Production Supervisor: Andrew Ensor
Marketing Manager: Molly Parke
Art Director: Lucy Krikorian
Text Design: Linda M. Robertson
Copy Editor: Bruce F. Emmer
Photo Research: Naomi Kornhauser
Cover Design: Sara Gates
Cover Art: Concentric Boxes, © Philip James Corwin/Corbis
Composition: Achorn International, Inc.
Printing and Binding: RR Donnelley and Sons

President: Joan E. Feinberg
Editorial Director: Denise B. Wydra
Editor in Chief: Karen S. Henry
Director of Development: Erica T. Appel
Director of Marketing: Karen R. Soeltz
Director of Editing, Design, and Production: Marcia Cohen
Assistant Director of Editing, Design, and Production: Elise S. Kaiser
Managing Editor: Shuli Traub

Acknowledgments

Acknowledgments and copyrights are continued at the back of the book on pages 780–85, which constitute an extension of the copyright page.

It is a violation of the law to reproduce these selections by any means whatsoever without the written permission of the copyright holder.

Preface

....●

Why This Book?

This third edition of *Making Sense: A Real-World Rhetorical Reader* remains anchored in the kinds of reading, thinking, and writing we all—teachers and students alike—do every day. After all, whether in conversations, e-mails, letters, memos, notes to colleagues, or the many other forms of discourse, we all describe, define, tell stories, classify groups of people or things, provide examples, make comparisons, analyze processes, analyze causes and consequences, and argue. Thus, everyday language—yours and your students'—provides a foundation for your teaching and for the reading and writing your students will be doing for this course. Using *Making Sense*, your students will simply build on what they already know and already do fairly well.

The "modes of discourse" covered in this text are nine rhetorical methods everyone uses to make sense of the world: the ways we work out problems, make decisions, and come to understandings. Thus, whether we're teachers or students, we can use them as strategies of invention, ways of shaping an entire essay or of invigorating just one paragraph—both inside and outside the classroom, in civic and other public contexts.

Making Sense takes these time-tested traditional rhetorical methods in exciting new directions by revealing how they underlie a surprising range of daily real-world discourse—both verbal and visual, in print and online. In doing so, the book links the kinds of reading and writing students do for school to the ways they encounter and use language and images in the world outside the classroom. In addition, a thematic focus on literacy helps students think critically about the meaning and importance of reading and writing both in their own lives and in a wider cultural context. To help them put all these insights into practice, the extensive prompts and other assignments get students writing sooner and more often than other rhetorical readers, and frequently in collaboration with others.

What's Special about This Book?

A unique focus on "real-world" examples. Dozens of brief examples of specific rhetorical methods in the chapter introductions include a postcard to the author, a weather forecast, the Sierra Club Web site, a pizza shop menu, a Red Cross ad soliciting blood donations, a letter to Dear Abby, a public service announcement from the Peace Corps, a foodie's blog, a restaurant review, and many other kinds of nonacademic or public writing, often drawn from online sources or incorporating visuals. One of these examples opens each chapter, helping students see how they are already familiar with — and comfortable using — the nine classic rhetorical methods, whether to solve a problem, tell a story, answer a question, or explain a process.

Engaging contemporary readings. The seventy reading selections, including one student essay in each chapter, have been chosen with an eye toward stimulating student interest and offering instructors more options outside the "canonical" range of most other rhetorical readers. Along with traditional favorites by writers like N. Scott Momaday, Malcolm X, Annie Dillard, Maya Angelou, and Amy Tan, each chapter includes recent pieces by newer or lesser-known authors on topics such as student excuses for turning in assignments late (Carolyn Foster Segal's "The Dog Ate My Flash Drive and Other Tales of Woe"), traditional journalism versus its satirical and amateur competitors (Greg Beato's "Amusing Ourselves to Depth: Is *The Onion* Our Most Intelligent Newspaper?" and Nicholas Lemann's "Journalism without Journalists"), and unintended consequences of the Chinese government's one-child-per-family policy (Taylor Clark's "Plight of the Little Emperors").

More opportunities for writing and collaboration than any other rhetorical reader. Going beyond the usual questions and assignments that accompany readings, *Making Sense* provides activities throughout each chapter introduction that stimulate students to begin writing as soon as they are introduced to the rhetorical method. Beginning with one about the chapter-opening example, these activities focus on issues of literacy, academic and public writing, visual analysis, and the different purposes for using the chapter's method. Many questions and assign-ments in each chapter call on students to work with one or more class-mates, and each chapter introduction ends with a revision checklist to help students analyze their own drafts or those of their peers in terms of the chapter's guidelines.

A thematic emphasis on literacy. Building on my own research inter-ests, the book brings home to students the centrality of reading and writ-ing in their lives both in and out of the classroom, in academic and public spheres. Each chapter begins with a writing prompt to focus students' at-tention on some issue of literacy and includes at least one selection on a literacy–related topic, from a narrative about learning a new language to an exemplification of one student's practical literacies.

A focus on the reading–writing connection. The first chapter shows students how active reading can contribute to skilled, purposeful writing. Among other features, it introduces students to strategies for critical read-ing (previewing, annotating, summarizing) and invention (freewriting, brainstorming, clustering) and includes a model analysis of an essay ex-cerpt and a visual "text." This chapter also traces the development of a model student essay from invention activities to peer analysis of a draft to revisions and choice of illustrations for a final draft. Then, in the intro-duction to each rhetorical–method chapter, a "How Do You Read?" section advises students on how to approach a text based on the chapter's method, pointing out the main features to look for and the ways in which such a text can succeed or fail in fulfilling its intended rhetorical purpose for a specific audience.

Sustained attention to visual rhetoric. More than eighty photo-graphs, drawings, ads, product labels, cartoons, computer screen shots, and other images — at least six per chapter — feature prominently as ac-companiments to text readings as well as in the main text of the book. Study questions, along with advice provided in the introduction to the book and to each chapter ("Reading and Using Visuals"), help students learn to analyze visual elements critically, judge the rhetorical effective-ness of images both as readers and writers, and see how they can use them in their own writing. In addition, a number of the prompts at the end of the chapter introductions, the readings, and the chapter ask stu-dents to consider incorporating visuals into their own writing.

Help with research and documentation. An appendix extends this discussion of the reading–writing connection by helping students under-stand how to use and incorporate source materials (their reading) into their writing and by providing source–citation guidelines and examples based on the new seventh edition of the *MLA Handbook for Writers of*

Research Papers (2009). To provide additional examples and practice in these skills, several of the readings (including one of the new student essays) include source citations, and a number of the writing assignments invite or require research.

What's New in the Third Edition?

Fifty-one new reading selections. Constituting more than two-thirds of the total, the new selections include Scott Russell Sanders's reflective description of his childhood home in Ohio, Barack Obama's Memorial Day speech at a national cemetery, excerpts from Malcolm Gladwell's *Outliers* and Connie Eble's scholarly study of college-student slang, Atul Gawande's *New Yorker* article on solitary confinement in U.S. prisons, Amy Tan's comparison of her "Englishes" with those of her mother, and Keith Bradsher's "The Ascent of Wind Power." The topics of the six new student essays, half of the total, range from the lesser-known sides of gonzo journalist Hunter S. Thompson to the differences between summer and school-term reading. Many of the new essays deal with contemporary topics of particular interest to today's students: for example, Nicholas Carr analyzes the ways Google has affected our thinking and research, both in school and in the public sphere, and two readings provide both a classification of questions for job interviews and an analysis of how to go about the process of interviewing for a job.

A new focus on academic and public writing. Starting with the introductory chapter, students are now asked to think about how the kinds of writing done in the classroom and in academic contexts more generally can be seen as both distinct from and on a continuum with writing done for the "real world." They are also asked to carry out writing tasks that help them learn these distinctions.

- Each of the introductions to the main chapters now features **a brief discussion explaining and illustrating how the chapter's rhetorical pattern is used in academic writing.** For example, the "Methods" section of an article about a botanical research project illustrates process analysis, and the "Discussion" section of a sociological study on differences in health patterns between ethnic groups illustrates comparison and contrast.

- **A new concluding chapter, "Academic and Public Writing: Synthesizing Strategies and Sources,"** calls attention to the ways writers combine both the rhetorical methods and a diversity of source materials to write for academia and for the public, especially when their writing is based on personal experience as well as research. The chapter opens with an explanation of the range of writing that occurs in the span between academic and public writing, engages students in the overlapping and distinctive features of the genres, and launches them in their own writing, both academic and public. Two model essays on wind power, one a student essay and the other written for the *New York Times*, show how academic and public writers may draw on different kinds of research and display it in markedly different ways. Because each of the essays has a different purpose and is aimed at a different audience, students are led through the research, drafting, and source-citing process that each author took in order to achieve his or her rhetorical goals.

- The thematically paired readings that appear in each main chapter are accompanied by **an assignment** following the second reading **that calls for a specific kind of academic or public writing for a specified purpose and audience.**

New paired readings. In Chapters 2–9, two of the readings in each chapter are now thematically linked and labeled as such, with the topics including "Waiting Tables" (Maya Angelou's "Finishing School" and Barbara Ehrenreich's "Serving in Florida"), "Narcissism on the Net," and "The Lies We Tell." The argument chapter, in addition to updated casebooks on college athletics and on the draft and national service, now offers three new sets of paired arguments: one made up of the Declaration of Independence and the Declaration of Sentiments by the 1848 Seneca Falls Conference, and the other two taking opposing positions on legalizing marijuana and on banning assault weapons. For each pairing, in addition to the academic or public writing assignment mentioned above, students are asked to compare the readings to assess their rhetorical effectiveness or comment on other features.

More guidance for critical reading. To help students build the reading skills they need to become more successful writers, the first reading in each chapter is now annotated to point out the features of the chapter's rhetorical method as well as other key features such as thesis statements and transitions.

What Comes with the Book?

Making Sense doesn't stop with a book. Online, you'll find both free and affordable premium resources to help students get even more out of the book and your course. You'll also find convenient instructor resources, such as downloadable sample syllabi, classroom activities, and even a nationwide community of teachers. To learn more about or order any of the products below, contact your Bedford/St. Martin's sales representative, e-mail sales support (sales_support@bfwpub.com), or visit the Web site at bedfordstmartins.com/makingsense/catalog.

● Student Resources

Send students to free and open resources, upgrade to an expanding collection of innovative digital content, or package a stand–alone CD-ROM for free with *Making Sense*.

Re:Writing, the best free collection of online resources for the writing class, offers clear advice on citing sources in *Research and Documentation Online* by Diana Hacker, thirty sample papers and designed documents, and over nine thousand writing and grammar exercises with immediate feedback and reporting in *Exercise Central.* Updated and redesigned, *Re:Writing* also features five free videos from *VideoCentral* and three new visual tutorials from our popular *ix visual exercises* by Cheryl Ball and Kristin Arola. *Re:Writing* is completely free and open (no codes required) to ensure access to all students. Visit bedfordstmartins.com/rewriting.

VideoCentral is a growing collection of videos for the writing class that captures real–world, academic, and student writers talking about how and why they write. Writer and teacher Peter Berkow interviewed hundreds of people — from Michael Moore to Cynthia Selfe — to produce fifty brief videos about topics such as revising and getting feedback. *VideoCentral* can be packaged with *Making Sense* at a significant discount. An activation code is required. To learn more, visit bedfordstmartins .com/videocentral. To order *VideoCentral* packaged with the print book, use ISBN–10: 0–312–64351–9 or ISBN–13: 978–0–312–64351–5.

Re:Writing Plus gathers all of Bedford/St. Martin's premium digital content for composition into one online collection. It includes hundreds of model documents, the first ever peer–review game, and *VideoCentral*. *Re:Writing Plus* can be purchased separately or packaged with the print book at a significant discount. An activation code is required. To learn more, visit bedfordstmartins.com/rewriting. To order *Re:Writing Plus* packaged with the print book, use ISBN–10: 0–312–62428–X or ISBN–13: 978–0–312–62428–6.

i·series on CD-ROM presents multimedia tutorials in a flexible format — because there are things you can't do in a book. To learn more, visit bedfordstmartins.com/makingsense/catalog.

- *ix visual exercises* helps students put into practice key rhetorical and visual concepts. To order *ix visual exercises* packaged with the print book, use ISBN–10: 0–312–62427–1 or ISBN–13: 978–0–312–62427–9.

- *i·claim: visualizing argument* offers a new way to see argument — with six tutorials, an illustrated glossary, and over seventy multimedia arguments. To order *i·claim: visualizing argument* packaged with the print book, use ISBN–10: 0–312–62426–3 or ISBN–13: 978–0–312–62426–2.

- *i·cite: visualizing sources* brings research to life through an animated introduction, four tutorials, and hands-on source practice. To order *i·cite: visualizing sources* packaged with the print book, use ISBN–10: 0–312–62425–5 or ISBN–13: 978–0–312–62425–5.

● Instructor Resources

You have a lot to do in your course. Bedford/St. Martin's wants to make it easy for you to find the support you need—and to get it quickly. To find everything available with *Making Sense*, visit bedfordstmartins .com/makingsense/catalog.

Resources for Teaching Making Sense, the instructor's manual for the book, is available in a PDF that can be downloaded from the Bedford/ St. Martin's online catalog. In addition to chapter overviews and teaching tips, the manual includes sample syllabi and suggestions for classroom activities.

Teaching Central offers the entire list of Bedford/St. Martin's print and online professional resources in one place. You'll find landmark reference works, sourcebooks on pedagogical issues, award-winning collections, and practical advice for the classroom — all free for instructors.

Bits collects creative ideas for teaching a range of composition topics in an easily searchable blog. A community of teachers — leading scholars, authors, and editors — discusses revision, research, grammar and style, technology, peer review, and much more. Take, use, adapt, and pass the ideas around. Then, come back to the site to comment or share your own suggestions.

Content cartridges for the most common course management systems — Blackboard, WebCT, ANGEL, and Desire2Learn — allow you to easily download digital materials from Bedford/St. Martin's for your course.

Who Helped?

Making Sense was once again reinvigorated during meetings with wise and creative Joan Feinberg, who continues to guide Bedford/St. Martin's with unparalleled grace and success. Valuable assistance in planning this revision also came from Denise Wydra, editorial director; Karen Henry, editor in chief for English; Steve Scipione, executive editor; Karita dos Santos, marketing manager; Karen Melton Soeltz, director of marketing; Erica T. Appel, director of development; and John Elliott, my constant intellectual companion and editor extraordinaire, whose gentlemanly tone makes granting his requests for more (and more) writing and re-writing almost a pleasure. Together, John and I worked closely with Jessica Enoch, whose brilliant suggestions for new readings, together with her keen insights into public writing (in all its guises) and her ability to write well and revise even better made her my perfect partner for producing the third edition of this textbook. I remain ever grateful to Jess for once again contributing her scholarly and pedagogical expertise to this project and, especially, for her friendship. She continues to teach, write, and research with enthusiasm, success, and a remarkable measure of joy.

Thanks, too, to Rosalyn Collings Eves, who used her keen intellect and wise pedagogy to revise and update the instructor's manual for this edition.

In addition, I am grateful to Cecilia Seiter, associate editor, who helped locate readings and visuals; Sue Brekka, who oversaw the huge task of chasing down permissions; Naomi Kornhauser, who carried out the art research, carefully selecting images that complement the essays; and project editor Jessica Skrocki Gould, who took over the manuscript where John left off, carefully overseeing the copyediting, typesetting, and proofreading.

I also want to thank my teaching colleagues who took the time out of their already busy lives to review the second edition of *Making Sense*, offering me their insights and advice for shaping the revision: Alan Brown, University of West Alabama; Stuart C. Brown, New Mexico State University; Stanley J. Dale, DeVry University; Dr. Sally Emmons–Featherston, Rogers State University; Linda G. Foss, Centralia College; Yuemin He, Northern Virginia Community College; Liz Kleinfeld, Red Rocks Community College; Karen Courtney Leyba, Rock Valley College; Cheryl R. Lyda, Idaho State University; Lisa Martin, Piedmont Technical College; Troy D. Nordman, Butler Community College; Catherine C. Olson, Tomball College; Arthur L. Rogers II (Chip), Rogers State University; Georgeanna Sellers, High Point University; Kristi Siegel, Mount Mary College; Alfred Taylor, Valencia Community College; Brian Walker, Pulaski Technical College; and Anthony Wilson, LaGrange College.

I'm especially grateful to Jon Olson, who makes my everyday life better in every way, and to Eddie, Helen, and Imogen, who make every day of the future look brighter.

Cheryl Glenn

Contents

PAIRED READINGS: A Boy's Life

4 Exemplification   203

Appendix: Using and Documenting Sources   **759**

Glossary of Terms   **774**

Acknowledgments   **780**

Index   **786**

chapter 1

INTRODUCTION: THE READING-WRITING CONNECTION

When I got [my] library card, that was when my life began.
— RITA MAE BROWN

The ability to read awoke inside me some long dormant craving to be mentally alive.
— MALCOLM X

Writing is an exploration. You start from nothing and learn as you go.
— E. L. DOCTOROW

Good writing facilitates the making of connections in a way that inspires openheartedness, thinking, talking, and action.

Good writing enlarges readers' knowledge of the world, or empowers readers to act for the common good, or even inspires other good writing.
— MARY PIPHER

Every day, you read and write in order to make sense of the world around you. You might go online to read your favorite blog, learn about your local politician's environmental policy, or research a topic for your history class. And when you're online, you're often writing as well, whether you're updating your Facebook page, sending a text message, or posting to a message board. You're reading and writing when you're offline too: browsing the newspaper, following road signs, taking notes in class. Your days are filled with language that enables you to engage the world around you and listen to, learn from, and respond to others.

Making Sense invites you to look at how you're using all this reading and writing, to think about your own **literacy** — but not just in terms of your basic ability to read, write, and see. Rather, it helps you imagine your literacy in a much broader sense: how you participate in the world by both interpreting and producing verbal and visual messages. In asking you to think about your literacy in this way, this book prompts you to analyze and produce various kinds of **public writing** — the written and visual materials you see every day, materials that allow writers to inform, persuade, and entertain their audiences. Thus, this book offers you the opportunity to cultivate the active reading and writing practices necessary for you to become a perceptive and thoughtful participant in the world around you.

As you gain the literacy skills of active participation through reading and composing various kinds of public writing, you will become a more perceptive and thoughtful reader and writer in your academic courses as well. For academic reading and writing are not far removed from the more public reading and writing you do in the "real" world. As you'll see in each of the chapters in this book, the kinds of reading and writing you deal with on a daily basis outside the classroom are very similar to the kinds of reading and writing you'll do inside the classroom. Just as journalists use narration in their newspaper stories and bloggers craft narratives in their daily posts, scientists use narration in their lab reports and students of history compose narratives for their end–of–term research projects. As you make your way through this book, you'll read about and experiment with both academic and public writing, leaning how to perform effectively in both situations. The work you'll do in this class, then, should prepare you to become an active and engaged participant who uses your reading and writing to direct and shape your academic career as well as your life in your workplace, your community, and the world beyond.

To those ends, *Making Sense* introduces you to nine basic methods of communication that we all rely on in both academic and public settings: description, narration, exemplification, classification and division, comparison and contrast, process analysis, cause–and–consequence analysis, definition, and argument. Each of these nine methods is **rhetorical** in that it uses language for a specific purpose in a way that leads to the creation of knowledge. These are the **rhetorical methods** we've all used since we were young, whether we're explaining, working out problems, making decisions, coming to an understanding, or making a case. In fact, you already bring to this course a good deal of rhetorical skill: you already know how to gauge the way you perceive and produce verbal and visual language according to the particular **rhetorical situation** — the intended audience, the purpose, the topic, the medium (oral, written, electronic), the time, and the place. You may not always gauge perfectly; your perception may not always be accurate, and your production may not always be successful, but you often interpret and choose language in ways that are appropriate to the rhetorical situation. You already know how to use language to make sense.

Building on the rhetorical knowledge you already have and regularly use, *Making Sense* will guide you as you create, select, and organize information in ways that describe an issue, narrate an entertaining story, explain a complex process, analyze your options, explore the consequences of a decision, or prove a point. *Making Sense* will help you become more conscious of exactly how words help you think through all kinds of language situations, especially those in academic settings.

Whether you're expected to read critically in preparation for class discussion, keep a journal, respond to someone else's rough draft, or plan and submit a formal academic essay, *Making Sense* will help you all the way, building on the literacy skills and rhetorical experiences you have spent your whole life developing. No matter what the assignment, when you use *Making Sense*, you'll be reading, writing, thinking, and talking about it — tapping your literacy background and your rhetorical skills — from beginning to end, from process to product.

. . . .

Looking at Your Own Literacy   Reflect on the various kinds of public and academic writing you produce and encounter during the day.

Write for five minutes, reflecting on all of the ways you participate in your world through reading and writing. Everything counts, from making a grocery list and text-messaging a friend to reading a chapter in your sociology textbook to browsing the Web. After you have accounted for your investments in both public and academic reading and writing, consider the range and depth of your participation. What do you value? What interests and excites you? What did you learn about your literacy practices? Be prepared to share your findings with the rest of the class.

. . . .

What's Reading Got to Do with Writing?

Why read in a class on writing?

Reading and writing are the basic components of literacy — as well as of contemporary rhetorical skills. Good readers are most often good writers, and vice versa, so you'll want to be both, in college and after. If you're like most first-year students, you're no doubt interested in improving in every way to meet the challenges of your new college curriculum. Most likely you'll find yourself doing much more reading than you did in high school, and your writing obligations will be greater as well. And you'll be expected to read and write more skillfully, making careful observations and asking many questions. *Making Sense* offers you opportunities to read and analyze models of good writing, to explore visual images and the ways they relate to verbal texts, to practice thinking about your own writing, and to respond to thought-provoking questions and assignments.

I hope that you'll come to see your literacy development (that is, your development as a reader and writer) as an unfolding, ever-improving process of growth and understanding — each time you analyze and discuss the readings, write to crystallize your thinking, share and discuss your drafts, and revise them until your words take the form that best articulates your intended meaning.

Reading Actively and Critically

Look at the picture on page 6 of the father and child reading together. Although the baby cannot decode the printed page, he is nevertheless *reading actively*. How do we know? First of all, the book is mostly in the baby's lap, not the father's. The baby seems to know instinctively to hold his hands and arms out of the way of the book so he and his father can see the words and pictures. But the most compelling evidence that this baby is reading actively is that he is reaching out to turn the page and move on to the next part of the text. This baby has already entered the active world of literacy, and he is learning how to "get into" a text in ways that are productive and appropriate to his age.

When you read actively, you read productively, efficiently, and in age–appropriate ways. You may no longer sit on a parent's lap to read, but you might still catch yourself reading aloud in order to make sense of a difficult text. You might also like to talk with someone else about what you're reading — just as the baby does. Your reading strategies are every bit as age–appropriate, then, as the baby's.

Reading actively means constantly interacting with the text as though you are in conversation with it. You start out by looking at an ac-companying image, if there is one. Then you read the introductory ma-terials and try to make sense of the rhetorical situation: the connections among the author, the text itself, and the audience for the text. That is, you start out by asking questions like these:

What do I know about this author?

What else has this author written?

Why is the author writing about this subject?

Who is the intended audience?

What does the title mean? Does it announce the intended subject, or is it intended to arouse interest?

How does the image connect with the text?

Reading actively means looking over the headings, taking the time to figure out the meanings of unfamiliar words and references by using a dictionary or examining the context. It means considering where and when the piece appears (and where and when it was first published, if necessary) and what that context means for your full understanding. Finally, reading actively means bringing your own observations to the text, connecting it with other reading you've done and the experiences you've had.

Active readers are critical readers; they approach the text inquisitively and carefully with an eye toward judging its strengths and weaknesses. Active readers ask questions like these:

- What is the gist of this text?
- What's important in it?
- How does it compare, contrast, or connect in some other way with other pieces I've read on the same subject?
- Does it hold my attention? How easy is it to follow?
- Are terms clearly defined? Does the author provide enough details and examples?
- What does the author think, and why does he or she hold that opinion?
- What do I think, and why do I hold my opinion?
- What are the key points the author makes or the main impression he or she creates?
- Do the points or impression seem convincing, given the information the author provides?
- Do the points or impression seem convincing, given my own knowledge about the subject?

To answer questions like these, active readers make sense of the text by getting into it in earnest: writing in the margins, underlining, adding checkmarks and asterisks. In short, active readers are engaged readers, raising significant questions and making significant connections between the text itself and the broader rhetorical situation.

Practical Reading Strategies

Reading actively and critically involves skills that people do not develop casually. Often one person in particular (a teacher, parent, or relative) took the time to teach a young reader these skills and then practiced with the reader until the skills became automatic. But all people must work at developing them. The following reading strategies form the basis for reading well — and they can be acquired, practiced, and perfected at any age.

Preview   Stop, look, and listen to a text before reading it in earnest. Focus on the title, the author, the headings, the introduction. Look to see what the text might be trying to tell you. Read aloud if you care to. Use visuals to become familiar with the text as well. Locate the parts of the text the visuals relate to, and read the captions. Consider, too, when and where the piece first appeared. Readers who have a good idea of where they're heading rarely get lost along the way.

Annotate   Don't just listen to the text; talk back to it as well. As you read, pose questions in the margins of the text, drawing arrows to connect supporting or opposing ideas. When the text pushes in a certain direction, push back, jotting down your questions, disagreements, and comments. If the text is online, most word–processing systems offer annotating capabilities that invite you to respond on the screen.

Summarize   Learn to perform one of the toughest but most rewarding reading tasks of all: summarizing the main points of what you read or see. Identify the author's purpose, audience, main point, and support. The better your reading skills, the better your summarizing skills — and vice versa.

Connect   Most important is to connect with what you read — emotionally or intellectually. In other words, you have to find a relationship with the text (through some facet of your personality, interests, or life experience) in order to hear it — and then to talk back to it. You may find yourself connecting with the author, specifically with the ways he or she has kept your attention, taught, pleased, or moved you. Or you may connect immediately with a visual for reasons you'll want to analyze. If you find yourself disagreeing strongly with the text or being completely bored by it, think about what features or passages make you feel disconnected to it.

Respond   Respond to the text: talk back, write back. You might respond on the page itself, or you might record your responses elsewhere — in a journal or on a class Listserv, for example. Or you might get together with classmates to talk about the reading, responding among yourselves. If the text is in a public, nonacademic setting like a newspaper or an online magazine or discussion forum, you might send a letter to the editor or post a comment.

Review   When you're finished reading, go back to the beginning, reconsidering the title, the author, the headings, the introduction, and the conclusion. By doing so, you'll recover a better sense of their importance to the full text. When you review a visual, you'll see how the parts work together to create an impact.

Here's an excerpt from *Where We Stand: Why Class Matters*, in which the writer, bell hooks, describes her memories of her childhood in Kentucky. If we apply the preceding reading strategies to this excerpt, the text might look something like this:

In the backyard vegetables grew. Scarecrows hung to chase away
Scarecrows, a field — this must have been a big backyard!
birds who could clear a field of every crop. My task was to learn

how to walk the rows without stepping on growing things. Life was

everywhere, under my feet and over my head. The lure of life was everywhere in everything. The first time I dug a fishing worm and

watched it move in my hand, feeling the sensual grittiness of min-
This image is so vivid that even someone who's never dug up a worm can identify with it.
gled dirt and wet, I knew that there is life below and above — always
This is the second sentence in a row she's said "life is everywhere" — let's move on!
life — and it lures and intoxicates. The chickens laying eggs were

such a mystery. We laughed at the way they sat. We laughed at the
Why not describe the chickens and their sounds?
sounds they made. And we relished being chosen to gather eggs.

One must have tender hands to hold eggs, tender words to soothe

chickens as they roost. *This repetition of "tender hands, tender words" gives a soothing sensation.*

Making Sense of Visuals

We are constantly surrounded by visual images, from the photographs in the morning paper and advertisements in our favorite magazines to the emoticons of our text messages ;-) and the graphic novels we read. Whether these visuals narrate stories, describe a scene or a person, compare and contrast two things, explain the steps in a process, define a concept, or argue a point, they use rhetorical methods just like those used in verbal texts. And as with spoken or written words, their overall success depends on how well they balance considerations of purpose, audience, and situation.

Because contemporary life has become increasingly a visual as well as a verbal one, *Making Sense* helps you develop the necessary skills for looking at — really seeing — and responding to visuals, for "reading" them actively and critically. At a time when a plastic yellow bracelet means that wearers LiveStrong and fight cancer, when a bitten apple signals cutting-edge personal technology, and when YouTube videos become key features of our presidential political campaigns, it's time for all of us to develop our visual literacy. *Making Sense* therefore uses visuals as "texts" for study and analysis, both as complements to written selections and as examples of various rhetorical methods in and of themselves. You'll find questions and writing assignments that ask you to consider how a particular visual works to fulfill its rhetorical goal. (You'll also learn how to use visuals to enhance your own verbal texts, as discussed on pages 27–28.) Just as you analyze the components of a verbal text, you'll analyze visual texts in terms of their rhetorical properties, asking questions like these:

- What is the overall purpose of the visual? How well does it achieve this purpose?
- Who is the intended audience? How does the visual appeal to this audience?

- Who or what company is the "author" of the visual? Is the author clearly identified?
- How is the visual arranged? What elements of it are emphasized — and deemphasized? What is not shown? How effective is the arrangement?
- Which smaller or more subtle elements of the visual support or extend the overall purpose?
- Is the visual accompanied by verbal text? If so, what is said? What goes unsaid? How are the visual and the text related?

You bring to this course years of successful experience in making sense of visuals. Some of you may have even had a special course in visual literacy. Regardless of your background in this area, no matter how expert or amateur you think you may be, you can build on your experiences as you make sense of this textbook and this course, improving your visual literacy and rhetorical capacities along the way.

The Readings and Visuals in Making Sense

As I've said repeatedly, reading and writing are literacy skills that are impossible to separate; thus, the verbal and visual selections in this textbook are so closely linked to the writing activities that it's hard to talk about one without the other. But I'll try.

The readings and visuals have been selected on the basis of their familiarity to you in some cases and their newness to you in others, but they have also been selected in terms of their rhetorical situation, including the author, subject, intended audience, purpose, and method of development. Every reading and visual is meant to provoke your interest, critical thinking, and response — in both speech and writing. In other words, none of these readings or visuals serves as a perfect model that you should try to imitate; instead, all the readings and visuals promote work on *your own* thinking and writing. (I'll talk more about the individual and group writing activities in the following section.)

As you look through this book, you'll see the names of writers that you might already know: Malcolm X, David Sedaris, Barbara Ehrenreich, Amy Tan, Barack Obama, Malcolm Gladwell, Deborah Tannen, and Jimmy Carter, for example. You'll also find examples from professional and student writers that you don't yet know. Many of the essays and examples are taken from sources that are familiar to you (*Consumer Reports*, *Rolling Stone*, *Vanity Fair*, *Latina*, the *New York Times*, *Slate.com*, and *Newsweek*), whereas other excerpts and examples come from the kinds of sources you'll continue to encounter in and after college (urban newspapers, novels, academic writing, autobiography, American ethnic literatures, creative nonfiction, Web-based journals, and so on). You'll also come across visuals, some that you've seen on billboards, in magazines and newspapers, on the

Web, or in other textbooks, and others that are new to you. For instance, you'll see a daily newspaper's line graph that reveals the rising costs of healthy foods and advertisements that persuade people to join the Peace Corps, buy a motor scooter, and give blood to the Red Cross. You'll also find blog postings, other excerpts from Web pages, and articles from on-line magazines.

Whether familiar or not, all the readings and visuals were selected especially for the ways they can help you develop your literacy skills as first-year college students and later as college graduates. Each chapter opens with a visual or a short reading that provides an immediate, familiar, nonacademic example of the rhetorical method of the chapter. Whether the chapter opens with an advertisement, a postcard, instructions, or a dictionary definition, it moves on to a full explanation of the rhetorical method at hand, including more verbal and visual examples. As you read the explanation, you are asked to reflect on your own literacy, to begin analyzing the method, and to try your own hand at using it. Following the introductory explanation are eight or nine (sometimes more) reading selections, including one focusing on a visual, one written by a college student, and sometimes one that is a poem or piece of fiction. These selections show the chapter's method (as well as other methods) at work in different ways, and each one is followed by questions and assignments that ask you to focus on particular aspects of the reading and apply what you've learned to essays of your own.

I'll show you how the readings work in *Making Sense* by using the following excerpt, which is followed by the same kinds of questions and writing assignments you'll find throughout this book:

> I was eight years old. At that moment in my life, nothing was more important to me than baseball. My team was the New York Giants, and I followed the doings of these men in the black-and-orange caps with all the devotion of a true believer. Even now, remembering that team — which no longer exists — I can reel off the names of nearly every player on the roster. Alvin Dark, Whitey Lockman, Don Mueller, Johnny Antonelli, Monte Irvin, Hoyt Wilhelm. But none was greater, none more perfect [or] more deserving of worship than Willie Mays, the incandescent Say Hey kid.
>
> That spring, I was taken to my first big-league game. Friends of my parents had box seats at the Polo Grounds, and one April night a group of us went to watch the Giants play the Milwaukee Braves. I don't know who won, I can't recall a single detail of the game, but I do remember that after the game was over my parents and their friends sat talking in their seats until all the other spectators had left. It got so late that we had to walk across the diamond and leave by the center-field exit, which was the only one still open. As it happened, that exit was right below the players' locker rooms.
>
> Just as we approached the wall, I caught sight of Willie Mays. There was no question about who it was. It was Willie Mays, already out of uniform and standing there in his street clothes not ten feet away from

me. I managed to keep my legs moving in his direction and then, mustering every ounce of my courage, I forced some words out of my mouth. "Mr. Mays," I said, "could I please have your autograph?"

He had to have been all of twenty-four years old, but I couldn't bring myself to pronounce his first name.

His response to my question was brusque but amicable. "Sure, kid, sure," he said. "You got a pencil?" He was so full of life, I remember, so full of youthful energy, that he kept bouncing up and down as he spoke.

I didn't have a pencil, so I asked my father if I could borrow his. He didn't have one, either. Nor did my mother. Nor, as it turned out, did any of the other grownups.

The great Willie Mays stood there watching in silence. When it became clear that no one in the group had anything to write with, he turned to me and shrugged. "Sorry, kid," he said. "Ain't got no pencil, can't give no autograph." And then he walked out of the ballpark into the night.

I didn't want to cry, but tears started falling down my cheeks, and there was nothing I could do to stop them. Even worse, I cried all the way home in the car. Yes, I was crushed with disappointment, but I was also revolted at myself for not being able to control those tears. I wasn't a baby. I was eight years old, and big kids weren't supposed to cry over things like that. Not only did I not have Willie Mays' autograph, I didn't have anything else, either. Life had put me to the test, and in all respects I had found myself wanting.

After that night, I started carrying a pencil with me wherever I went. It became a habit of mine never to leave the house without making sure I had a pencil in my pocket. It's not that I had any particular plans for that pencil, but I didn't want to be unprepared. I had been caught empty-handed once, and I wasn't about to let it happen again.

If nothing else, the years have taught me this: if there's a pencil in your pocket, there's a good chance that one day you'll feel tempted to start using it. As I like to tell my children, that's how I became a writer.

— Paul Auster, "Why Write?"

Of course, becoming a writer is more complicated than just remembering to carry a pencil. Still, Auster's story is charming and effective. Now take a few minutes to do the following:

1. Underline one phrase, sentence, or passage in Auster's piece that seemed familiar to you. In the margin, jot down the main reason it is familiar.

2. Circle one phrase, sentence, or passage that feels "foreign" to you. In the margin, write out the reason why. You might not know who Willie Mays is; you might be bored by all sports; you might not be interested in writing. Whatever you write, try to tell the truth about yourself and your reaction.

3. Compare the information provided by the visual and the text.

4. On a separate piece of paper, write for five minutes about a particular disappointment, challenge, or success you've had as a writer. Concentrate on one event, if you can, the way Auster does.

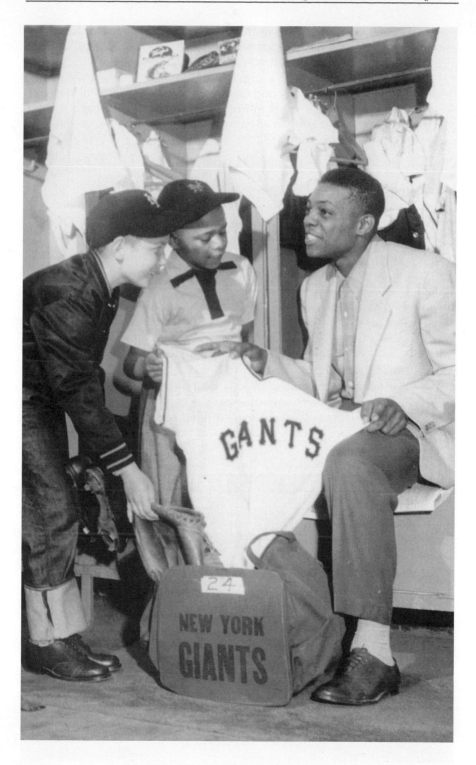

5. Share your writing with two or three classmates. Among your group, decide what your stories have in common and how they differ. Prepare a short report to share with the rest of the class.

6. Draft a two- to three-page essay based on the preceding in-class writing in which you connect a specific incident in your life with your development as a writer. Or if you'd rather, draft a two- to three-page essay in which you connect your development as a reader with your development as a writer.

Writing Well

You've been writing since you were a small child. Maybe you and your parents *thought* it was scribbling or coloring, but all those scribbles were nothing more or less than writing. The urge to make one's mark is a primitive urge, one that nearly every human being embraces early on. In fact, small children usually "write" before they read. Think back on all the "writing" you did as a child: in coloring books, on chalkboards and sidewalks, on sides of buildings, on walls and windows. The baby in the photo below cannot "write," but still he wants to get out his markers and put his marks on a surface. These are his first steps toward developing his writing life, the writing part of his literacy.

Now that you're in college, you'll be putting your mark on many paper surfaces — and electronic interfaces — as you continue to develop your college literacy. Essays, reports, bibliographies, exams, summaries,

proposals, analyses, e-mail, abstracts, articles, memos, résumés, letters, questions, journals: these are just some of the things you'll have occasion to write in college (and, most likely, at work). *Making Sense* will help you learn some of the basic organizational patterns of thinking and writing that you'll need to use in producing them. The examples, explanations, reading and writing questions, and guidelines will help prepare you for a lifetime of writing well.

But instead of explaining how this textbook will promote your development as a writer, a topic I'll return to eventually, right now I'd like to ask you a few questions about that same subject: your writing and the way you do it. Take out a piece of paper, and write out short answers to the following questions:

1. How do you typically go about preparing for a writing assignment? Describe the steps you take, including rereading the assignment, asking questions about it, talking to instructors or friends, jotting down ideas, gathering information, and so on. How far in advance of the due date do you usually begin working on the assignment?

2. What would be your ideal place to write? Would it be solitary and silent, or would it provide background noise? Describe the places you'll actually be doing your writing for this course, and then discuss their suitability for you. Do you begin on paper or on the screen?

3. Describe your typical drafting or writing process. Do you finish a draft in one sitting, or do you need to take breaks? When you get stuck, what do you do to get moving again? Is your process efficient? Are there specific steps you could take to improve your efficiency?

4. What does revising mean to you? Do you ever revise, and if so, what specifically do you do when you revise (insert, delete, move around information; check punctuation; proofread for typos and misspellings)? Why do you revise?

5. Finally, how do you respond to the evaluation of your writing? What do you read first — the grade itself or the teacher's comments? Do you want an explanation of your grade immediately, or do you understand how you earned that grade? Do you refer to your teacher's comments on previous assignments as you work on your current assignment?

After you answer all these questions, you might want to draft a short essay (three to four pages) in which you describe yourself as a beginning college writer. You may discover details about your writing life that you have never been aware of before.

What's Rhetoric Got to Do with Writing?

As I said earlier in this chapter, rhetoric is purposeful language that leads to the creation of knowledge, and the most effective language is always appropriate language. In other words, it's always gauged according to the rhetorical situation (the audience, the purpose, the context for meaning). Your goal in this course is to learn how to compose texts that are purposeful, appropriate, and effective. The following rhetorical considerations will help you develop successful writing strategies.

● **Understanding the Writing Task**

Start by making sense of your overall rhetorical situation. Are you creating a Web page for a student organization? putting together a job application? reviewing a movie? responding to a blog? Have you been assigned to keep the minutes of a meeting? write up lab results? describe a painting? analyze an essay? We all face many daily writing tasks that enable us to contribute to conversations and have a say in our lives. Some of these tasks are self–initiated, and some are prompted by others. Whatever the rhetorical situation, you have to figure out an effective way to handle the task.

. . . .

Try Your Hand   To begin using *Making Sense* in the way it is intended, stop now and consider the answer you gave for question 1 on page 15. Break into groups of two or three, and discuss your original answers. What do you all do the same? How is each of you different in your preparation? What do your classmates do that you forgot to mention? How might you improve your preparation by learning from your classmates? Now revise your original response, adding to, deleting from, or rearranging the answer you wrote out. How *do* you typically prepare for a writing assignment? Break into groups of two or three, and compare your revised responses. Then prepare to share your group's responses with the rest of the class.

. . . .

Now that you're actively thinking about your own process of writing and considering the strategies of your classmates, you'll have an easier time improving on the writing you do for college, no matter how strong the skills you bring to this course and this textbook. In fact, you're probably already self–conscious about your strengths as a writer.

. . . .

Try Your Hand   Write for three or four minutes, responding to the following questions:
1. At what part of your writing process are you most efficient and effective?
2. What is the most enjoyable part of the process?
3. What is the least effective part of your writing process?
4. What is the least enjoyable part?

Break into groups of two or three, and compare your answers. What did you learn from one another about the similarities and differences of your writing processes? How can you individually benefit from this knowledge? Be prepared to share your group's responses with the rest of the class.

· ·

You may already know that when you are faced with a specific writing assignment, you'll need to read that assignment carefully and talk back to it before beginning to carry it out. But you might not realize that you'll want to watch for particular words of guidance, such as *inform, explain, describe, define, entertain, persuade, prove, compare,* or *argue.* These words signal what you should do and help you focus on your purpose; sometimes they even tell you which organizational method to follow.

More often, though, your writing assignments will provide little, if any, specific purpose or direction. They may include only a subject and the vaguest of directions: "Write about your first week in college"; "Write a research paper focusing on the reasons you feel diversity requirements are important or inappropriate"; "Describe the labor that your most recent job entailed." In these writing situations, you'll need to figure out a way to transform the assignment into one you can and want to write about: "What information about that job might interest my audience?" "Do I want to entertain my readers or just inform them?" "What organizational pattern might work best in describing the job?" "Is there a story I can tell to help explain it?" Once you figure out your angle, you'll feel as though it's your topic rather than one generated by your instructor.

· ·

Try Your Hand   In preparation for making sense of your college-level writing assignments, take a minute to write out what each of the following terms means to you:

inform	describe	entertain	analyze	define
persuade	prove	compare	argue	explore
convince	evaluate	propose	formulate	classify
observe	report	explain		

Working with one or two classmates, compare your answers. Discuss your group's response with the rest of the class. You may be surprised by the range of definitions you and your classmates give these important academic terms.

· ·

● Focusing on Your Purpose, Audience, and Subject

Why are you writing? Did you initiate this writing, or was it assigned by your instructor, your boss, or someone else? Are you writing to provide information about something for someone? to entertain someone? to urge someone to do something? And who is this "someone" you are writing for and this "something" you are writing about?

Knowing your purpose is important because if you have only a vague idea (or no idea) of what you want to accomplish, it's easy to achieve the wrong purpose — one you definitely didn't intend — or to leave your readers bored or confused. For example, if your economics professor asks you to analyze how the political systems of Mexico and the United States influence those countries' economies, you probably should not focus on trying to prove that the U.S. political system is better than that of Mexico, or vice versa. Your professor has asked you to explain something, not to make an argument, and may not find it acceptable if (without asking) you write with a different purpose.

But even if the writing task is flexible enough to allow you to choose your own purpose or to combine different purposes, like the assignment about your most recent job, you need to think about purpose in order to guide your writing and avoid just stringing together random ideas about the subject. Once you have a good idea of your overall purpose, you can start thinking more specifically: Would a humorous or a serious approach be more likely to achieve your purpose of persuading your classmates that the student activity fee is unfair? Do you just need to give readers a general understanding of what your job involved, or is it important that you explain all the details?

If you're applying for a job, you have a pretty good idea who will read your application (your audience). If you're sending an e-mail to your mom and dad, you know, too. In the first situation, you're more than likely writing for a general audience of personnel directors, but in the second case, you're writing for a specific audience, people you know by name and face.

Sometimes, though, when you're writing for an academic assignment, it's harder to decide who (besides your instructor) your audience really is. Should you write directly to your instructor, who may know more about the subject than you do? Should you address your classmates, who may be working with the same materials? Or should you assume a more general audience of readers who may be interested in your topic but have little expertise in it? If you're writing for a class, ask your instructor what audience you need to assume and address.

When you have a sense of who your readers are, then think about what they are like. How old, what sex, how educated are they? What are their values and beliefs? What do they already know about your topic? What do they want to know more about? What is their attitude toward the topic and toward you as a writer? Do they know anything about you? Do they have expectations about you or the topic that you need to fulfill?

Answering these questions will help you decide what tone to take, information to include, terms to use, and points to make. The audience is a crucial element of the rhetorical situation — and connecting with it is crucial to all successful writing.

. . . .

Try Your Hand   Working with a classmate, discuss the role that audience has played in your writing.

1. What specific audience have school assignments asked you to address — the instructor? classmates? others?

2. How much thought do you give to the audience as you write? Can either of you remember an experience of writing with particular attention to a specific audience?

3. Does your audience affect your choice of writing by hand or using a computer?

4. Prepare a joint report for the rest of the class.

. . . .

When your instructor offers you a writing topic as broad as a temporary job or the sociology of the family, your job is to narrow down the subject to one that interests you (at the same time that you're considering a purpose for your writing and imagining a specific audience). You might start this subject-focusing process by asking a series of questions:

What is it?

What caused it?

What are its consequences?

What is it like?

What is it a part of?

What are its parts?

Who is involved in it?

Questions like these help you think about your subject in a variety of ways. Your answers will bring to the fore various features of the larger subject that you might want to concentrate on. (Your answers might also help you get a foothold on a purpose and an imagined audience.) Imagine that Paul Auster (pp. 11–12) took the general subject of "writing" before narrowing it down to "personal experiences as a writer." From there he might have moved on to "writing experience as a young person" before finally focusing on that particular interchange with Willie Mays and what meaning the pencil (or lack thereof) has held for him.

You might also decide to freewrite on one of those smaller subjects (see page 23 for an explanation of freewriting) or talk with one of your classmates about it, just to see what comes forth. But focusing on your subject cannot be separated from focusing on your purpose, which means that you may have to work simultaneously to tweak the assignment, narrowing or stretching it to suit your interest, experience, and knowledge. Auster focused his subject down to the much–needed pencil. And he decided that his purpose would be to explain how he became a writer. So don't be afraid to ask your instructor if you may customize your assignment to fit your own situation or preferences; after all, one size does *not* fit all. Besides, you're going to be writing for the rest of your life, so you might as well learn now how to imagine the kind of writing you *want* to do.

For example, if you have been asked to write about environmental issues on campus, you might decide to create a pamphlet for the residents of your dorm (a specific audience), giving tips (a specific purpose) as to how they might choose a more "green" lifestyle (a specific subject). If the assignment is about your job experience, you might choose to describe your nannying position briefly but focus most of your rhetorical energy on the consequences of holding that job: you now realize that rich families are not necessarily happy families; you want to move rapidly into a "real" career; you are more grateful than ever for the way your own parents raised you.

. . . .

Try Your Hand   Now that we're discussing your individual interests and life as a writer, take a minute or two to consider the following questions:

1. What have you been taught about writing, either directly or indirectly, that has helped or hindered your development as a writer?
2. How has your writing improved over the years? Why has it improved?
3. What kinds of writing do you expect to do in the future?
4. What kinds of writing do you hope to do? What in particular do you want to learn how to do?
5. What kinds of writing do you hope to avoid?

Prepare to share your responses with the rest of the class.

. . . .

Practical Writing Strategies

Once you have an overview of your rhetorical situation, you can move on to practical strategies for accomplishing each of the steps to successful writing.

● **Generating Ideas**

Where do ideas come from? Some of your best ideas will come from your own experience and observation; others will come from conversation with others or from your reading and research. To tap those sources, you might want to try some of the following activities.

Journal writing may be the most familiar of all the invention activities. Many instructors ask students to record their ideas, thoughts, and feelings about their composition class or about topics they might want to write on. Other instructors ask you to keep a reading journal, a response to your class assignments. But besides offering up subjects and purposes for writing and responses to other people's writing, journal writing has another significance: keeping a journal can change your feelings about writing, forever, for the better! Because a journal is a record of your *reactions*, not your actions, you can let your thoughts flow. If you allow yourself to record your thoughts, rather than your body and its movements, and if you read some excerpts of good journals kept by writers such as Francisco Urondo, Rita Valdivia, Virginia Woolf, or Anne Frank, you'll soon see that a journal can be every bit as interesting and thought-provoking as good fiction. For example, in preparation for writing an essay about a job, Jennifer Favorite, one of my students at Penn State, wrote the following journal entry.

A Journal Entry

My time in Connecticut as a nanny for a wealthy family was like nothing else I'd ever experienced, yet it fit all the stereotypical descriptions of nannying. I learned so much about the damage that wealth can do to people and their families. The experience forced me to reexamine how much I valued my upbringing just as much as I cultivated my desire to dissect the people I lived with for a year. The children I worked with had lots of qualities that shocked me at first: they were disrespectful, rude, ill mannered, and highly competitive, especially with each other. Their parents bought them almost anything they wanted and were incredibly lazy when it came to discipline. It was as if the parents wanted children, but only for bragging rights. They seemed to want nothing to do with the ins and outs of actually teaching children to be good people. Even so, the children were not necessarily complete monsters. They are all incredibly bright and talented, especially in sports. But it was what they *lacked* that made them so difficult to manage.

Some instructors ask students to keep a double-entry notebook, writing down notes of fact on one side of the page or screen and personal responses on the other side. Favorite's journal writing could easily be organized that way, because she so clearly thinks that the parents themselves are responsible for "difficult" children.

Brainstorming requires only that you jot down all the ideas that come to mind, as they come. As Favorite worked to get a foothold on how she might write about her nannying job, she brainstormed and came up with the following ideas.

Brainstorming

family dynamics	spoiled children	Connecticut
parental discipline	socialization	child care
middle-class	upper-class	societal expectations
parental neglect	emotional development	overachieving
overscheduled	pretension	executive lifestyle
idea of the elite	overspending	maintaining a façade
mother-daughter rivalry	father-son rivalry	sense of entitlement
class nights	parental expectations	child stress
exclusivity	sibling rivalry	

Sometimes just doing as Favorite has done, putting random thoughts on paper (or on a screen), can get you started on the assignment by providing details you can develop.

Clustering is a way to map out your ideas visually. Write your subject or a phrase about it in the center of a piece of paper and circle it, the way Favorite has done here with the word *nannying*. Then think of other ideas related to the central idea, write them around it, circle them, and draw lines to show the connections, as Favorite has done with *kids*, *child care*, and *parents*. Then think of ideas related to these ideas and repeat the process. As one idea leads to another, as various ideas radiate outward from the nucleus idea and its associations, you'll see patterns and details emerging that can provide you with a structure and support for your

Clustering

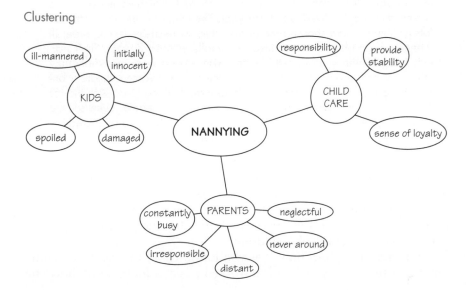

writing task. Or you may discover that you want to focus on just one part of the cluster that is especially interesting or important.

Freewriting is the easiest exercise of all, because all you do is write — without stopping — on whatever comes to your mind. You'll want to start out by writing down the topic you're considering — but then let your mind and hand go, writing for five minutes or so nonstop. *Nonstop* — that's the key. (And nonstop means that you might get off the subject.) You'll be surprised at how many ideas pop into your mind within those five minutes. And when you reread what you've written, you may discover insights into your subject that you never expected.

Here's what Favorite freewrote about her nannying job.

Freewriting

Sometimes I hated the kids I worked with in Connecticut, but most of the time I felt sorry for them. Their parents were never around, their mother has some kind of self-image disorder, their father is distant and overbearing at the same time, and the only real connection they have to some sort of real-world thinking is me — their nanny, who can barely stand the thought of sticking out the one year she's signed up for. I wonder if these kids have a hard time attaching to a yearly nanny and then detaching. It seems as though the process has left them armored, less reachable as human beings. The youngest son didn't even say goodbye to me when I left. He told me he was glad I was leaving because now he wouldn't be grounded from the computer anymore. He's going to be the most screwed up of the three children, I feel sure. And it's very sad. But after a year of nannying these kids, I'm pretty sure that the damage has already been done and is cemented in their psychological makeup. Sad but true. What's saddest of all, though, is that the parents don't even think of spending time with their kids to try to undo some of the damage or to change their behavior. As soon as school gets out in the summer, the children are off to camp for eight weeks straight. And as soon as camp is over, school starts again within a week or two. I asked the little girl if she'd rather go to camp or spend the time with her parents, and she said camp was more fun. I'm not sure these kids even realize that their parents are neglectful. I think they will, though, someday, when they're older. And that knowledge might be the most damaging thing of all.

In freewriting, Favorite discovered her sympathy for the children as well as her ability to identify the reasons for their unpleasant behavior.

Looping combines freewriting and clustering. First freewrite for five minutes on a subject. As you read over what you've written, circle the dominant idea or the best idea, the one you want to develop. Then loop back, freewriting for five minutes on that idea only and then again circling an idea you want to pursue further. Keep going with this exercise, maybe even giving yourself a break of an hour or so, until you land on an idea that might serve as the purpose and subject of your essay.

Here's how Favorite used looping to think and write about her job as a nanny.

Looping

I see the children as damaged goods. That's what they are. Every child is essentially a blank slate, and it's up to the parents to fill the slate with good ideas. But since these parents are too lazy to segregate the good from the bad, these children have absorbed more of the latter than the former. They've adopted the bad language they hear in R-rated movies; they act toward one another with spite and hatred, just as they've seen adults act on television; they are completely ignorant of proper table manners in general since their parents never reinforced these ideas. They are damaged in an almost tragic way because they have had so little to do with their own damage. And since they live such a privileged lifestyle, the damage seems to be magnified because they don't have any excuses, like no money, no social life, no education, no opportunity. These kids have everything — everything material, that is. They do not know the meaning of saving for an item; instant gratification is all they know. They feel entitled to all they desire, be it an ice cream cone or a new computer or a sleepover with friends. They are damaged in that they do not know how to process negative responses from others. It is a foreign concept to them, and instead of reacting logically, they react in a primitive way through screaming and anger. Their development as emotionally maturing human beings is stunted.

After writing this paragraph, Favorite looked over it and realized that her dominant idea was "damage." Later she returned to freewriting, starting with this dominant idea and expanding on it.

Questioning is another useful exercise for getting started. You may have heard of the classic questions a news story should answer: "Who?" "What?" "When?" "Where?" "Why?" and "How?" Those are still good places to start. You can think about your subject and ask questions such as "What happened/is happening/will happen?" "Who or what did/does/will do it?" "Where and when did/does/will it happen?" "How and why did/does/will it happen?" The following questions and answers are Favorite's.

Questioning

Who? Rich people who have children they're too busy (or too rich) to bother with.

What? The result is bratty children and a hired child–wrangler.

When? One year, when I was 22 and the kids were 9, 10, and 11.

Where? and **Why?** I wanted to live in the East, with rich people who traveled and did interesting things. These rich people needed someone they could pay to spend time with their wild children.

How? I applied to a nanny agency where the children's mother worked.

Coming up with ideas about your subject can be easy if you try one or more of the preceding activities. In fact, taking the time to do so will help you move from a general subject to a specific topic and a purpose for writing.

● **Deciding on a Tentative Thesis**

Spending time on generating ideas can also help you formulate a tentative **thesis,** the main idea you will develop in your writing. Usually your final thesis will appear in your introduction as a **thesis statement;** but even if the tentative thesis ends up changing drastically or the final thesis ends up being implied rather than stated directly, you need to formulate a thesis for yourself at an early stage to serve as a guide in organizing and drafting. As you move through several invention exercises, you might find yourself returning to one idea that seems to control your writing and thinking — that's probably the basis for your thesis. In addition, these activities may help you determine which thesis you can most easily support with the details that you've come up with while you're generating material about your subject.

Looking over the ideas she had generated, Jennifer Favorite decided on the tentative thesis "My year as a nanny for an extremely wealthy, extremely dysfunctional family showed me that the ways parents act — or fail to act — toward their children can make them very damaging models for the children's development." If you look at her final draft starting on page 36, you can see that she has essentially stayed with this thesis in her introductory paragraph, moving the information in the first part of the thesis into different sentences and ending up with the thesis statement in the last sentence of the paragraph: "And the moral you take away will be that children learn from their parents, especially those lessons that cause lifelong damage."

● **Organizing Your Ideas**

Some 2,000 years ago, Aristotle announced that every argument must include a beginning, a middle, and an end — advice that still holds true for all writing. *Making Sense* provides models of many good ways to organize an essay, from chronological and emphatic (p. 61, 138) to inductive and deductive (see Chapter 10), depending on the overall purpose for your writing. Just as reading and writing go together, purpose and organization do, too.

One of the most common ways to organize information involves the outline. *Scratch outlining* offers you a quick way to begin organizing your information (and it simultaneously supports the generation of more material). Favorite scratched out the following outline as she was experimenting with ways she might divide up and approach the subject of nannying.

Scratch Outlining

Nannying

I. Parents
   −Responsibilities
      socialization
      nurturing
      providing good examples
      commitment to good development
   −Failures
      reliance on others to socialize, nurture, all of the above
      seldom around the children
      force children into too many activities
      unwilling to change children's behavior
II. Children
   −Strengths
      intelligent
      well provided for
      talented
      athletic
   −Weaknesses
      stubborn
      lack strong emotional health
      lack of manners
      unaware of how to respond properly to a challenge

Favorite's scratch outline helped her narrow and begin to organize her topic. She found that by analyzing the responsibilities and failures of the parents and the strengths and weaknesses of the children, she could better understand and explain the nature and outcome of their family dynamics. When you read Favorite's first and final drafts (see pp. 30 and 36), though, you'll see that she eventually decided to organize the body of her essay largely by describing each of the family members in terms of his or her individual strengths and (mostly) weaknesses.

Generally speaking, you need to familiarize yourself with four patterns of organization, any of which can be used as the organizing principle of an outline: (1) chronological, in order of time; (2) spatial, in order of location; (3) emphatic, in order of importance or interest; and (4) level of detail, from general to specific. Some organizational patterns naturally unfold from the rhetorical method you're using, and you'll see just how such connections play out when you read the following chapters.

For instance, when you're writing *descriptions*, you'll probably use spatial organization most often. Most *narratives* or stories are arranged chronologically, but you might find yourself using flashbacks to events that took place before the time of the narrative and flashforwards to later events as well. Writing that uses *exemplification* usually moves from general assertion to specific examples, and sometimes vice versa — and you'll often want to arrange the examples themselves in chronological, emphatic, or some other kind of purposeful order. You'll also want to perform *classification and division* according to a general principle before putting your information into specific categories or breaking it down into specific parts; similarly, *comparison and contrast* will establish a general basis for comparing two or more subjects and then present specific points of similarity and difference, either whole by whole or part by part. A *process analysis* will use a strict chronological organization, whereas in an *analysis of causes and effects*, you'll choose between presenting the causes or the effects of the event in chronological or emphatic order. Whenever you write a *definition*, though, you'll link your organizational pattern to your purpose, following any one of the patterns for a description, process, comparison, exemplification, or definition. Finally, *argument* requires you to pay careful attention to the ordering of material. You might call on all the general organizational patterns as you introduce your argument, refute opposing arguments, and draw your conclusion.

Because most of the rhetorical methods offer options rather than strict requirements for organization, and because almost any essay uses more than one method, only you can decide if your entire essay or just a certain section of it would benefit from any one organizational pattern in particular. No matter which overall pattern you choose, you'll want to be sure that you include an introduction that engages your readers' interest, a clear and purposeful thesis (usually in the form of an explicit statement), plenty of supporting or illustrative details, and a conclusion that extends your thesis by answering the question "So what?" *Making Sense* will give you lots of practice in fulfilling all these features of a successful piece of writing.

● Drafting

When you've organized your ideas in the way that seems best, you're ready to begin drafting. Often you'll be able to lift passages directly from your freewriting or journal entries; at other times you'll find yourself inspired by what you've written while generating ideas and will be easily able to translate it into essay-quality material. In the first draft of Favorite's essay, which starts on page 30, you can see how she drew from her generating exercises and then moved ahead with her draft.

● Using Visuals

With technology making it easy to download images from the Web and scan them into word-processing programs (and with college writing increasingly being submitted online instead of on paper), more and more students are including visuals in their essays. Each chapter of *Making Sense* offers guidelines for choosing visuals for writing that follow the chapter's rhetorical method. In general, if you are considering using visuals, think about the following questions as you do so:

1. Will your instructor object to visuals? Some may prefer that you make your points with words alone.

2. What kinds of visuals would most enhance your essay — photographs? cartoons? bar or line graphs? pie charts? diagrams or other drawings? screen shots?

3. What purpose do you want the visuals to serve? Do you want them to strengthen your argument? help explain a complex process? set a mood?

4. Can the visuals stand on their own, or do you need to include labels, captions, or references to the visuals within the text?

Often a visual can help you focus your subject or your purpose. As you can see on page 30, Jennifer Favorite downloaded an image from the television show *Supernanny* from the Web. This image set up an implicit contrast between her own unpleasant experience as a nanny and the world of the television show, in which the nanny arrives on the scene and solves all of the problems in the household, leaving the family in a much better state than when she started. Favorite wrote that she was continually influenced by that particular visual. In her final draft (p. 36), Favorite used two visuals: the photograph and a cartoon, downloaded from the Web, that suggested an experience more like her own.

If you know that you want to include visuals, you may find that it's more efficient to locate several possibilities as you draft and revise so that when you're finished you can choose among them. If you put off looking for the visuals until the very end, you may not find any that really fit what you've written. It's better to let the visuals and the writing work together from an early stage.

If you want to use visuals that you did not create yourself and your essay is going to be posted or distributed on the Internet, you should request permission from the creator or owner to use them, because visuals are usually protected by copyright laws. You don't need to request permission if your essay will be submitted only to your instructor and classmates and only in print form. In either case, though, you should mention the sources of the visuals in the main text, in a caption or label, or perhaps (if the visuals are just intended to set a mood) in a note at the beginning or end of the essay.

If you look at Jennifer Favorite's final draft, you can see that she identified the source of the photograph in a caption and the source of the cartoon in the text. Your instructor may also want you to include the sources in a Works Cited list at the end of your essay (see the Appendix). Favorite's instructor didn't require such a list because her essay didn't include any outside sources other than visuals. In *Making Sense*, you will see that many of the visuals include captions or labels, others are referred to in the text, and still others stand on their own, but the sources of those that were not created by the author or the publisher are credited starting on page 780.

● **Collaborating**

Many of the things you read on a daily basis are the direct result of collaborations — between writers, between writers and editors, among writers and editors and publishers, among writers and their coworkers, among writers and their family members and friends. Every newspaper, textbook, novel, cookbook, guidebook, Web site, scientific proposal, and credit card statement is a collaboration of some sort. When you're writing, you will want to take advantage of the same opportunities that professional writers regularly use to talk with other people about their writing and work with others to strengthen it, asking and answering questions that will lead to your best work.

Making Sense offers you many opportunities to learn how to collaborate on projects where you are individually responsible for producing a final draft and those where a group creates it. It offers you daily opportunities to talk with the people in your class, to meet in pairs or small groups to compare your responses to the reading selections, to help one another with your reading and writing tasks. Step by step, then, you'll work together to read and respond to essays, generate ideas, evaluate rough drafts, and polish almost–final drafts. Every chapter includes guided activities for reading, writing, and revising that help make peer evaluations successful and rewarding, and you'll soon see how much better you read and write when you have a group of friends to help you.

Guidelines for Group Work.   Successful collaboration is not hard to achieve; the general guidelines are as follows.

1. Whether your instructor assigns you to a group or you form your own, try to keep it small, for the sake of convenience.

2. Arrange for regular places and times to meet, whether online or in a coffee shop. Attend all the meetings — your group needs you.

3. Set specific tasks for each meeting, and review them at the end of the meeting to make sure you haven't forgotten anything.

4. When you meet, stay on task, no matter how tempting it is to talk about the latest football game or sorority party. When you know you'll accomplish your goals, you'll look forward to your group meetings.

5. Divide up duties in order to make your meetings efficient as well as effective. Let one group member keep the time schedule, the amount of time you spend on each person's essay. Assign another member to keep everyone on task, whether you're focusing on organizing, support, or final editing.

6. Take time to evaluate group dynamics, concentrating on what *you* can do to improve the collaboration.

A Response to a Draft.   After Jennifer Favorite drafted her essay, she asked one of her classmates, Rey Saavedra, to respond to her draft. As you can see, he annotated the text to highlight what he saw as its strong points as well as places where she needed to revise or add or delete material. He also summarized his reaction to the draft in a few paragraphs on page 34.

I Played the Nanny

Great opening; right away you're inviting
readers to identify with you.

Walk awhile in my shoes:ˇ you've just finished a yearlong job as a

nanny for three children aged 9, 10, and 11. You cannot believe the

things you experienced and saw; in fact, you like to refer to your

time in this extremely wealthy, extremely dysfunctional family as a

What sorts of things? You might mention some of the
worst of them right now, in order to hook your reader.

sociological experiment of sorts.ˇ You also acknowledge it was

This sounds awkward.

<u>as if</u>ˇ<u>being</u> an observer and ancillary member of a living theater, a

I'm getting confused by all the comparisons to experiments,
acting, being a spectator—maybe settle on just one?

human spectacle that is fit to be explored.ˇ

Any character study of the household dynamic in this spectacle

would be best begun by examining the patriarch of the family.

Father is a high-ranking executive for a major television network who

is home two to three days per week, on average. This character is the

What's a rogue horse, and what does it have to do with a theater?

rogue horse of this living theater._ He frequently enters chomping

This is quite a vivid image—very effective!

on a gigantic cigar and bellowing for his childrens' affections._

Brash, pompous, and rude are his most redeeming qualities. He

claims to love his children, but will describe his daughter to you as

"a little bitch." Father frequently professes undying adoration for his

wife, loudly, in front of you, yet careful observation and pricked-up

ears will tell you he's most certainly carrying on with his ex-wife.

The role of Mother is played by a polite yet vacant woman who

exhibits momentary displays of caring but seems always to be

This opening topic sentence seems stronger and more

focused than the one in the previous paragraph.   complications—or contradictions?

focused on other tasks._ She is her own little gem of complications._

Fifteen years younger than Father, Mother lives on a steady diet of

Does the age difference make a big difference? (By the way, how old

is the ex-wife?) What point do you want to make about her diet?

popcorn, yogurt, and vanilla ice cream. _You are frequently woken

around six in the morning to the sound of the Stairmaster motor

churning below you, alerting you to Mother's first round of exercise

This essay has great sound effects!

for the day. _Rounds two and three will be completed while Mother

is at work for her nanny agency (yes, the very same one that

What connections do you want to make between her diet and her exercise schedule? And

her age? I'm unclear about her role at the nanny agency. Is she an executive there? Your

sentence sounds almost like Mother works as a nanny, and I know you don't mean that.

employs you)._ Mother has also dabbled in chewing tobacco at one

time, most certainly for the purpose of helping her to purge her

Mother was bulimic? How do you know? Did she tell you, as though you weren't even im-

portant enough to be private in front of? Or were you supposed to be her nanny as well?

Her confidante? "Vittles" sounds too informal, as if you're trying for humor—it doesn't

seem to fit in with your overall tone of disgust and amazement.

vittles._

The three child members of this troupe can be grouped into

in?

Sons and Daughter. Elder Son and Younger Son are at_ constant

battle. Their years competing in myriad sports have cultivated their battle skills to the point where Younger Son's coaches plead

with Mother and Father to curb his ruthlessly competitive

Why do you think the Sons become more competitive instead of bored or exhausted? Do
they earn extra points with their parents by being competitive on the sports field and
with each other? Also, you need an example or two of the Younger's "ruthlessly competi-
tive nature."

nature.∧The Sons share an unhealthy obsession with instant mes-

saging, exploding with beastlike behavior when asked to leave

the computer to complete homework or eat a meal. Each Son

tells you on numerous occasions to "shut up," and neither Son

avoid?

takes seriously any warning to arrest the use∧of offensive lan-

Do you want to connect this verbal behavior with the competition
idea? Or is there an idea that arches over both of them?

guage in your presence.∧Younger Son is positively brilliant, yet

These kids sound simply repulsive. Is there any way you could shape your
paragraph in terms of all of their material and intellectual advantages ver-
sus their emotional disadvantages? I think the "bleak future" idea is an im-
portant point. In fact, these kids have a pretty bleak present, if you ask me.

his lack of decorum and emotional depth betray a bleak future.∧

Both Sons take glee in torturing Daughter, who is the middle

Would this sentence sound better at the beginning of the
next paragraph? Here it just seems to trail off at the end.

child in this cast of characters.∧

Daughter is pleasant and darling to look at but can exhibit the

What makes her darling?

cunning and insincerity of a well–seasoned politician.∧She has been

hardened by years of pummeling by the Sons and will assert herself

brothers? parents? nanny?

forcefully in any argument against any opponent.∧The other side of

Daughter's personality sees herself adopting you as her newest

confidante and permanent playmate as soon as you come on stage in

So like Mother, Daughter is a bundle of contradictions? The Sons sound like their sneaky,
aggressive Father.

this family drama.∧Like the Sons, Daughter is overbooked with

sports and other activities and struggles to live the life of a normal

What would that normal life be like? How do bright
and personable equate with dramatic? What do you
want the topic sentence of this paragraph to be?   *best actor?*

∧ten–year–old. She is bright and personable, the true∧dramatic of the

family. However, it troubles you to know that Daughter refuses to sleep in her own bed at night, preferring instead to occupy the floor

Why does it trouble you? Why does she claim to want to sleep there?
Why do the parents let her? What do the brothers do about this?

next to the marital bed in the master bedroom.↴

I love the idea of the nanny as wrangler. That might be another option for your opening.

Your role in this living theater will be to act as a sort of wrangler. ↴

Part referee, part instructor, part exorcist to the demons ~~living~~ inside

each child, you must be as athletic as the children themselves,

What do you mean by this phrase?

constantly juggling activities, <u>playing both defensive and</u>↴<u>offensive</u>

<u>positions.</u> The stresses are considerable, and the victories are

hard-won. You have an occasional moment of camaraderie with

the Children, be it watching them thrill with delight at a cartoon

beheading or gingerly answering Elder Son's wild inquiries into the

nature of sex. You must also play the part of chef extraordinaire,

They're not "tots," they're closer to teenagers. Also, this sentence seems out of place
here unless you mean your performance in the chef role was one of your victories.

catering to the divergent palates of each temperamental tot.↴Overall,

this role is one of many highs and lows, and you are careful to assert

yourself and to keep your equanimity. You are determined to fulfill

There seem to be lots of things left unsaid in this paragraph.
But your perseverance comes across very clearly.

your contract with this theater to its completion.↴

Near the end of your run in the living theater of this family, you

You need to explain this "existential" idea

has been?   more if you're going to introduce it here.

realize the entire experience to↴be an existential↴one: what are the

put up?

effects of the actions you took, of the defenses you <u>played;</u>↴did you

Is this the right word?

in fact <u>affect</u>↴any lasting change in the lives of these children? It is

nearly impossible to tell, although the family's reactions to you near

the end leave you feeling vindicated. Father has acknowledged your

talents, Mother has thanked you for your resolve, Elder Son has

Are the commas OK in this sentence? (I always have trouble remembering the rules.)

turned to you for life advice,↴Daughter has admitted her fondness

for you, Younger Son has laughed at your attempts at humor.

The show has not ended badly, but the family characters will remain

This sentence seems too upbeat, given the "bleak" picture you've painted.
steadfast in their roles. ‸ As the outsider, you take your final bow. You

are finished now. You close the curtain on this play and raise the

curtain to another, a play far removed from the world of a nanny, a
It isn't an actor who closes and raises the curtain, is it? Maybe try
a different theater idea — but the end of the sentence is great!
play with you perhaps in the starring role. ‸

Here are Rey Saavedra's comments:

Jen,

First of all, I think you've got lots of good information to work with already, especially statements that just need to be developed in more detail.
I've marked the places that I think need more explanation. Second, I'd be careful with the theater metaphor. I'd keep it — that's for sure. I'd just be careful
that I was using all the comparisons correctly and being consistent. (I think
Maria is a theater major; she'd probably be able to help you.) If you keep the
theater metaphor, try to connect it more clearly with an overall purpose and
thesis — at the end of the introduction it's not very clear where you're going.

Third, I think you need to strengthen your opening. As I read over your
title and looked at the picture (it's from the reality TV show *Supernanny*,
right?), I couldn't help thinking about the show and how different your experience is from the Supernanny's. She swoops down on a dysfunctional family
every week, observes their many faults, shows both parents and children how
to right their wrongs, and then leaves the house with the family in perfect accord. I wonder if you might compare your experience with the show, which ideal-
izes what a nanny can do. Doing that might hook your readers. And if you did
that, you might have better luck introducing the characters in the way you've
set up your essay. Or if you didn't want to do anything like that, you might
give some statistics on the number of nannies that are advertised for yearly
in the U.S. I also found myself wondering what kinds of families hire nannies. In
other words, how different was your experience from the typical experience?

Last, I want to tell you that the second-person approach you used is
terrific. I was really impressed how easily you used "you." I haven't read very
many essays that do that — it's unusual.

If you'd like, I'll read your revision,

Rey

● Revising, Editing, and Proofreading

Getting responses to your draft, as important as they are, is only part
of the work you need to do for the last steps in getting your essay into
its final, polished form: revising, editing, and proofreading. All three
of these steps involve making changes in your draft, and they usually overlap to a considerable extent. But it's still useful to think about
them separately as three different ways in which you need to read your
own draft actively and critically, asking the same kinds of questions that

others responding to it did or that you would in reading something written by someone else. If you deliberately try to focus on each step at some point, it will help keep your attention from straying into other areas and prevent you from forgetting some things you need to do.

Essentially, these three steps involve focusing on three different levels of your rhetorical task. **Revising,** which literally means "seeing again," deals with the broadest issues: how well your draft achieves your purpose; how successfully you've addressed your specific audience; how clear your thesis is; whether you've met the requirements of the overall rhetorical method you're using; how effective your organization, introduction, and conclusion are; whether you've included too little or too much detail. *Making Sense* can give you a lot of help with this part of the writing process, because each chapter includes a checklist that summarizes the kinds of things you need to pay attention to in writing using that chapter's rhetorical method. (For example, look at "Checking Over Descriptive Writing" on page 140.) You can use these questions not only in revising your own draft but also in reviewing a classmate's.

In **editing,** you focus on issues that are smaller in scale but equally important (some of which are also covered in the chapter checklists): the length, structure, and variety of your paragraphs and sentences; your choice of words; the transitions between your ideas; the effectiveness and accuracy of your punctuation. Finally, **proofreading** focuses on the kinds of surface-level problems that are so important to the first visual impression your writing makes on readers: typos, misspellings, word spacing. The spell checkers in most word-processing programs can help with proofreading, although they don't catch everything; you'll still need to go through what you hope will be your final draft to check for these kinds of problems. (For editing, on the other hand, grammar checkers are themselves more often wrong than right in identifying "errors.")

To see what Jennifer Favorite did in these steps, compare her first draft with the final draft that begins on page 36. She followed several suggestions Rey Saavedra made, the most important being improvement of her use of the theater metaphor and strengthening her introduction. She also changed a number of words and phrases he had questioned, and responded to his questions about commas and the visual by changing the commas to semicolons and adding a caption. Favorite herself realized that she needed to add more details about the family members and include a stronger thesis statement that was more like her original tentative thesis, one that more clearly achieved her purpose of conveying the sadness of the situation she had been a part of. Saavedra's remark about one of her topic sentences led her to look at all of them more closely and edit them to tie them in to the thesis. And her spell checker corrected *childrens'* to *children's* in the second paragraph. As I mentioned earlier, she also decided to add a second visual, a cartoon.

Although this book shows only Favorite's first draft and her final essay, you'll often need to work through multiple drafts before you achieve
something that makes perfect sense to you, your instructor, your classmates, and whoever else will be reading your writing. (For example, this
book went through four or five drafts on its way to publication.) The
good news is that computers have made revising, editing, and proofreading physically faster and easier than ever before. In fact, it's often
impossible to tell when one "draft" ends and another begins — you can
keep cutting and pasting, tinkering with words and sentences, and asking
classmates for a response until you're ready to submit the essay, without
ever stopping to print a hard copy.

I Played the Nanny

Supernanny, Mary Poppins, The Sound of Music — all productions with

nannies in starring roles. If you are like I was a year ago, when I ap-

plied for a position as a nanny, this is the kind of role that you imagine

for yourself. You imagine the supporting cast as well: one or two lov-

ing (if distant) parents and several good-hearted (if mischievous) chil-

dren. But life doesn't resemble show business, you soon discover — or

rather, in this case it looks and feels less like a situation comedy than

a Shakespearean tragedy (without the physical fatalities). In your year

caring for three children aged 9, 10, and 11, you find that the plot and

characters in this real-life production are nothing like you expected.

You are, for the most part, sharing the set with cold and inaccessible

parents and with ill-mannered and permanently defiant children. Al-

though such a situation is not what the nanny agency had described

throughout the application and interview process, it does turn out to

be the sad norm among all the other nannies you met. You were all

assured that you'd be part of a family, but you come to realize that

families can be dysfunctional in ways you'd never dreamed of. You

end up feeling less like Julie Andrews than like Juliet's nurse. Cast

in what you hoped would be a major role, you turn out with a part

that's even more demanding than you'd bargained for — but much

On the reality television show *Supernanny*, the title character takes just a few days to right all the wrongs in a seemingly dysfunctional family. By the end of the show, misbehaving children are well behaved and frazzled parents are organized and in charge. From what I've experienced and heard about, happy endings like these are rare in families that hire nannies.

less rewarding. At the same time, since you've joined a show already long in its run, you also watch the plot unfold from the perspective of the audience, becoming an appalled onlooker at a human spectacle. And the moral you take away will be that children learn from their parents, especially those lessons that cause lifelong damage.

Perhaps the most damaging lessons are those taught by the patriarch of the family. A high-ranking executive for a major television network who is home two to three nights each week, on average, Father is the "stage hog" of this domestic drama. He frequently enters chomping on a gigantic cigar and bellowing for his children's affections. Brash, pompous, and rude are the most positive descriptive terms for him. Although he announces that he loves his children, he tells you privately that his daughter is "turning into a little bitch."

When he's around, the children compete for his attention, however brief, and his favor, vying for the role of most–loved offspring. Father encourages this sibling rivalry by pushing them to excel in sports and academics and conducting overbearing lectures when any child challenges or falters in his or her assigned role. He particularly likes proving his children wrong and arguing them down like the attorney he was trained to be. (When Father is onstage, your role is to stand to the side and silently watch the drama unfold.) When his company's photographer wants the family to pose, Father grabs his wife and children around him and roars that *this* is a family! Publicly and loudly, Father frequently assures you (and everyone else) that he adores his current, much–younger wife. Yet it doesn't take long for you to figure out that he seems to have an undying adoration for his former wife as well.

The role of Mother is played by a polite, rather vacant woman, who occasionally can emote maternal feelings. Despite Father's alleged adoration of her, the two exchange very little affection or even dialogue. In fact, Mother is focused on herself most of the time and seems happiest when Father is absent. If you venture any inquiry into Mother's tastes or personal history, she gives you banal and terse responses. If you say anything about your own life, Mother rarely responds at all, let alone acknowledges your statement with a question. But despite her seemingly placid emotional life, your observation reveals that she is truly complicated. Mother lives on a steady diet of dry popcorn, low–fat yogurt, and premium vanilla ice cream. You are frequently awakened around six in the morning to the sound of the Stairmaster motor churning below you, alerting you to Mother's first round of exercise for the day. Rounds two and three will be completed during breaks from her job as owner of a nanny agency (yes, the very same one that employs you). And at night, she will be back into the ice cream. Well, exercise is undoubtedly better than bulimia, which Mother used to rely on, using chewing tobacco as her purgative. What gives Mother pleasure besides her slim figure? Not her children. Like Father, she is rarely around the house or the children, preferring instead to let you act as chauffeur and role model for the younger generation while she naps behind the scenes, alone. Sometimes, though, she comes onstage to applaud or threaten the children, depending on their performances and her mood.

Among the junior members of this troupe, Elder Son and Younger Son wage constant battle. Their years of rigorous, elite training both at home and in myriad sports have cultivated their combat skills to the point where Younger Son's coaches plead with Mother and Father to help him curb his ruthlessly competitive nature. A basketball game between the Sons will soon dissolve into a screaming fisticuffs where you, the intervener, are faced with insult (and, on occasion, injury). Elder Son refuses defeat by his just-as-capable brother and retaliates with unmitigated violence whenever his tenuous dominance is threatened. The Sons' shared obsession with instant messaging further fuels their competition, as they argue over the one computer relegated to the children. When you ask your so-called charges to leave the computer to complete homework or eat a meal, the Sons explode with bestial nastiness. Both feel free to tell you to "shut up," and neither thinks of avoiding offensive language in your presence. You believe the Sons have learned much of their behavior from the violent and vulgarity-filled television programs they have been allowed to watch and from their parents' own practices. Younger Son is brilliant, yet his lack of personal control and emotional depth foretell a bleak future. Elder Son can display occasional moments of warmth, but his superior attitude eradicates any hope of lasting improvement. In spite of all the material advantages heaped upon them by Mother and Father, the Sons remain unappreciative of these advantages and absolutely resistant to any accompanying social lessons. When their ever–changing cast of friends visit, the Sons invariably get into a grim fight. As a result, those who visit rarely return.

Despite the pleasure they take in fighting each other, the Sons take special satisfaction in torturing Daughter, the middle child and unequivocally the most gifted performer on this living stage. Daughter is darling to look at, a young beauty who wears the finest clothes a child can own. Outsiders and Father, in particular, praise her freely for her beauty and people–pleasing personality. While displaying intelligence and charm in public, however, she privately exhibits the cunning and insincerity of a cynical politician. Hardened by years of brotherly abuse, she asserts herself forcefully in any disagreement, with child or adult. And the lies she regularly tells are delivered with bright steady eyes and a cheerful sweet voice. Her uglier activities are usually reserved for backstage performances. To your face, she wheedles you to be her newest confidante and playmate, at least for the duration of your one–year run. During that run, Daughter steals most scenes, dazzling you and her parents with her dancing, singing, and joke–telling abilities, exhausting herself to win over her audiences. Like the Sons, she is too busy attracting attention and participating in too many sports and lessons to live the life of a regular ten–year–old. Instead of sleepovers, Daughter attends late–night piano lessons, acting courses, and soccer practices. Instead of riding bikes with girls her own age, she rides in the car with her nanny to the next of her closely booked activities. Daughter seems confident and capable to all her public audience, but you know that privately she fights her insecurities. Her constant struggle to please Father and Mother, to get their attention and approval, has resulted in a deep–seated self–doubt. And you know that she slips into bed every single night with Mother, or both her parents when Father is at home. There is no resistance to this practice, and Mother and Father do nothing to help her overcome her fears and insecurities. Interestingly, the most time Daughter ever gets to spend with either of her parents is when she is sleeping with them.

Although it's tempting to (try to) perform the role of healer in this fractured family, you are forced instead into the less rewarding role of wrangler. Part referee, part instructor, part exorcist to the demons coursing through each child, you must be as aggressively athletic as the children themselves, constantly cross-training, switching off between defensive and offensive positions, regardless of the sport or activity. After all, Mother and Father have consistently removed themselves from most duties of a director; preoccupied with their own performances, they've abandoned you to a position of sole responsibility for the junior members of the cast (just like the nanny in Robert Mankoff's cartoon from the *New Yorker* on the next page). Your authority is challenged endlessly, and you must just as endlessly justify your responsibility, experience, and knowledge to these argumentative and perpetually resistant children. Any attempt on your part to undo an offensive behavior results immediately in an argument: "We don't have to do what you say; Mom and Dad let us (*fill in the blank*)." In the meantime, Mother and Father continually pledge their support to your efforts while doing nothing concrete to assist you. You're on your own, no speaking lines already written or assigned. In addition, you find you've had to develop new skills in lie detection and surveillance to look after these children. (After all, their parents have always participated in elaborate schemes designed to fool, from Father's devotion to two wives to Mother's eating disorders.) No homework sheet or written assignment can go unchecked. You must also play the part of chef extraordinaire, catering to the unique palate of each demanding charge. Whatever the scene, the mental and physical stresses are intense and the victories hard–won. Your role demands that you develop your survival skills, for you're determined to fulfill your contract.

Near the end of your run, you wonder how successful your performance has really been. What will be the effects of the actions you took, of the efforts you made; did you in fact achieve any lasting change in the lives of these children? It is nearly impossible to tell, although the family's reactions to you near the end leave you feeling vindicated, if only momentarily. Father has sparingly acknowledged your talents; Mother has thanked you for your resolve; Elder Son has turned to you for advice about life; Daughter has admitted a fondness for you; Younger Son has laughed at your attempts at humor. The show has not ended in disaster, but the family actors still seem all too typecast in their roles. The damage that was done before you arrived will remain — but not for your lack of persistence. As the outsider, the good nanny, the supporting character who's had to offer far too much

"They can't see you right now—would you like a bottle while you're waiting?"

A *New Yorker* cartoon depicts the all–too–common situation of parents using a nanny to keep their distance from their children.

support, you take your final bow. You exit the stage of this drama and

step onto another, a stage on which you really are the star.

Favorite's finished essay is a descriptive one: she moves from describing one character to the next. Yet within her overall description she taps the rhetorical power of narration, cause-and-consequence analysis, comparison and contrast, and exemplification, mixing the rhetorical methods. Her organization is emphatic overall, ending with a description of herself because the nanny is the most important character in her description. But within the individual paragraphs she moves from emphatic to chronological to spatial patterns of organization.

Favorite opens the essay with a "hook," mentioning three shows that feature nannies in starring roles, three shows with happy endings. In her introduction, she compares these stage and screen nannies with the actual nannies she knows (including herself), few of whom have managed to achieve such happy endings in the families they serve. In fact, Favorite's thesis statement is that the parents, no matter how neglectful or negative their behavior, are the role models the children emulate. Each of the remaining paragraphs now opens with a focused topic sentence that extends the thesis statement. And each paragraph includes details of various kinds (stories, examples, comparisons and contrasts) that bring the topic sentence to life. Favorite closes her essay with a question that grows out of her thesis statement: Has she been able to compensate to any significant extent for the parents' faults? She concludes that she has done the best job she can but that if she wants a role where she can thrive, rather than merely survive, she'll have to star in a show of her own making.

Making Sense with Your Writing

Now that you've seen the steps and strategies a writer needs to work through to achieve a rhetorical purpose — to create knowledge by making sense of a subject — let me return to my explanation of how this book will help you do this. In each chapter, *Making Sense* asks you to question the readings and your own writing in ways that will help you define a purpose and audience, decide on a thesis, develop supporting details, organize them into a series of related, purposeful paragraphs, choose an appropriate vocabulary and style, and write strong introductions and conclusions. As I mentioned earlier, every chapter also offers you help for revising; after you've drafted a text, you can turn to the checklist, respond to the questions, and apply your responses to your writing. You can also use these questions to respond to your classmates' writing or to have them respond to yours. In fact, a great many of the activities and assignments in *Making Sense* ask you to work with one or more classmates, giving you practice in the collaboration that's often so crucial to writing successfully. And each chapter offers suggestions for thinking about how to use specific kinds of visuals to enhance your writing and help you achieve your rhetorical goals.

As I hope you will see, the emphasis of *Making Sense* is on *your* development as a college–level reader, writer, and thinker — and sometimes a speaker as well. It includes many opportunities for in–class writing, speaking, and conversation as well as for self-evaluation, peer evaluation, and group evaluation of your writing. In every case, you will be working toward improving your literacy and your rhetorical skills; you'll also be improving your essays for your instructor's evaluation. But *Making Sense* isn't teacher–centered; it's student–centered, focused on improving your writing process as well as your written products.

Even though much of *Making Sense* focuses on the work you will do in class, it is important to remember that there are not great differences between academic and public (or "real–world") reading and writing. The literacy skills you fine-tune throughout this semester should help you succeed both in and out of class. The goal of *Making Sense* is for you to become an effective writer and reader who is able to analyze and contribute to conversations in every situation you encounter.

· ·

Try Your Hand   To reflect one more time on your feelings about writing, take a few minutes to write out answers to the following questions:

1. What does it mean to be a writer?
2. Do you think of yourself as a writer (or a particular kind of writer)? If so, when did you first begin to think of yourself that way?
3. Have you ever described yourself to others as a writer (or a particular kind of writer)? Can you remember the first time you did so?
4. Do you think of yourself as part of a community (or multiple communities) of writers? Who makes up your community or communities?
5. Does your writing include visuals?

· ·

Finally

I hope you have some fun using *Making Sense*. The readings, visuals, questions, writing assignments, and group work are all intended to help you continue to develop your verbal and visual literacy skills as a college student and a citizen. My greatest hope is that you become more self-conscious and confident about your own thinking, reading, and writing as you work your way through this text and make sense of the world beyond it. Best of luck in college — and let me know how I can help you.

Cheryl Glenn < cjg6@psu.edu >

chapter 2

NARRATION

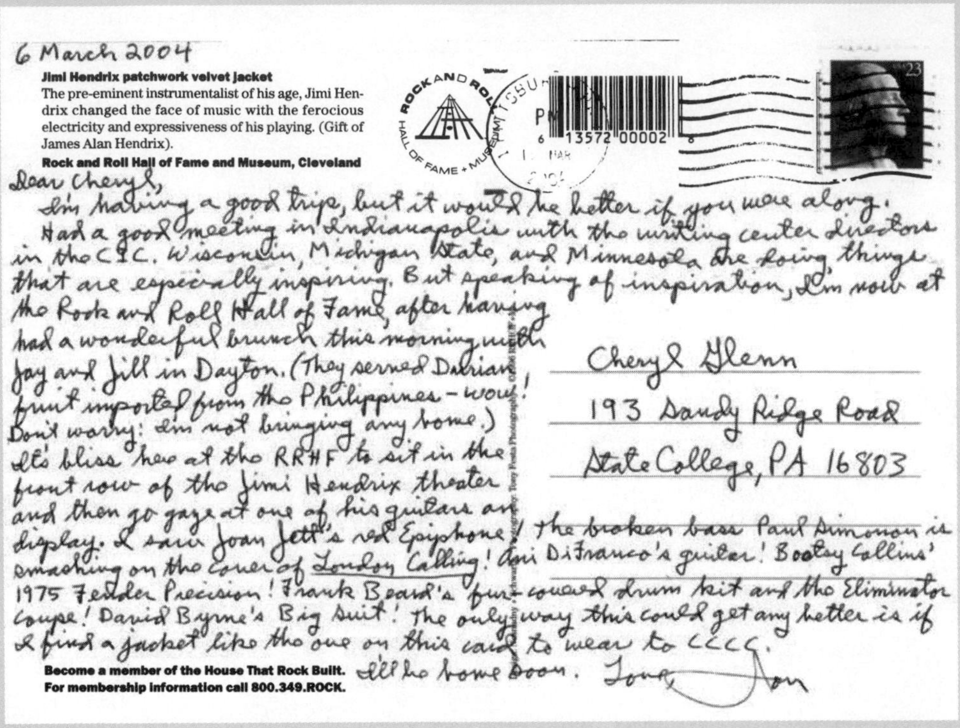

6 March 2004

Jimi Hendrix patchwork velvet jacket
The pre-eminent instrumentalist of his age, Jimi Hendrix changed the face of music with the ferocious electricity and expressiveness of his playing. (Gift of James Alan Hendrix).
Rock and Roll Hall of Fame and Museum, Cleveland

Dear Cheryl,

I'm having a good trip, but it would be better if you were along. Had a good meeting in Indianapolis with the writing center directors in the CIC. Wisconsin, Michigan State, and Minnesota are doing things that are especially inspiring. But speaking of inspiration, I'm now at the Rock and Roll Hall of Fame, after having had a wonderful brunch this morning with Jay and Jill in Dayton. (They served Durian fruit imported from the Philippines — wow! Don't worry: I'm not bringing any home.) It's bliss here at the RRHF to sit in the front row of the Jimi Hendrix theater and then go gaze at one of his guitars on display. I saw Joan Jett's red Epiphone she's smashing on the cover of London Calling! the broken bass Paul Simonon is Ani DiFranco's guitar! Bootsy Collins' 1975 Fender Precision! Frank Beard's fur-covered drum kit and the Eliminator Coupe! David Byrne's Big Suit! The only way this could get any better is if I find a jacket like the one on this card to wear to CCCC. I'll be home soon. Love, Jon

Cheryl Glenn
193 Sandy Ridge Road
State College, PA 16803

Become a member of the House That Rock Built.
For membership information call 800.349.ROCK.

*P*ostcards are an everyday kind of communication, casually sent and received. Yet despite their informality, most postcards are written and read with certain expectations:

- *A beginning that sets a scene:* "Dear Cheryl, I'm having a good trip, but it would be better if you were along."
- *A setting:* the Rock and Roll Hall of Fame and Museum, Cleveland, Ohio.
- *A middle that tells a story:* "Had a good meeting in Indianapolis with the writing center directors in the CIC. Wisconsin, Michigan State, and Minnesota are doing things that are especially inspiring. But speaking of inspiration, I'm now at the Rock and Roll Hall of Fame, after having had a wonderful brunch with Jay and Jill in Dayton. (They served durian fruit imported from the Philippines—wow! Don't worry: I'm not bringing any home.) It's bliss here at the RRHF to sit in the front row of the Jimi Hendrix theater and then go gaze at one of his guitars on display. I saw Joan Jett's red Epiphone! The broken bass Paul Simonon is smashing on the cover of *London Calling!* Ani DiFranco's guitar! Bootsy Collins' 1975 Fender Precision! Frank Beard's fur-covered drum kit and the Eliminator Coupe! David Byrne's Big Suit!"
- *An ending that brings the story to a close:* "The only way this could get any better is if I find a jacket like the one on this card to wear to CCCC. I'll be home soon. Love, Jon."
- *Characters:* Jay, Jill, Jon.
- *Description:* especially inspiring presentations, fruit imported from the Philippines, fur-covered drum kit.

Even if you don't know Jon and Cheryl or Jay and Jill, even if you've never been to Cleveland, let alone the Rock and Roll Hall of Fame and Museum, the message on the postcard probably makes sense to you because it is an example of **narration** — it tells a story — and you understand how narration works. We use the components of narration — chronological order, characters, dialogue, setting, and description — as we gossip over lunch, explain the reasons we're late for a meeting, and talk about our vacation plans.

. . . .

Looking at Your Own Literacy What kinds of postcards have you received or sent? What were the occasions for sending those postcards? What kinds of narratives did they contain? Besides postcard narratives, what other kinds of narratives do you often tell or write? Write for a few minutes about the kinds of stories they are, why and how you deliver them, and who your audience is.

. . . .

FIVE-DAY FORECAST

TODAY	TONIGHT	SUNDAY

Accumulating snow, mixing with rain late.	Windy and cold with more flurries.	Windy and cold with clouds and flurries.
36	20	28 | 18

MONDAY	TUESDAY	WEDNESDAY

Mostly sunny, but chilly.	Increasing clouds with periods of snow.	A mix of clouds and sun.
36 | 20	40 | 30	42 | 28

LOCAL SUMMARY

Snow this morning will accumulate 1-3 inches by afternoon, at which time it may change over to rain or drizzle. Heavier snow is likely in northern Pennsylvania. Snow will end tonight, and it will become very windy and cold. The wind will persist on Sunday with plenty of clouds and some flurries possible.

What Is Narration?

Because human beings are natural storytellers, narration is the most common method of communication. In fact, we use it and hear it so often that we don't think about it as narration. But all kinds of public writing, including newspapers, television comedies and dramas, news programs, movies, comic strips, lab reports, histories, biographies, diaries, and letters depend on the conventions of narration to tell what happened, is happening, or will happen — and to whom. And as you already know from sending and receiving postcards and e-mails, entertaining your friends with jokes, seeing movies, and reading novels, an effective narrative is often much more than a simple report or forecast of events. By creating or retelling a sequence of occurrences, a speaker, writer, or filmmaker can use narration to argue a point, create a mood, or provide an example.

Because we need narration in order to make sense of the world, we often use it as the primary way of organizing a piece of writing or an oral presentation. At other times, we tuck in a short narrative, or **an-ecdote,** to make a point within another kind of writing or speech. For instance, when an announcer on the Weather Channel is describing the icy weather that is expected in a certain area and encouraging people to stay home, she might relate a short narrative about a bad traffic accident caused by icy road conditions. The drivers involved in the accident, however, will no doubt tell their stories at greater length in a police or insurance report, with details about the series of events, setting, and characters. Finally, the newspaper forecast on page 48 reveals how a narration about the weather could work on a smaller but similarly effective scale.

Thinking about Narration

1. Look over the written text in the five-day forecast for central Pennsylvania. How is the information arranged? How does each day's forecast connect with the previous day's forecast? How is the local summary narrated differently from the main forecast?

2. What narrative do the pictures of the five-day forecast tell? How is that visual narrative the same as or different from the verbal narrative?

Why Use Narration?

When you use narration, you usually have one or more of four basic purposes: to report information, to support an argument, to provide an example, or to set a mood.

Every day, you communicate primarily by relating a sequence of incidents. Sharing stories is an important way to establish and maintain friendships, whether you're telling another parent about potty training your child or describing to your roommate the thrills of your recent whitewater rafting trip. In fact, many people who live alone say they would like to have someone to whom they can recount the events of their day. On a more practical level, explaining to a mechanic what's wrong with your car or rescheduling a class in the registrar's office also requires that you report a series of incidents to explain what you want or need.

Not all narratives reporting information are delivered orally; many appear in newspaper articles, history books, scientific reports, and other printed and electronic forms. For instance, in *The Mind at Work*, Mike Rose investigates the intellectual nature of what many define as blue-collar jobs (waiting on tables, carpentry, construction). Here he offers a sketch or report of his mother's career as a waitress in California before delving into the intellectual skills needed to do this work.

Narration to Report Information

At first she waitressed in a series of coffee shops in downtown L.A., the largest stretch at Coffee Dan's on heavily trafficked Broadway. Then she moved to Norm's, a "family-style" chain, working for nearly a decade at the shop on Sunset and Vermont, by major medical facilities and corporate offices, like that for Prudential. She spent her last ten years at the Norm's in Torrance, amid a more lower-middle-class, local merchant, and retirement clientele. During her time at Coffee Dan's and Norm's Sunset, my father would slip into grave illness and, for the last years of his life, be bedridden. I proceeded through elementary and high school. Mustering what immediate help she could, she struggled to balance work, caretaking, and child rearing. This period, roughly from 1952 to the early sixties, was another period of severe hardship. As my mother put it simply: "Dad was ill, and you were little. . . . I *had* to get work."

— MIKE ROSE, *The Mind at Work*

In this narrative, Rose reports the most basic information about his mother's work experience: where she worked, what kind of restaurants she worked in, whom she served. But even though Rose includes mostly objective information, he helps readers come to know his mother as a dedicated waitress and loving mother through both the many jobs she held and the one piece of dialogue in this excerpt: "Dad was ill, and you were little. . . . I *had* to get work."

· ·

Try Your Hand   Reflect on the working life of one of your family members. Compose a narrative of this life that focuses primarily on objective information about this person's career. Then create a second narrative that fleshes out this report, using telling details and descriptions. Compare these narratives, thinking specifically about the instances when one type of narrative might be more appropriate than the other.

· ·

A narrative can also provide powerful, convincing support for an argument. In a letter reprinted in the newspaper column "Dear Abby," one writer narrates a series of events that support her main point: people should pay attention to any symptoms of emotional distress in those who are close to them.

Narration to Provide Support for an Argument

Dear Abby,

    Two months ago my youngest sister called me — collect again — sobbing that she felt alone and frightened in the world. She asked if we could meet for tea or if I could visit her. As a mother of twins and self-employed, I reminded her that having tea in a cafe is a luxury I cannot afford.

Last month she called me again. She wanted to spend Saturday night with us and make a pancake breakfast "for old times' sake." She told me she missed me and felt blue. (Abby, Saturday nights are reserved for my husband.)

Two weeks ago, my sister invited me to a matinee — her treat. She tearfully informed me that she was not sleeping well (she was being treated for depression and chronic fatigue syndrome). I told her, "Working people don't go to matinees, but when you get your life together, you'll know what 'chronic-living-life-fatigue' is."

My little sister will never call again. She took her life last week.

My sister had some of the best medical help available, and I know she was ultimately responsible for her own life. But I also know that I'll never again brush her hair out of her sleepy blue eyes or trade my blouse for her mauve lipstick or tell her that she's not fat — she's beautiful.

Most of all, I will never forgive myself for not realizing how suicidal my sister was. Perhaps this letter will prevent others from making the mistakes I made.   — *Lesson Learned in the Worst of Ways*

This narrative could also support a broader argument: one person's illness, whether physical or mental, hurts more than just the patient. Narratives like this one appear in advice columns every day, with people using them to support a claim, a complaint, an assertion.

. . . .

Try Your Hand   Think of a lesson you've learned or an opinion you've developed as the result of a personal experience. Recall first the most memorable experiences of your life, remembering how you responded to them. Then choose and focus on a particular experience that led you to form one strong opinion. In a page or so, narrate your experience in a way that supports your opinion.

. . . .

A narrative can also provide examples to support or illustrate a generalization. In *Better Together: Restoring the American Community*, Robert Putnam and Lewis Feldstein study how people across the country are connecting with one another, creating community, and building relationships. In one of their chapters, Putnam and Feldstein focus on the online network Craigslist and make the general claim that Craigslist *creates* community, particularly in the city of San Francisco. To offer support for this generalization about Craigslist, Putnam and Feldstein tell the story of Katherine Rose.

Narration to Provide Examples of a Generalization

The high level of activity on the San Francisco site may be one factor arguing in favor of Craigslist as community or, at the very least, as deeply embedded in community. Craigslist has a presence in San Francisco. It has become a feature of the city's social landscape, something many people (especially but not exclusively those in their twenties and early thirties) use and discuss, something people who live there know about, part of the culture they share. The experience of one new user, Katherine Rose, shows how widely it is known and how closely it is identified with San Francisco. When Rose graduated from an East Coast university in the spring of 2002, she and some school friends decided to move to San Francisco. None of them had jobs lined up, but they trusted they would find work when they got there. Having grown up in the Boston area, Rose wanted the experience of living somewhere else.

She remembers, "As soon as I told people, 'I'm moving to San Francisco. I have to find an apartment,' they said, 'Have you looked on craigslist?' My mother's college roommate, who lives in Oakland, also suggested craigslist."

Once in San Francisco (she and her roommates rented a Russian Hill apartment they located through the site), Rose found that "everyone here says, 'Look at Craigslist' for jobs, for furniture, for whatever you need." Many Web sites that are familiar to Internet enthusiasts seem to be invisible or unknown to the culture at large. In San Francisco, craigslist is an exception.   — ROBERT PUTNAM and LEWIS FELDSTEIN, *Better Together: Restoring the American Community*

After using Rose's narrative to support their generalization about Craigslist, Putnam and Feldstein go on to investigate other ways in which Craigslist brings people together by connecting soccer players with soccer players, readers with readers, and theater lovers with theater lovers.

. . . .

Try Your Hand   Putnam and Feldstein focus on Craigslist and consider how this online site offers users a sense of community, but there are many other ideas about what the Internet is and what it does. While some people see it as driven by corporate interests and consumerism, others see it as a way to explore foreign worlds and cultures. Now it's your turn to enter this conversation. Create a general claim about the Internet, thinking specifically about how it functions and how it affects its users. Then compose a narrative that supports your generalization.

. . . .

Finally, a writer can use narrative writing simply to convey a mood or impression. For example, restaurant reviewers often take their readers through each step of their dining experience, from entering the restaurant to drinking an after-dinner coffee. Relating the experience in narrative form helps re-create the mood of the restaurant as wild and wacky, somber and formal, down-home and plentiful in its portions, or swanky and worth the expense. In the following restaurant review, Pittsburgh's *City Paper* food editors Angelique Bamberg and Jason Roth compose a narrative about their dining experience at Nicky's Thai Kitchen in Verona, Pennsylvania.

Narration to Convey a Mood or Impression

From the appetizer list, we chose steamed dumplings, which were *shumai*-style pouches, not pierogi-style half-moons, their delicate wrappers gathered at the tops like little drawstring purses. Within was a pork filling so moist and finely ground, it had almost the character of a paste. With an intensely gingery flavor, and a sauce that perfectly married sweet and sour, these were among the best Asian dumplings we recall tasting.

A generous portion of *tom yum* soup arrived next, steaming and aromatic in an appealing comma-shaped bowl. The plenteous chicken and mushrooms were tender, while the onion was still crunchy, and tomato added bright, fresh flavor to a hot — in both meanings of the word — broth that awakened the senses.

On one of — we hoped — the last nights of wintry weather this year, Angelique ordered *massaman* curry, a hearty, stick-to-your-ribs, stewlike dish of beef, peanuts and potatoes. Smooth and thickened with peanut butter, the broth was both sweet and savory, but with the intense flavors of a well-seasoned curry. The ingredients provided soft, chewy, and crunchy textures in every bite.

Chicken black came in a rum sauce, raising the question: Do they cook with alcohol in Thailand? If they don't, they should. Nicky's use of it transformed what looked like a generic Asian brown sauce into a sweet, richly flavored base for tender chicken, earthy shiitake slices, and handfuls of zingy ginger matchsticks.

Finally, we can never resist *pad Thai*. We were glad we didn't: Nicky's had such depth of that distinctive sweet-sour-salty pad Thai flavor that Jason thought it must be slathered in sauce. But an examination of the bottom of the bowl revealed nothing but well-coated noodles. The shrimp were beautifully cooked to their peak of fresh, briny flavor. The peanuts and bean sprouts grounded the dish and added crunch. And the noodles themselves (a bit narrower than usual) were tender without mushiness.

If we've overused the word "intense" in this review, please forgive us. It's the overwhelming impression that every dish at Nicky's gave: more flavor, and more flavors than we're used to, even at Thai restaurants that we love. And all this without overwhelming the native tastes of the fresh ingredients or creating clashing flavors. Verona, it turns out, is the next best thing to Thailand. And, happily, a heck of a lot closer for the return visits we're sure to make.

— Angelique Bamberg and Jason Roth, review of Nicky's Thai Kitchen

The mood that Bamberg and Roth create focuses on the mouthwatering details of their meal, and it's no surprise both reviewers ultimately give the restaurant four stars, their highest rating. From the steamed dumplings to the pad Thai, the sweet and savory flavors and interesting textures make the meal and the restaurant memorable and even remarkable, persuading any reader that a visit to Nicky's would be a real treat!

Try Your Hand   We've all experienced a memorable meal, and how we describe the meal and its events often creates a mood for readers or listeners, helping them understand if the meal was delicious or disgusting, the service impressive or disappointing, the company boring or fascinating. Take a few minutes to identify and then reflect on a memorable meal that you've had. Compose a narrative of this meal, making sure to convey the mood of the meal to your readers.

Narration can also be used to give directions for a process or to analyze a process that has already occurred. Chapter 7, Process Analysis, demonstrates a number of process-writing techniques, including those that incorporate narrative elements of chronology, characters, description, dialogue, and setting. And as you'll see as you work through the other chapters in the book, narration can be used with other methods as well — as part of an argument or writing that uses exemplification and especially as part of a cause-and-consequence analysis.

How Do You Use Narration in Academic Writing?

Narration functions as a key writing strategy in academic contexts. Like writers working in more "public" environments, students and professional scholars alike call on narration to report information, provide support for an argument, illustrate a generalization, or even convey a mood or impression. Academic contexts also offer opportunities for writers either to compose texts that rely primarily on narration or to combine this rhetorical method with other methods with the goal of crafting an effective writing project. For instance, in a history course, you might depend entirely on narration to tell the story of the battle at Gettysburg or to relay the events that led to Martin Luther King Jr.'s "I Have a Dream" speech. In a chemistry course, however, you may call on narration as a subordinate structuring device when you compose the "procedures" portion of a lab report.

David Wallace Adams, a scholar of Native American education, calls on narration when he examines the history of the Native American boarding school experience in *Education for Extinction: American Indians and the Boarding School Experience.* Throughout the text and in this particular example, he uses narration to enable readers to understand the troubling school experiences of Native students. Here he recounts Luther Standing Bear's experience in reading class.

Narration in Academic Writing

Luther Standing Bear would never forget the day his teacher decided to test her students' proficiency at reading by asking each student to stand and read a designated paragraph from the class text. "One after another the pupils read as called upon and each one in turn sat down bewildered and discouraged." When Standing Bear's turn came he read the paragraph thinking he had committed no errors. However, upon the teacher's question, Are you sure you made no errors? Standing Bear read it a second time. And then a third, a fourth, and fifth, each time receiving no affirmation from the teacher. What had begun as an unpleasant exercise was turning into sheer torture.

> Even for the sixth and seventh times I read. I began to tremble and I could not see my words plainly. I was terribly hurt and mystified. But for the eighth and ninth times I read. It was growing more terrible. Still the teacher gave no sign of approval, so I read for the tenth time! I started on the paragraph for the eleventh time, but before I was through, everything before me went black and I sat down thoroughly cowed and humiliated for the first time in my life and in front of the whole class!

At the weekly Saturday evening assembly, where Pratt regularly singled out individuals for praise or criticism, Standing Bear was certain the superintendent would humiliate him, but quite the opposite occurred. After speaking about the importance of having self-confidence, Pratt called attention to the fact that Luther Standing Bear had valiantly read a passage eleven times in succession without a single error.

— David Wallace Adams, *Education for Extinction: American Indians and the Boarding School Experience*

Standing Bear's educational experience does not stand alone in Adams's text. Adams repeatedly uses narration to offer readers countless examples of student educational experiences, ultimately persuading readers to see how deeply problematic the boarding school experiment was for Native students. Narration then functions as a vital rhetorical method throughout Adams's academically oriented writing.

As you progress through your academic career, it will be important for you to judge when and where to employ narration in your writing. Choosing the most effective rhetorical strategy for a particular writing situation is the mark of a sophisticated and adept writer and student. To know *when* to employ narration, pay close attention to the writing prompts provided by your instructor. If your English instructor asks you to reflect on a significant experience in your life, narration would be an appropriate choice for this writing assignment. If your history instructor asks you to set out the chain of events that led up to a significant moment in history, you would likely employ narration. And if your anthropology instructor asks you to engage in ethnographic work, studying an individual's or group's daily activities and ways of life, you might use narration to complete this project. Your job as a writer and a student, then, is to identify the rhetorical moments when narration is the most effective and appropriate choice to complete the task at hand.

. . . .

Analyzing Narration in Academic Writing   Take a moment to review three to four of your syllabi for your other classes, focusing particularly on moments when you are asked to respond to prompts with writing. When is narration an appropriate response? How do you know? When *isn't* narration an appropriate response? How do you know? Take notes of your findings and be prepared to share them with the class.

. . . .

How Do You Read a Narrative?

Knowing how to read narratives carefully and critically is the first step in learning how to write your own. When you take the time to read narratives in this way, you become more sensitive to the features that make them successful. Strong narratives are shaped by a sequence of events, events that usually involve people who speak. Therefore, an effective narrative needs to make the sequence of events clear and the characters and their dialogue interesting.

More specifically, though, you need to read a narrative with an eye to how well it fulfills its purpose (or multiple purposes): to report information, support an argument, provide an example, or set a mood. Remember, too, that how effective a narrative is may also depend to a large extent on who the intended readers are. As you read, then, you'll always want to keep in mind questions like the following: If the narrative is intended mainly to report information, is the information clear? Or is the sequence of events confusing or the amount of information too sketchy or too detailed to hold readers' interest? Will the intended readers feel that this narrative supports the writer's argument, or will many of them see it as weak or biased? Does the writer's language set the mood that he or she seems to intend? If so, how? If not, why not?

Look back at the "Dear Abby" letter (pp. 50–51). As you read the opening paragraph, see how it introduces the two main characters ("my youngest sister" and "me") and launches a sequence of events with "Two months ago." Notice that each of the next two paragraphs also begins with an expression of time that makes it easy to follow the progression of events in the narrative: "Last month" and "Two weeks ago." All three of these paragraphs are also structured the same way: the first sentence tells about the younger sister's call, the next sentence or two say how the younger sister wanted to get together, and the last sentence tells how the writer refused. With this parallel structure, the writer establishes a clear pattern of events that reveals the relationship between the sisters — the younger one depressed, lonely, frightened, apparently not working, and reaching out for contact, the older one a busy self–employed wife and mother who not only refuses the contact but admonishes her sister for seeking it. Then, abruptly, there is a much shorter paragraph with just two short sentences that bring the story to a tragic climax: "My little sister will never call again. She took her life last week." The rest of the narrative consists of the writer's reflections in the aftermath of this tragic sequence of events and a direct statement of her purpose and intended audience: "Perhaps this letter will prevent others from making the mistakes I made." While setting a mood of sadness and remorse, this narrative makes a powerful argument that repeated pleas for emotional support should not be dismissed, even by those who think they're just too busy with their own lives.

Most narratives you'll need to write won't be as dramatic or tragic as this one, and the events won't usually lend themselves to the kind of repeated paragraph structure that makes this narrative so compelling. Nor will you usually want or need to state your purpose and address your audience so directly. But even if you're writing a story that's intended to be funny or just informative, using clear time signals and shaping the narrative around a clear climax or turning point will help your readers follow the sequence of events and engage their interest. Notice also that the writer includes a couple of brief pieces of dialogue, one from each of the sisters, to help give the flavor of their relationship.

When reading any narrative, you'll also want to pay careful attention not only to what the characters say and do but also to what is unspoken and undone. What the author leaves out, in terms of actions and words, can be every bit as important as what is included. For instance, what role, if any, did their parents play in the sisters' lives? Had the sisters had this kind of relationship ever since childhood? When you consider both what is included and what is excluded, you'll get a clearer sense of the author's viewpoint. You'll begin to shape an opinion on what impression the author wants to make and whether that impression is balanced or deliberately slanted. As far as we know, the older sister's admonishments grew out of a frustration with (or maybe jealousy of) her younger sister's seemingly carefree life, so readers wonder about the source of the younger sister's chronic fatigue syndrome — as well as the reason it and the depression aren't mentioned until a parenthetical reference in the third paragraph. And although the writer acknowledges that she wasn't ultimately responsible for her sister's suicide, she seems to be portraying herself in the worst possible light. Is her remorse distorting her memory? Thinking about issues like these — how much your audience wants or needs to know, how much you want to reveal about yourself or other characters, and which details of the events will best serve your purpose — will help you as you consider what to include and what to leave out in your own narratives.

How Do You Write a Narrative?

Narratives can be the most absorbing and satisfying kind of writing to experience, whether they are read or watched on a screen, and writing them can be just as engaging. The key to writing an effective narrative can be expressed in one word: *choose.* When you are thinking about the incidents in a narrative, you'll no doubt come up with more ideas than you can use in the final draft. So as you decide on the story you want to tell — and why — you'll need to choose the most important details, characters, and dialogue and make certain that the setting and organizational pattern work to your best advantage. Whether you are writing a paragraph- or essay-length narrative, these suggestions will help you.

● Determining Your Purpose

The first step is to decide what your purpose is — not only whether you are trying to argue a point or create a mood, for example, but exactly what the point or mood is. Do you want your narrative to be the central focus of the piece of writing? If so, are you trying to explain how you came to know racism, sexism, or some other aspect of American culture? or how you realized that your parents were not perfect? or how your young son learned to keep trying despite initial failures? Alternatively, will the sequence of incidents support another type of writing? If, for example, your overall purpose is to support a thesis that your school's campus needs more parking facilities, you might weave in a short narrative that recounts a time when a classmate arrived on campus at 7:00 A.M. to find a parking spot before her 8:00 A.M. class and could not find even one empty space in the lot for her parking permit category. To make your argument effective, you would not rely just on this anecdote but would need to supply some statistical evidence as well.

African American writer bell hooks, for instance, opens one of her books with an incident, a short narrative, that illustrates how racism works and how strongly she feels about it.

> I am writing this essay sitting beside an anonymous white male that I long to murder. We have just been involved in an incident on an airplane where K, my friend and traveling companion, has been called to the front of the plane and publicly attacked by white female stewardesses who accuse her of trying to occupy a seat in first class that is not assigned to her. Although she had been assigned the seat, she was not given the appropriate boarding pass. When she tries to explain they ignore her. They keep explaining to her in loud voices as though she is a child, as though she is a foreigner who does not speak airline English, that she must take another seat. They do not want to know that the airline has made a mistake. They want only to ensure that the white male who has the appropriate boarding card will have a seat in first class. Realizing

our powerlessness to alter the moment we take our seats. K moves to coach. And I take my seat next to the anonymous white man who quickly apologizes to K as she moves her bag from the seat he has comfortably settled in. I stare him down with rage, tell him that I do not want to hear his liberal apologies, his repeated insistence that "it was not his fault." I am shouting at him that it is not a question of blame, that the mistake was understandable, but that the way K was treated was completely unacceptable, that it reflected both racism and sexism.

— BELL HOOKS, *Killing Rage: Ending Racism*

This short narrative pulls readers into hooks's text, providing an effective opening for a book on the prevalence of racism and the reasons it must be ended.

● Considering Your Audience

Closely tied to the purpose of your narrative is the audience for it. In fact, your audience is often the most important consideration in many of the decisions you make about your writing. Are you narrating the day's events for your private journal, writing an autobiographical sketch that some of your classmates will read, or recounting for your instructor a story about people neither of you know? Recognizing who the members of your audience are will help you calibrate the length of your narrative, decide on the amount of background detail you will provide or personal information you will disclose, and choose an effective organizational pattern.

If you're writing about the day's events in your private journal, you might include "insider information," emotional or personal details that will help you remember the events when you reread your entry at a later date. However, if you're writing for public consumption, you may need to include the kind of background information that you usually take for granted, and you may decide to do without details that you are uncomfortable revealing.

For example, consider the restaurant review from Pittsburgh's *City Paper*. Bamberg and Roth are writing to a local audience who could conceivably go to Nicky's for dinner. Their complete review is suited to this task. The review opens with directions for finding the restaurant, which is "located in a storefront just off the main drag of the little riverfront town of Verona." Referring to Nicky's as "much nicer than the stereotypical hole-in-the-wall," the reviewers continue with a narration of their meal and mention that they, along with their readers, will make many "return visits." If however, Bamberg and Roth were writing for a broader audience, such as readers of *Food and Wine* magazine, they might not include such specific information regarding the location of the restaurant or the great addition this restaurant is making to the Pittsburgh dining scene. For this more general audience, a restaurant reviewer might place the narrative in a different context: how Thai restaurants are growing in popularity across the country or what new trends are happening in Asian cooking.

● Establishing a Point of View

All good narratives offer readers a steady point of view. In hooks's excerpt, for instance, the use of consistent first-person pronouns (*I, we, me, my*) and present-tense verbs contributes to the viewpoint of an adult woman who is describing a disturbing altercation. When you write a narrative, you, too, will need a steady point of view. You might ask yourself the following questions: Who is telling my story? Is the telling consistent?

. . . .

Try Your Hand   Consider a disagreement with someone that you have had recently. Compose a narrative of the disagreement from your perspective. Then compose the same narrative from the perspective of the person with whom you disagreed. Try as hard as you can to treat that person's perspective in a fair and thoughtful way.

. . . .

● Using Dialogue

Most narratives include characters, and those characters often speak. Your initial draft might include an overly detailed (maybe even artificial) conversation. But as you compose and revise, you'll come to see the importance of keeping only necessary dialogue and nonverbal communication. In an excerpt from her book about working in low-wage jobs, Barbara Ehrenreich's use of dialogue reveals the concerns of her coworker Carlie, who is African American. This particular exchange gives insight into what Ehrenreich calls "all the little evidences of disrespect" that come Carlie's way, as well as the racial tensions at their workplace.

> We're eating our lunch side by side in the break room when a white guy in a maintenance uniform walks by and Carlie calls out, "Hey you," in a friendly way, "what's your name?"
> "Peter Pan," he says, his back already to us.
> "That wasn't funny," Carlie says, turning to me. "That was no kind of answer. Why did he have to be funny like that?" I venture that he has an attitude, and she nods as if that were an acute diagnosis. "Yeah he got an attitude all right."
> "Maybe he's having a bad day," I elaborate, not because I feel an obligation to defend the white race but because her face is so twisted with hurt.
> — BARBARA EHRENREICH, *Nickel and Dimed: On (Not) Getting By in America*

Whatever dialogue seems necessary to your narrative, make sure that it is accurate or, if you are relying on your memory or imagination, that it sounds authentic. Say the dialogue out loud to yourself to make sure that it sounds genuine.

● Organizing a Narrative

As with other types of writing, effective narratives have a purposeful pattern of organization. The organizational structure you choose for a narrative is directly related to your purpose and to the effect you want the story to create. Do you want to tell about a significant experience? a humorous one? Are you using your narrative to argue a thesis or to develop a mood? Regardless of the purpose, you should decide on an organizational pattern that will fulfill the purpose and help you make your point.

Virtually all narration follows a pattern of **chronological organization,** telling about events essentially in the order they happened and often building to a **climax** (the highest, or turning, point) that supports your assertion, "proves" your thesis, or establishes the mood you want to create. Within this basic framework, though, many variations are possible. Sometimes writers open a narrative by making an assertion and backing it up with a narrative example. Author Richard Wright does just that; he supports his assertion with a story that relates events from the beginning straight through to the end.

An Assertion Backed Up with a Narrative Example

My first lesson in how to live as a Negro came when I was quite small. We were living in Arkansas. Our house stood behind the railroad tracks. Its skimpy yard was paved with black cinders. Nothing green ever grew in that yard. The only touch of green we could see was far away, beyond the tracks, over where the white folks lived. But cinders were good enough for me and I never missed the green growing things. And anyhow cinders were fine weapons. You could always have a nice hot war with huge black cinders. All you had to do was crouch behind the brick pillars of a house with your hands full of gritty ammunition. And the first woolly black head you saw pop out from behind another row of pillars was your target. You tried your very best to knock it off. It was great fun.

I never fully realized the appalling disadvantages of a cinder environment till one day the gang to which I belonged found itself engaged in a war with the white boys who lived beyond the tracks. As usual we laid down our cinder barrage, thinking that this would wipe the white boys out. But they replied with a steady bombardment of broken bottles. We doubled our cinder barrage, but they hid behind trees, hedges, and the sloping embankments of their lawns. Having no such fortifications, we retreated to the brick pillars of our homes. During the retreat a broken milk bottle caught me behind the ear, opening a deep gash which bled profusely. The sight of blood pouring over my face completely demoralized our ranks. My fellow combatants left me standing paralyzed in the center of the yard, and scurried for their homes. A kind neighbor saw me and rushed me to a doctor, who took three stitches in my neck. . . .

From that time on, the charm of my cinder yard was gone. The green trees, the trimmed hedges, the cropped lawns grew very meaningful, became a symbol. Even today when I think of white folks, the hard, sharp outlines of white houses surrounded by trees, lawns, and hedges are present somewhere in the background of my mind. Through the years they grew into an overreaching symbol of fear.
—RICHARD WRIGHT, "The Ethics of Living Jim Crow"

Notice that Wright concludes with a restatement of his initial assertion. Ending with a restatement or not stating the assertion until the end are two common patterns in narration.

In other cases, instead of using a strictly chronological order, you might want to open or interrupt your narrative with a **flashback,** a glimpse of the past that illuminates the present. In her profile of Olympic swimmer Michael Phelps, Susan Casey investigates how Phelps has become such a successful athlete. In the opening pages of her *Sports Illustrated* article, she uses flashback to narrate a swim meet in which Phelps competed in early 2008. Notice how the present–tense verbs put readers in this moment, almost as if they are seeing Phelps swim this event.

Phelps shrugs off his black North Face puffa; removes the hip-hop mainline from his ears. This is a short-course meet, and the pool is only 25 yards long rather than the Olympic size of 50 meters. Short course is intimate and showy; long course is imposing and grand — the traditional distance of world records. As the fastest qualifier, Phelps is introduced last, and as he steps onto the block he snaps his arms across his chest three times, a prerace ritual. Even though he's sporting a new Fu Manchu mustache, the scene is very familiar.   — SUSAN CASEY, "8 the Quest"

Casey concludes her article with a **flashforward,** propelling readers to the 2008 Olympics and Phelps's entrance onto the starting blocks.

Eight years ago Phelps dived into the water for his first Olympic race. Since then he has had eight years of training, eight years of planning, eight years of waiting. Eight years to grow in every conceivable way. And though no one can be sure what will happen, we know this: Come 8/8/08 Michael Phelps will be more ready than he has ever been. The next day, when the swimming begins, he will walk to his block and wipe it with his towel. He'll be listening to hip-hop, and then he will stop. He'll snap his arms three times, and his mind will slip into that instant, and everything else will fall away. And as he stands on the block he'll glance at that cross on the bottom of the pool, and it will look oddly pristine to him, as though he's never seen it before. He'll step forward. He'll reach down. And then he will go.

Although we now know that Phelps did indeed achieve his goal, winning eight gold medals and becoming the most decorated Olympic athlete of all time, at the time this article was published, Casey's use of

flashforward positioned readers at the edge of their seats, anxiously waiting to see how fast Phelps will go.

Whether you start at the beginning of your narrative or use flashback
or flashforward, make sure that your organizational pattern contributes
to the purpose of your narrative (to report information, support an argument, provide an example, or set a mood). As you lead readers through
your narrative, you can help them by using **transitions,** words or phrases
that guide readers clearly from one incident to the next. Words such as
first, then, afterward, when, second, finally, and *before* and phrases such as *the next
day, in the years to follow,* and *in time* all help your readers move through the
story without becoming confused. In his 2007 article on the relationship
between food and health, Michael Pollan relies on transitions to recount
how scientific understandings have changed over the years:

> Last winter came the news that a low-fat diet, long believed to protect
> against breast cancer, may do no such thing — this from the monumental,
> federally financed Women's Health Initiative, which has also found no
> link between a low-fat diet and rates of coronary disease. The year be-
> fore we learned that dietary fiber might not, as we had been confidently
> told, help prevent colon cancer. Just last fall two prestigious studies on
> omega-3 fats published at the same time presented us with strikingly dif-
> ferent conclusions. While the Institute of Medicine stated that "it is uncer-
> tain how much these omega-3s contribute to improving health" (and they
> might do the opposite if you get them from mercury-contaminated fish),
> a Harvard study declared that simply by eating a couple of servings of
> fish each week (or by downing enough fish oil), you could cut your risk
> of dying from a heart attack by more than a third — a stunningly hope-
> ful piece of news. It's no wonder that omega-3 fatty acids are poised to
> become the oat bran of 2007, as food scientists micro-encapsulate fish
> oil and algae oil and blast them into such formerly all-terrestrial foods as
> bread and tortillas, milk and yogurt and cheese, all of which will soon,
> you can be sure, sprout fishy new health claims. (Remember the rule?)
> — MICHAEL POLLAN, "Unhappy Meals"

Pollan's transitional phrases (*Last winter, The year before, Just last fall*) make
it easy for readers to see how confusing (and frustrating) it can be for
people to make healthful dietary choices.

As you tell your story, choose the appropriate verb tense along with
transitions to help readers understand where you are in the narrative and
where you're going. In the preceding excerpt about diet and health, Pollan
primarily uses the simple past tense (*came, learned, published, presented, declared*)
to indicate actions that happened in the past. Compare Pollan's use of the
simple past tense with bell hooks's use of a wide variety of verb forms in
her narrative. For example, she uses three different present tense forms to
describe a series of events: present progressive tense (*am writing*) to indicate
what she is doing at that moment; simple present tense (*long, accuse*) to describe a current event; and present perfect tense (*have been involved, has been
called*) to call attention to something that began in the past but is ongoing.

"Reading" and Using Visuals in Narrative

Many narratives use visuals. If you consider the "before" and "after" photographs in ads for any hair–growth, muscle–building, or weight-loss product, you'll see how just two pictures can tell a story. Greeting cards often carry drawings or cartoons that narrate how two people met, why they fell in love, why they miss each other, and so on. All these kinds of images can enhance your written narratives as well. Bar graphs or line graphs can also support a narrative by tracing the history or the projected future of statistical trends. Even if a visual doesn't help explain your information or support your argument, it can help create a mood.

Evolution.

If you want to use visuals in writing an academic assignment, it is a good idea to check with your instructor beforehand. You also need to consider whether to include labels or captions (if the visuals do not already include them) and whether to refer to the visuals in your written text or let them stand on their own.

As with words, you want to choose visuals for your narratives carefully so that they help you achieve your purpose and appeal to your readers rather than distracting, boring, or confusing them. To succeed in these goals, you need to learn how to "read" visuals critically in the same way you do written narratives. For example, the series of drawings captioned "Evolution" accompanied an advertisement for the Alexander Technique, a unique form of physical reeducation widely used in music and drama schools to improve

Understanding and Using Narration

Analyzing Narratives

1. Reread the "Dear Abby" letter on pages 50–51. **Working with two or three classmates,** jot down the incidents that support the writer's thesis. Discuss whether the same story could support any other thesis, and prepare a brief presentation for the rest of the class.

the way a person uses his or her body. Proponents of the Alexander Technique argue that humans start out in life with naturally good posture, but the way we study, read, work on a computer, and play sports damages our posture so that we simply forget the best ways to stand, sit, and walk. The Alexander Technique is designed to reteach us these skills.

The visual tells this story as it fulfills its purposes of providing information (how and why posture declines) and making an argument (the Alexander Technique will improve posture). The narrative spans millions of years, as you can see, from the earliest *Pliopithecus* and *Ramapithecus* to the upright Cro-Magnon (a spear-carrying hunter with good posture) to the modern man, whose posture is damaged first by agricultural work, then by industrial work, and finally by bending over a computer. The silent characters in this visual narrative of human evolution convey the effects of tools on posture—in chronological order.

Notice how this visual implies that with each advance in technology or "civilization" beyond the hunting stage, humans have regressed further back toward the condition of chimpanzees, an unflattering comparison that presumably might encourage some readers to raise their eyes from the magazine (or the computer screen) and take a critical look at their own posture. The balanced structure of the series of drawings, gradually rising to a high point in the middle and then descending again, also creates a visually pleasing shape that draws the viewer's eye. (The shape of the chimpanzee at the beginning is even balanced by the shape of the computer user at the end.) But the visual itself does not argue that the Alexander Technique will improve posture, and there's always the possibility that some readers who don't believe in evolution might even be put off by it. Whenever you look at a visual that seems intended as a narrative — and especially if you're thinking of using it as part of a written narrative — carefully consider its details, the overall effect the details create, and how well this effect achieves a particular purpose for the intended audience.

2. Review the use of dialogue in the excerpt by Putnam and Feldstein on pages 51–52. What is the purpose of this dialogue? How does it support or detract from the authors' purpose?

3. Reread Mike Rose's narrative (p. 50), focusing on his choice of transitions. What transitions does he use? How do these transitions help to move the narrative along?

4. **Working with two or three classmates,** return to the Rose excerpt in which Rose offers a basic chronological narrative of his mother's working life. Pinpoint places where Rose might have elaborated on her life and career. What does Rose leave unmentioned? Why does Rose choose *not* to include certain facts about his mother and her work? How do these choices affect the narrative?

5. Return to your draft about the lesson you learned as a result of a memorable personal experience (p. 51). Number the events in your narrative; underline the characters and description; mark any dialogue. Then consider the purpose of the assignment, and decide whether these narrative elements in your draft help fulfill that purpose.

Planning and Writing Narratives

1. Reread the excerpt from Richard Wright's "The Ethics of Living Jim Crow" on pages 61–62 to remind yourself how a chronological pattern of organization can work. Then write out, in order, a list of everything that has happened in your composition class so far today. Who spoke? Who read? Who wrote? How much did each person do? to what overall effect? How might the information you've gathered be shaped into a narrative? **Trade your information with a classmate,** and discuss the ways each of your lists might become a narrative.

2. Complete and respond to this sentence: "The first day of college is _____." (You could choose to focus on the first day of orientation, of registration for classes, or of classes themselves.) You might write about the first day being scary, exhausting, or confusing — or exciting, surprising, or exhilarating. Choose *one* descriptive term to set the mood, and begin writing down ideas, incidents, characters, snippets of dialogue — whatever you remember from your first day that might be useful in a narrative essay. **Share your list with two or three classmates,** noting any ideas they give you that might work successfully in your essay. Working as a group, revise the thesis (controlling idea) for each group member's essay.

3. Look over your notes for the preceding question, and delete any details, characters, or dialogue that won't help develop the thesis statement by creating a particular mood. Referring to these notes and the following guidelines for checking over narrative writing, draft a two- to three-page narrative essay that supports your thesis statement about the first day of school.

4. How do you identify yourself? When you think about who you are, do you think of your age, sex, ethnicity, race, or class? your religion, occupation, or hometown? something else? Choose one of these aspects of yourself that you remember becoming conscious of at a specific time. Draft a two- to three-page narrative essay about this point in your life and the ways you've lived since then that confirm or enhance this identity. Revise your draft, using the following guidelines for checking over narrative writing.

5. Draft a three- to four-page retrospective account of your college life. From your imagined point of view on graduation day, describe your

college years in the way you hope they turn out and will be regarded by others. If you prefer, write in the third person. What will have been the purpose of your education? What will have been your most important struggles and successes? Who will be the major characters? As you write, remember to consult the following guidelines for checking over narrative writing.

✔ Checking Over Narrative Writing

1. What is the main purpose of your narrative? Are you aiming just to record an informative sequence of incidents, or is your purpose to support a thesis, provide an example, or create a mood? How well have you achieved that purpose?

2. What is the thesis of your narrative? Is it stated or implied? Does anything in the narrative distract from or contradict the thesis?

3. Who is the audience for this narrative? What limitations or responsibilities do the audience members place on you? Have you provided any background information they need? more than they need? Have you revealed personal information you might have preferred to keep to yourself?

4. What order are you using for the incidents in your narrative? Are you using chronological order? Number the incidents in your narrative *in the order they occurred*. Now use letters to indicate the order in which you have written about these incidents. Have you used flashback or flashforward? If so, is the technique effective? Might your readers be confused by it?

5. Have you used verb tenses correctly? Underline all the verbs and verb phrases. Do you use the present tense for incidents that are happening now? past or present perfect tense for incidents that happened in the past? and past perfect tense to indicate incidents that occurred before other events in the past?

6. Draw a circle around all the transitional words and phrases. Now read through your narrative. Are there other places where transitions would help your readers follow it more easily?

7. Do you use dialogue in your narrative? If so, does it help achieve your overall purpose?

8. If you're using visuals, do they help fulfill your overall purpose? Do you need to add labels, captions, or references in the written text?

READINGS

MALCOLM X
Prison Studies

Born Malcolm Little in Omaha, Nebraska, Malcolm X (1925–1965) is best known as a black militant leader who articulated concepts of race pride and black nationalism. As a child, he and his family faced racism on a daily basis, including having their house burned down by the Ku Klux Klan; his father's murder and his mother's confinement in a mental institution further disrupted his childhood. In 1946, Malcolm was imprisoned on burglary charges, and it was there — in prison — that his life changed for the better. He learned to read fluently and converted to the Nation of Islam, a faith that professes the superiority of black people. Eventually, after a visit to Africa, he separated himself from the Nation of Islam and abandoned his antiwhite stance, but shortly thereafter, on February 21, 1965, he was assassinated. Three members of the Nation of Islam were convicted of the crime, although controversy over the verdict continues. The following essay is from *The Autobiography of Malcolm X* (1964), which Malcolm wrote in collaboration with Alex Haley.

> **Preview**   As you read, consider how Malcolm X's narrative functions to support a particular argument. What argument is Malcolm X making through this narrative?

Many who today hear me somewhere in person, 1 or on television, or those who read something I've said, will think I went to school far beyond the eighth grade. This impression is due entirely to my prison studies.

Malcolm X uses a flash-back to return to the moment when his prison studies began.

It had really begun back in the Charlestown 2 Prison, when Bimbi first made me feel envy of his stock of knowledge. Bimbi had always taken charge of any conversation he was in, and I had tried to emulate him. But every book I picked up had few sentences which didn't contain anywhere from one to nearly all of the words that might as well have been in Chinese. When I just skipped those words, of course, I really ended up with little idea of what the book said. So I had come to the Norfolk Prison Colony still going through only book-reading motions. Pretty soon, I would have quit even these motions, unless I had received the motivation that I did.

In this paragraph, he establishes a consistent point of view with first-person pronouns.

3   I saw that the best thing I could do was get hold of a dictionary — to study, to learn some words. I was lucky enough to reason also that I should try to improve my penmanship. It was sad. I couldn't even write in a straight line. It was both ideas together that moved me to request a dictionary along with some tablets and pencils from the Norfolk Prison Colony school.

4   I spent two days just riffling uncertainly through the dictionary's pages. I'd never realized so many words existed! I didn't know which words I needed to learn. Finally, to start some kind of action, I began copying.

5   In my slow, painstaking, ragged handwriting, I copied into my tablet everything printed on that first page, down to the punctuation marks.

6   I believe it took me a day. Then, aloud, I read back, to myself, everything I'd written on the tablet. Over and over, aloud to myself, I read my own handwriting.

Malcolm X offers a dramatic climax: he begins to read his own writing, and his prison studies have begun in earnest.

7   I woke up the next morning, thinking about those words — immensely proud to realize that not only had I written so much at one time, but I'd written words that I never knew were in the world. Moreover, with a little effort, I also could remember what many of these words meant. I reviewed the words whose meanings I didn't remember. Funny thing, from the dictionary first page right now, that "aardvark" springs to my mind. The dictionary had a picture of it, a long-tailed, long-eared, burrowing African mammal, which lives off termites caught by sticking out its tongue as an anteater does for ants.

Consider the chronological sequence of events that he creates in this paragraph and the next one.

8   I was so fascinated that I went on — I copied the dictionary's next page. And the same experience came when I studied that. With every succeeding page, I also learned of people and places and

events from history. Actually the dictionary is like a miniature encyclopedia. Finally the dictionary's A section had filled a whole tablet — and I went on into the B's. That was the way I started copying what eventually became the entire dictionary. It went a lot faster after so much practice helped me to pick up handwriting speed. Between what I wrote in my tablet, and writing letters, during the rest of my time in prison I would guess I wrote a million words.

I suppose it was inevitable that as my word- 9
base broadened, I could for the first time pick up a book and read and now begin to understand what the book was saying. Anyone who has read a great deal can imagine the new world that opened. Let me tell you something: from then until I left the prison, in every free moment I had, if I was not reading in the library, I was reading on my bunk. You

Malcolm X during a Nation of Islam rally in New York City in 1963.

couldn't have gotten me out of books with a wedge. Between Mr. Muhammad's teachings, my correspondence, my visitors — usually Ella and Reginald — and my reading of books, months passed without my even thinking about being imprisoned. In fact, up to then, I never had been so truly free in my life.

10   As you can imagine, especially in a prison where there was heavy emphasis on rehabilitation, an inmate was smiled upon if he demonstrated an unusually intense interest in books. There was a sizable number of well-read inmates, especially the popular debaters. Some were said by many to be practically walking encyclopedias. They were almost celebrities. No university would ask any student to devour literature as I did when this new world opened to me, of being able to read and understand.

Malcolm X speaks directly to his audience here.

11   I read more in my room than in the library itself. An inmate who was known to read a lot could check out more than the permitted maximum number of books. I preferred reading in the total isolation of my own room.

12   When I had progressed to really serious reading, every night at about ten P.M. I would be outraged with the "lights out." It always seemed to catch me right in the middle of something engrossing.

13   Fortunately, right outside my door was a corridor light that cast a glow into my room. The glow was enough to read by, once my eyes adjusted to it. So when "lights out" came, I would sit on the floor where I could continue reading in that glow.

14   At one-hour intervals the night guards paced past every room. Each time I heard the approaching footsteps, I jumped into bed and feigned sleep. And as soon as the guard passed, I got back out of bed onto the floor area of that light-glow, where I would read for another fifty-eight minutes — until the guard approached again. That went on until three or four every morning. Three or four hours of sleep a night was enough for me. Often in the years in the streets I had slept less than that.

He includes another event that extends and deepens readers' understanding of his literacy development.

15   I have often reflected upon the new vistas that reading opened to me. I knew right there in prison that reading had changed forever the course of my

He returns to the present moment and reflects on his prison studies.

life. As I see it today, the ability to read awoke inside me some long dormant craving to be mentally alive. I certainly wasn't seeking any degree, the way a college confers a status symbol upon its students. My homemade education gave me, with every additional book that I read, a little bit more sensitivity to the deafness, dumbness, and blindness that was afflicting the black race in America. Not long ago, an English writer telephoned me from London, asking questions. One was, "What's your alma mater?" I told him, "Books." You will never catch me with a free fifteen minutes in which I'm not studying something I feel might be able to help the black man.

Other than "lights out," this is the only use of dialogue in the essay. Consider its importance.

Every time I catch a plane, I have with me a   16
book that I want to read — and that's a lot of books these days. If I weren't out here every day battling the white man, I could spend the rest of my life reading, just satisfying my curiosity — because you can hardly mention anything I'm not curious about. I don't think anybody ever got more out of going to prison than I did. In fact, prison enabled me to study far more intensively than I would have if my life had gone differently and I had attended some college. I imagine that one of the biggest troubles with colleges is there are too many distractions, too much panty-raiding, fraternities, and boola-boola and all of that. Where else but in prison could I have attacked my ignorance by being able to study intensely sometimes as much as fifteen hours a day?

Reading Closely

1. **With three or four classmates,** discuss what you learned about life in prison and the opportunities for reading there that you didn't know before you read this narrative. What surprised you the most? What pleased you the most? Prepare a group response to share with the rest of the class.

2. What is this narrative about? In no more than two paragraphs, retell Malcolm X's narrative. Then condense your paragraphs to one, leaving in only the crucial information.

3. What specific details does the visual offer? How do those details enhance the essay?

Considering Larger Issues

1. Early on, Malcolm X tells his readers that his skill at using language gives a mistaken impression of his formal education. Who is his audience for this remark? For whom does this narrative seem to be written? What might be his purpose in referring to the gap between his use of language and his formal education?

2. What is the overall purpose of this narrative? How is that purpose related to the audience?

3. Who are the characters in this narrative? How are they portrayed, and to what effect? How does their dialogue support Malcolm X's overall purpose?

4. What is the thesis of this narrative? Write it out in one sentence. Now, **work with three or four classmates** to share your sentences and come to a group decision on the thesis. Write out your group's decision as well as the incidents and descriptions that help to support or illustrate that thesis. Be prepared to share your ideas with the rest of the class.

5. COMBINING METHODS. Malcolm X's story about prison life is a powerful literacy narrative. But it's also an analysis of *causes and effects*. Mark the passages that analyze causes and consequences, and explain how these passages help fulfill the overall purpose of the narrative. Be prepared to share your ideas with the rest of the class.

Thinking about Language

1. Define the following words or phrases, either by using the essay context (numbers in parentheses refer to paragraphs in the essay) or by turning to your dictionary. Be prepared to share your answers with the rest of the class.

   emulate (2)   rehabilitation (10)   feigned (14)
   riffling (4)   engrossing (12)   dormant (15)
   burrowing (7)   corridor (13)

2. How many paragraphs does Malcolm X use in this essay? How many sentences are in each paragraph? How many words are in each paragraph? in each sentence? What are the averages? Paragraph length and sentence length are two ways an author establishes his or her own style. What do these averages tell you about Malcolm X's writing style? What is the effect on the reader?

Writing Your Own Narratives

1. Malcolm X's quest for greater literacy is one that all college students embark upon, if not to the same degree. Think about what you hope to gain from your undergraduate education. Make notes about the series of steps that lie ahead of you. What would you sacrifice, or what might you be sacrificing, for this education? In an essay of three to four pages, write a

narrative that recounts your gains as well as any losses (such as losing touch with certain friends or family) as you became an educated American. Refer to "Checking Over Narrative Writing" on page 67.

2. Draft a three- to four-page narrative that traces the educational progress — or lack thereof — of one of your parents. Determine a specific purpose for your narrative early on. Then develop a thesis statement that grows out of that purpose, making sure that each incident in the narrative supports the thesis. Consider what your parent gained — and lost — in the process. You may want to invent some dialogue and include a visual or two as a way to make your essay come alive. Be sure to refer to the guidelines for checking over narrative writing on page 67.

SAM LEGER
Moving On

● Sam Leger (b. 1990) wrote this essay for his first-year writing class at the University of New Hampshire. He plans to combine his business major with pre-med classes with the goal of attending medical school and focusing on osteopathic medicine. In the essay, Leger reflects on a particularly memorable summer day that prompted him to begin setting the course for his future.

Preview   Given the title, what do you imagine to be the topic for this narrative essay?

Twelve thirty in the afternoon. I awoke to the familiar sound of the ga- 1 rage door slamming shut. My bedroom was just as I like it. Not a quiver of light penetrated the wall of quilts I rigged to overlap the curtains. The fan was spinning at full tilt, mixing the stale, humid air just enough to keep me from waking up in a soggy mess of sweat. Shoes, pants, and all species of miscellany littered the barely visible shag carpet. As I kicked the sheets off my bed and stumbled to the door, I paused to reflect on how utterly mundane the summer was turning out to be. With a sigh, I blinked sleep out of my eyes and proceeded to pour a bowl of Reese's Puffs, pop in three waffles, and begin cracking the eggs for what was soon to be a delicious omelette.

My kitchen can be a lonely place when there's no one else in the 2 house. Red walls, concept art, and wine bottles neatly decorate the space, décor that seems to invite rich laughter and intelligent conversation. But that day there was neither laughter nor conversation. Just a lonely, chubby twelve-year-old making a breakfast far too large for a single person. As I sat down to enjoy my meal, the phone rang. My heart raced with the thought of the potential social interaction on the other end of the line. My dash to the phone was perhaps the fastest I'd moved in weeks.

"Hello," I panted in a charming middle-of-puberty voice. 3

"Hey, Sam," said my friend Alex with stifled excitement in his voice. 4 "You wanna do something?" The conversation entailed at least ten more minutes of the "I don't know, what do you want to do?" exchange and eventually tapered to an end with a resolution to meet at the nearby Beaver Pond on our bikes.

Ah, sweet victory! Social interaction at long last! Leaving the house 5 in partial wreckage, I trotted to the garage, flipped up the kickstand, and sped off down the street. It was a postcard kind of a day outside. The mechanical drone of lawn mowers and the rhythmic spitting of sprinkler systems came together to create an orchestra that provided the soundtrack for what was going to be an epic bicycle adventure. As I passed the fields and the farms of South Hooksett, a gentle breeze carried the smell of a neighbor's barbecue and the sounds of kids splashing in a nearby pool.

I arrived at the pond. Out of breath from my quarter-mile bike ride, 6 I sat on a rock and surveyed my domain. Swiveling my head in the summer heat, my vision halted on a foreboding sign across the street that read: PRIVATE ROAD, NO TRESPASSING. A well-known topic of neighborhood lore, this driveway belonged to an old recluse.

The man's private property was the last unexplored area of land in 7 my town. With this sole exception, I have literally seen and experienced every last foot of woods and road on my side of the Merrimack River. There was some tension between the sign and me. I felt as though it was the only thing standing between me and the closure of solving whatever great mystery was beyond that man's driveway. Despite the sign's warning, I couldn't help but consider disobeying it. I had to disobey it.

My thoughts were interrupted by Alex and our friend Mike skid- 8 ding to a halt on the Beaver Pond gravel. Mike came decked out in his usual assortment of expensive-looking Fox Racing gear. This detail would have gone unnoticed except for two things. One, Mike was not, is not, and barring any direct miracle, will never be a motocross racer. And two, Mike wore this outfit almost every time we rode bikes, which, bear in mind, were bicycles, not dirt bikes. Alex was the lucky one among the trio. Unlike poor Mike and me, he didn't inherit the fat-kid gene and endeavored to prove his superior athleticism and bravery at every possible juncture. His bike was like a slow, exhausted mule, hee-hawing at every turn and generally unreliable due to a lack of maintenance. He had one of those mop-top haircuts that he violently head-twitched and brushed away every time it obstructed his vision, which was every thirty seconds or so. I was shocked that he hadn't given himself whiplash yet.

"Hey, Sam," they said in chorus. 9

"So what do you want to do now?" Mike asked between deep gulps 10 from his Camel Pack. I nodded, Clint Eastwood style, toward the sign. It took only seconds for Alex to tear over to the head of the driveway, ready to break the law. Reluctantly, I followed him, leaving Mike to fret alone about what a terrible idea this was. "Guys, we can't go down there, that's someone's *private property*. It says 'no trespassing' right on the sign." Fully understanding that Mike was about to launch into some far-fetched story about how his uncle or cousin got the electric chair for doing something like this a few years ago, Alex and I thought fast.

"What do you say we just go and have a look around?" Alex 11 whispered.

"Good idea. Then we won't have to listen to this kid blabber on," 12 I said with bravado, whereupon we raced down the driveway, leaving Mike to continue his speech alone.

The farther we went down the long, winding driveway, the colder 13 and darker it got as the woods thickened around us. Occasionally, the

sun managed to poke through the dense canopy. During one such instance, I chanced a look back and was relieved to see a panicking Mike
ripping down the driveway at ramming speed. When I turned my head
back around, I saw it.

Towering before us was the dilapidated edifice that was home to the   14
old man. All it needed was some rolling fog and perhaps the far-off cry
of a pack of wolves, and I could easily have found myself in your run-of-
the-mill horror film. We were all speechless, except for Mike, who continued to give voice to the imminent doom that awaited us. Frantically,
we backed away, keeping our eyes fixed on the house as if it were a rabid
dog. "Um . . . it kind of looks like no one's home." Alex said quickly and
quietly. I'll never remember whose idea it was to keep looking around,
but I'm almost certain it wasn't Mike's. As we rounded the back of the
house, we were all drawn to a particularly sparse corner of woods at the
edge of the backyard.

"It looks like an ATV trail," Alex said. "You go first, Mike."   15

"Don't even joke, Alex! I've got to go back anyway, to my house, be- 16
cause . . . my mom said I have to be home by two o'clock."

"No way," Alex rebutted. "We only left at one thirty."   17

"Both of you shut up. I'll go first." As soon as those words left my   18
mouth, I regretted having uttered them. I did not want to be the fearless
leader of our illegal expedition. But peer pressure does strange things to
people, so in I went, Mike and Alex seemingly attached to my hip. We
sped down the narrow path. To our left stood hundreds of grimacing
trees. To our right lay an immense bog that stretched to the edge of our
vision. There was an eerie silence on the trail, broken only by the occasional bellow of a bullfrog and the grinding of our tires against the cold
earth. The path ahead was dark.

After we crossed a brook bridged primitively by a couple of decrepit, 19
nail-ridden two-by-fours, we ascended a steep hill toward what appeared
to be an opening in the woods.

"Guys, guys, I've got . . . to . . . to walk. I can't . . . can't do this . . . this 20
hill anymore," Mike gasped.

"OK, you . . . you win, Mike," I gasped in agreement.   21

"You guys suck," laughed Alex, bounding with his usual limitless en- 22
ergy. As Alex rolled farther up the hill, he froze in place, eyes hooked on
something out of our view.

Tall grass gave way to a rust-eaten wrought-iron fence, forever guard- 23
ing some ten or twenty ancient-looking gravestones. The once-elegant
angels that adorned them were beaten down by the elements to faded
stubs. Down a small embankment beside the cemetery sat an abandoned
trailer. Its door was half open, moving slightly in the gentle breeze. Broken glass, tire rims, and empty propane tanks were scattered among the
leaves. I couldn't see inside the trailer, nor did I want to, but in the presence of my friends, I had a stubborn and unshakable mask of confidence.

I flipped the kickstand on my bike and crept stealthily closer, once 24
again picturing every horror movie I had ever seen in the back of my
mind. I was that unassuming main character who was about to open
a door that was better off closed. Wind rustled the tall grass about my
ankles. I picked up a stick and pried the heavy door open. The trailer
released a pungent, musty odor. It was dark inside. As my eyes adjusted
to the dim light, I could make out tattered orange curtains dotted with
faded yellow flowers that hung over the windows. There was a fold-out
table in the back covered with closed boxes and bowling trophies. Outdated clothing was piled on what was left of the original vinyl seats. The
sides from what had been a row of cabinets were suspended from the
ceiling, which, itself was in bad shape, dotted frequently by large, brown
water stains. The trailer gave off a creepy vibe, but honestly, it was not
all that bad. The creepiness was complemented nicely by a broken-faced
porcelain doll that sat in the corner next to a lone bowling trophy. The
moment I laid eyes on the doll, I backed up, left the trailer, and was back
on my bike, still pretending to be perfectly calm.

After Alex had satiated his curiosity about the trailer, we continued 25
on. The remaining mile of our journey was a blur to me. Perhaps because
I was pumping like Lance Armstrong—all I could think about was that
doll, staring at me from the corner with half a face.

After saying goodbye to Alex and Mike, I pedaled home with an air 26
of triumph about me. If I did nothing else for the next month or so, the
summer still would've been a victory.

I got ready for bed that night half expecting the bones of whoever 27
was buried in the graveyard in the woods to be waiting in my closet for
the cover of darkness. It had been a long day, certainly the most stimulating of that summer and of many summers to come. Hooksett has
produced some good, solid memories, most of them slightly fuzzy and
possibly embellished but still good. I was expecting to toss and turn long
into the night, harassed by the thoughts of what I had seen down that
private road before drifting into an uneasy sleep hours later. But as I
hopped into bed, I felt an overwhelming sense of calm.

That man's private road truly was the last part of the neighborhood 28
where I hadn't set foot. I had officially seen and done everything. There
was nothing left to fear, nothing left to be anxious about, nothing left
to question. I had seen everything Hooksett had to offer. It was time for
change, but how? In the next couple of minutes before I fell asleep, I gave
thought to ideas that had never crossed my mind. Which high school
would I go to? College? What will I do for a car? Why does my mom still
make my bed? And so on.

It was at this pivotal time of reflection that I began taking a bit more 29
initiative. After leaving the bike adventures and dependency that ruled
my twelve years of life behind, it was finally time to move on.

Reading Closely

1. Name the characters in this essay, and list their characteristics, using textual evidence to support your answer.
2. What do you think the author's purpose is in writing this essay? What textual evidence can you use to support your answer?
3. What is the point of view in this essay? Which specific passages support your answer? If the story were told from a third-person point of view, what additional information might you expect? What if it were told from Mike's point of view?
4. Examine the dialogue in this essay. Why do you suppose Leger uses dialogue when he does? What is the effect of this dialogue on you, the reader?
5. Sketch a quick outline of this essay. Does your outline reveal any specific organizational strategy on the part of the author? If so, what is that strategy, and how does it support the purpose of the essay?

Considering Larger Issues

1. The preview question asked you to anticipate why the essay was called "Moving On." After reading the essay, why do you think the writer chose this title?
2. What part of the narration did you find particularly compelling? Why? What made this passage significant to you?
3. **Working with a classmate,** identify the climax or turning point of this essay. Why do you consider this point the climax?
4. COMBINING METHODS. Along with narration, Leger also depends on *description* to achieve his purpose. Identify the passages where he uses description. How does this rhetorical method work together with his use of narration?

Thinking about Language

1. Define the following words or phrases, either by using the essay context or by turning to your dictionary. Be prepared to share your answers with the rest of the class.

miscellany (1)	foreboding (6)	grimacing (18)
mundane (1)	juncture (8)	embankment (23)
concept art (2)	bravado (12)	stealthily (24)
drone (5)	canopy (13)	satiated (25)
epic (5)	edifice (14)	embellished (27)

2. Identify the transition words or phrases that Leger uses. How do these elements help move readers from one moment to the next?

Writing Your Own Narratives

1. Leger's essay is about moving from one part of his life to the next. At the end of the essay, we learn that Leger realizes the need to "move on" to other things. Identify a time in your life when you realized you needed to "move on," and write a three- to four-page narrative essay that reflects on this moment. Be sure to include relevant characters and dialogue as well as detailed description to create an effective and compelling narrative. As you draft and revise, refer to the guidelines for checking over narrative writing on page 67.

2. Leger's narrative includes elements of adventure. Reflect on a time in your life when you went on an adventure. Then compose a three- to four-page essay in which you tell the story of this adventure, using the various elements of narration (setting, dialogue, characters, transitions, and so on). As you develop your narrative, identify the climax or turning point in the story. Also consider the most effective point of view for your essay and the telling details that will bring your story to life. Refer to the guidelines for checking over narrative writing on page 67 as you draft and revise.

DAVID SEDARIS
Me Talk Pretty One Day

David Sedaris (b. 1957) taught writing at the Art Institute of Chicago for two years before making a splash on the national scene as a radio commentator, essayist, playwright, and humorist. A regular commentator on National Public Radio's *Morning Edition* and a contributor to the *New Yorker* and *Esquire* magazines, Sedaris has also written nearly ten plays with his sister Amy, including *Incident, One Woman Shoe, The Little Frieda Mysteries, Stump the Host,* and *Stitches.* He has also published several best-selling essay collections, including *Barrel Fever* (1994); *Me Talk Pretty One Day* (2000), from which the following essay is taken; *Dress Your Family in Corduroy and Denim* (2004); and *When You Are Engulfed in Flames* (2008). In 2001, Sedaris received the Thurber Prize for American Humor and was named *Time* magazine's Humorist of the Year. In 2004, he received Grammy nominations for Best Spoken Word Album and Best Comedy Album. Sedaris currently lives in Paris.

> **Preview** As you read, pinpoint the climax of the essay, thinking specifically about the cues that lead you to believe this is the essay's climax.

At the age of forty-one, I am returning to school and have to think of myself as what my French textbook calls "a true debutant." After paying my tuition, I was issued a student ID, which allows me a discounted entry fee at movie theaters, puppet shows, and Festyland, a far-flung amusement park that advertises with billboards picturing a cartoon stegosaurus sitting in a canoe and eating what appears to be a ham sandwich.

I've moved to Paris with hopes of learning the language. My school is an easy ten-minute walk from my apartment, and on the first day of class I arrived early, watching as the returning students greeted one another in the school lobby. Vacations were recounted, and questions were raised concerning mutual friends with names like Kang and Vlatnya. Regardless of their nationalities, everyone spoke in what sounded to me like excellent French. Some accents were better than others, but the students exhibited an ease and confidence I found intimidating. As an added discomfort, they were all young, attractive, and well dressed, causing me to feel not unlike Pa Kettle* trapped backstage after a fashion show.

The first day of class was nerve-racking because I knew I'd be expected to perform. That's the way they do it here — it's everybody into the language pool, sink or swim. The teacher marched in, deeply tanned from a recent vacation, and proceeded to rattle off a series of administrative announcements. I've spent quite a few summers in Normandy, and I took a monthlong French class before leaving New York. I'm not

---

* **Pa Kettle:** a country-bumpkin character in many movies of the 1940s and 50s.

completely in the dark, yet I understood only half of what this woman was saying.

"If you have not *meimslsxp* or *Igpdmurct* by this time, then you should   4
not be in this room. Has everyone *avzkiubjxow?* Everyone? Good, we shall begin." She spread out her lesson plan and sighed, saying, "All right, then, who knows the alphabet?"

It was startling because (a) I hadn't been asked that question in a   5
while and (b) I realized, while laughing, that I myself did *not* know the alphabet. They're the same letters, but in France they're pronounced differently. I know the shape of the alphabet but had no idea what it actually sounded like.

"Ahh." The teacher went to the board and sketched the letter *a*. "Do   6
we have anyone in the room whose first name commences with an *ahh?"*

Two Polish Annas raised their hands, and the teacher instructed them   7
to present themselves by stating their names, nationalities, occupations, and a brief list of things they liked and disliked in this world. The first Anna hailed from an industrial town outside of Warsaw and had front teeth the size of tombstones. She worked as a seamstress, enjoyed quiet times with friends, and hated the mosquito.

"Oh, really," the teacher said. "How very interesting. I thought that ev-   8
eryone loved the mosquito, but here, in front of all the world, you claim to detest him. How is it that we've been blessed with someone as unique and original as you? Tell us, please."

The seamstress did not understand what was being said but knew   9
that this was an occasion for shame. Her rabbity mouth huffed for breath, and she stared down at her lap as though the appropriate comeback were stitched somewhere alongside the zipper of her slacks.

The second Anna learned from the first and claimed to love sunshine   10
and detest lies. It sounded like a translation of one of those Playmate of the Month data sheets, the answers always written in the same loopy handwriting: "Turn-ons: Mom's famous five-alarm chili! Turnoffs: insecurity and guys who come on too strong!!!!"

The two Polish Annas surely had clear notions of what they loved   11
and hated, but like the rest of us, they were limited in terms of vocabulary, and this made them appear less than sophisticated. The teacher forged on, and we learned that Carlos, the Argentine bandonion player, loved wine, music, and, in his words, "making sex with the womens of the world." Next came a beautiful young Yugoslav who identified herself as an optimist, saying that she loved everything that life had to offer.

The teacher licked her lips, revealing a hint of the saucebox we would   12
later come to know. She crouched low for her attack, placed her hands on the young woman's desk, and leaned close, saying, "Oh yeah? And do you love your little war?"

While the optimist struggled to defend herself, I scrambled to think   13
of an answer to what had obviously become a trick question. How often

is one asked what he loves in this world? More to the point, how often is one asked and then publicly ridiculed for his answer? I recalled my mother, flushed with wine, pounding the tabletop late one night, saying, "Love? I love a good steak cooked rare. I love my cat, and I love . . ." My sisters and I leaned forward, waiting to hear our names. "Tums," our mother said. "I love Tums."

The teacher killed some time accusing the Yugoslavian girl of master- 14 minding a program of genocide, and I jotted frantic notes in the margins of my pad. While I can honestly say that I love leafing through medical textbooks devoted to severe dermatological conditions, the hobby is be- yond the reach of my French vocabulary, and acting it out would only have invited controversy.

When called upon, I delivered an effortless list of things that I detest: 15 blood sausage, intestinal pâtés, brain pudding. I'd learned these words the hard way. Having given it some thought, I then declared my love for IBM typewriters, the French word for *bruise*, and my electric floor waxer. It was a short list, but still I managed to mispronounce *IBM* and assign the wrong gender to both the floor waxer and the typewriter. The teach- er's reaction led me to believe that these mistakes were capital crimes in the country of France.

"Were you always this *palicmkrexis?*" she asked. "Even a *fiuscrzsa ticiwel-* 16 *mun* knows that a typewriter is feminine."

I absorbed as much of her abuse as I could understand, think- 17 ing — but not saying — that I find it ridiculous to assign a gender to an inanimate object incapable of disrobing and making an occasional fool of itself. Why refer to crack pipe or Good Sir Dishrag when these things could never live up to all that their sex implied?

The teacher proceeded to belittle everyone from German Eva, who 18 hated laziness, to Japanese Yukari, who loved paintbrushes and soap. Italian, Thai, Dutch, Korean, and Chinese — we all left class foolishly be- lieving that the worst was over. She'd shaken us up a little, but surely that was just an act designed to weed out the deadweight. We didn't know it then, but the coming months would teach us what it was like to spend time in the presence of a wild animal, something completely unpredictable. Her temperament was not based on a series of good and bad days but, rather, good and bad moments. We soon learned to dodge chalk and protect our heads and stomachs whenever she approached us with a question. She hadn't yet punched anyone, but it seemed wise to protect ourselves against the inevitable.

Though we were forbidden to speak anything but French, the 19 teacher would occasionally use us to practice any of her five fluent languages.

"I hate you," she said to me one afternoon. Her English was flawless. 20 "I really, really hate you." Call me sensitive, but I couldn't help but take it personally.

After being singled out as a lazy *kfdtinyfm*, I took to spending four 21
hours a night on my homework, putting in even more time whenever we
were assigned an essay. I suppose I could have gotten by with less, but I
was determined to create some sort of identity for myself: David the hard
worker, David the cut–up. We'd have one of those "complete this sentence" exercises, and I'd fool with the thing for hours, invariably settling
on something like "A quick run around the lake? I'd love to! Just give me
a moment while I strap on my wooden leg." The teacher, through word
and action, conveyed the message that if this was my idea of an identity,
she wanted nothing to do with it.

My fear and discomfort crept beyond the borders of the classroom 22
and accompanied me out onto the wide boulevards. Stopping for a coffee, asking directions, depositing money in my bank account: these things
were out of the question, as they involved having to speak. Before beginning school, there'd been no shutting me up, but now I was convinced
that everything I said was wrong. When the phone rang, I ignored it. If
someone asked me a question, I pretended to be deaf. I knew my fear
was getting the best of me when I started wondering why they don't sell
cuts of meat in vending machines.

My only comfort was the knowledge that I was not alone. Huddled 23
in the hallways and making the most of our pathetic French, my fellow
students and I engaged in the sort of conversation commonly overheard
in refugee camps.

"Sometime me cry alone at night."   24

"That be common for I, also, but be more strong, you. Much work 25
and someday you talk pretty. People start love you soon. Maybe tomorrow, okay."

Unlike the French class I had taken in New York, here there was no 26
sense of competition. When the teacher poked a shy Korean in the eyelid with a freshly sharpened pencil, we took no comfort in the fact that,
unlike Hyeyoon Cho, we all knew the irregular past tense of the verb *to
defeat*. In all fairness, the teacher hadn't meant to stab the girl, but neither did she spend much time apologizing, saying only "Well, you should
have been *vkkdyo* more *kdeynfulh*."

Over time it became impossible to believe that any of us would ever 27
improve. Fall arrived and it rained every day, meaning we would now be
scolded for the water dripping from our coats and umbrellas. It was mid-
October when the teacher singled me out, saying, "Every day spent with
you is like having a cesarean section." And it struck me that, for the first
time since arriving in France, I could understand every word that someone was saying.

Understanding doesn't mean that you can suddenly speak the lan- 28
guage. Far from it. It's a small step, nothing more, yet its rewards are intoxicating and deceptive. The teacher continued her diatribe and I settled
back, bathing in the subtle beauty of each new curse and insult.

"You exhaust me with your foolishness and reward my efforts with 29
nothing but pain, do you understand me?"

The world opened up, and it was with great joy that I responded, 30
"I know the thing that you speak exact now. Talk me more, you, plus,
please, plus."

Reading Closely

1. "The teacher marched in, deeply tanned from a recent vacation, and proceeded to rattle off a series of administrative announcements." This sentence resonates with the teacher's power in this narrative. Locate other
   passages in Sedaris's narration where he refers to the teacher's power.
   How many times does he refer to it?
2. What are the stages Sedaris goes through to learn French? Which stages
   seem to be positive ones? negative ones? What other stages does he
   describe?
3. What are the benefits of Sedaris's decision to learn French? to endure
   language school? What are the unpleasant consequences of his decision?
   What would you like—or not like—about the literacy experience he has
   chosen?
4. What is Sedaris's purpose in writing this essay? What specific events,
   characters, dialogue, and settings help support your answer?

Considering Larger Issues

1. What is the setting for this narration, and what significance does it have
   for Sedaris's overall purpose? What is his purpose?
2. Think about the audience for Sedaris's wickedly funny writing. What
   kinds of people would enjoy his writing and his subject? Locate the details and incidents that he uses to interest such an audience. Be prepared
   to share your response with the rest of the class.
3. What is the thesis of Sedaris's narration? Write it out in one sentence.
   How do mentions of his teacher, his classmates, and himself help support
   and develop his thesis? Prepare a brief report for the rest of the class.
4. Besides the teacher, who are the other characters in this essay? What
   do they say? How does Sedaris use these characters and their dialogue to
   support his main point and carry out his purpose for writing the
   essay?
5. COMBINING METHODS. How does Sedaris *compare* his literacy in English with
   his literacy in French? What is the overall effect of these comparisons?
6. Write for a few minutes about the power a teacher has, drawing from
   your own experiences with teachers. **Working with two or three students,** read your responses aloud and compare them. Then prepare a
   group response to share with the rest of the class.

Thinking about Language

1. Throughout his essay, Sedaris demonstrates the limits of any vocabulary, especially of his French vocabulary. Choose two of the following terms from Sedaris's English vocabulary and define them, either from the context of the essay or from your dictionary. Be prepared to share your answers with the rest of the class.

debutant (1)	genocide (14)	temperament (18)
saucebox (12)	dermatological (14)	diatribe (28)
masterminding (14)	deadweight (18)	

2. Underline all the words in this essay that you cannot define. Then circle the words you need to define in order to understand a passage. **Work with two or three classmates** to define the words you have circled, determining their meaning either from context or by using your dictionary.

3. Locate all the terms and phrases in the essay that signify transition. How often does Sedaris use transitions? Does he ever imply the passage of time or a change in location? If so, identify the places where he does so. How does his use of transitional words or phrases move his essay forward?

4. Jot down the descriptive words and phrases Sedaris uses to distinguish one classmate from another. Translate Sedaris's description into your own words, describing each classmate in a way that individualizes him or her.

Writing Your Own Narratives

1. Sedaris's goal is to speak French fluently. What career, health, family, academic, or athletic goal have you set for yourself? What specific steps have you taken to reach that goal? Which steps have been easy or just as you expected? Which steps have been surprisingly difficult or different from what you expected? What have you learned on the way to achieving your goal?

   After responding to these questions, draft a three- to four-page narrative essay about the process of striving for or reaching your specific goal. What is the purpose of your narrative? What thesis do you want your narrative to support? Order the steps carefully, and consider including important characters besides yourself and revealing dialogue as well as key details about the setting. Your final draft should include only the steps, characters, dialogue, and other details that help make your point. Refer to "Checking Over Narrative Writing" on page 67.

2. Freewrite for a few minutes about a time when you trusted someone because of that person's status or position. The authority figure might have been a teacher, doctor, nurse, dentist, member of the clergy, coach, firefighter, police officer, salesclerk, or car mechanic. What was good — or bad — about your experience with this person? What did you learn from it? Use your freewriting as the basis for a three- to four-page narrative

about this experience with trust and authority. As you draft and revise, refer to the guidelines for checking over narrative writing on page 67.

3. Consider the importance of psychology in the practice of teaching. **Working alone or with a classmate,** write down all the reasons you can think of for the importance of enthusiasm, empathy, and kindliness in teachers' relations with their students. Are these sensibilities less important than, more important than, or just as important as technical skill and knowledge? Decide on a thesis statement and provide some examples that support it, either from personal experience or from the experiences of other students you know. Then write a three- to four-page essay in which you support your thesis by weaving in these short narratives, referring to "Checking Over Narrative Writing" on page 67.

JEFF DRAYER
Bedside Terror

After publishing *The Cost-Effective Use of Leeches and Other Musings of a Medical School Survivor* (1998), Jeff Drayer (b. 1971) has continued to write essays about his life as a physician. "Bedside Terror," which appeared on the online periodical www.salon.com in June 2000, recounts his inexperience as an intern. "Bedside Terror" reveals how much information and how many procedures interns still need to learn — for the sake of the patients, other medical personnel, and the interns' own professional and personal growth. As you read the essay, consider whether you've ever been knowingly treated by an intern — and what difference that made.

> **Preview**   Consider how Drayer uses narration to convey suspense and worry in his essay.

This summer thousands of med school graduates will be unleashed on 1 unsuspecting patients, and I know why the public should be scared.

June 5, 2000, I tore down the last flight of stairs and burst into the 2 hallway. A crowd of people turned as I rushed, white coat flapping behind me like a superhero's cape, into their midst. They parted readily, forming a narrow trail for me to pass into the room, wherein raged a small tornado of activity. At the eye lay an enormous, pale, heaving man.

"He's in V-tach, Doctor," a nearby nurse informed me breathlessly. 3 "Oxygen sats down in the 80s." From nowhere an EKG appeared in my hand. I held it up and frowned thoughtfully. And as I stared at the series of lines and curves that held volumes of critical information about this dying man's cardiac function, one throbbing thought pulsed its way to the very front of my brain: I have no idea what the hell I'm doing.

Only 10 minutes before I had been sound asleep, dreaming that 4 dream in which I live in a far-off land where people can have all the bowel movements they want and I don't have to report them to my resident. Suddenly, there was this terrible, insane beeping, the kind that didn't stop no matter how many times I hit my alarm clock or tried to check my laundry.

It had been my beeper, of course. And when I groggily answered it, 5 only to get some woman asking for the intern on call, I became irate. After all, didn't she know I was just a med student?

But then, as I looked around at the sterile beige call room and the 6 hard plastic hospital bed beneath me, I came to a realization. That graduation ceremony a month before. That Oath. Maybe I was the intern on call. Shit.

The Association of American Medical Colleges estimates that 18,391 7 people like me — fresh from medical school — will be unleashed on the

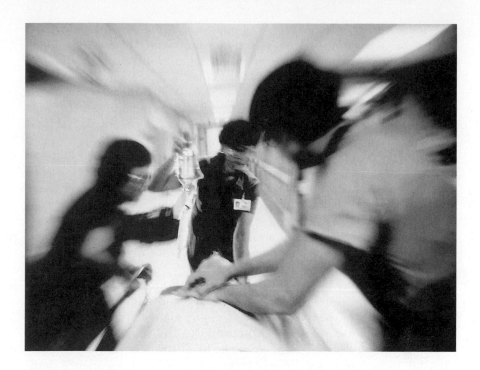

patients of this country on July 1. We will infiltrate local hospitals, clinics and medical centers near you. Despite the four years we spent memorizing textbooks and not sleeping, many will feel, like I did on that day, completely ill-prepared to be a doctor.

Contrary to popular belief, there are no actual classes in med school 8 on how to perform medical interventions. Sure, we sat for hours on end learning all the atoms in the pyridine ring and their fascinating relation to the pentose shunt. But spinal taps, Pap smears, staunching the uncontrollable bleeding caused by a zealous nurse-practitioner — these we simply had to pick up along the way. And if, through bad luck, poor timing or sheer lack of interest, we did not witness a particular procedure, such as draining an abscess, well, there was nothing you could do.

BEDSIDE TERROR

So there I stood, with 300 pounds of cirrhotic liver slowly degenerat- 9 ing from decades of alcohol abuse and emphysematous lungs worn down by thousands of packs of cigarettes, quivering violently next to me. I closed my eyes and tried to remember that graph from physiology class four years before, the one about cardiac output or something. It felt so nice to have my eyes closed.

"You want a liter of fluids?" a tall nurse asked, the way my mom used   10
to "ask" me if I wanted some broccoli as she heaped it onto my plate.
Startled, I nodded mutely and turned to see a blond nurse hauling in
paddles, glass vials and other vaguely familiar things.

"Should I put some gel on his chest?" she asked. It didn't sound like it   11
could hurt and she seemed so excited about it, so I nodded again. A large
nurse began to draw some blood, and after several moments asked if I'd
like her to draw some blood. I nodded once more.

Suddenly, two paddles appeared in my hand, just as I'd seen so many   12
times on television, and once in that class we had to take a few weeks
before. Did I want to put them on the patient's chest, the blond nurse
asked, in order to assess his cardiac rhythm? Another nod as the cold
steel contacted the cooling flesh.

"Still V-tach," someone announced. I squinted at the monitor and   13
tried to remember whether ventricular tachycardia was a squiggly pattern or a sawtooth pattern.

"Everyone stand back and let the doctor shock him!" the tall nurse   14
yelled. I looked around—it was just me and the patient, alone in the
middle of a circle of people, like the losers in some children's game. The
tall nurse looked me in the eye: "You're all clear."

I sure didn't feel all clear, though. In fact, I felt pretty confused.   15
After all, there I was, the lone M.D. responsible for this patient's dete-
riorating medical condition. True, there were two residents elsewhere in
the hospital with a year or two more experience than I, but their job
was simply to answer any questions I had, and I didn't particularly
think that a 10-minute telephone conversation was in order at the
moment.

Besides, I had enough knowledge floating around in the part of my   16
head that used to contain baseball statistics to pass the national boards. I
should be able to handle this, shouldn't I?

People have always told me that there was more to medicine than   17
just pure knowledge, but I had never believed them, until this very minute. They had said that the difference between being a medical student
and an intern was the ability to take what little knowledge you had
gained and put it all together. Was this true? Closing my eyes, I took a
deep breath.

I opened them again to see the paddles still clutched in my hands.   18
Put it all together, I thought. Ventricular tachycardia—the part of the heart
that pumped the blood to the rest of the body was spasming uncon-
trollably such that very little blood got pushed anywhere. How do you
stop that? I could not remember.

"Doctor? You're clear." Clear? Clear. I looked down at the paddles—   19
there was only one button on each. With nothing else to do, I pushed,
unleashing a terrible "ker-CHUNK!" I looked back at the monitor, as the
sawteeth gave way to a spiky pattern. Spiky I knew, was good.

"Pressure's back to 100 over 60," someone announced, dialing a phone. 20 "You want me to call intensive care?" I nodded, happy to know that this patient would soon be in a place where he wasn't my responsibility and could have all the arrhythmias he wanted. A smiling nurse handed me the chart and suggested I sign the orders. "Great work, doctor," she said, her eyes like saucers. I hadn't done a single thing, or even said a word. I nodded one last time.

Throughout medical school, there are two rules that are constantly 21 being pounded into each student's moist, softened brain. The first is that it's OK to admit that you don't know something. This is based on the idea that nobody knows everything, and if you don't know the answer, it's much better to admit to it rather than go off half-cocked and possibly screw something up like an idiot.

The second rule is that no matter what, under no circumstances 22 should you ever ever admit that you don't know something. The idea behind this is that we're doctors, damn it, and we need to act—after all this training, we have to know something and it's better to take your best guess and go with it (full-cocked) instead of just standing around doing nothing like an idiot.

It was the first rule that found a special place in my heart; in fact, I 23 perfected it. Because if you don't know something as a student, you have a built-in excuse: You're still learning. But somehow, there's this idea that once you make the jump to doctor, you have all the answers. Heck, that had always been my impression, based mostly on the events portrayed on "St. Elsewhere." I just figured all this knowledge and the ability to use it would occur magically with no explanation, much in the way the liver, I'm told, controls how well your blood clots.

But as it turned out, I was no different the day after graduation than 24 I was the day before. It's true, I had a brand new diploma and could legally be sued for a whole new set of reasons. But when I found myself leafing through my textbook of internal medicine, I realized that even though I was officially a doctor, I still hadn't heard of half the diseases. My heart then began to race and I broke out in a sweat, which I knew were the symptoms of something, though I couldn't quite put my finger on it. All I knew was that after four years and $142,863, I felt hopelessly, frighteningly unprepared.

After all, medical school had given us what it could, but what it could 25 not teach us was what it's like to have to care for a patient with no back-up. It never told us how it feels to be the last line of defense between a dying man and death.

Yet as I stood watching the patient's bed being wheeled toward the 26 intensive care unit, I realized that I had indeed learned something in medical school. And though it didn't seem like much at the time, it was, perhaps, the most valuable lesson I would ever get. Until you know everything there is to know, it's OK to listen to others who are more experienced, and learn from them. Maybe some doctors would pretend to know it all, but I could keep the humility of the med student alive.

Reading Closely

1. The author relates a series of incidents involving "an enormous, pale, heaving man" (paragraphs 2–3, 9–14, 18–20). What do you learn from this series of incidents?

2. **Working with two or three classmates,** compare your responses to "Bedside Terror." What did you learn from this essay that you didn't know before? What information made you want to know more? Share your findings with the rest of the class.

3. What information do you get from the photograph on page 89 that you don't get from the essay? What information or emotions are enhanced when you consider the photograph and the essay together? How do the visual and verbal language fulfill the author's purpose?

Considering Larger Issues

1. Decide on the main purpose of Drayer's narrative: to report events, create a mood, or argue a point. Prepare a brief response to share with the rest of the class.

2. Determine the point Drayer is making. How do the incidents in his essay work to support his point? Prepare a brief response to share with the rest of the class.

3. This essay appeared on the Web at www.salon.com under the heading "Health." Who are the readers of salon.com? Describe them in terms of age, sex, income, interests, and any other characteristics you can think of. How might the readers of salon.com change if you consider only readers of the "Health" section in particular?

4. COMBINING METHODS. Mark the passages that use *descriptive* details, make *comparisons*, or *analyze consequences*. What is the effect of each of these passages? Prepare to share your findings with the rest of the class.

Thinking about Language

1. "Bedside Terror" is a play on the common phrase "bedside manner," which is used to describe how well doctors relate to their patients. What is the effect of replacing the word *manner* with *terror*?

2. The title of the essay helps create a mood of fear. Locate all the words and phrases in "Bedside Terror" that suggest fear. Write them out.

3. Locate all the words and phrases throughout the essay that suggest rushing. Write them out.

4. **Working with two classmates,** compare the language that suggests fear and the language that suggests rushing. Discuss why both kinds of words are necessary to the success of this narrative, and report your conclusions to the class.

Writing Your Own Narratives

1. Look through books, manuals, and magazines until you locate a narrative that simply reports events in an unemotional or even bland way. **Working with two or three classmates,** discuss whether any of you could actually reproduce those events by reading that narrative account. As a group, draft a narrative that recounts those events, but enhance it with invented descriptive details so that you can also establish a mood. Prepare to share your group's results with the rest of the class.

   Use your group's narrative as the basis for a two- to three-page individual narrative essay that reports events at the same time that it establishes a mood. As you draft and revise, refer to the guidelines for checking over narrative writing on page 67.

2. One point that Drayer's essay makes is that book knowledge does not always translate into practical knowledge. Sometimes a person needs to practice alongside someone more experienced in order to learn. Draft a two- to three-page narrative essay that supports this thesis. Use the guidelines for checking over narrative writing on page 67.

MAYA ANGELOU
Finishing School

Born Marguerita Johnson in 1928 in St Louis, Maya Angelou spent much of her time while growing up with her Arkansas grandmother. Early on, Angelou made a career as a singer and actress and then as a film director, a civil rights leader, and a journalist. Author of over a dozen best-selling books, from *I Know Why the Caged Bird Sings* (1969) to *Letter to My Daughter* (2008), she is also an acclaimed poet, educator, dancer, editor, and public speaker. In 1993, she became the second poet in U.S. history to recite an original work ("On the Pulse of the Morning") for a presidential inauguration. Angelou teaches at Wake Forest University, where she has been the Reynolds Professor of American Studies since 1981. "Finishing School" is excerpted from *I Know Why the Caged Bird Sings.*

> **Preview** As you read, reflect on why Angelou chose to title this narrative "Finishing School."

Recently a white woman from Texas, who would quickly describe her- 1 self as a liberal, asked me about my hometown. When I told her that in Stamps my grandmother had owned the only Negro general merchandise store since the turn of the century, she exclaimed, "Why, you were a debutante." Ridiculous and even ludicrous. But Negro girls in small Southern towns, whether poverty-stricken or just munching along on a few of life's necessities, were given as extensive and irrelevant preparations for adulthood as rich white girls shown in magazines. Admittedly the training was not the same. While white girls learned to waltz and sit gracefully with a tea cup balanced on their knees, we were lagging behind, learning the mid-Victorian values with very little money to indulge them. . . .

We were required to embroider and I had trunkfuls of colorful dish- 2 towels, pillowcases, runners and handkerchiefs to my credit. I mastered the art of crocheting and tatting, and there was a lifetime's supply of dainty doilies that would never be used in sacheted dresser drawers. It went without saying that all girls could iron and wash, but the finer touches around the home, like setting a table with real silver, baking roasts and cooking vegetables without meat, had to be learned elsewhere. Usually at the source of those habits. During my tenth year, a white woman's kitchen became my finishing school.

Mrs. Viola Cullinan was a plump woman who lived in a three-bedroom 3 house somewhere behind the post office. She was singularly unattractive until she smiled, and then the lines around her eyes and mouth which made her look perpetually dirty disappeared, and her face looked like the mask of an impish elf. She usually rested her smile until late afternoon when her women friends dropped in and Miss Glory, the cook, served them cold drinks on the closed-in porch.

The exactness of her house was inhuman. This glass went here and 4
only here. That cup had its place and it was an act of impudent rebellion
to place it anywhere else. At twelve o'clock the table was set. At 12:15
Mrs. Cullinan sat down to dinner (whether her husband had arrived or
not). At 12:16 Miss Glory brought out the food.

It took me a week to learn the difference between a salad plate, a 5
bread plate and a dessert plate.

Mrs. Cullinan kept up the tradition of her wealthy parents. She 6
was from Virginia. Miss Glory, who was a descendant of slaves that had
worked for the Cullinans, told me her history. She had married beneath
her (according to Miss Glory). Her husband's family hadn't had their
money very long and what they had "didn't 'mount to much."

As ugly as she was, I thought privately, she was lucky to get a hus- 7
band above or beneath her station. But Miss Glory wouldn't let me say
a thing against her mistress. She was very patient with me, however,
over the housework. She explained the dishware, silverware and servants' bells. The large round bowl in which soup was served wasn't a
soup bowl, it was a tureen. There were goblets, sherbet glasses, ice–cream
glasses, wine glasses, green glass coffee cups with matching saucers, and
water glasses. I had a glass to drink from, and it sat with Miss Glory's on
a separate shelf from the others. Soup spoons, gravy boat, butter knives,
salad forks and carving platter were additions to my vocabulary and in
fact almost represented a new language. I was fascinated with the novelty,
with the fluttering Mrs. Cullinan and her Alice–in–Wonderland house.

Her husband remains, in my memory, undefined. I lumped him with 8
all the other white men that I had ever seen and tried not to see.

On our way home one evening, Miss Glory told me that Mrs. 9
Cullinan couldn't have children. She said that she was too delicate–boned.
It was hard to imagine bones at all under those layers of fat. Miss Glory
went on to say that the doctor had taken out all her lady organs. I reasoned that a pig's organs included the lungs, heart, and liver, so if Mrs.
Cullinan was walking around without those essentials, it explained why
she drank alcohol out of unmarked bottles. She was keeping herself
embalmed.

When I spoke to Bailey about it, he agreed that I was right, but he 10
also informed me that Mr. Cullinan had two daughters by a colored lady
and that I knew them very well. He added that the girls were the spitting
image of their father. I was unable to remember what he looked like, although I had just left him a few hours before, but I thought of the Coleman girls. They were very light–skinned and certainly didn't look very
much like their mother (no one ever mentioned Mr. Coleman).

My pity for Mrs. Cullinan preceded me the next morning like the 11
Cheshire cat's smile. Those girls, who could have been her daughters,
were beautiful. They didn't have to straighten their hair. Even when they
were caught in the rain, their braids still hung down straight like tamed

snakes. Their mouths were pouty little cupid's bows. Mrs. Cullinan didn't know what she missed. Or maybe she did. Poor Mrs. Cullinan.

For weeks after, I arrived early, left late and tried very hard to make 12 up for her barrenness. If she had her own children, she wouldn't have had to ask me to run a thousand errands from her back door to the back door of her friends. Poor old Mrs. Cullinan.

Then one evening Miss Glory told me to serve the ladies on the 13 porch. After I set the tray down and turned toward the kitchen, one of the women asked, "What's your name, girl?" It was the speckled–faced one. Mrs. Cullinan said, "She doesn't talk much. Her name's Margaret."

"Is she dumb?"   14

"No. As I understand it, she can talk when she wants to but she's 15 usually quiet as a little mouse. Aren't you, Margaret?"

I smiled at her. Poor thing. No organs and couldn't even pronounce 16 my name correctly.

"She's a sweet little thing, though."   17

"Well, that may be, but the name's too long. I'd never bother myself. 18 I'd call her Mary if I was you."

I fumed into the kitchen. That horrible woman would never have 19 the chance to call me Mary because if I was starving I'd never work for her. . . .

That evening I decided to write a poem on being white, fat, old and 20 without children. It was going to be a tragic ballad. I would have to watch her carefully to capture the essence of her loneliness and pain.

Shelley Morrison and Megan Mullally played a maid and her mistress on the sitcom *Will & Grace.*

The very next day she called me by the wrong name. Miss Glory and 21
I were washing up the lunch dishes when Mrs. Cullinan came to the
doorway. "Mary?"

Miss Glory asked, "Who?"   22

Mrs. Cullinan, sagging a little, knew and I knew. "I want Mary to go 23
down to Mrs. Randall's and take her some soup. She's not been feeling
well for a few days."

Miss Glory's face was a wonder to see. "You mean Margaret, ma'am. 24
Her name's Margaret."

"That's too long. She's Mary from now on. Heat that soup from last 25
night and put it in the china tureen and, Mary, I want you to carry it
carefully."

Every person I knew had a hellish horror of being "called out of 26
his name." It was a dangerous practice to call a Negro anything that
could be loosely construed as insulting because of the centuries of their
having been called niggers, jigs, dinges, blackbirds, crows, boots and
spooks.

Miss Glory had a fleeting second of feeling sorry for me. Then as she 27
handed me the hot tureen she said, "Don't mind, don't pay that no mind.
Sticks and stones may break your bones, but words . . . You know, I been
working for her for twenty years."

She held the back door open for me. "Twenty years. I wasn't much 28
older than you. My name used to be Hallelujah. That's what Ma named
me, but my mistress give me 'Glory,' and it stuck. I likes it better too."

I was in the little path that ran behind the houses when Miss Glory 29
shouted, "It's shorter too."

For a few seconds it was a tossup over whether I would laugh (imag- 30
ine being named Hallelujah) or cry (imagine letting some white woman
rename you for her convenience). My anger saved me from either out-
burst. I had to quit the job, but the problem was going to be how to do
it. Momma wouldn't allow me to quit for just any reason.

"She's a peach. That woman is a real peach." Mrs. Randall's maid was 31
talking as she took the soup from me, and I wondered what her name
used to be and what she answered to now.

For a week I looked into Mrs. Cullinan's face as she called me Mary. 32
She ignored my coming late and leaving early. Miss Glory was a little an-
noyed because I had begun to leave egg yolk on the dishes and wasn't
putting much heart in polishing the silver. I hoped that she would complain to our boss, but she didn't.

Then Bailey solved my dilemma. He had me describe the contents of 33
the cupboard and the particular plates she liked best. Her favorite piece
was a casserole shaped like a fish and the green glass coffee cups. I kept
his instructions in mind, so on the next day when Miss Glory was hanging
out clothes and I had again been told to serve the old biddies on the porch,
I dropped the empty serving tray. When I heard Mrs. Cullinan scream,

"Mary!" I picked up the casserole and two of the green glass cups in readi- ness. As she rounded the kitchen door I let them fall on the tiled floor.

I could never absolutely describe to Bailey what happened next, be- 34 cause each time I got to the part where she fell on the floor and screwed up her ugly face to cry we burst out laughing. She actually wobbled around on the floor and picked up shards of the cups and cried, "Oh, Momma. Oh, dear Gawd. It's Momma's china from Virginia. Oh, Momma, I sorry."

Miss Glory came running in from the yard and the women from the 35 porch crowded around. Miss Glory was almost as broken up as her mis- tress. "You mean to say she broke our Virginia dishes? What we gone do?"

Mrs. Cullinan cried louder. "That clumsy nigger. Clumsy little black 36 nigger."

Old speckled–face leaned down and asked, "Who did it, Viola? Was it 37 Mary? Who did it?"

Everything was happening so fast, I can't remember whether her ac- 38 tion preceded her words, but I know that Mrs. Cullinan said, "Her name's Margaret, goddamn it, her name's Margaret." And she threw a wedge of broken plate at me. It could have been the hysteria which put her aim off, but the flying crockery caught Miss Glory right over her ear and she started screaming.

I left the front door wide open so all the neighbors could hear.   39

Mrs. Cullinan was right about one thing. My name wasn't Mary.   40

Reading Closely

1. What were Angelou's duties at the Cullinan home?
2. Why was Mrs. Cullinan so exacting about housekeeping?
3. What passages in the narrative help you trace the changes Mrs. Cullinan goes through in her treatment of and attitude toward Angelou?
4. What does the scene from *Will & Grace* on page 96 suggest about the rela- tion between maids and their employers? How effectively does this vi- sual enhance Angelou's narrative?

Considering Larger Issues

1. What is the overall purpose of this narrative? How do the title, the char- acters, the setting, and the sequence of events work together to fulfill that purpose?
2. **Working with another classmate or two,** analyze Angelou's use of dialogue in this narrative. Which passages are most effective in helping her fulfill her purpose? Which ones most illuminate the contrast between Angelou's home life and working life? to what effect?

3. **COMBINING METHODS.** Angelou uses *description* and *comparison and contrast* to enhance her narrative. Mark the relevant passages, and explain their power to improve the narrative.

Thinking about Language

1. Using a dictionary or the context of the selection, define the following terms, preparing to share your answers with the rest of the class.

liberal (1)	impish (3)	ballad (20)
debutante (1)	impudent (4)	construed (26)
ludicrous (1)	embalmed (9)	fleeting (27)
tatting (2)	Cheshire cat (11)	a peach (31)
sacheted (2)	pouty (11)	dilemma (33)
perpetually (3)	barrenness (12)	

2. What can you say about the differences between a soup bowl and a tureen or among a goblet, sherbet glass, ice-cream glass, wineglass, and water glass? What about the differences between a soup spoon and a tablespoon or a butter knife and a carving knife? What does this knowledge — or lack thereof — say, if anything, about you? What did it say about Angelou?

3. What does the title, "Finishing School," mean for this narrative? What specific passages help you understand how Angelou is using that term? What specific vocabulary is necessary for passing "courses" in this school? Be prepared to share your answers with the rest of the class.

Writing Your Own Narratives

1. Like Angelou, we've all experienced a time in our life when someone treated us unfairly, as though we were "lower" than that person. Draft a three- to four-page essay in which you narrate your story of unfair treatment, making sure to include a title, a setting, a cast of characters, and a sequence of events. As you draft, decide on a specific audience (which could even be the person who treated you unfairly) and a specific purpose (which might be to report the information, make an argument, or set a mood). Refer to the guidelines for checking over narrative writing on page 67.

2. You may have an experience with name-calling to relate, one that's painful for you to remember, whether you were the one doing the name-calling or the victim of it. Draft a three- to four-page essay in which you narrate your name-calling story, making sure to include characters, descriptive details, and a sequence of events. You should have a specific audience in mind as well as an overall purpose. Refer to the guidelines for checking over narrative writing on page 67.

BARBARA EHRENREICH
Serving in Florida

● Barbara Ehrenreich (b. 1941) is a political activist and writer. Tackling issues from health care and class to citizenship and war, she has written or cowritten nineteen books and numerous articles, columns, and editorials. Ehrenreich has contributed to such publications as the *New York Times, Mother Jones, Atlantic, Ms., Progressive,* and *Time,* and she won the National Book Critics Circle Award for *Fear of Falling: The Inner Life of the Middle Class* (1989). She has also taught essay writing at the Graduate School of Journalism at the University of California at Berkeley. "Serving in Florida" comes from her book *Nickel and Dimed: On (Not) Getting By in America* (2001). In this book, she writes about her journalistic experiment: working as a waitress, housecleaner, and retail salesperson and trying to live on a "living" wage. This essay focuses on her experiences as a waitress in Florida at a restaurant she calls Jerry's, which was part of a "well-known national chain."

Preview   Both Ehrenreich and Angelou focus attention on issues of work. How is Ehrenreich's experience similar to and different from Angelou's?

Picture a fat person's hell, and I don't mean a place with no food. Instead there is everything you might eat if eating had no bodily consequences — the cheese fries, the chicken–fried steaks, the fudge–laden desserts — only here every bite must be paid for, one way or another, in human discomfort. The kitchen is a cavern, a stomach leading to the lower intestine that is the garbage and dishwashing area, from which issue bizarre smells combining the edible and the offal: creamy carrion, pizza barf, and that unique and enigmatic Jerry's scent, citrus fart. The floor is slick with spills, forcing us to walk through the kitchen with tiny steps, like [a person] in leg irons. Sinks everywhere are clogged with scraps of lettuce, decomposing lemon wedges, water–logged toast crusts. Put your hand down on any counter and you risk being stuck to it by the film of ancient syrup spills, and this is unfortunate because hands are utensils here, used for scooping up lettuce onto the salad plates, lifting out pie slices, and even moving hash browns from one plate to another. The regulation poster in the single unisex rest room admonishes us to wash our hands thoroughly, and even offers instructions for doing so, but there is always some vital substance missing — soap, paper towels, toilet paper — and I never found all three at once. You learn to stuff your pockets with napkins before going in there, and too bad about the customers, who must eat, although they don't realize it, almost literally out of our hands. 1

The break room summarizes the whole situation: there is none, because there are no breaks at Jerry's. For six to eight hours in a row, you never sit except to pee. Actually, there are three folding chairs at a table 2 immediately adjacent to the bathroom, but hardly anyone ever sits in this, the very rectum of the gastroarchitectural system. Rather, the function of the peri-toilet area is to house the ashtrays in which servers and dishwashers leave their cigarettes burning at all times, like votive candles, so they don't have to waste time lighting up again when they dash back here for a puff. Almost everyone smokes as if their pulmonary well-being depended on it — the multinational mélange of cooks; the dishwashers, who are all Czechs here; the servers, who are American natives — creating an atmosphere in which oxygen is only an occasional pollutant. My first morning at Jerry's, when the hypoglycemic shakes set in, I complain to one of my fellow servers that I don't understand how she can go so long without food. "Well, I don't understand how *you* can go so long without a cigarette," she responds in a tone of reproach. Because work is what you do for others; smoking is what you do for yourself. I don't know why the antismoking crusaders have never grasped the element of defiant self-nurturance that makes the habit so endearing to its victims — as if, in the American workplace, the only thing people have to call their own is the tumors they are nourishing and the spare moments they devote to feeding them. . . .

Customers arrive in human waves, sometimes disgorged fifty at a 3 time from their tour buses, puckish and whiny. Instead of two "girls" on the floor at once, there can be as many as six of us running around in our brilliant pink-and-orange Hawaiian shirts. Conversations, either with customers or with fellow employees, seldom last more than twenty seconds at a time. On my first day, in fact, I am hurt by my sister servers' coldness. My mentor for the day is a supremely competent, emotionally uninflected twenty-three-year-old, and the others, who gossip a little among themselves about the real reason someone is out sick today and the size of the bail bond someone else has had to pay, ignore me completely. On my second day, I find out why. "Well, it's good to see *you* again," one of them says in greeting. "Hardly anyone comes back after the first day." I feel powerfully vindicated — a survivor — but it would take a long time, probably months, before I could hope to be accepted into this sorority. . . .

Years ago, the kindly fry cook who trained me to waitress at a Los 4 Angeles truck stop used to say: Never make an unnecessary trip; if you don't have to walk fast, walk slow; if you don't have to walk, stand. But at Jerry's the effort of distinguishing necessary from unnecessary and urgent from whenever would itself be too much of an energy drain. The only thing to do is to treat each shift as a one-time-only emergency: you've got fifty starving people out there, lying scattered on the battlefield, so get out there and feed them! Forget that you will have to do this again tomorrow, forget that you will have to be alert enough to dodge the drunks on the drive home tonight — just burn, burn, burn! Ideally, at some point you enter what servers call a "rhythm" and psychologists term a "flow state" where signals pass from the sense organs directly to the muscles, bypassing the cerebral cortex, and a Zen–like emptiness sets in. I'm on a 2:00 – 10:00 P.M. shift now, and a male server from the morning shift tells me about the time he "pulled a triple" — three shifts in a row, all the way around the clock — and then got off and had a drink and met this girl, and maybe he shouldn't tell me this, but they had sex right then and there and it was like *beautiful*.

But there's another capacity of the neuromuscular system, which is 5 pain. I start tossing back drugstore–brand ibuprofens as if they were vitamin C, four before each shift, because an old mouse–related repetitive-stress injury in my upper back has come back to full–spasm strength, thanks to the tray carrying. In my ordinary life, this level of disability might justify a day of ice packs and stretching. Here I comfort myself with the Aleve commercial where the cute blue–collar guy asks: If you quit after working four hours, what would your boss say? And the not–so–cute blue–collar guy, who's lugging a metal beam on his back, answers: He'd fire me, that's what. But fortunately, the commercial tells us, we workers' can exert the same kind of authority over our painkillers that our bosses exert over us. If Tylenol doesn't want to work for more than four hours, you just fire its ass and switch to Aleve.

True, I take occasional breaks from this life, going home now and 6 then to catch up on e–mail and for conjugal visits (though I am careful to "pay" for everything I eat here, at $5 for a dinner, which I put in a jar), seeing *The Truman Show* with friends and letting them buy my ticket. And I still have those what–am–I–doing–here moments at work, when I get so homesick for the printed word that I obsessively reread the six–page menu. But as the days go by, my old life is beginning to look exceedingly strange. The e–mails and phone messages addressed to my former self come from a distant race of people with exotic concerns and far too much time on their hands. The neighborly market I used to cruise for produce now looks forbiddingly like a Manhattan yuppie emporium. And when I sit down one morning in my real home to pay bills from my past life, I am dazzled by the two– and three–figure sums owed to outfits like Club Body Tech and Amazon.com.

Management at Jerry's is generally calm and "professional," with two 7 exceptions. One is Joy, a plump, blowsy woman in her early thirties who once kindly devoted several minutes of her time to instructing me in the correct one–handed method of tray carrying but whose moods change disconcertingly from shift to shift and even within one. The other is B.J., aka B.J. the Bitch, whose contribution is to stand by the kitchen counter and yell, "Nita, your order's up, move it!" or "Barbara, didn't you see you've got another table out there? Come *on*, girl!" Among other things, she is hated for having replaced the whipped cream squirt cans with big plastic whipped–cream–filled baggies that have to be squeezed with both hands — because, reportedly, she saw or thought she saw employees trying to inhale the propellant gas from the squirt cans, in the hope that it might be nitrous oxide. On my third night, she pulls me aside abruptly and brings her face so close that it looks like she's planning to butt me with her forehead. But instead of saying "You're fired," she says, "You're doing fine." The only trouble is I'm spending time chatting with customers: "That's how they're getting you." Furthermore I am letting them "run me," which means harassment by sequential demands: you bring the catsup and they decide they want extra Thousand Island; you bring that and they announce they now need a side of fries, and so on into distraction. Finally she tells me not to take her wrong. She tries to say things in a nice way, but "you get into a mode, you know, because everything has to move so fast."

I mumble thanks for the advice, feeling like I've just been stripped 8 naked by the crazed enforcer of some ancient sumptuary law: No chatting for *you*, girl. No fancy service ethic allowed for the serfs. Chatting with customers is for the good-looking young college-educated servers in the downtown carpaccio and ceviche joints, the kids who can make $70–$100 a night. What had I been thinking? My job is to move orders from tables to kitchen and then trays from kitchen to tables. Customers are in fact the major obstacle to the smooth transformation of information into food and food into money — they are, in short, the enemy. And the painful thing is that I'm beginning to see it this way myself. There are the traditional asshole types — frat boys who down multiple Buds and then make a fuss because the steaks are so emaciated and the fries so sparse — as well as the variously impaired — due to age, diabetes, or literacy issues — who require patient nutritional counseling. The worst, for some reason, are the Visible Christians — like the ten-person table, all jolly and sanctified after Sunday night service, who run me mercilessly and then leave me $1 on a $92 bill. Or the guy with the crucifixion T-shirt (SOMEONE TO LOOK UP TO) who complains that his baked potato is too hard and his iced tea too icy (I cheerfully fix both) and leaves no tip at all. As a general rule, people wearing crosses or WWJD? ("What Would Jesus Do?") buttons look at us disapprovingly no matter what we do, as if they were confusing waitressing with Mary Magdalene's original profession.

I make friends, over time, with the other "girls" who work my shift: 9 Nita, the tattooed twenty-something who taunts us by going around saying brightly, "Have we started making money yet?" Ellen, whose teenage son cooks on the graveyard shift and who once managed a restaurant in Massachusetts but won't try out for management here because she prefers being a "common worker" and not "ordering people around." Easygoing fiftyish Lucy, with the raucous laugh, who limps toward the end of the shift because of something that has gone wrong with her leg, the exact nature of which cannot be determined without health insurance. We talk about the usual girl things — men, children, and the sinister allure of Jerry's chocolate peanut-butter cream pie — though no one, I notice, ever brings up anything potentially expensive, like shopping or movies. The only recreation ever referred to is partying, which requires little more than some beer, a joint, and a few close friends. Still, no one is homeless, or cops to it anyway, thanks usually to a working husband or boyfriend. All in all, we form a reliable mutual-support group: if one of us is feeling sick or overwhelmed, another one will "bev" a table or even carry trays for her. If one of us is off sneaking a cigarette or a pee, the others will do their best to conceal her absence from the enforcers of corporate rationality.

But my saving human connection — my oxytocin receptor, as it were — 10 is George, the nineteen-year-old Czech dishwasher who has been in this country exactly one week. We get talking when he asks me, tortuously, how much cigarettes cost at Jerry's. I do my best to explain that they cost over a dollar more here than at a regular store and suggest that he just take one from the half-filled packs that are always lying around on the break table. But that would be unthinkable. Except for the one tiny earring signaling his allegiance to some vaguely alternative point of view, George is a perfect straight arrow — crew-cut, hardworking, and hungry for eye contact. "Czech Republic," I ask, "or Slovakia?" and he seems delighted that I know the difference. "Vaclav Havel," I try, "Velvet Revolution, Frank Zappa?" "Yes, yes, 1989," he says, and I realize that for him this is already history.

My project is to teach George English. "How are you today, George?" I 11 say at the start of each shift. "I am good, and how are you today, Barbara?" I learn that he is not paid by Jerry's but by the "agent" who shipped him over — $5 an hour, with the agent getting the dollar or so difference between that and what Jerry's pays dishwashers. I learn also that he shares an apartment with a crowd of other Czech "dishers," as he calls them, and that he cannot sleep until one of them goes off for his shift, leaving a vacant bed. We are having one of our ESL sessions late one afternoon when B.J. catches us at it and orders "Joseph" to take up the rubber mats on the floor near the dishwashing sinks and mop underneath. "I thought your name was George," I say loud enough for B.J. to hear as she strides off back to the counter. Is she embarrassed? Maybe a little, because she greets me back at the counter with "George, Joseph — there are so many of them!" I say nothing, neither nodding nor smiling, and for this I am punished later, when I think I am ready to go and she announces that I need to roll fifty more sets of silverware, and isn't it time I mixed up a fresh four-gallon batch of blue-cheese dressing? May you grow old in this place, B.J., is the curse I beam out at her when I am finally permitted to leave. May the syrup spills glue your feet to the floor. . . .

In line with my reduced living conditions, a new form of ugliness 12 arises at Jerry's. First we are confronted — via an announcement on the computers through which we input orders — with the new rule that the

hotel bar, the Driftwood, is henceforth off-limits to restaurant employees. The culprit, I learn through the grapevine, is the ultraefficient twenty-three-year-old who trained me — another trailer home dweller and a mother of three. Something had set her off one morning, so she slipped out for a nip and returned to the floor impaired. The restriction mostly hurts Ellen, whose habit it is to free her hair from its rubber band and drop by the Driftwood for a couple of Zins before heading home at the end of her shift, but all of us feel the chill. Then the next day, when I go for straws, I find the dry-storage room locked. It's never been locked before; we go in and out of it all day — for napkins, jelly containers, Styrofoam cups for takeout. Vic, the portly assistant manager who opens it for me, explains that he caught one of the dishwashers attempting to steal something and, unfortunately, the miscreant will be with us until a replacement can be found — hence the locked door. I neglect to ask what he had been trying to steal but Vic tells me who he is — the kid with the buzz cut and the earring, you know, he's back there right now.

I wish I could say I rushed back and confronted George to get his side 13
of the story. I wish I could say I stood up to Vic and insisted that George be given a translator and allowed to defend himself or announced that I'd find a lawyer who'd handle the case pro bono. At the very least I should have testified as to the kid's honesty. The mystery to me is that

there's not much worth stealing in the dry-storage room, at least not in any fenceable quantity: "Is Gyorgi here, and am having 200 — maybe 250 — catsup packets. What do you say?" My guess is that he had taken — if he had taken anything at all — some Saltines or a can of cherry pie mix and that the motive for taking it was hunger.

So why didn't I intervene? Certainly not because I was held back by   14 the kind of moral paralysis that can mask as journalistic objectivity. On the contrary, something new — something loathsome and servile — had infected me, along with the kitchen odors that I could still sniff on my bra when I finally undressed at night. In real life I am moderately brave, but plenty of brave people shed their courage in POW camps, and maybe something similar goes on in the infinitely more congenial milieu of the low-wage American workplace. Maybe, in a month or two more at Jerry's, I might have regained my crusading spirit. Then again, in a month or two I might have turned into a different person altogether — say, the kind of person who would have turned George in.

But this is not something I was slated to find out. When my month-   15 long plunge into poverty was almost over, I finally landed my dream job — housekeeping. I did this by walking into the personnel office of the only place I figured I might have some credibility, the hotel attached to Jerry's, and confiding urgently that I had to have a second job if I was to pay my rent and, no, it couldn't be front-desk clerk. "All *right*," the personnel lady fairly spits, "so it's *housekeeping*," and marches me back to meet Millie, the housekeeping manager, a tiny, frenetic Hispanic woman who greets me as "babe" and hands me a pamphlet emphasizing the need for a positive attitude. The pay is $6.10 an hour and the hours are nine in the morning till "whenever," which I am hoping can be defined as a little before two. I don't have to ask about health insurance once I meet Carlotta, the middle-aged African American woman who will be training me. Carlie, as she tells me to call her, is missing all of her top front teeth.

On that first day of housekeeping and last day — although I don't yet   16 know it's the last — of my life as a low-wage worker in [this town], Carlie is in a foul mood. We have been given nineteen rooms to clean, most of them "checkouts," as opposed to "stay-overs," and requiring the whole enchilada of bed stripping, vacuuming, and bathroom scrubbing. When one of the rooms that had been listed as a stay-over turns out to be a checkout, she calls Millie to complain, but of course to no avail. "So make up the motherfucker," she orders me, and I do the beds while she sloshes around the bathroom. For four hours without a break I strip and remake beds, taking about four and a half minutes per queen-sized bed, which I could get down to three if there were any reason to. We try to avoid vacuuming by picking up the larger specks by hand, but often there is nothing to do but drag the monstrous vacuum cleaner — it weighs about thirty pounds — off our cart and try to wrestle it around the floor. Sometimes

Carlie hands me the squirt bottle of "Bam" (an acronym for something that begins, ominously, with "butyric" — the rest of it has been worn off the label) and lets me do the bathrooms. No service ethic challenges me here to new heights of performance. I just concentrate on removing the pubic hairs from the bathtubs, or at least the dark ones that I can see.

I had looked forward to the breaking–and–entering aspect of clean- 17 ing the stay–overs, the chance to examine the secret physical existence of strangers. But the contents of the rooms are always banal and surprisingly neat — zipped–up shaving kits, shoes lined up against the wall (there are no closets), flyers for snorkeling trips, maybe an empty wine bottle or two. It is the TV that keeps us going, from Jerry to Sally to *Hawaii Five-O* and then on to the soaps. If there's something especially arresting, like "Won't Take No for an Answer" on Jerry, we sit down on the edge of a bed and giggle for a moment, as if this were a pajama party instead of a terminally dead–end job. The soaps are the best, and Carlie turns the volume up full blast so she won't miss anything from the bathroom or while the vacuum is on. In Room 503, Marcia confronts Jeff about Lauren. In 505, Lauren taunts poor cheated–on Marcia. In 511, Helen offers Amanda $10,000 to stop seeing Eric, prompting Carlie to emerge from the bathroom to study Amanda's troubled face. "You take it, girl," she advises. "I would for sure."

The tourists' rooms that we clean and, beyond them, the far more ex- 18 pensively appointed interiors in the soaps begin after a while to merge. We have entered a better world — a world of comfort where every day is a day off, waiting to be filled with sexual intrigue. We are only gate-crashers in this fantasy, however, forced to pay for our presence with backaches and perpetual thirst. The mirrors, and there are far too many of them in hotel rooms, contain the kind of person you would normally find pushing a shopping cart down a city street — bedraggled, dressed in a damp hotel polo shirt two sizes too large, and with sweat dribbling down her chin like drool. I am enormously relieved when Carlie announces a half–hour meal break, but my appetite fades when I see that the bag of hot dog rolls she has been carrying around on our cart is not trash salvaged from a checkout but what she has brought for her lunch.

Between the TV and the fact that I'm in no position, as a first dayer, 19 to launch new topics of conversation, I don't learn much about Carlie except that she hurts, and in more than one way. She moves slowly about her work, muttering something about joint pain, and this is probably going to doom her, since the young immigrant housekeepers — Polish and Salvadoran — like to polish off their rooms by two in the afternoon, while she drags the work out till six. It doesn't make any sense to hurry, she observes, when you're being paid by the hour. Already, management has brought in a woman to do what sounds like time–motion studies and there's talk about switching to paying by the room. She broods, too, about all the little evidences of disrespect that come her way, and not

only from management. "They don't care about us," she tells me of the
hotel guests: in fact, they don't notice us at all unless something gets
stolen from a room — "then they're all over you." We're eating our lunch
side by side in the break room when a white guy in a maintenance uniform walks by and Carlie calls out, "Hey you," in a friendly way, "what's
your name?"

"Peter Pan," he says, his back already to us.   20

"That wasn't funny," Carlie says, turning to me. "That was no kind of   21
answer. Why did he have to be funny like that?" I venture that he has an
attitude, and she nods as if that were an acute diagnosis. "Yeah, he got a
attitude all right."

"Maybe he's a having a bad day," I elaborate, not because I feel any   22
obligation to defend the white race but because her face is so twisted
with hurt.

When I request permission to leave at about 3:30, another house-   23
keeper warns me that no one has so far succeeded in combining housekeeping with serving at Jerry's: "Some kid did it once for five days, and
you're no kid." With that helpful information in mind, I rush back to
number 46, down four Advils (the name brand this time), shower, and
attempt to compose myself for the oncoming shift. So much for what
Marx termed the "reproduction of labor power," meaning the things a
worker has to do just so she'll be ready to labor again. The only unforeseen obstacle to the smooth transition from job to job is that my tan
Jerry's slacks, which had looked reasonably clean by 40-watt bulb last
night when I hand washed my Hawaiian shirt, prove by daylight to be
mottled with catsup and ranch-dressing stains. I spend most of my hour-
long break between jobs attempting to remove the edible portions of the
slacks with a sponge and then drying them over the hood of my car in
the sun.

I can do this two-job thing, is my theory, if I can drink enough caf-   24
feine and avoid getting distracted by George's ever more obvious suffering. The first few days after the alleged theft, he seemed not to understand
the trouble he was in, and our chirpy little conversations had continued.
But the last couple of shifts he's been listless and unshaven, and tonight
he looks like the ghost we all know him to be, with dark half-moons
hanging from his eyes. At one point, when I am briefly immobilized by
the task of filling little paper cups with sour cream for baked potatoes, he
comes over and looks as if he'd like to explore the limits of our shared
vocabulary, but I am called to the floor for a table. I resolve to give him all
my tips that night, and to hell with the experiment in low-wage money
management. At eight, Ellen and I grab a snack together standing at
the mephitic end of the kitchen counter, but I can only manage two or
three mozzarella sticks, and lunch had been a mere handful of McNuggets. I am not tired at all, I assure myself, though it may be that there is
simply no more "I" left to do the tiredness monitoring. What I would see

if I were more alert to the situation is that the forces of destruction are already massing against me. There is only one cook on duty, a young man named Jesus ("Hay-Sue," that is), and he is new to the job. And there is Joy, who shows up to take over in the middle of the shift dressed in high heels and a long, clingy white dress and fuming as if she'd just been stood up in some cocktail bar.

Then it comes, the perfect storm. Four of my tables fill up at once.   25 Four tables is nothing for me now, but only so long as they are obligingly staggered. As I bev table 27, tables 25, 28, and 24 are watching enviously. As I bev 25, 24 glowers because their bevs haven't even been ordered. Twenty-eight is four yuppyish types, meaning everything on the side and agonizing instructions as to the chicken Caesars. Twenty-five is a middle-aged black couple who complain, with some justice, that the iced tea isn't fresh and the tabletop is sticky. But table 24 is the meteorological event of the century: ten British tourists who seem to have made the decision to absorb the American experience entirely by mouth. Here everyone has at least two drinks — iced tea *and* milk shake, Michelob *and* water (with lemon slice in the water, please) — and a huge, promiscuous orgy of breakfast specials, mozz sticks, chicken strips, quesadillas, burgers with cheese and without, sides of hash browns with cheddar, with onions, with gravy, seasoned fries, plain fries, banana splits. Poor Jesus! Poor me! Because when I arrive with their first tray of food — after three prior trips just to refill bevs — Princess Di refuses to eat her chicken strips with her pancake and sausage special since, as she now reveals, the strips were meant to be an appetizer. Maybe the others would have accepted their meals, but Di, who is deep into her third Michelob, insists that everything else go back while they work on their starters. Meanwhile, the yuppies are waving me down for more decaf and the black couple looks ready to summon the NAACP.

Much of what happens next is lost in the fog of war. Jesus starts going   26 under. The little printer in front of him is spewing out orders faster than he can rip them off, much less produce the meals. A menacing restlessness rises from the tables, all of which are full. Even the invincible Ellen is ashen from stress. I take table 24 their reheated main courses, which they immediately reject as either too cold or fossilized by the microwave. When I return to the kitchen with their trays (three trays in three trips) Joy confronts me with arms akimbo: "What *is* this?" She means the food — the plates of rejected pancakes, hash browns in assorted flavors, toasts, burgers, sausages, eggs. "Uh, scrambled with cheddar," I try, "and that's — " "No," she screams in my face, "is it a traditional, a super-scramble, an eye-opener?" I pretend to study my check for a clue, but entropy has been up to its tricks, not only on the plates but in my head, and I have to admit that the original order is beyond reconstruction. "You don't know an eye-opener from a traditional?" she demands in outrage. All I know, in fact, is that my legs have lost interest in the current venture and have announced their intention to fold. I am saved by a yuppie (mercifully not one of mine) who chooses this moment to charge into the kitchen to bellow that his food is twenty–five minutes late. Joy screams at him to get the hell out of her kitchen, *please*, and then turns on Jesus in a fury, hurling an empty tray across the room for emphasis.

I leave. I don't walk out, I just leave. I don't finish my side work or   27
pick up my credit card tips, if any, at the cash register or, of course, ask Joy's permission to go. And the surprising thing is that you *can* walk out without permission, that the door opens, that the thick tropical night air parts to let me pass, that my car is still parked where I left it. There is no vindication in this exit, no fuck–you surge of relief, just an overwhelming dank sense of failure pressing down on me and the entire parking lot. I had gone into this venture in the spirit of science, to test a mathematical proposition, but somewhere along the line, in the tunnel vision imposed by long shifts and relentless concentration, it became a test of myself, and clearly I have failed. Not only had I flamed out as a housekeeper/server, I had forgotten to give George my tips, and, for reasons perhaps best known to hardworking, generous people like Gail and Ellen, this hurts. I don't cry, but I am in a position to realize, for the first time in many years, that the tear ducts are still there and still capable of doing their job.

Reading Closely

1. **With three or four classmates,** discuss the specific aspects of Ehrenreich's narrative that were most compelling, pinpointing the places in the text that were especially moving, frustrating, or outrageous. Prepare a group response to share with the rest of the class.

2. Reflect on Ehrenreich's use of detailed language in this essay. What effect do these details have on you as a reader?

3. Identify the places in the essay in which Ehrenreich incorporates dialogue. What is the purpose of her use of dialogue?

4. Look at the photograph on page 105. How does it support or detract from the purpose of Ehrenreich's narrative?

Considering Larger Issues

1. What is the purpose of Ehrenreich's essay and her journalistic experiment? How do you know? Does she achieve her purpose?

2. Given Ehrenreich's experiences, why is it difficult to survive on a so-called living wage? What difficulties did she face? How did she try to overcome those difficulties? What ultimately led to her failure?

3. Who are the characters in the narrative? What purpose do these characters serve in terms of the essay's overarching argument?

4. **COMBINING METHODS.** Ehrenreich relies on narrative technique throughout "Serving in Florida." But she also incorporates *description* and *exemplification* in this essay. Identify the places in the essay where Ehrenreich uses these methods, and reflect on the ways they support both the narrative structure and the overarching purpose of the essay.

5. **PAIRED READINGS.** Both Ehrenreich and Angelou focus attention on issues of work. How is Ehrenreich's experience similar to and different from Angelou's?

Thinking about Language

1. Using a dictionary or the context of the selection, define the following terms, preparing to share your answers with the rest of the class.

cavern (1)	ethic (8)	milieu (14)
offal (1)	serfs (8)	avail (16)
carrion (1)	raucous (9)	ominously (16)
admonish (1)	oxytocin receptor (10)	Marx (23)
gastroarchitectural	miscreant (12)	mephitic (24)
system (2)	pro bono (13)	akimbo (26)
hypoglycemic (2)	congenial (14)	entropy (26)
sumptuary (8)		

2. Identify the transitions Ehrenreich uses throughout her essay. What transitions does she choose? How do they move along the action of the essay?

Writing Your Own Narratives

1. Ehrenreich's essay deals with her work experience as a waitress in Florida, focusing attention on the difficulties she faced on (and off) the job. Draft a three- to four-page narrative in which you reflect on a job experience you have had. Think specifically about what you want to say about this job: Was it difficult or easy? Was your boss a tyrant or a mentor? Did you become great friends or enemies with your coworkers? Once you decide on a purpose for your narrative, identify an event (or events) that will reflect this purpose. Like Ehrenreich, use details, characters, and dialogue to achieve your goal. Be sure to refer to the guidelines for checking over narrative writing on page 67.

2. At the heart of Ehrenreich's essay is her attempt to "stay afloat" by juggling two low-paying jobs that are taxing on her body, heart, and mind. We have all had experiences where we juggled too many things at once. Some of us find ways to keep everything in the air, and many of us have to take a few balls out of the act just to keep ourselves sane. Draft a three- to four-page essay in which you narrate a "juggling" experience in your life. How did you handle the stress? What was the ultimate result? Focusing on a clear sequence of events will make for an effective narrative, as will including a consistent point of view and strong transitional

words and phrases. Be sure to refer to the guidelines for checking over narrative writing on page 67.

3. PUBLIC WRITING. Both Ehrenreich and Angelou narrate experiences from their working situations by reflecting on pivotal moments that defined what it meant for them to work at a particular place or for a particular person. In this public writing assignment, compose a two- to three-page narrative article about working situations in your community. Envision this writing project as one that would appear in your local newspaper under the headline "Snapshots of Work in _____."

To compose your narrative, interview a person who works at a local institution in your community, asking him or her to relate to you a particularly telling experience that defines what it means to work at his or her place of employment. Take careful notes throughout the interview, focusing on moments of dialogue, characters, and the details he or she recalls. As you write your "snapshot," you'll need to make decisions about the organizational strategy for the narrative, the most effective point of view, and the climax of the story. Remember, too, that your audience is your community, so you'll want to accommodate their interests and reading expectations. Refer to the guidelines for checking over narrative writing as you draft and revise. Once all of your classmates have completed their assignments, share them with one another — or even create a class newspaper — so the entire class can learn of the various working experiences in your community.

ALFREDO CELEDÓN LUJÁN
Piñón Hunting

Alfredo Celedón Luján (b. 1949) was raised in northern New Mexico and is a graduate of New Mexico State University and the Bread Loaf School of English. He is a career educator, now teaching at Monte del Sol Charter School in Santa Fe, New Mexico. Luján's works have been published in *English Journal, Council Chronicle, California English, La Herencia del Norte, New Mexico Humanities Review, A Work of ARTE, Southwest Review, Sin Fronteras/Writers without Borders, Santa Fe New Mexican, Bread Loaf Teacher Magazine,* and *Puerto del Sol.* He is a National Endowment for the Humanities Fellow.

> **Preview** Consider how Luján establishes a consistent point of view throughout the essay.

My dad owned a 1959 white over brown Ford Fairlane. It had a chrome 1 continental kit on the back bumper for the spare tire. It was a low rider over the back wheels. The Fairlane had chrome fender skirts to match with the continental kit. It was a cool family car. My mom, dad, brother, sister and I took it everywhere — to Albuquerque on the long two lane highway, to Los Angeles on Route 66, to pick *piñónes** on Old Santa Fe Trail.

When we went *piñón* hunting, we would get up early — *de madrugada** — 2 as the sun was rising. Mom packed a lunch. It was usually *tortilla con carnitas** or *con bologna* sandwiches, boiled eggs, cokes, Black Cherry Can 'O' Pops, some green *chile, manzanitas*, tomates del jardín**, and ice water in an orange jug. Dad would get the car ready. He put an empty 25 pound flour sack, 4 empty Hills Brothers coffee cans, and a *tarpolio** in the trunk.

We got there early to get the best trees. We'd find a good tree loaded 3 with pine cones and *piñón* – the oblong, dark brown seeds that grow in the cones. We would walk up to the tree slowly, almost like we were stalking it . . . we didn't want to trample on any good *piñón* that had already dropped to the ground. The four of us kneeled about ten feet away from the tree in a semi-circle and picked our way up to the trunk. When we first started dropping the *piñónes* into the cans, they sounded like hail hitting a tin roof, but soon that sound stopped when the cans started to get full. Mom's can got filled the fastest. Dad said she picked fast because she was a typist — she could pick *piñón* with both hands. We'd dump the full cans into the flour sack and start again. Little by little we worked

---

* **piñón** (plural: **piñónes**): pine nuts
* **de madrugada:** at dawn
* **con carnitas:** with a little bit of meat
* **manzanitas:** little apples
* **del jardín:** from the garden
* **tarpolio:** tarpaulin

our way up to the tree, where we picked between the pine needles, and where the pine needles pricked our knees. By that time we might have picked 2 or 3 pounds altogether. Then, when we were sure that we had picked the best *piñón* under that tree, we'd put the *tarpolio* under it, and dad would climb the tree and go between the branches. He would stand on one branch and grab another one above him with both his hands. He would shake like crazy, and it would start drizzling *piñón* and pine needles on the *tarpolio*. It sounded like rain falling on a tent in the forest. He'd do it to another two branches and another two until he had shaken the whole tree. We then picked all the good *piñón* from the *tarpolio*. After that it was time for our boiled eggs and green *chile* snack. After breakfast we would do another tree, and then it would be time for our *tortilla con carnitas* lunch. After lunch we would do another tree or two until we got tired.

One time, when we were picking *piñón*, my brother was digging 4 around the roots of a tree with a stick.   He found a hole under a root, and then we heard him yell, "*A la* . . ." We ran over there and found that he had uncovered a squirrel's nest. It looked like there was a ton of *piñón* in there. I figured we'd have enough *piñón* for at least a couple of years. But dad didn't take the squirrel's *piñón*. He made us cover the hole with branches instead. He said that squirrel had worked very hard to gather that much *piñón*. It was his family's food for the winter, and wouldn't be fair for us to take it, dad said. He had made us cover it so no other *piñón* hunters would find it.

After a day of *juntando* piñón*, we'd load all of our stuff on the fancy 5 Ford Fairlane and go home. We usually went home with 10 to 15 pounds.

At home we would put the flour sack with *piñón* in the broom closet. 6 The next time we went *piñón* hunting, we took a new sack. We'd empty it into the other sack when we got home. Eventually we'd end up with two or three 25 pound sacks of *piñón* in the broom closet. That would be enough for the winter.

On "special" nights, like on Sundays when we watched *Bonanza* on 7 TV, mom would get a pound of *piñón* and put it in the sink to wash. All of the pine needles and dust and *vano* piñón* would float to the top, and she would take it out of the water with a paper towel and throw it into the garbage can. Then she would let the water out of the sink and turn on the faucet to rinse out the washed *piñón*. She would then put it on a flat cookie sheet and sprinkle salt on it while she warmed up the oven. Then she would roast it. The whole house would smell like roasting *pi-ñón*. There was nothing better than eating warm *piñón* on a special night.

The next day my brother and I would take the leftover *piñón* to school 8 in our pockets and eat it during class. It was almost like eating sunflower seeds, but it was a million times better. One time a teacher tried to take

---

* ***juntando:*** hunting
* ***vano:*** empty

my *piñón* away from me because I was annoying him by cracking it in class. I told him I wouldn't eat it any more, but that wasn't good enough, he wanted me to give it to him. No way, José. I had worked very hard to gather that much *piñón*. I told him I wouldn't give it to him. He gave me a slip of paper and told me to go to the principal's office for disobeying. What*ever, ese**. I ate more *piñónes* and thought of the squirrel on my way to the principal's office.

Reading Closely

1. What significance do *piñónes* and *piñón* hunting have in the life of Luján and his family? What do these treats represent to him? How does Luján signal this significance throughout his narration?

2. What parallel is Luján making between his disobedience at school and the squirrel's nest?

Considering Larger Issues

1. Luján combines three short narrations to compose this essay. Pinpoint the beginning and end of each of these narrations, and consider how they work together to achieve his overarching purpose for the essay. What is this purpose?

---

* ***ese:*** man

2. **Working with another classmate or two,** analyze the essay's introduction. Why does Luján choose to begin the essay in this way? How does this choice reinforce the purpose of the essay?

3. COMBINING METHODS. To create this narrative, Luján also calls on *description* and *process analysis*. Mark the passages that use these methods, and examine how they support the overall purpose of the narrative.

Thinking about Language

1. Using a dictionary or the context of the selection, define the following terms, preparing to share your answers with the rest of the class.

continental kit (1)	Route 66 (1)	*Bonanza* (7)
fender skirts (1)	stalking (3)	

2. Throughout the essay, Luján uses a number of Spanish terms (*piñónes, de madrugada, juntando*). What effect do these language choices have on the essay? How do they reinforce or detract from the essay's purpose or the intended mood of the narrative?

3. Many readers might not know what *piñónes* are. Pinpoint the place in the essay at which readers should be able to figure out the meaning of the term. To what extent (if any) does the photograph on page 115 help them do so? How does it enhance your understanding of Luján's narrative?

4. Analyze Luján's essay for transition words. How do these words help structure the essay's sequence of events?

Writing Your Own Narratives

1. Luján's narrative centers on the *piñón* hunting he did with his family. Draft a three- to four-page essay in which you narrate an outing you went on with your family. Like Luján, choose a simple, everyday experience rather than an extraordinary one, and craft that narrative so that your simple family outing becomes compelling. Your narrative should include a setting, characters, and a sequence of events. You might even consider including relevant dialogue. As you draft your essay, direct your writing to an interested audience and then fine-tune the purpose of your narration given your choice of readers. Refer to the guidelines for checking over narrative writing on page 67.

2. Luján concludes his essay by narrating his act of disobedience toward his teacher. Because he would not hand over the delicious *piñónes* he worked so hard to gather, he was sent to the principal's office. At one time or another, we've all been disobedient, for good or not-so-good reasons. Draft a three- to four-page essay in which you narrate your own act of disobedience, making sure to include characters, descriptive detail, and a careful sequence of events. You might even experiment with flashback or flashforward. You should have an overall purpose and audience in mind as you write. Refer to the guidelines for checking over narrative writing on page 67.

✳ Additional Suggestions for Writing

1. Draft a three- to four-page narrative essay in which you argue a thesis that relates education to identity. As you argue, you may find that you're also explaining a process and maybe even creating a mood. Consider modeling your essay on one of the narratives in this chapter, imitating the writer's strategies for making and supporting his or her points. Refer to the guidelines for checking over narrative writing (p. 67) as you draft and revise.

2. Several essays in this chapter explore issues of class. What makes someone a member of the upper class, middle class, or lower class: money, education, social status, occupation, or race? What are the effects of these distinctions? How do you behave, how have you behaved, and how would you like to behave in response to class distinctions? Drawing on your responses to these questions, draft a three- to four-page narrative essay in which you explore issues of class that you have experienced. You may find yourself using comparison and contrast or cause and consequence as you write. Remember that the guidelines for checking over narrative writing can be found on page 67.

3. Draft a three- to four-page narrative essay on the subject of online courses. If you have ever taken (or are now taking) an online, computer-mediated, or distance-learning course, use that course as the basis for your narrative essay. Freewrite for ten minutes about your experience, jotting down ideas on paper as they come to mind. From those ideas, try to determine a purpose for your essay, and from that purpose, a tentative thesis. Depending on your audience, your narration might also draw on *cause-and-effect analysis, process analysis, comparison and contrast,* and *argumentation.*

chapter 3

DESCRIPTION

Tell Me More

The Smitten Kitchen, in its latest physical incarnation is a 42 square foot (whimper) circa-1935 sort of half-galley kitchen with a 24 foot footprint, a single counter, tiny stove, checkered floor and a noisy window at the end to the avenue below.

What you'll see here is: A lot of comfort foods stepped up a bit, things like bread and birthday cakes made entirely from scratch and tutorials on everything from how to poach an egg to how to make tart doughs that don't shrink up on you, but also a favorite side dish (zucchini and almonds) that takes less than five minutes to make.

What we're wary of is: Excessively fussy foods and/or pretentious ingredients. We don't do truffle oil, Himalayan pink salt at $10 per quarter-ounce or single-origin chocolate that can only be found though Posh Nosh-approved purveyors. We think food should be accessible, and are certain that you don't need any of these things to cook fantastically.

The Writer, Cook, Photographer and Occasional Dishwasher

Deb is the kind of person you might innocently ask what the difference is between summer and winter squash and she'll go on for about twenty minutes before coming up for air to a cleared room and you soundly snoring. It's taken some time, but she's finally realized that there are people out there that might forgive her for such food, cooking and ingredient-obsessed blathering and possibly, even come back for more.

When she's not prattling on about galley and grub, Deb is a freelance writer focusing on topics from technology to the daily grind, and freelance photographer with a focus on travel and, of course, food.

The Husband

Alex gets billing as assistant photographer, majority-part dishwasher, cheering section and sometimes editor of grammar and spelling. He's a great cook on the too-rare occasion his wife lets him help with anything but reaching bowls on top shelves. He likes salt, shellfish, things wrapped, stuffed or balanced on bacon, steak frites, dried cranberries, milk chocolate, Bloody Marys, pretty much anything pickled, and Deb, although she is usually not.

When Alex is not putting out smitten kitchen fires, he manages things like information technology and other stuff that makes most people's eyes glaze over. But not Deb's.

*B*loggers write about everything imaginable: politics, sports, travel, technology, arts and crafts, celebrities, and ordinary daily life. As you may know, *blog* is short for *Web log*, and a blog functions as a log or journal for writers to post their thoughts for online audiences who might share their interests. Bloggers often include an "About" page or paragraph so readers can learn more about the writer as well as his or her interests, background, experiences, motivations for writing, and personal investments. In composing this "About" text, the writer often relies on description.

On the facing page are some sections of the "About" page for smittenkitchen.com, a blog that chronicles the culinary adventures of Deb, the primary writer and chef, and her husband, Alex. Here Deb begins by describing where all the cooking takes place (42-square-foot galley kitchen with a tiny stove, checkered floor, and noisy window) and the kinds of food that get cooked there ("comfort foods stepped up a bit"). Following the kitchen description (and a description of the site itself that is not shown on the facing page) are descriptions of Deb and Alex. Unlike the kitchen description, these do not detail the physical characteristics of the couple. Instead we learn about their backgrounds, skills, and personalities. Deb is a food enthusiast (and a talker) whose regular work is freelance writing and photography. Alex is obviously second in command—he's the main dishwasher, copy editor, and bowl retriever who likes a wide variety of foods and works in IT management. Through these few selected descriptive details, Deb gives readers a good sense of who she and her husband are and what their kitchen is like.

Looking at Your Own Literacy   If you already have a blog, how do you describe yourself on your "About" page? Why do you include these details and not others about yourself? How are these descriptions shaped by your readers' interests? If you don't blog, imagine that you do. What would you blog about? Why? What would you include in your "About" page? Why include these descriptions of yourself? How would these descriptions be shaped by your readers' interests?

What Is Description?

Every day, we use **description** to depict in words the details of what we see, hear, smell, taste, touch, or sense in some less physical way — or in our imagination. Description is such an indispensable element in our daily thinking and conversation that we often use it unconsciously. Just think of the descriptions you encounter in textbooks and assignments at school, the memos and e-mails you read at work, and the newspaper articles and television programs that tell you about the day's events. When you're alert to descriptions, to the ways writers and speakers try to appeal to your five senses, you'll realize how prevalent description really is.

Sometimes an entire piece of writing is devoted to description, but more often a writer uses description, visuals, and other kinds of writing to fulfill a broader purpose. Explanatory descriptions, for example, lead us through a process or help us make decisions. Repair manuals are filled with descriptions, as are gardening guides, bird–watching handbooks, and much advertising. Some particularly lush descriptions, such as those of national parks, museums, or other tourist attractions, persuade us to visit a place. Other descriptions of people or places simply entertain us, like a good story does. Whether you are explaining your pet's symptoms to the veterinarian, sending a postcard from a vacation spot, writing up a lab report, or compiling your birthday wish list, you have reasons every day to describe something.

When you are writing descriptions, your job is to transfer your own perceptions into a lasting image or impression for the reader. One way to create these images and impressions is to write with vivid details: either **sensory details** that appeal to the physical senses (sight, hearing, smell, taste, and touch) or details that appeal to your reader's emotional, physical, or intellectual **sensibilities** (such as prudence, nostalgia, empathy, kindness, and aesthetic taste). Writers create such sensations in descriptions all around you, from the "hot new colors" for athletic wear and the "refreshing citrus scents" in a new shampoo to the "bacteria–fighting power" of a mouthwash and the "natural crunch" of a breakfast cereal. On items as mundane as the label of your shampoo bottle or the packaging of your toothbrush, descriptions help you perceive the product in the way the writer wants you to perceive it.

The description of the running shoe on page 123 may seem mundane. But it actually teaches readers a good deal of important information: What is the most important part of the shoe and why? What functions do the different parts of the shoe serve? Such information will be especially important for these readers as they choose which running shoes will best suit their athletic needs.

. . . .

Thinking about Description

1. Imagine your dream job. How would you describe it? What would be the job description for this job? Now think of the job skills and experiences that would qualify you for this job. Describe the kind of work you'd need to do so you would meet (and exceed) the expectations of a hiring committee.

2. Review the "Anatomy of a Running Shoe" on page 123. Judging by the language used in the description, who is the intended audience? What sensibilities does the writer expect the audience to have? How is the writer appealing to these sensibilities?

. . . .

Anatomy of a Running Shoe

As running shoes have gotten more complicated, so has the terminology used to describe them. The glossary below will help you understand the basic parts of a running shoe.

Upper: The part of the shoe that wraps around and over the top of the foot. It's most of what you see when you look at a running shoe.

Heel counter: A firm cup that is encased in the upper and surrounds the heel. It controls rear-foot motion.

Outsole: The undersurface of the shoe, usually made from carbon rubber.

Midsole: The most important part of a shoe, it is the cushioning layer between the upper and the outsole. It is usually made of ethylene vinyl acetate (EVA), polyurethane (a synthetic rubber that's heavier and longer-lasting than EVA), or a combination of the two. Dual-density midsoles have a firmer material on the inside of the shoe. This helps limit pronation. Many shoe companies also put patented technologies in their midsoles, such as gel and high-tech plastics.

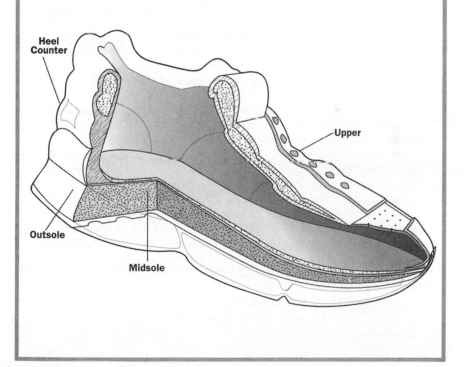

Heel Counter

Upper

Outsole

Midsole

Why Use Description?

The three most common purposes of description are to inform, to entertain, and to argue a point. If you are writing a description, you will need to decide on your purpose (or purposes, if you have more than one) and then choose those details that best help you achieve that purpose.

Every day, descriptions that inform help you make decisions, even small ones such as which coat to wear. For example, you might look at the forecast in the weather section of the morning paper: "Today, intervals of clouds, snow, and high wind. High 36, low 24." These descriptive details provide you with the information you need to decide whether to wear a winter coat, a light jacket, or just a T-shirt. You might also use these details to describe the weather in an e-mail message to a friend who is coming to visit. By conveying details about the weather to him, you will provide him with the information he needs for packing.

Good informative descriptions are loaded with details. In the following paragraph, creative nonfiction writer Bret Lott carefully and concisely describes a home movie of himself, his brother, and his mother from years ago.

Description to Inform

This much is fact: There is a home movie of the two of us sitting on the edge of the swimming pool at our grandma and grandpa's old apartment building in Culver City. The movie, taken sometime in early 1960, is in color, though the color has faded, leaving my brother Brad and me milk white and harmless children, me a year and a half old, Brad almost four, our brown hair faded to only the thought of brown hair. Our mother, impossibly young, sits next to me on the right of the screen. Her hair, for all the fading of the film, is coal black, shoulder length, and parted in the middle, curled up on the sides. She has on a bathing suit covered in purple and blue flowers, the color in them nearly gone. Next to me on the left of the screen is Brad, in his white swimming trunks. I am in the center, my fat arms up, bent at the elbows, fingers curled into fists, my legs kicking away at the water, splashing and splashing. I am smiling, the baby of the family, the center of the world at that very instant, though my little brother, Tim, is only some six or seven months off, and my little sister, Leslie, the last child, just three years distant. The pool water before us is only a thin sky blue, the bushes behind us a dull and lifeless light green. There is no sound.   – BRET LOTT, "Brothers"

Through Lott's descriptions, readers almost witness the movie themselves. Although this description seems merely informative, explaining to readers the basic details of the movie, Lott builds on this description to reflect on his relationship with his brother and how their relationship has changed over the years.

· ·

Try Your Hand   Find a picture or video of you and someone important to you. First, describe the picture or video as Lott does, including the basic informative details and explaining to readers exactly what the picture or video looks and sounds like. Then tell the story behind this picture or video: What moment is being captured?

· ·

Perhaps the most familiar kinds of descriptions are those intended to entertain. Whether they are found in the opening lines of a novel or essay, a radio announcer's play–by–play of a sports event, or a travel guide's account of exotic scenery, descriptive details give us pleasure. For example, when Barbara Kingsolver explains to readers how the physical space of her home inspires and shapes her writing process, she entertains readers with rich descriptions of her southern Appalachian home and its surrounding beauty.

Description to Entertain

I have places where all my stories begin.

One is a log cabin in a deep, wooded hollow at the end of Walker Mountain. This stoic little log house leans noticeably uphill, just as half the tobacco barns do in this rural part of southern Appalachia, where even gravity seems to have fled for better work in the city. Our cabin was built of chestnut logs in the late 1930s, when the American chestnut blight ran roughshod through every forest from Maine to Alabama, felling mammoth trees more extravagantly than the crosscut saw. Those of us who'll never get to see the spreading crown of an American chestnut have come to understand this blight as one of the great natural tragedies in our continent's history. But the pragmatic homesteaders who lived in this hollow at that time simply looked up and saw a godsend. They harnessed their mule and dragged the fallen soldiers down off the mountain to build their home.

Now it's mine. Between May and August, my family and I happily settle our lives inside its knobby, listing walls. We pace the floorboards of its porch while rain pummels the tin roof and slides off the steeply pitched eaves in a limpid sheet. I love this rain; my soul hankers for it. Through a curtain of it I watch the tulip poplars grow. When it stops, I listen to the woodblock concerto of dripping leaves and the first indignant Carolina wrens reclaiming their damp territories. Then come the wood thrushes, heartbreakers, with their minor-keyed harmonies as resonant as poetry. A narrow beam of sun files between the steep mountains, and butterflies traverse this column of light, from top to bottom to top again, like fish in a tall aquarium. My daughters hazard the damp grass to go hunt box turtles and crayfish, or climb into the barn loft to inhale the scent of decades-old tobacco. That particular dusty sweetness, among all other odors that exist, invokes the most reliable nostalgia for my own childhood; I'm slightly envious and have half a mind to run after the girls

with my own stick for poking into crawdad holes. But mostly I am glad to
watch them claim my own best secrets for themselves.

— Barbara Kingsolver, *Small Wonder*

Kingsolver's descriptions make her home come alive in readers' minds,
calling on almost all of their senses as a means for them to understand
this place and its serene beauty. With Kingsolver, readers hear the "concerto of dripping leaves" and the poetic "minor-keyed harmonies of the
wood thrushes." They can smell the "decades-old tobacco" in the barn and
feel the "knobby" walls of the cabin. And of course, they can see sunbeams
filing between "steep mountains." Through such a beautifully rich description, readers not only gain a sense of what this place looks, smells, feels,
and sounds like but also gain insight into Kingsolver's state of mind: this
is a serene and comforting place for her — a place that touches her soul.

If you are writing a description of a person or place, you will discover
that providing your own response to details about physical appearance and
personality as well as the details themselves creates a well-rounded portrait. Like Kingsolver, you should include expected details ("deep, wooded
hollow"; "chestnut logs"; "damp grass") as well as unexpected details ("the
first *indignant* Carolina wrens"; the butterflies who traverse the sunbeams
"like fish in a tall aquarium") to make your description memorable.

· ·

Try Your Hand   Take a moment to think about the place where you do
most of your writing. Is it your dorm room? your kitchen table? the library? a writing lab? Relying on descriptive details, paint a picture of
this place for other students in the class. Like Kingsolver, use different
kinds of details so they can see, hear, feel, smell, and maybe even taste
what this place is like. After you've composed your description, consider
whether this place is conducive to writing. Is it too loud? too bland? just
right? Why? Be prepared to share your writing with the class.

· ·

Description can often seem to be just a sensory rush of seemingly
objective details that transports readers into the presence of a person or
a place. But description can also be used as argument. In writing and in
conversation, the emotional charge of a few well-chosen descriptive details can change the opinions or actions of our readers or listeners. Consider this excerpt from a flyer intended to discourage smoking.

Description to Argue a Point

When a smoker takes a typical long drag on a cigarette, he follows
with a deep inhalation that pulls the smoke into the farthest recesses of
the lungs. It is as if every one of the hundreds of thousands of air sacs
is clamoring to be filled with the tar-bearing, nicotine-laden, gaseous
mixture.

> In this process, the sticky tar with many chemical constituents, including several cancer-causing agents, is deposited on the mucous membrane of the entire bronchial system — air passages of the lungs.
> — AMERICAN CANCER SOCIETY

The passage goes on to trace the physiological process by which the elements in cigarette smoke lead to the development of lung cancer. It is the descriptive details in the opening sentences, though, that catch readers' attention and perhaps cause them to change their actions by appealing to — or offending — all their physical senses. Details ranging from sight (the images of a smoker taking a drag and of tar being deposited on mucous membranes) to smell and taste and even sound ("clamoring" air sacs) and touch ("sticky" tar) work together to persuade readers of the direct correlation between smoking and illness.

. . . .

Try Your Hand Think of the descriptive details that teachers, parents, community leaders, advertisements, and health books have used to try to persuade you not to smoke, binge-drink, engage in unprotected sex, or participate in other potentially harmful activities. Or if you are a parent, think of details you have used with your children. Choose one of these potentially harmful activities, and make a list of vivid sensory details that describe its dangers. Draft a descriptive paragraph using details that might persuade one of your classmates not to engage in the activity.

. . . .

How Do You Use Description in Academic Writing?

In academic contexts, students and scholars use description to inform readers about a person, place, phenomenon, or event, and they call on description to persuade readers to see the validity of a particular perspective. Academic writers compose rich descriptions that rely on sensory details and that appeal to readers' emotional, physical, or intellectual sensibilities. As students, you will encounter (or may already have encountered) a number of situations in which you will be asked to observe something and then describe it. For example, when you take part in experiments in your science classes, you are often asked to record your observations in your lab reports, describing for readers what you see, hear, smell, and (sometimes) taste. These descriptions are necessary for you to assess chemical reactions (chemistry), mechanical processes (physics and engineering), physiological properties (anatomy), or behavioral patterns (psychology).

Academic writers in anthropology also rely heavily on description. To learn about the diverse cultures of the world, anthropologists study these cultures and their people, often living in these cultural communities as a means to gain deep and detailed knowledge about the values, relationships, ways of life, and language practices of these communities. Description is one of the primary rhetorical methods these scholars use in their work because before drawing conclusions about these cultural communities, they need to describe them as thoroughly as they can.

Anthropologist Margaret Reynolds uses description in her study of women in a religious community. In *Plain Women: Gender and Ritual in the Old Order River Brethren*, Reynolds observes women's place and participation in the community, focusing particularly on their dress and culinary traditions. In the following example, Reynolds describes her observations of these women's dress and then draws conclusions from her observations.

Description in Academic Writing

The cape dress embodies modesty for River Brethren women. Hemlines vary, but a common standard is midway between ankle and knee (although younger women have opted recently for a longer dress length). The dress consists of a long, gathered or pleated skirt sewn onto the waistband of the long-sleeved, high-necked bodice. Since the cape covers the dress front, it also conceals buttons, zippers, or snaps that fasten the dress bodice underneath the cape. Snaps or pins secure the cape front opening. The points of the triangular cape are sewn fast to the apron waistband in the front. One point of the cape extends down the back, and either hangs loose or is tucked into the back waistband. A portion of the bodice that extends below the apron band is known as the peplum, or "frill," as most River Brethren women refer to it. Most women wear dress sleeves full length, to the wrist, or no less than three-quarter length.

These details of dress differ from those of some Lancaster County Amish women, who wear their hemlines at about knee-length and their sleeves shortened above the elbow. Sister Deborah points out that in these aspects of dress, Old Order River Brethren are more conservative than the Amish, who are popularly thought to be the most orthodox in dress. This seems to be a point of considerable significance to the group.

River Brethren women wear the cape to cover the neckline and bosom and to provide modesty for nursing. The cape fully covers the bodice, and some women fashion it to lap over the shoulders a few extra inches. Others vary the width of the cape for greater modesty. The "half apron" (or waistband apron) and the bib apron for work are the types most commonly worn over the dress. Originally used as a protection for other clothing, the apron became a symbol of servitude and, eventually, a covering for modesty. The apron and the cape are worn to conceal the lines of the female form. A sister is never seen in public without her apron. Many Amish wear aprons of contrasting material to emphasize the separate character of each garment. The Old Order River Brethren cape and apron are of matching material. Most River Brethren women sew the cape and apron together (a progressive practice, compared to the Amish and members of other groups, who pin them together). Old Order River Brethren women fasten the apron at the waist with a belt or sash that extends from one side all the way around the waist to the opposite side. They attach the sash at the side of the waist by a hook or pin.

— Margaret Reynolds, *Plain Women:*
Gender and Ritual in the Old Order River Brethren

Before Reynolds explains the function and symbolism of these women's dress (aprons are a symbol of servitude and a covering for modesty), she describes what the dress looks like: hemlines are "midway between ankle and knee"; skirts are "gathered or pleated"; the cape "hangs loose or is tucked into the back waistband."

As in all rhetorical situations, you will need to assess when to use description in your academic writing. If your professors ask you to record, observe, portray, illustrate, or, of course, describe a situation, person, place, or event, they most likely want you to respond by offering deep and rich detailed descriptions. While composing your descriptions, you'll want to choose carefully which details to include, selecting only those features or characteristics pertinent to the discussion at hand. Reynolds, for instance, does not describe the women's physical characteristics because they are not relevant to her study. She just focuses on their clothing — the subject of her examination. Finally, academic writing projects might also provide you with the opportunity to call on two or even three rhetorical methods. In the example, Reynolds not only describes and analyzes, but also compares women in the Old Order River Brethren community with women in the Lancaster County Amish community.

. . . .

Analyzing Description in Academic Writing   Review a textbook in one of your other classes. When does the writer of the textbook use description in this academic setting? Why? What purpose does the description serve?

. . . .

How Do You Read a Description?

In order to write effective descriptions, you'll first need to learn to read descriptive writing closely and critically. Reading critically means analyzing, evaluating, and questioning as you read in order to determine the techniques that contribute to a successful piece of writing (and the problems that can work against success), no matter which rhetorical method of development you're considering. As the next section explains, in the case of description, the sensory details of the writing should work together to give a clear overall impression that is appropriate for the intended purpose and audience. For example, if the description is intended to be mainly informative, is it clear? Or does it seem confusing, contradictory, incomplete, or either too detailed or not detailed enough for the intended readers? If the purpose is to entertain, is the description vivid or flat? And if it's meant to be argumentative, will the audience find the details believable, or might they seemed biased or too skimpy?

To achieve a critical understanding of the piece under review, start out by considering the title (if it has one) and how that title orients you to what follows and how it might suggest its purpose. Bret Lott's title, "Brothers" (p. 124), for example, provides you with a point of reference as you begin the essay. Although the description of the movie includes his mother, the title suggests that the focus of the essay will be on Lott and his brother. In a longer piece, you'd need to evaluate the contributions of the introduction and conclusion to the description, locating the author's thesis and main points to see what part each of these features plays in revealing and supporting the overall purpose. You'd then need to read through the body of the text again, this time more closely, to see how (or whether) the use of descriptive details creates an overall impression that fulfills the purpose.

Lott's description, for example, is informative as well as entertaining and includes both sensory details and details that appeal to readers' sensibilities. Although Lott seems simply to describe what is happening in the movie, he offers readers a nostalgic scene of childhood, innocence, and even love. Readers are transported to a beautiful summer day when a young boy and his brother played in the pool. Lott's details assume a more general audience: those interested in reading about this family scene and this relationship between brothers. Kingsolver, by contrast, makes a number of assumptions about her readers by composing her description as she does. Readers of Kingsolver's essay are also transported to an idyllic scene. Through her description, though, Kingsolver assumes that her audience has at least a minimal knowledge of nature and geography. By not explaining or more deeply describing such terms as crawdad holes, Carolina wrens, wood thrushes, and tulip poplars, Kingsolver assumes that readers will know (or will learn) to what she is referring.

Finally, assess every description in terms not only of what the author says but also what is unsaid. Sometimes details that are not mentioned (where Kingsolver lives for the remainder of the year; the person who is taking Lott's home video) can be just as important to the overall impression as those that are, so you'll always want to try to imagine what could be missing and why.

. . . .

Try Your Hand   With a classmate, identify both the sensory details Lott employs in his description and the details that reach out to readers' sensibilities. What assumption is Lott making about his audience through these details and descriptions?

. . . .

How Do You Write a Description?

Whether its purpose is to inform, to entertain, to argue, or to achieve some combination of these goals, a description must create a dominant impression by using the right amount of detail, effective descriptive language, and an appropriate organizational pattern. In choosing details, language, and an organizational pattern, a writer also needs to think about the audience — the knowledge, expectations, and attitudes of those who will be reading the description.

● **Determining Your Purpose**

You will need to think about whether your description will fulfill one purpose or multiple purposes and whether it will be the main focus of your essay or play a smaller part in a larger piece of writing. These factors may influence, for example, how many or which details you choose to include. For instance, if you're using description to help compose an argument, you might follow the lead of Mimi Swartz. In the following passage from "How Green Is My Bayou?" an article published in *Texas Monthly,* Swartz relies on description to make an argument about the "greening" of Houston. She acknowledges that while many readers may think of Houston as a polluted and dirty city, she wants them to see how it's changed for the better.

Description to Argue a Point

What has happened since [2000] has been an all-out effort to change Houston's identity. Consider Discovery Green, the lovely new park across from the George R. Brown Convention Center, which even on weekdays is filled with giddy kids, dogs, and parents, cavorting in the fountains, picnicking by the pond, or just relaxing under the oaks, people-watching. On Interstate 10, on the west side of town, pine saplings and blooming crape myrtles have replaced billboards. The refurbished promenade and reflective pool at Hermann Park evoke Paris (well, almost). Landscaped hike-and-bike trails along Buffalo Bayou lead to secret gardens downtown; at night they glow with either blue or white lights, depending on the phase of the moon. (Incidentally, canoeing that same route no longer requires a gas mask or a wet suit.) Off Beltway 8, the once weedy flood-control field that is now Arthur Story Park fills up in the morning with people practicing tai chi. New public buildings must meet the latest LEED (Leadership in Energy and Environmental Design) certification standards—the national benchmark for energy efficiency—and, except for libraries and new fire stations, are supposed to be cooled to no lower than 76 degrees. Luxurious green homes sell for $1 million and up, while in Montgomery County, Land Tejas is building green housing starting at $170,000.   — MIMI SWARTZ, "How Green Is My Bayou?"

This descriptive passage uses vivid and telling details to help readers *see* Houston in a new (greener) light. Of course, Swartz's attention to audience connects closely to her purpose. Since she is writing to readers of *Texas Monthly*, her readers are most likely Texans familiar with Houston and its reputation as a wasteful and polluted city. By describing changes to specific places — places her readers probably know well — Swartz offers a compelling argument about how "green" Houston has become.

● Considering Your Audience

As seen in the passage by Mimi Swartz, closely tied to your purpose is your audience. Even if you don't know your readers by sight or name, you'll still need to consider the characteristics of the persons who will read your description and how these characteristics might influence your decision regarding the details you include or leave out. The online magazine ConsumerReports.org offers specific kinds of descriptions of products given the needs and expectations of its readers. This site supplies reviews of products from digital cameras to hybrid cars, helping readers decide which products to buy and which to avoid. The detailed descriptions included in the reviews help readers make informed decisions about their purchases. The following review of the hybrid Nissan Versa is just one example.

Budget Cars: Nissan Versa

Nissan's smallest car has a very roomy rear seat, comfortable ride, and well-finished interior. It's available as a hatchback or sedan. The tall roofline allows easy access. The relatively refined 1.8-liter engine isn't that powerful. A less expensive 1.6-liter is also available. The six-speed manual is a bit clunky, but the optional CVT and conventional automatic perform well. Fuel economy isn't impressive for a subcompact, however. The ride is relatively comfortable and quiet, but handling isn't particularly agile. Stopping distances are long without the optional antilock brakes. Curtain air bags are standard. Reliability is average for the hatchback, worse for the sedan.   — CONSUMERREPORTS.ORG, Review of Nissan Versa

Notice that the detailed descriptions included in this review are geared toward readers wanting to learn about the car's basic features, as well as its efficiency and reliability. Readers do not just learn of the positive characteristics of the car: the "very roomy" rear seat, the "tall" roofline; the "relatively refined" 1.8–liter engine. They also learn about the negative qualities: the manual transmission that's "a bit clunky" and the fuel economy that "isn't impressive for a subcompact." It is important to note what the reviewer of the Versa expects from readers of the magazine. By not defining a term like CVT, the reviewer assumes that buyers have done their homework and have already acquired a good deal of knowledge about these cars.

● Creating a Dominant Impression

The **dominant impression** you want a description to make on your readers is the quality of the subject that you want to convey to them or the attitude toward it that you want them to share. To create such an impression, you need to choose details that are directed to your specific audience, details that can "show" rather than just "tell" those readers exactly what you mean. In addition, you need to organize your description in a way that strongly reinforces the dominant impression.

Often you will state that dominant impression in a **thesis**, a one-sentence declaration of the main idea of your description. A thesis — which can refer to a paragraph, a longer passage, or an entire essay — sums up your subject, the perspective you're taking on the subject, and your purpose in writing the description.

In the passage from *Texas Monthly*, Swartz states her thesis in the first sentence of the paragraph: "What has happened since has been an all-out effort to change Houston's identity." The descriptions that follow support this thesis by showing readers how the city has become less gray and more green.

Although every description should have a clear sense of subject and purpose, not every one needs an explicit thesis. Sometimes an implied thesis can convey the description's mood or overall impression as well as its purpose indirectly. In his essay "Finders Keepers: The Story of Joey Coyle," author Mark Bowden offers a description of Coyle's neighborhood in South Philadelphia. While this description does not offer an explicit thesis, it does create a dominant impression for readers that suggests the passage's implicit thesis.

> His home on Front Street was at the tattered edge of the tight weave of South Philly's streets, away from its strong, nurturing core. East of Front Street is a wasteland: weedy, trash-piled lots, junkyards, old brick warehouses defaced with graffiti, rusting hulks of old boxcars in forlorn rows alongside the newer cars that come and go, fenced-in lots around the

trucking yards and dwindling industrial works along the Delaware River waterfront. Over this bleak expanse, the air is tinged gray and tastes of ash. Just behind the row of houses on Joey's block loomed the giant concrete underside of Interstate 95, which threw a perpetual shadow wider than a city block.

— MARK BOWDEN, "Finders Keepers: The Story of Joey Coyle"

Readers cannot miss the dominant impression or the implied thesis of this passage. Marked by "weedy, trash–piled lots"; "grotesque junk heaps"; the "perpetual shadow" of the highway; and the gray and ash–tasting air, Coyle's neighborhood is not a welcoming one. Here we see how the implied thesis is suggested by means of selection, organization, focus, and force of the descriptive details. Like Bowden's description, the antismoking flyer on pages 126–127 contains no explicit thesis, but the main idea behind the description is perfectly clear: smoking cigarettes starts a chain of events that can lead to lung cancer.

One other important consideration in creating a dominant impression is deciding how much descriptive detail to include. Because you're already familiar with the subject you're describing, you may tend either to include every single bit of information about it or to provide too few details. It's hard to figure out the right amount of detail by yourself, so don't hesitate to ask a friend or classmate to read your draft and tell you where you go overboard on detail and where you need to add more.

● Using Descriptive Language

Descriptive writing calls for descriptive language, either objective or subjective. **Objective description** tells about something (an event, person, place, animal, inanimate object) without evaluating it or revealing the writer's personal feelings about it. Writers who want to emphasize the accuracy and trustworthiness of their writing — most journalists, scientists, and technical writers — rely on objective description. Objective description relies on **denotative language,** words that sound neutral and do not carry any emotional associations. **Subjective description,** by contrast, shifts the emphasis from the facts to the writer's reactions and responses to those facts. It often uses **connotative language,** words that suggest evaluations and emotional responses. For example, an urban neighborhood might be described either with the denotative label *low-income* or the connotative label *slum*, a word that carries associations not just of low incomes but also of crime, decay, and squalor.

Writers often choose the type of descriptive language according to their particular purpose and audience. A political scientist, for example, might use *low-income* in an article for a scholarly journal about her latest research project, an article intended to inform an audience of other political scientists. But she might use *slum* in a letter to the editor of the local newspaper in which she tries to persuade a more general audience that the city government should provide better housing or police protection for the neighborhood's residents.

In fact, rarely is a description purely objective or subjective. It is almost impossible to be totally objective, to "let the facts speak for themselves." At the same time, even the most subjective description needs to be grounded in objective facts in order to make sense, to be meaningful to readers. To write a successful description, a writer often needs to use both types so that the overall description stands the test of (objective) reality or (subjective) meaning. In choosing whether to use objective or subjective description, or both, and how much of each, you will have to identify your purpose and the relationship you want to establish with your readers.

Using both objective and subjective description, writer David Foster Wallace describes radio talk show host John Ziegler in his *Atlantic* essay, "Host."

Objective and Subjective Description

Dressed, as is his custom, for golf, and wearing a white-billed cap w/ corporate logo, Mr. Ziegler is seated by himself in the on-air studio, surrounded by monitors and sheaves of Internet downloads. He is trim, clean-shaven, and handsome in the somewhat bland way that top golfers and local TV newsmen tend to be. His eyes, which off-air are usually flat and unhappy, are alight now with passionate conviction. Only some of the studio's monitors concern Mr. Z's own program; the ones up near the ceiling take muted, closed-caption feeds from Fox News, MSNBC, and what might be C-SPAN. To his big desk's upper left is a wall-mounted digital clock that counts down seconds. His computer monitors' displays also show the exact time.

Across the soundproof glass of the opposite wall, another monitor in the Airmix room is running an episode of *The Simpsons*, also muted, which both the board op and the call screener are watching with half an eye.

Pendent in front of John Ziegler's face, attached to the same type of hinged, flexible stand as certain student desk lamps, is a Shure-brand broadcast microphone that is sheathed in a gray foam filtration sock to soften popped p's and hissed sibilants. It is into this microphone that the host speaks.   — David Foster Wallace, "Host"

The objective details inform readers of Ziegler's physical appearance: he's dressed for golf, wearing a white cap with a corporate logo; he's trim and clean–shaven. Objective details also describe the room to readers: there is a microphone on the desk, a digital clock on the wall, studio monitors showing Fox News, MSNBC, and *The Simpsons*. But Wallace includes subjective details as well. Ziegler is "handsome in the

"Reading" and Using Visuals in Description

Many times, writers use visuals to anchor their descriptions. Photographs, drawings, or other kinds of images can strengthen the dominant impression of the descriptive writing, provide an organizational format (particularly a spatial one), and help the writer keep the point of view consistent. If you want to use visuals in writing for an academic assignment, it is a good idea to check with your instructor beforehand. You also need to consider whether to include labels or captions (if the visuals do not already include them) and whether to refer to the visuals in your written text or to let them stand on their own.

To use visuals effectively in descriptive writing, you'll need to learn how to "read" them critically in the same way that you do written descriptions—to judge what their intended purpose and

somewhat bland way that top golfers and local TV newsmen tend to be." Off-air, his eyes are "flat and unhappy"; on-air, they are "alight" with "passionate conviction." The interplay of objective and subjective details provides a tantalizing opening to this biographical sketch. Readers continue, wondering what about Ziegler's show makes his eyes shift from "flat" to "passionate."

Descriptive language also often includes **figurative language,** a type of subjective language that departs from the denotative meaning of a word or phrase for the sake of emphasis. Most often, figurative language involves a comparison between two unlike things. For instance, to describe Hermann Park in Houston, Swartz compares the park to Paris, and to explain the rainfall in her Appalachian hollow, Kingsolver defines it as a curtain. These **metaphors,** indirect comparisons of one thing to another, enable readers to gain a fuller sense of this place (the park) and this phenomenon (the rainfall) by comparing them to places (Paris) and objects (curtains) with which readers are familiar. A **simile** is a much more direct comparison connecting two unlike things with the words *like, as,* or *than.* Once again, Kingsolver uses simile

audience are, how well they achieve this purpose for this audience, and why. Consider for a moment the accompanying visual. Photographs of prolific Native American (Kiowa) writer N. Scott Momaday often accompany announcements of his lectures and other appearances—but to what purpose? What descriptive details can you glean from this visual representation of the literary figure?

Considered a foremost authority on the native peoples and cultures of the American Southwest, Momaday's appearance complements his reputation. His sport coat, plaid shirt, and necktie suggest that he (or perhaps his publisher or publicity agent) wants to present a combination of respectability and informality. Momaday's pose, with his hand on his chin, is a traditional visual way to suggest intellect and shows off his large silver-and-turquoise bracelet and ring, reminders of the American Indian heritage that is the focus of his writing. Whenever you look at a visual that seems intended as a description—and especially if you're thinking of using it as part of a written description—carefully consider its details and how well they work together to achieve a particular purpose for the intended audience.

in her description of her home and its surroundings, writing that the butterflies she sees flying through beams of sunlight are "like fish in a tall aquarium." The excerpt from the antismoking flyer contains an especially striking simile: "It is as if every one of the hundreds of thousands of air sacs is clamoring to be filled." Whenever you write a description, consider whether metaphors or similes can make it more effective.

● *Organizing Your Description*

Because descriptive writing generally focuses on visual details, it most often follows some variation on a **spatial organizational** pattern, with the details arranged according to their location. By arranging your description spatially, you are ordering information from a particular physical **point of view** (the assumed eye and mind of the writer). In this example, Charlotte Hogg uses spatial order to describe her hometown library.

Spatial Organization

The library looked the same that day as it has every day since. To the right of the door are magazine racks; to the left, the librarian's desk. To the left of that is the children's section, its own little square area of books, but not quite separate, since volunteer librarians like my grandma watch from the desk.

Spatial order is not the only possibility, however. Writers might choose to use a pattern of **chronological organization** to reflect how events they are describing occurred over time. Here the writer would explain what happened first, second, third, and so on. When Marjorie Garber describes "orders" of dogs, she uses a pattern of **emphatic organization**; she includes details that move from large dogs to small ones, for she has decided to concentrate on size.

Emphatic Organization

An owner of big dogs myself, I was inclined at first to admire the large ones above the small. The giant Schnauzers, an improbable and handsome crew; the Briards, with stuffed-toy good looks in a jumbo size; the all-white Great Pyrenees and the all-black Newfies. To me the Chinese cresteds, hairless except for strategic poufs, looked like tiny but determined cheerleaders, with pompoms at foot and head. The Maltese all seemed to be *en femme*, with bow in hair and silky coats brushing the ground, and they traversed the diagonal runway like little Miss Americas in training. But some small breeds proved unexpectedly endearing; I fell in love with the border terriers, a breed I'd never noticed in the flesh (or the fur?) before.   —Marjorie Garber, *Dog Love*

Garber names all the big dogs she likes at the beginning of the paragraph, and then she catalogues the small dogs she doesn't much like. Finally, though, she moves to the small dogs she finds herself admiring: "But some small breeds proved unexpectedly endearing." By organizing her description according to size, Garber builds up to a surprise, something unexpected for her as well as for her readers: she loves border terriers.

The Garber passage is a good reminder that just as in choosing your descriptive details and language, in deciding on an organizational pattern you may want to take into account not only your purpose but also your audience. You might consider an order that reflects the audience's physical or mental point of view rather than your own, moving from most familiar (to them) to least familiar, from most remote (from them) to closest, from least persuasive (to them) to most persuasive. Whatever organizational method you use, be sure to remain consistent to one point of view, as Garber does—unless, of course, you are deliberately recording multiple viewpoints of the same subject. Finally, a brief description, such as the review of the Nissan Versa, might not need an explicit organizational pattern.

Analyzing Description

1. **Together with another classmate,** reread Barbara Kingsolver's description of her home in an Appalachian hollow. Discuss with your classmate the words and images that make this description so effective. Next, writing individually, describe your campus, calling on some of the strategies Kingsolver uses to compose her description. Once you've completed your description, compare it with your classmate's. What similarities and differences do you see? What subjective and objective language did you call on? What metaphors and similes did you use?

2. Reread Mimi Swartz's description of Houston. Analyze the passage for objective and subjective as well as connotative and denotative language. What effect do these choices suggest about the passage's dominant impression?

3. Reread Bret Lott's description of the home movie of him, his brother, and his mother. What organizational strategy does he use for this description? Why do you think he made this choice?

4. Who is the audience for the antismoking flyer excerpted on pages 126–27? Is the audience composed of potential smokers, nonsmokers, or smokers? Is the writer being objective or subjective in describing the consequences of smoking? Which descriptive details will get the most attention from the audience?

Planning and Writing Descriptions

1. Write a brief description of what you're wearing today. Try to be as objective as possible; don't evaluate your clothes, shoes, jewelry, backpack, or handbag — just describe them. Then write a paragraph on how your attire represents the type of person you want to appear to be. Is there a discrepancy between what you're wearing today and the type of person you want people to think you are? Write another paragraph about this discrepancy, if there is any. If there's no discrepancy, then write a paragraph about your ability to represent yourself by what you wear.

2. Mimi Swartz's description of Houston is based on the change that has happened to the city. Houston used to be polluted and dirty, but now the city is "green" — filled with beautiful parks, new trails, and secret gardens. Think about a place familiar to you that has changed over the years, for the better or for the worse. Describe what this place was then and what it is now. Call on objective and subjective as well as connotative and

denotative details to compose your description. Also consider the organizational strategy that will best enable you to describe this place and the way it has changed.

3. Do you wish you had more time for one particular activity — such as writing letters or e-mail, visiting relatives, studying more diligently, working longer hours, watching television, or browsing the Web? Draft a three- to four-page essay in which you describe your current lifestyle in order to explain why you do not engage more frequently in that activity. Be sure to refer to the following guidelines for checking over descriptive writing.

4. Write a quick description of the place where you now sleep. You don't have to write complete sentences; just jot down every detail you can think of. Then freewrite for five minutes, describing your sleeping place and making connections between that space and the person you are right now. You might decide to use this freewriting as the basis for a full-length essay of two to three pages. **Working with a classmate,** read over your description, using the following guidelines for checking over descriptive writing.

✔ Checking Over Descriptive Writing

1. What is the main purpose of your description — to inform, to entertain, or to persuade? How well does your description fulfill that purpose?

2. Who is the audience for your description? Have you taken the audience into account in choosing details, language, and organizational pattern?

3. What quality or atmosphere of your subject do you want to convey to your readers, or what attitude toward it do you want them to share? Does the dominant impression of your draft convey that quality or atmosphere or encourage that attitude? Do you need more descriptive details? fewer? Do any of the details you do provide contradict (or distract from) the impression you intend to convey? Does your description include an explicit thesis statement? If not, would an explicit thesis strengthen the dominant impression?

4. Is your description intended to be primarily objective (emphasizing the person or thing you're describing), subjective (emphasizing your own opinions and response), or a combination of both? What details did you use to achieve this goal, and how well did you succeed? Do you need to add or substitute more neutral, denotative language? more emotional, connotative language?

5. Which details did you include that appeal to each of the senses: smell, taste, sight, touch, sound? Which details appeal to emotional or intellectual

sensibilities, such as compassion or a desire for adventure? Are there other senses or sensibilities you might appeal to?

6. Have you used appropriate comparisons (similes and metaphors)? Where else might a comparison enliven your description?

7. How have you organized your description? Does the organizational pattern contribute to the dominant impression you intended, or might another pattern work better? What is your viewpoint? Is it consistent?

8. If you're using visuals, what specific details in them help fulfill your overall purpose? Do you need to add labels, captions, or references in the written text?

READINGS

GAVIN REMBER
Closing Doors

Gavin Rember wrote the following essay as an undergraduate at the University of Denver, where he was majoring in mass communication and hoping to pursue a career in photojournalism. Rember's purpose is to inform his readers about the realities of the Denver Department of Social Services, both as a physical place and as a benefactor. Rember has no positive memories of the Social Services office, yet he and his mother relied on its benefits for a number of years.

> **Preview**   As you read, consider what the title, "Closing Doors," has to do with the essay.

These three descriptive images immediately place readers in the welfare office, enabling them to see and hear what this place is like.

Rember relies on both objective details using denotative language (*white metal railings, plastic chairs*) and subjective details using connotative language (*sprawled ominously, hideous shrubs, stained, throbbing*). Although he does not use metaphors and similes, he makes a comparison of the office façade to something with slightly sinister connotations.

A lonely child screams for her mother. A couple bickers in Spanish; the woman begins to sob. I sit in silence, trying to drown out the noise. These sights and sounds represent the instability of my childhood. Years later, in the sanctuary of my bedroom, I recall the discomfort of the welfare office. 1

The Denver Department of Social Services office was located in a strip mall, behind a Vietnamese market and a restaurant called The Organ Grinder. Skydeck Liquors, Kim Hong Jewelry, Plaza Mexico Salon Eldorado, and other small businesses scattered the mall. A vast asphalt parking lot sat ominously before the strip mall, which sprawled nearly half the length of a city block. Hideous shrubs grew near the entrance — an attempt at landscaping gone horribly awry. The exterior façade was all glass. It had a reflective coating, which gave an effect similar to that of a two-way mirror. White metal 2 railings rose from the steps and ancient rust stained the sidewalk at their base.

3   Inside the building, everything seemed inconsistent. The waiting area was filthy, unorganized, and overcrowded. Plastic chairs awaited the welfare-hopefuls, after they took a number. A large indicator above the counter would tell which number the overworked staff was serving, a dismal reminder of the crying, throbbing, aching mass of humanity yet to be served. The carpet, a dingy blue, clashed with its surroundings. The blandness of the building and its furnishings radiated with the blandness of government. The one exception could be found in the walls, which were painted a bright white and a gaudy purple. These flashy colors gave the impression that the social services facility was child-friendly.

> Note the organizational strategy in this paragraph and the one preceding it; Rember first describes the outside of the building and then the inside.

4   However, the Department of Social Services was not child-friendly. Perhaps that's one of the reasons I hated it so much. A sign in the waiting room read: "PARENTS PLEASE SILENCE YOUR CHILDREN." Another demanded, "PLEASE KEEP CHILDREN OFF COUNTER TOPS." The government offered no day care services of any kind. Parents brought their children to the office, making them sit for hours waiting to see a caseworker. Fortunately I had to visit only a few times.

> Note how he uses exemplification (the two signs, the lack of day care) to support his general description of the department as not child-friendly.

5   The visions of people I encountered there remain clear in my mind. The office was always full of people, many of whom were Hispanic or Vietnamese immigrants who spoke little or no English. The screams of infants and cries of toddlers echoed throughout the building. Out of view of the social workers, abusive parents with few parenting skills would rebuke, spank, or hit their children.

6   The caseworker assigned to my mother and me was a middle-aged white woman. She wore a red nylon jacket with red-and-white striped cuffs, brown pants, and a white shirt. Perhaps she held a second job driving a bus, I guessed from her clothing. Her lifeless gaze told a sad story. She hated her job, but years of it had desensitized her from its depressing reality.

7   I hated this place. To me, it symbolized the height of my family's instabilities. It shrouded me in embarrassment: not only having to visit the

> This paragraph expresses Rember's thesis.
> (continued)

Note how the details and descriptions in the preceding paragraphs have prepared us for this assertion.

Rember uses cause-and-effect analysis to explain why he and his mother had to go to the social services office.

In paragraphs 9–12, he uses narration to provide background for his description. Note the transition words and phrases he uses to move readers through these stages of his life.

office, but the humiliation of having to use food stamps at the grocery store. By using them, I felt we were telling everyone that we were a family of limited means, that we were poor.

I know my mother didn't want to take me 8 along. She resented what I had to go through by being there. She had little choice. I'm an only child of a single mom. My mother's an artist; her work often reflects crucial parts of her life, and in turn, a great deal of it reflects me. She's painted all of her life, and she is extremely talented. However, like many artists, her income fluctuates dramatically. One year we relied on food stamps, and the next we traveled to Europe.

Because my mother's income was so incon- 9 sistent, we moved around quite a bit. In all, I've gone to over 10 different schools and lived in just as many houses. Despite the moving, I had a good childhood. After I was born (at St. Luke's Hospital in Denver), we moved in with my great aunt in Greeley. Shortly after, we went west to Rifle, a small ranching town an hour east of the Utah–Colorado border. My mom painted, and I attended school. We lived in several houses in Rifle and then moved to Glenwood Springs in 1985. We lived there for several years, moving from place to place many times.

In 1988, rent rose so high that we were forced 10 to move again. We lived in a tent for two months that summer until we found a house in New Castle, a small town on the Colorado River, located about 150 miles west of Denver. My mother had no success with her art there and felt that moving to the city was the best choice. We had only lived in New Castle for a year and had no real reason to stay. We packed up our two dogs, three cats, and the rest of our belongings and left for Denver.

We found a house for rent in north Denver and 11 moved in. I started school that September, and we started our life over once again. Because of financial instability, we were forced to go on food stamps. Every month, my mom and I would go to the Denver Department of Social Services to pick them up. The Social Services office was the most depressing place I have ever been in my life.

12   Through all of this, my bedroom was a place of refuge. The safety of my room always welcomed me. There I could be alone, far from the screaming children and chaos of the Social Services office. But it wasn't until we bought our first house in 1991 that I had a true sanctuary. Previous houses weren't homes; they were temporary places to stay for a year or less. The house we bought on Adams Street was permanent. I could live there without the threat of leaving looming above me.

13   Recently, I went back to the Social Services office on Alameda and Federal. I parked and walked to the building. Above the entrance, the sign still reads: "Denver Department of Social Services." Posted on the inside of a door, a piece of paper reads: "DENVER HUMAN SERVICES DEPARTMENT WILL BE CLOSED AT THIS LOCATION PERMANENTLY."

14   The railing leading to the stairs rattled with icy gusts of wind. The once-prominent bushes dwindled in the chilly September sun. Old dry hoses snaked their way between the dying plants. I moved toward the window. The reflective covering peeled inward from the edges, allowing me to see into sections of the glass. Inside, the blue carpet remained. Dark spots on the floor revealed where desks and other large furnishings had once been. In one of the rooms, a solitary wooden chair faced outward toward the window. The chair, like many other artifacts inside, seemed out of place. A dusty yellow computer monitor sat sideways beside the chair, its power cord intertwined with unused phone cords.

> This description of the office is much different from the one Rember offers in the opening paragraphs. How does this description reinforce the argument he is making at the conclusion of the essay?

15   Back in my car, I sat in silence — with no noise to drown out my thoughts. In the distance, a young boy ran across the parking lot. I watched as he disappeared behind a building. I looked back at the Social Services office. The doors weren't simply closed on the outside. For me they had closed a chapter that signified the instability of my life. My hatred for this place had diminished. The uneasiness I had once felt was replaced with a sense of tranquillity. It was the tranquillity I needed to find peace in my life.

Reading Closely

1. How does Rember connect his description of the Denver Department of Social Services office with the supposed values of that office?

2. Rember recounts his experiences in this office as representing the "instability" of his childhood. What details does he provide at the beginning of the essay that lead you to think in terms of instability?

3. What, if anything, do you learn about the writer as you read his essay? What is your impression of him? What words or phrases contribute to this impression? **With a classmate,** compare your findings.

Considering Larger Issues

1. What is the purpose of this essay? What details and information help you grasp the purpose? Who might be the intended audience? What does Rember assume the audience already knows about the Department of Social Services? About the (child-unfriendly) atmosphere of a social services office? How are purpose and audience connected in this essay?

2. How does Rember organize his essay? Try outlining it or mapping it out. What other organizational patterns could he have used? Which pattern do you think would be the most effective? Why? **Working with one or two classmates,** discuss your findings and prepare a group response to share with the rest of the class.

3. COMBINING METHODS. Rember's essay provides not only descriptive details but also a *comparison and contrast* between periods of instability and stability in his life. Mark those passages of comparison and contrast. What other subjects does he compare and contrast? Prepare to discuss your findings with the rest of the class.

Thinking about Language

1. **Working with a classmate,** use the context of the essay and your dictionary to define any of the following words you do not know. How does Rember's use of these words contribute to the dominant impression of the essay?

sanctuary (1)	desensitized (6)	artifacts (14)
ominously (2)	fluctuates (8)	intertwined (14)
dingy (3)	refuge (12)	instability (15)
gaudy (3)	chaos (12)	tranquillity (15)

2. Reread Rember's essay, and circle or list all the evaluative (subjective) words or phrases he uses. What types of things does he evaluate?

3. How does Rember use transitional words or phrases to help you understand the time elements of his essay? Underline all these transitions. How does he use transitions to signify space as well?

Writing Your Own Descriptions

1. Watch a television program that is at least thirty minutes long. As you watch the program, write down details of dialogue, setting, characters, facial expressions, and so on. As you take notes, try to begin placing your responses and descriptions into various categories (dialogue, setting, and so on). As soon as the program is over, turn the television off. Review and organize your notes into categories of description; think about the ways the details in each category help create a dominant impression. Finally, draft a two- to three-page review of the program you watched; introduce the dominant impression early on in your review, and then demonstrate how the various elements of the program contributed to that impression. Refer to the guidelines for checking over descriptive writing (p. 140) as you draft and revise.

2. Rember's essay is about moving beyond an initial feeling. Think back to your own early impressions of a person you're currently living with or a person you're close to. Try to remember what happened during your first encounter. Describe these events and your perceptions of this person in as much detail as possible. Draft without stopping to edit (yet). Read over your writing, checking to see if the details you have included convey a dominant impression. Can you translate that dominant impression into a thesis statement and then into a two- to three-page descriptive essay? **Consider working with a classmate** as you revise your draft, relying on the guidelines for checking over descriptive writing on page 140.

SUSAN ORLEAN
The American Man, Age Ten

Susan Orlean (b. 1955) is a staff writer for the *New Yorker* and has also written for *Rolling Stone, Outside, Vogue,* and *Esquire* magazines. In addition, she has written several books, including *Saturday Night* (1990); *The Orchid Thief* (2000), which was made into the Academy Award–winning movie *Adaptation; My Kind of Place* (2004); and *Lazy Little Loafers* (2008). The following essay is taken from her 2001 collection *The Bullfighter Checks Her Makeup.*

Preview   How would you describe a ten-year-old American boy? Keep this description in mind as a basis for comparison as you read Orlean's essay.

If Colin Duffy and I were to get married, we would have matching superhero notebooks. We would wear shorts, big sneakers, and long, baggy boy T-shirts depicting famous athletes every single day, even in the winter. We would sleep in our clothes. We would both be good at Nintendo Street Fighter II, but Colin would be better than me. We would have some homework, but it would never be too hard and we would always have just finished it. We would eat pizza and candy for all of our meals. We wouldn't have sex, but we would have crushes on each other and, magically, babies would appear in our home. We would win the lottery and then buy land in Wyoming, where we would have one of every kind of cute animal. All the while, Colin would be working in law enforcement—probably the FBI. Our favorite movie star, Morgan Freeman, would visit us occasionally. We would listen to the same Eurythmics song ("Here Comes the Rain Again") over and over again and watch two hours of television every Friday night. We would both be good at football, have best friends, and know how to drive; we would cure AIDS and the garbage problem and everything that hurts animals. We would hang out a lot with Colin's dad. For fun, we would load a slingshot with dog food and shoot it at my butt. We would have a very good life.

Here are the particulars about Colin Duffy: He is ten years old, on the nose. He is four feet eight inches high, weighs seventy-five pounds, and appears to be mostly leg and shoulder blade. He is a handsome kid. He has a broad forehead, dark eyes with dense lashes, and a sharp, dimply smile. I have rarely seen him without a baseball cap. He owns several, but favors a University of Michigan Wolverines model, on account of its pleasing colors. The hat styles his hair into wild disarray. If you ever managed to get the hat off his head, you would see a boy with a nimbus of golden-brown hair, dented in the back, where the hat hits him.

Colin lives with his mother, Elaine; his father, Jim; his older sister, 3
Megan; and his little brother, Chris, in a pretty pale blue Victorian house
on a bosky street in Glen Ridge, New Jersey. Glen Ridge is a serene and
civilized old town twenty miles west of New York City. It does not have
much of a commercial district, but it is a town of amazing lawns. Most
of the houses were built around the turn of the century and are set back
a gracious, green distance from the street. The rest of the town seems
to consist of parks and playing fields and sidewalks and backyards — in
other words, it is a far cry from South-Central Los Angeles and from
Bedford–Stuyvesant and other, grimmer parts of the country where a
very different ten–year–old American man is growing up today.

There is a fine school system in Glen Ridge, but Elaine and Jim, who 4
are both schoolteachers, choose to send their children to a parents' cooperative elementary school in Montclair, a neighboring suburb. Currently,
Colin is in fifth grade. He is a good student. He plans to go to college, to
a place he says is called Oklahoma City State College University. OCSCU
satisfies his desire to live out west, to attend a small college, and to study
law enforcement, which OCSCU apparently offers as a major. After four
years at Oklahoma City State College University, he plans to work for
the FBI. He says that getting to be a police officer involves tons of hard
work, but working for the FBI will be a cinch, because all you have to
do is fill out one form, which he has already gotten from the head FBI
office. Colin is quiet in class but loud on the playground. He has a great
throwing arm, significant foot speed, and a lot of physical confidence. He
is also brave. Huge wild cats with rabies and gross stuff dripping from
their teeth, which he says run rampant throughout his neighborhood,
do not scare him. Otherwise, he is slightly bashful. This combination of
athletic grace and valor and personal reserve accounts for considerable
popularity. He has a fluid relationship to many social groups, including
the superbright nerds, the ultra–jocks, the flashy kids who will someday
become extremely popular and socially successful juvenile delinquents,
and the kids who will be elected president of the student body. In his
opinion, the most popular boy in his class is Christian, who happens to
be black, and Colin's favorite television character is Steve Urkel on *Family Matters*, who is black, too, but otherwise he seems uninterested in or
oblivious to race. Until this year, he was a Boy Scout. Now he is planning
to begin karate lessons. His favorite schoolyard game is football, followed
closely by prison dodgeball, blob tag, and bombardo. He's crazy about
athletes, although sometimes it isn't clear if he is absolutely sure of the
difference between human athletes and Marvel Comics action figures. His
current athletic hero is Dave Meggett. His current best friend is named
Japeth. He used to have another best friend named Ozzie. According to
Colin, Ozzie was found on a doorstep, then changed his name to Michael
and moved to Massachusetts, and then Colin never saw him or heard
from him again.

He has had other losses in his life. He is old enough to know people   5
who have died and to know things about the world that are worrisome.
When he dreams, he dreams about moving to Wyoming, which he has
visited with his family. His plan is to buy land there and have some sort
of ranch that would definitely include horses. Sometimes when he talks
about this, it sounds as ordinary and hard-boiled as a real estate appraisal; other times it can sound fantastical and wifty and achingly naive,
informed by the last inklings of childhood — the musings of a balmy real
estate appraiser assaying a wonderful and magical landscape that erodes
from memory a little bit every day. The collision in his mind of what he
understands, what he hears, what he figures out, what popular culture
pours into him, what he knows, what he pretends to know, and what he
imagines makes an interesting mess. The mess often has the form of what
he will probably think like when he is a grown man, but the content of
what he is like as a little boy.

He is old enough to begin imagining that he will someday get mar-   6
ried, but at ten he is still convinced that the best thing about being married will be that he will be allowed to sleep in his clothes. His father once
observed that living with Colin was like living with a Martian who had
done some reading on American culture. As it happens, Colin is not especially sad or worried about the prospect of growing up, although he
sometimes frets over whether he should be called a kid or a grown-up;
he has settled on the word *kid-up*. Once, I asked him what the biggest advantage to adulthood will be, and he said, "The best thing is that grown-
ups can go wherever they want." I asked him what he meant, exactly, and
he said, "Well, if you're grown up, you'd have a car, and whenever you felt
like it, you could get into your car and drive somewhere and get candy."

Colin loves recycling. He loves it even more than, say, playing with little   7
birds. That ten-year-olds feel the weight of the world and consider it
their mission to shoulder it came as a surprise to me. I had gone with
Colin one Monday to his classroom at Montclair Cooperative School. The
Co-op is in a steep, old, sharp-angled brick building that had served for
many years as a public school until a group of parents in the area took it
over and made it into a private, progressive elementary school. The fifth-
grade classroom is on the top floor, under the dormers, which gives the
room the eccentric shape and closeness of an attic. It is a rather informal
environment. There are computers lined up in an adjoining room and
instructions spelled out on the chalkboard — BRING IN: (1) A CUBBY WITH YOUR
NAME ON IT, (2) A TRAPPER WITH A 5-POCKET ENVELOPE LABELED SCIENCE, SOCIAL
STUDIES, READING/LANGUAGE ARTS, MATH, MATH LAB/COMPUTER; WHITE LINED PAPER; A PLAS-
TIC PENCIL BAG; A SMALL HOMEWORK PAD, (3) LARGE BROWN GROCERY BAGS — but there
is also a couch in the center of the classroom, which the kids take turns
occupying, a rocking chair, and three canaries in cages near the door.

It happened to be Colin's first day in fifth grade. Before class began, 8 there was a lot of horsing around, but there were also a lot of conversations about whether Magic Johnson had AIDS or just HIV and whether someone falling in a pool of blood from a cut of his would get the disease. These jolts of sobriety in the midst of rank goofiness are a ten–year–old's specialty. Each one comes as a fresh, hard surprise, like finding a razor blade in a candy apple. One day, Colin and I had been discussing horses or dogs or something, and out of the blue he said, "What do you think is better, to dump garbage in the ocean, to dump it on land, or to burn it?" Another time, he asked me if I planned to have children. I had just spent an evening with him and his friend Japeth, during which they put every small, movable object in the house into Japeth's slingshot and fired it at me, so I told him that I wanted children but that I hoped they would all be girls, and he said, "Will you have an abortion if you find out you have a boy?"

At school, after discussing summer vacation, the kids began choos- 9 ing the jobs they would do to help out around the classroom. Most of the jobs are humdrum — putting the chairs up on the tables, washing the chalkboard, turning the computers off or on. Five of the most humdrum tasks are recycling chores — for example, taking bottles or stacks of paper down to the basement, where they would be sorted and prepared for pickup. Two children would be assigned to feed the birds and cover their cages at the end of the day.

I expected the bird jobs to be the first to go. Everyone loved the 10 birds; they'd spent an hour that morning voting on names for them (Tweetie, Montgomery, and Rose narrowly beating out Axl Rose, Bugs, Ol' Yeller, Fido, Slim, Lucy, and Chirpie). Instead, they all wanted to recycle. The recycling jobs were claimed by the first five kids called by Suzanne Nakamura, the fifth–grade teacher; each kid called after that responded by groaning, "Suzanne, aren't there any more recycling jobs?" Colin ended up with the job of taking down the chairs each morning. He accepted the task with a sort of resignation — this was going to be just a job rather than a mission.

On the way home that day, I was quizzing Colin about his world- 11 views.

"Who's the coolest person in the world?"   12
"Morgan Freeman."   13
"What's the best sport?"   14
"Football."   15
"Who's the coolest woman?"   16
"None. I don't know."   17
"What's the most important thing in the world?"   18

"Game Boy." Pause. "No, the world. The world is the most important 19 thing in the world."

• • •

Danny's Pizzeria is a dark little shop next door to the Montclair 20
Cooperative School. It is not much to look at. Outside, the brick facing
is painted muddy brown. Inside, there are some saggy counters, a splin-
tered bench, and enough room for either six teenagers or about a dozen
ten–year–olds who happen to be getting along well. The light is low. The
air is oily. At Danny's, you will find pizza, candy, Nintendo, and very few
girls. To a ten–year–old boy, it is the most beautiful place in the world.

One afternoon, after class was dismissed, we went to Danny's with 21
Colin's friend Japeth to play Nintendo. Danny's has only one game, Street
Fighter II Champion Edition. Some teenage boys from a nearby middle
school had gotten there first and were standing in a tall, impenetrable
thicket around the machine.

"Next game," Colin said. The teenagers ignored him. 22

"Hey, we get next game," Japeth said. He is smaller than Colin, scrappy, 23
and, as he explained to me once, famous for wearing his hat backward
all the time and having a huge wristwatch and a huge bedroom. He
stamped his foot and announced again, "Hey, we get next game."

One of the teenagers turned around and said, "Fuck you, *next game*," 24
and then turned back to the machine.

"Whoa," Japeth said. 25

He and Colin went outside, where they felt bigger. 26

"Which street fighter are you going to be?" Colin asked Japeth. 27

"Blanka," Japeth said. "I know how to do his head–butt." 28

"I hate that! I hate the head–butt," Colin said. He dropped his voice 29
a little and growled, "I'm going to be Ken, and I will kill you with my
dragon punch."

"Yeah, right, and monkeys will fly out of my butt," Japeth said. 30

Street Fighter II is a video game in which two characters have an 31
explosive brawl in a scenic international setting. It is currently the most
popular video arcade game in America. This is not an insignificant
amount of popularity. Most arcade versions of video games, which end
up in pizza parlors, malls, and arcades, sell about two thousand units. So
far, some fifty thousand Street Fighter II and Street Fighter II Championship Edition arcade games have been sold. Not since Pac-Man, which was
released the year before Colin was born, has there been a video game
as popular as Street Fighter. The home version of Street Fighter is the
most popular home video game in the country, and that, too, is not an
insignificant thing. Thirty–two million Nintendo home systems have
been sold since 1986, when it was introduced in this country. There is
a Nintendo system in seven of every ten homes in America in which a
child between the ages of eight and twelve resides. By the time a boy
in America turns ten, he will almost certainly have been exposed to
Nintendo home games, Nintendo arcade games, and Game Boy, the hand-
held version. He will probably own a system and dozens of games. By

ten, according to Nintendo studies, teachers, and psychologists, game prowess becomes a fundamental, essential male social marker and a schoolyard boast.

The Street Fighter characters are Dhalsim, Ken, Guile, Blanka, E. Honda, 32 Ryu, Zangief, and Chun Li. Each represents a different country, and they each have their own special weapon. Chun Li, for instance, is from China and possesses a devastating whirlwind kick that is triggered if you push the control pad down for two seconds and then up for two seconds, and then you hit the kick button. Chun Li's kick is money in the bank, because most of the other fighters do not have a good defense against it. By the way, Chun Li happens to be a girl — the only female Street Fighter character.

I asked Colin if he was interested in being Chun Li. There was a long 33 pause. "I would rather be Ken," he said.

The girls in Colin's class at school are named Cortnerd, Terror, Spacey, 34 Lizard, Maggot, and Diarrhea. "They do have other names, but that's what we call them," Colin told me. "The girls aren't very popular."

"They are about as popular as a piece of dirt," Japeth said. "Or, you 35 know that couch in the classroom? That couch is more popular than any girl. A thousand times more." They talked for a minute about one of the girls in their class, a tall blonde with cheerleader genetic material, who they allowed was not quite as gross as some of the other girls. Japeth said that a chubby, awkward boy in their class was boasting that this girl liked him.

"No way," Colin said. "She would never like him. I mean, not that he's 36 so . . . I don't know. I don't hate him because he's fat, anyway. I hate him because he's nasty."

"Well, she doesn't like him," Japeth said. "She's been really mean to 37 me lately, so I'm pretty sure she likes me."

"Girls are different," Colin said. He hopped up and down on the balls 38 of his feet, wrinkling his nose. "Girls are stupid and weird."

"I have a lot of girlfriends, about six or so," Japeth said, turning con- 39 templative. "I don't exactly remember their names, though."

The teenagers came crashing out of Danny's and jostled past us, so 40 we went inside. The man who runs Danny's, whose name is Tom, was leaning across the counter on his elbows, looking exhausted. Two little boys, holding Slush Puppies, shuffled toward the Nintendo, but Colin and Japeth elbowed them aside and slammed their quarters down on the machine. The little boys shuffled back toward the counter and stood gawking at them, sucking on their drinks.

"You want to know how to tell if a girl likes you?" Japeth said. "She'll 41 act really mean to you. That's a sure sign. I don't know why they do it, but it's always a sure sign. It gets your attention. You know how I show a girl I like her? I steal something from her and then run away. I do it to get their attention, and it works."

They played four quarters' worth of games. During the last one, a 42
teenager with a quilted leather jacket and a fade haircut came in, pushed
his arm between them, and put a quarter down on the deck of the
machine.

Japeth said, "Hey, what's that?"   43

The teenager said, "I get next game. I've marked it now. Everyone 44
knows this secret sign for next game. It's a universal thing."

"So now we know," Japeth said. "Colin, let's get out of here and go 45
bother Maggie. I mean Maggot. Okay?" They picked up their backpacks
and headed out the door.

Psychologists identify ten as roughly the age at which many boys experi- 46
ence the gender–linked normative developmental trauma that leaves
them, as adult men, at risk for specific psychological sequelae often manifest as deficits in the arenas of intimacy, empathy, and struggles with
commitment in relationships. In other words, this is around the age when
guys get screwed up about girls. Elaine and Jim Duffy, and probably most
of the parents who send their kids to Montclair Cooperative School, have
done a lot of stuff to try to avoid this. They gave Colin dolls as well
as guns. (He preferred guns.) Japeth's father has three motorcycles and
two dirt bikes but does most of the cooking and cleaning in their home.
Suzanne, Colin's teacher, is careful to avoid sexist references in her presentations. After school, the yard at Montclair Cooperative is filled with as
many fathers as mothers — fathers who hug their kids when they come
prancing out of the building and are dismayed when their sons clamor
for Supersoaker water guns and war toys or take pleasure in beating up
girls.

In a study of adolescents conducted by the Gesell Institute of 47
Human Development, nearly half the ten–year–old boys questioned said
they thought they had adequate information about sex. Nevertheless,
most ten–year–old boys across the country are subjected to a few months
of sex education in school. Colin and his class will get their dose next
spring. It is yet another installment in a plan to make them into new, improved men with reconstructed notions of sex and male–female relationships. One afternoon I asked Philip, a schoolmate of Colin's, whether he
was looking forward to sex education, and he said, "No, because I think
it'll probably make me really, really hyper. I have a feeling it's going to be
just like what it was like when some television reporters came to school
last year and filmed us in class and I got really hyper. They stood around
with all these cameras and asked us questions. I think that's what sex
education is probably like."

At a class meeting earlier in the day: 48

Colin's teacher, SUZANNE: Today was our first day of swimming class, 49
and I have one observation to make. The girls went into their locker
room, got dressed without a lot of fuss, and came into the pool area. The

boys, on the other hand, the *boys* had some sort of problem doing that rather simple task. Can someone tell me what exactly went on in the locker room?

KEITH: There was a lot of shouting.   50

SUZANNE: Okay, I hear you saying that people were being noisy and shouting. Anything else?   51

CHRISTIAN: Some people were screaming so much that my ears were killing me. It gave me, like, a huge headache. Also, some of the boys were taking their towels, I mean, after they had taken their clothes off, they had their towels around their waists and then they would drop them really fast and then pull them back up, really fast.   52

SUZANNE: Okay, you're saying some people were being silly about their bodies.   53

CHRISTIAN: Well, yeah, but it was more like they were being silly about their pants.   54

Colin's bedroom is decorated simply. He has a cage with his pet parakeet, Dude, on his dresser, a lot of recently worn clothing piled haphazardly on the floor, and a husky brown teddy bear sitting upright in a chair near the foot of his bed. The walls are mostly bare, except for a Spider-Man poster and a few ads torn out of magazines he has thumbtacked up. One of the ads is for a cologne, illustrated with several small photographs of cowboy hats; another, a feverish portrait of a woman on a horse, is an ad for blue jeans. These inspire him sometimes when he lies in bed and makes plans for the move to Wyoming. Also, he happens   55

to like ads. He also likes television commercials. Generally speaking, he likes consumer products and popular culture. He partakes avidly but not indiscriminately. In fact, during the time we spent together, he provided a running commentary on merchandise, media, and entertainment:

"The only shoes anyone will wear are Reebok Pumps. Big T-shirts are 56 cool, not the kind that are sticky and close to you, but big and baggy and long, not the kind that stop at your stomach."

"The best food is Chicken McNuggets and Life cereal and Frosted 57 Flakes."

"Don't go to Blimpie's. They have the worst service." 58

"I'm not into Teenage Mutant Ninja Turtles anymore. I grew out of 59 that. I like Donatello, but I'm not a fan. I don't buy the figures anymore."

"The best television shows are on Friday night on ABC. It's called 60 TGIF, and it's *Family Matters, Step by Step, Dinosaurs,* and *Perfect Strangers,* where the guy has a funny accent."

"The best candy is Skittles and Symphony bars and Crybabies and 61 Warheads. Crybabies are great because if you eat a lot of them at once you feel so sour."

"Hyundais are Korean cars. It's the only Korean car. They're not that 62 good because Koreans don't have a lot of experience building cars."

"The best movie is *City Slickers,* and the best part was when he saved 63 his little cow in the river."

"The Giants really need to get rid of Ray Handley. They have to get 64 somebody who has real coaching experience. He's just no good."

"My dog, Sally, costs seventy-two dollars. That sounds like a lot 65 of money but it's a really good price because you get a flea bath with your dog."

"The best magazines are *Nintendo Power,* because they tell you how 66 to do the secret moves in the video games, and also *Mad* magazine and *Money Guide* — I really like that one."

"The best artist in the world is Jim Davis." 67

"The most beautiful woman in the world is not Madonna! Only 68 Wayne and Garth think that! She looks like maybe a . . . a . . . slut or something. Cindy Crawford looks like she would look good, but if you see her on an awards program on TV she doesn't look that good. I think the most beautiful woman in the world probably is my mom."

Colin thinks a lot about money. This started when he was about nine and 69 a half, which is when a lot of other things started — a new way of walking that has a little macho hitch and swagger, a decision about the Teenage Mutant Ninja Turtles (con) and Eurythmics (pro), and a persistent curiosity about a certain girl whose name he will not reveal. He knows the price of everything he encounters. He knows how much college costs and what someone might earn performing different jobs. Once, he asked me what my husband did; when I answered that he was a lawyer, he snapped,

"You must be a rich family. Lawyers make $400,000 a year." His preoccupation with money baffles his family. They are not struggling, so this is not the anxiety of deprivation; they are not rich, so he is not responding to an elegant, advantaged world. His allowance is five dollars a week. It seems sufficient for his needs, which consist chiefly of quarters for Nintendo and candy money. The remainder is put into his Wyoming fund. His fascination is not just specific to needing money or having plans for money: It is as if money itself, and the way it makes the world work, and the realization that almost everything in the world can be assigned a price, has possessed him. "I just pay attention to things like that," Colin says. "It's really very interesting."

He is looking for a windfall. He tells me his mother has been notified 70 that she is in the fourth and final round of the Publisher's Clearinghouse Sweepstakes. This is not an ironic observation. He plays the New Jersey lottery every Thursday night. He knows the weekly jackpot; he knows the number to call to find out if he has won. I do not think this presages a future for Colin as a high-stakes gambler; I think it says more about the powerful grasp that money has on imagination and what a large percentage of a ten-year-old's mind is made up of imaginings. One Friday, we were at school together, and one of his friends was asking him about the lottery, and he said, "This week it was $4 million. That would be I forget how much every year for the rest of your life. It's a lot, I think. You should play. All it takes is a dollar and a dream."

Until the lottery comes through and he starts putting together the 71 Wyoming land deal, Colin can be found most of the time in the backyard. Often, he will have friends come over. Regularly, children from the neighborhood will gravitate to the backyard, too. As a technical matter of real-property law, title to the house and yard belongs to Jim and Elaine Duffy, but Colin adversely possesses the backyard, at least from 4:00 each afternoon until it gets dark. As yet, the fixtures of teenage life — malls, video arcades, friends' basements, automobiles — either hold little interest for him or are not his to have.

He is, at the moment, very content with his backyard. For most in- 72 tents and purposes, it is as big as Wyoming. One day, certainly, he will grow and it will shrink, and it will become simply a suburban backyard and it won't be big enough for him anymore. This will happen so fast that one night he will be in the backyard, believing it a perfect place, and by the next night he will have changed and the yard as he imagined it will be gone, and this era of his life will be behind him forever.

Most days, he spends his hours in the backyard building an Evil 73 Spider-Web Trap. This entails running a spool of Jim's fishing line from every surface in the yard until it forms a huge web. Once a garbage-man picking up the Duffys' trash got caught in the trap. Otherwise, the Evil Spider-Web Trap mostly has a deterrent effect, because the kids in the neighborhood who might roam over know that Colin builds it back there. "I do it all the time," he says. "First I plan who I'd like to catch in it, and then we get started. Trespassers have to beware."

One afternoon when I came over, after a few rounds of Street Fighter 74 at Danny's, Colin started building a trap. He selected a victim for inspiration — a boy in his class who had been pestering him — and began wrapping. He was entirely absorbed. He moved from tree to tree, wrapping; he laced fishing line through the railing of the deck and then back to the shed; he circled an old jungle gym, something he'd outgrown and abandoned a few years ago, and then crossed over to a bush at the back of the yard. Briefly, he contemplated making his dog, Sally, part of the web. Dusk fell. He kept wrapping, paying out fishing line an inch at a time. We could hear mothers up and down the block hooting for their kids; two tiny children from next door stood transfixed at the edge of the yard, uncertain whether they would end up inside or outside the web. After a while, the spool spun around in Colin's hands one more time and then stopped; he was out of line.

It was almost too dark to see much of anything, although now and again 75 the light from the deck would glance off a length of line, and it would glint and sparkle. "That's the point," he said. "You could do it with thread, but the fishing line is invisible. Now I have this perfect thing and the only one who knows about it is me." With that, he dropped the spool, skipped up the stairs of the deck, threw open the screen door, and then bounded into the house, leaving me and Sally the dog trapped in his web.

Reading Closely

1. If Orlean had omitted Colin's age, how would we know that she's writing about a ten-year-old boy?
2. What details capture the "American" part of the title? Write a few minutes about how Orlean relates being ten, a boy, a man — *and* an American.
3. Write one paragraph summarizing this essay. **Trade paragraphs with a classmate,** and annotate your partner's paragraph with information from the essay that you've gleaned but your partner hasn't. Then work together to prepare a brief, unified report for the rest of the class.
4. What is Orlean's purpose in writing this description?

Considering Larger Issues

1. Does Orlean's essay have a one-sentence thesis statement? If so, what is it? If her thesis is implied, write out what it might be.
2. Who is Orlean's audience for this story? How might it fit within a collection of essays titled *The Bullfighter Checks Her Makeup*?
3. What is the dominant impression of this essay? Mark the specific descriptive details that enhance this impression. Which words, phrases, or

events seem to adhere to a ten–year–old boy's sensibilities? to those of a "man"? Be prepared to share your answers with the rest of the class.

4. What specific details in the photograph on page 155 enhance Orlean's description of this "man"? of this ten–year–old?

5. COMBINING METHODS. How does Orlean use *exemplification* to enhance her description? In other words, how does she assert a point and back it up with many examples? Which passages are more concerned with providing examples than with describing?

6. PAIRED READINGS. Orlean and Rember describe the lives of two young boys by writing from different points of view. Identify and compare the points of view that each writer employs in his or her essay. Why do you think each writer chose to write from this point of view? Why does the point of view suit the purpose and message of the essay?

Thinking about Language

1. Using the context of the essay and your dictionary, define any of the following terms that are unfamiliar to you. Be prepared to share your answers with the rest of the class.

nimbus (2)	sobriety (8)	avidly (55)
bosky (3)	prowess (31)	indiscriminately (55)
rampant (4)	normative (46)	windfall (70)
valor (4)	trauma (46)	deterrent (73)
wifty (5)	sequelae (46)	contemplated (74)
musings (5)	partakes (55)	transfixed (74)

2. The essay ends, "With that, he dropped the spool, skipped up the stairs of the deck, threw open the screen door, and then bounded into the house, leaving me and Sally the dog trapped in his web." What is the overall effect of ending the essay this way?

Writing Your Own Descriptions

1. Think about a ten–year–old (or fifteen–year–old or twenty–year–old) you've known or the ten–year–old you once were. Using "The American Man, Age Ten" as a model, draft a two- to three–page description of that person. As you begin drafting this essay, consider the various ways you might arrange the information. List descriptive details, keeping in mind the dominant impression that all the details suggest. What aspects of the dominant impression can you develop? Can you arrange those aspects from least to most important? Is there a chronology to the details? Would a spatial organization best serve your purpose? Write out a thesis statement. As you draft, be sure to refer to the guidelines for checking over descriptive writing on page 140.

2. **Working with a classmate who is writing about someone the same age,** trade your drafts. Write out the dominant impression of your classmate's essay, underlining words or phrases that bring the impression

into focus. Number the descriptive details in the order your classmate has placed them, and decide if rearranging them would strengthen the essay's overall effect. Discuss the effectiveness of the thesis as well. After the two of you have worked together, revise your own essay, referring to the guidelines for checking over descriptive writing on page 140.

3. ACADEMIC WRITING. Orlean and Rember offer detailed descriptions of two (very different) boys' lives. In various academic classes, you will be asked to compose similar kinds of detailed descriptions. For instance, in your history class, you might be assigned to write a sketch of a historical person. Your instructor might ask you to describe the early life of a well-known historical person, such as Malcolm X or Elizabeth Cady Stanton, as a means to learn more about him or her. Or your instructor could ask you to describe the life of an ordinary person at a particular time. As one example, you could be asked to compose a sketch of a resident of Laredo, Texas, at the turn of the twentieth century, with the goal of your learning more about the place, the period, and details of people's life experience at that time.

In this three- to four-page essay, compose a sketch of a person you might write about for your history class. The historical person you choose is up to you — it's your decision whether to investigate and describe the life of a famous or of an unknown person. The goal of the assignment is to rely on the skills you learned in this chapter as you compose, so you'll want to consider how you might employ objective and subjective descriptions, denotative and connotative language, and figurative language. You'll need to choose the most effective point of view for your sketch as well as the most logical organizational pattern. And finally, library research should play a significant role in completing this project. You'll want to consult at least five sources during your research so that your description is both thorough and detailed. Refer to the guidelines for checking over descriptive writing on page 140 as you draft and revise.

SCOTT RUSSELL SANDERS
Buckeye

Distinguished professor of English at Indiana University, Scott Russell Sanders (b. 1945) spent his childhood and adolescent years in Tennessee and Ohio. He attended Brown University, majoring in English and physics, and then earned his Ph.D. in English from the University of Cambridge. He has written over twenty books, including *Staying Put: Making a Home in a Restless World* (1994), *Hunting for Hope: A Father's Journeys* (1999), and *Wilderness Plots: Tales about the Settlement of American Land* (2007). *A Private History of Awe* (2006) was nominated for the Pulitzer Prize. The following essay was published in the collection *Landscapes with Figures: The Nonfiction of Place* (2007).

> **Preview**   Consider the title "Buckeye." As you read, think about why Sanders chose this title. What function does it serve in terms of the purpose of the essay?

Years after my father's heart quit, I keep in a wooden box on my desk 1
the two buckeyes that were in his pocket when he died. Once the size of plums, the brown seeds are shriveled now, hollow, hard as pebbles, yet they still gleam from the polish of his hands. He used to reach for them in his overalls or suit pants and click them together, or he would draw them out, cupped in his palm, and twirl them with his blunt carpenter's fingers, all the while humming snatches of old tunes.

"Do you really believe buckeyes keep off arthritis?" I asked him more 2
than once.

He would flex his hands and say, "I do so far." 3

My father never paid much heed to pain. Near the end, when his 4
worn knee often slipped out of joint, he would pound it back in place with a rubber mallet. If a splinter worked into his flesh beyond the reach of tweezers, he would heat the blade of his knife over a cigarette lighter and slice through the skin. He sought to ward off arthritis not because he feared pain but because he lived through his hands, and he dreaded the swelling of knuckles, the stiffening of fingers. What use would he be if he could no longer hold a hammer or guide a plow? When he was a boy he had known farmers not yet forty years old whose hands had curled into claws, men so crippled up they could not tie their own shoes, could not sign their names.

"I mean to tickle my grandchildren when they come along," he told 5
me, "and I mean to build doll houses and turn spindles for tiny chairs on my lathe."

So he fondled those buckeyes as if they were charms, carrying them 6
with him when our family moved from Ohio at the end of my childhood,

bearing them to new homes in Louisiana, then Oklahoma, Ontario, and Mississippi, carrying them still on his final day, when pain a thousand times fiercer than arthritis gripped his heart.

The box where I keep the buckeyes also comes from Ohio, made by 7 my father from a walnut plank he bought at a farm auction. I remember the auction, remember the sagging face of the widow whose home was being sold, remember my father telling her he would prize that walnut as if he had watched the tree grow from a sapling on his own land. He did not care for pewter or silver or gold, but he cherished wood. On the rare occasions when my mother coaxed him into a museum, he ignored the paintings or porcelain and studied the exhibit cases, the banisters, the moldings, the parquet floors.

I remember him planing that walnut board, sawing it, sanding it, 8 joining piece to piece to make foot stools, picture frames, jewelry boxes. My own box, a bit larger than a soap dish, lined with red corduroy, was meant to hold earrings and pins, not buckeyes. The top is inlaid with pieces fitted so as to bring out the grain, four diagonal joints converging from the corners toward the center. If I stare long enough at those converging lines, they float free of the box and point to a center deeper than wood.

I learned to recognize buckeyes and beeches, sugar maples and shagbark 9 hickories, wild cherries, walnuts, and dozens of other trees while tramping through the Ohio woods with my father. To his eyes, their shapes, their leaves, their bark, their winter buds, were as distinctive as the set of a friend's shoulders. As with friends, he was partial to some, craving their company, so he would go out of his way to visit particular trees, walking in a circle around the splayed roots of a sycamore, laying his hand against the trunk of a white oak, ruffling the feathery green boughs of a cedar.

"Trees breathe," he told me. "Listen."   10

I listened, and heard the stir of breath.   11

He was no botanist; the names and uses he taught me were those he 12 had learned from country folks, not from books. Latin never crossed his lips. Only much later would I discover that the tree he called ironwood, its branches like muscular arms, good for axe handles, is known in the books as "hophorn beam"; what he called tuliptree or canoewood, ideal for log cabins, is officially the yellow poplar; what he called hoop ash, good for barrels and fence posts, appears in books as hackberry.

When he introduced me to the buckeye, he broke off a chunk of the 13 gray bark and held it to my nose. I gagged.

"That's why the old-timers called it stinking buckeye," he told me. 14 "They used it for cradles and feed troughs and peg legs."

"Why for peg legs?" I asked.   15

"Because it's light and hard to split, so it won't shatter when you're 16 clumping around."

He showed me this tree in late summer, when the fruits had fallen 17 and the ground was littered with prickly brown pods. He picked up one, as fat as a lemon, and peeled away the husk to reveal the shiny seed. He laid it in my palm and closed my fist around it so the seed peeped out from the circle formed by my index finger and thumb. "You see where it got the name?" he asked.

I saw: what gleamed in my hand was the eye of a deer, bright with 18 life. "It's beautiful," I said.

"It's beautiful," my father agreed, "but also poisonous. Nobody eats 19 buckeyes, except maybe a fool squirrel."

I knew the gaze of deer from living in the Ravenna Arsenal, in 20 Portage County, up in the northeastern corner of Ohio. After supper we often drove the Arsenal's gravel roads, past the munitions bunkers, past acres of rusting tanks and wrecked bombers, into the far fields where we counted deer. One June evening, while mist rose from the ponds, we counted three hundred and eleven, our family record. We found the deer in herds, in bunches, in amorous pairs. We came upon lone bucks, their antlers lifted against the sky like the bare branches of dogwood. If you were quiet, if your hands were empty, if you moved slowly, you could leave the car and steal to within a few paces of a grazing deer, close enough to see the delicate lips, the twitching nostrils, the glossy, fathomless eyes.

The wooden box on my desk holds these grazing deer, as it holds the 21 buckeyes and the walnut plank and the farm auction and the munitions bunkers and the breathing forests and my father's hands. I could lose the box, I could lose the polished seeds, but if I were to lose the memories I would become a bush without roots, and every new breeze would toss me about. All those memories lead back to the northeastern corner of Ohio, the place where I came to consciousness, where I learned to connect feelings with words, where I fell in love with the earth.

It was a troubled love, for much of the land I knew as a child had 22 been ravaged. The ponds in the Arsenal teemed with bluegill and beaver, but they were also laced with TNT from the making of bombs. Because the wolves and coyotes had long since been killed, some of the deer, so plump in the June grass, collapsed on the January snow, whittled by hunger to racks of bones. Outside the Arsenal's high barbed fences, many of the farms had failed, their barns caving in, their topsoil gone. Ravines were choked with swollen couches and junked washing machines and cars. Crossing fields, you had to be careful not to slice your feet on tin cans or shards of glass. Most of the rivers had been dammed, turning fertile valleys into scummy playgrounds for boats.

One free-flowing river, the Mahoning, ran past the small farm near 23 the Arsenal where our family lived during my later years in Ohio. We owned just enough land to pasture three ponies and to grow vegetables for our table, but those few acres opened onto miles of woods and creeks and secret meadows. I walked that land in every season, every weather, following animal trails. But then the Mahoning, too, was doomed by a government decision; we were forced to sell our land, and a dam began to rise across the river.

If enough people had spoken for the river, we might have saved it. If 24 enough people had believed that our scarred country was worth defend- ing, we might have dug in our heels and fought. Our attachments to the land were all private. We had no shared lore, no literature, no art to root us there, to give us courage, to help us stand our ground. The only maps we had were those issued by the state, showing a maze of numbered lines stretched over emptiness. The Ohio landscape never showed up on postcards or posters, never unfurled like tapestry in films, rarely filled even a paragraph in books. There were no mountains in that place, no waterfalls, no rocky gorges, no vistas. It was a country of low hills, cut over woods, scoured fields, villages that had lost their purpose, roads that had lost their way.

"Let us love the country of here below," Simone Weil urged. "It is real; 25 it offers resistance to love. It is this country that God has given us to love. He has willed that it should be difficult yet possible to love it." Which is the deeper truth about buckeyes, their poison or their beauty? I hold with the beauty; or rather, I am held by the beauty, without forgetting the poison. In my corner of Ohio the gullies were choked with trash, yet cedars flickered up like green flames from cracks in stone; in the evening bombs exploded at the ammunition dump, yet from the darkness came the mating cries of owls. I was saved from despair by knowing a few men and women who cared enough about the land to clean up trash, who planted walnuts and oaks that would long outlive them, who imagined a world that would have no call for bombs.

How could our hearts be large enough for heaven if they are not large 26 enough for earth? The only country I am certain of is the one here below. The only paradise I know is the one lit by our everyday sun, this land of difficult love, shot through with shadow. The place where we learn this love, if we learn it at all, shimmers behind every new place we inhabit.

A family move carried me away from Ohio thirty years ago; my school- 27 ing and marriage and job have kept me away ever since, except for visits in memory and in flesh. I returned to the site of our farm one cold No- vember day, when the trees were skeletons and the ground shone with the yellow of fallen leaves. From a previous trip I knew that our house had been bulldozed, our yard and pasture had grown up in thickets, and the reservoir had flooded the woods. On my earlier visit I had merely

gazed from the car, too numb with loss to climb out. But on this November day I parked the car, drew on my hat and gloves, opened the door,
and walked.

I was looking for some sign that we had lived there, some token of 28
our affection for the place. All that I recognized, aside from the contours
of the land, were two weeping willows that my father and I had planted
near the road. They had been slips the length of my forearm when we set
them out, and now their crowns rose higher than the telephone poles.
When I touched them last, their trunks had been smooth and supple, as
thin as my wrist, and now they were furrowed and stout. I took off my
gloves and laid my hands against the rough bark. Immediately I felt the
wince of tears. Without knowing why, I said hello to my father, quietly at
first, then louder and louder, as if only shouts could reach him through
the bark and miles and years.

Surprised by sobs, I turned from the willows and stumbled away 29
toward the drowned woods, calling to my father. I sensed that he was
nearby. Even as I called, I was wary of grief's deceptions. I had never seen
his body after he died. By the time I reached the place of his death, a furnace had reduced him to ashes. The need to see him, to let go of him, to
let go of this land and time, was powerful enough to summon mirages; I
knew that. But I also knew, stumbling toward the woods, that my father
was here.

At the bottom of a slope where the creek used to run, I came to an 30
expanse of gray stumps and withered grass. It was a bay of the reservoir
from which the water had retreated, the level drawn down by engineers
or drought. I stood at the edge of this desolate ground, willing it back to
life, trying to recall the woods where my father had taught me the names
of trees. No green shoots rose. I walked out among the stumps. The grass
crackled under my boots, breath rasped in my throat, but otherwise the
world was silent.

Then a cry broke overhead, and I looked up to see a red-tailed hawk 31
launching out from the top of an oak. I recognized the bird from its
band of dark feathers across the creamy breast and the tail splayed like
rosy fingers against the sun. It was a red-tailed hawk for sure; and it was
also my father. Not a symbol of my father, not a reminder, not a ghost,
but the man himself, right there, circling in the air above me. I knew this
as clearly as I knew the sun burned in the sky. A calm poured through
me. My chest quit heaving. My eyes dried.

Hawk and father wheeled above me, circle upon circle, wings barely 32
moving, head still. My own head was still, looking up, knowing and being known. Time scattered like fog. At length father and hawk stroked the
air with those powerful wings, three beats, then vanished over a ridge.

The voice of my education told me then and tells me now that I did 33
not meet my father, that I merely projected my longing onto a bird. My
education may well be right; yet nothing I heard in school, nothing I've

read, no lesson reached by logic has ever convinced me as utterly or stirred me as deeply as did that red–tailed hawk. Nothing in my education prepared me to love a piece of the earth, least of all a humble, battered country like northeastern Ohio; I learned from the land itself.

Before leaving the drowned woods, I looked around at the ashen 34 stumps, the wilted grass, and for the first time since moving from this place I was able to let it go. This ground was lost; the flood would reclaim it. But other ground could be saved, must be saved, in every watershed, every neighborhood. For each home ground we need new maps, living maps, stories and poems, photographs and paintings, essays and songs. We need to know where we are, so that we may dwell in our place with a full heart.

Reading Closely

1. Review the descriptions of Sanders's father. What kind of man does Sanders depict him to be? How does Sanders's use of objective and subjective language help create this image?
2. **Working with a classmate,** identify the ways Sanders depicts the landscape and the changes in the landscape over the years. What is significant about these changes? What is Sanders trying to say about these changes?

Considering Larger Issues

1. What is the purpose of this essay? How does Sanders rely on description to achieve this purpose?
2. Is the thesis of this essay stated or implied? What is the thesis? How is the thesis supported by the dominant impression conveyed throughout the essay?
3. Why would Sanders choose to title his essay "Buckeye"? What is significant about this title? How does it correspond to the essay's purpose?
4. COMBINING METHODS. Sanders relies on description in this essay, but he also calls on the rhetorical methods of *comparison and contrast* and *narration*. Analyze Sanders's use of these rhetorical methods. How do they enable him to achieve his purpose?

Thinking about Language

1. **Working with a classmate,** use the context of the essay and your dictionary to define any of the following words you do not know. How does Sanders's use of these words contribute to the dominant impression of the essay?

buckeye (1)	botanist (12)	contours (28)
mallet (4)	munitions bunkers (20)	supple (28)
lathe (5)	amorous (20)	furrowed (28)
pewter (7)	fathomless (20)	stout (28)
parquet floors (7)	unfurled (24)	desolate (30)

2. Identify ten uses of figurative language in Sanders's descriptions of his father and the landscape and nature surrounding his home. What function do these metaphors and similes serve? How do they support the purpose of the essay?

3. Identify the places in the essay where Sanders uses dialogue. What function does this dialogue serve?

Writing Your Own Descriptions

1. Sanders's essay could be read as a meditation on the buckeye, which we might say represents both the beauty and the unsightliness of the landscape that surrounded Sanders's childhood home. Identify an object that you think represents you in some way. Consider how this object reflects the complexity of your personality. Compose a two- to three-page descriptive essay about the object, offering rich and descriptive details that enable readers to understand its significance to you and how it conveys your personality. Be sure to rely on objective and subjective as well as connotative and denotative language. Experiment with stating your thesis or offering an implied thesis through your use of description. Refer to the guidelines for checking over descriptive writing (p. 140) as you draft and revise.

2. When Sanders describes his father, he does not paint a detailed picture of exactly what his father looked like. Instead, Sanders focuses on characteristics of his father that were distinctive to *him*: the man's hands and his love of nature. In a two- to three-page essay, describe someone you know, focusing only on those features that say something meaningful to you about that person. First, compose a thesis statement about the person, and then choose details and features that support your claim about him or her. Make sure all of your details and descriptions as well as your use of objective and subjective language work together to create a dominant impression. **Consider working with a classmate** as you revise your draft, relying on the guidelines for checking over descriptive writing (p. 140).

SARAH M. BROOM

A Yellow House in New Orleans

● New Orleans native Sarah M. Broom is executive director of Village Health Works, a nonprofit organization headquartered in New York that provides quality health care to the people of Burundi, consistently ranked as one of the poorest countries in the world. Her work has appeared in the *New York Times Magazine, New America Media, O: The Oprah Magazine*, and other publications. "A Yellow House in New Orleans" was published in 2008 in the *Oxford American*, a magazine featuring writing and art by Southerners or about the South. Broom is currently writing a book about the life of the house that is the subject of her essay.

> **Preview**   What do you know about New Orleans? How might this knowledge influence your reading of this essay?

All that is left now of that yellow house is a piece of concrete slab in the   1
backyard where Mom hung clothes out to dry, and where, as children, we jumped rope with telephone cord. The house was demolished by the city, and not one of us twelve children was there to see it go. My mother, Ivory Mae Soulé, called me at home in New York, and told me the story in three lines:

"Someone said they went over to the old house and those people   2
had knocked it down.

"They say that land clean as a whistle now.   3
"They say it look like nothing was ever there."   4
I do not agree with that last line of hers. I went and saw it for myself.   5
For the first time in my life I'd brought someone not of my immediate family to the house I grew up in. We stood facing a fifty–foot–long bur-row in the ground beginning near the curb and running, shadowlike, the length of where the house used to be. My friend asked where certain rooms were, where Ivory and my banjo–playing dad, Simon, once slept. I tried to pinpoint them, but found myself confused.

"No, *that* was the kitchen."   6
He asked where might the door have been because, like me, he   7
had the blaring feeling that it was wrong to be standing outside a fam-ily house, unable to enter into its commotion and introduce yourself by name: David and Sarah, here, together. There used to be three doors to this house: the front (into the living room); the side (into the kitchen); and the back (into the den).

No place to go now but into deep ground.   8

It is a bone–cold Harlem day. Sitting across from me on the windowsill   9
are two artifacts belonging to the New Orleans ground that once held the yellow house I grew up in, into, and then out of. Half of a yellow, blue–

The house where the author grew up: 4121 Wilson Avenue, New Orleans East.

speckled plastic fleur–de–lis wall decoration, and a silver spoon — bent and overused to paper–thin. Once, the spoon went missing in my duplex. I found it washed in a drawer among utensils, and thought: *No, you do not belong in there with all the others, you have not come from where they've come*, be-fore putting it back on the windowsill.

They have been there ever since; nearly eight months have gone by. 10 I have not known what to do with them. I still do not. But I am leaving this place here on West 119th Street for Bujumbura, Burundi, and they cannot stay. I've put them in a Ziploc bag and placed them inside a box with "Misc–Fragile" written on top. Where, if at all, might I store these two things?

Just three months before Katrina, I had a premonition, so I sat down 11 and wrote:

> There is a narrow yellow paneled house in New Orleans that's got a lean to it, a lean, that is, toward falling. It's on the short, nearly for-gotten end of Wilson Avenue, which should really be called a street since there is nothing grandiose about it. Though if it were called its true, true name, this story would not be begging its way to the page. The Broom clan, five girls and seven boys, lived on the side of the street where there are only three remaining houses. Ours is the one begging to fall. And I don't blame it.

When I wrote that, I did indeed want the house to go, but mostly 12 from my mind, wanted to somehow be free of its lock and chain of mem-ory, but still imagined it could be rebuilt. Did not, could not, foresee wa-ter bum–rushing it.

I have photos of the way the storm pimp–slapped, and made fun of 13 the house, but only showed them once, to a New York friend, before em-barrassment had me stashing the photos underneath the bed. My worry: People might be able to see that the house was raggedy even before the storm.

I grew up in New Orleans East, the area of the city developed as suburbs 14 by a private company of the same name. To get to the yellow house if you were leaving the French Quarter area, where tourists mostly spend the night, you'd drive on Interstate 10 for ten minutes before exiting at I–90/Chef Menteur Highway. Before the storm, you'd see women stand-ing in front of Natal's (pronounced *Nay-Tells*) Super Market talking with each other, some of them wearing thin, pink house slippers with their toes hanging off, Newport cigarettes dancing off the edge of their lips. Now you will see nearly no one. You will drive past Causey's soul–food restaurant and see a tour bus parked at the counter.

Our house was what New Orleanians call camelback shotgun: nar– 15 row and running horizontal with no hallway, and with a second floor of only one room added onto the back, the kind of house old folks say spirits love because they can move through easily. There were no doors separat-ing rooms, so my seamstress mom put up curtains that fluttered or fell as we kids ran through. Mom's room was separated from the kitchen by a pink woolen blanket that we badly needed on our beds during winter-time when the collective drafts had us gathered around the oven. Some-one always walked away with a burnt leg from trying to get too close to the heat.

My Creole mother raised her children with flair. She herself was 16
raised by my grandmother Amelia, who, even once she got Alzheimer's
and couldn't remember my name, still held a fork with her pinkie finger
extended out and to the side in the way of a queen. Amelia taught us to
move about with stride, to do whatever it was we wanted to do, to pack
mental lunches wherever it was we were going.

My mom had taste. She grew up on Roman Street, uptown, and 17
seemed obsessed with other people's houses. Not the grand St. Charles
Avenue mansions of New Orleans, but the simple and clean homes. Those
across the highway, even, on the other side of Wilson, where the houses
were mostly brick. But she bought our house with $3,200 in cash in 1961.
And that stood for something.

Mom loves pretty things. She crocheted gorgeous, marigold–colored 18
blankets for the girls' twin beds, and concerned herself with the particulars
of how we looked when we left the house. She sewed most all of our clothes
so perfectly that no one could tell they were homemade. She planted vi-
brant gardens outside our house, and she demanded we stay out of the
living room, with its champagne–colored settee trimmed with dark wood
carvings, its gold candelabras, its gold and faux–crystal chandelier, and its
French windows that opened out. My grandmother made a white ceramic
statue of one of our cats, Persia, which sat on the floor beside two side
tables with harp–shaped bases that were hell to polish. If we happened to
have a visitor, like, say, the insurance man, this would be where he'd wait.
But even with this one good room, none of our friends could come over.

We understood this through subtlety, my mother's way. "You know 19
this house not all that comfortable" is how she might say it. And so you
asked once, twice if you were hardheaded, then never again.

My dad had never finished the upstairs that was the boys' room, so 20
there were still wall bearings instead of wall to stare into. "Your daddy
didn't want to spend the money to do things right," my mother would say.
"Instead of taking up the kitchen floor if it had a hole in it, like anybody
with sense, he'd just take boards and put over the hole so one part be up
all crazy–like and so you'd be walking up and down across the floor."

That's how things were fixed when Dad was alive. Once he died, 21
when I was six months old, things continued on in that way, or not at
all. The small bathroom where Mom discovered Dad on the toilet after
his brain aneurysm in June of 1980 seemed to fold in on itself: Its dark
blue–painted walls peeling; the socket hanging from the wall with pieces
of electrical tape showing; the sink collapsing.

"A house has to be maintained," says my brother Simon now, after 22
the fact, but back then when he was in the Army, the house felt like falling apart and the older children didn't fix it back up. My brother Eddie
left for marriage. Another brother found drugs. Others were running after women or seeking work in order to get them. And then it was just
five daughters, and Byron, the youngest boy.

My sister Karen's amateur-carpenter boyfriend once tried putting a   23
brown tribal-patterned linoleum on the kitchen floor, but the corners
started curling a few years too soon. One minute you'd be walking
around barefoot and gliding on the linoleum Mom had polished, then
two steps later suddenly feel yourself walking on wood patches where
the linoleum had come up. In due time, the floor got to be so holey that
rats had easier access to bread than at any other house on the block.
When I was a small girl playing hopscotch, Oak Heaven trailer park had
been right next door separated from us by a fence. Mom says the rats
came to live with us when those trailers were knocked down. However
they came, they did, and enough of them to make so much noise in the
next room while you were trying to read James Baldwin or sleep that you
didn't dare get up out of bed to see what they were doing. You'd know in
the morning, anyway.

Karen's boyfriend also built a kitchen cabinet but never got around   24
to making its doors. Mom ended up making curtains. She did the best
she could: white linen on the bottoms; fruit-themed valances on the tops.
"I like things nice," she will say.

This same boyfriend tore down the den walls to redo the paneling,   25
but then he and my sister broke up, so that the room where the family watched the Saints lose football games closed down, too, becoming a
storage room that leaked rain.

The plumbing was never right. We had buckets underneath the   26
kitchen sink catching dishwater. The kitchen cabinets had big holes that
led to the outside, which Mom patched up with foil after hearing somewhere that rats couldn't chew through it. They did.

The bathroom near the rear of the house was the only room with a   27
lock. I took full advantage of that, especially when I wanted to get away
from my older brother Troy, whose nerves were always bad. He had a
pointy ear and I fixated on it. The more his leg shook when he sat, the
madder you could get him. At those moments, I'd yell, "Ear, ear, ear!" to
rile him up, and sure enough, he (a grown man) would chase me (eight
or nine) through the house. I'd lock myself in the bathroom, and since
he'd wait a long time for me, yelling, "Wait till you come out, lil gawl," I
memorized its insides. I learned right then and there the geography of
hiding.

The faucets on the bathtub broke after we started using pliers to turn   28
the water on and off. When this happened, we'd have to boil water on
the kitchen stove and carry it through the bedroom and into the bath,
saying, "Watch out, watch out now," as warning.

Some nights we'd return home to find termites, or flying cockroaches,   29
gathered in our rooms and I'd stay up nearly the whole night watching
them fly, crawl, and fly.

To describe the house fully in its coming-apart feels maddening, like   30
trying to pinpoint the one thing that ruins a person's personality.

• • •

Years ago, in childhood, when friends asked if they could drop me home 31
from school, I'd go into a panic thinking maybe then they'd want to come
in and use the bathroom. I'd rather walk, or take the bus even in sopping
rain. If someone insisted on giving me a ride, I'd lie about needing to go
to the grocery store so I could be dropped off at the corner instead of in
front of the house.

I lost my best high-school friend, Tiffany Cage, who couldn't under- 32
stand why she was never invited over when I was at her apartment at
least once a week. Her place wasn't lavish, but it wasn't falling apart either. When she started demanding visits, I'd lie: *You will come* or *We have
company now* or *You will come.*

I just did not know how to be true about it yet.   33

Lynette, the makeup artist, and my closest sister in age, avoided hav- 34
ing a slumber party for so long that she also lost a playmate, Kristie Lee.
Thirty years after the fact, Lynette says: "I knew what would happen if
you made friends. So I stopped making them. It meant that people were
going to want to come into your life, and they weren't gonna come nowhere near that house. Not even if it took everything in me."

So there was this house that I belonged to, and then there was me 35
with my loud personality and private-school training. I'd been pulled
from public school after I began cutting classes out of boredom. Tuition
at the private school was more than my nurse-aid mother could afford,
but we paid in bits and pieces.

Mom dropped me off mornings in our white Chevy Nova, and I 36
remember never wanting her to get too close to the archway of campus.
"Just let me out here" is what I'd say the moment we entered the parking lot.

Once school let out, the return home was always more painful than 37
the initial leaving. Just like now.

The school bus would drop me off on the long side of Wilson 38
Avenue. Returning to the yellow house meant having to walk a ways before arriving and on the way a great many number of things might happen. Many of them were fun but then there were those times I passed
by parked police cars and saw women's heads bobbing up and down
in the driver's seat and knew exactly what was going on, and then was
taken with the wonder of that and the question of why we were living
in a city where police took lunch breaks in such peculiar ways. This feels
like telling on my city, but it is true. Then at the corner of Chef Menteur
and Wilson I'd wait on the neutral ground (as New Orleanians call the
median) in my red-and-gray uniform skirt, white button-down shirt, and
burgundy vest, before crossing over to walk the fifty or so steps home.

Home: Where I was only called by my French middle name, Monique. 39
On my very first day of school, Mom pulled me aside, and instructed me
thus: "When those people ask your name, be sure to tell them Sarah. Never

Monique." And so I did. And still I do. I went by my proper name, Sarah, outside the house. Monique inside. When classmates called asking for Sarah, my fisherman brother Carl said, "Who that?" Sarah and Monique, such different titles, in sound, in length, in feel. I've got to let you know this because I have felt for so long that those two names did not like each other, that each had conspired, somehow, against the other. That the classified, proper one told the raw, lots-of-space-to-move-around-in one that it was better than she. And to this day, no one within my family calls me Sarah, unless they are making fun.

Home: Where Mom taught us to clean maniacally so that even in the   40
falling-down house, she was always mopping floors using ammonia and bleach (which she calls Sure-Clean, no matter the brand), taping things together, trying to make everything presentable. "You've got to make whatever place you live in look decent" is what she'd say as I stood in my plaid skirt watching her. The house seemed like the biggest, rowdiest child, with Mom always bent trying to clean it, to dress it well. And yet she hadn't strength enough. The house kept falling down all around us.

When I went back to New Orleans the first time, thirty-five days past   41
the storm, there were birds living in my childhood home. So that when I approached it, with its broken-out windows, they flew away en masse. It was a flurry of flight — like the scrambling of overweight thieves at the sound of gunfire.

The house looked as though a furious and mighty man crouching   42
underneath had lifted it from the foundation and thrown it slightly left, off base. And once he'd done that, it was like he'd gone inside, to my lavender-walled bedroom, extended both arms, and pressed outward until the walls expanded, buckled, and then folded back inside themselves.

The house had split in half. And the yellow siding that cost in the   43
thousands of dollars, and which Mom paid for over seventy-two months, where it had not blown away, was suspended like icicles.

The front door was wide open; a skinny tree had angled its way in-   44
side. I entered the living room and took baby steps forward, afraid the weight of me might collapse it. The farthest I went was into the middle of the living room. It was all dust, wood chips, waterlines, but then also the light switch by the front door. Cream-colored with gold script around the edges. Pretty.

Somehow the house just looked more like itself. It was really so   45
small. And sitting there all curvy-looking. I knew right then that it had fallen so that something in me could open up.

For so long, I have held that yellow house inside me. I have been at   46
times shaken when it came to letting people near me because it would mean letting them near the unadulterated one, the *real* yellow house. I was a kid raised well (with class and hope but little money) and who

grew up in a raggedy house. I never did need to be one or the other. I mean, who does not know that they are more than just a single adjective? But back then when I was eight, twelve, fifteen, I had no idea about the stupefying nature of dichotomy.

Or that, if one is able, one might, one day, return to stand facing everything you originally left looking for. 47

Mom is living now in Saint Rose, Louisiana, but recently visited me in Harlem. We three: My sister Lynette, Mom, and I went to the Metropolitan Museum of Art to glimpse the "After the Flood" exhibit. As I slowly made my way around the bend, Mom said, "Got a picture down there make you think of the old house." I wanted to run and see, but did not. 48

Eventually, I stood facing the image. The color, yes, like our house, except that it was wider and the innards were spilling out. The yellow house always kept its dilapidation secret, lest the Broom clan's business be all over the streets. 49

Back home, I researched the demolition of our house, and found an article from the *New Orleans Times-Picayune* headlined "Red Danger List": 1,975 properties deemed "in imminent danger of collapse." I scrolled down fifty-one pages before seeing it: 4121 Wilson Avenue, New Orleans, 70126, our old address. 50

Yellow House, I wonder how you felt to be bursting open, at last, your secrets out, proclaimed, free, falling this way and that, at least momentarily, before being obliterated, swept up into flying dust. Gone. 51

Reading Closely

1. Identify the objective details about the house. Then review the essay for the subjective descriptions. Compare these objective and subjective details. How do they work together and reinforce one another to support a dominant impression? Define in one sentence the dominant impression conveyed through these descriptive details.

2. Broom spends a good deal of time discussing how the different inhabitants of the house (her brothers and sisters, her father and mother, even the rats) changed its interior. Pinpoint the various changes these inhabitants made to the house, focusing specifically on the descriptions Broom uses to convey these changes. What effect does each inhabitant (or group of inhabitants) have on the house? How do they change it for the better? for the worse? As readers learn about the changes the inhabitants made, what do readers also learn about the inhabitants themselves?

3. Sarah Broom, the author of this essay, took the photograph on page 169 herself. Why do you think she or the editors of the *Oxford American* chose this particular visual to illustrate her article? How does it extend or complicate the descriptions she provides in her writing?

Considering Larger Issues

1. What is the thesis of this essay? Is the thesis stated or implied?

2. What is the purpose of the essay? How is the audience expected to respond to this essay?

3. Broom's description of her home is in direct response to the devastation that Hurricane Katrina wreaked on New Orleans. **Working with a classmate,** consider the effect of the hurricane on her home. What was her home like before this natural disaster? What is it like now?

4. **Working with a classmate,** consider the organization of this essay. What is the organizing principle for the entire essay? What organizational strategy does Broom use when she is describing the house in paragraphs 15–31?

5. COMBINING METHODS. Just as Broom relies on description in this essay, she also uses *narration* to tell readers the events that happened in the house. Identify the places in the essay where Broom uses narration. How does narration support the purpose and thesis of the essay?

Thinking about Language

1. Use the context of the essay and your dictionary to define any of the following words you do not know.

burrow (5)	grandiose (11)	en masse (41)
fleur-de-lis (9)	Creole (16)	dichotomy (46)
Burundi (10)	Alzheimer's (16)	dilapidation (49)
premonition (11)	settee (18)	obliterated (51)

2. Review the dialogue that Broom uses in this essay. What effect does it have on the dominant impression she is trying to create?

Writing Your Own Descriptions

1. The subject of Broom's essay is her childhood home. Draft a two- to three-page essay about the home (or one of the homes) where you spent your childhood. As you write, you might also consider how this home changed over the years: Did your family make improvements? Did anything fall into disrepair? Like Broom, call on both objective and subjective details to describe your home, and use both connotative and denotative language to make your description as detailed as possible for your readers. Remember to also use sensory details to help readers understand what your home looked, smelled, sounded, and felt like. In addition, consider your organizational strategy, what pattern (spatial, emphatic) will work best for your purposes. Refer to the guidelines for checking over descriptive writing (p. 140) as you draft and revise.

2. As Broom describes her home, she also describes her relatives and friends who lived in and visited it. Readers learn about her grandmother's etiquette and her mother's love for "pretty things." Building on the descrip-

tion of your childhood home in the preceding assignment, compose another two- to three-page essay describing the family members who shared your home as well as relatives and friends who frequented it. Experiment with figurative language as you compose your descriptions. Refer to the guidelines for checking over descriptive writing (p. 140) as you draft and revise.

3. Now that you've composed almost six pages of description — two to three pages describing your home and two to three pages describing your family, relatives, and friends — combine these descriptions into a single four-page essay. Reflect on the dominant impression you want to convey to readers as well as the thesis that will drive the essay. As you write, carefully choose the elements from both previous essays that you will include in this new essay. All of the descriptions should work together to support the thesis. Refer to the guidelines for checking over descriptive writing (p. 140) as you draft and revise.

N. SCOTT MOMADAY
The Way to Rainy Mountain

Writer, teacher, and painter Navarre Scott Momaday writes eloquently about American Indian life in the United States. Born in 1934 of Kiowa ancestry, Momaday grew up in Lawton, Oklahoma, where he attended Native American schools. He graduated from the University of New Mexico in 1958 and received his Ph.D. from Stanford University in 1963. Momaday has taught writing at the University of Arizona. In 2007, he was named poet laureate of Oklahoma and was also awarded the National Medal of the Arts by President George W. Bush. Momaday's books include the Pulitzer Prize–winning *House Made of Dawn* (1968), *The Way to Rainy Mountain* (1969), *The Man Made of Words: Essays, Stories, Passages* (1997), *In the Bear's House* (1999), and several collections of poetry. The following essay is excerpted from the introduction to *The Way to Rainy Mountain*, an entertaining book that has an informative purpose: to help readers understand the American Indians' connection to the land. As you read the first paragraph, pay careful attention to the way Momaday uses specific details to lead up to its final phrase: "this . . . is where Creation was begun."

> **Preview**   What do you know about American Indians' connection to the land?

A single knoll rises out of the plain in Oklahoma, north and west of the Wichita Range. For my people, the Kiowas, it is an old landmark, and they gave it the name Rainy Mountain. The hardest weather in the world is there. Winter brings blizzards, hot tornadic winds arise in the spring, and in summer the prairie is an anvil's edge. The grass turns brittle and brown, and it cracks beneath your feet. There are green belts along the rivers and creeks, linear groves of hickory and pecan, willow and witch hazel. At a distance in July or August the steaming foliage seems almost to writhe in fire. Great green–and–yellow grasshoppers are everywhere in the tall grass, popping up like corn to sting the flesh, and tortoises crawl about on the red earth, going nowhere in the plenty of time. Loneliness is an aspect of the land. All things in the plain are isolate; there is no confusion of objects in the eye, but *one* hill or *one* tree or *one* man. To look upon that landscape in the early morning, with the sun at your back, is to lose the sense of proportion. Your imagination comes to life, and this, you think, is where Creation was begun. 1

I returned to Rainy Mountain in July. My grandmother had died in the spring, and I wanted to be at her grave. She had lived to be very old and at last infirm. Her only living daughter was with her when she died, and I was told that in death her face was that of a child. 2

I like to think of her as a child. When she was born, the Kiowas were living that last great moment of their history. For more than a hundred years they had controlled the open range from the Smoky Hill River to the 3

Red, from the headwaters of the Canadian to the fork of the Arkansas and Cimarron. In alliance with the Comanches, they had ruled the whole of the southern Plains. War was their sacred business, and they were among the finest horsemen the world has ever known. But warfare for the Kiowas was preeminently a matter of disposition rather than of survival, and they never understood the grim, unrelenting advance of the U.S. Cavalry. When at last, divided and ill–provisioned, they were driven onto the Staked Plains in the cold rains of autumn, they fell into panic. In Palo Duro Canyon they abandoned their crucial stores to pillage and had nothing then but their lives. In order to save themselves, they surrendered to the soldiers at Fort Sill and were imprisoned in the old stone corral that now stands as a military museum. My grandmother was spared the humiliation of those high gray walls by eight or ten years, but she must have known from birth the affliction of defeat, the dark brooding of old warriors.

Her name was Aho, and she belonged to the last culture to evolve in 4 North America. Her forebears came down from the high country in western Montana nearly three centuries ago. They were a mountain people, a mysterious tribe of hunters whose language has never been positively classified in any major group. In the late seventeenth century they began a long migration to the south and east. It was a long journey toward the dawn, and it led to a golden age. Along the way the Kiowas were befriended by the Crows, who gave them the culture and religion of the Plains. They acquired horses, and their ancient nomadic spirit was suddenly free of the ground. They acquired Tai–me, the sacred Sun Dance doll, from that moment the object and symbol of their worship, and so shared in the divinity of the sun. Not least, they acquired the sense of destiny, therefore courage and pride. When they entered upon the Southern Plains, they had been transformed. No longer were they slaves to the simple necessity of survival; they were a lordly and dangerous society of fighters and thieves, hunters and priests of the sun. According to their origin myth, they entered the world through a hollow log. From one point of view, their migration was the fruit of an old prophecy, for indeed they emerged from a sunless world.

Although my grandmother lived out her long life in the shadow of 5 Rainy Mountain, the immense landscape of the continental interior lay like memory in her blood. She could tell of the Crows, whom she had never seen, and of the Black Hills, where she had never been. I wanted to see in reality what she had seen more perfectly in the mind's eye, and traveled fifteen hundred miles to begin my pilgrimage.

Yellowstone, it seemed to me, was the top of the world, a region of 6 deep lakes and dark timber, canyons and waterfalls. But, beautiful as it is, one might have the sense of confinement there. The skyline in all directions is close at hand, the high wall of the woods and deep cleavages of shade. There is a perfect freedom in the mountains, but it belongs to the eagle and the elk, the badger and the bear. The Kiowas reckoned their stature by the distance they could see, and they were bent and blind in the wilderness.

Descending eastward, the highland meadows are a stairway to the 7 plain. In July the inland slope of the Rockies is luxuriant with flax and buckwheat, stonecrop and larkspur. The earth unfolds and the limit of the land recedes. Clusters of trees and animals grazing far in the distance cause the vision to reach away and wonder to build upon the mind. The sun follows a longer course in the day, and the sky is immense beyond all comparison. The great billowing clouds that sail upon it are shadows that move upon the grain like water, dividing light. Farther down, in the land of the Crows and Blackfeet, the plain is yellow. Sweet clover takes hold of the hills and bends upon itself to cover and seal the soil. There the Kiowas paused on their way; they had come to the place where they must change their lives. The sun is at home in the plains. Precisely there does it have the certain character of a god. When the Kiowas came to the land of the Crows, they could see the dark lees of the hills at dawn across the Bighorn River, the profusion of light on the grain shelves, the oldest deity ranging after the solstices. Not yet would they veer southward to the caldron of the land that lay below; they must wean their blood from the northern winter and hold the mountains a while longer in their view. They bore Tai–me in procession to the east.

A dark mist lay over the Black Hills, and the land was like iron. At the 8 top of a ridge I caught sight of Devil's Tower upthrust against the gray sky as if in the birth of time the core of the earth had broken through its crust and the motion of the world was begun. There are things in nature that engender an awful quiet in the heart of man; Devil's Tower is one of them. Two centuries ago, because they could not do otherwise, the Kiowas made a legend at the base of the rock. My grandmother said:

> Eight children were there at play, seven sisters and their brother. Suddenly the boy was struck dumb; he trembled and began to run upon his hands and feet. His fingers became claws, and his body was covered with fur. Directly there was a bear where the boy had been. The sisters were terrified; they ran, and the bear after them. They came to the stump of a great tree, and the tree spoke to them. It bade them climb upon it, and as they did so, it began to rise into the air. The bear came to kill them, but they were just beyond its reach. It reared against the tree and scored the bark all around with its claws. The seven sisters were borne into the sky, and they became the stars of the Big Dipper.

From that moment, and so long as the legend lives, the Kiowas have kins- men in the night sky. Whatever they were in the mountains, they could be no more. However tenuous their well–being, however much they had suf- fered and would suffer again, they had found a way out of the wilderness.

My grandmother had a reverence for the sun, a holy regard that 9 now is all but gone out of mankind. There was a wariness in her, and an ancient awe. She was a Christian in her later years, but she had come a long way about, and she never forgot her birthright. As a child she had been to the Sun Dances; she had taken part in those annual rites, and by them she had learned the restoration of her people in the presence of Tai-me. She was about seven when the last Kiowa Sun Dance was held in 1887 on the Washita River above Rainy Mountain Creek. The buffalo were gone. In order to consummate the ancient sacrifice — to impale the head of a buffalo bull upon the medicine tree — a delegation of old men journeyed into Texas, there to beg and barter for an animal from the Goodnight herd. She was ten when the Kiowas came together for the last time as a living Sun Dance culture. They could find no buffalo; they had to hang an old hide from the sacred tree. Before the dance could begin, a company of soldiers rode out from Fort Sill under orders to disperse the tribe. Forbidden without cause the essential act of their faith, hav- ing seen the wild herds slaughtered and left to rot upon the ground, the Kiowas backed away forever from the medicine tree. That was July 20, 1890, at the great bend of the Washita. My grandmother was there. Without bitterness, and for as long as she lived, she bore a vision of deicide.

Now that I can have her only in memory, I see my grandmother in 10 the several postures that were peculiar to her: standing at the wood stove on a winter morning and turning meat in a great iron skillet; sitting at the south window, bent above her beadwork, and afterwards, when her vision had failed, looking down for a long time into the fold of her hands; go- ing out upon a cane, very slowly as she did when the weight of age came upon her; praying. I remember her most often at prayer. She made long, rambling prayers out of suffering and hope, having seen many things. I was never sure that I had the right to hear, so exclusive were they of all mere custom and company. The last time I saw her she prayed standing by the side of her bed at night, naked to the waist, the light of a kerosene lamp moving upon her dark skin. Her long, black hair, always drawn and braided in the day, lay upon her shoulders and against her breasts like a shawl. I do not speak Kiowa, and I never understood her prayers, but there was something inherently sad in the sound, some merest hesitation upon the syllables of sorrow. She began in a high and descending pitch, exhausting her breath to silence; then again and again — and always the same intensity of effort, of something that is, and is not, like urgency in the human voice. Transported so in the dancing light among the shadows of her room, she seemed beyond the reach of time. But that was illusion; I think I knew that I should not see her again.

Reading Closely

1. In what ways is Momaday's experience different from his grandmother's experience? Draw a line down the center of a piece of paper, and record

the experiences of the narrator on one side and of the grandmother on the other. Be prepared to present your findings to the rest of the class.

2. On a sheet of paper, make five columns, one for each of the senses: sight, smell, hearing, touch, taste. Then list all the words and phrases in this essay that evoke each sense. For which sense do you find the largest number of descriptive words and phrases? Which sense does Momaday rely on most heavily in this essay?

Considering Larger Issues

1. What is Momaday's thesis? Is it implied or explicitly stated?

2. Descriptive essays may have several purposes. The main purpose of Momaday's essay is to entertain; his secondary purpose is to inform. Make a list of the specific words, phrases, and organizational strategies that Momaday uses to fulfill his dual purposes.

3. Who is the intended audience for this essay? How does the author's main purpose intersect with the knowledge and interests of this target audience? Write out your answers to these questions, and then **compare them with those of one or two classmates.** Prepare a small-group report to share with the rest of the class.

4. What part does Momaday's use of myth (the children, bear, and stars) play in his essay?

5. What is the dominant impression of Momaday's essay? **Working with two or three classmates,** write a one-page report stating the dominant impression and listing the descriptive strategies Momaday has used to achieve this impression.

6. COMBINING METHODS. In which passages does Momaday move from an emphasis on descriptive detail to an emphasis on *narration*, on storytelling? Mark those passages.

Thinking about Language

1. Use the context of the essay and your dictionary to define the following terms. Be prepared to share your answers with the rest of the class.

knoll (1)	forebears (4)	caldron (7)
writhe (1)	nomadic spirit (4)	upthrust (8)
headwaters (3)	luxuriant (7)	engender (8)
preeminently (3)	lees (7)	tenuous (8)
disposition (3)	profusion (7)	deicide (9)
pillage (3)	solstices (7)	postures (10)

2. What specific descriptive language does Momaday use to evoke loneliness? Write out the comparisons or connotative language that conveys this feeling.

3. What specific language does Momaday use to describe his grandmother? Write out the denotative and connotative language about her. How do the connotations provide an emotional element to the description?

Writing Your Own Descriptions

1. Freewrite for five minutes about a familiar place — either one that you'd like to return to just once more or one that you want never to experience again. Using this writing as a starting point, draft a three- to four-page essay in which you describe the sensations you experience when you think about returning to that familiar place. What smells, textures, sights, sounds, and tastes does that place call to mind? What emotional or intellectual sensibilities does it evoke? If you've gone there regularly over a long period, your feelings about it now might be very different from your earlier ones. Recalling those early memories and sensory impressions might help enrich your current feelings about that familiar place. Guidelines for checking over descriptive writing can be found on page 140.

2. Drawing on your freewriting about a familiar place, draft a three- to four-page essay in which you describe this place both from your point of view and from the point of view of someone who has different feelings about the place. You and your mother, for instance, might have markedly different memories of a camping spot: you may remember a carefree scene in the woods, whereas she may have worried about the family's safety or may have felt overworked with camp chores. Or the situation might be reversed: even though you might dread visiting your childhood home because it has changed so much, your children might be thrilled to hunt for treasure in the dusty and damp, cluttered basement. You could start the essay with one point of view and then move to the other, or the points of view could interweave and overlap. In other words, your organizational pattern may vary.

   Consider asking a classmate to read your draft, marking all the sections that express your point of view, the sections that convey the other person's point of view, and the sections in which the two views overlap.

   As you revise your draft, concentrate on strengthening the dominant impression. Make sure the essay fulfills your main purpose, whether it is to inform, to entertain, or to persuade. Refer to the guidelines for checking over descriptive writing on page 140.

3. If you've enjoyed visiting online places or communities, you might want to write about one. Freewrite for five to ten minutes about this cyberplace, and then decide on a purpose for writing about it. Be sure to connect your purpose with a specific audience. As you draft and revise your three- to four-page essay, refer to the guidelines for checking over descriptive writing on page 140.

ANNIE DILLARD

The Deer at Providencia

Pittsburgh native Annie Dillard (b. 1945) has written poetry, essays, fiction, criticism, and a memoir, including the Pulitzer Prize–winning *Pilgrim at Tinker Creek* (1975), *Living by Fiction* (1982), *Teaching a Stone to Talk* (1982), *An American Childhood* (1984), and *The Maytrees* (2007). "The Deer at Providencia," taken from *Teaching a Stone to Talk*, exemplifies some of Dillard's best writing: it is an artfully informative description of a part of the natural world. As you read the essay, consider not only how Dillard uses description to dominate her informative piece but also how — and to what effect — she employs narration and comparison and contrast to convey her ideas about different kinds of suffering and responses to suffering.

> **Preview**   Before you read the entire essay, read just the first paragraph and then write for five minutes about how it seems to prepare you for what will follow.

There were four of us North Americans in the jungle, in the Ecuadorian 1 jungle on the banks of the Napo River in the Amazon watershed. The other three North Americans were metropolitan men. We stayed in tents in one riverside village, and visited others. At the village called Providencia we saw a sight which moved us, and which shocked the men.

The first thing we saw when we climbed the riverbank to the village of 2 Providencia was the deer. It was roped to a tree on the grass clearing near the thatch shelter where we would eat lunch.

The deer was small, about the size of a whitetail fawn, but appar- 3 ently full-grown. It had a rope around its neck and three feet caught in the rope. Someone said that the dogs had caught it that morning and the villagers were going to cook and eat it that night.

This clearing lay at the edge of the little thatched hut village. We 4 could see the villagers going about their business, scattering feed corn for hens about their houses, and wandering down paths to the river to bathe. The village headman was our host; he stood beside us as we watched the deer struggle. Several village boys were interested in the deer; they formed part of the circle we made around it in the clearing. So also did four businessmen from Quito who were attempting to guide us around the jungle. Few of the very different people standing in this circle had a common language. We watched the deer, and no one said much.

The deer lay on its side at the rope's very end, so the rope lacked slack 5 to let it rest its head in the dust. It was "pretty," delicate of bone like all deer, and thin-skinned for the tropics. Its skin looked virtually hairless, in fact, and almost translucent, like a membrane. Its neck was no thicker than my wrist; it was rubbed open on the rope, and gashed. Trying to paw itself free of the rope, the deer had scratched its own neck with its hooves. The raw underside of its neck showed red stripes and some bruises bleeding inside the muscles. Now three of its feet were hooked in the rope under its jaw. It could not stand, of course, on one leg, so it could not move to slacken the rope and ease the pull on its throat and enable it to rest its head.

Repeatedly the deer paused, motionless, its eyes veiled, with only its 6 rib cage in motion, and its breaths the only sound. Then, after I would think, "It has given up; now it will die," it would heave. The rope twanged; the tree leaves clattered; the deer's free foot beat the ground. We stepped back and held our breaths. It thrashed, kicking, but only one leg moved; the other three legs tightened inside the rope's loop. Its hip jerked; its spine shook. Its eyes rolled; its tongue, thick with spittle, pushed in and out. Then it would rest again. We watched this for fifteen minutes.

Once three young native boys charged in, released its trapped legs, 7 and jumped back to the circle of people. But instantly the deer scratched up its neck with its hooves and snared its forelegs in the rope again. It was easy to imagine a third and then a fourth leg soon stuck, like Brer Rabbit and the Tar Baby.

We watched the deer from the circle, and then we drifted on to lunch. Our 8 palm-roofed shelter stood on a grassy promontory from which we could see the deer tied to the tree, pigs and hens walking under village houses, and black-and-white cattle standing in the river. There was even a breeze.

Lunch, which was the second and better lunch we had that day, was hot 9 and fried. There was a big fish called *doncella*, a kind of catfish, dipped whole in corn flour and beaten egg, then deep fried. With our fingers we pulled soft fragments of it from its sides to our plates, and ate; it was delicate fish-flesh, fresh and mild. Someone found the roe, and I ate of that too — it was fat and stronger, like egg yolk, naturally enough, and warm.

There was also a stew of meat in shreds with rice and pale brown 10 gravy. I had asked what kind of deer it was tied to the tree; Pepe had answered in Spanish, "*Gama.*" Now they told us this was *gama* too, stewed. I suspect the word means merely game or venison. At any rate, I heard that the village dogs had cornered another deer just yesterday, and it was this deer which we were now eating in full sight of the whole article. It was good. I was surprised at its tenderness. But it is a fact that high levels of lactic acid, which builds up in muscle tissues during exertion, tenderizes.

After the fish and meat we ate bananas fried in chunks and served 11 on a tray; they were sweet and full of flavor. I felt terrific. My shirt was wet and cool from swimming; I had had a night's sleep, two decent walks, three meals, and a swim — everything tasted good. From time to time each one of us, separately, would look beyond our shaded roof to the sunny spot where the deer was still convulsing in the dust. Our meal completed, we walked around the deer and back to the boats.

That night I learned that while we were watching the deer, the others 12 were watching me.

We four North Americans grew close in the jungle in a way that was 13 not the usual artificial intimacy of travelers. We liked each other. We stayed up all that night talking, murmuring, as though we rocked on hammocks slung above time. The others were from big cities: New York, Washington, Boston. They all said that I had no expression on my face when I was watching the deer — or at any rate, not the expression they expected.

They had looked to see how I, the only woman, and the youngest, 14 was taking the sight of the deer's struggles. I looked detached, apparently, or hard, or calm, or focused, still. I don't know. I was thinking. I remember feeling very old and energetic. I could say like Thoreau that I have traveled widely in Roanoke, Virginia. I have thought a great deal about carnivorousness; I eat meat. These things are not issues; they are mysteries.

Gentlemen of the city, what surprises you? That there is suffering here, or 15 that I know it?

We lay in the tent and talked. "If it had been my wife," one man said 16 with special vigor, amazed, "she wouldn't have cared *what* was going on; she would have dropped *everything* right at that moment and gone in the village from here to there to there, she would not have *stopped* until that animal was out of its suffering one way or another. She couldn't *bear* to see a creature in agony like that."

I nodded.   17

Now I am home. When I wake I comb my hair before the mirror above 18 my dresser. Every morning for the past two years I have seen in that mirror, beside my sleep-softened face, the blackened face of a burnt man. It is a wire-service photograph clipped from a newspaper and taped to my mirror. The caption reads: "Alan McDonald in Miami hospital bed." All you can see in the photograph is a smudged triangle of face from his eyelids to his lower lip; the rest is bandages. You cannot see the expression in his eyes; the bandages shade them.

The story, headed MAN BURNED FOR SECOND TIME, begins: 19

"Why does God hate me?" Alan McDonald asked from his hospital bed.
"When the gunpowder went off, I couldn't believe it," he said. "I just couldn't believe it. I said, 'No, God couldn't do this to me again.'"

He was in a burn ward in Miami, in serious condition. I do not even know if he lived. I wrote him a letter at the time, cringing.

He had been burned before, thirteen years previously, by flaming gas- 20
oline. For years he had been having his body restored and his face remade
in dozens of operations. He had been a boy, and then a burnt boy. He had
already been stunned by what could happen, by how life could veer.

Once I read that people who survive bad burns tend to go crazy; they 21
have a very high suicide rate. Medicine cannot ease their pain; drugs just
leak away, soaking the sheets, because there is no skin to hold them in.
The people just lie there and weep. Later they kill themselves. They had
not known, before they were burned, that the world included such suffering, that life could permit them personally such pain.

This time a bowl of gunpowder had exploded on McDonald. 22

> "I didn't realize what had happened at first," he recounted. "And
> then I heard that sound from 13 years ago. I was burning. I rolled to
> put the fire out and I thought, 'Oh God, not again.'
> "If my friend hadn't been there, I would have jumped into a canal
> with a rock around my neck."

His wife concludes the piece, "Man, it just isn't fair."

I read the whole clipping again every morning. This is the Big Time here, 23
every minute of it. Will someone please explain to Alan McDonald in his
dignity, to the deer at Providencia in his dignity, what is going on? And
mail me the carbon.

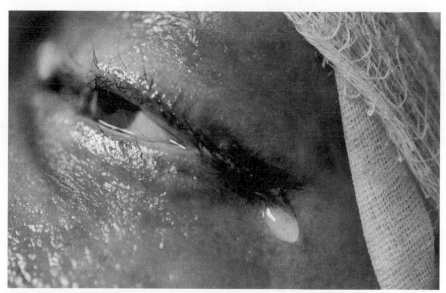

A student who was badly burned in a dormitory fire at a college in New Jersey looks
out at the world through his bandages. This photograph was awarded a Pulitzer
Prize.
Star-Ledger Photographs © The Star-Ledger, Newark, NJ

When we walked by the deer at Providencia for the last time, I said to   24
Pepe, with a pitying glance at the deer, *"Pobrecito"* — "poor little thing." But I
was trying out Spanish. I knew at the time it was a ridiculous thing to say.

Reading Closely

1. Dillard describes her fine jungle meal of fish, roe, deer, and fried bananas,
   even as she reminds her readers of the suffering deer. What impression
   do these intermixed details of taste and suffering convey to you?

2. Why does Dillard mention the men's reactions to her reaction to the
   deer? What is the point of these comparisons? How does the essay benefit from them? Prepare two sentences to report to the rest of the class.

3. Specifically, how does the photograph of the burn victim on page 187
   enhance Dillard's essay? What passages become more vivid when compared to the photograph?

Considering Larger Issues

1. Who might be the audience for this essay? In other words, what kind of
   person likes to read essays about travel and nature? In what ways does
   Dillard appeal to that audience in her essay?

2. **Working with two or three classmates,** discuss why Dillard writes
   about a captured deer and a burn victim. What is her purpose in discussing these two figures one after the other? Condense your conversation into two sentences, and report on your discussion to the rest of the
   class.

3. COMBINING METHODS. Underline the descriptive passages in the essay,
   bracket the *narrative* passages, and star any passages that set up a *comparison and contrast.* You may be able to work paragraph by paragraph. Prepare to discuss your findings with the rest of the class.

4. COMBINING METHODS. What purposes do the *narrative* and *comparison-and-
   contrast* passages help fulfill? How is the larger informative purpose of the
   essay enhanced by these short narratives and comparisons?

Thinking about Language

1. Using the context of the essay and your dictionary, define any of the following terms that are unfamiliar to you. Be prepared to share your answers with the rest of the class.

metropolitan (1)	membrane (5)	lactic acid (10)
thatch (2)	promontory (8)	carnivorousness (14)
translucent (5)	roe (9)	carbon (23)

2. What specific descriptive language does Dillard use to evoke the sense of
   suffering? Which suffering seems more painful to you as a reader: that of
   the soon-to-be-butchered deer or of the burn victim? Why?

3. Which passages in this essay seem to be developed with objective details and denotative language? Which ones are developed with subjective details and connotative language? Why do you think Dillard uses objective and subjective language in the way that she does?

Writing Your Own Descriptions

1. Draft a three- to four-page essay in which you describe in rich detail one of your favorite meals, punctuating that description with a narration of how your meal came into being (how the food met its death, was harvested, was prepared by another person, or was selected or purchased). You may want to describe the meal in one draft and then narrate its origins in another draft before you begin weaving the two parts of the essay together. The overall purpose is to demonstrate how much or how little thought we give to the ways our meals get to our plates. Be sure to appeal to the five senses throughout. Also refer to "Checking Over Descriptive Writing" on page 140.

2. Dillard writes about her apparently detached reaction to the suffering deer and her stronger, almost unaccountable reaction to Alan McDonald's suffering. What evidence in the text can you find that accounts for her different reactions? What else might account for them? Write a three- to four-page essay about an experience of your own that is comparable to Dillard's in either watching the deer or reading about McDonald. Describe your experience using both objective and subjective details. Use narration as necessary to tell your story, and compare how you felt at the time with how you currently feel about that situation. Have your feelings evolved, or have they remained unchanged? As you draft and revise, refer to "Checking Over Descriptive Writing" on page 140.

BARRIE JEAN BORICH

What Kind of King

Barrie Jean Borich (b. 1959) has been awarded many literary prizes for her prose and poetry, which have been published in the books *Restoring the Color of Roses* (1993) and *My Lesbian Husband: Landscapes of a Marriage* (1999) as well as in literary journals such as *The Ruminator Review, The Gettysburg Review, 13th Moon, The Greenfield Review, Sinister Wisdom,* and *Sing Heavenly Muse!* Borich currently teaches creative writing and related courses at Hamline University. She lives with her partner, Linnea Stenson, in Minneapolis. "What Kind of King" first appeared in a 1999 issue of *The Gettysburg Review.*

Preview   As you read, consider this question: How does dress describe (and not describe) who we are?

We are standing in J.C. Penney's men's department when I realize what 1 sort of king I have married. She is holding up ties, one with fluorescent triangles and intersecting lines, a pop art geometry assignment, the other a delicate Victorian print with inlaid roses that shimmer under the too-white department store lights.

"I'm leaning toward this one," Linnea says, lifting up the geometry les- 2 son. The harsh lights above her head highlight the gray in her hair. We are surrounded here by the base elements needed to conjure up what is commonly called a man — hangers hung with navy blue, forest green, and magnet gray suits and the caramel brown and unadorned black leather of men's accessories under glass. Paracelsus, who inspired those Renaissance alchemists who wanted to cure the world with the medicine of trans-formation, declared that *to conjure* meant "to observe anything rightly, to learn and understand what it is." Linnea conjures herself between the neat department store racks, and I am suddenly aware that for some time now she has been buying all of her clothes in the men's department, even her classic black wing tips. Even her white tube socks with the red or green stripe along the top. Even the silk boxers she sleeps in, or wears under her clothes on special occasions. Even her everyday underwear, the bright red, green, and blue bikini briefs that come in a clear plastic tube, tagged with a color photograph of a hard-jawed man of northern European descent, thick, blond hair on his chest, a long, muscled swimmer's body.

I wonder what I am to understand about our bodies when I observe 3 the two of us. I look at myself, my heavy eyeliner and mauve lipstick, a silk scarf tied around my throat that matches the leopard print of my gloves. Under my shirt I wear a satin underwire bra. I look at Linnea, noticing that the only items she buys outside of the men's department are her plain cotton and lycra sports bras, the kind designed to hold the breasts still and out of the way. They are more comfortable than the Ace bandages women passing as men once used to bind their breasts, but with similar effect, the aim to draw attention away from the possibility of a bust line, never to lift and separate. In the days before gay liberation, women could be arrested, charged with transvestism, for wearing fewer than three articles of women's clothing. On any day of the week, Linnea does not pass that test. Friends ask me why it matters what any of us wear. Our clothes, they say, are just the facile presentation of our surfaces. The real person is within, contained in the intangible soul. I want to agree, and then I find myself daydreaming about a leopard print dress of silk georgette I saw in a mail-order catalog, or I watch Linnea, a woman with a Ph.D. in literature, her face pursed in concentration as she tries to choose between two silk neckties stretched across her outstretched palms, and I feel certain there is something more than a surface at stake.

Here at J.C. Penney's, among the racks and cabinets of what is called   4 men's clothing, I can imagine Linnea in another time and place. She has an unremarkable singing voice, but is a fine dancer. She has been known to pull off a terrific lip synch and, unlike me, who has always had a hard time talking to strangers and who has never been able to swallow just one of anything intoxicating, Linnea is a model social drinker and can strike up a conversation with almost anybody. She would be great working in any kind of watering hole. She could have easily been one of the butches who worked as drag king impresarios in the mob-run show bars in New York, the Village, in the 1940s. She would be elegant on stage in a fine tailored tux, her hair cut short just as it is now, but slicked back smooth with Brylcream or Rose's Butch Wax. She would change her name for the stage to Lenny, or maybe Johnny, after her Italian grandfather from Hell's Kitchen, a gentle man tattooed from head to ankle. In the Village drag shows, Johnny/Linnea would be the king with the approachable face, handsome in her command of the gentlemanly arts, the mystery date all the ladies dream of, their faces lit amber in the boozy candlelight, Johnny/Linnea waltzing out before the bare-bulbed footlights, just as airborne as Kelly or Astaire, escorting Dietrich in a sea-blue sheath, dipping a reluctant Bette Davis or twirling a taffeta-clad Ginger Rogers under her arm.*

But what is it I see when I conjure up the image of Linnea on a drag   5 king stage? The old European fairy tales say the kings are the ones above

---

* **Gene Kelly** (1912–1996) was a Hollywood actor, dancer, and choreographer, best known for his work in *Singin' in the Rain.* **Fred Astaire** (1899–1987) was a sophisticated and debonair dancer and actor, most famous for his dancing partnership with the wholesome yet glamorous **Ginger Rogers** (1911–1995). **Marlene Dietrich** (1901–1992) was a German-born star of U.S. stage and screen whose stunning beauty had a certain bisexual appeal. **Bette Davis** (1908–1989) was a leading lady of Hollywood, known for her portrayal of strong and complex characters—and for her memorable eyes.

Marlene Dietrich.

all the rest, the rulers of countries and people, but there are kings of property and also those who possess a kingdom of self-knowledge, the low-rent regents of self-rule who have always known who they are. A drag king is no one's boss, an illusionary monarch, a magician with the alchemist's amber light in her eyes. Some kinds of kings are easy to see — the military leaders, the oil barons, the presidents, prime ministers, and prom kings. There's the King of Pop, the King of Rock, the Elvis impersonators swinging their hips in their beaded white jumpsuits. There's the cartoon king selling fast-food burgers, King Kong scaling the Empire State Building again, the terrified lion wailing all the way to Oz, "If I were the king of the forrrrrrest." There's the King of the Road, the King of Kings, the King's English. There's Linnea and my king-sized King Koil mattress. There's that merry old soul King Cole. There's King Midas, the King of the Hill, the King of Swing, and the Customer is King. I wonder what, if anything, this catalog of kings has in common with Linnea in her two-toned wing tips and creased trousers. Does she share some qualities with the kingly crested birds, the kingfisher, the ruby crowned kinglet? Is she the chessboard king? The laminated paper King of Hearts, ruler of the sub-conscious? The King of Pentacles, protector against evil spirits, a reliable husband but also a patriarch? What I see is the everyday checkerboard king, the player who has made it, panting, all the way to the other side of the board and now can move in whatever direction she chooses. So she does. She is a woman who wears men's clothes, except they aren't men's clothes to her, just her clothes, the clothes she likes.

At J.C. Penney's she hands me the geometry lesson tie. I move in, squint 6 to focus, then hold it back at arm's length again. "No," I tell her. "It's too awful. It hurts my eyes."

I hand it back to Linnea, who falls away from me in a long sigh. "So 7 you really hate it?"

Behind the glass counter a thin-boned woman clerk watches our ex- 8 change, a steady smile on her orangy lips. This Penney's is in a suburban shopping mall. I can't tell if she knows what kind of king her customer is, won't know unless she says the words, *thank you sir* or *thank you ma'am*. I have yet to meet a lesbian who doesn't recognize Linnea as one of her own kind, but straight people often address her as a man, and when we walk through the gay cruising zones of Minneapolis, Chicago, San Francisco, I watch the eyes of gay men fall from her face to her crotch and back up to her eyes, with just a fast glance toward me to wonder, I can only suppose, if I am his sister, his fag hag, or his wife of convenience. What people see depends on the context, on what they want to see, on what they are afraid to see.

I think of an old friend of mine, a woman proud to show off her un- 9 shaved legs, "untraditional beauty," she called it, wearing short striped skirts with big Doc Marten boots. She put up with every kind of heckling for years, but it was a department store clerk who finally did her in. One day, walking through a downtown Minneapolis store (with so many gay male employees some departments might be mistaken for an exclusive men's club) my friend passed by a young woman working behind the polished glass cosmetic case. The woman had thin tweaked eyebrows, pores smothered under foundation cream, and a twitch, some violent itch to spit at a queer. She leaned over the glistening glass and actually shouted: "Look. A transvestite!"

My friend's breasts were not bound. She was a woman wearing many 10 more than three pieces of women's clothing, despite her way of walking, in the long gait she learned in the military — unisex boots, yes, but also Hanes Her Way panties, a crop top bra, a black-and-white flared mini-skirt, a black scoop-necked top from the junior women's department, slouch socks from women's hosiery, red sunglasses from the women's wall of the optical shop. Her furry legs, her soldier stride, her British-made punk-boy boots — do three male props make her a masquerading

woman? Would she be arrested? My friend stopped dead and said simply, "I'm a lesbian," then continued on her way. When she got home she
called the store to complain. But the skin around her eyes was too pale
when she told me the story. She believed in being visible, in being out of
the closet even under bleach bright department store lights, but this was
too much exposure, a bad sunburn. Sometimes you have to cover up.
The next day she shaved.

In fairy tales it is common for a king to come upon his bride in dis-   11
guise, masquerading as a beggar, a frog, a swan. The night I started falling for Linnea, I was the house manager for a lesbian theater, and she
was a volunteer usher. We were still in our mid–twenties, and it was
Saturday night. She was wearing a gray tuxedo with full tails and black
velvet trim. I was wearing a little Jackie O suit — narrow skirt, bolero
length jacket — made from a black knit fabric with a sunspot design sewn
in with glittering amber thread. We had run into each other before — at
parties, at the grocery store. We had never been unattached at the same
time until now, but I had been watching her, been having fleeting day-
dreams of leaning into her embrace. I had warned friends not to date
her first. When we talked I felt jolted into a full habitation of my body,
surrounded by a bell of amber sunset, my skin glowing the color of that
resin gem said to cure all ailments of the flesh.

That night in the theater there was an elemental pull between us. I   12
couldn't keep myself from touching her elbow, her shoulder, her collar.
When she offered to help me set up the box office, I accepted, but it was
slow going. We kept stopping and staring, watching each other's faces, a
flimsy aluminum card table or a battered steel cash box floating like a
Ouija board between us, until we both just laughed. I laughed because
it was ridiculous — we had work to do, I had to find something to cover
the table, had to sell tickets, had to ignore her. She laughed, she told me
later, because she thought I was so pretty in my Jackie O suit.

This night was the last in a series of shows I had been working on   13
for over two years, with all of my closest friends, a group of lesbian actors, writers, and techies who had stumbled together through so much
bad gossip, so many misbegotten love affairs, we needed to hire a professional mediator before we could finish what we had begun. My plan
was to creep up to the front to watch this last show up close, but when
we stood at the back of the auditorium as the house lights dimmed,
Linnea let one arm fall over my shoulders and whispered, "This is it." She
meant the show, the end of something, but I heard more. *This is it*: the
next part of my life was beginning. In that moment of total darkness before the stage lights came up, I leaned back into her, that golden brown
bell descending again, my muscles falling limp as she held me up. Had
she had the nerve to keep her arm flung across my shoulders, I would
have stayed by her side, eyes closed, magnetized, ignoring the show until
the house lights came back up again. But she pulled her arm away, and

I was muscle and bone again, still hovering near but too shy to touch, wondering when we would really get together

The next time I saw her was at an actual masquerade. Linnea was Patsy 14 Cline, the crowd favorite of the women's lip-synch show at Sappho's Lounge, Tuesday nights when a downtown gay drag stage was trans- formed into a lesbian dance bar. That night's performance also featured a Janis Joplin in a floppy felt hat, limp blond hair, patched jeans, and a tie-dyed T-shirt, who dropped hard to her knees at the climax of "Take it. Take another little piece of my heart." There was a short, square, fair- skinned woman in a plain black tux and sand-colored crew cut, Whitney Houston's polar opposite, who leaned into the words of "The Greatest Love of All" so earnestly she nearly knocked the unattached mike off the four-foot-tall stage. Two other women wore vintage black dresses and bright bleached hair — one a big girl, over six feet, the other short and thin-waisted — and performed a number in which Doris Day sang a duet with herself. Another woman squinted without her glasses and wore a flouncy white Ginger Rogers gown as she spun around the stage like a folk dancer to the tune of "Fernando's Hideaway." The sheer hem of her dress fluttered like a flock of magician's doves.

I didn't see Linnea until she stepped between the glittering tinsel 15 curtain strings. She wore a ruffled red dress that cinched tight around the waist then belled out to her knees, a plain brown wig that had been set in curlers and ratted, three-inch heels, and lipstick a brighter red than the dress. She was perfect, a Patsy Cline concentrate, a refracted and am- plified twin, in the same way any gender illusionist is so much more than the real Judy Garland or Diana Ross or Barbra Streisand could ever be. I had never seen anything like it before, a woman impersonating a drag queen. When Patsy/Linnea twisted her hips while mouthing "I Fall to Pieces" through red lips, into an unwired mike, all the girls in the au- dience screamed, and I fell a little further into fascination.

But when I approached her after the show to gush over her perfor- 16 mance, I was confused to find nothing between us but dead air. Soon, however, I began to understand: she couldn't recognize me from inside her disguise. "I *was* Patsy Cline," she told me later. "Linnea wasn't there, couldn't be there, inside those clothes." Surrounded by the red bar fog and the hot thump from the DJ's speakers, she smiled at me politely with red lips that seemed to throb too in the pulsing light. A backstage star nodding generously to a subject fan. I was dizzy with deprivation, the molecules of my body pulling, scattering, spinning, but unacknowledged, uncaught. In the old European stories, the king rescues the soiled queen- to-be, curled up like a feral cat in front of a cold hearth, or redeems the selfish princess who only reluctantly shares her dinner with the croaking frog, her unrecognized lover. But I couldn't wait for Linnea to recognize me. I needed to make a move; I had to conjure my king.

I knew I was going to see Linnea at a party soon after, so I planned   17
my wardrobe carefully. I chose an old pair of jeans, dyed green, the knees
worn through, my sex–catching clothes. Ass–snug and knee–revealing,
the pants had belonged to a woman I went out with only a few times. I
borrowed them one night after she and I were soaked in a thunderstorm
during a long walk around a dark city lake. She was pretty enough to
have been a high school prom queen. I had never been involved with
such a girlie–girl before then; all my former lovers tended to live a few
degrees closer to the guy side of the scale. Walking with her was a bit
like wandering in a mirror — not that we looked so much alike. She was
shorter, had smoother features, fuller breasts, no ethnic nose, no south
Chicago accent. The similarity was from a deeper place, as if we were
broadcasting from the same pole. This woman and I went for lots of long
walks, and I began to feel like an image from those soft–focus greeting
cards you see in the drug store, two women in Victorian sheaths and
heavy streams of hair, riding a bicycle together through the too–green
countryside, bare skin touching, one nipple almost showing, one woman's hair falling over the other's shoulder as she leans forward to whis-
per. I was attracted to the sameness, the echo, and she seemed to like me
too, so for a little while I thought we might be able to tune each other
in. But then she stopped returning my calls. I was not heartbroken, but a
little miffed, so I kept her pants.

These were the jeans I wore to the party, along with the sunspot   18
jacket of my Jackie O suit. Linnea wore tight jeans, cowboy boots, a wide
belt. All night we circled each other in our friend's kitchen, my body
shifting inside my clothes like the shapes we used to make in grade
school science class with metal filings and a little red magnet. Later we
heard friends had laid bets. Would I take her to my two–room apartment
with the whistling radiators? Would we do it right in front of the house
on the hard bench seat of Linnea's pickup? But she was too much the
gentleman for that. She promised to call. We each left alone.

During the week before our first date, I was a planet without an or-   19
bit. I wandered through shopping malls, looking for a costume to impress
her, but found nothing. As the week dripped by, I found myself sweating
when others shivered, was bundled up in wool shawls and fake fur coats
while others complained the heat was turned up too high.

Years later Linnea took me to see the famous magician Harry   20
Blackstone Jr. He stood on an empty stage in a white tie and black tails
and levitated a burning light bulb over the astonished, upturned faces of
the crowd. Audience volunteers offered proof there were no wires, while
Blackstone circled the stage, keeping the bulb ever above their heads, an
incandescent vision. Anyone watching Linnea and me during our first
kiss would have seen something similar, a suspended moment, amber
lit and hovering. I wore black Capri pants and a little cashmere sweater
from the 1950s. Linnea wore jeans and cowboy boots and a man's dress

shirt, just pressed. We stood close next to a steaming radiator, on the bright white stage of my bare–walled apartment. My body floated before her, quivering in its own glow. The slightest furl of her fingers pulled me closer.

A decade has passed since that first kiss, and last week a woman 21 we both know said to me, "I've noticed over all this time that you and Linnea have shifted the way you look, to opposite poles." Have we? I wear lipstick more often these days. I used to think it was too much trouble. The sunspot skirt doesn't fit, but I still wear the jacket. Linnea owns more suits, more ties, but she is older too. She takes dressing up more seri– ously. She doesn't do lip–synch shows anymore, though we named our amber–haired dog Patsy Cline. Linnea used to wear women's underpants (she refuses to call them panties), but switched because she likes how men's underwear feels against her skin. It is the same with men's shirts, men's pants. Linnea also abandoned her thin ribbed white cotton man's undershirts for sports bras because of gravity's demands on her upper body, and I recently bought a Wonderbra, the movie–star cleavage push– up kind, to wear with a velveteen dress I rented for a gay wedding. We have both put on some weight, so our undergarment needs have shifted. That is the main change.

When Linnea first started dating me, some women warned her not 22 to. "She seems strange," they told her. "Look how she dresses." I did al– ways wear a few more than three items of women's clothing in the years most lesbians honored androgyny, and they may have been referring to my denim miniskirt, my black eyeliner, or my Jackie O suit. Linnea just smiled. She knew from chemistry which base elements yearn for each other. These days lesbians speak with another kind of certainty, separating our genders from our genitals, lining up beneath a myriad of headings: *butch* or *femme; femmy-butch* or *butchy-femme; femme top* or *butch bottom; femme-to-femme* or *butch-on-butch; transgender* or plain old *lesbian femi- nist*. And there are scientists now that tell us the old simple division of the world into easy categories, man or woman, boy or girl, is not precise enough to describe what may be five or more discernible sexes. But I don't trust science to be expressive enough to catalog the variations in a magnetic field that pull some to their opposite, others to their mir– ror, others to a mosaic of variations between the two. The clothes avail– able for us to wear may be to some a utilitarian surface, something to cover and protect the skin, to others another industry designed to profit from our confusion about our bodies, but to me, to Linnea, they are the choices we feel compelled to choose, our connection to some hum in the distance of existence to which we feel drawn as strongly as we are pulled to each other.

But on this day, at J.C. Penney's, we masquerade as regular shoppers. 23 What I haven't told her yet is that I love her men's clothes because of how they make me feel, Queen Moon to her Sun King. I don't think it is commonly known that you don't have to be heterosexual to conjure such a feeling. "Buy the rose tie," I tell her. "You'll see."

"So you really hate the other one," she says, glancing back at it over   24 her shoulder.

"This one is so nice," I say. I hold it against her chest, my knuckles   25 grazing her breasts, and I feel that old amber levitation, the pull of positive and negative poles, even on this cluttered stage, beneath this too-bright and unfocused light. Over Linnea's shoulder I see the clerk watching us, biting her orange lips, her head cocked the way our dog Patsy's head tilts when she doesn't understand what we are trying to tell her. I am not sure what she observes in us. I would kiss Linnea right here, but getting kicked out of Penney's might ruin the feeling.

In Sanskrit the word for magnetized rock, the lodestone, is *chumbaka,*   26 "the kisser." In Chinese it is *t' su chi,* "loving stone." The central image of the alchemists was marriage, the union of opposites. They weren't talking about women who broadcast from different poles, but then they were men among men and not talking about women at all. The lodestone is also a conjuring rock. We see ourselves rightly. We learn and understand what we are, king and queen of our own desire. At Penney's, Linnea turns from me, but the kissing current keeps on flowing. She steps away for a moment, but only to buy this rose–stitched tie.

Reading Closely

1. Besides the clothing information, what details in this essay reveal the relationship between the narrator and Linnea?

2. Take a few minutes to list all the things that male and female clothes buyers and clothes wearers have in common. Then write for a few minutes about the distinct ways in which members of the two genders deal with clothing differently. What details does Borich include that indicate how clothing for "what is commonly called a man" and "what is commonly called a woman" is alike and different? What are the similarities and differences between Linnea and the narrator? between Linnea and all the other cross–dressers in this essay? What might be Borich's purpose in giving her readers this information?

3. What is this essay really about? In other words, what is Borich's purpose? Write one paragraph summarizing the entire essay. Then **trade paragraphs with a classmate,** and annotate your partner's paragraph with information from the piece that you've gleaned but your partner hasn't. Finally, work together to prepare a brief, unified report for the rest of the class or for a small group.

4. How does the photograph of Marlene Dietrich enhance the overall essay? What specific details enhance specific passages of the essay?

Considering Larger Issues

1. Does Borich have a one–sentence thesis? If so, write it out. If her thesis is implied, write out what it might be.

2. Who is Borich's audience? Who might have been her intended audience when she wrote this essay? Who is her audience now?

3. Consider how well the vocabulary Borich uses and the incidents she describes reflect the needs and interests of her intended audience and of her current audience. **Working with one or two classmates,** list all the vocabulary and incidents that you feel are especially appropriate to either audience. Prepare a group response to share with the rest of the class.

4. COMBINING METHODS. Which passages in the essay seem to be more concerned with *narrating*, with telling a story, than with providing descriptive details? Mark those passages. Prepare to share your findings with the rest of the class.

5. COMBINING METHODS. Which passages in Borich's essay seem to be concerned with explaining the normality, the everydayness, of a lesbian relationship? How does the author *compare and contrast* a lesbian relationship with a heterosexual one?

Thinking about Language

1. Does any of Borich's language or vocabulary make you uncomfortable? Does any of it seem outdated? inappropriate? offensive? Write out any words and phrases that bother you, note which paragraph they're in, and then define any of them that are unfamiliar to you, using the context or a dictionary. Prepare to share your findings with the rest of the class, including the reason you listed each of the terms.

2. Using the context or a dictionary, define the following words: *impresarios* (4), *patriarch* (5), *feral* (16), *utilitarian* (22).

3. Underline all the comparisons (metaphors and similes) Borich employs to energize her essay, beginning with "what sort of king I have married" and "the geometry lesson" and continuing with "boozy candlelight" and "just as airborne as Kelly or Astaire." What effect do such comparisons have on the tone of the essay?

4. **Working with one or two classmates,** determine the dominant impression Borich is creating in this essay. Identify the specific descriptive language, and map out the organizational pattern that contributes to this impression. Prepare to share your group's findings with the rest of the class.

Writing Your Own Descriptions

1. In preparation for writing a two- to three–page essay describing one of your relatives who is different from you in several significant ways — age,

education, sex, and so on — list all the ways the two of you are alike, the things you have in common. Then list the ways you are definitely different from each other. List phrases replete with physical, emotional, intellectual, professional, academic, aesthetic, and/or athletic details.

Look over the details in the lists you wrote about your relative. What dominant impression do those details suggest? Is this the impression you want your readers to have? If so, start drafting your essay; if not, go back and add details to or delete them from the lists.

As you begin drafting the essay, consider the various ways you might choose to arrange the information. What aspects of the dominant impression can you develop? Can you arrange those aspects from least to most important? Is there a chronology of details? Would some variation on a spatial arrangement best serve your purpose? Write out a thesis statement. As you draft and revise, be sure to refer to the guidelines for checking over descriptive writing on page 140.

2. **Working with a classmate,** trade your drafts describing a relative. Each of you should write out the dominant impression that the other's essay creates, underlining particular words or phrases that bring the impression into focus. Number the descriptive details in the order your classmate has used them, and decide if rearranging them would strengthen the overall effect. Discuss the effectiveness of the thesis as well. After you've worked together, revise your essay, referring to the guidelines for checking over descriptive writing on page 140.

3. Draft a three- to four-page essay in which you describe someone whom you've gotten to know fairly well, either in person or online. The essay will be more interesting if you write about your first impression of this person (based on his or her looks, clothing, speech, writing style, and so on) and then recount what you've since learned about him or her. Although your essay will be mostly descriptive, it will also have elements of comparison and contrast, analysis of causes and consequences, definition, and narration. As you draft and revise, be sure to refer to the guidelines for checking over descriptive writing on page 140.

✳ Additional Suggestions for Writing

1. Drawing on the readings in this chapter, draft a three- to four-page essay that describes the experience of being an outsider. Of course, as you convey the idea of outsider status with various descriptive details, you will also be defining it accordingly. You might review the classified ad at the beginning of the chapter, Borich's essay about the lives of a lesbian couple, Broom's description of her home life, Rember's description of doors that close, or Sanders's memories of his father. In what ways do each of these readings describe, imply, and define "outsiderness" on some level? and to what purpose? Remember that the guidelines for checking over descriptive writing can be found on page 140.

2. Describe a typical meal with someone (or a group of people) you eat with frequently, using subjective and objective details, denotative and connotative language, and metaphors and similes that evoke all five senses and various sensibilities. Where do you eat? What do you eat? How do you behave while you eat? As you draft and revise, refer to the guidelines for checking over descriptive writing on page 140.

3. Draft a three- to four-page essay in which you describe a first meeting with one particular person. What was your initial visual impression? What details do you need to include to convey that visual impression? Which details are subjective, and which are objective? What is your dominant impression of that first meeting? What actions took place that might help you convey that dominant impression?

   First, develop your description of the meeting by coming up with details and examples. Then arrange the information you have generated so that each paragraph leads naturally into the next one. Make sure that you begin paragraphs with transitional sentences that remind readers of information from the previous paragraph and introduce new information to be covered in the next paragraph. Is your thesis explicit or implied? Write it out.

chapter 4

EXEMPLIFICATION

The acclaimed
New York Times
bestseller

STEPHEN KING

— A MEMOIR OF THE CRAFT —

On Writing

SIERRA CLUB
FOUNDED 1892

EXPLORE, ENJOY AND PROTECT THE PLANET
EXPLORE, ENJOY AND PROTECT THE PLANET
EXPLORE, ENJOY AND PROTECT THE PLANET

Search our websites | SEARCH

| About | Goals | News | Local | Outings | Join, Renew, Give | Take Action |

Member Center | Log-in | Register | Tell a Friend

Resilient Habitats & Safeguarding Communities

Submit Your Comments Today: Take Action
Don't Drill Our Coasts!

The Minerals Management Service (MMS) pushed through a
5-year drilling program which would open the majority of our
coasts to offshore drilling. Secretary Salazar has put a halt
on this unbalanced plan by extending the public comment
period through September. Send a message today that our
coasts are off limits!

Protect Our Wild Borderlands   Take Action
from the Border Wall

Stop the Border Wall and protect communities and wildlife.

Protect the Grand Canyon from   Take Action
Uranium Mining!

One million acres around the Grand Canyon are threatened
by uranium mining. Please support permanent protections for
this area and support the Grand Canyon Watershed
Protection Act.

Support America's Red Rock   Take Action
Wilderness Act

Urge Congress to support and co-sponsor "America's Red
Rock Wilderness Act" (ARWA), a bill that will protect nearly
10 million acres of Utah's magnificent redrock canyon lands.

Curbing Carbon & Green Transportation

Support the EPA's Stand against   Take Action
Big Oil and Coal

The endangerment finding was officially published last
Friday, meaning we now have 60 days to fill the Public
Register with enough comments to give the EPA the support
it needs to take on Big Oil and Coal.

Congress: Strengthen our Energy   Take Action
Bill!

The passage of the American Clean Energy & Security Act is
truly a historic victory for clean energy. Now it's up to
Congress to make sure we pass a strong energy bill. Send a
message today!

New Clean Energy Bill Makes a   Take Action
Strong Start

Tell Congress to make polluters pay for the carbon pollution
that causes global warming and implement requirements for
renewable energy, energy efficiency and clean fuels. Contact
your Representative today!

Protect EPA's Authority to   Take Action
Regulate Under the Clean Air Act

U.S. Rep Waxman (D-CA), recently laid out a plan to address

*E*very day, people invest themselves in political causes in the hope of making positive change in the world. Those interested in environmental concerns, for instance, might become members of the Sierra Club—the nation's largest grassroots environmental organization. The Sierra Club's Web site does not just discuss general ways for members to achieve change, however. As the visual on page 204 shows, the site offers a number of specific examples of ways members can get involved, take action, and make their voices heard. Most of the examples ask members to become activists by using their writing skills. From writing to Congress to urge support for "America's Red Rock Wilderness Act" to lobbying the State Department to create more "clean" energy jobs, the Sierra Club uses **exemplification** — it provides examples — for members to involve themselves in the environmental issues they find important.

. . . .

Looking at Your Own Literacy   What political issues interest you? How might you engage these issues by using your writing skills? Be specific in your response; pinpoint at least three examples of ways you might enter into these discussions.

. . . .

What Is Exemplification?

Each day, we make generalizations about people, places, or things, generalizations based on what we've read, seen, or experienced. We might assert that Italian food is fattening, that college athletes don't graduate, that English majors easily find jobs. We might say that Hollywood marriages are shaky, that Michael Moore's films are biased, that the Pittsburgh Steelers are always strong. All these generalizations may be true, but unless we back them up with concrete examples — stories, facts, statistics, ideas — chances are our listeners or readers won't immediately believe us, won't understand us, or won't be interested in our point. We need examples of the caloric components of specific Italian foods, graduation statistics, Moore's story lines, and the Steelers' defensive power. Specific examples make all sorts of conversation and public writing come alive and ring true.

In writing, exemplification can be the dominant rhetorical method of development for an entire essay or a supporting method within a work developed with any other method, from narration to argument. For instance, when I write a strong letter of recommendation for a student, I always provide examples of the student's strengths. For a student who wanted an internship at the Museum of Contemporary Photography in Chicago, I opened one paragraph with a generalization that she had planned her career seriously and then I backed up my generalization with examples.

A Generalization Backed Up with Examples

Just a glance at her résumé will show you how seriously she's planned for her career in art. Even as she worked as a bookstore cashier in order to finance her undergraduate studies at Penn State, she found the time and opportunity to work as a curator's assistant at Penn State's own Palmer Museum of Art, one of those jewels one sometimes finds on a college campus. During the summer between her junior and senior years of college, she lived with her grandparents in Cincinnati, Ohio, and worked as an intern at the Cincinnati Art Museum. After graduating Phi Beta Kappa in art history, Jennifer spent the summer in Paris, perfecting her French and studying in the museums. In late summer, she took off for Greenwich, Connecticut, where she worked as a nanny for the school year. While her young charges were in school, Jennifer worked three days a week as assistant to the curator at the Bruce Museum of Arts and Sciences. Jennifer is a young woman who knows what she's after, what she's doing, and how she'll do it. She is impressive.

. . . .

Thinking about Exemplification

1. Look over the Web page from the Sierra Club (p. 204) that features ways for members to get involved in environmental issues. What is your response to this page? What features of it would encourage you to read or deter you from reading further about these issues and then acting on them?

2. **Working with a classmate,** brainstorm about the activist causes that student groups engage in on campus. Make a list of these causes. For each example, explain how the student groups act on these issues. What forms does their activism take? How would you judge the effectiveness of the groups and their modes of activism?

. . . .

Why Use Exemplification?

Human beings tend to generalize, but listeners or readers want and need examples before they will pay much attention to any generalization or believe the person who's making it. Therefore, we use exemplification every day to illustrate or support the generalizations we make. More specifically, exemplification helps us achieve four specific purposes: to explain and clarify, to analyze, to argue, or to add interest.

Examples help explain and clarify a generalization. For instance, if someone said she wanted to "save the environment," she would need to clarify this statement by explaining her specific environmental concerns and the particular things she wants to "save." The Sierra Club's Web site offers some specific ways to "save the environment," and the May 2007

"Green Issue" of *Vanity Fair* uses other examples to clarify the generalization that musicians are fighting global warming by taking up different forms of activism.

Exemplification to Explain and Clarify

You can go electric and still be green — as these rockers will attest. [Jackson] Browne and [Bonnie] Raitt were the trailblazers, founding members of MUSE (Musicians United for Safe Energy), the group that organized the famous "No Nukes" concerts of 1979. Unmellowed by age, Browne remains an avid activist who owns a wind-powered house and is working with the Gibson guitar company to promote its SmartWood guitars, the sales of which help benefit the Rainforest Alliance. Raitt, through her Green Highway program and Web site, sets up tents at her concerts to educate fans about alternative-energy solutions. Browne and Raitt's bluesman pal Keb' Mo' has joined them in supporting the Songbird Foundation, which promotes the preservation of tropical-songbird habitats and encourages sustainable coffee farming in the forests where the birds live. [Jack] Johnson, as much a surf hunk as a singer-songwriter, co-founded the Kokua Hawaii Foundation to support environmental education in his home state. The Canadian firebrand [Alanis] Morissette champions solar power and has teamed up with her countryman Keanu Reeves to narrate *The Great Warming*, a Canuck companion piece to *An Inconvenient Truth*. Inscrutable synth boffin and Eurythmic Dave Stewart has emerged as an unlikely promoter of Greenpeace and has put together a new, socially conscious multi-media company, called Weapons of Mass Entertainment. Lollapalooza main man [Perry] Farrell has lent his organizational skills to Global Cool, a new nonprofit devoted to reducing carbon dioxide emissions by one billion tons a year; with his current group, Satellite Party, he's recorded a new song — "Woman in the Window," built around a snippet of Jim Morrison spoken-word verse — that serves as Global Cool's anthem. As for [Chuck] Leavell, Rock Snobs like to name-drop him as the consummate southern-rock session pro, a man who's played keyboards with the Allman Brothers and the Black Crowes (not to mention the Rolling Stones) — but who knew he was also a dedicated campaigner for sustainable forestry? Moonlighting as the noble proprietor of the Charlane Plantation, in his native Georgia, he has twice been named that state's Tree Farmer of the Year.

> — *Vanity Fair*, "The Soundtrack of Change"

. . . .

Try Your Hand   Imitating *Vanity Fair*'s "Green Issue," identify a general claim you hear about global warming or the fight against it: for example, ocean temperatures are rising; recycling efforts have increased; animal populations are dwindling; environmental groups are gaining popularity on college campuses. Then do some research, if necessary, and provide specific examples that support or question this claim.

. . . .

We also use exemplification when we want to analyze, either for ourselves or for an audience. In a column that appears every Sunday in *Parade* magazine, Marilyn vos Savant, who is listed in the *Guinness Book of World Records'* Hall of Fame for "Highest IQ," answers questions and analyzes processes, causes, or consequences for the folks who write in to her. The following exchange between vos Savant and Donald Anderson illustrates the use of examples in process analysis, for Anderson explicitly asks vos Savant to analyze and explain the process of sex determination.

Exemplification to Analyze

You wrote that an embryo, regardless of the genetic sex determined at conception, will become feminized unless "key masculinizing influences occur. Every embryo — male (XY) *and* female (XX) — contains structures capable of developing into either male or female sex organs. Only if certain activity occurs properly can any XY embryo head in the direction of becoming all male. If it does not occur, all embryos head in the direction of becoming females, almost by default."

I'm very surprised. I thought the sex determined at conception was definitive. What "activity" must occur to make an XY embryo stay masculine?   — DONALD ANDERSON, Des Plaines, Ill.

It surprised plenty of other readers too. There are *many* activities required at highly specific times for normal sexual differentiation, regardless of the genetic sex.

For example, all embryos have sexually indeterminate gonads, which develop into either testicles or ovaries. A "testis-organizing" activity helps the Y chromosome turn them into testes. Later, the testes must secrete an inhibiting substance to make certain ducts atrophy (otherwise, they become female fallopian tubes). They also must secrete testosterone to stimulate the development of other ducts instead (which will become the male *vas deferens*).

The biological organism is sensitive and complex indeed, and so are the causes of all sorts of sexual variance.   — MARILYN VOS SAVANT

Until he had read vos Savant's discussion of the potential for every embryo to develop into an individual of either sex, Anderson thought he'd understood embryonic sexual development. So he asks vos Savant to explain the process more fully. She does, providing a clear example at every step: first, "all embryos have sexually indeterminate gonads." Second, "a 'testis–organizing' activity helps the Y chromosome turn [those gonads] into testes." Vos Savant goes on to provide examples for each of the remaining steps in the process.

. . . .

Try Your Hand   Processes are easier to understand when examples accompany each step. Think of a process you have mastered. Write out the name of the process and the basic steps you follow when you perform it. Then go back and provide an example — an anecdote, fact, or other illustration — for each step, a specific example that brings that step alive.

• •

In writing, as in conversation, we also use examples when trying to convince someone to consider our point of view; assertions alone are usually not enough to bring the listener or reader to our way of thinking. In the following excerpt, Lisa Guernsey argues for the importance of the children's TV show *Sesame Street* even though it now routinely finds itself at the bottom of national rankings. To make this argument, she cites examples that prove how the show has positively influenced children's lives.

Exemplification to Argue

The tough topics aren't only political. Following the attacks of 9/11, the 33rd-season premiere found Elmo struggling to deal with his fear after he sees a grease fire break out at a lunch counter. He's reassured after he visits with real-life firefighters in Harlem. With that storyline, *Sesame Street* did more to acknowledge its audience's unsettled feelings than many adult shows did, even some set in Manhattan, including *Friends* and *Sex and the City*. In 1982, Will Lee, the man who played Mr. Hooper, died suddenly of a heart attack. The show decided to tackle the issue of death with an episode on Big Bird's distress and confusion over losing his friend.   — LISA GUERNSEY, "*Sesame Street*: The Show That Counts"

It's not difficult to be convinced of Guernsey's argument, especially since many of us have our own memories of *Sesame Street* episodes that shaped our lives.

• •

Try Your Hand   Reflect on your memories of *Sesame Street* or another television show you watched as a child. Write for five minutes about what you remember about the show, thinking specifically about particular episodes that were especially memorable. Why do these episodes stand out to you?

• •

Sometimes examples do nothing more than add interest. For instance, the award–winning author Tim O'Brien provides long lists of examples to illustrate the many belongings carried by U.S. soldiers fighting in the Vietnam War.

Exemplification to Add Interest

The things they carried were largely determined by necessity. Among the necessities or near necessities were P-38 can openers, pocket knives, heat tabs, wrist watches, dog tags, mosquito repellent, chewing gum, candy, cigarettes, salt tablets, packets of Kool-Aid, lighters, matches, sewing kits, Military Payment Certificates, C rations, and two or three canteens of water. Together, these items weighed between fifteen and twenty pounds, depending upon a man's habits or rate of metabolism. Henry Dobbins, who was a big man, carried extra rations; he was especially fond of canned peaches in heavy syrup over pound cake. Dave Jensen, who practiced field hygiene, carried a toothbrush, dental floss, and several hotel-size bars of soap he'd stolen on R&R in Sydney, Australia. Ted Lavender, who was scared, carried tranquilizers until he was shot in the head outside the village of Than Khe in mid-April. By necessity, and because it was SOP [standard operating procedure], they all carried steel helmets that weighed five pounds including the liner and camouflage cover. They carried the standard fatigue jackets and trousers. Very few carried underwear. On their feet they carried jungle boots — 2.1 pounds — and Dave Jensen carried three pairs of socks and a can of Dr. Scholl's foot powder as a precaution against trench foot. Until he was shot, Ted Lavender carried six or seven ounces of premium dope, which for him was a necessity. Mitchell Sanders, the RTO [radio telephone operator] carried condoms. Norman Bowker carried a diary. Rat Kiley carried comic books. Kiowa, a devout Baptist, carried an illustrated New Testament that had been presented to him by his father, who taught Sunday school in Oklahoma City, Oklahoma. As a hedge against bad times, however, Kiowa also carried his grandmother's distrust of the white man, his grandfather's old hunting hatchet. Necessity dictated. Because the land was mined and booby-trapped, it was SOP for each man to carry a steel-centered, nylon-covered flak jacket, Simonov carbines and black-market Uzis and .38 caliber Smith & Wesson handguns and 66 mm LAWs and shotguns and silencers and blackjacks and bayonets and C-4 plastic explosives. Lee Strunk carried a slingshot; a weapon of last resort, he called it. Mitchell Sanders carried brass knuckles. Kiowa carried his grandfather's feathered hatchet. Every third or fourth man carried a Claymore antipersonnel mine — 3.5 pounds with its firing device. They all carried at least one M-18 colored smoke grenade — twenty-four ounces. Some carried CS or teargas grenades. Some carried white-phosphorus grenades. They carried all they could bear, and then some, including a silent awe for the terrible power of the things they carried.   — TIM O'BRIEN, *The Things They Carried*

O'Brien's list of the things the soldiers carried exemplifies the burdens of war, adding interest — and building tension — until the final and deadliest examples. In this excerpt from his novel, O'Brien matter-of-factly recounts the "things"; yet the danger and fearsomeness of the Vietnam War are implicit in every item, in every mention of weaponry and firearms.

· ·

Try Your Hand   Think back to your last big move. Maybe it was just a few weeks ago, when you moved onto campus. Maybe it was years ago, when you and your family moved across the country. Think about the logistics of the move, and then write a list of all the things you carried (either by hand, in huge boxes, or in a van). If you have never moved or don't remember moving, make a list of all the things you took on a vacation or an outing, such as a picnic.

. . . .

How Do You Use Exemplification in Academic Writing?

Like Guernsey and vos Savant, scholars and students in various disciplines use exemplification to clarify, analyze, argue, and add interest. In your English literature class, for example, it would be difficult to prove your argument about *Wuthering Heights*'s Heathcliff without providing examples and support from the novel. Similarly, your history professor most likely expects you to use exemplification when she asks you to pinpoint moments in the late nineteenth century when African Americans asserted their rights to education. And finally, your marketing professor wants you to identify examples when he asks you to compose a paper on the effectiveness or ineffectiveness of shampoo campaigns.

In the following excerpt from the academic journal *Political Science Quarterly*, political scientists Peggy Lopipero, Dorie E. Apollonio, and Lisa A. Bero rely on exemplification to make an argument about the ways the tobacco industry attempted to thwart federal restrictions on public smoking on airplanes in the 1970s and 1980s. (This excerpt omits the footnotes the authors provided for their sources.)

Exemplification in Academic Writing

The tobacco industry attempted to hide its involvement in letter-writing campaigns throughout the airline smoking policy process. Letters were generated by the industry's own employees and related individuals and organizations (for example, the Tobacco Institute, tobacco companies and associations, wholesalers, distributors, advertisers, law firms, tobacco farmers and unions, and subsidiaries). Figure 1 [see p. 212] shows excerpts of examples of the various covert letter-writing requests found in the tobacco industry's files, from the first proceeding to establish smoking sections in 1972 through the congressional adoption of a smoking ban in 1987. Requests repeatedly indicated that any association with the tobacco industry be hidden. The industry was also aware that the correspondence needed to be sufficiently varied to "avoid the appearance of a tightly organized campaign."

— Peggy Lopipero, Dorie E. Apollonio, and Lisa A. Bero, "Interest Groups, Lobbying, and Deception: The Tobacco Industry and Airline Smoking"

The examples the authors provide offer *visual* proof that the tobacco companies did indeed engineer deceptive letter–writing campaigns with the

```
MR. BRESNAHAN:

      Attached are five drafts of "letters"
to the C.A.B. opposing the rule to require
airlines to segregate smokers.

      Could you get some of the agency
people to write these -- by hand -- on
non-company letterheads, using home
addresses, and ask each one to get one
or two more, similar, but not exactly
the same.
```

```
If you decide to write, you should use your own words and
you will be writing as a private individual.  For that
reason, you should not use company stationery nor state
that you are connected with B&W.
```

```
IN PREPARING YOUR LETTER, PLEASE USE PLAIN PAPER OR PERSONAL LETTERHEAD AND A
PLAIN ENVELOPE.  DO NOT USE PHILIP MORRIS LETTERHEAD OR ENVELOPES.
```

Figure 1.

hope that government leaders would think there was greater resistance to smoking restrictions on planes than there actually was. Without the letters as examples, the authors' argument would not be nearly as persuasive.

As you write your way through your classes, you'll want to determine when is the most effective time to use exemplification. As you've read throughout the chapter, writers use examples all the time, but it is up to you to reflect on each writing situation and ask if exemplification would help you accomplish your purpose. Could you deepen your argument by offering an example? Would an example (or two) help to clarify your idea? How might an example help you better analyze a problem? And how might you simply add interest by offering readers interesting and evocative examples?

How Do You Read Exemplification?

Examples that are concrete, real, or striking make for the strongest, most effective support of any generalization, no matter what their purpose or intended audience. To use exemplification effectively in your writing, you'll need to learn how to read essays with a critical eye using exemplification by other writers. By concentrating on several key features of essays that use exemplification successfully, you'll be able to evaluate the ones you read and plan out the ones you write.

First of all, read carefully to establish what generalization the author is making — as well as why and to whom. What belief, understanding, or feeling does the author want you to take away from the examples? Take another look at the excerpt from Tim O'Brien's *The Things They Carried*. A prize-winning novelist, O'Brien is undoubtedly using exemplification here to add interest to his story, which is aimed at readers of fiction. In this case, he might be writing more specifically for readers interested in fiction about war; many of his readers are no doubt Vietnam War buffs or even veterans, who read both fiction and nonfiction about that war. Therefore, as O'Brien develops his generalization and the examples to support it, he works to fulfill his overall purpose (adding interest) with his audience in mind.

O'Brien's generalization is clear: "The things they carried were largely determined by necessity." Once you've extracted the generalization from the reading, assess it to determine whether it sounds clear or plausible — or if it seems confusing, too sweeping, or biased in some way. O'Brien's generalization seems to be clear and plausible: it doesn't seem to be a controversial assertion, and he qualifies or limits it with "largely." However, when you know or suspect that the generalization *does* argue a point (as in the excerpt from Lisa Guernsey on page 209), you'll want to keep that bias in mind as you read through the examples and judge how effective they are in achieving that purpose.

"Can openers, pocket knives, heat tabs, wrist watches, dog tags, mosquito repellent, . . ." — O'Brien's first examples do indeed sound like a list of necessities. By the time he finishes this part of the list, he mentions that "these items weighed between fifteen and twenty pounds," a statement that both supports the "necessary" quality of the things the soldiers carried and adds interest to the passage. But then O'Brien moves into examples of individual soldiers, each of whom carries things that are personal necessities. These examples pack more emotion — and add more interest — than the initial ones of can openers and pocket knives because they personalize the men who fought in Vietnam. Finally, O'Brien moves into examples of the weapons they carried, including both high-tech standard-issue ones and low-tech personalized ones. By arranging his examples in this way, by saving the most essential and most serious things they carried for the end, the writer achieves the maximum emotional impact. Notice how he ends with a generalization that extends the meaning of his original one — that the burdens the soldiers had to carry were almost unbearable not only physically but emotionally as well. When in your reading you encounter examples that stir your emotions — or just your curiosity — try to understand how and why the writer uses those examples.

How Do You Write Using Exemplification?

Coming up with a generalization and examples to support it may sound like an easy task — and it can be. But like any other kind of writing, exemplification makes demands on the writer. Because it can be used for any subject and purpose, you'll want to begin by carefully determining your subject and your purpose: What generalization do you want to exemplify — and why? You'll also need to consider your audience, develop appropriate examples, and arrange those examples effectively.

● Considering Your Subject

Did you come up with your subject, or was it assigned to you? For example, has your sociology professor asked you to identify and cite evidence of patterns of alcohol consumption on your campus? Has your music professor asked you to provide examples as part of a historical analysis of patriotic songs and lyrics? Has your cultural anthropology instructor asked you to write about examples of racism and sexism that you've experienced or observed? If you are writing about an assigned topic, you probably already have a generalization ("Alcohol consumption on this campus is a major safety issue"), but you may need to narrow it or revise it in some other way, depending on the assignment ("Although students are drinking less beer and wine, consumption of other, more potent alcoholic beverages has increased sharply in recent years"). If writing about this subject is your own idea, then you will need to focus on a generalization about the subject that you can back up or illustrate with examples.

● Considering Your Purpose

Whether writing an essay or passage using exemplification was your idea or your instructor's, you should determine the purpose of your examples before you begin developing them. Why do you want to exemplify this particular generalization? In this excerpt from RollingStone.com, writer Jonathan Lethem asks the question "What makes a great singer?" To answer this question and achieve his purpose, Lethem offers examples of a numbers of singers whose voices shocked and surprised listeners.

Exemplification to Explain and Clarify

This points to what defines great singing in the rock-and-soul era: that some underlying tension exists in the space between singer and song. A bridge is being built across a void, and it's a bridge we're never sure the singer's going to manage to cross. The gulf may reside between vocal texture and the actual meaning of the words, or between the singer and band, musical genre, style of production or the audience's expectations. In any case, there's something beautifully uncomfortable at the root of the vocal style that defines the pop era. The simplest example comes at the moment of the style's inception, i.e., Elvis Presley: at first, listeners thought that the white guy was a black guy. It's not too much of an exaggeration to say that when Ed Sullivan's television show tossed this disjunction into everyone's living rooms, American culture was thrilled by it but also a little deranged, in ways we haven't gotten over yet. If few vocal styles since have had the same revolutionary potential, it wasn't for want of trying. When the Doors experimented with how rock & roll sounded fronted by sulky bombast, or the Ramones or Modern Lovers offered the sound of infantile twitching, a listener's first response may have been to regard their approaches as a joke. Yet that joke is the sound of something changing in the way a song can make us feel. In the cafe where I write this, Morrissey just came over the speakers, and it's pretty unmistakable that he came through the Doors Jim Morrison opened. Janis Joplin's voice howled in the wilderness for decades before Lucinda Williams came along to claim its tattered and glorious implications. In doing so, she deepened them.   — Jonathan Lethem, "What Makes a Great Singer?"

It is clear that Lethem's purpose is to explain to readers the qualities that make a great singer. His overarching claim, however, is a bit unclear at first: a great singer is one who can negotiate a certain kind of tension between singer and song, one who can cross a "void" and "build a bridge." Since these claims might seem vague to readers, Lethem's examples are crucial to helping readers understand what he means: Elvis's voice crossed racial lines, the Doors' lead singer was a "sulky bombast," and the Ramones sounded at first like "infantile twitching." Your purpose also shapes your thesis statement.

● Considering Your Audience

Of course, writers need to make sure their examples meet the needs and expectations of their audience. Lethem's use of exemplification makes perfect sense given his *Rolling Stone* readership, and we can see how Lethem accommodates and addresses his audience throughout the excerpt. Because he trusts that his readers are knowledgeable about the music world, he does not offer detailed explanations of his examples. He even goes so far as to *leave out* information, assuming that readers will understand his references. For instance, he does not need to tell readers who the sulky bombast and lead singer of the Doors was (Jim Morrison), and he doesn't describe what "infantile twitching" actually sounds like. He assumes that readers will know, and he's right: most hard-core music enthusiasts would not need further explanation for either of these examples. Lethem's excerpt makes it clear, then, that the purpose of a piece of writing must be closely aligned with the expectations of the audience. In your writing, you want to make sure that your examples not only fit your purpose but also are appropriate for your audience.

● **Considering Specific Examples**

Once you have a generalization about your subject, you'll need to make a list of as many examples as you can think of. **Anecdotes** (brief stories), facts, statistics, and ideas can all serve as examples that support or illustrate a generalization. In the following excerpt from *Eats, Shoots & Leaves*, British writer Lynne Truss uses an anecdote to bolster her claim that there is a growing indifference to correct punctuation.

> An Anecdote Used as an Example
>
> Everywhere one looks, there are signs of ignorance and indifference. What about that film *Two Weeks Notice*? Guaranteed to give sticklers a very nasty turn, that was—its posters slung along the sides of buses in letters four feet tall, with no apostrophe in sight. I remember, at the start of the *Two Weeks Notice* publicity campaign in the spring of 2003, emerging cheerfully from Victoria Station (was I whistling?) and stopping dead in my tracks with my fingers in my mouth. Where was the apostrophe? Surely there should be an apostrophe on that bus? If it were "one month's notice" there would be an apostrophe (I reasoned); yes, and if it were "one week's notice" there would be an apostrophe. Therefore "two weeks' notice" requires an apostrophe! Buses that I should have caught (the 73; two 38s) sailed off up Buckingham Palace Road while I communed thus at length with my inner stickler, unable to move or, indeed, regain any sense of perspective.   — Lynne Truss, *Eats, Shoots & Leaves*

Marc Ambinder uses facts (historical facts in particular) to support his argument that communications technologies have changed American politics.

> Facts Used as an Example
>
> Improvements to the printing press helped Andrew Jackson form and organize the Democratic Party, and he courted newspaper editors and publishers, some of whom became members of his Cabinet, with a zeal then unknown among political leaders. . . .
>
> Franklin Delano Roosevelt used radio to make his case for a dramatic redefinition of government itself, quickly mastering the informal tone best suited to the medium. In his fireside chats, Roosevelt reached directly into American living rooms at pivotal moments of his presidency. . . .
>
> And of course John F. Kennedy famously rode into the White House thanks in part to the first televised presidential debate in U.S. history, in which his keen sense of the medium's visual impact, plus a little makeup,

enabled him to fashion the look of a winner (especially when compared with a pale and haggard Richard Nixon).   — MARC AMBINDER, "HisSpace"

Andrew Martin uses statistics to support his generalization that cutting back on food waste could help reduce the country's hunger problems.

Statistics Used as Examples

Of course, eliminating food waste won't solve the problems of world hunger and greenhouse-gas pollution. But it could make a dent in this country and wouldn't require a huge amount of effort or money. The Department of Agriculture estimated that recovering just 5 percent of the food that is wasted could feed four million people a day; recovering 25 percent would feed 20 million people. The Department of Agriculture said it was updating its figures on food waste, and officials there weren't yet able to say if the problem has gotten better or worse.
—ANDREW MARTIN, "One Country's Table Scraps, Another Country's Meal"

Finally, Mary Carmichael uses hypothetical situations to illustrate her generalization about what causes stress in our lives.

Hypothetical Situations Used as Examples

In humans, almost anything can start the stress response. Battling traffic, planning a party, losing a job, even gaining a job — all may get the stress hormones flowing as freely as being attacked by a predator does. Even the prospect of future change can set off our alarms. We think, therefore we worry.   — MARY CARMICHAEL, "Who Says Stress Is Bad for You?"

As you list various kinds of examples, you'll see that some of them are only loosely related to your generalization. In fact, you may find that your list of examples calls for a narrower or slightly different generalization. Also keep in mind that your audience and purpose will influence which kinds of examples (anecdotes, facts, statistics) are most appropriate. Whichever kinds and however many you list, choose only those that are directly **relevant** to your generalization, those that support or illustrate at least one aspect of it. Examples that are used to make an argument must also be **representative** of the whole group covered by the generalization. For instance, if you're writing about current alcohol consumption on your campus, you won't want to include an anecdote from 2005, which would not be relevant, or to concentrate only on fraternity houses, which might not be representative. If you do, you should revise your generalization to reflect your focus.

There are no hard-and-fast rules for how many examples to provide, but keep in mind that you usually need a range of examples for any one generalization, especially one making an argument. In other words, draft more examples than you need and, as you revise, choose only those

"Reading" and Using Visuals in Exemplification

As you use exemplification in writing, you may find that words are not enough. To support your generalization or explain your verbal examples, you may need to use a visual or a group of visuals. Women's fashion magazines, for instance, usually carry an article that features descriptions of the latest look, whether it's low-slung pants, round-toe pumps, chandelier earrings, or even ponytails. But to teach readers how to carry out this new look, the magazine must include a series of photographs of the actual articles or of models displaying the actual look. For instance, in the accompanying display from *Latina* magazine, fashion editor Victoria Sánchez-Lincoln provides a wide range of examples that support her generalization that blue is the season's "color of cool."

To choose and use visuals effectively for exemplification, you can benefit from studying how other writers have used visuals. Given that the purpose of exemplification in the *Latina* visual is simply to add interest (and not to provide an exhaustive list of examples or to argue that red is also a "cool color"), the editor successfully does just that. For an audience made up of young women, she provides an array of clothing and accessories oriented toward them, including one item labeled "Great buy: $10." Notice that the visual examples provide a pleasing mixture of stripes, solids, and prints, of curves and straight lines. For this audience of young women, many of whom are still unsure of their own fashion instincts, Sánchez-Lincoln also provides a list of written examples of how to incorporate the new blue fashions into a wardrobe, suggesting that navy blue can serve as a neutral color the same way black does, that pairing turquoise with blue can create a pleasant surprise, and that lighter-colored jeans would look best with the halter top.

Cities heavily involved with the tourist industry use visuals in a similar way. Every tourist bureau circulates a photographic extravaganza, both in print brochures and in animated Web sites, that exemplifies all the reasons tourists should visit its city — for the fancy restaurants, musical entertainment, zoos, theme parks, skiing, scuba diving, botanical gardens, and so on. Remember that bar graphs, line graphs, or pie charts can support or serve as statistical examples. Even if a visual isn't needed to explain your information or support your argument, it can add interest.

If you want to use visuals in writing for an academic assignment, it is a good idea to check with your instructor beforehand. You also need to consider whether to include labels or captions (if the visuals do not already include them) and whether to refer to the visuals in your written text or let them stand on their own.

You've got rhythm...

And we've got blues. Check out our soulful picks in the color of cool

Fashion pages edited by Victoria Sánchez-Lincoln

Cascade Blues necklace ($16) and Fiesta earrings ($8: 800/MERVYNS for both items)

DKNY Jeans halter ($34: select Macy's stores)

Express shorts ($35: expressfashion.com or 877/415-4551)

Great buy: $10

Wet Seal sunglasses ($10: wetseal.com)

Guess Footwear sandals ($98: 800/39-GUESS or guess.com)

Putu by J. MacLear bag at D.P. Accessories ($42: 203/847-7103)

Sisley top ($34: 800/535-4491)

How to wear it

- Add another neutral to your wardrobe: Navy can be as basic as black; it goes with everything and is never boring.

- Teeny blue hot pants a bit too extreme? Find just-as-bold tropical prints on beach skirts or cabana pants, perfect for covering up after a day at *la playa. Latina's* golden rule: Let them hang low on your sexy hips!

- Be surprising. Go exotic and bright by pairing your blue pick with turquoise.

- Sure, you can wear jeans with this sexy halter (which enhances your bust with its horizontal stripes). Just pick lighter-wash denim jeans for the strongest impact.

LATINA JULY 2003   41

that will help prove your generalization to the most skeptical member of your audience, explain it to the most confused, or interest the most bored.

● Arranging All the Parts

If exemplification is the framework for your entire essay, then each paragraph will need to be related to your thesis, to the generalization you are trying to illustrate or prove. For instance, if you are responding to your professor's assignment about alcohol consumption, your entire essay should support whatever generalization about drinking alcohol you come up with. If you generalize that alcohol abuse on your campus is increasing, you'll need specific examples (probably including anecdotes, statistics, and facts) of such problems as binge drinking, drinking contests, underage drinking, alcohol-related traffic accidents, on-campus accidents (falling off balconies, passing out in public or in dorm rooms), alcohol-related academic difficulties, inappropriate sexual activity caused by alcohol, and so on.

The more examples you include, the more important it is to arrange them in some kind of meaningful order so that the reader doesn't lose sight of the connection between them — the generalization. For instance, you may want to arrange them chronologically (along a time line), the way vos Savant does on page 208 and Ambinder does on page 216. You may want to arrange them emphatically, starting with the least serious kinds of alcohol abuse and placing the most serious at the end. Or you may want to group them into examples dealing with beer and wine and those dealing with hard liquor, if this distinction seems important in understanding patterns of alcohol abuse. You may want to begin with anecdotes and move on to statistics and facts, reverse this order, or alternate between types of examples to avoid monotony. Regardless of the method you select for organizing your examples, you'll need to use transitional words and phrases (*for instance, likewise, an even more serious episode of binge drinking,* . . .) to guide readers smoothly from one to the next.

If you need to use exemplification in an essay that uses a different primary pattern (comparison and contrast or description, for example), you'll still need to organize the examples effectively — chronologically, emphatically, or in some other way — within your paragraph or passage. You'll also need to decide where your generalization should go in relation to the examples. It will usually come first, but sometimes — especially in an introductory paragraph or passage — you may want to use one or more examples to lead up to it. And after a series of examples or even just one long example, it's a good idea to remind readers of your generalization and, if possible, extend the point you're making with it. This is what Gretel Ehrlich does in the following passage, where she is writing about a particular kind of man, the cowboy.

> The iconic myth surrounding him is built on American notions of heroism: the index of a man's value as measured in physical courage. Such ideas have perverted manliness into a self-absorbed race for cheap thrills. In a rancher's world, courage has less to do with facing danger than with acting spontaneously — usually on behalf of an animal or another rider. If a cow is stuck in a boghole he throws a loop around her neck, takes his dally (a half hitch around the saddle horn), and pulls her out with horsepower. If a calf is born sick, he may take her home, warm her in front of the kitchen fire, and massage her legs until dawn. One friend, whose favorite horse was trying to swim a lake with hobbles on, dove under water and cut her legs loose with a knife, then swam her to shore, his arm around her neck lifeguard-style, and saved her from drowning. Because these incidents are usually linked to someone or something outside himself, the westerner's courage is selfless, a form of compassion. — GRETEL EHRLICH, "About Men"

In this passage, Ehrlich makes a generalization about the courage of cowboys, focusing on the idea of acting spontaneously. She then uses three examples, each more dramatic than the previous one, to bring it to life. She concludes by restating the idea she introduced almost as an afterthought in the original generalization: a cowboy's courage usually benefits not himself but others.

Understanding and Using Exemplification

Analyzing Exemplification

1. In *Vanity Fair*'s "Soundtracks of Change," the article lists the work that musicians are doing to fight global warming. Note each musician's contribution, and then compose another list of how other musicians you're familiar with might add to this list.

2. On page 216, Marc Ambinder uses the examples of Andrew Jackson, Franklin Delano Roosevelt, and John F. Kennedy to make his claim that technology has changed politics in general and elections more particularly. Thus as he relies on exemplification, he's also interested in cause-and-effect analysis. In what specific ways did these technologies affect political movements and presidential elections?

3. In the excerpt by Tim O'Brien on page 209, he uses vocabulary specific to his subject matter, such as "R&R" and "SOP." **Working with a classmate** and using your dictionary or the context, define any words in this excerpt that you don't know.

Planning and Writing Essays Using Exemplification

1. In her *Newsweek* article, Mary Carmichael offers a short list of hypothetical situations that cause stress in people's lives. Writing for no more than five minutes, make your own list of things that cause stress in your life. Once you've composed your list, reflect on it, identify the three "stressors" that are most stressful for you, and spend ten minutes writing about why they are stressful. Once you've finished, **share your writing with a classmate**, comparing the various things that "stress us out."

2. Turn to page 209 and copy — word for word — the excerpt from Tim O'Brien's essay "The Things They Carried." (When you copy by hand, the words, phrases, and rhythms stay in your mind longer than if you were to type them.) Now write a passage of approximately the same length, copying his style as closely as possible, about the things you and your friends carry in college.

3. In the excerpt on page 209, Lisa Guernsey argues that *Sesame Street* revolutionized children's television. To support her claim, Guernsey cites examples from the show that suggest just how revolutionary it was. Reflect on a television show that was or has been particularly influential to you, thinking specifically about particular episodes that shaped your thinking. Compose a two- to three-page essay that makes a claim about the significance of this program and, like Guernsey, use examples from episodes to support your argument. As you draft and revise, follow the guidelines for checking over the use of exemplification.

4. On page 221, Gretel Ehrlich uses exemplification to counter stereotypical ideas about cowboys and argue for her own view of this figure. Identify a stereotypical figure (such as cheerleader, computer geek, goth, or jock). Modeling your essay on Ehrlich's work, compose a two- to three-page essay that relies on exemplification to counter the stereotypes about this figure. As you draft and revise, refer to the guidelines for checking over the use of exemplification.

✔ Checking Over the Use of Exemplification

1. What is the generalization that you need to illustrate or support?

2. What is the purpose of your examples? to explain or clarify the generalization? to analyze it? to argue for it? to add interest? Do all your examples help fulfill this purpose?

3. Who is your audience? Are all your examples appropriate for that audience?

4. List all your examples. Are there enough of them? Are there too many? Are they all relevant to the generalization? If your generalization makes an argument, are the examples representative? Does your generalization need to be narrowed?

5. How are your examples arranged? Will the arrangement be effective in holding your readers' attention? Have you used transitional words and phrases to guide readers from one example to the next? Do readers need to be reminded of your generalization in your conclusion or at any point along the way?

6. If you're using visuals, do they help fulfill your overall purpose? Do you need to add labels, captions, or references in the written text?

READINGS

BRENT STAPLES

Just Walk On By: A Black Man Ponders His Power to Alter Public Space

Brent Staples (b. 1951) received a Ph.D. in psychology from the University of Chicago in 1982 and has drawn on his background in that field throughout his career as a leading print journalist. He's best known for his essays on culture and politics, which have appeared in the *Chicago Sun-Times*, the *Chicago Reader*, the *New York Times*, and *Down Beat*, *Harper's*, and *Ms.* magazines. A member of the editorial board of the *New York Times* since 1990, Staples has also published a memoir, *Parallel Time: Growing Up in Black and White*, which appeared in 1994. The following essay first appeared in *Harper's* in 1986, and a slightly different version appeared in *Parallel Time*.

> **Preview** What does it mean to "alter public space"? As you read Staples's essay, consider the ways that a particular kind of person—for example, a white woman, a gay man, a devout Christian, a person with a disability, or a homeless person—can change the emotional climate of a particular place.

Staples opens the essay with a riveting example. What is its effect?

My first victim was a woman — white, well dressed, probably in her late twenties. I came upon her late one evening on a deserted street in Hyde Park, a relatively affluent neighborhood in an otherwise mean, impoverished section of Chicago. As I swung onto the avenue behind her, there seemed to be a discreet, uninflammatory distance between us. Not so. She cast back a worried glance. To her, the youngish black man — a broad six feet two inches with a beard and billowing hair, both hands shoved into the pockets of a bulky military jacket — seemed menacingly close. After a few more quick glimpses,

1

she picked up her pace and was soon running in earnest. Within seconds she disappeared into a cross street.

2   That was more than a decade ago. I was twenty-two years old, a graduate student newly arrived at the University of Chicago. It was in the echo of that terrified woman's footfalls that I first began to know the unwieldy inheritance I'd come into — the ability to alter public space in ugly ways. It was clear that she thought herself the quarry of a mugger, a rapist, or worse. Suffering a bout of insomnia, however, I was stalking sleep, not defenseless wayfarers. As a softy who is scarcely able to take a knife to a raw chicken — let alone hold one to a person's throat — I was surprised, embarrassed, and dismayed all at once. Her flight made me feel like an accomplice in tyranny. It also made it clear that I was indistinguish-able from the muggers who occasionally seeped into the area from the surrounding ghetto. That first en-counter, and those that followed, signified that a vast, unnerving gulf lay between nighttime pedestri-ans — particularly women — and me. And I soon gathered that being perceived as dangerous is a haz-ard in itself. I only needed to turn a corner into a dicey situation, or crowd some frightened, armed person in a foyer somewhere, or make an errant move after being pulled over by a policeman. Where fear and weapons meet — and they often do in urban America — there is always the possibility of death.

Staples provides a series of brief examples to support a generali-zation.

3   In that first year, my first away from my home-town, I was to become thoroughly familiar with the language of fear. At dark, shadowy intersections, I could cross in front of a car stopped at a traffic light and elicit the thunk, thunk, thunk, thunk of the driver — black, white, male, or female — hammer-ing down the door locks. On less traveled streets after dark, I grew accustomed to but never com-fortable with people crossing to the other side of the street rather than pass me. Then there were the standard unpleasantries with policemen, doormen, bouncers, cab-drivers, and others whose business it is to screen out troublesome individuals before there is any nastiness.

In this paragraph, another series of examples develops the generalization of how Staples realized that his presence created fear. Note that the last sentence includes examples within an example.

4   I moved to New York nearly two years ago and I have remained an avid night walker. In central

Manhattan, the near-constant crowd cover mini-
mizes tense one-on-one street encounters. Elsewhere — in SoHo, for example, where sidewalks are
narrow and tightly spaced buildings shut out the
sky — things can get very taut indeed.

After dark, on the warrenlike streets of Brook- 5
lyn where I live, I often see women who fear the
worst from me. They seem to have set their faces
on neutral, and with their purse straps strung
across their chests bandolier-style, they forge ahead
as though bracing themselves against being tack-
led. I understand, of course, that the danger they
perceive is not a hallucination. Women are particularly vulnerable to street violence, and young black
males are drastically overrepresented among the
perpetrators of that violence. Yet these truths are
no solace against the kind of alienation that comes
of being ever the suspect, a fearsome entity with
whom pedestrians avoid making eye contact.

It is not altogether clear to me how I reached 6
the ripe old age of twenty-two without being conscious of the lethality nighttime pedestrians attributed to me. Perhaps it was because in Chester,
Pennsylvania, the small, angry industrial town
where I came of age in the 1960s, I was scarcely no-
ticeable against a backdrop of gang warfare, street
knifings, and murders. I grew up one of the good
boys, had perhaps a half-dozen fistfights. In retrospect, my shyness of combat has clear sources.

Staples uses a differ-
ent set of examples
here to support a new
generalization about
the tough guys he has
seen "locked away"
and buried.

As a boy, I saw countless tough guys locked 7
away; I have since buried several, too. They were babies, really — a teenage cousin, a brother of twenty-
two, a childhood friend in his mid-twenties — all
gone down in episodes of bravado played out in the
streets. I came to doubt the virtues of intimidation
early on. I chose, perhaps unconsciously, to remain
a shadow — timid, but a survivor.

Note how the topic
sentences of Staples's
paragraphs work to
introduce the examples
that follow.

The fearsomeness mistakenly attributed to me in 8
public places often has a perilous flavor. The most
frightening of these confusions occurred in the late
1970s and early 1980s, when I worked as a journalist
in Chicago. One day, rushing into the office of a
magazine I was writing for with a deadline story in
hand, I was mistaken for a burglar. The office manager called security and, with an ad hoc posse, pur-

sued me through the labyrinthine halls, nearly to
my editor's door. I had no way of proving who I was.
I could only move briskly toward the company of
someone who knew me.

9   Another time I was on assignment for a local
paper and killing time before an interview. I entered a jewelry store on the city's affluent Near
North Side. The proprietor excused herself and returned with an enormous red Doberman pinscher
straining at the end of a leash. She stood, the dog
extended toward me, silent to my questions, her
eyes bulging nearly out of her head. I took a cur-
sory look around, nodded, and bade her good
night.

A transitional phrase
helps move readers
from one example to
the next.

10   Relatively speaking, however, I never fared as
badly as another black male journalist. He went to
nearby Waukegan, Illinois, a couple of summers
ago to work on a story about a murderer who was
born there. Mistaking the reporter for the killer, police officers hauled him from his car at gunpoint
and but for his press credentials would probably
have tried to book him. Such episodes are not uncommon. Black men trade tales like this all the
time.

11   Over the years, I learned to smother the rage I
felt at so often being taken for a criminal. Not to do
so would surely have led to madness. I now take
precautions to make myself less threatening. I move
about with care, particularly late in the evening. I
give a wide berth to nervous people on subway
platforms during the wee hours, particularly when
I have exchanged business clothes for jeans. If I
happen to be entering a building behind some
people who appear skittish, I may walk by, letting
them clear the lobby before I return, so as not to
seem to be following them. I have been calm and
extremely congenial on those rare occasions when
I've been pulled over by the police.

Examples clarify
Staples's claim about
the precautions he takes
to make himself less
threatening.

12   And on late-evening constitutionals I employ
what has proved to be an excellent tension-reducing
measure: I whistle melodies from Beethoven and
Vivaldi and the more popular classical composers.
Even steely New Yorkers hunching toward nighttime destinations seem to relax, and occasionally
they even join in the tune. Virtually everybody

seems to sense that a mugger wouldn't be warbling bright, sunny selections from Vivaldi's *Four Seasons*. It is my equivalent of the cowbell that hikers wear when they know they are in bear country.

Reading Closely

1. How does Staples's essay make you feel? Does it remind you of any experiences you have had? If so, how?

2. What is Staples's purpose in writing this essay? What has he learned as a result of the experience he describes? And how does what he's learned connect with his overall purpose for writing?

3. Rewrite the opening paragraphs from the white woman's point of view. What details are you including? What feelings are you experiencing? What are you seeing, thinking, or planning?

Considering Larger Issues

1. As he explains the feelings of a black man in public places, what point is Staples making? How does he exemplify this point? Make a brief list of his anecdotes, examples, and facts. Does he prove his point? **Working with three or four classmates,** prepare a group response for the rest of the class.

2 COMBINING METHODS. Mark all the passages in this essay that are *narratives, descriptions,* or *cause-and-effect analyses*. How does Staples use each of these methods to support his main point? How does each method work differently yet effectively?

3. This essay was originally published in *Harper's*, a monthly magazine that includes readings on politics, culture, literature, and the arts. Characterize a typical member of Staples's intended audience. What information in the essay supports your description?

   Since its original publication, the essay has appeared in a large number of anthologies for college writing courses. Describe a typical member of this second audience. Are Staples's examples equally effective for both audiences? Why or why not?

Thinking about Language

1. Relying on the context of the essay or your dictionary, define the following words, preparing to share your answers with the rest of the class.

uninflammatory (1)	taut (4)	ad hoc (8)
wayfarers (2)	bandolier (5)	labyrinthine (8)
tyranny (2)	lethality (6)	berth (11)
dicey (2)	bravado (7)	constitutionals (12)

2. List all the words and phrases that Staples uses to create an atmosphere of danger, vulnerability, and risk. **Working with two or three class-mates,** compare your answers. Prepare a group response to share with the rest of the class.

Writing Your Own Essays Using Exemplification

1. Using Staples's essay as a model, draft a paragraph of at least six sen-tences that focuses on your own experiences in public space. Perhaps you feel unsafe walking or exercising in secluded — or even populated — areas, day or night, because of your size, sex, looks, race, or some other characteristic. Or you may not worry at all about yourself in public; you may feel stronger and safer than others. Or perhaps you worry that your presence is threatening.

   From those six sentences, compose a generalization about your pres-ence in public space, and then support it with specific examples, includ-ing facts, anecdotes, statistics, or ideas. You may need to conduct library or Web research in order to locate enough examples. As you expand your list into a three- to four-page essay, be sure to refer to the guide-lines for checking over the use of exemplification on pages 222–23.

2. Think about a specific person you know. Make a generalization about that person's public presence — for example, as vulnerable, unapproachable, confident, inviting, or threatening — and draft a three- to four-page essay in which you develop that generalization with examples. **Consider work-ing with one or two classmates.** Be sure to refer to the guidelines for checking over the use of exemplification (pp. 222–23) as you draft and revise.

3. Using Staples's essay as a model, draft a paragraph of at least six sen-tences that focuses on your experience presenting yourself in cyberspace. You may want to focus on your experience in a chat room, with a blog or newsgroup, or even just with e-mail and instant messaging. How do you try to present yourself to your online readers? Is it deliberately dif-ferent from the presence you create (or try to create) in "real time"? How do readers react to your online presence, and how do their reactions compare with those of people you interact with in real time? Include at least two specific examples in your paragraph. After you've written it, make a generalization about your online presence, connecting it with an overall purpose.

EVA PAYNE
Handy

Eva Payne (b. 1951) returned to college after the last of her three children enrolled in kindergarten. Like many returning students, Payne worried that she'd forgotten too much, that younger students would work circles around her, that she was taking a huge risk. These worries proved to be unfounded. As an English major, she graduated from Oregon State University with honors. She is now chair of the English Department at Chemeketa Community College in Salem, Oregon. The following essay was part of her application for membership in the Oregon chapter of Mortar Board, a national undergraduate honorary society.

Preview   As you read her brief essay, consider what Payne's purpose might be for using exemplification.

May 1994

I grew up as the little sister of two smart siblings. My older sister was   1
valedictorian of her graduating class and won a full scholarship to Eastern Washington State College. My brother was an electronic whiz kid, a ham radio operator by the time he was twelve. I was the one that the high school counselor told, "Plan a career where you will work with your hands; you aren't college material."

I believed him and worked for twenty years to become good with my   2
hands. I trained my hands to take shorthand at 120 words per minute and type at 70 words per minute. My hands can make the best pie crust you have ever tasted. I can raise green beans and make raspberry jelly with my hands. I learned to drive a fire truck, operate a pumper, and drag a two-inch line into a burning building. I've cleared airways and felt ribs splinter beneath my hands while giving CPR. My hands have given comfort to desperate people in the back of ambulances. I learned to tie bowline knots and rappel down the sides of buildings, make croissants, train a dog, make children laugh, and sew dresses—all with my hands.

Then my husband encouraged me to go to college. I thought of lots of   3
excuses to stay home—home where I did things so well and seldom failed. He convinced me to try, saying I could always withdraw if it looked like I was in over my head. I registered as a home economics major; it sounded like something I could do with my hands. I had always worked with my hands, as a dishwasher, a carhop, a truck driver, a waitress, a cook, a secretary, a bookkeeper, a firefighter, a wife, and as a mother. I know that I am a handy person. I discovered at Oregon State that the advice my high school counselor gave me twenty-five years ago was only half of the story. I am "college material," and my life has been enormously enriched by my discovery that I am mentally as well as manually dexterous.

Reading Closely

1. What examples does Payne provide to prove that she's handy? Can these examples be classified in any way? How?

2. From the evidence in the reading, how can you account for Payne's success in college? What did she do between high school and college that might have helped her? Does your life compare with hers in any way? Do you know anyone whose life story is similar to Payne's? Write out your responses.

3. What is Payne's purpose in writing this essay? What examples help her fulfill that purpose?

4. Look closely at the visual on page 231. What do you imagine this woman can do? What details support your answer?

Considering Larger Issues

1. **Working with two or three classmates,** answer the following questions. Other than the members of the Mortar Board selection committee, who else might be Payne's audience for this essay? How does she appeal to her audience? What details in her essay appeal to you? Prepare your group's responses for the rest of the class.

2. Have you ever been told that you weren't the right type, or the right "material," for something or that you were better suited for something else? In what ways did you succeed—or fail—because of, or in spite of, what others said about you?

3. COMBINING METHODS. Payne sets up a *comparison and contrast* between being manually and mentally dexterous, but her examples are all of manual dexterity. How does her comparison and contrast help develop her overall *generalization*? Would her essay have been strengthened or weakened by including examples of her mental dexterity? Or does the essay itself provide a sufficient example?

Thinking about Language

1. Payne uses a number of lists. Underline each of them. What is the overall effect of these lists?

2. How do Payne's lists reflect her topic?

Writing Your Own Essays Using Exemplification

1. Make a list of generalizations that fit you. Choose one, and then use a prewriting technique (see the Introduction, pp. 20–25) to come up with a list of examples that support this generalization. Draft a three- to four-page autobiographical essay with a one-word title in which you generalize about yourself—and prove your generalization. The guidelines for checking over the use of exemplification can be found on pages 222–23.

2. Using your response to question 2 under Considering Larger Issues as a starting point, draft a three- to four-page essay using exemplification in which you show how someone's observation about you turned out to be wrong—or right. You may want to choose a pivotal experience in your life that proved the point, but in any case be sure to include several examples that show that the observation was correct or that disprove it decisively. **Consider working with two or three classmates,** referring to the guidelines for checking over the use of exemplification (pp. 222–23) as you draft and revise.

PHIL LEITZ

The Greatest Automotive
Flops of the Last 25 Years

Contributing author and blogger for the online magazine CarandDriver.com, Phil Leitz writes about a variety of subjects including car accessories, car shows, new-model debuts, and automotive failures and disappointments. Leitz could not have composed this essay about the greatest flops of the past twenty-five years without using exemplification and a good deal of humor.

> **Preview**   How would you define an automotive flop? Do any specific cars come to mind when you hear that expression?

"Failure is the condiment that gives success its flavor." — TRUMAN CAPOTE

"My other Maserati is also a piece of shit." — bumper sticker seen on a Chrysler's TC by Maserati in Berkeley, California

As nouns go, "flop" is a good one — short, peppy, and to the point. Merriam-Webster's online dictionary defines a flop as "an act or sound of flopping," or "a complete failure." It implies a cheeky, jovial kind of bad, a light-hearted crappiness of fate that goes beyond simple notions of success or defeat. 1

By the same token, in the automotive world, a flop isn't necessarily a bad car. Bad cars come and go all the time, but flops are something more — they're an unholy convergence of economic, corporate, and design conditions; a perfect storm of bad luck, bad planning, and — *say what?* — engineering. Four-wheeled flops don't have to be miserable to drive or vomitous to look at (although it certainly helps); they just have to be a no-questions-asked sales disaster. 2

With that in mind, we give you the greatest vehicular face-plants of the past quarter-century. Welcome to the big, floppy machine — try not to touch anything. 3

VECTOR (1971–PRESENT)

Vector Motors founder Jerry Wiegert has been compared to P. T. Barnum, his company to Never-Never Land, and his cars to — well, most of the things said about his cars have been suspiciously positive or virtually unprintable. Such is the fate of the odd and boastful. 4

The Vector Motors Corporation was established in the early 1970s with the stated aim of producing an affordable American supercar. Its first running prototype, built in 1980, sported outlandish looks and a twin-turbocharged, 650-hp Chevrolet V-8. Wiegert claimed that the car, dubbed the W2, would see production the following year and cost $125,000. To no one's surprise, the first customer Vector, a modified version 5

of the W2 known as the W8, didn't appear until almost nine years later. Just 22 cars were built, and by the end of production, list price approached half a million dollars.

Vector was acquired by an Indonesian manufacturing conglomerate 6 in 1993, and Wiegert was forcibly removed from command. A host of abortive projects followed, including the Lamborghini–powered M12, a machine that British journalist Jeremy Clarkson once called "very probably the worst car in the entire world." Wiegert recently regained control of Vector, and according to the company's Web site, a new, 1800–hp "hypercar" is currently undergoing development.

We'll leave it to you to interpret what that means. As Barnum once 7 said, "Without promotion, something terrible happens—nothing!"

STERLING (1987–91)

Leave it to the Brits to floppify anything even remotely identifiable as a Honda 8 product. The Sterling brand was created as a way for the much–maligned Austin Rover Group to reenter the American market, and on paper, it made sense: Take a Rover 800—which was really just a rebodied Acura Legend—rebadge it, and sell it through a network of independent dealers under a new, made–up brand. The hope was that such a plan would keep people from making any connection to the last U.S.-market Rover, a horrible little turd blossom called the SD1. Japanese reliability, British interior ambience, and a lack of preconceived notions? How could you lose?

Quite easily, as it turned out. Predictably, the problem lay in the 9 car itself—the first Sterlings were nothing short of unreliable, hastily screwed–together nightmares. (Apparently, Japanese engineering doesn't work if you assemble it with equal parts wood glue and indifference. Who knew?) When build quality improved a few years later, it was a case of too little, too late. Rover left America for the third time in 20 years in 1991, muttering something along the lines of "It's not you, it's me." America listened to its friends and didn't call Rover back.

CHRYSLER'S TC BY MASERATI (1989–91)

Arrogance, thy name is Lee Iacocca. In the late 1980s, the Chrysler chair- 10
man and perpetual huckster turned a friendship with Alejandro de
Tomaso, then president of Maserati, into the most shudder-worthy example of corporate avarice ever to roll off an assembly line. Chrysler's TC
by Maserati was little more than a Milan-built K-car with a few pricey
underhood components and some styling hackery, a wrinkly grandmother dressed up in custom running shoes and ill-fitting hot pants. The
Maserati trident plastered on the grille just added insult to injury.

To be fair, Iacocca's brainchild wasn't without its pluses. For 1989, 11
the TC sported a 200-hp, 2.2-liter turbocharged four-cylinder with a
Maserati-designed 16-valve cylinder head. A five-speed Getrag manual
was also available that year, and Fichtel & Sachs dampers took care of
wheel control. But by and large, the TC was a dud. In 1990 and 1991,
Chrysler ditched the turbo four for a Mitsubishi-built V-6, neutering the
Italian connection even further. Just over 7,000 examples were sold over
the course of three years.

Comedian Patton Oswalt once called the Kentucky Fried Chicken 12
Famous Bowls— a heap of corn, mashed potatoes, and chicken lumped
into a plastic container— a "failure pile in a sadness bowl." Consider the
TC the vehicular equivalent.

SUBARU SVX (1991–97)

Ah, the Italians. *When in doubt*, that cherished Italian maxim goes, *design* 13
something beautiful. If you can't be bothered to come up with anything beautiful, it
continues, *then at least design something desperately weird and pawn it off on some-*
one else.

The SVX was most definitely a case of the latter. Subaru's most dis- 14
tinctive car— and considering the company gave birth to the 356cc 360
and the three-cylinder Justy, that's saying a lot— came from the pen of
legendary Italian designer Giorgetto Giugiaro. Yep, the same man who
gave us the BMW M1, the Mark I Volkswagen Golf, and the Maserati
Ghibli also gave us this wacky-windowed wonder. Perhaps the lunch
menu that day included a bit too much grappa.

The SVX was intended to be the car on which the "new" Subaru 15
would be built, a revolutionary achievement that banished all thoughts
of the marque's often quirky past. A 230-hp, 3.3-liter, 24-valve flat-six
lived under the hood, and a highly evolved, electronically managed all-
wheel-drive system put power to the ground. Four-wheel steering was
available in Japan, and Giugiaro's sweeping lines resulted in a drag coef-
ficient of just 0.29. Unfortunately, tech wizardry wasn't enough to overcome awkward styling and a high (almost $25,000 in 1992) price, and sales
never took off. The SVX was a good car dragged down into floptastic
floppiness by the hubris of its maker.

JAGUAR X-TYPE (2001–08)

For a brief— and I do mean *brief*— period of time in the early part of this decade, this scribe worked at a Jaguar dealership as a parts guy. Most of my time was spent learning the million and one ways that an X-type could fall apart. Engines seized, interiors collapsed, transmissions exploded, and driveshafts— oh, the countless, countless driveshafts— ate their U-joints so regularly that you could set your watch by them. At a time when Jaguar reliability was finally approaching respectable, the all-wheel-drive X-type was the lone, laughable holdout. It was obnoxiously underbuilt, remarkably overpriced, and about as charming as a hernia. 16

The X-type was Coventry's business-case company saver, an entry-level sports sedan for the wooden-drawing-room set. It was built on the bones of Jaguar parent Ford's Mondeo/Contour, and it was intended to resurrect Coventry's financial fortunes, providing the dignified marque with a way to snag young, affluent buyers. What the bean counters neglected to consider, however, was that young, affluent buyers are not lobotomy patients. A tarted-up economy sedan sold at luxury-car prices is still just a tarted-up economy sedan, especially if it tries to self-immolate every time you turn the key. 17

There was also an impossibly unpopular wagon version. The dealer that I worked for had one that sat on the lot for— I am not making this up— two years. 18

LINCOLN BLACKWOOD (2001–02)

Psst— hey, pal! Yeah, you! You wanna buy a truck, right? Tell you what I'm gonna do: Hows about we find you a *special* truck, one just for you and your *refined tastes*, see? You like luxury? We got luxury: This beauty may look like a crew-cab F-150, but it's a Lincoln, and it drives like one, sure as I'm standin' here. You look like a Lincoln kind of guy, you know that? You know Tony Soprano was a Lincoln guy? You want a cigar? I got some Cubans in my coat. Hold on. 19

Check out the cargo box: It's lined in carpet and gen-yoo-wine *stainless* steel. That's *stainless*— means it can't be stained. You can't carry nuthin' *heavy* or *dirty* in it without uglying it up, but it makes for a nice trunk, see? And that bed cover? It's power-operated! Opens to a 45-degree angle, it does! That's real, honest-to-God imitation African *wenge* wood on the sides of the bed, there— them Lincoln folks photographed it and reproduced it in vinyl and everything, and I got a cousin Sal over in Jersey who says it don't fade fer nuthin', not even when you get some blood on it. Only 3,000 of these dealies were made this year, and it only costs $52,000, and it only comes in black, and . . . 20

What? Why you walkin' away? Was it somethin' I said? I thought we had a deal! You want I should show you the LED lights in the trunk? 21

GMC ENVOY XUV (2003–05)

On paper, the plan was ingenious: Build a retractable roof and a movable, 22
watertight partition into the back half of an SUV. One minute, you have
lockable, covered cargo space; the next, you're hauling Christmas trees
and grandfather clocks and hosing out the back half of the car. Makes
sense, right?

Still, the General missed the boat on this one. The pickup–slash–SUV 23
concept was sound—witness the success of the Chevrolet Avalanche—but
for the Envoy XUV, the devil lay in the details. Strike one: The XUV was
made by slicing and dicing an extended-wheelbase GMC Envoy, which is
basically just a Chevrolet TrailBlazer, a.k.a. "The Mid–Size SUV That Time
Forgot." (Heavy, bumbling chassis? Check. Fisher–Price interior and the fuel
mileage of a 747? Check.) Strike two: Whereas the Envoy was merely unattractive, the XUV was hideous. Strike three: Impracticality. Even with folding
seats, an open roof, and a lay–down tailgate, the XUV couldn't haul much
more than an ordinary Envoy could. Thankfully, it was more expensive.

Oh, wait. That's not good.   24

CHEVROLET SSR (2003–06)

It's a convertible. It's a pickup. It's a car. It's yet another example of how 25
the American people refuse to pay for anything even remotely corporate
where hot-rod culture is concerned. Yep, that's right: It's the Chevrolet
SSR, and we can hear you yawning already.

You would think that GM executives would have taken a lesson from 26
the much–maligned Plymouth Prowler, an awkward–looking, underpow-
ered, and overpriced factory hot rod that failed miserably following a
relatively short production life. The SSR—an awkward–looking, under-
powered, and overpriced factory hot rod that arrived just one year after
the Prowler's death—also failed miserably and in short order. What on
earth prompted the General to retread such potentially floppy ground,
and so soon? Was it something in Detroit's water?

To GM's credit, the company at least attempted to right a few of the 27
Prowler's wrongs. The SSR may have been built on the same platform as
the Chevrolet TrailBlazer, but a 300–hp, 5.3–liter V–8 lived between the
truck's deep–draw fenders, not a puny V–6. After customers and journalists
complained of sluggish performance, the 4,700–pound, $40,000–plus SSR
was gifted with a 390–hp, 6.0–liter V–8 and an optional six–speed manual.
It wasn't enough, however, to overpower the *uncustom* convertible truck
rod's inherent dorkiness. Few cried when the SSR was axed.

CHRYSLER CROSSFIRE (2004–08)

What do you get when you combine a bunch of rehashed, last–generation 28
Mercedes–Benz chassis components with overwrought styling and a
bit of D–town pride? This bright–eyed hunk of weirdness, that's what.

The Crossfire fell victim to that most heinous of sporty–car sins: It 29
did nothing uniquely. Its chassis was borrowed from the 1997–to–2004
Mercedes–Benz SLK, and like the SLK, the Crossfire was a decent, if not
brilliant, sporting GT. Potential buyers were put off by the art–deco looks
and the $35,000–plus buy–in, and many simply bought an SLK instead.
Or an Infiniti G35 or a BMW 3–series, both of which were more fun to
drive than the Crossfire, and neither of which looked like a dog in the
middle of a life–altering dump. (Incidentally, whose bright idea was it to
name a car after multidirectional gunfire, anyway? In what world do you
want a car whose name implies that it might go off in any direction at
any moment, killing innocent bystanders?)

How's this for flop: In the second year of Crossfire production, 30
Chrysler actually resorted to dumping excess inventory on Overstock
.com. Flop, flop, *flopperoo.*

DODGE DURANGO HYBRID/CHRYSLER ASPEN HYBRID (2009)

What we have here is the very definition of the phrase "dead on arrival." 31
First, Chrysler blessed us with the second–generation Dodge Durango, a
truckish, forgettable SUV with all the road manners of a rudderless *Queen
Mary.* When Durango sales took a powder, Auburn Hills introduced the
world to the Chrysler Aspen, a Durango slathered in plastic chrome and
fake wood and arguably the least necessary vehicle in history. And last,
this past summer, amid much fanfare, Chrysler birthed a hybrid version
of each. Two months later, all four models were extinct. (Dodge does plan
on building another Durango in the near future.)

The Duraspen (Aspango?) hybrids were the first showroom divi– 32
dends of Chrysler's involvement in the Global Hybrid Cooperation, the
manufacturing consortium responsible for the powertrain technology in
GM's hybrid SUVs and the upcoming BMW X6 hybrid. Like GM's sport–
ute hybrids, the Chryslers reportedly were being built at a loss. When the

economy began to nosedive, Chrysler announced the upcoming closure of the Duraspen's sole production plant, citing slumping SUV sales as the main cause.

Fuel–friendly Aspango, we hardly knew ye. *Vaya con Dios*, sweet flop.   33

Reading Closely

1. In this essay, Leitz defines a flop in the automotive world as "an unholy convergence of economic, corporate, and design conditions; a perfect storm of bad luck, bad planning, and . . . engineering." Review the examples of flops he goes on to describe. How do the examples in his essay fit, support, and extend this definition?

2. Leitz uses humor to discuss the many car flops over the past twenty–five years. Identify places in the text where he relies on humor to make his point. What makes these moments humorous?

3. Review the visuals used in this reading. Why is it important to include them in the essay? How does each visual exemplify the point Leitz makes about the corresponding car model?

Considering Larger Issues

1. What is the purpose of this essay? What evidence in the text can you point to in support of your answer?

2. Given that this essay was published on CarandDriver.com, how would you describe the audience for it? Why would this audience be interested in the subject of car flops? How do you imagine this audience responding to the essay?

3. Leitz is certainly writing to car enthusiasts. If you fall into this category, how did you respond to this essay? If you're not a car enthusiast, how did you respond? What examples were difficult to understand? Identify places in the text that confused or frustrated you. What specific knowledge do you need to have to understand fully the points Leitz is trying to make?

4. COMBINING METHODS. In addition to exemplification, Leitz also relies on the methods of *narration, description, cause-and-effect analysis,* and *comparison and contrast*. **Working with two or three classmates,** identify places in the essay where he uses these methods. What purposes do they serve?

Thinking about Language

1. Make a list of all of the car–related language that Leitz uses in the essay. Which terms did you know? Which were unfamiliar? Given your level of automotive expertise, what effect do these language choices have on how readable you found the essay?

2. Using the context of the essay or your dictionary, define the following *non-car-related* terms. Be prepared to share your answers with the rest of the class.

convergence (2)	ambience (8)	coefficient (15)
vomitous (2)	huckster (10)	hubris (15)
conglomerate (6)	hackery (10)	heinous (29)
maligned (8)	marque (15)	

Writing Your Own Essays Using Exemplification

1. Cars are not the only things that "flop." For ten minutes, freewrite on flops you've experienced in your life. They do not all have to be in the same category, meaning you don't have to think only of, say, meals that flopped (although you could). Your writing might range from exercise regimens and art classes to movies and TV shows. Then reflect on what you've written and identify a category that interests you. For instance, you might consider flops in your athletic career or flops you've witnessed in pop culture. Once you identify a category of interest, list five examples that support and extend your point about this category and its flops. Then draft a three- to four-page essay that, first, defines what you mean by a flop in this category and, second, uses exemplification to support this definition. As you revise, refer to "Checking Over the Use of Exemplification" on pages 222–23.

2. Question 1 in the Thinking about Language section asks you to identify the terms Leitz uses that distinguish him as an expert in the automotive community. Whether or not you are an expert on cars, you have expertise in other areas and in other communities. Brainstorm for ten minutes about an area of your expertise, identifying terms that distinguish you as an expert. Then define ten terms particular to this community. As you define, you'll also want to explain why it is important for members of this community to know these terms. Finally, compose a two- to three-page essay that first describes the community in which you are an expert and then defines the ten terms you've selected as examples of what one has to know to be an expert in this community. As you revise, refer to "Checking Over the Use of Exemplification" on pages 222–23.

BARACK OBAMA

Memorial Day, Abraham Lincoln National Cemetery

Forty-fourth president of the United States, Barack Obama was born in Honolulu, Hawaii, in 1961. He attended Occidental College, Columbia University, and Harvard Law School. Before his election to the U.S. Senate from Illinois in 2004, he worked as a community organizer, a civil rights lawyer, and a law professor at the University of Chicago. In January 2009, he took office as the first African American president of the United States. In the following speech, Senator Obama speaks at the 2005 Memorial Day commemoration at the Abraham Lincoln National Cemetery in Elwood, Illinois.

Preview Think about the context of this speech. Why is Obama speaking at the Abraham Lincoln National Cemetery on Memorial Day?

Thank you for allowing me the honor of joining you here today. 1

This is my first time visiting the Abraham Lincoln National Cemetery, 2 and as I was driving through I thought to myself that the staff and the volunteers who have made this possible should feel very proud of the work they're doing—this is a beautiful place for our veterans to come home to.

Among red maples and sturdy oaks, over 10,000 Americans now lay 3 here, resting peacefully under an endless Illinois sky.

They rest in silence. On a typical day, except for scattered footsteps or 4 the soft gurgling of a stream, I imagine you could walk row after row of headstones without hearing a single sound.

It isn't until you come across another visitor—a widow watering 5 the plant she brought for her husband; a little girl planting a flag at her father's headstone; a mother shedding tears on the wreath she will lay for her son—that you realize something: in this place we have come to associate with the quiet of death, the memories of loved ones speak to us so strongly that when we stop and listen, we can't help but hear life.

And once a year on this day, in the fullness of spring, in the presence 6 of those who never really leave us, it is life that we honor. Lives of courage, lives of sacrifice, and the ultimate measure of selflessness—lives that were given to save others.

What led these men and women to wear their country's uniform? 7

What is it that leads anyone to put aside their own pursuit of happi- 8 ness, to subordinate their own sense of survival, for something larger— something greater?

Behind each stone is one of these stories, a personal journey that 9 eventually led to the decision to fight for one's country and defend

241

Senator Barack Obama and New Mexico Governor Bill Richardson greet Marine Corps veterans at the Veterans Memorial Park in Las Cruces, New Mexico, on Memorial Day 2008.

the freedoms we enjoy. Most of the Americans who rest here were like my grandfather, a World War II vet who volunteered after Pearl Harbor, fought in Patton's Army, but was lucky enough to come back in one piece, and went on to live well into his twilight years.

My grandfather never boasted about it. He treated the fact that he served in the military like it was only a matter of fact. 10

And so it is easy for us to forget sometimes that, like my grandfather, the men and women resting here, whose service spans a century of conflict from the Civil War to the war in Iraq, chose their path at a very young age. 11

These were kids who went to war. 12

They had a whole life ahead of them — birthdays and weddings, holidays with children and grandchildren, homes and jobs and happiness of their own. And yet at one moment or another, they felt the tug. Maybe it was a President's call to save the Union and to free the slaves. Maybe it was the day of infamy that awakened a nation to the dangers of Fascism. Or maybe it was the morning we saw our security disappear when the twin towers collapsed. 13

And at that moment, whatever the moment was, these men and women thought of a mom or a dad, a husband or a wife, or a child not yet born. They thought of a landscape, or a way of life, or a flag, or the 14 words of freedom they'd learned to love. And they determined that it was time to go. They decided: "I must serve so that the people I love may live—happily, safely, freely."

Oliver Wendell Holmes once remarked that "to fight out a war, you 15 must believe something and want something with all your might."

The Americans who lay here believed.   16

And when they waved goodbye to their families—some for the last 17 time—they held those beliefs close as they crossed the ocean toward an unknown destiny.

And they made us very proud.   18

No matter how many veterans you may meet or how many stories of 19 heroism you may hear, every encounter reminds you that through their service, these men and women have lived out the ideals that stir our na-tion—honor, duty, sacrifice.

They're people like Seamus Ahern, whom I met during the cam- 20 paign at a V.F.W. hall in East Moline, Illinois. He told me about how he'd joined the Marines because his country had given so much to him, and he felt that as a young person he needed to give something back. We became friends and we kept in touch over e-mail while he was in Iraq. One day he sent me an e-mail that said, "Im sorry I haven't written more often—I've been a little busy over here in Falujah." I had to reply, "I don't think it's necessary to apologize."

They're people like Major Tammy Duckworth, a helicopter pilot with 21 the Illinois Army Guard. Four months ago, she lost both of her legs when a rocket was shot through the floor of her Black Hawk helicopter over Iraq. And yet last month she came to the United States Senate to testify about ways we can improve the process of rehabilitating injured vets, and as we speak she has already begun training so that she can fly again for her country one day.

They're the people I had the honor of meeting at Walter Reed Medi- 22 cal Center in Washington. Young men and women who may have lost limbs or broken their backs or severed their nerves but have not lost the will to live or the pride they feel in having served their country. They have no time for self-pity but wish only to recuperate as quickly as they can and meet the next challenge.

It is this quintessentially American optimism that stands out in our 23 veterans. To meet these men and women gives you a clear sense of the quality of person we have serving in the United States Armed Forces.

No wonder, then, that when these men and women come home from 24 war, they return to parades and salutes, the arms of loved ones, and the waving flags of children.

But today, on Memorial Day, we also remember that some come 25 home in a different way. The news of their impending arrival is delivered with a soft knock on the door. Their return comes with the sound of a twenty-one gun salute and the lonely notes of taps.

I won't pretend that simple words of condolence could ever ease 26
the pain of the loss for the families they leave behind. I am the father of two little girls, and when I see the parents who have come
here today to lay wreaths for the children they lost, my heart breaks
with theirs.

But I will say to those parents that here in Illinois and all across 27
America, other children and other parents look to your children and their
service as a shining example of what's best in this land.

During the Civil War, President Lincoln took a moment to sit down 28
and personally write a condolence letter to a Mrs. Bixby of Massachusetts
after he had learned that she lost five of her sons in battle. In that letter,
the President wrote: "I pray that our Heavenly Father may assuage the
anguish of your bereavement, and leave you only the cherished memory
of the loved and lost, and the solemn pride that must be yours to have
laid so costly a sacrifice upon the altar of freedom."

Here on this hallowed ground and in ceremonies across the na- 29
tion, we choose this day to solemnly honor those costly sacrifices—
sacrifices that were made on the fields of Gettysburg, the beaches of Normandy, the deserts of Iraq, and so many other distant lands. It makes our
hearts heavy; our heads bow in respect.

But amid the quiet of this spring day in Elwood, we also hear life. 30
And as we are called by the memories of those who found the courage to
lay down a life so that others may live, we thank God for blessing us with
the privilege of knowing such heroic sons and daughters of America.

Reading Closely

1. What is the purpose of this speech? **Working with a classmate,** identify and list the examples Obama uses in this speech. How do these examples support Obama's purpose?

2. Throughout the speech, Obama offers examples of veterans he has
   known throughout his life. Review these examples. How do they offer an
   implicit definition of a veteran? What definition of *veteran* does Obama
   offer here?

3. Look at the photograph on page 242. How does Obama's body language
   reinforce or challenge the overarching message of his speech?

Considering Larger Issues

1. Given the purpose of this speech, do you find it effective? Why or why
   not?

2. Consider the list of examples you identified in question 2 under Reading
   Closely. Which examples (if any) did you find particularly compelling?
   Why?

3. Whom do you imagine to be the audience for this speech? What are Obama's listeners' expectations for it? How does he meet (or fail to meet) their expectations?

4. COMBINING METHODS. **Working with a classmate,** identify the methods of development Obama uses in addition to exemplification. What effect do these methods have on the purpose of the speech? How do they help (or hinder) Obama from achieving this purpose?

Thinking about Language

1. Identify the dominant impression Obama is attempting to convey through this speech. Make a list of the words that enable him to create this impression.

2. Throughout the essay, Obama chooses not to use complicated language. Why do you think he makes this choice? As you respond to this question, think specifically about the purpose, occasion, and audience for the speech.

Writing Your Own Essays Using Exemplification

1. In question 2 of the Reading Closely section, you considered how Obama defines the term *veteran* through the examples in his speech. Most of us know someone who is a veteran. In a two- to three-page essay, describe this person, explaining how he or she is an example of what it means to be a veteran in your eyes. In other words, this essay asks you to offer a general claim about the term *veteran* and then to compose an extended example showing how one person's experiences support this definition. To create an effective essay, you'll need to offer specific details about this person and his or her experience in the armed forces. As you draft and revise, refer to "Checking Over the Use of Exemplification" on pages 222–23.

2. Listening to speeches at a cemetery is one way that people recognize Memorial Day. Reflect on the Memorial Days you've experienced in your life. How have you observed this day? Make a list of the Memorial Days you remember, carefully describing what you did. After you've made your list, write a sentence or two making a generalization about how you've experienced Memorial Day throughout your life. Then write a two- to three-page essay that first states this generalization and then supports it with examples of Memorial Day memories from your life. If your experience is unlike the day Obama and his audience experienced, you might explain how and why.

DAVID BROWNE

On the Internet, It's All about "My"

David Browne (b. 1960) received his bachelor of arts degree in journalism from New York University and is now a renowned music critic. In addition to writing three books, *Goodbye Sonic Youth, Amped,* and *Dream Brother,* he's worked as a contributing editor for *Rolling Stone* and *Entertainment Weekly* while also publishing articles in magazines such as *Wired* and *Sports Illustrated.* In 1990, he was awarded the Music Journalism Award for Excellence. In this article, published in the *New York Times* in April 2008, Browne relies on exemplification to explore the various ways the word *my* has pervaded the social and cultural scene in the United States.

> **Preview**   How do you see the word functioning in society today? Given the examples you've identified, what is the significance of this term?

It's not you, it's me. Actually, on the Internet, it's "my." 1

The Web is awash in sites that begin with that most personal of pro- 2 nouns, and not simply MySpace. A few quick clicks will connect you to MyCoke, MyIBM, MySubaru, MyAOL—even MyClick, a mobile-phone marketing company.

Collectively, they amount to a new world of Web sites designed to 3 imply a one-on-one connection with a corporation or large business.

Last month, as part of a nationwide effort to reinvent itself, Starbucks 4 started My Starbucks Idea to solicit consumer feedback on its stores, products and image problems. If the '70s were dubbed the Me Decade, this era could well be the My Decade.

The rise of sites with the "my" prefix is an outgrowth of an increas- 5 ingly customized world of technology, such as the iPod and TiVo. "Marketing says, 'We all want to be individuals and this brand will help you express your individuality,'" said Nick Bartle, a director of behavioral planning at the advertising agency BBDO. "These 'my' Web sites are the logical extension of that strategy."

But they illustrate how corporations are striving to show that they 6 can be as intimately connected to their customers as in-vogue social networking sites. They're not just impersonal businesses; they are your close, intimate friends.

"Companies are trying to connect with consumers in more meaning- 7 ful ways," said Pete Blackshaw, a vice president at Nielsen Online Strategic Services, which monitors Web activity. "They're trying to emulate consumer behavior. Everyone's trying to be more authentic and connect with consumers on their terms. They can look more real, sincere and authentic."

The "my" trend is even a factor in the presidential election, particu- 8 larly the Democratic primary in Pennsylvania on April 22. Senator Hillary Rodham Clinton's Web site now includes a section called "My Pennsylvania," where supporters are asked to contribute ideas on how she should campaign in that state. The site contrasts with Senator Barack Obama's repeated use of the word "you" in speeches.

"He's a 'you' guy, empowering the people," said Jay Jurisich, the crea- 9 tive director of Igor, a naming and branding company in San Francisco. "With Hillary, it's 'I'm entitled to this. It's all about me.' It really is the 'you' candidate vs. the 'my' candidate."

In one way or another, many "my" sites aim to emulate homegrown 10 Web sites or trends. The My Starbucks Idea site is devoted to chat rooms that have the unfussy look of homemade blogs; there, Starbucks loyal- ists can grouse about the chairs in stores or the lack of free Wi-Fi con- nections. The www.MyCoke.com site links to a Second Life–style virtual environment, where customers can roam and create avatars — a "subtly branded experience," in the words of Doug Rollins, group director of dig- ital platforms at Coca-Cola.

The "my" prefix has become an easy and increasingly popular short- 11 hand for suggesting that bond between consumers and corporations. Matthew Zook of ZookNIC, a business that analyzes domain names, said domains that start with "my" more than tripled between 2005 and 2008, to 712,000 from 217,000. According to the government's Patent and Trademark Office, the number of trademark applications to register marks that in- clude the word "my" increased to 1,943 last year from 382 in 1998. Through March of this year, the number of applications has soared to 530.

"My" is the latest in a line of prefixes that have ebbed and flowed on 12 the Web. A decade ago, everything was "e" — from eTrade to eBay — and "i," as in iPod or iPhone, has become synonymous with all things Apple.

Among the earliest known "my" entries is the comparison-shopping 13 site www.MySimon.com, which filed for trademark in 1998. Mr. Jurisich said that Microsoft may have inadvertently played a role in this trend. "In the '90s, all these people were trying to find domain names and staring at their Windows computers, which had 'my documents' and 'my music,'" he said. "Everyone thought, 'Let's try "my."' It was very natural." (Of course, the success of MySpace, taking off in 2004, may have increased the barrage.)

For all its ubiquity, the concept of corporations trying to get up close 14 with consumers is sometimes greeted warily by even those in the mar- keting community. "It's a cold, calculated and impersonal attempt to be personal," said Mr. Jurisich, who says his firm shuns "my" URLs. "It's about making Big Brother into little brother. No one in their right mind should think, oh, the corporate entity really cares about me personally. But I can only assume that enough people fall for it that companies don't ditch it." (In a recent survey conducted by OTX, a consumer market research firm, one-third of respondents agreed that a Web site with a "my" function meant "the company cares about me.")

Another major benefit for companies behind those Web pages is the 15 personal data, including e-mail addresses and preferences, that customers provide when registering at one of the sites. "It's all about the database and getting that personal information," said Shelley Zalis, the founder of OTX. "That's what everyone wants."

At www.MyCokeRewards.com, Mr. Rollins of Coca-Cola said, the 16 company seeks to "collect data through survey questions and through categories and passions." Then, he said, the company creates new content and offers new rewards (redeemed through the purchase of Coca-Cola products) based "on what was created by you." Although Mr. Rollins declined to cite numbers for the site, he said MyCokeRewards is one of the company's "most robust return-investment models."

According to Alexandra Wheeler, director of digital strategies for Star- 17 bucks, the 150,000 customers who have posted responses at My Starbucks Idea since March have led to tangible results at stores, like the introduction of a "splash stick" to prevent spillage from coffee cups.

Yet people in marketing and business also agree that the "my" prefix 18 could have a limited shelf life if it is overused. Already, the phenomenon is spreading beyond the Web: Two years ago, when Fox Broadcasting began a new television network from stations left over from the WB-UPN merger, it named this creation MyNetworkTV. "People have been very quick to grab it," said Dean Crutchfield, an executive at Wolff Olins, a branding agency. "I'm concerned it will get bastardized, and the uniqueness and sense of purpose it has will be lost in a sea of copycats."

"It's the word today," said Ms. Zalis of OTX. "But I don't know how 19 long today will last."

Few in the industry are sure what the next word or prefix will be. Mr. 20 Jurisich said he had toyed with "exo," as in "outside," but said no client went for it. Said Ms. Zalis, "In the very near future, it's not going to be about 'my'. It'll be 'we'. It'll be the collective 'me', whatever that is."

"In our research, values like participation now vastly outrank self- 21 interest," said Mr. Bartle of BBDO. "People want to be connected and part of a community."

Mr. Crutchfield agreed, but said that coming up with the appropriate 22 prefix to convey those values will be tricky. "I see a trend back to the 'we' state," he said. "But it can't be 'We Business.'"

For now, Mr. Crutchfield said, he hopes the "my" prefix will hang on 23 a bit longer. His next Web project, intended for 2012 and being created in tandem with the International Olympics Committee, is My Olympics.

Reading Closely

1. Review the examples Browne uses in the essay. What is their purpose? Do they function to explain and clarify, to analyze, to argue, to add interest, or some combination of these purposes?

2. What *kinds* of examples does Browne use in the essay? anecdotes? facts? statistics? hypothetical situations? Why do you think he relies on the kinds of examples that he does?

3. Given Browne's assessments, what is the "my" prefix supposed to do? Why are companies using it, and to what effect?

Considering Larger Issues

1. What is the purpose of this essay? Who is its intended audience? What evidence in the text supports your answers? How does the purpose meet the needs and interests of the audience?

2. What is Browne's thesis statement? How does it reflect his purpose?

3. What is your response to the "my" prefix? Does it affect you the way Browne says companies expect it to? **Working with two or three classmates,** discuss your individual responses to these questions, noting similarities and differences. Be prepared to share them with the rest of the class.

4. COMBINING METHODS. While Browne relies on exemplification throughout the essay, he also calls on *description* to discuss more fully the "my" examples he cites. Identify the places in the text where Browne uses description. How does this rhetorical method aid his purpose?

Thinking about Language

1. Using the context of the essay or your dictionary, define the following terms. Be prepared to share your answers with the rest of the class.

   awash (2)   avatars (10)   bastardized (18)
   in-vogue (6)   ubiquity (14)   tandem (23)
   emulate (10)   tangible (17)

2. In this essay, Browne makes an argument about what the "my" prefix means in today's society. **Working with a classmate,** review the essay, considering the specific word choices Browne uses throughout the essay that enable him to make his claim. Create a list of all of the words. Then examine when and where Browne uses these words. How is Browne reinforcing his point sentence by sentence, paragraph by paragraph?

Writing Your Own Essays Using Exemplification

1. In his essay, Browne claims we are living in a "my" moment. Making a claim similar to Browne's, choose a term that you think defines this moment in history. Then list as many examples as you can from your everyday life that confirm your choice. Once you've completed the list, compose a two- to three-page essay that relies on exemplification to make a claim about the present moment. As you draft and revise, refer to "Checking Over the Use of Exemplification" on pages 222–23.

2. For a few hours, sit back and examine a place you frequent in your everyday life: the student union, a coffee shop, a workplace, a park, a gym, or your dorm floor. Take notes on the activities happening in these spaces, the people you see there, the kinds of conversations you hear, the general atmosphere (such as tense, relaxed, bored, or hectic). After reviewing your notes about what goes on in this space, compose a three- to four-page essay in which you make a generalization about this space and then support this generalization with examples. Consider the following questions as you write: What do your examples tell you about this space? What kind of space is it? How would you define and describe it to others? Which examples most effectively support your claim? As you draft and revise, refer to "Checking Over the Use of Exemplification" on pages 222–23.

3. One of the arguments Browne makes in this essay is that companies are using the Internet to make an intimate connection with users, and one of the ways they do this is by using the "my" prefix. Consider your own experience online. Do you think companies are attempting to make a connection with you? As you think through this question, explore the sites you visit frequently, taking notes as to how they are or are not making a connection with you through means *other than* the "my" prefix. Once you've finished your research, compose a three- to four-page essay in which you agree or disagree with Browne by calling on online examples other than the "my" prefix. Refer to "Checking Over the Use of Exemplification" on pages 222–23 as you draft and revise.

CHRISTINE ROSEN

Virtual Friendship
and the New Narcissism

● Christine Rosen (b. 1974) is senior editor of the *New Atlantis,* a scholarly journal about science and technology, and a fellow at the Ethics and Public Policy Center in Washington, D.C. An expert in technology, the history of eugenics, the fertility industry, and bioethics, she has authored or coauthored four books and published articles and opinion pieces in such periodicals as the *Washington Post,* the *New England Journal of Medicine,* the *New Republic,* the *New York Times,* and the *National Review.* In the following article, Rosen explores the ways online social networking sites like Facebook and MySpace have affected how participants understand and express friendship.

> **Preview**   What do you know about sites like Facebook and MySpace? How (if at all) do these sites shape your friendships?

For centuries, the rich and the powerful documented their existence and 1 their status through painted portraits. A marker of wealth and a bid for immortality, portraits offer intriguing hints about the daily life of their subjects — professions, ambitions, attitudes, and, most importantly, social standing. Such portraits, as German art historian Hans Belting has argued, can be understood as "painted anthropology," with much to teach us, both intentionally and unintentionally, about the culture in which they were created.

Self-portraits can be especially instructive. By showing the artist both 2 as he sees his true self and as he wishes to be seen, self-portraits can at once expose and obscure, clarify and distort. They offer opportunities for both self-expression and self-seeking. They can display egotism and modesty, self-aggrandizement and self-mockery.

Today, our self-portraits are democratic and digital; they are crafted 3 from pixels rather than paints. On social networking websites like MySpace and Facebook, our modern self-portraits feature background music, carefully manipulated photographs, stream-of-consciousness musings, and lists of our hobbies and friends. They are interactive, inviting viewers not merely to look at, but also to respond to, the life portrayed online. We create them to find friendship, love, and that ambiguous modern thing called connection. Like painters constantly retouching their work, we alter, update, and tweak our online self-portraits; but as digital objects they are far more ephemeral than oil on canvas. Vital statistics, glimpses of bare flesh, lists of favorite bands and favorite poems all clamor for our attention — and it is the timeless human desire for attention that emerges as the dominant theme of these vast virtual galleries.

Although social networking sites are in their infancy, we are seeing 4 their impact culturally: in language (where *to friend* is now a verb), in politics (where it is *de rigueur* for presidential aspirants to catalogue their virtues on MySpace), and on college campuses (where *not* using Facebook can be a social handicap). But we are only beginning to come to grips with the consequences of our use of these sites: for friendship, and for our notions of privacy, authenticity, community, and identity. As with any new technological advance, we must consider what type of behavior online social networking encourages. Does this technology, with its constant demands to collect (friends and status), and perform (by marketing ourselves), in some ways undermine our ability to attain what it promises — a surer sense of who we are and where we belong? The Delphic oracle's guidance was *know thyself*. Today, in the world of online social networks, the oracle's advice might be *show thyself*.

MAKING CONNECTIONS

The earliest online social networks were arguably the Bulletin Board Systems of the 1980s that let users post public messages, send and receive private messages, play games, and exchange software. Some of those BBSs, like The WELL (Whole Earth 'Lectronic Link) that technologist Larry Brilliant and futurist Stewart Brand started in 1985, made the transition to the World Wide Web in the mid-1990s. (Now owned by Salon.com, The WELL boasts that it was "the primordial ooze where the online community movement was born.") Other websites for community and connection emerged in the 1990s, including Classmates.com (1995), where users register by high school and year of graduation; Company of Friends, a business-oriented site founded in 1997; and Epinions, founded in 1999 to allow users to give their opinions about various consumer products. 5

A new generation of social networking websites appeared in 2002 with the launch of Friendster, whose founder, Jonathan Abrams, admitted that his main motivation for creating the site was to meet attractive women. Unlike previous online communities, which brought together anonymous strangers with shared interests, Friendster uses a model of social networking known as the "Circle of Friends" (developed by British computer scientist Jonathan Bishop), in which users invite friends and acquaintances — that is, people they already know and like — to join their network. 6

Friendster was an immediate success, with millions of registered users by mid-2003. But technological glitches and poor management at the company allowed a new social networking site, MySpace, launched in 2003, quickly to surpass it. Originally started by musicians, MySpace has become a major venue for sharing music as well as videos and photos. It is now the behemoth of online social networking, with over 100 million registered users. Connection has become big business: in 2005, Rupert Murdoch's News Corporation bought MySpace for $580 million. 7

Besides MySpace and Friendster, the best-known social networking 8 site is Facebook, launched in 2004. Originally restricted to college students, Facebook—which takes its name from the small photo albums that colleges once gave to incoming freshmen and faculty to help them cope with meeting so many new people—soon extended membership to high schoolers and is now open to anyone. Still, it is most popular among college students and recent college graduates, many of whom use the site as their primary method of communicating with one another. Millions of college students check their Facebook pages several times every day and spend hours sending and receiving messages, making appointments, getting updates on their friends' activities, and learning about people they might recently have met or heard about.

There are dozens of other social networking sites, including Orkut, 9 Bebo, and Yahoo 360°. Microsoft recently announced its own plans for a social networking site called Wallop; the company boasts that the site will offer "an entirely new way for consumers to express their individuality online." (It is noteworthy that Microsoft refers to social networkers as "consumers" rather than merely "users" or, say, "people.") Niche social networking sites are also flourishing: there are sites offering forums and fellowship for photographers, music lovers, and sports fans. There are professional networking sites, such as LinkedIn, that keep people connected with present and former colleagues and other business acquaintances. There are sites specifically for younger children, such as Club Penguin, which lets kids pretend to be chubby, colored penguins who waddle around chatting, playing games, earning virtual money, and buying virtual clothes. Other niche social networking sites connect like-minded self-improvers; the site 43things.com encourages people to share their personal goals. Click on "watch less TV," one of the goals listed on the site, and you can see the profiles of the 1,300 other people in the network who want to do the same thing. And for people who want to join a social network but don't know which niche site is right for them, there are sites that help users locate the proper online social networking community for their particular (or peculiar) interests.

Social networking sites are also fertile ground for those who make 10 it their lives' work to get your attention—namely, spammers, marketers, and politicians. Incidents of spamming and spyware on MySpace and other social networking sites are legion. Legitimate advertisers such as record labels and film studios have also set up pages for their products. In some cases, fictional characters from books and movies are given their own official MySpace pages. Some sports mascots and brand icons have them, too. Procter & Gamble has a Crest toothpaste page on MySpace featuring a sultry-looking model called "Miss Irresistible." As of this summer, she had about 50,000 users linked as friends, whom she urged to "spice it up by sending a naughty (or nice) e-card." The e-cards are emblazoned with Crest or Scope logos, of course, and include messages such as "I wanna get fresh with you" or "Pucker up baby—I'm getting fresh." A P&G marketing officer recently told the *Wall Street Journal* that from a business perspective, social networking sites are "going to be one giant living dynamic learning experience about consumers."

As for politicians, with the presidential primary season now under- 11 way, candidates have embraced a no–website–left–behind policy. Senator Hillary Clinton has official pages on social networking sites MySpace, Flickr, LiveJournal, Facebook, Friendster, and Orkut. As of July 1, 2007, she had a mere 52,472 friends on MySpace (a bit more than Miss irresistible); her Democratic rival Senator Barack Obama had an impressive 128,859. Former Senator John Edwards has profiles on twenty–three different sites. Republican contenders for the White House are poorer social networkers than their Democratic counterparts; as of this writing, none of the GOP candidates has as many MySpace friends as Hillary, and some of the leading Republican candidates have no social networking presence at all.

Despite the increasingly diverse range of social networking sites, the 12 most popular sites share certain features. On MySpace and Facebook, for example, the process of setting up one's online identity is relatively simple: provide your name, address, e–mail address, and a few other pieces of information and you're up and running and ready to create your online persona. MySpace includes a section, "About Me," where you can post your name, age, where you live, and other personal details such as your zodiac sign, religion, sexual orientation, and relationship status. There is also a "Who I'd Like to Meet" section, which on most MySpace profiles is filled with images of celebrities. Users can also list their favorite music, movies, and television shows, as well as their personal heroes; MySpace users can also blog on their pages. A user "friends" people—that is, invites them by e–mail to appear on the user's "Friend Space," where they are listed, linked, and ranked. Below the Friends space is a Comments section where friends can post notes. MySpace allows users to personalize their pages by uploading images and music and videos; indeed, one of the defining features of most MySpace pages is the ubiquity of visual and audio clutter. With silly, hyper flashing graphics in neon colors and clip–art style images of kittens and cartoons, MySpace pages often resemble an overdecorated high school yearbook.

By contrast, Facebook limits what its users can do to their profiles. 13 Besides general personal information, Facebook users have a "Wall" where people can leave them brief notes, as well as a Messages feature that functions like an in–house Facebook e–mail account. You list your friends on Facebook as well, but in general, unlike MySpace friends, which are often complete strangers (or spammers), Facebook friends tend to be part of one's offline social circle. (This might change, however, now that Facebook has opened its site to anyone rather than restricting it to college and high school students.) Facebook (and MySpace) allows users to form groups based on mutual interests. Facebook users can also send "pokes"

"Why can't you use Facebook, like everybody else?"

to friends; these little digital nudges are meant to let someone know you are thinking about him or her. But they can also be interpreted as not-so-subtle come-ons; one Facebook group with over 200,000 members is called "Enough with the Poking, Let's Just Have Sex." . . .

WON'T YOU BE MY DIGITAL NEIGHBOR?

According to a survey recently conducted by the Pew Internet and Amer- 14 ican Life Project, more than half of all Americans between the ages of twelve and seventeen use some online social networking site. Indeed, media coverage of social networking sites usually describes them as vast teenage playgrounds — or wastelands, depending on one's perspective. Central to this narrative is a nearly unbridgeable generational divide, with tech-savvy youngsters redefining friendship while their doddering elders look on with bafflement and increasing anxiety. This seems anec-dotally correct; I can't count how many times I have mentioned social networking websites to someone over the age of forty and received the reply, "Oh yes, I've heard about that MyFace! All the kids are doing that these days. Very interesting!"

Numerous articles have chronicled adults' attempts to navigate the 15 world of social networking, such as the recent *New York Times* essay in which columnist Michelle Slatalla described the incredible embarrassment she caused her teenage daughter when she joined Facebook: "everyone in the whole world thinks its super creepy when adults have facebooks," her daughter instant-messaged her. "unfriend paige right now. im serious. . . . i will be soo mad if you dont unfriend paige right now. actually." In fact, social networking sites are not only for the young. More than half of the visitors to MySpace claim to be over the age of 35. And now that the first generation of college Facebook users has graduated, and the site is open to all, more than half of Facebook users are no longer students. What's more, the proliferation of niche social networking sites, including those aimed at adults, suggests that it is not only teenagers who will nurture relationships in virtual space for the foreseeable future.

What characterizes these online communities in which an increas- 16 ing number of us are spending our time? Social networking sites have a peculiar psychogeography. As researchers at the Pew project have noted, the proto-social networking sites of a decade ago used metaphors of *place* to organize their members: people were linked through virtual cities, communities, and homepages. In 1997, GeoCities boasted thirty virtual "neighborhoods" in which "homesteaders" or "GeoCitizens" could gather—"Heartland" for family and parenting tips, "SouthBeach" for socializing, "Vienna" for classical music aficionados, "Broadway" for theater buffs, and so on. By contrast, today's social networking sites organize themselves around metaphors of the *person*, with individual profiles that list hobbies and interests. As a result, one's entrée into this world generally isn't through a virtual neighborhood or community but through the revelation of personal information. And unlike a neighborhood, where one usually has a general knowledge of others who live in the area, social networking sites are gatherings of deracinated individuals, none of whose personal boastings and musings are necessarily trustworthy. Here, the old arbiters of community—geographic location, family, role, or occupations—have little effect on relationships.

Also, in the offline world, communities typically are responsible for 17 enforcing norms of privacy and general etiquette. In the online world, which is unfettered by the boundaries of real-world communities, new etiquette challenges abound. For example, what do you do with a "friend" who posts inappropriate comments on your Wall? What recourse do you have if someone posts an embarrassing picture of you on his MySpace page? What happens when a friend breaks up with someone—do you defriend the ex? If someone "friends" you and you don't accept the overture, how serious a rejection is it? Some of these scenarios can be resolved with split-second snap judgments; others can provoke days of agonizing.

Enthusiasts of social networking argue that these sites are not merely 18 entertaining; they also edify by teaching users about the rules of social space. As Danah Boyd, a graduate student studying social networks at the University of California, Berkeley, told the authors of *MySpace Unraveled*, social networking promotes "informal learning. . . . It's where you learn social norms, rules, how to interact with others, narrative, personal and group history, and media literacy." This is more a hopeful assertion than a proven fact, however. The question that isn't asked is how the technology itself—the way it encourages us to present ourselves and interact—limits or imposes on that process of informal learning. All communities expect their members to internalize certain norms. Even individuals in the transient communities that form in public spaces obey these rules, for the most part; for example, patrons of libraries are expected to keep noise to a minimum. New technologies are challenging such norms— cell phones ring during church sermons; blaring televisions in doctors' waiting rooms make it difficult to talk quietly— and new norms must develop to replace the old. What cues are young, avid social networkers learning about social space? What unspoken rules and communal norms have the millions of participants in these online social networks internalized, and how have these new norms influenced their behavior in the offline world?

Social rules and norms are not merely the strait-laced conceits of a 19 bygone era; they serve a protective function. I know a young woman— attractive, intelligent, and well-spoken— who, like many other people in their twenties, joined Facebook as a college student when it launched. When she and her boyfriend got engaged, they both updated their relationship status to "Engaged" on their profiles and friends posted congratulatory messages on her Wall.

But then they broke off the engagement. And a funny thing hap- 20 pened. Although she had already told a few friends and family members that the relationship was over, her ex decided to make it official in a very twenty-first century way: he changed his status on his profile from "Engaged" to "Single." Facebook immediately sent out a feed to every one of their mutual "friends" announcing the news, "Mr. X and Ms. Y are no longer in a relationship," complete with an icon of a broken heart. When I asked the young woman how she felt about this, she said that although she assumed her friends and acquaintances would eventually hear the news, there was something disconcerting about the fact that everyone found out about it instantaneously; and since the message came from Facebook, rather than in a face-to-face exchange initiated by her, it was devoid of context— save for a helpful notation of the time and that tacky little heart. . . .

THE NEW TAXONOMY OF FRIENDSHIP

There is a Spanish proverb that warns, "Life without a friend is death 21 without a witness." In the world of online social networking, the warning might be simpler; "Life without hundreds of online 'friends' is virtual death." On these sites, friendship is the stated *raison d'être*. "A place for friends" is the slogan of MySpace. Facebook is a "social utility that connects people with friends." Orkut describes itself as "an online community that connects people through a network of trusted friends." Friendster's name speaks for itself.

But "friendship" in these virtual spaces is thoroughly different from 22 real-world friendship. In its traditional sense, friendship is a relationship which, broadly speaking, involves the sharing of mutual interests, reciprocity, trust, and the revelation of intimate details over time and within specific social (and cultural) contexts. Because friendship depends on mutual revelations that are concealed from the rest of the world, it can only flourish within the boundaries of privacy; the idea of public friendship is an oxymoron.

The hypertext link called "friendship" on social networking sites is   23
very different: public, fluid, and promiscuous, yet oddly bureaucratized. Friendship on these sites focuses a great deal on collecting, managing, and ranking the people you know. Everything about MySpace, for example, is designed to encourage users to gather as many friends as possible, as though friendship were philately. If you are so unfortunate as to have but one MySpace friend, for example, your page reads: "You have 1 friends," along with a stretch of sad empty space where dozens of thumbnail photos of your acquaintances should appear.

This promotes a form of frantic friend procurement. As one young   24
Facebook user with 800 friends told John Cassidy in *The New Yorker*, "I always find the competitive spirit in me wanting to up the number." An associate dean at Purdue University recently boasted to the *Christian Science Monitor* that since establishing a Facebook profile, he had collected more than 700 friends. The phrase universally found on MySpace is "Thanks for the add!"— an acknowledgment by one user that another has added you to his list of friends. There are even services like FriendFlood.com that act as social networking pimps: for a fee, they will post messages on your page from an attractive person posing as your "friend." As the founder of one such service told the *New York Times* in February 2007, he wanted to "turn cyberlosers into social-networking magnets."

The structure of social networking sites also encourages the bureau-   25
cratization of friendship. Each site has its own terminology, but among the words that users employ most often is "managing." The Pew survey mentioned earlier found that "teens say social networking sites help them manage their friendships." There is something Orwellian about the management-speak on social networking sites: "Change My Top Friends," "View All of My Friends," and for those times when our inner Stalins sense the need for a virtual purge, "Edit Friends." With a few mouse clicks one can elevate or downgrade (or entirely eliminate) a relationship.

To be sure, we all rank our friends, albeit in unspoken and intuitive   26
ways. One friend might be a good companion for outings to movies or concerts; another might be someone with whom you socialize in professional settings; another might be the kind of person for whom you would drop everything if he needed help. But social networking sites allow us to rank our friends publicly. And not only can we publicize our own preferences in people, but we can also peruse the favorites among our other acquaintances. We can learn all about the friends of our friends— often without having ever met them in person.

STATUS-SEEKERS

Of course, it would be foolish to suggest that people are incapable of 27 making distinctions between social networking "friends" and friends they see in the flesh. The use of the word "friend" on social networking sites is a dilution and a debasement, and surely no one with hundreds of MySpace or Facebook "friends" is so confused as to believe those are all real friendships. The impulse to collect as many "friends" as possible on a MySpace page is not an expression of the human need for companionship, but of a different need no less profound and pressing: the need for status. Unlike the painted portraits that members of the middle class in a bygone era would commission to signal their elite status once they rose in society, social networking websites allow us to *create* status — not merely to commemorate the achievement of it. There is a reason that most of the MySpace profiles of famous people are fakes, often created by fans: celebrities don't need legions of MySpace friends to prove their importance. It's the rest of the population, seeking a form of parochial celebrity, that does.

But status-seeking has an ever-present partner: anxiety. Unlike a 28 portrait, which, once finished and framed, hung tamely on the wall signaling one's status, maintaining status on MySpace or Facebook requires constant vigilance. As one 24-year-old wrote in a *New York Times* essay, "I am obsessed with testimonials and solicit them incessantly. They are the ultimate social currency, public declarations of the intimacy status of a relationship. . . . Every profile is a carefully planned media campaign."

The sites themselves were designed to encourage this. Describing 29 the work of B. J. Fogg of Stanford University, who studies "persuasion strategies" used by social networking sites to increase participation, *The New Scientist* noted, "The secret is to tie the acquisition of friends, compliments and status — spoils that humans will work hard for — to activities that enhance the site." As Fogg told the magazine, "You offer someone a context for gaining status, and they are going to work for that status." Network theorist Albert-László Barabási notes that online connection follows the rule of "preferential attachment" — that is, "when choosing between two pages, one with twice as many links as the other, about twice as many people link to the more connected page." As a result, "while our individual choices are highly unpredictable, as a group we follow strict patterns." Our lemming-like pursuit of online status via the collection of hundreds of "friends" clearly follows this rule.

What, in the end, does this pursuit of virtual status mean for com- 30 munity and friendship? Writing in the 1980s in *Habits of the Heart*, sociologist Robert Bellah and his colleagues documented the movement away from close-knit, traditional communities to "lifestyle enclaves," which were defined largely by "leisure and consumption." Perhaps today we have moved beyond lifestyle enclaves and into "personality enclaves" or "identity enclaves" — discrete virtual places in which we can be different (and sometimes contradictory) people, with different groups of like-minded, though ever-shifting, friends.

BEYOND NETWORKING

This past spring, Len Harmon, the director of the Fischer Policy and Cul- 31
tural Institute at Nichols College in Dudley, Massachusetts, offered a new course about social networking. Nichols is a small school whose students come largely from Connecticut and Massachusetts; many of them are the first members of their families to attend college. "I noticed a lot of issues involved with social networking sites," Harmon told me when I asked him why he created the class. How have these sites been useful to Nichols students? "It has relieved some of the stress of transitions for them," he said. "When abrupt departures occur — their family moves or they have to leave friends behind — they can cope by keeping in touch more easily."

So perhaps we should praise social networking websites for stream- 32
lining friendship the way e-mail streamlined correspondence. In the nineteenth century, Emerson observed that "friendship requires more time than poor busy men can usually command." Now, technology has given us the freedom to tap into our network of friends when it is con-venient for us. "It's a way of maintaining a friendship without having to make any effort whatsoever," as a recent graduate of Harvard explained to *The New Yorker*. And that ease admittedly makes it possible to stay in contact with a wider circle of offline acquaintances than might have been possible in the era before Facebook. Friends you haven't heard from in years, old buddies from elementary school, people you might have (should have?) fallen out of touch with — it is now easier than ever to reconnect to those people.

But what kind of connections are these? In his excellent book *Friend-* 33
ship: An Exposé, Joseph Epstein praises the telephone and e-mail as tech-nologies that have greatly facilitated friendship. He writes, "Proust once said he didn't much care for the analogy of a book to a friend. He thought a book was better than a friend, because you could shut it — and be shut of it — when you wished, which one can't always do with a friend." With e-mail and caller ID, Epstein enthuses, you can. But social networking sites (which Epstein says "speak to the vast loneliness in the world") have a different effect: they discourage "being shut of" people. On the contrary, they encourage users to check in frequently, "poke" friends, and post comments on others' pages. They favor interaction of greater quantity but less quality.

This constant connectivity concerns Len Harmon. "There is a sense 34
of, 'if I'm not online or constantly texting or posting, then I'm missing something,'" he said of his students. "This is where I find the generational impact the greatest — not the use of the technology, but the *overuse* of

the technology." It is unclear how the regular use of these sites will affect behavior over the long run—especially the behavior of children and
young adults who are growing up with these tools. Almost no research
has explored how virtual socializing affects children's development. What
does a child weaned on Club Penguin learn about social interaction?
How is an adolescent who spends her evenings managing her MySpace
page different from a teenager who spends her night gossiping on the
telephone to friends? Given that "people want to live their lives online,"
as the founder of one social networking site recently told *Fast Company*
magazine, and they are beginning to do so at ever-younger ages, these
questions are worth exploring.

The few studies that have emerged do not inspire confidence. Re- 35
searcher Rob Nyland at Brigham Young University recently surveyed 184
users of social networking sites and found that heavy users "feel less socially involved with the community around them." He also found that "as
individuals use social networking more for entertainment, their level of
social involvement decreases." Another recent study conducted by communications professor Qingwen Dong and colleagues at the University of
the Pacific found that "those who engaged in romantic communication
over MySpace tend to have low levels of both emotional intelligence and
self-esteem."

The implications of the narcissistic and exhibitionistic tendencies of 36
social networkers also cry out for further consideration. There are opportunity costs when we spend so much time carefully grooming ourselves online. Given how much time we already devote to entertaining
ourselves with technology, it is at least worth asking if the time we spend
on social networking sites is well spent. In investing so much energy into
improving how we *present* ourselves online, are we missing chances to
genuinely *improve* ourselves?

We should also take note of the trend toward giving up face-to-face 37
for virtual contact—and, in some cases, a preference for the latter. Today,
many of our cultural, social, and political interactions take place through
eminently convenient technological surrogates—Why go to the bank if
you can use the ATM? Why browse in a bookstore when you can simply
peruse the personalized selections Amazon.com has made for you? In
the same vein, social networking sites are often convenient surrogates
for offline friendship and community. In this context it is worth considering an observation that Stanley Milgram made in 1974, regarding
his experiments with obedience: "The social psychology of this century
reveals a major lesson," he wrote. "Often it is not so much the kind of
person a man is as the kind of situation in which he finds himself that
determines how he will act." To an increasing degree, we find and form
our friendships and communities in the virtual world as well as the real
world. These virtual networks greatly expand our opportunities to meet
others, but they might also result in our valuing less the capacity for

genuine connection. As the young woman writing in the *Times* admitted, "I consistently trade actual human contact for the more reliable high of smiles on MySpace, winks on Match.com, and pokes on Facebook." That she finds these online relationships more *reliable* is telling: it shows a desire to avoid the vulnerability and uncertainty that true friendship entails. Real intimacy requires risk— the risk of disapproval, of heartache, of being thought a fool. Social networking websites may make relationships more reliable, but whether those relationships can be humanly satisfying remains to be seen.

Reading Closely

1. In this essay, Rosen weighs what she considers the benefits and drawbacks of online social networking sites. What are the benefits, in her view? What are the drawbacks? After listing the benefits and drawbacks that Rosen finds, consider the overarching argument of the essay. What is Rosen saying about the kinds of virtual friendships that are created on social networking sites?

2. Rosen uses section headings to separate her points of discussion. In each section, underline as many examples as you can. What purpose do these examples serve? How do they reinforce the purpose of the individual sections? How do the examples reinforce the overarching argument of the essay?

3. **Working with a classmate,** review the examples you underlined for question 2. What *kinds* of examples does Rosen rely on throughout the essay? Anecdotes? Facts? Statistics? Hypothetical situations? What purpose do these various examples serve?

4. What connections can you make between the cartoon on page 255 and Rosen's essay? What does the cartoon say about the kind of narcissism Rosen is writing about?

Considering Larger Issues

1. What did you learn in this essay? What was new for you?

2. Drawing from your experience with social networking sites, where do you agree and disagree with Rosen?

3. PAIRED READINGS. Compare Rosen's essay with the previous essay by David Browne, "On the Internet, It's All About 'My'." What connections do you see between these two essays? What are both authors saying about the possibilities and problems inherent in the Internet and the connections it affords?

4. COMBINING METHODS. In addition to exemplification, Rosen calls on *comparison and contrast* as well as cause–and–effect analysis to make her point. **Working with a classmate,** identify the places in the essay where

Rosen uses these methods of development. What purpose do these methods serve? How do they support the main argument of the essay?

Thinking about Language

1. Using the context of the essay or your dictionary, define the following terms. Be prepared to share your answers with the rest of the class.

narcissism (title)	legion (10)	oxymoron (22)
self–aggrandizement (2)	ubiquity (12)	bureaucratized (23)
pixels (3)	proliferation (15)	philately (23)
stream of consciousness (3)	psychogeography (16)	Orwellian (25)
		parochial (27)
ambiguous (3)	proto–social (16)	enclaves (30)
ephemeral (3)	aficionados (16)	exhibitionistic (36)
de rigueur (4)	deracinated (16)	opportunity costs (36)
Delphic oracle (4)	transient (18)	
behemoth (7)	taxonomy (21)	
niche (9)	*raison d'être* (21)	

2. Chapter 1, Description, discusses how writers choose to use specific terms throughout an essay that work to make a dominant impression on readers—a particular quality of their subject or attitude toward it. What dominant impression is Rosen attempting to convey? Identify terms throughout the essay that Rosen uses to create and confirm this impression.

Writing Your Own Essays Using Exemplification

1. If you participate in a social networking site, examine your page, and consider how—or whether—it enables you to create and maintain friendships. As you review your page, take notes, listing examples of your experiences online and reflecting on how your experiences match (or don't match) Rosen's analyses. Review your notes and then create a generalization about how social networking sites have affected your friendships. Once you've taken your notes and composed your generalization, draft a three- to four-page essay in which you make an argument about friendships on social networking sites. Rely on examples from your experiences to make your point. As you compose, be sure to refer to the guidelines for checking over the use of exemplification on pages 222–23.

2. In paragraph 18, Rosen briefly describes the rules of etiquette that exist on social networking sites. If you participate on one of these sites, think about the rules of etiquette that users must follow. Review your site or your participation on it to identify concrete examples that confirm that these rules exist. Then compose a two- to three-page essay that makes a generalization about the rules of etiquette on the site and gives examples to support it. As you draft and revise, refer to "Checking Over the Use of Exemplification" on pages 222–23.

3. **ACADEMIC WRITING.** Both Browne and Rosen analyze how the Internet is affecting interpersonal and social relationships. In a three- to four-page academic essay, reflect on how the Internet has affected the educational environment— from the perspective of teachers rather than students. Your first step will be to conduct research: You'll want to explore work by scholars that investigates such topics as online and distance learning, plagiarism, multimodal learning, student collaboration, and student writing. Identify as many examples as possible that illustrate the varied concerns teachers must consider as they educate students in the increasingly digital world of the twenty–first century. Then, compose a research essay that is geared toward an audience of scholars and students of education. You should rely on exemplification to survey the various educational possibilities and problems relating to the digital world. As you draft your essay, pay particular attention to finding a logical organization to guide your presentation of examples. Refer to "Checking Over the Use of Exemplification" on pages 222–23 as you draft and revise.

✳ Additional Suggestions for Writing

1. Write a generalization about someone you know well who has a public persona. List all the examples you can think of that clarify or explain your generalization. **Working with a classmate,** review your generalization and your list, discussing any changes you may want to make to either one. Then draft a two- to three-page essay in which you develop your generalization and begin to link it to your subject's public persona, making connections between the private person whom you know well and the public person whom everyone else sees. Remember that the guidelines for checking over the use of exemplification can be found on pages 222–23.

2. Pretend that you are responding to a sociology professor's assignment about alcohol consumption or another activity that is potentially unhealthy or dangerous. Make a list of such activities that you have participated in, witnessed, or heard about. After you make your list, **work with a classmate** to compare and merge lists. Then draft a three- to four-page essay in which you generalize about one of those activities and provide examples — including anecdotes, facts, or statistics — that support your generalization. You may want to conduct library or Internet research, interview people who currently or formerly participated in the activity, or relate personal anecdotes. As you draft, revise, and assess examples, be sure to refer to the guidelines for checking over the use of exemplification on pages 222–23.

chapter 5

CLASSIFICATION
AND DIVISION

PIZZA	18"	16"	14"
Cheese	$13.99	$11.99	$9..99
Extra Topping	$2.00	$1.75	$1.50
Half Topping	$1.00	$.90	$.80
Veggie Pizza	$18.50	$16.50	$14.50
Meatlovers	$19.50	$17.50	$15.50
Brother's Supreme	$21.50	$19.50	$17.50
Hawaiian Pizza	$16.99	$14.49	$11.99
White Pizza	$16.99	$14.49	$11.99

SLICE of CHEESE PIZZA..............................*$1.85*
TOPPING on SLICE...*$.45*
Veggie or Meaty Slice...................................*$3.00*

AVAILABLE TOPPINGS

Pepperoni- Sausage- Meatballs- Ham- Salami-
Capicola- Chicken- Bacon-Bits- Black Olives-
Onions- Mushrooms- Tomatoes- Banana or
Jalapeno Peppers-Pineapple- Green Peppers-
Broccoli- Spinach- Anchovies- Extra Cheese

SICILIAN

Sicilian Pizza Pie	(16"x14")	$15.99
Each Topping		$2.00
1/2 Topping		$1.00
Sicilian by the Slice		$1.99
Each Topping on Slice		$.50

STROMBOLIS & CALZONES

Strombolis = Mozzarella Cheese + Toppings
Calzones = Blend of Cheeses + Toppings

MADE to ORDER	STM.	CAL.
12" 2-Toppings of your choice	$10.99	$11.99
Each extra topping	$1.25	$1.25
12" Vegetarian	$12.99	$13.99
12" Meatlovers	$13.99	$14.99
12" Steak	$12.99	$13.99

Ready to go Stromboli

Made with Ham-Pepperoni-Cheese	$ 4.99
Cup of sauce	$.50

DRINKS

16oz.....$1.65   22oz.....$1.85   Pitcher....$5.29
Snapples......Red Bull....... Brothers Spring Water....

When college students head for their favorite pizza place, they usually grab a menu, even if they already know what they want to order. When they arrive at Brothers N.Y. Style Pizzeria in State College, Pennsylvania, they see that the menu begins with the heading "Pizza," the most important item Brothers sells. Below it are listings and prices for three different sizes of pizzas and six different kinds of each size, ranging from cheese to veggie to Hawaiian (plus the charges for an extra topping and a "half topping"). Next, the "Available Toppings" section lists nineteen items, ranging from pepperoni and sausage to pineapple and extra cheese. Elsewhere on the menu, mozzarella sticks, garlic knots, buffalo wings, and so on are listed under "Side Orders"; "Salads" lists tossed, garden, chef, and four others. In fact, all of the restaurant's offerings are classified into the categories of "Pizza," "Available Toppings," "Sicilian," "Strombolis & Calzones," "Drinks," "Salads," "Side Orders," "Subs," and "Wedges." Whoever designed the menu uses classification and a closely related method, division, to help customers make sense of what Brothers Pizza has to offer.

Throughout our lives, we encounter and compose different kinds of public writing that rely on classification and division. Many times, when we use these methods, we don't even give them much thought. When we go to a restaurant, we choose what we want to eat and drink from specific categories on the menu. When we check our e-mail, we navigate the divisions on the site's Web page, most likely by tabbing the Inbox, Sent, and Trash categories. And when we compose our résumés, we create different categories that provide evidence of our expertise and qualifications: objectives, education, honors and activities, and work experiences. As readers and writers, then, we have countless occasions to interpret and produce classification and division for various situations and purposes.

· ·

Looking at Your Own Literacy Think back to a time when you were classified—and labeled—on the basis of your reading, writing, or speaking ability. Take a few minutes to reflect on your place in the classification and division, and write about how you felt and what you learned about being labeled.

· ·

What Are Classification and Division?

Classification and division are different ways of thinking and talking about information, but they are a kind of mirror image of each other, and they usually work in tandem. **Classification** is the process of sorting specific things into more general categories; **division** is the process of breaking a general whole into more specific parts, which are often categories. We encounter classification and division when, for example, we go shopping on iTunes. This site classifies its material into different sections: "iTunes Store," "New and Noteworthy," and "Quick Links." But then each of these sections is divided into categories: for example, "New and Noteworthy" is divided into music, movies, TV shows, and so on. This process of classification and division happens offline too, of course. We expect grocery stores to use classification and division to help us locate the product we want: typically, all the products in the store are classified by type— produce, meat, dairy, and so on— and all the products within each category are classified into subtypes. For instance, the meats are classified into chicken, pork, beef, and lamb; cured, fresh, and frozen. And the store is divided into sections and subsections for each type and subtype.

Our examinations of iTunes and the grocery store demonstrate one of the purposes of classification and division: to inform and teach. But these methods can also be used to please or entertain and to argue. In the most general sense, they offer a way to put an array of items into groups and then to label each group— or to define and label groups and then put items into each one.

We routinely make sense of our world by sorting incidents, people, places, steps, and topics into categories and then labeling the categories. Each time you put away your groceries, you classify them. You put frozen foods into the freezer, items that need to be kept cold into the refrigerator, and products that can be kept at room temperature, such as cereals or flour, into the pantry or cupboards. Whenever you sort items according to their similarities and differences— whether you're separating your clothes from your roommate's at the Laundromat, deciding which of your many friends to invite to your small party, or filling out your schedule according to required courses for your particular major and courses that are general requirements— you are using classification.

Division is slightly different. Instead of sorting a number of items into categories, you're dividing one item into its parts (and often analyzing the connections among the parts). Instead of looking at something from the bottom up, you're looking from the top down. Think back to your groceries— let's say you bring in several bags of items that need to be put away. And let's say that instead of thinking of the situation in terms of the groceries— taking each item out of the bag and deciding where to put it (how to classify it)— you instead think in terms of your kitchen and its physical parts: the refrigerator, the freezer, and the pantry or cupboards. You move to each part in turn, taking the items that go in that part out of the shopping bags and putting those items away before moving on to the next part. By mentally dividing up the kitchen, you've divided up all the groceries.

In fact, when most of us put away groceries, we use classification and division simultaneously. Maybe we put the shopping bags down in front of whatever part of the kitchen is closest to the door— say, the pantry— and look into the bags for items that belong in that part (division). Before we finish putting those away, we notice that the ice cream is starting to melt, and we rush to get it into the freezer (classification). While we're there, we look in the bags for other items that belong in that part (division), and so on. Whether as physical processes or writing strategies, classifying and dividing usually go hand in hand.

When classification and division constitute the dominant pattern in a whole essay, each section of the essay is about a category or a main part. If you were writing an essay about your summer job in a fast-food restaurant, for instance, you might open by dividing the menu (or classifying the items on it) into sandwiches, meal deals, drinks, and desserts. Then you might move into a discussion of your work as a sandwich maker, discussing hamburgers, cheeseburgers, fish sandwiches, superfattening and double hamburgers, and kiddy burgers. You could move from one classification of food to the next, describing each of the items that you prepared, until you've fleshed out an entire essay.

You can also use classification and division in a supporting passage or paragraph. For instance, if you're writing a narrative about buying a used car or an analysis of the process, you might mention two classes of used cars: smart choices and big risks. In a certain paragraph, you might list some smart choices in a sentence or two and give the reasons why you think so. In the same paragraph or in another one, you might do the same for the big risks. Such information would bring your essay alive and make it more interesting to your readers, maybe even entertaining or persuading them at the same time.

The annual auto issue of *Consumer Reports* contains all sorts of information that is presented using classification and division. The lists on page 272 appeared in the 2008 issue of *Consumer Report's Buying Guide* as a part of the section on used cars.

- -

Thinking about Classification and Division

1. Read over the classification from *Consumer Reports*. What is the overall purpose of this classification? How easy is it to read and understand?

2. Do you own or have you driven one of the cars listed in the *Consumer Reports* guide? If so, which one? Write a quick response to *Consumer Reports* based on your experience with this car. If you don't have experience with any of these cars, classify a car or another kind of product you do know about as either reliable or to be avoided, and explain why.

- -

Why Classify and Divide?

When we use classification and division, we often do so simply with an informative purpose, whether we are classifying or dividing the contents of a store, a kitchen, or popular music charts. For example, in

CR Good Bets & Bad Bets

CR Good Bets These models, listed alphabetically, have performed well in CONSUMER REPORTS road tests and have had several years of better–than–average reliability according to our 2006 survey results. **CR Bad Bets** These vehicles showed multiple Used Car Verdicts that were much worse than average, according to our 2006 survey results. They consistently had more problems than other models overall.

GOOD BETS	Lexus LS	Toyota RAV4	Land Rover
Acura Integra	Lexus RX	Toyota Sequoia	Discovery, LR3
Acura MDX	Lexus SC	Toyota Sienna	Lincoln Aviator
Acura RL	Lincoln Town Car	Toyota Tundra	Lincoln Navigator
Acura RSX	Mazda Millenia	————————	Mercedes–Benz CLK
(except '06)	Mazda MX–5 Miata	**BAD BETS**	Mercedes–Benz
Acura TL	Mazda Protegé	BMW 7 Series	M–Class (V8)
Acura TSX	Mazda3	BMW X5 (V8)	Mercedes–Benz
Buick Regal	Nissan Altima	Chevrolet Astro	S–Class (V8)
Chevrolet Prizm	Nissan Maxima	Chevrolet Blazer	Mercedes–Benz SL
Honda Accord	Nissan Pathfinder	Chevrolet Express	Nissan Armada
Honda Civic	Pontiac Vibe	Chevrolet S–10 (4WD)	Nissan Titan
Honda Civic	Scion xB	Chevrolet Venture,	Oldsmobile Bravada
Hybrid	Subaru Forester	Uplander	Oldsmobile Cutlass
Honda CR–V	Subaru Impreza	Chrysler Town &	Oldsmobile
Honda Element	Subaru Impreza WRX	Country (AWD)	Silhouette
Honda Odyssey	Subaru Legacy	Dodge Grand	Pontiac Aztek
Honda Pilot	Subaru Outback	Caravan (AWD)	Pontiac Trans Sport.
Honda Prelude	Toyota 4Runner	GMC Jimmy	Montana,
Honda S2000	Toyota Avalon	GMC Sonoma (4WD)	Montana SV6
Infiniti FX	Toyota Camry	GMC Safari	Volkswagen Cabrio
Infiniti G20	Toyota Camry Solara	GMC Savana	Volkswagen
Infiniti G35	Toyota Celica	Infiniti QX56	Jetta (turbo gas)
Infiniti i30, i35	Toyota Corolla	Jaguar S–Type	Volkswagen
Infiniti QX4	Toyota Echo	Jaguar X–Type	Jetta (V6)
Lexus ES	Toyota Highlander	Jeep Grand	Volkswagen New
Lexus GS	Toyota Land Cruiser	Cherokee	Beetle (4–cyl.)
Lexus GX	Toyota Matrix	Kia Sedona	Volkswagen Touareg
Lexus IS	Toyota Prius	(except '06)	Volvo XC90 (6 cyl.)

the following excerpt, Roberto Suro classifies Latino gathering places called *cantinas*, drawing on the experiences of Houston police sergeant Art Valdez, who patrols Magnolia, Houston's Latino district.

Classification to Inform

Valdez can do a typology of Magnolia's cantinas as precisely as if he were categorizing butterflies by genus and species, except that it is a human caste system he describes. At one end, there are the raucous dance halls, some of them big Quonset huts, where younger men, mostly

Mexican and mostly illegals, are drawn by the abundant bar girls, most of them now young Salvadorans, who will dance and perhaps do more, depending on the money. When there are fights, they are usually over women.

Then there are the simple bars frequented by older men who remain tied to home, whatever their immigration status. They mostly drink without women and listen to little *conjuntos*, which are minstrel groups with a few guitars and maybe an accordion that play old songs. And now there are the new places that play salsa and other sounds with tropical rhythms rarely heard when the barrio was populated predominately by mountain and desert people.

At the other end of the spectrum are the fancy places with neon lights outside and bouncers in slick suits where Mexican-Americans go. The music is eclectic, some rock, a lot of country and western, but mostly *tejano*, a kind of country-rock combination that originated in south Texas and is sung in Spanish. The customers are English-speaking young people in their twenties and thirties out on dates. Most have come back to the old neighborhood from new suburban barrios. Valdez does not bother with them.   — ROBERTO SURO, "Houston: Cantina Patrol"

In these brief paragraphs, Suro informs his readers about the various kinds of cantinas in Houston and the kind of patron who frequents each kind. When he discusses "the fancy places," he divides that category further, according to the kind of music that is played there.

· ·

Try Your Hand   Undoubtedly, you socialize somewhere: restaurants, dorm lounges, church functions, clubs, coffee shops, bookstores, gyms. Using Suro's categories, or categories like his, try to classify the kinds of places you frequent. If you can divide one of those categories further, do so. If you notice that another classmate is writing about the same kinds of places, compare your reponses and prepare to report to the rest of the class.

· ·

Classification and division are also used to entertain, to give pleasure to readers. In this article from Penn State's student newspaper, the *Collegian*, a writer entertains her readers by considering the five most influential people she has met throughout her time at school and then classifies them into categories.

Classification to Entertain

I won't deny this. When I first arrived at Penn State, I asked someone in all seriousness, "What is a JoePa?"

Besides the boy on the third floor in Snyder residence hall who informed me that JoePa was not a thing but a person, there were others who educated, inspired, and motivated me through my college years. Just like the main character in Mitch Albom's book *The Five People You*

Meet in Heaven, I've narrowed my long list down to five individuals whose influences have changed me the most at Penn State.

The Professor Who Makes You Think.   When my ENGL 30 (Honors English) professor first assigned Don Delillo's *White Noise,* a satire on postmodern American culture, I thought of it as just another book to purchase. But when complex topics like media saturation and consumerism were touched on, I began to take a closer look at my life, not only for the class but also because I felt compelled to. This teacher made it clear to never stop questioning the truth because if we do, there's nothing else to prove, and then what's the purpose of anything?

The Die-Hard Partier.   Like any college, there are students who go out every night, rain or shine. However, I was uptight. I cringed at the smell of cheap beer and preferred staying in rather than ruining a pair of shoes at a house party. Then I made a friend who knew where to go out at night and invited me along. Sooner than later, I started making friends and stopped pouting in the corner. This friend taught me that three excused absences from class exist for a reason and Vladimir vodka wasn't that bad when you mixed it with Capri Sun. More important, he taught me to stop taking myself too seriously and to embrace the revelry college has to offer.

The College Romance.   There is a significant disparity between high school and college relationships. I'd compare it to upgrading from Tasti Delite—watered down and artificial—to homemade ice cream—authentic and fulfilling. In high school you are a "couple," two people who think and act as a single and often thoughtless unit. By the time college rolls around, it's a stronger connection that involves two distinct individuals. My college relationship taught me to never take advantage of feelings that you're certain won't fade and to always respect one another whether you're dating or not because it's more serious than an average high school fling.

The Friend You Thought You'd Never Be Friends With.   College inevitably puts you face-to-face with people who are from unfamiliar territory. Lines drawn from previous high school social groupings dissolve, and everyone is granted a second chance to hand-pick whom they want to be associated with. For me, this happened at the *Collegian.* With all of us working in close quarters and under tight deadlines, you can't help but become friends and discover you have more in common than you originally thought.

The Newspaper Editor.   True, not every Penn State student can relate to this, but anyone who has had a peer mentor can relate. When it came time to write my first story on a tight deadline, I panicked. Thankfully, I had an editor who sat with me and worked out the kinks with a patience that I strive to emulate today. She calmly made suggestions and praised me when I deserved it. As an editor now, I always think back to working underneath this individual, and I've learned patience and fairness is never forgotten.

I learned from these five individuals that college is about taking yourself out of a comfortable situation and making each day new and unpredictable through meeting and learning from different kinds of people.

One of the characters in Albom's book said that while in heaven, "Strangers are just family you have yet to come to know." College is just as good as eternal paradise to figure that one out.

— Nicole Sciotto, "The Five People You Meet in College"

As Sciotto notes, these five people are those who influenced her the most while she was at Penn State. There were of course others she encountered during her time there, and if she had considered a different question, she would have created different categories and classifications. For example, if she had considered the five people at Penn State who *challenged* her the most, she might have come up with a different classification system. Professors might still make Sciotto's list, but she might also have included her roommate, who questioned her ability to be neat and organized; an old friend from high school, who reminded her of what life was like at home before she got to college; or her academic adviser, who pushed her to take classes that were outside of her "comfort zone."

Try Your Hand   Who are the five people who have influenced you the most since you arrived at college? Who are the five people who have challenged you the most? Draw a line down the middle of a page, and list the five most influential people on one side and the five most challenging people on the other. Then spend ten minutes writing descriptions of the people on the list. Extend your thinking by reflecting on the specific characteristics that prompt you to categorize one person as influential and another as challenging.

Classification and division can also be used to argue a point or convince a reader to consider a particular opinion. For example, by classifying crimes by type—vehicle thefts, larcenies, break-ins, robberies, rapes, and murders—and then dividing an area into neighborhoods, a writer might reveal that certain neighborhoods have more crime of a certain type. The information that such a classification and division reveals can then be used to persuade readers that one neighborhood should initiate a neighborhood watch program, another should have regular police patrols, and yet another should be avoided altogether, if possible.

In fact, the act of classifying and dividing can itself make an argument. In the United States, there's a tradition of classifying all the residents into various racial categories—whether for police reports, job or college applications, or marriage and driver's licenses. For example, in 1980, there were four racial categories in the U.S. census: American Indian or Alaskan Native, Asian or Pacific Islander, Black, and White. By 2000, the number of categories had grown to six: American Indian or Alaska

Native, Asian, Black or African American, Native Hawaiian or Other Pacific Islander, White, and Some Other Race, for those who did not identify with any of the other five categories. In addition, respondents in 2000 were given the options of selecting more than one race and of listing their "ethnicity" as "Hispanic or Latino" or "Not Hispanic or Latino"; those who listed Hispanic or Latino could also specify an ethnicity such as Mexican or Cuban, and some of the racial categories also offered options for subcategories. Not surprisingly, the classifications will most likely be revised again for the 2010 census.

Inez Peterson takes up the issue of racial categorization when she writes about the difficulties of answering a colleague (who is also a writer) who asked "what part Indian she is." The woman who asked "should know better than to ask such an ignorant question," writes Peterson, whose response follows.

> What I do know is that if we divide ourselves, we are doing the work of the dominant culture; there is no need for them to keep us down, for we do it to ourselves. What is true too: if I had no need of this generosity of spirit, to include all of us, the mixed-bloods, the traditions, the urbans, the full-bloods, I might be just as exclusive as my author-colleague.
>
> I do not enjoy the privileged status of only one race, nor can I claim a traditional upbringing. My grandmother died believing it best not to pass on her Salish tongue. My white father abandoned his children and their mother, leaving nothing but his blood in my veins and a twisted belief in the ongoing nature of absented love. I do not know my own traditions.
>
> However, if I do not allow myself the right to dance intertribals, or sit in on non-Quinault sweat house ceremonies, or participate in rituals not specific to the Northwest, is not this the expected acquiescence of assimilation? Because my untaught mother taught me no tradition whatsoever, am I to refuse when a loving older Kiowa woman wants to teach me about fringing shawls? If I should exclude myself from belonging on the basis of my nontraditional upbringing and of the color of my skin, it would bring about unbearable loneliness. . . .
>
> And so when she asked me, "What part Indian are you?" I said, "I think it is my heart."   —INEZ PETERSON, "What Part Moon?"

Peterson helps readers see the insignificance of percentages (What part _____ are you?) and of those categorizations so prevalent on standard applications and forms. To choose to identify herself as an Indian seems, finally, more important to her than to have the "right" skin or hair color or the traditions or skills of an Indian. Nevertheless, although she refuses to divide herself into parts, racial classifications still linger in her essay in her own mind as well as the minds of others. She does not argue that "Indianness" does not exist, that it is not a category. Instead, she argues that it resides not in "blood" or rituals but in the heart.

· ·

Try Your Hand   Which racial category — or categories — do you mark when you're filling out an application? How might you subdivide your particular category or categories, given your heritage? Which identification feels most appropriate to you or "fits you the best"? Why?

· ·

How Do You Use Classification and Division in Academic Writing?

Just as writers who compose more public–oriented writing use classification and division, so do writers composing for academic audiences. As a student, you have used and will use classification and division throughout your academic career. In biology classes, you'll study and create scientific taxonomies that classify organisms into phylum, class, order, family, tribe, genus, species, and so on. In marketing classes, you'll analyze potential users of a product, dividing them into groups by age, gender, interests, and geographic region. And in art history courses, you'll learn about art through classifications of time such as the Greco–Roman, Romantic, and Modern periods.

In the following excerpt from an article in an academic journal, psychologists Lindsey M. O'Brennan, Catherine P. Bradshaw, and Anne L. Sawyer survey the scholarship on bullying at the elementary, middle, and high school levels. As they survey past studies, they classify this research into categories, showing how these studies come together to explore issues related to bullying such as "retaliatory attitudes," "aggressive–impulse behavior problems," "internalizing symptoms," "peer relationships," and "perceptions of belongingness and safety." This excerpt presents the introduction to this section of their article and to the first two of these issues.

Classification and Division in Academic Writing

Social-Emotional Problems Associated with Frequent Involvement in Bullying

Despite its prevalence, bullying has traditionally been viewed by many adults and school personnel as a normative developmental experience (Bradshaw et al., 2007). However, there is emerging evidence that children who are frequently involved in bullying are at an increased risk for social and emotional problems. Furthermore, the types of social-emotional problems experienced appear to vary depending on the student's type of involvement in bullying, as a bully, victim, or bully/victim (Nansel et al., 2004; Tobin, Schwartz, Gorman, & Abou-ezzeddine, 2005). In the following sections, we consider prior research on specific social-emotional problems and how it may be related to different types of involvement in bullying.

Retaliatory Attitudes. Although few studies have specifically examined retaliatory attitudes among youth involved in bullying, a number of researchers have found that aggressive youth are more likely than nonaggressive children to display attitudes and beliefs supporting aggressive retaliation (Bradshaw, O'Brennan, & Sawyer, 2008; Guerra, Huesmann, & Spindler, 2003). Such attitudes supporting violence, in turn, place youth at heightened risk for reacting aggressively in social situations (Huesmann & Guerra, 1997). The available research on school shootings also suggests a link between prior victimization and retaliatory violence (Leary et al., 2003), such that youth involved in bullying may be more likely than their peers to respond aggressively to interpersonal threats.

Aggressive-Impulsive Behavior Problems.   Similarly, perpetrators of aggressive behavior have been found to display higher levels of aggressive-impulsive behavior than other youth (Olweus, 1993; Smokowski & Kopasz, 2005). The extant research suggests that students who bully display both proactive (i.e., instrumental, deliberate, goal-directed behavior) and reactive (i.e., defensive, protective response) forms of aggression (Crick & Dodge, 1994), whereas victims of bullying display reactive rather than proactive aggression (Camodeca & Goossens, 2005). Similar to bullies, students classified as bully/victims also tend to exhibit problems regulating their emotions and show a proclivity toward acting impulsively (Mynard & Joseph, 1997). A study by Schwartz (2000), for example, indicated that bully/victims were rated by their teachers as hyperactive and disruptive, and having difficulties controlling their anger when provoked by their peers.   — Lindsey M. O'Brennan, Catherine P. Bradshaw, and Anne L. Sawyer, "Examining Developmental Differences in the Social-Emotional Problems among Frequent Bullies, Victims, and Bully/Victims"

The classification work that O'Brennan, Bradshaw, and Sawyer do here is often called a literature review — a review of the written accounts of previous research on a topic. The purpose of such reviews is to make readers aware of the work that's been done in the field and what's left to do. The article then goes on to offer the authors' own findings.

In your courses, it will be important for you to assess when to rely on the rhetorical method of classification and division. Obviously, an assignment may explicitly ask you to classify or divide. But you would also turn to classification and division if your professor asks you to *categorize* behaviors, terms, actions, or moments. Assignments that prompt you to consider *kinds* or *types* or that ask you to *break* or *separate* an idea, text, material object, or action into *parts* might also call for classification and division. Pay attention to the key words in the assignment. They should give you clues as to which rhetorical method to choose as you begin your thinking and writing process.

. . . .

Analyzing Classification and Division in Academic Writing

Reflect on a time when you've used classification and division for an academic assignment. In what class was the assignment? What purpose did this rhetorical method serve?

. . . .

How Do You Read Classification and Division?

It's usually easy to spot an essay or a passage that consists of classification or division—either a collection of people, ideas, or things are being put into categories, or one idea or thing is being broken into distinct parts. But noticing the organizational pattern is only one aspect of reading a classification and division *critically*, which is a key skill you need to develop in order to write one yourself. Reading critically means looking closely to analyze how successful the classification or division is, not only in general but also in terms of its specific purpose and intended audience. For example, do the categories or parts make sense, or do they seem to overlap or leave out some important part of the subject? Are they clear, entertaining, or persuasive, or do they seem confusing, dull, or unconvincing to potential readers? As you learn to read classifications and divisions in these ways, chances are you'll also be getting better at writing them as well.

To get an idea of what a critical reading involves, look back at Roberto Suro's classification of Houston's cantinas on pages 272–73. How does the author organize the subject—and more important, why? Suro classifies all the cantinas in town in order to inform—specifically, to explain how different social classes, nationalities, and genders of native and immigrant Spanish speakers can be found at specific kinds of cantinas. An author's purpose won't always be presented in a clear thesis statement, but Suro's essay opens with an explicit one that states his explanatory purpose: "Valdez can do a typology of Magnolia's cantinas as precisely as if he were categorizing butterflies by genus and species, except that it is a human caste system he describes." Although the title of this particular essay, "Houston: Cantina Patrol," provides little hint about its content, the titles and introductions of other essays might help orient you to the writers' principles of organization and purpose.

Notice that the key feature of each of Suro's cantina categories is the patrons, whom he groups by nationality, age, and gender. As he develops these categories, he enriches the description of each one with details of the cantinas' appearance and atmosphere as well as additional details about the patrons, such as their immigration status and the music they enjoy. In general, each of his categories seems clearly defined and clearly distinguished from the others, except that in the second paragraph it's not entirely clear whether "the new places that play salsa and other sounds with tropical rhythms" make up a different category from "the simple bars frequented by older men" or just a newer subcategory. Notice also that Suro defines two of the Spanish words he uses, *conjuntos* and *tejano*, while leaving *barrio* and *salsa* undefined. What does this difference suggest? He seems to be writing for readers who have some general familiarity with Latino culture but not a detailed knowledge of Latino musical styles.

Finally, as you read a classification or division critically, you'll want to think not only about the information the author supplies but also about what has been left unsaid. What information might Suro have omitted from his classification? For example, are there cantinas with a predominantly gay or lesbian clientele? Are cantinas (or specific kinds of cantinas) located in residential neighborhoods, commercial areas, or elsewhere? And would including that information enhance or detract from his essay? Could Houston's cantinas be classified differently—geographically, for instance? And if they were, would that new organizational pattern better fulfill the author's purpose or be easier for readers to follow? Asking questions like these will help you think about all the factors that go into an effective classification or division and understand better how to write one.

How Do You Write Using Classification and Division?

Keep the following guidelines in mind as you begin writing using classification or division or a combination of the two. As you generate ideas, draft, and revise, you'll want to make sure that you have established and carried out a clear purpose, are making choices appropriate for your particular audience, and are following a consistent principle of classification or division so that your categories or parts don't overlap or leave anything out. Following these guidelines will help you decide on the most effective way to organize the categories or parts and the appropriate amount of detail to devote to each one. You'll also want to make sure that you conclude by extending the point you're making through classification or division and that you consider whether visuals such as charts, graphs, photographs, or drawings might enhance it.

● Determining Your Purpose

First, you'll need to determine why you are imposing your organizational pattern on this group of items. Your first-year writing instructor might ask you to classify the different types of students at your school in a humorous way (that is, to entertain). Your history professor might ask you to organize the various causes of World War I into categories as part of an assignment to decide which causes were most important (to argue). Or your social psychology professor might have you divide the pressures college students face into different kinds in order to train you to analyze human behavior (to inform). If you can determine *why* you are classifying and dividing students, causes, or pressures, you'll have the basis for your audience analysis, your thesis statement, your method of arranging categories or parts, your choice of details, and your conclusions.

Do you want to teach and explain? Jay Heinrichs acts on this purpose in his popular book *Thank You for Arguing* when he teaches his readers the differences between arguing and fighting by classifying examples from everyday life and pop culture.

Classification to Explain

You succeed in an argument when you persuade your audience. You win a fight when you dominate the enemy. A territorial dispute in the backseat of a car fails to qualify as argument, for example, unless each child makes the unlikely attempt to persuade instead of scream. ("I see your point, sister. However, have you considered the analogy of the international frontier?")

At the age of two, my son, George, became a devotee of what rhetoricians call "argument by the stick"; when words failed him, he used his fists. After every fight I would ask him: "Did you get the other kid to agree with you?" For years he considered that to be a thoroughly stupid question, and maybe it was. But eventually it made sense to him: argument by the stick — fighting — is no argument. It never persuades, it only inspires revenge or retreat. . . .

On the other hand, when George Foreman tries to sell you a grill, he makes an argument: persuasion that tries to change your mood, your mind, or your willingness to do something.

Homer Simpson offers a legitimate argument when he demonstrates our intellectual superiority to dolphins: "Don't forget — we invented computers, leg warmers, bendy straws, peel-and-eat shrimp, the glory hole, *and* the pudding cup."

Mariah Carey pitches an argument when she sings, "We belong together," to an assumed ex-boyfriend; she tries to change his mind (and judging by all the moaning in the background, get some action).

Daughter screaming at her parents: *fight.*
Business proposal: *argument.*
Howard Dean saying of Republicans, "A lot of them have never made an honest living in their lives": *fight.*
Yogi Berra saying, "It's not the heat, it's the humility": *argument.*

The basic difference between an argument and a fight: an argument, done skillfully, gets people to want to do what you want. You fight to win; you argue to achieve agreement.   —JAY HEINRICHS, *Thank You for Arguing*

The main purpose here is to explain to readers the differences between fighting and arguing: "You fight to win; you argue to achieve agreement," and Heinrichs's own argument becomes more clear when he classifies examples of each form of debate.

Heinrichs's classifications do not just inform, however; they also entertain. If entertainment is your main purpose, you might take as a model Ken Brower's article in the March 2009 issue of *National Geographic*, which delights readers by describing the beauty of the blue whale in the wild. To achieve his purpose, he relies on division to offer readers a picture of what it's like to see a whale, starting with the first moment he sees the whale's blow to the last moment he captures a view of its "flukeprint."

Division to Entertain

The first we saw of a whale was almost always its blow.

When the sun was behind us, we sometimes saw a prismatic scatter of color in the explosive expansion of spray and vapor — a few milliseconds of rainbow — before the color shimmered out and the spout faded to white.

Whenever a blue whale surfaced to blow nearby, I was struck by the blowhole — a pair of nostrils countersunk atop the tapering mound of the splash guard, built up almost into a kind of nose on the back of the head. Other baleen whales have splash guards too, but not like this. This nose was almost Roman. It seemed disproportionately large, even for the biggest of whales. Its size explained that loud, concussive exhalation — less a breath than a detonation — and its size explained the 30-foot spout. It was a mighty blow, followed quickly by a mighty inhalation.

The second thing we saw of the whale was its back.

The blue whale is "a light bluish gray overall, mottled with gray or grayish white," as one field guide describes it, and the back is often, indeed, this advertised color, but just as often, depending on the light, the back shows as silvery gray or pale tan. Whichever the color, the back always has a glassy shine. When you are close, you see the water sluicing off the vast back, first in rivulets and sheets, and then in a film that flows in lovely, pulsed patterns downhill to the sea.

If blue whales above water are only putatively blue, then below the surface they go indisputably turquoise. *Balaenoptera musculus* is a pale whale, and when seen through the blue filter of the ocean, its pallor goes turquoise or aquamarine. This view of the whale, downward through 20 to 50 feet of water, is for me the most haunting and evocative.

If the most beautiful hue of the blue whale is turquoise, then the most beautiful form, the finest sculpture, is in the flukes. In the first week of our tagging efforts, the tail always seemed to be waving goodbye. "Ta-ta," it signaled. "Nice try. Better luck next time." When a whale showed its flukes — when the two palmate blades poised high in the air — we would break off the chase, because elevated flukes meant a deep dive.

But sometimes we saw the flukes close under the surface. They were huge, wider than the boat, and in motion they were hypnotically lovely. "In no living thing are the lines of beauty more exquisitely defined than in the crescentic borders of these flukes," Melville writes in *Moby Dick*.

The last thing we saw of the whale was its "flukeprint."

When a whale or dolphin swims at shallow depths, turbulence from its flukes rises to form a circular slick on the surface: the footprint or flukeprint. The flukeprints of blue whales are large and surprisingly persistent. The smooth patch lingers long after the whale is gone. "It's a measure of how much energy is in the stroke," Mate told me one afternoon when he caught me staring at one of these slicks. The circle of the flukeprint is perfectly smooth, except for a few faint curves that mark the continued upwelling of energy. Eventually the chop of the ocean begins to erode the slick from the outside inward, but only slowly.

—KEN BROWER, "Still Blue"

By educating and entertaining his readers, Brower persuades them to value the beauty of the blue whale, and also to see the value of preserving and protecting its habitat. You, too, may want to use classification and division to help you argue a point. By classifying or dividing in specific ways, you can encourage readers to adopt your point of view or change their behavior.

For example, someone who made a comment to a blog posting about People for the Ethical Treatment of Animals (PETA) used a classification of four levels of human (or humane) attitudes toward treatment of animals. Beginning with the attitude that "wanton cruelty for no purpose to animals that can feel pain is wrong," the classification proceeds through the attitude that "no pain we can avoid causing them is OK" to the attitude of what the commenter calls "the real crazies, where animal life is more important than human." The fourth and final category is the attitude of PETA, "a whole level of crazy beyond that." For each level or category of attitude, the writer gives details about it and examples of the consequences that would supposedly result from adopting it, ranging from banning overcrowded factory farming at the first level to "feral cats and dogs wandering everywhere and eventually attacking people" at the last one.

Clearly, the purpose of this classification is to make the first two categories seem reasonable and the last two "crazy." Whether or not you agree with this particular writer, you can see how classifying and dividing in this way can contribute to a powerful argument. For example, if you're making an argument about grading policies at your college, you might classify professors in groupings from "easy" (or even "too easy") to "average," "hard," or "too hard" in order to argue that there are too many professors in certain groups relative to others.

When you've answered the question "What is my point, exactly, in creating these categories or parts?" you've come close to determining your **thesis statement** (the controlling idea) for your classification or division.

● Considering Your Audience

Had Jay Heinrichs written his book for an academic audience instead of a popular audience, chances are his excerpt would be much different. Even though he would have used the same categories (fighting and arguing), he might have chosen different examples to explain his classifications: instead of Mariah Carey and Homer Simpson, perhaps Socrates and Kenneth Burke. In addition, he might have incorporated more scholarship from studies of argument (rhetoric) to support his claims and to create common ground with his readers. This kind of support isn't necessary for a more popular audience, who would most likely be less familiar with or less interested in recent scholarship in rhetorical studies.

When you're writing an essay based on or making use of classification and division, be sure to consider your audience carefully. Decide who your readers are and how best to pitch your writing to those readers. For instance, if you're writing a column for the student newspaper to inform readers about various kinds of restaurants on or near campus, you might decide to classify them on the basis of price or type of food. If your column is about where to go for a special occasion, however, you'll want to reenvision your readers as celebrants; therefore, you might want to make your classification more persuasive in purpose, describing upscale restaurants and clubs and their individual atmospheres and specialties. Audience analysis is closely related to purpose: as you consider *how* to achieve your purpose, you'll need to consider the effect these strategies will have on your readers.

● Defining the Categories or Parts

To be successful, a classification or division must follow a **ruling principle** for the categories or parts—a uniform way of grouping the information. For example, the principle ruling the list of physicians in the Yellow Pages is their medical specialty. Under this principle, the list is *consistent*—every category is a medical specialty. It is *exclusive*—the listings don't overlap, and no physician is listed in more than one. And it is *complete*—every physician is listed.

When you set up categories and parts, you'll want to be sure to meet these three qualifications. For example, if you were writing the newspaper column about restaurants, you wouldn't want to mix categories such as "full meals under $10" and "full meals $10 to $20" with ones such as "Italian" and "informal." This classification is not consistent or exclusive; because the ruling principle is price for the first two categories, type of food for the third, and atmosphere for the fourth, a single restaurant could fall into two or even three categories. Any of these principles might work perfectly well for your column, but they can't be combined.

Or say that you were writing a paper for a political science class and making an argument based on a survey of students at your school about their political affiliation. If your survey covered only Republicans and Democrats, your classification would be incomplete and your argument would be weakened because some students are probably independents or supporters of smaller parties—not to mention those who have no interest in politics at all.

As this example suggests, we often tend to classify or divide things into only two opposing groups—black or white, male or female, conservative or liberal. Sometimes this is useful, but be careful not to oversimplify a classification or division by creating too few categories or parts.

● **Arranging All the Parts**

You need to keep all these considerations in mind as you draft an essay or passage using classification or division, but your purpose and your thesis statement, in particular, will actually determine the organizational pattern. You might find a good reason to move chronologically; logically, based on the way one category or part relates to the next; or emphatically, starting with the least important category or part and ending with the most important — which could be the largest, the most complex, the most entertaining, or the most persuasive.

In a classification and division that extends over several paragraphs or a whole essay, you'll want to introduce each of the categories or parts with a **topic sentence** that not only reflects your thesis statement but also previews the ways you will develop that category or part. As you move from one category or part to the next, use **transitions** — words or phrases that take the reader along with you: "*At one end*, there are the raucous dance halls, . . ."; "*However*, have you considered the analogy of the international frontier?"

Student writer Jessica Moyer uses the opening paragraph of her essay to indicate to her readers that her ideas will be organized emphatically.

> As I sit here and think about the friends that I have had or do have in my life, I am amazed at the eclectic opportunities and diversities that each of my friendships has offered me, whether they were developed in high school, at college, or through work. I am a complex person with many different and sometimes seemingly contradictory personality traits, yet my personality as a whole can be divided into three very distinct but general categories: the academic side, the work side, and the social side. I seem to have one specific friend for each side of my personality, as well as a best friend who is in a category all her own.
>
> —JESSICA MOYER, "My Circle of Friends"

Moyer makes clear the reason for this organizational pattern. She is saving the best for last; her best friend is "in a category all her own."

Ken Brower divides his description of the blue whale into its various parts by using chronological order, meaning that he describes the parts in the sequence in which he and his crewmates saw them. To arrange his description in this way, Brower chooses effective transitional words: "The *first* we saw of the whale was almost always its blow"; "The *second* thing we saw of the whale was its back"; "The *last* thing we saw of the whale was its 'flukeprint.'"

● **Providing Details**

The details and examples that you use in explaining each category or part help keep your classification or division appropriately balanced, consistent, and complete. For instance, if you're writing a newspaper

"Reading" and Using Visuals in Classification and Division

This chapter introduction uses a number of visuals, from the Brothers Pizza menu (p. 268) and the *Consumer Reports* used car guide (p. 272) to the accompanying U.S. Census Bureau map that designates the percentage of Spanish speakers by county as reported in the 2000 census. Each of these visuals is a model of classification or division, yet they all look different, have different purposes, and make different points. You can also use various kinds of visuals to enhance your own classifications and divisions, but to understand how to do so most effectively, you need to learn how to "read" visuals closely and critically the same way you do written classifications and divisions. Learning to do this kind of analysis will help you understand what kinds of visuals and what details and arrangements of them are most effective (and which ones are not effective) in achieving your purpose, appealing to your audience, and supporting the points you're making in your written text.

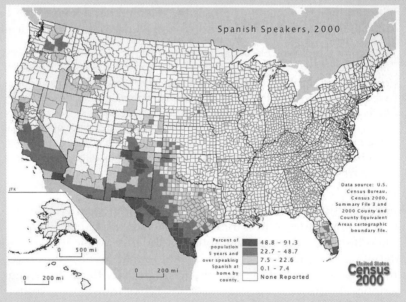

The census map of Spanish speakers in the United States offers a good deal of information, and by studying it carefully and critically, readers can learn much from its classifications and divisions. The first step in reading the map is to note—from the title at the top and the key at the bottom—that it divides the country into concentrations of Spanish speakers. Although we can see from the dark lines how the country is divided into states, the important divisions are the smaller areas that designate the *counties* in each state. (Both the key and the brief note on the right of the map offer this information.) Notice that the county divisions on the map are designated by specific colors—colors that represent the concentration of Spanish speakers in each county: the darker the color, the higher the concentration of Spanish speakers. Counties designated by the darkest color have a concentration between 48.8 and 91.3 percent, while those designated by the lightest color have a concentration between 0.1 and 7.4 percent. Finally, observe that a few areas of the map are left white. This doesn't mean there are no Spanish speakers in the county. As the key explains, the counties colored white are those in which there were no Spanish speakers *reported*, which does not necessarily mean there were none *present*.

The classifications and divisions on this map are interesting in their own right, but it's important to consider what this visual *does* and *can do* for writers and readers. First, think about how much more efficiently this map conveys information than a purely verbal explanation would. It would take pages of tedious text to explain the concentrations of Spanish speakers in almost every county in the country. The map, by contrast, conveys this information almost instantly. After assessing the key and the short informational text on the map, readers can easily see where high and low concentrations of Spanish speakers are. They can choose any place that interests them—their home county or part of a state, for instance—and quickly see the percentage of the population that speaks Spanish.

But it's also interesting to consider how writers might employ this visual to make an argument. For instance, someone interested in programs to teach English to immigrants might identify places of interest and need by learning where the highest concentrations of Spanish speakers reside and then lobby for more classes in that area. Or residents or government officials in Washington state, for example, might use the map to argue that their state should receive more funding for translating public documents, since some counties in this state have proportionally just as many Spanish speakers as counties in California, Texas, and Florida.

As you prepare your own classifications and divisions, consider using visuals of some kind, reviewing the ones throughout this book in order to determine which kind might work best for your writing project. As you can see, visuals can emphasize or clarify points you want the reader to understand or agree with, or they can make your classification or division more entertaining. If you want to use visuals in writing for an academic assignment, it is a good idea to check with your instructor beforehand. You also need to consider whether to include labels or captions (if the visuals do not already include them) and whether to refer to the visuals in your written text or to let them stand on their own.

column on various kinds of student eateries—on-campus, off-campus, and private residential—you might want to include details from all types of eating places on campus: the dormitories, the rathskeller, the fraternity and sorority houses, the café run by the school of restaurant management, and so on. All the details also bring your categories to life.

The amount and kinds of details you need to provide depend on your subject, your audience, and your purpose. For instance, you may need to give more explanation or examples for categories or parts that are larger, more complex, more important to your purpose, or less familiar to your readers. In any case, it's a good idea to vary the discussion of different categories or parts just to avoid monotony, especially if there are more than two or three of them.

Look again at the excerpt by Roberto Suro in which he classifies Magnolia's cantinas into four categories: "raucous dance halls," "simple bars," "new places," and "fancy places." His use of detail is what makes these categories come alive, helping readers see the distinctions among them. At the "raucous dance halls," there are younger Mexicans and dancing bar girls. Older men frequent the simple bars, where they "drink without women and listen to *conjuntos*." The new bars play salsa and tropical music. And the fancy bars have bouncers, fancy lights, *tejano* music, and a Mexican-American clientele. These details allow Suro to capture for readers the specific identity of each cantina.

● Considering Your Conclusion

Why are you classifying or dividing this subject? What did your classification or division reveal to you? What do you want your readers to know, understand, enjoy, or do as a result of reading it? As you consider how to conclude your essay or passage using classification or division, you'll need to ask yourself these questions. Don't merely restate the thesis. You can make your conclusion purposeful and effective by carrying the thesis further and making an additional point.

Nicole Sciotto's conclusion to her *Collegian* article about the five people you meet in college carries forward the tone of the essay yet also makes a point:

> I learned from these five individuals that college is about taking yourself out of a comfortable situation and making each day new and unpredictable through meeting and learning from different kinds of people. One of the characters in [Mitch] Albom's book [*The Five People You Meet in Heaven*] said that while in heaven, "Strangers are just family you have yet to come to know." College is just as good as eternal paradise to figure that one out.

In her conclusion, Sciotto begins by summarizing what she has learned from the five influential people she met in college. She then returns to the book she references in her introduction, *The Five People You Meet in Heaven*. By returning to Albom's text, Sciotto does not simply repeat his point but extends it, connecting it to her own objectives: college is the place to "figure out" and come to know strangers as family.

Understanding and Using Classification and Division

Analyzing Classification and Division

1. What did you learn from Roberto Suro's explanation of cantinas on pages 272–73 that you didn't already know? What did you learn about your own ability to translate places such as "cantinas" into categories?

2. **Working with another classmate,** write out the ruling principle and the consistent and exclusive categories that Suro uses. Discuss how his classification helps you both understand and appreciate Magnolia's nightlife. Be prepared to share your answers with the rest of your class.

3. **Working with one or two classmates,** discuss how Inez Peterson handles classification in the excerpt on page 276. What is her ruling principle? What are her consistent and exclusive categories? Share your small group's responses with the rest of the class.

4. **Working with another student,** devise a brief response to the Peterson excerpt on identity. What do the two of you think of Peterson's ideas? What issues did you think about as you read the excerpt? Have they ever occurred to you before? If so, when? Why do they seem important? How are your responses alike and different? Prepare a joint response to share with the rest of the class.

Planning and Writing Essays Using Classification and Division

1. Review your responses to the "Try Your Hand" prompt on page 275, in which you considered the five most influential and the five most challenging people you've met since you've been at college. Choose one category with which to work (either the most influential or most challenging people), and compose a two- to three-page essay that uses Sciotto's article as a model. As you draft and revise, refer to "Checking Over the Use of Classification and Division" on page 290.

2. In the excerpt from *Thank You for Arguing* on page 281, Jay Heinrichs classifies popular examples of debate into the categories of "fight" and "argument." Think of a debate you've been involved in recently. How would you classify it? Given Heinrichs's distinctions, was it a fight or an argument? Compose a two- to three-page essay in which you first describe the debate and then discuss why it should be classified as a fight or an argument, thinking about how its features fit the definitions Heinrichs provides. Refer to "Checking Over the Use of Classification and Division" on page 290 as you draft and revise.

3. Reflect on the languages you speak. Think broadly. You might, for instance, speak fluent Spanish, Russian, or Chinese. But you might also be fluent in a kind of Pittsburghese or Appalachian dialect. Don't forget the languages you speak online; texting is a language all its own. After brainstorming your fluency in these various languages, compose a two- to three-page essay in which you classify the languages you speak, discussing the communities in which you practice them and the significance they hold in your life. Be sure to refer to "Checking Over the Use of Classification and Division" below.

4. How would you classify the dozen or so restaurants closest to your campus? What might be the purpose of such a classification? What other ruling principles can you think of to classify the same group of restaurants? Choose one ruling principle to develop into a three- to four-page essay. How does the ruling principle relate to your purpose? Be sure to refer to "Checking Over the Use of Classification and Division" below.

✔ Checking Over the Use of Classification and Division

1. Why are you writing about this group of items or this particular item? What is your purpose? Does your thesis statement reflect that purpose?

2. Who is your audience? Have you taken your audience into consideration in defining parts or categories and providing details about them?

3. What is your ruling principle? Are your categories or parts consistent and exclusive, or is there overlap among them? Are they complete, or are there items or pieces that they don't cover? If you have only two categories or parts, are you oversimplifying?

4. How have you organized the categories or parts? Is the arrangement effective? Have you used topic sentences and transitional words or phrases to help the reader follow your points and move from one category or part to the next?

5. What details and examples have you provided for each category or part? Underline them. Do any categories or parts need more explanation? Do any have too much?

6. What does your classification or division show the reader? What is the point of your conclusion? Underline your conclusion. Does it merely restate the thesis, or does it make an additional point in an effective way?

7. Have you used any visuals as part of your classification or division? If so, do they help make your points more effectively? Do you need to add labels, captions, or references to the visuals in the text? If you have not used any visuals, should you?

READINGS

BILL BRYSON
Varieties of English

Born in Des Moines, Iowa, in 1951, Bill Bryson has traveled across America and around the world, writing books such as *The Lost Continent* (1990), *A Walk in the Woods* (1999), and *In a Sunburned Country* (2001) about his adventures. In addition to his travel writing, Bryson has a deep interest in language and dialect, and he explores this topic in *Mother Tongue* (2001), *Bill Bryson's Dictionary of Troublesome Language* (2004), and *Bryson's Dictionary for Writers and Editors* (2008). The following essay is taken from *Mother Tongue*; in it, Bryson uses classification and division to consider how language and dialect work to categorize people across the country according to their region, their social ties, and their class status.

> **Preview** How does your language and dialect classify and categorize you?

1 Whether you call a long cylindrical sandwich a hero, a submarine, a hoagy, a torpedo, a garibaldi, a poor boy, or any of at least half a dozen other names tells us something about where you come from. Whether you call it cottage cheese, Dutch cheese, pot cheese, smearcase, clabber cheese, or curd cheese tells us something more. If you call the playground toy in which a long plank balances on a fulcrum a dandle you almost certainly come from Rhode Island. If you call a soft drink tonic, you come from Boston. If you call a small naturally occurring object a stone rather than a rock you mark yourself as a New Englander. If you have a catch rather than play catch or stand on line rather than in line clearly you are a New Yorker. Whether you

Note how Bryson uses exemplification to introduce his essay.

Bryson states the relationship between idiolect and classification.

Bryson uses comparison to show differences between the number of idiolects in the United States as opposed to England.

call it pop or soda, bucket or pail, baby carriage or baby buggy, scat or gesundheit, the beach or the shore—all these and countless others tell us a little something about where you come from. Taken together they add up to what grammarians call your *idiolect*, the linguistic quirks and conventions that distinguish one group of language users from another.

A paradox of accents is that in England, where 2 people from a common heritage have been living together in a small area for thousands of years, there is still a huge variety of accents, whereas in America, where people from a great mix of backgrounds have been living together in a vast area for a relatively short period, people speak with just a few voices. As Simeon Potter puts it: "It would be no exaggeration to say that greater differences in pronunciation are discernible in the north of England between Trent and Tweed [a distance of about 100 miles] than in the whole of North America." Surely we should expect it to be the other way around. In England, the prolonged proximity of people ought to militate against differences in accent, while in America the relative isolation of many people ought to encourage regional accents. And yet people as far apart as New York State and Oregon speak with largely identical voices. According to some estimates almost two thirds of the American population, living on some 80 percent of the land area, speak with the same accent—a quite remarkable degree of homogeneity.

Some authorities have suggested that once there 3 was much greater diversity in American speech than now. As evidence, they point out that in *Huckleberry Finn*, Mark Twain needed seven separate dialects to reflect the speech of various characters, even though they all came from much the same area. Clearly that would not be necessary, or even possible, today. On the other hand, it may be that thousands of regional accents exist out there and that we're simply not as alert to them as we might be.

The study of dialects is a relatively recent thing. 4 The American Dialect Society was founded as long ago as 1889, and the topic has been discussed by authorities throughout this [twentieth] century. Even so, systematic scientific investigation did not begin until well into this century. Much of the most important initial work was done by Professor Hans Kurath of the University of Michigan, who produced the seminal *Word Geography of the Eastern United States* in 1949. Kurath carefully studied the minute variations in speech to be found along the eastern seaboard—differences in vocabulary, pronunciation, and the like—and drew lines called isoglosses that divided the country into four main speech groups: Northern, Midland, Southern, and New England. Later work by others enabled these lines to be extended as far west as Texas and the prairie states. Most authorities since then have accepted these four broad divisions.

5   If you followed Kurath's isoglosses carefully enough, you could go to a field in, say, northern Iowa and stand with one foot in the Northern dialect region and the other foot in the Midland region. But if you expected to find that people on one side of the line spoke a variety of American English distinctively different from people on the other side, you would be disappointed. It is not as simple as that. Isoglosses are notional conveniences for the benefit of geographical linguists. There is no place where one speech region begins and another ends. You could as easily move the line in that Iowa field 200 yards to the north or 14 miles or perhaps even 100 miles and be no less accurate. It is true that people on the Northern side of the line *tend* to have characteristics of speech that distinguish them from people on the Midland side, but that's about as far as you can take it. Even within a single region speech patterns blur and blur again into an infinitude of tiny variations. A person in Joliet sounds quite different from a person in Texarkana, yet they are both said to live in the Midland speech area. Partly to get around this problem, Midland is now usually subdivided into North Midland and South Midland, but we are still dealing with huge generalities.

6   So only in the very baldest sense can we divide American speech into distinct speech areas. Nonetheless these speech areas do have certain broad characteristics that set them apart from one another. People from the Northern states call it frosting. To southerners it's icing. Northerners say "greasy."

Bryson discusses why linguistic classifications don't line up neatly with geographic ones.

Bryson divides the country into regions and explains the language variations of specific areas. Notice his use of exemplification in this paragraph as well.

Others say "greezy." In the East groceries are put in a bag, in the South in a poke, and everywhere else in a sack—except in one small part of Oregon where they rather mysteriously also say poke. Northerners tend to prefer the "oo" sound to the "ew" sound in words like *duty, Tuesday* and *newspaper,* saying "dooty" instead "dewty" and so on. The Northern and Northern Midland accents are further distinguished by a more clipped pattern, as evidenced by a pronounced tendency to drop words at the beginning of sentences, as in "This your house?" and "You coming?" People from the same area have less ability to distinguish between rounded vowel sounds like "ö" and "ah" such as exist between *cot* and *caught.* In the South, on the other hand, there is a general reluctance or inability to distinguish clearly between *fall* and *foal, oil* and *all, poet* and *pour it, morning* and *moaning, peony* and *penny, fire* and *far, sawer* and *sour, courier* and *Korea, ahs* and *eyes, are* and *hour,* and many others.

Sometimes these speech preferences can pinpoint speakers to a fairly precise area. People in South Carolina, for instance, say "vegetubbles," but in North Carolina it's "vegetibbles." North Carolinians also give themselves away when they say, "She's still in the bed" and "Let's do this one at the time." People in Philadelphia don't say *attitude,* they say "attytude," and they don't have a downtown, they have a center city, which is divided not into blocks but squares. In one small area of eastern Virginia people tend to say *about* and *house* as Canadians do, saying (roughly) "aboot" and "hoose." These linguistic pockets are surprisingly numerous. In southern Utah, around St. George, there's a pocket where people speak a peculiar dialect called—no one seems quite sure why—Dixie, whose principal characteristics are the reversal of "ar" and "or" sounds, so that a person from St. George doesn't park his car in a carport, but rather porks his core in a corepart. The bright objects in the night sky are stores, while the heroine of *The Wizard of Oz* is Darthy. When someone leaves a door open, Dixie speakers don't say, "Were you born in a barn?" They say, "Were you barn in a born?"

Add all these regional peculiarities together and it might be possible to trace any one person

with considerable precision. A sufficiently sophisticated computer could probably place with reasonable accuracy, sometimes to within a few miles,
almost any English–speaking person depending on
how he pronounced the following ten words: *cot,
caught, cart, bomb, balm, oil, house, horse, good,* and *water.* Just four of these words— *bomb, balm, cot,* and
caught — could serve as regional shibboleths for almost every American, according to the dialectologist W. Nelson Francis. When an American airline
received anonymous telephone threats, the linguistics authority William Labov of the University
of Pennsylvania was able to identify the caller as
coming from within a seventy–five–mile radius of
Boston. His testimony helped to clear a man from
greater New York accused of the crime.

9   Although the main dialect boundaries run
from east to west, dividing America into a kind of
linguistic layer cake, some important speech differences in fact run from north to south. People along
the East Coast tend to pronounce words such as *foreign* and *horrible* as "fahrun" and "harruble," whereas
people further west, whether from the North or
South, tend to say "forun" (or "forn") and "horruble."
People along much of the eastern seaboard can
distinguish between words that are elsewhere in
America strictly homonyms: *horse* and *hoarse, morning* and *mourning, for* and *four.* . . .

> Bryson offers another
> kind of linguistic clas-
> sification by region.

10   Why do we have all these regional variations?
Why do people in Boston and New York call white
coffee "regular" when everywhere else regular coffee is black? Why do people in Texas say "arn" for
iron? Why do so many people in New York say
"doo–awg" for *dog*, "oo–awf" for *off*, "kee–ab" for *cab*,
"thoid" for *third*, "erster" for *oyster*? There is certainly
no shortage of theories, some of which may be
charitably described as being less than half–baked.
Charlton Laird, generally a shrewd and reliable observer of the vagaries of English, writes in *The Miracle of Language*: "'The New York City variant of *doy*
for *die, boy* for *buy, thoid* for *third* suggests forms in
Yorkshire, which are reflections of the strong influence of old York upon the New York." That is just
nonsense; people in Yorkshire simply do not speak
that way and never have. Robert Hendrickson in

American Talk cites the interesting theory, which he attributes to a former professor of Hofstra University, that the New York accent may come from Gaelic. The hallmark of the New York accent is of course the "oi" diphthong as in *thoidy-thoid* for *thirty-third* and *moider* for *murder*, and Hendrickson points out that *oi* appears in many Gaelic words, such as *taoiseach* (the Irish term for prime minister). However, there are one or two considerations that suggest this theory may need further work. First, *oi* is not pronounced "oy" in Gaelic; *taoiseach* is pronounced "tea–sack." Second, there is no tradition of converting "ir" sounds to "oi" ones in Ireland, such as would result in *murder* becoming *moider*. And third, most of the Irish immigrants to New York didn't speak Gaelic anyway.

Note the way Bryson's topic sentence introduces two new kinds of classification systems.

But there are other factors at work, such as history and geography. The colonists along the eastern seaboard naturally had closer relationships with England than those colonists who moved inland. That explains at least partly why the English of the eastern seaboard tends to have so much in common with British English — the tendency to put a "yew" sound into words like *stew* and *Tuesday*, the tendency to have broader and rounder "a" and "o" sounds, the tendency to suppress "r" sounds in words like *car* and *horse*. There are also similarities of vocabulary. *Queer* is still widely used in the South in the sense of strange or odd. *Common* still has a pejorative flavor (as in "She's so common") that it lacks elsewhere in America. Ladybugs, as they are known in the North, are still called ladybirds in the South and sidewalks in some areas are called pavements, as they are in Britain. All of these are a result of the closer links between such East Coast cities as Boston, Savannah, and Charleston and Britain. 11

This topic sentence signals another shift in discussion and introduces yet another classification system.

Fashion comes into it too. When the custom arose in eighteenth–century Britain of pronouncing words like *bath* and *path* with a broad *a* rather than a flat one, the practice was imitated along the eastern seaboard, but not further inland, where people were clearly less susceptible to considerations of what fashionable society thought of them. In Boston, the new fashion was embraced to such an extent that up to the middle of the last century, ac- 12 cording to H. L. Mencken, people used the broad *a* in such improbable words as *apple, hammer, practical,* and *Saturday*.

13   Related to all these factors is probably the most important, and certainly the least understood, factor of all, social bonding, as revealed in a study by William Labov of the University of Pennsylvania, probably America's leading dialectologist. Labov studied the accents of New York City and found that they were more complicated and diverse than was generally assumed. In particular he studied the sound of *r*'s in words like *more, store,* and *car*. As recently as the 1930s such *r*'s were never voiced by native New Yorkers, but over the years they have come increasingly to be spoken — but only sometimes. Whether or not people voiced the *r* in a given instance was thought to be largely random. But Labov found that there was actually much more of a pattern to it. In a word, people were using *r*'s as a way of signaling their social standing, rather like the flickerings of fireflies. The higher one's social standing, the more often the *r*'s were flickered, so to speak. Upper–middle–class speakers pronounced the *r* about 20 percent of the time in casual speech, about 30 percent of the time in careful speech, and 60 percent of the time in highly careful speech (when asked to read a list of words). The comparable figures for lower–class speakers were 10 percent for the first two and 30 percent for the third. More than that, Labov found, most people used or disregarded *r*'s as social circumstances demanded. He found that sales assistants in department stores tended to use many more *r*'s when addressed by middle–class people than when speaking to lower–class customers. In short, there was very little randomness involved.

14   Even more interestingly, Labov found that certain vowel sounds were more specific to one ethnic group or another. For instance, the tendency to turn *bag* into something more like "be-agg" and *bad* into "be-add" was more frequent among second-generation Italians, while the tendency — and I should stress that it was no more than that — among lower–class Jewish speakers was to drawl certain "o" sounds, turning *dog* into "doo-awg," *coffee* into

www.CartoonStock.com

"coo–awfee." The suggestion is that this is a kind of hypercorrection. The speakers are unconsciously trying to distance themselves from their parents' foreign accents. Yiddish speakers tended to have trouble with certain unfamiliar English vowel sounds. They tended to turn *cup of coffee* into "cop of coffee." The presumption is that their children compensated for this by overpronouncing those vowels. Hence the accent.

So while certain distinctive pronunciations like 15 "doo–er" (or "doo–ah") for *door*, "oo–off" for *off*, "kee–ab" for *cab*, "moider" for *murder*, and so on are all features of the New York accent, almost no native New Yorker uses more than a few of them.

Outside New York, regional accents play an 16 important part in binding people together— sometimes in unexpected ways. On Martha's Vineyard the "ou" sound of *house* and *loud* was traditionally pronounced "həus" and "ləoud." With the rise of tourism, the normal, sharper American "house'" pronunciation was introduced to the island and for a while threatened to drive out the old sound. But a study reported by Professor Peter Trudgill in *Sociolinguistics* found that the old pronunciation was on the increase, particularly among people who had left the island to work and later come back. They were using the old accent as a way of distinguishing themselves from off–islanders.

Dialects are sometimes said to be used as a 17 shibboleth. People in Northern Ireland are naturally attentive to clues as to whether a person is Catholic or Protestant, and generally assume that if he has a North Down or east Belfast accent he is Protestant, and that if he has a South Armagh or west Belfast accent he is Catholic. But the differences in accent are often very slight—west Belfast people are more likely to say "thet" for *that*, while people in east Belfast say "hahn" for *hand*—and not always reliable. In fact, almost the only consistent difference is that Protestants say "aitch" for the eighth letter of the alphabet while Catholics say "haitch," though whether this quirk "has been used by both the IRA and the UDR to determine the fate of their captives," as the *Story of English* suggests, is perhaps doubtful. It is after all difficult to imagine circumstances in which a captive could be made to enunciate the letter *h* without being aware of the crucial importance for his survival of how he pronounced it.

18   Dialects are not just matters of localities and regions. There are also occupational dialects, ethnic dialects, and class dialects. It is not too much to say, given all the variables, that dialects vary from house to house, indeed from room to room within each house, that there are as many dialects in a language as there are speakers. As Mario Pei has noted, no two people in any language speak the same sounds in precisely the same way. That is of course what enables us to recognize a person by his voice. In short, we each have our own dialect. . . .

Bryson offers three other ways to classify dialects.

19   With all their grammatical intricacies and deviations from standard vocabulary, dialects can sometimes become almost like separate languages. . . . In America, a case is sometimes made to consider Cajun a separate tongue. Cajun is still spoken by a quarter of a million people (or more, depending on whose estimates you follow) in parts of Louisiana. The name is a corruption of *Acadian*, the adjective for the French-speaking inhabitants of Acadia (based on Nova Scotia, but taking in parts of Quebec and Maine) who settled there in 1604 but were driven out by the British in the 1750s. Moving to the isolated bayous of southern Louisiana, they continued to speak French but were cut off from their linguistic homeland and thus forced to develop their own vocabulary to a large extent. Often it is more colorful and expressive than the parent tongue. The Cajun for hummingbird, *sucfleur* ("flower-sucker"), is clearly an improvement on the French *oiseaumouche*. Other Cajun terms arc *rat du bois* ("rat of the woods")

Note Bryson's uses of an extended example to support his claim about dialects as separate languages.

for a possum and *sac à lait* ("sack of milk") for a type of fish. The Cajun term for the language they speak is Bougalie or Yats, short for "Where y'at?" Their speech is also peppered with common French words and phrases: *merci, adieu, c'est vrai* ("it's true"), *qu'est-ce que c'est* ("what is it"), and many others. The pronunciation has a distinctly Gallic air, as in their way of turning long "ā" sounds into "eh" sounds so that *bake* and *lake* become "behk" and "lehk." And finally, as with most adapted languages, there's a tendency to use nonstandard grammatical forms: *bestest* and *don't nobody know*.

Bryson offers another extended example to further support his argument.

A similar argument is often put forward for 20 Gullah, still spoken by up to a quarter of a million people mostly on the Sea Islands of Georgia and South Carolina. It is a peculiarly rich and affecting blend of West African and English. Gullah (the name may come from the Gola tribe of West Africa) is often called Geechee by those who speak it, though no one knows why. Those captured as slaves suffered not only the tragedy of having their lives irretrievably disrupted but also the further misfortune of coming from one of the most linguistically diverse regions of the world, so that communication between slaves was often difficult. If you can imagine yourself torn from your family, shackled to some Hungarians, Russians, Swedes, and Poles, taken halfway around the world, dumped in a strange land, worked like a dog, and shorn forever of the tiniest shred of personal liberty and dignity, then you can perhaps conceive the background against which creoles like Gullah arose. Gullah itself is a blend of twenty-eight separate African tongues. So it is hardly surprising if at first glance such languages seem rudimentary and unrefined. As Robert Hendrickson notes in his absorbing book *American Talk,* "The syntactic structure, or underlying grammar, of Gullah is . . . extraordinarily economical, making the language quickly and readily accessible to new learners." But although it is simple, it is not without subtlety. Gullah is as capable of poetry and beauty as any other language.

One of the first serious investigations into Gul- 21 lah was undertaken by Joel Chandler Harris, known for his Uncle Remus stories. Harris, born in 1848 in Eatonton, Georgia, was a painfully shy newspaperman with a pronounced stammer who grew up deeply ashamed that he was illegitimate. He became fascinated with the fables and language of former slaves during the period just after the Civil War and recorded them with exacting diligence in stories that were published first in the *Atlanta Constitution* and later compiled into books that enjoyed a considerable popularity both in his lifetime and after it. The formula was to present the stories as if they were being told by Uncle Remus to the small son of a plantation owner. Among the best known were *Nights with Uncle Remus* (1881), *The Tar Baby* (1904), and *Uncle Remus and Br'er Rabbit* (1906). All of these employed the patois spoken by mainland blacks. But Harris also produced a series of Gullah stories, based on a character called Daddy Jack. This was a considerably different dialect, though Harris thought it simpler and more direct. It had—indeed still has—no gender and no plurals. *Dem* can refer to one item or to hundreds. Apart from a few lingering West African terms like *churrah* for splash, *dafa* for fat, and *yeddy* or *yerry* for hear, the vocabulary is now almost entirely English, though many of the words don't exist in mainstream English. *Dayclean*, for instance, means "dawn" and *trut mout* (literally "truth mouth") means "a truthful speaker." Other words are truncated and pronounced in ways that make them all but unidentifiable to the uninitiated. *Nead* is Gullah for underneath. Learn is *lun*, thirsty is *tusty*, the other is *turrer*, going is *gwan*.

22   Without any doubt, the most far-flung variety of English is that found on Tristan da Cunha, a small group of islands in the mid-Atlantic roughly halfway between Africa and South America. Tristan is the most isolated inhabited place in the world, 1,500 miles from the nearest landfall, and the local language reflects the fact. Although the inhabitants have the dark looks of the Portuguese who first inhabited the islands, the family names of the 300-odd islanders are mostly English, as is their language—though with certain quaint differences reflecting their long isolation from the rest of the world. It is often endearingly ungrammatical. People don't say "How are you?" but "How you is?" It also has many wholly local terms. *Pennemin*

is a penguin; *watrem* is a stream. But perhaps most strikingly, spellings are often loose. Many islanders are called Donald, but the name is always spelled Dondall. Evidently one of the first users misspelled it that way generations ago and the spelling stuck.

Reading Closely

1. What surprised you in this essay? Identify the places in the text that surprised you. What did you learn about language variety and dialect?
2. **Working with a classmate,** review Bryson's use of topic sentences. How do they work to provide both a link between ideas and a preview for what's to come?
3. Bryson refers to scholars who study language and dialect. What does he say are the reasons for and goals of these investigations?
4. One way that Bryson classifies language variety is by geographic location. Look at the cartoon on page 298. What does it say about the ways language varies in smaller geographic regions like restaurants, for instance?

Considering Larger Issues

1. What might be the purpose of Bryson's essay — to argue, entertain, or inform? Use textual evidence to support your answer.
2. Who is the audience for this essay? What clues in the text help you make this assessment?
3. Why is it important to investigate the ways language differences can be classified? What larger conversations about language, education, and intelligence does Bryson's essay engage? Why are these conversations significant or not?
4. COMBINING METHODS. How does Bryson use *cause-and-effect analysis* in this essay? Mark the passages that use this method of development. How does this method work with classification and division? How does it contribute to the overall argument?

Thinking about Language

1. Use the context of the essay or your dictionary to define the following words. Be prepared to share your answers with the rest of the class.

cylindrical (1)	seminal (4)	drawl (14)
fulcrum (1)	isoglosses (4)	hypercorrection (14)
grammarians (1)	shibboleth (8)	enunciate (17)
idiolect (1)	linguistics (8)	rudimentary (20)
paradox (2)	vagaries (10)	patois (21)
homogeneity (2)	diphthong (10)	truncated (21)
dialect (3)		

2. Bryson uses humor throughout the essay. Pinpoint places in the text that you found humorous. What language does Bryson use to contribute to the humor?

Writing Your Own Essays Using Classification and Division

1. Spend a few days observing and listening to the languages and dialects being used in your area or on your campus. Take careful notes of your observations, recording the ways people speak. Choose three people who use different languages or dialects. Interview these people, asking them about their language background and use. Once you've completed your interviews, write a three- to four-page essay in which you classify the types of language used in your area, using your interview subjects as examples. As you draft and revise, refer to the guidelines for checking over the use of classification and division on page 290.

2. Bryson classifies language and dialect in terms of region, but he also considers how history, fashion, social bonding, and social class create language categories. Reflect on your own language choices (your dialect). Compose a two- to three-page essay in which you discuss how your language use classifies you in a category (or categories) not based on geographic location. Like Bryson, use exemplification to make your points more effective and convincing. As you draft and revise, refer to the guidelines for checking over the use of classification and division on page 290.

BILL PRATT

Interview Questions: Most Common, Illegal, and Questions You Should Never Ask

Economist Bill Pratt holds an M.B.A. in finance and has worked for the federal government and as a vice president of Citigroup. He now writes books about finance primarily for college-age audiences. His works include *Extra Credit: The 7 Things Every College Student Needs to Know about Credit, Debt, and Ca$h* (2008) and *The Graduate's Guide to Life and Money* (2009). In addition to his writing, Pratt travels around the country speaking to high school and college audiences about topics ranging from finances to career choices. The following essay, published in the March 10, 2009, issue of *Young Money* magazine, is an excerpt from *The Graduate's Guide to Life and Money.*

> **Preview**   Have you ever been on an interview? What questions did the interviewer ask you? How did you handle the experience?

Last week we looked at how to begin your interview and ensure you arrive on time. This week we will look at some sample interview questions, including illegal ones, and the four types of questions to NEVER ask during your interview.

Smile and firmly shake the interviewer's hand. If the interviewer is of the opposite sex, wait for him or her to extend his or her hand first. If you do extend your hand first, don't worry about it. The worst move would be to pull your hand back and make yourself look weak. If the interviewer begins to fumble around for a copy of your resume, or appears to not have a copy handy, offer him or her one.

There are two types of questions at an interview: the questions the interviewer asks you and the questions you will ask the interviewer. We will discuss both types of questions as well as those that should not be asked.

At the end of the interview, you will usually have the opportunity to ask a few questions. If you don't want the job, don't ask questions. Since you did your research, you probably know a few things of interest about the company that were not brought up during the interview. Ask about them. For instance, "I read recently that the company has more than 100 employees. Are all of the employees at this location?" The point is, you did your homework on the company, and you want them to know it.

Below are some possible questions the interviewer may ask:

- Where do you see yourself in five years?
- Do you have any difficulty working with others?
- Why do you want to work here?
- Why should we hire you?

- How well do you handle stress?
- What are your strengths?
- What are your weaknesses?
- What is your biggest pet peeve?
- What do you think of your previous employer?
- What did you like most about your last job?
- What did you like least about your last job?
- What was the last book you read? What did you learn?
- What starting salary do you expect?
- Do you prefer to work independently or with others?
- Where else have you applied?
- Why did you leave your last job?
- Why did you choose your major?
- How does your experience and education relate to this job?
- Describe a situation where you had to deal with a difficult customer.
- Give me an example where you tried something new and it worked.
- Give me an example where you tried something new and it failed.

Of course, **some questions are illegal.** Do not get too defensive 6
right away, because sometimes the interviewer is not intentionally trying

to ask these questions as a means to make a hiring decision; he or she may simply be trying to make small talk. Sometimes the person doing the interview is just as nervous as you are. If one of the following illegal questions is asked, respond professionally. Either turn it back into a question, or respond by merely brushing across the answer and mentioning how it will not affect your performance.

Illegal questions include the following: 7

- Are you married?
- How old are you?
- What religion do you practice?
- Do you have children?
- Are you planning to have children?

A good response to one of the illegal questions may be, "I pride myself in separating my work life from my family responsibilities."

Next are some questions you may want to ask the interviewer: 8

- When do you expect to make a decision on this position?
- Am I replacing someone who moved on from this position or is it a new position?
- What is the expected career track with this position?

There are also a few questions you should not ask the inter- 9
viewer:

- What type of salary can I expect?
- What kind of benefits do you offer?
- Do I get a discount on any of your products?
- Can I wear blue jeans on Fridays?

When the interviewer is ready to discuss salary and benefits, he or she will bring it up. If the interviewer does not mention it, don't worry about it until you are called back after the interview. If you are offered the job without having discussed any of the benefits, then you should bring this up before accepting the offer. You should also try to get an offer in writing. The easiest way to approach this topic is to ask your employer if the company will be sending you the offer in the mail. If not, then ask him or her to do so.

Next week we will look at the one thing you MUST do after an inter- 10
view, and a sample of what it should look like.

Reading Closely

1. What is the purpose of this essay? What clues in the text reveal this purpose?

2. Pratt chooses to write in the second person throughout the essay, directing his message to "you." Why do you think Pratt makes this choice? Is it effective?

3. What ruling principle does Pratt use to classify his essay about interview questions? Why does this ruling principle make sense given his audience and purpose? What other ruling principle possibilities might Pratt have chosen for this topic?

4. How does the visual on page 305 support—or why does it not support—the overarching purpose of Pratt's essay?

Considering Larger Issues

1. Look at the questions that the interviewer might ask. Pick two questions that stand out to you. Why would the interviewer ask these questions? What is he or she trying to learn by asking them?

2. Look at the illegal questions. Why are these classified as illegal? Why is it important that interviewers *not* ask such questions?

3. Look at the questions the interviewee might ask the interviewer. Why are these good questions to ask? What do they say about the interviewee as a potential employee?

4. Look at the questions the interviewee should *not* ask the interviewer. Why should the interviewee avoid these questions? What do these questions say about the interviewee as a potential employee?

5. COMBINING METHODS. How does Pratt use *exemplification* throughout the essay? How does this method of development reinforce the purpose of the essay?

Thinking about Language

1. **Working with a classmate,** review the arrangement of the essay. How does Pratt organize his classifications? What textual cues and signposts does he use to create this organizational pattern? What is its effect on the reader?

2. Identify and list the transition words Pratt uses in the essay. How do these specific words help move the essay along?

Writing Your Own Essays Using Classification and Division

1. Reflect on the work experiences you've had. Write for ten minutes about these experiences, thinking about the range of work you've done. Once you've finished writing, classify your experiences using a ruling principle that makes sense to you. You might, for instance, choose to classify your experiences from least to most challenging. Or you might choose to classify your experiences according to the kind of gratification you received (financial, emotional, educational, intellectual). Once you choose your

ruling principle, draft a three- to four-page essay that elaborates on how you've classified your work experiences. As you draft and revise, refer to the guidelines for checking over the use of classification and division on page 290.

2. In a three- to four-page essay, consider your career goals by first identifying the career you'd like to enter and then classifying the various types of experiences that would prepare you for this career. To help you compose this essay, research this career and interview one person who already works in this capacity. As you research, focus on questions like these: What kind of work do people in this career do? What kinds of preparation help potential candidates achieve this career goal (summer internships, volunteer work, part-time jobs)? What majors, minors, and academic work (clubs, research assistantships) would help you achieve your career goals? Then draft your essay, using the ruling principle of preparation to guide your writing. Make sure that you explain fully the types of preparation you might need, the reasons why this preparation would be helpful, and the kind of work you'd do in each type of preparatory experience. As you draft and revise, refer to the guidelines for checking over the use of classification and division on page 290.

SUZANNE GROVE

Hunter S. Thompson—Three Ways

● Suzanne Grove (b. 1987) wrote this essay when she was a student at the University of Pittsburgh. Her career goal is to teach English at the high school or possibly collegiate level. In addition, Grove hopes to continue writing both fiction and nonfiction and someday publish books in both of these genres. She uses as inspiration for her writing the works of e.e. cummings, F. Scott Fitzgerald, Nick Hornby, and Hunter S. Thompson. In the following essay, Grove works to rewrite the stereotypical image of Thompson by persuading readers to see beyond this image to the other sides of this acclaimed but misunderstood journalist.

> **Preview**   What (if anything) do you know about Hunter S. Thompson and his best-known work, *Fear and Loathing in Las Vegas?*

In a 1978 episode of *Omnibus,* the British Broadcasting Corporation (BBC) 1
television documentary series, Hunter S. Thompson readies himself for his interview perched on a white lawn chair, his forehead shaded by a casino dealer visor with the words "Fabulous LAS VEGAS" scrawled across the flap in white lettering. The camera pulls back as he pours a bottle of whiskey into an ice–filled glass and then catches him panicking when he drops a bag of some unnamed drug into the grass beneath his feet. Throughout the interview, Thompson shifts uncomfortably, his face alternating among expressions of intense concentration, annoyance, and sincerity. When the interviewer, in an attempt to bring Thompson's wandering mind back to the interview, asks whether he feels "pressure to live up to the image you've created," Thompson smiles, sighs, and cocks his head to the side as if he's heard that one before ("Fear and Loathing").

This initial, familiar image of the incisive journalist living outside 2
society and gobbling up drugs is the image that haunted Thompson and overshadowed much of his life and work. But there were two other, equally impressive sides to this man: the aspiring novelist and the political analyst. Although not nearly as well known to the public, the other sides of Thompson were equally if not more important in his own eyes and deserve to be remembered.

American–born Hunter S. Thompson (1937–2005) created gonzo 3
journalism, a genre of reportage in which the journalist becomes part of the story itself, writing subjectively and in the first person about his or her experiences. It often requires that the reporter fictionalize events and details in order to convey a truthful message. Among Thompson's best-known gonzo journalism pieces are *Hell's Angels: The Strange and Terrible Saga of the Outlaw Motorcycle Gangs,* in which Thompson travels and lives with Hell's Angels cyclists for over a year, and "The Hashbury Is the Capital of the Hippies," in which he writes of San Francisco's hippie drug culture.

But his most famous contribution to the gonzo genre remains *Fear and Loathing in Las Vegas.*

Fear and Loathing engraved Thompson's image on the American cul-   4
tural landscape—or at least the image of his main character, and sometimes alter ego, Raoul Duke. When the book was made into a 1988 movie,
Johnny Depp's portrayal of Raoul Duke catapulted the character, as well
as Thompson himself, to iconic status. Both the book and movie are first-
person narrations, documenting a journalist's assignment to the Mint 500
auto race in Las Vegas, which accounts for the tendency of readers and
viewers alike to conflate the drug-using, joy-riding Duke with Thompson.
In the opening pages of *Fear and Loathing*, Thompson offers an inventory
of the drug stash that Duke shares with his attorney:

> The sporting editors had . . . given me $300 in cash, most of which
> was already spent on extremely dangerous drugs. The trunk of the
> car looked like a mobile police narcotics lab. We had two bags of
> grass, seventy-five pellets of mescaline, five sheets of high-powered
> blotter acid, a salt shaker half full of cocaine, and a whole galaxy of
> multi-colored uppers, downers, screamers, laughers . . . and also a
> quart of tequila, a quart of rum, a case of Budweiser, a pint of raw
> ether and two dozen amyls. (4)

Through Duke, Thompson clearly paints an image of a writer on the
edge—one whose drug life and work life were one and the same.

Duke and Thompson, however, were not one, despite the fact that   5
Thompson's public image—of a delusional, strangely attired man standing awkwardly in a drug-induced haze, a press pass swinging from his
neck, calling journalistic ethics into question—was so closely aligned
with his real self. Thompson's own drug use did not come anywhere
close to that of the fictional Duke, who constantly remained in an altered
state, taking monstrous doses of everything from LSD to mescaline. Although no one but Thompson knows the extent of his own drug use, he
seems to have been more conservative (otherwise, he'd have been dead
long before age 50). In his letters, Thompson admitted that he had experimented with nearly every illegal substance available to him, and he
made regular references to drugs and drug use in his later years. In 2008,
Jann Wenner, cofounder of *Rolling Stone*, told a National Public Radio interviewer that "Hunter was a drug addict . . . he admitted it . . . and sadly
towards the end it took him over and it destroyed him" ("Portrait"). The
media have fed the public a steady dose of *only* this image—a hybrid of
real Thompson and the fictional Duke—and people have greedily consumed it and rubbed their bellies with a sly grin, refusing to so much
as glance at the real Thompson, whom they believe to be an unsightly
blemish on America.

But Thompson was far more than a man on the proverbial drug-   6
crazed edge. Some of the most important parts of his personality have
been deemphasized and often pushed aside. Specifically, Thompson's life

Hunter S. Thompson as photographed in 1976 (left) and at an unidentified date (right)

was marked by his passion for two things: his desire to spend his days writing fiction and become the next F. Scott Fitzgerald and his wish to explore American politics through writing.

Perhaps the greatest representation of Thompson's identity that re- 7 mains absent from his stereotypical image involves his passion for fiction writing. Though usually referred to as a journalist, Thompson much preferred writing and creating new forms of fiction. Back in his twenties, he had already announced that journalism was just a job, while fiction writing was his ambition. In 1965, at the age of 28, Thompson wrote to Pulizer Prize winner William J. Kennedy:

> I should have quit journalism . . . and hit the fiction for all I was worth. And if I'm ever to be worth anything I honestly think it will have to be in the realm of fiction, [which is] the only way I can live with my imagination, point of view, instincts, and all those other intangibles that make people nervous in my journalism. (Kennedy xix).

Even though Thompson was never able to "quit" journalism, he dedi- 8 cated a good part of his writing life to cultivating the fiction writer in himself. At night, after finishing his journalistic writing, Thompson set about working on *The Rum Diary*, which was inspired by his time working as a reporter and stringer in Puerto Rico. But despite his work, his constant rewrites and edits, no agent or publisher wanted the novel (it was published only after Thompson's death). Still, Thompson continued chasing after his dream of becoming a published fiction writer. He wrote his friends, particularly Kennedy, about literary theory and his own stories, and he encouraged his friends to read certain novels and authors, especially F. Scott Fitzgerald.

If Thompson had been alive in the 1920s, or if F. Scott Fitzgerald hadn't died three years after Thompson's birth, Thompson surely would have written to Fitzgerald as well. Just as Jay Gatsby reaches out for the green light radiating from the end of Daisy Buchanan's dock in Fitzgerald's novel *The Great Gatsby*, Thompson spent most of his young adulthood reaching out for the kind of literary skill Fitzgerald's writing displayed. Thompson was determined to become the Fitzgerald of his generation and depict the decline of the American dream, just as Fitzgerald had done during the Jazz Age. In a 1957 letter to Susan Haselden, one of his romantic interests, Thompson wrote, "I shall return to my story, which I am counting on to bring me fame, fortune, and recognition as the new F. S. Fitzgerald" (*Proud Highway* 56). In another letter to Haselden, written only a couple of weeks later, Thompson states, "Actually, I am already the new Fitzgerald: I just haven't been recognized yet" (57). 9

Thompson first cultivated his love of Fitzgerald's works in 1956 while serving in the U.S. Air Force at Eglin Air Force Base (*Proud Highway* 29). From that point forward, he mentioned Fitzgerald in dozens of letters and began emulating Fitzgerald's style. Thompson had an intense dedication to crafting himself as a serious fiction writer, as evidenced by his copying the entirety of *The Great Gatsby*, Ernest Hemingway's *The Sun Also Rises*, and other works on his typewriter in order to better understand his favorite authors' rhythms and styles. In a 1997 interview on *The Charlie Rose Show*, Thompson said, "If you type out somebody's work, you learn a lot about [the person]. . . . Typing out parts of Faulkner, Hemingway, Fitzgerald . . . I wanted to learn from the best, I guess, and that was one way to do it. I was quite serious." Thompson not only learned about technique from these prolific writers but also became inspired by the content of their works. 10

Like Fitzgerald, Thompson was deeply invested in the ideal of the American dream and what he saw as its decline. Through his writings, Thompson was devoted to critiquing and analyzing the United States — its government, its culture, and its people. Thompson's development of this interest resulted in a stunning sort of elegy to the death of the American dream in *Fear and Loathing in Las Vegas*, as well as several other pieces observing and commenting on American society. He also voiced this interest in his correspondence. Thompson ended a letter to friend Clifford Ridley, "We will have to get together on my return so I can tell you how I'm going to write what America means" (*Proud Highway* 371). 11

This dedicated interest in America and "what America means" reveals the third side of Thompson, a part of his life that is relatively unknown to the public and absent from his public image. He deeply embedded him- 12 self into American politics at an early age. In 1970, at 33 years old, he took an active role when he ran (unsuccessfully) for sheriff of Pitkin County, Colorado. As a political junkie, Thompson constantly kept abreast of national affairs, often writing friends with his opinions on government figures and events. He was outspoken about his hatred for Richard Nixon and, in later years, his dislike of George W. Bush and his administration.

Unlike his hugely popular *Fear and Loathing in Las Vegas*, Thompson's lesser- 13 known journalistic works consistently had an overt political theme. For his book *Fear and Loathing on the Campaign Trail, 1972*, he covered that year's presidential election. He also wrote about the 1983 invasion of Grenada by U.S. armed forces and authored *Better than Sex: Confessions of a Political Junkie* (1995) about the 1992 presidential election and Bill Clinton. Thompson's last piece to be published in *Rolling Stone*, "Fear and Loathing, Campaign 2004," dealt with his experiences on the campaign trail with John Kerry.

Through these and other politically minded articles, in publica- 14 tions ranging from *Playboy* to the *New York Times Magazine*, Thompson became recognized as a political influence and analyst, to the point that the narrator of the BBC documentary credited him with influencing the youth vote for Jimmy Carter in 1976. Moreover, in a review of *Gonzo*, another documentary film about Thompson, NPR critic John Powers said, "Thompson's political writing, especially *Fear and Loathing on the Campaign Trail, 1972*, reminds us that campaign coverage was once far more ambitious than it now is" ("Portrait").

Thompson's love for politics wasn't unrequited. As Douglas Brinkley 15 noted in a *Rolling Stone* article, several politicians delivered eulogies at Thompson's funeral in 2005. John Kerry said, "I met Hunter in the days of the Vietnam Veterans Against the War. Then, last summer I offered him the vice presidency in jest. He's missed." George McGovern called him "a man of deep goodness and justice and compassion and idealism." Pat Buchanan said, "There was no one quite like Hunter. He was on the edge and beyond the edge and he was very funny." Thompson's political pieces most certainly gained him the respect, or at least notice, of those who, having careers in politics, were privileged to recognize Thompson's political contributions.

A more in-depth look at the life and works of Hunter S. Thompson 16 reveals that his mark on America was not merely one of the drug-crazed gadfly, stumbling outside the city limits of Las Vegas, Nevada. In great contrast, Thompson spent most of his days writing and working toward changing the landscape of American literature and political thought. Unfortunately, the public still focuses more on his experiments with drugs than his efforts to become a great fiction writer and enhance public discussion about American life and politics. For those willing to look beyond the gonzo persona, Thompson was a man of vigor and intelligence, who used his tremendous talent to create a unique literary voice and insightful political analysis.

WORKS CITED

Brinkley, Douglas. "Football Season Is Over." *Rolling Stone* 8 Sept. 2005: n. pag. *Rolling Stone*. Web. 1 Aug. 2008.

"Fear and Loathing in Gonzovision." *Omnibus*. BBC. 1978. *Fear and Loathing in Las Vegas*. Criterion Collection, 2003. DVD.

Kennedy, William J. "The Curse of the Bronze Plaque." Foreword. *The Proud Highway: Saga of a Desperate Southern Gentleman, 1955–1967*. By Hunter S. Thompson. Ed. Douglas Brinkley. xv–xx. New York: Ballantine, 1998. Print.

"A Portrait of the Great 'Gonzo'" Narr. John Powers. *Fresh Air*. National Public Radio. 18 July 2008. Radio.

Thompson, Hunter S. *Fear and Loathing in Las Vegas: A Savage Journey to the Heart of the American Dream*. 2nd ed. New York: Vintage, 1998. Print.

Thompson, Hunter S. Interview by Charlie Rose. *The Charlie Rose Show*. PBS. 13 June 1997. *Charlie Rose*. Web. 1 Aug. 2008.

Thompson, Hunter S. *The Proud Highway: Saga of a Desperate Southern Gentleman, 1955–1967*. Ed. Douglas Brinkley. New York: Ballantine, 1998. Print.

Reading Closely

1. What is the thesis of this essay? Underline the thesis statement. How does classification and division enable Grove to support this thesis?

2. What is the purpose of this essay?

3. What ruling principle does Grove use to achieve the purpose and support the thesis?

4. Review the photographs on page 311. How do they reflect different "sides" of Thompson? How might you place them in the categories that Grove establishes in her essay?

Considering Larger Issues

1. Why is it important to consider the "other" sides of Hunter S. Thompson?

2. **Working with a classmate,** review Grove's use of topic sentences. How do these sentences enable Grove to organize her essay and argue her case?

3. Review Grove's use of sources in this essay. What kinds of sources does she use? What purpose do these sources serve, and how do they contribute to the success of the essay?

4. COMBINING METHODS. In her essay, Grove uses *comparison and contrast, description*, and *narration* in addition to classification and division. Identify the places in the text where she uses these methods. What effect do they have on the purpose of the essay?

Thinking about Language

1. Use the context of the essay or your dictionary to define the following words. Be prepared to share your answers with the rest of the class.

    subjectively (3)   proverbial (6)   elegy (11)
    engraved (4)   stringer (8)   abreast (12)
    alter ego (4)   Jazz Age (9)   unrequited (15)
    iconic (4)   prolific (10)   persona (16)
    conflate (4)

2. Identify the words Grove uses to describe the three sides of Thompson in this essay. How do these terms help her to achieve her purpose?

Writing Your Own Essays Using Classification and Division

1. In her essay, Grove argues that readers need to reconsider Thompson's dominant and most recognizable image by seeing two other sides to this figure. Model a three- to four-page essay on Grove's work. Identify a figure like Thompson, one whom you believe is misunderstood. Then consider the other sides of this figure that most people would not know. Be sure to be detailed in your explanation of both the dominant image of your figure and the other sides that you want readers to see. As you draft and revise, refer to the guidelines for checking over the use of classification and division on page 290.

2. Categorize the stereotypes that you encounter in your daily life. Compose a three- to four-page essay that discusses these stereotypes, elaborating on the effect — negative or positive — they may have on the individuals to whom these stereotypes apply. As you draft and revise, refer to the guidelines for checking over the use of classification and division on page 290.

CAROLYN FOSTER SEGAL

The Dog Ate My Flash Drive, and Other Tales of Woe

Carolyn Foster Segal (b. 1950) is an English professor at Cedar Crest College in Allentown, Pennsylvania, where she specializes in American literature, poetry, creative writing, computer-enhanced English, and women's film. Her print publications include poems in *Buffalo Spree Magazine; Phoebe: A Journal of Feminist Scholarship, Theory, and Aesthetics;* and *The Bucks County Writer.* The following essay first appeared in the *Chronicle of Higher Education,* a newspaper for college faculty and administrators, in 2000, under the title "The Dog Ate My Disk, and Other Tales of Woe." With the author's permission, it was updated slightly for this edition of *Making Sense* to reflect changes in computer technology.

> **Preview**   What does the title tell you this essay is about? Do you have any school-related excuses that are equivalent to a dog eating a flash drive?

Taped to the door of my office is a cartoon that features a cat explain- 1 ing to his feline teacher, "The dog ate my homework." It is intended as a gently humorous reminder to my students that I will not accept excuses for late work, and it, like the lengthy warning on my syllabus, has had absolutely no effect. With a show of energy and creativity that would be admirable if applied to the (missing) assignments in question, my students persist, week after week, semester after semester, year after year, in offering excuses about why their work is not ready. Those reasons fall into several broad categories: the family, the best friend, the evils of dorm life, the evils of technology, and the totally bizarre.

The Family.   The death of the grandfather/grandmother is, of course, 2 the grandmother of all excuses. What heartless teacher would dare to question a student's grief or veracity? What heartless student would lie, wishing death on a revered family member, just to avoid a deadline? Creative students may win extra extensions (and days off) with a little careful planning and fuller plot development, as in the sequence of "My grandfather/grandmother is sick"; "Now my grandfather/grandmother is in the hospital"; and finally, "We could all see it coming — my grandfather/grandmother is dead."

Another favorite excuse is "the family emergency," which (always) 3 goes like this: "There was an emergency at home, and I had to help my family." It's a lovely sentiment, one that conjures up images of Louisa May Alcott's little women rushing off with baskets of food and copies of *Pilgrim's Progress,* but I do not understand why anyone would turn to my most irresponsible students in times of trouble.

The Best Friend.   This heartwarming concern for others extends 4 beyond the family to friends, as in, "My best friend was up all night and I had to (a) stay up with her in the dorm, (b) drive her to the hospital, or (c) drive to her college because (1) her boyfriend broke up with her, (2) she was throwing up blood [no one catches a cold anymore; everyone throws up blood], or (3) her grandfather/grandmother died."

At one private university where I worked as an adjunct, I heard an interesting spin that incorporated the motifs of both best friend and dead relative: "My best friend's mother killed herself." One has to admire the cleverness here: A mysterious woman in the prime of her life has allegedly committed suicide, and no professor can prove otherwise! And I admit I was moved, until finally I had to point out to my students that it was amazing how the simple act of my assigning a topic for a paper seemed to drive large numbers of otherwise happy and healthy middle-aged women to their deaths. I was careful to make that point during an off week, during which no deaths were reported.

The Evils of Dorm Life.   These stories are usually fairly predictable; almost always feature the evil roommate or hallmate, with my student in the role of the innocent victim; and can be summed up as follows: My roommate, who is a horrible person, likes to party, and I, who am a good person, cannot concentrate on my work when he or she is partying.

WILT

**"I lost my taste for his homework when
it came burned on a CD."**

www.CartoonStock.com

Variations include stories about the two people next door who were running around and crying loudly last night because (a) one of them had
boyfriend/girlfriend problems; (b) one of them was throwing up blood;
or (c) someone, somewhere, died. A friend of mine in graduate school
had a student who claimed that his roommate attacked him with a hammer. That, in fact, was a true story; it came out in court when the bad
roommate was tried for killing his grandfather.

The Evils of Technology. The computer age has revolutionized 7
the student story, inspiring almost as many new excuses as it has Internet
businesses. Here are just a few electronically enhanced explanations:

- The computer wouldn't let me save my work.
- The printer wouldn't print.
- The printer wouldn't print this file.
- The printer wouldn't give me time to proofread.
- The printer made a black line run through all my words, and I know you
  can't read this, but do you still want it, or wait, here, take my flash drive.
  File name? I don't know what you mean.
- I swear I attached it.
- It's my roommate's computer, and she usually helps me, but she had to
  go to the hospital because she was throwing up blood.
- I did write to the Listserv, but all my messages came back to me.
- I just found out that all my other Listserv messages came up under a
  diferent name. I just want you to know that its really me who wrote all
  those messages, you can tel which ones our mine because I didnt use the
  spelcheck! But it was yours truely :) Anyway, just in case you missed those
  messages or dont belief its my writting, I'll repeat what I sad: I thought the
  last movie we watched in clas was borring.

The Totally Bizarre. I call the first story "The Pennsylvania Chain 8
Saw Episode." A commuter student called to explain why she had missed
my morning class. She had gotten up early so that she would be wide
awake for class. Having a bit of extra time, she walked outside to see her
neighbor, who was cutting some wood. She called out to him, and he
waved back to her with the saw. Wouldn't you know it, the safety catch
wasn't on or was broken, and the blade flew right out of the saw and
across his lawn and over her fence and across her yard and severed a
tendon in her right hand. So she was calling me from the hospital, where
she was waiting for surgery. Luckily, she reassured me, she had remembered to bring her paper and a stamped envelope (in a plastic bag, to
avoid bloodstains) along with her in the ambulance, and a nurse was
mailing everything to me even as we spoke.

That wasn't her first absence. In fact, this student had missed most 9
of the class meetings, and I had already recommended that she withdraw from the course. Now I suggested again that it might be best if

she dropped the class. I didn't harp on the absences (what if even some of this story were true?). I did mention that she would need time to recuperate and that making up so much missed work might be difficult. "Oh, no," she said, "I can't drop this course. I had been planning to go on to medical school and become a surgeon, but since I won't be able to operate because of my accident, I'll have to major in English, and this course is more important than ever to me." She did come to the next class, wearing — as evidence of her recent trauma — a bedraggled Ace bandage on her left hand.

You may be thinking that nothing could top that excuse, but in fact I have 10 one more story provided by the same student, who sent me a letter to explain why her final assignment would be late. While recuperating from her surgery, she had begun corresponding on the Internet with a man who lived in Germany. After a one-week, whirlwind Web romance, they had agreed to meet in Rome, to rendezvous (her phrase) at the papal Easter Mass. Regrettably, the time of her flight made it impossible for her to attend class, but she trusted that I — just this once — would accept late work if the pope wrote a note.

Reading Closely

1. What categories does Segal provide for students' excuses? Do these categories seem believable? What about the examples within each category?

2. After reading this essay, how do you think Segal handles late work in her own courses?

3. Review the cartoon on page 317. How does it capture the ways that this age-old excuse (or lie) about missing homework has changed over the years? What other common or popular excuses do students give their teachers? How does the cartoon prompt you to think about how these old favorites might change given time and new contexts?

Considering Larger Issues

1. Who is the audience for this essay? What is Segal's purpose? How do her audience and purpose intersect?

2. What is Segal's tone in this essay? How is it related to her audience and purpose — and more important, how is her tone appropriate to the topic?

3. Would Segal need to change the tone if she were writing to students taking her course? Why or why not? Explain. Rewrite one paragraph as though it were directed at students.

4. COMBINING METHODS. How does Segal use *definition, comparison and contrast,* and *cause-and-effect analysis* to develop her argument? Mark the specific passages that use methods other than classification and division. **Working with a classmate,** compare your responses and prepare to report your findings to the rest of the class.

Thinking about Language

1. Use the context of the essay or your dictionary to define the following terms. Be prepared to share your answers with the rest of the class.

   feline (1)   adjunct (5)   harp (9)
   veracity (2)   motifs (5)   papal (10)

2. Refer to question 2 under Considering Larger Issues. What specific words or phrases reflect Segal's tone? How would you rewrite any of those phrases to convey a more sympathetic tone?

Writing Your Own Essays Using Classification and Division

1. **Working with two or three classmates,** discuss the excuses you've each given teachers for late homework, absences, or other problems. Work together to group your excuses into categories, remembering to organize according to a ruling principle. Using your notes from this group activity, draft individual two- to three-page essays in which you recount the categories of and reasons for your excuses. Your audience will be other students, and your purpose will be to entertain. As you draft and revise, refer to the guidelines for checking over the use of classification and division on page 290.

2. Reread Segal's essay, annotating her points as you read. Use your annotations as the basis for a three- to four-page classification-and-division essay about student excuses that speaks to teachers from a student's point of view. Your essay might focus on the ways teachers are unfeeling, unforgiving, or gullible — or sympathetic, tolerant, or fair and impartial — in enforcing uniform deadlines for all students. Yours can be a positive, a neutral, or a defensive response to Segal. Refer to the guidelines for checking over the use of classification and division (p. 290) as you draft and revise.

STEPHANIE ERICSSON
The Ways We Lie

San Francisco native Stephanie Ericsson (b. 1953) has published widely and for many years, but she is probably best known for her four autobiographical books, the first two of which focus on her recovery from addiction — *Shame Faced: The Road to Recovery* and *Women of AA: Recovering Together* (both in 1985) — and the last two on her eventual recovery from her husband's sudden death — *Companion through the Darkness: Inner Dialogues on Grief* (1993) and *Companion into the Dawn: Inner Dialogues on Loving* (1994).

"The Ways We Lie" first appeared in 1992 in *Utne Reader*, a magazine that covers a wide range of social, political, and lifestyle topics. Ericsson's essay was the cover story for an issue focused on the political ramifications of questions surrounding the honesty of public figures (such as President Bill Clinton, then newly elected, and Anita Hill, who had recently accused Supreme Court nominee Clarence Thomas of sexual harassment). It was reprinted in *Companion into the Dawn.*

> **Preview**   Do you ever lie? When? What kinds of lies do you tell?

The bank called today and I told them my deposit was in the mail, even though I hadn't written a check yet. It'd been a rough day. The baby I'm pregnant with decided to do aerobics on my lungs for two hours, our three-year-old daughter painted the living-room couch with lipstick, the IRS put me on hold for an hour, and I was late to a business meeting because I was tired.

I told my client that traffic had been bad. When my partner came home, his haggard face told me his day hadn't gone any better than mine, so when he asked, "How was your day?" I said, "Oh, fine," knowing that one more straw might break his back. A friend called and wanted to take me to lunch. I said I was busy. Four lies in the course of a day, none of which I felt the least bit guilty about.

We lie. We all do. We exaggerate, we minimize, we avoid confrontation, we spare people's feelings, we conveniently forget, we keep secrets, we justify lying to the big-guy institutions. Like most people, I indulge in small falsehoods and still think of myself as an honest person. Sure I lie, but it doesn't hurt anything. Or does it?

I once tried going a whole week without telling a lie, and it was paralyzing. I discovered that telling the truth all the time is nearly impossible. It means living with some serious consequences: The bank charges me $60 in overdraft fees, my partner keels over when I tell him about my travails, my client fires me for telling her I didn't feel like being on time, and my friend takes it personally when I say I'm not hungry. There must be some merit to lying.

But if I justify lying, what makes me any different from slick politicians 5
or the corporate robbers who raided the S&L industry? Saying it's okay to
lie one way and not another is hedging. I cannot seem to escape the voice
deep inside me that tells me: When someone lies, someone loses.

What far-reaching consequences will I, or others, pay as a result of 6
my lie? Will someone's trust be destroyed? Will someone else pay *my*
penance because I ducked out? We must consider the *meaning of our actions.* Deception, lies, capital crimes, and misdemeanors all carry meanings. *Webster's* definition of *lie* is specific:

1: a false statement or action especially made with the intent to deceive;

2: anything that gives or is meant to give a false impression.

A definition like this implies that there are many, many ways to tell a 7
lie. Here are just a few.

THE WHITE LIE

A man who won't lie to a woman has very little consideration for her
feelings.   — BERGEN EVANS

The white lie assumes that the truth will cause more damage than a 8
simple, harmless untruth. Telling a friend he looks great when he looks
like hell can be based on a decision that the friend needs a compliment
more than a frank opinion. But, in effect, it is the liar deciding what is
best for the lied to. Ultimately, it is a vote of no confidence. It is an act of
subtle arrogance for anyone to decide what is best for someone else.

Yet not all circumstances are quite so cut-and-dried. Take, for in- 9
stance, the sergeant in Vietnam who knew one of his men was killed in
action but listed him as missing so that the man's family would receive
indefinite compensation instead of the lump-sum pittance the military
gives widows and children. His intent was honorable. Yet for twenty years
this family kept their hopes alive, unable to move on to a new life.

FAÇADES

Et tu, Brute?   — CAESAR

We all put up façades to one degree or another. When I put on a suit 10
to go to see a client, I feel as though I am putting on another face, obey-
ing the expectation that serious businesspeople wear suits rather than
sweatpants. But I'm a writer. Normally, I get up, get the kid off to school,
and sit at my computer in my pajamas until four in the afternoon. When
I answer the phone, the caller thinks I'm wearing a suit (though the UPS
man knows better).

But façades can be destructive because they are used to seduce others 11
into an illusion. For instance, I recently realized that a former friend was

a liar. He presented himself with all the right looks and the right words and offered lots of new consciousness theories, fabulous books to read, and fascinating insights. Then I did some business with him, and the time came for him to pay me. He turned out to be all talk and no walk. I heard a plethora of reasonable excuses, including in–depth descriptions of the big break around the corner. In six months of work, I saw less than a hundred bucks. When I confronted him, he raised both eyebrows and tried to convince me that I'd heard him wrong, that he'd made no com- mitment to me. A simple investigation into his past revealed a crowded graveyard of disenchanted former friends.

IGNORING THE PLAIN FACTS

Well, you must understand that Father Porter is only human.

— A Massachusetts Priest

In the '60s, the Catholic Church in Massachusetts began hearing com- 12 plaints that Father James Porter was sexually molesting children. Rather than relieving him of his duties, the ecclesiastical authorities simply moved him from one parish to another between 1960 and 1967, actually providing him with a fresh supply of unsuspecting families and innocent children to abuse. After treatment in 1967 for pedophilia, he went back to work, this time in Minnesota. The new diocese was aware of Father Porter's obsession with children, but they needed priests and recklessly believed treatment had cured him. More children were abused until he was relieved of his duties a year later. By his own admission, Porter may have abused as many as a hundred children.

Ignoring the facts may not in and of itself be a form of lying, but 13 consider the context of this situation. If a lie is *a false action done with the intent to deceive,* then the Catholic Church's conscious covering for Porter created irreparable consequences. The church became a co–perpetrator with Porter.

DEFLECTING

When you have no basis for an argument, abuse the plaintiff.

— Cicero

I've discovered that I can keep anyone from seeing the true me by 14 being selectively blatant. I set a precedent of being up–front about inti- mate issues, but I never bring up the things I truly want to hide; I just let people assume I'm revealing everything. It's an effective way of hiding.

Any good liar knows that the way to perpetuate an untruth is to de- 15 flect attention from it. When Clarence Thomas exploded with accusations that the Senate hearings were a "high–tech lynching," he simply switched the focus from a highly charged subject to a radioactive subject. Rather than defending himself, he took the offensive and accused the country of racism. It was a brilliant maneuver. Racism is now politically incorrect in official circles—unlike sexual harassment, which still rewards those who can get away with it.

Some of the most skilled deflectors are passive–aggressive people 16 who, when accused of inappropriate behavior, refuse to respond to the accusations. This you–don't–exist stance infuriates the accuser, who, understandably, screams something obscene out of frustration. The trap is sprung and the act of deflection successful, because now the passive–aggressive person can indignantly say, "Who can talk to someone as unreasonable as you?" The real issue is forgotten and the sins of the original victim become the focus. Feeling guilty of name–calling, the victim is fully tamed and crawls into a hole, ashamed. I have watched this fighting technique work thousands of times in disputes between men and women, and what I've learned is that the real culprit is not necessarily the one who swears the loudest.

OMISSION

The cruelest lies are often told in silence.   — R. L. STEVENSON

Omission involves telling most of the truth minus one or two key 17 facts whose absence changes the story completely. You break a pair of glasses that are guaranteed under normal use and get a new pair, without mentioning that the first pair broke during a rowdy game of basketball. Who hasn't tried something like that? But what about omission of information that could make a difference in how a person lives his or her life?

For instance, one day I found out that rabbinical legends tell of an– 18 other woman in the Garden of Eden before Eve. I was stunned. The omission of the Sumerian goddess Lilith from Genesis—as well as her demonization by ancient misogynists as an embodiment of female evil—felt like spiritual robbery. I felt like I'd just found out my mother was really my stepmother. To take seriously the tradition that Adam was created out of the same mud as his equal counterpart, Lilith, redefines all of Judeo–Christian history.

Some renegade Catholic feminists introduced me to a view of Lilith 19 that had been suppressed during the many centuries when this strong goddess was seen only as a spirit of evil. Lilith was a proud goddess who defied Adam's need to control her, attempted negotiations, and when this failed, said adios and left the Garden of Eden.

This omission of Lilith from the Bible was a patriarchal strategy to 20 keep women weak. Omitting the strong–woman archetype of Lilith from Western religions and starting the story with Eve the Rib has helped keep Christian and Jewish women believing they were the lesser sex for thousands of years.

STEREOTYPES AND CLICHÉS

Where opinion does not exist, the status quo becomes stereotyped
and all originality is discouraged.   — BERTRAND RUSSELL

Stereotype and cliché serve a purpose as a form of shorthand. Our   21
need for vast amounts of information in nanoseconds has made the stereotype vital to modern communication. Unfortunately it often shuts
down original thinking, giving those hungry for the truth a candy bar of
misinformation instead of a balanced meal. The stereotype explains a situation with just enough truth to seem unquestionable.

All the "isms"—racism, sexism, ageism, et al.—are founded on and   22
fueled by the stereotype and the cliché, which are lies of exaggeration, omission, and ignorance. They are always dangerous. They take a
single tree and make it a landscape. They destroy curiosity. They close
minds and separate people. The single mother on welfare is assumed to
be cheating. Any black male could tell you how much of his identity
is obliterated daily by stereotypes. Fat people, ugly people, beautiful
people, old people, large-breasted women, short men, the mentally ill,
and the homeless all could tell you how much more they are like us
than we want to think. I once admitted to a group of people that I had a
mouth like a truck driver. Much to my surprise, a man stood up and said,
"I'm a truck driver, and I never cuss." Needless to say, I was humbled.

GROUPTHINK

Who is more foolish, the child afraid of the dark, or the man afraid
of the light?   — MAURICE FREEHILL

Irving Janis, in *Victims of Groupthink*, defines this sort of lie as a psy-   23
chological phenomenon within decision-making groups in which loyalty
to the group has become more important than any other value, with
the result that dissent and the appraisal of alternatives are suppressed. If
you've ever worked on a committee or in a corporation, you've encountered groupthink. It requires a combination of other forms of lying—
ignoring facts, selective memory, omission, and denial, to name a few.

The textbook example of groupthink came on December 7, 1941. From   24
as early as the fall of 1941, the warnings came in, one after another, that
Japan was preparing for a massive military operation. The navy command
in Hawaii assumed Pearl Harbor was invulnerable—the Japanese weren't
stupid enough to attack the United States' most important base. On the
other hand, racist stereotypes said the Japanese weren't smart enough
to invent a torpedo effective in less than 60 feet of water (the fleet was
docked in 30 feet); after all, U.S. technology hadn't been able to do it.

On Friday, December 5, normal weekend leave was granted to all the   25
commanders at Pearl Harbor, even though the Japanese consulate in Hawaii
was busy burning papers. Within the tight, good-ole-boy cohesiveness

of the U.S. command in Hawaii, the myth of invulnerability stayed well entrenched. No one in the group considered the alternatives. The rest is history.

OUT–AND–OUT LIES

The only form of lying that is beyond reproach is lying for its own sake.   — Oscar Wilde

Of all the ways to lie, I like this one the best, probably because I get 26 tired of trying to figure out the real meanings behind things. At least I can trust the bald–faced lie. I once asked my five–year–old nephew, "Who broke the fence?" (I had seen him do it.) He answered, "The murderers." Who could argue?

At least when this sort of lie is told it can be easily confronted. As the 27 person who is lied to, I know where I stand. The bald–faced lie doesn't toy with my perceptions — it argues with them. It doesn't try to refashion reality, it tries to refute it. *Read my lips.* . . . No sleight of hand. No guessing. If this were the only form of lying, there would be no such things as floating anxiety or the adult–children–of–alcoholics movement.

DISMISSAL

Pay no attention to that man behind the curtain! I am the Great Oz!
                                                                    — The Wizard of Oz

Dismissal is perhaps the slipperiest of all lies. Dismissing feelings, 28 perceptions, or even the raw facts of a situation ranks as a kind of lie that can do as much damage to a person as any other kind of lie.

The roots of many mental disorders can be traced back to the dis– 29 missal of reality. Imagine that a person is told from the time she is a tot that her perceptions are inaccurate. *"Mommy, I'm scared."* "No you're not, darling." *"I don't like that man next door; he makes me feel icky."* "Johnny, that's a terrible thing to say; of course you like him. You go over there right now and be nice to him."

I've often mused over the idea that madness is actually a sane reaction 30 to an insane world. Psychologist R. D. Laing supports this hypothesis in *Sanity, Madness and the Family,* an account of his investigation into the families of schizophrenics. The common thread that ran through all of the families he studied was a deliberate, staunch dismissal of the patient's perceptions from a very early age. Each of the patients started out with an accurate grasp of reality, which, through meticulous and methodical dismissal, was demolished until the only reality the patient could trust was catatonia.

Dismissal runs the gamut. Mild dismissal can be quite handy for for– 31 giving the foibles of others in our day–to–day lives. Toddlers who have just learned to manipulate their parents' attention sometimes are dismissed out of necessity. Absolute attention from the parents would require so much energy that no one would get to eat dinner. But we must be careful and attentive about how far we take our "necessary" dismissals. Dismissal is a dangerous tool, because it's nothing less than a lie.

DELUSION

We lie loudest when we lie to ourselves.   — ERIC HOFFER

I could write the book on this one. Delusion, a cousin of dismissal, 32 is the tendency to see excuses as facts. It's a powerful lying tool because it filters out information that contradicts what we want to believe. Alcoholics who believe that the problems in their lives are legitimate reasons for drinking rather than results of the drinking offer the classic example of deluded thinking. Delusion uses the mind's ability to see things in myriad ways to support what it wants to be the truth.

But delusion is also a survival mechanism we all use. If we were to 33 fully contemplate the consequences of our stockpiles of nuclear weapons or global warming, we could hardly function on a day–to–day level. We don't want to incorporate that much reality into our lives because to do so would be paralyzing.

Delusion acts as an adhesive to keep the status quo intact. It shame- 34 lessly employs dismissal, omission, and amnesia, among other sorts of lies. Its most cunning defense is that it cannot see itself.

• • •

The liar's punishment . . . is that he cannot believe anyone else.
                    — GEORGE BERNARD SHAW

These are only a few of the ways we lie. Or are lied to. As I said ear- 35 lier, it's not easy to entirely eliminate lies from our lives. No matter how pious we may try to be, we will still embellish, hedge, and omit to lubricate the daily machinery of living. But there is a world of difference between telling functional lies and living a lie. Martin Buber once said, "The lie is the spirit committing treason against itself." Our acceptance of lies becomes a cultural cancer that eventually shrouds and reorders reality until moral garbage becomes as invisible to us as water is to a fish.

How much do we tolerate before we become sick and tired of be- 36 ing sick and tired? When will we stand up and declare our *right* to trust? When do we stop accepting that the real truth is in the fine print? Whose lips do we read this year when we vote for president? When will we stop being so reticent about making judgments? When do we stop turning over our personal power and responsibility to liars?

Maybe if I don't tell the bank the check's in the mail I'll be less toler- 37 ant of the lies told me every day. A country song I once heard said it all for me: "You've got to stand for something or you'll fall for anything."

Reading Closely

1. Without looking back at the essay, list as many of Ericsson's ways of lying as you can remember. Which one "stung" you? Why?

2. Why does Ericsson believe that lies are necessary? Which kinds of lies do you believe are so?

3. Which kinds of lies do you tell the most? Which do you most detest hearing? Why? Be prepared to share your answers with the rest of the class.

Considering Larger Issues

1. **With a classmate or two,** discuss questions of honesty currently circulating in the news. Which athletes, actors, politicians, or others are being questioned about lying? What is your opinion of their truth-telling?

2. PAIRED READINGS. Place Ericsson's essay in conversation with Segal's "The Dog Ate My Flash Drive, and Other Tales of Woe." How are these writers addressing the questions of lying and truth-telling? What differences do you see in their approaches to this issue? What similarities do you see? What perspectives about lying do you gain by reading these two essays together?

3. What evidence in the text helps you determine whether Ericsson is a dedicated liar or a dedicated writer investigating lying? Be prepared to share your answer with the rest of the class.

4. What is Ericsson's purpose in writing this essay, and what audience is she writing it for? Is she primarily trying to explore her own feelings? discourage her readers from telling lies? rouse them to action against liars and "acceptance of lies" in public life? Point to the evidence in the essay that supports your answers.

5. COMBINING METHODS. Mark the places where Ericsson uses *exemplification* to support her classification and division of "The Ways We Lie." Do you think she gives enough examples for each type of lying? Are all of the examples effective? Why or why not?

Thinking about Language

1. Using a dictionary or the context of the essay, define the following terms. Be prepared to share your answers with the rest of the class.

haggard (2)	ecclesiastical (12)	renegade (19)
travails (4)	irreparable (13)	groupthink (23)
penance (6)	blatant (14)	dissent (23)
pittance (9)	culprit (16)	catatonia (30)
façades (10)	omission (17)	gamut (31)
plethora (11)	misogynists (18)	

2. What differences can you discern among the following words: *deception, lies, capital crimes,* and *misdemeanors?*

Writing Your Own Essays Using Classification and Division

1. What are the merits of lying? Using Ericsson's essay as a model of classification and division, draft a three- to four-page essay in which you categorize the advantages of lying within social interactions. Or if you prefer, categorize the merits of telling the truth. Remember to consult the guidelines for checking over the use of classification and division on page 290.

2. On the basis of your response to question 1 under Considering Larger Issues, draft a three- to four-page essay about kinds of lying, dishonesty, or cheating that are currently appearing in the media. Whether you decide to use real public figures, characters in television shows or movies, or both, remember to include a ruling principle, consistent and exclusive categories, and vivid details and examples. Do some online research, if necessary, to find details and examples, and illustrate your essay with at least two visuals. Refer to the guidelines for checking over the use of classification and division on page 290.

3. ACADEMIC WRITING. Both Ericsson and Segal reflect on and classify lies for public audiences, considering the various ways people lie and the ways audiences respond to these lies. Such classifications can also occur in academic contexts. In political science courses, for example, in exploring controversies that occur during various presidential administrations, you might need to classify the lies that presidents, White House officials, or members of Congress have told the American public. In a six- to eight-page essay, classify the different kinds of lies that U.S. government officials have told and reflect on how these lies affected international affairs, domestic policy, or the American people's trust. So that you gain a deep understanding of the controversies that have occurred throughout U.S. history, you'll need to conduct a good deal of library and online research. As you draft and revise, refer to the guidelines for checking over the use of classification and division on page 290.

AMY TAN
Mother Tongue

Amy Tan (b. 1952) is a California native who grew up surrounded by strong influences of both Chinese and American culture. She attended high school in Switzerland and went to eight different colleges before earning a master's degree in linguistics from San Jose State University. Before her literary career took off, Tan held a variety of jobs, ranging from tending bar and counseling the developmentally disabled to working as a corporate communications specialist. Realizing she was becoming a workaholic, she began writing stories about the intersection of her parents' traditional life in China with her own life as an Americanized Chinese American woman. When her first novel, *The Joy Luck Club* (1989), won both the *Los Angeles Times* Book Award and the National Book Award, she was able to devote herself full-time to writing. Since *The Joy Luck Club*, she has published *The Kitchen God's Wife* (1991), *The Moon Lady* (1992), *The Chinese Siamese Cat* (1994), *One Hundred Secret Senses* (1995), *The Bonesetter's Daughter* (2000), and *Saving a Fish from Drowning* (2005), as well as a collection of essays called *The Opposite Side of Fate* (2003).

"Mother Tongue," which first appeared in the literary journal *Threepenny Review* (1990), is dedicated to her mother and illustrates Tan's linguistic expertise and training. It also exemplifies a successful mixed-method essay.

> **Preview**   What is your "mother tongue"? What language—or what kind of language—do you speak at home, with close family members? How is that language different from the one you speak at school?

I am not a scholar of English or literature. I cannot give you much more than 1 personal opinions on the English language and its variations in this country or others.

I am a writer. And by that definition, I am someone who has always 2 loved language. I am fascinated by language in daily life. I spend a great deal of my time thinking about the power of language—the way it can evoke an emotion, a visual image, a complex idea, or a simple truth. Language is the tool of my trade. And I use them all—all the Englishes I grew up with.

Recently, I was made keenly aware of the different Englishes I do use. I 3 was giving a talk to a large group of people, the same talk I had already given to half a dozen other groups. The nature of the talk was about my writing, my life, and my book, *The Joy Luck Club*. The talk was going along well enough, until I remembered one major difference that made the whole talk sound wrong. My mother was in the room. And it was perhaps the first time she had heard me give a lengthy speech, using the kind of English I have never used with her. I was saying things like "The intersection of memory upon imagination" and "There is an aspect of my fiction that relates to thus-and-thus"—a speech filled with carefully wrought grammatical phrases, burdened, it suddenly seemed to me, with nominalized forms, past perfect tenses, conditional phrases, all the forms of standard English that I had learned in school and through books, the forms of English I did not use at home with my mother.

Just last week, I was walking down the street with my mother, and I again found myself conscious of the English I was using, the English I do use with her. We were talking about the price of new and used furniture and I heard myself saying this: "Not waste money that way." My husband was with us as well, and he didn't notice any switch in my English. And then I realized why. It's because over the twenty years we've been together I've often used that same kind of English with him, and sometimes he even uses it with me. It has become our language of intimacy, a different sort of English that relates to family talk, the language I grew up with.

So you'll have some idea of what this family talk I heard sounds like, I'll quote what my mother said during a recent conversation which I videotaped and then transcribed. During this conversation, my mother was talking about a political gangster in Shanghai who had the same last name as her family's, Du, and how the gangster in his early years wanted to be adopted by her family, which was rich by comparison. Later, the gangster became more powerful, far richer than my mother's family, and one day showed up at my mother's wedding to pay his respects. Here's what she said in part:

"Du Yusong having business like fruit stand. Like off the street kind. He is Du like Du Zong—but not Tsung-ming Island people. The local people call putong, the river east side, he belong to that side local people. That man want to ask Du Zong father take him in like become own family. Du Zong father wasn't look down on him, but didn't take seriously, until that man big like become a mafia. Now important person, very hard to inviting him. Chinese way, came only to show respect, don't stay for dinner. Respect for making big celebration, he shows up. Mean give lots of respect. Chinese custom. Chinese social life that way. If too important won't have to stay too long. He come to my wedding. I didn't see, I heard it. I gone to boy's side, they have YMCA dinner. Chinese age I was nineteen."

You should know that my mother's expressive command of English belies how much she actually understands. She reads the *Forbes* report, listens to *Wall Street Week*, converses daily with her stockbroker, reads all of Shirley MacLaine's books with ease—all kinds of things I can't begin to understand. Yet some of my friends tell me they understand 50 percent of what my mother says. Some say they understand 80 to 90 percent. Some say they understand none of it, as if she were speaking pure Chinese. But to me, my mother's English is perfectly clear, perfectly natural. It's my mother tongue. Her language, as I hear it, is vivid, direct, full of observation and imagery. That was the language that helped shape the way I saw things, expressed things, made sense of the world.

Amy Tan and her mother

Lately, I've been giving more thought to the kind of English my mother 8 speaks. Like others, I have described it to people as "broken" or "fractured" English. But I wince when I say that. It has always bothered me that I can think of no way to describe it other than "broken," as if it were damaged and needed to be fixed, as if it lacked a certain wholeness and soundness. I've heard other terms used, "limited English," for example. But they seem just as bad, as if everything is limited, including people's perceptions of the limited English speaker.

I know this for a fact, because when I was growing up, my mother's 9 "limited" English limited *my* perception of her. I was ashamed of her English. I believed that her English reflected the quality of what she had to say. That is, because she expressed them imperfectly her thoughts were imperfect. And I had plenty of empirical evidence to support me: the fact that people in department stores, at banks, and at restaurants did not take her seriously, did not give her good service, pretended not to understand her, or even acted as if they did not hear her.

My mother has long realized the limitations of her English as well. 10 When I was fifteen, she used to have me call people on the phone to pretend I was she. In this guise, I was forced to ask for information or even to complain and yell at people who had been rude to her. One time it was a call to her stockbroker in New York. She had cashed out her small portfolio and it just happened we were going to go to New York the next week, our very first trip outside California. I had to get on the phone and say in an adolescent voice that was not very convincing, "This is Mrs. Tan."

And my mother was standing in the back whispering loudly, "Why 11 he don't send me check, already two weeks late. So mad he lie to me, losing me money."

And then I said in perfect English, "Yes, I'm getting rather concerned.   12
You had agreed to send the check two weeks ago, but it hasn't arrived."

Then she began to talk more loudly. "What he want, I come to New   13
York tell him front of his boss, you cheating me?" And I was trying to
calm her down, make her be quiet, while telling the stockbroker, "I can't
tolerate any more excuses. If I don't receive the check immediately, I am
going to have to speak to your manager when I'm in New York next
week." And sure enough, the following week there we were in front of
this astonished stockbroker, and I was sitting there red-faced and quiet,
and my mother, the real Mrs. Tan, was shouting at his boss in her impec-
cable broken English.

We used a similar routine just five days ago, for a situation that was   14
far less humorous. My mother had gone to the hospital for an appointment, to find out about a benign brain tumor a CAT scan had revealed a
month ago. She said she had spoken very good English, her best English,
no mistakes. Still, she said, the hospital did not apologize when they said
they had lost the CAT scan and she had come for nothing. She said they
did not seem to have any sympathy when she told them she was anxious
to know the exact diagnosis, since her husband and son had both died
of brain tumors. She said they would not give her any more information
until the next time and she would have to make another appointment for
that. So she said she would not leave until the doctor called her daughter. She wouldn't budge. And when the doctor finally called her daughter,
me, who spoke in perfect English—lo and behold—we had assurances
the CAT scan would be found, promises that a conference call on Monday would be held, and apologies for any suffering my mother had gone
through for a most regrettable mistake.

I think my mother's English almost had an effect on limiting my pos-   15
sibilities in life as well. Sociologists and linguists probably will tell you
that a person's developing language skills are more influenced by peers.
But I do think that the language spoken in the family, especially in immigrant families which are more insular, plays a large role in shaping
the language of the child. And I believe that it affected my results on
achievement tests, IQ tests, and the SAT. While my English skills were
never judged as poor, compared to math, English could not be considered my strong suit. In grade school I did moderately well, getting perhaps B's, sometimes B-pluses, in English and scoring perhaps in the
sixtieth or seventieth percentile on achievement tests. But those scores
were not good enough to override the opinion that my true abilities lay
in math and science, because in those areas I achieved A's and scored in
the ninetieth percentile or higher.

This was understandable. Math is precise; there is only one correct   16
answer. Whereas, for me at least, the answers on English tests were always a judgment call, a matter of opinion and personal experience.
Those tests were constructed around items like fill-in-the-blank sentence

completion, such as, "Even though Tom was _____, Mary thought he was _____." And the correct answer always seemed to be the most bland combinations of thoughts, for example, "Even though Tom was shy, Mary thought he was charming," with the grammatical structure "even though" limiting the correct answer to some sort of semantic opposites, so you wouldn't get answers like "Even though Tom was foolish, Mary thought he was ridiculous." Well, according to my mother, there were very few limitations as to what Tom could have been and what Mary might have thought of him. So I never did well on tests like that.

The same was true with word analogies, pairs of words in which you 17 were supposed to find some sort of logical, semantic relationship—for example, "*Sunset* is to *nightfall* as _____ is to_____." And here you would be presented with a list of four possible pairs, one of which showed the same kind of relationship: *red* is to *spotlight, bus* is to *arrival, chills* is to *fever, yawn* is to *boring*. Well, I could never think that way. I knew what the tests were asking, but I could not block out of my mind the images already created by the first pair, "*sunset* is to *nightfall*"—and I would see a burst of colors against a darkening sky, the moon rising, the lowering of a curtain of stars. And all the other pairs of words—red, bus, spotlight, boring—just threw up a mass of confusing images, making it impossible for me to sort out something as logical as saying: "A sunset precedes nightfall" is the same as "a chill precedes a fever." The only way I would have gotten that answer right would have been to imagine an associative situation, for example, my being disobedient and staying out past sunset, catching a chill at night, which turns into feverish pneumonia as punishment, which indeed did happen to me.

I have been thinking about all this lately, about my mother's English, 18 about achievement tests. Because lately I've been asked as a writer, why there are not more Asian Americans represented in American literature. Why are there few Asian Americans enrolled in creative writing programs? Why do so many Chinese students go into engineering? Well, these are broad sociological questions I can't begin to answer. But I have noticed in surveys—in fact, just last week—that Asian students, as a whole, always do significantly better on math achievement tests than in English. And this makes me think that there are other Asian-American students whose English spoken in the home might also be described as "broken" or "limited." And perhaps they also have teachers who are steering them away from writing and into math and science, which is what happened to me.

Fortunately, I happen to be rebellious in nature and enjoy the chal- 19 lenge of disproving assumptions made about me. I became an English major my first year in college, after being enrolled as pre-med. I started writing nonfiction as a freelancer the week after I was told by my former boss that writing was my worst skill and I should hone my talents toward account management.

But it wasn't until 1985 that I finally began to write fiction. And at 20
first I wrote using what I thought to be wittily crafted sentences, sentences that would finally prove I had mastery over the English language.
Here's an example from the first draft of a story that later made its way
into *The Joy Luck Club*, but without this line: "That was my mental quan-
dary in its nascent state." A terrible line, which I can barely pronounce.

Fortunately, for reasons I won't get into today, I later decided I should 21
envision a reader for the stories I would write. And the reader I decided
upon was my mother, because these were stories about mothers. So with
this reader in mind—and in fact she did read my early drafts—I began to write stories using all the Englishes I grew up with: the English I
spoke to my mother, which for lack of a better term might be described
as "simple"; the English she used with me, which for lack of a better term
might be described as "broken"; my translation of her Chinese, which
could certainly be described as "watered down"; and what I imagined to
be her translation of her Chinese if she could speak in perfect English,
her internal language, and for that I sought to preserve the essence, but
neither an English nor a Chinese structure. I wanted to capture what language ability tests can never reveal: her intent, her passion, her imagery,
the rhythms of her speech and the nature of her thoughts.

Apart from what any critic had to say about my writing, I knew I had 22
succeeded where it counted when my mother finished reading my book
and gave me her verdict: "So easy to read."

Reading Closely

1. What is your immediate response to this essay's title? Respond to Tan's
   enumeration of the different Englishes she and many other people use,
   particularly with family members, and list them. Did any of these Englishes surprise, offend, or puzzle you? How many of them do you use?

2. Compare your responses to question 1 **with those of two or three
   classmates.** Where do you and your classmates agree and disagree with
   one another? Prepare a group response for the rest of the class.

3. What does the photograph on page 332 suggest about Tan's relationship
   with her mother? How does this visual add to or complicate the understanding you gained about their relationship through reading the essay?

Considering Larger Issues

1. Who is the audience for Tan's essay? What is her purpose in writing this
   essay? How do audience and purpose intersect for Tan?

2. What connections does Tan make between speaking and writing? Why
   does she emphasize the importance of knowing which English you're
   using?

3. Referring to your list of the different Englishes (question 1, under Reading Closely), discuss the real differences and similarities of these Englishes. How does Tan's narrative voice soften the process of learning and using these different Englishes, particularly in terms of their intimate or businesslike quality? In other words, what sorts of narratives and examples does she provide for the reasons she and her mother speak a range of Englishes? What examples does she provide for the consequences of using each English?

4. Tan uses herself and her mother as examples throughout this essay. Despite her reliance on two characters, how might Tan be speaking to the politics of language use in the United States? What do you know about the politics of who's saying what—and how—in U.S. culture? Write for five minutes in response to these questions.

5. COMBINING METHODS. Besides classification and division, what other methods of writing and thinking does Tan use to develop this essay? **Break into small groups of two or three classmates,** with each group looking over the essay for places where Tan uses *description, definition, narration, comparison and contrast, process analysis, cause-and-effect analysis,* or *argumentation.* Report your group's finding to the rest of the class.

Thinking about Language

1. Use the context of the essay or your dictionary to define the following terms. Be prepared to share your answers with the rest of the class.

keenly (3)	wince (8)	benign (14)
nominalized (3)	empirical (9)	insular (15)
conditional phrases (3)	guise (10)	semantic (17)
transcribed (5)	portfolio (10)	quandary (20)
expressive (7)	impeccable (13)	nascent (20)

2. What is the overall effect of the final paragraph: "Apart from what any critic had to say about my writing, I knew I had succeeded where it counted when my mother finished reading my book and gave me her verdict: 'So easy to read'"? What is Tan explicitly saying? What is she implying? To what overall effect? Why does she make this single sentence a separate paragraph?

3. How would you describe Tan's tone? How does her tone relate to her audience and purpose?

Writing Your Own Essays Using Classification and Division

1. Think of a way to classify your use of language. What categories do you come up with? What examples can you provide for each category? Draft a three- to four-page essay in which you recount your language use. Make sure that your thesis statement reflects your purpose. The guidelines for checking over the use of classification and division can be found on page 290.

2. Listen for a few days to how your friends or family members (a group of twelve or so people) use one or more languages or dialects. Then draft a three- to four-page essay in which you analyze the language use of this group, classifying the members into categories based on a ruling principle related to their language choices, such as vocabulary, style, and appropriateness. As you draft and revise, **consider working with a classmate,** and refer to "Checking Over the Use of Classification and Division" on page 290.

✳ Additional Suggestions for Writing

1. Make a list of all the television talk shows you can think of. **Ask your roommate or a classmate** to help you add to your list. How might you classify and divide these shows so that your categories are exhaustive and exclusive?

   Work with two classmates to expand your list, focus on a purpose for your classification and division, and decide on examples for each category. Then draft a three- to four-page essay that classifies and divides television talk shows. Revise your draft, using comments from your classmates and referring to "Checking Over the Use of Classification and Division" (p. 290) before preparing your final essay.

2. Reflect on your writing process, dividing this process into parts. For instance, your process might follow a traditional trajectory: prewriting, drafting, peer reviewing, drafting, editing, and so on. But it most likely will be unique to you. You might begin the writing process by going for a run, or you might need to conduct your editing in the student lounge where there's noise around you. In this two- to three-page essay, divide your writing process into parts, elaborating on what you do in which part of the process and how it helps you move the process along. The guidelines on page 290 should help you with your drafting and revisions.

chapter 6

COMPARISON
AND CONTRAST

*E*very day, many of us have to make decisions about what we eat. Should we fix a healthful meal at home, grab a quick snack, take time to eat at a restaurant, or buy fast food to eat on our way to school? We often make these decisions by using the rhetorical method of comparison and contrast. For example, you might prefer to fix your own meal, rather than eat at a restaurant, because you have more control over the situation. When you cook, you're in charge of the quality of the food you eat, the method of preparation, the overall cost, and the convenience, whereas eating at a restaurant requires that you depend on the waitstaff's timing, the chef's cooking skills, and the restaurant's menu choices and prices. On the other hand, stopping at the restaurant can save you time (if not money), let you invite someone to join you for a meal without having to cook or clean up, and allow you to try foods you don't know how to prepare.

The New York City subway poster that introduces this chapter enters into this discussion about preferred foods by asking readers to compare and contrast which meal is the wiser choice: the burger, large fries, and regular soda or the burger, small fries, and diet soda. The poster uses only a small amount of text because it expects readers to have enough knowledge about calorie requirements — and arithmetic — to be able to make the comparison on their own. The super-sized meal might look inviting, but it uses up more than half the daily calorie requirements. The smaller meal, on the other hand, uses only about one-third of the daily requirements while providing nearly the same taste sensations. If readers are truly concerned about what they're eating in terms of calories and nutrition, they should consider buying the smaller, less-caloric meal — or skipping fast food altogether.

Looking at Your Own Literacy   Reflect on the ads you see in newspapers and magazines, on Web sites, and on TV. Think about how one of these ads uses comparison and contrast, and write for five minutes about how it does so. What is the goal of this advertisement? What is its persuasive effect?

What Are Comparison and Contrast?

When you hear "compare and contrast," you may think of an artificial exercise used only in academic settings, but comparison and contrast are actually among the most important methods we use to make sense of the world. We use **comparison** when considering how two or more things are alike, to see what they have in common (for example, both Honda's Smart car and its Metropolitan model are fuel efficient). We use **contrast**, on the other hand, to show how two or more things are different (for example, the Metropolitan is *more* fuel efficient than the Smart car).

Every day, we call on comparison and contrast to evaluate information and find the answers we need. We notice a sign in the grocery store that says, "National brand $4.00, OUR brand $3.00"; we try on several pairs of athletic shoes before making a purchase because we want to buy the best pair; and we trace two possible routes on a map in order to determine the best way out of a city. In each of these situations, we first establish a **basis for comparison,** the shared feature or features of the two or more things we are comparing (for example, the convenience of the route, the versatility of the shoes, and so on), what they have in common. Then we decide on the **points of comparison,** the features that we will compare or contrast (Which route has less traffic? Which route flows into the beltway? Which route is longer?).

We can also use comparison and contrast as the overall organizational pattern for a piece of writing or as a supporting passage within another organizational pattern, such as classification and division, definition, or exemplification. We use comparison and contrast to help us understand or explain one relationship, situation, object, or personality in terms of another. In fact, one particular kind of comparison, called **analogy,** draws a likeness between one thing and something entirely different, usually something more familiar or less abstract. Here's an example of an analogy written by a student.

An Analogy

Writing a paper is like spring cleaning. The first phase of cleaning is like researching: you have to look through lots of material, deciding what to keep and what to throw away. The goal is to keep only what is useful. Once you've gotten rid of all the junk, you'll need to organize whatever you have left. Organization is the key to a clean house, as well as a well-written paper. Once everything is in its place, it's time to buff and polish — clean up your prose, fix your spelling, tidy sloppy sentences.

In *An Inconvenient Truth,* Al Gore uses comparison and contrast to show how the environment has changed over time. The visuals on page 343 reveal the drastic changes in Swiss glaciers from the early 1900s to today.

· ·

Thinking about Comparison and Contrast

1. What argument does Gore make by asking readers to compare and contrast these visuals? What conclusions are readers supposed to draw?

2. Gore does not use a lot of text to help readers make sense of this comparison. Why does he make this choice?

3. Are you persuaded by this comparison? Why or why not?

· ·

Throughout the Alps we are witnessing a similar story. Here is an old postcard from Switzerland depicting a scenic glacier early in the last century.

Here is the same site today.

TSCHIERVA GLACIER, SWITZERLAND, 1910

TSCHIERVA GLACIER, 2001

Below is the famous Hotel Belvedere, situated on the Rhone Glacier in Switzerland.

Here is the same site nearly a century later. The hotel is still there — but the glacier is not.

HOTEL BELVEDERE, RHONE GLACIER, SWITZERLAND, 1906

HOTEL BELVEDERE, RHONE GLACIER, 2003

Why Use Comparison and Contrast?

Comparison and contrast are fundamental ways of thinking about any situation. They help us make sense of the world by revealing information. Although you often employ these methods when speaking and writing, rarely do you set out to compare and contrast. Instead, your topic, purpose, and audience will naturally lead you to use comparison and contrast. Whenever you are being asked or asking others to consider the merits, advantages and disadvantages, or similarities and differences of two or more things, you're being called on to compare and contrast. And you'll want to establish your purpose from the very beginning. The main purposes for which comparison and contrast are used include explaining, evaluating choices, persuading, and entertaining.

To explain his complicated feelings about ownership of land, David Mas Masumoto compares and contrasts himself with his childhood friend Jessie Alvarado, whose family worked the farmland that Masumoto's family owned.

Comparison and Contrast to Explain

In 1966, while in the sixth grade at Del Rey Elementary School, I sat next to Jessie Alvarado. We had what, I later learned, was a symbiotic relationship. We'd cheat on tests together — he'd open a book so I could read the needed information, and then he copied my response. I provided the answers, he took the risks.

But that was before they told me he was Mexican and I was Japanese. Our cultures were different they said; he ate tortillas and I ate rice at home. We each had "our own thing" and belonged in different worlds despite both living in this small farm community just south of Fresno, California.

That was before they told me that my family was the farmers, and his family was the farm workers. We owned the land; he came to work for us. Nature rewarded us differently. While we talked about profits, Jessie's family spoke of hard-earned wages. We worked in all four seasons in our fields; he came to labor seasonally. My family would pass the land to the next generation. His family's dream was for the next generation to get out of the fields. We were supposed to be on opposite sides, even though we both sweated and itched the same each summer as we picked peaches in one-hundred-degree heat.

That was before they told me he was poor and I was rich. It made me feel guilty yet confused as a kid growing up.

—David Mas Masumoto, "Belonging on the Land"

Masumoto establishes his basis for comparison when he mentions his "symbiotic relationship" with Jessie Alvarado. Just as these two sixth graders had one, so did their fathers: one owned the land; the other worked it. Then Masumoto acknowledges what the boys had in common: they cheated together, both lived near Fresno, and both picked peaches each summer. Their differences were their cultural backgrounds (Mexican and Japanese), what they ate at home, and—most important—how their families earned a living. His purpose is to explore his discomfort with the discrepancies between their lives.

. . . .

Try Your Hand Think back to a friendship you established early in life, only to discover that you two were "supposed" to be different. Using comparison or contrast, explain in two sentences your relationship with your friend. Share your written thoughts with a classmate to see if your comparison or contrast is clear.

. . . .

Often we use comparison and contrast to help ourselves or others make choices. In the following excerpt, Debbe Geiger considers the ban on her children's text-messaging instituted by her husband. Comparing the benefits and drawbacks of texting as a mode of communication, Geiger decides where she sits inside this family debate.

Comparison and Contrast to Make Choices

The truth is, I like texting with my kids. It makes me feel hip to communicate with them in a way they actually respond to. I liked being able to find out where they were, who they were with, and if their plans had changed and to tell them when they needed to come home, without having to talk on the phone. I would text my son an "I love you" when I knew he was home from school. He'd immediately send me one back, and I knew he was safe. That was important to me because he's not a big talker.

However, there is plenty about texting I don't like. I didn't like that my daughter rarely spoke to her friends in New York anymore, relying only on texting to communicate. And I certainly do not like hearing about kids who send around half-naked pictures of themselves. They're too young to fully grasp the ramifications such actions hold for the future. And the overuse and misuse show they're not mature enough to use these expensive gadgets responsibly.

— DEBBE GEIGER, "When Dad Banned Text-Messaging"

To make her decision, Geiger lists the positives and negatives she sees in her children's use of texting. Positives: she communicates with them *and* gets a response; she keeps in touch when plans change without having to talk on the phone; she knows where her children are and that they are safe. Negatives: her daughter isn't talking, just texting; there's the probability of her children encountering illicit images and pictures; she's not sure they're mature enough to handle this responsibility. After weighing these positives and negatives, Geiger makes her decision. She writes, "Whenever the subject [of the texting ban] comes up, my husband calmly shakes his head no and stands his ground. I leave the room. I don't want to disagree with him in front of our children, but I secretly hope he'll come around."

· ·

Try Your Hand What do you think of Geiger's decision? Given her points of comparison, was her decision a surprise to you? From your perspective, what are the benefits and drawbacks of texting? In a single paragraph, write about how you'd enter into this debate.

· ·

Insurance agents can be among the most persuasive comparers and contrasters. When trying to sell you a policy, good agents often ask if they can compare coverage and then contrast rates and deductibles with your current policy. They are trying to underbid your current carrier — or at least compete with it. They want to persuade you to do business with their company.

But people use comparison and contrast to persuade their audience to do other things besides buy a product. In the following excerpt, nineteenth-century black female activist Sojourner Truth relies on this combined rhetorical method to argue for women's rights. In her 1851 speech given at the Women's Rights Convention in Akron, Ohio, Truth compares herself — a strong and able woman who was once a slave — to the genteel and fragile vision of women many people held at the time as a means to counter the idea that women were not physically or mentally capable of exercising full rights as citizens.

Comparison and Contrast to Persuade

What's all this here talking about? That man over there says that women need to be helped into carriages, and lifted over ditches, and to have the best place everywhere. Nobody ever helps me into carriages, or over mud puddles or gives me any best place (*and raising herself to her full height and her voice to a pitch like rolling thunder, she asked*), and aren't I a woman? Look at me! Look at my arm! (*And she bared her right arm to the shoulder, showing her tremendous muscular power.*) I have plowed, and planted, and gathered into barns, and no man could head me — and aren't I a woman? I could work as much and eat as much as a man (when I could get it), and bear the lash as well — and aren't I a woman? I have borne thirteen children and seen them almost all sold off into slavery, and when I cried out with a mother's grief, none but Jesus heard — and aren't I a woman? Then they talk about this thing in the head — what's this they call it? (*"Intellect," whispered someone near.*) That's it, honey. What's that got to do with woman's rights or Negroes' rights? If my cup won't hold but a pint and yours holds a quart, wouldn't you be mean not to let me have my little half-measure full? (*And she pointed her significant finger and sent a keen glance at the minister who had made the argument. The cheering was long and loud.*)

— SOJOURNER TRUTH

Here Truth uses both verbal and physical arguments to make claims about women's capabilities. By comparing and contrasting herself to the "womanly ideal," she persuades her audience to see that she is indeed a woman, but not one who needs to be cared for or coddled. And by challenging generally accepted ideas about women's frailty through her own experiences and physicality, Truth hopes that her audience will see that this contradiction occurs in other instances and applies to other women.

··

Try Your Hand   In this excerpt, Truth compares herself to an ideal or stereotype to challenge the stereotype. Consider how this argumentative strategy could be used in other instances. When might you employ this strategy in your life circumstances? How would the comparison play out?

··

Finally, comparison and contrast can be used to entertain. We don't have to make a decision or change our mind; we can just simply enjoy. In the following excerpt, fashion expert Josh Patner addresses Michelle Obama (whose husband had then been elected president but not yet inaugurated) about the frequent comparisons of her to Jacqueline Kennedy, with sense of style as the basis of comparison.

Comparison and Contrast to Entertain

By now, I imagine you must find the comparisons to Jacqueline Kennedy flattering but tiring. At 44, you will be the youngest first lady since Camelot; the comparisons are inevitable. That doesn't make them accurate.

Like Kennedy, you clearly understand the power of clothes to telegraph messages. In the midst of Sarah Palin's Wardrobegate, you wore inexpensive J. Crew separates on *The Tonight Show*, telling Jay Leno, "You can get a lot of great stuff online." ("All Politics Aside . . . this outfit gets our vote" reads a current J. Crew ad, an effort to cash in on your endorsement.) Another savvy choice: You wore evening pajamas by Isabel Toledo for a fundraiser hosted by *Vogue* Editor-in-Chief Anna Wintour in New York last June. Toledo is an insider's designer; all black was a smart choice for meeting fashion deities (and the pope.)

Like Jackie Kennedy, you understand that dressing for your audience is important. But that's where the comparison ends. Where Kennedy's wardrobe was constant, a calculated piece of stagecraft, your style is more casual and more spontaneous. Which makes it much more interesting.

Jackie's White House wardrobe was essentially custom work from one designer, Oleg Cassini; you buy off the rack. Jackie bought clothes and returned them after wearing them. What you wear, you own. Jackie often spent tens of thousands of dollars in one shot; no one could accuse you of lavish spending.   —JOSH PATNER, "Fashion Advice for Michelle Obama"

Although there is not much at stake in this discussion, it is interesting and entertaining for readers to consider the similarities and differences between these two fashion icons. As Patner explains, Obama and Kennedy are similar in that both recognize "the power of clothes to telegraph messages" and "that dressing for your audience is important." But once we get beyond these similarities, there are also some real style differences between the two: while Kennedy's wardrobe was "a calculated piece of stagecraft," achieved with what Patner considers essentially expensive rented costumes, Obama's is more "casual and spontaneous"—and much less extravagant. And it is this "off-the-rack" spontaneity that he finds exciting to observe.

How Do You Use Comparison and Contrast in Academic Writing?

Academic situations offer the same opportunities to employ comparison and contrast as more public, nonacademic situations. In your years as a student, you've most likely noticed this fact. Teachers often assign comparison-and-contrast essays because they ask the student to gain a deep and thorough knowledge of two topics—so deep that the student can distinguish similarities and differences between the two. For instance, if your history teacher asked you to compare and contrast the Vietnam era political groups the hawks and the doves, you would need to know both groups so well that you could explain how they differed in terms of their ideological stance, position on the war, and activist engagements.

But comparison and contrast are also used in academic environments as a means of investigation—a way for scholars and students to pursue a topic they have a question about and arrive at an answer they did not know before they began the investigation. For example, sociologist James Nazroo and his colleagues conducted a study on the differences in the health of three ethnic groups in the United States (black Americans, Caribbean Americans, and white Americans) and two in England (Caribbean English and white English). This comparison is an important one because, they hypothesize, it should reveal how migration histories and socioeconomic conditions in different contexts lead to differences in health and economic status. In the following excerpt, we see the conclusions they draw from their comparative study.

Comparison and Contrast in Academic Writing

This paper has used independent, but similarly designed, surveys in England and the US to compare the health of five ethnic groups — Black American; Caribbean American; white American; white English; and Caribbean English — with the intention of exploring how the context of migration and post-migration circumstances might influence health inequalities between Black and white groups. Our main health measure, self-assessed general health, revealed a stark contrast between the situations in England and the US. The Caribbean English group have worse health than the white English group, while in the US the Caribbean American group has a very similar health profile to the white American group. In addition, there were marked differences in health between the groups in the US compared with those in England, with those in the US having better health than their English equivalents. Finally, the Black American group had worse health than the white American group, although this difference was not statistically significant. Although there were differences for the reports of diagnosed conditions, as would be expected for specific diseases and different healthcare systems, findings for these were broadly the same as for self-assessed general health.

This pattern of findings for health was also found for markers of economic inequality, including income, employment and education. On the whole, the white groups were better off than the Black groups in both countries, but while the Caribbean English profile matched that of the Black American profile (with the exception of level of education), the Caribbean American group was better off than their Black American and Caribbean English counterparts (with a profile close to that of the white American group). An exploration of migration effects revealed that the Caribbean American group were more likely than the Caribbean English group to be first generation, and to have migrated more recently. Generation was shown to be strongly related to social and economic inequalities, with the 'second' generation in both countries on the whole better off for economic markers, but more likely to report exposure to racism and discrimination.
—James Nazroo, James Jackson, Saffron Karlsen, and Myriam Torres,
"The Black Diaspora and Health Inequities in the U.S. and England"

The comparison reveals not only whom health agencies might pay attention to as they create health intervention practices but also what these agencies should be attentive to (migration patterns and generation) as they apply these different intervention practices.

As you compose comparison-and-contrast essays throughout your academic career, you might also envision these writing projects as moments of exploration. How can you use these rhetorical methods of development not only to showcase knowledge but also to pursue it? Comparing and contrasting come alive when they are envisioned as inquiry and investigation, when they become an opportunity to learn something new by placing topics in conversation with one another.

Analyzing Comparison and Contrast in Academic Writing

Reflect on your coursework this semester. When do you see opportunities for comparison and contrast? What would you learn through the investigation process? Like Nazroo and colleagues, offer a hypothesis regarding this investigation.

How Do You Read Comparison and Contrast?

As with any other kind of writing, the first step in learning how to write an effective comparison-and-contrast essay is knowing how to read one critically. Once you've established that you're reading this type of writing, make a habit of examining it closely to see how the writer sets up the comparison or contrast and how successful it is—both in general terms and for the author's specific purpose and audience. Are the things being compared or contrasted clear, or are they vague or confusing? Does the writer help you see similarities or differences you hadn't recognized, or does he or she strain to find or exaggerate ones that hardly exist? Whether the purpose of the comparison and contrast is to explain, evaluate a choice, entertain, or argue a point, how well does the writing do so for the intended readers (whose identity you may have to figure out)?

Look back at the passage by David Mas Masumoto on page 344, and consider first the title, "Belonging on the Land." It alerts you that the passage deals somehow with a feeling of connection to some land, although it doesn't suggest what will be compared or contrasted. Whether you can glean information from the title or not, keep reading, paying special attention to the effect of the introduction:

> In 1966, while in the sixth grade at Del Rey Elementary School, I sat next to Jessie Alvarado. We had what, I later learned, was a symbiotic relationship.

Here the title and introduction work together to prepare you for the purpose of the comparison and contrast, which seems to be explanatory, maybe even entertaining. At the beginning of the next paragraph, however, the author suddenly shifts to his main point. The thesis at the end of this paragraph, "We each had 'our own thing' and belonged in different worlds," will sustain the rest of the passage, informing the reader of the differences between the two boys.

Notice how Masumoto organizes the contrasts between his two subjects. They appear one after another in three paragraphs, each beginning with the phrase "that was before they told me," and are often stated in short, blunt ways: "he was Mexican and I was Japanese," "We owned the land; he came to work for us." But the effect isn't monotonous because Masumoto uses different sentence structures and lengths and twice acknowledges similarities: "despite both living in this small farm community," "even though we both sweated and itched the same." Also notice that he starts with the least significant contrasts (ethnicity, diet), gradually develops the economic differences between the two families, and leads up to the most important contrast of all, where Masumoto states his personal feelings: "he was poor and I was rich. It made me feel guilty yet confused. . . ."

As you evaluate the comparisons and contrasts authors make, you'll also want to consider what others could have been made but weren't. In this case, you might wonder what Jessie felt about the boys' relationship—whether he too was confused or harbored any feelings of resentment, or if he might have taken advantage of his relationship with David. Think about what else is left unsaid as well: for instance, sometimes the writer's intended audience is obvious, but in this excerpt, Masumoto gives us few clues about whom he sees as his audience: people interested in issues of social or economic class differences? children who don't yet recognize such differences? landowners? farmworkers? What is *not* expressed can be every bit as important as what is there.

How Do You Write Using Comparison and Contrast?

Besides the rhetorical elements that we're considering in every chapter— purpose, audience, thesis— writing that compares and contrasts has unique elements: the basis and points of comparison. These provide the framework for two characteristic organizational patterns.

● Determining Your Purpose

The first question you should ask yourself is "Why am I making this comparison and contrast?" Did your history instructor assign you to compare and contrast two books on the war in Iraq and to recommend one over the other (to evaluate a choice)? Are you applying for a grant to study abroad for a semester and being asked to sketch out the advantages and disadvantages of doing so (to argue)? Does an exam for an art course ask you to explain the similarities and differences between the Cubist and Expressionist painters (to explain)? Whether you're writing for school, for your job, or in some other context, you'll use comparison and contrast to explain something, to evaluate a choice, to argue a point, or just to entertain. Sometimes these purposes overlap, but you'll always have one dominant purpose that you need to keep in mind.

● Considering Your Audience

After establishing your purpose, your second question should be "For whom am I writing this comparison and contrast?" Are you writing for your teacher? yourself? your parents? a friend? a boss? Are you writing to your girlfriend to try to convince her the two of you should be friends first (but lovers second) instead of being "just friends"? Are you writing to your parents to explain the differences between placing your children in school-sponsored as opposed to church-sponsored day care? Are you e-mailing your adviser to explore the pros and cons of majoring in dance, your first love, as opposed to the more practical physical therapy?

Audience and purpose work hand in hand to affect other features of your comparison and contrast: the basis and points of comparison, how much emphasis you give one point over another, and the order in which points are presented. If you are trying to decide where to place your children in day care, you will no doubt weigh such points of comparison as cost, distance from home and work, staff, equipment, and atmosphere. Although cost might be your most immediate concern, your spouse might be more concerned with staff and equipment and your employer with how distance affects your work schedule. Your parents might be more interested in the religious or educational atmosphere (and be more willing to help you out financially, depending on which option you choose). You will want to gauge the elements of your comparison and contrast to fit your audience; therefore, it's vital to have a sense of that audience as you draft and revise.

● Considering the Basis and Points of Comparison

What features or elements of your subject have you chosen to compare? If you're comparing your own academic success with that of a high school classmate who made the same grades, who works about the same number of hours, and who, like you, has a small child to care for, then you are comparing two "like" things. But if you are comparing your success with that of a genius who isn't a parent and has never had to hold a job, then you're "comparing apples and oranges"—a phrase we use when two very different things are being compared without any rational basis.

Points of comparison grow out of your initial basis for comparison. If you are comparing the advantages and disadvantages of attending a two-year as opposed to a four-year college, your basis is that both kinds of school provide higher education, and you may want to establish such points of comparison as cost, course offerings, faculty, and distance from home. But those points are obvious. You will sometimes need to move beyond the obvious—for instance, what the lifetime potential payoffs for a degree from each kind of college are or whether you would be more likely to go on for a bachelor's degree if you started at one or the other. If you're applying to college or transferring from one kind to the other, or if you're applying for scholarship support, you may find yourself developing these points in your letter of application or your statement of purpose. In every comparison and contrast, you'll want to identify several appropriate and well-supported points of comparison so that your thesis is adequately supported and your conclusion is indisputable.

● Considering Your Thesis Statement

Your purpose and your basis for comparison will come together in your thesis statement. An effective thesis statement answers the question "What do I want this comparison and contrast to do?" If you're comparing two literary characters or two sports figures, for instance, why are you doing so? Do you want to explain something to readers? to evaluate a choice for them? to argue a point to them? to entertain them? Your thesis should also indicate whether you will concentrate on similarities, differences, or both. Finally, a strong thesis statement makes a point about your subjects so that your comparison is more than just an empty exercise.

Not all thesis statements are just one sentence long. For instance, when Lisa Miller explains the "new culture war" over abortion by comparing and contrasting how the political left and right talk about their attempts to reduce abortion, she uses a two-sentence-long thesis statement to focus on her main point.

A Two-Sentence Thesis Statement

<u>Beneath all the optimism, though, tensions continue to simmer, and it can seem that differences between the old culture wars and the new ones are merely differences in tone and tactics, not in ideology. In previous eras, warriors fought with rhetorical bludgeons; now they use newfangled semantic weapons so sharp they could split a hair.</u> On both sides, people say they want abortion reduction. But listen carefully to how they say it. On the left, the so-called common ground advocates talk about reducing the need for abortion. With this language, they are saying — in code — that *Roe* must continue to stand. (When one abortion-reduction bill was introduced in the last session of Congress, women's groups prevailed at the very last minute to change its name from the Reducing Abortion and Supporting Parents Act to the Reducing the Need for Abortion and Supporting Parents Act. "This step proved necessary in order to find common ground among many in the pro-choice and pro-life communities," says Rachel Laser, culture director of Third Way, which helped write the bill.) On the right, folks talk about reducing the number of abortions, signaling a belief that fighting *Roe* must remain a priority. ("Reducing the number would involve some legal issues," says Frank Page, former head of the Southern Baptist Convention. "People on the left would be violently opposed to anything that would restrict a woman's right to an abortion.") The way you talk about your desire for common ground, it turns out, signals whose side you're actually on. The left wants to reduce demand for abortion; the right wants to reduce supply.

—LISA MILLER, "The Culture War of Words"

Miller's thesis statement conveys the purpose of her comparison: to demonstrate the semantic differences between the new culture wars over abortion.

● Arranging and Developing the Comparison

Writing that compares and contrasts has traditionally been organized in one of two ways: (1) the writer makes a point-by-point case for subject A and then does the same for subject B (and subject C if necessary, and so on), emphasizing each subject, or (2) the writer compares and contrasts each point of subject A with the corresponding point of subject B and then moves on to the next point, with the emphasis on the points of comparison themselves rather than the subjects.

If you're writing a short, simple comparison and contrast, with only a few points of comparison, the first organizational pattern might be the better one for your purpose. You'll want to open with an introduction including a thesis statement and move quickly to your first subject. Even a thesis statement as simple as "Living in Corvallis, Oregon, is every bit as desirable as living in State College, Pennsylvania" can work if you are responding to folks who wonder how you could possibly enjoy living in two drastically different locations. You could talk about the geography of Corvallis, the size of the town and suburbs, the university, and the weather and then talk about these same points for State College, following the same order. Therefore, taking them one at a time, you could prove that these two cities are both desirable places in which to live.

If you're developing a longer, more complicated comparison and contrast, however, the second organizational pattern will probably be a better choice, because the first requires readers to hold all the points of the first subject in their minds while waiting to read about those of the second subject. You could use a similar thesis statement but then discuss each of the points of comparison one at a time in relation to both subjects. For instance, you could write, "Even though Corvallis, Oregon, and State College, Pennsylvania, are on opposite sides of the United States, they offer uncannily similar ways of life." Then, using the points of comparison as the main ideas of your topic sentences, you would introduce each point in turn, discussing both cities in each paragraph and using transitional words or phrases to move between one subject and the other and from one point to the next.

You'll want to support all your points with an adequate but not necessarily equal amount of detail. Relevant details will bring your comparison and contrast to life and make it purposeful—clear, convincing, or entertaining. But providing exactly the same amount or kinds of detail in the same order for each point or each subject can make your writing sound mechanical and monotonous. So try to introduce some variation, such as giving more detail for points that are more important, complex, or unexpected. In addition, unless you're deliberately exaggerating for humorous effect, your claims of similarity or difference shouldn't sound forced or overstated, especially if you're making an analogy. Don't be afraid to acknowledge that your subjects are alike in some ways and different in others.

● Reaching a Conclusion

Whatever organizational pattern you choose, you should end with a concluding paragraph (or two) that moves beyond the mere restatement of the thesis to answer the important question "So what?" In "The Culture War of Words," Lisa Miller brings home her comparison by explaining the effects of the semantic differences between the left and the right, thinking specifically about how these differences affect policy decisions and activist work.

"Reading" and Using Visuals in Comparison and Contrast

You can diagram your comparison and contrast to make sure you have covered all the points of comparison in the case of all your subjects. The following illustration shows how you might diagram the essay about life in Corvallis, Oregon, and State College, Pennsylvania:

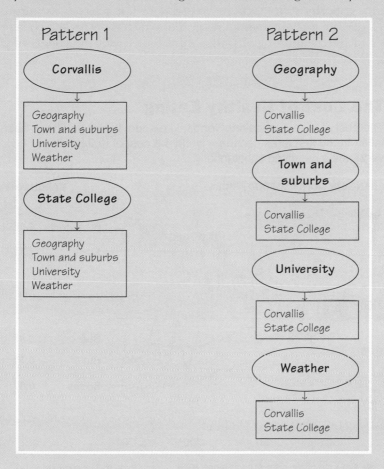

In addition, writers often use visuals in presenting a comparison or contrast to readers. Visuals such as bar graphs, line graphs, pie charts, ads like the one on page 340, and "before and after" photos quickly reveal how two or more subjects size up in comparison with each other. Whether you want to indicate Republican and Democratic voting preferences according to age or state, the daily ranges in temperature of two cities, or unemployment rates across a period of months or years, visuals can help explain your information and make your point.

To choose or compose visuals that will work effectively, though, you need to analyze the information that a visual contains or the point that it makes as well as how it conveys that information or point. You need not only to be able to "read" a visual but also to read it critically, to judge how well or poorly it achieves its purpose. Consider the accompanying line graph, which displays the changing costs of five healthful and unhealthful foods over the course of the past three decades.

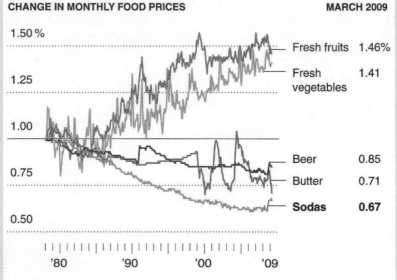

The Cost of Healthy Eating

The cost of many unhealthful foods, like soda, butter and beer, has fallen in the last three decades, while the cost of fruits and vegetables has risen substantially.

CHANGE IN MONTHLY FOOD PRICES   **MARCH 2009**

Fresh fruits   1.46%

Fresh   1.41
vegetables

Beer   0.85

Butter   0.71

Sodas   **0.67**

'80   '90   '00   '09

Lines show change in price of items since 1978, relative to overall inflation as measured by the Consumer Price Index. The price of vegetables, for example, has risen 40 percent faster than the overall index.

Source: Bureau of Labor Statistics, via Haver

What does this line graph show, and how well does it show it? The heading on the upper left indicates that the column of numbers below the label and the horizontal lines below each number measure the range of change in monthly food prices. The rows of vertical marks and numbers below the lines represent the years under investigation, 1978–2009. The labels and pointers on the right side identify the specific categories of food whose prices the graph tracks, and the text at the bottom tells readers that what the graph measures is not the actual rates of price changes but the relationship between these rates and the overall rate of inflation, as measured by the federal Consumer Price Index. Finally, on the far right the heading "March 2009" indicates the end point of the time period the graph covers, and the column of numbers below the heading provides the numerical values of the price changes for the specific kinds of food.

Each of the five jagged lines on the graph represents a different category of food, and the text sets up a comparison between two healthful categories (fresh fruits and vegetables) and three deemed unhealthful (beer, butter, and sodas). One look at the graph reveals that in relation to each other as well as to consumer goods in general, the healthful foods have dramatically increased in price since the late 1970s, while the unhealthful ones have become significantly cheaper. The reader can also tell that prices for fresh fruits and fresh vegetables tend to go up and down quite a bit from month to month, often in opposite directions from each other. Butter remained fairly stable in price for the first twenty years and then began fluctuating rapidly, whereas prices of sodas have declined almost steadily from year to year over the entire period.

How might a reader or writer use this graph? To begin, one might use the graph as an incentive to ask more questions, conduct further research, and create more comparisons. What about other foods that fall into the healthful and unhealthful categories? Have their price changes followed the same patterns? Answering these questions would require more research — research that would, for example, investigate how the prices of foods like whole-grain and organic products compare over time to the prices of processed breads and snacks such as potato chips and pretzels.

Another research topic that the graph might inspire has to do with comparing the relative diets and health of people at different income levels. For instance, because of the price differences between healthful and unhealthful foods, are lower-income people less healthy than higher-income people because they cannot often afford fresh fruits or vegetables? Answering this question would require another research investigation that would include identifying data on the eating and food-purchasing habits of people in these economic categories, as well as information about their relative health. The results of the research would be interesting indeed, as they might — or might not— provide support for an argument that the government should subsidize the production of more healthful foods at lower prices.

Or a writer might decide to investigate the patterns in price changes for individual items, such as why fresh fruits often seem to rise in price when fresh vegetables drop and vice versa, or why in the late 1990s butter prices suddenly became unstable but beer prices leveled off. Thus visuals like "The Cost of Healthy Eating" not only require close examination to understand the comparisons they are making, but also have the potential to prompt compelling questions in readers' minds that can inspire more research and writing.

Understanding and Using Comparison and Contrast

Analyzing Comparison and Contrast

1. Who is the intended audience for the "Choose less. Weigh less" poster that opened this chapter? What supporting arguments can you offer for your answer?

2. What do you think of Lisa Miller's comparison (p. 353) between the left and right's war of words over abortion? What are your thoughts on the differences between the two groups' language and political choices?

3. According to the excerpt by David Mas Masumoto (p. 344), what are the terms by which young friends are often compared and contrasted? **Working with a classmate,** enumerate the ways. Prepare to report your findings to the rest of the class.

Planning and Writing Essays Using Comparison and Contrast

1. Look again at the "Choose less. Weigh less" poster that opened this chapter. Write a few paragraphs about your eating choices, comparing and contrasting the possibilities available to you. How do you make decisions about where, what, and how much you eat? What is your basis for comparison? What are your points of comparison? How do you make "smart" choices?

2. Often we engage in comparison and contrast to make a decision. For example, how did you come to attend this school? Make a list of the colleges where you were accepted; then list the features you considered as you compared them, such as location, cost, financial assistance, academic programs, physical appearance, and student population. Draft a two- to three-page essay in which you explain your decision to attend this college. If you didn't choose among several colleges, explain how you came to choose one of the courses you're taking this term instead of one or more others that you considered. As you work, refer to the following guidelines for checking over the use of comparison and contrast.

3. **Working with a classmate,** plan a comparison–and–contrast essay about the two of you. What might be the basis for your comparison? What points would you compare or contrast? Most important, what would be a realistic purpose for comparing and contrasting yourselves? After you have answered these questions, draft a two- to three-page essay relying on the input of your classmate and the following guidelines for checking over the use of comparison and contrast.

✔ Checking Over the Use of Comparison and Contrast

1. What is the purpose of your comparison and contrast? Is it to explain, to evaluate a choice, to persuade, or to entertain? Do you achieve that purpose?
2. Who is the audience? Have you taken the audience into consideration in developing the comparison and contrast?
3. What is the thesis statement? Underline it. Does it make a strong point?
4. What is the basis for comparison? Do the subjects you are comparing have at least one point in common?
5. What are the points of comparison? Have you considered points that go beyond the obvious?
6. How have you organized the comparison and contrast — according to pattern 1 or pattern 2 (p. 355)? Is the organization easy to follow? If not, would the other pattern make it easier to follow?
7. Is there appropriate supporting detail for each subject and point? Is there too much information on one subject or point and not enough on others? Or is the supporting detail so similar as to be monotonous?
8. How do you move readers from one subject and one point of comparison to the next? Underline the transitional words or phrases that you have used. Are there other places where transitions are needed?
9. If you are using visuals, do they clearly convey the points you want them to make? Do you need to add labels, captions, or references in the written text?
10. What's the point of your comparison and contrast? Does the conclusion go beyond your thesis to answer the question "So what?"

READINGS

SUZANNE BRITT
Neat People vs. Sloppy People

North Carolina native Suzanne Britt (b. 1946) teaches part-time at Meredith College in Raleigh, North Carolina, and has published essays and columns in *Authors Ink*, the *Cleveland Plain Dealer*, the *Charlotte Observer*, and a range of other magazines and newspapers. Her books include a history of Meredith College, two writing textbooks, and two collections of essays, *Skinny People Are Dull and Crunchy like Carrots* (1982) and *Show and Tell* (1983); the following essay first appeared in the latter.

> **Preview**   If people can be divided into the two basic categories that Britt focuses on, in which category do you belong, neat or sloppy? What specific evidence can you supply for your answer?

Britt offers her thesis statement here.

I've finally figured out the difference between neat 1 people and sloppy people. The distinction is, as always, moral. Neat people are lazier and meaner than sloppy people.

Britt's basis for comparison is morality. This topic sentence enables her to move into the specifics about how sloppy people are morally superior to neat people. She arranges her essay subject by subject, discussing sloppy people first.

Sloppy people, you see, are not really sloppy. 2 Their sloppiness is merely the unfortunate consequence of their extreme moral rectitude. Sloppy people carry in their mind's eye a heavenly vision, a precise plan, that is so stupendous, so perfect, it can't be achieved in this world or the next.

Sloppy people live in Never–Never Land. Some- 3 day is their métier. Someday they are planning to alphabetize all their books and set up home catalogs. Someday they will go through their wardrobes and mark certain items for tentative mending and certain items for passing on to relatives of similar shape and size. Someday sloppy people will make

family scrapbooks into which they will put newspaper clippings, postcards, locks of hair, and the
dried corsage from their senior prom. Someday they
will file everything on the surface of their desks,
including the cash receipts from coffee purchases
at the snack shop. Someday they will sit down and
read all the back issues of *The New Yorker.*

4   For all these noble reasons and more, sloppy
people never get neat. They aim too high and wide.
They save everything, planning someday to file, order, and straighten out the world. But while these
ambitious plans take clearer and clearer shape in
their heads, the books spill from the shelves onto the
floor, the clothes pile up in the hamper and closet,
the family mementos accumulate in every drawer,
the surface of the desk is buried under mounds of
paper, and the unread magazines threaten to reach
the ceiling.

5   Sloppy people can't bear to part with anything.
They give loving attention to every detail. When
sloppy people say they're going to tackle the surface of a desk, they really mean it. Not a paper will
go unturned; not a rubber band will go unboxed.
Four hours or two weeks into the excavation, the
desk looks exactly the same, primarily because the
sloppy person is meticulously creating new piles of
papers with new headings and scrupulously stopping to read all the old book catalogs before he
throws them away. A neat person would just bull-
doze the desk.

Here Britt transitions to
a discussion of the
negative characteristics
of neat people.

6   Neat people are bums and clods at heart. They
have cavalier attitudes toward possessions, including family heirlooms. Everything is just another
dust-catcher to them. If anything collects dust, it's
got to go and that's that. Neat people will toy with
the idea of throwing the children out of the house
just to cut down on the clutter.

7   Neat people don't care about process. They like
results. What they want to do is get the whole thing
over with so they can sit down and watch the ras-
slin' on TV. Neat people operate on two unvarying
principles: Never handle any item twice, and throw
everything away.

8   The only thing messy in a neat person's house
is the trash can. The minute something comes to a

neat person's hand, he will look at it, try to decide if it has immediate use and, finding none, throw it in the trash.

Notice in this paragraph and the next three how Britt uses strong topic sentences to introduce new arguments that support her thesis.

Neat people are especially vicious with mail. 9 They never go through their mail unless they are standing directly over a trash can. If the trash can is beside the mailbox, even better. All ads, catalogs, pleas for charitable contributions, church bulletins, and money–saving coupons go straight into the trash can without being opened. All letters from home, postcards from Europe, bills, and pay-checks are opened, immediately responded to, then dropped in the trash can. Neat people keep their receipts only for tax purposes. That's it. No sentimental salvaging of birthday cards or the last letter a dying relative ever wrote. Into the trash it goes.

Neat people place neatness above everything, 10 even economics. They are incredibly wasteful. Neat people throw away several toys every time they walk through the den. I knew a neat person once who threw away a perfectly good dish drainer because it had mold on it. The drainer was too much trouble to wash. And neat people sell their furniture when they move. They will sell a La–Z–Boy re-cliner while you are reclining in it.

11   Neat people are no good to borrow from. Neat people buy everything in expensive little single portions. They get their flour and sugar in two-pound bags. They wouldn't consider clipping a coupon, saving a leftover, reusing plastic nondairy whipped cream containers, or rinsing off tin foil and draping it over the unmoldy dish drainer. You can never borrow a neat person's newspaper to see what's playing at the movies. Neat people have the paper all wadded up and in the trash by 7:05 A.M.

12   Neat people cut a clean swath through the organic as well as the inorganic world. People, animals, and things are all one to them. They are so insensitive. After they've finished with the pantry, the medicine cabinet, and the attic, they will throw out the red geranium (too many leaves), sell the dog (too many fleas), and send the children off to boarding school (too many scuff-marks on the hardwood floors).

Reading Closely

1. Britt divides people into two general categories: neat and sloppy. But she also connects each of these categories with other personal attributes.

What are they? Are the connections believable? What support can you give for your answers? Be prepared to share your answers with the rest of the class.

2. In her opening paragraph, Britt writes, "The distinction is, as always, moral." How exactly does she develop the morality issues in her comparison and contrast?

3. What specific points of comparison does Britt use to create distinctions between neat and sloppy people?

4. What comparisons and contrasts can you draw between the two photographs on pages 362 and 363? Do you think they support Britt's analysis of the moral differences between neat people and sloppy people? Or do they call it into question?

Considering Larger Issues

1. Britt uses opposites as a way to categorize people. **Working with a classmate or two,** develop a third category of people to which you can compare and contrast both neat and sloppy people. Name the category and the specific behaviorial and "moral" characteristics of that group. Be prepared to share your group response with the rest of the class.

2. What do you see as the purpose for Britt's essay? Who is her intended audience? How are the two related?

3. Are there any similarities between neat and sloppy people that Britt has left unmentioned?

4. Where on the spectrum between serious and humorous do you rank Britt's essay? What specific passages support your answer? Be prepared to share your response with the rest of the class.

5. **COMBINING METHODS.** Mark the places where Britt uses *cause-and-effect analysis.* How do these passages enhance her essay?

Thinking about Language

1. Using a dictionary or the context of the essay, define the following terms:

moral rectitude (2)	meticulously (5)	salvaging (9)
stupendous (2)	scrupulously (5)	swath (12)
métier (3)	cavalier (6)	organic (12)
excavation (5)	unvarying (7)	inorganic (12)

2. In paragraph 4, Britt uses three fairly short sentences followed by a very long one. What effect does this sequence create, and how does it relate to the point she's making in this paragraph?

Writing Your Own Essays Using Comparison and Contrast

1. Using Britt's essay as a model, draft a three- to four-page essay in which you divide people into two groups who exhibit opposite characteristics: fast and slow, honest and dishonest, hardworking and lazy, extroverted and introverted, or some other set of easy opposites. If you consider Britt's essay to be serious, then write a serious essay. If you consider it to be humorous, then try humor. Be sure to refer to the guidelines for checking over the use of comparison and contrast on page 359.

2. Movies, television shows, and sports events all feature people who are compared and contrasted: *Harry Potter's* Harry Potter and Lucius Malfoy; *Twilight's* Edward Cullen and Jacob Black; *Lost's* John Locke and Jack Shepherd; *The Office's* Jim Halpert and Dwight Schrute; Oprah Winfrey and Ellen DeGeneres; LeBron James and Kobe Bryant; Venus Williams and Serena Williams; Peyton Manning and Tom Brady. Choose two people or types of people who share a basis for comparison, and draft an essay of three to four pages comparing and contrasting them for a specific purpose. Be sure to refer to the guidelines for checking over the use of comparison and contrast on page 359.

DAVE BARRY
Guys vs. Men

Associated with the *Miami Herald* since 1983, Dave Barry (b. 1947) is one of the most widely syndicated columnists in the United States. He is best known for his humorous writings, but his commentary also earned him a 1988 Pulitzer Prize. Besides writing a daily newspaper column, Barry is lead guitarist for the Rock Bottom Remainders and has published a number of best-selling books, among them *Dave Barry Is Not Taking This Sitting Down* (2000), *Tricky Business* (2002), *Boogers Are My Beat* (2003), and *Dave Barry's History of the Millennium (So Far)* (2006). With coauthor Ridley Pearson, Barry has also written a number of children's books, including *Peter and the Starcatchers* (2006), *Peter and the Shadow Thieves* (2006), and *Escape from the Carnivale* (2006). The following selection was first published as the introduction *to Dave Barry's Complete Guide to Guys* (1995).

> **Preview** Write for a few minutes about the differences you see between "guys" and "men."

This is a book about guys. It's *not* a book about men. There are already 1 way too many books about men, and most of them are *way* too serious.

Men itself is a serious word, not to mention *manhood* and *manly.* Such 2 words make being male sound like a very important activity, as opposed to what it primarily consists of, namely, possessing a set of minor and frequently unreliable organs.

But men tend to attach great significance to Manhood. This results in 3 certain characteristically masculine, by which I mean stupid, behavioral patterns that can produce unfortunate results such as violent crime, war, spitting, and ice hockey. These things have given males a bad name.[1] And the "Men's Movement," which is supposed to bring out the more positive aspects of Manliness, seems to be densely populated with loons and goobers.

So I'm saying that there's another way to look at males: not as ag- 4 gressive macho dominators; not as sensitive, liberated, hugging drummers; but as *guys.*

And what, exactly, do I mean by "guys"? I don't know. I haven't 5 thought that much about it. One of the major characteristics of guyhood is that we guys don't spend a lot of time pondering our deep innermost feelings. There is a serious question in my mind about whether guys actually *have* deep innermost feelings, unless you count, for example, loyalty to the Detroit Tigers, or fear of bridal showers.

But although I can't define exactly what it means to be a guy, I can 6 describe certain guy characteristics, such as:

---

[1] Specifically, "asshole."

GUYS LIKE NEAT STUFF

By "neat," I mean "mechanical and unnecessarily complex." I'll give 7
you an example. Right now I'm typing these words on an *extremely* powerful computer. It's the latest in a line of maybe ten computers I've owned,
each one more powerful than the last. My computer is chock full of RAM
and ROM and bytes and megahertzes and various other items that enable a computer to kick data–processing butt. It is probably capable of
supervising the entire U.S. air–defense apparatus while simultaneously
processing the tax return of every resident of Ohio. I use it mainly to
write a newspaper column. This is an activity wherein I sit and stare at
the screen for maybe ten minutes, then, using only my forefingers, slowly
type something like:

Henry Kissinger* looks like a big wart.   8

I stare at this for another ten minutes, have an inspiration, then am- 9
plify the original thought as follows:

Henry Kissinger looks like a big fat wart.   10

Then I stare at that for another ten minutes, pondering whether I 11
should try to work in the concept of "hairy."

This is absurdly simple work for my computer. It sits there, humming 12
impatiently, bored to death, passing the time between keystrokes via
brain–teaser activities such as developing a Unified Field Theory of the
universe and translating the complete works of Shakespeare into rap.[2]

In other words, this computer is absurdly overqualified to work for 13
me, and yet soon, I guarantee, I will buy an *even more powerful* one. I won't
be able to stop myself. I'm a guy.

Probably the ultimate example of the fundamental guy drive to have 14
neat stuff is the Space Shuttle. Granted, the guys in charge of this program *claim* it has a Higher Scientific Purpose, namely to see how humans function in space. But of course we have known for years how
humans function in space: They float around and say things like: "Looks
real good, Houston!"

No, the real reason for the existence of the Space Shuttle is that it 15
is one humongous and spectacularly gizmo–intensive item of hardware.
Guys can tinker with it practically forever, and occasionally even get it
to work, and use it to place *other* complex mechanical items into orbit,
where they almost immediately break, which provides a great excuse to
send the Space Shuttle up *again*. It's Guy Heaven.

Other results of the guy need to have stuff are Star Wars, the recre- 16
ational boating industry, monorails, nuclear weapons, and wristwatches

---

* **Henry Kissinger** (b. 1923): foreign policy adviser to President Richard Nixon and
U.S. secretary of state, 1973–77.

[2] To be or not? I got to *know.*
    Might kill myself by the end of the *show.*

that indicate the phase of the moon. I am not saying that women haven't been involved in the development or use of this stuff. I'm saying that, without guys, this stuff probably would not exist; just as, without women, virtually every piece of furniture in the world would still be in its original position. Guys do not have a basic need to rearrange furniture. Whereas a woman who could cheerfully use the same computer for fifty-three years will rearrange her furniture on almost a weekly basis, sometimes in the dead of night. She'll be sound asleep in bed, and suddenly, at 2 A.M., she'll be awakened by the urgent thought: *The blue-green sofa needs to go perpendicular to the wall instead of parallel, and it needs to go there RIGHT NOW.* So she'll get up and move it, which of course necessitates moving other furniture, and soon she has rearranged her entire living room, shifting great big heavy pieces that ordinarily would require several burly men to lift, because there are few forces in Nature more powerful than a woman who needs to rearrange furniture. Every so often a guy will wake up to discover that, because of his wife's overnight efforts, he now lives in an entirely different house.

(I realize that I'm making gender-based generalizations here, but my   17
feeling is that if God did not want us to make gender-based generalizations, She would not have given us genders.)

GUYS LIKE A REALLY POINTLESS CHALLENGE

Not long ago I was sitting in my office at the *Miami Herald*'s Sunday   18
magazine, *Tropic*, reading my fan mail,[3] when I heard several of my guy coworkers in the hallway talking about how fast they could run the forty-yard dash. These are guys in their thirties and forties who work in journalism, where the most demanding physical requirement is the ability to digest vending-machine food. In other words, these guys have absolutely no need to run the forty-yard dash.

But one of them, Mike Wilson, was writing a story about a star high   19
school football player who could run it in 4.38 seconds. Now if Mike had written a story about, say, a star high school poet, none of my guy coworkers would have suddenly decided to find out how well they could write sonnets. But when Mike turned in his story, they became *deeply* concerned about how fast they could run the forty-yard dash. They were so concerned that the magazine editor, Tom Shroder, decided that they should get a stopwatch and go out to a nearby park and find out. Which they did, a bunch of guys taking off their shoes and running around barefoot in a public park on company time.

This is what I heard them talking about, out in the hall. I heard Tom,   20
who was thirty-eight years old, saying that his time in the forty had

---

[3] Typical fan letter: "Who cuts your hair? Beavers?"

been 5.75 seconds. And I thought to myself: This is ridiculous. These are middle-aged guys, supposedly adults, and they're out there *bragging* about their performance in this stupid juvenile footrace. Finally I couldn't stand it anymore.

"Hey!" I shouted. *"I could beat 5.75 seconds."*   21

So we went out to the park and measured off forty yards, and the   22 guys told me that I had three chances to make my best time. On the first try my time was 5.78 seconds, just three-hundredths of a second slower than Tom's, even though, at forty-five, I was seven years older than he. So I just *knew* I'd beat him on the second attempt if I ran really, really hard, which I did for a solid ten yards, at which point my left hamstring muscle, which had not yet shifted into Spring Mode from Mail-Reading Mode, went, and I quote, "pop."

I had to be helped off the field. I was in considerable pain, and I was   23 obviously not going to be able to walk right for weeks. The other guys were very sympathetic, especially Tom, who took the time to call me at home, where I was sitting with an ice pack on my leg and twenty-three Advil in my bloodstream, so he could express his concern.

"Just remember," he said, *"you didn't beat my time."*   24

There are countless other examples of guys rising to meet pointless   25 challenges. Virtually all sports fall into this category as well as a large part of U.S. foreign policy. ("I'll bet you can't capture Manuel Noriega!"* "Oh YEAH??")

GUYS DO NOT HAVE A RIGID
AND WELL-DEFINED MORAL CODE

This is not the same as saying that guys are bad. Guys *are* capable   26 of doing bad things, but this generally happens when they try to be Men and start becoming manly and aggressive and stupid. When they're being just plain guys, they aren't so much actively *evil* as they are *lost.* Because guys have never really grasped the Basic Human Moral Code, which I believe was invented by women millions of years ago when all the guys were out engaging in some other activity, such as seeing who could burp the loudest. When they came back, there were certain rules that they were expected to follow unless they wanted to get into Big Trouble, and they have been trying to follow these rules ever since, with extremely irregular results. Because guys have never *internalized* these rules. Guys are similar to my small auxiliary backup dog, Zippy, a guy dog[4] who has been told numerous times that he is *not* supposed to (1) get

---

* **Manuel Noriega** (b. 1934): Panamanian dictator removed from power by armed U.S. intervention in 1989.

[4] I also have a female dog, Earnest, who *never* breaks the rules.

into the kitchen garbage or (2) poop on the floor. He knows that these are the rules, but he has never really understood *why*, and sometimes he gets to thinking: Sure, I am *ordinarily* not supposed to get into the garbage, but obviously this rule is not meant to apply when there are certain extenuating[5] circumstances, such as (1) somebody just threw away some perfectly good seven-week-old Kung Pao Chicken, and (2) I am home alone.

And so when the humans come home, the kitchen floor has been   27
transformed into Garbage-Fest USA, and Zippy, who usually comes rushing up, is off in a corner disguised in a wig and sunglasses, hoping to get into the Federal Bad Dog Relocation Program before the humans discover the scene of the crime.

When I yell at him, he frequently becomes so upset that he poops on   28
the floor.

Morally, most guys are just like Zippy, only taller and usually less hairy.   29
Guys are *aware* of the rules of moral behavior, but they have trouble keeping these rules in the forefronts of their minds at certain times, especially the present. This is especially true in the area of faithfulness to one's mate. I realize, of course, that there are countless examples of guys being faithful to their mates until they die, usually as a result of being eaten by their mates immediately following copulation. Guys outside of the spider community, however, do not have a terrific record of faithfulness.

I'm not saying guys are scum. I'm saying that many guys who con-   30
sider themselves to be committed to their marriages will stray if they are confronted with overwhelming temptation, defined as "virtually any temptation."

Okay, so maybe I *am* saying guys are scum. But they're not *mean-*   31
spirited scum. And few of them—even when they are out of town on business trips, far from their wives, and have a clear-cut opportunity—will poop on the floor.

GUYS ARE NOT GREAT AT COMMUNICATING THEIR INTIMATE FEELINGS, ASSUMING THEY HAVE ANY

This is an aspect of guyhood that is very frustrating to women. A guy   32
will be reading the newspaper, and the phone will ring; he'll answer it, listen for ten minutes, hang up, and resume reading. Finally his wife will say: "Who was that?"

And he'll say: "Phil Wonkerman's mom."   33

(Phil is an old friend they haven't heard from in seventeen years.)   34

And the wife will say, "Well?"   35

And the guy will say, "Well what?"   36

---

[5] I am taking some liberties here with Zippy's vocabulary. More likely in his mind, he uses the term *mitigating*.

And the wife will say, "What did she *say?*"   37

And the guy will say "She said Phil is fine," making it clear by his   38
tone of voice that, although he does not wish to be rude, he is trying to
read the newspaper, and he happens to be right in the middle of an important panel of "Calvin and Hobbes."

But the wife, ignoring this, will say, "That's *all* she said?"   39

And she will not let up. She will continue to ask district–attorney–style   40
questions, forcing the guy to recount the conversation until she's satisfied
that she has the entire story, which is that Phil just got out of prison after
serving a sentence for a murder he committed when he became a drug
addict because of the guilt he felt when his wife died in a freak submarine accident while Phil was having an affair with a nun, but now he's
all straightened out and has a good job as a trapeze artist and is almost
through with the surgical part of his sex change and recently became
happily engaged to marry a prominent member of the Grateful Dead, so
in other words he is fine, which is *exactly* what the guy told her in the first
place, but is that enough? No. She wants to hear *every single detail.*

Or let's say two couples get together after a long separation. The two   41
women will have a conversation, lasting several days, during which they
discuss virtually every significant event that has occurred in their lives
and the lives of those they care about, sharing their innermost thoughts,
analyzing and probing, inevitably coming to a deeper understanding of
each other, and a strengthening of a cherished friendship. Whereas the
guys will watch the play–offs.

This is not to say the guys won't share their feelings. Sometimes   42
they'll get quite emotional.

"That's not a FOUL??" they'll say.   43

Or: "YOU'RE TELLING ME THAT'S NOT A FOUL???"   44

I have a good friend, Gene, and one time, when he was going   45
through a major medical development in his life, we spent a weekend
together. During this time Gene and I talked a lot and enjoyed each other's company immensely, but—this is true—the most intimate personal
statement he made to me is that he has reached Level 24 of a video game
called "Arkanoid." He had even seen the Evil Presence, although he refused to tell me what it looks like. We're very close, but there is a limit.

You may think that my friends and I are Neanderthals, and that a   46
lot of guys are different. This is true. A lot of guys don't use words at *all.*
They communicate entirely by nonverbal methods, such as sharing bait.

Are you starting to see what I mean by "guyness"? I'm basically talking   47
about the part of the male psyche that is less serious and/or aggressive
than the Manly Manhood part, but still essentially very male. My feeling is that the world would be a much better[6] place if more males would

---

[6] As measured by total sales of [my] book.

Example Chart

Men	Guys
Vince Lombardi	Joe Namath
Oliver North	Gilligan
Hemingway	Gary Larson
Columbus	Whichever astronaut hit the first golf ball on the Moon
Superman	Bart Simpson
Doberman pinschers	Labrador retrievers
Abbott	Costello
Captain Ahab	Captain Kangaroo
Satan	Snidely Whiplash
The pope	Willard Scott
Germany	Italy
Geraldo	Katie Couric

stop trying so hard to be Men and instead settle for being Guys. Think of the historical problems that could have been avoided if more males had been able to keep their genderhood in its proper perspective, both in themselves and in others. ("Hey, Adolf, just because you happen to possess a set of minor and frequently unreliable organs, that is no reason to in–vade Poland.") And think how much happier women would be if, instead of endlessly fretting about what the males in their lives are thinking, they could relax, secure in the knowledge that the correct answer is: *very little.*

Yes, what we need, on the part of both genders, is more understand–   48
ing of guyness. And that is why I wrote this book. I intend to explore in detail every major facet of guyhood, including the historical facet, the sociological facet, the physiological facet, the psychosexual facet, and the facet of how come guys spit so much. Every statement of fact you will read in this book is either based on actual laboratory tests, or else I made it up. But you can trust me. I'm a guy.

Stimulus–Response Comparison Chart: Women vs. Men vs. Guys

Stimulus	Typical Woman Response	Typical Man Response	Typical Guy Response
An untamed river in the wilderness.	Contemplate its beauty.	Build a dam.	See who can pee the farthest off the dam.
A child who is sent home from school for being disruptive in class.	Talk to the child in an effort to de–termine the cause.	Threaten to send the child to a mil–itary academy.	Teach the child how to make armpit farts.
Human mortality	Religious faith	The pyramids	Bungee–jumping

Reading Closely

1. Define *guy* and *man*, according to Dave Barry. What details does Barry provide about how each of them lives his life?

2. How would you relate the characteristics of these two groups of males within U.S. culture? Discuss your responses **with several classmates,** determining whether you all read Barry's piece in similar or different ways. Share your group's findings with the rest of the class.

3. How does the information organized in either chart extend Barry's examples?

Considering Larger Issues

1. What is the purpose of this introduction? Who is Barry's audience? How does his audience affect his purpose, and how does his purpose influence the way he addresses his audience? Write out your answers, supplying evidence from the selection as support.

2. How exactly do the two charts near the end enhance the thesis? What is Barry's thesis?

3. Determine the organizational pattern, and make an outline of the selection that shows the pattern of organization. As you look over your outline and the selection, consider why Barry uses this particular organizational pattern. Be prepared to share your response with the rest of the class.

4. **COMBINING METHODS.** How does Barry use *cause-and-effect analysis* to support his comparison and contrast? Mark the specific cause-and-effect passages, and discuss their impact with your classmates.

Thinking about Language

1. Referring to the context or to your dictionary, define the following terms. Be prepared to share your answers with the rest of the class.

loons (3)	gender-based (17)	forefronts (29)
dominators (4)	hamstring (22)	recount (40)
megahertzes (7)	internalized (26)	Neanderthals (46)
burly (16)	extenuating (26)	nonverbal (46)

2. How might Barry define *maturity*? What are the various ways he illustrates this term in the selection? Write out your answers, and prepare to share them with the rest of the class.

3. **Working with two or three classmates,** discuss the initial effect of the opening paragraph as well as its overall effect after you've read the entire selection. What evidence from Barry's text supports your responses? How would you describe the style of Barry's opening? Share your responses with the rest of the class.

Writing Your Own Essays Using Comparison and Contrast

1. Attend or watch a sporting event **with a group of students** (or others) that includes both sexes. Pay careful attention to the ways various spectators respond, taking copious and very careful notes as you observe how others watch the game. Can you compare and contrast your findings in any meaningful way? Did the men react differently from the guys? Did the women respond differently from either or both of those two male groups? Draft a two- to three-page essay in which you compare and contrast the behavior of either the men and the guys or the males and the females. Be sure to follow the guidelines in "Checking Over the Use of Comparison and Contrast" (p. 359).

2. Can women be broken down into two groups comparable to "men" and "guys"? If so, draft a three- to four-page essay, modeled after Barry's, in which you compare and contrast these two groups of women. Make assertions about each group, and support your assertions with examples and details. Be sure to establish clear points of comparison. If your examples can be ironic and humorous, like Barry's, so much the better. As you draft and revise, be sure to follow the guidelines in "Checking Over the Use of Comparison and Contrast" (p. 359).

DEBORAH TANNEN
Cross Talk

● Deborah Tannen (b. 1945) came to national attention in 1990 with the publication of *You Just Don't Understand* and consolidated her reputation as an expert in the ways people communicate — or fail to communicate — with *Talking from 9 to 5* (1993), *Gender and Discourse* (1994), *The Argument Culture* (1998), *I Only Say This Because I Love You* (2002), and *You're Wearing That? Understanding Mothers and Daughters in Conversation* (2006). But long before she became famous among the general public, this professor of linguistics at Georgetown University had established herself as a brilliant and prolific academic scholar by carefully exploring the connections between language and the situations in which it is used. Tannen's specialty is sociolinguistics, the study of the intersection between society and language (between class and language, gender and language, ethnicity and language, race and language, geographic location and language). The following essay, "Cross Talk," is excerpted from *You Just Don't Understand*.

> **Preview** As you read, consider if — and if so, where — Tannen inserts her own opinion as she compares and contrasts.

A woman who owns a bookstore needed to have a talk with the store 1 manager. She had told him to help the bookkeeper with billing, he had agreed, and now, days later, he still hadn't done it. Thinking how much she disliked this part of her work, she sat down with the manager to clear things up. They traced the problem to a breakdown in communication.

She had said, "Sarah needs help with the bills. What do you think 2 about helping her out?" He had responded, "OK," by which he meant, "OK, I'll think about whether or not I want to help her." During the next day he thought about it and concluded that he'd rather not.

This wasn't just an ordinary communication breakdown that could 3 happen between any two people. It was a particular sort of breakdown that tends to occur between women and men.

Most women avoid giving orders. More comfortable with decision- 4 making by consensus, they tend to phrase requests as questions, to give others the feeling they have some say in the matter and are not being bossed around. But this doesn't mean they aren't making their wishes clear. Most women would have understood the bookstore owner's question, "What do you think about helping her out?" as assigning a task in a considerate way.

The manager, however, took the owner's words literally. She had 5 asked him what he thought; she hadn't told him to *do* anything. So he felt within his rights when he took her at her word, thought about it and decided not to help Sarah.

Women in positions of authority are likely to regard such responses 6 as insubordination: "He knows I am in charge, and he knows what I want; if he doesn't do it, he is resisting my authority."

There may be a kernel of truth in this view—most men are inclined   7
to resist authority if they can because being in a subordinate position
makes them intensely uncomfortable. But indirect requests that are transparent to women may be genuinely opaque to men. They assume that
people in authority will give orders if they really want something done.

These differences in management styles are one of many manifesta-   8
tions of gender differences in how we talk to one another. Women use
language to create connection and rapport; men use it to negotiate their
status in a hierarchical order. It isn't that women are unaware of status or
that men don't build rapport, but that *the genders tend to focus on different goals.*

THE SOURCE OF GENDER DIFFERENCES

These differences stem from the way boys and girls learn to use   9
language while growing up. Girls tend to play indoors, either in small
groups or with one other girl. The center of a girl's social life is her best
friend, with whom she spends a great deal of time sitting, talking and exchanging secrets. It is the telling of secrets that makes them best friends.
Boys tend to play outdoors, in larger groups, usually in competitive
games. It's doing things together that makes them friends.

Anthropologist Marjorie Harness Goodwin compared boys and girls   10
at play in a black inner–city neighborhood in Philadelphia. Her findings,
which have been supported by researchers in other settings, show that the
boys' groups are hierarchical: high–status boys give orders, and low–status
boys have to follow them, so they end up being told what to do. Girls'
groups tend to be egalitarian: girls who appeared "better" than others or
gave orders were not countenanced and in some cases were ostracized.

So while boys are learning to fear being "put down" and pushed   11
around, girls are learning to fear being "locked out." Whereas high–status
boys establish and reinforce their authority by giving orders and resisting doing what others want, girls tend to make suggestions, which are
likely to be taken up by the group.

CROSS–GENDER COMMUNICATION IN THE WORKPLACE

The implications of these different conversational habits and con-   12
cerns in terms of office interactions are staggering. Men are inclined to
continue to jockey for position, trying to resist following orders as much
as possible within the constraints of their jobs.

Women, on the other hand, are inclined to do what they sense their   13
bosses want, whether or not they are ordered to. By the same token,
women in positions of authority are inclined to phrase their requests as
suggestions and to assume they will be respected because of their authority. These assumptions are likely to hold up as long as both parties are
women, but they may well break down in cross–gender communication.

© Scott Adams/Dist. by United Feature Syndicate, Inc.

When a woman is in the position of authority, such as the bookstore 14
owner, she may find her requests are systematically misunderstood by
men. And when a woman is working for a male boss, she may find that
her boss gives bald commands that seem unnecessarily imperious because most women would prefer to be asked rather than ordered. One
woman who worked at an all-male radio station commented that the
way the men she worked for told her what to do made her feel as if she
should salute and say, "Yes, boss."

Many men complain that a woman who is indirect in making re- 15
quests is manipulative: she's trying to get them to do what she wants
without telling them to do it. Another common accusation is that she is
insecure: she doesn't know what she wants. But if a woman gives direct
orders, the same men might complain that she is aggressive, unfeminine,
or worse.

Women are in a double bind: *If we talk like women, we are not respected. If* 16
we talk like men, we are not liked.

We have to walk a fine line, finding ways to be more direct with- 17
out appearing bossy. The bookstore owner may never be comfortable by
directly saying, "Help Sarah with the billing today," but she might find
some compromise such as, "Sarah needs help with the billing. I'd appreciate it if you would make some time to help her out in the next day or
two." This request is clear, while still reflecting women's preferences for
giving reasons and options.

What if you're the subordinate and your boss is a man who's offend- 18
ing you daily by giving you orders? If you know him well enough, one
potential solution is "metacommunication"—that is, talk about communication. Point out the differences between women and men, and discuss
how you could accommodate to each other's styles. (You may want to
give him a copy of this article or my book.)

But if you don't have the kind of relationship that makes metacom- 19
munication possible, you could casually, even jokingly, suggest he give
orders another way. Or just try to remind yourself it's a cross-cultural
difference and try not to take his curtness personally.

HOW TO HANDLE A MEETING

There are other aspects of women's styles that can work against us in 20
a work setting. Because women are most comfortable using language to
create rapport with someone they feel close to, and men are used to talking in a group where they have to prove themselves and display what
they know, a formal meeting can be a natural for men and a hard nut
to crack for women. Many women find it difficult to speak up at meetings; if they do, they may find their comments ignored, perhaps later to
be resuscitated by a man who gets credit for the idea. Part of this is simply due to the expectation that men will have more important things to
contribute.

But the way women and men tend to present themselves can aggra- 21
vate this inequity. At meetings, men are more likely to speak often, at
length and in a declamatory manner. They may state their opinions as
fact and leave it to others to challenge them.

Women, on the other hand, are often worried about appearing to 22
talk too much—a fear that is justified by research showing that when
they talk equally, women are perceived as talking more than men. As a
result, many women are hesitant to speak at a meeting and inclined to
be succinct and tentative when they do.

DEVELOPING OPTIONS

Working on changing your presentational style is one option; an- 23
other is to make your opinions known in private conversation with the
key people before a meeting. And if you are the key person, it would be
wise to talk personally to the women on your staff rather than assuming
all participants have had a chance to express themselves at the meeting.

Many women's reticence about displaying their knowledge at a meet- 24
ing is related to their reluctance to boast. They find it more humble to
keep quiet about their accomplishments and wait for someone else to
notice them. But most men learn early on to display their accomplishments and skills. And women often find that no one bothers to ferret out

their achievements if they don't put them on display. Again, a woman risks criticism if she talks about her achievements, but this may be a risk she needs to take, to make sure she gets credit for her work.

I would never want to be heard as telling women to adopt men's 25 styles across the board. For one thing, there are many situations in which women's styles are more successful. For example, the inclination to make decisions by consensus can be a boon to a woman in a managerial position. Many people, men as well as women, would rather feel they have influence in decision–making than be given orders.

Moreover, recommending that women adopt men's styles would be 26 offensive, as well as impractical, because women are judged by the norms for women's behavior, and doing the same thing as men has a very different, often negative, effect.

A STARTING POINT

Simply knowing about gender differences in conversational style 27 provides a starting point for improving relations with the women and men who are above and below you in a hierarchy.

The key is *flexibility*; a way of talking that works beautifully with one 28 person may be a disaster with another. If one way of talking isn't working, try another, rather than trying harder to do more of the same.

Once you know what the parameters are, you can become an ob– 29 server of your own interactions, and a style–switcher when you choose.

Reading Closely

1. What's this selection about? In one paragraph, summarize the entire passage.

2. What reasons does Tannen give or imply for the source of differences between the ways men and women use language?

3. **Working with a classmate,** list all the common purposes men and women have for using language. Then, using information from the reading, list the ways Tannen says men use language and then list the ways she says women use language. Do you think that what Tannen writes is true? Can you think of any exceptions to her generalizations? Report your responses to the class.

4. Which of Tannen's generalizations about gender differences in language does the Dilbert cartoon strip on page 377 demonstrate — or disprove?

Considering Larger Issues

1. Who is Tannen's audience for this essay? What evidence from the essay supports your answer? Write out your answers.

2. What is the purpose of Tannen's essay? **Working with a classmate,** compare responses and, together, determine the purpose.

3. Assuming that Tannen's scholarly opinions about the ways men and women use language are correct, what are some aspects about your own use of language that you might like to change? List some ways that you currently use language. Then, alongside each point, write the way you'd like to change it. What might be the consequences of your change?

4. PAIRED READINGS. In the preceding essay, Dave Barry compares and contrasts guys and men. In this essay, Tannen compares and contrasts men and women. Compare and contrast these two essays, considering how both writers treat questions of gender and gender difference.

5. COMBINING METHODS. In what ways does Tannen use comparison and contrast to fulfill the overall purpose of her essay? Mark the passages in which she uses *description, narration,* and *exemplification* to support that overall purpose.

Thinking about Language

1. Using the context of the selection or your dictionary, define each of the following terms. Be prepared to share your answers with the rest of the class.

insubordination (6)	ostracized (10)	inequity (21)
transparent (7)	systematically (14)	declamatory (21)
opaque (7)	bald (14)	succinct (22)
manifestations (8)	imperious (14)	reticence (24)
rapport (8, 20)	double bind (16)	ferret out (24)
hierarchical (10)	metacommunication (18)	boon (25)
egalitarian (10)	resuscitated (20)	parameters (29)
countenanced (10)		

2. What specific language (specialized words, terms, phrases) does Tannen use that convinces her readers of her professionalism and expertise? List and define these words, terms, and phrases, and compare your list and definitions with those of your classmates.

3. To reach readers beyond the academic world, Tannen had to modify her writing style from that of a professor. Reviewing the excerpt, whom do you think she writes like, if not a professor? What does this example of her writing sound like? **Working with one or two classmates,** write out the words, phrases, and sentences that support your answers to these questions.

Writing Your Own Essays Using Comparison and Contrast

1. Using your responses to questions 3 and 4 under Considering Larger Is-sues, draft a three- to four-page essay in which you compare your use of language with the way it is used by a member of the opposite sex or by someone from another generation or culture. Map out the points of com-

parison, and tell your side of the language story. Your essay will be especially pointed if you offer suggestions for improving communication in your conclusion. Refer to the guidelines on page 359, "Checking Over the Use of Comparison and Contrast."

2. Draft a three- to four-page self-portrait based mostly on your use of language. In what ways, if any, is your use of language affected by whether you are a man or woman? How do the specific ways you use language help or hinder you? Compare and contrast your current language use with how you would like to use language to your advantage. As you draft and revise, refer to the guidelines for checking over the use of comparison and contrast on page 359.

3. PUBLIC WRITING. While Barry compares guys to men, Tannen compares the language practices of men and women. Both writers, though, use comparison and contrast to create public texts that explore questions of gender. Compose a six- to eight-page manual for students at your college or university that helps them understand specific groups of men and women on your campus. You might compare people *within* a gender, as Barry does, by comparing women who participate in two different sports or men who belong to two different fraternities or clubs. Or you may compare gendered differences, as Tannen does, examining how men in your dorm behave as opposed to women, or how female science students study as opposed to male science students. The key for your manual is to explain these differences to an interested audience by using detailed information, rich descriptions, and specific examples. As you draft and revise, refer to the guidelines on page 359, "Checking Over the Use of Comparison and Contrast."

LYNN TAN

Reading for Pleasure: A Comparison of Summer Reading and Reading for School

Lynn Tan (b. 1987) graduated in 2008 from the University of Pittsburgh as an English literature major. After moving to Houston, Tan took education courses in an alternative certificate program and is now teaching in the city's public schools. Her long-term plans are to become certified in English as a Second Language and possibly earn a master's degree in counseling. Tan's essay investigates how her reading practices change from the summer months to the academic year. To achieve this investigation, Tan compares and contrasts these reading practices and considers the benefits of both styles.

> **Preview**   How would you characterize the way you read during the summer? How does your summer reading compare to your reading during the academic year?

About a month into every new semester, something strange happens. All 1 the excitement I initially felt about learning dissipates as midterms and paper deadlines draw near. Finding myself suddenly buried under a pile of books, I begin thinking back to my summer days. What happened to those long, peaceful afternoons spent reading magazines and browsing books at Barnes & Noble or unwinding after work with a short story or two? What has suddenly made reading a burden, a chore, a thing to dread? What happened to reading for fun?

That's where the piled-up textbooks come in. They are material evi- 2 dence that the reading I do for school and the reading I do on my own are two very different activities. During the summer, when my time is less structured, reading occurs at a relaxed pace. I may read a couple pages of a tantalizing novel during dinner or skim a random chapter from an art history book before going to bed. If I come across a confusing passage in one of those texts, I may pause and mull over it for a while, but I do it without worrying about a deep, thorough understanding of everything I read. To me, summer is a time to relax at the same time that I keep my mind fresh and alert. My summer expectations are to gain pleasure and knowledge from what I read — without exerting too much energy or making myself nervous. With such humane expectations in mind, I seldom feel frustrated while reading. If I do not finish a book before the next term begins (which sometimes happens when I choose longer works, such as Leo Tolstoy's *Anna Karenina* or Howard Zinn's *A People's History of the United States*, for example), I don't get discouraged; I simply remind myself that there is always next summer.

In stark contrast is the reading I do for school. It's not so casual — and 3 it's very, very structured. During school, I read strictly to learn. To maximize learning, I must read a certain amount of books I did not choose by deadlines I did not set. I must also complete assignments — papers, exams, and presentations — that prove I have read carefully and gained a deep understanding of what I have read. With so much at stake, I cannot stop reading every time I hit a confusing passage or skip over chapters that bear boring titles, practices I admit I do during my summer reading. If I did that in my school reading, I would miss important details that might lead to an interesting discussion question or paper topic. There-fore, the higher expectations placed on me as a student call for a reading style that is more alert, more concentrated, and aimed only at drawing meaning from what I read (with little or no attention given to reading for pleasure).

My reading style in school also involves critical thinking and a much 4 closer interaction with texts. For example, to keep me focused and to check my understanding, I ask myself questions as I read: Who are the main characters? How do they relate to one another? What is the sig-nificance of the setting or time in which this story takes place? What are some important themes I have come across so far? Such questions guard against boredom by motivating me to keep reading in search of answers. When I come across any confusing moments in a text, places where I am not sure why a character behaves in a certain way, I write down the page number where the confusion occurred, along with a question that expresses my confusion, in a notebook. Then I continue reading while keeping my eyes open for a chapter, paragraph, or sentence that may clear up my confusion or at least make it more meaningful.

This careful "pause, think, and move on" pattern of school reading 5 requires patience and determination. Unlike the popular magazines, memoirs, and celebrity biographies I read during the summer (which for the most part are easy to interpret), the texts I read for school tend to be those that literary critics throughout the centuries have worked to inter-pret and understand. The meanings are not so explicit, for example, in the works of Shakespeare, in which language often carries double mean-ing. Thus gaining a good understanding of what I read takes some extra intellectual digging — hard work that can be frustrating at times but also produces a deeper learning experience.

The type of reading I do during the summer is, in a sense, more plea- 6 surable because the expectations for interpretation are much lower. After all, many of the books on my summer reading list (*Peony in Love, The Kite Runner, Outliers*) are "quick reads" that provide instant gratification and es-capism. Conversely, the reading I do for school may not be as automati-cally entertaining because the texts are typically difficult and my learning goals are more demanding. So does this difference simply make one kind of reading (summer reading) pleasurable and the other (school reading) difficult? one type lazy and the other studious? What names do I give to these two types of reading?

Perhaps a definition of reading may also help define the types of   7
reading I engage in. The *Elements (and Pleasures) of Difficulty*, written by
Mariolina Salvatori and Patricia Donahue, gives this definition of reading: "Can be passive or active. Passive reading is a process of absorption.
Active reading is a process of interpretation and reflection, whereby a
reader constructs meaning, establishes significance, and reflects on the
limits of his or her understanding" (A128). At this point in my analysis, I
think I can say with confidence that the type of reading I do in the summer is largely passive. During the summer, I "absorb" information from
books and magazines under the assumption that some of what I read
will simply stick in my mind without any reflection. Yet when I think
back to the more difficult texts I have read during the summer (*Pride and
Prejudice, White Noise*), I find that I can recall interesting elements — an unusual use of language, a romance or fight between two characters, or a
surprise ending — but I cannot explain their significance. Thus while I
can "absorb" facts of knowledge, I cannot "absorb" understanding.

Earlier I mentioned that I experienced no frustration while reading   8
passively. Yet perhaps that is because the frustration that comes from
passive reading occurs after the activity of reading is over — when a
friend asks my opinion of a particular book I have just finished and all
I can say is, "I thought it was interesting, but I don't remember why" or
"I loved it, even though I barely remember the characters or plot." Active
reading that I do during school, which includes the activities of interpretation, reflection, and the "construction of meaning," may ultimately be
more rewarding than passive reading because it encourages me to confront the "limits of my understanding," to discover what, exactly, makes a
text interesting, boring, confusing, or frustrating to me. Active reading involves gaining a deeper understanding of texts, but it also involves gaining a deeper understanding of who I am and why I think the way I do.

For instance, many of the most challenging texts I have read in school   9
deal with the universal themes of life, death, and fate. When I read the
texts of Shakespeare, Dante, and Homer actively, moving through and
beyond the strange language, elaborate plots, and historical and cultural
differences between their authors, I find that each one includes a significantly different view of life. By interpreting these views, I also come to
questions about my own: Do I agree with Dante in *The Divine Comedy* that
life is governed by reason, or do I agree more with Shakespeare in *The
Tempest* that life is more unpredictable? What are my views about fate? By
inviting me to engage in a dialogue with the different perspectives presented in texts, active reading also helps me identify and possibly rethink
my own assumptions and values.

In the film *Slacker* (1991), which presents a day in the life of some in-   10
triguing Texan underachievers, a young woman confronts her boyfriend
while he is giving her another one of his lessons on ethics. She accuses
him of drawing his argument from books he has read but never thought

over himself. "It's like you just pasted together these bits and pieces from your 'authoritative sources.' I don't know. I'm beginning to suspect there's nothing really in there," she says, poking his chest. In a sense, she is accusing him of being a passive reader. Yet she also touches on one of the greatest pleasures that arises from active reading: it affords us a chance to form our own opinions after carefully assessing the opinions of other authors, our so-called authoritative sources. Thus while it might be tempting to simply absorb and accept everything I read, especially when I have a lot of reading to do, I must also remember that doing the difficult work of active reading promises a reading experience ultimately more fulfilling than even the best bookstore browsing can offer. Passive reading can stimulate the mind, but active reading helps it grow.

WORKS CITED

Salvatori, Mariolina Rizza, and Patricia Donahue. *The Elements (and Pleasures) of Difficulty*. New York: Pearson, 2005. Print.
Slacker. Dir. Richard Linklater. Detour, 1991. Film.

Reading Closely

1. What is the purpose of this essay?
2. What is the basis for comparison? What are the points of comparison?
3. Review the topic sentences of this essay and then think about how it is organized. How does Tan choose to arrange her comparison and contrast? How do the topic sentences enable her to achieve this arrangement?
4. What purpose does Tan's reference to Salvatori and Donahue's book *Elements (and Pleasures) of Difficulty* serve in her comparison?

Considering Larger Issues

1. What is your response to this essay? How do your experiences with reading during the summer and the academic year compare with Tan's?
2. It seems that Tan is working through her comparison as she composes her essay. In the opening paragraphs, she seems to appreciate summer reading more than school reading. By the conclusion, she flips this assessment, arguing that school reading is more rewarding. **Working with a classmate**, consider her decision to develop her essay in this way. What might be other options for arguing her case? Do you find her arrangement effective? Why or why not?
3. COMBINING METHODS. How does Tan use the methods of *description, definition,* and *exemplification*? How do these methods help her achieve her purpose?

Thinking about Language

1. Using the context of the selection or your dictionary, define each of the following terms. Be prepared to share your answers with the rest of the class.

   dissipates (1)   memoir (5)   escapism (6)
   tantalizing (2)   explicit (5)   authoritative (10)
   mull (2)   gratification (6)

2. What specific terms does Tan employ as she explores the differences between school and summer reading? How does she move from analyzing summer reading to analyzing school reading?

Writing Your Own Essays Using Comparison and Contrast

1. Building on your response to question 1 under Considering Larger Issues, reflect on the differences between your reading practices during the summer months and those during the academic year. What differences and similarities do you see? Compose a three- to four-page essay in which you respond to Tan's essay by assessing your reading practices during the summer and during the school year. Use exemplification and description to add emphasis to your essay. Refer to the guidelines on page 359, "Checking Over the Use of Comparison and Contrast," as you draft and revise.

2. Instead of comparing reading practices during the summer and academic months as Tan does, compose a three- to four-page essay in which you compare and contrast your reading practices in two of your classes. How are your reading practices different in your engineering or economics class as opposed to your English or history class? What different strategies do you rely on? Be specific in the ways you describe these reading strategies, explaining *how* you go about reading for these classes. As you draft and revise, refer to the guidelines for checking over the use of comparison and contrast on page 359.

GREG BEATO
Amusing Ourselves to Depth

San Francisco native Greg Beato is a contributing editor and columnist for *Reason,* an online magazine. He also regularly publishes his work in *Las Vegas Weekly.* His writings on pop culture have appeared in over seventy publications around the world. In this 2007 essay, Beato compares and contrasts the satirical newspaper *The Onion* with more traditional newspapers, using this rhetorical method to consider why *The Onion* is so successful while many of its peers are failing.

> **Preview**   Have you read *The Onion* before? What did you think of this newspaper? How does it compare to more conventional newspapers?

In August 1988, college junior Tim Keck borrowed $7,000 from his mom, 1 rented a Mac Plus, and published a 12-page newspaper. His ambition was hardly the stuff of future journalism symposiums: He wanted to create a compelling way to deliver advertising to his fellow students. Part of the first issue's front page was devoted to a story about a monster running amok at a local lake; the rest was reserved for beer and pizza coupons.

Almost 20 years later, *The Onion* stands as one of the newspaper in- 2 dustry's few great success stories in the post-newspaper era. Currently, it prints 710,000 copies of each weekly edition, roughly 6,000 more than *The Denver Post,* the nation's ninth-largest daily. Its syndicated radio dispatches reach a weekly audience of 1 million, and it recently started producing video clips too. Roughly 3,000 local advertisers keep *The Onion* afloat, and the paper plans to add 170 employees to its staff of 130 this year.

Online it attracts more than 2 million readers a week. Type *onion* into 3 Google, and *The Onion* pops up first. Type *the* into Google, and *The Onion* pops up first.

But type "best practices for newspapers" into Google, and *The Onion* 4 is nowhere to be found. Maybe it should be. At a time when traditional newspapers are frantic to divest themselves of their newsy, papery legacies, *The Onion* takes a surprisingly conservative approach to innovation. As much as it has used and benefited from the Web, it owes much of its success to low-tech attributes readily available to any paper but nonetheless in short supply: candor, irreverence, and a willingness to offend.

While other newspapers desperately add gardening sections, ask 5 readers to share their favorite bratwurst recipes, or throw their staffers to ravenous packs of bloggers for online question-and-answer sessions, *The Onion* has focused on reporting the news. The fake news, sure, but still the news. It doesn't ask readers to post their comments at the end of stories, allow them to rate stories on a scale of one to five, or encourage citizen-satire. It makes no effort to convince readers that it really does

POLITICS

Nation Descends Into Chaos As Throat Infection Throws Off Obama's Cadence

JULY 14, 2009 | ISSUE 45•29

This cough led directly to 1,400 overturned cars and three major prison riots.

understand their needs and exists only to serve them. *The Onion's* journalists concentrate on writing stories and then getting them out there in a variety of formats, and this relatively old-fashioned approach to newspapering has been tremendously successful.

Are there any other newspapers that can boast a 60 percent increase 6 in their print circulation during the last three years? Yet as traditional newspapers fail to draw readers, only industry mavericks like *The New York Times'* Jayson Blair and *USA Today's* Jack Kelley have looked to *The Onion* for inspiration.

One reason *The Onion* isn't taken more seriously is that it's actually 7 fun to read. In 1985, the cultural critic Neil Postman published the influential *Amusing Ourselves to Death*, which warned of the fate that would befall us if public discourse were allowed to become substantially more entertaining than, say, a Neil Postman book. Today newspapers are eager to entertain — in their Travel, Food, and Style sections, that is. But even as scope creep has made the average big-city tree killer less portable than a 10-year-old laptop, hard news invariably comes in a single flavor: Double Objectivity Sludge.

Too many high priests of journalism still see humor as the enemy of 8 seriousness: If the news goes down too easily, it can't be very good for you. But do *The Onion* and its more fact-based acolytes, *The Daily Show* and *The Colbert Report*, monitor current events and the way the news media report on them any less rigorously than, say, the *Columbia Journalism Review* or *USA Today*?

During the last few years, multiple surveys by the Pew Research Cen- 9
ter and the Annenberg Public Policy Center have found that viewers of
The Daily Show and *The Colbert Report* are among America's most informed
citizens. Now, it may be that Jon Stewart isn't making anyone smarter;
perhaps America's most informed citizens simply prefer comedy over the
stentorian drivel the network anchormannequins dispense. But at the
very least, such surveys suggest that news sharpened with satire doesn't
cause the intellectual coronaries Postman predicted. Instead, it seems to
correlate with engagement.

It's easy to see why readers connect with *The Onion*, and it's not just 10
the jokes: Despite its "fake news" purview, it's an extremely honest publication. Most dailies, especially those in monopoly or near–monopoly
markets, operate as if they're focused more on not offending readers (or
advertisers) than on expressing a worldview of any kind.

The Onion takes the opposite approach. It delights in crapping on 11
pieties and regularly publishes stories guaranteed to upset someone:
"Christ Kills Two, Injures Seven in Abortion–Clinic Attack." "Heroic PETA
Commandos Kill 49, Save Rabbit." "Gay Pride Parade Sets Mainstream Acceptance of Gays Back 50 Years." There's no predictable ideology running
through those headlines, just a desire to express some rude, blunt truth
about the world.

One common complaint about newspapers is that they're too nega- 12
tive, too focused on bad news, too obsessed with the most unpleasant
aspects of life. *The Onion* shows how wrong this characterization is, how
gingerly most newspapers dance around the unrelenting awfulness of
life and refuse to acknowledge the limits of our tolerance and compassion. The perfunctory coverage that traditional newspapers give disasters
in countries cursed with relatability issues is reduced to its bare, dismal
essence: "15,000 Brown People Dead Somewhere." Beggars aren't grist for
Pulitzers, just punch lines: "Man Can't Decide Whether to Give Sandwich
to Homeless or Ducks." Triumphs of the human spirit are as rare as veg-
ans at an NRA barbecue: "Loved Ones Recall Local Man's Cowardly Battle
with Cancer."

Such headlines come with a cost, of course. Outraged readers have 13
convinced advertisers to pull ads. Ginger Rogers and Denzel Washington,
among other celebrities, have objected to stories featuring their names,
and former *Onion* editor Robert Siegel once told a lecture audience that
the paper was "very nearly sued out of existence" after it ran a story with
the headline "Dying Boy Gets Wish: To Pork Janet Jackson."

But if this irreverence is sometimes economically inconvenient, it's 14
also a major reason for the publication's popularity. It's a refreshing an-
tidote to the he–said/she–said balancing acts that leave so many dailies
sounding mealy–mouthed. And while *The Onion* may not adhere to the
facts too strictly, it would no doubt place high if the Pew Research Center
ever included it in a survey ranking America's most trusted news sources.

During the last few years, big–city dailies have begun to introduce   15
"commuter" papers that function as lite versions of their original fare.
These publications share some of *The Onion*'s attributes: They're free,
they're tabloids, and most of their stories are bite–sized. But while they
may be less filling, they still taste bland. You have to wonder: Why stop
at price and paper size? Why not adopt the brutal frankness, the willingness to pierce orthodoxies of all political and cultural stripes, and apply
these attributes to a genuinely reported daily newspaper?

Today's publishers give comics strips less and less space. Editorial   16
cartoonists and folksy syndicated humorists have been nearly eradicated.
Such changes have helped make newspapers more entertaining — or
at least less dull — but they're just a start. Until today's front pages can
amuse our staunchest defenders of journalistic integrity to severe dys-
pepsia, if not death, they're not trying hard enough.

Reading Closely

1. What is the thesis of Beato's essay?
2. What are the points of comparison in this essay?
3. What other publications or news sources are similar to *The Onion*? What
   characteristics do they share?
4. How does the visual on page 388 support or detract from Beato's claims
   about *The Onion?*

Considering Larger Issues

1. Given Beato's comparison of *The Onion* with traditional newspapers,
   how would you describe both kinds of news sources? Describe *The
   Onion* and its characteristics. Describe traditional newspapers and their
   characteristics.
2. What is the purpose of the essay? Identify the evidence in the essay that
   supports your claim.
3. **With two or three classmates,** discuss what it would be like if newspapers like the *New York Times* or *Washington Post* actually adopted *The
   Onion*'s reporting and writing styles. What benefits or drawbacks do you
   see to their doing so?
4. Why does Beato title his essay "Amusing Ourselves to Depth"? How does
   this title prepare readers for what's to come?
5. COMBINING METHODS. How does Beato use *cause-and-effect analysis, definition,* and *exemplification*? Mark the places in the essay where Beato relies
   on these methods. How do these methods support the purpose of the
   essay?

Thinking about Language

1. Using a dictionary or the context of the essay, define the following terms. Be prepared to share your answers with the rest of the class.

symposiums (1)	invariably (7)	gingerly (12)
amok (1)	acolytes (8)	perfunctory (12)
divest (4)	stentorian (9)	mealy–mouthed (14)
candor (4)	drivel (9)	orthodoxies (15)
irreverence (4)	anchormannequins (9)	syndicated (16)
ravenous (5)	purview (10)	dyspepsia (16)
mavericks (6)	pieties (11)	

2. What tone does Beato establish throughout his essay? How do his language choices contribute to this tone? Identify specific examples to support your claim.

Writing Your Own Essays Using Comparison and Contrast

1. Review your student newspaper, identifying its distinctive characteristics. Then compare this newspaper to another newspaper. You might choose to compare it to a local or nationwide publication or to another student newspaper at your college, but the objective is for you to identify the basis for comparison and points of comparison as a means to consider the similarities and differences between the two. Then draft a two– to three–page essay in which you explore this comparison, considering the strengths of your student newspaper and the ways in which it might borrow from the other publication as a means to improve the work it's attempting to do. As you draft and revise, refer to the guidelines for checking over the use of comparison and contrast on page 359.

2. What sources do you read, listen to, or watch to get your news? Freewrite about these sources, describing the characteristics of each as well as your reasons for reading, listening to, or watching them. Then compare and contrast these news sources. What are their similarities? What are their differences? Draft a three– to four–page essay in which you develop this comparison of your preferred news sources. As you compose, you'll want to pinpoint a basis for comparison and the points of comparison to help you make clear distinctions among the sources. Refer to the guidelines for checking over the use of comparison and contrast on page 359.

MALCOLM JONES
Who Was More Important: Lincoln or Darwin?

Malcolm Jones has been a contributing editor to the Arts section of *Newsweek* magazine since 1989. He is a reporter, book reviewer, and feature writer on topics having to do with culture. Jones also edits *Newsweek*'s Web site. Prior to joining *Newsweek*, Jones was an editorial writer for the *Greensboro Daily News* (in North Carolina) and the book editor for the *St. Petersburg Times* in Florida. In this essay, published in *Newsweek* in March 2009, Jones compares two contemporaries, Abraham Lincoln and Charles Darwin, considering which man more greatly affected his own and future times.

Preview In his title, Jones asks, "Who was more important: Lincoln or Darwin?" What is your initial response to this question? Why?

How's this for a coincidence? Charles Darwin and Abraham Lincoln were 1 born in the same year, on the same day: Feb. 12, 1809. As historical facts go, it amounts to little more than a footnote. Still, while it's just a coincidence, it's a coincidence that's guaranteed to make you do a double take the first time you run across it. Everybody knows Darwin and Lincoln were near–mythic figures in the 19th century. But who ever thinks of them in tandem? Who puts the theory of evolution and the Civil War in the same sentence? Why would you, unless you're writing your dissertation on epochal events in the 19th century? But instinctively, we want to say that they belong together. It's not just because they were both great men, and not because they happen to be exact coevals. Rather, it's because the scientist and the politician each touched off a revolution that changed the world.

As soon as you do start comparing this odd couple, you discover 2 there is more to this birthday coincidence than the same astrological chart (as Aquarians, they should both be stubborn, visionary, tolerant, free–spirited, rebellious, genial but remote and detached— hmmm, so far so good). Two recent books give them double billing: historian David R. Contosta's *Rebel Giants* and *New Yorker* writer Adam Gopnik's *Angels and Ages*. Contosta's joint biography doesn't turn up anything new, but the biographical parallels he sets forth are enough to make us see each man afresh. Both lost their mothers in early childhood. Both suffered from depression (Darwin also suffered from a variety of crippling stomach ailments and chronic headaches), and both wrestled with religious doubt. Each had a strained relationship with his father, and each of them lost children to early death. Both spent the better part of their 20s trying to settle on a career, and neither man gave much evidence of his future greatness until well into middle age: Darwin published *The Origin of*

Species when he was 50, and Lincoln won the presidency a year later. Both men were private and guarded. Most of Darwin's friendships were conducted through the mail, and after his five-year voyage on *HMS Beagle* as a young man, he rarely left his home in the English countryside. Lincoln, though a much more public man, carefully cultivated a bumpkin persona that encouraged both friends and enemies to underestimate his considerable, almost Machiavellian skill as a politician.

It is a measure of their accomplishments, of how much they changed 3 the world, that the era into which Lincoln and Darwin was born seems so strange to us now. On their birth date, Thomas Jefferson had three weeks left in his second term as president. George III still sat on the throne of England. The Enlightenment was giving way to Romanticism. At the center of what people then believed, the tent poles of their reality were that God created the world and that man was the crown of creation. Well, some men, since the institution of slavery was still acceptable on both sides of the Mason–Dixon line— it would not be abolished in New York state, for example, until 1827, and while it had been illegal in England since 1772, it would not be abolished in English colonies until 1833. And Darwin, at least at the outset, was hardly even a scientist in the sense that we understand the term— a highly trained specialist whose professional vocabulary is so arcane that he or she can talk only to other scientists.

Darwin, the man who would almost singlehandedly redefine biologi- 4 cal science, started out as an amateur naturalist, a beetle collector, a rockhound, a 22-year-old rich-kid dilettante who, after flirting with the idea of being first a physician and then a preacher, was allowed to ship out with the *Beagle* as someone who might supply good conversation at the captain's table. His father had all but ordered him not to go to sea, worrying that it was nothing more than one of Charles's lengthening list of aimless exploits— years before, Dr. Darwin had scolded his teenage son, saying, "You care for nothing but shooting, dogs, and rat catching, and you will be a disgrace to yourself and all your family." How could the father know that when the son came ashore after his five-year voyage, he would not only have shed his aimlessness but would have replaced it with a scientific sense of skepticism and curiosity so rigorous and abiding that he would be a workaholic almost to the day he died? Darwin was also in the grip of an idea so subversive that he would keep it under wraps for another two decades. But the crucial thing is that he did all this by himself. He became the very model of a modern major scientist without benefit of graduate school, grants or even much peer review. (It's hard to get a sympathetic hearing when your work, if successful, is clearly going to knock the blocks out from under civilization.) Darwin may have been independently wealthy, but in terms of his vocation, he was a self-made man.

Lincoln was self-made in the more conventional sense— a walk- 5 ing, talking embodiment of the frontier myth made good. Like Darwin,

Lincoln was not a quick study. Both men worked slowly to master a subject. But both had restless, hungry minds. After about a year of schooling
as a boy—and that spread out in dribs and drabs of three months here
and four months there—Lincoln taught himself. He mastered trigonom-
etry (for work as a surveyor); he read Blackstone on his own to become
a lawyer. He memorized swaths of the Bible and Shakespeare. At the age
of 40, after he had already served a term in the U.S. House of Representatives, he undertook Euclidean geometry as a mental exercise. After a
while, his myth becomes a little much—he actually was born in a log
cabin with a dirt floor—so much that we begin looking for flaws, and
they're there: the bad marriage, some maladroit comments on racial in-
feriority. Then there were those terrible jokes. But even there, dammit,
he could be truly witty: "I have endured a great deal of ridicule without
much malice; and have received a great deal of kindness, not quite free
from ridicule. I am used to it."

Perhaps the most mysterious aspect of this riddlesome man was just   6
how he managed, somewhere along the way, to turn himself into one of
the best prose writers America has produced. Lincoln united the North
behind him with an eloquence so timeless that his words remain fresh
no matter how many times you read them. Darwin wrote one of the few
scientific treatises, maybe the only one, worth reading as a work of literature. Both of them demand to be read in the original, not in paraphrase,
because both men are so much in their prose. To read them is to know
these elusive figures a little better. Given their influence on our lives,
these are men you want to know.

Darwin seems to have been able to think only with a pen in his   7
hand. He was a compulsive note taker and list maker. He made an extensive list setting down the pros and cons of marriage before he proposed to his future wife. His first published work, *The Voyage of the Beagle*,
is a tidied-up version of the log he kept on the five-year trip around the
world, and he is unflaggingly meticulous in his observations of the plant
and animal life he saw or collected along the way. To live, for Darwin,
meant looking and examining and then writing down what he saw and
then trying to make sense of it.

In the *Beagle* log and his journals, Darwin is something like a cub   8
reporter, asking questions, taking notes, delighting in the varieties of life
he discovers, both alive and in the fossil record, in South America, Australia or the Cape Verde Islands. With Darwin there is no Eureka moment
when he suddenly discovers evolution. But by the time he left the *Beagle*
in 1836, he was plainly becoming convinced that, contrary to the prevailing wisdom, life is not static—species change and evolve. Shortly before
the voyage was over, he mulled over what he had seen on the Galápagos:
"When I see these islands in sight of each other, and possessed of but a
scanty stock of animals, tenanted by these birds, but slightly differing in
structure and filling the same place in Nature, I must suspect they are

only varieties. . . . If there is the slightest foundation for these remarks the zoology of the [Galápagos] will be well worth examining; for such facts would undermine the stability of Species." What he did not have was a controlling mechanism for this process. It was not until two years later that he conceived the idea of natural selection, after reading economist Thomas Malthus on the competition for resources among humans brought on by the inexorable demands of overpopulation. There he had it: a theory of everything that actually worked. Species evolve and the ones best adapted to their environment thrive and leave more offspring, crowding out the rest.

As delighted as he was with his discovery, Darwin was equally hor- 9
rified, because he understood the consequences of his theory. Mankind was no longer the culmination of life but merely part of it; creation was mechanistic and purposeless. In a letter to a fellow scientist, Darwin wrote that confiding his theory was "like confessing a murder." Small wonder that instead of rushing to publish his theory, he sat on it—for 20 years. He started a series of notebooks in which he began refining his theory, recording the results of his research in fields as disparate as animal husbandry and barnacles. Over the next five or six years, he went through notebook after notebook, including one in which he began to pose metaphysical questions arising from his research. Do animals have consciences? Where does the idea of God come from?

This questioning spirit is one of the most appealing facets of Darwin's 10
character, particularly where it finds its way into his published work. Reading *The Origin of Species*, you feel as though he is addressing you as an equal. He is never autocratic, never bullying. Instead, he is always willing to admit what he does not know or understand, and when he poses a question, he is never rhetorical. He seems genuinely to want to know the answer. He's also a good salesman. He knows that what he has to say will not only be troubling for a general reader to take but difficult to understand—so he works very hard not to lose his customer. The book opens not with theory but in the humblest place imaginable: the barnyard, as Darwin introduces us to the idea of species variation in a way we, or certainly his 19th-century audience, will easily grasp—the breeding of domestic animals. The quality of Darwin's mind is in evidence everywhere in this book, but so is his character—generous, open-minded and always respectful of those who he knew would disagree with him, as you might expect of a man who was, after all, married to a creationist.

Like Darwin, Lincoln was a compulsive scribbler, forever jotting down 11
phrases, notes and ideas on scraps of paper, then squirreling the notes away in a coat pocket, a desk drawer—or sometimes his hat—where they would collect until he found a use for them in a letter, a speech or a document. He was also a compulsive reviser. He knew that words heard are not the same as words read. After delivering his emotional farewell speech in Springfield, Ill., in 1861, he boarded the train for Washington

and, if the shakiness of his handwriting is any indication, immediately began revising his remarks prior to publication.

The Gettysburg Address apparently gestated in a somewhat similar fashion. The winter and spring of 1863 were one of the lowest points for the Union. In the West, Grant was bogged down in his protracted siege of Vicksburg. In the East, the South won decisively at Chancellorsville. Since the Emancipation Proclamation had been issued on Jan. 1, people in the North were wondering aloud just what it was they were fighting for. Was it to preserve the Union, or was it to abolish slavery? Lincoln was keenly aware that he needed to clarify the issue. The Northern victory at Gettysburg in early July gave him the occasion he was seeking.   12

Some witnesses at Gettysburg claimed to recall applause during the speech, but most did not, and Lincoln was already taking his seat before many in the audience realized he had finished. This was a time when speeches could last for four hours. Edward Everett, who preceded the president on the program, had confined his remarks to two hours. Lincoln said what he had to say in two minutes. Brevity is only one of the several noteworthy aspects of what is surely one of the greatest speeches ever made. Of much greater importance are what the president said and how he said it.   13

With his first 29 words, Lincoln accomplished what he had come to Gettysburg to do — he defined the purpose of the war for the Union: "Four score and seven years ago our fathers brought forth on this continent a new nation, conceived in Liberty and dedicated to the proposition that all men are created equal." He could have put this sentence in the form of an argument — the equality of all men was one of the things the war was about. Instead, he states his argument as fact: the nation was founded on the principle of equality; this is what we fight to preserve. There is a hint of qualification — but only a hint — in the word *proposition*: equality is not a self-evident truth; it is what we believe in. In the next paragraph, he continues this idea of contingency: "Now we are engaged in a great civil war, testing whether that nation, or any nation so conceived and so dedicated, can long endure." In other words, republican democracy hangs in the balance. Before the speech, none of this was taken for granted, even in the North. In 272 words, he defined the national principle so thoroughly that today no one would think of arguing otherwise.   14

Lincoln's political genius stood on two pillars: he possessed an uncanny awareness of what *could* be done at any given moment, and he had the ability to change his mind, to adapt to circumstances, to grow. This is Lincoln in 1838, addressing the Springfield Young Men's Lyceum on a citizen's obligations to the legal system with such lines as "Let reverence for the laws be breathed by every American mother to the lisping babe that prattles on her lap." Here he is not quite 30 years later in the Second Inaugural of 1865 (there's a mother and child in this one, too, but what   15 a difference): "With malice toward none; with charity for all; with firm-ness in the right, as God gives us to see the right, let us strive on to finish the work we are in; to bind up the nation's wounds; to care for him who shall have borne the battle, and for his widow, and his orphan—to do all which may achieve and cherish a just and a lasting peace, among our-selves and with all nations."

This is the language of the Bible, and if the rhetoric does not con-   16 vince us of that, Lincoln mentions God six times in one paragraph. But what kind of God? Lincoln's religious history is perhaps the most tangled aspect of his life. His law partner, William Herndon, swore Lincoln was an atheist, and to be sure, there are plenty of boilerplate references to the Almighty scattered through Lincoln's speeches. But as the war wears on, and the speeches grow more spiritual, they become less conventional. Lincoln was a believer, but it is hard to say just what he believed. He speaks often of the will of God, but just as often adamantly refuses to de-cipher God's purpose. And he never, ever claims that God is on his side.

The God of the Second Inaugural is utterly inscrutable: "The Almighty   17 has His own purposes." One of those purposes, Lincoln then suggests, may be to punish both North and South for permitting the offense of slavery. Then he delivers what biographer David Herbert Donald has called "one of the most terrible statements ever made by an American public official": "Fondly do we hope, fervently do we pray, that this mighty scourge of war may speedily pass away. Yet if God wills that it continue until all the wealth piled by the bondsman's two hundred and fifty years of unrequited toil shall be sunk, and until every drop of blood drawn with the lash shall be paid by another drawn with the sword, as was said three thou-sand years ago, so still it must be said 'the judgments of the Lord are true and righteous altogether.'" It is here, just when he has brought his audi-ence to the edge of the cliff, that Lincoln spins on his heel in one of the great rhetorical 180s of all time and concludes, "With malice toward none; with charity for all . . ." Even today, reading that conclusion after what's come before is like coming out of a tunnel into bright sunshine—or out of a war that claimed more than 600,000 lives. Lincoln understood that language could heal, and he knew when to use it.

Lincoln, no less than Mark Twain, forged what we think of today as   18 the American style: forthright, rhythmic, muscular, beautiful but never pretty. As Douglas L. Wilson observes in *Lincoln's Sword*, his brilliant analy-sis of the president's writing, Lincoln was political, not literary, but he was, every bit as much as Melville or Thoreau, "perfecting a prose that expressed a uniquely American way of apprehending and ordering expe-rience." What Lincoln says and how he says it are one. You cannot imag-ine the Gettysburg Address or the Second Inaugural in words other than those in which they are conveyed.

Lincoln and Darwin were both revolutionaries, in the sense that   19 both men upended realities that prevailed when they were born. They

seem—and sound—modern to us, because the world they left behind
them is more or less the one we still live in. So, considering the joint
magnitude of their contributions—and the coincidence of their con-
joined birthdays—it is hard not to wonder: who was the greater man?
It's an apples-and-oranges—or Superman-vs.-Santa—comparison. But if
you limit the question to influence, it bears pondering, all the more if you
turn the question around and ask, what might have happened if one of
these men had not been born? Very quickly the balance tips in Lincoln's
favor. As much of a bombshell as Darwin detonated, and as great as his
book on evolution is (E. O. Wilson calls it "the greatest scientific book
of all time"), it does no harm to remember that he hurried to publish
The Origin of Species because he thought he was about to be scooped by
his fellow naturalist Alfred Russel Wallace, who had independently come
up with much the same idea of evolution through natural selection. In
other words, there was a certain inevitability to Darwin's theory. Ideas
about evolution surfaced throughout the first part of the 19th century,
and while none of them was as cogent as Darwin's—until Wallace came
along—it was not as though he was the only man who had the idea.

  Lincoln, in contrast, is sui generis. Take him out of the picture, and   20
there is no telling what might have happened to the country. True, his
election to the presidency did provoke secession and, in turn, the war
itself, but that war seems inevitable—not a question of if but when.
Once in office, he becomes the indispensable man. As James McPher-
son demonstrates so well in the forthcoming *Tried by War: Abraham
Lincoln as Commander in Chief,* Lincoln's prosecution of the war was crucial
to the North's success—before Grant came to the rescue, Lincoln was his
own best general. Certainly we know what happened once he was assassinated: Reconstruction was administered punitively and then abandoned, leaving the issue of racial equality to dangle for another century.
But here again, what Lincoln said and wrote matters as much as what
he did. He framed the conflict in language that united the North—and
inspires us still. If anything, with the passage of time, he only looms
larger—more impressive, and also more mysterious. Other presidents,
even the great ones, submit to analysis. Lincoln forever remains just beyond our grasp—though not for want of trying: it has been estimated
that more books have been written about him than any other human
being except Jesus.

  If Darwin were not so irreplaceable as Lincoln, that should not gain-   21
say his accomplishment. No one could have formulated his theory any
more elegantly—or anguished more over its implications. Like Lincoln,
Darwin was brave. He risked his health and his reputation to advance
the idea that we are not over nature but a part of it. Lincoln prosecuted a
war—and became its ultimate casualty—to ensure that no man should
have dominion over another. Their identical birthdays afford us a superb opportunity to observe these men in the shared context of their

time—how each was shaped by his circumstances, how each reacted to the beliefs that steered the world into which he was born and ultimately how each reshaped his corner of that world and left it irrevocably changed.

Answer: Lincoln.

Reading Closely

1. What are the points of comparison in this essay?

2. **Working with a classmate,** review the arrangement of the essay. How does Jones organize his comparison?

3. Reread the introduction of the essay. What do you think of this introduction? How successful is Jones's attempt to grab his readers' attention and simultaneously to begin his comparison?

4. Review Jones's use of quotation throughout the essay. What kinds of quotations does he use? How do these quotations affect the purpose of the essay?

Considering Larger Issues

1. What did you learn about Lincoln and Darwin as you read? What do you find significant about both figures?

2. Jones concludes by arguing that Lincoln was more important. Do you agree? Why or why not? What evidence persuaded you to make this decision?

3. COMBINING METHODS. Identify the places in the essay where Jones relies on *narration* and *description*. How do these strategies reinforce the purpose of the essay?

Thinking about Language

1. Using a dictionary or the context of the essay, define the following terms. Be prepared to share your answers with the rest of the class.

mythic (1)	swaths (5)	protracted (12)
epochal (1)	maladroit (5)	contingency (14)
coevals (1)	paraphrase (6)	uncanny (15)
bumpkin (2)	unflaggingly (7)	boilerplate (16)
Machiavellian (2)	inexorable (8)	inscrutable (17)
Mason–Dixon line (3)	mechanistic (9)	scooped (19)
arcane (3)	husbandry (9)	sui generis (20)
naturalist (4)	metaphysical (9)	Reconstruction (20)
rockhound (4)	autocratic (10)	gainsay (21)
dilettante (4)	gestated (12)	

2. Consider Jones's topic sentences and transitions. What word choices and strategies does Jones rely on as he moves from one paragraph to the next?

Writing Your Own Essays Using Comparison and Contrast

1. Like Jones, compare two contemporaries of any period: Malcolm X and Martin Luther King Jr., Madonna and Michael Jackson, Tiger Woods and Michael Phelps. Draft a three- to four-page essay in which you compare these figures, considering how each figure affected his or her time. Of course, as you choose your pair, you'll want to make sure there is a basis of comparison (civil rights, music, sports). Once you establish the basis of comparison, identify points of comparison to explore the similarities and differences between these figures. As you write and revise, refer to the guidelines for checking over the use of comparison and contrast on page 359.

2. In Jones's essay, he addresses the writing styles of Darwin and Lincoln. Choose two writers you admire, compare their writing styles, and draft a three- to four-page essay that explores this comparison. Identify points of comparison as you compose. As Jones does, use quotations from these writers' work to support your claims about their writing. As you write and revise, refer to the guidelines for checking over the use of comparison and contrast on page 359.

✱ Additional Suggestions for Writing

1. Often we engage in comparison and contrast to make a decision. For example, how did you decide on a college major, area of concentration, or degree program? If you haven't already decided, how are you deciding? Make a list of the possibilities you considered or are considering; then list the features of each one that are most and least desirable. Personal interest, aptitude, reputation of the faculty, career and earning potential—these are some of the features you may have considered or may want to consider. (You might have to research some of them.) Reduce your list of possibilities to the top two, and then draft a two-page comparison-and-contrast essay that reveals information as it explains your decision or helps focus on your future decision. Be sure to refer to "Checking Over the Use of Comparison and Contrast" (p. 359) as you draft.

2. In college you have to read and write—a lot. These skills usually develop together, yet some people like reading more than writing, or vice versa. Draft a two- to three-page essay in which you compare and contrast your feelings about reading and writing. You may want to consider both school-related and personal reading and writing, or you may choose to concentrate on one or the other. Regardless of your purpose and pattern of organization, be sure to explain your attitudes in terms of a comparison and contrast. As you work, refer to the guidelines for checking over the use of comparison and contrast on page 359.

chapter 7

PROCESS ANALYSIS

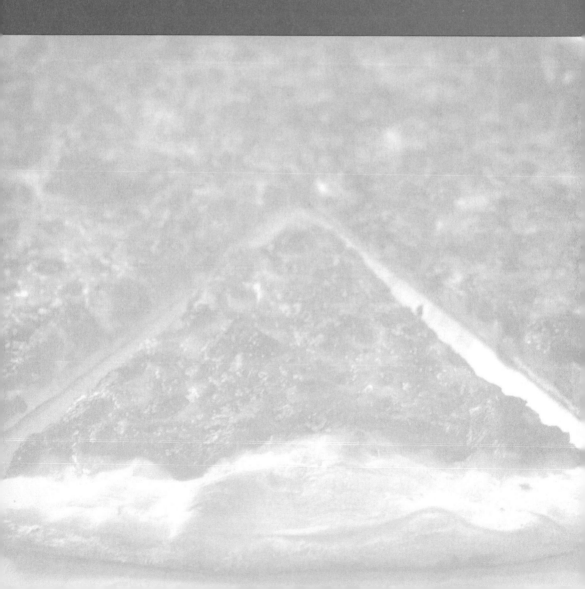

Gabe —

I went to Garth's house for dinner. There is pizza in the frige for you to eat.

To heat up pizza: (try one or the other)

Garth's Way:	Our Way:
- put pizza slices on plate to left. ⬅	- put pizza slices on metal tray to right. ➡
- put plastic wrap over it	- put on top rack of oven.
- heat in microwave on [Auto Cook] then [1]	- push ① upper oven ② 200 ③ start/enter
	- when oven beeps, take pizza out.
DO NOT put metal tray in microwave (will catch on fire ⚡).	NO PLASTIC WRAP OR IT WILL MELT IN OVEN.

- Have carrots with meal ⬆
- have MILK with meal
- DO NOT EAT IN TV ROOM !!!

If your friends are here, call me at Garth's (234-9014) so I can come home + watch you OR go to their house after dinner + LEAVE A NOTE WHERE YOU ARE!!
- Clean up after yourself !!

— Lydia

*E*very day, people leave notes for others, explaining how to complete a process. In this case, Lydia is writing to her younger brother, Gabe, giving him directions for two possible ways to heat up leftover pizza (as well as what to eat and drink with his pizza and how to behave). Like Gabe, we often know what we want to do, but we're not sure how to do it. We need an analysis of the process, and in Gabe's case, Lydia has analyzed two alternative processes for achieving the same result. Whether he decides to try "Garth's way" by using the microwave or "our way" by using the regular oven, Gabe has all the information he needs to complete the process. Whether we're explaining how to heat up pizza or how to drive to someone's house, how our eyes perceive color or how a bill in Congress becomes a law, we are analyzing a process.

Looking at Your Own Literacy   When was the last time you left an instructional note for someone — or when one was left for you? What was that note about? How detailed and clear were the instructions?

What Is Process Analysis?

A **process** is a series of actions that always leads to the same result, no matter how many times it's repeated. The purpose of **process analysis** is to explain the process by breaking it down into a fixed order of steps. Like narration, process analysis is chronological — it's organized according to time — but narration is concerned with a onetime event. A process analysis, on the other hand, is concerned with an event that is replicable, that can be duplicated. For instance, if you're changing a tire on your motorcycle, you'd be better off following clearly ordered, step-by-step instructions than listening to a friend tell a story about a time she changed the tire on her motorcycle. You need to know exactly what to do, in what order, how the steps in the process relate to one another, and how each step leads to the desired outcome. You need a process analysis, not a story.

Every day, we analyze processes to understand the world around us. You already know the steps in a wide variety of processes, such as setting the time on a watch, cleaning your contact lenses, logging on to your computer, or preparing a particular food. In fact, you often know the steps so well that you don't even think about them anymore; you just do them. But most of us are always interested in learning how to do something else, from how to study successfully or write competently to how to negotiate relations with coworkers and classmates and maintain friendships. In fact, process analysis has become such an important part of our lives that it is big business: books analyzing processes are always among the best–sellers. Consider the following popular titles: *God Is My Broker: A Monk-Tycoon Reveals the 7½ Laws of Spiritual and Financial Growth; 8 Weeks to Optimum Health: A Proven Program for Taking Full Advantage of Your Body's Natural Healing Power;* and *The Motley Fool Investment Guide: How the Fool Beats Wall Street's Wise Men and How You Can Too.* Interestingly, books about how to make money are always among the top sellers.

Although such books may or may not actually help you make money or stay healthy, process analysis can also be pleasurable and interesting for its own sake. Many people buy cookbooks just to read recipes they never make themselves; others buy weight–loss books, investment magazines, or car–repair manuals to read about processes they are curious about but don't perform on a regular basis, if ever. But whenever we have to explain a process to someone else, we consciously break it into easy–to–follow steps, like those on a box of Anchor Purity Wrap All–Purpose Food Film, a brand of plastic sheeting used to wrap food.

CUTTER BOX ASSEMBLY INSTRUCTIONS
1. Remove anti-slip rubber pads and secure to bottom of box.
2. Verify film unwind is in direction indicated.
3. Feed film through slot on top of box.

SEE BLADE PAD FOR LOCK-TOP ASSEMBLY INSTRUCTIONS

Warning: Sharp Cutter Edge

Thinking about Process Analysis

1. Look over the visual and written instructions for assembling the box used to cut the film. What is your first impression?

2. Why do the instructions include a picture?

3. What purpose do the words serve? Rewrite the instructions using words only.

Why Use Process Analysis?

A process analysis can have one—or both—of two explanatory purposes. A **directive process analysis** is often a set of step–by–step instructions for a customer, patient, worker, or some other person to follow, like the instructions for assembling the food wrap box. But a process analysis can be more than just a set of instructions: a writer can use it to explain the mysteries of how something happens or is done or to persuade an audience of the advantages or disadvantages of doing it or of doing it one way as opposed to another. Writers of such **infor-mative process analyses,** which explain how something works or is done, don't necessarily expect or want readers to carry out the process themselves.

A directive process analysis is usually instructional, the kind of advice you might find in a weight–loss book, investment guide, or cookbook. The writer's goal is for the reader to be able to learn and replicate the process. In the following excerpt, Jane De Mouy instructs readers on how to eat "Baltimore's soul food": Chesapeake Bay blue crab.

A Directive Process Analysis

Begin by pulling off the spindly legs on each side of the crab. Some people like to suck small bits of meat out of these, but you're better off concentrating on bigger pickin's: the pincer claws. Break these off and snap at the joint. Crack the hard claw firmly but gently with your mallet, or the handle end of a crab knife. If you hit too hard, you'll smash the meat. Break the shell apart to reveal the claw meat, and dig out your first tasty bite of this wonderful feast.

Flip the hard body of the crab on its red back, revealing its ivory, ribbed apron underneath. Slip a knife point under the key-like spoke of the apron and lift. You'll see greenish matter called the "devil," and the lungs, a web of thin spongy fingers of tissue. Discard the devil and lungs. The mustard-colored pudding is the crab's fat. Similar to a lob-ster's tomalley, it's edible if you like the rich taste.

Now, with your knife, cut the cartilage in two down the center. Sip your beer. You're after the crab's prize—nuggets of lump meat as big as your thumb, if your critter has full-season size on him; the object is to extract the meat without destroying the lump. There are as many techniques for this as there are feasters, but one efficient method is to cut away the outer edges of the crab's body, then slice across the top of the cartilage to create a lid. Remove the lid to expose the crab in its shell chamber. Inserting your knife into the shell cavity, pry out the lump of crab and savor. After the first one, you'll pick up speed. After half a dozen or so, you'll understand why spicy, succulent blue crabs are Balti-more's soul food.   —JANE DE MOUY, "A Crab Cracker's How-To"

Try Your Hand Identify a delicacy like Baltimore's crabs that is well known in a place where you live or have lived, and instruct outsiders as to the best way to enjoy this particular food. Using De Mouy as a model, write for five minutes explaining the process. Once you're fin-ished, share your writing with a classmate.

Whether directive or informative, process analysis can provide in-struction and pleasure as well as satisfy intellectual curiosity. For in-stance, most children want to know how Santa Claus, the Easter bunny, and the tooth fairy operate and where babies come from. They may have no intention of doing anything with this information; they simply want to know the things that grown-ups know. So they turn to process analysis, gleaning information from older siblings, friends, and books.

Of course, children are not the only ones who want explanations for how things came to be or how they work. Adults often look to informational process analyses as a way to learn and explain complex information. *Wired* magazine writer Jonah Lehrer uses this rhetorical method, along with visual cues, to inform readers about the scientific process called mapping the brain, in which scientists industrialize and streamline the anatomical study of the brain to create a complex atlas of this all-important organ.

An Informative Process Analysis

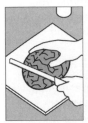 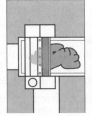 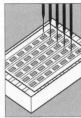 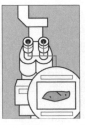 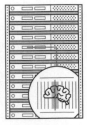

1. As soon as the institute receives a fresh human brain—fewer than 15 specimens will ultimately be used to create the atlas—it's immediately hand-sliced into 5-mm slabs, which are frozen.

2. Using a machine called a microtome, technicians shave each slab into thousands of transparent slices only a few microns thick. These are mounted on 2- x 3-inch bar-coded glass slides.

3. In a process called in situ hybridization, specialized robots work round the clock using fragments of RNA to probe each sample for a particular gene, which is stained with colored dye.

4. Robotic microscopes equipped with high-speed loaders take digital photographs of each slide. The intensity of dye color is used to quantify the amount of gene expression in the tissue.

5. The complete atlas, correlated by both gene and location, is stored on the institute's servers. Powerful tools to explore the data will be available for free to all researchers at brain-map.org.

—JONAH LEHRER, "Scientists Map the Brain, Gene by Gene"

Lehrer's excerpt is certainly informative, but even though the steps are carefully laid out and explained, it's doubtful he expects ordinary readers to be able to replicate this process.

. . . .

Try Your Hand   Write a brief process analysis for your classmates, one that is both directive and informative. You might, for instance, write about how a peer might enjoy the sights and sounds of your hometown. You should tell your reader where to go and in what order.

You'll also want to provide detailed information about each stop, explaining the location and its significance.

. . . .

Informational process analysis is more versatile than directional process analysis: you can use it to share information, such as how to drop a class; you can use it to entertain readers with information on, say, dog training, skydiving, or race car driving; or you can use it to argue that a particular process is the most successful, quickest, safest, or best one to follow or advocate. Some best–selling books fit both the directive and informational categories of process analysis: the writer claims that if you "buy my books and follow my program," you'll be able to lose weight, win friends, or become rich. Julie Morgenstern makes a similar claim in *Making Work Work*, when she educates readers as to how they might become more productive at their jobs. Her process analysis includes one easy (or perhaps not-so-easy) step: turning off the e-mail.

A Directive and Informative Process Analysis

Change the rhythm of the workday by starting out with your own drumbeat. The most dramatic, effective way to boost your productivity is to completely avoid e-mail for the first hour of the day. Instead, devote that first hour every day to your most critical task. When you devote your first hour to concentrated work—a dash—the day starts with *you* in charge of *it* rather than the other way around. It's a bold statement to the world (and yourself) that you can take control, pull away from the frenetic pace, and create the time for quiet work when you need it. In reality, if you don't consciously create the space for the dashes, they won't get done. . . .

To make your first-hour policy work, decide the night before exactly what you are going to tackle during that hour. Ask yourself, If tomorrow flies out of control, what *one* task (not two or three) would I be thrilled to get done—what can I do to earn my salary by 10 A.M.? Deciding the evening before will give you a chance to mull it over in your sleep and on your commute to the office that morning. Once you arrive, you can hit the ground running, Instead of wasting half of your precious hour figuring out what you should do. Try it. Turn off your e-mail alarm, turn on your voice mail, and walk into your office with a single focus—completing that critical task. Don't drop in on a friend. Put on your blinders and tear into your task. The energy you'll feel from accomplishing it will fuel you all day long.   —JULIE MORGENSTERN, *Making Work* Work

Morgenstern's suggestions are both directional and informative to readers.

. . . .

Try Your Hand   In her book, Morgenstern helps readers learn how to become the most productive they can be. Reflect on a particularly productive day at work or at school. Write for five minutes about the
(continued)

(*continued*)
process that led to this productivity. How did the day begin? What did
you do? How did you accomplish the tasks you set out for yourself?

How Do You Use Process Analysis in Academic Writing?

Writers composing in many academic contexts use process analysis
to achieve their purposes. For example, an art historian might explain the
process by which a painter creates a work in a particular medium, such
as a fresco, or uses perspective to create the illusion of three dimensions
on a flat surface. But scientists are the group of academic writers who
probably use process analysis the most, to explain the procedures — the
processes — of their experiments. An integral part of the scientific method,
the "procedures" section of a scientific journal article allows readers to
see how the scientists conducted the study — the order in which they
performed their actions and the process through which they arrived at
their results. The goal of the procedures section is that other researchers
can, if they choose, replicate the process, testing the results and learning
from their colleagues' work. So that scientists can effectively share their
findings, they need to be sure their procedures section is thorough, con-
cise, and clear.

In the following example from the journal *Ecology*, three scientists explain the procedure of an experiment in which they investigate how the
life cycle of four species of shrubs that grow in a dry Mediterranean climate is affected by the timing of when their seedlings emerge after brush
fires.

Process Analysis in Academic Writing

In October 1996, after the first autumn rains and on windless days, we
burned the three plots. Plots were previously delimited by a 5 m wide fire-
break in which the vegetation was eliminated by mechanical brushing. The
fires were ignited in the upper part of each plot with the fire fronts being made
in a continuous line downhill.

Immediately after fire and for the next three years, seedling recruitment,
survival, growth (height), and fecundity (number of flowers per plant) of all
species presented in four $2 \times 0.5 \text{ m}^2$ subplots established within each experimental plot were monitored (fire scenario). Germinating seedlings were
tagged monthly at first, then once every two months and then each season.
An additional sampling was made in autumn of 2005 (9 years after fire).
Biomass estimation of each plant at each time was derived through specific
allometric relationships between height and basal diameters from individuals
harvested in an adjacent area.

> — MARTIN DE LUIS, MIGUEL VERDÚ, and JOSÉ RAVENTÓS, "Early
> to Rise Makes a Plant Healthy, Wealthy, and Wise"

In performing their experiments, these ecologists found that the earlier a plant emerged, the better chance it had of survival. If other ecologists want to test this finding, all they need to do is replicate the process de Luis and his colleagues lay out in their procedures section.

• •

Analyzing Process Analysis in Academic Writing   Reflecting on science classes you are taking or have taken, think about times when you've performed and then have written up an experiment. What challenges did you find in composing your procedures section? What changes did you need to make to your writing style?

• •

How Do You Read a Process Analysis?

The heading for this section — "How Do You Read a Process Analysis?" — suggests that you're about to read just that: a process analysis of how to read a process analysis. Actually this section is about learning to read a process analysis *critically*, not just understanding what one means but also judging its effectiveness — and you don't have to follow a specific series of steps to do so. But if you make a habit of reading a process analysis in this way — thinking about how well it explains the process and achieves other purposes the writer intends for a specific audience — you'll glean more information from it and will be better able to write your own process analyses with success.

If there's a title or heading, that's where you'll start, to see if it provides a clue to how the author wants you to read the process analysis. Take another look at the process analysis that opens this chapter (p. 404). The heading, "Gabe," indicates that Gabe is being addressed by an author (Lydia), but it's not until you read the introduction and the thesis that Lydia's purpose is revealed: "I went to Garth's house for dinner. There is pizza in the fri[d]ge for you to eat. To heat up pizza: (try one [way] or the other)." As you know, there are two basic types of process analysis, descriptive and informative, and Lydia makes clear that hers is an *informative* one. She wants Gabe to be able to do more than just understand the process of heating up pizza; she expects him to be able to replicate the process, to heat up his own pizza — as well as to do or not do certain other things.

Whether a process analysis is descriptive or informative, it can serve one of three overall purposes: to explain a process, to entertain readers with an explanation, or to argue the positive or negative attributes of a particular process. Although Lydia mentions a negative feature of each pizza-heating process for Gabe to avoid, she concentrates on fulfilling an explanatory purpose. As she does, she includes a number of necessary details that enhance her step-by-step explanation.

One key aspect of reading a process analysis critically is to evaluate how knowledgeable and experienced the author appears to be in terms of this process. Lydia seems to be both, as she explains two ways for Gabe to heat up his pizza: "Garth's way" and "our way." Apparently, she's set up the kitchen so that he can either "put pizza slices on plate to left ←" or "put pizza slices on metal tray to right →." And she's set up the explanation so that the two possible processes are shown side by side, with an underlined heading for each alternative, a line between them, and each step and substep clearly indicated with dashes or numbers. Because she's giving the steps in list form from top to bottom, Lydia doesn't need to indicate the relationship between them with words or phrases like "first," "next," or "after five minutes." When you're writing a process analysis in full sentences and paragraphs, however, it's usually a good idea to begin each step with some indication of how it relates to the previous one.

Notice also how Lydia draws special attention to key tasks in the process that Gabe should do—or things he should avoid—with capital letters, underlining, exclamation points, or combinations of these. For her audience—a child—signals like these may be a good idea, although it's worth noting that the more they're used, the less attention readers will pay to them. When you're writing for an adult audience, try to find other ways to emphasize the key points you want to make in your analysis. For example, you might start out the sentence about the most crucial step in the process with "Most important, be sure to . . ."

Finally, as you read a process analysis, think not just about what the writer says but what he or she doesn't say. For example, Lydia doesn't tell Gabe where to find the plastic wrap or the carrots, remind him to use a pot holder to take the metal tray out of the oven, or specify what cleaning up involves. Presumably, he's old enough and familiar enough with the kitchen that she feels he doesn't need these instructions (or maybe she just ran out of space on the page). By thinking about what the writer leaves out, you may be able to learn something about writing your own process analyses without confusing or boring readers with too much detail or puzzling them by omitting necessary information.

How Do You Write a Process Analysis?

Whether it's directive or informative, your process needs to be explanatory. Therefore, you'll want to select and arrange the details about the process with care, explaining the steps thoroughly and accurately so that they can be replicated or easily understood. From writing out directions for making egg salad to explaining how a fossil is formed, you'll also need to consider your audience and purpose, arrange the steps in the process carefully, and add transitions to make the order of the steps clear for your readers.

● Considering the Process

What process are you concentrating on? Will you cover all of this process or only part of it? For instance, if your goal is to teach your brother how to make pizza, you'll have to consider how much of this process you (and he) can handle in the first lesson. In other words, where will you start? Where will you end? It's easier to write a process analysis if you limit the scope of the process you are explaining. If you decide to start by teaching your brother how to make a simple pizza, you'll probably begin with a ready-made crust or with a mix. A later lesson, based on the earlier one, might begin with making pizza dough from scratch.

● Considering Your Audience

No matter what kind of process analysis you are writing, you will always need to think carefully about the best way to present the process to your audience. What does your audience already know about the topic? What terms or phrases will you need to define or explain? If your brother is the audience and making a simple pizza is the process you are explaining, you'll need to determine how much or how little he already knows about cooking. If he already knows how to mix dough, you can start with letting the dough rise. But he may not understand the necessity of punching down dough to release the air bubbles, a detail that a more experienced baker would know. Considering how much your audience knows, or doesn't know, will help you determine how many steps you need to break down the process into and how much detail to include in each step.

Considering your audience will also help you decide which **point of view** to use: first-, second-, or third-person point of view. When the process analysis is directive—when the audience may actually be carrying out the process—writers often use second-person point of view; in other words, they speak directly to "you." In the note on page 404, Lydia writes directly to Gabe, explaining the process of heating up pizza and always using or implying "you": "You, Gabe, should put pizza slices on the plate to the left"; "You, Gabe, should not put the metal tray in the microwave." She is explaining a process, directing Gabe, and giving commands. In the excerpt on page 409, Julie Morgenstern also addresses her audience using "you." "When you devote your first hour to concentrated work—a dash—the day starts with *you* in charge of *it* rather than the other way around." Such a choice makes sense for an advice book: Morgenstern needs to create a personal relationship with her readers, and by using "you," she speaks directly to them.

When the process analysis is informational, writers often resort to first-person ("I" or "we") or third-person ("he," "she," "it," "they") point of view. In the example of academic writing on pages 410–11, the authors use the first person ("we burned") in the first sentence and then switch not only to the third person but also to passive voice ("was eliminated," "were ignited," "were monitored"), which does not mention who carried out the process. This point of view seems an appropriate choice for a scientific article, creating objective distance both between the writers and their topic and between the writers and their audience.

● Considering Your Purpose

The point of view you choose to use connects your topic and your audience to your purpose — what you want the audience to do with the explanation provided in your analysis. In many cases, your purpose will be determined by a class assignment, a specific request for information, or a request for a solution to a problem. Perhaps your brother-in-law has asked you how to take the subway from the airport to downtown, or your geology professor has asked you to explain how sediment turns into rock. Maybe your daughter wants to know how to get chocolate stains out of her white cotton blouse, or a coworker has asked how to deal with a customer's complaint. In other cases, only you will decide on your purpose for writing. You may write out the pizza-heating directions because you want your brother to be able to fix his own supper. You may want to analyze the complex process of applying for off-campus housing in order to argue that it should be simplified. You may simply want your readers to be able to replicate the steps you've written down for them; but especially if you are writing an informative process analysis, you may also want the audience to appreciate the steps in the process themselves for their beauty, their efficiency, the skill they require — or to recognize how inefficient, unpleasant, or ridiculous the process is.

Whatever your purpose, it should help you focus your **thesis statement,** which provides a general overview of the process and its significance. For example, in an article for the women's magazine *Latina*, author Mimi Valdez writes about the powerful benefits of boxing:

> That's the great thing about a boxing workout: Just as you're almost spent doing one thing, you move on to another, which seems easier because it involves fresh moves and muscles.

She develops this thesis as she describes the process of training to box:

> Jason explains the pace of the workout — train three minutes, rest for one — just like in rounds of boxing. We begin jumping rope to warm up. If you have pretty good endurance — if you don't collapse after two flights of stairs — rope skipping isn't hard to master. But by the last set, I'm so

tired that my skills fly out the window, with me longing to escape with them. Then we switch gears, heading over to the mirror to shadowbox, to learn the proper stance for throwing punches. . . .

Just as I get the maneuvers (or think I have), Jason moves me to the punching bags. He puts boxing gloves on me, and I try to translate what I learned about punching onto the jumpy little speed bag, but apparently it knows more about dodging punches than I do about throwing them. We switch to the big, hanging punching bag, which is attached with elastic to both the ceiling and floor. I'm trying to throw two left jabs and a right while circling the bag and keeping my form. Instead, I'm all over the place, not making a dent. And the bag stays where it is, still as a stone. "Don't worry about strength, " Jason says. "The first day is all about form."
                                                    — MIMI VALDEZ, "Mimi Throws Her Punches"

Written to demonstrate the benefits of boxing to a female audience, Valdez's article contains a sidebar with a more specific purpose, telling readers how to find an instructor:

If you prefer working one-on-one with a trainer, locate a boxing gym in the yellow pages. Make sure it has a strong female membership, so you'll feel comfortable there. Before you commit to join, ask if they have a fitness program you can try for a month, working out with an instructor three or four times a week. The cost will be anywhere from $100 to $200 monthly. Otherwise, check out your local fitness center to see if they have aerobic classes in boxing — it's fun to do it in a group. Often called Cardio Boxing, these aerobic classes build your heart and lung capacity as well as muscle strength, especially firming the arms, shoulders, and back. Whichever you choose, one-on-one or a class, don't forget: Always warm up and stretch before exercise, and cool down afterward.

As you can see, a writer can have two different purposes for writing about a process and can address two or more different audiences. In the quoted passages, Valdez seems merely to want to interest her female readers in her exercise regimen. But in the sidebar, she's more specific about both her purpose and her audience: she wants to help those who are interested begin the exercise program for themselves. Both careful audience analysis and an awareness of purpose are crucial as you develop your process analysis.

● Considering Your Method of Organization

Like narration, a process analysis is presented as a chronological sequence of actions or steps. But unlike narration, a process analysis usually has a fixed order: the steps are always the same; the results are always the same. Therefore, when Valdez describes her boxing workout, she's describing the general sequence of actions (steps or groups of steps) in any boxing workout. She skips rope, practices maneuvers, shadow-boxes, punches the speed bag and the big bag, goes one-on-one with Jason, and then does lunges and sit-ups, reminded by her boxing instructor that "boxers do complete workouts." The results of complete workouts are the same as well: when she leaves after an hour, she feels "great." But when she wakes up the next morning, she feels "pretty sore all over, but particularly sore in my arms and shoulders."

When readers already understand some steps of the process or don't need to know them at all, a process analysis may condense a long series of steps into just a few short steps. In the analysis on page 417, Shutterfly .com wants readers to know how easy it is to turn pictures from their digital cameras into holiday cards. As you read each step in the three-step process, you'll see that the writer assumes that the reader has a digital camera and knows how to use it and how to upload pictures.

Process analysis visuals can move readers step by step, or they can include all the steps in one visual, as in the Shutterfly ad.

● Considering the Necessary Details

To explain a process successfully, writers need to include clear, pertinent details for each step. In her description of a boxing workout, Mimi Valdez includes a number of vivid, specific details.

Clear, Specific Details in a Process Analysis

I'm all riled up and I concentrate. There is a proper formation for your body to be in before you can throw punches. For example, right-handers should have the right leg behind, left in front; right toes slightly pointed out; knees bent so that your weight is evenly balanced in the stance. I make a few left jabs (short, quick punches) at Jason's grin in the mirror. Noticing how my elbows fly up each time, he shows me how my fighting-mad punching is making me vulnerable. I should be keeping my chin down and my elbows in at my sides, throwing punches straight from there. If I don't, and instead I lift my elbows, it signals to the other boxer that my punch is coming.

Valdez wants her readers to understand exactly how the practice is done; she wants them to know that one misstep or mispunch can undo all her careful training. Including such vivid details also helps bring her process analysis to life, making it interesting to read.

● Providing Transitions

As you lead your readers through the steps of your process analysis, be sure to include transitional words or phrases that help them understand the progression. In the following account of bronze casting, Nancy Ellis moves her readers through a complicated yet well-explained process: the transformation of Estella Loretto's eight-foot-tall clay figure, *Morning Prayer*, into a bronze sculpture.

CREATE THE MOST
WONDERFUL
CARD OF THE YEAR.

It's time to share beautiful holiday photo cards with your friends and family. Our collection of styles let you find the holiday cheer that's right for you.

Greeting Cards

Classic. Traditional designs that are both timeless and elegant. They're everything you want in a great holiday card.

Fun. Bright designs and playful illustrations that show off your holiday personality and everything that's right with the season.

Photo Cards

Designer Cards

Modern. Expressive and stylish designs that bring out the beauty in your pictures. These cards are a great way to start a new tradition while showing that holiday spirit.

⑤

TIPS FOR THE BEST HOLIDAY PHOTO CARDS.

- If you're taking pictures outside, make sure the sun is behind the person with the camera. And think about early morning light or afternoon sun to spruce up your pics with warmer tones.

- The holiday season is busy enough. Try to avoid holiday patterns on clothes by putting everyone in solid colors.

- Don't forget about using a great candid picture from the year. They can be just as beautiful as professional portraits.

- Think about adjusting your photos to black and white on our site. It's more distinctive and works well with every style of card.

- Get creative. Tell your story through a collage or write a funny caption.

*April 2008 InfoTrends

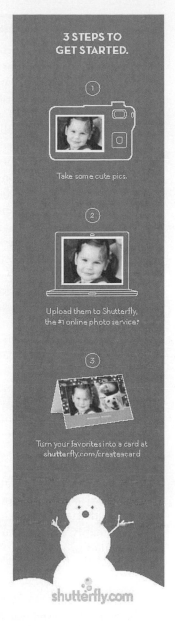

3 STEPS TO GET STARTED.

① Take some cute pics.

② Upload them to Shutterfly, the #1 online photo service.*

③ Turn your favorites into a card at shutterfly.com/createacard

shutterfly.com

"Reading" and Using Visuals in a Process Analysis

An effective process analysis often includes visuals. When we follow a directional process analysis, we like—and often need—to see that process in pictures. For that reason, home and car repair manuals, science books, and cookbooks use many visuals to explain a system or process from start to finish. Good cookbooks and specialized magazines are especially valuable for their photographs and drawings of individual processes (chopping, dicing, wallpapering, pitching, putting) and of finished products (casseroles, walls, gardens). And good doctors and pharmacists always try to ensure that you know how to take your medication. Although visuals more commonly accompany directional process analyses, they are also an important enhancement to many informational process analyses, making them more interesting, more easily understood, and more helpful.

To use visuals effectively in your own process analyses, you need to study ones used by other writers to see how clearly they convey information in visual form and, specifically, how well they do so for their particular purpose and audience. The accompanying visual, for example, is part of a folding pocket guide for installing drywall that features instructions in English, in Spanish, and in pictures. Perhaps the most interesting feature of this visual is how much information is omitted. This guide is intended for someone who already knows how to install drywall—not for someone who wants to learn how to do it. Drywall installation is a skilled job involving careful measuring, cutting, hanging, patching, sanding, and finishing. This series of pictures, then, serves only as a sketch of the key steps in the job, something the worker and supervisor can look at or point to for reference. Experienced drywall workers will bring much more knowledge and know-how to the installation than this visual provides. For instance, the third panel includes a picture of a "mud tray/*bandeja para resanar*" with no explanation of how it is involved in the process, but presumably workers familiar with drywall installation won't need an explanation.

Transitions in Process Analysis

Because Estella lived with this large clay woman in her studio for so many months as the artwork progressed, observing her from all angles and especially in the morning light, she knew instinctively when the sculpture was complete and ready for the mold-maker. For this critical part of the process, she chose Brett Chromer, a Santa Fe sculptor who has extensive experience making molds for other artists.

Chromer first decides where he will put the shims — ultimately, the seams— into the clay (*Morning Prayer* was cast in 17 separate sections).

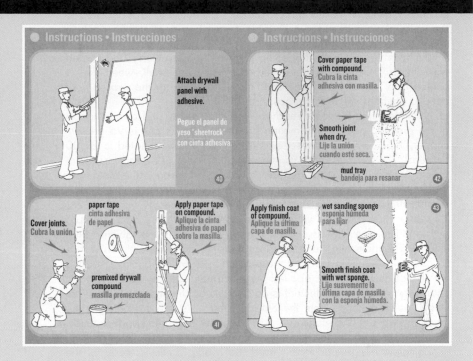

As you can see, the visual explanation can be a more efficient reference than a verbal one, particularly when there is a language barrier. Although a supervisor and a worker might not speak the same language, both of them can understand the pictures and will already understand the general process. Notice that some of the smaller items involved in drywall installation — such as the roll of paper tape and the wet sanding sponge — are also shown "blown up" to a larger size so that they can be identified more easily. Other panels of this pocket guide show pictures of other tools and supplies involved in drywall installation, along with their English and Spanish names.

Next, layers of silicone rubber material are brushed over the original, creating a mold — a perfect imprint of the original that will be used for casting all other pieces in the edition. "Keys" are permanently affixed to the last coating of rubber, so the separated parts of the "mother mold" always can be accurately reassembled. After a final coat of plaster has set, the mold is broken open and the original artwork is removed, and the mold is ready for Shidoni [a foundry in Santa Fe].

At the foundry, wax is layered with a brush into the rubber mold, creating a perfect wax copy of the original. It is the wax reproduction that will be used to create another mold into which the molten bronze will be poured. Wax bars, called sprues, and a wax pour cup are attached to the work, along with sumps and gates, to create a system of channels to allow bronze to flow bottom to top.

The wax copy is now dipped in a colloidal silica slurry and coated with stucco, creating a second ceramic mold. This shell, when dry, is heated in a kiln to 1,600 degrees Fahrenheit, causing the wax to flush out and giving name to this process, lost wax.

Now, *Morning Prayer* is ready for the most visual and dramatic part of the process: pouring the molten bronze (Shidoni's mix is 95 percent copper, 1 percent manganese, and 4 percent silicone, heated to 2,000 degrees). The ceramic molds are heated and placed in a sand pit, where bronze from the furnace is ladled into them. When cool, the molds are broken off with hammers and pneumatic tools, and the bronze sculpture is sandblasted before being sent to the metal shop. Here *Morning Prayer's* 17 sections are carefully welded back together and the seams "chased" with grinders. The fully assembled bronze sculpture is now given a final cleansing sandblast so that it will accept the patina.

Estella is deeply involved in the patination of *Morning Prayer*, during which hot chemicals are applied to its bronze surface, oxidizing and changing color. Her excitement is contagious as she supervises this final stage, with assistance from the Shidoni staff. "It's like a painting," she explains, working the sculpture's skin with finer and finer grades of steel pads. "I like a soft, warm, radiant look."

Completely engrossed in this hard, hot work, Estella is ready for the first coating of wax over the finished face of *Morning Prayer*. She stands back. "It's like having a baby," she says. "You can't rush any part of the process." Climbing back up on the ladder, she looks directly into the eyes of *Morning Prayer*.

Estella is obviously thrilled with this first edition of *Morning Prayer*, which is cast, like most of her monumental pieces, in an edition of seven. There were some difficult issues to be resolved — Estella re-sculpted her face at one point, seeking a more subtle, more serene smile — during the period of nearly a year that it took to bring *Morning Prayer* from original concept to completion.   —Nancy Ellis, "The Art of Casting Bronze"

The transitional words and phrases ("first," "next," "after a final coat," "at the foundry," "now," "here") and the specific details ("17 separate sections"; "wax is layered with a brush into the rubber mold"; "wax bars . . . and a wax pour cup are attached to the work . . . to create a system of channels to allow bronze to flow bottom to top"; "heated in a kiln to 1,600 degrees"; "95 percent copper, 1 percent manganese, and 4 percent silicone") all work to help us follow Ellis's account of these steps.

Ellis's concluding sentences reconfirm her artistic appreciation of the process, an appreciation she wants her readers to share: "'You can tell how happy she is,' says Estella, her own eyes brimming with tears. 'She's so happy; it almost makes me cry.'" Ellis's process analysis is both directive and informational, a replicable process to be understood and appreciated.

Understanding and Using Process Analysis

Analyzing Process Analysis

1. Reread Jane De Mouy's crab-eating analysis on page 407. Who is the audience for this analysis? How do you know?

2. Julie Morgenstern's excerpt (p. 409) offers just one piece of advice as to how readers might be more productive at work. **Working with two or three classmates,** consider other processes that might be included in Morgenstern's book. How would these steps allow for greater productivity at work or at school?

Planning and Writing Essays Using Process Analysis

1. Think for a minute: What processes are you really good at? Which one could you teach to someone else? The process can be as simple as shifting gears in a car or making a pot of tea, as unexpected as preparing the perfect bath, or as adventurous as snowboarding without a hitch. Jot down a few ideas for process analysis papers, and then write about each possible topic for a few minutes. Which topic seems the most promising? Can you remember all the necessary steps, in order? Can you weave in the necessary details and explanations? Would a visual or two help readers understand the process better?

    Trade papers with a classmate, and help each other decide which idea might work best for each of you. Try to help each other come up with a thesis statement that reflects the basic purpose of the essay.

2. Look over the syllabus for this class. Jot down what you need to do in order to succeed in the class, based on both the requirements and expectations listed on the syllabus and your own sense of your strengths and weaknesses. Now try to break down the process of taking this course, numbering the steps. Next to each step, add the details and necessary information explaining that particular step. What might be the thesis statement of such an essay? Who, besides your instructor, might be your audience?

3. Share the ideas about succeeding in this particular class that you generated in response to question 2. **Working with two or three classmates,** write down all the steps that you agree on. In a separate list, write down the steps that were unique to each of you. (You might show the lists to your instructor and ask him or her to complete or improve on them.) In what ways are your thoughts about success the same? different? In what ways are the steps for success the same? different?

4. Look over your notes for question 1 in this section. What process have you decided you'd most like to develop into an essay? With your classmates as your audience, draft a three- to four-page process analysis essay that develops your thesis statement. **Share your draft with one or two classmates** to get their responses before you revise it for submission. Refer to the following guidelines for checking over the use of process analysis.

5. Go back to the notes you gathered on how best to succeed in this course for questions 2 and 3. Taking into consideration what your classmates advised, what your instructor may have advised, what the syllabus says, and what your own academic abilities and achievements are, draft a two-page process analysis essay that sets out a plan for success in your first-year writing course. Your instructor will be your audience, and your thesis statement will focus on your plans for achieving success in this course. Refer to the following guidelines for checking over the use of process analysis.

✔ Checking Over the Use of Process Analysis

1. What is the purpose of your process analysis? Is it directional or informational? In one sentence, write out the specific purpose; in other words, what's in it for the reader?

2. What is your thesis? If you cannot locate a thesis statement, write out the main idea of your essay.

3. Who are your readers? What do they already know about the process? How much background information do they need? Have you defined any terms that they probably won't know? Should you add more details to your explanation? streamline your explanation? break the process down into more steps? condense it into fewer steps?

4. Have you ordered your process analysis chronologically? Is the sequence of steps clear and complete?

5. Underline all the transitional words or phrases. Do they lead readers clearly from one step or group of steps to the next?

6. What is the purpose of your conclusion? Do you want your readers to feel a sense of confidence that they can reproduce the process? Or do you want them to appreciate the details of the process?

7. Does your process analysis include visuals? How exactly do the visuals enhance the verbal part of the analysis? Do you need to add captions, labels, or references to the visuals in the text?

READINGS

ED GRABIANOWSKI
How Online Dating Works

● Ed Grabianowski, a freelance writer, is a native of Buffalo who attended Kansas State University and the State University of New York at Plattsburgh. In the following essay, published on the Web site HowStuffWorks.com, Grabianowski investigates the complex and sometimes rewarding process of online dating. His goal is to help readers decide whether or not they want to participate in this process. If readers decide to jump into the world of online dating, Grabianowski will show them how.

> **Preview** What is your perception of online dating? Who participates in these dating sites and why?

INTRODUCTION TO HOW ONLINE DATING WORKS

1 One of the basic human impulses is to develop a romantic relationship—and maybe even fall in love. But there are a lot of obstacles that might keep someone from meeting the love of his or her life in today's world. Maybe dating co-workers is against company policy. Perhaps you hate the bar scene. You might not be in the right mood to meet your soul mate while you're trekking through the grocery store.

2 People of all ages, lifestyles and locations have been facing this problem for decades. In the last 10 years or so, a new solution has arrived to help lonely hearts find their soul mates: online dating.

3 Online dating is simply a method of meeting people, and it has advantages and disadvantages. The variety of dating sites is constantly growing, with many sites focused on very specific groups

Before Grabianowski discusses the process of online dating, he defines what it is.

423

or interests. There are sites for seniors, sites for Muslims, sites for fitness-oriented people, sites for people just looking for friends and sites for people who are interested in more adult activities. In this article, we'll be focusing on the most basic type of dating site—one that works to bring two people together for a romantic relationship. While this article applies to the majority of popular dating sites, the rules and practices of any given individual site may differ.

Once you decide you're going to give it a shot, 4 the first thing you need to do is create your profile. See the next page to get started, and learn what online dating is like, find out how (and if) it works and get some helpful tips on making your online dating experience safe and successful.

ONLINE DATING: CREATING A PROFILE

When you first arrive at an online dating site, you 5 can browse through profiles without entering any information about yourself. The amount of information you can see about each user depends on the site. Some sites allow users to restrict access to their profiles to paying members. Photos might not be displayed unless you have a paid membership. This helps preserve anonymity, since a co-worker or family member can't accidentally stumble across your profile. They'd have to pay for a membership to see a picture of the person they're reading about.

When it's time to make your own profile, you'll 6 start with some basic information. Are you a man or a woman? Are you looking to meet a man or a woman? What age range are you interested in? Where do you live? (Some sites just ask for a ZIP code, while others may allow you to choose from a list of cities.) This is generally the same information you provide to perform a simple search, or "browse."

Basic profile information may also include your 7 birthdate and a valid e-mail address. Site administrators will communicate with you through this address, and some sites allow messages from users to be sent to your e-mail anonymously. When they send you a message, it is routed through the site's

Consider how Grabianowski's section headings help organize the essay and direct the reader's attention.

Grabianowski uses "you" to establish his point of view and speak directly to his readers.

system and redirected to your e-mail without the other user ever seeing your address. Some sites use their own internal messaging system. If you're especially concerned about privacy, it's easy enough to create a free e-mail account somewhere and use it solely for your online dating contacts.

8   **Indicating your physical attributes** is usually the next step. Height, weight, hair and eye color and body type are common pieces of data, while some sites ask about piercings and tattoos. At this point, the process becomes increasingly detailed. Interests and activities, favorite sports, authors, music or movies, how you like to spend weekends—these topics are all fair game. More personal questions might involve whether or not you have children, whether or not you want children, your religious beliefs and your political views. Pets, occupation, income and living situation are usually on the list as well.

9   Next, you'll be asked to answer many of these same questions a second time, but instead of indicating your own traits, you'll be **describing your ideal date.** The site will then use this information and the information you provided about yourself to find suitable matches that you might want to contact. Most sites will also allow you to **write about yourself** in a more freeform manner—a chance to get across more of your personality than a series of pull-down lists can offer.

10   **Posting a photo** of yourself is another important step. Most sites report a huge increase in responses to ads that have photos posted. There will usually be guidelines as to what sorts of photo you can post, and there might be an approval process before it actually gets posted. In general, avoid posting revealing photos, don't post photos with people other than yourself in them and don't post glossy, "glam" photos. Although you want to look your best, try and make sure the photo is accurate to how you currently look. If you're 35, your high school yearbook photo isn't a good choice. If you recently dyed your hair purple, try to get a photo that reflects that.

11   There's one last rule that needs to be mentioned, and it's an important one: **Don't put personal identification information in your profile.** This

Notice how Grabianowski's topic sentences function to move readers from one step of the process to the next.

Grabianowski uses boldface type to emphasize key information.

includes your address, phone number, Social Security number, full name or place of employment. You might meet people on the site that you'll want to share some of that information with down the line, but it should never be public knowledge.

Now, let's go through some helpful tips on creating a profile that encourages people to contact you.   12

**ONLINE DATING:
CREATING A *GOOD* PROFILE**

If you browse through a typical dating site, you will   13
see hundreds of ads from people who are "looking for Mr. Right." Nearly everyone "enjoys a night out on the town, but also likes a quiet evening at home." It would be difficult to find someone who doesn't like a good sense of humor in a date.

Begin with the subject. Inject some humor   14
into your subject line or include one of your interests. "Bogart fan seeking unusual suspects." "Come sail away with this boating enthusiast/Styx fan." This is the first thing people will see, and it needs to stand out from the crowd.

When it comes to the profile itself, make sure   15
you **fill out the whole thing.** Take your time and put some thought into it. It may seem tedious or difficult to describe yourself, but leaving sections blank or putting in short, generic answers makes it look like you aren't really interested. Avoid phrases like "I wouldn't normally use one of these dating services, but my friends put me up to this." Remember, your target audience is other people who are using this dating service. You don't want to start off by insulting them.

Think of specific aspects of your personality   16
that you want to highlight. Then don't just state them—**demonstrate them.** Instead of "I enjoy Stanley Kubrick films," say, "The other night I was watching *A Clockwork Orange*, and I found myself thinking it would be a lot more fun to watch and discuss it with someone else." Humor is especially important. Not everyone shares the same sense of humor, so saying "I'm a funny person" isn't sufficient. "I love quoting lines from Monty Python sketches and Simpsons episodes" gives other users a better grasp of your personality.

Here and in paragraph 27, Grabianowski uses one-sentence transitional paragraphs to move readers from one section to the next.

Grabianowski's use of imperative verbs offers readers direct, no-nonsense advice as to how to participate in the online dating process.

17   Another key to success is **knowing what you want** and putting it in your profile. You'll get more responses from people who are looking for the same thing you are, whether you want to settle down with a long-term relationship or just want a date for Friday night. "I think there is more of a mental connection first by online dating," said one user, a teacher from New York. "Also, you know what you're looking for, not what your friends think would be 'perfect' for you."

18   Last, but not least, **mind your grammar.** Poor grammar and spelling doesn't lead to a good first impression, so take the time to get it right.

ONLINE DATING: MAKING CONTACT

19 If you've decided to become a paying member of a dating site, you can start contacting other users if their profile appeals to you. These messages don't have to be very elaborate, since you've already put a lot of information into your profile. Something along the lines of "Hey, I saw your profile and it seems like we have some common interests. Take a look at my profile, and if you're interested, send me a message" is probably sufficient. You might send messages to several people at once, or you might contact one at a time — it's up to each user.

20   From there, you simply wait. Some people will write back to let you know they're not interested, while others will simply ignore your message. In some cases, the person you wrote to might not be visiting the site anymore. But a few of your contacts will eventually respond, and other people will start contacting you after they see your profile. How long it takes depends on the site and the individual user. Reports from dating-site users range from one who cited a ratio of "about a million to one" contacts to actual dates to another who had two dates almost immediately and is still dating one of them.

Note the use of transitions here and in the next few paragraphs to move readers from one step to the next.

21   Before long, you'll have e-mailed back and forth with someone you're interested in meeting face to face. In the next section, we'll plan a date for maximum safety and success.

22   The amount of time between that first e-mail and a first in-person date varies from person to person. That's one of the benefits of online dating — you

can take your time if you want to and really get to know someone well before you ever meet. Or you can plan a date right away and find out if there's any chemistry. Either way, it's important to keep safety in mind, along with a few other things to make sure your first date goes smoothly.

It's important to **talk to your date on the** 23 **phone** before you meet. Even if you've been conversing via e-mail for weeks, just one call can avoid a lot of problems. If the blonde, 24–year–old, female swimsuit model you've been writing to turns out to be a 13–year–old boy playing a joke, a phone call is a good way to find out.

Once it comes time to plan the actual date, 24 choose a **neutral, public setting** and arrive there independently. There are some dangerous people in the world, and even though they may be thankfully rare, it's still not a good idea to take a long hike into an isolated area with someone you don't know. Going to someone's house can be risky, too, for both men and women. In one case, a man went to meet a women he met online, and when he arrived, she pulled a knife and took his wallet.

Specific suggestions include a coffee shop, a 25 busy restaurant, a college sports game or a movie theater. The key is to make sure there will be plenty of other people around. Make sure you let someone know where you'll be going and what time you plan to return. A little caution never hurt anybody.

Of course, the vast majority of dates will turn 26 out to be perfectly normal, safe people. However, quite a few of them can be boring, annoying or just plain unattractive. For this reason, plan for a short first date. Dinner or a few cups of coffee won't take more than an hour or so, so even the worst date will be over soon enough. If all goes well, you can plan for more lengthy dates in the future.

Next, we'll see how online dating sites put 27 people together.

ONLINE DATING: THE SCIENCE OF MATCHMAKING

Once you've filled out a profile, online dating sites 28 will provide a list of matches — people they think you are compatible with. How do they decide who matches up with whom?

29   Sometimes, the process is very simple. Each profile has a list of attributes or interests that members check off. The more matching attributes that two profiles have, the higher "match percentage" the site will assign to it. Some sites, like match.com, allow users to specify how important each attribute is. Each matching attribute is assigned a different weight depending on how important it is to the user. For example, if you prefer blondes, but really have nothing against brunettes and redheads, then you can rank that attribute as very low. If it's very important to you that your date has a college degree, you can rank that very high. Then the site will match you with a highly educated brunette sooner than a blonde who didn't finish high school.

30   Some sites use very complex personality surveys and mathematical algorithms to match partners. Online matchmaking site eHarmony.com uses "29 key dimensions that help predict compatibility and the potential for relationship success." Their system was developed by Dr. Neil Clark Warren, who studied thousands of marriages to develop his "predictive model of compatibility."

31   Do such scientific methods work? Obviously, the dating sites claim they do. However, scientific personality tests completed with the guidance of a trained researcher do not have 100 percent accuracy (it's closer to 75 percent). And when you're sitting alone in your living room filling out a personality profile on a Web site, there is an even greater chance that the resulting matches will not be perfect. When you multiply the chance for inaccuracy by the number of users on a given dating site, complicated matching systems are probably not working much better than basic attribute-and-interest matching.

32   Fortunately, the main advantage of online dating is that it gives each user control over whom they contact and with whom they subsequently communicate. It might take more work than relying on the site's matching system, but browsing through profiles yourself may ultimately be the best way to find the right person.

The last stage in the online dating process: the matchmaking.

Specific facts and figures for online dating are 33 hard to come by. For obvious reasons, each individual site tends to inflate membership numbers and success rates in its promotional materials. There are close to 100 million single adults in the United States alone. Of those, 40 million use online dating services. FriendFinder.com claims over 11 million members. eHarmony.com claims responsibility for more than 9,000 marriages.

On the other hand, there are those who think 34 the online dating industry may have reached its saturation point. According to an article in the *Christian Science Monitor*, consumer spending on these sites declined slightly in the fourth quarter of 2004, indicating that growth for online dating sites may be stagnant.

While some of the numbers may be fuzzy, one 35 thing is certain — the use of online dating services continues in huge numbers. According to *Online Media Daily*, consumer spending on personals and dating sites rose by 8 percent in the first half of 2005, topping $245 million.

For more information on online dating and re- 36 lated topics, check out the links on the next page.

Reading Closely

1. In his essay, Grabianowski breaks the larger process of online dating into smaller processes. What are these supporting processes? Why is it important to discuss them?

2. Identify the *kind* of process analysis Grabianowski uses. Is it directive, informative, or a mixture? How do you know?

3. What kind of research did Grabianowski conduct to write this essay? Identify specific places in the text to support your answer. What sources did he consult? What is the effect of this research?

Considering Larger Issues

1. What do you think of the advice offered in this essay? What do you find valuable? What might readers disregard?

2. **Working with a classmate,** analyze the organizational strategy Grabianowski chooses for this essay. Why do you think he used this organization? How does it fit the purpose of the essay?

3. COMBINING METHODS. Identify places in the essay where the writer uses *exemplification* and *cause-and-effect analysis*. How do these rhetorical methods support the purpose of the essay?

Thinking about Language

1. Use the context of the essay and your dictionary to define any of the following terms you do not know.

trekking (1)	Styx (14)	sufficient (19)
anonymity (5)	tedious (15)	compatible (28)
freeform (9)	generic (15)	attributes (29)
pull–down (9)	Stanley Kubrick (16)	algorithms (30)
Bogart (14)		

Writing Your Own Essays Using Process Analysis

1. What is your experience with the dating process? Do most people use online sites, or does the dating process happen through other means? Respond to these questions by composing a three- to four–page essay that analyzes the dating process you know best. Use exemplification, description, and narration to add detail and depth to your essay. The guidelines on page 422 for checking over the use of process analysis should help you as you draft and revise.

2. People often need to follow a complementary or inverse process in seeking out someone to begin a relationship: the process of breaking up a relationship. In fact, the process of breaking up is often one of the most calculated and thought-out processes daters go through. In a two- to three–page essay, compose a guide for daters on "how to break up," setting out the specific steps the "breaker" should take as she or he ends the relationship with the "breakee." As you identify each step in the process, elaborate on the advice you give by offering helpful tips, imagined or real-life scenarios, and useful recommendations on what to avoid. Use description, exemplification, and narration to deepen your analysis. Refer to "Checking Over the Use of Process Analysis" on page 422 as you draft and revise.

MONSTER.COM
How to Interview

The motto of Monster.com is "find your calling." So it's no surprise that this popular employment Web site not only lists thousands of job openings but also offers interested readers tips on how they might find their calling and get the job they want. Monster.com helps readers achieve their goals through numerous process-related articles, from "How to Buy a Business" and "How to Start a Baby Boutique" to "How to Write a Business Plan" and "How to Write a Mission Statement." The following article gives helpful suggestions for anyone participating in a job search: "How to Interview."

> **Preview**   What do you already know about the interviewing process? How did you gain this information?

Today's job marketplace is hyper-competitive. There can be dozens or 1 even hundreds of people vying for one quality position. If you want to land that dream job, you will need to know some specific tips that will keep you head and shoulders above the rest of the pack. Interviewing for a job is not most people's favorite situation. In effect, an interview is where one is evaluated by an employer. In many cases, in order to land that job, you can't crack under the pressure, you have to be strong and sell yourself. Here are some tips to remember for the next time you interview.

So, you are looking for a job, have sent in your résumé and finally 2 have been called in to interview for the position. The good news is that your chances of landing the job have just gone up; the bad news is that you are not through the woods yet. While being called for an interview reduces the amount of people that you are in competition with, it also raises the stakes as well. Where maybe a hundred people send in a résumé for a job, an interview usually thins the competition to about 3 to 10 applicants. If you really want to land the job, here are some things to keep in mind.

BE PREPARED

Being prepared cannot be emphasized enough. Preparation is essential to 3 doing well on an interview and landing a job. You don't want to come off to your interviewer as if you just stepped in off the street. Preparation can come in many different forms; the most apparent ones are discussed below.

Know about the company — interviewers want to see that you 4 don't just want a job, but want to work for their company.

Be prepared to talk about yourself — make sure you are ready 5 to talk about yourself. This is an interview, so if you don't want to talk about your past, future goals or your skill set, don't bother showing up.

Be prepared to ask smart questions — interviews are not inter- 6
rogations. There should be a back and forth of communication and ideas.
You should not only be answering questions, but asking intelligent questions. Before arriving for the interview, memorize or write down a few
questions that interest you.

FIRST IMPRESSIONS

Once you are called in for an interview, you will need to sell yourself in a 7
short period of time to someone that you have never met before. Human
resource recruiters are quite skilled at arrival and judging others. There are
winning candidates and candidates that are total losers. Your mission is to
come off as a winner. You should show yourself in a good light and present yourself as an excellent candidate. Here are some tips on making a
great first impression.

Show up on time — One of the worst things that you can do is 8
show up late to an interview. A late interviewer tells the recruiter that you
don't take the job seriously, you are not punctual and are unmotivated to
find a new job. If you are running late or are experiencing traffic or an
unforeseen event, call ahead. Nine out of 10 times calling ahead will not
put any negative consequences on your chances of employment.

Dress to impress — One of the most important pieces to the puzzle 9
of making a good first impression is to dress to impress. Dressing well
for an interview means that you are wearing smart business attire and
are well groomed. This shows that you care how you look, have confidence and will be a good representative for the company if you are hired.
During the summer months, many job applicants sometimes dress down.
Dressing down can only hurt your chances of landing a job. Always dress
appropriately. If you have the slightest doubts about an outfit, choose another outfit to wear.

Be confident — It is imperative that you show confidence when you 10
show up for your interview. No one is impressed by someone who is very
meek or extremely shy. You don't have to be obnoxious or act super cool,
but be the best that you can be.

Greet the recruiter properly — Believe it or not, the way you greet 11
the recruiter matters. A nice proper hello with a smile and a decent hand-
shake will do the trick. Never frown, look down or look away when meeting someone. Also, it is good to stand up and show interest. The recruiter
is a person, and it is not only what you say that matters, but also how you
make the other person feel.

DURING THE INTERVIEW

Now that you are done with the meet and greet and have given the re- 12
cruiter a good first impression of yourself, the interview begins. Some

applicants freeze up and get very self-conscious. No one likes being judged, and while the interview process is exactly this, there are ways to avoid the common pitfalls and instead shine during the interview process.

Be prepared— Make sure you have done your homework and are well prepared for the interview. This means that you should have researched the company beforehand, understood its products or services and know a few interesting facts about the company. What you want to convey to the employer is that you are genuinely interested in working for this company. Anyone can find a job, but human resource recruiters want to hire people who genuinely want to work for their firm.   13

Answer questions clearly and completely— Obviously, the interview process involves the job recruiter asking you questions. It is very important that you answer these questions clearly and be thorough with your answers. It is extremely easy to tell when someone is lying, so be honest and forthcoming. Many questions that recruiters ask are obvious questions and are quite common. You can easily prepare beforehand for many of these obvious questions. Some of the most common questions asked by recruiters are: 14

"Your resume says that you were previously a waiter.
Can I assume that you're comfortable taking orders?"

www.CartoonStock.com

- What are your strengths and weaknesses?
- Why do you want to work for this organization?
- Why are you leaving your current or last position?
- What would you like to achieve at your new position if hired?
- Do you work well with others or prefer to work on your own?
- What are your successes and failures?
- What kind of salary range are your looking to be in?
- What are your credentials (education, special training, etc.)
- Do you have any hobbies?

ASK QUESTIONS DURING THE INTERVIEW

Try to think of the interview as a conversation instead of an interroga-   15
tion. Many job applicants receive high marks by the recruiter if they ask
insightful and intelligent questions. You should be very engaging in the
interview. This shows the recruiter that you are genuinely interested in
the position. While questions are good, make sure they are intelligent;
asking questions just for sake of asking is a waste of time for both you
and the recruiter. Some of the questions you might want to ask an interviewer are:

- What are you looking for in an employee?
- What is the reason for the open position (is it due to growth or
  turnover)?
- Could you describe some of the challenges this position offers?
- Could you describe the working environment, work culture, etc.?
- Could you describe some of the benefits of working for your
  company?
- When will the job be available (are you looking to hire someone as soon
  as possible or in the next few months)?

AFTER THE INTERVIEW

Once the interview is complete, it is wise to do a couple of things. You   16
should write the recruiter a thank-you letter and follow up with the recruiter. These days, a job applicant might have to go through 3 interviews
to land a job. It is important to stay on the recruiter's radar as being a
high-quality applicant. Many times, after an interview is over, recruiters
will state that if they are interested they will give you a call; other times
they will try to schedule you for a second interview.

　If a recruiter doesn't give you a definite vote of confidence once the   17
interview is over, it doesn't mean that you didn't do well or you aren't
a good applicant. Many times, there are other things working in the

background. Some departments wait to the last possible moment to fill positions; other times a key executive who gives the green light to hire might be out of the office. If you are not hired, don't consider yourself a failure. There are plenty more jobs out in the marketplace.

Reading Closely

1. How does the article walk readers through the interview process? What steps does it provide?
2. What kind of process analysis is this, directive or informative? How do you know?
3. What is the method of organization for the essay? Is this organizational choice effective? Why or why not?
4. Review the cartoon on page 434. Given the advice offered in this essay, how should the interviewee answer the question posed by the interviewer?

Considering Larger Issues

1. What did you learn from this essay? How might it help you in your future interviews?
2. **Working with a classmate,** extend four pieces of advice the writer offers in this essay. For example, you might elaborate on what it means to "know about the company," thinking about the kinds of research job seekers should conduct. Or you might be more specific about what it means to "dress for success."
3. COMBINING METHODS. How does the writer use *exemplification* and *classification and division* in this essay? How do these methods help the writer achieve his or her purpose?

Thinking about Language

1. What point of view does the writer establish in this essay? How does he or she achieve this point of view through specific language choices?
2. The writer uses imperative verbs (*be prepared, answer questions clearly and completely*) throughout the essay to give advice to readers. What effect does this choice have on the purpose of the essay?

Writing Your Own Essays Using Process Analysis

1. Reflect on a time when you've interviewed for something you were trying to get. Your interview may have been for a particular job or internship or even a volunteer position, award, or scholarship. How did you pre-

pare for this interview? Compose a two- to three-page essay that analyzes your interview preparation process, thinking specifically about your individual actions. For instance, you may have eaten a special breakfast to get ready, or you may have brought along a "good luck" charm. Include all of this specific information to add interest to your essay. Refer to "Checking Over the Use of Process Analysis" on page 422 as you draft and revise.

2. Identify a person in the profession you would like to enter. Interview that person, asking about the process he or she went through to reach this position, focusing on the specific steps that led to getting the job. Draft and revise a three- to four-page process analysis essay that describes this person's employment process. Supplement your analysis with detailed description and narration. Use the guidelines on page 422 to check over your use of process analysis.

RACHEL DILLON
Mission Possible

● When Rachel Dillon (b. 1980) wrote this essay, she was an undergraduate secondary education major at Penn State University, specializing in English and communication. She is now teaching high school English in Pittsburgh. If you've ever faced a research paper assignment, then you know the worry that Dillon felt throughout the process.

> **Preview**   If you've ever been assigned a research project, what was your first reaction? your second reaction? What steps did you go through to meet your deadline?

"Your mission, whether you choose to accept it or not, is to write a re-   1
search paper." To most college students, this mission seems impossible; it's a specialized kind of skill that they've never developed. Who knows how to write a research paper? And even if they know how to write one, who'd want to? The research paper assignment brings fear and loathing to nearly every student, everywhere. No wonder so many students resist learning the process of research writing, and with the ever-growing supply of research papers on the Internet, seek out quick solutions for their problem:

> ***Research Papers for Sale!*** Visit here to download research papers for sale! **Writing Assistance!** The only service through which your writing project is personally directed by a former college instructor, Harvard graduate & Ph.D.: "Quality is our top priority!" Confidential. Since 1975.

> ***Need Help with Your Research Project?*** An extensive database of research projects on all subjects at the click of your mouse. Low-priced and top-quality.

No matter how enticing these advertisements seem to be, they are clever booby traps that will lead you away from the mission at hand, and ultimately to plagiarism and failure. In order to successfully accomplish this mission, then, all special agents must develop the research and writing skills necessary for the assignment. (After all, research writing is a crucial stage in their college-level intellectual development.) So if you are willing to attempt this mission, be prepared to follow a detailed process as you defy the odds and accomplish the mission of writing a research paper. The impossible mission becomes possible when you follow my process from beginning to end.

I was assigned my mission on the first day of my class "Women's   2
Rhetorics and Feminist Pedagogies." It was right there, on the syllabus, which said that 25% of my final grade would be based on a research proj-

ect. That didn't seem so bad except that the syllabus also said that I'd have to develop my project over the course of the semester; I'd have to submit various parts of my research early on. And the professor kept emphasizing that each of us had to find a way to "own" our topics. Until then, I had never made any connection between doing research and owning the topic. Among the various pages of the syllabus, I found long explanations of those early research–related assignments: research topic lists, annotated bibliographies, a research project overview, all due before the final project due date. With the task of finding and researching a topic and the additional burden of making it "my own," the research paper assignment was a mission that overwhelmed and frightened me. I knew that if I was to carry out this mission, I'd have to prepare, so I followed a process and prevailed.

The first step in overcoming my anxiety was choosing a topic that 3 fulfilled the requirements for the project and also interested me. If I was to make this project mine, I had to really care about what I was writing about. So I began reading and researching women speakers and writers, especially those who were practicing feminism. Suddenly, I remembered Kathy Acker, whose work I'd come across when I was preparing a unit plan on Nathaniel Hawthorne's *Scarlet Letter* for the high school English class I was student–teaching. Author of such works as *Blood & Guts in High School* and *Don Quixote*, Acker wrote feminist responses to canonical male writers, to Nathaniel Hawthorne, in particular. Her writings were edgy and sexy, the kind of contemporary writing that I thought my high school students would enjoy and could use for access into Hawthorne's more old–fashioned writing and plot. The second step I took in my research project was reading additional works by Acker and as much scholarship on her writings as I could manage. Just as soon as I became familiar with her and her work, I began to list possible topics, angles I could take on her for my research paper. I was feeling confident.

The next step, though, was probably the most difficult for me, and 4 it might be for you, too: narrowing down the subject. I knew I couldn't read and write about every work ever written by Acker; likewise, it would be impossible for me to find every piece of commentary on her. In order to clearly define what the topic and thesis statement of my paper might be, I had to consider the goal of this project, which my teacher had provided in the syllabus: the paper must focus on a course–related issue. I looked back at the required readings for the course and thought about how Kathy Acker might best fit into "Women's Rhetorics and Feminist Pedagogies." I decided to focus on the specific ways Acker successfully resisted "classic" texts, in particular *The Scarlet Letter*, which I knew I would be expected to teach at the high school level very soon. Just as soon as I was able to narrow down my topic in a way that met the teacher's objectives, I was also able to narrow down my research and work. I began reading and researching only those of Acker's writings that spoke directly to *The Scarlet*

Letter. I took notes and organized them according to their chronological relevance to the novel. Then I began developing supporting ideas. After I was sure to have at least ten bibliographic sources and a thesis statement with enough information to support it, I sat down to write my first draft.

Many special agents fumble the mission at this point because they do not understand the steps that drafting entails. Once the actual writing is under way it is crucial to get peer feedback at an early stage. After I had a solid start on my draft, I met with other students in my English class, and we began to read each other's papers and discuss the direction our research projects were taking. We gave and received feedback, and then we each returned to our computers — that's where I began to revise my earlier draft according to the good advice I'd received. (It was hard for me to learn how to use my peers, but once we got into the habit of helping each other, we stayed together all term.) The success of the revision step (or steps) will vary based on the quality of the feedback received. If the feedback is of high quality, the writer may have more work to do than if the feedback is weak. One writer might discover that she has far too much material and too broad a focus, while another may learn that he needs to supply even more supporting material, which means more reading and research on the topic. In any case, it will probably be necessary to reorganize the paper if the peer feedback is any good. To continue the revising process, I had to work alone for a while to be sure that the paper was organized in the most effective way (in my case, chronologically), with an introduction, thesis (controlling idea), and the supporting points following, ending with the conclusion. 5

After completing the second draft of my paper, I continued my revisions by discussing the draft with both the professor and teaching assistant (the graduate student also assigned to the course). Both offered feedback and tips — different in their focus and advice — that would help ensure the success of the mission. It was back to the computer for me, time to revise for a third draft. After I felt satisfied with this draft, I met again with the members of my peer group for some final feedback. This session was beneficial to me, as they found errors in spelling, punctuation, and sentence structure that I had missed. I'd been too focused on the substance of my research to think about the surface of my paper. After receiving their feedback, I headed back to my computer for the last time, to fix any typos or grammatical errors. And reading my paper one final time, I realized, with satisfaction, that the impossible was now possible. By following through the process of preparing, drafting, and revising, I was able to write an A research paper. Mission accomplished! 6

Reading Closely

1. What details does Dillon include that reveal information about her as a student, a future teacher, and/or a reader?

2. What are the steps of the process that Dillon is analyzing? Write them out.

Considering Larger Issues

1. What is Dillon's purpose for writing this essay? What textual evidence can you provide to support your answer?
2. Who is Dillon's audience? What specific information in the essay helps you determine her audience?
3. What is Dillon's thesis statement?
4. COMBINING METHODS. Dillon *analyzes cause and effect* in parts of her essay. Mark the passages in which she uses this method, and then, **working with two or three classmates,** discuss why she does so. What overall effect does the cause–and–effect analysis have? Prepare to share your responses with the rest of the class.

Thinking about Language

1. Use the context of the essay or your dictionary to define the following terms. Be prepared to share your answers with the rest of the class.

loathing (1)	pedagogies (2)	edgy (3)
rhetorics (2)	annotated (2)	commentary (4)
feminist (2)	canonical (3)	peer feedback (5)

2. List the technical terms or phrases relating to a research assignment that Dillon includes.

Writing Your Own Essays Using Process Analysis

1. What school–related process have you carried out successfully? It could be a school only process or one related to successful balancing of responsibilities at school and at home. What are the steps of this process? Which steps are unique to your experience and abilities, and which ones are replicable by others? Draft a three– to four–page essay in which you write about the successful use of the process. Make sure all the steps and details you include help develop your thesis statement about this process. If a visual would enhance your essay, include one. Refer to "Checking Over the Use of Process Analysis" (p. 422).
2. Look back at the chapter–opening example, Lydia's instructions to Gabe for reheating pizza (p. 404). Writing from Gabe's point of view, draft a two–page essay in which you explain to your older sister how to do some household or everyday activity, one that a ninth–grade boy would know how to do. Refer to "Checking Over the Use of Process Analysis" (p. 422).

ANNE LAMOTT
Shitty First Drafts

San Francisco native Anne Lamott (b. 1954) is a fiction and nonfiction writer who tackles topics such as religion, alcoholism, and single motherhood. In addition to contributing articles to numerous magazines, Lamott has also published *All New People* (1999), *Traveling Mercies: Some Thoughts on Faith* (2000), *Operating Instructions: A Journal of My Son's First Year* (2005), and *Grace (Eventually)* (2008). In the following essay, taken from *Bird by Bird: Instructions on Writing and Life* (1995), Lamott explains the process of how she gets from the first draft of writing to the final draft.

Preview   What is your writing process? How would you explain the steps you take to move from first to final draft?

Now, practically even better news than that of short assignments is the idea of shitty first drafts. All good writers write them. This is how they end up with good second drafts and terrific third drafts. People tend to look at successful writers who are getting their books published and maybe even doing well financially and think that they sit down at their desks every morning feeling like a million dollars, feeling great about who they are and how much talent they have and what a great story they have to tell; that they take in a few deep breaths, push back their sleeves, roll their necks a few times to get all the cricks out, and dive in, typing fully formed passages as fast as a court reporter. But this is just the fantasy of the uninitiated. I know some very great writers, writers you love who write beautifully and have made a great deal of money, and not one of them sits down routinely feeling wildly enthusiastic and confident. Not one of them writes elegant first drafts. All right, one of them does, but we do not like her very much. We do not think that she has a rich inner life or that God likes her or can even stand her. (Although when I mentioned this to my priest friend Tom, he said you can safely assume you've created God in your own image when it turns out that God hates all the same people you do.)

Very few writers really know what they are doing until they've done it. Nor do they go about their business feeling dewy and thrilled. They do not type a few stiff warm-up sentences and then find themselves bounding along like huskies across the snow. One writer I know tells me that he sits down every morning and says to himself nicely, "It's not like you don't have a choice, because you do — you can either type, or kill yourself." We all often feel like we are pulling teeth, even those writers whose prose ends up being the most natural and fluid. The right words and sentences just do not come pouring out like ticker tape most of the time. Now, Muriel Spark is said to have felt that she was taking dictation from God every morning— sitting there, one supposes, plugged into a Dictaphone, typing away, humming. But this is a very hostile and aggressive position. One might hope for bad things to rain down on a person like this.

For me and most of the other writers I know, writing is not rapturous. In fact, the only way I can get anything written at all is to write really, really shitty first drafts.

The first draft is the child's draft, where you let it all pour out and then let it romp all over the place, knowing that no one is going to see it and that you can shape it later. You just let this childlike part of you channel whatever voices and visions come through and onto the page. If one of the characters wants to say, "Well, so what, Mr. Poopy Pants?" you let her. No one is going to see it. If the kid wants to get into really sentimental, weepy, emotional territory, you let him. Just get it all down on paper because there may be something great in those six crazy pages that you would never have gotten to by more rational, grown-up means. There may be something in the very last line of the very last paragraph on page six that you just love, that is so beautiful or wild that you now know what you're supposed to be writing about, more or less, or in what direction you might go— but there was no way to get to this without first getting through the first five and a half pages.

I used to write food reviews for *California* magazine before it folded. (My writing food reviews had nothing to do with the magazine folding, although every single review did cause a couple of canceled subscriptions. Some readers took umbrage at my comparing mounds of vegetable puree with various ex-presidents' brains.) These reviews always took two days to write. First I'd go to a restaurant several times with a few opinionated, articulate friends in tow. I'd sit there writing down everything anyone said that was at all interesting or funny. Then on the following Monday I'd sit down at my desk with my notes and try to write the review. Even after I'd been doing this for years, panic would set in. I'd try to write a lead, but instead I'd write a couple of dreadful sentences, XX them out, try again, XX everything out, and then feel despair and worry settle on my chest like an x-ray apron. It's over, I'd think calmly. I'm not going to be able to get the magic to work this time. I'm ruined. I'm through. I'm toast. Maybe, I'd think, I can get my old job back as a clerk-typist. But probably not. I'd get up and study my teeth in the mirror for a while. Then I'd stop, remember to breathe, make a few phone calls, hit the kitchen and chow down. Eventually I'd go back and sit down at my desk, and sigh for the next ten minutes. Finally I would pick up my one-inch picture frame, stare into it as if for the answer, and every time the answer would come: all I had to do was to write a really shitty first draft of, say, the opening paragraph. And no one was going to see it.

WRITER'S BLOCK

www.CartoonStock.com

So I'd start writing without reining myself in. It was almost just typing, 6 just making my fingers move. And the writing would be terrible. I'd write a lead paragraph that was a whole page, even though the entire review could only be three pages long, and then I'd start writing up descriptions of the food, one dish at a time, bird by bird, and the critics would be sitting on my shoulders, commenting like cartoon characters. They'd be pretending to snore, or rolling their eyes at my overwrought descriptions, no matter how hard I tried to tone those descriptions down, no matter how conscious I was of what a friend said to me gently in my early days of restaurant reviewing. "Annie," she said, "it is just a piece of *chicken*. It is just a bit of *cake*."

But because by then I had been writing for so long, I would eventually 7 let myself trust the process — sort of, more or less. I'd write a first draft that was maybe twice as long as it should be, with a self-indulgent and boring beginning, stupefying descriptions of the meal, lots of quotes from my black-humored friends that made them sound more like the Manson girls than food lovers, and no ending to speak of. The whole thing would be so long and incoherent and hideous that for the rest of the day I'd obsess about getting creamed by a car before I could write a decent second draft. I'd worry that people would read what I'd written and believe that the accident had really been a suicide, that I had panicked because my talent was waning and my mind was shot.

The next day, I'd sit down, go through it all with a colored pen, take 8 out everything I possibly could, find a new lead somewhere on the second page, figure out a kicky place to end it, and then write a second draft. It always turned out fine, sometimes even funny and weird and helpful. I'd go over it one more time and mail it in.

Then, a month later, when it was time for another review, the 9 whole process would start again, complete with the fears that people would find my first draft before I could rewrite it.

Almost all good writing begins with terrible first efforts. You need 10 to start somewhere. Start by getting something—anything—down on paper. A friend of mine says that the first draft is the down draft—you just get it down. The second draft is the up draft—you fix it up. You try to say what you have to say more accurately. And the third draft is the dental draft, where you check every tooth, to see if it's loose or cramped or decayed, or even, God help us, healthy.

Reading Closely

1. Would you characterize Lamott's process analysis as informative or directive? Why?

2. What is the purpose of Lamott's essay? How do you know? What cues in the text help you draw this conclusion?

3. In addition to her own writing process, Lamott also writes about other writers' writing processes. What are these processes? How are they different from Lamott's?

4. Lamott claims that writer's block is a common problem. How does the cartoon on page 444 add depth to this claim?

Considering Larger Issues

1. Do you find it helpful to read about Lamott's writing process? Why or why not? What, if anything, did you learn about writing by reading Lamott's essay?

2. PAIRED ESSAYS. Compare Lamott's essay with Rachel Dillon's "Mission Possible." How are these processes different? How are they similar?

3. Reflect on your own writing style, thinking about how you move through your drafting process. **Working with a classmate,** compare your drafting processes. How are they the same? How are they different?

4. COMBINING METHODS. Identify the places in the text where Lamott uses *exemplification, description,* and *narration.* How do these rhetorical methods enable Lamott to achieve her purpose?

Thinking about Language

1. Use the context of the reading or your dictionary to define the following terms. Be prepared to share your answers with the rest of the class.

dewy (2)	Dictaphone (2)	overwrought (6)
ticker tape (2)	rapturous (3)	stupefying (7)
dictation (2)	umbrage (5)	incoherent (7)

2. Identify the metaphors Lamott uses in this essay. What effect do they have on her writing style?

Writing Your Own Essays Using Process Analysis

1. Drawing on your responses to the Preview prompt and question 3 under Considering Larger Issues, draft a two- to three-page essay that explains your writing process. Like Lamott, use description, narration, and exemplification to add depth and detail to your process analysis. As you draft and revise, refer to the guidelines for checking over the use of process analysis on page 422.

2. Students often weigh the benefits and drawbacks of writing a paper for a course or taking a test. In a three- to four-page essay, first explain the process you use to compose an essay for a course, and then explain the process you use to study for an exam. Once you've analyzed these processes, compare them, thinking about which process you find more challenging, rewarding, or enjoyable. Refer to the guidelines for checking over the use of process analysis on page 422 as you draft and revise.

3. PUBLIC WRITING. Helping people through various writing tasks is something writers do all the time. Go to any bookstore, and you'll find guides on how to compose job-related documents like a résumé or press release; more personal writing like condolence or thank-you letters; and, of course, school-related documents like essays for college admission. Compose a guide for high school students on how to write an essay for college admission. You'll want to open your guide with general advice on the essay-writing process as well as the specific demands of college admission essays. Then you'll want to walk your readers through particular elements of the drafting, revising, and editing processes. To elaborate on each step in the process, draw from your own or others' experiences. In addition, you'll also want to include advice regarding the dos and don'ts of the process. Your guide should be six to eight pages long. Refer to "Checking Over the Use of Process Analysis" on page 422 as you draft and revise your guide.

JESSICA MITFORD

The Embalming of Mr. Jones

Jessica Mitford (1917–1996) was born into a wealthy, aristocratic English family. Her early life was one of leisure and gentility, but she eventually rebelled against the atmosphere of sheltered ignorance in which she was brought up. She went to Spain to support the anti-Fascists during the country's civil war in the 1930s and later immigrated to the United States, where she continued her activism in left-wing politics and also took up investigative journalism.

Mitford had a productive life as a writer. Besides newspaper articles, she wrote fiction, autobiography, and other nonfiction that explored topics ranging from her own upbringing to the U.S. funeral, obstetrics, and prison systems; her books include *Daughters and Rebels* (1960), *The American Way of Death* (1963), *Kind and Unusual Punishment* (1973), *A Fine Old Conflict* (1976), and *The American Way of Birth* (1992). The following excerpt is from *The American Way of Death*.

Preview   What is your experience with "the American way of death"?

Embalming is indeed a most extraordinary procedure, and one must 1 wonder at the docility of Americans who each year pay hundreds of millions of dollars for its perpetuation, blissfully ignorant of what it is all about, what is done, how it is done. Not one in ten thousand has any idea of what actually takes place. Books on the subject are extremely hard to come by. They are not to be found in most libraries or bookshops.

In an era when huge television audiences watch surgical operations 2 in the comfort of their living rooms, when, thanks to the animated cartoon, the geography of the digestive system has become familiar territory even to the nursery school set, in a land where the satisfaction of curiosity about almost all matters is a national pastime, the secrecy surrounding embalming can, surely, hardly be attributed to the inherent gruesomeness of the subject. Custom in this regard has within this century suffered a complete reversal. In the early days of American embalming, when it was performed in the home of the deceased, it was almost mandatory for some relative to stay by the embalmer's side and witness the procedure. Today, family members who might wish to be in attendance would certainly be dissuaded by the funeral director. All others, except apprentices, are excluded by law from the preparation room.

A close look at what does actually take place may explain in large 3 measure the undertaker's intractable reticence concerning a procedure that has become his major *raison d'être.** Is it possible he fears that public information about embalming might lead patrons to wonder if they really want this service? If the funeral men are loath to discuss the subject

---

* **raison d'être:** reason for being, reason to exist

outside the trade, the reader may, understandably, be equally loath to go on reading at this point. For those who have the stomach for it, let us part the formaldehyde curtain. . . .

The body is first laid out in the undertaker's morgue—or rather, 4 Mr. Jones is reposing in the preparation room—to be readied to bid the world farewell.

The preparation room in any of the better funeral establishments has 5 the tiled and sterile look of a surgery, and indeed the embalmer–restorative artist who does his chores there is beginning to adopt the term "derma-surgeon" (appropriately corrupted by some mortician-writers as "demi-surgeon") to describe his calling. His equipment, consisting of scalpels, scissors, augers, forceps, clamps, needles, pumps, tubes, bowls, and basin, is crudely imitative of the surgeon's, as is his technique, acquired in a nine- or twelve-month post–high-school course in an embalming school. He is supplied by an advanced chemical industry with a bewildering array of fluids, sprays, pastes, oils, powders, creams, to fix or soften tissue, shrink or distend it as needed, dry it here, restore the moisture there. There are cosmetics, waxes, and paints to fill and cover features, even plaster of Paris to replace entire limbs. There are ingenious aids to prop and stabilize the cadaver: a Vari-Pose Head Rest, the Edwards Arm and Hand Positioner, the Repose Block (to support the shoulders during the embalming), and the Throop Foot Positioner, which resembles an old-fashioned stocks.

Mr. John H. Eckels, president of the Eckels College of Mortuary Sci-6 ence, thus describes the first part of the embalming procedure: "In the hands of a skilled practitioner, this work may be done in a comparatively short time and without mutilating the body other than by slight incision—so slight that it scarcely would cause serious inconvenience if made upon a living person. It is necessary to remove all the blood, and doing this not only helps in the disinfecting, but removes the principal cause of disfigurements due to discoloration."

Another textbook discusses the all-important time element: "The ear-7 lier this is done, the better, for every hour that elapses between death and embalming will add to the problems and complications encountered. . . ." Just how soon should one get going on the embalming? The author tells us, "On the basis of such scanty information made available to this profession through its rudimentary and haphazard system of technical research, we must conclude that the best results are to be obtained if the subject is embalmed before life is completely extinct—that is, before cellular death has occurred. In the average case, this would mean within an hour after somatic death." For those who feel that there is something a little rudimentary, not to say haphazard, about this advice, a comforting thought is offered by another writer. Speaking of fears entertained in early days of premature burial, he points out, "One of the effects of embalming by chemical injection, however, has been to dispel fears of live

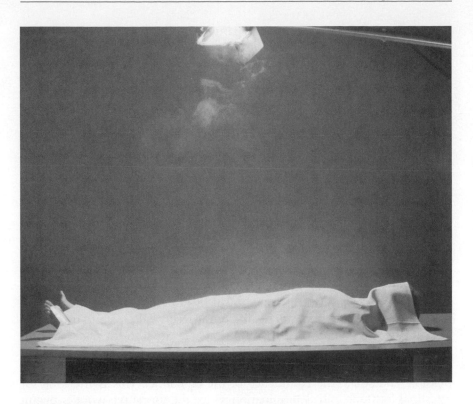

burial." How true; once the blood is removed, chances of live burial are indeed remote.

To return to Mr. Jones, the blood is drained out through the veins   8 and replaced by embalming fluid pumped in through the arteries. As noted in *The Principles and Practices of Embalming*, "Every operator has a favorite injection and drainage point — a fact which becomes a handicap only if he fails or refuses to forsake his favorites when conditions demand it." Typical favorites are the carotid artery, femoral artery, jugular vein, sub-clavian vein. There are various choices of embalming fluid. If Flextone is used, it will produce a "mild, flexible rigidity. The skin retains a vel-vety softness, the tissues are rubbery and pliable. Ideal for women and children." It may be blended with B. and G. Products Company's Lyf-Lyk tint, which is guaranteed to reproduce "nature's own skin texture . . . the velvety appearance of living tissue." Suntone comes in three separate tints: Suntan; Special Cosmetic Tint, a pink shade "especially indicated for young female subjects"; and Regular Cosmetic Tint, moderately pink.

About three to six gallons of a dyed and perfumed solution of form-   9 aldehyde, glycerin, borax, phenol, alcohol, and water is soon circu-lating through Mr. Jones, whose mouth has been sewn together with a "needle directed upward between the upper lip and gum and brought out through the left nostril," with the corners raised slightly "for a more pleasant expression." If he should be buck–toothed, his teeth are cleaned with Bon Ami and coated with colorless nail polish. His eyes, meanwhile, are closed with flesh–tinted eye caps and eye cement.

The next step is to have at Mr. Jones with a thing called a trocar. This   10 is a long, hollow needle attached to a tube. It is jabbed into the abdomen, poked around the entrails and chest cavity, the contents of which are pumped out and replaced with "cavity fluid." This done, and the hole in the abdomen sewed up, Mr. Jones's face is heavily creamed (to protect the skin from burns which may be caused by leakage of the chemicals), and he is covered with a sheet and left unmolested for a while. But not for long—there is more, much more, in store for him. He has been embalmed, but not yet restored, and the best time to start restorative work is eight to ten hours after embalming, when the tissues have become firm and dry.

The object of all this attention to the corpse, it must be remembered,   11 is to make it presentable for viewing in an attitude of healthy repose. "Our customs require the presentation of our dead in the semblance of normal- ity . . . unmarred by the ravages of illness, disease or mutilation," says Mr. J. Sheridan Mayer in his *Restorative Art*. This is rather a large order since few people die in the full bloom of health, unravaged by illness and unmarked by some disfigurement. The funeral industry is equal to the challenge: "In some cases the gruesome appearance of a mutilated or disease–ridden subject may be quite discouraging. The task of restoration may seem im- possible and shake the confidence of the embalmer. This is the time for intestinal fortitude and determination. Once the formative work is begun and affected tissues are cleaned or removed, all doubts of success vanish. It is surprising and gratifying to discover the results which may be obtained."

The embalmer, having allowed an appropriate interval to elapse, re-   12 turns to the attack, but now he brings into play the skill and equipment of sculptor and cosmetician. Is a hand missing? Casting one in plaster of Paris is a simple matter. "For replacement purposes, only a cast of the back of the hand is necessary; this is within the ability of the average operator and is quite adequate." If a lip or two, a nose or an ear should be missing, the embalmer has at hand a variety of restorative waxes with which to model replacements. Pores and skin texture are simulated by stippling with a little brush, and over this cosmetics are laid on. Head off? Decapitation cases are rather routinely handled. Ragged edges are trimmed, and head joined to torso with a series of splints, wires, and sutures. It is a good idea to have a little something at the neck—a scarf or high collar—when time for viewing comes. Swollen mouth? Cut out tissue as needed from inside the lips. If too much is removed, the surface contour can easily be restored by padding with cotton. Swollen necks and cheeks are reduced by removing tissue through vertical incisions made down each side of the neck. "When the deceased is casketed, the pillow will hide the suture incisions . . . as an extra precaution against leakage, the suture may be painted with liquid sealer."

The opposite condition is more likely to be present itself—that of 13 emaciation. His hypodermic syringe now loaded with massage cream, the embalmer seeks out and fills the hollowed and sunken areas by injection. In this procedure the backs of the hands and fingers and the underchin area should not be neglected.

Positioning the lips is a problem that recurrently challenges the inge- 14 nuity of the embalmer. Closed too tightly, they tend to give a stern, even disapproving expression. Ideally, embalmers feel, the lips should give the impression of being ever so slightly parted, the upper lip protruding slightly for a more youthful appearance. This takes some engineering, however, as the lips tend to drift apart. Lip drift can sometimes be remedied by pushing one or two straight pins through the inner margin of the lower lip and then inserting them between the two front upper teeth. If Mr. Jones happens to have no teeth, the pins can just as easily be anchored in his Armstrong Face Former and Denture Replacer. Another method to maintain lip closure is to dislocate the lower jaw, which is then held in its new position by a wire run through holes which have been drilled through the upper jaws at the midline. As the French are fond of saying, *il faut souffrir pour être belle.**

If Mr. Jones has died of jaundice, the embalming fluid will very likely 15 turn him green. Does this deter the embalmer? Not if he has intestinal fortitude. Masking pastes and cosmetics are heavily laid on, burial garments and casket interiors are color-correlated with particular care, and Jones is displayed beneath rose-colored lights. Friends will say, "How *well* he looks." Death by carbon monoxide, on the other hand, can be rather a good thing from an embalmer's viewpoint: "One advantage is the fact that this type of discoloration is an exaggerated form of a natural pink coloration." This is nice because the healthy glow is already present and needs but little attention.

The patching and filling completed, Mr. Jones is now shaved, washed, 16 and dressed. Cream-based cosmetic, available in pink, flesh, suntan, brunette, and blonde, is applied to his hands and face, his hair is shampooed and combed (and, in the case of Mrs. Jones, set), his hands manicured. For the horny-handed son of toil special care must be taken; cream should be applied to remove ingrained grime, and the nails cleaned. "If he were not in the habit of having them manicured in life, trimming and shaping is advised for better appearance—never questioned by kin."

Jones is now ready for casketing (this is the present participle of the 17 verb "to casket"). In this operation his right shoulder should be depressed slightly "to turn the body a bit to the right and soften the appearance of lying flat on the back." Positioning the hands is a matter of importance, and special rubber positioning blocks may be used. The hands should be cupped slightly for a more lifelike, relaxed appearance. Proper placement of the body requires a delicate sense of balance. It should lie as high as

---

* *il faut souffrir pour être belle:* it is necessary to suffer in order to be beautiful

possible in the casket, yet not so high that the lid, when lowered, will hit the nose. On the other hand, we are cautioned, placing the body too low "creates the impression that the body is in a box."

Jones is next wheeled into the appointed slumber room where a few   18
last touches may be added—his favorite pipe placed in his hand or, if he was a great reader, a book propped into position. (In the case of little Master Jones a Teddy bear may be clutched.) Here he will hold open house for a few days, visiting hours 10 A.M. to 9 P.M.

Reading Closely

1. What is your immediate response to Mitford's essay? Be prepared to share your response with rest of the class.
2. What did you learn about embalming that you didn't know before you read this process analysis?
3. What are the individual steps in the process that Mitford is analyzing? Is her analysis directional, informational, or both? **Work with three or four classmates** to come up with an answer and the reasons for it.
4. What stage in the embalming process does the visual depict?

Considering Larger Issues

1. Who is the audience for Mitford's essay? How does audience affect the kind of process analysis this is, and vice versa?
2. What details does Mitford use to help fulfill her purpose in writing? What exactly is her purpose?
3. What specific information does Mitford include or not include to create an informational process analysis? a directional process analysis? What kinds of information are necessary for each kind of process analysis?
4. COMBINING METHODS. In which passages does Mitford use *description? narration?* Mark those passages, and account for their importance to the overall essay.

Thinking about Language

1. Define the following words using the context of the essay or your dictionary. Be prepared to share your answers with the rest of the class.

docility (1)	loath (3)	rudimentary (7)
perpetuation (1)	formaldehyde (3)	somatic (7)
inherent (2)	reposing (4)	trocar (10)
mandatory (2)	augers (5)	intestinal fortitude (11)
apprentices (2)	distend (5)	sutures (12)
intractable (3)	mutilating (6)	jaundice (15)
reticence (3)		

2. Reread the first two paragraphs. What effect did they have on you when you first read them? What is their overall effect on the essay? What do they reveal about the author's style (her distinctive tone and use of language)?

Writing Your Own Essays Using Process Analysis

1. If you have ever grieved for someone who died, or if you attended the funeral or memorial service, what steps did you go through — from learning about the death to recovering from your grief? Draft a three- to four-page directional and informative analysis of this process, using your classmates as your audience. Be sure to focus on one part of this process — breaking it down into steps or groups of steps — that your audience could replicate. Refer to "Checking Over the Use of Process Analysis" on page 422.

2. Mitford's tone in this essay is ironic: Americans are "blissfully ignorant" of what goes on behind "the formaldehyde curtain." Using Mitford's essay and her tone as a model, draft a three- to four-page process analysis of something with which you're familiar but of which others are blissfully ignorant. Try to have some fun as you draft your essay, providing details that might surprise your readers and perhaps an amusing visual or two. **Consider working with one or two classmates** to make sure that you include enough detail to fulfill your purpose. Your process analysis should be informational. Refer to "Checking Over the Use of Process Analysis" (p. 422).

BERNICE WUETHRICH

Getting Stupid

● Before joining the staff of Burness Communications in 2000, Bernice Wuethrich
was an exhibition writer and editor for the Smithsonian Institution's National
Museum of Natural History as well as a freelance science writer. Her essays
have appeared in *New Scientist, Science, Science News, and Smithsonian Magazine;* she has
also coauthored the book *Dying to Drink: Confronting Binge Drinking on College Campuses* (2000). The following article appeared in the March 2001 issue of *Discover.*

Preview   What kind of topic might "Getting Stupid" be about?

The most recent statistics from the U.S. Substance Abuse and Mental   1
Health Services Administration's National Household Survey on Drug
Abuse indicate that nearly 7 million youths between the ages of 12 and
20 binge-drink at least once a month. And despite the fact that many
colleges have cracked down on drinking, Henry Wechsler of the Harvard School of Public Health says that two of every five college students
still binge-drink regularly. For a male that means downing five or more
drinks in a row; for a female it means consuming four drinks in one session at least once in a two-week period.

Few teens seem to worry much about what such drinking does to   2
their bodies. Cirrhosis of the liver is unlikely to catch up with them for
decades, and heart disease must seem as remote as retirement. But new
research suggests that young drinkers are courting danger. Because their
brains are still developing well into their twenties, teens who drink excessively may be destroying significant amounts of mental capacity in
ways that are more dramatic than in older drinkers.

Scientists have long known that excessive alcohol consumption   3
among adults over long periods of time can create brain damage, ranging from a mild loss of motor skills to psychosis and even the inability
to form memories. But less has been known about the impact alcohol
has on younger brains. Until recently, scientists assumed that a youthful
brain is more resilient than an adult brain and could escape many of the
worst ills of alcohol. But some researchers are now beginning to question
this assumption. Preliminary results from several studies indicate that the
younger the brain is, the more it may be at risk. "The adolescent brain is
a developing nervous system, and the things you do to it can change it,"
says Scott Swartzwelder, a neuropsychologist at Duke University and the
U.S. Department of Veterans Affairs.

Teen drinkers appear to be most susceptible to damage in the hip-   4
pocampus, a structure buried deep in the brain that is responsible for
many types of learning and memory, and the prefrontal cortex, located
behind the forehead, which is the brain's chief decision maker and voice

of reason. Both areas, especially the prefrontal cortex, undergo dramatic change in the second decade of life.

Swartzwelder and his team have been studying how alcohol affects the [5] hippocampus, an evolutionary old part of the brain that is similar in rats and humans. Six years ago, when Swartzwelder published his first paper suggesting that alcohol disrupts the hippocampus more severely in adolescent rats than in adult rats, "people didn't believe it," he says. Since then, his research has shown that the adolescent brain is more easily damaged in the structures that regulate the acquisition and storage of memories.

Learning depends on communication between nerve cells, or neu- [6] rons, within the hippocampus. To communicate, a neuron fires an electrical signal down its axon, a single fiber extending away from the cell's center. In response, the axon releases chemical messengers, called neurotransmitters, which bind to receptors on the receiving branches of neighboring cells. Depending on the types of neurotransmitters released, the receiving cell may be jolted into action or settle more deeply into rest.

But the formation of memories requires more than the simple fir- [7] ing or inhibition of nerve cells. There must be some physical change in the hippocampus neurons that represents the encoding of new information. Scientists believe that this change occurs in the synapses, the tiny gaps between neurons that neurotransmitters traverse. Repeated use of synapses seems to increase their ability to fire up connecting cells. Laboratory experiments on brain tissue can induce this process, called long-term potentiation. Researchers assume that something similar takes place in the intact living brain, although it is impossible to observe directly. Essentially, if the repetitive neural reverberations are strong enough, they burn in new patterns of synaptic circuitry to encode memory, just as the more often a child recites his ABCs, the better he knows them.

Swartzwelder's first clue that alcohol powerfully disrupts memory in [8] the adolescent brain came from studying rat hippocampi. He found that alcohol blocks long-term potentiation in adolescent brain tissue much more than in adult tissue. Next, Swartzwelder identified a likely explanation. Long-term potentiation — and thus memory formation — relies in large part on the action of a neurotransmitter known as glutamate, the brain's chemical kingpin of neural excitation. Glutamate strengthens a cell's electrical stimulation when it binds to a docking port called the NMDA receptor. If the receptor is blocked, so is long-term potentiation, and thus memory formation. Swartzwelder found that exposure to the equivalent of just two beers inhibits the NMDA receptors in the hippocampal cells of adolescent rats, while more than twice as much is required to produce the same effect in adult rats. These findings led him to suspect that alcohol consumption might have a dramatic impact on the ability of adolescents to learn. So he set up a series of behavioral tests.

First, Swartzwelder's team dosed adolescent and adult rats with alco- [9] hol and ran them through maze-learning tests. Compared with the adult rats, the adolescents failed miserably. To see whether similar results held true for humans, Swartzwelder recruited a group of volunteers aged 21 to 29 years old. He couldn't use younger subjects because of laws that forbid drinking before age 21. He chose to split the volunteers into two groups: 21 to 24 years old and 25 to 29 years old. "While I wouldn't argue that these younger folks are adolescents, even in their early twenties their brains are still developing," Swartzwelder says. After three drinks, with a blood–alcohol level slightly below the National Highway Traffic Safety Administration's recommended limit—.08 percent—the younger group's learning was impaired 25 percent more than the older group's.

Intrigued by these results, Swartzwelder's colleague Aaron White, a   10 biological psychologist at Duke, set out to discover how vulnerable the adolescent brain is to long–term damage. He gave adolescent and adult rats large doses of alcohol every other day for 20 days—the equivalent of a 150–pound human chugging 24 drinks in a row. Twenty days after the last binge, when the adolescent rats had reached adulthood, White trained them in a maze–memory task roughly akin to that performed by a human when remembering the location of his car in a parking garage.

Both the younger and older rats performed equally well when sober.   11 But when intoxicated, those who had binged as adolescents performed much worse. "Binge alcohol exposure in adolescence appears to produce long–lasting changes in brain function," White says. He suspects that early damage caused by alcohol could surface whenever the brain is taxed. He also suspects that the NMDA receptor is involved, because just as alcohol

in the system inhibits the receptor, the drug's withdrawal overstimulates it—which can kill the cell outright.

Students who drink heavily sometimes joke that they are killing a few   12
brain cells. New research suggests that this is not funny. Some of the evidence is anatomical: Michael De Bellis at the University of Pittsburgh Medical Center used magnetic resonance imaging to compare the hippocampi of subjects 14 to 21 years old who abused alcohol to the hippocampi of those who did not. He found that the longer and the more a young person had been drinking, the smaller his hippocampus. The average size difference between healthy teens and alcohol abusers was roughly 10 percent. That is a lot of brain cells.

De Bellis speculates that the shrinkage may be due to cell damage   13
and death that occurs during withdrawal from alcohol. Withdrawal is the brain's way of trying to get back to normal after prolonged or heavy drinking. It can leave the hands jittery, set off the classic headache, generate intense anxiety, and even provoke seizures, as neurons that had adjusted to the presence of alcohol try to adjust to its absence. Because alcohol slows down the transmission of nerve signals — in part by stopping glutamate from activating its NMDA receptors — nerve cells under the influence react by increasing the number and sensitivity of these receptors. When drinking stops, the brain is suddenly stuck with too many hyperactive receptors.

Mark Prendergast, a neuroscientist at the University of Kentucky, re-   14
cently revealed one way these hyperactive receptors kill brain cells. First, he exposed rat hippocampal slices to alcohol for 10 days, then removed the alcohol. Following withdrawal, he stained the tissue with a fluorescent dye that lit up dead and dying cells. When exposed to an alcohol concentration of about .08 percent, cell death increased some 25 percent above the baseline. When concentrations were two or three times higher, he wrote in a recent issue of *Alcoholism: Clinical and Experimental Research*, the number of dead cells shot up to 100 percent above the baseline.

Prendergast says that the younger brain tissue was far more sensi-   15
tive. Preadolescent tissue suffered four to five times more cell death than did adult tissue. In all cases, most of the death occurred in hippocampal cells that were packed with NMDA receptors. To home in on the cause, he treated another batch of brain slices with the drug MK–801, which blocks NMDA receptors. He reasoned that if overexcitability during alcohol withdrawal was causing cell death, blocking the receptors should minimize the carnage. It did, by about 75 percent.

Now Prendergast is examining what makes the receptors so lethal.   16
By tracking radioactive calcium, he found that the overexcited receptors open floodgates that allow calcium to swamp the cell. Too much calcium can turn on suicide genes that cause the neuron to break down its own membrane. Indeed, that is exactly what Prendergast observed during

alcohol withdrawal: Overactive receptors opened wide, and the influx of calcium became a raging flood.

Prendergast says that four or five drinks may cause a mild with- 17 drawal. And, according to Harvard's Wechsler, 44 percent of college students binge in this manner. More alarming, 23 percent of them consume 72 percent of all the alcohol that college students drink.

Recent human studies support a conclusion Prendergast drew from his 18 molecular experiments: The greatest brain damage from alcohol occurs during withdrawal. At the University of California at San Diego and the VA San Diego Health Care System, Sandra Brown, Susan Tapert, and Gregory Brown have been following alcohol-dependent adolescents for eight years. Repeated testing shows that problem drinkers perform more poorly on tests of cognition and learning than do nondrinkers. Furthermore, "the single best predictor of neuropsychological deficits for adolescents is withdrawal symptoms," says principal investigator Sandra Brown.

The psychologists recruited a group of 33 teenagers aged 15 and 16, 19 all heavy drinkers. On average, each teen had used alcohol more than 750 times—the equivalent of drinking every day for two and a half years. Bingeing was common: The teens downed an average of eight drinks at each sitting. The researchers matched drinkers with nondrinkers of the same gender and similar age, IQ, socioeconomic background, and family history of alcohol use. Then, three weeks after the drinkers had their last drink, all the teens took a two-hour battery of tests.

The teens with alcohol problems had a harder time recalling infor- 20 mation, both verbal and nonverbal, that they had learned 20 minutes earlier. Words such as *apple* and *football* escaped them. The performance difference was about 10 percent. "It's not serious brain damage, but it's the difference of a grade, a pass or a fail," Tapert says. Other tests evaluated skills needed for map learning, geometry, or science. Again, there was a 10 percent difference in performance.

"The study shows that just several years of heavy alcohol use by 21 youth can adversely affect their brain functions in ways that are critical to learning," Sandra Brown says. She is following the group of teenagers until they reach age 30, and some have already passed 21. "Those who continue to use alcohol heavily are developing attentional deficits in addition to the memory and problem-solving deficits that showed up early on," Brown says. "In the past we thought of alcohol as a more benign drug. It's not included in the war on drugs. This study clearly demonstrates that the most popular drug is also an incredibly dangerous drug."

Brown's research team is also using functional magnetic resonance 22 imaging to compare the brain function of alcohol abusers and nondrinkers. Initial results show that brains of young adults with a history of alcohol dependence are less active than the brains of nondrinkers during tasks that require spatial working memory (comparable to the maze task that White conducted on rats). In addition, the adolescent drinkers seem to exhibit greater levels of brain activity when they are exposed to alcohol–related stimuli. For instance, when the drinkers read words such as *wasted* or *tequila* on a screen, the nucleus accumbens—a small section of the brain associated with craving—lights up.

The nucleus accumbens is integral to the brain's so-called pleasure 23 circuit, which scientists now believe undergoes major remodeling during adolescence. Underlying the pleasure circuit is the neurotransmitter dopamine. Sex, food, and many drugs, including alcohol, can all induce the release of dopamine, which creates feelings of pleasure and in turn encourages repetition of the original behavior. During adolescence, the balance of dopamine activity temporarily shifts away from the nucleus accumbens, the brain's key pleasure and reward center, to the prefrontal cortex. Linda Spear, a developmental psychobiologist at Binghamton University in New York, speculates that as a result of this shift in balance, teenagers may find drugs less rewarding than earlier or later in life. And if the drugs produce less of a kick, more will be needed for the same effect. "In the case of alcohol, this may lead to binge drinking," she says.

During adolescence, the prefrontal cortex changes more than any other 24 part of the brain. At around age 11 or 12, its neurons branch out like crazy, only to be seriously pruned back in the years that follow. All this tumult is to good purpose. In the adult brain, the prefrontal cortex executes the thought processes adolescents struggle to master: the ability to plan ahead, think abstractly, and integrate information to make sound decisions.

Now there is evidence that the prefrontal cortex and associated areas 25 are among those most damaged in the brains of bingeing adolescents. Fulton Crews, director of the Center for Alcohol Studies at the University of North Carolina at Chapel Hill, has studied the patterns of cell death in the brains of adolescent and adult rats after four–day drinking bouts. While both groups showed damage in the back areas of the brain and in the frontally located olfactory bulb, used for smell, only the adolescents suffered brain damage in other frontal areas.

That youthful damage was severe. It extended from the rat's olfactory 26 bulb to the interconnected parts of the brain that process sensory information and memories to make associations, such as "this smell and the sight of that wall tell me I'm in a place where I previously faced down an enemy." The regions of cell death in the rat experiment corresponded to the human prefrontal cortex and to parts of the limbic system.

The limbic system, which includes the hippocampus, changes 27 throughout adolescence, according to recent work by Jay Giedd at the National Institute of Mental Health in Bethesda, Maryland. The limbic system not only encodes memory but is also mobilized when a person is hungry or frightened or angry; it helps the brain process survival impulses. The limbic system and the prefrontal cortex must work in concert for a person to make sound decisions.

Damage to the prefrontal cortex and the limbic system is especially 28 worrisome because they play an important role in the formation of an adult personality. "Binge drinking could be making permanent long-term changes in the final neural physiology, which is expressed as personality and behavior in the individual," Crew says. But he readily acknowledges that such conclusions are hypothetical. "It's very hard to prove this stuff. You can't do an experiment in which you change people's brains."

Nonetheless, evidence of the vulnerability of young people to al- 29 cohol is mounting. A study by Bridget Grant of the National Institute on Alcohol Abuse and Alcoholism shows that the younger someone is when he begins to regularly drink alcohol, the more likely that individual will eventually become an alcoholic. Grant found that 40 percent of the drinkers who got started before age 15 were classified later in life as alcohol dependent, compared with only 10 percent of those who began drinking at age 21 or 22. Overall, beginning at age 15, the risk of future alcohol dependence decreased by 14 percent with each passing year of abstention.

The study leaves unanswered whether early regular drinking is merely 30 a marker of later abuse or whether it results in long-term changes in the brain that increase the later propensity for abuse. "It's got to be both," Crew says. For one thing, he points out that studies of rats and people have shown that repeated alcohol use makes it harder for a person — or a rat — to learn new ways of doing things, rather than repeating the same actions over and over again. In short, the way alcohol changes the brain makes it increasingly difficult over time to stop reaching for beer after beer after beer.

Ultimately, the collateral damage caused by having so many Ameri- 31 can adolescents reach for one drink after another may be incalculable. "People in their late teens have been drinking heavily for generations. We're not a society of idiots, but we're not a society of Einsteins either," says Swartzwelder. "What if you've compromised your function by 7 percent or 10 percent and never known the difference?"

Reading Closely

1. What details does Wuethrich include that reveal her expertise in science writing?
2. What are the steps of the process that Wuethrich is analyzing? Is hers a directional or informational process analysis?
3. How does the visual enhance (or why does it fail to enhance) Wuethrich's text?

Considering Larger Issues

1. What is Wuethrich's purpose? How do you know? What is her thesis statement?

2. Who is Wuethrich's audience? What specific information in the essay helps you determine that audience?

3. **Working with three or four classmates,** respond to the following questions: What big and small processes is Wuethrich analyzing? Which process is her main topic?

4. COMBINING METHODS. How does Wuethrich use *cause-and-effect analysis* to explain the relationships between the bigger and smaller processes? between her main topic and the related smaller topics?

Thinking about Language

1. Using the context of the essay or your dictionary, define the following terms. Some of the technical terms are defined in the context. Be prepared to share your answers with the rest of the class.

binge–drink (1)	receptors (6)	socioeconomic (19)
psychosis (3)	synapses (7)	benign (21)
resilient (3)	reverberations (7)	tumult (24)
hippocampus (4)	maze–memory	integrate (24)
prefrontal cortex (4)	task (10)	
neurons (6)	cognition (18)	

2. List the technical terms or phrases that Wuethrich includes.

Writing Your Own Essays Using Process Analysis

1. Wuethrich's essay analyzes what happens when teenagers binge–drink. Although hers is a process analysis, it's also an analysis of causes and effects. Do some research on a process with which you are unfamiliar, one that is connected with an occupation—farming, sewing, truck driving, birthing sheep, accounting, repairing machinery, merchandising, and so on. Using Wuethrich's essay as a starting point, draft a three– to four–page essay analyzing that occupational process, and extend your analysis to include consequences or effects. Include some visuals to help readers follow the process. Refer to the guidelines for checking over the use of process analysis (p. 422) as you draft and revise.

2. Think about a process that you know well, related, perhaps, to a sport, hobby, pastime, or job. See if you can compare it to some other activity not usually linked with it. Then draft a three– to four–page essay in which you use an analogy to the secondary process to explain the primary process. **Consider working with three or four classmates** to discuss and review your essays while you draft. Refer to "Checking Over the Use of Process Analysis" (p. 422).

✱ Additional Suggestions for Writing

1. Identify a process of student life that is often troublesome: staying on a budget, negotiating living arrangements with a roommate, finding an honest and inexpensive car repair shop, registering for classes, getting good advice from a reliable adviser, and so on. Draft a three- to four-page directional process essay that will help your classmates with this problem. Refer to "Checking Over the Use of Process Analysis" (p. 422).

2. Ceremonies of all kinds are an important part of any culture: weddings, funerals, graduations, religious and political rites. Concentrate on one U.S. ceremony in particular and on the ways your own ethnicity, gender, or religion adds texture to the ceremony. Analyze the process of this ceremony, making sure that your three- to four-page essay has a thesis statement. Refer to "Checking Over the Use of Process Analysis" (p. 422).

3. Draft a three- to four-page essay in which you explain the process of enjoying a particular meal or of gaining someone's respect. Be sure to break the process down into steps in order to make it clear for your readers. Refer to "Checking Over the Use of Process Analysis" (p. 422).

4. **Working with one or two classmates,** discuss the processes you each know how to do on a computer—and the ones you do not. Think of a computer application or process that you know well, and break it down into a directional process essay for your classmates. You might consider how to research a topic on the Web, how to install a software application, how to run the defragmenter, or how to check for viruses. Whichever process you choose, make sure that the members of your group can follow your process and replicate it, if necessary. Your final essay should be two to three pages long. Refer to "Checking Over the Use of Process Analysis" (p. 422).

chapter 8

CAUSE-AND-EFFECT
ANALYSIS

Your parents made a better life for someone else. Now it's your turn.

800.424.8580
www.peacecorps.gov

Life is calling. How far will you go?

PEACE CORPS

our parents made a better life for someone else. Now it's your turn." This public service announcement attempts to persuade young people to join the ranks of the Peace Corps. It achieves this purpose by asking readers first to remember how their parents have positively affected their lives and then to consider how they might have similar effects on other people's lives, presumably those of people like the little boy in the photo. The Peace Corps, the ad suggests, will enable readers to create positive change in the world. By prompting readers to reflect in this way, the Peace Corps calls readers to engage in **cause–and–effect analysis:** What caused my life to be the way it is? How can I cause other people's lives to be better?

. . . .

Looking at Your Own Literacy Write for five minutes considering these questions: Who has positively affected your life? How? In what specific ways have you positively affected the lives of others?

. . . .

What Is Cause-and-Effect Analysis?

We think about causes and effects constantly: when we worry about getting in shape, plan to lose weight, attempt to calm cranky children, try to make peace with our roommates or our partners, or look for ways to succeed in school. We try to discover the reasons for a particular situation (flabbiness, too–tight jeans, crying, frustration, mediocre grades), and we determine or predict the consequences of that particular situation or action (our own unhappiness and dissatisfaction, a quieter child, a happier relationship, a better grade). Every day, we figure out *why* things occur and what happens as a result.

Like process analysis, cause–and–effect analysis links events along a time line. But the purpose of process analysis is to explain *how* things happen, so readers can understand the process and, in many cases, repeat it if they want to. Cause–and–effect analysis explains *why* things happen or predicts that certain events (or certain sets of events) will lead to particular effects (or a particular set of effects). Thus, cause–and–effect analysis can reveal a complex array of causes and predict a complex array of effects. Whether it deals with single or multiple causes or effects, the analysis generally uses a chronological pattern of organization, with causes usually preceding effects (although analyses that deal with a past series of events sometimes use reverse chronological order to trace effects back to their causes).

Whether we're enrolling in the Peace Corps, diagnosing a child's illness, researching the causes of divorce, collecting data on the effects of

teen violence, or assessing a financial investment opportunity, we are analyzing causes or effects. Of course, public writing projects such as the PSA for the Peace Corps calls for such analysis, but so do academic writing assignments. A typical writing assignment in a history class is to ascertain the causes of a particular war or the effects of an economic depression; in a chemistry lab, the instructor may want a report on the effects of a chemical interaction; in a literature course, students might analyze the influence of one poet on another.

The ad on page 466 is based on a cause–and–effect analysis aimed at an audience of people who want to save money.

. . . .

Thinking about Cause-and-Effect Analysis

1. Look over the ad. What effects does the ad promise that packing your lunch will have on the reader?

2. How does the ad work visually to make its point?

. . . .

Why Use Cause-and-Effect Analysis?

Whether used as the primary or a secondary method in a piece of writing, a cause–and–effect analysis can serve one or more of four main purposes: to entertain, to inform, to speculate, and to argue. For some analyses, a writer might focus on just the causes of a situation (such as a disease, a natural disaster, or high school dropout rates), whereas in other cases, a writer might concentrate on only the effects of a situation (such as crime, epidemics, increasing longevity, or contentment). In this chapter, you'll be asked to analyze causes and effects separately as well as in combination.

Newspaper columnist Dave Barry is a prolific analyzer of causes and effects. His purpose is almost always to entertain his loyal readers, as he does in the following excerpt from a column that originally appeared in 2004.

Cause-and-Effect Analysis to Entertain

I started lifting weights. But not for the reason you think. You think I want to look "cut" and "ripped" and have bulging muscles like the ones on male underwear models, who for some reason are always shown posing outdoors, looking sullen, as if a group of even more muscular models stole their pants.

You think I want to have muscles like that, so women will look at me and think: "Wow! I would like to see *his* syndicated column!" But you are wrong. I'm lifting weights for sensible medical reasons, which I learned about from the highest possible medical authority: the Internet. If you ever experience a medical symptom, such as itching, you don't need to waste time sitting in a doctor's waiting room reading 1997 issues of *Redbook*.

Instead, you can go to the Internet, and with just a few mouse clicks, you'll discover the reassuring truth: There might be a worm in your brain.

Really. According to a site called Medline Plus ("Trusted Health Information for You"), sponsored by the National Medical Library *and* the National Institutes of Health, itching can be a symptom of a condition called "visceral larva migrans" (literally, "a worm in your brain"). And before I get a bunch of nasty letters from irate physicians attacking me for unnecessarily scaring people, let me note that another symptom of brain worm is—and this is a direct quote from Medline Plus—"irritability."

—Dave Barry, "A Healthy Dose of Pain"

With his customary humor, Barry analyzes why he's begun weight lifting. The cause is not to garner appreciation and interest from women; no, the reason is health–related: he's lifting for "sensible medical reasons"—something he's learned while doing research on the Web. This cause–and–effect analysis leads him to another one: what happens when you do this kind of Web–based research? Well, it can cause you to make some pretty preposterous diagnoses, like believing that an itching sensation means that you have a worm in your brain.

· ·

Try Your Hand   Barry's column explains to readers that his motivation for weight lifting is not a desire for attention but concern for his health. In essence, he's writing about clarifying the causes of his actions. Write for five minutes about a time when you needed to clarify your motivations for a particular action or practice. How did you explain the *real* cause for this behavior?

· ·

In an article originally published in *Science* magazine in 2003, Jocelyn Kaiser writes an informative analysis of one cause of the decline in the number of migratory songbirds.

Cause-and-Effect Analysis to Inform

Migratory songbirds have become scarcer in recent decades, in part because their tropical wintering grounds are being degraded and many birds don't survive the winter. A new study uses a chemical marker in birds' blood to suggest that this habitat loss has a ripple effect in surviving birds that extends well into the breeding season, when the birds may be a continent away.

The American redstart, a warbler, spends winters in the Caribbean, Central America, and northern South America and summers in temperate forests in the United States and Canada. There the birds mate and produce up to five chicks. Redstarts that winter in poor habitat produce fewer chicks and their chicks fledge later, a team led by graduate student Ryan Norris of Queens University in Kingston, Ontario, reported here [Savannah, Georgia] earlier this month at the annual meeting of the Ecological Society of America.

The finding builds on earlier work linking winter habitat with a bird's health when it arrives to breed. But "nobody has demonstrated" a direct link between winter habitat and breeding success until now, says avian ecologist Susan Hannon of the University of Alberta in Edmonton. "This adds another potential problem [birds] have to deal with," along with threats such as fragmentation of northern forests, which attracts cowbirds that replace redstart eggs with their own.

A few years ago, Peter Marra of the Smithsonian Environmental Research Center in Edgewater, Maryland, and co-workers developed a chemical technique that can identify the kind of habitat in which a bird over-wintered. Because plants use different pathways for photosynthesis, those that grow in richer, wetter tropical habitats — such as mangroves and wet lowland forests — contain less of the carbon-13 isotope than do plants in drier areas, such as scrub. Insects eat the plants, birds eat the insects, and the habitat leaves a carbon-13 signature in the birds' blood. Marra's team used this marker to show that redstarts arrive up north sooner and in better physical condition when they have spent the winter in a richer habitat.

In the new study, Norris, his adviser Marra, and co-workers show that better winter habitat translates into better breeding success. Norris spent two summers monitoring about 90 male and female redstarts nesting north of Lake Ontario. He found a striking correlation between carbon-13 levels in the birds' blood and breeding success: Males that had better winter diets not only arrived earlier at the breeding grounds but also sired slightly more young. Effects were even stronger for females: Those that arrived from better habitats produced up to two more chicks and fledged them up to a month earlier than did females that wintered in sparser grounds.

"Negative effects in one season can be negative again in another season," Norris says. He says this "carryover" effect underscores the fact that conserving migratory birds will require saving wet tropical forests and mangroves, which are rapidly being lost to logging and development.

— JOCELYN KAISER, "Lean Winters Hinder Birds' Summertime Breeding Efforts"

Kaiser's cause–and–effect analysis explains all the reasons that winter habitats make a difference in the breeding habits of songbirds. She provides new scientific findings and includes quotes from experts to support her thesis, "migratory songbirds have become scarcer in recent decades, in part because their tropical wintering grounds are being degraded and many birds don't survive the winter." In addition to identifying one of the biological and environmental causes for this growing scarcity of songbirds, she also identifies a consequence of that scarcity: the need to stop the rapid loss of wet tropical forests and mangroves.

· ·

Try Your Hand   Do you accept Kaiser's explanation? Why or why not? What is her purpose? Who might be her audience?

· ·

People speculate on the causes and effects of certain phenomena all the time, from the weather or the gender of an unborn baby to the success of a sports team before the season starts. In the following excerpt, *New York Times* contributor Matt Richtel speculates on the effects of working out of the home as a blogger.

Cause-and-Effect Analysis to Speculate

A growing work force of home-office laborers and entrepreneurs, armed with computers and smartphones and wired to the hilt, are toiling under great physical and emotional stress created by the around-the-clock Internet economy that demands a constant stream of news and comment.

Of course, the bloggers can work elsewhere, and they profess a love of the nonstop action and perhaps the chance to create a global media outlet without a major up-front investment. At the same time, some are starting to wonder if something has gone very wrong. In the last few months, two among their ranks have died suddenly.

Two weeks ago in North Lauderdale, Fla., funeral services were held for Russell Shaw, a prolific blogger on technology subjects who died at 60 of a heart attack. In December, another tech blogger, Marc Orchant, died at 50 of a massive coronary. A third, Om Malik, 41, survived a heart attack in December.

Other bloggers complain of weight loss or gain, sleep disorders, exhaustion and other maladies born of the nonstop strain of producing for a news and information cycle that is as always-on as the Internet.

To be sure, there is no official diagnosis of death by blogging, and the premature demise of two people obviously does not qualify as an epidemic. There is also no certainty that the stress of the work contributed to their deaths. But friends and family of the deceased, and fellow information workers, say those deaths have them thinking about the dangers of their work style.

— MATT RICHTEL, "In Web World of 24/7 Stress, Writers Blog till They Drop"

Richtel acknowledges that his claims are speculative when he writes, "to be sure, there is no official diagnosis of death by blogging." But the possible effects of blogging that he sees are significant. Three bloggers suffered heart attacks in a matter of months — a medical problem that could very well be linked to (or caused by) these bloggers' round–the–clock work life combined with the constant pressure to produce.

· ·

Try Your Hand   Reflect on the effects of your work style, whether it be the work you do for school or your employment outside of class (or both). How does your work affect your mental and physical health as well as your social life?

· ·

When we speculate, we are often guessing, estimating, or predicting certain causes and/or effects. But cause–and–effect analysis can also be used to make an argument. For instance, in her essay "Forging *El Mundo*

Zurdo: Changing Ourselves, Changing the World," activist writer Ana-Louise Keating uses cause–and–effect analysis to argue about the destructiveness of racial categories.

Cause-and-Effect Analysis to Argue

Out of all the categories we today employ, "race" is the most destructive. "Race" is, for sure, one of the "master's tools," one of the most insidious tools of all. We've been trained to classify and evaluate ourselves and those we meet according to racialized appearances: we look at a person's body, classify her, insert him into a category, make generalizations, and base our interactions on these racialized assumptions. These assumptions rely on and reinforce monolithic, divisive stereotypes that erase the incredible diversity within each individual and within each so-called "race." But racial categories are not — and never have been — benign; rather, they were developed by those in power (generally property-owning men of Northern European descent) to create a hierarchy that grants privilege and power to specific groups of people while simultaneously oppressing and excluding others. Racialized categories originated in histories of oppression, exclusion, land theft, body theft, soul theft, physical/psychic murder, and other crimes against specific groups of human beings. These categories were motivated by economics and politics, by insecurity and greed — not by innate biological or divinely created differences. When we refer to "race" or to specific "races," we are drawing on and therefore reinforcing this violent history as well as the "white" supremacism buttressing the entire system.

> — AnaLouise Keating, "Forging *El Mundo Zurdo*: Changing Ourselves, Changing the World"

· ·

Try Your Hand   Keating points to a number of causes for and effects of racial categories. She does not, though, offer specific examples of what she means. Write for five minutes, identifying specific examples that would support (or question) her argument.

· ·

How Do You Use Cause-and-Effect Analysis in Academic Writing?

From advertisements and public service announcements to editorials and blogs, public writing is full of examples of cause–and–effect analysis. So too is academic writing. As mentioned in the opening pages of this chapter, you have probably already composed cause–and–effect analyses in your history classes, chemistry labs, and literature courses at a number of points in your academic career. And this rhetorical method only becomes more important as you proceed. The most experienced scholars often employ this method as a means to inform, speculate, and argue (and sometimes to entertain as well).

The following excerpt offers an example of scholars using cause–and–effect analysis in a scholarly publication for an academic audience. In an article for the journal *Sociology*, sociologists Nabil Khattab and Steve Fenton ask, "What makes young adults happy?" To answer this question about causation, Khattab and Fenton surveyed 1,100 young adults, asking them what contributes to their overall "life satisfaction," or LS. In the following excerpt, the authors assert that their study identified a number of unexpected causes in addition to the "employment satisfaction" (ES) that previous research had found to be the determining factor for happiness among young people.

Cause-and-Effect Analysis in Academic Writing

Although we have seen that ES played an important role in determining LS among young men and women, other factors had a stronger and a more direct effect on LS than ES; these included "sense of life control" and "living with a partner" among men and "sense of life control" and "satisfied with home" among women. This may challenge some classical and contemporary arguments about the relationship between employment and life satisfaction. Our analysis suggests that the effect of demoralizing work and fragmentation, including risks of unemployment and insecurity, is cancelled out and/or balanced by sense of control over life on the one hand and by the very close association between social relations (living with partner) and LS.

— NABIL KHATTAB and STEVE FENTON, "What Makes Young Adults Happy? Employment and Nonwork as Determinants of Life Satisfaction"

You can see that Khattab and Fenton's causal analysis presents new insights in sociological research. Their study revealed that besides satisfaction with work, a sense of control over one's life and satisfaction at home were equally or even more important factors that led to happiness.

Your instructors will often ask you to conduct cause–and–effect analyses like Khattab and Fenton's. You should be able to identify the need to write this kind of essay by the terminology instructors use in their assignment descriptions. Of course, if an instructor asks you to pinpoint causes and effects, you'll know what to do. But there are other key words and phrases that would suggest that cause–and–effect analysis is the most appropriate method for the writing situation — for example: How does X *influence* Y (cause)? What are the *consequences* of A (effect)? Where did B *come from* (cause)? What *led to* G (cause)? What are the *symptoms* of H (effect)? What were the *results* or *outcomes* of this phenomenon (effect)?

. . . .

Analyzing Cause-and-Effect Analysis in Academic Writing   Reflect on the range of cause–and–effect essays you've composed throughout your academic career. Which did you find to be the most productive, worthwhile, exciting, or interesting? Why? Be prepared to share your answers with the class.

. . . .

How Do You Read Cause-and-Effect Analysis?

Knowing how to be a critical reader of examples of cause-and-effect analysis will enable you to write your own with more skill and confidence. By looking closely at such an analysis, you can evaluate it in a number of ways. For example, do the causes or effects, as presented by the author, seem plausible? If the analysis discusses multiple causes of something, is it clear how they're related or which one is most important? And how well does the analysis achieve its specific purpose—to entertain, inform, speculate, or argue a point—for its specific audience? Writing a cause-and-effect essay is a complex task, and taking a detailed look at how other writers deal with the distinctive challenges of such an essay will help you see both strategies to take advantage of and pitfalls to avoid.

Look, for instance, at the passage by Jocelyn Kaiser on pages 468–69. The title, "Lean Winters Hinder Birds' Summertime Breeding Efforts," alerts you that it's a causal analysis and suggests that the overall purpose of the essay is informative or argumentative, not humorous or speculative. Notice that the introduction consists of two sentences, a first sentence that introduces a cause—the loss of tropical winter habitat by migratory songbirds—and then a second sentence that states the effect or consequence of this cause: "this habitat loss has a ripple effect in surviving birds that extends well into the breeding season." The next paragraphs go on to explain the migration and breeding patterns of the American redstart, the specific effects that the research team found were related to poor winter habitats, and the scientific significance of this finding. The rest of the passage explains the details of the research, including how the researchers measured the quality of the birds' habitat and how this quality is related to their success in breeding, and concludes with a statement from the research leader about the causes of the habitat loss and what he sees as the effects of the scientific findings.

This is a fairly simple, straightforward causal analysis, which clearly presents just one cause (habitat loss) producing two effects (fewer chicks and later fledging). As Kaiser explains in her final paragraph, however, the cause is also an effect that can be traced back to its own causes—"wet tropical forests and mangroves . . . are rapidly being lost to logging and development"—which implies yet another cause-and-effect relationship: conserving the birds requires saving the forests and mangroves. Often a writer will present a much more complex web of causes and effects than this one, requiring very careful thought and organization to be clear to readers. The most important cause won't always be the same as the most apparent one; in fact, they may not even be closely related. Seeing how—or whether—other writers make these distinctions clear will help you see how to clarify them in your own cause-and-effect analyses.

In your critical reading, you also need to pay attention to the language the author uses. Notice that the language of this passage is not highly technical, but Kaiser does assume that her audience (readers of *Science* magazine) has some familiarity with scientific concepts and terminology like *degraded habitats, avian, photosynthesis, fledge,* and *fragmentation* of forests. When you write a cause–and–effect analysis of your own, be sure to take your audience into account both in your language and in other ways, such as how much background information readers will need to understand the logical connections between particular causes and effects. Notice also in the second sentence that Kaiser uses the word *suggest,* rather than *prove* or *establish,* to refer to what the study found. It's often difficult or impossible to prove beyond doubt that one thing is caused by another or will have certain effects, so it's a good idea not to sound overconfident when making such a claim.

As you read an author's claims about causes or effects, pay careful attention also to the supporting evidence that is provided — or the lack of it. In Kaiser's analysis, she carefully sets out the evidence for the researchers' findings in her fourth and fifth paragraphs. Sometimes, though, authors assert causes or effects without bothering to support those assertions. There might be plenty of supporting evidence, but the author didn't think or choose to use it. At other times, the author either hasn't done enough homework on the situation or wants you to believe there's a causal relationship when none exists.

In fact, one final important thing to consider in reading a cause–and–effect analysis (or any other kind of writing) is what the author has left out. You'll need to think especially about whether the author has omitted not just evidence but entire causes or effects altogether. In Kaiser's essay, for example, she doesn't mention whether there could be — or whether the researchers considered — possible causes other than tropical habitat loss for the finding that redstarts with more of the carbon–13 marker in their blood were less successful in breeding. Perhaps this case has no other plausible or likely explanation. But when you're writing such an analysis, always think carefully about what other causes or effects the audience may expect you to mention; if you believe they're unlikely, you may need to explain why you think so, in addition to explaining the causes or effects that you do believe are important.

How Do You Write Using Cause-and-Effect Analysis?

Like any writing assignment, cause–and–effect analysis demands that you pay careful attention to a number of concerns: your subject, purpose, audience, thesis statement, and method of organization. In addition, this method requires that you take particular care in figuring out and explaining relationships among the different causes and effects you discuss and in choosing the language you use.

● Considering Your Subject

What event or situation are you analyzing? What causes or effects can you think of immediately? Is it a subject that is complex or unfamiliar enough that you should consult sources to find other possible causes or effects? You may find that discussing your subject with one or two class-mates will help you answer these questions.

● Determining Your Purpose

What do you want your readers to do as a result of your analysis? Do you want them to laugh, understand your subject more fully, ponder the future, or change their behavior or way of thinking about the subject? As you determine which of the four purposes (to entertain, inform, specu-late, or argue a point) your analysis will have, you'll also need to deter-mine whether to concentrate on the *causes* of something, as Kaiser does when she accounts for one reason that some American redstarts are less successful at breeding than others, or on the *effects* of something, as Barry does when he discusses the effects of looking for medical advice online. Keeping your purpose in mind will help you stay on course, concentrat-ing on either causes or effects — or perhaps finding a way to do both by establishing a causal chain, the way Richtel does when he recounts how blogging at home leads to stressful working conditions that may result in a heart attack.

● Considering Your Audience

Who is your audience? Like every other kind of writing, cause-and-effect analysis demands that you consider your purpose in light of your audience, and vice versa. Whether you are writing a causal or an effect analysis, you'll want to consider specific characteristics of your audience: age, education, experience, attitudes, and so on. How informed are mem-bers of your audience about the event or situation that you are analyzing? What causes or effects might they be expecting you to mention? Every audience has needs and expectations that you will want to address in terms of your overall purpose and the particular details you provide.

● Thinking Critically about Different Causes or Effects

In every cause-and-effect analysis, you'll discover a jumble of differ-ent causes. Your job is to untangle them, using two basic methods. For causes, you will need to distinguish (1) the **primary cause,** the most important one, from the **contributory causes,** and (2) the **immediate cause,** the one directly producing the event, from less obvious **remote causes.** In terms of effects, you will want to distinguish (1) the **primary effect** from the **secondary effects** and (2) the **immediate effect** from the **remote effects.**

1. Let's say that you're exhausted. Sometimes you feel too tired to get out of bed and go to class. You've felt this way for several weeks now, and you're beginning to worry. Your mother says it's because you're studying too hard, working too many hours, and partying too much on the weekends. So you cut back on your studying (something's got to give, right?), but you're still pooped. You drag yourself over to the student health center and tell the doctor all the reasons you're tired. When she tells you that you have mononucleosis, you know immediately that mono is the primary cause of your exhaustion and that studying, working, and partying are only contributory causes. As you treat the primary cause—your illness—you will be treating the contributory causes as well. No more school or work or play for you—you're home on the sofa, recovering.

2. Or you could look at the situation in another way. You know you're tired on a Monday morning because you stayed out so late on Friday and Saturday nights. Indeed, partying (keeping late hours, eating junk food, and dancing) is the immediate cause of your malaise. But the remote causes are that you're not getting enough rest during the week because you attend classes, have a lot of homework, and work twenty hours a week as a cafeteria server. The most remote cause of all is your mono, a factor you never suspected.

Although often considered separately, these two types of causes are not mutually exclusive: sometimes you'll discover that the immediate cause is also the primary cause. If you are focusing on causes, you'll need to think critically about the various causes of an event or situation in order to arrive at a controlling idea that you can express in your thesis statement.

What about the effects of having mononucleosis? The primary effect is your exhaustion, but the secondary effects could be that you must drop a course or two—or even leave school because you need time to rest and recover. The immediate effect, again, is your exhaustion, but the remote effects could be that your resistance to disease remains low for years to come, that you end up taking a year longer to finish your degree, and that your time away from school gives you an opportunity to rethink and change your major.

To visualize these causes and effects that are linked with mononucleosis, consider the following diagrams:

CAUSES

Studying hard

Working many hours

Partying on the weekend

Being exposed to the virus

SITUATION/EVENT

Mononucleosis

SITUATION/EVENT

Mononucleosis

EFFECTS

Exhaustion

Dropping a class or two

Dropping out of school for a term

SITUATION/EVENT

Dropping out of school
for a term

EFFECTS

Reevaluating your chosen major

Changing schools

If your analysis reveals a series of related events, you may be uncovering a **causal chain,** in which one situation or event causes another situation or event, which results in yet another situation or event. In this case, you may find yourself analyzing both causes and effects in your essay. For example, the causal chain of mononucleosis could look something like this:

Partying on the weekends →

Exposure to the virus →

Mononucleosis →

Exhaustion →

Sleeping →

Missing classes →

Failing classes →

Dropping out for a term →

Recovering at home →

Reevaluating your plans →

Changing your major

One particular pitfall in untangling causes and effects is confusing them with chronology—that is, assuming that just because one event preceded another, the first caused the second (or, from another perspective, that the second was a consequence of the first). For example, to establish the first link in the casual chain illustrated here, you would have to establish clearly that your partying was indeed what exposed you to the mononucleosis virus. Certainly you could have been exposed at a party or a club, but you could also have been exposed in many other settings — the classroom, the dorm, the library, your job. If you went out partying several times with two people who came down with mono shortly before you did, that fact might enable you to say that your partying *probably* caused your exposure to the virus. In many cases, however, two events or situations that appear at first to have a cause–and–effect relationship prove to be completely unrelated. So you will always need to analyze each individual event or situation that could be understood as a cause or a consequence and then analyze its relationship to what precedes or follows it.

● Considering Your Thesis Statement

After considering your purpose, your audience, and the causes and/or effects of the event or situation, what conclusions have you reached? Have you decided to concentrate on causes, effects, or both? If you are focusing on causes, will you differentiate between primary and contributory causes or between immediate and remote causes — or both? Whatever your focus, your thesis statement should introduce your subject, suggest the reason you're analyzing it, and state the idea about causes and/or effects that you want your readers to accept. For example, you might write a thesis statement like one of the following:

1. I blamed myself for being lazy and stretched too thin with school, work, and play, but only when I went to the student health center did I discover I was suffering from an undiagnosed case of mononucleosis.

2. Because my mononucleosis went undiagnosed for too long, I was unable to remain in school.

3. Even though mononucleosis is a terrible disease, my bout with it provided me with time to rethink my life's goals.

● Arranging All the Parts

How are you organizing your analysis? You might open your essay with a description of the event or situation you are analyzing and then introduce your thesis statement. For example, you might open with something like the following:

> I was constantly exhausted, often too tired to go to class, let alone do my homework. So during the week, I rested up for my usual weekend of socializing. Only after collapsing at a dance club and being rushed to the hospital did I discover the cause of my weekday exhaustion: I had a severe case of mononucleosis.

After this introduction, however, you'll need to decide whether you should explain the causes or effects of the event or situation in **chrono–logical order** or **emphatic order.** Do you want to narrate the causes that led up to your illness in chronological order, almost like a process analysis? Or would it be more effective to order the causes emphatically, from least to most important?

In general, chronological order (or reverse chronological order) is most effective if you are focusing on the distinction between immediate and remote causes or effects, because that distinction is related to time. Emphatic order (or reverse emphatic order) is most effective if you are focusing on the distinction between primary and contributory causes or between primary and secondary effects, because those distinctions are related to importance. Whatever organizational pattern you decide on, however, remember to stay with that pattern throughout your analysis. Moving back and forth between the two patterns — or not following any pattern at all — will confuse your readers and weaken the impact of your analysis.

● Considering Your Language

Cause–and–effect analysis is often complex or controversial. To help readers follow your analysis and convince them to accept the causes or effects you are presenting, you'll need to choose your words carefully. First, your thesis statement should clearly indicate whether you will focus on causes, effects, or both. You might write something like "I had always been a strong student, but when my grades began to fall, I had to find out the reasons why" or "When I came down with mononucleosis my first term at college, the effects proved far–reaching" or "Students should make every effort to avoid mononucleosis because the effects are terrible."

Second, unless you're absolutely certain about the causes or effects of an event or situation, using language such as *probably, most likely,* and *might well be* will enhance your credibility with readers, particularly if you're speculating about future effects: "Although mononucleosis is a viral infection, it can probably be avoided if you follow some basic rules for good health."

Third, using clear transitional words or phrases will help your readers follow your line of thinking. Words and phrases such as *first of all* and *second; one cause, a contributing factor,* and *most important;* or *therefore, as a result,* and *brings about yet another* also help indicate which cause you think is primary or immediate or what the effects are. The best way to find out if your transitional language is working is to ask a classmate to read your draft and tell you where problems following your analysis were encountered.

Finally, your language signals your tone. If your goal is to entertain, you might want to include some Dave Barry–like exaggeration, making

"Reading" and Using Visuals in Cause-and-Effect Analysis

Visuals of various kinds can help clarify or breathe life into your cause–and–effect analysis. If you think readers might have trouble following a complex chain of interrelated causes or effects, for example, you might want to include a diagram like the ones on page 477.

More complex diagrams or other kinds of visuals can also be useful for cause–and–effect analysis, but creating or choosing effective ones requires thought and skill. To learn how to do this, make a habit of noticing visuals that illustrate cause–and–effect relationships and then "reading" them critically in the same way you would read such an analysis in words. That is, consider how well the specific parts of the images work together with the text to establish clear relationships between causes and effects that are effective for the writer's specific purpose and audience.

For example, look at the diagram shown here, developed by a group seeking to explain the causes and effects of domestic abuse.

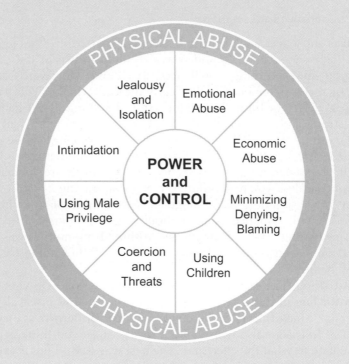

Notice that instead of using arrows to show how one thing leads to another, as in the diagrams on page 477, this diagram places "POWER and CONTROL" in the center of a circle, as the root cause of all abuse. From this center—from the abuser's need for power and control—radiate the effects: the immediate effects of various kinds of nonphysical abuse and the more remote effect of physical abuse. Using this circular arrangement keeps the focus on the root cause in the center and on the ultimate effect on the rim, both of which are also emphasized by being set in larger type and in all capital letters. Various kinds of nonphysical abuse often precede physical abuse and may pave the way for it, this layout suggests. This diagram does not emphasize nonphysical abuse, however, or give any indication of whether some forms of it are more common than others or more likely to lead to physical abuse.

The visual qualities of the diagram suggest several things about its intended audience and purpose. Because it uses terms like "Economic Abuse" and "Using Male Privilege" without explaining them, it's apparently intended for readers who either already have some understanding of the dynamics of domestic abuse or are reading a verbal explanation of these dynamics along with the diagram. If you were using a similar diagram in your own cause-and-effect analysis, in the text of your essay you would need to explain any terms like this that your readers aren't likely to be familiar with. Also notice that the diagram seems intended more to help people understand domestic abuse in a broad, abstract context rather than, say, to alert women who are experiencing nonphysical abuse from their male partners that there is a risk that it may lead to physical abuse. For such women, a writer might instead choose a visual that highlighted the various kinds of nonphysical abuse under a heading like "Is He Going to Get Violent? Eight Danger Signs."

Although diagrams showing the relationships between causes and effects can be especially useful in a cause-and-effect analysis, other kinds of visuals—photographs, cartoons, graphs, and so on—can also help you illustrate your points. Always check with your instructor, though, before submitting visuals with an academic assignment. In addition, think about whether you need to add labels or captions to any visuals and whether you should refer to them in your written text or let them stand on their own.

one sweeping assertion after another. If you are dead serious, you will need to use an objective tone and include convincing facts, statistics, and other details. If you are working with a writing group, your fellow group members can help you calibrate your language to suit your purpose.

● Considering Your Conclusion

Conclusions offer you an opportunity to push your own thinking as well as that of your audience a bit further than your thesis statement was able to do. What do you want your readers to take away with them? What did the analysis reveal to you, and what do you want it to reveal to them? What are its larger or long–term implications? Answering these questions will help you write a meaningful conclusion, one that goes beyond a mere restatement of your introduction.

Understanding and Using Cause-and-Effect Analysis

Analyzing Cause-and-Effect Analysis

1. Review the diagram on domestic abuse (p. 480). The image gives readers a sense of how each kind of abuse contributes to (or causes) domestic abuse. However, the visual does not get specific in explaining what each category means and how it leads to domestic abuse. **Working with a classmate,** choose three categories. Explain what these categories mean, using detailed description and exemplification. Then discuss the causal relationship between the category and the overarching issue of domestic abuse.

2. Review the opening visual on page 464 of this chapter. Who is the audience for this public service announcement? How do you know? Be specific in your assessments.

Planning and Writing Essays Using Cause-and-Effect Analysis

1. Look at the Keating excerpt on page 471. How have racial categories affected your life and the lives of those around you? What have been the effects of these categorizations? Compose a two–page essay that examines these effects. As you write, consider the primary and secondary effects as well as the immediate and remote ones.

2. Think for a minute about a problem or a special talent you have. Maybe you're shy, behind in your classwork, overcommitted, out of shape, or out of money; maybe you're highly motivated, popular, or particularly witty. Make a list of both the causes and the effects of your problem or gift. Which list provides you with more information about your problem or talent?

Concentrating on the richer list, begin planning an essay in which you develop the causes or effects with specific examples. As you generate ideas for your essay, try to draft a meaningful thesis statement.

3. Drawing on your response to question 1 or question 2, draft a three- to four-page essay in which you expand your analysis, focusing on the primary or immediate cause or effect. Refer to the following guidelines for checking over the use of cause–and–effect analysis.

4. If you're a sports fan, watch a game on TV, taking careful notes so that you will be able to explain the causes of the outcome. Your notes will probably be descriptive and chronological. After the game is over, decide which of the causes is the most important (primary) one, which one might be immediate, and how you plan to arrange your information. Draft a three- to four-page essay in which you argue the causes of the outcome. Include specific examples from the game that help you make your points, and refer to the following guidelines for checking over the use of cause–and–effect analysis.

✔ Checking Over the Use of Cause-and-Effect Analysis

1. What event or situation are you analyzing? Are you concentrating on its causes, its effects, or both? Identify your thesis statement. Does it clearly identify your focus?

2. Why are you writing about this event or situation? To entertain? inform? speculate? argue a point? Does the thesis statement reflect this purpose? Does the rest of the essay?

3. Who is the audience for this analysis? Have you taken your readers' needs and expectations into account throughout the essay?

4. What causes or effects of the event or situation have you identified? Have you clearly connected each of the causes or effects with the event or situation? Can you think of any additional causes or effects you should include?

5. Have you identified specific causes as primary or contributory or as immediate or remote? Have you identified the effects as primary or secondary or as immediate or remote? Do you have any second thoughts about your classifications? Have you included language like *probably* or *most likely* where appropriate?

6. In what order have you presented the causes or effects: chronological or emphatic? Is this order effective, or would the other order work more effectively?

7. What transitional words or phrases have you included to help readers move from one cause or effect to the next? Underline them. Are there other places where transitions are needed?

8. What point have you made in your conclusion? Do you move beyond your thesis statement by drawing larger or longer–term implications?

9. If you're using visuals, do they support your thesis and purpose? Will your audience have any trouble understanding them? Do you need to add labels, captions, or references in the written text?

READINGS

TAYLOR CLARK
Plight of the Little Emperors

Taylor Clark is a graduate of Dartmouth College. His work has appeared in the online magazine *Slate* as well as Portland, Oregon's alternative weekly magazine, *Willamette Week*. He has also published *Starbucked: A Double Tall Tale of Caffeine, Commerce, and Culture* (2007). In this essay, which appeared in *Psychology Today* in 2008, Clark analyzes the effects of what he calls "hypereducation" on Chinese youth.

Preview　What do you imagine "hypereducation" is? What might be the causes of hypereducation of young people in China? What effects might it have?

1　When Dawei Liu was growing up in the coastal city of Tai'an during the 1990s, all of his classmates— 95 percent of whom were only children— received plenty of doting parental support. One student, however, truly stood out from the rest. Every day, this boy went from class to class with an entourage of one: his mother, who had given up the income of her day job to monitor his studies full-time, sitting beside him constantly in order to ensure perfect attention. "The teacher was OK with it," Liu shrugs. "He might not focus as much on class if his parent wasn't there."

Note Clark's use of narration in the opening paragraph to set the scene of this cause-and-effect analysis.

2　　Across China, stories of parents going to incredible lengths to give their only children a competitive edge have become commonplace. Throughout Jing Zhang's youth in Beijing, her parents took her to weekly résumé-boosting painting classes, waiting outside the school building for two hours each time, even in winter. Yanming Lin enjoyed perfect silence in her family's one–room Shanghai apartment throughout her five–plus hours of nightly homework; besides nixing the television, her mother kept perpetual watch over her to make sure she stayed on task. "By high school, my parents knew I could control myself and only do homework," Lin says. "Because I knew the situation."

Clark pinpoints a possible cause of "hypereducation": the *gao kao.*

The situation for urban young people in today's 3 China, from preschoolers on up, is this: Your entire future hinges on one test, the national college entrance exam — China's magnified version of the SAT. The Chinese call it *gao kao,* or "tall test," because it looms so large. If students do well, they win spots at China's top universities and an easy route to a middle–class lifestyle. If not, they must confront the kind of tough, blue–collar lives their parents faced. With such high stakes, families dedicate themselves to their child's test prep virtually from infancy. "Many people come home to have dinner and then study until bed," says Liu. "You have to do it to go to the best university and get a good job. You must do this to live."

Here Clark discusses the intended effects of China's only-child policy.

When China began limiting couples to one child 4 30 years ago, the policy's most obvious goal was to contain a mushrooming population. For the Chinese people, however, the policy's greater purpose was to turn out a group of young elites who would each enjoy the undivided resources of their whole family — the so–called *xiao huangdi,* or "little emperors." The plan was to "produce a generation of high–quality children to facilitate China's introduction as a global power," explains Susan Greenhalgh, an expert on the policy.

Clark offers his thesis here.

But while these well–educated, driven achievers are fueling the nation's economic boom, their generation has become too modern too quickly, glutted as it is with televisions, access to computers, cash to buy name brands, and the same expectations of middle–class success as Western kids.

Clark begins to consider the effects of China's hypereducated children.

The shift in temperament has happened too fast 5 for society to handle. China is still a developing nation with limited opportunity, leaving millions of ambitious little emperors out in the cold; the country now churns out more than 4 million university graduates yearly, but only 1.6 million new college–level jobs.

Even the strivers end up as security guards. China may be the world's next great superpower, but it's facing a looming crisis as millions of overpressurized, hypereducated only children come of age in a nation that can't fulfill their expectations.

6   This culture of pressure and frustration has sparked a mental–health crisis for young Chinese. Many simmer in depression or unemployment, unwilling to take jobs they consider beneath them. Millions, afraid to face the real world, escape into video games, which the government considers a national epidemic. And a disturbing number decide to end it all; suicide is now China's leading cause of death for those aged 20 to 35. "People in China— especially parents and college students— are suddenly becoming aware of huge depression and anxiety problems in young people," says Yu Zeng, a 23–year–old from Sichuan province. "The media report on new campus suicides all the time."

Another effect of hypereducation: a mental-health crisis.

7   "In this generation, every child is raised to be at the top," says Vanessa Fong, a Harvard education professor and author of *Only Hope: Coming of Age under China's One-Child Policy.* "They've worked hard for it, and it's what their parents have focused their lives on. But the problem is that the country can't provide the lifestyle they feel they deserve. Only a few will get it." China's accomplished young elites are celebrated on billboards as the vanguard of the nation, yet they're quickly becoming victims of their own lofty expectations.

8   Bringing up a high–achieving child in a crowded and impoverished city like Hohhot, parents sometimes have to get creative. Since the government issued minuscule rations of milk, for instance, Yu Wang's parents scraped together the money to buy a sheep and kept it with relatives outside the city. Every day, Wang's father cycled 40 minutes to fetch fresh milk for his son. Out of his parents' meager monthly salary of 45 RMB (about $6), 35 RMB went to Wang's education— including a packed slate of piano, painting, guitar, and even dancing classes.

Note Clark's use of exemplification in this paragraph

9   The pressure to succeed was all the greater given that his parents' own dreams had been dashed during China's Cultural Revolution, when Mao Zedong closed schools and sent difficult–to–control intellectuals to

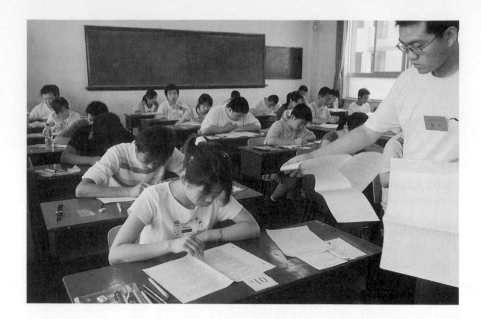

be "reeducated" by working the fields. Wang's father spent eight years herding goats. His own dreams destroyed, he poured all his hopes and ambitions into his son. "Because of the Cultural Revolution, my parents literally wasted 10 years," explains Wang, 29, who was among the first Chinese only kids born under the one-child policy. "I was explicitly told that they had lost a lot in their lives, so they wanted me to get it back for them."

In recent years, however, Chinese parents have 10 sometimes blurred the line between sacrifice and slavery in aiding their child's success: Mothers carry their child's backpack around; couples forgo lunch so their kid can have plentiful snacks or new Nikes. Vanessa Fong recalls meeting one mother who resisted hospitalization for her heart and kidney troubles because she feared it might interfere with her daughter's *gao kao* preparation; when Fong gave the mother money for medication, it mostly went to expensive food for her daughter.

Clark points to another possible cause of hyper-education.

Parents go to such lengths in part because Chi- 11 nese culture has always emphasized success, but also for a more pressing reason: Traditionally, children support their parents in old age. With only one child to carry the load, parents' fortunes are tied to their child's, and they push (and pamper) the little ones accordingly. "In China, the term for a one-child family is a 'risky family,'" says Baochang Gu, a demography professor at Beijing's Renmin University who advises the Chinese government on the one-child policy. "If something happened to that child, it would be a disaster. So from the parents' point of view, the spoiling is all necessary to protect them."

12   Since the policy's inception, the Chinese have worried that the extreme combination of discipline and indulgence would result in maladjusted kids, self-centered brats who can't take criticism and don't understand sharing. Asked if he wished he'd had siblings, one 22-year-old from Sichuan province replied, "Does this mean everything I have would have to be cut in half or shared? No, I don't want that."

13   Yet despite the stereotype, the research has revealed no evidence that only kids have more negative traits than their peers with siblings—in China or anywhere else. "The only way only children are reliably different from others is they score slightly higher in academic achievement," explains Toni Falbo, a University of Texas psychology professor who has gathered data on more than 4,000 Chinese only kids. Sure, some little emperors are bratty, but no more than children with siblings.

Clark questions the claim that the cause of the psychological situation of young Chinese is the one-child policy.

14   This isn't to say Chinese only kids are pictures of mental health—it's just that their psychological issues stem not from a lack of siblings but from the harsh academic competition and parental prodding that pervade their lives. Susan Newman, a New Jersey psychologist and only-child expert, says the notion that little emperors are bossy, self-obsessed little brats is simply part of the greater myth of only kids as damaged goods. "Pinning their problems on having no siblings is really making them a scapegoat," she says. Being an only child is not the problem.

15   Chinese parents bemoan their only child's desire for instant gratification, excessive consumption, and a life free of hardship, but such complaints are just proof that the policy worked: The children are like little Americans. "These kids have the same dreams as all middle-class kids: to go to college, to get white-collar jobs, to own their own home, to have Nikes

Here Clark uses comparison, likening the Chinese to "little Americans."

and name brands," says Fong. "They expect things that are normal in developed countries, but by China's standards, are unheard of."

Another effect of hypereducation: a rise in suicide rates.

Yu Zeng remembers hearing of the first suicide at 16 his school in 2005, when he was a junior at Sichuan University. By the next year, three more of his class-mates had leapt to their deaths from campus build-ings, and Zeng noticed a wave of news stories about suicides—all of them for a similar, perplexing reason. "It was after they got a bad grade on a test," Zeng says. "They think to die is better than to have that bad mark."

In the pressurized world of Chinese academics, 17 any setback can seem fatal. Last January, for example, one 17–year–old Beijing girl tried to kill herself after learning that a paperwork snafu might prevent her from registering for the *gao kao*. Suicide has become China's fifth most common cause of death over-all, with young urban intellectuals at highest risk. A study by the Society Survey Institute of China con-cluded that over 25 percent of university students have had suicidal thoughts, compared to 6 percent in the United States.

The number of Chinese college graduates per 18 year has nearly tripled in the last half–decade—from 1.5 million in 2002 to 4.1 million in 2007—which means more than 2 million grads a year end up with expensive diplomas, but no job. With so few top positions available and so many seekers, urban only children must study constantly just to have a shot. Out of Yanming Lin's five hours of schoolwork per night, four hours went to "voluntary" homework designed to boost test scores. "That one grade be-comes the only standard to justify you as a person," says Zeng. "If you have a good personality or maybe you're good in math but not Chinese, all of that is your downfall, because it's all about your grade."

The extra homework is not required by the 19 teacher, explains Lin. "But all the other students do the extra homework, so if you do not do it you will lag behind." At one top Beijing kindergarten, stu-dents must know pi to 100 digits by age 3.

Many young only children opt for escape from 20 reality through online gaming worlds. Every day, the nation's 113,000 Internet cafes teem with twitchy, solitary players—high school and university students, dropouts, and unemployed graduates—an alarming number of whom remain in place for days without food or sleep. Official estimates put the number of Chinese Internet addicts at over 2 million, and the government considers it such a serious threat that it deploys volunteer groups to prowl the streets and prevent teens from entering Internet cafes.

21   The mostly male youth who turn to virtual realms find there a place to realize ambitions that are frustrated in real life, says Kimberly Young, a psychologist and Internet addiction expert who has advised Chinese therapists. "With the click of a button, they go from a 19-year-old with no social life to a great warrior in World of Warcraft," Young says. "Why bother doing things in the real world when they can be in this game and be fulfilled?" Burnt-out and overtaxed, even kids who did well on the *gao kao* turn into virtual dropouts, choosing the respite of computer games over the university spots they worked so hard to win. Without a parent to push them, many stop going to class. "In Chinese universities, so many just give up," says Howe, a college student from Chengdu.

> Note how Clark uses this topic sentence to introduce another effect of hypereducation.

22   Faced with bleak prospects, elite only children often don't know how to cope; they've been brought up to do only one thing: succeed. Indeed, in a 2007 survey on stress in young people by the Chinese Internet portal Sina.com, most respondents—56 percent—blamed their misery on the gap between China's developing-world reality and their own high expectations. "They have trouble adjusting to the idea that they're going to be working-class," says Fong.

23   For the frustrated, depressed, and anxious Chinese kids buckling under the constant pressure—the news agency Xinhua estimates there are 30 million Chinese under 17 with significant mental-health problems—finding someone to talk to can be tough. Taught to strive and achieve from an early age, they've never had the time for heart-to-heart chats. "It's not like American universities where you have many friends," says Yu Zeng. "At Chinese universities, you compete for limited resources and everyone is concerned about themselves. And if you wanted to talk

to your parents, they wouldn't understand. When they were your age, they were reading Mao's little red book." Plus, the conversation would be strained even if you did find a sympathetic ear. "In the 20th century, the term 'depression' didn't even exist in China," Toni Falbo says. "It couldn't be talked about because there was no vocabulary for it yet."

Nor is professional help readily available. When 24 Mao cracked down on intellectuals during the Cultural Revolution, he decimated the nation's already thin psychological establishment. "Back then, every mental problem was seen as anti–socialist," says Kai-ping Peng, a University of California, Berkeley, professor who was among the first generation of Chinese psychologists to receive formal clinical training, in the late 1970s. "If you were depressed, they thought you were politically impure and sent you to a labor camp." For decades, Chinese psychiatrists dealt exclusively in pills and electroshock, and until recently, China had just a handful of university psychology programs—which is why Peng believes there are only about 2,000 qualified therapists at work there today for a population of 1.3 billion.

Clark discusses how Chinese universities are trying to address the negative effects of hypereducation.

But as universities work to churn out qualified 25 psychologists and as teens and twenty–somethings realize they need more help with their unrealistic expectations than with their grades, Peng grows optimistic. "People in China have more knowledge about mental health today," he says. "Now there are books and popular magazines about it, and the training infrastructure gets better all the time." Cities are also experimenting with crisis hotlines. China's inaugural suicide–prevention line debuted in 2003; it received more than 220,000 calls over its first two years.

Meanwhile, Chinese officials are taking steps to 26 ease the pressure on young students. Schools no longer publicly announce each student's exam scores and class rank, for one, and the government is also asking parents to let their precious little emperors actually *play* every once in a while.

Besides, all of that studying can only take you 27 so far. "On your résumé, you can't put, '1988 to 2001: studied 10 hours every day,'" laughs Howe, the Chengdu student. "You have to actually do stuff."

Reading Closely

1. What is the purpose of this essay?

2. **With a classmate,** identify the primary, contributory, immediate, and remote causes of hypereducation, as well as its primary, secondary, immediate, and remote effects.

3. Create an outline of the essay, showing how Clark progresses from beginning to middle to end. What organizational strategy does he use?

4. What kind of research did Clark conduct to compose this essay? Identify each source he consulted (books and interview subjects), and consider why he chose these sources. How does this research contribute to the effectiveness of the essay?

5. Review the photograph on page 488. What details does it offer about Chinese education that the essay does not?

Considering Larger Issues

1. Why was this essay published in *Psychology Today*? Who is the audience for this publication? Why would this audience be interested in this topic?

2. Given your answer to question 1, what might be the audience's possible response to this cause–and–effect analysis?

3. COMBINING METHODS. As the annotations indicate, Clark supplements his cause–and–effect analysis with *exemplification, narration,* and *comparison and contrast.* How do these methods develop his purpose?

Thinking about Language

1. Using the context of the essay or your dictionary, define the following words and phrases. Be prepared to share your answers with the rest of the class.

doting (1)	scapegoat (14)	teem (20)
glutted (4)	bemoan (15)	decimated (24)
vanguard (7)	snafu (17)	churn (25)
demography (11)	pi (19)	infrastructure (25)
prodding (14)		

2. Considering Clark's audience, identify the terms in the essay that speak directly to their concerns.

Writing Your Own Essays Using Cause-and-Effect Analysis

1. In his essay, Clark identifies a number of causes for the hypereducation of Chinese youth. Now consider the causes of your own educational path. What caused you to make the decisions you did? Why did you decide to

attend a particular high school or college? Why did you choose your major or the classes you are now taking? Compose a three- to four-page essay in which you identify and describe the causes of your education. Think specifically about the primary and contributory as well as immediate and remote causes. Refer to "Checking Over the Use of Cause–and–Effect Analysis" on pages 483–84 as you draft and revise.

2. Identify a positive or negative educational experience that you've had. What were the effects of this experience? How did it change your educational path, your attitudes toward a particular subject, or your interests in a specific issue? Compose a three- to four-page essay in which you identify and analyze the effects of this educational experience. Think specifically about the primary and contributory as well as immediate and remote effects. As you draft and revise, refer to "Checking Over the Use of Cause–and–Effect Analysis" on pages 483–84.

JACK McCALLUM
Steroids in America: The Real Dope

Jack McCallum, a graduate of Muhlenberg College, joined the *Sports Illustrated* staff in 1981. While basketball is his primary writerly interest, he's also written on topics such as game fixing, dogfighting, and gambling. McCallum is the author of *Seven Seconds or Less: My Season on the Bench with the Runnin' and Gunnin' Phoenix Suns* (2006) and the coauthor (with Jon Wertheim) of a pro basketball novel called *Foul Lines* (2006). In this essay, published in the March 2008 issue of *Sports Illustrated*, McCallum examines the causes of steroid use among average Americans.

> **Preview**   What do you know about steroid use among average Americans? What do you think causes it?

Athletes who take performance-improving drugs make all the headlines. But the culture of personal physical enhancement has pushed use of steroids and HGH everywhere — from Hollywood to the music industry to your next-door neighbor who doesn't want to grow old. Don't blame only the jocks.

We are a juiced nation.   1

We are a nation on dope.   2

We are a nation looking for enhancement, a way to age gracefully,   3 perform better and longer, and, at the outer edge, vanquish what was once considered that alltime undefeated opponent known as aging. We do that by Botoxing our wrinkles, lifting our faces, reconstructing our noses, despidering our veins, tucking our tummies, augmenting our breasts and taking a little pill to make sure we're ready when, you know, the right time presents itself. We also do it by injecting human growth hormone (HGH) and testosterone, America's new golden pharmaceutical couple.

Numbers are hard to come by because much of the flow of these   4 drugs is illegal, but Dr. Mark Gordon, one of 20,000 members of the American Academy of Anti-Aging Medicine, cites a 2004 study that found that more than $1 billion was spent annually on legal HGH. "And it's safe to assume it's gone up in the last four years," Gordon says. The Mayo Clinic reports that 2.4 million testosterone prescriptions were filled by U.S. pharmacies in 2004, more than twice the number filled in 2000. Mayo also estimates that three million people in the U.S. use anabolic steroids, the synthetic versions of testosterone that are illegal when they are used for nonmedical reasons such as building an impressive physique and increasing endurance for training. John Romano, senior editor at *Muscular Development*, the top seller among the dozens of magazines that cover powerlifting and bodybuilding, estimates that 15 million Americans use performance-enhancing drugs (PEDs).

    Yet to judge by the blanket coverage given the bizarre Roger Clemens– 5
Brian McNamee pas de deux,* Congress's incessant (and in many cases
politically motivated) effort to ferret out drug cheats among athletes; the
table–pounding vows of various politicians to *get drugs out of sports!*; and
the never–ending BALCO–Barry saga,* one might conclude that PEDs
are the exclusive province of professional athletes. When George Bush
mentioned steroids in his January 2004 State of the Union speech, he
set the societal agenda. "The use of performance–enhancing drugs like
steroids in baseball, football and other sports is dangerous," thundered
the President. "It sends the wrong message that there are shortcuts to
accomplishment and that performance is more important than character. So tonight I call on team owners, union representatives, coaches
and players to take the lead, to send the right signal, to get tough and
to get rid of steroids now." Massive applause followed.
    O.K., performance–enhancing drugs . . . bad. Athletes who use them . . . 6
bad. Influencing kids to use them . . . bad. On to the next problem.
    That politicians have locked in on sports is understandable at one 7
level (beyond the obvious fact that a nationally televised Clemens hearing will draw more attention than, say, an antitrust debate on C–Span).
Athletic achievement is made to be measured and is available for instant
analysis when performances improve, even incrementally. Athletes
stand on pedestals, and pedestals are made to be toppled. A kind of
moral ceiling hangs over sports, as degraded as that ceiling might've become in the 3,000 years since a bunch of Greeks began throwing javelins
and racing chariots. *Play by the rules. Play fair. Level playing field.*
    But what's happened is that the subject of PEDs has been conveniently 8
compressed and poured into a small airtight bottle at which politicians
and society at large can throw stones. We did roughly the same thing with
cocaine in the '80s, when you might've thought that baseball players and
an unfortunate 22–year–old named Len Bias were the only ones snorting
the drug, along with a godless Hollywood elite, of course.
    The truth is, sports do not define the culture— they reflect it. So- 9
ciety's image of the ideal body is shaped largely by forces outside the

---

    * **Roger Clemens–Brian McNamee pas de deux:** During a congressional in-
vestigation of drug use by professional baseball players, seven–time Cy Young
Award–winner Roger Clemens was accused by his trainer, Brian McNamee, of using steroids. In testimony before the House Committee on Oversight and Government Reform
in 2008, the two offered competing stories, and there was no resolution as to the truth of
the matter.
    * **BALCO–Barry saga:** Seven–time MVP of the National Baseball League, Barry
Bonds has been involved in the Bay Area Laboratory Co–Operative (BALCO) scandal
since 2003. In 2000, his trainer, Greg Anderson, who worked at BALCO, was charged
with supplying steroids to athletes and indicted by a federal grand jury. Bonds testified
before the grand jury, pleading innocence, but was indicted on counts of obstruction of
justice and perjury in 2007.

chalked lines. And the belief that life can be improved, even extended, by drugs comes not from sports but from the burgeoning field known as antiaging medicine.

The music industry, hip-hop in particular, has glamorized the bad 10 and buff body, which many kids embrace as a model. We didn't need the well-publicized probe into HGH and steroid prescriptions allegedly sent by an Orlando pharmacy to rappers to notice that Timbaland and 50 Cent are among the many rappers who are as powerfully muscled as blocking backs. Or as NBA superstars. "In the rap business," says one well-placed music-industry source, "guys look at an athlete like LeBron James, who's built like a tank, and they say, 'I want to look like LeBron.'" And that's how the record companies want them to look. The source confirms that steroid and HGH use "is absolutely happening in the [rap] industry" and puts the percentage of users—an educated guess, he admits—at "about one third." . . .

PED use in the hip-hop world is as much about preparing for the 11 job as simply trying to look good. The beast is a ripped physique, one that plays well in music videos, and the beast must be fed. The source describes one artist whom MTV would not feature because he was over-weight. He was told to get in the gym. And, if he's like many other art-ists, he'll get in the gym, but he'll also get on the juice. It's a cycle of narcissistic necessity.

Perhaps the most prominent name in the Orlando investigation 12 was that of Mary J. Blige, an eight-time Grammy winner. Through a spokesman, Blige has denied steroid or HGH use. She did sing backup on a new Jay-Z song, *You're Welcome*, in which he addresses PEDs. Sort of. ("You would think I was on 'roids, I been hittin' so long, and I'm a big-headed boy/Nah we ain't on HGH, though I might pick up some weight when I'm runnin' through your state.") The 37-year-old Blige has the chiseled look that began taking over music back in the '80s. That's when rockers started showing up in tight-fitting T-shirts with buff bodies and arms of steel, and the Sweet Baby James paradigm, soulful and skinny, was pretty much chased off the stage.

Few segments of society depend as heavily on physical appearance as 13 Hollywood, and it turns out that Sylvester Stallone, who may one day give us *Rambo: The Assisted-Living Years*, needed more than one-handed pushups and raw eggs at dawn to stay cut. Last May in Australia the 61-year-old Stallone paid $10,600 to settle a charge of criminal drug possession after he was found to have 48 vials of HGH and several vials of testosterone. Stallone has since acknowledged that he takes HGH and testosterone regularly, and legally. "Everyone over 40 years old would be wise to investigate it [HGH and testosterone use] because it increases the quality of your life," Stallone told *Time* last month.

Adds a prominent Hollywood plastic surgeon, who requested ano- 14 nymity because he has many clients in the industry, "If you're an actor

Sylvester Stallone has acknowledged regular legal use of human growth hormone and testosterone.

in Hollywood and you're over 40, you are doing HGH. Period. Why wouldn't you? It makes your skin look better, your hair, your finger-nails, everything."

Chuck Zito—former Hells Angel, former bodyguard to the stars, 15 former Hollywood stuntman and beefcake extra, former sinister pres-ence on HBO's *Oz*—was an enthusiastic steroid and HGH user for three years during his acting days earlier this decade. "It's just something everybody did," says Zito, "and they're still doing it. It's ridiculous that we only talk about it in sports. You think these actors who suddenly get big for a movie, then go back to normal get like that by *accident*? You put 30 pounds of muscle on and you expect everybody to believe that just happened?"

While we affect that same "I'm shocked, *shocked*" response to steroid 16 and HGH use that Captain Renault did to reports of gambling in *Casa-blanca*, steroids are all over the culture. *Bigger, Stronger, Faster*, a docu-mentary about steroid use, was well received at this year's Sundance Film Festival. You might suspect that a football player on NBC's *Friday Night Lights* would dip into the steroid pool— Smash, the star running back, turned to them after a bad game in a 2006 episode— but if you watched the Lifetime movie *Love Thy Neighbor*, you also saw a young soccer-playing girl accused of using Winstrol, a popular anabolic ste-roid. In 1994 Ben Affleck starred in a made-for-TV movie called *A Body to Die For: The Aaron Henry Story.* After taking PEDs in an effort to bulk up and make his high school football team, Affleck/Aaron suffers a bad case of 'roid rage, losing his hair and developing acne. Willem Dafoe's Norman Osborn in the *Spider-Man* movies brought 'roid rage to a new level when he transmogrified into the Green Goblin. Search for *steroids* and *HGH* on the Internet Movie Database website and dozens of movies and TV episodes pop up.

It's uncertain whether hip–hop artists will find the irony amus-   17 ing, but PEDs seem to be a part of life among the police as well. In a 2007 probe the names of 27 New York City officers and at least two dozen from the Jersey City force were found among those who pur- chased HGH or steroids. (None has been charged.) The prosecutor's office in Mercer County, New Jersey, is investigating a group of officers, mostly from Trenton, who are accused of illegally buying HGH. The investiga- tion prompted the Trenton department to draft a policy to follow when it suspects an officer of using PEDs.

Gene Sanders, a police psychologist in Spokane, has estimated   18 that 25% of officers in urban settings take steroids, many as a defense against street criminals. "How do I deal with people who are in better shape than me and want to kill me?" Sanders told ABC News as a way of explaining steroid use by the thin blue line.*

Steroids may also be a major part of prison culture. And not just on   19 one side of the bars. In a story that would be humorous if it weren't so ugly, Florida's then secretary of prisons, over a two–year period beginning in 2006, fired 90 people, most of them guards, for infractions that included the importation and sale of steroids for the primary purpose of beefing up for interdepartmental softball games. There were also postgame orgies. All in all, it sounds like the makings of a Cinemax movie.

More than softball is at stake in an ongoing civil case against Black-   20 water, the controversial security firm that supplies private guards to pro- tect U.S. officials in Iraq. A lawsuit filed in November alleges that one quarter of Blackwater's guards take steroids and that the use of such "judgment–altering substances" was a factor in at least two incidents in which Iraqi civilians were killed. "Not to belittle the importance of ste- roid abuse in sports," says Susan Burke, the lead counsel for family mem- bers of civilians who were killed, "but this is an instance in which it may have led to death. It's obvious that when people have guns and their jobs involve being armed, it's critical to ensure that they are not on steroids."

---

*   **the thin blue line:** an expression police officers use to symbolize their work, implying that their (typically blue) uniforms preserve a fragile barrier between good and evil or order and chaos. In 2007, police officer David Johnson published *Falling off the Thin Blue Line*, in which he recounts how his use of steroids developed into an underground (and illegal) business in which he helped to supply other users with steroids, syringes, and needles.

Blackwater says that steroids are not tolerated among its personnel. Meanwhile, a 2007 U.S. military police raid of the living quarters of a similar firm in Iraq, Crescent Security Group, turned up steroids.

At the heart of the incessant hunt for PEDs in sports is the message 21 that the President was conveying in his State of the Union speech: Kids who hear about pro athletes using performance–enhancing drugs will use them too. It is always about *our nation's youth*, as if that were one heterogeneous group that marches in lockstep, buying its steroids and its Will Ferrell movie tickets in bulk.

The assumption that kids blindly emulate their sports stars is not 22 just simplistic, it's also wrong. In a poll of teenagers commissioned by SI last month, 99% of the respondents said they would not use steroids just because a pro athlete does. Other studies have consistently shown that the majority of kids who use PEDs do so to enhance their looks, not to bowl over a free safety at the goal line or get something extra on their fastball.

If there is some knuckle–dragging musclehead out there who advo- 23 cates unlimited PED use by minors, he has not yet surfaced. Zito is an unapologetic past user — "There's no difference between someone taking a steroid and someone having their face lifted" — but draws the line with teenagers. "Your body is still growing," he says, "and you should let it grow without drugs." Dan Duchaine was an anabolic–steroid pioneer who in 1982 wrote the *Underground Steroid Handbook*, a tract that offered a detailed breakdown of every PED known at the time as well as a guide on how to use the drugs. In the book's second edition he wrote, "I don't think children (teenagers included) should take steroids because all but one or two of the drugs can stop bone growth prematurely." *Muscular Development*'s Romano, who says that he has "not one single regret" from a steroid–loaded past and would entertain the notion of adding anabolic steroids to his HGH and testosterone regimen, says he would not consider giving his eight–year–old son HGH or steroids until the boy has reached adulthood.

That, of course, doesn't mean large numbers of kids aren't using 24 them, though it's difficult to determine how many. In the SI poll, 0.3% admitted taking steroids, and 0.3% said they took HGH. But Dr. Charles Yesalis, a retired Penn State professor and a recognized authority on steroids, estimates that "at least half a million and probably closer to three quarters of a million children in this country have used these drugs in their lifetime." Adds Yesalis, "The teens I've talked to say [steroids and HGH] are as easy to get as marijuana." The Mayo Clinic has published information that one tenth of U.S. steroid users are teenagers, which by its estimate would put the figure at 300,000.

A major concern about kids and PEDs is the manner in which the 25 youngsters procure the drugs. "Because steroids and growth hormone have been pushed underground," says Romano, "kids are buying them off the Internet. Or from their older brother, or the guy at the gym. And the stuff they're getting is the imported junk from Mexico, the rejected veterinary crap. If they were using the best of the best stuff, that would be bad enough, but it's worse because they're using the bad stuff." Harrison G. Pope Jr., a professor of psychiatry at Harvard Medical School, an avid weightlifter and a coauthor of *The Adonis Complex: The Secret Crisis of Male Body Obsession*, doesn't believe that steroid use among teenagers is epidemic. But he agrees that the street purchase of PEDs is a major problem, ascribing it to what he calls "the most secret culture of any drug."

Indeed, steroids evolved through clandestine experimentation in dark gyms by men who, even as they displayed their freakish musculature, rarely talked publicly about how they got that way. Zito still kicks himself for having lied on the *Howard Stern Show* several years ago when asked if he was juicing. "I never lie to my friends," he says, "but I lied that day. When you were asked about steroids back then, you lied." 26

Predictably, when athletes in mainstream sports discovered PEDs, they too kept the secrets within the confines of the locker room, if not to themselves. Workout buddies sometimes exchanged stories — what *did* Roger tell Andy? — but often it didn't go any further than that. Steroid use was strictly "Don't ask, don't tell," even when averaged-sized players began to mysteriously inflate. Athletes had a lot more to lose than Zito, and their secrets got out only when publicity hounds like Jose Canseco started singing or subpoenas started flying. Even within the bodybuilding industry, outspoken PED proponents like Romano are rare. He says that the physician who prescribes his testosterone and growth hormone has made him swear that he will never utter his name in an interview, even though the prescriptions are dispensed lawfully. 27

With secrecy comes hypocrisy, and the hypocrisy surrounding PEDs is mind-boggling. Take the rappers, for whom admitting acts of lawlessness, such as PED use, would seem to be part of the drill. But Timbaland trumpets the bodybuilding and weightlifting regimen that turned him from a 300-pound blubber factory into a buff bodybuilder. The most intriguing part of 50 Cent's story is his transformation from 12-year-old Queens drug dealer Curtis James Jackson III to a 32-year-old workout freak. He even has his own flavor of Vitamin Water, and last year Coca-Cola bought the company that manufactures his drink for $4.1 billion. How would all that jibe with performance-enhancing drugs? "You don't want to be a faker," says the industry source. "That's the game." 28

Or take California governor Arnold Schwarzenegger, who despite having used steroids to help him become a seven-time winner of the Mr. Olympia title, bodybuilding's top prize, was named by George H. W. Bush in 1990 to head the President's Council on Physical Fitness and Sports. By all accounts Schwarzenegger (who says he stopped using steroids well before it became illegal to sell or possess them without a prescription, in '90) worked tirelessly and brought unprecedented attention to the 29

California Governor Arnold Schwarzenegger congratulates a winner at the Arnold Sports Festival.

council, decrying steroid use all the while. But there was the overmuscled Ah–nold model for all to see. The governor continues to say that PEDs have no place in sport, yet tacitly endorses their use with his annual Arnold Sports Festival, a carnival of muscle porn in Columbus, Ohio, that includes bodybuilding contests and an expo featuring supplements pushed by cartoonishly sculpted hulks. "Even though performance-enhancing drugs have been part of his life," said one exhibitor at last week's festival who requested anonymity, "what can Arnold do? He has to say he's against them."

To a large degree, that describes the position of many Americans, 30 certainly those in Congress and within the sports establishment: They have to say that they're against performance enhancers; they have to bang the gavel and declare, as Delaware senator Joe Biden did in 2004 during a hearing on drugs in sports, "There is something simply un-American about [using PEDs]!"

But it's not un–American. It's *entirely* American, that search for an 31 edge, that effort to be all you can be, that willingness to push the envelope. That's what Andy Pettitte was doing when he took HGH. That's what Debbie Clemens was doing when she took HGH. That's what male collegiate cheerleaders are doing when they bulk up on anabolic steroids so they can lift more weight, or more female cheerleaders, according to author Kate Torgovnick in her new book, *Cheer!* That's what a rapper is doing when he receives a package of PEDs at his hotel. That's what Schwarzenegger was doing when he loaded himself with steroids years ago. That's what Kevin and Peggy Hart are doing in the privacy of their bedroom with their HGH and their "test," now as familiar a morning ritual as tea and toast.

We are entering a brave new world. A serious academic and research 32 war rages between those who say that HGH and testosterone are natural substances that need to be replenished when the body's supply runs low and those who proclaim such a philosophy as quackery. "There are very basic questions we're trying to get answers to," says Gary Gaffney, associate professor of psychiatry at the University of Iowa's College of Medicine. He is against doctors prescribing HGH and testosterone for anti-aging reasons, and even dislikes the term. "Is aging a disease? Should it be treated?" Gaffney believes there hasn't been nearly enough testing on the potential long-term effects of HGH- and testosterone-replacement therapies. And his message is being heard. "If you could prove to me that HGH is not harmful," says Dallas Mavericks owner Mark Cuban, "I'd be the first in line to get some. But I don't know that."

Dr. Gordon, who in a book promoted the phrase "interventional 33 endocrinology," largely because he recognizes that antiaging raises so many eyebrows, comes from the opposite perspective. "Isn't my dispensing medication to lower blood pressure an antiaging [effort]?" Gordon says. "Otherwise, you'll die, and I call that true antiaging. It's the same thing with testosterone and HGH."

Crucial medical questions are being debated by serious medical 34 people, yet we seem determined to hear them only in the limited context of Roger Clemens's injected buttocks. Pro sports shouldn't stand apart from discussions about performance-enhancing drugs, but they shouldn't frame them either. Who is George Mitchell, a former politician who conducted baseball's steroid investigation, to be asking for legislation to make HGH a controlled substance on par with anabolic steroids, as he did recently? Has he been spending secret time in a research lab all these years? We need to realize that someday, perhaps not far down the road, the names of Clemens, Bonds, Mitchell and Rep. Henry Waxman will be mere footnotes in a story that goes far beyond baseball clubhouses and congressional hearing rooms.

Reading Closely

1. What is the thesis of McCallum's essay? Identify the place in the essay where he states this thesis.

2. Review the introductory sentences, thinking specifically about McCallum's use of "we." Why does he begin the essay in this way? What is the effect on the reader?

3. Review the research McCallum conducted to compose this essay. What sources does he use? How do these sources support the thesis and purpose of the essay?

4. Review the photographs on pages 498 and 502. How do these images contribute to (or detract from) the causal argument McCallum is making in the essay?

Considering Larger Issues

1. What are the causes of steroid use, according to McCallum? How does he support his claims?

2. **Working with a classmate,** consider how McCallum's argument disrupts dominant understandings about the causes of steroid use in America. How, then, does his causal argument suggest changes to the ways the country should address steroid use?

3. What in this essay surprised or especially interested you? What did you learn?

4. In addition to identifying what may be surprising causes of steroid use, what other issues does McCallum raise in this essay?

5. COMBINING METHODS. Besides cause–and–effect analysis, what other rhetorical methods does McCallum use? How do these methods contribute to the purpose of the essay?

Thinking about Language

1. Using the context of the essay or your dictionary, define the following words and phrases. Be prepared to share your answers with the rest of the class.

vanquish (3)	physique (11)	procure (25)
augmenting (3)	narcissistic (11)	clandestine (26)
anabolic (4)	paradigm (12)	musculature (26)
synthetic (4)	transmogrified (16)	subpoenas (27)
pas de deux (5)	irony (17)	hypocrisy (28)
ferret (5)	alleges (20)	tacitly (29)
incrementally (7)	incessant (21)	gavel (30)
burgeoning (9)	heterogeneous (21)	interventional
probe (10)	emulate (22)	endocrinology (33)

2. This essay was published in *Sports Illustrated* magazine. Identify passages in which McCallum chooses language that he assumes his sports–loving audience would know and understand.

Writing Your Own Essays Using Cause-and-Effect Analysis

1. McCallum argues that one of the causes of steroid use in America is obsession with the perfect body. Besides steroid use, what are other effects

of this obsession? Compose a three- to four-page essay that examines one of these effects. Like McCallum, you should conduct library research to support your claims. As you draft and revise, consult the guidelines for checking over your cause-and-effect analysis on pages 483–84.

2. McCallum counters the claim that professional sports are to blame for widespread steroid use among everyday Americans. Identify one professional athlete or team, and discuss how this person's or this team's behavior on and off the playing field positively or negatively affects everyday Americans. Be specific in your analysis, using detailed description, narration, and exemplification to support your claims. Consult the guidelines for checking over your cause-and-effect analysis on pages 483–84 as you draft and revise.

ROBYN SYLVES

Credit Card Debt among College Students: Just What Does It Cost?

Robyn Sylves wrote this essay while she was an undergraduate at Penn State University. She has since graduated with a major in English, a minor in sociology, an emphasis in publishing, and a certificate through the university's World Campus in "Writing Social Commentary." Sylves worked her way through college at her family's restaurant, the Boalsburg Steakhouse, where she started as a dishwasher and worked her way up to management. She plans to continue her education sometime in the future. In the meantime, she continues to work at the restaurant and is also a freelance writer.

> **Preview**   As a student, what do you see as the causes and effects of credit card debt? Be prepared to share your answers with the rest of the class.

College administrators like to say that alcohol is the number one vice 1 of their undergraduates. But in fact, an even bigger problem may be something that gets far less attention: credit card debt. Credit cards are dangled in front of undergraduates like free money, money that students do not actually have to earn or borrow or save. It's free — or at least that's how it seems. On their first trip to the campus bookstore, freshmen are bombarded by freebies — calling cards, water bottles, hats, the list goes on — that they can have "just for applying!" Representatives swarm the sidewalks with clipboards, applications, and sales pitches to provide new students with financial freedom. In all of the bustle, who really stops to read the fine print? Is it surprising to learn that credit card debt has led to health problems, conflicts with friends and family, long-term credit problems, academic failure, and in extreme cases, suicide?

Colleges and universities are like silent partners in the credit card 2 business. Many have multimillion-dollar deals with the credit card companies so that students can have their college logo embossed on their personal Visa or MasterCard. Does your school have a building adorned with the name of a credit card company, such as Penn State University's MBNA Career Center? It might: More than 700 colleges and universities have contracts with MBNA, the largest independent issuer of credit cards, under which they receive financial incentives in return for providing MBNA with information about students (Carlson). University officials are quick to preach about the sins of college that will haunt students for life, yet they say little about the damage that charging textbooks, late-night pizza, concert tickets, and spring break trips can do to a person's financial future.

Experts point to several factors for excessive credit card debt among 3 college students. High on the list is students' lack of financial literacy. The

credit card representatives on campus, the preapproved applications that arrive in the mail several times a week, and the incessant phone offers for credit cards tempt students into opening accounts before they really can understand what they are getting themselves into. The people marketing these cards depend on the fact that many students don't realize what an annual percentage rate is. Credit card companies count on applicants failing to read the fine print, which tells them how after an "introductory" period the interest rate on a given card can increase two to three times. The companies also don't want students to know that every year people send money (interest) to these companies that there is no need to send. That annual fee that credit card companies love to charge can be waived. I think that many people, students and nonstudents alike, might be surprised how often and easily it can disappear if people call the company to say they don't want to pay it.

Today's society, with its need for instant gratification, also pressures 4
young people to accumulate excessive credit card debt. No one wants to
wait in a world where the Internet and cell phones provide instant connection to anywhere. Even test scores arrive instantly: students can find
out their scores on the GRE (Graduate Record Examination) as soon as
they finish taking it. Why stand in line even when shopping? With a few
mouse clicks and a credit card, your purchase can arrive at your door as
soon as the next day. Like everyone else, students are more likely to buy
now and pay later than to save to afford purchases.

The third major contributor to high credit card debt among college 5
students, one that is more specific to students who say their cards are
"only for emergencies," is a student's overly broad definition of what constitutes an emergency—such as the need for that late-night pizza. Steve
Bucci, a debt adviser for Bankrate.com and president of Consumer Credit
Counseling Service of Southern New England, has a rule of thumb for
people like this: "If you can eat it, drink it, or wear it, then it's not an
emergency" (qtd. in Lazarony). We can assume that spring break packages and DVDs are also included in that list.

In fact, students today "are being socialized to perceive consumer 6
credit as a generational entitlement rather than an earned privilege," according to a statement prepared for a United States Senate committee
hearing in 2002 on financial literacy among college students. Caught between the rising costs of higher education and outside pressures from
peers, media, and marketing, students are turning to "plastic" money
more often and accruing higher amounts of personal debt. In 2002, Penn
State's *Daily Collegian* newspaper reported on a study that found that by
2001, more than three-fourths of all undergraduates had at least one
credit card, and almost a third of card holders had four or more cards.
"Nearly one in four students with credit debt owes more than $3,000, and
almost 10 percent owe $7,000 or more," the article noted (Charsar). Unfor-
tunately, it isn't as uncommon as one might think to find undergraduates
who have accumulated more than $20,000 in credit card debt. Fig. 1 illus-
trates the findings presented at the Senate committee hearing, using data
from a survey of students at George Mason University in April 2002.

When the U.S. financial services industry was deregulated in the early 7
1980s, credit card companies changed their attitude toward young people.
Selling college students on credit cards went from a risky business to a
marketing madhouse. In fact, teenagers are now the largest marketing
target for these companies, which recognize that teens and college students are the group with the largest disposable income. Full-time students
are nearly always guaranteed approval of their credit card applications
because companies know that students can turn to their parents or use
student loans to pay balances. The George Mason University study backs
up this belief, showing that many students are using student loans to pay
their credit card bills (see Fig. 2).

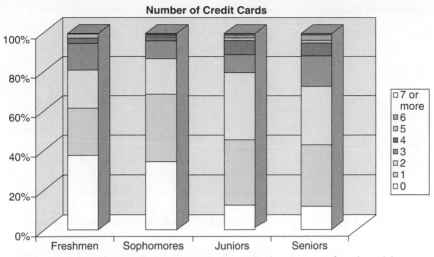

Fig. 1. As undergraduates obtain more credit cards, the amount of student debt climbs.

Source: United States, Cong., Senate, Committee on Banking, Housing and Urban Affairs; "Prepared Statement of Dr. Robert D. Manning"; Hearing on the Importance of Financial Literacy among College Students, 5 Sept. 2002; Web, 21 May 2004; table 1.

Today more than 20 percent of students open their credit card ac- 8 counts while still in high school, compared to a mere 11 percent in 1994. Data from the George Mason study shows a growing trend of young people opening credit card accounts at a younger age (see Fig. 3).

Just as the reasons behind debt vary, so do the penalties. Lucky stu- 9 dents might get a lecture and a strict budget enforced by parents. For others, the road is rougher. High debt may force them to cut back to part-time student status in order to have time for a job or even a second job. Of course, this drop in class time can translate into less financial aid, which means less money for rent, bills, and credit card payments. What can a student do? Take a semester off? Move home? Quit school altogether? Some students get into big trouble by sending each credit card company a few dollars "whenever," trying to pay—but not always succeeding in paying—the minimum monthly amount due on multiple cards. They think that once they graduate and get a good job, the money will come rolling in and their financial faults from student days will all be forgiven. It's not that simple. Instead of building their credit, they've turned something potentially positive into something as bad as, if not worse than, no credit at all—bad credit. When they reach this point, no bank will give them a loan to buy a car to get to school or work. They can't buy a house because no lending agency is going to give them a

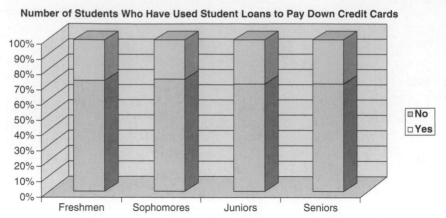

Fig. 2. Between 60 and 70 percent of college students have used student loans to help pay off their credit card debt.

Source: United States, Cong., Senate, Committee on Banking, Housing and Urban Affairs; "Prepared Statement of Dr. Robert D. Manning"; Hearing on the Importance of Financial Literacy among College Students, 5 Sept. 2002; Web, 21 May 2004; table 2.

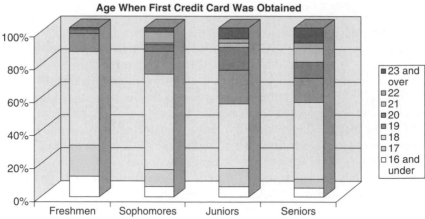

Fig. 3. As with cell phones, today many students get their first credit card while still in high school.

Source: United States, Cong., Senate, Committee on Banking, Housing and Urban Affairs; "Prepared Statement of Dr. Robert D. Manning"; Hearing on the Importance of Financial Literacy among College Students, 5 Sept. 2002; Web, 21 May 2004; table 3.

mortgage. They could even have trouble renting an apartment because many rental companies and most utilities run credit checks on potential customers. More than 800,000 Americans file for bankruptcy annually, and a growing number of the people who are filing are under the age of 25. Filing for bankruptcy can remain on your credit report for as long as 10 years, making it harder to build good credit as an adult.

So how does all this happen? How does it get to this point? It's as easy to run into problems with credit cards as it is to use them. Not understanding penalties, fees, and interest rates can ruin people's credit just as fast as if they stopped paying their bills altogether. By not being responsible with credit, as well as not being informed and educated on the subject, young adults make mistakes that they will carry with them for years to come.

Many consumer credit experts have suggested that parents and educators should teach teens about safe credit just as they teach them about safe sex and safe driving. Knowing what an APR (annual percentage rate) is and what it means sounds like kid stuff, but that's exactly what it has to be. In an attempt to open students' eyes, Bankrate.com suggests cardholders get the answers to these simple questions before even considering applying for a credit card:

- Is there an introductory rate, what is it, and how long does it last?
- After that, what will my rate be?
- Is there an application fee?
- Are there processing fees?
- Is there an annual fee?
- Is there a late fee?
- Is there an over-the-limit fee?
- Are there any other fees, like account termination fees or balance transfer fees?
- When and how can a variable rate be changed?
- When and how can a fixed rate be changed?
- What is the grace period before interest is applied?
- How will you inform me of any changes in my contract?
- Will the company inform me if I am about to go over my limit?
- If I go over my limit, what happens?
- What is the company policy if I have trouble paying my bill? ("Key Questions")

Many books and other resources are available to help students become financially aware, but by asking these questions and reviewing applications with parents, students increase their chances for a successful financial future. A study of Penn State's Erie campus that was cited in the 2002 Senate committee hearing showed that students who use credit cards cosigned or paid for by parents spend much less money than those who open and manage credit accounts on their own.

Whether or not parents, teachers, legislators, or even the credit card 13 companies make it a point to educate young people about using credit wisely, the choice to open an account is ultimately the student's. With the growing numbers of young adults holding credit cards and the increasing levels of debt among those under 25, the problem of student credit card debt is not one that will disappear overnight. An undergraduate quoted in statement given at the Senate committee hearing offered an insider's point of view:

> I believe credit card use by students is alarming. How do students who generally don't work pay back credit card bills . . . [?] I think that there should be restrictions and legislation on credit card solicitations on college campus[es]—college administrators, student government council[,] et cetera, have a responsibility to protect and educate students on the evils of credit card companies seeking student sign-ups. Also, I think credit card knowledge and awareness should be part of the College 101/1st-year orientation class to help prevent this epidemic sweeping across college campuses. My mom was once a bank loan lender and she noted to me the sadness of the number of people who were denied loans because of poor credit ratings established as young college students.

No matter how students learn about building and maintaining 14 healthy credit, these may be among the more important lessons they learn, ones that can be useful in other aspects of life as well as beneficial to their credit report. Students must always read the fine print to know what they're getting into. They should learn as much as they can about the rules related to the credit cards they use. They need to be assertive in asking questions and doing research. Above all, students should think hard about how and when they use their credit. College is a place where young people should be able to make some mistakes, but accruing bad credit is a mistake that can and should be avoided at all costs. Much of what students learn in college will stick with them for life. What they learn about building credit—good or bad—will also stick with them for life.

WORKS CITED

Carlson, Michael. "Campus Rules Tightening." *New Mexico Daily Lobo.* U of New Mexico, 28 Aug. 2003. Pt. 1 of a series, Credit Card Companies Target Students. Web. 17 May 2004.

Charsar, Nicole. "Student Credit Card Debt Has Increased, Study Says." *Daily Collegian.* Penn State U, 31 Oct. 2002. Web. 20 May 2004.

"Key Questions to Ask before You Sign Up." *Bankrate.com.* Bankrate, Inc., 19 Mar. 2003. Web. 16 May 2004.

Lazarony, Lucy. "College Students: Prepare for Credit Card Deluge." *Bankrate.com.* Bankrate, Inc., 27 Aug. 1999. Web. 17 May 2004.

United States. Cong. Senate. Committee on Banking, Housing and Urban Affairs. "Prepared Statement of Dr. Robert D. Manning." Hearing on the Importance of Financial Literacy among College Students. 5 Sept. 2002. Web. 21 May 2004.

Reading Closely

1. **Working with one or two classmates,** map out the various causes of student credit card debt: primary, contributory, immediate, and remote. Do any of the causes overlap? Which ones? Which causes stand alone? Prepare a group response that you can share with the rest of the class.

2. Now map out the effects of student credit card debt: primary, secondary, immediate, and remote. Answer the same set of follow-up questions that you answered in question 1, again preparing a group response for the class.

3. What specific information did you gain from each of the bar graphs? How did that information enhance or further explain the information in the essay?

4. The photograph on page 507 shows a man making an online purchase. What are some of the reasons people make online purchases? What is the primary reason? What are the primary and secondary effects of on-line purchasing?

Considering Larger Issues

1. What is Sylves's purpose in writing this essay? Who is her audience? How do purpose and audience intersect in this essay?

2. After reading Sylves's essay, where do you think blame for student credit card debt should be assigned? Why? Be prepared to share your response with the rest of the class.

3. Judging from your own experience and that of your friends, in what ways do students follow or resist their parents' spending patterns? How do these patterns affect credit card debt for both parents and students?

4. This essay was written in 2004. Judging from your own experience and your knowledge of other college students, has the credit card situation at colleges changed in the intervening years? Or has it remained essentially the same? What differences or similarities do you see when you compare the current situation at your school (or among students you know, wherever they attend college) with Sylves's analysis? If you see significant differences, what do you see as their causes?

5. COMBINING METHODS. Mark the places where Sylves uses *exemplification* to support her cause-and-effect analysis. Do you think she provides enough

examples to support her points? **Working with one or two class-mates,** decide if there are any places where adding examples would have strengthened her essay, and report your findings to the class.

Thinking about Language

1. Using the context of the essay or a dictionary, define the following words and phrases. Be prepared to share your answers with the rest of the class.

incentives (2)	consumer credit (6)	deregulated (7)

preapproved appli-
    cations (3)
	generational enti-
	    tlement (6)
		minimum (9)
		APR (11)

incessant (3)	accruing (6)	cosigned (12)
instant gratification (4)		

2. Define "financial literacy," using information from Sylves's essay, your own experience, and any research you care to do. Be prepared to share your definition with the rest of the class.

Writing Your Own Essays Using Cause-and-Effect Analysis

1. Credit card debt is a big problem, and not just on college campuses or for young people. Draft a three- to four-page essay in which you explore the causes and effects of someone's credit card or other financial decisions, good or bad. The person can be either you or someone you know well. Just be sure that you can supply enough detail to write an analysis that sets out clear causes and effects and has a clear purpose (informative, entertaining, speculative, or argumentative). Be sure to refer to the guidelines for checking over a cause–and–effect analysis on pages 483–84.

2. The author of this essay opens with examples of dire effects: "health problems, conflicts with friends and family, long–term credit problems, academic failure, and in extreme cases, . . . suicide." Draft a three- to four-page essay in which you chart either the dire effects of a bad set of decisions or actions or the positive effects (the kind that too often go unnoticed) of good decisions. You can write about either yourself or someone else, as long as your essay is detailed, purposeful (informative, entertaining, speculative, or argumentative), and aimed at a specific audience. Refer to the guidelines for checking over a cause–and–effect analysis on pages 483–84.

MALCOLM GLADWELL
The 10,000-Hour Rule

Born in England in 1963 and raised in Canada, Malcolm Gladwell graduated from the University of Toronto with a degree in history. From 1987 to 1999, he worked as a reporter for the *Washington Post*, covering business- and science-related topics. In 1996, he became a staff writer for the *New Yorker* magazine, where he won a National Magazine Award in 1999 for his profile of Ron Popeil, an American inventor and marketing personality. In addition to numerous magazine articles, Gladwell has published three books, all of which were best-sellers: *The Tipping Point: How Little Things Make a Big Difference* (2000), *Blink: The Power of Thinking without Thinking* (2005), and *Outliers: The Story of Success* (2008). He was named one of *Time* magazine's 100 Most Influential People in 2005. In the following essay, which is an excerpt from *Outliers*, Gladwell explores the causes of success by using the Beatles and Bill Gates as subjects for analysis.

Preview   As you see it, what are the causes of success?

For almost a generation, psychologists around the world have been engaged in a spirited debate over a question that most of us would consider to have been settled years ago. The question is this: is there such a thing as innate talent? The obvious answer is yes. . . . Achievement is talent plus preparation. The problem with this view is that the closer psychologists look at the careers of the gifted, the smaller the role innate talent seems to play and the bigger the role preparation seems to play.

Exhibit A in the talent argument is a study done in the early 1990s by the psychologist K. Anders Ericsson and two colleagues at Berlin's elite Academy of Music. With the help of the Academy's professors, they divided the school's violinists into three groups. In the first group were the stars, the students with the potential to become world-class soloists. In the second were those judged to be merely "good." In the third were students who were unlikely to ever play professionally and who intended to be music teachers in the public school system. All of the violinists were then asked the same question: over the course of your entire career, ever since you first picked up the violin, how many hours have you practiced?

Everyone from all three groups started playing at roughly the same age, around five years old. In those first few years, everyone practiced roughly the same amount, about two or three hours a week. But when the students were around the age of eight, real differences started to emerge. The students who would end up the best in their class began to practice more than everyone else: six hours a week by age nine, eight hours a week by age twelve, sixteen hours a week by age fourteen, and up and up, until by the age of twenty they were practicing—that is, purposefully and single-mindedly playing their instruments with the intent to get better—well over thirty hours a week. In fact, by the age of twenty, the elite performers had each totaled ten thousand hours of practice. By contrast, the merely good students had totaled eight thousand hours, and the future music teachers had totaled just over four thousand hours.

Ericsson and his colleagues then compared amateur pianists 4 with professional pianists. The same pattern emerged. The amateurs never practiced more than about three hours a week over the course of their childhood, and by the age of twenty they had totaled two thousand hours of practice. The professionals, on the other hand, steadily increased their practice time every year, until by the age of twenty they, like the violinists, had reached ten thousand hours.

The striking thing about Ericsson's study is that he and his col- 5 leagues couldn't find any "naturals," musicians who floated effortlessly to the top while practicing a fraction of the time their peers did. Nor could they find any "grinds," people who worked harder than everyone else, yet just didn't have what it takes to break the top ranks. Their research suggests that once a musician has enough ability to get into a top music school, the thing that distinguishes one performer from another is how hard he or she works. That's it. And what's more, the people at the very top don't work just harder or even much harder than everyone else. They work much, *much* harder.

The idea that excellence at performing a complex task requires a 6 critical minimum level of practice surfaces again and again in studies of expertise. In fact, researchers have settled on what they believe is the magic number for true expertise: ten thousand hours.

"The emerging picture from such studies is that ten thousand 7 hours of practice is required to achieve the level of mastery associated with being a world-class expert — in anything," writes the neurologist Daniel Levitin. "In study after study, of composers, basketball players, fiction writers, ice skaters, concert pianists, chess players, master criminals, and what have you, this number comes up again and again. Of course, this doesn't address why some people get more out of their practice sessions than others do. But no one has yet found a case in which true world-class expertise was accomplished in less time. It seems that it takes the brain this long to assimilate all that it needs to know to achieve true mastery."

This is true even of people we think of as prodigies. Mozart, for 8 example, famously started writing music at six. But, writes the psychologist Michael Howe in his book *Genius Explained*,

> by the standards of mature composers, Mozart's early works are not outstanding. The earliest pieces were all probably written down by

his father, and perhaps improved in the process. Many of Wolfgang's childhood compositions, such as the first seven of his concertos for piano and orchestra, are largely arrangements of works by other composers. Of those concertos that only contain music original to Mozart, the earliest that is now regarded as a masterwork (No. 9, K. 271) was not composed until he was twenty–one: by that time Mozart had already been composing concertos for ten years.

The music critic Harold Schonberg goes further: Mozart, he argues, actually "developed late," since he didn't produce his greatest work until he had been composing for more than twenty years.

To become a chess grandmaster also seems to take about ten years. 9 (Only the legendary Bobby Fischer got to that elite level in less than that amount of time: it took him nine years.) And what's ten years? Well, it's roughly how long it takes to put in ten thousand hours of hard practice. Ten thousand hours is the magic number of greatness. . . .

The other interesting thing about that ten thousand hours, of 10 course, is that ten thousand hours is an *enormous* amount of time. It's all but impossible to reach that number all by yourself by the time you're a young adult. You have to have parents who encourage and support you. You can't be poor, because if you have to hold down a part–time job on the side to help make ends meet, there won't be time left in the day to practice enough. In fact, most people can reach that number only if they get into some kind of special program . . . or if they get some kind of extraordinary opportunity that gives them a chance to put in those hours.

• • •

Let's test the idea with two examples, and for the sake of simplicity, let's 11 make them as familiar as possible: the Beatles, one of the most famous rock bands ever; and Bill Gates, one of the world's richest men.

The Beatles—John Lennon, Paul McCartney, George Harrison, and 12 Ringo Starr— came to the United States in February of 1964, starting the so–called British Invasion of the American music scene and putting out a string of hit records that transformed the face of popular music.

The first interesting thing about the Beatles for our purposes is how 13 long they had already been together by the time they reached the United States. Lennon and McCartney first started playing together in 1957, seven years prior to landing in America. (Incidentally, the time that elapsed between their founding and their arguably greatest artistic achievements — *Sgt. Pepper's Lonely Hearts Club Band* and *The Beatles* [White Album]— is ten years.) . . . In 1960, while they were still just a struggling high school rock band, they were invited to play in Hamburg, Germany.

"Hamburg in those days did not have rock–and–roll music clubs. 14 It had strip clubs," says Philip Norman, who wrote the Beatles biography *Shout!* "There was one particular club owner called Bruno, who was originally a fairground showman. He had the idea of bringing in rock groups to play in various clubs. They had this formula. It was a huge nonstop show, hour after hour, with a lot of people lurching in and the other lot lurching out. And the bands would play all the time to catch the passing traffic. In an American red–light district, they would call it nonstop striptease.

"Many of the bands that played in Hamburg were from Liverpool," 15 Norman went on. "It was an accident. Bruno went to London to look for bands. But he happened to meet an entrepreneur from Liverpool in Soho who was down in London by pure chance. And he arranged to send some bands over. That's how the connection was established. And eventually the Beatles made a connection not just with Bruno but with other club owners as well. They kept going back because they got a lot of alcohol and a lot of sex."

And what was so special about Hamburg? It wasn't that it paid 16 well. It didn't. Or that the acoustics were fantastic. They weren't. Or that the audiences were savvy and appreciative. They were anything but. It was the sheer amount of time the band was forced to play.

Here is John Lennon, in an interview after the Beatles disbanded, 17 talking about the band's performances at a Hamburg strip club called the Indra:

> We got better and got more confidence. We couldn't help it with all the experience playing all night long. It was handy them being foreign. We had to try even harder, put our heart and soul into it, to get our-selves over.
>
> In Liverpool, we'd only ever done one–hour sessions, and we just used to do our best numbers, the same ones, at every one. In Ham-burg, we had to play for eight hours, so we really had to find a new way of playing.

Eight hours?   18

Here is Pete Best, the Beatles' drummer at the time: "Once the 19 news got out about that we were making a show, the club started pack-ing them in. We played seven nights a week. At first we played almost nonstop till twelve–thirty, when it closed, but as we got better the crowds stayed till two most mornings."

Seven days a week?   20

The Beatles ended up traveling to Hamburg five times between 21 1960 and the end of 1962. On the first trip, they played 106 nights, five or more hours a night. On their second trip, they played 92 times. On their third trip, they played 48 times, for a total of 172 hours on stage. The last two Hamburg gigs, in November and December of 1962, involved another 90 hours of performing. All told, they performed for 270 nights in just over a year and a half. By the time they had their first burst of success in 1964, in fact, they had performed live an estimated twelve hundred times. Do you know how extraordinary that is? Most bands

The Beatles performing in Munich, Germany, in 1966. According to Gladwell, it was their extensive, demanding early performance schedule in another German city, Hamburg, that made them so good.

today don't perform twelve hundred times in their entire careers. The Hamburg crucible is one of the things that set the Beatles apart.

"They were no good onstage when they went there and they were   22 very good when they came back," Norman went on. "They learned not only stamina. They had to learn an enormous amount of numbers — cover versions of everything you can think of, not just rock and roll, a bit of jazz too. They weren't disciplined onstage at all before that. But when they came back, they sounded like no one else. It was the making of them."

* * *

Let's now turn to the history of Bill Gates. His story is almost as well   23 known as the Beatles'. Brilliant, young math whiz discovers computer programming. Drops out of Harvard. Starts a little computer company called Microsoft with his friends. Through sheer brilliance and ambition and guts builds it into the giant of the software world. That's the broad outline. Let's dig a little bit deeper.

Gates's father was a wealthy lawyer in Seattle, and his mother was   24 the daughter of a well-to-do banker. As a child Bill was precocious and easily bored by his studies. So his parents took him out of public school and, at the beginning of seventh grade, sent him to Lakeside, a private school that catered to Seattle's elite families. Midway through Gates's second year at Lakeside, the school started a computer club.

"The Mothers' Club at school did a rummage sale every year, and   25
there was always the question of what the money would go to," Gates
remembers. "Some went to the summer program, where inner–city
kids would come up to the campus. Some of it would go for teachers.
That year, they put three thousand dollars into a computer terminal
down in this funny little room that we subsequently took control of. It
was kind of an amazing thing."

It was an "amazing thing," of course, because this was 1968. Most   26
colleges didn't have computer clubs in the 1960s. Even more remarkable
was the kind of computer Lakeside bought. The school didn't have its
students learn programming by the laborious computer–card system,
like virtually everyone else was doing in the 1960s. Instead, Lakeside installed what was called an ASR–33 Teletype, which was a time–sharing
terminal with a direct link to a mainframe computer in downtown
Seattle. "The whole idea of time–sharing only got invented in nineteen
sixty–five," Gates continued. "Someone was pretty forward–looking." . . .
Bill Gates got to do real–time programming *as an eighth grader in 1968.*

From that moment forward, Gates lived in the computer room. He   27
and a number of others began to teach themselves how to use this
strange new device. Buying time on the mainframe computer the
ASR was hooked up to was, of course, expensive— even for a wealthy
institution like Lakeside— and it wasn't long before the $3,000 put up by
the Mothers' Club ran out. The parents raised more money. The students
spent it. Then a group of programmers at the University of Washington formed an outfit called Computer Center Corporation (or C–
Cubed), which leased computer time to local companies. As luck would
have it, one of the founders of the firm— Monique Rona— had a son at
Lakeside, a year ahead of Gates. Would the Lakeside computer club,
Rona wondered, like to test out the company's software programs on
the weekends in exchange for free programming time? Absolutely! After
school, Gates took the bus to the C–Cubed offices and programmed
long into the evening.

C–Cubed eventually went bankrupt, so Gates and his friends be-   28
gan hanging around the computer center at the University of Washington. Before long, they latched onto an outfit called ISI (Information
Sciences Inc.), which agreed to let them have free computer time in
exchange for working on a piece of software that could be used to au-
tomate company payrolls. In one seven–month period in 1971, Gates
and his cohorts ran up 1,575 hours of computer time on the ISI mainframe, which averages out to eight hours a day, seven days a week.

"It was my obsession," Gates says of his early high school years.   29
"I skipped athletics. I went up there at night. We were programming
on weekends. It would be a rare week that we wouldn't get twenty or
thirty hours in. There was a period where Paul Allen and I got in trouble

Bill Gates in the 1980s.

for stealing a bunch of passwords and crashing the system. We got kicked out. I didn't get to use the computer the whole summer. This is when I was fifteen and sixteen. Then I found out Paul had found a computer that was free at the University of Washington. They had these machines in the medical center and the physics department. They were on a twenty–four–hour schedule, but with this big slack period, so that between three and six in the morning they never scheduled anything." Gates laughed. "I'd leave at night, after my bedtime. I could walk up to the University of Washington from my house. Or I'd take the bus. That's why I'm always so generous to the University of Washington, because they let me steal so much computer time." (Years later, Gates's mother said, "We always wondered why it was so hard for him to get up in the morning.")

One of the founders of ISI, Bud Pembroke, then got a call from the tech- 30 nology company TRW, which had just signed a contract to set up a computer system at the huge Bonneville Power station in southern Washington State. TRW desperately needed programmers familiar with the particular software the power station used. In these early days of the computer revolution, programmers with that kind of specialized experience were hard to find. But Pembroke knew exactly whom to call: those high school kids from Lakeside who had been running up thousands of hours of computer time on the ISI mainframe. Gates was now in his senior year, and somehow he managed to convince his teachers to let him decamp for Bonneville under the guise of an independent study project. There he spent the spring writing code, supervised by a man named John Norton, who Gates says taught him as much about programming as almost anyone he'd ever met.

Those five years, from eighth grade through the end of high school, 31 were Bill Gates's Hamburg, and by any measure, he was presented with an extraordinary series of opportunities.

Opportunity number one was that Gates got sent to Lakeside. How 32 many high schools in the world had access to a time-sharing terminal in 1968? Opportunity number two was that the mothers of Lakeside had enough money to pay for the school's computer fees. Number three was that, when that money ran out, one of the parents happened to work at C-Cubed, which happened to need someone to check its code on the weekends, and which also happened not to care if weekends turned into weeknights. Number four was that Gates just happened to find out about ISI, and ISI just happened to need someone to work on its payroll software. Number five was that Gates happened to live within walking distance of the University of Washington. Number six was that the university happened to have free computer time between three and six in the morning. Number seven was that TRW happened to call Bud Pembroke. Number eight was that the best programmers Pembroke knew for that particular problem happened to be two high school kids. And number nine was that Lakeside was willing to let those kids spend their spring term miles away, writing code.

And what did virtually all of those opportunities have in common? 33 They gave Bill Gates extra time to practice. By the time Gates dropped out of Harvard after his sophomore year to try his hand at his own software company, he'd been programming practically nonstop for seven consecutive years. He was *way* past ten thousand hours. How many teenagers in the world had the kind of experience Gates had? "If there were fifty in the world, I'd be stunned," he says. "There was C-Cubed and the payroll stuff we did, then TRW — all those things came together. I had a better exposure to software development at a young age than I think anyone did in that period of time, and all because of an incredibly lucky series of events."

•   •   •

If we put the stories of the Beatles and Bill Gates together, I think we get a 34 more complete picture of the path to success. Gates and the Beatles are all undeniably talented. Lennon and McCartney had a musical gift of the sort that comes along once in a generation. That much is obvious.

But what truly distinguishes their histories is not their extraordinary 35 talent but their extraordinary opportunities. The Beatles, for the most random of reasons, got invited to go to Hamburg. Without Hamburg, the Beatles might well have taken a different path. "I was very lucky," Bill Gates said at the beginning of our interview. That doesn't mean he isn't brilliant or an extraordinary entrepreneur. It just means that he under–stands what incredible good fortune it was to be at Lakeside in 1968.

All the outliers we've looked at so far were the beneficiaries of some   36
kind of unusual opportunity. Lucky breaks don't seem like the exception
with software billionaires and rock bands and star athletes. They seem like
the rule.

Reading Closely

1. What is the purpose of Gladwell's essay? What point is he trying to make
   about success?
2. In addition to examining the successful careers of Bill Gates and the
   Beatles, Gladwell also cites K. Anders Ericsson's study of musicians. What
   does he attempt to prove by citing this study?
3. What caused the Beatles' success, according to Gladwell?
4. What caused Bill Gates's success?
5. What do each of Gladwell's examples (the musicians Ericsson studied,
   the Beatles, and Bill Gates) have in common? What components of their
   success stories do they share?
6. Review the photographs on pages 519 and 521. Which one does a better
   job of reflecting the causal relationship that Gladwell describes in the
   essay? Use evidence from the photographs to support your claim.

Considering Larger Issues

1. **Working with a classmate,** discuss how Gladwell's argument about
   success confirms or counters your ideas about the causes of success. Be
   prepared to share your findings with the rest of the class.
2. COMBINING METHODS. In addition to cause–and–effect analysis, Gladwell
   incorporates the rhetorical methods of *exemplification, narration, comparison
   and contrast,* and *process analysis* into this essay. Identify the places where
   Gladwell integrates these methods into the essay. How do they work to
   support the overarching purpose of the analysis?

Thinking about Language

1. Using the context of the essay or your dictionary, define the following
   words and phrases. Be prepared to share your answers with the rest of
   the class.

innate (1)	lurching (14)	laborious (26)
single–mindedly (3)	acoustics (16)	automate (28)
neurologist (7)	crucible (21)	decamp (30)
prodigies (8)	precocious (24)	outliers (36)
incidentally (13)	rummage sale (25)	

2. The title of Gladwell's book is *Outliers: The Story of Success*. Does the term *outlier* fit the Beatles and Bill Gates? What is Gladwell arguing by calling them outliers?

Writing Your Own Essays Using Cause-and-Effect Analysis

1. One of the arguments Gladwell is making in his essay is that luck plays a big part in people's success. Reflect on a successful moment in your life, and compose a three- to four-page essay that analyzes all the factors that caused this success. As Gladwell does, you want to consider the primary, contributory, immediate, and remote causes. In addition to your purposeful actions, consider how luck may have contributed to your success. As you draft and revise, consult "Checking Over the Use of Cause-and-Effect Analysis" on pages 483–84.

2. In his essay, Gladwell does not reflect on his own success, although he could have. Instead, he identifies other successful people and investigates their paths to success. For a three- to four-page essay, investigate a person you believe to be successful. If it is someone you know, interview him or her. If it is a historical or prominent figure, conduct research on the person. In either case, try to uncover the specific causes of their success. As you identify these causes, place the person's success story in the context of Gladwell's essay. Did elements of luck contribute? Did the person have an unprecedented amount of time to practice his or her skill or access necessary materials? Consult "Checking Over the Use of Cause-and-Effect Analysis" on pages 483–84 as you draft and revise.

ATUL GAWANDE
Hellhole

Atul Gawande (b. 1965) earned his bachelor's degree at Stanford University, his master's at Oxford University, and his doctorate at Harvard Medical School. A surgeon, he teaches at Harvard's Medical School and its School of Public Health while also practicing medicine at the Dana Farber Cancer Institute and at Brigham and Women's Hospital. In addition to his work as a professor and doctor, Gawande is a regular contributor to the *New Yorker* magazine. He has written two books having to do with medical issues and the medical profession: *Complications: A Surgeon's Notes on an Imperfect Science* (2002), which was a finalist for the National Book Award, and *Better: A Surgeon's Notes on Performance* (2007), which was named one of Amazon.com's ten best books in 2007 and a *New York Times* best-seller. In 2006, Gawande received a MacArthur Genius Award for his research and writing. In the following essay, which was published in the March 2009 issue of the *New Yorker*, Gawande departs from medical discussions to examine the effects of long-term solitary confinement on prison inmates.

> **Preview**   What do you know about solitary confinement of prison inmates? Why do you think the prison system uses this form of incarceration?

Human beings are social creatures. We are social not just in the trivial 1 sense that we like company, and not just in the obvious sense that we each depend on others. We are social in a more elemental way: simply to exist as a normal human being requires interaction with other people.

Children provide the clearest demonstration of this fact, although 2 it was slow to be accepted. Well into the nineteen–fifties, psychologists were encouraging parents to give children *less* attention and affection, in order to encourage independence. Then Harry Harlow, a professor of psychology at the University of Wisconsin at Madison, produced a series of influential studies involving baby rhesus monkeys.

He happened upon the findings in the mid–fifties, when he decided 3 to save money for his primate–research laboratory by breeding his own lab monkeys instead of importing them from India. Because he didn't know how to raise infant monkeys, he cared for them the way hospitals of the era cared for human infants — in nurseries, with plenty of food, warm blankets, some toys, and in isolation from other infants to prevent the spread of infection. The monkeys grew up sturdy, disease-free, and larger than those from the wild. Yet they were also profoundly disturbed, given to staring blankly and rocking in place for long periods, circling their cages repetitively, and mutilating themselves.

At first, Harlow and his graduate students couldn't figure out what 4 the problem was. They considered factors such as diet, patterns of light exposure, even the antibiotics they used. Then, as Deborah Blum recounts

in a fascinating biography of Harlow, *Love at Goon Park*, one of his researchers noticed how tightly the monkeys clung to their soft blankets. Harlow
wondered whether what the monkeys were missing in their Isolettes was a
mother. So, in an odd experiment, he gave them an artificial one.

In the studies, one artificial mother was a doll made of terry cloth; the   5
other was made of wire. He placed a warming device inside the dolls to
make them seem more comforting. The babies, Harlow discovered, largely
ignored the wire mother. But they became deeply attached to the cloth
mother. They caressed it. They slept curled up on it. They ran to it when
frightened. They refused replacements: they wanted only "their" mother. If
sharp spikes were made to randomly thrust out of the mother's body when
the rhesus babies held it, they waited patiently for the spikes to recede and
returned to clutching it. No matter how tightly they clung to the surrogate
mothers, however, the monkeys remained psychologically abnormal.

In a later study on the effect of total isolation from birth, the re-   6
searchers found that the test monkeys, upon being released into a group
of ordinary monkeys, "usually go into a state of emotional shock, characterized by . . . autistic self-clutching and rocking." Harlow noted, "One
of six monkeys isolated for three months refused to eat after release and
died five days later." After several weeks in the company of other monkeys, most of them adjusted—but not those who had been isolated for
longer periods. "Twelve months of isolation almost obliterated the animals socially," Harlow wrote. They became permanently withdrawn, and
they lived as outcasts—regularly set upon, as if inviting abuse.

The research made Harlow famous (and infamous, too — revulsion at 7 his work helped spur the animal–rights movement). Other psychologists produced evidence of similarly deep and sustained damage in neglected and orphaned children. Hospitals were made to open up their nurseries to parents. And it became widely accepted that children require nurturing human beings not just for food and protection but also for the normal functioning of their brains.

We have been hesitant to apply these lessons to adults. Adults, af- 8 ter all, are fully formed, independent beings, with internal strengths and knowledge to draw upon. We wouldn't have anything like a child's dependence on other people, right? Yet it seems that we do. We don't have a lot of monkey experiments to call upon here. But mankind has produced tens of thousands of human ones, including in our prison system. And the picture that has emerged is profoundly unsettling.

Among our most benign experiments are those with people who volun- 9 tarily isolate themselves for extended periods. Long–distance solo sailors, for instance, commit themselves to months at sea. They face all manner of physical terrors: thrashing storms, fifty–foot waves, leaks, illness. Yet, for many, the single most overwhelming difficulty they report is the "soul–destroying loneliness," as one sailor called it. Astronauts have to be screened for their ability to tolerate long stretches in tightly confined isolation, and they come to depend on radio and video communications for social contact.

The problem of isolation goes beyond ordinary loneliness, how- 10 ever. Consider what we've learned from hostages who have been held in solitary confinement — from the journalist Terry Anderson, for example, whose extraordinary memoir, *Den of Lions*, recounts his seven years as a hostage of Hezbollah in Lebanon.

Anderson was the chief Middle East correspondent for the Associated 11 Press when, on March 16, 1985, three bearded men forced him from his car in Beirut at gunpoint. He was pushed into a Mercedes sedan, covered head to toe with a heavy blanket, and made to crouch head down in the footwell behind the front seat. His captors drove him to a garage, pulled him out of the car, put a hood over his head, and bound his wrists and ankles with tape. For half an hour, they grilled him for the names of other Americans in Beirut, but he gave no names and they did not beat him or press him further. They threw him in the trunk of the car, drove him to another building, and put him in what would be the first of a succession of cells across Lebanon. He was soon placed in what seemed to be a dusty closet, large enough for only a mattress. Blindfolded, he could make out the distant sounds of other hostages. (One was William Buckley, the C.I.A. station chief who was kidnapped and tortured repeatedly until he weakened and died.) Peering around his blindfold, Anderson could see a bare light bulb dangling from the ceiling. He received three unpalatable meals a day — usually a sandwich of bread and cheese, or cold rice with canned vegetables, or soup. He had a bottle to urinate in and was allotted one five- to ten-minute trip each day to a rotting bathroom to empty his bowels and wash with water at a dirty sink. Otherwise, the only reprieve from isolation came when the guards made short visits to bark at him for breaking a rule or to threaten him, sometimes with a gun at his temple.

He missed people terribly, especially his fiancée and his family. He was despondent and depressed. Then, with time, he began to feel something more. He felt himself disintegrating. It was as if his brain were grinding down. A month into his confinement, he recalled in his memoir, "The mind is a blank. Jesus, I always thought I was smart. Where are all the things I learned, the books I read, the poems I memorized? There's nothing there, just a formless, gray-black misery. My mind's gone dead. God, help me." 12

He was stiff from lying in bed day and night, yet tired all the time. He dozed off and on constantly, sleeping twelve hours a day. He craved activity of almost any kind. He would watch the daylight wax and wane on the ceiling, or roaches creep slowly up the wall. He had a Bible and tried to read, but he often found that he lacked the concentration to do so. He observed himself becoming neurotically possessive about his little space, at times putting his life in jeopardy by flying into a rage if a guard happened to step on his bed. He brooded incessantly, thinking back on all the mistakes he'd made in life, his regrets, his offenses against God and family. 13

His captors moved him every few months. For unpredictable stretches of time, he was granted the salvation of a companion — sometimes he shared a cell with as many as four other hostages — and he noticed that his thinking recovered rapidly when this occurred. He could read and concentrate longer, avoid hallucinations, and better control his emotions. "I would rather have had the worst companion than no companion at all," he noted. 14

In September, 1986, after several months of sharing a cell with another hostage, Anderson was, for no apparent reason, returned to solitary confinement, this time in a six-by-six-foot cell, with no windows, and light from only a flickering fluorescent lamp in an outside corridor. The guards refused to say how long he would be there. After a few weeks, he felt his mind slipping away again. 15

"I find myself trembling sometimes for no reason," he wrote. "I'm afraid I'm beginning to lose my mind, to lose control completely." 16

One day, three years into his ordeal, he snapped. He walked over to a wall and began beating his forehead against it, dozens of times. His head was smashed and bleeding before the guards were able to stop him. 17

Some hostages fared worse. Anderson told the story of Frank Reed, a fifty-four-year-old American private-school director who was taken hostage and held in solitary confinement for four months before being put in with Anderson. By then, Reed had become severely withdrawn. He lay motionless for hours facing a wall, semi-catatonic. He could not follow 18 the guards' simplest instructions. This invited abuse from them, in much the same way that once isolated rhesus monkeys seemed to invite abuse from the colony. Released after three and a half years, Reed ultimately required admission to a psychiatric hospital.

"It's an awful thing, solitary," John McCain wrote of his five and a half 19 years as a prisoner of war in Vietnam— more than two years of it spent in isolation in a fifteen–by–fifteen–foot cell, unable to communicate with other P.O.W.s except by tap code, secreted notes, or by speaking into an enamel cup pressed against the wall. "It crushes your spirit and weakens your resistance more effectively than any other form of mistreatment." And this comes from a man who was beaten regularly; denied adequate medical treatment for two broken arms, a broken leg, and chronic dys-entery; and tortured to the point of having an arm broken again. A U.S. military study of almost a hundred and fifty naval aviators returned from imprisonment in Vietnam, many of whom were treated even worse than McCain, reported that they found social isolation to be as torturous and agonizing as any physical abuse they suffered.

And what happened to them *was* physical. EEG studies going back to 20 the nineteen–sixties have shown diffuse slowing of brain waves in pris-oners after a week or more of solitary confinement. In 1992, fifty–seven prisoners of war, released after an average of six months in detention camps in the former Yugoslavia, were examined using EEG–like tests. The recordings revealed brain abnormalities months afterward; the most se-vere were found in prisoners who had endured either head trauma suf-ficient to render them unconscious or, yes, solitary confinement. Without sustained social interaction, the human brain may become as impaired as one that has incurred a traumatic injury.

On December 4, 1991, Terry Anderson was released from captivity. 21 He had been the last and the longest–held American hostage in Lebanon. I spoke to Keron Fletcher, a former British military psychiatrist who had been on the receiving team for Anderson and many other hostages, and followed them for years afterward. Initially, Fletcher said, everyone experi-ences the pure elation of being able to see and talk to people again, espe-cially family and friends. They can't get enough of other people, and talk almost non–stop for hours. They are optimistic and hopeful. But, after-ward, normal sleeping and eating patterns prove difficult to reestablish. Some have lost their sense of time. For weeks, they have trouble manag-ing the sensations and emotional complexities of their freedom.

For the first few months after his release, Anderson said when I 22 reached him by phone recently, "it was just kind of a fog." He had done many television interviews at the time. "And if you look at me in the pic-tures? Look at my eyes. You can tell. I look drugged."

Most hostages survived their ordeal, Fletcher said, although relation- 23 ships, marriages, and careers were often lost. Some found, as John McCain did, that the experience even strengthened them. Yet none saw solitary confinement as anything less than torture. This presents us with an awkward question: If prolonged isolation is—as research and experience have confirmed for decades—so objectively horrifying, so intrinsically cruel, how did we end up with a prison system that may subject more of our own citizens to it than any other country in history has?

Recently, I met a man who had spent more than five years in isola- 24
tion at a prison in the Boston suburb of Walpole, Massachusetts, not far from my home. Bobby Dellelo was, to say the least, no Terry Anderson or John McCain. Brought up in the run–down neighborhoods of Boston's West End, in the nineteen–forties, he was caught burglarizing a shoe store at the age of ten. At thirteen, he recalls, he was nabbed while robbing a Jordan Marsh department store. (He and his friends learned to hide out in stores at closing time, steal their merchandise, and then break out during the night.) The remainder of his childhood was spent mostly in the state reform school. That was where he learned how to fight, how to hot–wire a car with a piece of foil, how to pick locks, and how to make a zip gun using a snapped–off automobile radio antenna, which, in those days, was just thick enough to barrel a .22–calibre bullet. Released upon turning eighteen, Dellelo returned to stealing. Usually, he stole from office buildings at night. But some of the people he hung out with did stickups, and, together with one of them, he held up a liquor store in Dorchester.

"What a disaster that thing was," he recalls, laughing. They put the 25
store's owner and the customers in a walk–in refrigerator at gunpoint, took their wallets, and went to rob the register. But more customers came in. So they robbed them and put them in the refrigerator, too. Then still more customers arrived, the refrigerator got full, and the whole thing turned into a circus. Dellelo and his partner finally escaped. But one of the customers identified him to the police. By the time he was caught, Dellelo had been fingered for robbing the Commander Hotel in Cambridge as well. He served a year for the first conviction and two and a half years for the second.

Three months after his release, in 1963, at the age of twenty, he and a 26
friend tried to rob the Kopelman jewelry store, in downtown Boston. But an alarm went off before they got their hands on anything. They separated and ran. The friend shot and killed an off–duty policeman while trying to escape, then killed himself. Dellelo was convicted of first–degree murder and sentenced to life in prison. He ended up serving forty years. Five years and one month were spent in isolation.

The criteria for the isolation of prisoners vary by state but typically 27
include not only violent infractions but also violation of prison rules or association with gang members. The imposition of long–term isolation— which can be for months or years— is ultimately at the discretion of prison administrators. One former prisoner I spoke to, for example, re-

called being put in solitary confinement for petty annoyances like refusing to get out of the shower quickly enough. Bobby Dellelo was put there for escaping.

It was an elaborate scheme. He had a partner, who picked the lock 28 to a supervisor's office and got hold of the information manual for the microwave-detection system that patrolled a grassy no man's land between the prison and the road. They studied the manual long enough to learn how to circumvent the system and returned it. On Halloween Sunday, 1993, they had friends stage a fight in the prison yard. With all the guards in the towers looking at the fight through binoculars, the two men tipped a picnic table up against a twelve-foot wall and climbed it like a ladder. Beyond it, they scaled a sixteen-foot fence. To get over the razor wire on top, they used a Z-shaped tool they'd improvised from locker handles. They dropped down into the no man's land and followed an invisible path that they'd calculated the microwave system would not detect. No alarm sounded. They went over one more fence, walked around a parking lot, picked their way through some woods, and emerged onto a four-lane road. After a short walk to a convenience store, they called a taxi from a telephone booth and rolled away before anyone knew they were gone.

They lasted twenty-four days on the outside. Eventually, somebody 29 ratted them out, and the police captured them on the day before Thanksgiving, at the house of a friend in Cambridge. The prison administration gave Dellelo five years in the Departmental Disciplinary Unit of the Walpole prison, its hundred-and-twenty-four-cell super-maximum segregation unit.

Wearing ankle bracelets, handcuffs, and a belly chain, Dellelo was 30 marched into a thirteen-by-eight-foot off-white cell. A four-inch-thick concrete bed slab jutted out from the wall opposite the door. A smaller slab protruding from a side wall provided a desk. A cylindrical concrete block in the floor served as a seat. On the remaining wall was a toilet and a metal sink. He was given four sheets, four towels, a blanket, a bedroll, a toothbrush, toilet paper, a tall clear plastic cup, a bar of soap, seven white T-shirts, seven pairs of boxer shorts, seven pairs of socks, plastic slippers, a pad of paper, and a ballpoint pen. A speaker with a microphone was mounted on the door. Cells used for solitary confinement are often windowless, but this one had a ribbonlike window that was seven inches wide and five feet tall. The electrically controlled door was solid steel, with a seven-inch-by-twenty-eight-inch aperture and two wickets — little door slots, one at ankle height and one at waist height, for shackling him whenever he was let out and for passing him meal trays.

As in other supermaxes — facilities designed to isolate prisoners from 31 social contact — Dellelo was confined to his cell for at least twenty-three hours a day and permitted out only for a shower or for recreation in an outdoor cage that he estimated to be fifty feet long and five feet wide, known as "the dog kennel." He could talk to other prisoners through the steel door of his cell, and during recreation if a prisoner was in an adjacent cage. He made a kind of fishing line for passing notes to adjacent cells by unwinding the elastic from his boxer shorts, though it was contraband and would be confiscated. Prisoners could receive mail and as many as ten reading items. They were allowed one phone call the first month and could earn up to four calls and four visits per month if they followed the rules, but there could be no physical contact with anyone, except when guards forcibly restrained them. Some supermaxes even use food as punishment, serving the prisoners nutra–loaf, an unpalatable food brick that contains just enough nutrition for survival. Dellelo was spared this. The rules also permitted him to have a radio after thirty days, and, after sixty days, a thirteen–inch black–and–white television.

"This is going to be a piece of cake," Dellelo recalls thinking when the 32 door closed behind him. Whereas many American supermax prisoners— and most P.O.W.s and hostages— have no idea when they might get out, he knew exactly how long he was going to be there. He drew a calendar on his pad of paper to start counting down the days. He would get a radio and a TV. He could read. No one was going to bother him. And, as his elaborate escape plan showed, he could be patient. "This is their sophisticated security?" he said to himself. "They don't know what they're doing."

After a few months without regular social contact, however, his ex- 33 perience proved no different from that of the P.O.W.s or hostages, or the majority of isolated prisoners whom researchers have studied: he started to lose his mind. He talked to himself. He paced back and forth compulsively, shuffling along the same six–foot path for hours on end. Soon, he was having panic attacks, screaming for help. He hallucinated that the colors on the walls were changing. He became enraged by routine noises— the sound of doors opening as the guards made their hourly checks, the sounds of inmates in nearby cells. After a year or so, he was hearing voices on the television talking directly to him. He put the television under his bed, and rarely took it out again.

One of the paradoxes of solitary confinement is that, as starved as 34 people become for companionship, the experience typically leaves them unfit for social interaction. Once, Dellelo was allowed to have an in–person meeting with his lawyer, and he simply couldn't handle it. After so many months in which his primary human contact had been an occasional phone call or brief conversations with an inmate down the tier, shouted through steel doors at the top of their lungs, he found himself unable to carry on a face–to–face conversation. He had trouble following both words and hand gestures and couldn't generate them himself. When he realized this, he succumbed to a full–blown panic attack.

Craig Haney, a psychology professor at the University of California 35 at Santa Cruz, received rare permission to study a hundred randomly selected inmates at California's Pelican Bay supermax, and noted a number of phenomena. First, after months or years of complete isolation, many prisoners "begin to lose the ability to initiate behavior of any kind—to organize their own lives around activity and purpose," he writes. "Chronic apathy, lethargy, depression, and despair often result. . . . In extreme cases, prisoners may literally stop behaving," becoming essentially catatonic.

Second, almost ninety percent of these prisoners had difficulties with 36 "irrational anger," compared with just three percent of the general population. Haney attributed this to the extreme restriction, the totality of control, and the extended absence of any opportunity for happiness or joy. Many prisoners in solitary become consumed with revenge fantasies.

"There were some guards in D.D.U. who were decent guys," Dellelo told 37 me. They didn't trash his room when he was let out for a shower, or try to trip him when escorting him in chains, or write him up for contraband if he kept food or a salt packet from a meal in his cell. "But some of them were evil, evil pricks." One correctional officer became a particular obsession. Dellelo spent hours imagining cutting his head off and rolling it down the tier. "I mean, I know this is insane thinking," he says now. Even at the time, he added, "I had a fear in the background—like how much of this am I going to be able to let go? How much is this going to affect who I am?"

He was right to worry. Everyone's identity is socially created: it's 38 through your relationships that you understand yourself as a mother or a father, a teacher or an accountant, a hero or a villain. But, after years of isolation, many prisoners change in another way that Haney observed. They begin to see themselves primarily as combatants in the world, people whose identity is rooted in thwarting prison control.

As a matter of self-preservation, this may not be a bad thing. Accord- 39 ing to the Navy P.O.W. researchers, the instinct to fight back against the enemy constituted the most important coping mechanism for the prisoners they studied. Resistance was often their sole means of maintaining a sense of purpose, and so their sanity. Yet resistance is precisely what we wish to destroy in our supermax prisoners. As Haney observed in a review of research findings, prisoners in solitary confinement must be able to withstand the experience in order to be allowed to return to the highly social world of mainline prison or free society. Perversely, then, the prisoners who can't handle profound isolation are the ones who are forced to remain in it. "And those who have adapted," Haney writes, "are prime candidates for release to a social world to which they may be incapable of ever fully readjusting."

Dellelo eventually found a way to resist that would not prolong his 40 ordeal. He fought his battle through the courts, filing motion after motion in an effort to get his conviction overturned. He became so good at submitting his claims that he obtained a paralegal certificate along the way. And, after forty years in prison, and more than five years in solitary, he got his first-degree-homicide conviction reduced to manslaughter. On November 19, 2003, he was freed.

Bobby Dellelo is sixty–seven years old now. He lives on Social Secu– 41
rity in a Cambridge efficiency apartment that is about four times larger
than his cell. He still seems to be adjusting to the world outside. He lives
alone. To the extent that he is out in society, it is, in large measure, as a
combatant. He works for prisoners' rights at the American Friends Service Committee. He also does occasional work assisting prisoners with
their legal cases. Sitting at his kitchen table, he showed me how to pick a
padlock — you know, just in case I ever find myself in trouble.

But it was impossible to talk to him about his time in isolation with– 42
out seeing that it was fundamentally no different from the isolation that
Terry Anderson and John McCain had endured. Whether in Walpole or
Beirut or Hanoi, all human beings experience isolation as torture.

The main argument for using long–term isolation in prisons is that it pro– 43
vides discipline and prevents violence. When inmates refuse to follow the
rules — when they escape, deal drugs, or attack other inmates and corrections officers — wardens must be able to punish and contain the miscon-
duct. Presumably, less stringent measures haven't worked, or the behavior
would not have occurred. And it's legitimate to incapacitate violent ag-
gressors for the safety of others. So, advocates say, isolation is a necessary
evil, and those who don't recognize this are dangerously naïve.

The argument makes intuitive sense. If the worst of the worst are re– 44
moved from the general prison population and put in isolation, you'd expect
there to be markedly fewer inmate shankings and attacks on corrections
officers. But the evidence doesn't bear this out. Perhaps the most careful
inquiry into whether supermax prisons decrease violence and disorder
was a 2003 analysis examining the experience in three states — Arizona,
Illinois, and Minnesota — following the opening of their supermax prisons.
The study found that levels of inmate–on–inmate violence were unchanged,
and that levels of inmate–on–staff violence changed unpredictably, rising
in Arizona, falling in Illinois, and holding steady in Minnesota.

Prison violence, it turns out, is not simply an issue of a few bel– 45
ligerents. In the past thirty years, the United States has quadrupled its
incarceration rate but not its prison space. Work and education programs
have been cancelled, out of a belief that the pursuit of rehabilitation is
pointless. The result has been unprecedented overcrowding, along with
unprecedented idleness — a nice formula for violence. Remove a few
prisoners to solitary confinement, and the violence doesn't change. So
you remove some more, and still nothing happens. Before long, you find
yourself in the position we are in today. The United States now has five
percent of the world's population, twenty–five percent of its prisoners,
and probably the vast majority of prisoners who are in long–term solitary confinement.

It wasn't always like this. The wide–scale use of isolation is, almost 46
exclusively, a phenomenon of the past twenty years. In 1890, the United

States Supreme Court came close to declaring the punishment to be un-constitutional. Writing for the majority in the case of a Colorado murderer who had been held in isolation for a month, Justice Samuel Miller noted that experience had revealed "serious objections" to solitary confinement:

> A considerable number of the prisoners fell, after even a short con-finement, into a semi-fatuous condition, from which it was next to impossible to arouse them, and others became violently insane; oth-ers, still, committed suicide; while those who stood the ordeal bet-ter were not generally reformed, and in most cases did not recover sufficient mental activity to be of any subsequent service to the community.

Prolonged isolation was used sparingly, if at all, by most American 47 prisons for almost a century. Our first supermax—our first institution specifically designed for mass solitary confinement—was not estab-lished until 1983, in Marion, Illinois. In 1995, a federal court reviewing California's first supermax admitted that the conditions "hover on the edge of what is humanly tolerable for those with normal resilience." But it did not rule them to be unconstitutionally cruel or unusual, except in cases of mental illness. The prison's supermax conditions, the court stated, did not pose "a sufficiently high risk to all inmates of incurring a serious mental illness." In other words, there could be no legal objection to its routine use, given that the isolation didn't make *everyone* crazy. The ruling seemed to fit the public mood. By the end of the nineteen-nineties, some sixty supermax institutions had opened across the country. And new solitary-confinement units were established within nearly all of our ordinary maximum-security prisons.

The number of prisoners in these facilities has since risen to extraor- 48 dinary levels. America now holds at least twenty-five thousand inmates in isolation in supermax prisons. An additional fifty to eighty thousand are kept in restrictive segregation units, many of them in isolation, too, al-though the government does not release these figures. By 1999, the practice had grown to the point that Arizona, Colorado, Maine, Nebraska, Nevada, Rhode Island, and Virginia kept between five and eight percent of their prison population in isolation, and, by 2003, New York had joined them as well. Mississippi alone held eighteen hundred prisoners in supermax— twelve percent of its prisoners overall. At the same time, other states had just a tiny fraction of their inmates in solitary confinement. In 1999, for example, Indiana had eighty-five supermax beds; Georgia had only ten. Neither of these two states can be described as being soft on crime.

Advocates of solitary confinement are left with a single argument for 49 subjecting thousands of people to years of isolation: What else are we supposed to do? How else are we to deal with the violent, the disruptive, the prisoners who are just too dangerous to be housed with others?

· · ·

Is there an alternative? Consider what other countries do. Britain, for ex- 50
ample, has had its share of serial killers, homicidal rapists, and prisoners
who have taken hostages and repeatedly assaulted staff. The British also
fought a seemingly unending war in Northern Ireland, which brought
them hundreds of Irish Republican Army prisoners committed to violent resistance. The authorities resorted to a harshly punitive approach to
control, including, in the mid–seventies, extensive use of solitary confinement. But the violence in prisons remained unchanged, the costs were
phenomenal (in the United States, they reach more than fifty thousand
dollars a year per inmate), and the public outcry became intolerable.
British authorities therefore looked for another approach.

Beginning in the nineteen–eighties, they gradually adopted a strategy 51
that focused on preventing prison violence rather than on delivering an
ever more brutal series of punishments for it. The approach starts with the
simple observation that prisoners who are unmanageable in one setting
often behave perfectly reasonably in another. This suggested that violence might, to a critical extent, be a function of the conditions of incarceration. The British noticed that problem prisoners were usually people
for whom avoiding humiliation and saving face were fundamental and
instinctive. When conditions maximized humiliation and confrontation,
every interaction escalated into a trial of strength. Violence became a
predictable consequence.

So the British decided to give their most dangerous prisoners more 52
control, rather than less. They reduced isolation and offered them opportunities for work, education, and special programming to increase social
ties and skills. The prisoners were housed in small, stable units of fewer
than ten people in individual cells, to avoid conditions of social chaos
and unpredictability. In these reformed "Close Supervision Centres," prisoners could receive mental–health treatment and earn rights for more
exercise, more phone calls, "contact visits," and even access to cooking
facilities. They were allowed to air grievances. And the government set
up an independent body of inspectors to track the results and enable
adjustments based on the data.

The results have been impressive. The use of long–term isolation in 53
England is now negligible. In all of England, there are now fewer prisoners in "extreme custody" than there are in the state of Maine. And the
other countries of Europe have, with a similar focus on small units and
violence prevention, achieved a similar outcome.

In this country, in June of 2006, a bipartisan national task force, the 54
Commission on Safety and Abuse in America's Prisons, released its recommendations after a yearlong investigation. It called for ending long–
term isolation of prisoners. Beyond about ten days, the report noted,
practically no benefits can be found and the harm is clear— not just for
inmates but for the public as well. Most prisoners in long–term isolation
are returned to society, after all. And evidence from a number of studies

has shown that supermax conditions — in which prisoners have virtually no social interactions and are given no programmatic support — make it highly likely that they will commit more crimes when they are released. Instead, the report said, we should follow the preventive approaches used in European countries.

The recommendations went nowhere, of course. Whatever the evi- 55 dence in its favor, people simply did not believe in the treatment.

I spoke to a state-prison commissioner who wished to remain un- 56 identified. He was a veteran of the system, having been either a prison warden or a commissioner in several states across the country for more than twenty years. He has publicly defended the use of long-term isolation everywhere that he has worked. Nonetheless, he said, he would remove most prisoners from long-term isolation units if he could and provide programming for the mental illnesses that many of them have.

"Prolonged isolation is not going to serve anyone's best interest," he 57 told me. He still thought that prisons needed the option of isolation. "A bad violation should, I think, land you there for about ninety days, but it should not go beyond that."

He is apparently not alone among prison officials. Over the years, he 58 has come to know commissioners in nearly every state in the country. "I believe that today you'll probably find that two-thirds or three-fourths of the heads of correctional agencies will largely share the position that I articulated with you," he said.

Commissioners are not powerless. They could eliminate prolonged 59 isolation with the stroke of a pen. So, I asked, why haven't they? He told me what happened when he tried to move just one prisoner out of isolation. Legislators called for him to be fired and threatened to withhold basic funding. Corrections officers called members of the crime victim's family and told them that he'd gone soft on crime. Hostile stories appeared in the tabloids. It is pointless for commissioners to act unilaterally, he said, without a change in public opinion.

This past year, both the Republican and the Democratic Presiden- 60 tial candidates came out firmly for banning torture and closing the facility in Guantánamo Bay, where hundreds of prisoners have been held in years-long isolation. Neither Barack Obama nor John McCain, however, addressed the question of whether prolonged solitary confinement is torture. For a Presidential candidate, no less than for the prison commissioner, this would have been political suicide. The simple truth is that public sentiment in America is the reason that solitary confinement has exploded in this country, even as other Western nations have taken steps to reduce it. This is the dark side of American exceptionalism. With little concern or demurral, we have consigned tens of thousands of our own citizens to conditions that horrified our highest court a century ago. Our willingness to discard these standards for American prisoners made it easy to discard the Geneva Conventions prohibiting similar treatment of foreign prisoners of war, to the detriment of America's moral stature in the world. In much the same way that a previous generation of Americans countenanced legalized segregation, ours has countenanced legalized torture. And there is no clearer manifestation of this than our routine use of solitary confinement—on our own people, in our own communities, in a supermax prison, for example, that is a thirty-minute drive from my door.

Reading Closely

1. What argument is Gawande making about long-term solitary confinement for prison inmates?
2. What are the effects of solitary confinement on humans (and monkeys)?
3. How does cause-and-effect analysis help Gawande make this argument?
4. **With a classmate,** review the arrangement of this essay. Why does Gawande choose to wait until almost halfway through the essay to discuss the effects of solitary confinement on prison inmates? In other words, why does he discuss the effects of solitary confinement on monkeys and prisoners of war first?
5. What tone or mood does the drawing on page 526 create? How does this image support (or why does it detract from) the causal argument Gawande is making in his essay?

Considering Larger Issues

1. What about Gawande's essay surprised or especially interested you? Did his essay affect your thinking about solitary confinement? If so, how?
2. COMBINING METHODS. Gawande uses *description, narration, exemplification, definition,* and *process analysis* to support his cause–and–effect analysis. But the rhetorical method that most effectively supports his analysis is *comparison and contrast.* Identify the comparisons Gawande draws in this essay. How do they help him achieve his purpose?
3. Identify the place in the essay where Gawande discusses Britain's strategy for prison violence. What is this strategy? What are its effects? Why do you think Americans reject the British strategy for prison violence prevention?

Thinking about Language

1. Using the context of the essay or your dictionary, define the following words and phrases. Be prepared to share your answers with the rest of the class.

elemental (1)	aperture (30)	shankings (44)
benign (9)	contraband (31)	belligerents (45)
unpalatable (11)	paradoxes (34)	semi–fatuous (46)
neurotically (13)	succumbed (34)	punitive (50)
catatonic (18)	apathy (35)	unilaterally (59)
dysentery (19)	lethargy (35)	exceptionalism (60)
diffuse (20)	stringent (43)	demurral (60)
elation (21)	incapacitate (43)	countenanced (60)
circumvent (28)		

2. Gawande uses a number of emotionally charged words to persuade readers. Identify these terms and be ready to discuss how they move readers to see the negative effects of prison isolation.

Writing Your Own Essays Using Cause-and-Effect Analysis

1. Gawande states that even in the face of examples like Britain, the American people continue to support long–term solitary confinement for prisoners. Conduct research on the arguments made in opposition to Gawande's. In other words, research the arguments *for* solitary confinement. What do these advocates believe are the *benefits* of solitary confinement? Compose a three– to four–page essay that examines the positive and negative effects of solitary confinement, using Gawande's essay as just one among a number of sources. Conclude the essay by explaining where you stand in this debate. Consult the guidelines for checking over a cause–and–effect analysis on pages 483–84 as you draft and revise.

2. There are a number of other compelling controversies regarding treatment of prisoners besides the debate over solitary confinement. The rate of incarceration, access to medical and mental health care, and basic living conditions in the facilities are just a few of these issues. Identify one of these controversies, and consider the causes and effects of this issue on prisoners' lives as well as on the prison and legal system as a whole. You'll certainly want to conduct extensive research regarding your issue. As you draft and revise your essay, consult the guidelines for checking over a cause–and–effect analysis on pages 483–84.

CLAUDIA WALLIS
The Multitasking Generation

A graduate of Yale University with a degree in philosophy, Claudia Wallis began her career at *Time* magazine in 1979 as a medical writer. As she moved up the ranks at the publication, she contributed articles that focus on women's and children's issues, health, education, science, and lifestyle — more than twenty of them cover stories. In 1995, she founded *Time for Kids,* and she also edits "Connections," a special section in *Time* intended for its female readership. A former managing editor of the magazine, she is now its editor at large. In the following essay, published in *Time* in 2008, Wallis explores how "multitasking" affects American teens today.

> **Preview**   How do you multitask during the day? What effect is this practice having on your life?

It's 9:30 p.m., and Stephen and Georgina Cox know exactly where their children are. Well, their bodies, at least. Piers, 14, is holed up in his bedroom — eyes fixed on his computer screen — where he has been logged onto a MySpace chat room and AOL Instant Messenger (IM) for the past three hours. His twin sister Bronte is planted in the living room, having commandeered her dad's iMac — as usual. She, too, is busily IMing, while chatting on her cell phone and chipping away at homework. 1

By all standard space-time calculations, the four members of the family occupy the same three-bedroom home in Van Nuys, Calif., but psychologically each exists in his or her own little universe. Georgina, 51, who works for a display-cabinet maker, is tidying up the living room as Bronte works, not that her daughter notices. Stephen, 49, who juggles jobs as a squash coach, fitness trainer, event planner and head of a cancer charity he founded, has wolfed down his dinner alone in the kitchen, having missed supper with the kids. He, too, typically spends the evening on his cell phone and returning e-mails — when he can nudge Bronte off the computer. "One gets obsessed with one's gadgets," he concedes. 2

Zooming in on Piers' screen gives a pretty good indication of what's on his hyperkinetic mind. O.K., there's a Google Images window open, where he's chasing down pictures of Keira Knightley. Good ones get added to a snazzy Windows Media Player slide show that serves as his personal e-shrine to the actress. Several IM windows are also open, revealing such penetrating conversations as this one with a MySpace pal: 3

MySpacer: suuuuuup!!! (Translation: What's up?)
Piers: wat up dude
MySpacer: nmu (Not much. You?)
Piers: same

Naturally, iTunes is open, and Piers is blasting a mix of Queen, AC/ 4
DC, classic rock and hip–hop. Somewhere on the screen there's a Word
file, in which Piers is writing an essay for English class. "I usually fin–
ish my homework at school," he explains to a visitor, "but if not, I pop a
book open on my lap in my room, and while the computer is loading, I'll
do a problem or write a sentence. Then, while mail is loading, I do more.
I get it done a little bit at a time."

Bronte has the same strategy. "You just multitask," she explains. "My 5
parents always tell me I can't do homework while listening to music,
but they don't understand that it helps me concentrate." The twins also
multitask when hanging with friends, which has its own etiquette. "When
I talk to my best friend Eloy," says Piers, "he'll have one earpiece [of his
iPod] in and one out." Says Bronte: "If a friend thinks she's not getting my
full attention, I just make it very clear that she is, even though I'm also
listening to music."

The Coxes are one of 32 families in the Los Angeles area participating 6
in an intensive, four-year study of modern family life, led by anthropolo–
gist Elinor Ochs, director of UCLA's Center on Everyday Lives of Fami–
lies. While the impact of multitasking gadgets was not her original focus,
Ochs found it to be one of the most dramatic areas of change since she
conducted a similar study 20 years ago. "I'm not certain how the children
can monitor all those things at the same time, but I think it is pretty
consequential for the structure of the family relationship," says Ochs,
whose work on language, interaction and culture earned her a MacArthur
"genius" grant.

One of the things Ochs' team of observers looks at is what happens 7
at the end of the workday when parents and kids reunite — and what
doesn't happen, as in the case of the Coxes. "We saw that when the work–
ing parent comes through the door, the other spouse and the kids are so
absorbed by what they're doing that they don't give the arriving parent
the time of day," says Ochs. The returning parent, generally the father, was
greeted only about a third of the time, usually with a perfunctory "Hi."
"About half the time the kids ignored him or didn't stop what they were
doing, multitasking and monitoring their various electronic gadgets," she
says. "We also saw how difficult it was for parents to penetrate the child's
universe. We have so many videotapes of parents actually backing away,
retreating from kids who are absorbed by whatever they're doing."

Human beings have always had a capacity to attend to several things at 8
once. Mothers have done it since the hunter–gatherer era — picking ber–
ries while suckling an infant, stirring the pot with one eye on the toddler.
Nor is electronic multitasking entirely new: we've been driving while lis–
tening to car radios since they became popular in the 1930s. But there is
no doubt that the phenomenon has reached a kind of warp speed in the
era of Web–enabled computers, when it has become routine to conduct six

IM conversations, watch *American Idol* on TV and Google the names of last season's finalists all at once.

That level of multiprocessing and interpersonal connectivity is now 9 so commonplace that it's easy to forget how quickly it came about. Fifteen years ago, most home computers weren't even linked to the Internet. In 1990 the majority of adolescents responding to a survey done by Donald Roberts, a professor of communication at Stanford, said the one medium they couldn't live without was a radio/CD player. How quaint. In a 2004 follow-up, the computer won hands down.

Today 82% of kids are online by the seventh grade, according to the Pew 10 Internet and American Life Project. And what they love about the computer, of course, is that it offers the radio/CD thing and so much more—games, movies, e-mail, IM, Google, MySpace. The big finding of a 2005 survey of Americans ages 8 to 18 by the Kaiser Family Foundation, co-authored by Roberts, is not that kids were spending a larger chunk of time using electronic media—that was holding steady at 6.5 hours a day (could it possibly get any bigger?)—but that they were packing more media exposure into that time: 8.5 hours' worth, thanks to "media multitasking"—listening to iTunes, watching a DVD and IMing friends all at the same time. Increasingly, the media–hungry members of Generation M, as Kaiser dubbed them, don't just sit down to watch a TV show with their friends or family. From a quarter to a third of them, according to the survey, say they simultaneously absorb some other medium "most of the time" while watching TV, listening to music, using the computer or even while reading.

Parents have watched this phenomenon unfold with a mixture of awe 11 and concern. The Coxes, for instance, are bowled over by their children's technical prowess. Piers repairs the family computers and DVD player. Bronte uses digital technology to compose elaborate photo collages and create a documentary of her father's ongoing treatment for cancer. And, says Georgina, "they both make these fancy PowerPoint presentations about what they want for Christmas." But both parents worry about the ways that kids' compulsive screen time is affecting their schoolwork and squeezing out family life. "We rarely have dinner together anymore," frets Stephen. "Everyone is in their own little world, and we don't get out together to have a social life."

Every generation of adults sees new technology—and the social 12 changes it stirs—as a threat to the rightful order of things: Plato warned (correctly) that reading would be the downfall of oral tradition and memory. And every generation of teenagers embraces the freedoms and possibilities wrought by technology in ways that shock the elders: just think about what the automobile did for dating.

As for multitasking devices, social scientists and educators are just 13 beginning to assess their impact, but the researchers already have some strong opinions. The mental habit of dividing one's attention into many small slices has significant implications for the way young people learn, reason, socialize, do creative work and understand the world. Although such habits may prepare kids for today's frenzied workplace, many cognitive scientists are positively alarmed by the trend. "Kids that are instant messaging while doing homework, playing games online and watching TV, I predict, aren't going to do well in the long run," says Jordan Grafman, chief of the cognitive neuroscience section at the National Institute of Neurological Disorders and Stroke (NINDS). Decades of research (not to mention common sense) indicate that the quality of one's output and depth of thought deteriorate as one attends to ever more tasks. Some are concerned about the disappearance of mental downtime to relax and reflect. Roberts notes Stanford students "can't go the few minutes between their 10 o'clock and 11 o'clock classes without talking on their cell phones. It seems to me that there's almost a discomfort with not being stimulated—a kind of 'I can't stand the silence.'"

Gen M's multitasking habits have social and psychological implica- 14 tions as well. If you're IMing four friends while watching *That '70s Show*, it's not the same as sitting on the couch with your buddies or your sisters and watching the show together. Or sharing a family meal across a table. Thousands of years of evolution created human physical communication— facial expressions, body language—that puts broadband to shame in its ability to convey meaning and create bonds. What happens, wonders UCLA's Ochs, as we replace side-by-side and eye-to-eye human connections with quick, disembodied e-exchanges? Those are critical issues not just for social scientists but for parents and teachers trying to understand—and do right by—Generation M.

YOUR BRAIN WHEN IT MULTITASKS

Although many aspects of the networked life remain scientifically un- 15 charted, there's substantial literature on how the brain handles multitasking. And basically, it doesn't. It may seem that a teenage girl is writing an instant message, burning a CD and telling her mother that she's doing homework—all at the same time—but what's really going on is a rapid toggling among tasks rather than simultaneous processing. "You're doing more than one thing, but you're ordering them and deciding which one to do at any one time," explains neuroscientist Grafman.

Then why can we so easily walk down the street while engrossed 16 in a deep conversation? Why can we chop onions while watching *Jeopardy*? "We, along with quite a few others, have been focused on exactly this question," says Hal Pashler, psychology professor at the University of California at San Diego. It turns out that very automatic actions or what researchers call "highly practiced skills," like walking or chopping an onion, can be easily done while thinking about other things, although the decision to add an extra onion to a recipe or change the direction in which you're walking is another matter. "It seems that action planning—figuring out what I want to say in response to a person's question or which way I want to steer the car—is usually, perhaps invariably, performed sequentially" or one task at a time, says Pashler. On the other hand, producing the actions you've decided on—moving your hand on the steering wheel, speaking the words you've formulated—can be performed "in parallel with planning some other action." Similarly, many aspects of perception—looking, listening, touching—can be performed in parallel with action planning and with movement.

The switching of attention from one task to another, the toggling 17 action, occurs in a region right behind the forehead called Brodmann's Area 10 in the brain's anterior prefrontal cortex, according to a functional magnetic resonance imaging (fMRI) study by Grafman's team. Brodmann's Area 10 is part of the frontal lobes, which "are important for maintaining long-term goals and achieving them," Grafman explains. "The most anterior part allows you to leave something when it's incomplete and return to the same place and continue from there." This gives us a "form of multitasking," he says, though it's actually sequential processing. Because the prefrontal cortex is one of the last regions of the brain to mature and one of the first to decline with aging, young children do not multitask well, and neither do most adults over 60. New fMRI studies at Toronto's Rotman Research Institute suggest that as we get older, we have more trouble "turning down background thoughts when turning to a new task," says Rotman senior scientist and assistant director Cheryl Grady. "Younger adults are better at tuning out stuff when they want to," says Grady. "I'm in my 50s, and I know that I can't work and listen to music with lyrics; it was easier when I was younger."

But the ability to multiprocess has its limits, even among young 18 adults. When people try to perform two or more related tasks either at the same time or alternating rapidly between them, errors go way up, and it takes far longer—often double the time or more—to get the jobs done than if they were done sequentially, says David E. Meyer, director of the Brain, Cognition and Action Laboratory at the University of Michigan: "The toll in terms of slowdown is extremely large—amazingly so." Meyer frequently tests Gen M students in his lab, and he sees no exception for them, despite their "mystique" as master multitaskers. "The bottom line is that you can't simultaneously be thinking about your tax return and reading an essay, just as you can't talk to yourself about two things at once," he says. "If a teenager is trying to have a conversation on an e-mail chat line while doing algebra, she'll suffer a decrease in efficiency, compared to if she just thought about algebra until she was done. People

**"This project calls for real concentration.
Are you still able to monotask?"**

www.CartoonStock.com

may think otherwise, but it's a myth. With such complicated tasks [you]
will never, ever be able to overcome the inherent limitations in the brain
for processing information during multitasking. It just can't be, any more
than the best of all humans will ever be able to run a one-minute mile."

Other research shows the relationship between stimulation and per-   19
formance forms a bell curve: a little stimulation—whether it's coffee or
a blaring soundtrack—can boost performance, but too much is stressful
and causes a fall-off. In addition, the brain needs rest and recovery time
to consolidate thoughts and memories. Teenagers who fill every quiet
moment with a phone call or some kind of e-stimulation may not be
getting that needed reprieve. Habitual multitasking may condition their
brain to an overexcited state, making it difficult to focus even when they
want to. "People lose the skill and the will to maintain concentration, and
they get mental antsiness," says Meyer.

IS THIS ANY WAY TO LEARN?

Longtime professors at universities around the U.S. have noticed that 20
Gen M kids arrive on campus with a different set of cognitive skills and
habits than past generations. In lecture halls with wireless Internet access—
now more than 40% of college classrooms, according to the Campus Computing Project—the compulsion to multitask can get out of hand. "People
are going to lectures by some of the greatest minds, and they are doing
their mail," says Sherry Turkle, professor of the social studies of science and
technology at M.I.T. In her class, says Turkle, "I tell them this is not a place
for e–mail, it's not a place to do online searches and not a place to set up
IRC [Internet relay chat] channels in which to comment on the class. It's
not going to help if there are parallel discussions about how boring it is.
You've got to get people to participate in the world as it is."

Such concerns have, in fact, led a number of schools, including the 21
M.B.A. programs at UCLA and the University of Virginia, to look into
blocking Internet access during lectures. "I tell my students not to treat
me like TV," says University of Wisconsin professor Aaron Brower, who
has been teaching social work for 20 years. "They have to think of me
like a real person talking. I want to have them thinking about things
we're talking about."

On the positive side, Gen M students tend to be extraordinarily good 22
at finding and manipulating information. And presumably because modern childhood tilts toward visual rather than print media, they are especially skilled at analyzing visual data and images, observes Claudia
Koonz, professor of history at Duke University. A growing number of college professors are using film, audio clips and PowerPoint presentations
to play to their students' strengths and capture their evanescent attention. It's a powerful way to teach history, says Koonz. "I love bringing
media into the classroom, to be able to go to the website for Edward R.
Murrow and hear his voice as he walked with the liberators of Buchen-
wald." Another adjustment to teaching Generation M: professors are assigning fewer full–length books and more excerpts and articles. (Koonz,
however, was stunned when a student matter–of–factly informed her, "We
don't read whole books anymore," after Koonz had assigned a 350–page
volume. "And this is Duke!" she says.)

Many students make brilliant use of media in their work, embedding 23
audio files and video clips in their presentations, but the habit of grazing
among many data streams leaves telltale signs in their writing, according to
some educators. "The breadth of their knowledge and their ability to find
answers has just burgeoned," says Roberts of his students at Stanford, "but
my impression is that their ability to write clear, focused and extended narratives has eroded somewhat." Says Koonz: "What I find is paragraphs that
make sense internally, but don't necessarily follow a line of argument."

Koonz and Turkle believe that today's students are less tolerant of 24
ambiguity than the students they taught in the past. "They demand clar-

ity," says Koonz. They want identifiable good guys and bad guys, which she finds problematic in teaching complex topics like Hutu–Tutsi history in Rwanda. She also thinks there are political implications: "Their belief in the simple answer, put together in a visual way, is, I think, dangerous." Koonz thinks this aversion to complexity is directly related to multitasking: "It's as if they have too many windows open on their hard drive. In order to have a taste for sifting through different layers of truth, you have to stay with a topic and pursue it deeply, rather than go across the surface with your toolbar." She tries to encourage her students to find a quiet spot on campus to just think, cell phone off, laptop packed away.

GOT 2 GO. TXT ME L8ER

But turning down the noise isn't easy. By the time many kids get to col- 25 lege, their devices have become extensions of themselves, indispensable social accessories. "The minute the bell rings at most big public high schools, the first thing most kids do is reach into their bag and pick up their cell phone," observes Denise Clark Pope, lecturer at the Stanford School of Education, "never mind that the person [they're contacting] could be right down the hall."

Parents are mystified by this obsession with e-communication— 26 particularly among younger adolescents who often can't wait to share the most mundane details of life. Dominique Jones, 12, of Los Angeles, likes to IM her friends before school to find out what they plan to wear. "You'll get IMs back that say things like 'Oh, my God, I'm wearing the same shoes!' After school we talk about what happened that day, what outfits we want to wear the next day."

Turkle, author of the recently reissued *The Second Self: Computers and the* 27 *Human Spirit*, has an explanation for this breathless exchange of inanities. "There's an extraordinary fit between the medium and the moment, a heady, giddy fit in terms of social needs." The online environment, she points out, "is less risky if you are lonely and afraid of intimacy, which is almost a definition of adolescence. Things get too hot, you log off, while in real time and space, you have consequences." Teen venues like My-Space, Xanga and Facebook—and the ways kids can personalize their IM personas—meet another teen need: the desire to experiment with identity. By changing their picture, their "away" message, their icon or list of favorite bands, kids can cycle through different personalities. "Online life is like an identity workshop," says Turkle, "and that's the job of adolescents—to experiment with identity."

All that is probably healthy, provided that parents set limits on where 28 their kids can venture online, teach them to exercise caution and regulate how much time they can spend with electronics in general. The problem is that most parents don't. According to the Kaiser survey, only 23%

of seventh– to 12th–graders say their family has rules about computer activity; just 17% say they have restrictions on video–game time.

In the absence of rules, it's all too easy for kids to wander into un– wholesome neighborhoods on the Net and get caught up in the compulsive behavior that psychiatrist Edward Hallowell dubs "screen–sucking" in his new book, *CrazyBusy*. Patricia Wallace, a techno–psychologist who directs the Johns Hopkins Center for Talented Youth program, believes part of the allure of e–mail— for adults as well as teens— is similar to that of a slot machine. "You have intermittent, variable reinforcement," she explains. "You are not sure you are going to get a reward every time or how often you will, so you keep pulling that handle. Why else do people get up in the middle of the night to check their e–mail?"   29

GETTING THEM TO LOG OFF

Many educators and psychologists say parents need to actively ensure that their teenagers break free of compulsive engagement with screens and spend time in the physical company of human beings — a growing challenge not just because technology offers such a handy alternative but because so many kids lead highly scheduled lives that leave little time for old–fashioned socializing and family meals. Indeed, many teenagers and college students say overcommitted schedules drive much of their multitasking.   30

Just as important is for parents and educators to teach kids, preferably by example, that it's valuable, even essential, to occasionally slow down, unplug and take time to think about something for a while. David Levy, a professor at the University of Washington Information School, has found, to his surprise, that his most technophilic undergraduates — those majoring in "informatics" — are genuinely concerned about getting lost in the multitasking blur. In an informal poll of 60 students last semester, he says, the majority expressed concerns about how plugged–in they were and "the way it takes them away from other activities, including exercise, meals and sleep." Levy's students talked about difficulties concentrating and their efforts to break away, get into the outdoors and inside their head. "Although it wasn't a scientific survey," he says, "it was the first evidence I had that people in this age group are reflecting on these questions."   31

For all the handwringing about Generation M, technology is not really the problem. "The problem," says Hallowell, "is what you are not doing if the electronic moment grows too large"— too large for the teenager and too large for those parents who are equally tethered to their gadgets. In that case, says Hallowell, "you are not having family dinner, you are not having conversations, you are not debating whether to go out with a boy who wants to have sex on the first date, you are not going on a family ski trip or taking time just to veg. It's not so much that the video game is going to rot your brain; it's what you are not doing that's going to rot your life."   32

Generation M has a lot to teach parents and teachers about what 33
new technology can do. But it's up to grownups to show them what it
can't do, and that there's life beyond the screen.

Reading Closely

1. What is the purpose of this essay: to entertain? inform? speculate?
   argue?
2. According to Wallis, what are the effects of multitasking?
3. What kinds of research does Wallis call on in this essay? How does this
   research support her cause–and–effect analysis?
4. Evaluate Wallis's method of organization in this essay. Do you find it effective? Why or why not?
5. Review the cartoon on page 545. Identify a passage from Wallis's essay
   that speaks directly to the issue raised in the cartoon. Why did you make
   this connection between the cartoon and this passage?

Considering Larger Issues

1. This essay examines the effects of multitasking, but what do you see as
   its *causes*? Why are people so drawn to this practice?
2. **Working with a classmate,** reflect on the kinds of multitasking that
   happen in everyday college life. What are the effects of this multitasking?
3. The final section of the essay offers solutions to the multitasking problem. What do you think of these solutions?
4. COMBINING METHODS. Identify places in the essay where Wallis uses *exem
   plification, comparison and contrast*, and *description*. What do these rhetorical
   methods of development contribute to this essay?

Thinking about Language

1. Using the context of the essay or your dictionary, define the following
   words and phrases. Be prepared to share your answers with the rest of
   the class.

commandeered (1)	toggling (15)	burgeoned (23)
hyperkinetic (3)	anterior prefrontal	ambiguity (24)
consequential (6)	cortex (17)	mundane (26)
perfunctory (7)	mystique (18)	inanities (27)
interpersonal	bell curve (19)	intermittent (29)
connectivity (9)	habitual (19)	technophilic (31)
prowess (11)	compulsion (20)	informatics (31)
cognitive (13)	evanescent (22)	

2. What is the tone of this essay? Identify specific places in the text that support your answer. How does the tone further Wallis's purpose?

Writing Your Own Essays Using Cause-and-Effect Analysis

1. Building on your response to question 2 under Considering Larger Issues, compose a three- to four-page essay in which you explore the effects of multitasking that you see in your daily life. You might consider the multitasking that you do, or you might reflect on how the multitasking of others (your roommate, coworker, parent) affects you. As you draft and revise, refer to "Checking Over the Use of Cause–and–Effect Analysis" on pages 483–84.

2. Instead of thinking about multitasking, pinpoint a moment when you were focused on a particular project and did *not* multitask. Compose a two- to three-page essay in which you describe this project and the effects of your attention on it. You might especially discuss how you *avoided* multitasking so that you could focus intently on the issue at hand. Use description and narration to support your analysis. The guidelines for checking over the use of cause–and–effect analysis on pages 483–84 will help you as you draft and revise.

NICHOLAS CARR
Is Google Making Us Stupid?

Nicholas Carr (b. 1968) explores such topics as information technology and technological utopianism in his three books *Digital Enterprise: How to Reshape Your Business for a Connected World* (2001), *Does IT Matter? Information Technology and the Corrosion of Competitive Advantage* (2004), and *The Big Switch: Rewiring the World from Edison to Google* (2008). He also takes up these subjects in his blog, Rough Type. In the following essay, published in the *Atlantic* in 2008, Carr considers the effects of the Internet on human cognition.

> **Preview** Consider the question in Carr's title. How might Google be making (or not making) us stupid?

Stop, will you? Stop, Dave. Will you stop, Dave?" So the su- 1
per HAL pleads with the implacable astronaut Dave Bowman in
and weirdly poignant scene toward the end of Stanley Kubrick's
2001: A Space Odyssey. Bowman, having nearly been sent to a deep-space
the malfunctioning machine, is calmly, coldly disconnecting the
circuits that control its artificial brain. "Dave, my mind is going,"
forlornly. "I can feel it. I can feel it."

feel it, too. Over the past few years I've had an uncomfortable 2
sense that someone, or something, has been tinkering with my brain, re-
mapping the neural circuitry, reprogramming the memory. My mind isn't
going—so far as I can tell—but it's changing. I'm not thinking the way
I used to think. I can feel it most strongly when I'm reading. Immersing
myself in a book or a lengthy article used to be easy. My mind would get
caught up in the narrative or the turns of the argument, and I'd spend
hours strolling through long stretches of prose. That's rarely the case
anymore. Now my concentration often starts to drift after two or three

First published in the *Atlantic Monthly*

pages. I get fidgety, lose the thread, begin looking for something else to do. I feel as if I'm always dragging my wayward brain back to the text. The deep reading that used to come naturally has become a struggle.

I think I know what's going on. For more than a decade now, I've been spending a lot of time online, searching and surfing and sometimes adding to the great databases of the Internet. The Web has been a godsend to me as a writer. Research that once required days in the stacks or periodical rooms of libraries can now be done in minutes. A few Google searches, some quick clicks on hyperlinks, and I've got the telltale fact or pithy quote I was after. Even when I'm not working, I'm as likely as not to be foraging in the Web's info–thickets — reading and writing e–mails, scanning headlines and blog posts, watching videos and listening to podcasts, or just tripping from link to link to link. (Unlike footnotes, to which they're sometimes likened, hyperlinks don't merely point to related works; they propel you toward them.)

For me, as for others, the Net is becoming a universal medium, the conduit for most of the information that flows through my eyes and ears and into my mind. The advantages of having immediate access to such an incredibly rich store of information are many, and they've been widely described and duly applauded. "The perfect recall of silicon memory," *Wired*'s Clive Thompson has written, "can be an enormous boon to thinking." But that boon comes at a price. As the media theorist Marshall McLuhan pointed out in the 1960s, media are not just passive channels of information. They supply the stuff of thought, but they also shape the process of thought. And what the Net seems to be doing is chipping away my capacity for concentration and contemplation. My mind now expects to take in information the way the Net distributes it: in a swiftly moving stream of particles. Once I was a scuba diver in the sea of words. Now I zip along the surface like a guy on a Jet Ski.

I'm not the only one. When I mention my troubles with reading to friends and acquaintances — literary types, most of them — many say they're having similar experiences. The more they use the Web, the more they have to fight to stay focused on long pieces of writing. Some of the bloggers I follow have also begun mentioning the phenomenon. Scott Karp, who writes a blog about online media, recently confessed that he has stopped reading books altogether. "I was a lit major in college, and used to be [a] voracious book reader," he wrote. "What happened?" He speculates on the answer: "What if I do all my reading on the web not so much because the way I read has changed, i.e. I'm just seeking convenience, but because the way I THINK has changed?"

Bruce Friedman, who blogs regularly about the use of computers in medicine, also has described how the Internet has altered his mental habits. "I now have almost totally lost the ability to read and absorb a longish article on the web or in print," he wrote earlier this year. A pathologist who has long been on the faculty of the University of Michigan Medical School, Friedman elaborated on his comment in a telephone conversation with me. His thinking, he said, has taken on a "staccato" quality, reflecting the way he quickly scans short passages of text from many sources online. "I can't read *War and Peace* anymore," he admitted. "I've lost the ability to do that. Even a blog post of more than three or four paragraphs is too much to absorb. I skim it."

Anecdotes alone don't prove much. And we still await the long-term 7 neurological and psychological experiments that will provide a definitive picture of how Internet use affects cognition. But a recently published study of online research habits, conducted by scholars from University College London, suggests that we may well be in the midst of a sea change in the way we read and think. As part of the five-year research program, the scholars examined computer logs documenting the behavior of visitors to two popular research sites, one operated by the British Library and one by a U.K. educational consortium, that provide access to journal articles, e-books, and other sources of written information. They found that people using the sites exhibited "a form of skimming activity," hopping from one source to another and rarely returning to any source they'd already visited. They typically read no more than one or two pages of an article or book before they would "bounce" out to another site. Sometimes they'd save a long article, but there's no evidence that they ever went back and actually read it. The authors of the study report:

> It is clear that users are not reading online in the traditional sense; indeed there are signs that new forms of "reading" are emerging as users "power browse" horizontally through titles, contents pages and abstracts going for quick wins. It almost seems that they go online to avoid reading in the traditional sense.

Thanks to the ubiquity of text on the Internet, not to mention the 8 popularity of text-messaging on cell phones, we may well be reading more today than we did in the 1970s or 1980s, when television was our medium of choice. But it's a different kind of reading, and behind it lies a different kind of thinking—perhaps even a new sense of the self. "We are not only *what* we read," says Maryanne Wolf, a developmental psychologist at Tufts University and the author of *Proust and the Squid: The Story and Science of the Reading Brain.* "We are *how* we read." Wolf worries that the style of reading promoted by the Net, a style that puts "efficiency" and "immediacy" above all else, may be weakening our capacity for the kind of deep reading that emerged when an earlier technology, the printing press, made long and complex works of prose commonplace. When we read online, she says, we tend to become "mere decoders of information." Our ability to interpret text, to make the rich mental connections that form when we read deeply and without distraction, remains largely disengaged.

Reading, explains Wolf, is not an instinctive skill for human beings. 9 It's not etched into our genes the way speech is. We have to teach our

process, a series of discrete steps that can be isolated, measured, and op-timized. In Google's world, the world we enter when we go online, there's little place for the fuzziness of contemplation. Ambiguity is not an open-ing for insight but a bug to be fixed. The human brain is just an outdated computer that needs a faster processor and a bigger hard drive.

The idea that our minds should operate as high–speed data–processing 29
machines is not only built into the workings of the Internet, it is the net-work's reigning business model as well. The faster we surf across the Web—the more links we click and pages we view—the more opportuni-ties Google and other companies gain to collect information about us and to feed us advertisements. Most of the proprietors of the commercial Inter-net have a financial stake in collecting the crumbs of data we leave behind as we flit from link to link—the more crumbs, the better. The last thing these companies want is to encourage leisurely reading or slow, concen-trated thought. It's in their economic interest to drive us to distraction.

Maybe I'm just a worrywart. Just as there's a tendency to glorify techno– 30
logical progress, there's a countertendency to expect the worst of every new tool or machine. In Plato's *Phaedrus*, Socrates bemoaned the development of writing. He feared that, as people came to rely on the written word as a substitute for the knowledge they used to carry inside their heads, they would, in the words of one of the dialogue's characters, "cease to exercise their memory and become forgetful." And because they would be able to "receive a quantity of information without proper instruction," they would "be thought very knowledgeable when they are for the most part quite ignorant." They would be "filled with the conceit of wisdom instead of real wisdom." Socrates wasn't wrong—the new technology did often have the effects he feared—but he was shortsighted. He couldn't foresee the many ways that writing and reading would serve to spread informa-tion, spur fresh ideas, and expand human knowledge (if not wisdom).

The arrival of Gutenberg's printing press, in the 15th century, set off 31
another round of teeth gnashing. The Italian humanist Hieronimo Squar-ciafico worried that the easy availability of books would lead to intel-lectual laziness, making men "less studious" and weakening their minds. Others argued that cheaply printed books and broadsheets would under-mine religious authority, demean the work of scholars and scribes, and spread sedition and debauchery. As New York University professor Clay Shirky notes, "Most of the arguments made against the printing press were correct, even prescient." But, again, the doomsayers were unable to imagine the myriad blessings that the printed word would deliver.

So, yes, you should be skeptical of my skepticism. Perhaps those who 32
dismiss critics of the Internet as Luddites or nostalgists will be proved correct, and from our hyperactive, data–stoked minds will spring a golden age of intellectual discovery and universal wisdom. Then again, the Net isn't the alphabet, and although it may replace the printing press, it pro-

duces something altogether different. The kind of deep reading that a sequence of printed pages promotes is valuable not just for the knowledge we acquire from the author's words but for the intellectual vibrations those words set off within our own minds. In the quiet spaces opened up by the sustained, undistracted reading of a book, or by any other act of contemplation, for that matter, we make our own associations, draw our own inferences and analogies, foster our own ideas. Deep reading, as Maryanne Wolf argues, is indistinguishable from deep thinking.

If we lose those quiet spaces, or fill them up with "content," we will 33 sacrifice something important not only in ourselves but in our culture. In a recent essay, the playwright Richard Foreman eloquently described what's at stake:

> I come from a tradition of Western culture, in which the ideal (my ideal) was the complex, dense and "cathedral-like" structure of the highly educated and articulate personality—a man or woman who carried . . . a personally constructed and unique version of the entire heritage of the West. [But now] I see within us all (myself included) the replacement of complex inner density with a new kind of self—evolving under the pressure of information overload and the technology of the "instantly available."

As we are drained of our "inner repertory of dense cultural inheritance," Foreman concluded, we risk turning into "'pancake people'—spread wide and thin as we connect with that vast network of information accessed by the mere touch of a button."

I'm haunted by that scene in *2001*. What makes it so poignant, and 34 so weird, is the computer's emotional response to the disassembly of its mind: its despair as one circuit after another goes dark, its childlike pleading with the astronaut—"I can feel it. I can feel it. I'm afraid"—and its final reversion to what can only be called a state of innocence. HAL's outpouring of feeling contrasts with the emotionlessness that characterizes the human figures in the film, who go about their business with an almost robotic efficiency. Their thoughts and actions feel scripted, as if they're following the steps of an algorithm. In the world of *2001*, people have become so machinelike that the most human character turns out to be a machine. That's the essence of Kubrick's dark prophecy: as we come to rely on computers to mediate our understanding of the world, it is our own intelligence that flattens into artificial intelligence.

Reading Closely

1. What is the purpose of this essay?
2. Review the introduction and conclusion to the essay. What is the significance of Carr's beginning and ending by discussing Stanley Kubrick's

film *2001: A Space Odyssey*? What effect does this have on the purpose of the essay?

3. **Working with a classmate,** review the research Carr conducted for this essay. What sources did he consult? How do these sources support his cause–and–effect analysis?

4. What is the cartoon on page 551 trying to say? How is it contributing to, extending, or detracting from Carr's thesis?

Considering Larger Issues

1. How would you describe your reading practices? Has the Internet shaped the way you read? If so, in what ways? If not, why not?

2. COMBINING METHODS. Carr relies heavily on *comparison and contrast* to show how technological change has affected people's lives in small and significant ways. Identify all the comparisons he makes in the essay. How do they support the claims he's making about the effects of the Internet on our lives?

3. PAIRED READINGS. Both Carr's "Is Google Making Us Stupid?" and Claudia Wallis's "The Multitasking Generation" discuss the effects of technology on our lives. Compare the two essays. What are the similarities and differences in these authors' analyses of technology and its effects?

Thinking about Language

1. Using the context of the essay or your dictionary, define the following words and phrases. Be prepared to share your answers with the rest of the class.

implacable (1)	terse (11)	worrywart (30)
poignant (1)	aphorisms (12)	bemoaned (30)
pithy (3)	malleable (13)	gnashing (31)
conduit (4)	plastic (13)	broadsheets (31)
voracious (5)	subsuming (17)	sedition (31)
pathologist (6)	gewgaws (18)	debauchery (31)
staccato (6)	crazy quilt (19)	prescient (31)
consortium (7)	harried (19)	doomsayers (31)
ubiquity (8)	automatons (21)	Luddites (32)
commonplace (8)	terabytes (24)	nostalgists (32)
ideograms (9)		

2. Reflect on Carr's use of metaphor throughout the essay. How does his use of metaphor support the overall cause–and–effect analysis?

Writing Your Own Essays Using Cause-and-Effect Analysis

1. Carr writes that one of the effects of our reliance on artificial intelligence is the loss of contemplation and ambiguity (paragraph 28). In a three- to

four-page essay, consider the benefits (and drawbacks) of the practice of thinking deeply (contemplation) and the experience of uncertainty or "fuzziness" (ambiguity), focusing particularly on the effects that contemplation and ambiguity have on our lives. As you draft and revise, refer to "Checking Over the Use of Cause-and-Effect Analysis" on pages 483–84.

2. Carr focuses his remarks on the Internet and how it might be affecting our brain function. Choose another technology that you use on a daily basis (your cell phone or iPod, for example) and consider how it affects your life—in both positive and negative ways. You might support your analysis by integrating description, narration, and exemplification. Refer to "Checking Over the Use of Cause-and-Effect Analysis" on pages 483–84 as you draft and revise.

3. ACADEMIC WRITING. Both Carr and Wallis are writing to public audiences about the effects of technology and multitasking on cognition, attention, and social interaction. For a six- to eight-page academic essay, carry out a similar, but more specific, causal analysis, in this case about the effects of technology on students' writing and learning. Your audience for this project is your teacher and classmates. To get started on your research, identify journals, books, and reliable Web sites that discuss how educators view technology's effects on student writing and learning. Once you've conducted this research, review and synthesize what you've learned, thinking specifically about the following questions: How are writing and learning changing due to technological developments? What are the positive effects? The negative ones? What challenges do teachers and students face given this situation? As you answer these questions, draft your essay, using "Checking Over the Use of Cause-and-Effect Analysis" on pages 483–84 as a guide.

✱ Additional Suggestions for Writing

1. Draft a three- to four-page essay in which you analyze the causes that led you to become a college student. **Working with one or two classmates,** decide how to rank your primary or immediate cause and contributory or remote causes. Refer to "Checking Over the Use of Cause-and–Effect Analysis" on pages 483–84.

2. Look around you at the people in your classes, at your job, in your daily life. What kinds of judgments are you making about people on the basis of how they look? First make a list of the various "looks" you see every day, including clothing, hairstyle, grooming, footwear, coloring, and age, and of the accessories for each look. (See Chapter 5 for help with classifying.) Then determine the effects of these categories for yourself. What looks are you immediately attracted to? distrustful of? turned off by? Have you learned any important lessons about appearances being deceptive—or have your opinions about appearance been reinforced? Draft a three- to four-page essay in which you investigate the possible consequences of appearance. Refer to "Checking Over the Use of Cause-and–Effect Analysis" on pages 483–84.

3. Define *success*, and then think about the effects of success. As evidence, you might want to use your own life or the life of someone you know well: a parent, for instance. Or you may turn to the popular media and examine one of the many examples of success they offer on a daily basis. Then write a three- to four-page essay on the topic. Be sure to discuss immediate and more remote effects. As you plan, draft, and revise your essay, use the guidelines for checking over the use of cause–and–effect analysis (pp. 483–84) to make sure that your essay has a clear purpose and presents specific examples.

4. Examine yourself—as a writer, a student, a worker, a friend, or a spouse or partner. Open a four-page essay by describing yourself in one of these roles. How well do you fulfill your role? What are the causes of the success or failure you have had in this role? What are the effects? Take some time to develop a list of both the causes and the effects, and then choose one set of responses. Develop your essay by analyzing critically the causes or effects as primary or other (contributory or secondary) or as immediate or remote. **Working with one or two classmates,** discuss your conclusion about yourself as well as the conclusion of your essay. Refer to "Checking Over the Use of Cause-and–Effect Analysis" on pages 483–84.

5. Describe yourself as a college student, and chart the consequences of your decision to become one. What are the immediate effects and the remote or long-term ones? Which is the primary effect? Draft a two- to three-page speculative essay in which you analyze the effects of your getting a college education. As you draft and revise, refer to the guidelines for checking over the use of cause–and–effect analysis on pages 483–84.

chapter

9

DEFINITION

.fine \di-'fīn\ vb de·fined; de·fin·ing [ME, fr. L definire, fr. de- + -re to limit, end, fr. finis boundary, end] vt (14c) **1 a** : to determine identify the essential qualities or meaning of ⟨whatever ∼s us as hu- n⟩ **b** : to discover and set forth the meaning of (as a word) **c** : to ate on a computer ⟨∼ a window⟩ ⟨∼ a procedure⟩ **2 a** : to fix or rk the limits of : DEMARCATE ⟨rigidly defined property lines⟩ **b** o make distinct, clear, or detailed esp. in outline ⟨the issues aren't well defined⟩ **3** : CHARACTERIZE, DISTINGUISH ⟨you ∼ yourself the choices you make —Denison Univ. Bull.⟩ ∼ vi : to make a defi- ion — **de·fine·ment** \-'fīn-mənt\ n — **de·fin·er** \-'fī-nər\ n

fin·i·en·dum \di-ˌfi-nē-'en-dəm\ n, pl -da \-də\ [L, something to be ined, neut. of definiendus, gerundive of definire] (1871) : an expres- n that is being defined

fin·i·ens \di-'fi-nē-ˌenz\ n, pl de·fin·i·en·tia \di-ˌfi-nē-'en(t)-shē-ə prp. of definire] (1838) : an expression that defines : DEFINITION

·i·nite \'de-fə-nit, 'def-nət\ adj [L definitus, pp. of definire] (1553) **1** : aving distinct or certain limits ⟨set ∼ standards for pupils to meet⟩ **a** : free of all ambiguity, uncertainty, or obscurity ⟨demanded a ∼ wer⟩ **b** : UNQUESTIONABLE, DECIDED ⟨the quarterback was a ∼ o today⟩ **3** : typically designating an identified or immediately ntifiable person or thing ⟨the ∼ article the⟩ **4 a** of floral organs eing constant in number, usu. less than 20, and occurring in multi- s of the petal number ⟨stamens ∼⟩ **b** : CYMOSE ⟨a ∼ inflores- ce⟩ syn see EXPLICIT — **def·i·nite·ly** adv — **def·i·nite·ness** n

inite integral n (1834) : the difference between the values of the in- ral of a given function f(x) for an upper value b and a lower value a he independent variable x

·i·ni·tion \ˌde-fə-'ni-shən\ n [ME diffinicioun, fr. AF, fr. L defini- n-, definitio, fr. definire] (14c) **1** : an act of determining; specif : the mal proclamation of a Roman Catholic dogma **2 a** : a statement pressing the essential nature of something **b** : a statement of the aning of a word or word group or a sign or symbol ⟨dictionary ∼s⟩ a product of defining **3** : the action or process of defining **4 a** ae action or the power of describing, explaining, or making definite l clear ⟨the ∼ of a telescope⟩ ⟨her comic genius is beyond ∼⟩ **b** : clarity of visual presentation : distinctness of outline or detail ⟨im- ve the ∼ of an image⟩ (2) : clarity esp. of musical sound in repro- ction **c** : sharp demarcation of outlines or limits ⟨a jacket with dis- ct waist ∼⟩ — **def·i·ni·tion·al** \-'ni-shə-nᵊl\ adj

fin·i·tive \di-'fi-nə-tiv\ adj [ME diffinityf, fr. AF diffinitive, fr. L de- itivus, fr. definitus] (14c) **1** : serving to provide a final solution or to **l** a situation ⟨a ∼ victory⟩ **2** : authoritative and apparently ex- ustive ⟨a ∼ edition⟩ **3 a** : serving to define or specify precisely ∼s⟩ **b** : serving as a perfect example : QUINTESSENTIAL ⟨a ∼ bour- ois⟩ **4** : fully differentiated or developed ⟨a ∼ organ⟩ **5** of a post- stamp : issued as a regular stamp for the country or territory in ich it is to be used syn see CONCLUSIVE — **de·fin·i·tive·ly** adv — ·fin·i·tive·ness n

·nitive n (1951) : a definitive postage stamp — compare PROVISION-

·nitive host n (1901) : the host in which the sexual reproduction of arasite takes place — compare INTERMEDIATE HOST 1

fi·ni·tize \'de-fə-nə-ˌtīz, di-'fi-\ vt -tized; -tiz·ing (1876) : to make inite

fi·ni·tude \di-'fi-nə-ˌtüd, -ˌtyüd\ n [irreg. fr. definite] (1836) : PRECI- N, DEFINITENESS

·la·grate \'def-lə-ˌgrāt\ vb -grat·ed; -grat·ing [L deflagratus, pp. of lagrare to burn down, fr. de- + flagrare to burn — more at BLACK] vt . 1727) : to cause to deflagrate — compare DETONATE 1 ∼ vi : to rn rapidly with intense heat and sparks being given off — **def·la· a·tion** \def-lə-'grā-shən\ n

flate \di-'flāt, ˌdē-\ vb de·flat·ed; de·flat·ing [de- + -flate (as in in- ʼe)] vt (1891) **1** : to release air or gas from ⟨∼ a tire⟩ **2** : to reduce size, importance, or effectiveness ⟨∼ his ego with cutting remarks⟩ to reduce (a price level) or cause (a volume of credit) to contract ∼ to lose firmness through or as if through the escape of contained syn see CONTRACT — **de·fla·tor** also **de·fla·ter** \-'flā-tor\ n

fla·tion \di-'flā-shən, ˌdē-\ n (1891) **1** : an act or instance of deflat-

form of **2 a** : to spoil the looks of : DISFIGURE ⟨a face ∼ed by bitter- ness⟩ **b** : to mar the character of ⟨a marriage ∼ed by jealousy⟩ **3** : to alter the shape of by stress ∼ vi : to become misshapen or changed in shape — **de·form·able** \-mə-bəl\ adj

syn DEFORM, DISTORT, CONTORT, WARP means to mar or spoil by or as if by twisting. DEFORM may imply a change of shape through stress, injury, or some accident of growth ⟨his face was deformed by hatred⟩. DISTORT and CONTORT both imply a wrenching from the natural, nor- mal, or justly proportioned, but CONTORT suggests a more involved twisting and a more grotesque and painful result ⟨the odd camera an- gle distorts the figure in the photograph⟩ ⟨disease had painfully con- torted her body⟩. WARP indicates physically an uneven shrinking that bends or twists out of a flat plane ⟨warped floorboards⟩.

de·for·mal·ize \(ˌ)dē-'fȯr-mə-ˌlīz\ vt (1880) : to make less formal

de·for·ma·tion \ˌdē-fȯr-'mā-shən, ˌde-fər-\ n (15c) **1** : alteration of form or shape; also : the product of such alteration **2** : the action of deforming : the state of being deformed **3** : change for the worse — de·for·ma·tion·al \-shə-nᵊl\ adj

de·for·ma·tive \di-'fȯr-mə-tiv, dē-\ adj (1641) : tending to deform

de·formed adj (15c) : distorted or unshapely in form : MISSHAPEN

de·for·mi·ty \di-'fȯr-mə-tē, dē-\ n, pl -ties [ME deformite, fr. MF def- formeteit, fr. L deformitat-, deformitas, fr. deformis deformed, fr. de- + forma] (15c) **1** : the state of being deformed **2** : IMPERFECTION, BLEMISH; as **a** : a physical blemish or distortion : DISFIGUREMENT **b** : a moral or aesthetic flaw or defect

de·frag \dē-'frag\ vt defragged; defragging (1988) : DEFRAGMENT

de·frag·ment \(ˌ)dē-'frag-mənt\ vt (1985) : to reorganize separated fragments of related data on (a computer disk) into a contiguous ar- rangement — **de·frag·men·ta·tion** \-ˌfrag-mən-'tā shon, -ˌmen-\ n

de·frag·ment·er \-'frag-ˌmen-tər, -mən-\ n (1986) : software that de- fragments a computer disk

de·fraud \di-'frȯd, dē-\ vt [ME, fr. AF defrauder, fr. L defraudare, fr. de- + fraudare to cheat, fr. fraud-, fraus fraud] (14c) : to deprive of some- thing by deception or fraud syn see CHEAT — **de·fraud·er** \di-'frȯ- dər\ n

de·fray \di-'frā, dē-\ vt [MF deffroyer, fr. des- de- + frayer to expend, fr. OF, fr. frais, pl. of fret, frait expenditure, lit., damage by breaking, fr. L fractum, neut. of fractus, pp. of frangere to break — more at BREAK] (1536) **1** : to provide for the payment of : PAY **2** archaic : to bear the expenses of — **de·fray·able** \-ə-bəl\ adj — **de·fray·al** \-'frā(-ə)l\ n

de·frock \(ˌ)dē-'fräk\ vt (1581) **1** : to deprive (as a priest) of the right to exercise the functions of office **2** : to remove from a position of honor or privilege

de·frost \di-'frȯst, 'dē-\ vb (1895) **1** : to release from a frozen state ⟨∼ meat⟩ **2** : to free from ice ⟨∼ the refrigerator⟩: also : DEFOG ⟨∼ the windshield⟩ ∼ vi : to thaw out esp. from a deep-frozen state — de· frost·er n

deft \'deft\ adj [ME defte gentle — more at DAFT] (15c) : characterized by facility and skill syn see DEXTEROUS — **deft·ly** adv — **deft·ness** \'def(t)-nəs\ n

de·funct \di-'fəŋkt, dē-\ adj [L defunctus, fr. pp. of defungi to finish, die, fr. de- + fungi to perform — more at FUNCTION] (1599) : no longer living, existing, or functioning ⟨the committee is now ∼⟩ syn see DEAD

de·fund \(ˌ)dē-'fənd\ vt (1948) : to withdraw funding from

de·fuse \(ˌ)dē-'fyüz\ vt (1943) **1** : to remove the fuse from (as a mine or bomb) **2** : to make less harmful, potent, or tense ⟨∼ the crisis⟩

¹de·fy \di-'fī, dē-\ vt de·fied; de·fy·ing [ME, to renounce faith in, chal- lenge, fr. AF desfier, defier, fr. des- de- + fier to entrust, fr. VL *fidare, alter. of L fidere to trust — more at BIDE] (14c) **1** archaic : to chal- lenge to combat **2** : to challenge to do something considered impossi- ble : DARE **3** : to confront with assured power of resistance : DISRE- GARD ⟨∼ public opinion⟩ **4** : to resist attempts at : WITHSTAND ⟨the paintings ∼ classification⟩

²de·fy \di-'fī, 'dē-\ n, pl defies (1580) : CHALLENGE, DEFIANCE

deg abbr degree

dé·ga·gé \ˌdā-ˌgä-'zhā\ adj [F, fr. pp. of dégager to put at ease, fr. OF desgagier to redeem, fr. des- + gage pledge —

def·i·ni·tion (dĕf′ə-nĭsh′ən) *n. Abbr.* **def.** **1.** The act of stating a precise meaning or significance, as of a word, phrase, or term. **2.** The statement of the meaning of a word, phrase, or term. **3.** The act of making clear and distinct: *a definition of one's intentions.* **4.** The state of being closely outlined or determined: *"A way of liberation can have no positive definition."* (Alan W. Watts). **5.** A determining of outline, extent, or limits: *the definition of a nation's authority.* **6.** *Telecommunications.* The degree of clarity with which a televised image is received or a radio receives a given station. **7.** *Optics.* The clarity of detail in an optically produced image, as in a photograph, produced by a combination of resolution and contrast. [Middle English *diffinicioun,* from Old French *definition,* from Latin *dēfīnītiō,* from *dēfīnīre,* DEFINE.] —**def′i·ni′tion·al** *adj.*

*T*he act of stating a precise meaning or significance." "The statement of the meaning of a word." We rely on **definition** for successful, efficient communication. Not only do we need to know exactly what others mean when they speak or write to us, but we also want them to know exactly what we mean. When words have more than one meaning, as they often do in English, we need to make sure that the intended meaning is clear. If a word or term may be unfamiliar to our audience, we need to take the time to define it. Definition is especially important when we use words related to controversial or contested ideas. Terms such as *fairness, democracy, education,* and *human rights* have many different meanings to different people. Whenever we use such terms, we need to let listeners and readers know *exactly* how we are using them.

....

Looking at Your Own Literacy How do you define *literacy*? How can you measure it? How might your definition differ from that of your classmates?

....

What Is Definition?

The word *definition* calls to mind a dictionary, a book filled with the specific meanings of particular words—such as the *American Heritage Dictionary of the English Language,* where the definition on page 564 appears. But every day, we need to know the meanings of words and the boundaries and relationships between one word and another; in other words, we define words constantly to ourselves and to others. If your instructor tells you that you write with *ingenuity,* you may wonder what that word means, exactly, and whether it is positive or negative. *Ingenuity,* with its "in" prefix, might have a negative sense—or does it? The *American Heritage Dictionary* gives four definitions of *ingenuity.*

A Dictionary Definition

in·ge·nu·i·ty (ĭn′jə-nōō′ə-tē, -nyōō′ə-tē) *n., pl.* **-ties. 1.** Inventive skill or imagination; cleverness. **2.** The state of being ingeniously contrived. **3.** *Usually plural.* An ingenious or imaginative device. **4.** *Archaic.* Ingenuousness. [Latin *ingenuitās,* frankness, innocence (but influenced in meaning by INGENIOUS), from *ingenuus,* INGENUOUS.]

From this definition, with its use of **synonyms** (words that mean the same or nearly the same thing), you can tell that your instructor probably thinks your writing is skillful, imaginative, and clever—nothing negative. But you might also have picked up clues to your instructor's meaning from the way she spoke to you or the other comments written on your paper. If she says, "You write like an angel," she's using an **analogy** (a direct comparison between unlike things) to define your writing style.

Successful communication between instructors and students—or between friends, colleagues, or family members—is based on shared definitions of words. Even though we know that language naturally evolves and that the meanings of words change over time, as the *Oxford English Dictionary* (OED) so carefully demonstrates, the definition of words must be fairly stable, or communication will break down. Unlike Humpty Dumpty, we can't have words mean whatever we want them to mean:

> "But 'glory' doesn't mean 'a nice knockdown argument,'" Alice objected.
>
> "When I use a word," Humpty Dumpty said, in rather a scornful tone, "it means just what I choose it to mean — neither more nor less."
>
> "The question is," said Alice, "whether you *can* make words mean so many different things."   — LEWIS CARROLL, *Through the Looking-Glass*

We *can* make words mean different things—but only if our **language community,** the people with whom we speak most frequently, agrees to share the meaning with us. Words mean what our community agrees that they mean; words enter our common vocabulary or acquire new meanings when the members of our community begin to use a new word or to use a word in a new way. Therefore, we quickly catch on when we need to learn new words such as *netiquette, blogosphere,* and *digerati* or when

"Instead of 'It sucks' you could say, 'It doesn't speak to me.'"

words such as *cool* and *bad* acquire new meanings. But we have trouble communicating when the way *we* define a word is markedly different from the way others in our community define it.

Thinking about Definition

1. Look over the cartoon on page 566. How does the phrase "It sucks" differ from "It doesn't speak to me"? Would you define the two phrases the same way?

2. How does each phrase relate to the person who said it? What would be the effect of the woman saying "It sucks" or the boy saying "It doesn't speak to me?" Are these two people part of the same language community?

Why Use Definition?

Whether you are conveying information or arguing a point—the two general purposes of definition—definition is a powerful means of developing your ideas. First, when you define your terms, you immediately connect with your audience by clarifying exactly what you are—and are not—talking about. Second, by defining your terms, you filter out related ideas that you don't have the time or inclination to go into; instead, you focus on the concept or issue at hand.

For instance, if you are talking with a sales clerk about buying a new coat, the clerk will probably ask you to define the type of coat you need. Do you need a coat for winter or for cool summer nights? Do you need a rain-resistant coat or a warm coat? Do you need a long coat for walking to class or a shorter one for riding your bike? Definition can help you describe your needs or persuade yourself about them. It can also help you explain or understand an idea or a problem, compare and contrast, make choices, exemplify, or classify. ("I need a coat, but do I need a trench coat, a slicker, a parka, or a denim jacket? How badly do I need a coat?")

Every day we hear, read, and write definitions that are part of descriptions, arguments, comparisons and contrasts, and examples. Whether you are defining the concept of "a good buy" when you're shopping for a new car, defining the perfect potential partner to a friend, defining the kind of apartment you need as you look through the real estate section of the local newspaper, or responding to a question that asks you to define something on an essay exam, you are intentionally including—and excluding—information.

Most newspapers carry personal ads that define—by describing—the people who place the ads or their ideal potential partners. When you read these ads, you can usually tell who is included and excluded from the ad and what specific characteristics are sought or rejected:

> SWM, 25, 6'2", 190 lbs., blue eyes, enjoys horseback riding, hunting, housework, hiking, wishes to meet a slim, sassy, savvy, sentimental SWF 24–35, for friendship and fun.
>
> SBF, 23, 5'4", smoker, student, enjoys playing tennis, poetry, the park, seeking medium-build SM, 21+.
>
> Quiet and shy GWM, 30, 5'7", brown hair, blue eyes, nonsmoker, employed, likes hiking, going out, seeking employed, slim GAM, 25–40.

By defining themselves or their ideal partner in terms of descriptive qualities—age, race, interests, goals, and sexual orientations and preferences—the people who place these ads are providing the information that they think (or hope) will yield a fruitful response.

Try Your Hand   If you were looking for an ideal partner, how might you define yourself in a personal ad? How would you describe the person you were seeking?

Definitions also help us learn about or explain objects, concepts, situations, processes, and choices. The following excerpt explains what the term *Twitter* means to uninformed audiences.

Definition to Explain a Process

If you're the last person in the world to not know what Twitter is, here's a simple explanation: It allows you to post text messages to the web. You have a 140-character limit per posting, and you can follow other users (in aggregate or individually) and they can follow you. It's kind of like Facebook's status updates, but available for anyone to see. To read an individual user's Twitter page in some semblance of order is beside the point. Most individual Twitter pages resemble a poorly written blog.
—WILL LEITCH, "How Tweet It Is"

This explanation of Twitter enables readers to gain a quick sense of what this new technology is, what it allows users to do, and how it works. Of course, if readers were still curious, they could experiment with the technology itself, but this basic explanation helps them decide if they want to pursue their initial interest.

Try Your Hand   Identify a technological or social practice in which you have expertise but others may not. Define this practice to the uninformed in a way that helps them gain a basic sense of it.

Some definitions resonate with comparisons. *Love,* for instance, is a word with many definitions, each appropriate for a particular situation. If you were to ask a married couple why they married, for instance, they would probably say they were "in love." But what exactly is that feeling? As Henry A. Bowman and Graham B. Spanier point out, we use the term *love* in many ways, and without a great deal of precision. You might use the term in all the following ways: "I love my parents," "I love my partner," "I love God," "I love my country," "I love animals," "I love ice cream." But you don't love your mother in the same way you love ice cream. Nor do you have the same emotional experience with your country that you do with your partner.

Many of you may want to define *love* for one of your writing assignments. But to do so well, you'll need to compare situations and contexts for love. According to Bowman and Spanier, *love* has different meanings depending on the following factors:

- The background or experience of the person involved
- The nature of the love object (mother, partner, activity, object)
- The period in the individual's life
- The intensity of the individual's attraction to the love object
- The importance the individual places on being in love
  — HENRY A. BOWMAN AND GRAHAM B. SPANIER, *Modern Marriage*

If you compare these situations and contexts to find the definitions of *love*, you can use a specific definition that applies to a particular relationship or object.

Try Your Hand   Jot down a list of five or more people whom you love, note your relationship to each of them, and list the ways you love them. For each person, write a sentence that defines the kind of love you feel.

Definitions also exemplify when they include examples for a class or category. The following definition from a textbook uses exemplification.

Definition Using Exemplification

Structures seemingly without use and of reduced size are termed **vestigial organs.** They were at one time functional and necessary but appear to be in the process of disappearing. . . . The horse, rodents, and some other mammals have a large caecum or appendix as an accessory digestive chamber. In humans the appendix is a slender vestige about 6.5 cm long that seems to have little function and sometimes is a site of infection requiring surgical removal. The external ears of mammals are moved by special muscles; in humans, lacking need for such movement, the muscles are usually reduced and nonfunctional. In the inner angle of the human eye is a pinkish membrane . . . representing the transparent nictitating membrane, or third eyelid, to be seen in the cat, bird, frog, and other land vertebrates. The human "wisdom teeth," or posterior molars, are often smaller and more variable than the other molars and irregular as to time or manner of eruption; this suggests that they are becoming useless and may eventually disappear. A word of caution is necessary. An organ classed as vestigial and nonfunctional may, in fact, have an unknown, reduced, or changed function. The term, therefore, should be applied with reservation.

— TRACY STORER ET AL., *General Zoology*

. . . .

Try Your Hand   Think of a technical term from your major or another course that you can define best by exemplifying. Compare your definition with that of a classmate to see if you both have made your meanings clear.

. . . .

Definitions are a perfect way to classify, and classifying is a useful way to define a word. In the study of rhetoric, examples of persuasive language are classified into three categories: (1) legislators and other politicians use *deliberative rhetoric* to decide on the best course for the future, focusing on issues of expediency and inexpediency; (2) lawyers and judges use *judicial rhetoric* to make decisions about the past, focusing on issues of justice and injustice; and (3) speech writers and religious leaders use *epideictic rhetoric* to express their sense of the present occasion at a ceremony or memorial, focusing on issues of honor or dishonor. We can use these three kinds of rhetoric to classify any rhetorical event. Which kind of rhetoric is the president's annual State of the Union address? a knighting ceremony conducted by Great Britain's Queen Elizabeth? the indictment of Bernard Madoff for investment fraud?

. . . .

Try Your Hand   Provide one or more examples of each of the categories of rhetoric.

. . . .

How Does Definition Work?

Usually you'll develop a definition in two steps. First you'll classify the term by placing it in a broader category. Then you'll differentiate it from other terms in the same category by stating its distinguishing characteristics.

Term	*Class*	*Differentiation*
Evolution	is a process	in which something changes into a significantly different form, especially one that is more complex or sophisticated.
Adolescence	is a process	of growth between childhood and maturity.
A beauty makeover	is a process	of aesthetic and cosmetic improvement.

For instance, if a question on an essay exam asks you to define *evolution*, you might start by classifying the term as a process. But then you'll need to differentiate *evolution* from other processes *(maturation; mitosis; revolution)* by focusing on evolution's distinguishing characteristics: "a process in which something changes into a significantly different form, especially one that is more complex or sophisticated." That **sentence definition** describes *evolution*, but it could also describe *adolescence* or even *beauty makeover*. To define this concept adequately, you need to develop an **extended definition** by introducing additional differentiating features.

An Extended Definition

Evolution is a gradual process in which something changes into a significantly different form, especially one that is more complex or sophisticated. In biology, evolution is the theory that groups of organisms, such as species, may change with the passage of time so that descendants differ morphologically and physiologically from their ancestors.

You may also find yourself writing a **historical definition,** which is an extended definition that traces the different meanings a word has had over time. A historical definition shows when, where, and why the term was established and how it has been used. The *Oxford English Dictionary* is a reliable source of information about the history of words. The OED provides a long list of various definitions of *evolution*, including the relatively recent biological meanings that appear after five older meanings:

Evolution (evoliu· ʃən) . . .
6. *Biol.* **a.** Of animal and vegetable organisms or their parts: The process of developing from a rudimentary to a mature or complete state.
    1670 *Phil. Trans.* V 207[8] By the word Change [in Insects] is nothing else to be understood but a gradual and natural Evolution and Growth of the parts.   **1745** NEEDHAM *Microsc. Disc.* Intro. I Nature . . ever exerting its Fecundity in a successive Evolution of organized Bodies. **1791** E. Darwin. *Bot. Gar.* II. 8 *note*, The gradual evolution of the young animal or plant from its egg or seed. **1801** *Med. Jrnl.* V. 588 A series of experiments on the evolution of the Chick.   **1805** *Ibid.* XIV. 336 The formation and evolution of this part of the brain.   **1839** JOHNSTON in *Proc. Berw. Nat. Club* I. 201 Masses of eggs, in different stages of their evolution, are met with in the same nest.
    b. *Theory of Evolution:* the hypothesis (first propounded under that name by Bonnet 1762) that the embryo or germ, instead of being brought into existence by the process of fecundation, is a development or expansion of a pre-existing form, which contains the rudiments of all the parts of the future organism. Also called 'the theory of Preformation'; the latter name is now preferred to avoid confusion with the following sense.
    1831 [see Epigensis].   **1877** HUXLEY *Encycl. Brit.* VIII. 745.
    c. The origination of species of animals and plants, as conceived by those who attribute it to a process of development from earlier forms, and not to a process of 'special creation'. Often in phrases *Doctrine, Theory of Evolution.*

1832 PRINC. GEOL. II. II The testacea of the ocean existed first, until some of them by gradual evolution, were improved into those inhabiting land.

1852 DARWIN *Orig. Spec.* vii (1873) 201 At the present day almost all naturalists admit evolution under some form.   **1863** E. V. NEALE *Anal. Th. & Nat.* 185 The diversity of species has arisen by the evolution of one species out of another.   **1881** SIR J. HOOKER in *Nature* No. 619. 446 The doctrine of the orderly evolution of species under known law.

Beginning in 1670, writers used the word *evolution* in a biological sense, and the meaning itself has evolved further since that time.

Sometimes you'll need to write a **negative definition,** telling your readers not only what your word or term means but also what it does not mean. Someone who says "Success is not all it's cracked up to be" is using a negative definition. *Success* does not mean many of the things you might think it means: an interesting job, prestige, money, leisure, connections. The speaker's own success might bring her plenty of money, but at the cost of too much work, responsibility, and worry; too many hours spent in hotels, airports, and restaurants; and incredible loneliness. A negative definition starts out by limiting the term to what it is not. Writing for Slate.com, Taylor Clark uses negative definition to clarify readers' understandings of what a vegetarian is (and is not).

A Negative Definition

To demonstrate what a vegetarian really is, let's begin with a simple thought experiment. Imagine a completely normal person with completely normal food cravings, someone who has a broad range of friends, enjoys a good time, is carbon-based, and so on. Now remove from this person's diet anything that once had eyes, and *wham!* you have yourself a vegetarian. Normal person, no previously ocular food, end of story. Some people call themselves vegetarians and still eat chicken or fish, but unless we're talking about the kind of salmon that comes freshly plucked from the vine, this makes you an omnivore. A select few herbivores go one step further and avoid *all* animal products—milk, eggs, honey, leather—and they call themselves *vegan*, which rhymes with "tree men." These people are intense.   —TAYLOR CLARK, "Meatless like Me"

Clark uses negative definition to explain to readers that a vegetarian is *not* someone who eats anything that once had eyes. Vegetarians are *not* people who eat chicken or fish; they're called *omnivores*.

Finally, in some situations you might need to write a **stipulative definition,** one in which you limit—or stipulate—the scope of your discussion by telling your readers how you'll be using a term. In some important ways, a stipulative definition is both a sentence definition and a negative one. For example, in an article on Asian Americans in *Y* magazine, the editor in chief argues that "What does it mean to be Asian American?" is the most overused question in the Asian community, so she stipulates what she means when she uses the term *Asian American:* it's being "real to oneself." She writes that she's familiar with other ways the term is used: to describe a person's physical features; an inherited or a practiced culture of language, food, and religious customs; or "the pretentious attitude of those who consider themselves culturally superior while at the same time shunning their Asian traditions." But she can "do without" all those definitions, most of which carry an "undertoned social correctness," because she wants to concentrate on "being true to who you are."

The different kinds of definition all offer useful ways of thinking and writing about a given topic. Some definitions, like the ones you have already read in this chapter, are relatively short; they provide a quick idea of the boundaries of an individual concept, process, or object. These short definitions are the kind you'll often be expected to supply in your writing, especially when your audience is not as familiar with the subject as you are. If you're writing about funk music, for example, your instructor may not know what it is unless you insert a brief definition — or two: *Funk music,* which has an identifiable beat and rhythm in the bass lines and chorus chants, celebrates *funk* itself, the life force in all its sweaty carnality."

But other definitions can be much longer and more detailed. Essays, chapters, even entire books have been dedicated to defining one term or concept: *Modern Marriage; Heroines; Saints; Composition in the Twenty-First Century; Eloquence in an Electronic Age; Chaucer's Dante.* Your instructors will certainly not ask you to write book-length definitions, but they will want you to develop paragraphs and essays that use definition to inform and persuade.

How Do You Use Definition in Academic Writing?

It should not be a surprise to you that definition is used just as much in academic contexts as it is in more public contexts. In fact, you've most likely been asked to define terms in various courses throughout your academic career. As you probably know, definition is a vital rhetorical strategy in all academic fields because it enables scholars and students to clarify terms under discussion, introduce new terms into scholarly conversation, distinguish one term from another, and establish relationships among terms. Like those writing for more public audiences, academic writers create definitions through description, exemplification, comparison, and classification. And these academic writers, both scholars and students, also call on sentence definitions, extended definitions, historical definitions, negative definitions, and stipulative definitions to clarify and deepen readers' understanding.

In the following excerpt from the June 2008 issue of the academic journal *Business and Society,* scholars David Campbell and Richard Slack use definition to explain and then draw distinctions between two terms, *philanthropy strategy* and *strategic philanthropy*. These distinctions are necessary, for the subject of the article is to investigate the effects that companies' charitable (philanthropic) donations have on their decision making and investments.

Definition in Academic Writing

Post and Waddock (1995) drew a helpful distinction between "philanthropy strategy" ("The firm is orderly in the methods and procedures it uses to give money away"; Saiia et al., 2003, p. 185) and "strategic philanthropy" ("The corporate resources that are given have meaning and impact on the firm as well as the community that receives those resources"; Saiia et al., 2003, p. 185). Strategic philanthropy was later described by Thorne, Ferrell, and Ferrell (2003) as being the "synergistic use of a firm's resources to achieve both organisational and social benefits" (Thorne et al., 2003, p. 360). Thus, strategic philanthropy has a dual objective of corporate value added and charitable benevolence. Importantly, strategic philanthropy imputes to donors motives other than altruism in their engagement with charitable involvement (Burlinghame & Young, 1996).

—DAVID CAMPBELL and RICHARD SLACK, "Corporate 'Philanthropy Strategy' and 'Strategic Philanthropy': Some Insights from Voluntary Disclosures in Annual Reports"

Drawing on the work of other scholars, Campbell and Slack explain that while *philanthropy strategy* is the "methods and procedures [used] to give money away," *strategic philanthropy* offers another dimension to this process: it is a way of giving money that has "meaning and impact on the firm as well as the community that receives those resources." Strategic philanthropy, then, represents a more complex aspect or analysis of charitable donation than philanthropy strategy because it takes into account how the donation is intended to benefit not only the community it contributes to but also the corporation that provides the donation. Campbell and Slack go on to investigate whether and how companies' disclosure of their philanthropy strategies influences investor confidence and corporate investment decisions.

Although you've most likely composed definitions like this throughout your academic career, it is important to remember the key words in an assignment that would prompt you to define. Of course, if the assignment description asks you to define a term, that's what you should do. But you might also call on definition if the assignment asks you to compare and make distinctions between (or among) terms, as Campbell and Slack do; to identify the significant characteristics of a term; or to explain in detail what a term means. In addition, an assignment might also ask you to use definition in combination with another rhetorical method. For instance, you could be asked to define and analyze a process, to define and classify various ideas, or to define and provide an example.

....

Analyzing Definition in Academic Writing   Reflect on a time during your academic career when you've had to define a term. How did your instructor describe this assignment? How did you carry it out? What definitional strategies did you call on (stipulative, historical, negative, sentence, or extended definitions)? What connections did you make with other rhetorical methods such as exemplification, classification, comparison, description, argument, or process analysis?

....

How Do You Read a Definition?

To learn how to write definitions that are clear and effective for their particular purpose and audience, it helps to learn how to read definitions critically and to analyze and evaluate ones that you encounter. If you develop the habit of looking closely at the definitions you read, you'll learn to pose the kinds of questions that will help you write your own. For example, does the definition clearly distinguish what's being defined from things that are similar to it? Will the intended readers understand the difference? Does the definition apply under all circumstances or only at certain times or in certain places? Is it a definition that virtually everyone would agree on, or does it have an argumentative edge—and if so, how convincing will it be to the intended audience? How is the definition organized and developed?

Look back at the definition of *vestigial organs* on page 569. Notice that it opens with a brief sentence definition giving the classification of these organs ("Structures") and the two essential characteristics that differentiate these organs from others ("seemingly without use and of reduced size"). The second sentence extends this definition by putting these characteristics in an evolutionary context: vestigial organs, now useless and small, were once useful and larger. Next, the definition is developed by exemplification, four examples of organs that are apparently vestigial in humans—the appendix, external ear muscles, nictitating membrane, and wisdom teeth—and that in some cases are compared with their functional counterparts in other animals. The definition ends with a stipulation, a "word of caution" against applying the term too broadly to organs that may in fact not possess the characteristic of "uselessness."

As you might expect of a definition that appears in a science textbook, this one is intended simply to be informative; there is no disagreement among zoologists about how to define *vestigial organs*, although the writers do say that it's impossible to define particular organs as vestigial with absolute certainty. Notice also the language of this definition. In general, it's not difficult for the intended audience of college students to understand, but it's fairly formal and does include some terms that might confuse or puzzle readers. For example, in the first sentence, it's not entirely clear what "of reduced size" refers to. Are vestigial human organs smaller than these organs used to be, smaller than comparable organs in other animals, or both? And what exactly does it mean that wisdom teeth are "often . . . more variable than the other molars"? Asking questions like these will sharpen your ability to see both the strong and the weak points in the definitions you read and thus to write your own definitions with more confidence and success.

One other point to think about as you read a definition critically is to consider not just what it says but also what it doesn't say — what it leaves out. Some definitions, especially those that are intended to make an argument, deliberately use terms in a biased way, without any stipulation by the writer that he or she is doing so. A reader who doesn't accept this definition will be unlikely to accept the argument that it's making. And even definitions that are intended to be neutral and objective may fail to take into account some meanings of a term. For example, the definition of the word *definition* that appears on page 564 doesn't seem to include any meaning that covers the kind of "definition" you get from working out at a gym. Maybe this use of the word is too recent to have been reflected in a dictionary entry, or maybe those compiling the dictionary considered it too informal or temporary to include. When you write a definition, then, always try to think about whether your readers will be expecting a certain meaning and, if so, how you need to take their expectations into account.

How Do You Write Using Definition?

Whether you are writing a historical, negative, or stipulative definition, and whether it will be only a few sentences or paragraphs long or an entire essay, you will need to consider your purpose and audience and decide on the details that will clarify the term for your readers. If you are writing an essay, you will also need to choose an effective organizational method for presenting details.

● Determining Your Purpose

Before you begin writing an extended definition or using a brief definition to develop your essay, consider your purpose. Do you want to inform your readers with an **objective definition,** which emphasizes the object itself and can be applied to various situations? Or do you want to persuade your readers to agree with your **subjective definition,** which emphasizes your own opinions and response and the way you want to define the term for this particular piece of writing? If you and students from other campuses are defining what it means to be *college-educated*, chances are your definitions will inform your readers, using classification and comparison. But if you are defining *college-educated* for a lending or granting agency (whether it's your parents, a bank, a foundation, or a scholarship committee), your definition will probably need to persuade your readers of the benefits of this education so that you will receive money.

● Considering Your Audience

As the preceding example suggests, your purpose is often closely related to your audience. If you are writing your definition for a class, an instructor, or a supervisor, you will undoubtedly use different language and maybe even different examples and details from those you would use if you were writing a letter or an e-mail to a friend back home or across campus. When you consider audience, you need to think about what your readers may already know, or think they know, about your term or concept. You should also consider the tone you should take, the kinds of words you will use, and the information about the term or concept that you will include and exclude.

● Considering What Kind of Definition to Use

Once you know why and for whom you are defining the term or concept, you will need to determine the kind of definition that will work best for your audience and purpose. Do you need to write only a sentence-length definition as part of a larger essay, or do you need to write an extended definition that gives readers a wider understanding of the subject at hand? If you need to chart the evolution of a word or idea, you may decide that a historical definition best suits your needs. If you need to define a term or concept in order to argue or explain your point, you may need to write a stipulative definition so that you can define how *you* will be using the word in your discussion. You may find that your definition merits further thought and study, so you may want to conduct research at the library or on the Web.

● Considering Appropriate Examples and Details

In some ways, writing a definition can be easier than other kinds of writing for school or work; all you need to do is come up with the perfect examples and details (from your own experience and knowledge or from library or Web research) that will make the term or concept clear for your readers. For example, if you were defining *diabetes* for a general audience, you would first place the term in a class (physical disorders) and then provide the kind of information that distinguishes that disorder from other disorders in the class, as the following definition demonstrates.

"Reading" and Using Visuals for Definition

When we think of a definition, we automatically think of using words to define something. But many definitions can be enhanced or need to be accompanied by a visual or visuals. For instance, guide–books for bird–watching or wildflower identification always include visuals, especially when they are differentiating a specific bird or flower from other members of its class. In the following visual, *wood-peckers* are defined as a genus verbally, and then three specific species of woodpecker are defined visually as well as in words.

Often only visuals can help you understand the differences among a class (or genus) of things, whether they're woodpeckers, flowers,

WOODPECKERS

Judy Loven, USDA-APHIS-Wildlife Services

IDENTIFICATION

There are 21 species of woodpeckers found in the United States, seven of which are present in Indiana. Year-round Indiana woodpeckers include the downy (6¾" in length), hairy (9¼"), red-headed (9¼"), red-bellied (9¼"), pileated (16½") woodpeckers and the northern flicker (12½"). The yellow-bellied sapsucker (7¾") is a resident of Indiana during the winter months.

Woodpeckers have short legs with two sharp-clawed toes forward and two backward-pointed toes. These toes, along with their stiff tail feathers, allow them to cling to trees, utility poles, or wood siding. Their strong, pointed beak is used for digging insects from trees, excavating nesting cavities, and for "drumming." Since woodpeckers do not have true "songs," they use sharp calls and perform rhythmic tapping (better known as drumming) with their beaks on surfaces such as dead tree limbs, metal poles, and building siding to attract a mate or announce their territorial boundaries. Both male and female woodpeckers drum. It is primarily this drumming behavior that may cause serious problems for homeowners.

The downy (Figure 1a) and the hairy (Figure 1b) woodpeckers cause the most damage in Indiana. Both are identified by their white backs and black and white striped wing feathers. The downy is sparrow-size and has a short bill. The hairy woodpecker is robin-size. The downy also has black and white bars on the outer tail feathers while the hairy has entirely white tail feathers. In both species, the male has a red spot on the back of the head.

Figure 1a.
**DOWNY
WOODPECKER**

Figure 1b.
**HAIRY
WOODPECKER**

Figure 1c.
**PILEATED
WOODPECKER**

paintings, buildings, cars, bicycles, or athletic shoes. We so depend on visuals to help us define and understand definitions that we may tend to take them for granted. To learn how to use visuals effectively for definition, though, it will help if you learn to "read" visual definitions closely and critically, the same way that you would read a definition in words, to see how well they succeed in expressing the meaning of a term for the writer's specific purpose and audience.

The woodpecker visual, for example, appeared on the Web site of the Department of Entomology at Purdue University, as one of a series of pages offering advice about how to deal with various animals that cause damage to homes, gardens, crops, and other things created or cultivated by humans. As the text suggests, the main intended audience for this advice is the residents of Indiana, where Purdue is a state university. The third paragraph of the text identifies the two species of woodpeckers that cause the most damage in Indiana, the downy and the hairy woodpeckers, and defines each one as it explains the similarities and differences between them in size, color pattern, and length of bill. The three images at the bottom of the page illustrate these two species as well as the pileated woodpecker, which is discussed on the next page of the Web site.

Notice how Figures 1a and 1b reflect the differences in size and in the shape of the bill that the text says differentiate the downy and hairy woodpeckers, as well as the white backs and striped wing feathers that make them alike. Placing the two drawings next to each other helps call attention to the differences and likenesses. But the two black-and-white figures don't (or can't) show the different coloration of the tail feathers or the similar red spots on the back of the head. In fact, the next page of the Web site advises that "to accurately identify these and other woodpeckers, a field guide with color illustrations is recommended." When you use visuals as part of your own definitions, you will need to think about considerations like these — how large they need to be, whether they should be in color, or whether to show what you're defining in relation to other things in the same category or classification — as you decide how best to achieve your purpose for your specific audience.

Remember that if you want to use visuals in an academic writing assignment, it is a good idea to check with your instructor beforehand. You also need to consider what kind of labels or captions, like those in the woodpecker illustrations, to provide, if the visuals do not already include them.

Definition with Examples and Details

Diabetes is a disorder of the very engine of life, a subtle calamity at the molecular level. Its hallmark is a failure to metabolize glucose, the ubiquitous sugar molecule carried by the bloodstream to fuel every part of the body. Deprived of their prime energy supply, muscle and nerve cells slow their function, which is why early diabetes may manifest itself as lethargy and irritability. That was the experience of Maria DelMundo, 46, a Rochester, Minn., mother who weighed around 190 (she's 5 feet 2) when she stopped by her doctor's office for a checkup in 1991. "I just wasn't feeling good—tired and out of sorts," she recalls; in effect, she was undernourished even while eating her fill of the "buttery icing and whipped cream, French pastries and Häagen-Dazs" she loves.

— Jerry Adler and Claudia Kalb, "Diabetes: The Silent Killer"

This brief definition, excerpted from an extended–definition essay, shows how diabetes is a disease that deprives the body of energy by failing to metabolize glucose. As the writers continue, they extend the definition by including relevant details that describe the unique effects of the physical disorder called diabetes: "Deprived of their prime energy supply, muscle and nerve cells slow their function, which is why early diabetes may manifest itself as lethargy and irritability." Finally, the writers include a specific example of the disease in action: "'I just wasn't feeling good — tired and out of sorts,'" Maria DelMundo recalls; "in effect, she was undernourished even while eating her fill of the 'buttery icing and whipped cream, French pastries and Häagen-Dazs' she loves."

● Arranging All the Parts

There is no "right" way to organize a definition essay, but your organizational pattern should be linked to your purpose of either informing or persuading. Like all essays, a definition essay opens with an introduction that states (or implies) a thesis, moves into a well–developed body, and ends with a conclusion. To develop the body of your essay, you might find yourself organizing information spatially or visually, chronologically, emphatically, or according to points of comparison. But regardless of the organizational pattern you choose, you'll need to establish your own definition for the term or concept and then support your definition by using examples, descriptions, comparison and contrast, narratives, or other methods of development.

If you are informing your audience about diabetes, you might want to provide an initial definition for the disease and then move into explaining its causes and effects. For instance, Adler and Kalb explain the effects of the disease.

Definition Using Cause-and-Effect Analysis to Inform

Something terrible was happening to Yolanda Benitez's eyes. They were being poisoned; the fragile capillaries of the retina attacked from within and were leaking blood. The first symptoms were red lines, appearing vertically across her field of vision; the lines multiplied and merged into a haze that shut out light entirely.

If the purpose of your definition essay is to argue that the members of your diabetic audience should change their eating habits, you may want to focus on giving examples of preventive measures, as Adler and Kalb do.

Definition Using Exemplification to Argue

There's another surefire way [other than drugs] to control blood sugar and lessen the complications of diabetes; it calls for eating a healthy diet in the first place. A recurring theme in the conversations of diabetics is the foods they had to give up. Maria Menoza, a college janitor in Los Angeles, cut down from "six or seven tortillas a day" to two, after she was diagnosed . . . and gave up "tacos, sweets, chocolates and *pan dulce* [sweet bread]." "I can't eat what I want, and that makes me sad," she says.

Whatever methods of development and organization you use, be sure to include clear transitions so that readers can follow your explanation or argument. You'll want your conclusion to move beyond your introduction, pushing forward the thinking of your readers, helping them decide what to do with the information you've provided.

Understanding and Using Definition

Analyzing Definition

1. Reread the personal ads on page 568. How would you define *love* for each of the people who placed these ads? What are they looking for? What's their ideal partner like? Where are they now in their lives?

2. Reread the OED's historical definition of *evolution* on page 571. What did you learn from the definition that you didn't know before? How has this word itself evolved? Which meanings are outdated?

3. As you read for school and other purposes this week, identify definitions used to inform and ones used to argue a point. You'll find definitions in sports, computer, and fashion magazines; in your school and local newspapers; and in the novels and textbooks you're reading. Classify the various kinds of definitions, and write out what you think the author wanted you as the reader to do with the information.

Planning and Writing Definitions

1. **Working with two or three classmates,** look carefully at the definitions of potential partners in the personal ads on page 568. Rewrite one of those definitions in paragraph form, expanding on the telegraphic description that appeared in the newspaper to create an extended definition. Share your group response with the rest of the class.

2. Now rewrite your paragraph as a negative definition, one that defines not only who the right partner might be but, more important, who the right partner is not (who is excluded). Compare your original paragraphs and rewrites with the rest of the class.

3. Take a few minutes to write your own definition of *love*, using your responses from page 569 as a guide. After you've defined the term, take a few more minutes to consider your background or experience, the nature of your love object, the intensity of your feelings, and the importance of love in your life right now. Write out your responses to these factors, and then revise your definition of *love* accordingly.

4. A definition typically includes the class to which a term or concept belongs and the distinguishing characteristics that set it apart from other members of that class. **Working with two or three classmates,** select one or two of the following terms, and briefly define them by determining their class and distinguishing characteristics. Try to be objective. As you develop your definition, think about the features of the term you want to explain for your readers:

education	character
love	loyalty
family	childhood
middle age	failure
responsibility	success
security	happiness
satisfaction	bad words
sin	another word or term of your choice

Share your definitions with the rest of the class, and note your classmates' comments and suggestions. Then draft a two- to three-page essay defining one of your terms, using the guidelines for checking over the use of definition (p. 583). **Ask a classmate** to review your draft.

5. Choose one of the terms from the list in question 4, and write an extended, subjective definition essay, three to four pages long. Be sure to give your opinion on the meaning of the term, and try to persuade your reader to share that opinion. Use the guidelines for checking over the use of definition (p. 583), and **ask one or two classmates** to review your draft.

6. Building on your work for question 3 under Analyzing Definition, **break into small groups** and compare your definitions and interpretations of those definitions with those of your classmates. Share with the rest of the class several definitions on which your group agrees or disagrees. Use the information you gleaned from this exercise as the basis for a two- to three-page comparison-and-contrast or classification-and-division essay on the ways definition is used in writing intended for a mass audience. Refer to "Checking Over the Use of Definition" (p. 583).

7. Define yourself. But before you start, consider your audience. For whom do you want to define yourself? What parts of yourself do you want to define? What is your purpose in writing this definition? What characteristics will you definitely include—and exclude? Write a two- to three-

page essay of self-definition. Refer to "Checking Over the Use of Definition" on this page to decide how to revise your draft, and **ask one or two classmates** to give you feedback as well.

✔ Checking Over the Use of Definition

1. What is your purpose in writing this definition? Are you aiming to inform or argue a point? What details did you include that helped make the definition objective or subjective? Label each detail *objective* (O) or *subjective* (S).

2. Who is your intended audience? How much do members of your audience know or think they know about the concept you're defining? What is their attitude toward it? Have you taken their knowledge and attitudes into account in writing the definition?

3. Which kind of definition are you using? Have you written a sentence definition or an extended definition? a historical definition, a negative definition, or a stipulative definition?

4. What words or phrases did you use to classify your term? to distinguish it from other terms in the same class? Underline them.

5. What is the thesis statement of your definition? Have you drawn clear boundaries around your term or concept? What exactly are you including in and excluding from your definition?

6. How do your details and examples support your definition? What methods — description, comparison, classification, process analysis — did you use to develop and illustrate it? Do they help make your definition vivid and clear for your readers?

7. Did you consult any sources in writing your definition? If not, do you need to?

8. What organizational plan did you follow? Is it chronological, spatial, emphatic, or something else? Does it seem to work effectively? Did you provide clear transitions to help readers move from one part of your essay to the next?

9. What specific point does your conclusion make? How does it extend your thesis?

10. If you've used visuals, do they enhance your definition and help fulfill your purpose? Do you need to add labels, captions, or references to the visuals in the text? If you haven't used visuals, should you?

READINGS

BRIAN GREENE
Put a Little Science in Your Life

Brian Greene is a professor of mathematics and physics at Columbia University, where his primary area of research is string theory. In addition to his academic writing, Greene writes for more popular audiences, translating scientific findings for nonspecialist readers. His publications include the books *The Elegant Universe: Superstrings, Hidden Dimensions, and the Quest for the Ultimate Theory* (2000) and *The Fabric of the Cosmos: Space, Time, and the Texture of Reality* (2005). In the following essay, originally published in the *New York Times* in 2008, Greene defines the term *science* for another group of nonspecialist readers.

Preview   Define the term *science*. What does this term mean to you?

Greene uses narration to introduce readers to his discussion on the definition and relevance of science.

A couple of years ago I received a letter from an 1 American soldier in Iraq. The letter began by saying that, as we've all become painfully aware, serving on the front lines is physically exhausting and emotionally debilitating. But the reason for his writing was to tell me that in that hostile and lonely environment, a book I'd written had become a kind of lifeline. As the book is about science—one that traces physicists' search for nature's deepest laws—the soldier's letter might strike you as, well, odd.

Here is the thesis statement that Greene's definition will support.

But it's not. Rather, it speaks to the power- 2 ful role science can play in giving life context and meaning. At the same time, the soldier's letter emphasized something I've increasingly come to believe: America's educational system fails to teach science in a way that allows students to integrate it into their lives.

3   When we consider the ubiquity of cell phones, iPods, personal computers and the Internet, it's easy to see how science is woven into the fabric of our day-to-day activities. When we benefit from MRI devices, pacemakers and arterial stents, we can immediately appreciate how science affects the quality of our lives. When we assess the state of the world, and identify looming challenges like climate change, global pandemics, security threats and diminishing resources, we don't hesitate in turning to science to gauge the problems and find solutions.

4   And when we look at the wealth of opportunities hovering on the horizon — stem cells, genomic sequencing, longevity research, nanoscience, quantum computers, space technology — we realize how crucial it is to cultivate a general public that can engage with scientific issues; there's simply no other way that as a society we will be prepared to make informed decisions on a range of issues that will shape the future.

Note the use of exemplification in these paragraphs.

5   These are the standard reasons many would give in explaining why science matters.

6   But the reason science really matters runs deeper still. Science is a way of life. Science is a perspective. Science is the process that takes us from confusion to understanding in a manner that's precise, predictive and reliable — a transformation, for those lucky enough to experience it, that is empowering and emotional. To be able to think through and grasp explanations — for everything from why the sky is blue to how life formed on earth — not because they are declared dogma but rather because they reveal patterns confirmed by experiment and observation, is one of the most precious of human experiences. As a practicing scientist, I know this from my own work and study.

Greene offers his first definition of science here.

7   But I also know that you don't have to be a scientist for science to be transformative. I've seen children's eyes light up as I've told them about black holes and the big bang. I've spoken with high school dropouts who've stumbled on popular science books about the human genome project, and then returned to school with new-found purpose.

8   And in that letter from Iraq, the soldier told me how learning about relativity and quantum physics

in the dusty and dangerous environs of greater Baghdad kept him going because it revealed a deeper reality of which we're all a part.

Greene offers the conventional definition of science and then counters it with his own.

It's striking that science is still widely viewed as an isolated body of largely esoteric knowledge that sometimes shows up in the "real" world in the form of technological or medical advances. In reality, science is a language of hope and inspiration, providing discoveries that instill a sense of connection to our lives and our world.   9

I've spoken with so many people over the years whose encounters with science in school left them thinking of it as cold, distant and intimidating. What a shame. Like a life without music, art or literature, a life without science is bereft of something that gives experience a rich and otherwise inaccessible dimension.   10

Greene explains what it means to see science as he does.

It's one thing to go outside on a crisp, clear night and marvel at a sky full of stars. It's another to marvel not only at the spectacle but to recognize that those stars are the result of exceedingly ordered conditions 13.7 billion years ago at the moment of the big bang. It's another still to understand how those stars act as nuclear furnaces that supply the universe with carbon, oxygen and nitrogen, the raw material of life as we know it.   11

And it's yet another level of experience to realize that those stars account for less than 4 percent of what's out there — the rest being of an unknown composition, so-called dark matter and energy, which researchers are now trying to divine.   12

As every parent knows, children begin life as uninhibited, unabashed explorers of the unknown. From the time we can walk and talk, we want to know what things are and how they work — we begin life as little scientists. But most of us quickly lose our intrinsic scientific passion. And it's a profound loss.   13

A great many studies have focused on this problem, identifying important opportunities for improving science education. Recommendations have ranged from increasing the level of training for science teachers to curriculum reforms.   14

But most of these studies avoid an overarching systemic issue: In teaching students, we continually fail to activate rich opportunities for revealing the breathtaking vistas opened up by science, and in-   15 stead focus on the need to gain competency with science's underlying technical details.

16   In fact, many students I've spoken to have little sense of the big questions those technical details collectively try to answer: Where did the universe come from? How did life originate? How does the brain give rise to consciousness? Like a music curriculum that requires its students to practice scales while rarely if ever inspiring them by playing the great masterpieces, this way of teaching science squanders the chance to make students sit up in their chairs and say, "Wow, that's science?"

Note Greene's use of comparison here.

17   In physics, just to give a sense of the raw material that's available to be leveraged, the most revolutionary of advances have happened in the last 100 years—special relativity, general relativity, quantum mechanics—a symphony of discoveries that changed our conception of reality. More recently, the last 10 years have witnessed an upheaval in our understanding of the universe's composition, yielding a wholly new prediction for what the cosmos will be like in the far future.

18   These are paradigm-shaking developments. But rare is the high school class in which these breakthroughs are introduced. It's much the same story in classes for biology, chemistry and mathematics.

19   At the root of this pedagogical approach is a firm belief in the vertical nature of science: You must master A before moving on to B. Certainly, when it comes to teaching the technicalities—solving this equation, balancing that reaction, grasping the discrete parts of the cell—the verticality of science is unassailable.

20   But science is so much more than its technical details. And with careful attention to presentation, cutting-edge insights and discoveries can be clearly and faithfully communicated to students independent of those details; in fact, those insights and discoveries are precisely the ones that can drive a young student to want to learn the details. We rob science education of life when we focus solely on results and seek to train students to solve problems and recite facts without a commensurate emphasis on transporting them out beyond the stars.

Greene offers yet another definition of science.

21   Science is the greatest of all adventure stories, one that's been unfolding for thousands of years.

Greene offers his final definition of science.

Science needs to be taught to the young and communicated to the mature in a manner that captures this drama. We must embark on a cultural shift that places science in its rightful place alongside music, art and literature as an indispensable part of what makes life worth living.

It's the birthright of every child, it's a necessity   22
for every adult, to look out on the world, as the soldier in Iraq did, and see that the wonder of the cosmos transcends everything that divides us.

Reading Closely

1. From Greene's perspective, what is the conventional definition of science, and how is the subject taught in schools?
2. How does the opening narrative set the stage for Greene's definition essay?
3. Greene composes his essay using the first-person pronoun, *I*. What effect does this decision have on the reader? How does his particular perspective affect the success (or failure) of the essay?

Considering Larger Issues

1. What has your science education been like in school? How does it (or doesn't it) compare with Greene's description?
2. What would Greene's science classroom look like? What would students do?
3. **Working with a classmate,** review all the places (indicated in the annotations) where Greene defines the term *science*. How are these multiple definitions different from or similar to one another? What is the effect of the writer's offering these multiple definitions?
4. Who is the audience for this essay? Why is Greene writing about this topic to this particular audience?

Thinking about Language

1. Using the context of the essay or your dictionary, define the following words and phrases. Be prepared to share your answers with the rest of the class.

debilitating (1)	nanoscience (4)	esoteric (9)
ubiquity (3)	dogma (6)	intrinsic (13)
arterial stents (3)	black holes (7)	paradigm–shaking (18)
pandemics (3)	big bang (7)	commensurate (20)
genomic sequencing (4)	relativity (8)	

2. Underline the "scientific" terms that Greene uses throughout the essay. What are the effects of these terms on his audience?

Writing Your Own Essays Using Definition

1. In a three- to four-page essay, define *science education*. As Greene does, compose your definition by both reflecting on your experiences in science classes and imagining how science education might be improved. Be specific in your definition, explaining what science education should be for future students and giving examples of potential student projects and assignments. As you draft and revise, refer to the guidelines for checking over the use of definition on page 583.

2. In the opening paragraphs of Greene's essay, he argues that people should be more engaged with science and science education because of the important ways this field affects our everyday lives. Greene points out that we constantly rely on the scientific research that resulted in medical devices like MRIs and CT scanners, and we look to scientists to solve major world problems such as climate change and pandemics. In a three- to four-page essay, define a medical, social, or environmental concern of your choice (not necessarily a global one), and then explain the pivotal role scientific research plays in addressing it. For instance, you might want to investigate Alzheimer's disease. You would define the disease and how it affects those afflicted with it. Then you would discuss how scientists are working toward a cure for this disease. To compose your definition of the issue and the explanation of science's response to it, you'll need to conduct a good deal of research. As you do, be sure to identify resources that are reliable and credible. Refer to the guidelines for checking over the use of definition on page 583 as you draft and revise.

WILLIAM LAURENS RATHJE

How Garbage Got to Be an -Ology

Archaeologist William Laurens Rathje (b. 1945) is professor emeritus of anthropology at the University of Arizona and a consulting professor of anthropological sciences at Stanford University. In 1973, Rathje and his students began the Garbage Project, which sorted and studied discarded waste and landfills. His writings encompass publications about consumption and refuse disposal in both scholarly journals (*American Behavioral Scientist*) and popular magazines (*Atlantic, National Geographic*). With coauthor Cullen Murphy, Rathje also published *Rubbish: The Archaeology of Garbage* in 2001. In the following essay, published in *Municipal Solid Waste Management* magazine in 2002, Rathje defines his field of study as "garbology."

Preview   What do you imagine the field of garbology to be? What would this area of research and study include?

Every year, thousands of new words, such as "incentivize" and "dumb-   1
ing down," fight for that place in the word limelight we call the dictionary. But attaining "dictionary-worthiness" isn't easy. In fact, out of every thousand newly minted words, only a handful survive.

Imagine, then, my surprise when a word coined in the late 1970s   2
to describe the work of the Garbage Project became enshrined in the 1990s in that thoroughbred of dictionaries, the *Oxford English Dictionary*. The *American Heritage Dictionary* followed suit, and half a dozen more have piled on since.

The entry itself usually looks something like this: **gar·bol'o·gy** *n.*   3
[GARB(AGE) + –LOGY.]—**gar·bol'o·gist** *n.*; and the definition is "The study of a society by examining or analyzing its refuse."

OK, just about every noun seeking respect has dressed itself up in   4
the starched suffix *–ology*; for example, "hamburgerology." But most of these endeavors don't get as far as the *New Yorker* cartoon spoof with the word "cantaloupology" below a man looking intently at a cantaloupe. Why, then, did *garbology* make the prime cut?

Simply put, the word was right for the times. It epitomizes the way   5
garbologists — garbage people like you and me — have *made a difference* because we deal with garbage dilemmas in a systematic and scientific manner. But more important, it epitomizes a positive way our society has come to look at itself today . . . garbage and all.

The new vision of garbage began creeping into the American con-   6
sciousness on the first Earth Day in 1970, with its mantra that extolled recycling. Soon industry was touting incineration in the same glowing terms. During the next decade, sources as authoritative as *Science* magazine proclaimed there was "Gold in Garbage." The problem was perceived as rapidly growing mountains of discards; the solution was perceived as

recycling or burning it for a profit. What more could any red–blooded American ask?

There was only one hitch: All but a few of the thousands of idealistic 7 recyclers who opened their doors in April 1970 were quickly shaken out of business, and most of the big–enough–to–heat–Detroit–sized incinerators followed suit. Clearly, garbage was something important we didn't yet understand.

Meanwhile, without any hoopla, America's underground economy 8 had been stood on its head. The 1800s had been a boom time for rag pickers because household garbage was rife with old textiles that mills needed to produce paper. But early in this century, the freshly christened transcontinental railroad brought cheap lumber from the West to the East, not coincidentally, just as the mills figured out how to make paper out of wood.

That left garbage pickers without a valuable to pick, and the trade of 9 garbage scavenging languished until the 1970s. By then, battalions of pre-prepared foods and a newly inspired desire for fresh–looking produce flooded America with both profits and supermarket Dumpsters laden with not–consumer–acceptable–but–still–edible wastes, such as dented cans and slightly browning lettuce. The monetary incentives attached to re-cyclables also led the hungry underclass back to garbage. In fact, street people began to stake out personal territories where the garbage is rich in rewards.

But again, something was wrong. Yes, some of the waste was sal- 10 vaged, but why were the mountains of waste there in the first place, and why wasn't more of it benefiting millions of the even more needy? Again, it seemed we didn't understand garbage.

Meanwhile, there was a third type of interest in everyday discards 11 that became prominent in the early 1970s: garbage "peeping Toms." Since time immemorial, law enforcement organizations have searched through garbage for evidence. That technique was exploited by A. J. Weberman, a self-proclaimed "garbage guerrilla" who wrote a cover article for *Esquire* magazine in 1971. In it Weberman displayed refuse he had swiped from the homes of Bob Dylan, Neil Simon, and other celebrities of the day. Reporters quickly took up the practice of swiping refuse, and similar be-havior appeared on just about every cop and whodunit TV series, from *The Rockford Files* to *Law & Order*.

What probably kept this garbage avocation from surviving much past 12 the 1980s was simple: The artifacts hidden in celebrities' refuse were, by and large, the same kinds of mundane things we all throw away (Dylan's garbage contained soiled diapers and Simon's a half–eaten bagel). Besides, if you only sort through a bag or two, you probably won't find many astonishing insights. From my experience, those only come after sort-ing through thousands of samples and looking for non–person–specific patterns that characterize neighborhoods.

Meanwhile, such systematic sampling, sorting, and recording of gar- 13
bage appeared in what might seem a parallel universe to "peeping Tom"
refuse poking. Its roots stretch back more than 100 years to the first archaeologists who excavated ancient artifacts to shed light on humanity's
dim past. What archaeologists dug up was mostly old garbage, but the
passing centuries had tinged it with both grandeur and mystery. Using
discards, archaeologists opened a window on ancient human behavior.

It wasn't much of a leap to realize that our own fresh garbage pro- 14
vided an equally clear window onto our contemporary behavior, one
that reported what we actually did rather than what we just said we did.
The study of garbage was a "material sociology" of American society.

Early market researchers exploited it as such. In a now legendary 15
study, household refuse collected from Andover, MA, was searched for
Campbell's soup cans that had just appeared in markets. The cans weren't
found where expected, in the rubbish of the rich, who had servants to
make soup for them. Instead, the empty cans were spotted in the refuse of
the middle class, who had little free time and less help. To judge from their
garbage, the middle class enjoyed the convenience of canned soup . . .
and the marketing of convenience to everyday families began in earnest, restructuring the form and content of the most critical relationships
within American families.

When I started the Garbage Project's academic study of fresh MSW 16
[municipal solid waste] in Tucson, I wasn't thinking in such big-picture
terms. I just wanted to give freshmen at the University of Arizona a
chance to experience, hands-on, the panorama of behaviors archaeologists could reconstruct from everyday garbage.

We began by focusing on food waste because the large quantities we 17
recorded were so shocking. Then we expanded to diet and nutrition, recycling and household hazardous waste discards, brand loyalty and consumer responses to new products, and on and on.

Our unexpected discoveries attracted considerable media attention, 18
due in no small part, I'm sure, to the fact that clean-cut university students were hand-sorting and recording yucky garbage. But that made
the students and our results "real."

Now all the "meanwhiles" began to come together. Three were espe- 19
cially memorable to me.

The first occurred in 1971, well before the Garbage Project, when 20
Charles Kuralt interviewed a can-tosser named Frenchy Benguerel in
Kenwood, CA, as part of his "On the Road" series for *CBS Evening News*.
Kuralt didn't interview Frenchy as a garbageman or a "peeping Tom" but
as a chronicler of neighborhood lifestyles, concerned about waste and
recycling, but just as interested in the overall frequency of hair coloring
and alcohol containers.

Directly related to that image of Frenchy as a neighborhood sociolo- 21
gist is the *Grin and Bear It* cartoon that I believe coined the term *garbology*.

It pictured two bedraggled hobos picking through the contents of a garbage can, as one says, "'Garbology' is becoming a science, Arnold . . .
And, just think, we were pioneers in the field."

Finally, in the spring of 1987, the garbage barge sailed out from Long   22
Island and into history. The *Mobro 4000* was a riveting wake–up call. Before the garbage barge, when someone I sat next to on an airplane asked
me what I did, I would change the subject to avoid puzzled looks. After
the garbage barge, there was no problem. Everyone immediately got that
I–understand–why–studying–garbage–is–important look on their face.

We have the same look on our faces today. We all understand that to   23
make a difference—to recycle efficiently, to burn safely, and to cut down
on waste in all MSW management—we need systematic, scientific studies to design waste–handling systems and consumer education programs
that work as they are supposed to.

It seems that just about everyone is now a self–styled garbologist,   24
from Dumpster divers to people who test the strength of garbage cans.
And now and then don't all of us who place our garbage out for collection claim garbology expertise? In fact, the term has experienced such
wide circulation that it has appeared at a national spelling bee, on the
TV game show *Jeopardy*, and now and again in *Time* and other national
newsmagazines. I believe that this is a good sign for both garbage people
and our nation as a whole.

Even though it brings smiles, maybe even smirks, to people's faces,   25
the term *garbology* means that Americans are no longer turning a blind
eye to MSW. In fact, without exception, garbage is being taken far more
seriously—even die–hard litterers feel either more guilty or more afraid
of fines. At the same time, most of the lay public is aware of the basic
refuse problem and is becoming more garbage literate. Not everyone, by
far, knows what "postconsumer recycled content" or "source reduction"
means for sure, but they are beginning to believe that they should know.
After all, any self–respecting garbologist would know.

Reading Closely

1. What is the definition of *garbology*? What does a garbologist do?
2. What is the purpose of this essay? Identify places in the text that reveal
   this purpose.
3. Rathje classifies "garbage pickers" into distinct categories. What are these
   categories? What interest does each group have in garbage?

Considering Larger Issues

1. What did you learn while reading this essay? What surprised or interested you?

2. **Working with a classmate,** identify the audience for this essay. What is Rathje's message to this audience?

3. COMBINING METHODS. Although Rathje calls on a number of rhetorical methods throughout the essay, he relies heavily on *process analysis* to compose his definition of *garbology*. Identify the places in the text where Rathje uses process analysis, and discuss how this particular method supports Rathje's definition.

4. PAIRED READINGS. Both Rathje and Brian Greene, the author of the reading "Put a Little Science in Your Life," are attempting to define a field of study. Compare how these writers compose their definitions, thinking specifically about the strategies they use to define. What similarities and differences do you see?

Thinking about Language

1. Using the context of the essay or your dictionary, define the following words and phrases. Be prepared to share your answers with the rest of the class.

refuse (3)	idealistic (7)	immemorial (11)
epitomizes (5)	rag pickers (8)	bedraggled (21)
mantra (6)	rife (8)	barge (22)
extolled (6)	battalions (9)	Dumpster divers (24)
incineration (6)		

2. Underline the transitional words Rathje uses in this essay. How do these words help move readers from paragraph to paragraph?

Writing Your Own Essays Using Definition

1. Rathje argues, "It wasn't much of a leap to realize that our own fresh garbage provided an equally clear window onto our contemporary behavior." In other words, Rathje asserts that we are what we throw away. In a three- to four-page essay, reflect on *what* you throw away and *how* you do so, and consider how these materials and the ways you dispose of them define who you are. To research the essay, become a garbologist for two or three days, taking careful notes of what you throw away and how (for example, do you recycle, compost, take materials to large Dumpsters, or discard them in a trash can?). What do your findings say about you? How do they define you? As you compose, use the "Checking Over the Use of Definition" guidelines on page 583.

2. Rathje uses this essay to define the term *garbology*, and in doing so, he also defines the work of a garbologist. In a three- to four-page essay, identify a career (in, say, sports psychology, market research, architecture, or child care) that you are or may be interested in pursuing. Then define the kind of work people in this field do. What is a sports psychologist, market researcher, architect, or child care provider? What does this kind of professional do? Be detailed in your definition, moving beyond what

most audiences already know about this career. To expand your knowledge, conduct library research and interview someone already in the
field. Use the "Checking Over the Use of Definition" guidelines on
page 583 as you draft and revise.

3. PUBLIC WRITING. Both Rathje and Brian Greene ("Put a Little Science in
   Your Life") define a field of study in their essays. While Rathje defines
   garbology by providing a historical definition, Greene offers his definition of science by contrasting it with more popular understandings of
   the subject. In a three- to four-page essay, choose a field of study that
   you know well (not a kind of work, as in question 2), and compose a
   definition of this term for a nonspecialist, public audience. Whether you
   choose economics, social work, or history, offer a definition that might
   surprise and interest your readers. As you write, think about the following questions: What is the general perception of this field? What *don't*
   most people know about this field of study? What is interesting about it?
   What do practitioners of this field do that a nonspecialist audience might
   not know about? As you compose your essay, model it after Greene's,
   which was published in the Opinion section of the *New York Times*. Refer
   to "Checking Over the Use of Definition" on page 583 throughout the
   drafting and revising process.

JUDY BRADY
Why I Want a Wife

Judy Brady (b. 1937) earned a bachelor of fine arts degree from the University of Iowa and has published many articles and edited two books, *Women and Cancer* (1990) and *One in Three: Women with Cancer Confront an Epidemic* (1991). "Why I Want a Wife" first appeared in 1970 in *Motherload,* a feminist magazine, and reappeared in the premier issue of *Ms.* in 1972. It has been reprinted regularly in textbooks and anthologies ever since. As you read it, notice how Brady uses irony as she extends and develops her definition of a wife.

> **Preview** How do you define *wife?* How do you define *husband? partner?*

I belong to that classification of people known as wives. I am A Wife. 1
And, not altogether incidentally, I am a mother.

Not too long ago a male friend of mine appeared on the scene fresh 2
from a recent divorce. He had one child, who is, of course, with his ex-wife. He is looking for another wife. As I thought about him while I was ironing one evening, it suddenly occurred to me that I, too, would like to have a wife. Why do I want a wife?

I would like to go back to school so that I can become economically 3
independent, support myself, and if need be, support those dependent upon me. I want a wife who will work and send me to school. And while I am going to school I want a wife to take care of my children. I want a wife to keep track of the children's doctor and dentist appointments. And to keep track of mine, too. I want a wife to make sure my children eat properly and are kept clean. I want a wife who will wash the children's clothes and keep them mended. I want a wife who is a good nurturant attendant to my children, who arranges for their schooling, makes sure that they have an adequate social life with their peers, takes them to the park, the zoo, etc. I want a wife who takes care of the children when they are sick, a wife who arranges to be around when the children need special care, because, of course, I cannot miss classes at school. My wife must arrange to lose time at work and not lose the job. It may mean a small cut in my wife's income from time to time, but I guess I can tolerate that. Needless to say, my wife will arrange and pay for the care of the children while my wife is working.

I want a wife who will take care of *my* physical needs. I want a wife 4
who will keep my house clean. A wife who will pick up after my children, a wife who will pick up after me. I want a wife who will keep my clothes clean, ironed, mended, replaced when need be, and who will see to it that my personal things are kept in their proper place so that I can find what I need the minute I need it. I want a wife who cooks the meals, a wife who is a *good* cook. I want a wife who will plan the menus, do the necessary grocery shopping, prepare the meals, serve them pleasantly,

and then do the cleaning up while I do my studying. I want a wife who will care for me when I am sick and sympathize with my pain and loss of time from school. I want a wife to go along when our family takes a vacation so that someone can continue to care for me and my children when I need a rest and change of scene.

I want a wife who will not bother me with rambling complaints 5 about a wife's duties. But I want a wife who will listen to me when I feel the need to explain a rather difficult point I have come across in my course of studies. And I want a wife who will type my papers for me when I have written them.

I want a wife who will take care of the details of my social life. When 6 my wife and I are invited out by my friends, I want a wife who will take care of the babysitting arrangements. When I meet people at school that I like and want to entertain, I want a wife who will have the house clean, will prepare a special meal, serve it to me and my friends, and not interrupt when I talk about things that interest me and my friends. I want a wife who will have arranged that the children are fed and ready for bed before my guests arrive so that the children do not bother us. I want a wife who takes care of the needs of my guests so that they feel comfortable, who makes sure that they have an ashtray, that they are passed the hors d'oeuvres, that they are offered a second helping of the food, that their wine glasses are replenished when necessary, that their coffee is served to them as they like it. And I want a wife who knows that sometimes I need a night out by myself.

I want a wife who is sensitive to my sexual needs, a wife who makes   7
love passionately and eagerly when I feel like it, a wife who makes sure
that I am satisfied. And, of course, I want a wife who will not demand
sexual attention when I am not in the mood for it. I want a wife who
assumes the complete responsibility for birth control, because I do not
want more children. I want a wife who will remain sexually faithful to
me so that I do not have to clutter up my intellectual life with jealousies.
And I want a wife who understands that *my* sexual needs may entail
more than strict adherence to monogamy. I must, after all, be able to relate to people as fully as possible.

If, by chance, I find another person more suitable as a wife than the   8
wife I already have, I want the liberty to replace my present wife with
another one. Naturally, I will expect a fresh, new life; my wife will take
the children and be solely responsible for them so that I am left free.

When I am through with school and have a job, I want my wife to   9
quit working and remain at home so that my wife can more fully and
completely take care of a wife's duties.

My God, who *wouldn't* want a wife?   10

Reading Closely

1. In one sentence, define Brady's concept *of wife*. **Working with two or
   three classmates,** compare your definitions. How are they similar? dissimilar?

2. How does Brady also define the duties of the *mother* in the house? How
   are the duties of the wife and mother related?

3. Does the scene from the TV program *Family Guy* on page 597 support
   Brady's definitions, or does it suggest that expectations for wives have
   changed since 1970, when her article was written? What details from the
   scene support your answer?

Considering Larger Issues

1. Reread the headnote on page 596 to review the publication history of
   this essay. How does knowing that history help you establish the purpose and audience?

2. How does Brady develop her extended definition of *wife*? What distinguishing characteristics does she describe? What details, examples, or
   anecdotes does she use to bring these characteristics to life? Mark them
   in the text. Prepare to compare your responses and findings with the rest
   of the class.

3. COMBINING METHODS. How does Brady use *comparison and contrast* to enrich
   her definition *of wife*? Specifically what are the points of comparison between *husband* and *wife*? What is the effect of this comparison on her
   overall essay?

Thinking about Language

1. Using the context of the essay or your dictionary, define the following words. Be prepared to share your answers with the rest of the class.

   incidentally (1)   rambling (5)   entail (7)
   nurturant (3)   replenished (6)

2. Underline every use of the phrase *I want a wife*. How many times does Brady use that phrase in this relatively short essay? What is the effect of her refrain?

3. When writers use irony, they mean the opposite of what their words say. An author using irony often understates or exaggerates information in order to make a point. **Working with two or three classmates,** identify places in the essay where Brady understates or exaggerates. Prepare to present your group's findings to the rest of the class.

Writing Your Own Essays Using Definition

1. Write an essay of no more than two pages defining a type of person you encounter at school: professor, teaching assistant, secretary, cafeteria worker, janitor, and so on. You may draw on Brady's essay for examples of tone (irony) and supporting details (real–life examples), but embellish her style if you can with ideas based on your own experiences and observations. Refer to "Checking Over the Use of Definition" on page 583.

2. Prepare to write an essay that defines a word referring to a family member: *wife, husband, daughter, son, in-law, grandparent,* and so on. First jot down all the features of that role you can think of. Then list the three kinds of extended definitions: historical, negative, and stipulative. For each type of definition, which of your details could you use? Match the details with the type of definition. For which type have you come up with the most details? Which kind of definition, then, are you prepared to write? What might your thesis statement be?

   Look over the details that you have gathered. How do those details define your conception of that role? **Consider working with one or two classmates** to determine how your definitions differ or overlap and how your own definition is unique. Will you arrange your information by describing, explaining, classifying, or comparing? As you draft and revise your two– to three–page essay, refer to the guidelines for checking over the use of definition on page 583.

PAUL THEROUX
Being a Man

Paul Theroux (b. 1941) was born and raised in Massachusetts and then left for Italy after his 1963 graduation from the University of Massachusetts at Amherst. For the next few years he taught English at the University of Urbino and then at Soche Hille College in Malawi. Later he joined the faculty at the University of Singapore, where he began establishing his reputation as an American novelist and travel writer. His numerous books include *Waldo* (1966), *The Great Railway Bazaar* (1975), *The Mosquito Coast* (1982), *Millroy the Magician* (1993), *Hotel Honolulu* (2001), *Dark Star Safari* (2003), *Blinding Light* (2006), and *The Elephant Suite* (2007). The following essay, written in 1983, first appeared in his *Sunrise with Seamonsters* (1985).

> **Preview**   What reasons might cause someone to feel the need to write an essay on being a man? What could possibly be complicated about being a man?

There is a pathetic sentence in the chapter "Fetishism" in Dr. Norman 1 Cameron's book *Personality Development and Psychopathology*. It goes, "Fetishists are nearly always men; and their commonest fetish is a woman's shoe." I cannot read that sentence without thinking that it is just one more awful thing about being a man—and perhaps it is an important thing to know about us.

I have always disliked being a man. The whole idea of manhood in 2 America is pitiful, in my opinion. This version of masculinity is a little like having to wear an ill–fitting coat for one's entire life (by contrast, I imagine femininity to be an oppressive sense of nakedness). Even the expression "Be a man!" strikes me as insulting and abusive. It means: Be stupid, be unfeeling, obedient, soldierly and stop thinking. Man means "manly"—how can one think about men without considering the terrible ambition of manliness? And yet it is part of every man's life. It is a hideous and crippling lie; it not only insists on difference and connives at superiority, it is also by its very nature destructive—emotionally damaging and socially harmful.

The youth who is subverted, as most are, into believing in the mas- 3 culine ideal is effectively separated from women and he spends the rest of his life finding women a riddle and a nuisance. Of course, there is a female version of this male affliction. It begins with mothers encouraging little girls to say (to other adults) "Do you like my new dress?" In a sense, little girls are traditionally urged to please adults with a kind of coquettishness, while boys are enjoined to behave like monkeys towards each other. The nine–year–old coquette proceeds to become womanish in a subtle power game in which she learns to be sexually indispensable, socially decorative and always alert to a man's sense of inadequacy.

Femininity—being lady-like—implies needing a man as witness and 4
seducer; but masculinity celebrates the exclusive company of men. That
is why it is so grotesque; and that is also why there is no manliness
without inadequacy—because it denies men the natural friendship of
women.

It is very hard to imagine any concept of manliness that does not be- 5
little women, and it begins very early. At an age when I wanted to meet
girls—let's say the treacherous years of thirteen to sixteen—I was told to
take up a sport, get more fresh air, join the Boy Scouts, and I was urged
not to read so much. It was the 1950s and if you asked too many questions about sex you were sent to camp—boy's camp, of course: the night-
mare. Nothing is more unnatural or prison-like than a boy's camp, but if
it were not for them we would have no Elks' Lodges, no pool rooms, no
boxing matches, no Marines.

And perhaps no sports as we know them. Everyone is aware of how 6
few in number are the athletes who behave like gentlemen. Just as high
school basketball teaches you how to be a poor loser, the manly attitude towards sports seems to be little more than a recipe for creating
bad marriages, social misfits, moral degenerates, sadists, latent rapists
and just plain louts. I regard high school sports as a drug far worse than
marijuana, and it is the reason that the average tennis champion, say, is
a pathetic oaf.

Any objective study would find the quest for manliness essentially 7
right-wing, puritanical, cowardly, neurotic and fueled largely by a fear of
women. It is also certainly philistine. There is no book-hater like a Little
League coach. But indeed all the creative arts are obnoxious to the manly
ideal, because at their best the arts are pursued by uncompetitive and
essentially solitary people. It makes it very hard for a creative youngster,
for any boy who expresses the desire to be alone seems to be saying that
there is something wrong with him.

It ought to be clear by now that I have something of an objection to 8
the way we turn boys into men. It does not surprise me that when the
President of the United States [Ronald Reagan at the time] has his customary weekend off he dresses like a cowboy—it is both a measure of his
insecurity and his willingness to please. In many ways, American culture does little more for a man than prepare him for modeling clothes
in the L. L. Bean catalogue. I take this as a personal insult because for
many years I found it impossible to admit to myself that I wanted to be
a writer. It was my guilty secret, because being a writer was incompatible
with being a man.

There are people who might deny this, but that is because the Amer- 9
ican writer, typically, has been so at pains to prove his manliness that we
have come to see literariness and manliness as mingled qualities. But first
there was a fear that writing was not a manly profession—indeed, not a
profession at all. (The paradox in American letters is that it has always been

"I'm tired of being sensitive. I want to be an oaf again."

easier for a woman to write and for a man to be published.) Growing up,
I had thought of sports as wasteful and humiliating, and the idea of manliness was a bore. My wanting to become a writer was not a flight from
that oppressive role-playing, but I quickly saw that it was at odds with it.
Everything in stereotyped manliness goes against the life of the mind. The
Hemingway personality is too tedious to go into here, and in any case his
exertions are well-known, but certainly it was not until this aberrant behavior was examined by feminists in the 1960s that any male writer dared
question the pugnacity in Hemingway's fiction. All the bullfighting and
arm wrestling and elephant shooting diminished Hemingway as a writer,
but it is consistent with a prevailing attitude in American writing: one cannot be a male writer without first proving that one is a man.

It is normal in America for a man to be dismissive or even somewhat 10
apologetic about being a writer. Various factors make it easier. There is
a heartiness about journalism that makes it acceptable—journalism is
the manliest form of American writing and, therefore, the profession the

most independent–minded women seek (yes, it is an illusion, but that is my point). Fiction–writing is equated with a kind of dispirited failure and is only manly when it produces wealth—money is masculinity. So is drinking. Being a drunkard is another assertion, if misplaced, of manliness. The American male writer is traditionally proud of his heavy drinking. But we are also a very literal–minded people. A man proves his manhood in America in old–fashioned ways. He kills lions, like Hemingway; or he hunts ducks, like Nathanael West; or he makes pronouncements like, "A man should carry enough knife to defend himself with," as James Jones once said to a *Life* interviewer. Or he says he can drink you under the table. But even tiny drunken William Faulkner loved to mount a horse and go fox hunting, and Jack Kerouac roistered up and down Manhattan in a lumberjack shirt (and spent every night of [his novel] *The Subterraneans* with his mother in Queens). And we are familiar with the lengths to which Norman Mailer is prepared, in his endearing way, to prove that he is just as much a monster as the next man.

When the novelist John Irving was revealed as a wrestler, people took 11 him to be a very serious writer; and even a bubble reputation like Eric *(Love Story)* Segal's was enhanced by the news that he ran the marathon in a respectable time. How surprised we would be if Joyce Carol Oates were revealed as a sumo wrestler or Joan Didion active in pumping iron. "Lives in New York City with her three children" is the typical woman writer's biographical note, for just as the male writer must prove he has achieved a sort of muscular manhood, the woman writer—or rather her publicists—must prove her motherhood.

There would be no point in saying any of this if it were not generally 12 accepted that to be a man is somehow—even now in feminist–influenced America—a privilege. It is on the contrary an unmerciful and punishing burden. Being a man is bad enough; being manly is appalling (in this sense, women's lib has done much more for men than for women). It is the sinister silliness of men's fashions, and a clubby attitude in the arts. It is the subversion of good students. It is the so–called "Dress Code" of the Ritz–Carlton Hotel in Boston, and it is the institutionalized cheating in college sports. It is the most primitive insecurity.

And this is also why men often object to feminism but are afraid to 13 explain why: of course women have a justified grievance, but most men believe—and with reason—that their lives are just as bad.

Reading Closely

1. What is this essay about? Summarize it in one paragraph. Then summarize it in a single sentence.

2. How does Theroux define *being a man*? Exchange your one–sentence definitions **with a classmate.** Ask your classmate to revise your definition

while you edit the sentence that came your way. Share your sentences with the rest of the class.

3. How does the cartoon on page 602 relate to Theroux's point?

Considering Larger Issues

1. What do you think Theroux's purpose is for writing this essay? Who do you see as his intended audience? How does his audience affect his overall purpose, and vice versa?

2. What message do you think the author wants you to come away with?

3. What complications about being a man does Theroux cite? Do you agree with him? Which complications did he omit? Prepare to share your responses with the rest of the class.

4. COMBINING METHODS. In developing his definition of *being a man*, Theroux uses *cause-and-effect analysis*. Mark the passages in which he uses this method, and then discuss the overall effect of these passages on his essay.

Thinking about Language

1. Using the context of the essay or your dictionary, define the following terms. Be prepared to share your answers with the rest of the class.

pathetic (1)	Elks' Lodges (5)	aberrant (9)
fetishists (1)	belittle (5)	pugnacity (9)
manliness (2)	degenerates (6)	roistered (10)
connives (2)	latent (6)	publicists (11)
coquettishness (3)	puritanical (7)	clubby (12)
enjoined (3)	philistine (7)	subversion (12)
inadequacy (3)	mingled (9)	institutionalized (12)
grotesque (4)		

2. What is the effect of the last paragraph? Is it essential to the essay? Why or why not?

3. Unlike Brady's "Why I Want a Wife" (p. 596), there is nothing ironic in this essay. Theroux relates his experiences and observations in a straightforward way and with a measure of frustration. Mark all the places and list all the ways that Theroux's style expresses his disappointment and frustration. **Working with two or three classmates,** compare your responses, and prepare to present your group's findings to the rest of the class.

Writing Your Own Essays Using Definition

1. Take five minutes to write a short autobiography about "being a ____," filling in the blank with whatever role you identify with most: a man, a woman, a mother, a father, a laborer, a cook, a student, a leader, and so

on. After you are finished writing, underline all the features of your role that have stayed the same over a period of time, and circle the features that have changed. Make two columns, one for each set of features. What did you learn about your role from this exercise? Has your definition of your role changed over time? Write a two- to three-page essay defining your identifying role over time. Refer to the guidelines for checking over the use of definition (p. 583).

2. Using Theroux's essay as a starting point, draft a three- to four-page essay in which you define being a man. You may want to consider that role in terms of religion, politics, marriage and family, the women's movement, social class, racial or ethnic identity, or work. **Consider working with a classmate** and including visuals as you draft and revise, and be sure to refer to the guidelines for checking over the use of definition (p. 583).

MARY INKS
Dancing through the Learning Process

Mary Inks (b. 1984) wrote this essay when she was a student at Pennsylvania State University. After her undergraduate study, she went on to pursue a master of arts in professional writing and editing at West Virginia University. As an undergraduate and master's student, Inks worked as a tutor in the writing centers at both Penn State and West Virginia. She is now working toward a doctorate in rhetoric and composition.

Preview Think about a time when you were eager to learn something (in or out of school). How would you define your learning process in this situation?

What is learning, and what does it mean to learn? It is not surprising that 1 these are two questions college students often ask, since they are challenged to learn all the time in different classes, subjects, and contexts. But even though students often ask these questions, they are difficult ones to answer. Learning is a complex process to define; people learn at different rates, with different approaches, and at different levels of satisfaction. Adding to this complexity, students bring a wide range of experiences to their learning situations, making every learning experience unique to the individual. Nevertheless, understanding how people make progress up the learning curve can be simplified if we take a look at how learning happens in terms of hobbies, sports, or arts — learning situations where a wide range of learning approaches can be leveraged toward success. Learning to dance is a case in point, for the way people learn to dance compares with the way people learn in life, whether during their first year of college or their first years of life. Through this comparison, a basic definition of learning emerges: it is a gradual process that develops in stages, some of which may overlap, repeat, or continue forward, depending on people's interests.

Most people take dancing lessons because they want to: they've been 2 inspired to learn to dance by the music they enjoy or by the accomplished dancing of other people. These wanting–to–learn dancers (whether children or adults) often engage in the imitation–through–observation stage of learning: they tend to imitate dancers they watch without a base knowledge of the art or very much, if any, instruction. Basically, they observe dancers and attempt to move similarly, probably attempting to use their bodies in a new way. Without knowledge of how the dancers are using their bodies to produce the dance movements and how to express themselves through dance, beginners sometimes flail around, yet they're enjoying themselves. Although they may not completely understand the observations they are making, their imitations, their experience of making distinctive body movements to music, provide a good measure of learning as they strive to reproduce the art of dancing.

After this initial inspiration period, want-to-be dancers often go on to 3 receive formal instruction from a friend, parent, or teacher. Now they learn dance as an art form with specific moves and rhythms. During this formal instruction stage, people learn the fundamentals of maintaining good posture, holding their center to keep balance, pointing and flexing feet, and isolating body movements (head, shoulders, arms, ribs, hips, legs). Learning these fundamentals helps people understand how their body works and how to maintain proper dance placement throughout the dancing. Most important, people learn the proper way to do movements, which results in aesthetically pleasing dance form as well as injury-free dancing. In addition to proper form, choreography is another feature of formal dance instruction. Learning a combination of choreographed steps and styling helps people learn and then refine memorization techniques. Once they learn to memorize steps, they transfer these memorization techniques to other learning situations. Formal dance instruction requires dedicated work and practice from aspiring dancers, and the payoffs are quickly experienced by the dancers. Formal instruction also provides dancers with the analytical tools necessary for understanding how the people they imitate successfully execute their dance movements to the music, helping aspiring dancers better imitate their models. The information learned and the progress made during this stage provides aspiring dancers a crucial foundation on which to build their learning.

Learning cannot stop at the formal instruction stage, though. The 4
technical foundation learned acts as a launching pad for improvement
and development, especially with style. Experimenting with style (performance, musicality, and personality) allows dancers to improve their presentation, helping them appear polished, well rehearsed, and confident.
Furthermore, this foundation supports the learning of even more advanced dance steps. For instance, dancers can strive to complete three pir-
ouettes instead of only two or work to land more gracefully from a leap.
Eventually, technically correct dancing and styling become second nature.
No longer do dancers have to think about the proper way to move or
which steps work best with certain music—these things just happen.

At times, this more advanced stage reverts back to imitation and ex- 5
perimentation. As with many things, dancing has evolved, regresses, and
continues to change. People might become interested in learning different types of dance to extend their knowledge and skill. After learning one
type of dance early in life, such as ballet or jazz, some people want to expand their dance repertoire, learning other dances, such as ballroom or
salsa. In this case, some relearning may be required—not because people
forget how to move but because their bodies naturally lose flexibility, so
they need to reawaken their muscle memory. Posture and center remain
significant and similar, but people who haven't danced with a partner
need to learn those skills and the new style. When learning a subsequent
dance, dancers realize that although some features remain constant, new
skills must be learned and developed.

At first glance, students may wonder how learning to dance has any- 6
thing at all in common with the learning they do in college. If they realize that the process of learning to dance can be compared to learning to
read and write, they can see how one step of learning leads to the next.
For instance, initially, parents expose their children to picture books. The
child may look at words but not understand them; they look and "talk"
about the pictures. At some point, though, children begin to babble in
imitation of the talking adults, and after that stage, they may even begin to say the words they immediately recognize. Eventually (if all goes
as planned), young children learn many more words and the meanings
of those words. They can consume the printed word as they learn to
produce it, learning to write the letters and words they see in books. As
children increase their vocabulary and continue to read, their interest in
books may explode.

Students who learn to enjoy their reading may enroll in literature 7
courses, where they learn how to analyze and appreciate literature,
participate in discussions about it, and write about it. Learning at this
stage can serve not only as a development stage but also as a foundation stage. Literature courses that include reading and writing often lead
people onto further literary and rhetorical study in college, where they
can hone their analytical skills and learn to relate a piece of literature to
other imaginative works at the same time that they discover how authors

manage to achieve their purpose or establish a mood via their organizational, metaphoric, or character development.

This kind of progress indicates that learning has indeed occurred. 8 Learning, in this case, means that a person has demonstrated a sustained interest in a subject that grows over time. Although that interest might be directed toward different subinterests (like writing over reading or poetry over nonfiction), the person is continually learning. When students think of learning this way—as something enjoyable that provides a lifetime of pleasure—they begin to think of their college courses and experiences in a new way. Whether they're learning to appreciate literature or compose an essay, they're learning, just as a dancer moves along the learning curve when learning a new step or a new dance genre. No matter what the subject, learning entails "steps" for success, practice, and experimentation.

Reading Closely

1. How does Inks define the learning process in this essay? Pinpoint places in the text where she explicitly sets out her definition.

2. What is the purpose of Inks's definition? Is she writing to inform or argue?

3. Does Inks offer a subjective or objective definition of the learning process in her essay? Identify places in the text that support your claim.

4. Assess how Inks's use of detail helps her define the learning process. What details does she use? How do these details help (or hinder) this definition project?

5. Analyze the photograph on page 607. How does it extend (or detract from) Inks's analogy between dancing and learning?

Considering Larger Issues

1. Inks uses an extended metaphor to define the learning process, asserting that learning a school subject is like learning to dance. What do you think of this comparison? How does it resonate with your learning experiences?

2. **With a classmate,** review the arrangement of Inks's essay. What is her organizational strategy? How do you know? Identify places in the text that support your assessment.

3. COMBINING METHODS. Although Inks relies on a number of rhetorical methods throughout her essay, how, especially, does she use *process analysis* to compose her definition?

Thinking about Language

1. Using the context of the essay or your dictionary, define the following terms. Be prepared to share your answers with the rest of the class.

flail (2)	choreographed (3)	repertoire (5)
aesthetically (3)	pirouettes (4)	hone (7)

2. How would you describe the language Inks uses in her essay? Given these choices, what conclusions might we draw about her language community?

Writing Your Own Essays Using Definition

1. Inks uses an extended metaphor in her essay to claim that learning a school subject is like learning to dance. Whether you agree or disagree with Inks's choice of metaphor, identify another metaphor that would help define your particular learning process: for you, learning is like _____. Then compose a two- to three-page essay that develops and extends this metaphor. Your response to question 1 under the Considering Larger Issues section might help you to create your metaphor and compose your definition. Remember that your definition will gain depth through the use of details and examples, so be sure to include them in your essay. "Checking Over the Use of Definition" on page 583 should help you as you draft and revise.

2. Although Inks provides a general definition for learning in her essay, she also acknowledges that a person's learning process often changes given the specific learning situation. In a three- to four-page essay, identify two learning situations you have experienced, and define your learning process in each situation. As you define, compare these two processes and definitions of learning by considering the similarities and differences between them. In particular, you'll want to highlight how these processes share or don't share certain characteristics such as experimentation, practice, repetition, and observation, explaining why some characteristics are more important in one learning context than in the other. As you draft and revise, refer to "Checking Over the Use of Definition" on page 583.

NICHOLAS LEMANN

Amateur Hour:
Journalism without Journalists

● Nicholas Lemann is dean and professor of journalism at the Columbia University Graduate School of Journalism in New York. As a journalist and editor, he has worked for such publications as the *Washington Post*, the *Atlantic*, the *New Yorker*, and *Texas Monthly*. He is the author of three books: *The Promised Land: The Great Black Migration and How It Changed America* (1992), *The Big Test: The Secret History of the American Meritocracy* (2000), and *Redemption: The Last Battle of the Civil War* (2006). In the following article, published in the August 2006 issue of the *New Yorker*, Lemann defines the term *citizen journalism*, comparing the practices of citizen journalists to those of traditional journalists as he composes his definition.

> **Preview**   What do you know about journalism on the Internet? How does it compare to the kinds of journalism you read, see, or hear in traditional news outlets?

On the Internet, everybody is a millenarian. Internet journalism, accord-   1
ing to those who produce manifestos on its behalf, represents a world-historical development—not so much because of the expressive power of the new medium as because of its accessibility to producers and consumers. That permits it to break the long-standing choke hold on public information and discussion that the traditional media—usually known, when this argument is made, as "gatekeepers" or "the priesthood"—have supposedly been able to maintain up to now. "Millions of Americans who were once in awe of the punditocracy now realize that anyone can do this stuff—and that many unknowns can do it better than the lords of the profession," Glenn Reynolds, a University of Tennessee law professor who operates one of the leading blogs, Instapundit, writes, typically, in his new book, *An Army of Davids: How Markets and Technology Empower Ordinary People to Beat Big Media, Big Government, and Other Goliaths*.

The rhetoric about Internet journalism produced by Reynolds and   2
many others is plausible only because it conflates several distinct categories of material that are widely available online and didn't use to be. One is pure opinion, especially political opinion, which the Internet has made infinitely easy to purvey. Another is information originally published in other media—everything from Chilean newspaper stories and entries in German encyclopedias to papers presented at Micronesian conferences on accounting methods—which one can find instantly on search and aggregation sites. Lately, grand journalistic claims have been made on behalf of material produced specifically for Web sites by people who don't have jobs with news organizations. According to a study published

last month by the Pew Internet & American Life Project, there are twelve million bloggers in the United States, and thirty-four percent of them consider blogging to be a form of journalism. That would add up to more than four million newly minted journalists just among the ranks of American bloggers. If you add everyone abroad, and everyone who practices other forms of Web journalism, the profession must have increased in size a thousandfold over the last decade.

As the Pew study makes clear, most bloggers see themselves as en-   3 gaging only in personal expression; they don't inspire the biggest claims currently being made for Internet journalism. The category that inspires the most soaring rhetoric about supplanting traditional news organizations is "citizen journalism," meaning sites that publish contributions of people who don't have jobs with news organizations but are performing a similar function.

Citizen journalists are supposedly inspired amateurs who find out   4 what's going on in the places where they live and work, and who bring us a fuller, richer picture of the world than we get from familiar news organizations, while sparing us the pomposity and preening that journalists often display. Hong Eun-taek, the editor-in-chief of perhaps the biggest citizen-journalism site, Oh My News, which is based in Seoul and has a staff of editors managing about forty thousand volunteer contributors, has posted a brief manifesto, which says, "Traditional means of news gathering and dissemination are quickly falling behind the new paradigm. . . . We believe news is something that is made not only by a George W. Bush or a Bill Gates but, more importantly, by people who are all allowed to think together. The news is a form of collective thinking. It is the ideas and minds of the people that are changing the world, when they are heard."

That's the catechism, but what has citizen journalism actually brought   5 us? It's a difficult question, in part because many of the truest believers are very good at making life unpleasant for doubters, through relentless sneering. Thus far, no "traditional journalist" has been silly enough to own up to and defend the idea of belonging to an elite from which ordinary citizens are barred. But sometimes one will unwittingly toss a chunk of red meat to the new-media visionaries by appearing not to accord the Internet revolution the full measure of respect it deserves — as John Markoff, a technology reporter for the [*New York*] *Times*, did in 2003 in an interview with *Online Journalism Review*. Jeff Jarvis, a veteran editor, publisher, and columnist, and, starting in September, a professor at the City University of New York's new journalism school, posted the interview on his blog, BuzzMachine, with his own post-facto reactions added, so that it reads, in part, this way:

> MARKOFF: I certainly can see that scenario, where all these new technologies may only be good enough to destroy all the old standards

but not create something better to replace them with. I think that's
certainly one scenario.

JARVIS: Pardon me for interrupting, but that made no frigging
sense whatsoever. Can you parse that for me, Mr. Markoff? Or do
you need an editor to speak sense? How do new standards "destroy"
old standards? Something won't become a "standard" unless it is accepted by someone in power— the publishers or the audiences. This
isn't a game of PacMan.

MARKOFF: The other possibility right now— it sometimes seems
we have a world full of bloggers and that blogging is the future of
journalism, or at least that's what the bloggers argue, and to my
mind, it's not clear yet whether blogging is anything more than CB
radio.

JARVIS: The reference is as old–farty and out–of–date as the sentiment. It's clear that Markoff isn't reading weblogs and doesn't know
what's there.

Hey, fool, that's your *audience* talking there. You should want to
listen to what they have to say. You are, after all, spending your living writing for *them*. If you were a reporter worth a damn, you'd
care to know what the marketplace cares about. But, no, you're the
mighty NYT guy. You don't need no stinking audience. You don't
need ears. You only need a mouth.

To live up to its billing, Internet journalism has to meet high standards 6
both conceptually and practically: the medium has to be revolutionary,
and the journalism has to be good. The quality of Internet journalism
is bound to improve over time, especially if more of the virtues of traditional journalism migrate to the Internet. But, although the medium
has great capabilities, especially the way it opens out and speeds up the
discourse, it is not quite as different from what has gone before as its advocates are saying.

Societies create structures of authority for producing and distributing 7
knowledge, information, and opinion. These structures are always waxing
and waning, depending not only on the invention of new means of communication but also on political, cultural, and economic developments.
An interesting new book about this came out last year in Britain under
the daunting title *Representation and Misrepresentation in Later Stuart Britain:
Partisanship and Political Culture*. It is set in the late seventeenth and early
eighteenth centuries, and although its author, Mark Knights, who teaches
at the University of East Anglia, does not make explicit comparisons to
the present, it seems obvious that such comparisons are on his mind.

The "new media" of later Stuart Britain were pamphlets and peri- 8
odicals, made possible not only by the advent of the printing press but
by the relaxation of government censorship and licensing regimes, by
political unrest, and by urbanization (which created audiences for public
debate). Today, the best known of the periodicals is Addison and Steele's
Spectator, but it was one of dozens that proliferated almost explosively in

the early seventeen-hundreds, including *The Tatler, The Post Boy, The Medley,* and *The British Apollo.* The most famous of the pamphleteers was Daniel Defoe, but there were hundreds of others, including Thomas Sprat, the author of *A True Account and Declaration of the Horrid Conspiracy Against the Late King* (1685), and Charles Leslie, the author of *The Wolf Stript of His Shepherd's Cloathing* (1704). These voices entered a public conversation that had been narrowly restricted, mainly to holders of official positions in church and state. They were the bloggers and citizen journalists of their day, and their influence was far greater (though their audiences were far smaller) than what anybody on the Internet has yet achieved.

As media, Knights points out, both pamphlets and periodicals were 9 radically transformative in their capabilities. Pamphlets were a mass medium with a short lead time—cheap, transportable, and easily accessible to people of all classes and political inclinations. They were, as Knights puts it, "capable of assuming different forms (letters, dialogues, essays, refutations, vindications, and so on)" and, he adds, were "ideally suited to making a public statement at a particular moment." Periodicals were, by the standards of the day, "a sort of interactive entertainment," because of the invention of letters to the editor and because publications were constantly responding to their readers and to one another.

Then as now, the new media in their fresh youth produced a distinc- 10 tive, hot-tempered rhetorical style. Knights writes, "Polemical print . . . challenged conventional notions of how rhetoric worked and was a medium that facilitated slander, polemic, and satire. It delighted in mocking or even abusive criticism, in part because of the conventions of anonymity." But one of Knights's most useful observations is that this was a self-limiting phenomenon. Each side in what Knights understands, properly, as the media front in a merciless political struggle between Whigs and Tories soon began accusing the other of trafficking in lies, distortions, conspiracy theories, and special pleading, and presenting itself as the avatar of the public interest, civil discourse, and epistemologically derived truth. Knights sees this genteeler style of expression as just another political tactic, but it nonetheless drove print publication toward a more reasoned, less inflamed rhetorical stance, which went along with a partial settling down of British politics from hot war between the parties to cold. (Full-dress British newspapers, like the *Times* and the *Guardian,* did not emerge until the late eighteenth and early nineteenth centuries, well into this calmer period and long after Knights ends his story.) At least in part, Internet journalism will surely repeat the cycle, and will begin to differentiate itself tonally, by trying to sound responsible and trustworthy in the hope of building a larger, possibly paying audience.

American journalism began, roughly speaking, on the later Stuart 11 Britain model; during colonial times it was dominated by fiery political speechmakers, like Thomas Paine. All those uplifting statements by the Founders about freedom of the press were almost certainly produced with pamphleteers in mind. When, in the early nineteenth century, political parties and fast cylinder printing presses developed, American journalism became mainly a branch of the party system, with very little pretense to neutral authority or ownership of the facts.

A related development was the sensational penny press, which 12 served the big cities, whose populations were swollen with immigrants from rural America and abroad. It produced powerful local newspapers, but it's hard to think of them as fitting the priesthood model. William Randolph Hearst's New York papers, the leading examples, were flamboyant, populist, opinionated, and thoroughly disreputable. They influenced politics, but that is different from saying, as Glenn Reynolds says of the Hearst papers, that they "set the agenda for public discussion." Most of the formal means of generating information that are familiar in America today— objective journalism is only one; others are modern academic research, professional licensing, and think tanks— were created, in the late nineteenth and early twentieth centuries, explicitly to counter the populist inclinations of various institutions, one of which was the big media.

In fact, what the prophets of Internet journalism believe themselves 13 to be fighting against— journalism in the hands of an enthroned few, who speak in a voice of phony, unearned authority to the passive masses— is, as a historical phenomenon, mainly a straw man. Even after the Second World War, some American cities still had several furiously battling papers, on the model of *The Front Page*.* There were always small political magazines of all persuasions, and books written in the spirit of the old pamphlets, and, later in the twentieth century, alternative weeklies and dissenting journalists like I. F. Stone. When journalism was at its most blandly authoritative— probably in the period when the three television broadcast networks* were in their heyday and local newspaper monopoly was beginning to become the rule— so were American politics and culture, and you have to be very media-centric to believe that the press established the tone of national life rather than vice versa.

Every new medium generates its own set of personalities and forms. In 14 ternet journalism is a huge tent that encompasses sites from traditional news organizations; Web-only magazines like *Slate* and *Salon*; sites like

---

* ***The Front Page:*** a play by Ben Hecht and Charles MacArthur about a Chicago newspaper reporter trying to scoop his rival journalists on a sensational story involving an escaped convict who has been wrongly convicted of murder because of political corruption. A hit in its original 1928 Broadway production, it has been revived several times on Broadway and made into several film versions.

* **the three television broadcast networks:** ABC, CBS, and NBC, which controlled almost all television news coverage in the United States from the beginnings of TV broadcasting in the late 1940s until the rise of cable networks in the 1980s.

Daily Kos and NewsMax, which use some notional connection to the news to function as influential political actors; and aggregation sites (for instance, Arts & Letters Daily and Indy Media) that bring together an astonishingly wide range of disparate material in a particular category. The more ambitious blogs, taken together, function as a form of fast-moving, densely cross-referential pamphleteering—an open forum for every conceivable opinion that can't make its way into the big media, or, in the case of the millions of purely personal blogs, simply an individual's take on life. The Internet is also a venue for press criticism ("We can fact-check your ass!" is one of the familiar rallying cries of the blogosphere) and a major research library of bloopers, outtakes, pranks, jokes, and embarrassing performances by big shots. But none of that yet rises to the level of a journalistic culture rich enough to compete in a serious way with the old media—to function as a replacement rather than an addendum.

The most fervent believers in the transforming potential of Internet   15
journalism are operating not only on faith in its achievements, even if they lie mainly in the future, but on a certainty that the old media, in selecting what to publish and broadcast, make horrible and, even worse, ignobly motivated mistakes. They are politically biased, or they are ignoring or suppressing important stories, or they are out of touch with ordinary people's concerns, or they are merely passive transmitters of official utterances. The more that traditional journalism appears to be an old-fashioned captive press, the more providential the Internet looks.

Jay Rosen, a professor of journalism at New York University who   16
was the leading champion of "civic journalism" even before there was an Internet, wrote in the *Washington Post* in June that he started his blog, PressThink, because "I was tired of passing my ideas through editors who forced me to observe the silences they kept as professional journalists. The day after President Bush was re-elected in 2004, I suggested on my blog that at least some news organizations should consider themselves the opposition to the White House. Only by going into opposition, I argued, could the press really tell the story of the Bush administration's vast expansion of executive power. That notion simply hadn't been discussed in mainstream newsrooms, which had always been able to limit debate about what is and isn't the job of the journalist. But now that amateurs had joined pros in the press zone, newsrooms couldn't afford not to debate their practices."

In PressThink, Rosen now has the forum that he didn't before; and last   17
week he announced the launch of a new venture, called NewAssignment .Net, in which a "smart mob" of donors would pay journalists to pursue "stories the regular news media doesn't do, can't do, wouldn't do, or already screwed up." The key to the idea, in Rosen's mind, is to give "people formerly known as the audience" the assigning power previously

reserved for editors. "NewAssignment.Net would be a case of journalism without the media," he wrote on PressThink. "That's the beauty part."

Even before the advent of NewAssignment.Net, and even for people 18 who don't blog, there is a lot more opportunity to talk back to news organizations than there used to be. In their Internet versions, most traditional news organizations make their reporters available to answer readers' questions and, often, permit readers to post their own material. Being able to see this as the advent of true democracy in what had been a media oligarchy makes it much easier to argue that Internet journalism has already achieved great things.

Still: Is the Internet a mere safety valve, a *salon des refusés*,* or does it 19 actually produce original information beyond the realm of opinion and comment? It ought to raise suspicion that we so often hear the same menu of examples in support of its achievements: bloggers took down the 2004 *60 Minutes* report on President Bush's National Guard service and, with it, Dan Rather's career; bloggers put Trent Lott's remarks in apparent praise of the Jim Crow era front and center, and thereby deposed him as Senate majority leader.

The best original Internet journalism happens more often by acci- 20 dent, when smart and curious people with access to means of communication are at the scene of a sudden disaster. Any time that big news happens unexpectedly, or in remote and dangerous places, there is more raw information available right away on the Internet than through established news organizations. The most memorable photographs of the London terrorist bombing last summer were taken by subway riders using cell phones, not by news photographers, who didn't have time to get there. There were more ordinary people than paid reporters posting information when the tsunami first hit South Asia, in 2004, when Hurricane Katrina hit the Gulf Coast, in 2005, and when Israeli bombs hit Beirut this summer. I am in an especially good position to appreciate the benefits of citizen journalism at such moments, because it helped save my father and stepmother's lives when they were stranded in New Orleans after Hurricane Katrina: the citizen portions of the Web sites of local news organizations were, for a crucial day or two, one of the best places to get information about how to drive out of the city. But, over time, the best information about why the hurricane destroyed so much of the city came from reporters, not citizens.

Eyewitness accounts and information–sharing during sudden disas- 21 ters are welcome, even if they don't provide a complete report of what is going on in a particular situation. And that is what citizen journalism

---

* *salon des refusés:* an exhibition of works rejected by established authorities in a field.

is supposed to do: keep up with public affairs, especially locally, year in and year out, even when there's no disaster. Citizen journalists bear a heavy theoretical load. They ought to be fanning out like a great army, covering not just what professional journalists cover, as well or better, but also much that they ignore. Great citizen journalism is like the imagined Northwest Passage— it has to exist in order to prove that citizens can learn about public life without the mediation of professionals. But when one reads it, after having been exposed to the buildup, it is nearly impossible not to think, *This* is what all the fuss is about?

Oh My News seems to attract far more readers than any other citizen- 22 journalism site— about six hundred thousand daily by its own count. One day in June, readers of the English-language edition found this lead story: "Printable Robots: Advances in InkJet Technology Forecast Robotic Origami," by Gregory Daigle. It begins:

> From the diminutive ASIMO from Honda to the colossus in the animated film *Iron Giant*, kids around the world know that robots are cool yet complex machines. Advances in robotics fuel plans from NASA that read like science fiction movie scripts.
>   Back on Earth, what can we expect over the next few years in robot technology for the consumer?
>   Reprogram your Roomba? Boring.
>   Hack your Aibo robot dog? Been there.
>   Print your own robot? Whoa!

OhmyNews INTERNATIONAL

KOREA | WORLD | SCI&TECH | ART&LIFE | ENTERTAINMENT | SPORTS | GLOBAL WATCH | INTERVIEWS | CITIZEN JOURNALISM

Taliban Attacks Kabul Before Elections

International community in a security rethink mood

The latest rocket attack in Kabul on August 4, sent alarm bells ringing especially among the international community, here to monitor the presidential and the provincial council elections scheduled to take place on August 20.... (Bidhayak Das)

Homosexual Killings Traumatize Tel Aviv's Gay Community

Fears that two decades of gains have been eroded

Saturday night's bloody shooting attack of a gay youth support center in downtown Tel Aviv, during which two persons were murdered and another 10 were injured, has shattered Israeli society.... (Yehonathan Tommer)

Do you live in a news hotspot? No?

Send us your story. (Buzztracker Map)

OhmyNews at a glance

Change to Reader Comments: Registered Members

You'll need to login before posting on articles. Our Talk Back board is still open to anonymous comments....

* Important Changes to OMNI Payment System

On the same day, Barista of Bloomfield Avenue, the nom de Web of 23
Debbie Galant, who lives in a suburban town in New Jersey and is one of
the most esteemed "hyperlocal bloggers" in the country, led with a picture from her recent vacation in the Berkshires. The next item was "Haz-
ing Goes Loony Tunes," and here it is in its entirety:

> Word on the sidewalk is that Glen Ridge officialdom pretty much
> defeated the class of 2007 in the annual senior-on-freshman hazing
> ritual yesterday by making the rising seniors stay after school for
> several minutes in order to give freshmen a head start to run home.
> We have reports that seniors in cars, once released from school,
> searched for slow-moving freshman prey, while Glen Ridge police
> officers in cars closely tracked any cars decorated with class of 2007
> regalia. Of course, if any freshman got pummelled with mayonnaise,
> we want to know about it.

What is generally considered to be the most complete local citizen- 24
journalism site in the United States, the Northwest Voice, in Bakersfield,
California (which also has a print version and is owned by the big daily
paper in town), led with a story called "A Boost for Business Women,"
which began:

> So long, Corporate World.
>   Hello, business ownership — family time, and happiness.
>   At least, that's how Northwest resident Jennifer Meadors feels after
> the former commercial banking professional started her own business
> for Arbonne International, a skin care company, about eight months
> ago. So far, it's been successful, professionally and personally.

Another much praised citizen–journalism site is Backfence.com, head- 25
quartered in the suburbs of Washington, D.C. Last month, it sponsored a
contest to pick the two best citizen–journalism stories; the prize was a
free trip to a conference held by Oh My News, in Seoul. One winner was
Liz Milner, of Reston, Virginia, for a story that began this way:

> Among the many definitions of "hero" given in the *American Heritage*
> *Dictionary* is "a person noted for special achievement in a particular
> field." Reston is a community of creative people, so it seems only
> right that our heroes should be paragons of creativity. Therefore, I'm
> nominating Reston musician and freelance writer Ralph Lee Smith
> for the post of "Local Hero, Creative Category."
>   Through his performances, recordings, writings, teaching and mu-
> seum exhibitions, this 78–year–old Reston resident has helped bring
> new life to an art form that had been on the verge of extinction —
> the art of playing the mountain dulcimer. He has helped to popular-
> ize the repertoire for this instrument so that now mountain music is
> everywhere — even in slick Hollywood films.

In other words, the content of most citizen journalism will be familiar 26
to anybody who has ever read a church or community newsletter — it's

heartwarming and it probably adds to the store of good things in the world, but it does not mount the collective challenge to power which the traditional media are supposedly too timid to take up. Often the most journalistically impressive material on one of the "hyperlocal" citizen-journalism sites has links to professional journalism, as in the Northwest Voice, or Chi-Town Daily News, where much of the material is written by students at Northwestern University's Medill School of Journalism, who are in training to take up full-time jobs in news organizations. At the highest level of journalistic achievement, the reporting that revealed the civil-liberties encroachments of the war on terror, which upset the Bush Administration, has come from old-fashioned big-city newspapers and television networks, not Internet journalists; day by day, most in-dependent accounts of world events have come from the same tradi-tional sources. Even at its best and most ambitious, citizen journalism reads like a decent Op-Ed page, and not one that offers daring, brilliant, forbidden opinions that would otherwise be unavailable. Most citizen journalism reaches very small and specialized audiences and is proudly minor in its concerns. David Weinberger, another advocate of new-media journalism, has summarized the situation with a witty play on Andy Warhol's maxim: "On the Web, everyone will be famous to fifteen people."

Reporting— meaning the tradition by which a member of a distinct occu- 27
pational category gets to cross the usual bounds of geography and class, to go where important things are happening, to ask powerful people blunt and impertinent questions, and to report back, reliably and in plain language, to a general audience— is a distinctive, fairly recent invention. It probably started in the United States, in the mid-nineteenth century, long after the Founders wrote the First Amendment. It has spread— and it continues to spread— around the world. It is a powerful social tool, because it provides citizens with an independent source of information about the state and other holders of power. It sounds obvious, but re-porting requires reporters. They don't have to be priests or gatekeepers or even paid professionals; they just have to go out and do the work.

The Internet is not unfriendly to reporting; potentially, it is the best 28
reporting medium ever invented. A few places, like the site on Yahoo! op-erated by Kevin Sites, consistently offer good journalism that has a dis-tinctly Internet, rather than repurposed, feeling. To keep pushing in that direction, though, requires that we hold up original reporting as a vir-tue and use the Internet to find new ways of presenting fresh material— which, inescapably, will wind up being produced by people who do that full time, not "citizens" with day jobs.

Journalism is not in a period of maximal self-confidence right now, 29
and the Internet's cheerleaders are practically laboratory specimens of maximal self-confidence. They have got the rhetorical upper hand; tradi-

tional journalists answering their challenges often sound either clueless or cowed and apologetic. As of now, though, there is not much relation between claims for the possibilities inherent in journalist–free journalism and what the people engaged in that pursuit are actually producing. As journalism moves to the Internet, the main project ought to be moving reporters there, not stripping them away.

Reading Closely

1. How does Lemann define citizen journalism? What is a citizen journalist? What does such a person do?

2. What is the purpose of this essay? Identify passages in the essay that lead you to this conclusion.

3. Look through the essay and identify the outside sources Lemann uses. What kind of research did he conduct? What purpose do these sources serve?

4. In addition to *citizen journalism*, Lemann defines a number of other journalism–related terms. What are these terms, and how and *why* does he define them?

5. How does the image of the Oh My News Web page on page 618 extend and add depth to the definition of citizen journalism that Lemann offers in this essay?

Considering Larger Issues

1. **Working with a classmate,** identify the main issues in the debate between citizen journalists and traditional journalists. What arguments does each side make about journalism and its responsibility to the public?

2. What is Lemann's argument about citizen journalism? What is your response to this argument?

3. Lemann turns to historical examples to draw parallels between citizen journalism and forms of journalism that were popular in the past. What is the purpose of this historical examination?

4. COMBINING METHODS. Lemann relies on *comparison and contrast* to make distinctions between traditional journalism and online citizen journalism. What kinds of comparisons does he make? How effective do you find them?

Thinking about Language

1. Using the context of the essay or your dictionary, define the following terms. Be prepared to share your answers with the rest of the class.

millenarian (1)	waxing (7)	straw man (13)
manifestos (1)	waning (7)	dissenting (13)
punditocracy (1)	urbanization (8)	notional (14)
plausible (2)	proliferated (8)	addendum (14)
conflates (2)	lead time (9)	ignobly (15)
purvey (2)	vindications (9)	providential (15)
aggregation (2)	polemical (10)	oligarchy (18)
supplanting (3)	avatar (10)	deposed (19)
pomposity (4)	epistemologically (10)	dulcimer (25)
preening (4)	genteeler (10)	encroachments (26)
catechism (5)	penny press (12)	impertinent (27)
accord (5)	populist (12)	cowed (29)

2. Reflect on Lemann's word choice in this essay. The list of terms in question 1 might be a good start. Given his word choice, what assumptions is Lemann making about his audience?

Writing Your Own Essays Using Definition

1. In his essay, Lemann defines citizen journalism by comparing it to traditional journalistic methods and practices. Compose a two- to three-page essay on citizen journalism by taking a different approach. Identify one citizen-journalist site on the Web, and analyze the site for its distinctive characteristics. As you reflect on the site and draft your definition, consider how you might use explanation, description, classification, and even comparison to deepen your discussion. As a point of comparison, you might consult more traditional news sources, such as the *Washington Post* or the *New York Times*. The goal, though, is for you to define citizen journalism as you see it demonstrated on the site you've chosen. Refer to the guidelines for checking over the use of definition on page 583 as you draft and revise your essay.

2. One of the goals of Lemann's essay is to distinguish citizen journalism from traditional journalism by using definition. In a three- to four-page essay, choose two objects, concepts, practices, or issues that are related but different, and use definition to help to make the distinctions between the two. For example, you might choose to write about the differences between off-road mountain biking and grand tour bike racing, defining each kind of biking on its own terms and then in relation to the other. Or you may want to define what *active* citizenship means as opposed to *passive* citizenship. Ultimately, your goal is to clarify readers' understanding of these objects, concepts, practices, or issues. As you draft and revise, use the guidelines for checking over the use of definition on page 583.

CONNIE EBLE

Slang

Connie Eble is a professor of linguistics at the University of North Carolina, Chapel Hill, where she teaches classes on the structure and history of the English language and also conducts and publishes research on the topic of slang. Her articles have appeared in such publications as *Language in the U.S.A.*, *Needed Research in American English*, and *American History through Literature*. She has published two books, *College Slang* (1989) and *Slang and Sociability* (1996). In the following essay, which is a chapter from *Slang and Sociability*, Eble takes on the difficult project of defining the term *slang*.

Preview What does the term *slang* mean to you?

Slang is an ever changing set of colloquial words and phrases that speakers 1 use to establish or reinforce social identity or cohesiveness within a group or with a trend or fashion in society at large. The existence of vocabulary of this sort within a language is possibly as old as language itself, for slang seems to be part of any language used in ordinary interaction by a community large enough and diverse enough to have identifiable subgroups.

The origin of the word *slang* is unknown. Its resemblance in sound 2 and figurative meaning to the noun and verb *sling* and the occurrence of apparently the same root in Scandinavian expressions referring to language suggest that the term *slang* is a development of a Germanic root from which the current English *sling* is derived. Another conjecture is that *slang* has been formed by shortening from genitive phrases like *beggars' language* or *rogues' language*, in which the genitive suffix of the first noun attaches to the initial syllable of *language* and then the final syllable is lost. In its earliest occurrences in the eighteenth century, the word *slang* referred to the specialized vocabulary of underworld groups and was used fairly interchangeably with the terms *cant*, *flash*, and *argot*.

The social and psychological complexities captured in slang vo- 3 cabulary make the term difficult to define, leading Bethany Dumas and Jonathan Lighter to question whether the term is even usable for linguists. Dumas and Lighter reject the classical formula for definition and instead propose four identifying criteria for slang.

1. Its presence will markedly lower, at least for the moment, the dignity of formal or serious speech or writing.

2. Its use implies the user's special familiarity either with the referent or with that less statusful or less responsible class of people who have such special familiarity and use the term.

3. It is a tabooed term in ordinary discourse with persons of higher social status or greater responsibility.

4. It is used in place of the well-known conventional synonym, especially in order (a) to protect the user from the discomfort caused by the conventional item or (b) to protect the user from the discomfort or annoyance of further elaboration.

They conclude that "when something fits at least two of the criteria, a linguistically sensitive audience will react to it in a certain way. This reaction, which cannot be measured, is the ultimate identifying characteristic of true slang."

Here is a selection of Dumas and Lighter's examples.   4

Though their dissent was not always noisy or dramatic, many Americans felt the President was a *jerk* for continuing the war.

"What should we do with the prisoners, Lieutenant?"
"*Waste* 'em."

I'd like this job, sir, because the one I have now is *shit*.

According to the criteria, *jerk, waste,* and *shit* all qualify as slang. *Jerk* fulfills criteria 1, 2, and 4b; *waste*, criteria 1, 2, and 4a; and *shit*, criteria 1, 2, 3, and possibly 4b.

None of the four criteria is formal, for slang is not distinct in form. And   5 only number 3 may be said to be loosely based on meaning. But all four concern the social relationships of the participants, and the "ultimate identifying characteristic" is the consciousness of shared knowledge between speaker and hearer. Dumas and Lighter's formulation requires that the type of lexis called *slang* be recognized for its power to effect union between speaker and hearer. Whether or not the particulars of their operational definition are necessary or sufficient, in the final analysis Dumas and Lighter are right. Slang cannot be defined independent of its functions and use.

Despite the difficulty of defining the term, slang does have some con-   6 sistent characteristics. Foremost, slang is ephemeral. A constant supply of new words requires the rapid change characteristic of slang. Most slang items enjoy only a brief time of popularity, bursting into existence and falling out of use at a much more rapid rate than items of the general vocabulary. Sometimes a new slang form either replaces an earlier one or provides another synonym for a notion already named in slang, like *ramped, ranked, ted* (from *wasted*), and *toe* (from *torn*) for 'drunk'; *bogel* and *hang* for 'do nothing in particular'; *bumping* and *kegging* for 'exhilarating'; *squirrel kisser* and *tree nymph* for 'someone concerned with the environment'; or *red-shirted* and *latered* for 'jilted.' Sometimes new slang extends to new areas of meaning or to areas of meaning of recent interest to the group inventing the slang, like *Tom* (from *totally obedient moron*) for 'computer'; *dangling modifier* for 'a single, long, flashy earring'; *the five-year program* (or even the *six-year program*) for 'the time it takes to complete an undergraduate degree'; or *twinkie* (yellow on the outside, white on the inside) for 'an Asian who identifies with Caucasians or has a white girlfriend or boyfriend.'

The vocabulary of college students can illustrate the ephemeral and 7 innovative character of slang. One way to measure the ephemerality of student slang is to compare slang vocabulary at the same institution at different times. Two studies of this sort have been reported in *American Speech*. Slang items from Stanford University published in 1927 were found to be largely out of use just five years later: "In comparing the 'Stanford Expressions' of 1926 with those of 1931 I find a complete change. The place–names, and a very few characteristic Stanford words such as 'apple–polisher', 'bawlout', and 'rough' are the only words used as slang now— we use about fifty of the five hundred words typical of Stanford in 1926. This period of five years has had an astounding effect on our language!" . . .

My sampling of the slang of students at the University of North 8 Carolina at Chapel Hill over a fifteen–year period also attests to the rapid change in slang vocabulary. This study tabulates the overlap of different items collected in the fall of 1972, the fall of 1980, and the fall of 1987— the dates bounding the two complete seven–year generations of college students who graduated in 1973–79 and 1982–88. The size of the collections at the three points differs: about two hundred separate items from fall 1972 and from fall 1980, and five hundred from fall 1987.

A simple headword–plus–definition comparison of the three sets bears 9 out the ephemeral quality of the UNC–CH student vocabulary. Only four of the slightly fewer than two hundred items from 1972 were submitted with the same form and meaning in both 1980 and 1987, roughly 2 percent of the types in the 1972 and 1980 collections and less than 1 percent in the 1987 collection. An additional eight occur in both 1972 and in 1987 but not in 1980. That makes a total of twelve items reported in both 1972 and 1987, about 6 percent of the types for 1972 and 2 percent for 1987. Fifteen items occur both in 1972 and in 1980, for a retention rate of about 7 percent. Twenty of the two hundred slang items from 1980 are reported still in use in 1987, about 10 percent of the 1980 corpus and about 4 percent of the 1987 corpus. Thus, within a span of fifteen years the specific items of slang vocabulary reported by UNC–CH undergraduates obviously changed to a very large extent.

Some slang words, however, maintained their form and meaning in 10 this great flux. The four items that occur at all three sampling points are *bad* 'good'; *bummer* 'unpleasant experience'; *slide* 'easy course'; and *wheels* 'car'. Another eight occur in both 1972 and 1987 but were not submitted in 1980: *cool* 'good, in–the–know, sophisticated'; *do*, an all–purpose verb; *get real* 'be serious'; *gravy* 'easy'; *pound* 'drink heavily'; *shit*, an expression of anger or disappointment; *threads* 'clothing'; and *tough* 'good, admirable, attractive'.

A few additional items altered slightly in form or meaning. For ex- 11 ample, *bomb out* 'fail' also shortened to *bomb*, and *jam* 'make music, dance' shifted to mean also 'perform well'. Even adding such items with altered forms or shifted meanings to the twelve slang items that have the same form and definition in 1972 and 1987, the total percentage of college slang words in this collection that lasted over a fifteen–year span is still under 10 percent.

The small percentage of items that persisted should not be surprising, 12 for here slang shows the characteristics of the language as a whole, as it does in both its word–building and semantic processes. Looking back a thousand years in English, we find that the vast majority of words have changed. Frequently used Old English verbs such as *brucan* 'enjoy', *fremman* 'do', *hatan* 'call', and *niman* 'take' have been replaced by other verbs. Nouns of kinship such as Old English *eam* and *swigra* are now expressed in the phrases *maternal uncle* and *sister's son*. The common Old English adjective *faeger* 'fair' has changed to mean 'mediocre', and its earlier meaning is now expressed in words like *pretty* and *beautiful*. In Old English the pronoun *his* was both masculine and neuter; the language subsequently developed *its* for neuter reference. Only a few words have persisted unchanged in form and meaning, for example, *mid* and *edge* (spelled *ecg* in Old English but pronounced the same). What is remarkable about the ephemerality of slang is not the percentage of terms that change but the short span of time involved.

Another feature of the comings and goings of slang is that some slang 13 terms come back for a second and third life, the way that fashions do. For example, *cram* 'study hard at the last minute' was submitted as current in fall 1980 and fall 1987 but not in 1972 at North Carolina or in 1971 at Arkansas. *Dead soldier*, which has been part of military slang since the eighteenth century when it meant 'empty bottle,' emerged at North Carolina in 1987 with the more contemporary referent 'empty beer can'. *Out of sight* 'excellent, extraordinary' of the 1960s was felt at the time to be novel and fresh but was a reincarnation of the same form and meaning used in the Bowery in the 1890s and recorded in Stephen Crane's *Maggie: Girl of the Streets* in 1896. *Hot* 'sexually attractive' is currently in vogue for the umpteenth time, as well as *gravy* for 'an easy test or course.'

Although slang items come and go, it is easier to pinpoint, and in 14 some instances to explain, the comings than the goings. *Ghetto blaster, jambox*, and *third world briefcase* naturally did not come into the language before this past decade [1990s] because the 'portable stereo tape deck' had not been invented. Likewise, when a referent disappears, the slang item for it is likely to go. A striking example from college slang is the apparent loss of the most pervasive set of college slang items of the nineteenth century, words conveying the image of traveling the easy way — that is, being carried by a horse or pony — to refer to using a translation for Latin class. In the days when Latin was a required subject in British and American schools, *pony, horse*, and *trot* were widely known slang terms for 'a literal translation'. Because so few American college students are now compelled to study Latin, their slang no longer contains words for subverting the requirement. . . .

Ephemerality is often considered a particular attribute of slang. But   15
not all slang is ephemeral, and not all ephemeral vocabulary is slang.
Bones as slang for 'dice,' for example, was used by Chaucer in the fourteenth
century and is still slang. A comparison of words labeled slang in *Webster's
Second* (1934) and *Webster's Third* (1961) shows that many slang terms have
staying power, among them *beef* and *bitch* 'complain,' *buck* 'dollar,' *bull* 'talk
insincerely,' and *come again* 'repeat.' Maurer and High find that a number
of terms marked slang in Grose's 1785 *Classical Dictionary of the Vulgar Tongue*
are still around and still slang two hundred years later, for example,
knock off 'to quit work' and *plant* 'to lay, place, hide.' But when slang items
remain in the language for years, they often lose their slang status. Middle
English *bouse*, now spelled *booze*, persists in highly informal contexts, as
does *pooped* for 'exhausted,' first attested in the sixteenth century. Still other
slang items pass into the general vocabulary and bear little or no association with their earlier lives as slang, for example, the noun *rascal*, the verb
bluff, and the adjective *flimsy*. *Jeopardy* from gambling and *crestfallen* from
cockfighting have even acquired a learned tinge. . . .

Another often cited characteristic of slang is its group–identifying   16
function. It is well documented that social groups are fertile breeding
grounds for an idiosyncratic vocabulary to enhance their solidarity. Groups
that operate on the periphery of society, such as con artists or drug dealers, seem particularly adept at creating slang. However, association with
a group is not essential to slang. With the possibility of instant and widespread communication, the group–identifying functions of slang for the
population at large may be diminishing in favor of identification with a
style or an attitude rather than with a specific, easily delineated group. If
items like *idiot box* 'television set,' *loose cannon* 'someone who is uncon-
trolled and unpredictable,' *shrink* 'psychiatrist,' and *weirdo* 'a strange person' can be considered slang in the United States, they are a kind of
national slang and say little about group identification. Robert Chapman,
editor of the *New Dictionary of American Slang*, calls this type of slang "secondary" and predicts that in the future it will be the major type of slang
in America.

Slang must be distinguished from other subsets of the lexicon such   17
as regionalisms or dialect words, jargon, profanity and obscenity, and
colloquialism — although slang shares some characteristics with each of
these and can overlap them.

Slang is not geographically restricted vocabulary, like British *lift, servi-*   18
ette, and *zed* instead of the equivalent *elevator, napkin*, and *zee* of the United
States. Vocabulary that is typical of one region within the United States
is likewise not slang, such as the southern use of *you all* and *y'all* as a
second–person plural pronoun, or the use in the environs of New Orleans
of *neutral ground* for 'median strip in a divided street,' *batture* 'alluvial land
between the Mississippi River and the levee,' *banquette* 'sidewalk,' and *krewe*
'Mardi Gras social club.' Nevertheless, just like the standard vocabulary,

some slang items are associated with a particular region—for example, *bloke* with Britain and *guy* with America.

Slang is not jargon, the vocabulary used in carrying out a trade or profession or in pursuing an interest or hobby. *Ejecta* 'debris thrown by the explosion of a missile' and *jam* 'impair the enemy's electronic system' are military jargon; *cursor* 'movable indicator on a screen' and *mouse* 'box with buttons to move the cursor' belong to computer jargon; and *shot clock* and *zone defense* are basic jargon to basketball fans. But groups united by their work or a common interest can also develop a less precise slang vocabulary, which usually conveys feelings and attitudes and unity of spirit. *Chicken colonel* for 'full colonel' and *John Wayne* for 'militarily exemplary' are U.S. Army slang; *meatware* 'human body' is slang invented by computer users by analogy with the jargon *hardware* and *software*; basketball fans might call 'an official' a *zebra* or refer to a 'spectacular dunk' *as doing windows*. Sometimes words that start out as the jargon of a particular group become slang for a wider group. For example, *ice* 'diamonds' is no longer known by only jewel thieves; *gig* 'a job' is used by more than just hungry musicians, and *heavyweight* can refer to 'any important person', not just to a boxer in the highest weight classification. In other instances, words pass from the jargon of a group into the general vocabulary without ever being slang. For example, *input*, *output*, and *interface* are frequently used standard vocabulary items that gained their current popularity because of increased public exposure to the jargon of computer science. . . .

Slang is largely colloquial. It belongs to the spoken part of language 20 and is rarely written except in direct quotation of speech. But not all colloquial expressions are slang. *Shut up* for 'be quiet' is seldom written except in dialogue, but it is not slang. Neither are colloquial expressions like *stickup* and *throw up*, which contrast with neutral synonyms *robbery* and *vomit* and slang synonyms *heist* and *ralph*. In practice it is difficult to distinguish between colloquial and informal, which means vocabulary not suited to serious and important occasions. Slang words always diminish the formality of a conversation in which they occur, as in "Would you lend me some *bread?*" versus "Would you lend me some *money?*" But not all words with informal connotations are necessarily slang, like *decaf* 'decaffeinated coffee', *leak* 'unauthorized disclosure', *limo* 'limousine', or *warmups* 'clothing worn to keep the muscles warm before or during exercise.'

Although slang vocabulary carries a nuance of trendiness, Thomas J. 21 Creswell and Virginia McDavid, in a prefatory essay in *The Random House Dictionary of the English Language* of 1987, make a distinction between slang and vogue words. Vogue words are usually new combinations or new senses of already existing words that come to national prominence very quickly from nonjocular uses in government, business, education, entertainment, and the like. Some recent examples of vogue words are *behavior disorder, bottom line, damage control, user-friendly*, and *wellness program*. "Vogue expressions demonstrate that their users are socially or professionally *with it.*"

The Persian Gulf War brought several words into vogue in 1990 and 1991. Suddenly elementary school children in the United States could use correctly such words as *deployment, sortie,* and *scud missile,* and the slangy *mother of all* 'quintessence' got applied to everything from parades to pizzas.

Slang is also not an "improper" grammatical construction—like *Win-* stons *taste good like a cigarette should* or *between you and I*—or an objectionable form like *ain't* or *irregardless.* The use of a slang term rarely violates sentence structure. For example, the slang word *bogart* 'steal' takes the regular past tense ending and functions like a verb in "Joey *bogarted* my sweatpants again." Objections to the use of slang are matters of social appropriateness and not grammar. . . . 22

Slang is mainly words or groups of words, though body language 23 and the sounds used are often important in conveying the meaning of slang expressions. For instance, the term *L7* for 'a socially inept person, a *square*' should be accompanied by the thumb and index finger of one hand (shaped like an *L*) joining the index finger and thumb of the other (shaped like a 7) to form a square. Other expressions must be said with specific combinations of pitch, stress, and pauses. *Gouda, gouda, gouda,* a signal that someone who is *cheezy* (an *L7*) is approaching, is intoned in measured alternations of stressed and unstressed syllables to imitate a pulsing alarm. Although, for the most part, slang items conform to the general constraints on sound combinations that govern the English language, the venturesome spirit behind much slang includes playing with sounds. Onomatopoeia or echoism, mock dialect and foreign pronunciations, and rhyming account for many slang terms. The intonation with which something is said can indicate to the hearer that it is to be taken as slang: in their slang interpretations a *wicked* car, a *mean* machine, and a *bad* dress are all 'good.'

Syntax, or sentence structure, is not important in defining slang. Slang 24 expressions are not composed in word order sequences idiosyncratic to slang, and individual slang words and phrases typically fit into an appropriate grammatical slot in an established pattern. For example, the slang verb *bum out* 'cause or experience unpleasant feelings or bad reactions' behaves syntactically like any transitive phrasal verb.

That bad call *bummed out* the whole team.
That bad call *bummed* the whole team *out.*
That bad call *bummed* them *out.*

Nevertheless, UCLA students have found several features of "slang syntax" noteworthy and one or two idiosyncratic, for example, "an unusual affective use of the definite article," as in "Susan set me up with her big brother. She's *the* homie."

Users of American English who want to know whether a given word 25 is or is not slang are destined for disappointment. Dictionaries, the ordinary repositories of information about words, are ill equipped to record slang. In large part, slang is short–lived, slippery in meaning, characteristic of marginalized groups, oral, and, most important, defined by social context and situation—all characteristics that militate against slang's showing up frequently and consistently in the files on which dictionaries are based. Nevertheless, *slang* is a label in almost all contemporary American dictionaries of English, although just what the label means and its relationship to other usage labels can vary widely.

Reading Closely

1. How does Eble use negative definition to define *slang*? Identify the places in the essay where she uses negative definition, and explain the effect of this strategy.

2. How does Eble use comparison to define *slang*? Identify the places in the essay where she uses comparison, and explain the effect of this strategy.

3. **Working with a classmate,** compose a definition of *slang* based on the claims Eble makes in her essay. Try to identify all the components of her definition.

4. Who is the audience for Eble's essay? How do you know? What clues in the text support your claim?

Considering Larger Issues

1. What in the essay surprised, interested, or confused you?

2. Why is Eble interested in defining the term *slang*? What is her purpose in setting out this definition?

3. What kind of research does Eble use in her essay? How does this research shape her definition?

4. COMBINING METHODS. Besides comparison, Eble calls on the rhetorical methods of *exemplification, description,* and *classification and division* to define *slang*. Identify the places in the text where Eble uses these methods. How do they work in support of her overarching purpose?

Thinking about Language

1. Using the context of the essay or your dictionary, define the following terms. Be prepared to share your answers with the rest of the class.

colloquial (1)	tabulates (8)	jargon (17)
conjecture (2)	headword (9)	alluvial (18)
genitive (2)	corpus (9)	connotations (20)
referent (3)	semantic (12)	nonjocular (21)
tabooed (3)	kinship (12)	intoned (23)
lexis (5)	idiosyncratic (16)	onomatopoeia (23)
ephemeral (6)	periphery (16)	militate against (25)

2. Identify five slang terms in Eble's essay that were unfamiliar to you. What, if anything, surprised you about the meaning of these terms? Why do you think they were unfamiliar to you?

Writing Your Own Essays Using Definition

1. Identify a slang term that you use in everyday conversation, and compose a two- to three-page essay that takes up the following two tasks. First, confirm for readers that your term truly falls under the definition of slang by explaining how it meets the criteria that Eble sets out in her essay. Second, define your slang term, explaining in detail how and when you use it. As you define this term, discuss the contexts in which the term would make sense and the people who would understand and use this term. You might also discuss when using this term would be inappropriate or misunderstood. As you draft and revise your essay, refer to the guidelines for checking over and using definition on page 583.

2. In her essay, Eble focuses on slang terms used in college settings, discussing how terms have come in and out of use at the University of North Carolina, Chapel Hill, in particular. In a three- to four-page essay, identify ten slang terms that are specific to your own college campus. Define each of these terms for an audience of incoming first-year students at your school. Your goal is to help introduce your readers to life on your campus. As you define each term, you'll want to consider the context for its use. When, where, why, and how do you use this term? What do you need to know about the school or its campus, social scene, or academic life to understand what this term means and how it is used? What might confuse people about this term? How and with whom should (and shouldn't) they use this term? The guidelines for checking over and using definition on page 583 will help you as you draft and revise.

✱ Additional Suggestions for Writing

1. Consider writing an essay about a disease, disability, or other physical difference with which you are familiar. Begin by writing a one-sentence definition of that condition. Then write another sentence that states what the condition is *not*. Draft a three-page essay about this condition, defining it with a history, a set of causes, or a set of effects. You might use the Internet or the library to research the history of the condition in terms of its being understood or misunderstood, diagnosed or misdiagnosed. You might research the causes of the condition or its effects. Refer to "Checking Over the Use of Definition" on page 583 as you draft and revise.

2. Jot down a word that is painful for you, a word you would not want to be called, maybe a word you have been called. Write a few sentences about a situation where its use was or could be painful for you. Now consider what you might do or say to respond to this word.

    Draft a three- to four-page essay in which you develop your definition of that word, based on actual or hypothetical situations. **Ask a classmate** to review your draft to ensure that you've defined the terms of your discussion, developed a thesis statement, and carried out your purpose. As you draft and revise, refer to the guidelines for checking over the use of definition on page 583.

3. Watch television for at least thirty minutes, being on the lookout for different types of definitions. Listen carefully, and take notes about each example of a sentence definition, negative definition, historical definition, or stipulative definition that you see and/or hear.

    When and how do the words and visuals work together? What terms seem most successfully or accurately defined? Are any terms defined persuasively yet inaccurately? **Work with one or two classmates** to compare your findings before drafting a three- to four-page essay based on your findings. Ask someone in your writing group to give you comments as you draft and revise your essay. Be sure to refer to the guidelines for checking over the use of definition on page 583.

chapter 10

ARGUMENT

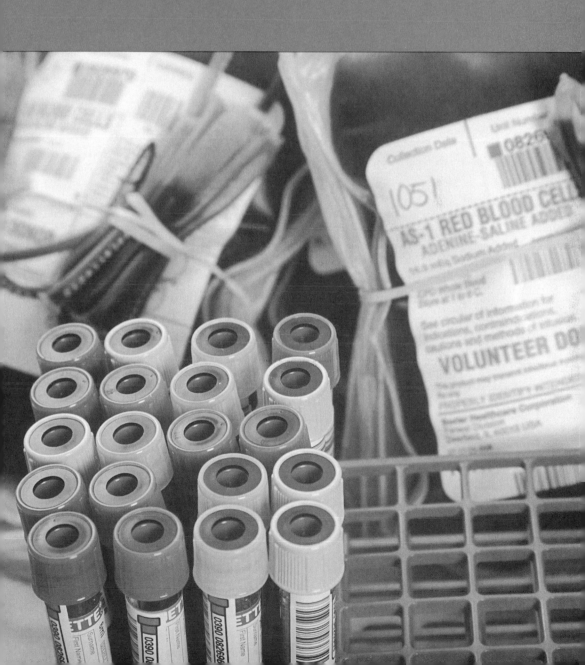

Why Give?

Every two seconds

someone in the United States needs blood. That's a lot of blood.

But only 5% of the eligible US population donates blood in any given year. Healthy donors are the only source of blood.

Currently there is no substitute.

Blood is needed for emergencies and for people who have cancer, blood disorders, sickle cell, anemia and other illnesses. Some people need regular blood transfusions to live.

Imagine if giving blood was part of everyone's life. Something you did on a regular basis, like eating at your favorite restaurant. What kind of difference would that make? For nearly 5 million people who receive blood transfusions every year, your donation can make the difference between life and death.

Giving blood is simple and convenient — see our top 10 reasons to give, browse categories on the left to learn about blood donation, or simply...

sign up to donate now!

click here ▸

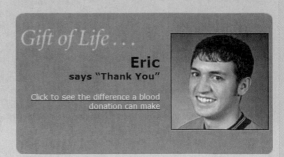

Gift of Life . . .

Eric
says "Thank You"

Click to see the difference a blood donation can make

Calculate your next donation date

Enter the date of your last whole blood donation* here:

[▾] [▾] , 2009 [▾]

[Calculate Now!]

*Whole blood donations only. Apheresis donations can be made every 3 days, up to 24 times per year.

Where do you fit?

Whether you are a donor or not, find out what donors like you think and do. Select the categories that best describe you:

Sex: [Female ▾]   Age: [18-24 ▾]

[Find Out!]

Why give blood? Because only 5 percent of eligible Americans donate, because there's no other source of blood than healthy donors, because it's needed in emergencies and for people battling diseases like cancer and sickle cell anemia, and because donors can make a real difference by saving someone's life. By raising the question and then answering it in these various ways, the Red Cross Web site offers an argument for healthy people to donate.

Arguments like the Red Cross's surround us; they're the essence of many intellectual, political, and financial discussions. They're also the essence of advertising. Every day, each of us is bombarded with arguments that range from which candidate to vote for or which school to attend to how to invest our money or how loud to play our favorite music. We are encouraged to read important books, see particular movies, sign up for a certain class, take better care of ourselves, or accept ourselves just the way we are. Sometimes arguments are quarrelsome, even unpleasant, but on the whole, they merely express a difference of opinion about a statement that is open to discussion or dispute.

In the course of our daily lives, we argue with ourselves about whether to accept or reject disputable statements: "I should not be expected to pick up my boss's dry cleaning"; "I can save money if I switch my car insurance to a different company"; or "My relationship with my partner will never improve." And not only do we constantly consider other people's arguments, but we also advance our own. Argument is not reserved for law courts or legislatures; it is used everywhere, every day.

. . . .

Looking at Your Own Literacy   Consider the last important issue you argued about. What was it? Why was it important to you? With whom were you arguing? What did you want that person to do? What was the result? Where did you learn how to argue? How would you like to improve your skills at arguing?

. . . .

What Is Argument?

Although a distinction is sometimes made between *argument* and *persuasion*, the terms are often used interchangeably. When the distinction is made, **argument** usually refers to expressing a point of view and then using logical reasoning to try to get an audience to accept that point of view as true or valid. **Persuasion** is usually defined as using emotion as well as reasoning to *change* an audience's point of view and often to move people to action. But because writing almost any extended expression of a point of view involves using both reason and emotion—and might change readers' minds or move them to action—in this chapter and this book, *argument* is used to cover all meanings of both terms.

Now, successful argument often does change a point of view, that's for sure, but its purpose is not always victory over an opponent. Rather, argument often invites exchange, cooperation, mutually beneficial decisions. The best arguments make points openly and honestly, addressing any opposition straight on and working for clarity and understanding all around. We use argument to help an audience understand our point of view. Whether or not we have anything to "win," we want to be heard and understood. And we want to understand others' points of view as well.

The writer who composed the Red Cross Web page that opens this chapter is not attempting to win a debate. Instead, the writer pinpoints a problem (the need for blood in the blood bank) and suggests a course of action that will solve that problem (blood donation). The writer's argument becomes especially compelling, however, when he or she offers a number of compelling *reasons* as to why people should donate. By explaining why the Red Cross needs blood and what blood donation can do, the writer works to convince readers that they should donate. In essence, this writer wants his or her message to be heard so that positive change happens in the world: greater numbers of people make blood donations, providing an irreplaceable resource for people who need it.

We ourselves use the techniques of argumentation every day to bring attention to and sell our ideas, opinions, and decisions to friends and colleagues. If we perceive a problem, we employ these techniques to explore and analyze complicated issues, to provide information that might eventually change someone's mind (say, about where to eat, whom to date, or where to vacation), and to invite and consider additional information. Whether you are watching an NBA game with friends, phoning a radio station, exchanging text messages, completing a written assignment, or reading comments posted on a blog, chances are you're encountering argument.

Thinking about Argument

1. Read the advertisement on the facing page. What is the problem that needs a solution?
2. What argument is the ad making about a solution?
3. Underline the words that appeal, positively or negatively, to readers' emotions. What emotional appeal does the image make?

Why Argue?

Whether you're describing an architectural style for your art history professor, comparing and contrasting two military leaders of the Vietnam War for your political science professor, or analyzing the benefits of

Photo: Roslyn Dickens

Without someone to share it, dinner is always a cold meal.

Close relatives move far away. Old friends become increasingly frail and homebound. For some seniors, loneliness and isolation erode all of life's joys.

With your help, UJA-Federation is there — providing community centers and programs where the elderly can find warmth, companionship, and a renewed appetite for life.

Give to UJA-Federation of New York.

UJA Federation
of New York

New York • Long Island • Westchester • Israel • Around the Globe • **1.212.836.1880** • **www.ujafedny.org/give**

the euro for your economics professor, chances are you're also using elements of argument. As a writer, you will use argument for three general and often overlapping purposes: to *express* or *defend* your own position or opinion, to *question* or *argue against* an established belief or course of action, or to *invite* or *convince* readers to change their position.

See how Robert Sapolsky argues that there's a direct link between wealth and health.

Argument to Defend a Position

Modern science has finally provided some information that should aid everyone in making lifestyle decisions. If you wish to live a long and healthy life, it is advisable to be wealthy. More specifically: Try not to be born into poverty, and if you have inadvertently made that mistake, change your station in life ASAP.

People have long known about what is called the socioeconomic status (SES) gradient in health. For example, in the United States the poorer you are, the more likely you are to contract and succumb to heart disease, respiratory disorders, ulcers, rheumatoid disorders, psychiatric disease, or a number of types of cancer. And this is a whopper of an effect: In some cases disease or mortality risk increases more than fivefold as you go from the wealthiest to the poorest segments of our society, with things worsening each step of the way.

—Robert Sapolsky, "How the Other Half Heals"

Sapolsky gets readers' attention with his initial assertion that modern science has discovered the connection between wealth and good health. He argues this point with additional information about who is most likely to contract various illnesses or disorders.

. . . .

Try Your Hand   If Sapolsky is correct, we should all try to change our socioeconomic status as soon as possible. But such a grand claim demands support. List some specific ways that having more money could lead to an improvement in a person's health. It might help to consider a specific case—the health of your parents or grandparents, perhaps.

. . . .

Now look at the following passage, in which Sallie Tisdale takes on the question of what's "wrong" with high schools in the United States. Going beyond blaming students or teachers, she questions the very idea of high school, arguing that as a system it has few, if any, redeeming qualities.

Argument to Question an Established Belief

Much of the commentary on what's wrong with high school today is framed as what's wrong with high school students, who are blamed for drop-out rates, low attendance, declining test scores, crime, pregnancy and everything from litter to vandalism. The sad fact is that almost everything about high school fails to work—yet the system itself, the very idea of high school, is rarely blamed.

. . . High school as we conceive it now is fundamentally bad—not a flawed system needing to be fixed, but a bureaucracy of the worst kind, directly counterproductive to education, made up of a million pieces of glue and tape, without a core. It can't simply be "fixed."

High school is chaos mixed with boredom—much of it thoughtless, a matter of many tiny decisions made over time. It is, I think, the only world that can be made by people who have not known other worlds; it is made up of piecemeal solutions that present themselves to people who have seen only similar solutions. It is so big, entrenched and familiar that real change will always seem radically amiss to a lot of people inside it. Real change here will be met with alarm by people who are utterly convinced nothing else would work but have never tried any other way.   —Sallie Tisdale, "Second Thoughts"

Tisdale continues her essay by enumerating some specific problems high school students face: boredom, noise, frustration, and so on. In each case, she traces the cause not to the students but to the structure of high school itself.

Try Your Hand   Try extending Tisdale's argument to consider some possible solutions to the problems she raises. List three ways that high school could be improved. Share your suggestions with one or two classmates, and then present the group's responses to the rest of the class.

Finally, argument is often used to invite or convince readers to reconsider or even change their position on an issue. One controversial issue in U.S. education today is linguistic diversity: What languages and dialects should students use at school, and what languages and dialects should be taught there? In the following excerpt, stage and film critic John Simon invites readers to consider (and perhaps be convinced of) his opinion that "good English is good for you."

Argument to Change Readers' Position

The usual basic defense of good English (and here, again, let us not worry about nomenclature—for all I care, you may call it "Standard English," "correct American," or anything else) is that it helps communication, that it is perhaps even a *sine qua non*° of mutual understanding. Although this is a crude truth of sorts, it strikes me as, in some ways, both more and less than a truth. Suppose you say, "Everyone in their right mind would cross on the green light" or "Hopefully, it won't rain tomorrow"; chances are very good that the person you say this to will understand you, even though you are committing obvious solecisms* or creating needless ambiguities. Similarly, if you write in a letter, "The

---

° ***sine qua non:*** a necessity
* **solecisms:** violations of accepted language use or grammar

baby has finally ceased it's howling" (spelling *its* as *it's*), the recipient will be able to figure out what was meant. But "figuring out" is precisely what a listener or reader should not have to do. There is, of course, the fundamental matter of courtesy to the other person, but it goes beyond that: why waste time on unscrambling simple meaning when there are more complex questions that should receive our undivided attention? If the many cooks had to worry first about which out of a large number of pots had no leak in it, the broth, whether spoiled or not, would take forever to be ready.   — JOHN SIMON, "Good English Is Good for You"

Simon spends the rest of the piece trying to convince his readers that the *only* good American language is "good English"; no other dialects, languages, or usages will do.

. . . .

Try Your Hand   What is your position on "correct" English? What dialects, languages, or usages do you feel are useful, even valuable, in America? How does your position overlap with or diverge from Simon's? Write out your position, and then write three reasons you hold that position.

. . . .

How Do You Use Argument in Academic Writing?

As noted, elements of argument are used all the time in academic contexts. Scholars and students rely on argument to express or defend a position or opinion, to question or argue against an established belief or course of action, or to invite or convince readers to change their position. In the following excerpt, professor of rhetoric Bo Wang offers an argument about the Chinese writer Lu Yin in the opening paragraphs of an article published in *Rhetoric Review*. Wang makes her argument by expressing her opinion that readers should shift their understanding of this early–twentieth–century woman writer.

Argument in Academic Writing

Lu Yin (1899–1935), a prolific modern Chinese writer who composed in a variety of genres, reached a large number of readers in the early twentieth century in an effort to expose social problems and encourage women to break down patriarchal norms. Her literary works, long denigrated and ignored, have recently received more recognition on both sides of the Pacific for her depiction of women's lives at the turn of the century. Her essays, fiction, and autobiography have been made available through reprinted editions. While several literary scholars have written about her as a fiction writer (for example, Qian; Dai and Meng; Zhang; Feng; Dooling), I want to contend that Lu Yin was not only a fiction writer but also a feminist rhetorician whose use of language in public exerted a significant impact on the thinking and attitude of the audiences of her time. Lu Yin both constructed a rhetorical theory that is empowering and modeled rhetorical strategies that women can use to fight against oppression and explore their roles and images in a modern society.

— Bo Wang, "Breaking the Age of Flower Vases"

It's not difficult to identify the place in the introductory paragraph where Wang articulates her argument about Lu Yin. She states her thesis in this way: "I *want to contend* that Lu Yin was not only a fiction writer but also a feminist rhetorician whose use of language in public exerted a significant impact on the thinking and attitude of the audiences of her time." Wang makes clear why this argument should be significant to the readers of *Rhetoric Review* — scholars and students interested in theories of argument and histories of rhetoric. First, Wang offers a new and different vision of Lu Yin: readers should see her not only as a fiction writer but also as a feminist rhetorician. Second, Wang's analysis contributes to disciplinary knowledge about rhetorical theory and practice. According to Wang, Lu Yin both constructed a rhetorical theory and modeled feminist rhetorical strategies. In the rest of her article, it's up to Wang to prove these claims by presenting her readers with strong, convincing evidence and supporting arguments.

When you make arguments in your courses, you'll want to use many of the strategies that Wang does in this paragraph. Like her, you'll want to articulate what your argument is by composing a clear thesis statement. You'll also want to follow Wang's example by explaining why readers should be interested in this argument. Making this particular explanation enables you to answer the "So what?" question that readers often have: "Why should I care about this argument?" You might also learn from another one of Wang's strategies. Notice how she does not downplay or criticize the work of other scholars who have argued for Lu Yin as a literary figure. Instead, Wang constructs her argument in a way that *builds on* these scholars' work; she simply wants to offer another perspective, another way to see and understand this writer.

· ·

Analyzing Argument in Academic Writing   Reflect on the last time you composed an argument for one of your classes. How did you create this argument? What difficulties or challenges did you have in composing this argument? How might the discussions in this chapter so far have helped you construct your argument?

· ·

How Do You Read an Argument?

In some ways, all spoken and written language is an argument. Every time a meaningful transaction occurs between a writer (or speaker) and reader (or listener), every time one person has successfully conveyed meaning to another person, a kind of argument takes place. Whether you're listening to your friend's description of her wedding gown, reading about someone's battle with leukemia, watching a television news report about the torture of prisoners, or listening to a radio ad enumerating all the reasons you should vote for a specific candidate in the next election, each of these speakers or writers is trying to express a point of view in such a way that you accept it. Because arguments are so prevalent, it's obviously important that you know how to read them closely and critically to evaluate how strong an argument is and decide to what extent you are persuaded by it. Close critical reading of arguments is also important for another reason — seeing the ways that others succeed (or don't succeed) in making their case will help you learn how to write your own arguments more effectively.

In most cases, the title and thesis statement of an argument will help orient you to the subject of the argument, the author's purpose for writing, and the intended audience. And the opening section of the argument will also often tell you how successfully the author connects with the audience. Look again at the Red Cross Web page on page 634. The title "Why Give?" informs you right away about the general subject of the argument. By using a question for the title, the writer makes a connection with the audience. That is, the author hopes the audience will be interested in not only the question but also its answer. Notice that after asking the question, the author provides the audience with a compelling statistic: "Every two seconds someone in the United States needs blood." Then the author continues the connection with the audience by making a comment that many readers may well be thinking: "That's a lot of blood."

As you read through the body of an argument, try to trace the progress of the author's reasoning to see if it makes good sense. In the case of the Red Cross page, the reasoning is simple: people with diseases and injuries need blood transfusions, and if healthy donors give blood, these people's lives might be saved. The author then asks the audience to consider their part in this process by imagining a scenario: "Imagine if giving blood was part of everyone's life. Something you did on a regular basis, like eating at your favorite restaurant." Here the author personalizes the argument for the audience, prompting people to think about how easy it is to become a blood donor.

When reading an argument, you'll also want to determine if the author has recommended any specific belief or course of action — appreciate the wedding gown, complain to officials about the treatment of prisoners, vote for candidate Smith. It's impossible to miss the course of action advocated through the Red Cross Web page: give blood. The site makes it easy for readers to give by guiding them to sign up and donate on the next page. The Red Cross's course of action seems simple and basic; just one click, and the audience shows just how persuasive the argument is. The positions or courses of action you advocate in your arguments might not be so straightforward, but in your arguments, you often want to consider how to solve the problem you've identified, persuading readers toward a particular solution or advocating that one solution is better or more effective than another.

One last thing to be aware of as you analyze an argument critically is what it does *not* say. In the Red Cross page, the author doesn't say anything about the blood donation process. There's no mention of needles, for instance, to put off those who might get queasy about that aspect of the donation. Nor does the page go into detail about blood banks, matching blood types, or problems that occur with blood transfusions. It makes sense not to bring up this information: by avoiding detailed or disheartening discussions, the author is able to focus on the basic information that if the audience gives blood, the Red Cross and the health care providers will take care of the rest. Still, although this is not the case for the Red Cross example, often the things an author leaves unmentioned *are* central to the effectiveness of an argument — and leaving out details or objections that readers need or expect to find may fatally weaken it. Think about this issue both when you're reading an argument and when you're writing one of your own.

How Do You Write an Argument?

When you argue a point in writing, you need to be concerned with a number of important issues that are generally more complex than issues related to any of the rhetorical methods discussed in earlier chapters. So if you can, work with a classmate or two as you write. You and your classmates can help each other stay on track and remain alert to problems and weaknesses in your arguments.

● Making a Claim

Once you decide what you're writing about, you'll need to consider your opinion on or belief about that subject and the **claim** you want to make about it — the position you want to take. The claim you make must necessarily be one of several claims that *could* be made with regard to this subject, and you should be aware of — and perhaps respond to — those other perspectives as you form your claim. In other words, your claim, which will become the basis of your **thesis statement,** must be **arguable.**

In the readings that follow, James L. Shulman and William G. Bowen argue that athletes should not receive such preferential treatment in college admissions as they now do. Lynda Rush claims that Shulman and Bowen base their argument on sloppy science. Andrew Wible argues that college athletics are a positive influence, both on campus and off. And William F. Shughart II argues that colleges and universities should create four-year degree programs in football and basketball, just like the degree programs in art, drama, and music. Of course, there are other perspectives for each of these claims, and the writers knew that when they made their arguments. None of them made claims that were not arguable: for instance, a claim like "college athletes have many boosters" or "some college athletes are also scholars."

● Determining Your Purpose

What is at stake? What are the possible consequences of your argument? Are you writing to express or defend your own beliefs? to question or argue against something? or to invite or convince someone to reconsider a position? For instance, you might write a letter to the editor of your school newspaper expressing your belief that the student union should stay open longer on the weekends. Or you might question your instructor's assumption that careful planning is essential to success in writing, especially in your case. You might even write to the chair of the English Department in an attempt to convince her to drop attendance requirements from the department's grading policy; in your view, undergraduate students are old enough to monitor their own academic progress. Any of these arguments might be successful; in other words, your belief might prevail.

On the other hand, if you assert that having multiple romantic partners can be physically safe, your purpose might be to open up a lively discussion, given the pressure in America to practice monogamy and safe sex. In this case, you probably shouldn't expect to convince all your readers to accept your argument, but you might succeed in being heard and understood.

● Considering Your Audience

Who will be reading your argument? Whose opinion would you like to influence or change? How do your readers feel—and how much do they know—about the issue you are addressing?

In argument even more than in other kinds of writing, your audience is almost inseparable from your purpose. In fact, your audience may even shape your purpose, depending on whether its members (1) already agree with you and want their beliefs to be confirmed (look back at the Sapolsky excerpt on page 638); (2) are willing to consider opinions, beliefs, or practices that differ from their own but will need to be convinced (Tisdale is counting on readers to do just that in the excerpt on pages 638–39); or (3) are hostile or deaf to your opinion and will be looking for faults in it (consider Simon's excerpt on pages 639–40). Regardless of how you imagine your audience's response to your argument, you'll need to establish **common ground,** stating a goal toward which you both want to work or a belief, assumption, or value that you both share.

With college writing, it is sometimes hard to decide what audience to address your argument to, because your instructor may seem to be your only audience — as well as your judge. But once you decide on a subject that you feel strongly about, you need to imagine the person you need to convince, the person whose actions or opinions you'd like to influence. You can address this imagined audience as you write, even if you suspect that your instructor is your only flesh-and-blood reader. If you address a specific audience, the instructor can assume that position. After all, you need to determine this specific audience in order to write your thesis statement and choose your supporting arguments, according to what that audience knows and how people feel about your subject. For instance, in the following excerpt, educator Etta Kralovec imagines an audience that is already interested in issues surrounding homework.

Establishing Common Ground with an Audience

The problem isn't homework per se, it's that homework is unfair. It plays on social inequities. Consider the differences between families: One kid goes home to two well-educated parents, a home library and computer access to massive databases. Another kid goes home to parents who work at night, have no computer and no books. Which kid is going to handle homework better and do better in school?

— Etta Kralovec, "Give Me a Break"

Kralovec establishes common ground immediately when she assures her readers that she is not objecting to homework itself. As she continues, she explains that the increasing load of homework assigned by many schools has become a burden to families and a way for "educators and politicians" to achieve "school reform on the cheap." She then addresses another claim that could be made for homework — that it teaches good study habits — and argues that children need guidance from teachers to learn these skills. Convincing most readers to agree with her proposal to make all "homework" into in-school activities is not Kralovec's purpose; rather, she wants the audience to reconsider their own ideas.

Kralovec makes her claim — that "homework" should be reconceived — to the broad readership of *People* magazine. As she attends to her purpose (questioning the value of homework as we know it) and to her audience (*People* readers), she also attends to three other essential features of argument that all writers must address: (1) the ways you appeal to your audience, (2) the way you arrange your material, and (3) your pattern of reasoning. There are also several common errors of logic you'll want to take care to avoid.

● Making Rhetorical Appeals

Just as you'll need to establish common ground with your audience, you'll need to use other strategies as well in order to appeal to them. The three basic kinds of strategies, called **rhetorical appeals,** are (1) the appeal of your own trustworthiness, or **ethos;** (2) the appeal of the reasoning in your argument, or **logos;** and (3) the appeal to the audience's emotions, or **pathos.**

The first of these appeals, the *ethical appeal*, demonstrates your character, credibility, and integrity as a writer and thinker, so that your audience will continue listening to you. Establishing common ground with the audience is one important part of the ethical appeal. You'll also need to show how knowledgeable you are about the issue you're discussing and to represent opposing viewpoints accurately and fairly even while disagreeing with them.

In an essay questioning the push to computerize classrooms, Jane Healy uses one of her introductory paragraphs to establish her ethos.

Establishing an Ethos

I have spent hundreds of hours in classrooms, labs, and homes, watching kids using new technologies, picking the brains of leaders in the field, and researching both off- and on-line. As a longtime enthusiast for and user of educational computing, I found this journey sometimes shocking, often disheartening, and occasionally inspiring. While some very exciting and potentially valuable things are happening between children and computers, we are currently spending far too much money with too little thought. It is past time to pause, reflect, and ask some probing questions.   —JANE M. HEALY, "Blundering into the Future: Hype or Hope?"

Logical appeals present reasons and evidence—facts, statistics, comparisons, anecdotes, expert opinions, personal experiences and observations—that illustrate or support your claim fairly, accurately, and knowledgeably. In another essay on classroom computerization, the authors appeal to logic.

Logical Appeals

Most schools have installed computers (the latest figures from Market Data Retrieval show the ratio of students to computers has fallen below 5 to 1). Most schools are wired and about 98 percent have Internet access; more than half have a home page on the Web, and about 70 percent of teachers claim regular use of computers. eLearning tools and the Internet are opening windows to the world for most pupils.
          —WILLIAM G. ZIMMERMAN JR. AND RICHARD H. GOODMAN,
          "Thinking Differently about Technology in Our Schools"

Finally, *pathetic appeals* are emotional appeals that clarify the issue by touching its human elements. Appealing to an audience's emotions is one of the most effective ways to move that audience toward your own feelings about an issue. For example, in a report to the president and Congress about expanding the use of the Internet for education, these authors use pathos to argue their thesis.

Pathetic Appeals

Millions still cannot access the Internet and do not understand how to use it to harness the global web of knowledge.

They do not know how to deal in information, the basic currency of the knowledge economy. They do not know how to find information, how to handle it, how to trade in it, how to invest it for their futures.

—WEB-BASED EDUCATION COMMISSION, "The Power of the Internet for Learning"

Naturally, your choice of logical and pathetic appeals can enhance or detract from your ethos, so you'll want to choose reasons, evidence, and emotional appeals that not only are effective in their own right but also support your credibility as a fair-minded writer.

For example, personal anecdotes can be powerful evidence, but if your own problems in, say, getting a student loan are the *only* evidence you cite for your argument that such loans are too hard to get, your audience may suspect that you are overgeneralizing from your own experience. On the other hand, citing statistic after statistic about loans without giving any individual examples may convince your readers, but at the cost of having them lose interest in your argument.

In the same way, you'll need to judge emotional appeals carefully. If the audience feels that you're relying on emotion to make up for a weakness in your logical case — or if you've misjudged your readers' own feelings about the issue — such appeals can backfire.

● Arranging All the Parts

Argument also requires that you pay careful attention to the arrangement of your essay, the ordering of your material. Every essay, of course, has an introduction, a body, and a conclusion, but an argumentative essay imposes special requirements for each section.

In your introduction, you'll want to orient your reader to your topic and, at the same time, establish it as worthy of consideration and yourself as a trustworthy writer. To get your readers' attention, you might open with a dramatic anecdote, a startling fact or statistic, or a brief historical overview. Your introduction should also establish your ethos in three ways: it should provide evidence of your goodwill, your good sense, and your good character. You may want to close your introduction with your thesis statement, the belief or opinion that you are arguing, as Lynda Rush does in the last sentence of her introduction (p. 665). (Using another organizational pattern, as discussed in the next section, you might save your thesis statement for the conclusion of your argument.)

Following the introduction is the body, in which you present the argument itself, providing reasons for your belief or opinion. Each reason must be supported with clear, relevant, and representative evidence that enhances the logic of your argument. Either before or after framing your opinion, you'll also need to mention and refute, or disprove, any opposing views — or admit their strong points — so that your audience knows that you are arguing from a basis of knowledge and understanding. As you move from one piece of evidence to the next, and between your own views and opposing ones, you'll need to use transitional words and phrases to help your readers follow your argument.

By the time you arrive at the conclusion of your argument, you will have laid out the importance of your subject, your own credibility as a thinker and writer, and a series of logical arguments. In your conclusion, then, you might want to use emotional appeals in order to connect, person to person, with your audience. (Of course, you may have included such appeals in earlier parts of the argument as well.) If you foresee potentially harmful or dangerous — or potentially beneficial or wonderful—consequences of a belief or an activity, now is the time to describe those consequences in a last attempt to encourage your readers to consider (if not commit to) a course of action.

If you have not stated your thesis explicitly in your introduction — and perhaps even if you have — you will want to do so in your conclusion. Notice how Shulman and Bowen conclude their essay about preferential admissions for college athletes with an explicit statement of the proposal they are making for change, a proposal they have only implied up to that point.

A Conclusion with an Explicit Thesis Statement

It seems clear that consideration should be given to changing the way in which at least some admissions offices approach the athletics side of the process of selecting a class. The admissions process should rely much less heavily on the coaches' lists, and less weight should be given to raw athletic talent and single-minded commitment to a sport—or what we can only call athletic "purposiveness." Rather, admissions staffs could be encouraged to revert to the practices of earlier days, when more weight was given to athletic talent seen in combination with other qualifications that made the applicant attractive to the institution—including a commitment to the educational purposes of the institution. The exceptional records achieved both in college and after graduation by the male athletes who entered in 1951 and the female athletes who entered in 1976 reflect the presence of the admissions approach we are advocating.

In sum, intercollegiate athletics has come to have too pronounced an effect on colleges and universities—and on society—to be treated with benign neglect. Failure to see where the intensification of athletics programs is taking us, and to adjust expectations, could have the unintended consequence of allowing intercollegiate athletics to become less and less relevant to the educational experiences of most students, and more and more at odds with the core missions of the institutions themselves. The objective should be to strengthen the links between athletics and educational missions—and to reinvigorate an aspect of college life so that it can be celebrated for its positive contributions, not condemned for its excesses or criticized for its conflicts with educational values.

      —JAMES L. SHULMAN AND WILLIAM G. BOWEN, "How the Playing Field
      Is Encroaching on the Admissions Office"

● Considering Patterns of Reasoning

There are two basic ways to frame an argument: deductively and inductively. Deductive arguments move from a generalized claim to a series of supporting examples, and inductive arguments move in the opposite direction, from a limited number of specific cases to a generalization. Sociolinguist Deborah Tannen uses a deductive pattern of reasoning to argue that men talk more than women.

Deductive Reasoning

Women are believed to talk too much. Yet study after study finds that it is men who talk more—at meetings, in mixed-group discussions, and in classrooms where girls or young women sit next to boys or young men. For example, communications researchers Barbara and Gene Eakins tape-recorded and studied seven university faculty meetings. They found that, with one exception, men spoke more often and, without exception, spoke for a longer time. The men's turns ranged from 10.66 to 17.07 seconds, while the women's turns ranged from 3 to 10 seconds. In other words, the women's longest turns were still shorter than the men's shortest turns.   —DEBORAH TANNEN, *You Just Don't Understand*

Tannen goes on to support her generalization with even more examples and studies of men talking more than women.

After explaining the theory that blushing occurs to show embarrassment, physician Atul Gawande provides two facts that call this theory into question.

Inductive Reasoning

One theory is that the blush exists to show embarrassment, just as the smile exists to show happiness. This would explain why the reaction appears only in the visible regions of the body (the face, the neck, the upper chest). But then why do dark-skinned people blush? Surveys find that nearly everyone blushes, regardless of skin color, despite the fact that in many people it is nearly invisible. And you don't need to turn red in order for people to recognize that you're embarrassed. Studies show that people detect embarrassment *before* you blush. Apparently, blushing takes between fifteen and twenty seconds to reach its peak, yet most people need less than five seconds to recognize that someone is embarrassed—they pick it up from the almost immediate shift in gaze, usually down and to the left, or from the sheepish, self-conscious grin that follows a half second to a second later. So there's reason to doubt that the purpose of blushing is entirely expressive.   — ATUL GAWANDE, "Crimson Tide"

"Reading" and Using Visuals in Argument

As you compose your essay, consider whether particular kinds of visuals — photographs, for instance — might enhance the pathetic appeal of your argument, just as diagrams, charts, and graphs might enhance its logical appeal. To learn to use visuals effectively as a tool for argument, make a habit of examining visuals you encounter to see how they go about making their point and how effective they are at doing so. That is, learn to "read" visual arguments with a critical eye, the same way you would written arguments, to judge how well they achieve their purpose for their intended audience.

Look, for example, at the poster on page 651, which was published by the Campus Health Service at the University of Arizona as part of a campaign to reduce binge drinking on campus. As you can see from a glance, the aim of the poster is to inform students about what "most" students on campus do. The ultimate (and unstated) argument is a logical one: since most students at the University of Arizona work hard and drink in moderation, readers of the poster should not feel that normal college student behavior means drinking heavily and disregarding schoolwork. In fact, they should feel comfortable being responsible, just like the majority of their peers. The visual and the verbal elements of the text work together to create this argument for readers.

The verbal text sets out the argument for the poster. The largest word that readers see is the one at the top, "most," which in the original poster is in white type on a red background. As readers move their eyes down the poster, they learn first that "most" refers to "UA students" and then what these students do: they "work hard" and "drink moderately." Notice how this dominant message not only appears in the largest type on the poster but also is emphasized other ways. These key words and phrases appear in boxes, with the oval ones echoing the shape of the Campus Health Service logo in the lower left corner, and their text is white rather than black, the other color choice for text on the poster. These visual choices for the text help draw readers' eyes to the dominant message of the poster. If they choose not to read on, they will still get a sense of the main argument. And notice that because "work hard" and "drink moderately" are visually separated from the words above them, they look like commands as well as a description of what most UA students do.

Now look at the bottom half of the poster, which elaborates on the claim that Arizona students do indeed work hard and drink in moderation. Readers learn that the average GPA for Arizona students is a B and that 64 percent of students have four or fewer drinks when

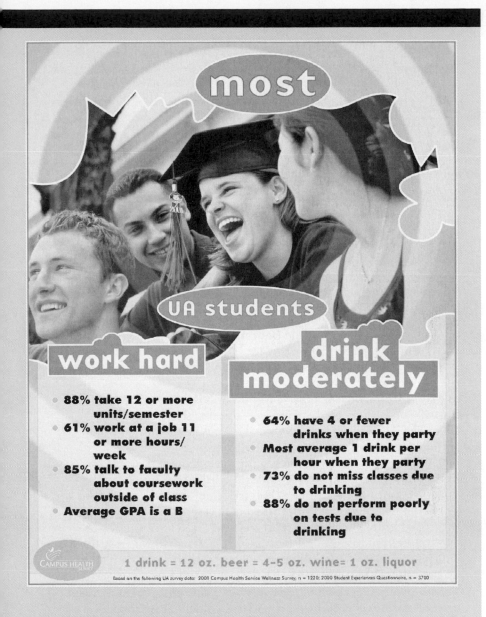

they attend a party. This information is impressive, but let's look again at how the presentation of the text also supports the project of the poster. The statistical information about working hard and drinking in moderation is separated into two columns, with each column placed within a boxed background. By looking at these columns, readers can easily see how each one provides specific examples of the general assertions about students' work and drinking habits. Within each column, the information is separated into lists by using bullets and indentation, so that the numerical parts of it stand out: "88%," "Average," "64%," "Most."

These strategies are important, especially if we remember that this argument takes the form of a poster. Students will be passing by while walking to class, to their dorms or dining facilities, or even to a party, so the author needs to make sure they can read it easily and quickly. The poster's columns, bullets, text size, and color all help the author achieve this goal. Notice, too, that the less important information — the Campus Health Service logo and the three definitions of a "drink" — appear in small type and more muted colors at the bottom. All the way at the bottom, in very small type, is the background information about the surveys on which the statistics are based, including their dates and the number of participants.

Now examine the most prominent visual element of the poster. The picture of the four students laughing and enjoying themselves, with one even wearing a graduation cap, also contributes significantly to the overall effectiveness of the argument. Given the text of the poster, what message is the visual sending? These students are part of the majority of the student body; they have fun (responsibly) while achieving their academic goals. The graduating student is proof of this latter claim. And the curving, jagged edges of the picture, like the text ovals and the "bull's-eye" background (pink and orange in the original), suggest that college life doesn't have to be all severe straight lines and right angles. We can imagine that the Campus Health Service expected the student audience would identify with this group of students, reemphasizing the argument: if you're a student at Arizona, don't think that you need to drink heavily to fit in. Instead, being "normal" at Arizona means cultivating responsible work and drinking habits.

If you are thinking of using visuals in an academic writing assignment, it's a good idea to check with your instructor beforehand.

These facts move toward Gawande's general claim, which appears at the very end of his essay: "So there's reason to doubt that the purpose of blushing is entirely expressive."

● Avoiding Logical Fallacies

Throughout your essay, you will want to use sound reasoning, avoiding errors of logic. If you use such **logical fallacies** (faulty reasoning), however innocently, you are sending up a warning flag to your readers that your thinking is not entirely trustworthy. Some of the most common logical fallacies are the following:

The *ad hominem* fallacy (a personal attack) targets the actual person who holds an opinion rather than the opinion itself. For example, "I won't vote for any politician that Rush Limbaugh supports" or "I'm not interested in global warming because I don't like Al Gore."

Begging the question (it's true because it's true) asks the audience simply to accept a statement as the truth when in actuality it is controversial. For example, "You and I both know that all lawyers are crooked"; "Of course, all interior walls should be painted off-white"; "All pornography is protected by the U.S. Constitution." Sometimes the logic is circular. The writer supports the supposedly controversial claim by restating the same claim in different words: "He is guilty of murdering his wife because he killed her"; "I am a Republican/Democrat because it is the best political party"; "Michigan lost the game because the other team kept scoring."

The *post hoc, ergo propter hoc* (literally, "after this, therefore because of this") fallacy assumes a cause-and-effect relationship just because one event happened after another. If you argue that your grandmother broke her hip because she fell, you might be ignoring the possibility that her hip had been weakened by osteoporosis and that in fact she fell because her hip gave way. If you argue that Oregon State had a winning football season because of its new coach, you may be overlooking the fact that some of the star players are juniors and seniors who were trained for several years by the former coach.

The *non sequitur* ("it does not follow") fallacy, like the preceding one, is also an error in cause-and-effect analysis. Non sequiturs are faulty conclusions about consequences: "Because more retired people are moving to this area, we need to build another hospital"; "I'm related to the mayor; vote for me for city council"; "The war in Iraq was very divisive politically, so we shouldn't intervene elsewhere."

Sweeping generalizations (jumping to conclusions) are the kind of overstatements almost everyone resorts to when they have not thought through an issue or action. For example, "AIDS is a gay disease"; "Welfare recipients don't want to work"; "The United States is being overrun by illegal immigrants."

The *false dilemma* (either–or) fallacy, imagining only and no more than two sides or solutions to an issue, might be the most common kind of illogical thinking. Controversial issues such as abortion, same-sex marriage, welfare, euthanasia, and affirmative action may seem to have only two sides, pro and con. But in every case the issues are complicated in terms of their causes and possible solutions.

In fact, few of the issues you will argue offer easy answers or solutions. As you write arguments, you will want to take care to move your readers ethically and logically toward your careful and possibly tentative conclusion.

Understanding and Using Argument

Analyzing Argument

1. **Working with two or three classmates,** come up with two examples of each of the logical fallacies on pages 652–54. Share your list with the rest of the class.

2. Reread the excerpt from John Simon's "Good English Is Good for You" on pages 639–40. Determine if he uses deductive or inductive argument; how he uses ethical, logical, and emotional rhetorical appeals; and if he slips into any logical fallacies.

3. Look back at the excerpt from Etta Kralovec's "Give Me a Break" on page 645. List as many reasons for having students do homework as you can think of. Given Kralovec's position on the subject, how might she respond to each of your reasons?

Planning and Writing an Argument

1. Complete this statement: "One thing I believe in strongly is _____." Now list every reason you can think of to support your view.

2. Who — what groups or individuals — might agree with you?

3. Now complete this statement: "Mine is not the only opinion on this subject, though, because other people believe _____ or _____."

4. List all the reasons you can think of that these people might hold these opinions.

5. **Share your list with a classmate** to see whether he or she can suggest any other opinions you've not thought of. These might be views you would need to acknowledge and perhaps refute in a written argument on this topic.

6. Draft a three- to four-page argument essay using as your topic the idea you tried out in question 1. On a separate sheet of paper, describe your audience. List the views you think your audience members may hold that are different from yours, and be sure to address them in your essay.

Assume that this audience is willing to listen to, maybe even consider seriously, your point of view. Refer to "Checking Over an Argument," below, as you draft and revise.

7. Look at the advertisement on page 637 (or select another advertisement that you think offers a clear argument) and analyze it, evaluating its power and noting its weaknesses. Draft a two- to three-page essay in which you discuss the audience, purpose, rhetorical appeals, and arrangement of this advertisement. Point out any logical fallacies that you notice. Your thesis statement should make an argument about the overall effectiveness of the ad. Refer to the following guidelines for checking over an argument as you draft and revise.

✔ Checking Over an Argument

1. What is the topic or issue? How is it arguable? What claim does the essay make about this topic? Underline the thesis statement of the argument.

2. What kinds of people make up the audience for this argument? What do you think their attitude is toward the issue? toward the essay's position? Does the argument take their attitudes into account?

3. Given the audience, what is the argument's purpose? Write out the purpose in one sentence. Does the argument reflect this purpose?

4. Does the introduction establish goodwill, good sense, and good character? Does it establish common ground with the audience? How, exactly?

5. What specific support is provided for the claim? Number the supporting points in the order that they are introduced. Are they all accurate? relevant? representative? In other words, are they used to their best advantage? After each number, write the kind of support it is: statistic, fact, personal experience or observation, comparison, and so on. What other kinds of support are needed?

6. Does the argument proceed deductively or inductively? Is this arrangement successful or not?

7. Can you identify any logical fallacies in the argument?

8. Does the essay acknowledge and respond to opposing viewpoints?

9. Circle all transitional words or phrases that move the reader from one point to the next. Are there other places where transitions are needed?

10. How does the conclusion appeal to the audience? What does it do to get readers to be sympathetic to the argument? How else could the conclusion establish an emotional link between you and the audience?

11. Do the visuals enhance the argument itself? How, specifically? Are captions, labels, or references to the visuals needed in the written text? If there are no visuals, should there be?

READINGS

Casebook:
College Athletics

JAMES L. SHULMAN AND WILLIAM G. BOWEN
How the Playing Field Is
Encroaching on the Admissions Office

James L. Shulman (b. 1965) is executive director of ARTstor, a project of the Andrew W. Mellon Foundation, which makes grants to institutions in education, cultural affairs, the performing arts, and environmental and public affairs. William G. Bowen (b. 1933) has been the president of the foundation since 1988 and was president of Princeton University from 1972 to 1988. He has written extensively on issues in higher education, especially affirmative action. The following article, which appeared in the *Chronicle of Higher Education* in January 2001, is excerpted from Shulman and Bowen's book *The Game of Life: College Sports and Educational Values* (2001).

> **Preview** How do you imagine college athletics encroaches on college admissions?

Shulman and Bowen use their opening to create common ground with their readers.	Faculty members often remark that the most discouraging aspect of teaching is encountering a student who just does not seem to care, who has to be cajoled into thinking about the reading, who is obviously bored in class, or who resists rewriting a paper that is passable but not very good. Such students are failing to take full advantage of the educational opportunities that colleges and universities are there to provide.

1

2   Uninspired students come in all sizes and shapes, and no one would suggest that athletes are uniformly different from other students in this regard. But the evidence presented does demonstrate a consistent tendency for athletes to do less well academically than their classmates — and, even more troubling, a consistent tendency for athletes to underperform academically not just relative to other students, but relative to how they themselves might have been expected to perform. Those tendencies have become more pronounced over time, and all-pervasive: Academic underperformance is now found among female athletes as well as male, among those who play the lower-profile sports as well as those on football and basketball teams, and among athletes playing at the Division III level as well as those playing in bowl games and competing for national championships.

3   In our research, we studied 30 academically selective colleges and universities. Being selective means that they receive many more applications from well-qualified students than they have places in their entering classes, and thus must pick and choose among applicants on a variety of criteria, including athletic talent. By national standards, the freshman classes that they admit have very strong academic qualifications — with SAT scores, for example, that are well above national norms, and with large numbers of high-school valedictorians and National Merit Scholarship winners.

Shulman and Bowen explain the study that propels their argument.

4   The institutions included Ivy League members — Columbia, Princeton, and Yale Universities, and the University of Pennsylvania — and women's colleges — Barnard, Bryn Mawr, Smith, and Wellesley. We also studied coed liberal-arts institutions: Denison and Wesleyan Universities, and Hamilton, Kenyon, Oberlin, Swarthmore, and Williams Colleges. Some of the others that we reviewed were private universities in the National Collegiate Athletic Association's Division I-A: Duke, Georgetown, Northwestern, Rice, Stanford, Tulane, and Vanderbilt Universities, and the University of Notre Dame. Others were Division I-A public institutions: Miami University of Ohio, Pennsylvania State University at University Park, the University of Michigan at Ann Arbor, and the University of North Carolina at

The authors' detailed description of their research helps them create a credible ethos.

Chapel Hill. In addition, we looked at Emory, Tufts, and Washington (Mo.) Universities.

A transitional question moves the reader from discussion of the study to discussion of its findings.

What did we find? Athletes who are recruited, 5 and who end up on the carefully winnowed lists of desired candidates submitted by coaches to the admissions offices of those selective institutions, now enjoy a very substantial statistical "advantage" in the admissions process. That advantage—for both male and female athletes—is much greater than that enjoyed by other targeted groups, such as underrepresented minority students and alumni children.

Shulman and Bowen offer a logical appeal here.

For example, at a representative nonscholarship 6 institution for which we have complete data on all applicants, recruited male athletes who applied to enter with the fall–1999 class had a 48–percent greater chance of being admitted than did male students at large, after taking differences in SAT scores into account. The corresponding admissions advantage enjoyed by recruited female athletes in 1999 was 53 percent. The admissions advantages enjoyed by minority students and legacies were in the range of 18 to 24 percent.

The questions in this paragraph help create both a logical and a pathetic appeal.

When recruited athletes make up such a sub– 7 stantial fraction of the entering class in at least some colleges, is there a risk that there will be too few places for other students, who want to become poets, scientists, or leaders of civic causes? Is there a possibility that, without realizing what is leading to what, the institutions themselves will become unbalanced in various ways? For example, will they feel a need to devote more and more of their teaching resources to fields like business and economics—which are disproportionately elected by athletes—in lieu of investing more heavily in less "practical" fields, such as classics, physics, and language study? Similarly, as one commentator put the question, what are the effects on those students interested in fields like philosophy? Could they feel at risk of being devalued?

In an ideal world, institutions would like to 8 see a diversity of majors, values, and career choices among all subgroups of students. Society is best served when the financial–services sector "inherits" some students who have a deep commitment to understanding history and culture, rather than mainly those with a narrower focus on earning a great deal of money as an end in itself. In the same way, academe benefits when some of those who pursue Ph.D.'s include students who also have learned some of the lessons about life that are gained on the playing field, rather than just students with a narrower focus on an arcane, if not obscure, realm of academic research. In short, the heavy concentration of male athletes, in particular, in certain fields of study raises real questions of institutional priorities and balance.

9   Moreover, high–school students, their parents, and their schools watch attentively for the signals that colleges send. The more that leading institutions signal *through their actions* how much they value athletic prowess, the greater the emphasis that potential applicants will place on those activities. The issuing of rewards based on sports accomplishments supports — and, in fact, makes real — the message that sports is the road to opportunity.

Shulman and Bowen create a logical appeal here.

10   As a result, young people in schools of all kinds — from prep schools to inner–city schools — are less likely to get a message that the way upward is to learn to write computer code or take chemistry seriously when it is not only the big–time–sports institutions but also the Ivies and the most selective liberal-arts colleges that place a large premium on athletic prowess, focus, and specialization. Athletics scholarships and tickets of admission to nonscholarship institutions provide a more powerful incentive than the promises contained in high-minded proclamations.

11   Taken together, such a signaling process has a powerful impact. We were told of one situation in which almost half of the students from a leading prep school who had been admitted to an Ivy League university were either outstanding hockey or lacrosse players, and not particularly noteworthy students. When asked at a recruiting session in a large city about the success of his prep school in placing its students in the most prestigious colleges, the school's representative gave the absolute number of students admitted to that Ivy League institution, hoped that no one would ask him how many of the admittees had been athletes, and went home

The authors use exemplification to support their claim in the topic sentence.

"I'm glad we won, and I hope that someday we'll have a
university that our football team can be proud of."

with mixed feelings about his presentation. The real issue, however, is not about how forthcoming the prep-school representative was in explaining his school's success in placing students, but the nature of the reality that underlies that "success."

The authors use a historical comparison to advance their argument.

In fact, the changes in the face of athletics between the 1950's and today can be related to a still broader shift in admissions philosophies. In the 1950's, much was said about the desirability of enrolling "well-rounded students." One consequence, among many others, was that athletes needed to have other attributes — to be ready to take advantage of the broad range of the institution's academic offerings, or to be interested in being part of the larger campus community, for example. Many   12 of them were class officers, not just team captains. We suspect that the subsequent success of a number of the athletes of this era in gaining leadership positions, including positions as chief executive officers, owes something to their having had a strong combination of attributes.

13   Sometime in the late 1960's or the 1970's, that admissions philosophy was altered in major ways. At some of the institutions with which we are familiar, the attack on the desirability of the well–rounded individual came from faculty members. One group of mathematicians objected vehemently to the rejection of candidates who had extremely high math aptitude scores but were not impressive in other respects. A new admissions mantra was coined; the search was on to enroll the "well–rounded class," rather than the well–rounded individual. The idea was that the super–mathematician should definitely be admitted, along with the super–musician and maybe even the super–gymnast. It was argued that, taken together, such an array of talented individuals would create an attractively diverse community of learners. For some years now, most admissions officers at academically selective institutions have talked in terms of the well–rounded class.

14   The mathematicians who lobbied for the admission of high–school students with off–the–scale mathematical potential were absolutely right. "Spiky" students of that kind belong in a great university with a great mathematics department. We are much more skeptical, however, that "spikiness" can be used to justify the admission of a bone–crushing fullback whose high–school grades are over the academic threshold but who otherwise does not seem a particularly good fit for the academic values that a college espouses. There are many types of spikiness, and the objective should be to assemble a well–rounded class with a range of attributes that resonate with the academic and service missions of the institution. Looked at from that perspective, the arguments for spiky mathematicians and for spiky golfers seem quite different.

Shulman and Bowen offer a different kind of comparison here to support their argument.

15   We also wonder how well some of the increasingly spiky athletes who entered the colleges that we studied in 1989 (and those who entered later)

will do in the long run. Not as well, we suspect, as their male predecessors who entered in the fall of 1951, and the female athletes who entered in 1976 — and who appear to have had, as the saying goes, "more arrows in their quivers."

The authors state their thesis here.

It seems clear that consideration should be given to changing the way in which at least some admissions offices approach the athletics side of the process of selecting a class. The admissions process should rely much less heavily on the coaches' lists, and less weight should be given to raw athletic talent and single-minded commitment to a sport — or what we can only call athletic "purposiveness." Rather, admissions staffs could be encouraged to revert to the practices of earlier days, when more weight was given to athletic talent seen in combination with other qualifications that made the applicant attractive to the institution — including a commitment to the educational purposes of the institution. The exceptional records achieved both in college and after graduation by the male athletes who entered in 1951 and the female athletes who entered in 1976 reflect the presence of the admissions approach we are advocating. 16

The authors rely on cause-and-effect analysis here to conclude their essay.

In sum, intercollegiate athletics has come to have too pronounced an effect on colleges and universities — and on society — to be treated with benign neglect. Failure to see where the intensification of athletics programs is taking us, and to adjust expectations, could have the unintended consequence of allowing intercollegiate athletics to become less and less relevant to the educational experiences of most students, and more and more at odds with the core missions of the institutions themselves. The objective should be to strengthen the links between athletics and educational missions — and to reinvigorate an aspect of college life so that it can be celebrated for its positive contributions, not condemned for its excesses or criticized for its conflicts with educational values. 17

Reading Closely

1. What specific information in this essay surprised you? Did any of the information alarm you?

2. What is your reaction to the following passage: "Athletes who are re-cruited . . . enjoy a very substantial statistical 'advantage' in the admis-sions process. That advantage — for both male and female athletes — is much greater than that enjoyed by other targeted groups, such as under-represented minority students and alumni children" (paragraph 5)? What is the basis for your reaction? Be prepared to share it with the rest of the class.

3. **Working with a classmate,** list all the examples and anecdotes the au-thors provide to support their assertions. Discuss your list to determine which ones do and do not work to advance the argument.

4. What is your reaction to the cartoon on page 660? What argument is it making? How does it relate to Shulman and Bowen's thesis?

Considering Larger Issues

1. "How the Playing Field Is Encroaching on the Admissions Office" ap-peared in the *Chronicle of Higher Education.* Who are the readers of that journal? Describe them.

2. What is Shulman and Bowen's purpose for this essay, particularly in terms of their *Chronicle* audience? What passages support your answer?

3. What is Shulman and Bowen's thesis? List the reasons they give to sup-port it. Why do you think they develop their argument inductively, wait-ing until their conclusion to state the thesis?

4. COMBINING METHODS. Shulman and Bowen use *cause-and-effect analysis* to ad-vance their argument in several other places besides their conclusion. Mark the passages that analyze causes and effects, and explain their ef-fect on the overall essay.

Thinking about Language

1. Use the context of the essay or your dictionary to define the following words and phrases. Be prepared to share your definitions with the rest of the class.

cajoled (1)	legacies (6)	mantra (13)
underperform (2)	arcane (8)	"spiky" (14)
winnowed (5)	obscure (8)	benign neglect (17)

2. What one word would you use to describe Shulman and Bowen's atti-tude toward their subject in this essay? What specific words and phrases express this attitude?

Writing Your Own Arguments

1. Whether or not you're a college athlete, you might be offended by Shulman and Bowen's essay. Draft a two- to three-page argument essay that defends an actual or hypothetical college admissions policy that

favors athletes. Use as much specific information and support for your thesis as possible, and refer to the guidelines for checking over an argument on page 655.

2. **Working with one or two classmates,** gather material for a short (two- to three-page) essay in response to Shulman and Bowen's. You might decide to divide up the research necessary to prove their argument wrong or to support them. Possible supporting or opposing information could include recruiting rules and violations, graduation rates of athletes in various programs, percentage of athletes given an admissions advantage in comparison to other targeted groups, and so on. You might focus on admissions at your own school or broaden your research to include the schools in your league, state, or region. You might then write individual essays or a coauthored group essay. Remember to use the guidelines for checking over an argument on page 655.

LYNDA RUSH
Assessing a Study of College Athletes

● Lynda Rush (b. 1953), a professor and chair of the Department of Economics at California State Polytechnic University, Pomona, wrote a letter to the editor of the *Chronicle of Higher Education* in response to the preceding essay, addressing head-on Shulman and Bowen's findings that athletes are favored in college admissions. Rush specializes in the economics of poverty and discrimination with an emphasis on gender issues.

Preview   What do you imagine a professor of economics might have to say about the Shulman and Bowen essay?

To the Editor:

James L. Shulman and William G. Bowen's *The Game of Life: College Sports and* 1 *Educational Values* will certainly stimulate a storm of activity in college admissions offices and high-school advising offices throughout the country. The authors attempt to make the case that student athletes are taking the place of more deserving students. Their nostalgia for the good old days of the gentleman athlete pursuing a liberal arts education in the 1950s has certainly colored their analysis. While their story may be cloaked in statistics and elaborate charts, it's an example of very sloppy social science.

The authors appear to discount the contributions and accomplish- 2 ments of student athletes. The most egregious omission is the impact on socioeconomic diversity that I suspect that athletes bring to the elite institutions included in the study. Today's student athletes may bear little resemblance to the gentlemen athletes of the fifties and the authors appear to be blind to the fact that this may be a benefit. Student athletes attending these elite institutions in the fifties were typically white, upper class, and male.

Over the last 50 years, intercollegiate athletic programs have opened 3 the doors of our elite colleges and universities to people of color, the working class, and women. The Civil Rights Movement and the passage of Title IX of the Education Amendments in 1972 broke down the barriers for minority and female athletes. Minorities were barely accepted in professional sports during the 1950's and were rarely if ever admitted to elite colleges and universities. Opportunities for women athletes to compete at the intercollegiate level did not even begin to percolate until the mid 1980's. The benefits of diversity are not easily calculated and are virtually ignored by the authors.

Shulman and Bowen include pages and pages of charts on mean 4 GPA's, SAT scores, etc., to support their hypothesis, but they generally

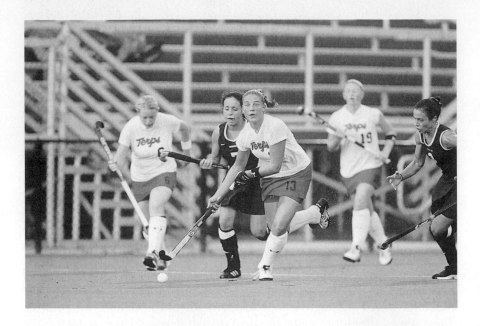

fail to include even the most basic statistical significance tests. Their conclusions are based on the mean values of the performance indictors, and they fail to discuss the distribution of the values (the standard deviations) or even basic test of significance (*t*-values). An exception to this practice is their reported finding that athletes tend to earn higher wages after college. The authors did mention that the statistical significance of these findings was marginal. Mean values are only a piece of the story, because extreme high or low values can skew the mean up or down. For example, a closer look at individual SAT scores may have shown that most athlete SAT scores were comparable to the general student population with the exception of a few very low scores.

Shulman and Bowen write disdainfully about the athlete's typical 5 major (economics or political science) and their financial success later in life. Athletes' GPAs are probably lower due to the hours allocated to athletic competition. The authors make an interesting comparison to grades of students active in other extracurricular activities. Students involved in non–athletic extracurricular activities have higher grades according to their analysis. However, the authors did not directly compare the actual time commitment of the two groups. The spillover benefits of athletic competition are less likely to be direct and are more likely to accrue over time. The study did not attempt to address these indirect benefits.

The Game of Life appears to be an exercise in elitism designed to stir up 6 controversy in the hallowed halls of some of our most prestigious institutions of higher learning. I would hope that its intended audience sees through the foggy lens of the authors. Their nostalgia for a time when student athletes with large trust funds competed on verdant lawns surrounded by walls of ivy is just that, nostalgia.

Lynda Rush
Chair
Department of Economics
Professor of Economics
California State Polytechnic University
Pomona, Calif.

Reading Closely

1. Why does Rush feel she must respond to Shulman and Bowen?
2. What is your initial response to Rush's argument? How much do you care about college admissions, particularly in terms of college athletes?
3. On what grounds does Rush criticize the findings of Shulman and Bowen? Do you think her grounds are valid? Why or why not?
4. How exactly does the photograph on page 666 enhance Rush's argument?
5. **Working with a classmate,** determine the basic issue that Shulman and Bowen and Rush set out in each of their essays. What solution does each of these essays propose? Be prepared to share your response with the rest of the class.

Considering Larger Issues

1. What is Rush's thesis? What assertions does she make to support or extend her thesis?
2. Who is her intended audience? What might she want the readers to do in terms of her argument?
3. COMBINING METHODS. Although hers is an argumentative essay, Rush uses *causal analysis* throughout. How successful is her causal analysis? Why do you think she uses it?

Thinking about Language

1. Use the context of the essay or your dictionary to define the following words and phrases. Be prepared to share your definitions with the rest of the class.

student athletes (1)	percolate (3)	allocated (5)
nostalgia (1)	hypothesis (4)	spillover (5)
gentleman athlete (1)	mean values (4)	elitism (6)
cloaked (1)	skew (4)	prestigious (6)
egregious (2)	disdainfully (5)	foggy lens (6)
socioeconomic (2)		

2. What is Rush's attitude toward her subject? What specific words, phrases, passages, and examples demonstrate her attitude?

Writing Your Own Arguments

1. If you are a sports fan, you might be interested in drafting a three- to four-page essay in which you argue for the importance of intercollegiate athletics. You might argue for the value of intercollegiate athletics to the school, the student body, the alumni, and/or the athletes themselves. (Your argument might be strengthened by factual information regarding attendance records, box-office receipts, and income from memorabilia.) You might want to consider directing your argument to an audience of readers who want to deemphasize intercollegiate athletics or abolish them altogether in order to emphasize academics. Refer to the guidelines for checking over an argument on page 655.

2. Take another side on the issue of college sports. Draft a three- to four-page essay in which you argue that intercollegiate athletics should be replaced with organized intramural sports in which all students would be required to participate or that women's sports should be given equal financial support and news coverage with men's sports. Whatever your argument, be sure to explain the advantages of your position. Refer to the guidelines for checking over an argument on page 655.

ANDREW WIBLE

Using the Athletic Department to Enhance the University

Andrew Wible (b. 1987) graduated from Penn State University in 2009 with a journalism major. During his undergraduate years, Wible was a sportswriter for the Penn State student newspaper, the *Daily Collegian*, and covered the football and men's basketball teams. His future plans include working in the fields of sports journalism or sports information.

Preview   What impact do athletics have on your campus?

When the Farmers High School of Pennsylvania first opened its doors 1
on 200 acres of donated farmland in 1859, cows outnumbered students
as campus occupants. Fast-forward a century and a half, and more than
45,000 students call Penn State, and its campus fifty times the original
size, home. And the main fuel for that rapid transformation has been the
Nittany Lion athletic department.

Penn State has become such a popular college destination that more 2
than 100,000 high school seniors submitted applications for the 2009–10
school year. Not coincidentally, the 5 percent rise in applicants just happened to come after the Nittany Lions' most successful combined football
and basketball seasons in more than a decade. But that rise in applicants
has also come with a rise in tuition and student fees. Given the current
financial downturn, Penn State has had to increase its tuition in order to
sustain its rate of growth. Meanwhile, Penn State's athletic department
generated $91.6 million in revenue last year. Critics of the programs look
at these numbers and argue that there's too much of an emphasis on
sports and that the money raised through athletics should be taken from
financially successful programs (football and basketball) and used to help
offset the costs for all students.

But those critics often forget that the athletic department is self- 3
sustaining and already gives back to the student body. From a purely
monetary perspective, the Bryce Jordan Center, home to Penn State's
women's and men's basketball teams, as well as most of the athletic offices, is actually owned by the university, which charges the athletic department rent. Then there's the millions of revenue dollars brought to
the university when more than 110,000 fans flock to campus during fall
Saturdays, turning State College into Pennsylvania's third largest city.

But Nittany Lion athletics mean much more to Penn State and the 4
student body than simply dollars and cents. There is the sense of pride
by being able to say "I'm a Penn Stater." And the famous "We Are . . .
Penn State" cheer is more than just a chant; it encompasses the feeling
that the players on the field or court aren't just playing for themselves

but for the entire student body and for everyone that has ever set foot on campus.

The money could go to help build new intramural fields or provide 5 affordable education to academically qualified students in financial need, but take away just a fraction of the athletic department's income, and nonrevenue sports will start hitting the chopping block. It's not right to force a golfer or field hockey player to give up a scholarship simply because a few members of the academic community feel it's not fair to the rest of the student body. These athletes have earned their scholarships and deserve to maintain them. If students and fans have a problem with the ever-growing world of college athletics, they will stop going to games and pouring money into the programs. But with record attendance levels, multimillion-dollar television deals, and rocketing revenue figures, it's obvious that the demand for college athletics is greater than ever.

At the same time, it's clear that the growth of athletic programs at 6 places like Penn State do not hinder students' academic performance. Penn State continues to grow academically. The university remains solidly ranked among the top fifty national universities and top fifteen public schools in the country. Penn State has even jumped spots in recent years. And those same athletes that have produced on the courts and fields to help Penn State's reputation grow nationally have also excelled in the classroom. Fifty-nine percent of Nittany Lion student athletes earned a 3.0 GPA or higher during the 2009 spring semester, with 23.7 percent earning dean's list honors. It's not as if the athletes are being exploited simply for their money-earning potential. For the 680 student athletes at Penn State, playing a sport teaches life skills such as self-discipline, teamwork, resiliency, persistence, and integrity. For example, former Penn State defensive lineman Rosey Grier used the instincts he learned while playing for the Nittany Lions to subdue attacker Sirhan Sirhan moments after the Robert Kennedy assassination.

Having the best of both the academic and athletic worlds is not only 7 possible; it is happening at Penn State and several other schools around the country. The importance of athletics to the culture and reputation of Penn State should never be downplayed. If it weren't for Nittany Lion athletics, the university would be only a shell of what it is today. There's a reason Penn State's football stadium is named after a former university president and part of the library is named after longtime football coach Joe Paterno (who coincidentally offered a sizable donation for a much-needed library expansion). Academics and athletics embrace each other, and because of this mutual appreciation, both are allowed to flourish.

There are schools where athletics dominate the campus to the point 8 where academics become an afterthought and administrators turn a blind eye to cheating in the classroom and on the recruiting trail. But that does not mean schools must automatically sacrifice graduation rates for wins. There are many colleges in America where administrators and

Penn State football coach Joe Paterno with player Kevin Cousins before the start of a game in 2006.

coaches act morally and excel on both levels. When viewed as a welcome addition to the academic landscape, athletics do nothing but enhance the entire learning environment. They teach valuable lessons to the athletes, as well as the fans, and give alumni some added accomplishments with which to identify and call their own.

When the athletic teams succeed, the university as a whole succeeds. 9 Be it through national publicity or increased donations or simply student pride, athletics are a positive extension of university life. Athletics may not have entirely made Penn State the major university it is today, but it is safe to say that without the successes of Nittany Lion athletics, there would be a lot fewer football fans and a lot more cows roaming State College.

Reading Closely

1. What is Wible's thesis in this essay? Cite textual evidence to support your claims.

2. **Working with a partner,** identify the appeals (logical, ethical, and pathetic) that Wible relies on in this essay. Pinpoint the places in the text where Wible uses these appeals, and discuss their effect on the overall argument.

3. Review the introduction and conclusion of Wible's essay. Why do you think he introduces and concludes the essay as he does?

4. Given Wible's point that part of the Penn State library is named for foot-ball coach Joe Paterno, whose large donation helped pay for the library's expansion, how does the photograph on page 671 enhance his argument?

Considering Larger Issues

1. Wible relies on one example (Penn State) to make his claims about college athletics. What are the benefits and drawbacks of relying on this one example?
2. What did you find persuasive about this essay? Why?
3. COMBINING METHODS. How does Wible use *cause-and-effect analysis* to discuss the benefits of a successful athletic program? Cite evidence from the text to support your answer.

Thinking about Language

1. How would you describe Wible's position in this debate about college athletics? What specific words or phrases describe his attitude and his ethos?
2. Wible is a Penn State alumnus. What sentences, phrases, and words reflect his relationship to the school?

Writing Your Own Arguments

1. In this essay, Wible focuses on Penn State University and the effects the athletic program has on the academic programs as well as the student body. In a three- to four-page essay, mount an argument about the ath-letic department at your school. Like Wible, you'll most likely need to do research regarding the financial connections between the athletic and aca-demic programs, the academic performance of student athletes compared to other students, the revenue generated by various sports, the ways in which sports help cultivate "school spirit," and the numbers of fans who come to athletic events. Your goal, though, is to make an argument about the role of athletics at your institution and the relationship the athletic program has to the student body and to academics. Refer to the guidelines for checking over argument on page 655 as you draft and revise.
2. In Wible's essay, he focuses on financially successful athletic programs such as basketball and football and does not discuss at length the sports that do not generate funds for the university, such as tennis, field hockey, or rowing. Compose a three- to four-page essay in which you reflect on the relevance of these sports programs to the student body and univer-sity, evaluating the role they play in college life. As you draft your essay, you might focus attention on one or two of these programs at your school by researching the programs themselves and even interviewing one of the student athletes or coaches. Refer to the guidelines for check-ing over argument on page 655 as you draft and revise.

Why Not a Football Degree?

William F. Shughart II (b. 1947) is F. A. P. Barnard Distinguished Professor of Economics and holder of the Robert M. Hearin Chair in Business Administration at the University of Mississippi. He has published numerous books, including *Modern Managerial Economics: Economic Theory for Business Decisions* (1994), *The Political Economy of the New Deal* (1998), *Economics of Budget Deficits* (2002), and *Policy Changes and Political Responses: Public Choice Perspectives on the Post-9/11 World* (with Robert D. Tollison, 2005). Given his economic expertise, it is no wonder that he sees college football from a financial perspective. "Why Not a Football Degree?" first appeared in the *Wall Street Journal* in 1990 and was updated by Shughart in 2007; it offers yet another solution to the problems generated by college athletics.

> **Preview** As you read the essay, consider the effectiveness of Shughart's use of logos — his logical reasoning.

The college football career of 2006's Heisman Trophy winner, Ohio State 1 University quarterback Troy Smith, nearly was cut short at the end of his sophomore year following allegations that he had accepted $500 from a Buckeye booster. He was barred from playing in the 2005 Alamo Bowl and the next season's opener against Miami (Ohio). Quarterback Rhett Bomar was dismissed from the University of Oklahoma's football team after it was disclosed that he had earned substantially more than justified by the number of hours worked during the summer of 2006 at a job arranged for him by a patron of OU athletics. As a result of charges that, from 1993 to 1998, Coach Clem Haskins paid to have more than 400 term papers ghost-written for 18 of his players, the postseason tournament victories credited to the University of Minnesota's basketball team were erased from the NCAA's record books and the program was placed on a four-year probation from which it has not yet recovered. In recent years, gambling and point-shaving scandals have rocked the basketball programs at Arizona State, Northwestern, and Florida; player suspensions and other penalties have been handed out for illegal betting on games by members of the Boston University, Florida State, and University of Maryland football teams.

Each of these events, which are only the latest revelations in a long 2 series of NCAA rule violations, has generated the usual hand-wringing about the apparent loss of amateurism in college sports. Nostalgia for supposedly simpler times when love of the game and not money was the driving force in intercollegiate athletics has led to all sorts of reform proposals. The NCAA's decision in the late 1980s to require its member institutions to make public athletes' graduation rates is perhaps the least controversial example. Proposition 48's mandate that freshman athletes must meet more stringent test score and grade point requirements to participate in NCAA–sanctioned contests than is demanded of entering non–student–athletes has been criticized as a naked attempt to discrimi–nate against disadvantaged (and mostly minority) high–school graduates who see college sports as a way out of poverty.

But whether or not one supports any particular reform proposal, 3 there seems to be a general consensus that something must be done. If so, why stop at half–measures? I hereby offer three suggestions for solv–ing the crisis in college athletics.

1. *Create four-year degree programs in football and basketball.* Many colleges 4 and universities grant bachelors' degrees in vocational subjects. Art, drama, and music are a few examples, but there are others. Undergradu–ates who major in these areas typically are required to spend only about one of their four years in introductory English, math, history and sci–ence courses; the remainder of their time is spent in the studio, the the–ater or the practice hall honing the creative talents they will later sell as professionals.

Although a college education is no more necessary for success in the 5 art world than it is in the world of sports, no similar option is available for students whose talents lie on the athletic field or in the gym. Ma–joring in physical education is a possibility, of course, but while PE is hardly a rigorous, demanding discipline, undergraduates pursuing a de–gree in that major normally must spend many more hours in the class–room than their counterparts who are preparing for careers on the stage. While the music major is receiving academic credit for practice sessions and recitals, the PE major is studying and taking exams in kinesiology, exercise physiology and nutrition. Why should academic credit be given for practicing the violin, but not for practicing a three–point shot?

2. *Extend the time limit on athletic scholarships by two years.* In addition to 6 practicing and playing during the regular football or basketball season, college athletes must continue to work to improve their skills and keep in shape during the off–season. For football players, these off–season ac–tivities include several weeks of organized spring practice as well as year–round exercise programs in the weight room and on the running track. Basketball players participate in summer leagues and practice with their teams during the fall. In effect, college athletes are required to work at their sports for as much as 10 months a year.

These time–consuming extracurricular activities make it extremely dif– 7 ficult for college athletes to devote more than minimal effort to the stud–ies required for maintaining their academic eligibility. They miss lectures and exams when their teams travel, and the extra tutoring they receive at athletic department expense often fails to make up the difference.

If the NCAA and its member schools are truly concerned about the 8 academic side of the college athletic experience, let them put their money where their collective mouth is. The period of an athlete's eligibility to participate in intercollegiate sports would remain at four years, but the two additional years of scholarship support could be exercised at any time during the athlete's lifetime. Athletes who use up their college eligibility and do not choose careers in professional sports would be guaranteed financial backing to remain in school and finish their undergraduate degrees. Athletes who have the talent to turn pro could complete their degrees when their playing days are over.

3. *Allow a competitive marketplace to determine the compensation of college* 9 *athletes.* Football and basketball players at the top NCAA institutions produce millions of dollars in benefits for their respective schools. Successful college athletic programs draw more fans to the football stadium and to the basketball arena. They generate revenues for the school from regular season television appearances and from invitations to participate in post-season play. There is evidence that schools attract greater financial support from public and private sources—for both their athletic and academic programs—if their teams achieve national ranking. There even is evidence that the quality of students who apply for admission to institutions of higher learning improves following a successful football or basketball season.

Despite the considerable contributions made to the wealth and welfare of his or her school, however, the compensation payable to a college athlete is limited by the NCAA to a scholarship that includes tuition, books, room and board, and a nominal expense allowance. Any payment above and beyond this amount subjects the offending athletic program to NCAA sanctions. In-kind payments to players and recruits in the form of free tickets to athletic contests, T-shirts, transportation and accommodations likewise are limited. These restrictions apply to alumni and fans as well as to the institutions themselves. The NCAA also limits the amount of money athletes can earn outside of school by curtailing the use of summer jobs as a means by which coaches and boosters can pay athletes more than authorized.

The illegal financial inducements reported to be widespread in collegiate football and basketball supply conclusive evidence that many college athletes are now underpaid. The relevant question is whether the current system of compensation ought to remain in place. Allowing it to do so will preserve the illusion of amateurism in college sports and permit coaches, athletic departments and college administrators to continue to benefit financially at the expense of the players. On the other hand, shifting to a market-based system of compensation would transfer some of the wealth created by big-time athletic programs to the individuals whose talents are key ingredients in the success of those programs.

It would also cause a sea change in the distribution of power among 12 the top NCAA institutions. Under the present NCAA rules, some of the major college athletic programs, such as Southern Cal, LSU and Florida in football, and Duke, North Carolina and Florida in basketball, have developed such strong winning traditions over the years that they can maintain their dominant positions without cheating.

These schools are able to attract superior high–school athletes sea-   13
son after season by offering packages of non–monetary benefits (well–
equipped training facilities, quality coaching staffs, talented teammates,
national exposure and so on) that increases the present value of an amateur athlete's future professional income relative to the value added by
historically weaker athletic programs. Given this factor, along with NCAA
rules that mandate uniform compensation across the board, the top institutions have a built–in competitive advantage in recruiting the best
and brightest athletes.

It follows that under the current system, the weaker programs are   14
virtually compelled to offer illegal financial inducements to players and
recruits if they wish to compete successfully with the traditional powers.
It also follows that shifting to a market–based system of compensation
would remove some of the built–in advantages now enjoyed by the top
college athletic programs. It is surely this effect, along with the reductions
in the incomes of coaches and the "fat" in athletic department budgets to
be expected once a competitive marketplace is permitted to work, that is
the cause of the objection to paying student–athletes a market–determined
wage, not the rhetoric about the repugnance of professionalism.

It is a fight over the distribution of the college sports revenue pie   15
that lies at the bottom of the debate about reforming NCAA rules. And
notwithstanding the high moral principles and concern for players usually expressed by debaters on all sides of the issue, the interests of the
athlete are in fact often the last to be considered.

Reading Closely

1. What background information does Shughart supply that explains his
   solution?
2. **Working with two classmates,** discuss the arrangement of Shughart's
   argument. What information does he include in his introduction, his
   thesis statement, his supporting argument, his attention to opposing
   views, and his conclusion? Mark the specific passages that compose each
   of those sections. Share your group's findings with the rest of the class.

Considering Larger Issues

1. What is Shughart's purpose? How does it differ from the purposes of
   each of the preceding essays, particularly in terms of his *Wall Street Journal*
   audience?
2. What is Shughart's thesis statement? What reasons does he provide to
   support or extend his thesis statement?
3. **Working with a classmate,** mark the specific passages that support
   each of Shughart's reasons. Be prepared to share your findings with the
   rest of the class.

4. Which kind of rhetorical appeal does Shughart rely on most heavily: ethos, logos, or pathos? Identify words, phrases, or passages that support your answer.

5. COMBINING METHODS. On what other rhetorical method does Shughart rely as he develops his argument? Mark the passages using that other method. Why do you suppose Shughart used it?

Thinking about Language

1. Use the context of the essay or your dictionary to define the following terms or phrases. Be prepared to share your definitions with the rest of the class.

ghostwritten (1)	respective (9)	sea change (12)
amateurism (2)	compensation (10)	mandate (13)
stringent (2)	inducements (11)	repugnance (14)
counterparts (5)	market–based	
kinesiology (5)	system (11)	

2. When Shughart mentions "half–measures" (paragraph 3), what is he referring to? How do the half-measures compare with his suggestions, which might be called "full measures"?

3. **Working with a classmate,** determine Shughart's attitude toward the subject of college sports. What specific words, phrases, or passages demonstrate his attitude? Share your group's response with the rest of the class.

Writing Your Own Arguments

1. Draft a two- to three-page essay in which you address each of Shughart's assertions. You may want to develop his argument and assertions further, or you may want to develop an argument that opposes his, perhaps point by point. In either case, you'll need to do some research about college sports on your campus, in your school's athletic league, or in your area of the country. Be sure to organize your argument so that it has an introduction, a thesis statement, supporting arguments, recognition of opposing arguments, and a conclusion. Refer to the guidelines for checking over an argument on page 655.

2. **Consider working with two or three classmates** to discuss various new degrees that colleges might offer based on student interest or experience and moneymaking potential. You may have to study college catalogues in order to see what degrees are already in place. Draft a three- to four-page essay in which you argue for one such degree. You may want to arrange your essay like Shughart's, introducing the background information necessary to help you establish your argument. Work with your group as you each draft and revise your essays, referring to the guidelines for checking over an argument on page 655.

Casebook:
The Draft and National Service

CHARLES B. RANGEL
Bring Back the Draft

● Charles B. Rangel (b. 1930) has been a Democratic member of the U.S. House of Representatives from New York since 1970, representing the Upper West Side and Harlem neighborhoods of New York City. His political career has focused on revitalizing poor neighborhoods and giving opportunities to the under-privileged. Since 2007, he has been chairman of the House Ways and Means Committee.

A combat veteran of the Korean War, Rangel was a vocal critic of President George W. Bush's decision to go to war with Iraq, and in early 2003, shortly before the war began, he introduced a bill in Congress to resume the military draft. The following essay, explaining his reasons for doing so, was published in the *New York Times* on December 31, 2002. He has advanced the idea several times since.

> **Preview**   What are your feelings about reinstating the draft?

President Bush and his administration have declared a war against terrorism 1
that may soon involve sending thousands of American troops into combat in Iraq. I voted against the Congressional resolution giving the president authority to carry out this war — an engagement that would dwarf
our military efforts to find Osama bin Laden and bring him to justice.

But as a combat veteran of the Korean conflict, I believe that if we 2
are going to send our children to war, the governing principle must be
that of shared sacrifice. Throughout much of our history, Americans have
been asked to shoulder the burden of war equally.

That's why I will ask Congress next week to consider and support 3
legislation I will introduce to resume the military draft.

Carrying out the administration's policy toward Iraq will require 4
long-term sacrifices by the American people, particularly those who have
sons and daughters in the military. Yet the Congress that voted over-
whelmingly to allow the use of force in Iraq includes only one member
who has a child in the enlisted ranks of the military — just a few more
have children who are officers.

I believe that if those calling for war knew that their children were 5
likely to be required to serve — and to be placed in harm's way — there
would be more caution and a greater willingness to work with the international community in dealing with Iraq. A renewed draft will help

bring a greater appreciation of the consequences of decisions to go
to war.

Service in our nation's armed forces is no longer a common experi- 6
ence. A disproportionate number of the poor and members of minority
groups make up the enlisted ranks of the military, while the most privileged Americans are underrepresented or absent.

We need to return to the tradition of the citizen soldier — with alter- 7
native national service required for those who cannot serve because of
physical limitations or reasons of conscience.

There is no doubt that going to war against Iraq will severely strain 8
military resources already burdened by a growing number of obligations.
There are daunting challenges facing the 1.4 million men and women in
active military service and those in our National Guard and Reserve. The
Pentagon has said that up to 250,000 troops may be mobilized for the invasion of Iraq. An additional 265,000 members of the National Guard and
Reserve, roughly as many as were called up during the Persian Gulf War
in 1991, may also be activated.

Already, we have long–term troop commitments in Europe and the 9
Pacific, with an estimated 116,000 troops in Europe, 90,000 in the Pacific
(nearly 40,000 in Japan and 38,000 in Korea) and additional troop commitments to operations in Afghanistan, Bosnia, Kosovo and elsewhere.
There are also military trainers in countries across the world, including
the Philippines, Colombia and Yemen.

We can expect the evolving global war on terrorism to drain our 10
military resources even more, stretching them to the limit.

The administration has yet to address the question of whether our 11
military is of sufficient strength and size to meet present and future commitments. Those who would lead us into war have the obligation to support an all–out mobilization of Americans for the war effort, including
mandatory national service that asks something of us all.

Reading Closely

1. What is your response to Rangel's argument? On what do you base your
   response?
2. How does Rangel establish his ethos in this essay? How does he use
   logos? pathos? Mark the passages that best establish those three appeals.

Considering Larger Issues

1. **Together with a classmate,** define Rangel's intended audience for this
   essay. What information in the essay helps you define the audience?
2. What is Rangel's purpose in writing this essay? What does he want his
   audience to do with his argument?

3. COMBINING METHODS. To develop his argument, Rangel uses *cause-and-effect analysis*. Concentrate on his analysis, and account for its effect in terms of supporting the argument, fulfilling the rhetorical appeals, and reaching the intended audience.

4. What questions did you have after reading this essay? In other words, what specifics about national service does the author leave unspoken? **Working with a classmate,** list all the places that Rangel talks about national service but doesn't mention who exactly should serve, where, and how. How might you and your classmate fill in the blanks? Be prepared to share your answers with the rest of the class.

Thinking about Language

1. **With a classmate,** use the context of the essay and a dictionary to define the following words and phrases. You'll see that some familiar words are being used in unfamiliar ways. Be prepared to share your definitions with the rest of the class.

terrorism (1)	shared sacrifice (2)	daunting (8)
engagement (1)	force (4)	mobilized (8)
dwarf (1)	disproportionate (6)	commitments (9)
governing principle (2)	citizen soldier (7)	mandatory (11)

2. What is the author's attitude toward war? What words and phrases express his attitude?

Writing Your Own Arguments

1. In a three- to four-page essay, respond to Rangel. You might argue that it's impossible, unnecessary, or unwise to reinstate the draft and develop a list of good reasons for your assertion. Or you might flesh out his argument, such as by arguing that the concept of national service needs to be broadened to include men and women of all social classes, physical abilities, religious convictions, and age. You'll need to conduct library and online research in order to supply convincing logical appeals. Be sure to refer to the guidelines for checking over an argument on page 655 as you draft and revise.

2. In an essay of three to four pages, argue for various ways that Americans should be allowed to accomplish their national service if it becomes a requirement. Such a paper will entail research on your part because you'll want to incorporate statistics, facts, experiences, and observations that support your argument. You'll also want to be sure to establish goodwill and common ground with readers, to enhance your credibility as a writer. You should assume an audience of traditional college-age young people for this essay. Refer to the guidelines for checking over an argument on page 655.

CHARLES MOSKOS AND PAUL GLASTRIS
Now Do You Believe We Need a Draft?

Charles Moskos (1934–2008) was a professor of sociology at Northwestern University. The *Wall Street Journal* once called him the country's "most influential military sociologist," a scholar who studies the military as a social structure and its relationship to the larger society. A peacetime draftee who served in the U.S. Army Combat Engineers in Vietnam, Moskos was the author of the "don't ask, don't tell" policy for gay and lesbian military personnel that was adopted in 1993. Paul Glastris is editor in chief of *Washington Monthly*, a liberal political magazine, and a senior fellow at the Western Policy Center in Washington, D.C. He was previously a correspondent and editor at *U.S. News & World Report* and a special assistant and senior speechwriter to President Bill Clinton. The following essay was originally published in the November 2001 issue of *Washington Monthly*.

Preview What specific knowledge do you have of the draft?

President Bush has said that the new war against terrorism will be "a 1 different kind of conflict." He is more right than he knows. Not only are we facing a uniquely shadowy enemy, one committed to inflicting mass civilian casualties on U.S. soil. But for the first time in our history we are entering a war of significant size and probable duration (administration officials have said it may last for "years") without drafting young men to fight the threat.

Not only are we not drafting our young men. We are not even planning 2 to draft them. Elected leaders are not even talking about the possibility of drafting them. That terrorists might poison municipal water supplies, spray anthrax from crop dusters, or suicidally infect themselves with smallpox and stroll through busy city streets is no longer considered farfetched. That we might need to draft some of our people to counter these threats — now that's considered farfetched, to the extent that it's considered at all.

America needs to wake up. We're at war. We need a draft. But be- 3 cause this is a new kind of conflict, we need a new kind of draft. A 21st century draft would be less focused on preparing men for conventional combat — which probably won't be that extensive in this war — than on the arguably more daunting task of guarding against and responding to terrorism at home and abroad. If structured right, this new draft might not be as tough to sell as you would think.

Churchill famously said that America could be counted on to do the 4 right thing, after exhausting all other possibilities. On the subject of the draft, we are rapidly reaching that point of exhaustion. A draft might be avoidable if enough Americans were volunteering to serve. But we're not. Soon after the events of September 11, newspapers reported that the phones in military recruitment offices were ringing off the hook.

Follow–up stories showed that all that clamor had brought virtually no new recruits. So far, our patriotism, though sincerely felt, has largely amounted to flag–waving and coat holding.

Perhaps we could get by without a draft if our all–volunteer military ⁵ had more than enough troops on hand. But it doesn't. The actions so far taken in Afghanistan, and the buildup to support those actions, have been relatively modest. Yet with personnel cut by a third since the end of the Cold War, the services were hard–pressed to meet ongoing missions even before September 11. There is already talk of pulling U.S. forces out of the Balkans, something the Bush administration wanted to do anyway. But it will not please our NATO allies, whose long–term support we will need in the fight against terrorism, and who will have to fill the gap with more troops of their own.

We are calling up large numbers of reservists, but because so many ⁶ of them work as police officers, firefighters, and emergency medical technicians, our municipalities are being drained of precisely the people we will need if (when) the terrorists return.

Indeed, it seems clear that we are going to need thousands more men ⁷ and women in uniform to deal with terrorist threats here at home. The president has appointed former Pennsylvania Governor Tom Ridge as his new homeland security "czar." The federal government will be taking over airport security, either providing the services directly or supervising

Young men burning their draft cards during a protest against the Vietnam War.

private firms providing it. However the restructuring shakes out, we are clearly going to need more federal armed personnel to guard dams, nuclear power plants, sports complexes, and U.S. embassies abroad; more border patrol and customs agents to keep terrorists and their weapons from entering the country; more INS agents to track down immigrants who have overstayed their visas; more coast guard personnel to inspect ships; more air marshals to ride on passenger jets; and more FBI agents to uncover terrorist cells still operating within and outside our borders.

Where are all these brave men and women going to come from? Cer- 8
tainly, America is rich enough, and the need vital enough, that we could afford to offer significant salaries to lure candidates. But even in a weak economy, there is a finite number of competent people willing to choose a career that requires wearing a uniform, performing often dull work, such as guard duty, with alertness, and being ready at any moment to risk one's life for others. A whole range of government agencies and private firms, from the U.S. Army to Brinks to local police departments, must compete for this limited labor pool. And the pool is probably not expanding.

Consider this: Between 1980 and 2000, surveys showed that the num- 9
ber of young people saying they would definitely not serve in the military rose from 40 to 64 percent. The only reason this change of attitude did not destroy military recruiting efforts is that the need for new recruits plummeted with the end of the Cold War. But the military is feeling the pinch nonetheless. The armed services have had to double starting pay to recruit half as many enlistees, and the quality of new recruits is not what it should be. The number of enlistees scoring in the top half of the armed forces qualification tests has dropped by a third since the mid-1990s. In fiscal year 2000, the Army took in some 380 recruits with felony arrest records, double the number in 1998. Desertions are also on the rise. Most telling, over one-third of those entering the military fail to complete their enlistments. Contrast this with the one in ten of draftees who did not complete his two-year obligation during the Cold War. Much better to have a soldier serve a short term honorably than to be discharged for cause.

NO PEELING POTATOES

Reinstituting the draft is the obvious way to meet the suddenly in- 10
creased manpower needs for military and homeland security. This fact would have seemed obvious to previous generations of Americans. That today we aren't even talking about a draft is a measure of the deep psychological resistance Americans have developed to anything that smacks of the state compelling anyone to do anything. Ideology plays a role here. In general, the left doesn't like the military, and the right doesn't like anything that interferes with the marketplace. When it comes to national needs, the left believes in something for nothing, the right in every man for himself.

The psychological resistance also gains comfort from arguments 11
made by the opponents of the draft and by the military hierarchy, which
also resists a return to conscription. (The military resists the draft largely
because it resists all change; it opposed ending the draft in 1973).

One argument is that today's military requires professional soldiers, 12
especially for overseas missions. Let's leave aside the fact that in World
War II, Korea, and Vietnam, most combat soldiers had only six months
of training before being sent to war. Let's also grant that because of today's high-tech weapons and complex war-fighting strategies, the actual
combat must be left to professional soldiers (though there is some reason
for skepticism here). Still, there are hundreds of thousands of vital military jobs — not peeling potatoes — that could be filled with short-term
draftees.

One example is peacekeeping. From experience with U.S. deploy- 13
ments in Bosnia and Kosovo, we know that combat troops tend to chafe
at peacekeeping duty when they are stuck on bases with nothing to do
and little opportunity to train with their weapons. But it's also clear that
military police thrive on such assignments, because they get to perform
the jobs they are trained for — patrolling neighborhoods, arresting trouble-
makers, intervening in disputes with a minimum of force. Military police
work doesn't require that many special skills. After two months of basic
and four months of special police training, new recruits are shipped off
to places like Tuzla, and they do just fine. The average tour of duty in
Bosnia or Kosovo: about six months. Short-term draftees, in other words,
could easily do these M.P. jobs, and many others besides. This would free
up more professional soldiers to fight the war on terrorism without requiring that the U.S. abandon other commitments.

Draftees would not have to be offered the relatively high wages and 14
benefits that it takes to lure voluntary recruits (an increasing number of
whom are married with families). This would leave more funds available to raise pay for the kinds of personnel that the military is having a
terribly hard time holding on to, such as computer specialists, mid-level
officers, and master sergeants. To put it baldly, we now have overpaid
recruits and underpaid sergeants. In the draft era, the pay ratio between
a master sergeant and a private was seven to one; today it is less than
three to one. Restoring something like the old balance is the best way to
upgrade retention in hard-to-fill skills and leadership positions.

All these arguments apply equally to the homeland security front. 15
There is no reason why conscripts, with professional supervision, can't
work as border guards, customs agents, anthrax inoculators, or disaster-
relief specialists. Federal law enforcement agencies and unions will deny
this with all their bureaucratic might, but it's true. It takes less than five
months to train someone to be a border guard. The FBI turns applicants
with law or accounting degrees into fully fledged agents after only four
months of training.

Other developed nations that have retained the draft typically use 16
conscripts for homeland security. In Israel, draftees serve in both the
regular military and as as lightly armed "guard police" along the Gaza
Strip. They also man the "home command," which provides security and
other services in the country's cities during emergencies, such as the Scud
missile attacks during the Gulf War. In France, which finally abandoned
its draft last year (believing that threats to its security had diminished),
conscripts worked alongside professional police in the Gendarmerie and
provided emergency airport security when terrorists set off bombs in the
Paris Metro in 1995. In Germany, most draft-age men choose to serve either in the military or in some form of civilian service, such as working
with the elderly. But about one in ten chooses to work in a state or federal police force, providing such things as border security, or they train
as volunteer firefighters and serve part-time for seven years.

One can imagine a similar three-tiered system of youth service in 17
America, with 18-month terms of duty for all citizens age 18 to 25. In this
new-style draft, conscripts would have what all Americans now demand:
choice. They could choose to serve in the military, in homeland security,
or in a civilian national service program like AmeriCorps (there's no reason women couldn't be drafted for the latter two categories). In return,
draftees would get GI Bill–style college scholarships, with higher awards
for those who accept more dangerous duty.

Americorps volunteers working at a construction site in New Orleans in the aftermath
of Hurricane Katrina.

Back in Vietnam days, opting to fulfill your draft requirement stateside 18
in, say, the National Guard, was considered a way to save your skin. That
won't be so true in the new war on terrorism. As we saw with the deaths
of firefighters in New York, homeland security duty can be dangerous.

THE SUCKER FACTOR

That brings up the second argument against the draft: that the sons 19
of the elite will find ways to avoid service. Of course, that's even truer
in an age of all–volunteer forces. But it's fair to ask: How can a draft be
made equitable?

The best way would be to require all young people to serve. One 20
reason more young people don't serve now is the fear that while they're
wearing the uniform, their peers will be out having fun and getting a leg
up in their careers. If everyone were required to serve, no one would feel
like a sucker. They might even enjoy the experience; surveys show that
most former draftees look back on their time in the service with fondness
and pride.

It's possible, however, that the country won't have the need for every 21
eligible young person to serve. What then? One answer is a lottery with
no student deferments. (Under Selective Service rules established after
Vietnam, college deferments are no longer allowed.)

Part of what makes Americans dubious of conscription is our mem– 22
ory of how the class–biased draft of the Vietnam War era helped drive
America apart. We tend to forget that the more equitable draft that existed during World War II and for 20 years afterwards helped bring the
country together. During the peaceful years of the 1950s — a time not unlike our own, when the threat of mass destruction hung in the air — most
Ivy League men had to spend two years in uniform, before or after college, working and bunking with others of very different backgrounds
and races (the military, remember, was about the only racially integrated
institution at the time).

This shared experience helped instill in those who served, as in the 23
national culture generally, a sense of unity and moral seriousness that we
would not see again — until after September 11, 2001. It's a shame that it
has taken terrorist attacks to awaken us to the reality of our shared national
fate. We should use this moment to rebuild institutions like the draft that
will keep us awake to this reality even as the memory of the attacks fades.

A 21st century draft might be more welcome than most of us real– 24
ize, especially among young people whose lives will be affected by it.
While national leaders and pundits have avoided the subject, a potential
return of the draft has been a hot topic of conversation among young
people since September 11. "If it's something they want us to do for our
country to keep us safe, then go for it," Ryan Aaron, a senior at U.S. Grant
High School in Oklahoma City, told *National Journal*. Another young man,

Julian Medina, a day laborer cleaning up office buildings near the still-smoldering World Trade Center, told the *Washington Post:* "If I have to, I'd fight to catch the man who did this." Not all young people are so gung ho; many, in fact, hate the idea. But at least they're talking about it. If their views can move from news pages to the editorial pages, and ultimately to the floors of Congress, then we could be on our way to a more secure and more unified America.

Reading Closely

1. What did you learn about the armed forces that you didn't know before reading this essay? Write out three things you've learned and one thing you'd like to know more about.
2. Map out the overall organization of the argument in terms of the introduction, the thesis statement, the supporting arguments, recognition of the opposition, and the conclusion. Which passages make up each of these organizational parts? Prepare to share your response with the rest of the class.

Considering Larger Issues

1. What is the thesis for this essay? Is it explicitly stated or only implied? What reasons do the authors give to support their thesis? What specific evidence do they provide to support each of their reasons? (You may find yourself drawing on your responses to question 2 under Reading Closely.)
2. Who is the audience for this essay? What words, passages, or examples help you establish the audience? How does knowing that this essay first appeared in *Washington Monthly* affect your answer?
3. Which passages and examples fulfill the rhetorical appeals of ethos, pathos, and logos?
4. COMBINING METHODS. The authors rely on *cause-and-effect analysis* to build their assertion that we need to reinstate the draft. Mark the passages that analyze causes and those that analyze effects, and explain why the authors chose to use them.
5. What specific information did you learn from the photographs and captions on pages 682 and 685 that enhanced or complicated the information in the essay?

Thinking about Language

1. **With a classmate,** use the context of the essay or your dictionary to define the following terms. Be prepared to share your definitions with the rest of the class.

uniquely (1)	cells (7)	chafe (13)
casualties (1)	lure (8)	intervening (13)
municipal (2)	finite (8)	baldly (14)
crop dusters (2)	pinch (9)	conscripts (15)
daunting (3)	enlistees (9)	inoculators (15)
clamor (4)	reinstituting (10)	GI Bill (17)
recruits (4)	ideology (10)	leg up (20)
hard–pressed (5)	conscription (11)	class–biased (22)
reservists (6)	skepticism (12)	bunking (22)

2. **With a classmate or two,** write a short paragraph that summarizes all the ways the authors support the opening sentence: "The new war against terrorism will be 'a different kind of conflict.'" What words, phrases, and passages in the essay illustrate this assertion? Share your paragraph with the rest of the class. Now condense your paragraph into a single sentence. Be prepared to share your group's sentence with the rest of the class. Also be prepared to discuss the language you marked that illustrates the assertion.

Writing Your Own Arguments

1. How can a U.S. college student connect with the idea of "a different kind of conflict"? How might this essay be an inspiration to you — or just the opposite? **With one or two classmates,** discuss possible responses to these questions. Then draft a three- to four–page essay in which you argue either for or against the importance of reinstating the draft for reasons of national security. Pay careful attention to the organization of your argument as well as to your use of the rhetorical appeals. Work with the guidelines for checking over an argument on page 655 as you and your classmates plan, draft, revise, and respond to each other's drafts.

2. The authors suggest a three–tiered system of national service, one limited to citizens 18 to 25 years old. Evaluate this suggestion by considering the following issues: whether short–term training could be enough to teach any job well (or make any job interesting), whether the choice among the three tiers would be fair to those in each tier, and whether you or anyone you know aged 18 to 25 would be interested in any of these tiers and why. In order to make a fair comparison, you'll want to conduct research into the current programs of voluntary U.S. national service, such as AmeriCorps and Teach for America. In addition, you'll want to research the experiences and actions (both positive and negative) of military personnel stationed in the Middle East, the Balkans, and elsewhere, as well as in the United States. (Consider, for example, whether a draft would have had any effect on the treatment of prisoners in the Iraq War.) You may also want to research compulsory national service programs in other countries, including those mentioned by the authors. Write a three- to four–page essay in which you evaluate Moskos and Glastris's recommendations. Refer to the guidelines for checking over an argument on page 655 as you draft and revise.

WALL STREET JOURNAL
Uncle Charlie Wants You!

Begun in 1889, the *Wall Street Journal* now has a circulation of two million print copies daily. Although it focuses primarily on news and opinion about business and financial issues, it does address other fields. The *Journal* published the following piece in its online Opinion Journal section in November 2006. The anonymous writer takes on the renewed argument offered by Congressman Charles Rangel to reinstitute the draft and argues instead that enlistment in the military should remain voluntary.

> **Preview** Who, in your mind, enlists in the military? What leads you to make this assessment?

Harlem Congressman Charles Rangel created a stir once again this week with his call for renewing the military draft. His own party leaders quickly disavowed any such plan, suggesting just how unpopular the idea is among most Americans. Yet the proposal deserves some further inspection before it vanishes, if only to expose its false assumptions about the current U.S. military.

A vocal Iraq war critic, Mr. Rangel told CBS News recently, "There's no question in my mind that this President and this Administration would never have invaded Iraq, especially on the flimsy evidence that was presented to the Congress, if indeed we had a draft and members of Congress and the Administration thought that their kids from their communities would be placed in harm's way."

In other words, Mr. Rangel's real argument is about class in America, not over the best way to fight Islamic terrorism overseas. He's suggesting that somehow only the poor serve in Uncle Sam's Army. But his views are both out of date and condescending to those who do serve. Alas, they are shared by many on the political left, who think that the military places an unfair burden on the working class.

In this mythology, the military is overly reliant on uneducated dupes from poor communities because those from more affluent backgrounds don't want to serve. But the truth is closer to the opposite, according to a recent Heritage Foundation report on the demographic characteristics of the military. It's titled "Who Are the Recruits?" and Mr. Rangel, a Korean War veteran, might want to read it before implying that the military doesn't look like America.

According to the report, which analyzed the most recent Pentagon enlistee data, "the only group that is lowering its participation in the military is the poor. The percentage of recruits from the poorest American neighborhoods (with one-fifth of the U.S. population) declined from 18 percent in 1999 to 14.6 percent in 2003, 14.1 percent in 2004, and

13.7 percent in 2005." Put another way, if military burdens aren't spread more evenly among socioeconomic groups in the U.S., it's because *the poor* are underrepresented.

Or consider education levels. In the general U.S. population, the high 6 school graduation rate is a little under 80%. But among military recruits from 2003–2005, nearly 97% had high school diplomas. The academic quality of recruits has also been rising this decade. According to Heritage, the military defines a "high quality" recruit as someone who scores above the 50th percentile on the Armed Forces Qualifying Test and has a high school degree. The percentage of high quality recruits had climbed to 67% in 2004 and 64% in 2005, up from 57% in 2001.

And what about race? In 2004, about 76% of the U.S. population was 7 white, which was only slightly above the 73% of military recruits (and 72% of Army recruits) who were white. Blacks made up 12.17% of the population in 2004, and made up 14.54% of recruits in 2004 and 13% in 2005. Hispanic Americans are also slightly overrepresented in the military compared to their share of the population, but also not to a degree that suggests some worrisome cultural chasm among the races.

The overall truth is that today's recruits come primarily from the 8 middle class, and, more importantly, they come willingly. This makes them more amenable to training and more likely to adapt to the rigors of military culture. An Army of draftees would so expand the number of recruits that training resources would inevitably be stretched and standards watered down. Meanwhile, scarce resources would be devoted to tens of thousands of temporary soldiers who planned to leave as soon as their year or two of forced service was up.

It's true that such training would help to shape up more young 9 Americans who could use a few weeks of Marine discipline at Parris Island, and if this is what Mr. Rangel has in mind he should say so. But the price would be a less effective fighting force, and precisely at a time when experience and technological mastery are more important than ever in a fighting force.

"The military doesn't want a draft," says Tim Kane, an Air Force vet- 10 eran and author of the Heritage study. "What the military wants is the most effective fighting force they can field. They want to win wars and minimize casualties. And you don't do that when you're forced to take less–educated, unmotivated people."

What about Mr. Rangel's point that conscription would have made 11 intervention in Iraq less likely? It's impossible to know, but this is a dangerous argument for the future in any case. The main reason for having an effective Army is to deter enemies by making them believe we have the will to fight if we must. Mr. Rangel is saying the U.S. needs a conscript Army precisely to show an adversary we'll never use it. This is a good way to tempt Iran, say, into provocations that could lead to larger conflicts in which we would have no choice but to fight.

Reading Closely

1. What argument is the writer making about the draft in this essay? How do you know? Identify places in the essay that support your answer.

2. What is Congressman Rangel's argument about the draft? Why would he make this argument?

3. What research does the writer conduct to compose this essay? Does this research help support the argument? Explain your answer.

4. Analyze the arrangement of the essay. What is the writer's organizational strategy? How does this arrangement support or detract from the overall argument of the essay?

Considering Larger Issues

1. What is your response to the writer's argument?

2. **Working with a classmate,** identify the appeals (ethical, logical, or pathetic) the writer relies on to make the argument. Cite evidence from the essay that supports your claim.

3. COMBINING METHODS. How does the writer use *exemplification* and *cause-and-effect analysis* in this essay? How do these rhetorical methods support or detract from the writer's argument?

Thinking about Language

1. Use the context of the essay or a dictionary to define the following terms. Be prepared to share your definitions with the rest of the class.

disavowed (1)	affluent (4)	amenable (8)
mythology (4)	demographic (4)	conscription (11)
dupes (4)	chasm (7)	provocations (11)

2. Review the transitions the writer uses to move readers from paragraph to paragraph. What kinds of transitions are they? Do you find them effective? Why or why not?

Writing Your Own Arguments

1. This essay does not elaborate on the benefits of a voluntary military force because the writer dedicates most of the essay to opposing Rangel's argument for a draft. For a three- to four-page essay, do research to identify and then evaluate the arguments for keeping enlistment in the military voluntary. Then create your own argument about whether or not you think these claims in favor of a voluntary military are valid. As you compose your essay, be sure to refer to the guidelines for checking over an argument on page 655.

2. Now that you've read three essays on the draft—Rangel's, Moskos and Glastris's, and the *Wall Street Journal's*, reflect on which arguments about

this topic you find most persuasive. Consider, too, arguments missing from all three essays. Compose a three- to four-page essay in which you add your voice to this debate, making your argument about the draft and national service. Remember, you don't necessarily have to side with one of the essays you've read; you can offer a different perspective on the debate or a new argument that none of the writers addressed. So that you are well informed on the issue, conduct additional research, especially as you explore your position. Be sure to refer to the guidelines for checking over an argument on page 655 as you draft and revise.

MAGGIE KOERTH

Women in the Draft: A Necessary Part of the Quest to End Discrimination

Maggie Koerth (b. 1981) wrote the following essay when she was a senior at the University of Kansas, majoring in journalism and anthropology. It was originally published in the *University Daily Kansan*, the student newspaper of the University of Kansas, in February 2003.

Preview What's your opinion on women in the draft? Do you think it's necessary for ending gender discrimination?

Women, what are you willing to do to gain gender equality? Stage a pro- 1 test? Lobby your congressman? How about go to war?

Chances are, most women on this campus would tell you they are 2 in favor of gender equality. We want all the beneficial effects that true equality will bring. Unfortunately, while we have been busy fighting for equal education and job opportunities, we have forgotten that true equality does not always equal fun.

On Jan. 7, U.S. Representative Charles Rangel proposed that the draft 3 be reinstated if our country goes to war with Iraq. When he did not propose that women be included in the draft, the most common reaction I heard from my peers was a sigh of relief.

In a way, this is understandable. Few people desperately want to 4 risk death on a battlefield, and the draft itself is not a popular institution. However, the draft is also one of the most glaring examples of state-sanctioned sexual discrimination in our country.

Every argument made by the Selective Service (www.sss.gov/wmbkgr 5 .htm) and by the Supreme Court (*Rostker* v. *Goldberg*, 453 U.S. 57) against the inclusion of women in the draft is based on the assumptions that women do not belong on the battlefield and that the military has no use for anyone who is not on the front lines. Both are untrue.

The Israeli armed forces have drafted both men and women since 6 1948 without any detriment to their ability to fight and win. For decades, those women aided their country by serving in technology, intelligence and other behind-the-scenes positions crucial to the military effort. Their work allowed more men to be moved to frontline positions.

According to the Israeli Defense Forces Web site, wwrw.idf.il/english/ 7 organization/chen/chen.stm, drafted women have been serving as para-military border police in combat positions since 1995. This is the equivalent of serving on the front lines.

Are Israeli women really that much more useful and capable than 8 American women? I doubt it.

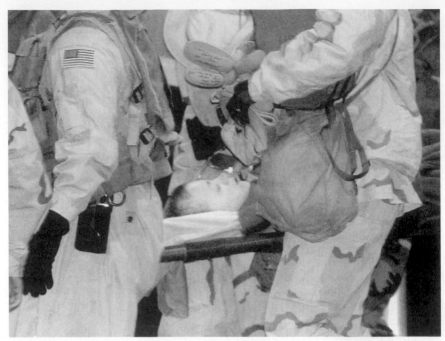

Jessica Lynch and Shoshana Johnson became symbols of the role of women soldiers in the Iraq War. Both were wounded and captured in the early weeks of combat before being rescued by U.S. troops; in the photo above, Lynch is carried off a military plane on a stretcher. Seven months later (in the photo below), she and Johnson were honored at *Glamour* magazine's Women of the Year awards ceremony.

So why have so many women ignored this issue? Why are there 9
not daily protests on Wescoe Beach demanding the military respect the
equality of the sexes?

It can't be because it's a hard point to argue.   10

Even those people who will never be convinced that women can 11
fight in a war must see how useful women can be to the support services
of the military, especially now that the military is so understaffed.

I am not asking women to believe the draft is a good thing. I am not 12
asking them to want to fight and die.

What I am telling women is that we cannot pick and choose what 13
equalities we want.

This is not a new problem. Gloria Steinem addressed the same issues 14
in 1970 in a *Washington Post* article called "Women's Liberation Aims to
Free Men Too."

To her, accepting all parts of equality would ultimately help both 15
sexes by equally distributing the pressure of traditionally sex–related
roles like military service.

"We want to liberate men from those inhuman roles as well," she 16
wrote. "We want to share the work and responsibility, and to have men
share equal responsibility for the children."

If we accept the discrimination of the draft, we accept the chauvinis- 17
tic images of an unreliable, delicate womanhood and a macho, war-
loving manhood. No amount of protesting for more "fun" rights will
erase that acceptance.

So ladies, stand up and fight for all your rights, even the unpopular 18
ones. Like the Selective Service ad says, "You can handle this."

Reading Closely

1. How does Koerth define "gender equality"?
2. How does she link gender equality with the draft?
3. What are three things you understand in her argument? What's one
   thing you want to know more about? Be prepared to share your question with the rest of the class.

Considering Larger Issues

1. Who is Koerth's audience for this essay? What does she want the audience to do?
2. **Working with a classmate,** identify the passages in which Koerth uses
   ethos, pathos, and logos. Be prepared to discuss the effectiveness of each
   of these passages with the rest of the class.

3. In making her logical appeals, Koerth refers to other sources of information. What are some of these sources? Explore them in order to evaluate their validity and relevance to her argument. Be prepared to share your answers with the rest of the class.

4. COMBINING METHODS. How does Koerth use *cause-and-effect analysis* to help shape her argument?

5. Which rhetorical methods other than argument do the photographs on page 694 feature? to what effect?

Thinking about Language

1. Use your dictionary or the context of the essay to define the following terms. Be prepared to share your definitions with the rest of the class.

gender equality (1)	discrimination (4)	support services
lobby (1)	detriment (6)	(11)
reinstated (3)	paramilitary (7)	chauvinistic (17)
state–sanctioned (4)		

2. Mark all the words and phrases that Koerth uses to emphasize the concept of "equality." What is the overall effect of her word choices? Could they have been more subtle? more explicit?

Writing Your Own Arguments

1. In a two- to three–page response to Koerth, engage each of her assertions. You'll need to consult the citations she mentions (the Web sites, court cases, and articles) in order to understand the supporting materials to which she refers. Your response could be the basis for a longer argument paper. Refer to the guidelines for checking over an argument on page 655.

2. If the United States required military or civilian national service of all 18– to 25–year–olds, what would you choose to do? Write a three– to four–page essay in which you argue for your personal plan and the reasons for it. You may find that you'll have to conduct Web–based or library research in order to come up with a plan, although the essays in this section may help you get started. If you are older than 25, write your essay in the form of advice to a specific younger person you know. Refer to the guidelines for checking over an argument on page 655.

THOMAS JEFFERSON
The Declaration of Independence

● Thomas Jefferson (1743–1826) started his career as a lawyer and served as governor of Virginia, a diplomat to France, and vice president to John Adams before becoming the third president of the United States in 1801. A "Renaissance man" who was, among other talents, a speaker of several languages, a musician, an inventor, a farmer, an architect, and the founder of the University of Virginia, Jefferson is perhaps most famous for crafting one of the most influential political documents of all time: the Declaration of Independence.

> **Preview**   Can you recite any of the Declaration of Independence by heart? Even if you cannot, what do you remember about it?

When in the course of human events, it becomes necessary for one people 1 to dissolve the political bonds which have connected them with another, and to assume among the powers of the earth, the separate and equal station to which the Laws of Nature and of Nature's God entitle them, a decent respect to the opinions of mankind requires that they should declare the causes which impel them to the separation.

We hold these truths to be self-evident, that all men are created 2 equal, that they are endowed by their Creator with certain unalienable rights, that among these are life, liberty and the pursuit of happiness. That to secure these rights, governments are instituted among men, deriving their just powers from the consent of the governed. That whenever any form of government becomes destructive to these ends, it is the right of the people to alter or to abolish it, and to institute new government, laying its foundation on such principles and organizing its powers in such form, as to them shall seem most likely to effect their safety and happiness. Prudence, indeed, will dictate that governments long established should not be changed for light and transient causes; and accordingly all experience hath shown, that mankind are more disposed to suffer, while evils are sufferable, than to right themselves by abolishing the forms to which they are accustomed. But when a long rain of abuses and usurpations, pursuing invariably the same object, evinces a design to reduce them under absolute despotism, it is their right, it is their duty, to throw off such government, and to provide new guards for their future security. Such has been the patient sufferance of these Colonies; and such is now the necessity which constrains them to alter their former systems of government. This history of the present king of Great Britain is a history of repeated injuries and usurpations, all having in direct object the establishment of an absolute tyranny over these States. To prove this, let facts be submitted to a candid world.

He has refused his assent to laws, the most wholesome and necessary 3
for the public good.

He has forbidden his Governors to pass laws of immediate and press- 4
ing importance, unless suspended in their operation till his assent should
be obtained; and when so suspended, he has utterly neglected to attend
to them.

He has refused to pass other laws for the accommodation of large 5
districts of people, unless those people would relinquish the right of representation in the legislature, a right inestimable to them and formidable
to tyrants only.

He has called together legislative bodies at places unusual, un- 6
comfortable, and distant from the depository of their public records, for
the sole purpose of fatiguing them into compliance with his measure.

He has dissolved representative houses repeatedly, for opposing with 7
manly firmness his invasions on the rights of people.

He has refused for a long time, after such dissolutions, to cause oth- 8
ers to be elected; whereby the legislative powers, incapable of annihila-
tion, have returned to the people at large for their exercise; the State
remaining in the meantime exposed to all the dangers of invasion from
without and convulsions within.

He has endeavoured to prevent the population of these states; for 9
that purpose obstructing the laws for naturalization of foreigners; refusing to pass others to encourage their migration hither, and raising the
conditions of new appropriations of lands.

He has obstructed the administration of justice, by refusing his as- 10
sent to laws for establishing judiciary powers.

He has made judges dependent on his will alone, for the tenure of 11
their offices, and the amount and payment of their salaries.

He has erected a multitude of new offices, and sent hither swarms of 12
officers to harass our people, and eat out their substance.

He has kept among us, in times of peace, standing armies without 13
the consent of our legislatures.

He has affected to render the military independent of and superior to 14
the civil power.

He has combined with others to subject us to a jurisdiction foreign 15
to our constitution, and unacknowledged by our laws; giving his assent
to their acts of pretended legislation:

For quartering large bodies of troops among us: 16

For protecting them, by a mock trial, from punishment for any mur- 17
ders which they should commit on the inhabitants of these States:

For cutting off our trade with all parts of the world: 18

For imposing taxes on us without our consent: 19

For depriving us in many cases of the benefits of trial by jury: 20

For transporting us beyond seas to be tried for pretended offences: 21

For abolishing the free system of English laws in a neighbouring 22 Province, establishing therein an arbitrary government, and enlarging its boundaries so as to render it at once an example and fit instrument for introducing the same absolute rule into these Colonies:

For taking away our Charters, abolishing our most valuable laws, and 23 altering fundamentally the forms of our governments:

For suspending our own legislatures, and declaring themselves in- 24 vested with power to legislate for us in all cases whatsoever.

He has abdicated government here, by declaring us out of his pro- 25 tection and waging war against us.

He has plundered our seas, ravaged our coasts, burnt our towns, and 26 destroyed the lives of our people.

He is at this time transporting large armies of foreign mercenaries to 27 complete the works of death, desolation and tyranny, already begun with circumstances of cruelty and perfidy scarcely paralleled in the most barbarous ages, and totally unworthy the head of a civilized nation.

He has constrained our fellow citizens taken captive on the high seas 28 to bear arms against their country, to become the executioners of their friends and brethren, or to fall themselves by their hands.

He has excited domestic insurrections amongst us, and has endeav- 29 oured to bring on the inhabitants of our frontiers, the merciless Indian savages, whose known rule of warfare, is an undistinguished destruction of all ages, sexes, and conditions.

In every stage of these oppressions we have petitioned for redress in 30 the most humble terms: our repeated petitions have been answered only by repeated injury. A prince whose character is thus marked by every act which may define a tyrant is unfit to be the ruler of a free people.

Nor have we been wanting in attention to our British brethren. We 31 have warned them from time to time of attempts by their legislature to extend an unwarrantable jurisdiction over us. We have reminded them of the circumstances of our emigration and settlement here. We have appealed to their native justice and magnanimity, and we have conjured them by the ties of our common kindred to disavow these usurpations, which would inevitably interrupt our connections and correspondence. They too have been deaf to the voice of justice and of consanguinity. We must, therefore, acquiesce in the necessity, which denounces our separation, and hold them, as we hold the rest of mankind, enemies in war, in peace friends.

We, therefore, the Representatives of the United States of America, in 32 General Congress assembled, appealing to the Supreme Judge of the world for the rectitude of our intentions, do, in the name, and by authority of the good people of these Colonies, solemnly publish and declare, That these United Colonies are, and of right ought to be, Free and Independent States; that they are absolved from all allegiance to the British Crown, and that all political connection between them and the state of Great Britain, is and ought to be totally dissolved; and that as Free and Independent States, they have full power to levy war, conclude peace, contract alliances, establish commerce, and to do all other acts and things which Independent States may of right do. And for the support of this declaration, with a firm reliance on the protection of Divine Providence, we mutually pledge to each other our lives, our fortunes, and our sacred honor.

Reading Closely

1. What truths are self-evident, according to this document?
2. List ten of the reasons Jefferson gives for declaring independence from Great Britain.
3. What reasons does Jefferson supply for declaring independence rather than working toward a more productive relationship with the British?
4. What did you learn about Britain's colonial rule during this period that you didn't know before?

Considering Larger Issues

1. Overall, what do you think is the purpose of Jefferson's argument: to express or defend his ideas, to question an idea, or to invite or convince his readers to change their point of view? What audience does he have in mind, and what does he want his readers to do with his argument? How successfully does the declaration fulfill its purpose? What specific passages help support your answers?
2. What is Jefferson's thesis? Where is it located in the declaration? Why do you think he placed it where he did?
3. **Together with a classmate or two,** determine the ways Jefferson establishes his ethos (goodwill, good sense, good character) in the introduction. What specific logical (or reasonable) support does Jefferson offer in the body of his argument? Is it all reasonable? Is his argument arranged deductively or inductively? How does he use emotion to connect with his readers in the conclusion? Write out your answers, and prepare to share them with the rest of the class.
4. COMBINING METHODS. To fulfill the purpose of his argument, Jefferson relies on *cause-and-effect analysis.* Outline the progression of his analysis. What information does he include for its logical appeal? its emotional appeal? What kinds of information might he be omitting?

Thinking about Language

1. Use the context of the declaration or a dictionary to define the following terms or phrases. Be prepared to share your definitions with the rest of the class.

impel (1)	sufferance (2)	appropriations (9)
self-evident (2)	candid (2)	swarms (12)
unalienable (2)	assent (3)	mercenaries (27)
deriving (2)	relinquish (5)	redress (30)
prudence (2)	inestimable (5)	unwarrantable (31)
transient (2)	formidable (5)	magnanimity (31)
disposed (2)	annihilation (8)	conjured (31)
usurpations (2)	endeavoured (9)	disavow (31)
evinces (2)	obstructing (9)	consanguinity (31)
despotism (2)	hither (9)	

2. Select one of the longer paragraphs (or a series of short paragraphs) and rewrite it, using more contemporary language. If your class can divide up the entire declaration, then you can all combine your translations, providing a paragraph–by–paragraph Declaration of Independence for the twenty–first century.

Writing Your Own Arguments

1. Draft a three– to four–page essay in which you declare your independence from something (school, job, drugs, junk food, e-mail) or someone (parents, family, partner, friend). Use either the original declaration or your class's update of the declaration as your model. Be sure to employ the rhetorical appeals, spending a good deal of time working on the logical appeals of your declaration. Argue for the reasons that you should be independent and that the thing or person should agree with your decision. Your challenge will be in determining your audience as well as in establishing goodwill and common ground in your introduction. Be sure to refer to the guidelines for checking over an argument on page 655.

2. Consider a grievance that you (or you and your friends) have. Write a two– to three–page essay in which you state your grievance and then argue for the way it should be resolved. Be sure to articulate your audience and purpose as you develop the ethos, pathos, and logos of your essay. Refer to the guidelines for checking over an argument on page 655 as you draft and revise.

ELIZABETH CADY STANTON

The Declaration of Sentiments

● Although the principal author of the following document is Elizabeth Cady
Stanton (1815–1902), the Declaration of Sentiments was a collaborative effort,
written by those who attended the First Women's Rights Convention in Seneca
Falls, New York. Held in July 1848, the convention brought women and men
from around the country together to discuss women's right to vote and their
equal treatment under the law. Throughout the convention, Stanton and
Lucretia Mott read the declaration, and participants suggested revisions and
additions. Of the 300 people who attended the convention, 100 signed the
Declaration (68 women and 32 men); among the signers were Stanton, Mott,
and Frederick Douglass, the prominent abolitionist.

> **Preview**   What do you already know about the women's suffrage move-
> ment in the nineteenth century?

When, in the course of human events, it becomes necessary for one por- 1
tion of the family of man to assume among the people of the earth a
position different from that which they have hitherto occupied, but one
to which the laws of nature and of nature's God entitle them, a decent
respect to the opinions of mankind requires that they should declare the
causes that impel them to such a course.

We hold these truths to be self-evident: that all men and women 2
are created equal; that they are endowed by their Creator with certain
inalienable rights; that among these are life, liberty, and the pursuit of
happiness; that to secure these rights governments are instituted, deriving their just powers from the consent of the governed. Whenever any
form of government becomes destructive of these ends, it is the right of
those who suffer from it to refuse allegiance to it, and to insist upon the
institution of a new government, laying its foundation on such principles,
and organizing its powers in such form, as to them shall seem most likely
to effect their safety and happiness.

Prudence, indeed, will dictate that governments long established 3
should not be changed for light and transient causes; and, accordingly,
all experience has shown that mankind are more disposed to suffer, while
evils are sufferable, than to right themselves by abolishing the forms to
which they were accustomed. But when a long train of abuses and usurpations, pursuing invariably the same object, evinces a design to reduce
them under absolute despotism, it is their duty to throw off such government and to provide new guards for their future security. Such has been
the patient sufferance of the women under this government, and such is
now the necessity which constrains them to demand the equal station to
which they are entitled.

The history of mankind is a history of repeated injuries and usur- 4
pations on the part of man toward woman, having in direct object the
establishment of an absolute tyranny over her. To prove this, let facts be
submitted to a candid world.

He has never permitted her to exercise her inalienable right to the 5
elective franchise.

He has compelled her to submit to law in the formation of which she 6
had no voice.

He has withheld from her rights which are given to the most igno- 7
rant and degraded men, both natives and foreigners.

Having deprived her of this first right as a citizen, the elective fran- 8
chise, thereby leaving her without representation in the halls of legislation, he has oppressed her on all sides.

He has made her, if married, in the eye of the law, civilly dead. 9

He has taken from her all right in property, even to the wages she 10
earns.

He has made her morally, an irresponsible being, as she can commit 11
many crimes with impunity, provided they be done in the presence of
her husband. In the covenant of marriage, she is compelled to promise
obedience to her husband, he becoming, to all intents and purposes, her
master—the law giving him power to deprive her of her liberty and to
administer chastisement.

He has so framed the laws of divorce, as to what shall be the proper 12
causes and, in case of separation, to whom the guardianship of the children shall be given, as to be wholly regardless of the happiness of the
women — the law, in all cases, going upon a false supposition of the supremacy of man and giving all power into his hands.

After depriving her of all rights as a married woman, if single and 13
the owner of property, he has taxed her to support a government which
recognizes her only when her property can be made profitable to it.

He has monopolized nearly all the profitable employments, and from 14
those she is permitted to follow, she receives but a scanty remuneration.
He closes against her all the avenues to wealth and distinction which he
considers most honorable to himself. As a teacher of theology, medicine,
or law, she is not known.

He has denied her the facilities for obtaining a thorough education, 15
all colleges being closed against her.

He allows her in church, as well as state, but a subordinate position, 16
claiming apostolic authority for her exclusion from the ministry, and, with
some exceptions, from any public participation in the affairs of the church.

He has created a false public sentiment by giving to the world a dif- 17
ferent code of morals for men and women, by which moral delinquencies
which exclude women from society are not only tolerated but deemed of
little account in man.

He has usurped the prerogative of Jehovah himself, claiming it as his 18 right to assign for her a sphere of action, when that belongs to her conscience and to her God.

He has endeavored, in every way that he could, to destroy her confidence in her own powers, to lessen her self-respect, and to make her willing to lead a dependent and abject life. 19

Now, in view of this entire disfranchisement of one-half the people 20 of this country, their social and religious degradation, in view of the unjust laws above mentioned, and because women do feel themselves aggrieved, oppressed, and fraudulently deprived of their most sacred rights, we insist that they have immediate admission to all the rights and privileges which belong to them as citizens of the United States.

In entering upon the great work before us, we anticipate no small 21 amount of misconception, misrepresentation, and ridicule; but we shall use every instrumentality within our power to effect our object. We shall employ agents, circulate tracts, petition the state and national legislatures, and endeavor to enlist the pulpit and the press in our behalf. We hope this Convention will be followed by a series of conventions embracing every part of the country.

RESOLUTIONS

Whereas, the great precept of nature is conceded to be that "man shall 22 pursue his own true and substantial happiness." Blackstone in his Commentaries remarks that this law of nature, being coeval with mankind and dictated by God himself, is, of course, superior in obligation to any other. It is binding over all the globe, in all countries and at all times; no human laws are of any validity if contrary to this, and such of them as are valid derive all their force, and all their validity, and all their authority, mediately and immediately, from this original; therefore,

Resolved, That such laws as conflict, in any way, with the true and 23 substantial happiness of woman, are contrary to the great precept of nature and of no validity, for this is "superior in obligation to any other."

Resolved, that all laws which prevent woman from occupying such a 24 station in society as her conscience shall dictate, or which place her in a position inferior to that of man, are contrary to the great precept of nature and therefore of no force or authority.

Resolved, that woman is man's equal, was intended to be so by the 25 Creator, and the highest good of the race demands that she should be recognized as such.

Resolved, that the women of this country ought to be enlightened in 26 regard to the laws under which they live, that they may no longer publish their degradation by declaring themselves satisfied with their present position, nor their ignorance, by asserting that they have all the rights they want.

Resolved, that inasmuch as man, while claiming for himself intel-   27
lectual superiority, does accord to woman moral superiority, it is preeminently his duty to encourage her to speak and teach, as she has an
opportunity, in all religious assemblies.

Resolved, that the same amount of virtue, delicacy, and refinement of   28
behavior that is required of woman in the social state also be required of
man, and the same transgressions should be visited with equal severity
on both man and woman.

Resolved, that the objection of indelicacy and impropriety, which is   29
so often brought against woman when she addresses a public audience,
comes with a very ill grace from those who encourage, by their attendance,
her appearance on the stage, in the concert, or in feats of the circus.

Resolved, that woman has too long rested satisfied in the circum-   30
scribed limits which corrupt customs and a perverted application of the
Scriptures have marked out for her, and that it is time she should move
in the enlarged sphere which her great Creator has assigned her.

Resolved, that it is the duty of the women of this country to secure to   31
themselves their sacred right to the elective franchise.

Resolved, that the equality of human rights results necessarily from   32
the fact of the identity of the race in capabilities and responsibilities.

Resolved, that the speedy success of our cause depends upon the   33
zealous and untiring efforts of both men and women for the overthrow
of the monopoly of the pulpit, and for the securing to woman an equal
participation with men in the various trades, professions, and commerce.

Resolved, therefore, that, being invested by the Creator with the same   34
capabilities and same consciousness of responsibility for their exercise,
it is demonstrably the right and duty of woman, equally with man, to
promote every righteous cause by every righteous means; and especially
in regard to the great subjects of morals and religion, it is self-evidently
her right to participate with her brother in teaching them, both in private and in public, by writing and by speaking, by any instrumentalities
proper to be used, and in any assemblies proper to be held; and this being a self-evident truth growing out of the divinely implanted principles
of human nature, any custom or authority adverse to it, whether modern
or wearing the hoary sanction of antiquity, is to be regarded as a self-
evident falsehood, and at war with mankind.

Reading Closely

1. What overall argument are Stanton and her collaborators making in their
   declaration? Cite examples from the text that support your answer.
2. Which kinds of appeals do Stanton and her collaborators rely on to compose their argument? Identify examples of these appeals.

3. How do Stanton and her collaborators choose to arrange their declaration? How does this arrangement affect the overall argument of the declaration?

4. What is the ultimate purpose of the Declaration of Sentiments? How do you know? Cite examples from the text that support your answer.

Considering Larger Issues

1. What surprised or especially interested you as you read the declaration?

2. PAIRED READINGS. Compare the Declaration of Sentiments with the Declaration of Independence. What similarities do you see? Why do you think the writers of the Declaration of Sentiments created these links to the Declaration of Independence?

3. **Working with a classmate,** choose two of the facts listed in the Declaration of Sentiments, and explain exactly what each grievance means. For instance, what do Stanton and her collaborators mean when they say, "He has made her, if married, civilly dead"?

4. **Working with a classmate,** choose two of the resolutions listed in the Declaration of Sentiments, and explain exactly what each one means. For instance, what do Stanton and her collaborators mean when they say, "Resolved, that it is the duty of the women of this country to secure themselves their sacred right to the elective franchise"?

5. COMBINING METHODS. How do Stanton and her collaborators use *comparison and contrast, cause-and-effect analysis,* and *process analysis* to help them compose their argument?

Thinking about Language

1. Use the context of the declaration or a dictionary to define the following terms or phrases. Be prepared to share your definitions with the rest of the class.

hitherto (1)	chastisement (11)	fraudulently (20)
impel (1)	supposition (12)	instrumentality (21)
inalienable (2)	scanty (14)	tracts (21)
prudence (3)	remuneration (14)	precept (22)
usurpations (3)	apostolic (16)	coeval (22)
invariably (3)	prerogative (18)	indelicacy (29)
despotism (3)	Jehovah (18)	circumscribed (30)
equal station (3)	abject (19)	zealous (33)
candid (4)	disfranchisement (20)	demonstrably (34)
elective franchise (5)	degradation (20)	hoary (34)
impunity (11)		

2. Stanton and her collaborators called their document a "declaration of sentiments." Why do you think they chose the word *sentiments*? What is the effect of this choice?

Writing Your Own Arguments

1. For this two- to three-page essay, compose a "declaration of sentiments" for the twenty-first century. Like the original declaration, first identify gender inequalities (favoring either males or females) that you see in your daily life, describing them in detail. Then craft arguments as to how they might be resolved. Remember that Stanton and her collaborators relied on cause-and-effect analysis to compose this argument. You should consider a similar strategy. Be sure to refer to the guidelines for checking over an argument on page 655 as you draft and revise your essay.

2. Compose a three- to four-page essay in which you choose one of the facts or resolutions in the Declaration of Sentiments and argue either that this situation has changed since the nineteenth century or that it has remained the same. For example, you might choose to explore the resolution about "the objection of indelicacy and impropriety, which is so often brought against woman when she addresses a public audience" and to argue that while women are indeed now able to speak publicly, they are still often held to a different standard than men in the public sphere. For instance, during the 2008 presidential campaign, the media often commented on Hillary Clinton's attire (and even at one point her low neckline). Or you might address the fact about "the laws of divorce" and argue that "in case of separation, to whom the guardianship of the children should be given" is no longer based on "a false supposition of the supremacy of man" but instead on the belief that children should usually remain with their mother.

    Be sure to choose a fact or resolution that is arguable (for example, no one would deny that women are now able to vote on the same terms as men) and to focus your argument not on what the current situation *should be* but on what it is—that is, on "facts," not "sentiments" or "resolutions." The key to this essay is that you use exemplification to support your claims and create a strong and convincing argument. As you draft and revise, refer to the guidelines for checking over an argument on page 655.

JOSEPH C. GFROERER, LI-TZY WU, AND MICHAEL A. PENNE

Marijuana Is a Gateway Drug

Joseph C. Gfroerer, Li-Tzy Wu, and Michael A. Penne are researchers for the Substance Abuse and Mental Health Services Administration in the U.S. Department of Health and Human Services. Separately, their research has ranged from investigating the effectiveness of drug treatment plans to the connections between alcohol and aggression and the risks to children from substance-abusing parents. The following essay is taken from a longer and more detailed study of marijuana use titled *Initiation of Marijuana Use: Trends, Patterns, and Implications* (2002).

Preview   What is a gateway drug? What problems does this kind of drug pose?

Marijuana is the most widely used illicit drug in the United States. Ac- 1 cording to the 2000 NHSDA [National Household Surveys on Drug Abuse], an estimated 14.0 million Americans were current (past month) marijuana users. This represents 6.3 percent of people aged 12 or older and 76 percent of current illicit drug users. Of all current illicit drug users, approximately 59 percent used only marijuana, 17 percent used marijuana and another illicit drug, and the remaining 24 percent used only an illicit drug other than marijuana in the past month.

The NHSDA and the Monitoring the Future (MTF) [survey] have shown 2 generally similar long-term trends in the prevalence of substance use among youths, regardless of substantial differences in methodology between the two primary surveys of youth substance use. Between 1999 and 2000, both the NHSDA and MTF found no significant changes in lifetime, past year, and current use of marijuana.

The MTF found that marijuana use rose particularly sharply among 3 8th graders in the 1990s, with annual prevalence tripling between 1991 and 1996 (from 6 to 18 percent). Starting a year later, marijuana use also rose significantly among 10th and 12th graders. Following the recent peak in 1996–1997, annual marijuana use declined somewhat in recent years.

MOST NEW MARIJUANA USERS ARE UNDER SEVENTEEN

Although the prevalence of marijuana use has been studied widely, rela- 4 tively few incidence (first use) data are available. In the first published analysis of national incidence trends, Gfroerer and Brodsky estimated the number of new users of marijuana and other drugs based on combined data of 1985 to 1991 NHSDAs. They found that fewer than half a million people per year began using marijuana before 1966 and that new use of marijuana began increasing after 1966, reaching a peak in 1973 and declining thereafter. Johnson [et al.] studied the incidence of alcohol, cigarettes and illicit drugs using data from the 1991 to 1993 NHSDAs. Their investigation found declining trends of marijuana initiation at all ages since at least the late 1970s. However, the mean age of marijuana initiates declined throughout most of the measurement period, from older than 19 years in the mid–1960s to younger than 18 years in the late 1980s and early 1990s. In addition, the rates of marijuana initiation at ages 12 to 17 (youths) and 18 to 25 (young adults) in the early 1990s were still much higher than corresponding rates in the early 1960s.

In recent years, youths aged 12 to 17 have constituted about two 5 thirds of the new marijuana users, with young adults aged 18 to 25 constituting most of the remaining third. Additionally, recent rates of new use among youths in 1996–1998 (averaging 86.4 initiates per 1,000 potential new users) were higher than they had ever been. Nonetheless, rates of new use for both youths and young adults decreased between 1998 and 1999. The average age of marijuana initiation has generally declined since 1965 and remained around 17 years after 1992. . . .

Little research exists on the predictors of marijuana initiation. Van 6 Etten and Anthony examined the initial opportunity to try marijuana and the transition from first opportunity to first marijuana use using data from the 1979 to 1994 NHSDAs. They found that an estimated 51 percent of U.S. residents had an opportunity to try marijuana. One striking finding is that 43 percent of those with an opportunity went on to first use marijuana within 1 year of the first opportunity (i.e., making a rapid transition). The

"Wish I could!"

www.CartoonStock.com

study also found that males were more likely than females to have an opportunity to use marijuana, but were not more likely to eventually use marijuana once an opportunity was presented. Research has also shown that the risk of initiating marijuana use is associated with age and birth cohort. Chen and Kandel found that the major risk period for initiation into marijuana was mostly over by age 20. Gfroerer and Epstein also found that marijuana initiation was unlikely to occur after age 21. Rates of first marijuana use were higher among younger people and cohorts born after World War II than older people and cohorts born before World War II.

The onset of marijuana use also is influenced by a variety of personal, 7 family, and community risk and protective factors, such as affiliation with drug-using peers, personality dimensions (e.g., unconventionality), and the parent-child bond.

MARIJUANA IS A GATEWAY DRUG

Marijuana has been hypothesized to be a gateway drug for other illicit 8 drug use. Studies by Kandel and other investigators have identified a developmental sequence of drug involvement among youths. Specifically, the initial use of alcohol and/or cigarettes typically precedes the use of marijuana, which then is followed by the involvement of other illicit drugs. By studying a sample of rural youths, Donnermeyer also found that early use of alcohol predicted early use of marijuana, which in turn was predictive of early use of other illicit drugs. Studies of age at initiation of drug use confirmed that initiation of alcohol or tobacco typically occurred before marijuana initiation.

Not only does early marijuana use signal an increased risk for hard 9 drug use by grade 10, but it also is associated with drug use problems, dependency, and treatment need. Among individuals with a history of marijuana dependence, the age at onset of marijuana dependence was younger in the adolescent-onset individuals compared with the adult-onset individuals, and the time from the first use to the onset of dependence also was shorter in the adolescent-onset individuals. Among middle school students, use of marijuana and other drugs before the age of 12 was found to be associated with engaging in greater numbers of health risk behaviors than among students whose age at onset was 12 years or older or the never users. Early marijuana use is associated with later adolescent problems that limit the acquisition of skills necessary for employment and increased risk of contracting the human immunodeficiency virus (HIV) and using illicit drugs. Gfroerer and Epstein used NHSDA data to examine the impact of marijuana initiation on future drug abuse treatment need and found age at first use of marijuana as the most significant predictor of treatment need in all four age groups.

The number of new marijuana users may have a significant impact 10 on the future demand for substance abuse treatment as some new users continue into heavier marijuana use or other illicit drug taking. Consequently, delaying the onset of marijuana initiation could be important in preventing the progression into heavy drug involvement and other drug-related health risk behaviors, as well as in decreasing the social burdens of illicit drug use.

Taken together, studies of marijuana initiation provide vital informa-   11
tion for focused prevention programs about the periods of heightened initiation risk, specify subgroups vulnerable to initial use, and generate estimates on treatment needs and future demand for substance abuse treatment.

Reading Closely

1. What is the effect of the use of statistics in the opening paragraphs? What are the writers attempting to accomplish through this strategy?
2. What appeals (of ethos, pathos, or logos) do the writers rely on most heavily? Be prepared to identify specific examples of these appeals.
3. What is the purpose of this essay? How do you know?
4. How does the cartoon on page 709 support—or why does it not support—the writers' argument that marijuana is a gateway drug?

Considering Larger Issues

1. **Working with a classmate,** identify the arguments the writers use to convince readers that marijuana is a gateway drug.
2. What is your response to the writers' arguments?
3. Review the arrangement of the essay. Once the writers offer their argument that marijuana is a gateway drug, what's their next step?
4. COMBINING METHODS. To support their argument, the writers also rely on *exemplification* and *cause-and-effect analysis.* Identify places in the text where the writers use these rhetorical methods. How do these methods support the purpose of the essay?

Thinking about Language

1. Use the context of the essay or your dictionary to define any of the following words you do not know. Be prepared to share your definitions with the rest of the class.

illicit (1)	initiates (4)	affiliation (7)
methodology (2)	cohort (6)	acquisition (9)
mean (4)	onset (7)	

2. What assessments can you make about the sentence structure and tone of the essay? Given these assessments, who is the audience for this essay? How is the audience expected to respond to this essay?

Writing Your Own Arguments

1. The writers argue that marijuana is a gateway drug, which means that a person who uses marijuana is likely to try other drugs. In other words, the writers are making an argument about a causal relationship: doing X leads to Y. In a three- to four-page essay, compose a causal argument in which you argue that X leads to Y. You will want to consult Chapter 8 on cause–and–effect analysis as you compose your argument, but now that you've become a student of argument, you'll want to bolster your causal analysis with the elements of argument. Therefore, you'll want to integrate the appeals of ethos, logos, and pathos into your essay; establish common ground with your audience; create a strong thesis statement; and avoid logical fallacies. As you compose your essay, refer to "Checking Over an Argument" on page 655.

2. In arguing that marijuana is a gateway drug, the writers of this essay make an implicit argument that marijuana use should continue to be illegal. In addition to this argument, what other arguments are used in favor of keeping marijuana illegal? To answer this question, conduct online and library research, identifying additional lines of argument. Although you may not agree with this position, compose a two- to three-page essay in which you argue for keeping marijuana illegal, setting out the various arguments advocates of this position make. If you disagree with this position, this exercise will help you know what these arguments are and fine-tune your counterarguments to them. You'll have the opportunity to advocate for marijuana legalization by responding to question 2 under Writing Your Own Arguments following the next essay. Refer to "Checking Over an Argument" on page 655 as you draft and revise your essay.

WILLIAM F. BUCKLEY JR.
Free Weeds

● Author, columnist, and commentator William F. Buckley Jr. (1925–2008), considered the father of the modern conservative movement in the United States, founded the magazine *National Review* in 1955 and also hosted the television talk show *Firing Line* from 1966 until 1999. Buckley was a graduate of Yale University, where he studied economics, history, and political science. As a writer, he published both fiction and nonfiction, beginning with his best-known book, *God and Man at Yale: The Superstitions of "Academic Freedom"* (1951) and ending with *The Rake* and *Cancel Your Own Goddam Subscription: Notes and Asides from the National Review* (both 2007). "Free Weeds" was originally published in the *National Review* in 2004.

Preview   What position would you expect a conservative to take on marijuana legalization?

Conservatives pride themselves on resisting change, which is as it should   1
be. But intelligent deference to tradition and stability can evolve into intellectual sloth and moral fanaticism, as when conservatives simply decline to look up from dogma because the effort to raise their heads and reconsider is too great. The laws aren't exactly indefensible, because practically nothing is, and the thunderers who tell us to stay the course can always find one man or woman who, having taken marijuana, moved on to severe mental disorder. But that argument, to quote myself, is on the order of saying that every rapist began by masturbating. General rules based on individual victims are unwise. And although there is a perfectly respectable case against using marijuana, the penalties imposed on those who reject that case, or who give way to weakness of resolution, are very difficult to defend. If all our laws were paradigmatic, imagine what we would do to anyone caught lighting a cigarette, or drinking a beer. Or   exulting in life in the paradigm—committing adultery. Send them all to Guantanamo?

Legal practices should be informed by realities. These are enlightening,   2
in the matter of marijuana. There are approximately 700,000 marijuana-related arrests made every year. Most of these—87 percent—involve nothing more than mere possession of small amounts of marijuana. This exercise in scrupulosity costs us $10–$15 billion per year in direct expenditures alone. Most transgressors caught using marijuana aren't packed away to jail, but some are, and in Alabama, if you are convicted three times of marijuana possession, they'll lock you up for 15 years to life. Professor Ethan Nadelmann, of the Drug Policy Alliance, writing in the *National Review*, estimates at 100,000 the number of Americans currently behind bars for one or another marijuana offense.

What we face is the politician's fear of endorsing any change in exist-   3
ing marijuana laws. You can imagine what a call for reform in those laws

would do to an upwardly mobile political figure. Gary Johnson, governor of New Mexico, came out in favor of legalization—and went on to private life. George Shultz, former secretary of state, long ago called for legalization, but he was not running for office, and at his age, and with his distinctions, he is immune to slurred charges of indifference to the fate of children and humankind. But Kurt Schmoke, mayor of Baltimore, did it, and survived a reelection challenge.

But the stodgy inertia most politicians feel is up against a creeping 4 reality. It is that marijuana for medical relief is a movement which is attracting voters who are pretty assertive on the subject. Every state ballot initiative to legalize medical marijuana has been approved, often by wide margins. Of course we have here collisions of federal and state authority. Federal authority technically supervenes state laws, but federal authority in the matter is being challenged on grounds of medical self–government. It simply isn't so that there are substitutes equally efficacious. Richard Brookhiser, the widely respected author and editor, has written on the subject for the *New York Observer*. He had a bout of cancer and found relief from chemotherapy only in marijuana—which he consumed, and discarded after the affliction was gone.

The court has told federal enforcers that they are not to impose their 5 way between doctors and their patients, and one bill sitting about in Congress would even deny the use of federal funds for prosecuting medical marijuana use. Critics of reform do make a pretty plausible case when they say that whatever is said about using marijuana only for medical relief masks what the advocates are really after, which is legal marijuana for whoever wants it.

That would be different from the situation today. Today we have ille- 6 gal marijuana for whoever wants it. An estimated 100 million Americans have smoked marijuana at least once, the great majority abandoning its use after a few highs. But to stop using it does not close off its availability. A Boston commentator observed years ago that it is easier for an 18-year-old to get marijuana in Cambridge than to get beer. Vendors who sell beer to minors can forfeit their valuable licenses. It requires less effort for the college student to find marijuana than for a sailor to find a brothel. Still, there is the danger of arrest (as 700,000 people a year will tell you), of possible imprisonment, of blemish on one's record. The obverse of this is increased cynicism about the law.

We're not going to find someone running for president who ad- 7 vocates reform of those laws. What is required is a genuine republican groundswell. It is happening, but ever so gradually. Two of every five Americans, according to a 2003 Zogby poll cited by Dr. Nadelmann, believe "the government should treat marijuana more or less the same way it treats alcohol: It should regulate it, control it, tax it, and make it illegal only for children."

Such reforms would hugely increase the use of the drug? Why? It is 8 de facto legal in the Netherlands, and the percentage of users there is the same as here. The Dutch do odd things, but here they teach us a lesson.

Reading Closely

1. What is Buckley's argument in this essay?
2. Who is Buckley's audience? What clues in the text help you decide?
3. What research did Buckley conduct to compose this essay? How does this research affect his argument?
4. What does Buckley mean when he writes in the opening paragraph, "General rules based on individual victims are unwise"?
5. How does the cartoon strip on page 714 support—or why does it not support—Buckley's argument?

Considering Larger Issues

1. What surprised or especially interested you in this essay?
2. In the conclusion, Buckley asserts that the Dutch can teach U.S. citizens a lesson. What lesson does he think they can teach?

3. **COMBINING METHODS.** Buckley relies on *exemplification* throughout this essay. How do these examples serve his argument?

4. **PAIRED ESSAY.** **Working with a classmate,** compare the arguments that Buckley makes about drug legalization with Gfroerer, Wu, and Penne's argument. What would these writers say to one another about drug legalization? Where would their positions differ? How does their interest in the topic differ?

Thinking about Language

1. Use the context of the essay or your dictionary to define any of the following words you do not know. Be prepared to share your definitions with the rest of the class.

deference (1)	paradigmatic (1)	supervenes (4)
intellectual sloth (1)	scrupulosity (2)	efficacious (4)
moral fanaticism (1)	expenditures (2)	plausible (5)
dogma (1)	inertia (4)	obverse (6)

2. What does Buckley mean when he calls for a "genuine republican groundswell"? How would a groundswell help him achieve the goal of his argument?

Writing Your Own Arguments

1. In the final paragraphs of Buckley's essay, he asserts a comparative argument: marijuana should be treated like alcohol. The government should "regulate it, control it, tax it, and make it illegal only for children." In a two- to three-page essay, respond to Buckley's comparison by considering these questions: To what extent and in what ways is marijuana like alcohol? Is this a realistic and appropriate comparison? What would daily life be like if marijuana were treated like alcohol? Your goal is to compose an argument that builds from Buckley's comparison by first considering whether this comparison makes sense and then imagining the benefits and drawbacks of treating marijuana like alcohol. As you make your argument, you'll most likely need to conduct additional research, so be sure to consult both online and traditional library resources. As you draft and revise, refer to the guidelines for checking over an argument on page 655.

2. Now that you have read two essays on marijuana legalization, compose a three- to four-page argumentative essay in which you assert your voice in this debate. Your goal, then, is to answer these questions: Should marijuana be legalized? Why or why not? And if so, to what exent? To determine your own position within this debate, you'll want not only to reflect on the positions of the writers above but also to do additional reading by conducting both online and traditional library research. Remember, don't simply voice agreement with the *exact* arguments made by Buckley or Gfroerer, Wu, and Penne: introduce new ideas and arguments into the debate. Your research will help you identify them. As you draft and revise, be sure to refer to the guidelines for checking over an argument on page 655.

TIMOTHY WHEELER
Assault-Weapons Ban, R.I.P.

Timothy Wheeler works in southern California as a surgeon and directs the Doctors for Responsible Gun Ownership project. As director of the project, Wheeler has created a network of over 1,400 health professionals who agree with and advocate for the legal and safe use of firearms. Wheeler has also published a number of articles in the *National Review,* a conservative magazine, that argue against gun control legislation. The following essay is one such article, which appeared in September 2004.

> **Preview** What is your understanding of the debate over the assault-weapons ban?

The 1994 federal assault-weapons ban officially dies tonight. It was a bad job from the beginning, a fraudulent piece of legislation pushed through by hard-line gun-control advocates during the glory days of the Clinton era. To get it through Congress, its backers had to agree to a ten-year sunset provision. The law passes quietly into history at midnight. 1

Until the last minute, apologists for the ban have tried desperately to breathe life back into it, predicting doom if Congress failed to extend the law. A frantic Sarah Brady from the Brady Campaign to Prevent Gun Violence (formerly known as Handgun Control, Inc.) was quoted in the *New York Times* as warning, "The assault weapons are coming, they're coming next week." 2

Perhaps the most pathetic attempt to spin the law's demise came from a list of medical organizations claiming in a September 7 press release that gun violence (public-health-speak for armed hoodlums on the job) is "an ongoing home-security problem." Nice try. 3

The medical groups were mostly the same players from the medical antigun advocacy of the 1990s. They all banded together under the Handgun Epidemic Lowering Plan (HELP Network), run out of Children's Memorial Hospital in Chicago. The group includes the American Academy of Pediatrics, the American College of Physicians, and Doctors Against Handgun Injury, all groups whose official policies call for doctors to urge their patients to get rid of their guns. 4

So strong is the denial of the HELP Network activists that they will continue to believe the world is ending, even though most Americans don't even know the law has expired. Here are a few predictions, based on the psychology of criminals and gun-control activists: 5

Gun crimes committed with "assault weapons" won't increase. Semiautomatic rifles never did catch on in a big way with career criminals, because they are too difficult to carry concealed. As a National Institute of Justice study noted in July, using a broad definition of the term, assault weapons were used in fewer than eight percent of gun crimes even before the ban. The 6 firearm of choice for armed criminals has always been the high–quality handgun.

The HELP crowd and other antigunners will nevertheless maintain to the end that 7 *the ban's end will touch off a crime wave of epic proportions.* The core delusion here is that all guns are evil. Gun–control advocates will therefore refuse to accept that their condemnation of "assault weapons" has no basis in fact. Even though as physicians they are trained in the scientific method, they will carry this conviction to the ends of their flat earth.

As the assault-weapon panic fades, gun-control activists will find another kind 8 *of gun to demonize.* In fact, they already have. On California Gov. Arnold Schwarzenegger's desk lies a bill to ban .50–caliber rifles, a target rifle fancied by well–to–do hobbyists. Gun controllers have ginned up a myth of .50–caliber rifles as the new weapon of choice for terrorists, just as as–sault weapons were supposedly preferred by criminals. In fact, there is only one reported case of a .50–caliber rifle ever having been used in a crime in the United States. Golf clubs are more frequently used as crime weapons than .50–caliber rifles.

Antigunners will deliberately continue to misrepresent "assault weapons" as ma- 9 *chine guns.* CNN did it back in May 2003, when it ran a piece on assault weapons but showed video of a machine gun. CNN was forced to is–sue a retraction when National Rifle Association executive vice president Wayne LaPierre pointed out the obvious lie.

ABC News did it again last week in a *World News Tonight* advocacy– 10 news piece by Bill Redeker on the expiration of the ban. The segment quoted Los Angeles Police Chief William Bratton, who warned, "We'll probably have more of these weapons in the United States than there are in Iraq in the hands of insurgents." Not true. Iraqi insurgents shoot fully automatic military rifles—the real thing. American target shooters and collectors whose guns were banned by the 1994 law only want to shoot their semiautomatic rifles, one bullet with each trigger pull.

Redeker further tried to mislead viewers into thinking machine guns 11 are legal again by showing video footage of a 1997 North Hollywood shootout. In one of the relatively few modern crimes involving machine guns, two bank robbers fired on police with fully automatic rifles, not with the guns now legal again.

Intentionally misrepresenting assault weapons as machine guns is 12 nothing new for the gun–control lobby. But if the public mood about the issue is any indication, the lie is exposed. Congressional leaders held fast to the end, citing their constituents' desires in letting the law die its programmed death.

The experiment failed. The myth of the deadly assault weapon can 13 now be laid to rest, a victim of its own falsity.

Reading Closely

1. In his essay, Wheeler is not explicitly arguing for or against assault–weapons legislation. What is his argumentative strategy? What kind of argument is he making? Identify evidence from the essay to support your answers.

2. How does Wheeler portray gun–control activists in this essay? Cite evidence from the essay to support your answer.

3. Who is Wheeler's audience in this essay? How does Wheeler want his audience to respond to his argument? Cite evidence from the text that leads you to make this assessment.

Considering Larger Issues

1. What do you think of Wheeler's argument and, more specifically, his predictions? Were you persuaded? Why or why not?

2. COMBINING METHODS. As part of his argument, Wheeler critiques what he says is gun–control activists' inability to classify guns, arguing that they do not know the difference between assault weapons and machine guns. **Working with a classmate,** identify the difference between these kinds of guns. Why does this classification matter to his argument?

3. Reflect on and evaluate the arrangement of the essay. What do you find effective or ineffective about Wheeler's organization?

4. Identify places in the essay where Wheeler uses ethical, logical, and pathetic appeals. Which appeals does he use most consistently? Why does he rely on these types of appeals?

Thinking about Language

1. Use the context of the essay or your dictionary to define any of the following words you do not know. Be prepared to share your definitions with the rest of the class.

fraudulent (1)	condemnation (7)	retraction (9)
sunset provision (1)	ginned up (8)	insurgents (10)
apologists (2)		

2. How would you describe the tone Wheeler uses in this essay? Identify the language choices he makes that help create the tone. What effect does this tone have on his ethos?

Writing Your Own Arguments

1. A significant part of Wheeler's essay and his argument is dedicated to his predictions of how people will respond to the legalization of assault weapons. In effect, he's predicting the *effects* of discontinuing the current policy. In a three– to four-page essay, compose an argument based on

predictions about either implementing or discontinuing a policy. The policy you choose is up to you, but your argument must center not on the policy itself but on what you predict will be the effects of beginning or ending it. For instance, you might decide to argue that the strict attendance policy in one of your classes should be lifted by predicting students' behavior and class atmosphere. In this case, you might argue that without the policy most students will still come to class, participate, and do well, while the rest won't come to class, will do poorly, but won't be disruptive to those trying to pay attention. Without the policy, therefore, you argue that the overall outcome will be better. Whatever policy you choose to argue about—and it does not have to be school-related—you'll want to make sure your predictions are reasonable and credible by supporting your claims with strong evidence. As you draft and revise your essay, refer to "Checking Over an Argument" on page 655.

2. In his essay, Wheeler makes a distinction between assault weapons and machine guns. In your essay, investigate the gun-control debate by exploring the various kinds of weapons under consideration. In particular, you'll want to research the bans that individuals and groups involved in the debate (hunters, law-enforcement groups, members of the NRA, gun-control advocates, Doctors for Responsible Gun Ownership) believe should and should not be placed on different kinds of weapons. Then choose a particular kind of weapon, and argue whether or not this weapon should be banned. To make your argument, you'll want to investigate the weapon itself and its potential danger (or lack thereof), as well as the arguments that surround its legal sale. Your essay should be three to four pages long. Refer to "Checking Over an Argument" on page 655 as you draft and revise your essay.

JIMMY CARTER
Assault-Gun Ban Should Be Reinstated

Jimmy Carter (b. 1924) was the thirty-ninth president of the United States, serving from 1977 to 1981. During his presidency, he negotiated a peace treaty between Israel and Egypt and established the Department of Energy and the Department of Education. Since he left office, Carter has focused on human rights and humanitarian efforts. He has been instrumental in helping countries work toward peace negotiations, fair elections, and disease prevention. In 2002, he received the Nobel Peace Prize. He has also continued to speak out on public issues in the United States, as in the following essay, which was originally published in the op-ed section of the *New York Times* on April 27, 2009. Carter grew up and now lives in rural Georgia, and in this piece, he engages the debate over the ban on assault weapons from the perspective of a hunter.

Preview What position might you expect a hunter to take in a debate about a ban on assault weapons? Why do you think Carter favors a ban?

The evolution in public policy concerning the manufacture, sale and possession of semiautomatic assault weapons like AK–47s, AR–15s and Uzis has been disturbing. Presidents Ronald Reagan, George H. W. Bush, Bill Clinton and I all supported a ban on these formidable firearms, and one was finally passed in 1994. 1

When the 10-year ban was set to expire, many police organizations — including 1,100 police chiefs and sheriffs from around the nation — called on Congress and President George W. Bush to renew and strengthen it. But with a wink from the White House, the gun lobby prevailed and the ban expired. 2

I have used weapons since I was big enough to carry one, and now own two handguns, four shotguns and three rifles, two with scopes. I use them carefully, for hunting game from our family woods and fields, and occasionally for hunting with my family and friends in other places. We cherish the right to own a gun, and some of my hunting companions like to collect rare weapons. One of them is a superb craftsman who makes muzzle-loading rifles, one of which I displayed for four years in my private White House office. 3

But none of us wants to own an assault weapon, because we have no desire to kill policemen or go to a school or workplace to see how many victims we can accumulate before we are finally shot or take our own lives. That's why the White House and Congress must not give up on trying to reinstate a ban on assault weapons, even if it may be politically difficult. 4

An overwhelming majority of Americans, including me and my hunting companions, believe in the right to own weapons, but surveys show 5

that they also support modest restraints like background checks, manda‐
tory registration and brief waiting periods before purchase.

A majority of Americans also support banning assault weapons. 6
Many of us who hunt are dismayed by some of the more extreme poli‐
cies of the National Rifle Association, the most prominent voice in op‐
position to a ban, and by the timidity of public officials who yield to the
group's unreasonable demands.

Heavily influenced and supported by the firearms industry, NRA 7
leaders have misled many gullible people into believing that our weap‐
ons are going to be taken away from us, and that homeowners will be
deprived of the right to protect ourselves and our families. The NRA
would be justified in its efforts if there was a real threat to our constitu‐
tional right to bear arms. But that is not the case.

Instead, the NRA is defending criminals' access to assault weapons 8
and use of ammunition that can penetrate protective clothing worn by
police officers on duty. In addition, while the NRA seems to have reluc‐
tantly accepted current law restricting sales by licensed gun dealers to
convicted felons, it claims that only "law‐abiding people" obey such re‐
strictions—and it opposes applying them to private gun dealers or those
who sell all kinds of weapons from the back of a van or pickup truck at
gun shows.

What are the results of this profligate ownership and use of guns 9
designed to kill people? In 2006, the Centers for Disease Control and Pre‐
vention reported more than 30,000 people died from firearms. In 2005,
every nine hours a child or teenager in the United States was killed in a
firearm‐related accident or suicide.

Across our border, Mexican drug cartels are being armed with ad‐ 10
vanced weaponry imported from the United States—a reality only the
NRA seems to dispute.

The gun lobby and the firearms industry should reassess their policies 11
concerning safety and accountability—at least on assault weapons—and
ease their pressure on acquiescent politicians who fear NRA disapproval at
election time. We can't let the NRA's political blackmail prevent the ban‐
ning of assault weapons—designed only to kill police officers and the
people they defend.

Reading Closely

1. Describe the problem or issue Carter is addressing in this essay.
2. What is Carter's argument in this essay?
3. How does Carter cultivate his ethos in this essay? Why might readers
    find him to be a credible spokesperson in this debate?
4. How does Carter describe the NRA and its position in the assault‐gun
    debate?

Considering Larger Issues

1. What research does Carter conduct for this essay? How does this research help him compose his logical appeals?

2. What do you think of Carter's argument? What's your position in this debate?

3. Who is the intended audience for Carter's essay? How does he want people to respond to his argument?

4. **Working with a classmate,** discuss the implications and intentions of the Second Amendment to the Constitution, guaranteeing the right to bear arms. What is the purpose of this amendment? What is its relevance in the debate about assault weapons?

5. PAIRED READINGS. Now that you've read both Carter's and Wheeler's essays on gun control, which argument do you find more persuasive? Why?

6. COMBINING METHODS. Carter uses *cause-and-effect analysis* to support his argument about assault weapons. Identify the places in the essay where he uses this rhetorical method. How does his use of this method affect his argument?

Thinking about Language

1. Use the context of the essay or your dictionary to define any of the following words you do not know. Be prepared to share your definitions with the rest of the class.

formidable (1)	timidity (6)	cartels (10)
muzzle-loading rifles (3)	gullible (7)	reassess (11)
reinstate (4)	profligate (9)	acquiescent (11)

2. Throughout the essay, Carter uses the plural pronouns *we* and *our*. To whom is he referring in using these pronouns? How do they affect his argument? What is their effect on the audience?

Writing Your Own Arguments

1. In a three- to four-page essay, build on your response to question 4 under Considering Larger Issues to make an argument for how you think the Second Amendment should guide gun legislation. To compose your essay, you'll need to conduct more detailed research on the Second Amendment itself and the various ways participants in the gun-control debate use it to support their arguments. Then put forward your own argument about how the Second Amendment should be used. What, in your opinion, is the correct interpretation of this amendment? Refer to "Checking Over an Argument" on page 655 as you draft and revise your essay.

2. PUBLIC WRITING. Review Carter's and Wheeler's arguments about the ban on assault weapons, and consider where you stand in this debate; then compose your own argument in the form of Carter's newspaper op-ed piece. As you consider your position, remember that there are more than

two sides to every argument, so explore other possibilities for argument in addition to those that Carter and Wheeler advocate. As you compose your op–ed piece, designate a *specific* newspaper in which your piece would appear, and then create common ground with that newspaper's readership. For instance, if you chose to write for your school newspaper, you'd want to consider how this issue is relevant to a college–age audience. On the other hand, if the newspaper you chose is your local newspaper in a small rural town, you'd need to speak to the interests of that readership. As you draft and revise your op–ed piece, refer to "Checking Over an Argument" on page 655.

✳ Additional Suggestions for Writing

1. Think back to a time when you were treated unfairly, maybe by a police officer, a professor, a boss, or a relative. Write a two- to three-page letter to that person in which you argue your point of view, taking special care to establish common ground and your goodwill, good sense, and good character. Refer to the guidelines on page 655 for checking over an argument.

2. Think of a movie that you like but that others are criticizing, maybe on the grounds of sentimentality, violence, artificiality, or predictability. Argue for reconsideration of that movie, demonstrating its positive qualities and addressing each of the criticisms of it. Be sure to imagine a particular audience, in this case an almost hostile one. You may want to research reviews or talk with your friends about their opinions before you begin writing your argument. You'll certainly want to watch the movie again before you start. As you draft and revise, refer to the guidelines on page 655 for checking over an argument.

3. Draft a three- to four-page essay in which you make an argument about the role of alcohol in your life. For example, you may want to defend its role in your life, argue that you should change that role, or make a factual argument that alcohol is more — or less — important to you than it is to other students. Before you begin writing, though, imagine an audience for such an essay: your parents, your partner, your roommate, your children. List all the reasons you have for holding your opinion, particularly in terms of your audience, and refer to the guidelines on page 655 for checking over an argument.

chapter 11

ACADEMIC AND PUBLIC WRITING: SYNTHESIZING STRATEGIES AND SOURCES

In slapstick comedy, the worst thing that could happen usually does: The person with a sore toe manages to stub it, sometimes twice. Such errors also arise in daily life, and research traces the tendency to do precisely the worst thing to ironic processes of mental control. These monitoring processes keep us watchful for errors of thought, speech, and action and enable us to avoid the worst thing in most situations, but they also increase the likelihood of such errors when we attempt to exert control under mental load (stress, time pressure, or distraction). Ironic errors in attention and memory occur with identifiable brain activity and prompt recurrent unwanted thoughts; attraction to forbidden desires; expression of objectionable social prejudices; production of movement errors; and rebounds of negative experiences such as anxiety, pain, and depression. Such ironies can be overcome when effective control strategies are deployed and mental load is minimized.

> —DANIEL M. WEGNER, "How to Think, Say, or Do
> Precisely the Worst Thing for Any Occasion"

*T*his paragraph is the introduction to a research review that appeared in *Science*, one of the top scientific journals in the world, which publishes only the most significant scientific discoveries. Renowned Harvard psychology professor Daniel M. Wegner knows that any article will be taken seriously if it appears in *Science*, even if the article's title itself does not appear to be highly scientific. On first read, Wegner's review of the research that has been done in a particular field is clearly an example of academic writing — the kind of formal writing that uses vocabulary specific to a scholarly discipline that appears in scholarly publications like *Science*. But a second read should reassure those who are not professional scholars or academics that they have managed to understand every word of the review, even if they had to stop and figure out the meaning of jargon like "movement errors." So the piece might also be an example of public writing — except how many people besides scientists actually read *Science*?

One key feature of all writing to consider is this: Who is the intended audience? What expectations does the writer have for the readers? What expectations do the readers have for the writing? Where does the writing appear? Is it available in print only in college libraries? Or can it be purchased at the newsstand? Is it available online to anyone who locates the site, or is the site subscription–only? Does the writer rely mostly on the rhetorical appeal of logos in an attempt to assure readers that the writing is "logical" and "objective," or does he or she bring pathos (emotional appeals) into play? And in what ways does the writer try to establish his or her ethos (credibility and reputation)? By answering these questions, you can begin to gain a sense of whether the intended audience is public or academic.

Other keys to understanding the distinction between public and academic writing are the writer's language, stylistic, and grammatical choices; the arrangement of the text (for instance, does it begin with an abstract?); the ways that sources are acknowledged; and the ways that any visual information is presented (is it referred to and discussed in the text or simply used for visual interest?). Academic authors do not write only for an academic audience; often they find ways to reach a public one as well, just as Wegner does. Yes, academic writing is specialized, but public writing can be as well. Just as the "most academic" kinds of writing are intended for a small, narrowly defined audience, public writing can also be aimed at a limited readership interested in a specific topic such as job opportunities for chemistry majors, a particular college community, feminist politics, the local farmers' market, the Catholic church, or backpacking.

. . . .

Looking at Your Own Literacy

1. What specialized books, magazines, and Web sites do you read? Make a list of the places where you regularly read about a particular topic— cooking, sports, fitness, fashion, travel, investing, or health, for instance. What terms specific to that topic are used in the materials you read? Make a list of twenty such terms. What advice would you give to someone unfamiliar with that topic who is reading about it for the first time? What are the differences between the way you read books, articles, and Web postings about the topic and the ways a newcomer might read them?

2. List the kinds of reading and writing you do on a daily basis. Given the distinctions between public and academic writing made in this text, how would you describe each of your daily reading and writing practices? As you reflect on your answer to this question, begin to think about the questions of writer and reader expectations, publishing venue, arrangement of text, acknowledgment of sources, and so on that were discussed in the text.

. . . .

Academic and Public Writing: What's the Difference?

By this point in your writing course, you've already learned a good deal about academic and public writing. Each chapter has explained and illustrated the ways a particular rhetorical method, such as narration or comparison and contrast, is used in both kinds of writing. In this chapter, you'll concentrate on the differences between academic and public writing as well as on the broad spectrum of writing between the two and the qualities that make *all* kinds of writing good writing. Indeed, many of the qualities of successful academic writing are the same as those of successful public writing: careful attention to purpose, audience, thesis, organization, word choice, and editing and proofreading.

● Characteristics of Academic Writing

Academic writing can be defined simply as the writing you do for your college classes and that professional scholars do when writing for each other. Depending on the career(s) you follow, you may need to do it after college as well. Thus academic writing is a blanket term for scholarly writing that shares specific characteristics — and yet it's adaptable enough to shape itself for the particular expectations of each discipline. You already know by now that the writing you read and produce differs from your history course to your sociology course and from your chemistry course to your health course. So as you gain expertise in the similarities across academic writing, you'll also want to be able to understand and identify the differences among various types. You don't want to write the same way for your English professors as you do for your chemistry professors.

So how do you go about assessing these differences? Pay attention to what you're reading, identifying the kinds of genres that writers in those disciplines use as well as the specific instructions for your assignments. Which classes ask for reports, abstracts, or essays? What do these genres look and sound like? Are there sections and subsections to the writing? Does the writer use first, second, or third person? How formal is the writing style? What voice (active or passive) does the writer choose? Compared with public writing, academic writing tends to have a more "impersonal," formal tone and to avoid first ("I") and especially second ("you") person, but in some disciplines and contexts they may be accepted or even expected. Likewise, in some kinds of academic writing — but not all — passive voice is preferred. If you're unsure of the genre and style of the academic discipline you're working in, ask your professor for examples of the kind of writing he or she is expecting. Such examples should give you another clue as to the expectations for the course.

. . . .

Try Your Hand   Compare the academic writing from two of your textbooks for different courses. What specific differences and similarities do you find between those books in terms of language, audience expectations, genres, and rhetorical methods of development? Be prepared to share your findings with the rest of the class.

. . . .

When writing in academic settings, writers expect their audience to have some mastery of or experience with the topic under discussion. Readers of academic writing also have expectations: they expect that the writer will engage them at a certain intellectual level, confirming or extending their understanding of the topic under discussion. Therefore, academic writing always functions inside specific language communities in which members know certain terms, proper names, processes, or practices. For instance, in the following excerpt from his research review, Wegner includes specialized terms and parenthetical references to his bibliographic citations:

Do we do the worst thing more often than other things? Fortunately for the proprietors of china shops, we do not. However, accumulating evidence on ironic processes of mental control (6) reveals conditions under which people commit precisely counterintentional errors. The prototypical error of this kind occurs when people are asked to keep a thought out of mind (e.g., "don't think about a white bear"). The thought often comes back. When asked to signal any return of that thought, people may indicate that it comes back about once per minute (7)—often to echo for yet longer periods (8) and, at the extreme, to return for days (9, 10). Some people are better at such thought suppression than others (11), but keeping a thought out of mind remains a challenge for most of us even when we have only arbitrarily tried to suppress it.

You can see the context of Wegner's language community by noting the terms and phrases he does not define for his readers in the excerpt and in the conclusion that follows: "ironic processes of mental control," "counterintentional errors," "prototypical errors," "not mentally loading," "artificial loads," and so on. He expects his readers to know these terms already, just as he expects them to have some understanding of how the mind works. And like much academic writing, Wegner's review includes headings such as "Taboos and Faux Pas: Worst Thoughts and Utterances" and "References and Notes," acknowledgment of references (from Edgar Allan Poe and Sigmund Freud to studies in professional journals and Wegner's own research), a procedure section that explains how exactly Wegner set up his laboratory experiments and reached his conclusions, and the conclusion itself, which follows.

Putting the Worst Behind Us

The ubiquity of ironic effects suggests we should consider it something of a treat when we control ourselves successfully. According to ironic process theory, however, successful control is likely to be far more prevalent than ironic error because people often use effective strategies for control and deploy them under conditions that are not mentally loading. Ironic effects are often small, and the experimental production of ironic errors often depends on the introduction of artificial loads, time pressures, or other means of magnifying ironic effects. Even such amplifiers of ironic error may be overcome, however, in certain individuals with talents of mental control. People who are susceptible to hypnotic suggestion, for example, and who are given suggestions to control thoughts show heightened mental control without ironic effects (60, 61).

The rest of us, however, who go through life without special talent for mental control, sometimes must turn to other tactics to overcome ironic error. Strategies people use to relax excessive striving for control, for example, show promise in reducing the severity of ironic effects. Potentially effective strategies include accepting symptoms rather than attempting to control them (62) and disclosing problems rather than keeping them secret (63). Therapies devised for improving mental control—or for helping people to relax it—remain largely untested, however, and there are enough ambiguities surrounding the translation of laboratory research into effective treatments that recommendations for clinical practice at this time are premature. Current research indicates only that, under certain conditions, we may be better able to avoid the worst in what we think, do, or say by avoiding the avoiding. Failing that, our best option is to orchestrate our circumstances so as to minimize mental load when mental control is needed.

Although academic writing is distinctive in terms of language and citations, its purpose, just like that of public writing, may be to explain, argue, compare, evaluate, or even entertain. As you know by now, academic writing taps all the rhetorical methods of development, often several methods in the same piece. But regardless of the rhetorical method used, the author tries to relay information in a way that sounds objective, logical, and reasonable. Explicit appeals to pathos or emotion are generally absent, and ethos is established mainly by the author's demonstration of having done careful, thorough research, supported by detailed source citations. Nevertheless, even though academic writing often sounds "scholarly," with extended technical explanations, it can also sound less formal and even engaging (as you will soon see). In addition, academic writing normally follows the conventions of grammar, mechanics, usage, format, and style. You may be familiar with the Modern Language Association (MLA) citation system, for instance, but as you can see, Wegner uses the citation system required by *Science*. As you write across the disciplines, you will probably be expected to conform to the conventions of those disciplines.

● Characteristics of Public Writing

Public writing differs from academic writing in one distinctive way: it is more often aimed at a general audience, readers who are interested in learning more about a subject, analyzing a process, or enjoying the author's ability to deliver information, whether that information is factual, artistically pleasing, exploratory, or argumentative. Whereas academic writing appears in academic circles (from college classes and professional meetings to scholarly journals and specialized books), public writing appears in the public sphere—in general newspapers and magazines, blogs, community newsletters, and the Web sites of many corporations, non-profit organizations, and government agencies, to give just a few examples (some of which also include academic writing). Unless you become a professional scholar, most of your writing after college will probably be public writing.

As in academic writing, writers and readers of public writing hold expectations for one another, although the expectations for this kind of writing are different. Readers expect to be able to progress through the text easily, without the obstructions of obscure references or undefined technical terms, so they can follow the writer's argument or discussion.

Likewise, writers strive to create an accessible and understandable text, for they know that their readers represent a broad variety of backgrounds, experiences, and education.

Like academic writing, public writing draws on all of the rhetorical methods of development, often mixing the methods in the same piece of writing, as well as mixing the methods with a good bit of personal information and personal references. Whether the author is using narration or exemplification, classification and division or argument, he or she works to deliver information in such a way that a wide range of readers will understand it.

The distinctions between public and academic writing in particular cases are sometimes absolutely clear. In general, however, it may be more useful to think of public and academic writing as the two ends of a spectrum, with the range of writing between them being vast and varied. Much public writing—newspaper stories and editorials, opinion pieces, public service announcements, community newsletters, online movie reviews—is indeed aimed at a broad community and a national or even global audience. But in professional and business settings, for instance, employees compose in-house documents, reports, proposals, memos, and letters for other employees within their specific setting—they are writing for neither an academic audience nor the general public. And technical writers create instruction manuals, software installation guides, repair logs, feasibility reports, and protocol analyses for narrowly defined audiences outside the writer's own professional setting. The specific purpose of such technical documents is to teach or explain, which is often fulfilled by the writer's translating technical language into language more easily understood by the general reader. Neighborhood watch groups compose reports on crime in their area (types, frequency, and locations), submitting those reports to the local police for the purpose of arguing for increased protection. Parent-teacher associations regularly put together pamphlets, often for the purpose of stimulating fundraising for specific projects: computers, new playground equipment, or materials for the school library. Personal writing of any kind that is intended to be read by anyone other than the writer—from journals and memoirs to online blogging and tweeting—can also be considered a form of public writing.

Thinking about Academic and Public Writing   Reread the paragraph that opens this chapter, underlining all the words and phrases that indicate to you that it's a piece of academic writing. Consider the reasons you underlined those specific words and phrases. What about them made them seem "academic" to you? Then go through the same paragraph and mark all the words and phrases that seem to be examples of public writing. Consider the reasons for your choices. Be prepared to share your answers with the class.

Why and How Is Academic Writing Used?

Academic writing is most often used to inform, explain, or argue a point, all within a specific discipline. When it's particularly well written, however, it can also entertain readers. Consider the example of internationally renowned physical anthropologist Pat Shipman, who often contributes scientifically rigorous yet accessible essays to the prestigious journal *American Scientist*. This publication is written for an audience of professional scientists or seriously interested amateurs who use its broad coverage of scientific developments as a way to keep up with their own and other fields. In her latest essay, "The Woof at the Door," Shipman compares and contrasts a "woof" and a "wolf" at the same time that she analyzes the evolutionary process that resulted in the differences between dogs and wolves. Following is the beginning of her essay, the bibliography of sources she used, and a brief paragraph giving her academic affiliation and contact information for readers who may wish to enter into conversation with her about her findings.

It's funny how much difference a single letter makes. A "woof" at the door is a very different thing from a wolf at the door. One is familiar, domestic, reassuring; the other is a frightening apparition of imminent danger. The distinction between our fond companions and the ferocious predator of northern climes goes back a long way.

Dogs are descended from wolves, probably the gray wolf. Some scientists argue that because dogs and wolves can and do interbreed, they shouldn't be considered to be separate species at all. They believe that domestic dogs are only a subspecies or variant of the gray wolf, *Canis lupus*, and ought to be called *Canis lupus familiaris* (the familiar or domestic wolf) instead of *Canis familiaris* (the familiar or domestic dog). Although the ability to interbreed and produce a fertile offspring is a tried-and-true criterion for recognizing that two populations are really variants of a single species, the reality is more nuanced. We cannot know whether dog-wolf hybrids will thrive and survive, or die out, in the long run. Modern wolves and dogs can be distinguished reasonably easily by their appearance. The most telling feature of dogs is the snout, which is significantly shorter and wider than wolves' snouts. Only a few dog breeds with extremely elongated, slender snouts, such as Irish wolfhounds, surpass wolves in "snoutiness."

But a crucial part of the difference we perceive is in the animals' manner and attitude toward humans. Domesticated dogs are just that: canids that live in the house or domicile of humans. They are genetically disposed to seek out human attention and approval and to accept human leadership. Wolves are not.

How did this important change come about? Probably in the distant past, humans took in a wolf cub, or even a whole litter of cubs, and provided shelter, food and protection. As the adopted cubs matured, some were aggressive, ferocious and difficult to handle; those probably ended up in the pot or were cast out. The ones that were more accepting of and

Prehistoric cave paintings rarely depict wolves or other carnivores. This water-color tracing of a cave painting was made by the archaeologist Abbé Henri Breuil in the early 1900s from the Grotte de Font-de-Gaume in France. The 17,000-year-old cave paintings number about 250 and mostly show bison and mammoths—only one is thought to be a wolf. Canids may have been domesticated by this point; it is possible that portraying wolves and humans was taboo.

more agreeable to humans were kept around longer and fed more. In time, humans might have co-opted the natural abilities of canids, using the dogs' keen noses and swift running skills, for example, to assist in hunting game. If only the most desirable dogs were permitted to breed, the genes encoding for "better" dogs would continue to be concentrated until the new domesticated species (or subspecies) was formed.

Bibliography

Germonpré, M., et al. 2009. Fossil dogs and wolves from Paleolithic sites in Belgium, the Ukraine and Russia: Osteometry, ancient DNA and stable isotopes. *Journal of Archaeological Science* 36:473–490.

Morey, D. F. 1994. The early evolution of the domestic dog. *American Scientist* 82:336–347.

Ostrander, E. A. 2007. Genetics and the shape of dogs. *American Scientist* 95:406–413.

Savolainen, P., et al. 2002. Genetic evidence for an East Asian origin of domestic dogs. *Science* 298:1610–1613.

Trut, L. N. 1999. Early canid domestication: The farm-fox experiment. *American Scientist* 87:160–169.

Vilà, C., et al. 1997. Multiple and ancient origins of the domestic dog. *Science* 276:1687–1689.

Pat Shipman is an adjunct professor of anthropology at the Pennsylvania State University. Address: Department of Anthropology, 315 Carpenter Building, Pennsylvania State University, University Park, PA 16802. Internet: pls10@psu.edu

Shipman refers to a number of outside sources in her well-documented essay, which her bibliography lists in conventional academic style. In addition to the prehistoric cave painting depicting a wolf or other carnivore, her essay also includes other clearly explained visuals: a chart that shows the differences in shape between wolves and dogs and photographs of prehistoric examples of *Canis lupus* teeth used as necklaces. As she continues her essay, she builds on several rhetorical methods of development: a narrative explanation of evidence of prehistoric dogs in the fossil record of the Upper Paleolithic Era, a comparative analysis of three fossil skulls of prehistoric dogs, and a process analysis as well as a cause–and–effect analysis of the evolutionary story from wolf to "woof." As you can see from this example, good academic writing doesn't have to be dry, dull, or abstract. It can be lively, interesting, and focused on familiar "real–world" topics like dogs and their relationship to humans.

Thinking about Academic and Public Writing

1. Return to "The Woof at the Door," and mark all the phrases and words that signal "academic" to you. Then mark all the phrases and words that signal "public." Consider the reasons you've made these distinctions, and be prepared to share your reasoning with the rest of the class.

2. Identify the ways Shipman employs the rhetorical appeals of ethos, logos, and pathos in her essay. What can you tell about Shipman's professional status from her writing? from her brief biographical paragraph? What can you tell from her bibliography?

3. Look over a magazine or Web site that you frequently enjoy reading. Locate an essay or article that is specialized and uses language specific to the field or topic, the way Shipman's article does. Whether the article is about biking, trip planning, career advice, or another topic of interest to you, read it carefully for the language it uses (some of which may need to be defined), the explanatory visuals that are included, and the rhetorical methods the author employs to make his or her points. Bring the article to class, along with your analysis, and be prepared to share your findings with the rest of the class.

Why and How Is Public Writing Used?

It might be easy to think of public writing as casual writing that uses simple language and sentence structures so that anyone has easy access to it. If you think of public writing in terms of the kinds of breezy articles

that appear in popular magazines, you'd be exactly right. In the following excerpt from an article in *National Geographic*, Garrison Keillor describes his visits to six state fairs:

> The state fair is a ritual carnival marking the end of summer and gardens and apple orchards and the start of school and higher algebra and the imposition of strict rules and what we in the north call the Long Dark Time. Like gardening, the fair doesn't change all that much.
>
> The big wheel whirls and the girls squeal and the bratwursts cook on the little steel rollers and the boys slouch around and keep checking their hair. It isn't the World's Columbian Exposition, the Aquarian Exposition, the Great Exhibition of the Works of Industry of All Nations, the Exposition Universelle, the Gathering of the Tribes, or the Aspen Institute. It's just us, taking a break from digging potatoes.
>
> The Ten Chief Joys of the State Fair are:
>
> 1. To eat food with your two hands.
> 2. To feel extreme centrifugal force reshaping your face and jowls as you are flung or whirled turbulently and you experience that intense joyfulness that is indistinguishable from anguish, or (as you get older) to observe other persons in extreme centrifugal situations.
> 3. To mingle, merge, mill, jostle gently, and flock together with throngs, swarms, mobs, and multitudes of persons slight or hefty, punky or preppy, young or ancient, wandering through the hubbub and amplified razzmatazz and raw neon and clouds of wiener steam in search of some elusive thing, nobody is sure exactly what.
> 4. To witness the stupidity of others, their gluttony and low-grade obsessions, their poor manners and slack-jawed, mouth-breathing, pop-eyed yahootude, and feel rather sophisticated by comparison.

5. To see the art of salesmanship, of barking, hustling, touting, and see how effectively it works on others and not on cool you.
6. To see designer chickens, the largest swine, teams of mighty draft horses, llamas, rare breeds of geese, geckos, poisonous snakes, a two-headed calf, a 650-pound man, and whatever else appeals to the keen, inquiring mind.
7. To watch the judging of livestock.
8. To observe entertainers attempt to engage a crowd that is moving laterally.
9. To sit down and rest amid the turmoil and reconsider the meaning of life.
10. To turn away from food and amusement and crass pleasure and to resolve to live on a higher plane from now on.

Keillor's writing seems effortless in its attention to detail, its ability to capture the spirit of a state fair, and its wry humor. His is public writing at its best, the kind of writing that tantalizes readers to want to read on, whether they have a subscription to *National Geographic* or happen to read it while waiting in the dentist's office.

Now consider the kind of public writing produced by neurologist Oliver Sacks, which is considered accessible by a wide range of readers even though it is a discipline-specific, jargon-laden, "academic" kind of writing. The following excerpt is the beginning of "Brilliant Light, a Chemical Boyhood," an autobiographical essay that appeared in the *New Yorker*, a publication known for the avid and wide-ranging intellectual curiosity of its readers. Sacks opens his essay, which explains his lifelong fascination with metals, with a meditation on the role metals play in his adult life:

> Something has got into me these last weeks—I do not know why. I have pulled out my old books (and bought many new ones), have set the little tungsten bar on a pedestal and papered the kitchen with chemical charts. I read lists of cosmic abundances in the bath. On cold, dismal Saturday afternoons, there is nothing better than curling up with a fat volume of Thorpe's Dictionary of Applied Chemistry, opening it anywhere, and reading at random. It was Uncle Tungsten's favorite book, and now it is one of mine. On depressive mornings, I like to work out atomic radii or ionization potentials with my Grape-Nuts—their charm has come back, and they will get me going for the day.

When Sacks refers to "atomic radii" and "ionization potentials," he's employing the language of chemistry, merging it with an everyday reference to Grape-Nuts, not specifying whether it's the chemistry or the cereal whose charm has returned to fuel his day.

Following his introduction, Sacks moves into the first section of his memoir:

> Many of my childhood memories are of metals: these seemed to exert a power on me from the start. They stood out, conspicuous against the heterogeneousness of the world, by their silveriness, their smoothness and weight. They seemed cool to the touch, and they rang when they were struck.

I also loved the yellowness, the heaviness of gold. My mother would take the wedding ring from her finger and let me handle it for a while, as she told me of its inviolacy, how it never tarnished. "Feel how heavy it is," she would add. "It's even heavier than lead." I knew what lead was, for I had handled the heavy, soft piping the plumber had left behind one year. Gold was soft, too, my mother told me, so it was usually combined with another metal to make it harder.

It was the same with copper—people mixed it with tin to produce bronze. Bronze! The very word was like a trumpet to me, for battle was the brave clash of bronze upon bronze, bronze spears on bronze shields, the great shield of Achilles. Or you could alloy copper with zinc, my mother said, to produce brass. All of us—my mother, my brothers, and I—had our own brass menorahs for Hanukkah. (My father, though, had a silver one.)

I knew copper, the shiny rose color of the great copper cauldron in our kitchen—it was taken down only once a year, when the quinces and crab apples were ripe in the garden and my mother would stew them to make jelly.

I knew zinc—the dull, slightly bluish birdbath in the garden was made of zinc—and tin, from the heavy tinfoil in which sandwiches were wrapped for a picnic. My mother showed me that when tin or zinc was bent it uttered a special "cry." "It's due to deformation of the crystal structure," she said, forgetting that I was five and could not understand her— and yet her words made me want to know more.

There was an enormous cast-iron lawn roller out in the garden—it weighed five hundred pounds, my father said. We, as children, could hardly budge it, but he was immensely strong and could lift it off the ground. It was always slightly rusty, and this bothered me, for the rust flaked off, leaving little cavities and scabs, and I was afraid the whole roller might corrode and fall apart one day, reduced to a mass of red dust and flakes. I needed to think of metals as stable, like gold—able to stave off the losses and ravages of time.

Sacks uses several rhetorical methods of development to explain his early fascination with metals: narration, exemplification, and definition. The narrative elements of his essay include characters, setting, and vivid dialogue. He arranges the events in his narration in order of importance, from least to most significant, using exemplification to emphasize the effect that different metals had on him as a boy and giving the most weight (five hundred pounds of weight, in fact) to iron.

· ·

Thinking about Academic and Public Writing

1. Reread the excerpt by Keillor, and determine what specific features of his piece distinguish it as public writing.

2. As you look over Keillor's writing, identify the terms or phrases that seem more intellectual or sophisticated than the language you might think is appropriate for an account of a state fair. Which of those words or phrases did you need to define as you read or to look up in a

dictionary? Be prepared to share your responses with the rest of the class.

3. What methods of rhetorical development does Keillor employ? How do each of those methods help Keillor make his point?

4. In your opinion, how do Keillor's and Sacks's essays compare in terms of where they lie along the axis of academic and public writing? Use textual evidence to support your answer.

5. Compare the two excerpts in terms of intended audience, purpose, and reliance on rhetorical appeals. Use textual evidence to support your answers.

How Do Academic and Public Writing on the Same Topic Compare?

By now, you realize that although academic and public writing each have distinctive features in terms of subject, audience, vocabulary, sentence structure, and venue (where the writing appears, whether in print or online), these two distinct types of writing also have much in common. The two essays that follow provide examples of academic and public writing: both are researched pieces on the topic of wind farming. The first essay, by undergraduate writer Catherine Leece, investigates the advantages of wind farming for small communities. Leece wrote this essay for her first-year honors composition course at Penn State University.

CATHERINE LEECE
Energy for the Community

Every time I visit my grandparents' house in Scotland, I spend a lot of 1 time walking around the old Royal Air Force runway that is now abandoned and overgrown. "I hope this place won't be forgotten," I think, but then I look up and realize that now there is no way that that could happen. Scattered around the airfield are seven giant wind turbines that electrify the surrounding community. The blades of these majestic machines rotate in the wind, and I can almost sense the energy that they are creating. Aside from the clean energy that they supply, these gentle giants have also supplied the area with monetary resources for community development, giving it economic and energetic independence from the rest of the country. Witnessing the Banff community's success with a program like this one made me realize that other small, rural, or even poor communities could benefit from the cultural, economic, and social changes that a similar program could bring. Implementing a local and sustainable energy source is a good way to encourage positive changes like autonomy and democracy, and it can promote the educational and developmental progress of a community like that of my grandparents.

TYPES OF ALTERNATIVE ENERGY

In 2000, Walter Youngquist noted that "no other substance can equal 2 the enormous impact which the use of oil has had on so many people, so rapidly, in so many ways, and in so many places around the world." Youngquist qualified his statement by also pointing out that the world's supply of oil is getting overused. Aside from the pollution that burning fossil fuels causes, it will soon cost so much to drill and refine the small amount of hard-to-reach oil that will be left that it will not be worth it. Fortunately, there are many other more sustainable options available, including water, solar, and wind power.

Water power, or hydroelectric power, captures the energy of moving water and immediately turns it into useful electricity ("Wind"). The 3 water used to create hydroelectric power is not consumed in the generation process, so this resource is renewable. Solar and wind power are very similar in that they also transform mechanical energy into electrical energy, and they are both much more sustainable than oil for the long-term.

Although Youngquist points out many of the controversial down- 4 sides of current alternative energy sources (which I will discuss shortly), he readily admits that a change will soon be necessary and that "delay in dealing with the issues will surely result in unpleasant surprises." At present, oil and natural gas constitute about 50 percent of our energy supply (Youngquist). As a result, much work lies ahead before renewable resources can even begin to replace fossil fuels. In fact, in order to have a sustainable energy income, we will have to expand our energy horizons to include these clean energy sources.

CURRENT ENERGY SITUATION IN SMALL, RURAL COMMUNITIES

Right now, there is a huge discrepancy between the energy situations 5 of developed and developing countries (Reddy 3435), and that discrepancy is causing social and economic divides that continue to give the governments of developed countries control over those of developing countries. As a necessary but hard–to–produce resource, energy is a commodity that allows the populations who control it to manipulate those populations who do not. Before any kind of alternative energy program can be implemented, however, the preexisting demographic, cultural, and economic characteristics of each population would have to be taken into account as well as the energy sources that are currently relied on (3435). Right now, these issues are being ignored, and the energy demands of small, rural, and poor countries fall between the cracks because their energy crisis is not being analyzed separately from that of larger, developed communities (3436).

In contrast to developed areas, poor or rural areas tend to rely heav- 6 ily on the use of inefficient energy, such as fuelwood or animate energy sources (human and animal energy, for example), which causes a large part of their culture and economy to revolve around the use of these sources (Reddy 3436). In a 1999 study of communities in India, the most utilized energy sources were fuelwood, human energy, kerosene, bullock energy, and electricity (3436), and unfortunately, these sources are all inefficient and unproductive. The large amounts of human labor required to generate enough electricity generally come from the women and children, whose day revolves around collecting fuelwood and water, and this delegation breeds gender discrepancies and sexism. Even worse, all this effort still results in low levels of energy efficiency and water consumption, creating a never-ending struggle for energy (3437).

In developed or urban areas, the laborious tasks of generating and 7 collecting energy are carried out by inanimate sources, like oil and power plants, creating huge disparities between societies with these resources (developed populations) and societies without them (developing populations). The previously mentioned study of Indian communities points out that despite the rising energy crisis in poor and rural areas, "the growing politically powerful urban population is generating an escalating urban energy demand that is eclipsing rural needs" (Reddy 3435). Because urban populations are so large and dense, they hold a strong influence over energy programs, and their energy demands are met while rural needs go unheard.

WHY SHOULD SMALL, RURAL COMMUNITIES EMPLOY ALTERNATIVE ENERGY?

As noted earlier, there is a huge energy discrepancy between rural 8 developing areas and urban, developed areas of the world. According to the World Bank, there are still 2 billion people who cook with traditional, unhealthy, inefficient energy sources like fuelwood and 1.7 billion people living without electricity (Reddy 3435), and all of these people live in underdeveloped, poor, or rural areas. The only way for these populations to achieve some level of equality with their larger counterparts is to achieve the same level of energetic success as them, and what would be even better is for developing areas to begin their development with sustainable energy sources. If they start off with renewable energy sources, they will not have to worry about switching to them after assimilating to nonrenewable resources. When developed countries, which rely heavily on fossil fuels, have to do this (probably sometime in the not–so–distant future), small and rural communities that "grow up" with renewable resources will be many steps ahead of them. An assessment by the Socio–Political Evaluation of Energy Deployment (SPEED) suggested wind energy as a good jumping–off point for the implementation of alternative energy programs. SPEED believes that wind energy has the potential to support development in rural areas (Stephens, Wilson, and Peterson 1224), and the U.S. Department of Energy's Energy Efficiency and Renewable Energy (EERE) program pointed out that the best sites for wind farms are often rural locations anyway. Even if these communities are not poor or struggling for survival, they can benefit immensely from local energy sources. For example, for farmers and ranch owners who live far away from the utility grid, having a local source of energy can save a lot of money ("Wind"); in addition, wind farm owners have to pay the land–owners to lease the property on which they build the turbines, benefiting the landowners economically. The EERE estimates that domestic wind power could supply enough energy to cheaply electrify the entire United States ("Wind"), demonstrating the incredible supply of energy that the wind holds if employed efficiently.

RURAL WIND FARM COMMUNITY IN BOYNDIE, SCOTLAND

One good example of a small community employing a local, re- 9 newable energy source is that of the seaside community of Boyndie, Scotland. My family was extensively involved in the deployment and development of a wind farm project, so the source of the following information is my uncle, Duncan Leece. About six years ago, my uncle, vice–chairman of the local community council, was contacted by an Italian energy company interested in building a wind farm on the land adjacent to his. The Boyndie community council and the energy corporation worked together for almost four years, and in the end, the council negotiated a two-part program that benefited the community as well as the energy company.

The first part of the program involved the setup of a trust fund by the Italian company. This fund is now controlled by the community council, and any local community group or project can apply for financial support from this fund. Community projects— such as school improvements, park restoration, and drama camps— have been funded by this trust, which will grow to £500,000 over twenty-five years. The second part of the program was created for the benefit of individuals that live within a twenty-mile radius of Boyndie. My uncle and four colleagues purchased a £750,000 share in the wind farm, which they then resold as £1 shares. Seven hundred locals invested an average of £1,000 each, and their expected return rate is 10 to 15 percent per year. After twenty-five years, the original investment should also be returned.

By involving the entire community in the decision-making and developmental process from the start, the Boyndie community was able to prevent "a lot of objection and myth" that could have developed around the construction of a wind farm. Although it still expects strict guidelines to be followed, the community is unanimously supportive of this program and its benefits, and now that many other areas are following their lead, Scotland is on its way to being completely energetically independent.

COUNTERARGUMENTS AND PROBLEMS

The critics of alternative energy sources make many points about the viability of alternative energy sources as a replacement for fossil fuels, the economic consequences of switching energy sources, and the actual pros and cons of certain alternative fuel sources. For example, Mario Giampetro, who did a study on the use of biomass as a viable alternative to oil, warned that it "is not even an advisable option to cover a significant fraction" of the current use of oil (qtd. in Youngquist). This statement reflects the downside of alternative energy use; right now it cannot replace oil for anything other than its electrical value.

Unfortunately, it is also often hard to implement localized energy programs, especially from renewable sources. As Stevens, Wilson, and Peterson point out, much of the research about incorporating "alternative emerging energy technologies" (1224) has not taken into account sociopolitical concerns at the subnational level (1225), making it impossible to efficiently implement alternative energy programs into smaller communities, especially economically or socially unstable ones. These factors must be understood before programs like the one in my grandparents' community can become commonplace.

Actual renewability is yet another factor that must be taken into account before alternative energy sources can be commonly used. Many people do not realize that there are some features of alternative energy sources that make them less renewable than one might think. For example, the use of wood, which is considered a renewable source, is slowly deforesting large areas of land, and corn crops, which are used to create an alternative to gasoline, quickly erode soil (Youngquist); both of these sources are therefore inefficient, and due to the destruction they cause, they are much less renewable than many people assume. Hydroelectric power also has its drawbacks, often causing flooding or damage to areas valuable to wildlife or human populations, and the sedimentation of reserves compromises its sustainability. The biggest drawback of solar and wind energy is that these sources are not constant (Youngquist). Certain latitudes may not get enough direct sunlight to support solar energy, and many areas do not have sufficient wind to profit from turbines (Youngquist). Even when used, these sources provide only electricity, so other alternatives are needed for things like gasoline and plastics. The fault of these counterarguments, however, is that many of them stem from a lack of research and knowledge on the subject. Concerns about the safety and efficiency of alternative energy sources as well as the economic and political concerns of trying to suddenly move away from oil hold back our nation as well as many others from participating in clean energy programs. Research and public education could overcome these drawbacks and help scientists create effective alternative energy programs. The research of Stevens, Wilson, and Peterson supports this theory, concluding that alternative energy research often overlooks important nontechnical aspects of energy programs that are heavily "influenced by varying perception and levels of awareness about the risks, benefits, and cost of emerging technologies" (1224). Even Youngquist, who pointed out the cons of alternative energy, strongly encourages us to make the cultural, social, and economic changes that will get us on our way to a major energy transition. As James Winebrake describes, we need a "technology roadmap" to help us make a plan for implementing new energy technologies (1). A plan like this would consider three variables: "what we desire," "what is preventing us from getting what we desire," and "how we can overcome those barriers" (1), ultimately leading to a sustainable energy program.

For developing or rural communities, utilizing local, renewable energy sources has the potential to bring about positive cultural, social, and economic changes. For example, communities that employ large amounts of human labor could instead use wind or solar energy for some tasks, thus relieving many women and children from strenuous labor and allowing them to concentrate on other things, like education. There is already a lot of information about the economic aspects of this kind of shift as well as how it would affect poor, developing communities, but I would like to expand that argument to any small or rural community that has the appropriate natural resources. Obviously, I concede to the fact that not all communities can employ renewable sources like wind or solar power, but that is no reason not to improve those that can benefit from new energy programs.

WORKS CITED

Leece, Duncan. Online interview. 25 Mar. 2009. Web.

Reddy, Amulya. "Goals, Strategies and Policies for Rural Energy." *Economic and Political Weekly* 34.49 (1999): 3435–45. Web. 4 Apr. 2009.

Stephens, Jennie, Elizabeth Wilson, and Tarla Rai Peterson. "Socio-Political Evaluation of Energy Deployment (SPEED): An Integrated Research Framework Analyzing Energy Technology Deployment." *Technological Forecasting and Social Change* 76.9 (2008): 1224–46. Web. 4 Apr. 2009.

"Wind and Hydropower Technologies Program." U.S. Department of Energy, 2006. Web. 8 Apr. 2009.

Winebrake, James. *Alternative Energy: Assessment and Implementation Reference Book.* New York: Fairmont, 2004. Print.

Youngquist, Walter. "Alternative Energy Sources." *Hubbert Peak of Oil Production,* 2000. Web. 6 Apr. 2009.

Analyzing Academic Writing

1. What question is Leece attempting to answer with her research and writing? Why does her question require serious research?
2. What is the significance to her of that question and its answer?
3. Reread Leece's essay, marking every place that she acknowledges sources. Which of her sources do you consider to be authoritative? Why?
4. How does Leece's own experience work as a reference source? Be prepared to share your answer with the rest of the class.
5. What is the purpose of her essay? What textual evidence can you use to support your answer?
6. How does Leece use the rhetorical appeals of ethos, pathos, and logos? Which appeal dominates her essay? Why might she have concentrated on that appeal?
7. Look at Leece's paragraphs and sentences. How would you describe their length and structure?

Journalist Keith Bradsher explored the topic of wind power for the *New York Times*, resulting in a newspaper article that is also carefully researched and composed. Unlike Leece's academic essay, though, the following article was widely distributed to the reading public.

KEITH BRADSHER
The Ascent of Wind Power

KHORI, India— Dilip Pantosh Patil uses an ox–drawn wooden plow to till 1
the same land as his father, grandfather and great–grandfather. But now
he has a new neighbor: a shiny white wind turbine taller than a 20–story
building, generating electricity at the edge of his bean field.

Wind power may still have an image as something of a plaything of 2
environmentalists more concerned with clean energy than saving money.
But it is quickly emerging as a serious alternative not just in affluent areas of the world but in fast–growing countries like India and China that
are avidly seeking new energy sources. And leading the charge here in
west–central India and elsewhere is an unlikely champion, Suzlon Energy, a homegrown Indian company.

Suzlon already dominates the Indian market and is now expanding 3
rapidly abroad, having erected factories in locations as far away as Pipe-
stone, Minn., and Tianjin, China. Four–fifths of the orders in Suzlon's
packed book now come from outside India.

Not even on the list of the world's top 10 wind–turbine manufactur- 4
ers as recently as 2002, Suzlon passed Siemens of Germany last year to
become the fifth–largest producer by installed megawatts of capacity. It
still trails the market leader, Vestas Wind Systems of Denmark, as well as
General Electric, Enercon of Germany and Gamesa Tecnológica of Spain.

Suzlon's past shows how a company can prosper by tackling the spe- 5
cial needs of a developing country. Its presence suggests a way of serving expanding energy needs without relying quite so much on coal, the
fastest–growth fossil fuel now but also the most polluting.

And Suzlon's future is likely to be a case study of how a manufac- 6
turer copes with China, both in capturing sales there and in confronting
competition from Chinese companies.

Suzlon is an outgrowth in many ways of India's dysfunctional power- 7
distribution system. Electricity boards owned by state governments
charge industrial users more than twice as much for each kilowatt–hour
as such customers pay in the United States— and they still suffer black-
outs almost every day, especially in northern India.

Subject to political pressures, the boards are often slow to collect 8
payments from residential consumers and well–connected businesses, especially before elections. As a result, they often lack the money to invest
in new equipment.

To stay open and prevent crucial industrial or computer processes 9
from stopping, a wide range of businesses— including auto parts factories and outsourcing giants— rely on still more costly diesel generators.

With natural gas prices climbing as well, wind turbines have become 10
attractive to Indian business. The Essar Group of Mumbai, a big industrial
conglomerate active in shipping, steel and construction, is now working

The Patils, father and son, plow a field below Indian wind towers.

on plans for a wind farm near Chennai, formerly Madras, after concluding that regulatory changes in India have made it financially attractive.

"The mechanisms didn't used to be there; now they are," said Jose 11
Numpeli, vice president for operations at Essar Power. The electricity
boards "know how to cost it, they know how to pay for it."

Roughly 70 percent of the demand for wind turbines in India comes 12
from industrial users seeking alternatives to relying on the grid, said Tulsi R.
Tanti, Suzlon's managing director. The rest of the purchases are made by
a small group of wealthy families in India, for whom the tax breaks for
wind turbines are attractive.

Wind will remain competitive as long as the price of crude oil re- 13
mains above $40 a barrel, Mr. Tanti estimated. To remain cost–effective

below $40 a barrel, wind energy may require subsidies, or possibly carbon–based taxes on oil and other fossil fuels.

Mr. Tanti and his three younger brothers were running a textile busi- 14 ness in Gujarat, in northwestern India, when they purchased a German wind turbine—only to find that they could not keep it running. So they decided to build and maintain turbines themselves, starting Suzlon in 1995 and later leaving the textile business.

To minimize land costs, wind farms are typically in rural areas, cho- 15 sen for the strength of the wind there as well as low prices for land. But that can mean culture shock.

"There were no big changes until the turbines came," Mr. Patil said, 16 pausing from plowing here with his father in this remote, hilly, tribal area 200 miles northeast of Mumbai, where oxen remain at the center of farm life and motorized vehicles are uncommon.

Doing business in rural areas of the developing world carries special 17 challenges. The new Suzlon Energy wind farm in Khori is a subject of national pride. More than 300 giant wind turbines, with 110–foot blades, snatch electricity from the air. But it has also struggled with the sporadic lawlessness that bedevils India.

S. Mohammed Farook, the installation's manager, was far from happy 18 one recent afternoon. At least 63 new turbines, worth $1.3 million apiece and each capable of lighting several thousand homes when the wind blows, could not be put into service because thieves had stolen their copper power cables and aluminum service ladders for sale as scrap.

The copper or aluminum fetches as little as $1 from black–market 19 scrap dealers. But each repair costs thousands of dollars in parts and staff time, in a country that is desperately short of electricity and technicians.

"I am crying inside," Mr. Farook said.   20

Despite such problems, Suzlon has expanded rapidly as global de- 21 mand for wind energy has taken off. Its sales and earnings tripled in the quarter ended June 30, as the company earned the equivalent of $41.6 million on sales of $202.4 million.

The demand for wind turbines has particularly accelerated in India, 22 where installations rose nearly 48 percent last year, and in China, where they rose 65 percent, although from a lower base. Wind farms are start- ing to dot the coastline of east–central China and the southern tip of India, as well as scattered mesas and hills across central India and even Inner Mongolia.

Coal is the main alternative in the two countries, and is causing 23 acid rain and respiratory ailments while contributing to global warm- ing. China accounted for 79 percent of the world's growth in coal con- sumption last year and India used 7 percent more, according to statistics from BP.

Worried by its reliance on coal, China has imposed a requirement 24 that power companies generate a fifth of their electricity from renewable sources by 2020. This target calls for expanding wind power almost as much as nuclear energy over the next 15 years. India already leads China in wind power and is quickly building more wind turbines.

Chinese and Indian officials are optimistic about relying much more 25 heavily on wind.

"I believe we may break through these targets — if not, we should 26 at least have no problem reaching them," said Zhang Yuan, vice general manager of the China Longyuan Electric Power Group, the renewable-energy arm of one of China's five state-owned electric utilities, China Guodian.

Kamal Nath, India's minister of commerce and industry, was even 27 more enthusiastic. "India is ideally suited for wind energy," he said. "The cost of it works well and we have the manufacturing capability."

International experts are more skeptical that wind will displace coal 28 to a considerable extent, saying that while electricity production from wind is likely to increase rapidly, the sheer scale of energy demands suggests that coal burning will expand even more.

Suzlon still sees plenty of opportunity in China and has decided to 29 build some of its latest designs in China for the market there, despite the risk of having them copied by Chinese manufacturers.

"Being an Asian leader," Mr. Tanti said, "we cannot afford to ignore 30 China."

A dozen Chinese manufacturers have jumped into wind-turbine 31 manufacturing as well. They have struggled with quality problems and have limited production capacity so far, resulting in long delivery delays.

But the Chinese producers already have an edge on price over im- 32 ported equipment, according to Meiya Power of Hong Kong, which owns and operates power plants in China and across Asia, and is considering a wind farm in windswept Inner Mongolia.

Mr. Tanti said that rapid innovation and design changes would allow 33 Suzlon to stay ahead of copycats. "It's a time-consuming process," he said, estimating that it would take two to three years for rivals to clone Suzlon turbines because they use unique or proprietary parts.

Suzlon manufactures its turbines at two factories in India, but has 34 begun test production at a just-completed turbine-blade factory in Minnesota, where it already supplies turbines for a wind farm operated by the Edison Mission Group and Deere & Company. It has also begun test production at a Chinese factory that will make both turbines and blades.

To reach the Suzlon wind farm here, the huge rotors travel by night 35 on special trucks for a 300-mile journey from northwestern India on a succession of paved and dirt roads.

Squatter huts have had to be removed along the way to allow the 36 long trucks to turn; Suzlon is not required to pay compensation but often makes donations in these cases, Mr. Farook said.

The truck crews also carry wooden poles to prop up electricity wires 37 across the road and pass underneath. The trucks sometimes attract gawkers, and live wires occasionally burn bystanders.

"With human error, it may touch human flesh," Mr. Farook said. "In 38 that case, we have to pay compensation."

Villagers in Khori said that thievery and even robberies by rock- 39 throwing gangs were nothing new, and were a problem long before Suzlon began setting up wind turbines. The company's response— stepping up patrols by security guards— has reduced everyday crime. That has made villagers more willing to rent land at the edge of their fields for the turbines.

At first, "we were really confused about what was going on," Mr. Patil 40 said. "But now we're O.K. on it."

· ·

Analyzing Public Writing

1. What question is Bradsher attempting to answer? Why does this question require serious research?

2. What is the significance of that question and its answer to the *New York Times*'s readers?

3. Reread Bradsher's article, marking every place where he acknowledges or demonstrates that he's done research. Which of his sources do you consider the most and the least authoritative? Why?

4. How does Bradsher's own experience work as a source?

5. How does Bradsher use the rhetorical appeals of ethos, pathos, and logos? Which appeal dominates the article? Why might Bradsher have concentrated on that appeal?

6. What is the purpose of this article? What textual evidence can you use to support your answer?

7. Look at Bradsher's paragraphs and sentences. How would you describe their length and structure?

· ·

· ·

Try Your Hand   Using your answers to the questions following Leece's essay and Bradsher's article, make a list of the ways you would go about either revising Leece's essay into a *New York Times* article or revising Bradsher's article into an academic essay. Be prepared to share your ideas with the rest of the class.

· ·

How Do You Do Academic and Public Writing?

Whenever you're doing either academic or public writing that entails research, you'll want to consider three basic aspects of researched writing that may differ from one kind of writing to another: conducting research, planning the essay (which involves synthesizing a variety of rhetorical methods), and synthesizing and acknowledging sources.

● Conducting Research

Look again at Leece's academic essay, which she carefully researched before and as she wrote it. You'll see that she conducted different kinds of research, tapping her own experience and observation (in what is called "naturalistic research"), interviewing people, reading academic books on the subject of wind power, and pulling information from reliable Web sources, such as academic journals and the U.S. Department of Energy. Given that her audience is an academic one and her purpose is to argue for the benefits of wind power, Leece made the right research decisions.

In comparison, the *New York Times* article, written for a much broader public audience and for a different purpose— to inform readers about the development of wind power in India and elsewhere— does not appear to be based on academic research sources. The writer, Keith Bradsher, seems to have visited India to research his story, by witnessing himself the success of wind power, studying the growth of Suzlon Energy, and interviewing various people (from farmer Dilip Pantosh Patil to the vice president for operations at Essar Power Group of Mumbai). He obviously also did research to be able to include numerical information such as the ranking of the world's leading wind-turbine manufacturers and the statistics on the growth of turbine construction and coal consumption in India and China, although he doesn't mention any specific sources for this kind of information other than a Suzlon executive and BP, the oil company.

Although you will not ordinarily need to travel to Scotland or India to do research for either academic or public writing, note that both Leece and Bradsher use personal observation and interviews effectively. But readers of academic writing usually expect the writer to have done additional, specifically "academic" research, whereas readers of most public writing usually do not (although they often expect more than observation and interviews). For academic writing, evidence of this specialized research is a key element in creating the writer's ethos, or credibility. For public writing, ethos usually depends more on other factors. Whenever you are faced with a writing task, then, think about the kinds of research your audience will expect you to do, and plan your work accordingly.

● Planning the Essay

In both academic and public writing, the researcher goes through the same process of determining a specific audience and purpose for the writing and of combining the rhetorical appeals (ethos, logos, pathos) and the various rhetorical methods of development in order to achieve that purpose for that audience. In her academic essay, Leece skillfully handles all of these considerations. You can see that she opens her essay with description and narration about her own personal experience and then moves quickly to explain her argumentative purpose for researching and writing: "Implementing a local and sustainable energy source is a good way to encourage positive changes like autonomy and democracy, and it can promote the educational and developmental progress of a community like that of my grandparents." Once she moves into the body of the essay, she begins using the research she did, using her good insights into which sources will persuade her academic audience.

In terms of rhetorical methods, the body of the essay first uses cause-and–effect analysis and comparison and contrast to discuss the need to switch from oil to alternative fuels and to compare these energy sources. The section "Current Energy Situation in Small, Rural Communities" contrasts both developed with developing countries and urban with rural populations in analyzing the effect these contrasts have on energy conditions and policies. As you continue looking over Leece's essay, you'll see that she taps other rhetorical methods of development as well, supporting those methods with her expert research. Toward the end of her essay, Leece addresses arguments counter to her own, dealing with each of them in a reasonable and researched way.

In "The Ascent of Wind Power," Bradsher opens with a brief description of the Patil family farming beneath wind turbines and moves quickly into exemplification, the method that is the central one for his entire article: Suzlon Energy is a leading example of the expansion of wind power in developing countries. To tell this story to his public audience, Bradsher relies on a number of brief narrations and examples, many of them based on personal interviews. He also compares and contrasts two leading developing countries, India and China, in their development of wind power and the growth in their coal consumption and includes a cause-and–effect analysis of how "Suzlon is an outgrowth in many ways of India's dysfunctional power–distribution system."

In addition to Bradsher's verbal use of rhetorical methods, his article includes two compelling visuals (one of which is reproduced here) that emphasize the contrast between human energy and wind energy. Notice also that his writing style, typical for a newspaper article, is slightly less formal than that of Leece. His paragraphs are markedly shorter, and many of his sentences are as well.

As you plan a piece of academic or public writing, think carefully about the issues of which rhetorical methods to use and how to synthesize them smoothly into a coherent text. For some kinds of academic and public writing, a certain method or combination of methods is expected or required. For example, a report on a research study you did for your psychology class will need to analyze the process by which the study was conducted, and a proposal to your college to change the system for assigning dorm rooms to students will need to contrast the characteristics of the current system with those of the proposed one, argue for the change, and maybe also provide some narratives or examples of problems it would eliminate. More often, though, you will have to make these decisions yourself, guided by your specific purpose (to inform, to argue) and audience (your instructor, other psychology students, the college housing department). Similarly, think about whether your writing situation, academic or public, calls for a formal style or a less formal one, long sentences and paragraphs or short ones, illustrations and what kinds, and so on.

● Synthesizing and Acknowledging Sources

In addition to the differences in the *kinds* of sources used by Leece and Bradsher, you can see sharp differences between the ways Leece *uses and acknowledges* her sources and the ways Bradsher does. For example, notice that near the beginning of her essay, Leece uses Walter Youngquist, an expert in energy issues, to make the argument that the earth is running out of oil. But she also notes that he "points out the controversial downsides of current alternative energy sources" and says she will discuss these later—which she does near the end of her essay, where she again uses Youngquist as a main source of information for her discussion of arguments against development of wind energy. For other parts of her essay, she makes good use of articles from the professional journal *Technological Forecasting and Social Change,* as well as from the U.S. Department of Energy Web site and *Economic and Political Weekly*, an Indian-based publication that she uses for information about the energy situation in developing countries (such as India) and rural areas.

Throughout her essay, Leece carefully cites these sources using MLA style, either within the text or in parenthetical references, and uses her personal (and family) experience mainly as a way to bring assertions to life (at the same time that she enhances her ethos and illuminates the pathos of her essay). She ends her academic essay with her list of Works Cited (credible sources that further enhance her ethos).

Bradsher's article is beautifully built on his research, yet as noted earlier, most of his sources are missing from the text. He acknowledges all of the direct quotations from the people he has interviewed, and he makes a gesture toward BP (formerly British Petroleum) as a source. (In the online version of the article, mention of BP was linked to the company's Web site, where readers could presumably check whether Bradsher was presenting the information from it accurately.) But because he's writing for the popular media and for a public audience, he is not expected to cite each and every bit of specific information he provides. Nor is he expected to supply a Works Cited list. Still, notice how he, like Leece, skillfully synthesizes different sources. For example, in two consecutive paragraphs, he quotes first an executive for a government–owned utility in China and then the minister of commerce and industry for India about their optimistic views of the future of wind power in their countries. The following paragraph, however, cites (with no formal acknowledgment) "international experts" who are skeptical about these claims.

In doing your own academic and public writing, work to synthesize any sources you have used, both with each other and with your own ideas, into a coherent, convincing whole. And think carefully about to what extent and exactly how your audience will expect you to acknowledge these sources. Academic writing like the psychology research report mentioned earlier is virtually always expected to use formal systems of source citation, whereas public writing may not require formal citations.

✱ Academic Writing Assignments

1. Consider the patterns of speech and silence in any of your classes. Why do some students dominate class discussion while others rarely, if ever, participate vocally? To answer this question, you may want to conduct careful classroom observations, as well as conduct library and online research on conversation patterns, silence in the classroom, and discussion patterns that allow you to analyze the discussion patterns in your classroom. As you draft your academic essay, you may want to consider such questions as who talks the most, who talks the least, who remains silent, who appears to be listening (or not), and who interrupts. You may also want to consider how issues of gender, race, class, and age influence these factors. Be sure to research, synthesize your sources, and document your essay according to the citation system your instructor requires.

2. Consider the reading and laboratory work you are doing for another course in another discipline: psychology, history, chemistry, math, or sociology, for example. What is a question you would like to answer about the content of this course? What kinds of research might you need to do in order to locate the information you need? After you have answered these questions, begin researching and drafting an academic essay for one of your other classes. Take care to synthesize your research findings into your own opinions, assertions, and examples; to cite your sources according to the system your instructor prefers; and to acknowledge every source. Pay careful attention to the rhetorical methods of development you need to employ.

3. Consider your own dietary habits and those of other people in your age group. What foods and drinks constitute that diet? How nutritious might that diet be? Using the quality of nutrition as the basis for your research, launch an investigation (using library and online resources, observation, interviews) into the dietary habits of your generation, which you can define as broadly or narrowly as you choose. Draft an academic essay on

this topic of generational eating habits in which you synthesize and acknowledge your sources, knitting them together with your own experiences and observations, to describe what people in your age group eat and the effects of that diet. Consider your audience to be experts in the field of health, college services, or nutrition. Be sure to document your essay according to the citation system your instructor requires.

✳ Public Writing Assignments

1. Taking the topic of classroom patterns of speech and silence described in question 1 under Academic Writing Assignments, research and write an essay for a general audience. You can depend on the library and online research you've done as well as on your classroom observations. In addition, however, you may want to conduct interviews with some of your classmates to see if their observations align with yours or to see what exactly they're noticing. Determine who might be the members of your audience, where and how you might deliver the information, which rhetorical methods you will employ, and how, exactly, you'll credit your research sources. Use Bradsher's article from the *New York Times* as a model.

2. What kinds of employment or service do you value but not want to do? It might be house cleaning, cooking, dishwashing, car repair, carpentry, restaurant service, or something else. Choose a job or service, and conduct research in the library, online, and in observation and interviews in order to determine the kinds of knowledge, training, and expertise required to perform it well. (You may be surprised to learn just "what it takes.") Draft an essay, aimed at a general audience, that explains the expertise and intelligence necessary to do this job well. As you write, consider your purpose, how you will synthesize and cite your research findings, which rhetorical methods of development you will employ, and how you will deliver your information.

3. Consider the financial, social, and intellectual effects of obtaining a college education — specifically, *your* college education. Relying on the rhetorical method of cause-and-effect analysis, write an essay that combines your personal response to the question of effects with information you've gained by conducting online and library research. Your audience will be interested readers, who will read your essay in a popular venue (such as your campus newspaper or your personal blog) that you will determine. Take care to synthesize and acknowledge your research according to your instructor's expectations.

USING AND DOCUMENTING SOURCES

The quality of your writing will often depend on how well you use and document the intellectual work of others. In many cases, you will decide to limit your sources to firsthand evidence — your own observations and experiences. Often, however, you will want or need to balance such firsthand evidence with secondhand evidence — library research, online research, or maybe interviews you conduct or questionnaires you administer.

The purpose of this appendix is twofold: first, to help you learn how to use sources to your advantage in the text of your essays, and second, to help you learn how to document clearly the sources you are using, both in your text and in your Works Cited list. All of the examples follow the style recommended by the Modern Language Association (MLA). If you find that you need additional information, refer to the seventh edition of the *MLA Handbook for Writers of Research Papers* (New York: MLA, 2009).

Summarizing and Paraphrasing

Summarizing and paraphrasing are two common ways of referring to the intellectual work of others without directly quoting the entire work. When you summarize a text, you condense that work or a substantial passage of it (which can be anything from a paragraph to several chapters) into a much shorter piece of writing within your own writing. For instance, if you need to refer to the plot of *Romeo and Juliet*, you might write a summary like the following:

> *Summary:* Many of the most romantic love stories, whether true or fiction, are based on the plot of William Shakespeare's late-sixteenth-century play *Romeo and Juliet*, a story of young lovers from feuding families. Romeo and Juliet manage to elope and hatch a plan for their life together, but through a series of unfortunate coincidences, they both die at the end of the play, to the sorrow of their reconciled families.

A summary should be as short as possible — a sentence or a couple of sentences. Within the summary, you should identify the author of the source and, if you are citing more than one work by that author in your essay, the title as well. If you are summarizing a specific passage, you will need to list the page number or numbers (or in the case of Shakespeare, the act and scene) of the part being summarized.

Another common way to use someone else's ideas or research is to paraphrase. Paraphrasing deals with a much shorter passage in the original work — a few sentences at most — and restates it in about the same number of words as the original. Though you rephrase the idea in your own words, you still need to give credit to the original source. Here is an example of a paraphrased idea from Bruce Catton's "Grant and Lee: A Study in Contrasts":

Quotation: "Thousands of tired, underfed, poorly clothed Confederate soldiers, long-since past the simple enthusiasm of the early days of the struggle, somehow considered Lee the symbol of everything for which they had been willing to die" (194).

Paraphrase: Catton shows that the Confederate troops, despite physical disadvantages that were increasingly discouraging, still found the inspiration and purpose to fight for the South through the figure of their General Lee (194).

Using and Integrating Quotations

In general, try to summarize and paraphrase most of the materials that you take from other sources, saving only the most compelling passages or bits of material to use as direct quotations. When you do use a quotation, the first rule is to be sure that you've copied it correctly, which is harder to do than you might think. All of us become familiar with the outside sources we are using— so familiar that we begin to leave out, add, or change words within the original quotation. The second rule of using quotations is to weave the quotation smoothly into the fabric of the sentence or paragraph. Rather than dropping the quotation into your work abruptly, introduce it with your own words. For instance, if you are arguing that allegiance to the cause represented by the figure of Robert E. Lee was the only reason the Confederate soldiers continued fighting a losing Civil War, you might write something like this:

The Confederate soldiers continued fighting a losing battle because they "considered Lee the symbol of everything for which they had been willing to die" (Catton 194).

Avoiding Plagiarism

Good writers use the work of others to their own advantage. But you cannot simply take another's words and ideas and put them into your own essay; you must be sure to document the source — to give that other writer credit for his or her thoughts and language. Plagiarism, the use of someone else's words or ideas without acknowledgment, is the theft of someone else's intellectual work; it does not matter if the theft is intentional or unintentional — the consequences for you are the same, from failing the essay or the course to being expelled from school. Therefore it is important that you acquaint yourself with the distinction between appropriate paraphrasing and quoting on the one hand and plagiarizing on the other. If you use an author's words or ideas without crediting him or her, the plagiarism is obvious. More subtle, however, would be if you credited the author but neither paraphrased the original language nor enclosed it in quotation marks.

If you decided to paraphrase the Bruce Catton quotation, for example, you would need to go far beyond the following:

> Catton shows that thousands of tired, underfed, poorly clothed Confederate soldiers, having lost the simple enthusiasm of the early days of the struggle, found in Lee the inspiration to fight on (194).

The language of this sentence is mostly that of the original Catton quote; it is not original language from you, the writer. As a result, a good deal of it would need to be enclosed in quotation marks. As it stands, the sentence constitutes plagiarism.

Ideas that are considered common knowledge do not need to be credited to a particular author or source. For example, you may have learned that former president Bill Clinton was born on August 19, 1946, from reading a biography of him, but that information is available in many sources and is not in dispute. Facts that could not be argued with are considered common knowledge.

MLA Style for Source Citations in the Text

The most common way of citing sources in the humanities is the style recommended by the Modern Language Association (MLA). The following examples explain the variety of ways you can use MLA style to cite the sources you are using. Remember, if you need further reference, consult the *MLA Handbook for Writers of Research Papers*, seventh edition.

In MLA style, citations in the text provide the reader with just enough information to find the source in a Works Cited list at the end of the essay or research paper. Unless you are referring to an entire work, these citations are placed in parentheses immediately following the source information they refer to. A parenthetical citation includes the page number or page range where the information can be found and sometimes the author and the title of the source as well. The following examples demonstrate the ways to use text citations for various kinds of sources.

A Work with One Author

If you have not mentioned the author in your sentence, place in parentheses the author's last name and the page number or page range of the material you are citing.

> The police of Beverly Hills have won awards for their fashionable uniforms four times since 1989 (Steinmetz 129).

If you do name the author in your sentence, you need only to include the page number or range in the parenthetical citation.

Steinmetz claims that in the real-life ZIP code 90210 area, "perception truly is reality" and "wealth is not displayed with more exuberance anywhere else" (128, 129).

A Work with Two or Three Authors

Use *and* before the name of the last author, and use commas after the names of the first and second authors if there are three.

David Snowdon studied the autobiographies of two hundred nuns and found that those whose emotions were most positive and detailed in their writing ended up living the longest and were the least likely to suffer from Alzheimer's later in life (Lemonick and Park 56).

A Work with More than Three Authors

List either the names of all the authors or the name of the first author followed by *et al.* ("and others" in Latin).

"Conscription without representation" became a rallying cry in the 1960s, when the voting age was twenty-one but a young man could be drafted into the army at eighteen (Wayne, Mackenzie, O'Brien, and Cole 316).

Despite the tragic cause that brought about the lowering of the voting age to eighteen, few eighteen- to twenty-one-year olds today actually vote (Wayne et al. 316).

An Entire Work

If you are referring to an entire work, you do not need to include page numbers.

The Solace of Open Spaces paints a picture of the West that contains more complicated characters than those Americans have met in John Wayne films and *Little House on the Prairie* reruns.

In "About Men," Gretel Ehrlich shows us both the limitations and the almost feminine humanity of the modern-day cowboy.

A Work in More than One Volume

List the volume number before the page number, and separate the two with a colon and a space.

Fields, Barber, and Riggs show that half of Cambodia's population died or fled the country within three years in the 1970s and that the Cambodian case is representative of several violent population dislocations that have occurred since World War II (2: 1041).

Two or More Works by the Same Author

If you do not name the author in your own text, in the parenthetical citation put a comma and the title of the work, or a shortened version of it, after the author's name and before the page number. If you do name the author in your own text, include just the title and the page number in the parenthetical citation.

> The Pima became the most obese group of people in the world after they were forced off of their land in central Arizona and their traditional diet changed markedly (Gladwell, "Pima Paradox" 36).

> The fast-food industry, Gladwell argues, originally intended to make people's lives more convenient and hence better, now plays a major role in the high death rate of Americans due to obesity ("Trouble" 24).

An Unsigned Work

If the title is not mentioned in your own text, include it or a shortened version of it in the parenthetical citation.

> Sheldrick experimented for twenty-eight years to find a formula that a baby elephant could digest as easily as its mother's milk ("Caring Hands" xv).

An Indirect Source

Use the notation *qtd. in* before the author of the indirect source.

> In preparing for the Louisiana Purchase expedition, Thomas Jefferson instructed Lewis and Clark to treat the Native Americans they met "in the most friendly and conciliatory manner which their own conduct will admit [and] allay all jealousies as to the object of your journey" (qtd. in Deverell and Hyde 163).

A Literary Work

Your reader will need to be able to find your source in any edition of the work, not just the one you are using. Therefore, for novels, list the chapter number after the page number, and separate the two with a semicolon. For a play or poem, list the line number instead of the page number. If the play contains parts or acts, list those and the line number, if given.

> Maggie, a girl who seemed to have "none of the dirt of Rum Alley . . . in her veins," is a classic Naturalist character, doomed to desperation and failure in a hostile urban environment (*Crane* 49; ch. 5).

> In one of the most famous poems of the Harlem Renaissance, Langston Hughes writes, "I've known rivers ancient as the world and older than the flow of / human blood in human veins. / My soul has grown deep like the rivers" ("Negro Speaks," lines 2–4).

Shepard suggests that his play is going to be an exploration of personal identity when the troubled and unstable Lee tells his recluse brother, Austin, "I always wondered what'd be like to be you" (*True West*, 1.4).

More than One Work

Cite both works in the order in which they appear in your text (if pertinent), and separate them with a semicolon.

In the 1990s a third of all children were born to unmarried mothers, suggesting not only that women are increasingly choosing to become single parents but that women who have not traditionally chosen this life course, including single, middle-class, educated women, are no longer willing to sacrifice their desire to parent (Kantrowitz and Wingert 48; Davis 72).

MLA List of Works Cited

Whenever you have cited the work of someone else in your text, you will need to provide a Works Cited list at the end of your essay or research project. The following examples provide guidelines for listing your sources correctly. Besides following the guidelines for each kind of source, remember that the Works Cited list should be arranged alphabetically, by the last names of the authors or editors. When a work has neither an author nor an editor, alphabetize by the first word of the title other than *A, An,* or *The.* MLA style now requires the medium of publication in all Works Cited entries. The medium usually appears at the end of the citation (but see specific models in this section, especially for electronic entries, for exact placement of the medium).

Your Works Cited page should be double-spaced, just like the rest of your essay or research project, with the same margins (format) as your essay. If a citation is longer than one line, indent each subsequent line half an inch (or five character spaces) — or use the "hanging indent" command on your computer.

● Books

The basic entry for a print book looks like this:

Author's last name, Author's first name [and Middle initial, if any]. *Title of the Book: Subtitle of the Book.* Place of publication: Publisher, year of publication. Medium.

If several places or years of publication are listed, use the first city or the most recent year. In general, use a shortened form of the publisher's name, such as "St. Martin's" for "St. Martin's Press" or "Random" for "Random House." For university presses, abbreviate "University" as "U" and "Press" as "P."

A Book with One Author

Dillard, Annie. *Teaching a Stone to Talk*. New York: Harper, 1982. Print.

A Book with Two or Three Authors

List authors in the order they appear on the title page. (Notice that the first author is listed last name first, but additional authors are listed in normal order.)

Hall, John A., and Charles Lindholm. *Is America Breaking Apart?* Princeton: Princeton UP, 1999. Print.

A Book with More than Three Authors

You may either list all of the authors in the order they appear on the title page or list the first author named and *et al.* ("and others"), not italicized. If you list all the others, you give them equal credit for their work. Notice that only the first author is listed last name first.

Gould, Eric, Robert DiYanni, William Smith, and Judith Stanford. *The Art of Reading*. 2nd ed. New York: McGraw, 1990. Print.

Gould, Eric, et al. *The Art of Reading*. 2nd ed. New York: McGraw, 1990. Print.

More than One Work by the Same Author or Authors

List the works alphabetically by title, and give the author's name only in the first entry. In subsequent entries, substitute three hyphens for the name.

Tannen, Deborah. *The Argument Culture: Moving from Debate to Dialogue*. New York: Random, 1998. Print.

---. *You Just Don't Understand*. New York: Morrow, 1990. Print.

A Book with an Editor

List the editor as you would an author, followed by *ed.* (which is not italicized).

Varenne, Herve, ed. *Symbolizing America*. Lincoln: U of Nebraska P, 1986. Print.

A Book with an Author and an Editor

List the author first, and give the editor's name, preceded by *Ed.*, after the title.

Catton, Bruce. *Reflections on the Civil War*. Ed. John Leekley. Garden City: Doubleday, 1981. Print.

A Later Edition

Cite the edition number after the title.

Zinsser, William. *On Writing Well: An Informal Guide to Writing Nonfiction*.
2nd ed. New York: Harper, 1980. Print.

A Work in a Series

After the publication information, list the medium and the series title.

McKay, Nellie, and Kathryn Earle, eds. *Approaches to Teaching the Novels
of Toni Morrison*. New York: MLA, 1997. Print. Approaches to Teaching
World Lit.

An Anthology

List the editor of the anthology as you would an author, followed by
ed. (not italicized).

Reed, Ishmael, ed. *MultiAmerica: Essays on Cultural Wars and Cultural Peace*.
New York: Viking-Penguin, 1997. Print.

A Selection from an Anthology

Follow the author, title of the selection, title of the anthology, editor,
and publication information with the page numbers of the selection.

Ozick, Cynthia. "A Drugstore in Winter." *Eight Modern Essayists*. Ed. William
Smart. 6th ed. New York: St. Martin's, 1995. 249–54. Print.

An Article in a Reference Work

Well-known reference works do not require publication information.
If the article has an author, begin your citation with the author's name. In
all other cases, list the title of the article, the title of the work, the edition,
and the date.

"Smith." *Encyclopedia of American Family Names*. 2nd ed. 2004. Print.

● Periodicals

The basic entry for a print periodical looks like this:

Author's last name, Author's first name [and Middle initial, if any]. "Title
of the Article." *Name of the Periodical* Other publication information
[such as volume and issue numbers, edition, date]: page numbers of
the article. Medium.

If an article is not printed on consecutive pages (for example, if it skips
from page 3 to page 14), list only the first page number followed by a plus
sign: 3+.

An Article in a Journal with Continuous Pagination throughout the Annual Volume

List the author's name, the title of the article, the title of the journal, the volume number followed by a period and the issue number (if there is one), and the date of publication, followed by a colon and the page numbers of the article. End with the medium.

> Helmer, Marguerite. "Media, Discourse, and the Public Sphere: Electronic Memorials to Diana, Princess of Wales." *College English* 63 (2001): 437–56. Print.

An Article in a Journal That Paginates Issues Separately

> Green-Anderson, Gail. "Writing in the World: Teaching about HIV/AIDS in English 101." *Teaching English in the Two-Year College* 28.1 (2000): 44–51. Print.

An Article in a Monthly or Bimonthly Magazine

List the month and year of the issue after the title of the magazine. Do not include volume or issue numbers. Abbreviate all months except May, June, and July.

> Wuethrich, Bernice. "Getting Stupid." *Discover* Mar. 2001: 56–63. Print.

An Article in a Weekly or Biweekly Magazine

List the date of the issue after the title of the magazine.

> Surowiecki, James. "Farewell to Mr. Fix-It." *New Yorker* 5 Mar. 2001: 41. Print.

An Article in a Newspaper

> Day, Sherri. "Two Groups Are at Odds over the Proper Way to Observe Malcolm X's Birthday." *New York Times* 17 May 2001, late ed.: B9. Print.

An Unsigned Article

Begin the entry with the title of the article. When alphabetizing the entry, ignore *A*, *An*, or *The* at the beginning of the title.

> "Open Up and Say 'Blaaaahhh.'" *Newsweek* 16 Apr. 2001: 10. Print.

A Review

List the reviewer's name first. Follow the title of the review with *Rev. of* (not italicized), the title of the work reviewed, and the name of the author, editor, director, or other creator of the work. End with the publication information for the periodical.

Lane, Anthony. "The Devil and Miss Jones." Rev. of *Bridget Jones's Diary*,
dir. Sharon Maguire. *New Yorker* 16 Apr. 2001: 90–91. Print.

● Nonperiodical Publications on CD-ROM, Diskette,
or Magnetic Tape

For publications in media that are published like books rather than as
periodically revised databases, list the author and title of the selection; the
title of the CD–ROM, diskette, or magnetic tape, italicized; the publication
information; and the medium of the publication.

Frost, Robert. "The Road Not Taken." *American Poetry*. Alexandria: Chadwyk-
Healey, 1995. CD-ROM.

● Online Sources

Because online sources do not exist in the stable and predictable forms
that most print sources do, they can be particularly difficult to cite in an
accurate and useful way. MLA style no longer requires you to list a URL
but instead requires you to give as much information to allow a reader to
find your source using standard search engines. The two general guidelines you should keep in mind are as follows: (1) if you can't find some
of the information for a citation, cite what is available to you, and (2) if
an online source also appears in print, list the information for the print
source first, followed by the information for the electronic version. Online
sources should include the following information:

• The author of the specific work you are citing, its title, and any print
  publication information.
• The name of the Web site, italicized, followed by the sponsor or
  publisher of the site (usually found near the copyright on the home
  page). If you can't find this information, use *N. p.* (not italicized).
• The date of publication or most recent update (use *n.d.* for "no date").
• The medium (*Web*).
• The date you accessed the work.

For works accessed through a library database, the name of the database
(in italics) follows any print publication information. After the database
name, list the medium (*Web*) and the date of access.

An Entire Web Site

Unless the site has an overall author, begin with its name, italicized.
Follow with the sponsor, the date of last update (if there isn't one listed,
use *n.d.* for "no date"), the medium (*Web*), and your date of access.

Common Cause. Common Cause, n.d. Web. 6 Aug. 2009.

A Document from a Web Site

Begin with the author of the document, if given, followed by its title, in quotation marks. Then give the information for the Web site.

"Fox News Channel: Fair and Balanced?" *Common Cause.* Common Cause,
    21 July 2004. Web. 6 Aug. 2009.

A Home Page for a Course

Begin with the name of the instructor, the title of the course, the Web site, the sponsor, and the date of the course. End with the medium and the date of access.

Wilkins, John. "Writing and Speaking about Physics and Astronomy." *Ohio
    State University.* Ohio State U, Mar.-June 2001. Web. 3 Nov. 2003.

A Home Page for an Academic Department

Include the name of the department, a description of the site such as "Dept. home page," the name of the site, the sponsor, the date of last update, the medium, and your date of access.

Mass Communications. Dept. home page. *Shaw University.* Shaw U, 2003.
    Web. 23 Apr. 2009.

A Personal Site

Begin with the name of the person who created the site; its title, italicized (or, if there is no title, the description "Home page"); its sponsor or publisher; and the date it was published or last updated. End with the medium and the date of access.

Fulton, Alice. Home page. Alice Fulton, 14 May 2004. Web. 11 July 2009.

A Scholarly Project

Include the editor (if any); the name of the project or Web site, italicized; the sponsoring institution; and the date of publication or last update. End with the medium and the date of access. If you are citing a specific document, begin with its author and the title, in quotation marks.

Surkan, Kim, ed. *Voices from the Gaps: Women Writers and Artists of Color.*
    U of Minnesota, 20 July 2009. Web. 14 Jan. 2010.

An Online Book

For a book that is published as part of a scholarly project, include the editor's name (if any). Include the publication information as for a print book, followed by the name of the Web site, the medium, and the date of access. To cite part of an online book, begin with the part you are citing. If the online book does not include page numbers, use *N. pag.*

> Cather, Willa. *My Antonia*. Ed. Charles Mignon. Lincoln: U of Nebraska P, 1994. *The Willa Cather Archive*. Web. 14 Jan. 2010.

> Lowell, Amy. "A Lady." *The New Poetry: An Anthology*. Ed. Harriet Monroe and Alice Corbin Henderson. New York: Macmillan, 1917. N. pag. *Bartleby.com: Great Books Online*. Web. 7 Nov. 2009.

An Online Government Publication

> United States. Dept. of Health and Human Services. Food and Drug Administration. *How to Understand and Use the Nutrition Facts Label*. Food and Drug Administration, 18 June 2009. Web. 29 Aug. 2009.

An Article in a Journal

Include the range or total number of pages, paragraphs, or other sections if they are numbered. End with the medium and date of access.

> Moore, Randy. "Writing about Biology: How Rhetorical Choices Can Influence the Impact of a Scientific Paper." *Bioscene: Journal of College Biology Teaching* 26 (2000): 23–25. Web. 14 Sept. 2009.

An Article in a Newspaper

List the author; the title of the article, in quotation marks; and the name of the Web site. Then list the publisher, the date of publication, the medium, and the date of access.

> Chass, Murray. "Bonds Hits 70th to Tie Home Run Record." *New York Times*. New York Times, 5 Oct. 2001. Web. 12 Nov. 2009.

An Article in a Magazine

List the author; the title of the article, in quotation marks; and the name of the Web site. Then list the publisher or sponsor of the site (usually found near the copyright information at the bottom of the home page), the date of publication, the medium, and the date of access.

> Last, Jonathan. "How to Market *Pearl Harbor* in Japan." *Slate*. Washington Post-Newsweek Interactive, 11 May 2001. Web. 16 May 2001.

A Review

> Conquest, Robert. "The Terror." Rev. of *Stalin: The Court of the Red Tsar* by Simon Sebag Montefiore. *TheAtlantic.com*. Atlantic Monthly Group, July-Aug. 2004. Web. 15 July 2004.

An Editorial

"AIDS in Africa." Editorial. *New York Times*. New York Times, 14 July 2004.
    Web. 17 July 2004.

A Letter to the Editor

Tucker, David. Letter. *Newsweek*. Newsweek, 19 July 2004. Web. 1 Aug.
    2004.

A Work Accessed through a Database or Library Subscription Service

List the publication information for the source and then give the name
of the database, italicized. End with the medium (*Web*) and the date of
access.

Ruskin, Gary. "The Fast Food Trap: How Commercialism Creates Overweight
    Kids." *Mothering* Nov.–Dec. 2003: 34+. *Infotrac OneFile*. Web. 3 May
    2004.

An E-Mail Message

List the author of the message followed by the subject line, if any, in
quotation marks. Include a description of the message that mentions the
recipient. End with the date and the medium (*E-mail*).

Rezny, Jane. "Re: Writing on the Edge." Message to the author. 3 Dec.
    2003. E-mail.

● Other Sources

A Film or Video Recording

Begin with the title of the work unless you are citing the contribution
of a specific person, such as a director, performer, producer, or screen-
writer. In that case, begin with the person's name. If you do not start with
the director's name, include it after the title, where you may also include
the names of other contributors. Then list the name of the distributor
and the year of release. End with the medium (*Film*). For a recording, end
with the film's original release date, the distributor, the year the recording
was released, and the medium (*DVD, Videocassette*).

Lee, Spike, dir. *She Hate Me*. Perf. Kerry Washington and Anthony Mackie.
    Sony, 2004. Film.

Malcolm X. Dir. Spike Lee. Perf. Denzel Washington. 1992. Warner, 2000.
    DVD.

A Television or Radio Program

List the episode title, in quotation marks; the title of the program, italicized; the name of the network; the call letters and city of the local station; the broadcast date; and the medium.

> "The One with the Cheap Wedding Dress." *Friends*. NBC. WNBC, New York. 15 Mar. 2001. Television.

A Sound Recording on Compact Disc

> Lopez, Jennifer. "I'm Real." *J. Lo*. Sony, 2001. CD.

> Bach, Johann Sebastian. *Goldberg Variations*. Perf. Murray Perahia. Sony, 2000. CD.

A Letter

For a letter published in a collection, cite the author; the title or subject of the letter, in quotation marks; the date of the letter; and publication information for the collection, ending with the medium. For a personal letter, list the author, the recipient (in the phrase *Letter to*), the date of the letter, and the medium (use *TS* for typescript and *MS* for manuscript or handwritten letters).

> Frost, Robert. "Letter to the Editor of the *Independent*." 28 Mar. 1894. *Selected Letters of Robert Frost*. Ed. Lawrence Thompson. New York: Holt, 1964. 19. Print.

> Quillen, Anna. Letter to the author. 25 Sept. 2001. TS.

An Interview

> Angelou, Maya. Interview by Terri Gross. *Fresh Air*. Natl. Public Radio. WNYC, New York. 5 July 1993. Radio.

> Clinton, William J. Interview by Jann Wenner. *Rolling Stone* 28 Dec. 2000: 84. Print.

> Shiflett, Mary. Personal interview. 8 Oct. 2001.

Glossary of Terms

academic writing   the writing that students do for their college classes and that professional scholars do when writing for each other; usually has a fairly formal and impersonal tone, relies mostly on logical rather than emotional appeals, and is written in the third person; carefully follows established conventions of grammar, style, format, and so on and documents source materials

analogy   a direct comparison between two unlike things, one of which is usually more familiar or less abstract than the other

anecdote   a short narrative that helps make a point within a piece of writing or speech

arguable   open for discussion and debate

argument   a rhetorical method that expresses a point of view and then uses logical reasoning to attempt to get an audience to accept the point of view as true or valid; often defined more broadly to include the use of both logical and emotional appeals and the effort to change listeners' or readers' point of view and move them to action

basis for comparison   the shared aspect of two or more things being compared; what the things have in common

causal chain   the idea that one situation or event causes another, which then causes another, and so on

cause–and–effect analysis   a rhetorical method that explains why certain events happen or predicts that certain events will lead to particular consequences

chronological order   the order in which events occur over time

chronological organization   the arrangement of parts of an essay in order of the time period they refer to

claim   a statement that asserts the writer's opinion on or belief about a subject, or the position the writer wants to take

classification   a rhetorical method that involves sorting specific things into more general categories

climax   the highest point or turning point in a narrative

common ground   the beliefs or values shared between the writer or speaker and the audience

comparison   a rhetorical method that shows how two or more things are alike

connotative language   words that suggest evaluations and emotional responses

contrast   a rhetorical method that shows how two or more things are different

contributory cause   a cause that contributes to an event but does not directly cause it

deductive arguments   arguments that move from a general claim to a specific statement or example

definition   a rhetorical method that states what a word or term means

deliberative rhetoric   legislative rhetoric used in deciding on the best course for the future, focusing on issues of expediency and inexpediency

denotative language   words that sound neutral and do not carry any emotional associations

description   a rhetorical method that depicts in words the details of what we see, hear, smell, taste, touch, or sense in some less physical way—or in our imagination

directive process analysis   a set of step-by-step instructions for a reader to follow

division   a rhetorical method that involves breaking a general whole into more specific parts

dominant impression   the quality of a subject that a writer wants to convey to readers, or the attitude toward a subject that a writer wants the readers to share

editing   checking a draft and making changes as necessary for such issues as the length, structure, and variety of paragraphs and sentences; the choice of words; the transitions between ideas; and the effectiveness and accuracy of the punctuation

emphatic order   an order based on relative importance

emphatic organization   the arrangement of parts of an essay in a sequence from the least to the most important

epideictic rhetoric   rhetoric used to express a sense of the occasion at a ceremony or memorial, focusing on issues of honor or dishonor

ethos   a rhetorical appeal that relies on the writer's or speaker's character and credibility to persuade an audience

exemplification   a rhetorical method that provides concrete examples — such as stories, expert opinions, or facts — to support a generalization

extended definition   a definition that expands on a sentence definition by differentiating the word or term from others and introducing additional features

figurative language   a type of subjective language that departs from the denotative meaning of a word or phrase for the sake of emphasis; the comparison of two unlike things by means of simile and metaphor

flashback   a technique in narration that gives the reader a glimpse of the past to illuminate the present

flashforward   a technique in narration that quickly takes readers to future events

historical definition   a definition that states where, when, why, and how a term came into being

immediate cause   the cause directly preceding an event

immediate effect   an effect that follows directly from an event

implied thesis   a thesis that conveys the writer's mood or overall impression, as well as purpose, but not directly; suggested by means of the selection, organization, focus, and force of the details in the writing

inductive arguments   arguments that move from specific examples to a generalization

informative process analysis   a process analysis that explains how something works, is done, or has happened without necessarily having readers follow the steps of the process themselves

judicial rhetoric   rhetoric that makes decisions about the past and focuses on issues of justice and injustice

language community   the people with whom one speaks most frequently

literacy   on a basic level, the ability to read and write; more broadly, how a person reacts to and interprets language in particular ways and produces and uses language to achieve certain goals

logical fallacies   arguments that are based on faulty reasoning or an error in judgment

logos   a rhetorical appeal that relies on reason or logic to persuade an audience, using facts, statistics, comparisons, narrative examples, documentation, personal experience, and observation

metaphor   an indirect comparison of one thing to another, such as "the snow covered the hills with a white blanket"

narration   a rhetorical method that tells a story

negative definition   a definition that distinguishes the meaning of a word or term by telling readers what it is not

objective definition   a definition that emphasizes what is being defined instead of the writer's feelings, opinions, or perspectives toward it

objective description   a method of description that tells about a subject without evaluating it

pathos   a rhetorical appeal to the emotions, values, and attitudes of an audience

persuasion   a form of communication that relies on emotion as well as reasoning to change the audience's point of view and move them to action

point of view   the assumed perspective from the mind and eye of the writer

points of comparison   the aspects of things that are being compared and contrasted (for example, when comparing two movies, points of comparison might be: which movie is funnier? more intellectual? more romantic? more action-packed?)

primary cause   the most important cause

primary effect   the most important effect

process   a series of actions that always leads to the same result, no matter how many times it is repeated

process analysis   a rhetorical method that explains a process by breaking it down into a fixed order of steps that produces a result

proofreading   checking a draft and changing it as necessary for surface-level problems such as typos and misspellings

public writing   writing that is aimed at a general rather than an academic or scholarly audience

relevant   specifically supporting or illustrating an aspect of a generalization

remote cause   a cause that is not as close in time to the event it causes as the immediate cause is

remote effect   an effect that does not occur immediately after an event but does eventually occur because of it

representative   typical of the whole group of items covered by a generalization

revising   the step of the writing process in which the writer looks at a draft and makes changes as necessary in light of how well it achieves its purpose; how successfully the writing addresses the specific audience; how clear the thesis is; whether the writer has met the requirements of the particular rhetorical method; how effective the organization, introduction, and conclusion are; and whether there is too little or too much information

rhetoric   language used for a specific purpose that leads to the creation of knowledge

rhetorical   making use of language for a specific purpose in a way that leads to the creation of knowledge

rhetorical appeals   strategies a writer or speaker uses to make an argument, including ethos, logos, and pathos

rhetorical method   any of the nine types of discourse described in this book, including narration, description, and exemplification

rhetorical situation   the conditions in which language is used, including the intended audience, purpose, topic, medium (oral, written, electronic), time, and place

ruling principle   the basis or criterion used to group items in a classification or division; must group items consistently (all items must be grouped according to the same principle), exclusively (there cannot be overlap in the grouping), and completely (no items can be omitted)

secondary effects   effects that occur because of an event but are less important than the primary effect

sensibilities   ethical, moral, and ideological inclinations, such as prudence, nostalgia, empathy, kindness, and aesthetic taste

sensory details   descriptions that appeal to a reader's physical senses (sight, hearing, taste, touch, smell)

sentence definition   a definition in one complete sentence that defines a term clearly and concisely

simile   a direct comparison connecting two unlike things with *like, as,* or *than,* such as "her voice was like honey"

spatial organization   the arrangement of information in an essay in an order related to its physical location

stipulative definition   a definition in which the writer specifies how a term will and will not be used

subjective definition   a definition that emphasizes the writer's opinions and responses and the way he or she wants to define the term for this particular occasion

subjective description   a method of description that emphasizes the writer's perspective on and personal reactions to what is being described

synonym   a word that has nearly the same meaning as another word

thesis   the main idea developed in a piece of writing

thesis statement   an explicit declaration (usually in one sentence) of the main idea of a piece of writing

topic sentence   a sentence within a paragraph, usually the first sentence, that states the main idea of the paragraph; usually reflects the thesis statement of the piece of writing and also previews the message of the sentences to follow

transitions   words or phrases that indicate to the reader a logical connection or change of direction between parts of a discussion, including *however, similarly, in contrast, in other words, first, second, third,* and *next*

Acknowledgments

Picture Credits

Page 6, courtesy of the author; **13,** AP/Wide World Photos; **14,** courtesy of the author; **30–37,** Everett Collection; **45,** Elliott Landy/The Image Works; **48,** Weather graphics courtesy of Accuweather, Inc., 385 Science Park Road, State College, PA 16801, (814) 237-0309, © 2009; **70,** AP/Wide World Photos; **89,** Larry Mulvehill/Photo Researchers; **96,** Everett Collection; **105,** David Woolley/Getty Images; **115,** Tom Leeson/Photo Researchers; **119,** © Scott Frances/Esto; **123,** Reprinted from RUNNER'S WORLD COMPLETE BOOK OF RUNNING by Amby Burfoot. Copyright © 1997 by Rodale, Inc. Permission granted by Rodale, Inc., Emmaus, PA 18098; **136,** Lore Denny; **155,** J.B. Grant/eStock Photo; **192,** Eugene Robert Richee/Getty Images; **203,** Barry Lewis/Alamy; **204,** Reproduced from sierraclub.org with permission of the Sierra Club; **212,** From the UCSF Legacy Tobacco Documents Library: http://legacy.library.ucsf.edu/tid/raa56e00, http://legacy.library.ucsf.edu/tid/rbw04f00, and http://legacy.library.ucsf.edu/tid/cfi22d00; **219,** Excerpt from the July 2003 issue of *Latina* magazine. Reprinted with permission from Latina Media Ventures LLC; **231,** Margaret Miller/Photo Researchers; **234,** © Dean Siracusa/Transtock/Corbis; **238,** Jeff Haynes/Getty Images; **242,** AP Images/Chris Carlson; **267–268,** courtesy of the author; **305,** iStockphoto; **311,** (left) Michael Ochs/Getty Images; (right) Jigsaw Productions/The Kobal Collection; **332,** Jim McHugh; **339,** Holly Harris/Getty Images; **340,** Reprinted with permission, NYC Department of Health and Mental Hygiene; **343,** Society for Ecological Research, Munich; **356,** The New York Times Agency; **362,** Geri Engberg/Stock Boston; **363,** © Catrina Genovese/Omni Photo Communications; **388,** Reprinted with permission of THE ONION. Copyright © 2009, by ONION, INC. www.theonion.com; **403,** Foodcollection/Getty Images; **406,** courtesy of Anchor Packaging; **408,** Illustrations by L–Dopa Design; **417,** courtesy of Shutterfly.com; **419,** courtesy of Sylvia Acevedo, CommuniCard, LLC; **449,** copyright 2009 Amethyst—Custom Medical Stock Photo, All Rights Reserved; **456,** Andrew Lichtenstein/The Image Works; **463,** David Boyer/National Geographic Image Collection; **464,** courtesy of the Peace Corps; **466,** American Institute of Certified Public Accountants; **488,** China Photos/Getty Images; **498,** AP Images/Vincent Thian; **502,** © Jay LaPrete/Icon SMI/Corbis; **507,** Bob Daemmrich; **519,** © Bettmann/Corbis; **521,** Doug Wilson/Getty Images; **526,** Drawing © 2009 Brad Holland, The New Yorker; **551,** Guy Billout; **597,** Photofest; **607,** Timothy A. Clary/Getty Images; **633,** Patti McConville/Alamy; **634,** courtesy of American Red Cross; **637,** reproduced with permission from United Jewish Appeal–Federation of Jewish Philanthropies of New York, Inc.; **651,** © The University of Arizona Campus Health Service, Health Promotion & Preventive Services; **666,** Chuck Solomon/Getty Images; **671,** Jim Rogash/Getty Images; **682,** Burt Glinn/Magnum Photos; **685,** Kayte M. Deioma/PhotoEdit; **694,** (top) AP Images/Michael Probst; (bottom) AP Images/Jennifer Graylock; **736,** Mary Evans/Photo Researchers; **738,** Joel Sartore/joelsartore.com; **749,** Scott Eells/Redux Pictures

Text

David Wallace Adams. Excerpt from *Education for Extinction: American Indians and the Boarding School Experience*, pp. 77–78. Copyright © 1995 by the University Press of Kansas. Used by permission. All rights reserved.

Jerry Adler and Claudia Kalb. "An American Epidemic: Diabetes." From *Newsweek*, Sept 4, 2000 issue, page 40. © 2000 Newsweek, Inc. All rights reserved. Used by permission and protected by the Copyright Laws of the United States. The printing, copying, redistribution, or retransmission of the Material without express written permission is prohibited.

American Heritage Dictionary. Definitions of "Definition" and "Ingenuity." From *American Heritage Dictionary of the English Language, New College Edition.* Copyright © 1981. Reprinted by permission of Houghton Mifflin Harcourt Brace.

Maya Angelou. "Finishing School." From *I Know Why the Caged Bird Sings* by Maya Angelou. Copyright © 1969 and renewed 1997 by Maya Angelou. Used by permission of Random House, Inc.

Paul Auster. Excerpt from "Why I Write." Copyright © 1994 Paul Auster. Reprinted with permission of the Carol Mann Agency.

Angelique Bamberg. Excerpt from "Nicky's Thai Kitchen." From *Pittsburgh City Paper*, April 10, 2008. pittsburgh.gyrosite.com. Reprinted by permission of Pittsburgh City Paper.

Dave Barry. "Introduction: Guys vs. Men." From *Dave Barry's Complete Guide to Guys*, by Dave Barry, copyright © 1995 by Dave Barry. Used by permission of Random House, Inc. "A Healthy Dose of Pain." Excerpt from "Just Call Me Studboy.com," *The Miami Herald*, September 26, 2004. http://www.rx8club.com/archive/index.php.t–40314.html. Reprinted by permission of the author.

Greg Beato. "Amusing Ourselves to Depth." From *Reason*, November 2007. http://www.reason.com/news/show/122453.html. Reprinted by permission.

Barrie Jean Borich. "What Kind of King." From *My Lesbian Husband*. Copyright © 1999, 2000 by Barrie Jean Borich. Reprinted with the permission of Graywolf Press, Minneapolis, MN. www.graywolfpress.org.

Mark Bowden. "Finders Keepers: The Story of Joey Coyle." *In Fact: The Best of Creative Non-Fiction*. Ed. Lee Gutkind. New York: W. W. Norton, 2005, 189–222. Reprinted by permission of the author.

Catherine Bradshaw and Annie Sawyer. "Examining Developmental Differences in the Social-Emotional Problems Among Frequent Bullies, Victims, and Bully/Victims." *Psychology in the Schools* 46.2 (2009): 100–115. Copyright © 2009 by John Wiley & Sons, Inc. Reproduced with permission of John Wiley & Sons, Inc.

Keith Bradsher. "The Ascent of Wind Power." From *The New York Times*, September 28, 2006. http://www.nytimes.com/2006/09/28/business/worldbusiness/28wind.html?pagewanted=print. Reprinted by permission.

Judy Brady. "Why I Want a Wife." From *Ms.* (1971). Copyright © 1971 Judy Brady. Reprinted with the permission of the author.

Suzanne Britt. "Neat People vs. Sloppy People." From *Show and Tell*, 1983. Reprinted by permission of the author.

Sarah M. Broom. "A Yellow House in New Orleans" and the picture of the yellow house. From *The Oxford American*, 2008. Copyright © 2008 Sarah M. Broom. Reprinted by permission of the author.

Ken Brower. Excerpt from "Still Blue." *National Geographic*, March 2009. Reprinted by permission.

David Browne. "On the Internet, It's All about 'My'." From *The New York Times*, April 20, 2008. Copyright © 2008 The New York Times, Inc. All rights reserved. Used by permission and protected by the Copyright Laws of the United States. The printing, copying, redistribution, or retransmission of the Material without express written permission is prohibited.

Bill Bryson. Chapter Seven, "Varieties of English." From *The Mother Tongue* by Bill Bryson. Copyright © 1990 by Bill Bryson. Reprinted by permission of HarperCollins Publishers.

William F. Buckley, Jr. "Free Weeds." From *National Review Online*, June 29, 2004. © 2004 by National Review Online, www.nationalreview.com. Reprinted by permission.

Amby Burfoot. "Anatomy of a Running Shoe." From Amby Burfoot, *Runner's World, The Complete Book of Running*. Copyright © 2004, 1997 by Rodale Inc. Illustrations copyright © 1997 by Robert Frawley. Reprinted by permission.

Nicholas Carr. "Is Google Making Us Stupid?" From *The Atlantic*, July/August 2008. Copyright © 2008 by Nicholas Carr. Reprinted with permission of the author. Originally appeared in *The Atlantic*.

Jimmy Carter. "Assault-Gun Ban Should Be Reinstated." From Startribune.com. May 1, 2009. Reprinted by permission.

Taylor Clark. "Plight of the Little Emperors." From *Psychology Today*, July 1, 2008. Reprinted by permission of the publisher.

Consumer Reports. "CR Good Bets & Bad Bets." From 2008 Consumer Reports Survey. © 2008 by Consumers Union of U.S., Inc., Yonkers, NY 10703-1057, a nonprofit organization.

Barbara Kingsolver. Excerpt from "Knowing Our Place" (pp. 1–21) from *Small Wonder Essays* by Barbara Kingsolver. Copyright © 2002 by Barbara Kingsolver. Reprinted by permission of HarperCollins Publishers.

Anne Lamott. "Shitty First Drafts." From *Bird by Bird* by Anne Lamott, copyright © 1994 by Anne Lamott. Used by permission of Pantheon Books, a division of Random House, Inc.

Catherine Leece. "Energy for the Community." Reprinted by permission of the author.

Jonah Lehrer. Figure from "Scientists Map the Brain, Gene by Gene." From *Wired Magazine*, 17(4). March 28, 2009. Copyright © 2009 Conde Nast Publications. All rights reserved. Originally published in *Wired*. Reprinted by permission.

Phil Leitz. "The Greatest Automotive Flops of the Last 25 Years – Feature. Bad cars come and go, but flops are forever." *Car and Driver*, February 2009. http://www.caranddriver.com/features/09q1/the_greatest_automotive_flops_of_the_last_25_years-feature. Reprinted by permission.

Nicholas Lemann. "Amateur Hour: Journalism Without Journalists." From *The New Yorker*, August 2006. Reprinted by permission of the author.

Jonathan Lethem. "What Makes a Great Singer." *Rolling Stone* issue 1066, November 27, 2008. © Rolling Stone LLC 2008. All Rights Reserved. Reprinted by permission.

Brett Lott. Excerpt from "Brothers" by Brett Lott. Copyright © 1993 by The Antioch Review, Inc. First appeared in *The Antioch Review*, vol. 51, no. 1. Reprinted by permission of the Editor.

Alfredo Celedón Luján. "*Piñón* Hunting." Reprinted by permission of the author.

Robert Mankoff. "They can't see you right now—would you like a bottle while you're waiting?" ID: 24972, cartoon published in *The New Yorker* February 15, 1993. © The New Yorker Collection, 1993, Robert Mankoff, from cartoonbank.com. All Rights Reserved.

Jack McCallum. "Steroids in America: The Real Dope." From *Sports Illustrated*, March 11, 2008. Reprinted by permission.

Lisa Miller. Excerpt from "The Culture War of Words." From *The Washington Post*, April 29, 2009. © 2009 by the Washington Post. All rights reserved. Used by permission and protected by the Copyright Laws of the United States. The printing, copying, redistribution, or retransmission of the Material without express written permission is prohibited.

Jessica Mitford. "The Embalming of Mr. Jones." From *The American Way of Death* by Jessica Mitford. Reprinted by permission of the Estate of Jessica Mitford. Copyright © 1963, 1978 by Jessica Mitford, all rights reserved.

N. Scott Momaday. Excerpt from the Introduction to *The Way to Rainy Mountain*. Reprinted by permission of the University of New Mexico Press.

Monsterguide. "How to Interview." Posted January 2, 2009. Reprinted by permission of Monsterguide.net.

Charles Moskos and Paul Glastris. "Now Do You Believe We Need a Draft?" From *The Washington Monthly*. November 2001. Copyright © 2001. Reprinted by permission of the author.

Susan Orlean. From *The Bullfighter Checks Her Makeup* by Susan Orlean, copyright © 2001 by Susan Orlean. Used by permission of Random House, Inc.

Oxford English Dictionary. Definition of "evolution." From *Oxford English Dictionary* by John Simpson. (1989). Used by permission of Oxford University Press.

Josh Patner. "Fashion Advice for Michelle Obama." From *Slate Magazine*, November 13, 2008. Reprinted by permission of the author.

Inez Peterson. "What Part Moon?" From *As We Are Now: Mixblood Essays on Race and Identity*. Copyright © 1997 by the Regents of the University of California Press.

Bill Pratt. "Interview Questions: Most Common, Illegal, and Questions You Should Never Ask." From *The Graduate's Guide to Life and Money*. Copyright © 2008 Bill Pratt. Reprinted with permission of the author.

Thesmittenkitchen.com. Screenshots from www.thesmittenkitchen.com. Reprinted by permission of Deb Perelman.

Abigal Van Buren. *Dear Abby*. "Sister of Suicide Victim Living with Guilt." February 15, 1998. Reprinted by permission of Universal Press Syndicate.

Vanity Fair. "Soundtrack of Change." From *Vanity Fair*, April 2009. Copyright © 2009 Condé Nast Publications. All rights reserved. Originally published in Vanity Fair. Reprinted by permission.

Marilyn vos Savant and Donald Anderson. Question and answer on "Sex Determination." From "Ask Marilyn" by Marilyn vos Savant, March 8, 1998. © 1998 Marilyn vos Savant. Initially published in *Parade Magazine*. All rights reserved.

The Wall Street Journal. "Uncle Charlie Wants You!" From *The Wall Street Journal*, November 25, 2006. Reprinted by permission of The Wall Street Journal, Copyright © 2006 Dow Jones & Company, Inc. All Rights Reserved Worldwide. License number 2265680163303.

David Foster Wallace. "Host." *Atlantic Monthly* 295.3 (April 2005): 51–77. Reprinted by permission of The Atlantic.

Claudia Wallis. "The Multitasking Generation." From *Time Magazine*, Mar. 19, 2006. Copyright TIME INC. Reprinted by permission. TIME is a registered trademark of Time Inc. All rights reserved.

Daniel M. Wegner. Excerpt from "How to Think, Say, or Do Precisely the Worst Thing for Any Occasion." From *The American Scientist*, July 3, 2009. Copyright © 2009 The American Scientist. Reprinted with permission from AAAS.

Timothy Wheeler. "Assault-Weapons Ban, R.I.P." From *National Review Online*, September 13, 2004. © 2004 by National Review Online, www.nationalreview.com. Reprinted by permission.

Alexander Wolff. Excerpt from "An Honest Wage." From *Sports Illustrated*, May 30, 1994. Reprinted by permission.

Bernice Wuethrich. "Getting Stupid." From *Discover Magazine*, March 2001. Reprinted by permission of the author.

Malcolm X and Alex Haley. Excerpt from *The Autobiography of Malcolm X* by Malcolm X and Alex Haley, copyright © 1964 by Alex Haley and Malcolm X. Copyright © 1965 by Alex Haley and Betty Shabazz. Used by permission of Random House, Inc.

Index

graphy is correct (*āgamār-*
only our own response to
aracteristic order will enable
.. If Kṛṣṇa is depicted as the
raja, it would be ridiculous to
nds, as though a model on
presented; for here art, by
eals with the natural rela-
ation is female to God"),
l not accept the tradition,
of our inability to pass
e.
unequal quality and
by decadence "charac-
her than the opposite
perfection in a work
the artist, such per-
ng a product of the
first consideration
be done, for it is
s to whether the
ded by a proper
not be over-
orks, whether
ge, the image
mage, which
ed, can still
in the sec-

superiority to discipline (*anācāra*) on behalf of the human artist, to idolize one who is still a man as something more than man, to glorify rebellion and independence, as in the modern deification of genius and tolerance of the vagaries of genius, is plainly preposterous, or as Muslims would say blasphemous, for who shall presume to say that he indeed knows Brahman, or truly and completely loves God? The ultimate liberty of spontaneity is indeed conceivable only as a workless manifestation in which art and artist are perfected; but what thus lies beyond contingency is no longer "art," and in the meantime the way to liberty has nothing whatever in common with any wilful rebellion or calculated originality; least of all has it anything to do with functional self-expression. Ascertained rules should be thought of as the vehicle assumed by spontaneity, in so far as spontaneity is possible for us, rather than as any kind of bondage. Such rules are necessary to any being whose activity depends on will, as expressed in India with reference to the drama: "All the activities of the angels, whether at home in their own places, or abroad in the breaths of life, are intellectually emanated; those of men are put forth by conscious effort; therefore it is that the works to be done by men are defined in detail," *Nāṭya Śāstra*, II, 5. As expressed by St Thomas (*Sum. Theol.*, I, Q. 59, A. 2), "there alone are essence and will identified where all good is contained within the essence of him who wills . . . this cannot be said of any creature." In tending toward an ultimate coincidence of discipline and will, the artist does indeed become ever less and less conscious of rules, and for the virtuoso intuition and performance are already apparently simultaneous; but at every stage the artist will delight in rules, as the master of language delights in grammar, though he may speak without constant reference to the treatises on syntax. It is of the essence of art to bring back into order the multiplicity of Nature, and it is in this sense that he "prepares all creatures to return to God."

It should be hardly necessary to point out that art is by definition essentially conventional (*saṁketita*); for it is only by convention that nature can be made intelligible, and only by signs and symbols, *rūpa*, *pratīka*, that communication is made possible. A good example of the way in which we take the conventionality of art for granted is afforded by the story of a famous master who was commissioned to paint a bamboo forest. With magnificent skill he paint entirely in red. The patron objected that this was natural. The painter enquired, "In what color should have been painted?" and the patron replied, "In bl course." "And who," said the artist, "ever saw a leaved bamboo?" [22]

The whole problem of symbolism (*pratīka*, "sypmorphic discussed by Śaṅkarâcārya, Commentary on th *Sūtras*, I, 1, 20. Endorsing the statement that " here to the harp, sing Him," he points out th refers to the highest Lord only, who is the ul even of worldly songs. And as to anthropom sions in scripture, "we reply that the high

ond the form by which the art was moved must have been immanent in every part of it, and is thus present in what survives of it, and this is why such works may be adequate to evoke in a strong-minded spectator a true aesthetic experience, such a one supplying by his own imaginative energy all that is lacking in the original production. More often, of course, what passes for an appreciation of decadent or damaged work is merely a sentimental pleasure based on associated ideas, *vāsanā qua* nostalgia.

There are two distinguishable modes of decadence in art, one corresponding to a diminished sensuality, the other reflecting, not an animal attachment to sensation, but a senescent refinement. It is essential to distinguish this attenuation or over-refinement of what was once a classical art from the austerity of primitive forms which may be less seductive, but express a high degree of intellectuality. Over-refinement and elaboration of apparatus in the arts are well illustrated in modern dramatic and concert production, and in the quality of trained voices and instruments such as the piano. All these means at the disposal of the artist are the means of his undoing, except in the rare cases where he can still by a real devotion to his theme make us forget them. Those accustomed to such comfortable arts as these are in real danger of rejecting less highly finished or less elaborate products, not at all on aesthetic grounds, but out of pure laziness and love of comfort. One thinks by contrast of the Bengālī *Yātrās* that "without scenery, without the artistic display of costumes, could rouse emotions which nowadays we scarcely experience," or, on the other hand, of utterly sophisticated arts like the Nō plays of Japan, in which the means have been reduced to a minimum, and though they have been brought to that high pitch of perfection that the theme demands, are yet entirely devoid of any element of luxury. These points of view have been discussed by Rabindranath Tagore in connection with the rendition of Indian music. "Our master singers," he says, "never take the least trouble to make their voice and manner attractive. . . . Those of the audience . . . whose senses have to be satisfied as well are held to be beneath the notice of any self-respecting artist," while "those of the audience who are appreciative are content to perfect the song in their own mind by the force of their own feeling." In other words, while the formal beauty is the essential in art, loveliness and convenience are, not indeed fortuitous, but in the proper sense of the word, accidents of art, happy or unhappy accidents as the case may be.

We are now in a position to describe the peculiarities of Oriental art with greater precision. The Indian or Far Eastern icon, carved or painted, is neither a memory image nor an idealization, but a visual symbolism, ideal in the mathematical sense. The "anthropomorphic" icon is of of the same kind as a *yantra*, that is, a geometrical representation of a deity, or a *mantra*, that is, an auditory representation of a deity. The peculiarity of the icon depends immediately upon these conditions, and could not be otherwise explained, even were we unaware that in actual practice it *is* the *mantra* and not the eye's intrinsic faculty that originates the image. Accordingly, the Indian icon fills the whole field of vision at once, all is equally clear and equally essential; the eye is not led to range from one point to another, as in empirical vision, nor to seek a concentration of meaning in one part more than in another, as in a more "theatrical" art. There is no feeling of texture or flesh, but only of stone, metal, or pigment, the object being an image in one or other of these materials, and not a deceptive replica (*savarṇa*) of any objective cause of sensation. The parts of the icon are not organically related, for it is not contemplated that they should function biologically, but ideally related, being the required component parts of a given type of activity stated in terms of the visible and tangible medium. This does not mean that the various parts are not related, or that the whole is not a unity, but that the relation is mental rather than functional. These principles will apply as much to landscape as to iconography.

In Western art the picture is generally conceived as seen in a frame or through a window, and so brought toward the spectator; but the Oriental image really exists only in our own mind and heart and is thence projected or reflected onto space. The Western presentation is designed as if seen from a fixed point of view, and must be optically plausible; Chinese landscape is typically represented as seen from more than one point of view, or in any case from a conventional, not a "real," point of view, and here it is not plausibility but intelligibility that is essential. In painting generally there is relievo (*natônnata, nimnônnata*), that is to say modelling in abstract light, painting being thought of as a constricted *mode* of sculpture; but never before the European influence in the seventeenth century any use of cast shadows, chiaroscuro, *chāyâtapa*, "shade and shine." Methods of representing space in art will always correspond more or less to contemporary habits of vision, and nothing more than this is required for art; perspective is nothing but the means employed to convey to the spectator the idea of three-dimensional space, and among the different kinds of perspective that have been made use of, the one called "scientific" has no particular advantage from the aesthetic point of view. On this point, Asaṅga, *Mahāyāna Sūtrâlaṁkāra*, XIII, 17, is illuminating: *citre . . . natônnataṁ nâsti ca, dṛśyate atha ca*, "there is no actual relief in a painting, and yet we see it there," an observation which is repeated from the same point of view in the *Laṅkâvatāra Sūtra*, Nanjio's ed., p. 91.[23] It would be thus as much beside the mark to conceive of a progress in art as revealed by a development in *Raumdarstellung* as to seek to establish a stylistic sequence on a supposed more or less close observation of Nature. Let us not forget that the mind is a part, and the most important part, of our knowledge of Nature, and that this point of view, though it may have been forgotten in Europe, has been continuously current in Asia for more than two thousand years.

Where European art naturally depicts a moment of time,

an arrested action or an effect of light, Oriental art represents a continuous condition. In traditional European terms, we should express this by saying that modern European art endeavors to represent things as they are in themselves, Asiatic and Christian art to represent things more nearly as they are in God, or nearer to their source. As to what is meant by representing a continuous condition, for example, the Buddha attained Enlightenment countless ages since, his manifestation is still accessible, and will so remain; the Dance of Śiva takes place, not merely in the Tāraka forest, nor even at Cidambaram, but in the heart of the worshipper; the Kṛṣṇa Līlā is not an historical event, of which Nīlakaṇṭha reminds us, but, using Christian phraseology, a "play played eternally before all creatures." This point of view, which was by no means unknown to the European schoolmen and is still reflected in India's so-called lack of any historical sense, Islam and China being here nearer to the world than India, though not so enmeshed in the world as modern Europe, constitutes the *a priori* explanation of the Indian adherence to types and indifference to transient effects. One might say, not that transient effects are meaningless, but that their value is not realized except to the degree that they are seen *sub specie aeternitatis*, that is *formaliter*. And where it is not the event but the type of activity that constitutes the theme, how could the East have been interested in cast shadows? Or how could the Śūnyavādin, who may deny that any Buddha ever really existed, or that any doctrine was ever actually taught, and so must be entirely indifferent as to the historicity of the Buddha's life, have been curious about the portraiture of Buddha? It would indeed be irrelevant to demand from any art a solution of problems of representation altogether remote from contemporary interest.

Little as it might have been foreseen, the concept of types prevails also in the portraiture of individuals, where the model is present (*pratyakṣa*) to the eye or memory. It is true that classical Indian portraits must have been recognizable, and even admirable, likenesses. We have already seen that *sādṛśya*, conformity of sense and substance, is essential in painting, and it has been pointed out that different, though closely related, terms, viz. *sadṛśī* and *su-sadṛśī*, are employed when the idea of an exact or speaking likeness is to be expressed.[24] The painted portrait (*pratikṛti*, *ākṛti*) functioned primarily as a substitute for the living presence of the original. One of the oldest treatises, the Tanjur *Citralakṣaṇa*, refers the origin of painting in the world to this requirement, and yet actually treats only the physiognomical peculiarities (*lakṣaṇa*) of types. Even more instructive is a later case, occurring in one of the *Vikramacaritra* stories: here the King is so much attached to the Queen that he keeps her at his side, even in council, but this departure from custom and propriety is disapproved of by the courtiers, and the King consents to have a portrait painted, as a substitute for the Queen's presence. The court painter is allowed to see the Queen; he recognizes that she is a *padminī*, that is, a "Lotus-lady," one of the four types under which women are classed according to physiognomy and character by Hindu rhetoricians. He paints her accordingly *padminī-lakṣaṇa-yuktam*, "with the characteristic marks of a Lotus-lady," and yet the portrait is spoken of not merely as *rūpam*, a figure, but even as *svarūpam*, "her intrinsic aspect." We know also, both in China and in India, of ancestral portraits, but these were usually prepared after death, and so far as preserved have the character of effigies (Chinese *ying-tu*, "diagram of a shade") rather than of speaking likenesses. In the *Pratimā-nāṭaka*, the hero, marvelling at the execution of the statues in an ancestral chapel, does not recognize them as those of his parents, and wonders if they are representations of deities. We even find a polemic against portraiture: "images of the angels are productive of good, and heaven-ward-leading, but those of men or other mortal beings lead not to heaven nor work weal," *Śukranītisāra*, IV, 4, 75 and 76. Chinese ancestral portraits are not devoid of individual characterization, but this represents only a slight, not an essential, modification of general formulae; the books on portraiture (*fu shên*, "depicting soul") refer only to types of features, canons of proportion, suitable accessories, and varieties of brush stroke proper for the draperies; the essence of the subject must be portrayed, but there is nothing said about anatomical accuracy. The painter Kuo Kung-ch'ên was praised for his rendering of very soul (*ching shên*, 2133, 9819) and mind (*i ch'u*, 5367, 3120) in a portrait; but there cannot be adduced from the whole of

Asia such a thing as a treatise on anatomy designed for use by artists.

The first effect produced on a modern Western spectator by these scholastic qualities of Oriental art is one of monotony. In literature and plastic art, persons are not so much distinguished as individuals as by what they do, in which connection it may be remembered that orthodoxy, for the East, is determined by what a man does, and not by his beliefs. Again, the productions of any one period are characterized far more by what is common to them all than by the personal variations. Because of their exclusively professional character and formal control, and the total absence of the conception of private property in ideas, the range of quality and theme that can be found in Oriental works of one and the same age or school is less than that which can be seen in European art at the present day, and besides this, identical themes and formulae have been adhered to during long periods. Where the modern student, accustomed to an infinite variety of choice in themes, and an infinite variety and tolerance of personal mannerisms, has neither accustomed himself to the idea of an unanimous style, nor to that of themes determined by general necessities and unanimous demand, nor learned to distinguish nuances in the unfamiliar stylistic sequences, his impatience can hardly be wondered at; but this impatience, which is not a virtue, must be outgrown. Here is involved the whole question of the distinction between originality or novelty and intensity or energy; it should be enough to say that when there is realization, when the themes are felt and art *lives*, it is of no moment whether or not the themes are new or old.

Life itself — the different ways in which the difficult problems of human association have been solved — represents the ultimate and chief of the arts of Asia; and it must be stated once for all that the forms assumed by this life are by no means empirically determined, but designed as far as possible according to a metaphysical tradition, on the one hand conformably to a divine order, and on the other with a view to facilitating the attainment by each individual of approximate perfection in his kind, that is, permitting him, by an exact adjustment of opportunity to potentiality, to achieve such realization of his entire being as is possible to him. Even town-planning depends in the last analysis upon considerations of this kind. Neither the society nor the specific arts can be rationally enjoyed without a recognition of the metaphysical principles to which they are thus related, for things can be enjoyed only in proportion to their intelligibility, speaking, that is, humanly and not merely functionally.

Oriental life is modelled on types of conduct sanctioned by tradition. For India, Rāma and Sītā represent ideals still potent, the *svadharma* of each caste is a *mode* of behavior, good form being *à la mode*; and until recently every Chinese accepted as a matter of course the concept of manners established by Confucius. The Japanese word for rudeness means "acting in an unexpected way." Here, then, life is designed like a garden, not allowed to run wild. All this formality, for a cultured spectator, is far more attractive than can be the variety of imperfection so freely displayed by the plain and blunt, or as he thinks, "more sincere," European. This external conformity, whereby a man is lost in the crowd as true architecture seems to be a part of its native landscape, constitutes for the Oriental himself a privacy within which the individual character can flower unhampered. This is most of all true in the case of women, whom the East has so long sheltered from necessities of self-assertion; one may say that for women of the aristocratic classes in India or Japan there has existed no freedom whatever in the modern sense, yet these same women, molded by centuries of stylistic living, achieved an absolute perfection in their kind, and perhaps Asiatic art can show no higher achievement than this. In India, where the "tyranny of caste" strictly governs marriage, diet, and every detail of outward conduct, there exists and has always existed unrestricted freedom of thought as to modes of belief or thought; a breach of social etiquette may involve excommunication from society, but religious intolerance is practically unknown, and it is a perfectly normal thing for different members of the same family to choose for themselves the particular deity of their personal devotion.

It has been well said that civilization is style. An immanent culture in this sense endows every individual with an outward grace, a typological perfection, such as only the rarest beings can achieve by their own effort, a kind of perfection which does not belong to genius; whereas a democracy, which requires of every man to save his own "face" and soul, actually condemns each to an exhibition of his own irregularity and imperfection, and this implicit acceptance of formal imperfection only too easily passes over into an exhibitionism which makes a virtue of vanity and is complacently described as self-expression.

We have so far discussed the art of Asia in its theological aspect, that is with reference to the scholastic organization of thought in terms of types of activity, and the corresponding arts of symbolism and iconography, in which the elements of form presented by Nature and redeemed by art are used as means of communication. The classical developments of this kind of art belong mainly to the first millennium of the Christian era. Its later prolongations tend to decadence, the formal elements retaining their edifying value, in design and composition, but losing their vitality, or surviving only in folk art, where the intensity of an earlier time expressing a more conscious will is replaced by a simpler harmony of style prevailing throughout the whole man-made environment. Eighteenth-century Siam and Ceylon provide us with admirable examples of such a folk style based on classical tradition, this condition representing the antithesis of that now realized in the West, where in place of vocation as the general type of activity we find the types of individual genius on the one hand, and that of unskilled labor on the other.

Another kind of art, sometimes called romantic or idealistic, but better described as imagist [25] or mystical, where denotation and connotation cannot be divided, is typically developed throughout Asia in the second millennium. In this kind of art no distinction is felt between what a thing "is" and what it "signifies." However, in thus drawing a distinction between symbolic and imagist art it must be very strongly emphasized that the two kinds of art are inseverably connected and related historically and aesthetically; for example, Kamakura Buddhist painting in the twelfth or thirteenth century is still iconographic, in Sung landscape and animal painting there is always an underlying symbolism, and, on the other hand, Indian animal sculpture at Māmallapuram in the seventh century is already romantic, humorous, and mystical. A more definite break between the two points of view is illustrated in the well-known story of the Zen priest Tan-hsia, who used a wooden image of the Buddha to make his fire — not however, as iconoclast, but simply because he was cold. The two kinds of art are most closely connected by the philosophy and practice of Yoga; in other words, a self-identification with the theme is always prerequisite. But whereas the theological art is concerned with types of power, the mystical art is concerned with only one power. Its ultimate theme is that single and undivided principle which reveals itself in every form of life whenever the light of the mind so shines on anything that the secret of its inner life is realized, both as an end in itself unrelated to any human purpose, and as no other than the secret of one's own innermost being. "When thou seest an eagle, thou seest a portion of genius"; "the heavens declare the glory of God"; "a mouse is miracle enough," these are European analogies; or St Bernard's *Ligna et lapides docebunt te, quod a magistris audire non posse.*

Here, then, the proximate theme may be any aspect of Nature whatsoever, not excluding human nature but "wherever the mind attaches itself," every aspect of life having an equal value in a spiritual view. In theory this point of view could be applied in justification of the greatest possible variety of individual choice, and interpreted as a "liberation" of the artist from associated ideas. However, in the more practical economy of the great living traditions we find, as before, that certain restricted kinds or groups of themes are adhered to generation after generation in a given area, and that the technique is still controlled by most elaborate rules, and can only be acquired in long years of patient practice (*abhyāsa*). Historical conditions and environment, an inheritance of older symbolisms, specific racial sensibilities, all these provide a better than private determination of the work to be done; for the artist or artisan, who "has his art which he is expected to practice," this is a means to the conservation of energy; for man generally, it secures a continued comprehensibility of art, its value as communication.

The outstanding aspects of the imagist or mystical art of Asia are the Ch'an or Zen [26] art of China and Japan, in which the theme is either landscape or plant or animal life;

Vaiṣṇava painting, poetry, and music in India, where the theme is sexual love; and Ṣūfī poetry and music in Persia, devoted to the praise of intoxication.

The nature of Ch'an Zen is not easy to explain. Its sources are partly Indian, partly Taoist, its development both Chinese and Japanese. Chinese Buddhist art is *like* Indian in general aspect, differing only in style; Ch'an-Zen art provides us with a perfect example of that kind of real assimilation of new cultural ideas which results in a development formally *unlike* the original. This is altogether different from that hybridization which results from "influences" exerted by one art upon another; influences in this last sense, though historians of art attach great importance to them, are almost always manifested in unconscious parody, — one thinks of Hellenistic art in India, or *chinoiseries* in Europe, — and in any case belong to the history of taste rather than to the history of art. At the same time that we recognize Indian sources of Ch'an-Zen art, it is to be remembered that Zen is also deeply rooted in Taoism; it is sufficiently shown by the saying of Chuang Tzŭ, "The mind of the sage, being in repose, becomes the mirror of the universe, the speculum of all creation," that China had always and independently been aware of the true nature of imaginative vision.

The Ch'an-Zen discipline is one of activity and order; its doctrine the invalidity of doctrine, its end an illumination by immediate experience. Ch'an-Zen art, seeking realization of the divine being in man, proceeds by way of opening his eyes to a like spiritual essence in the world of Nature external to himself; the scripture of Zen "is written with the characters of heaven, of man, of beasts, of demons, of hundreds of blades of grass, and of thousands of trees" (Dō-gen), "every flower exhibits the image of Buddha" (Du-gō). A good idea of Ch'en-Zen art can be obtained from the words of a twelfth-century Chinese critic, writing on animal painting: after alluding to the horse and bull as symbols of Heaven and Earth, he continues: "But tigers, leopards, deer, wild swine, fawns, and hares — creatures that cannot be inured to the will of man — these the painter chooses for the sake of their skittish gambols and swift shy evasions, loves them as things that seek the desolation of great plains and wintry snows, as creatures that will not be haltered with a bridle, nor tethered by the foot. He would commit to brushwork the gallant splendor of their stride; *this he would do and no more.*" [27] But the Ch'an-Zen artist no more paints from Nature than the poet writes from Nature; he has been trained according to treatises on style so detailed and explicit that there would seem to be no room left for the operation of personality. A Japanese painter once said to me, "I have had to concentrate on the bamboo for many, many years, still a certain technique for the rendering of the tips of bamboo leaves eludes me." And yet immediacy or spontaneity has been more nearly perfectly attained in Ch'an-Zen art than anywhere else. Here there is no formal iconography, but an intuition that has to be expressed in an ink painting where no least stroke of the brush can be erased or modified; the work is as irrevocable as life itself. There is no kind of art that comes nearer to "grasping the joy as it flies," the winged life that is no longer life when we have taken thought to remember and describe it; no kind of art more studied in method, or less labored in effect. Every work of Ch'an-Zen art is unique, and in proportion to its perfection inscrutable.

But Ch'an-Zen is by no means only a way to perfect experience, it is also a way to the perfecting of character. Ch'an-Zen represents all and more than we now mean by the word "culture": an active principle pervading every aspect of human life, becoming now the chivalry of the warrior, now the grace of the lover, now the habit of the craftsman. The latter point may be illustrated by Chuang Tzŭ's story of the wheelwright who ventured to criticize a nobleman for reading the works of a dead sage. In excusing his temerity, he explained: "Your humble servant must regard the matter from the point of view of his own art. In making a wheel, if I proceed too gently, that is easy enough, but the work will not stand fast; if I proceed too violently, that is not only toilsome, but the parts will not fit well together. It is only when the movements of my hand are neither too gentle nor too violent that the idea in my mind can be realized. Still, I cannot explain this in words; there is a skill in it which I cannot teach my son, nor can he learn it from me." The wheelwright pointed out, in other words, that perfection cannot be achieved by reading about it, but only in direct action.

Thus Ch'an-Zen is by no means an asceticism divorced from life, though there are many great Ch'an-Zen monasteries; Ch'an-Zen art presents no exception to the general rule in Asia, that all works of art have definite and commonly understood meanings, apart from any aesthetic perfection of the work itself. The meanings of Ch'an-Zen themes are such as have sometimes been expressed in European art by means of allegorical figures. Dragon and tiger, mist and mountain, horse and bull, are types of Heaven and Earth, spirit and matter; the gentle long-armed gibbon suggests benevolence, the peacock is symbolic of longevity, the lotus represents an immaculate purity. Let us consider the case of the pine tree and the morning glory, both favorite themes of Japanese art: "The morning glory blossoms only for an hour, and yet it differs not at heart from the pine, which may endure for a thousand years." What is to be understood here is not an obvious allegory of time and eternity, but that the pine no more takes thought of its thousand years than the morning glory of its passing hour; each fulfils its destiny and is content; and Matsunaga, the author of the poem, wished that his heart might be like theirs. If such associations add nothing directly to aesthetic quality, neither do they in any way detract from it. When at last Zen art found expression in scepticism,

> Granted this dewdrop world is but a dewdrop world,
> This granted, yet . . . [28]

there came into being the despised popular and secular

Ukiyoye [29] art of Japan. But here an artistic tradition had been so firmly established, the vision of the world so *approfondi*, that in a sphere corresponding with that of the modern picture postcard — Ukiyoye illustrated the theatre, the *Yoshiwara*, and the *Aussichtspunkt* — there still survived a purity and charm of conception that sufficed, however slight their essence, to win acceptance in Europe, long before the existence of a more serious and classical art had been suspected.

A mystical development took place in India somewhat later, and on different lines. In the anthropocentric European view of life, the nude human form has always seemed to be peculiarly significant, but in Asia, where human life has been thought of as differing from that of other creatures, or even from that of the "inanimate" creation only in degree, not in kind, this has never been the case. On the other hand, in India, the conditions of human love, from the first meeting of eyes to ultimate self-oblivion, have seemed spiritually significant, and there has always been a free and direct use of sexual imagery in religious symbolism. On the one hand, physical union has seemed to present a self-evident image of spiritual unity; on the other, operative forces, as in modern scientific method, are conceived as male and female, positive and negative. It was thus natural enough that later Vaiṣṇava mysticism, speaking always of devotion, *bhakti*, should do so in the same terms; the true and timeless relation of the soul to God could now only be expressed in impassioned epithalamia celebrating the nuptials of Rādhā and Kṛṣṇa, milkmaid and herdsman, earthly Bride and heavenly Bridegroom. So there came into being songs and dances in which at one and the same time sensuality has spiritual significance, and spirituality physical substance, and painting that depicts a transfigured world, where all men are heroic, all women beautiful and passionate and shy, beasts and even trees and rivers are aware of the presence of the Beloved — a world of imagination and reality, seen with the eyes of Majñūn.[30] If in the dance ("nautch") the mutual relations of hero and heroine imitated by the players display an esoteric meaning,[31] this is not by arbitrary interpretation or as allegory, but by a mutual introsusception. If in painting and poetry the daily life of peasants seemed to reflect conditions ever present in the pastoral Heaven of the Divine Cowherd, this is not a sentimental or romantic symbolism, but born of the conviction that "all the men and women of the world are His living forms" (Kabīr), that reality is here and now tangibly and visibly accessible. Here the scent of the earth is ever present: "If he has no eyes, nor nose, nor mouth, how could he have stolen and eaten curd? Can we abandon our love of Kṛṣṇa, to worship a figure painted on a wall?" (Sūr Dās.) Realities of experience, and neither a theory of design nor inspiration coming none knows whence, are the sources of this art; and those who cannot at least in fancy (vāsanā)[32] experience the same emotions and sense their natural operation cannot expect to be able to understand the art by any other and more analytical processes. For no art can be judged until we place ourselves at the point of view of the artist; so only can the determination be known by which its design and execution are entirely controlled.

A formal theory of art based on the facts as above outlined has been enunciated in India in a considerable literature on Rhetoric (*alaṁkāra*). It is true that this theory is mainly developed in connection with poetry, drama, dancing, and music, but it is immediately applicable to art of all kinds, much of its terminology employs the concept of color, and we have evidence that the theory was also in fact applied to painting.[33] Accordingly, in what follows we have not hesitated to give an extended interpretation to terms primarily employed in connection with poetry, or rather literature (*kāvya*), considered as the type of art.[34] The justification of art is then made with reference to use (*prayojana*) or value (*puruṣārtha*)[35] by pointing out that it subserves the Four Purposes of Life, viz. Right Action (*dharma*), Pleasure (*kāma*), Wealth (*artha*), and Spiritual Freedom (*mokṣa*). Of these, the first three represent the proximate, the last the ultimate, ends of life; the work of art is determined (*prativihita*) in the same way, proximately with regard to immediate use, and ultimately with regard to aesthetic experience. Art is then defined as follows: VAKYAṀ RASÂT-MAKAṀ KĀVYAM, that is, "ART IS EXPRESSION INFORMED BY IDEAL BEAUTY."[36] Mere narration (*nirvāha, itihāsa*), bare utility, are not art, or are only art in a rudimentary sense. Nor has art as such a merely informative value confined to its explicit meaning (*vyutpatti*): only the man of little wit (*alpabuddhi*) can fail to recognize that art is by nature a well-spring of delight (*ānanda-niṣyanda*), whatever may have been the occasion of its appearance.[37] On the other hand, there cannot be imagined an art without meaning or use. The doctrine of art for art's sake is disposed of in a sentence quoted in the *Sāhitya Darpaṇa* V, 1, Commentary: "All expressions (*vākya*), human or revealed, are directed to an end beyond themselves (*kārya-param*, 'another *facti-bile*'); or if not so determined (*atatparatve*) are thereby comparable only to the utterances of a madman." There-fore, "let the purpose (*kṛtârthatā*) of skill (*vaidagdhya*) be attained," *Mālatīmādhava*, I, 32 f. Again, the distinction of art (controlled workmanship, things well and truly made) from Nature (functional expression, *sattva-bhāva*) is made as follows: "the work (*karma*) of the two hands is an otherwise-determined (*parastāt-prativihitā*) element of natural being (*bhūta-mātrā*)," *Kauṣītaki Upaniṣad*, III, 5.

In this theory of art, the most important term is RASA, rendered above "Ideal Beauty," but meaning literally "tinc-ture" or essence, and generally translated in the present con-nection as "flavor"; aesthetic experience being described as the tasting of flavor (*rasâsvādana*) or simply as tasting (*svāda, āsvāda*), the taster as *rasika*, the work of art as *rasa-vat*.[38] It should also be observed that the word *rasa* is used (1) relatively, in the plural, with reference to the various, usually eight or nine, emotional conditions which may con-stitute the burden of a given work, love (*śṛṅgāra-rasa*) be-ing the most significant of these, and (2) absolutely, in the singular, with reference to the interior act of tasting flavor unparticularized. In the latter sense, which alone need be considered here, the idea of an aesthetic beauty to be tast*ed*, and knowable only in the activity of tast*ing*,[39] is to be clearly distinguished from the relative beauties or lovelinesses of the separate parts of the work, or of the work itself considered merely as a surface, the appreciation of all which is a matter of taste (*ruci*) or predilection.[40] The latter relative beauties will appear in the theme and aesthetic surfaces, in all that has to do with the proximate determination of the work to be done, its ordering to use; the formal beauty will be sensed in vitality and unity, design and rhythm, in no way depending on the nature of the theme, or its component parts. It is indeed very explicitly pointed out that any theme whatever, "lovely or unlovely, noble or vulgar, gracious or frightful, etc.," may become the vehicle of *rasa*.[41]

The definition of aesthetic experience (*rasâsvâdana*) given in the *Sāhitya Darpaṇa*, III, 2–3, is of such authority and value as to demand translation *in extenso*; we offer first, a very literal version with brief comment, then a slightly smoother rendering avoiding interruptions. Thus, (1) "Flavor (*rasaḥ*) is tasted (*āsvādyate*) by men having an innate knowledge of absolute values (*kaiścit-pramātṛbhiḥ*), in exaltation of the pure consciousness (*sattvôdrekāt*), as self-luminous (*svaprakāśaḥ*), in the mode at once of ecstasy and intellect (*ānanda-cin-mayaḥ*), void of contact with things knowable (*vedyântara-sparśa-śūnyaḥ*), twin brother to the

tasting of Brahma (*brahmâsvāda-sahôdaraḥ*), whereof the
life is a super-wordly lightning-flash (*lokôttara-camatkāra-prâṇaḥ*), as intrinsic aspect (*svâkāravat = svarūpavat*), in
indivisibility (*abhinnatve*) ": and (2) "Pure aesthetic experi-
ence is theirs in whom the knowledge of ideal beauty is innate; it is known intuitively, in intellectual ecstasy without
accompaniment of ideation, at the highest level of conscious
being; born of one mother with the vision of God, its life
is as it were a flash of blinding light of transmundane origin, impossible to analyze, and yet in the image of our very
being."

Neither of the foregoing renderings embodies any foreign
matter. On the other hand, only an extended series of alternative renderings would suffice to develop the full reference
of the original terms. *Pramātṛ* (from the same root as
pramāṇa, present also in English "metre") is *quis rationem
artis intelligit*; here not as one instructed, but by nature.
The notion of innate genius may be compared with Blake's
"Man is born like a garden ready planted and sown," and
"The knowledge of Ideal Beauty cannot be acquired, it is
born with us." But it must be understood that from the
Indian point of view, genius is not a fortuitous manifesta
tion, but the necessary consequence of a rectification of the
whole personality, accomplished in a previous condition of
being; cf. the notion of an absolute *pramāṇa* natural to
the Comprehensor, to the Buddha, see note 74, *infra*. The
"exaltation of *sattva*" implies, of course, abstraction from
extension, operation, local motion (*rajas*), and from inde-

termination or inertia (*tamas*). Aesthetic experience is a transformation not merely of feeling (as suggested by the word *aesthesis, per se*), but equally of understanding; cf. the state of "Deep Sleep," characterized by the expression *prajñāna-ghana-ānanda-mayi*, "a condensed understanding in the mode of ecstasy," discussed below, p. 133 and note 89. The level of pure aesthetic experience is indeed that of the pure angelic understanding, proper to the Motionless Heaven, Brahmaloka. With "like a flash of lightning," cf. *Bṛhadāraṇyaka Upaniṣad*, II, 3, 6 and *Kena Upaniṣad*, 29, where the vision of Brahman is compared to a "sudden flash of lightning," or "What flashes in the lightning." The vision is our very Being, *Ding an Sich, svâkāra*, and like our Being, beyond our individually limited grasp (*grahaṇa*) or conception (*saṁkalpa*); "you cannot see the seer of seeing," *Bṛhadāraṇyaka Upaniṣad*, III, 4, 2.[42]

In any case, "It is the spectator's own energy (*utsāha*) that is the cause of tasting, just as when children play with clay elephants"; the permanent mood (*sthāyi-bhāva*) is brought to life as *rasa* because of the spectator's own capacity for tasting, "not by the character or actions of the hero to be imitated (*anukārya*), nor by the deliberate ordering of the work to that end (*tatparatvataḥ*)."[43] Those devoid of the required capacity or energy are no better than the wood or masonry of the gallery.[44] Aesthetic experience is thus only accessible to those competent (*pramātṛ, rasika, sahṛdaya*). Competence depends "on purity or singleness (*sattva*) of heart and on an inner character (*antara-dharma*) or habit of obedience (*anuśīla*) tending to aversion of attention from external phenomena; this character and habit, not to be acquired by mere learning, but either innate or cultivated, depends on an ideal sensibility (*vāsanā*) and the faculty of self-identification (*yogyatā*) with the forms (*bhavana*) depicted (*varṇanīya*)." [45] Just as the original intuition arose from a self-identification of the artist with the appointed theme, so aesthetic experience, reproduction, arises from a self-identification of the spectator with the presented matter; criticism repeats the process of creation. An interesting case is that of the actor, or any artist, who must not be naturally moved by the passions he depicts, though he may obtain aesthetic experience from the spectacle of his own performance.[46]

Notwithstanding that aesthetic experience is thus declared to be an inscrutable and uncaused spiritual activity, that is virtually ever-present and potentially realizable, but not possible to be realized unless and until all affective and mental barriers have been resolved, all knots of the heart undone, it is necessarily admitted that the experience arises in relation to some specific representation. The elements of this representation, the work of art itself, can be and are discussed by the Hindu rhetoricians at great length, and provide the material and much of the terminology of analysis and criticism. For present purposes it will suffice to present these constituents of the work of art in a brief form; but it must not be forgotten that here only is to be found the tangible (*grāhya*) matter of the work of art, all that can be explained and accounted for in it, and that this all includes precisely that *a priori* knowledge which the spectator must possess or come to possess before he can pretend to competence in the sense above defined. The elements of the work of art are, then:

(1) Determinants (*vibhāva*), viz. the physical stimulants to aesthetic reproduction, particularly the theme and its parts, the indications of time and place, and other apparatus of representation — the whole *factibile*. The operation of the Determinants takes place by the operation of an ideal-sympathy (*sādhāraṇya*), a self-identification with the imagined situation.[47]

(2) Consequents (*anubhāva*), the specific and conventional means of "registering" (*sūcanā*) emotional states, in particular gestures (*abhinaya*).

(3) Moods (*bhāva*), the conscious emotional states as represented in art. These include thirty-three Fugitive or Transient (*vyabhicāri*) Moods such as joy, agitation, impatience, etc., and eight or nine Permanent (*sthāyi*) Moods, the Erotic, Heroic, etc., which in turn are the vehicles of the specific *rasas* or emotional colorings. In any work, one of the Permanent Moods must constitute a master motif to which all the others are subordinate; for "the extended development of a transient emotion becomes an inhibition of *rasa*," [48] or, as we should now express it, the work becomes sentimental, embarrassing rather than moving.

(4) The representation of involuntary physical reactions (*sattva-bhāva*), for example fainting.

All of these determinants and symbols are recognized collectively and indivisibly in aesthetic experience, the work of art being as such a unity; but they are recognized separately in subsequent analysis.

According to the related School of Manifestation (*Vyakti-vāda*) the essential or soul of poetry is called *dhvani*, "the reverberation of meaning arising by suggestion (*vyañjanā*)."[49] In grammar and logic, a word or other symbol is held to have two powers only, those of denotation (*abhidhā*) and connotation (*lakṣaṇā*); for example *gopāla* is literally "cowherd," but constantly signifies Kṛṣṇa. The rhetoricians assume for a word or symbol a third power, that of suggestion (*vyañjanā*), the matter suggested, which we should call the real content of the work, being *dhvani*, with respect to either the theme (*vastu*), any metaphor or other ornament (*alaṃkāra*), or, what is more essential, one of the specific *rasas*. In other words, *abhidhā*, *lakṣaṇā*, and *vyañjanā* correspond to literal, allegorical, and anagogic significance. *Dhvani*, as overtone of meaning, is thus the immediate vehicle of single *rasa* and means to aesthetic experience.[50] Included in *dhvani* is *tātparyārtha*, the meaning conveyed by the whole sentence or formula, as distinct from the mere sum of meanings of its separate parts. The School of Manifestation is so called because the perception (*pratīti*) of *rasa* is thought of simply as the manifestation of an inherent and already existing intuitive condition of the spirit, in the same sense that Enlightenment is virtually everpresent though not always realized. The *pratīti* of *rasa*, as it were, breaks through the enclosing walls (*varaṇa, āvaraṇa*) by which the soul, though predisposed by ideal sympathy (*sādhāraṇya*) and sensibility (*vāsanā*), is still immured [51] and restricted from shining forth in its true character as the taster of *rasa* in an aesthetic experience which is as aforesaid the very twin brother of the experience of the unity of Brahman.

In the later and otherwise more synthetic scheme of the *Sāhitya Darpaṇa*, the *rasa* and *dhvani* theories are not quite so closely linked, *dhvani* being now not so much the soul of all poetry as characteristic of the superior sort of poetry in which what is suggested outweighs what is literally expressed.

For the sake of completeness there need only be mentioned two earlier theories in which Ornament or Figures (*alaṁkāra*) and Style or Composition (*rīti*) are regarded respectively as the essential elements in art. These theories, which have not held their own in India, may be compared to the minor European conceptions of art as dexterity, or as consisting merely of aesthetic surfaces which are significant only as sources of sensation. This last point of view can be maintained consistently in India only from the standpoint of the naïve realism which underlies a strictly monastic prejudice against the world.

It remains to be pointed out that the *rasa* and *dhvani* theories are essentially metaphysical and Vedântic in method and conclusion, though they are expressed not so much in terms of the pure Vedânta of the Upaniṣads as in those of a later Vedânta combined with other systems, particularly the Yoga. The fully evolved Indian theory of beauty is in fact hardly to be dated before the tenth or eleventh century, though the doctrine of *rasa* is already clearly enunciated in Bharata's *Nāṭya Śāstra*, which may be anterior to the fifth century and itself derives from still older sources.

In any case, the conception of the work of art as determined outwardly to use and inwardly to a delight of the reason; the view of its operation as not intelligibly causal, but by way of a destruction of the mental and affective barriers behind which the natural manifestation of the spirit is concealed; the necessity that the soul should be already prepared for this emancipation by an inborn or acquired sensibility; the requirement of self-identification with the ultimate theme, on the part of both artist and spectator, as prerequisite to visualization in the first instance and reproduction in the second; finally, the conception of ideal beauty as unconditioned by natural affections, indivisible, supersensual, and indistinguishable from the gnosis of God— all these characteristics of the theory demonstrate its logical connection with the predominant trends of Indian thought, and its natural place in the whole body of Indian philosophy.

Consequently, though it could not be argued that any aesthetic theory is explicitly set forth in the Upaniṣads, it will not surprise us to find that the ideas and terminology of the later aesthetic are there already recognizable. For

example, in the *Bṛhadāraṇyaka Upaniṣad*, I, 4, 7, the world
is said to be differentiated or known in plurality by, and
only by, means of name and aspect, *nāmarūpa*, idea and
image; *ibid.*, III, 2, 3 and 5, "Voice (*vāc*) is an apprehender
(*graha*); it is seized by the idea (*nāma*) as an over-apprehender, then indeed by voice (*vāc*) one utters thoughts
(*nāmāni*)," and similarly "Sight (*cakṣu*) is an apprehender;
it is seized by aspect (*rūpa*) as an over-apprehender, then
indeed by the eye (*cakṣu*) one sees things (*rūpāṇi*)." [52]
Further, *ibid.*, III, 9, 20, "on the heart (*hṛdaya*) are aspects (*rūpāṇi*) based," and similarly in the case of speech.
As to the heart, "it is the same as Prajāpati, it is Brahman," *ibid.*, V, 3, and "other than that Imperishable, there
is none that (really) sees," *ibid.*, III, 8, 11. [53] Actual objects
(*rūpāṇi*) seen in space are really seen not as such, but only
as colored areas, the concept of space being altogether
mental and conventional. [54]

The Indian theory, in origins and formulation, seems at
first sight to be *sui generis*. But merely because of the specific idiomatic and mythical form in which it finds expression, it need not be thought of as otherwise than universal.
It does not in fact differ from what is implicit in the Far
Eastern view of art, or on the other hand in any essentials
from the Scholastic Christian point of view, or what is asserted in the aphorisms of Blake; it does differ essentially
from the modern non-intellectual interpretations of art as
sensation. What are probably the most significant elements
in the Asiatic theory are the views (1) that aesthetic ex-

perience is an ecstasy in itself inscrutable, but in so far as it can be defined, a delight of the reason, and (2) that the work of art itself, which serves as the stimulus to the release of the spirit from all inhibitions of vision, can only come into being and have being as a thing ordered to specific ends. Heaven and Earth are united in the analogy (*sādṛśya*, etc.) of art, which is an ordering of sensation to intelligibility and tends toward an ultimate perfection in which the seer perceives all things imaged in himself.

Chapter II

MEISTER ECKHART'S VIEW OF ART

Chapter II

MEISTER ECKHART'S VIEW OF ART

Docti rationem artis intelligunt, indocti voluptatem.
Quintilian, IX, 4.

THE Schoolmen composed no special treatise with the title 'Philosophy of Art.' . . . There is nevertheless a far-reaching theory of art to be found in their writings." [55] Amongst such there are none more universal, more profound, or more distinguished by vigor of statement and clarity of thought than those of Meister Eckhart, [56] whose *Sermons* might well be termed an Upaniṣad of Europe. Eckhart's preëminence is not of the order of genius; what is remarkable in him is nothing in kind, nothing individual or curious, but only a great energy or will that allows him to resume and concentrate in one consistent demonstration the spiritual being of Europe at its highest tension. Toward his theme he is utterly devout, and his trained mental powers are the author of his style, but otherwise, in his own words spoken with reference to the painter of portraits, "it is not himself that it reveals to us" (37); "What I give out is in me . . . as the gift of God" (143).

The real analogy between Eckhart's modes of thought and those which have long been current in India should make it easy for the Vedântist or Mahāyāna Buddhist to understand him, which would require a much greater effort on the part of a Protestant Christian or modern philosopher. In European readers, some knowledge of Scholastic thought and Christian theology must be taken for granted. Partly for the sake of Indian readers, and partly because the use of Oriental side by side with European technical terms cannot much longer be avoided by students of aesthetics or metaphysics, I have bracketed Sanskrit equivalents wherever they serve to explain or better define the meaning. For the rest, every word or passage enclosed by quotation marks is Eckhart's. I have not thought it necessary to distinguish his own words from those of the various doctors, masters, and heathen philosophers whom he sometimes quotes and endorses, this not being a study of Eckhart's sources. I have tried to arrange the available material logically, and where it has been necessary to develop the idea, to do so strictly in harmony with Scholastic ideas in general and Eckhart's phrases in particular, often using his own words even when this is not specifically indicated by the page references.

Eckhart's whole conception of human life in operation and attainment is aesthetic: it runs through all his thought that man is an artist in the analogy of the "exalted workman," and his idea of "sovran good" and "immutable delight" is that of a perfected art.[57] Art is religion, religion art, not related, but the same. No one can study theology without perceiving this; for example, the Trinity is an "arrangement" of God,[58] "articulate speech" (369), "de-

termined by formal notions" (268), "symmetry with supreme lucidity" (366). Eckhart is writing, not a treatise on
the arts as such, though he is evidently quite familiar with
them, but sermons on the art of knowing God. Ignorance
is "lack of knowledge . . . brutish" (13).

What is knowledge? Threefold: (1) of particulars and
generals, sensible, empirical, literal, indicative, *saṁvyavahārika-pratyakṣa*, (2) of universals, rational or intelligible,
allegorical, conventional, *parokṣa*, (3) of sameness, without
image or likeness, transcendental, anagogic, *aparokṣa* =
paramārthika-pratyakṣa (13, 32, 87–88, 166, 228, II, 183,
etc.; cf. Chapter V). Of these the first two (*avidyā*) are
relative, the last (*vidyā*) immediate and absolute, only to
be expressed in terms of negation.

To clarify his meaning, Eckhart makes constant allusion
to the practice of specific arts, to the art in the artist, and
to the perfecting of art and artist. Understanding may be
audibly or visibly perceived, in either case as an aesthetic
process. For example, "I see the lilies in the field, their
gaiety, their color, all their leaves" (143), just as any brute
perceives them; this is simply the recognition and relish-
ing of "creatures as creatures," "as they are in themselves,"
to be recognized and valued as to their uses. But "my inner
man relishes things not as creatures but as the gift of God"
(143), that is, as intelligible images, here with a specifically
edifying connotation. "And again, to my innermost man
they savor not of God's gift but of ever and aye. Even so
do all creatures speak God" (143), "I am come like the fra-

grance of a flower" (284); that is the overtone of meaning, suggestion, *dhvani*, unalloyed savoring, *rasa*. In all, these are the three aesthetic functions of denotation, connotation, and implication, corresponding to recognition, interpretation, and immediate understanding.

The soul has two powerful faculties, intellect and will, expressed in vision and love, which can be exercised in fruitful operation, outwardly or inwardly (166). Where things exist as intelligible images, as means of understanding and communication, intellectually, in the imagination, there lies man's way. It is here that things are known in unintelligible multiplicity and must be realized in intelligible unity, here that the use of things is understood, and that renunciation of all uses must be made: "to find nature herself all her likenesses have to be shattered and the further in the nearer the actual thing" (259), such renunciation and such shattering being of the essence of art, in which all things are seen alike without any sense of possession, not in their nature but in their being, quite disinterestedly.[59]

In outward operation, these powers of the soul, intellect and will, correspond to vocation, as with the artist (artifex), professor (doctor), or celebrant (priest), and to conduct as distinguished from specific skill. The artist is not a special kind of man, but every man is a special kind of artist. The vocations ("arranging this or that," 16) are so many different disciplines; conduct ("comforting another," 16) another discipline proper to all men alike. Every activity involves what we should now call an aesthetic process, a succession of problem, solution, and execution. Materials apart, whoever acts, acts in the same way, will following the intellect, whether he makes a house, or studies mathematics, or performs an office, or does good works.

Our modern system of thought has substituted for this division of labor a spiritual caste system which divides men into species. Those who have lost most by this are the artists, professionally speaking, on the one hand, and laymen generally on the other. The artist (meaning such as would still be so called) loses by his isolation and corresponding pride, and by the emasculation of his art, no longer conceived as intellectual, but only as emotional in motivation and significance; the workman (to whom the name of artist is now denied) loses in that he is not called, but forced to labor unintelligently, goods being valued above men. All alike have lost, in that art being now a luxury, no longer the normal type of all activity, all men are compelled to live in squalor and disorder and have become so inured to this that they are unaware of it. The only surviving artists in the Scholastic, Gothic sense, are scientists, surgeons, and engineers, the only ateliers, laboratories.

Just because Eckhart's treatment of aesthetics is not *ad hoc*, but takes for granted the point of view of a school, not in any private sense his own, it has a special value; we can have no doubt that it was actually in this fashion that cultured men in Paris and Cologne, in the twelfth and thirteenth centuries, when Christian art was at its zenith, thought of art and the specific arts. These same men in their collective capacity as the Church prescribed the themes of art and the more essential details of its iconography; the workman, sometimes a trained monk, more often a trained gildsman, added from the storehouse of tradition another element to form besides the skill of craft which he was expected to practice in his vocation. Thus intellect and will worked in unanimity. Is not the determination of this art — that in it which alone is common to the mind and to the product, that is, its imagery, not its style, still less any individual mannerism — a thing that must be understood if we would understand Christian art at all? I sometimes wonder if we really want to understand it. For on the one hand, from the histories of art one would suppose that the very form by which the art is moved from within can be neglected, and that nothing matters in it but the facts of history, accidents of provenance and influence, and problems of attribution — all those things with which the mediaeval workman was least of all concerned; and on the other hand, we have those who insist that the enjoyment of the work of art, admittedly its ultimate value (if we understand "enjoyment" rightly, which is the very problem of aesthetics, and cannot be assumed) demands no other preparatory discipline, being an unintelligible ecstasy (as may be granted), and can be taught (which is inadmissible) to those who aspire to the transcendent vision, but are only too ready to be persuaded that the mirror of the universe is the eye's intrinsic faculty (such readiness is "a trick the soul has, when indulging in comfortable intuitions of divinity," 447). The study of art, from a historical point of view, may be harmless in itself, yet no better than the satisfaction of a curiosity; the enjoyment of works of art merely as a pleasure of the eye or ear may be harmless in itself ("that a disagreeable noise should be as grateful to the ear as the sweet tones of a lyre is a thing I never shall attain to," II, 97), yet no more than an enhanced sensation. If this were all, aesthetic would be nothing more than a discussion of taste, and so indeed the experimental psychologists believe.

To speak of art exclusively in terms of sensation is doing violence to the inner man, the knowing subject; to extract from Eckhart's thought a theory of taste (*ruci*) would be doing violence to its unity. If I venture at all to extract from it a theory of art, this is not as an exercise in dialectics, but because it is required for the specific interpretation of Christian art, and because the Scholastic view is more than a great provincial school of thought; it represents a universal mode of thought, and this mode throws a light on the analogous theories that have prevailed in Asia, and should serve Western students as a means of approach to, and understanding of, Asiatic art.

The doctrine of types, ideas, forms, or images is of fundamental importance for the understanding of Eckhart's references to art. More rarely, the words semblance, likeness, symbol, effigy, pattern, and prototype are employed. Amongst all these, type and prototype, pattern, idea, and ideal are used only with reference to things known and seen intellectually (*parokṣa*), the others in the same sense or with reference to the image materially embodied (*pratyakṣa*). To begin with, what is an image in these two senses? An image "is anything known or born" (258), or anything both known and born or made. The Son, for example, is the Father's "own image abiding in himself . . . his immanent form," and at the same time "the exact likeness, the perfect image of his Father" (258) in a distinct Person. In the same way all creatures "in their preëxisting forms in God have been divine life for ever," only their material embodiment "when Nature is working in time and space" (71) being by birth and as it were God's handiwork: "these preëxisting forms are the origin or principle of the creation of all creatures, and in this sense they are types and pertain to practical knowledge" (253). They live in the "divine mind," the "hoard" which "is God's art" (461): "Intellect is the temple of God wherein he is shining in all his glory. Nowhere does God dwell more really than in this temple of his intellect's nature" (212) (*ālaya-vijñāna*), "quiddity or mode is the way into this temple" (*ibid.*). And like God's hoard "There is a power in the soul called mind (*vijñāna, saṁkalpa*); it is her storehouse of incorporeal forms and intellectual notions" (402); the ideas in this storehouse of the soul may seem either to be new or to be remembered (105), but in either case are as it were recollected (226, 295), for "all the words of his divine essence flow into the word in our mind in distinction of Person just as memory pours out treasure of images into the powers of the soul" (402). Another superficial distinction of ideas in kind can be made as between the ideas of natural species, as when one works with the "rose-form" (251) or the image of Conrad (128), and artificial ideas, arising "theoretically, as the house of wood and stone is designed in the architect's practical mind, who makes the house as much like his ideal as he can" (252), either kind being "in the practical power" as the "idea of the work" (252) to be done, if work is to be done, as well as abiding in the mind as objects of understanding and *a priori* means of rational communication. Either of these kinds of ideas is equally invention (*anuvitta*), a discovery amongst "the sum of all the forms conceived by man and which subsist in God himself, I having no property in them and no idea of ownership" (35, cf. 17); which point of view we all naturally endorse when we say that an idea has come to us, or that we have hit upon it, *eureka*, never that we have made it. At the best, we have prepared ourselves for it by emptying our conscience of all other creature images and fugitive emotions, accepting for the time being only the seal or imprint of this one thing. So the image is in the artist, not he in it; it is his whose image it is, not his who harbors it (52). When we find "just as the artist, inspired by his art, will carve in wood or paint on canvas or the wall" (II, 211), "art" means the idea of the theme, as it presents itself to him. The image in the object, in the artist's mind, and in the graven image are the same, though in the artist and in his work only according to his powers, not in its full perfection. In the graven image of anything it may be thought of not as introduced by the artist but as latent in the medium because of the appetite for form that matter has; for example, "when the artist makes a statue out of wood or stone he does not put the image in the wood, he chips away the wood which hides the form. He gives the wood nothing, he takes it away: carves it out where it is too thick, pares off overlay, and then there appears what was hidden" (II, 82) — an analogy of how God's image is ever present in the ground of the soul, but concealed by veils and hindrances (II, 81).

God's and man's ideas or types are thus not Platonic ideas external to intellect (in Essence there is no likeness or image, but only Sameness, *samatā*), nor immutable or general, but types of activity, forces, principles of work or becoming, living and particular — "to call a tree a tree is not to name it, for all the species are confused" (117), no two creatures being alike in their nature, for "every creature makes innate denial; the one denies it is the other" (249). Ideas are as many in number as there have been or ever can be things in time, "there are as many types as there are grades of nature to be typified" (252, 253); they cannot be more in number than this, because God's work is not by choice, there is nothing that he leaves undone, what he thinks is, what is is what he thinks, his creation is without means or succession. "Every nature emanates from its appropriate form" (477), but our conception of process and succession is merely "due to our gross senses" (365);

from God's point of view ideas are all known at once in perfection and in one form; from our temporal point of view ideas are free and variably becoming, or as we now say evolving. From any point of view, ideas or forms (*nāma*) are "living," not merely existing like standards fixed and deposited for safe-keeping — ideas not merely of static shapes, but ideas of acts (16).

"An icon in stone or on the wall, with no foundation to it (that is, materials apart, and) taken simply as form, is the same form as his whose form it is" (64). So then normally there will be nothing of the artist in the work except his skill: "the painter who has painted a good portrait therein shows his art; it is not himself that it reveals to us" (37). But if the painter paints his own portrait, as God does, then both his skill and his image will be in it, himself as he knows himself, but not his very self: "this reflects credit on the painter who embodies in it his dearest conception of his art and makes it the image of himself. The likeness of the portrait praises the author without words" (97). "If I paint my likeness on the wall, he who sees the likeness is not seeing me; but anyone who sees me sees my likeness and not my likeness merely but my child. If I really knew my soul, anyone who saw my conception of it would say it was my son, for I share therewith my energy and nature, and as here so it is in the Godhead. The Father understands himself perfectly clearly, so there appears to him his image, that is to say, his Son" (408) (the portrait and the corporeal man are both the man's conception of himself, they are "alike" in form, however different in aspect flesh and paint must be).

In this connection may be considered a difficult passage occurring in the exegesis of Genesis I, 26, "Let us make man in our image and likeness." Eckhart says, "Work comes from the outward and from the inner man, but the innermost man takes no part in it. In making a thing the very innermost self of a man comes into outwardness" (195), in which there seems to be some contradiction. The first is clear: the work as a substance in a given shape comes from the man's hands molding matter, and as form from the specific idea in him, as it is in his intellect, which does no work in molding matter, but only singles out the best it can according to its idiosyncrasy. Because the actual handiwork is done by the man's very body, it is only natural that there should be a trace of his physiognomy left in it, just as the axe which "brings about the workman's desired end" (II, 178) leaves its mark in the wood and could be identified thereby.[59] So then in touch and style the work somewhat reveals the man, that is as to the accidents of his being. That the very innermost self of a man also "comes into outwardness," according to Eckhart's own analogy, as "When God made man the very innermost heart of the Godhead was concerned in his making" (195, 436), and yet "God's works enclose a mere nothing of God, wherefore they cannot disclose him" (87, cf. *Bhagavad Gītā*, IX, 4 and 5). Or again, "Form is a revelation of essence" (38), in which there is neither image nor likeness; essence is in all things, and though it "gets not," yet "it moves movable things like creatures" (284). As Godhead to God, so is innermost man to workman, Godhead and innermost man being present in the work, one in being with it, but not operatively or intelligibly. In Eckhart's own work we see the man possessed of his ideas, and wrestling with his means, the "intractable" (119) and untaught German speech of his day; but in the ideas at last so vigorously expressed there is a "mere nothing of the man" as he is in God. For man to be in his handiwork as God is in his creation it would have to be as immanent life, the thing made would have to be alive and possessed of free will. If we do sometimes say that a work lives, this is only metaphorical, a sort of animism which projects our own living reactions into the thing as it is in itself.

That there is no life in man's handiwork underlies the Muḥammadan doctors' interdiction of representative art, the imitation of living forms being regarded as a blasphemy, inasmuch as the artist brings into being a pseudo-creation, as it were in mockery of God, who alone gives life. Nevertheless, as we have seen and shall further demonstrate, Christian art is not a mimicry of natural species, nor merely a source of pleasurable sensations, but is a manner of speaking about God and Nature: it no more trespasses upon God's dignity than when we speak of him or see of him or taste of him, using names or other images,[60] being only too well aware the while that "nothing true can be spoken of God" (8), "God is nameless" (246), "there is no knowing

him by likeness" (55), (who is *nirābhāsa, amūrta*), "a portrait of the highest seraph limned in black would be a better
likeness far than God portrayed as highest seraph; that were
a preëminent unlikeness" (46), and yet believing that there
is nothing "more useful and salutary to the soul than excursions in the science of the holy Trinity and unity" (392)
in which excursions we are naturally compelled to make use
of name and form, being "permitted to use the names his
saints have called him by" (70, cf. St Thomas, *Sum. Theol.*, I,
Q. 51, A. 3, "it is in no wise contrary to truth for intelligible things to be set forth in Scripture under sensible figures,
since it is not said for the purpose of maintaining that intelligible things are sensible, but in order that properties
of intelligible things may be understood according to similitude through sensible figures"). The demonstration of
iconoclasm is as follows: "they held their peace for fear
of lying" (237); "Anyone content with what can be expressed in words — God is a word, Heaven is a word — is
aptly styled an unbeliever" (339). But this is a sort of
asceticism or renunciation proper only to those who have
a vision of God without means and have earned the right
to say that all scripture is vain; otherwise, a denial of the
soul's powers, expressed in outward works, as a means to
edification and enlightenment, is by no means excusable.

Notwithstanding that man's handiwork is without life,
still the human maker is an analogy of the "exalted workman" (376), the divine architect, all-maker (Viśvakarma).
"Suppose some master of the arts. If he produces a work

of art he none the less preserves his arts within himself: the arts are the artist in the artist" (that is, in the man so called), just as "Things flowed forth finite into time while abiding in eternity" where they are "God in God" (285). "The idea of the work exists in the worker's practical mind as an object of his understanding, which regards it as expressing his idea to which he forms the material work" (252), that is, not in his mind as a *mode* of understanding, but as a thing already and directly understood, for "I make a letter of the alphabet like the image of that letter in my mind, not like my mind itself" (235). Every least detail of the work will correspond to details of form in the artist's mind: "no architect can carry in his head the plan of a whole house without the plans of all its details" (252).

Again, "the form, idea, or semblance of a thing, a rose, for instance, is present in my soul, and must be for two reasons. One is because from the appearance of its mental form (*jñāna-sattva-rūpa*) I can paint the rose in corporal matter, so there must be an image of the rose-form in my soul. The second reason is because from the subjective rose-idea I recognize the objective rose although I do not copy it (that is, do not copy the rose in painting). Just as I can carry in my mind the notion of a house I never mean to build" (252). "For the purpose of making a crock a man takes a handful of clay; that is the medium he works in. He gives it a form he has in him, nobler than his material" (68). And as to this form as it exists in the artist's mind, "Another power in the soul is that wherewith she thinks (*dhī, dhyai*). This power is able to picture in itself things which are not there, so that I can see things as well as with my eyes, or even better. I can see a rose in winter when there are no roses (cf. 116), therefore with this power the soul produces (*ākarṣati*) things from the non-existent (*hṛdaya-ākāśa*) like God who creates things out of nothing (*kha* = χάος)" (212, cf. 445). In any case "to be properly expressed a thing must proceed from within, moved by its form; it must come, not in from without, but out from within" (108).

In other words, just as "the soul is the form of the body," so the art in the artist is the form of the work: "the cutting of the wood is from the saw; but that it assumes at length the form of a bed is from the design of the art" (in the artist), "the form of the bed is not in the saw or the axe, but a certain movement toward that form," St Thomas, *Sum. Theol.*, I, Q. 110. A. 2 and Q. 118, A. 1, quoting also Avicenna, "all forms which are in matter proceed from the concept of the intellect."

The arising of the image is not by an act of will whether human or divine, but of attention (*dhāraṇā*) when the will is at rest; there can be nothing meritorious (17) in the possession of images, since an image "receives its being from the thing whose image it is, for it is a natural product . . . prior to the will, will following the image" (51, cf. 17). The aesthetic process is as follows: what I say "springs up in me, then I pause in the idea, and thirdly I speak it out" (222), or again, "First when a word is conceived in my mind it is a subtle, intangible thing; it is a true word when it takes shape in my thought. Later, as spoken aloud by my mouth, it is but an outward expression of the interior word" (80), "the mind sees and formulates and the will wills and memory holds it fast" (16). As to this abiding intention, or pause in the idea, "my wish of today is my purpose of tomorrow, the idea of which is kept alive (*sthita*) by my actual thinking (*vibhāvayati*) of it, just as, they said, God's works are done" (238). As to the work, "Working and becoming are the same. When the carpenter stops working, the house will stop becoming. Still the axe and stop the growth" (163); "Man requires many instruments for his external works; much preparation is needed ere he can bring them forth as he has imagined them" (5); the seeking intellect "spends perhaps a year or more in research on some natural fact, finding out what it is, only to work as long again stripping off what it is not" (17), but "angels . . . need less means for their works and have fewer images" (5).

As we have seen, the aesthetic process is threefold, the arising of the idea in germ, its taking shape before the mind's eye, and outward expression in work (80, 228). The first act is necessarily the effect of attention directed to a given object: the artist is commissioned, not to paint, but to paint something in particular, let us say a flower or an angel (*deva*) or other object. Eckhart takes the case of the host of angels, and though he does not refer to the third stage of actual execution, this would be an easy step. "A master was once questioned by his pupil about the angelic order. He answered him and said, Go hence and withdraw into thyself until thou understandest: give thy whole self up to it, then look, refusing to see anything but what thou findest there. It will seem to thee at first as though thou art the angels with them and as thou dost surrender to their collective being thou shalt think thyself [61] the angels as a whole with the whole company of angels" (216). So far, the process is identical with the Indian imager's *dhyāna-yoga*: and had an actual picture of the angels been required, it might have been added *dhyātvā kuryāt*, that is, "Having thus seen and surrendered to the presented form, begin the work." Had the painting been required to fill a given space, or had it been intended that the angels should stand in some particular relation to other figures in the picture, all this, being a part of the prescribed object, would have had its prototype in the perfected mental image. As to the picture itself, if one had been made, it is merely an arrangement of pigments, nor can my eye learn anything about the angels from its sensations of reflected light: only *I* can have some idea of them, and that not in or by sensation, but by their image, the same that was in the artist's mind, and now taken back from the picture into my mind, for "bodily hearing and sight are engineered in the mind" (93) and "If my soul knows an angel she knows him by some means and in an image, an image imageless, not in an image such as they are here" (112). "Before my eye can see the painting on the wall it must be filtered through the air and in a still more tenuous form borne into my phantasy to be assimilated by my understanding" (111).

Thus the artist's model is always a mental image. The eye (*māṁsa-cakṣu*) is nothing but a mirror: *it* may be said to see an object, such as a rose or stone or work of art, by virtue of some substantial kinship between them (104, 105, 116, 152, 212, 240); "it is a case of like to like" (258). But if I say *I* see, it is only as it were, for "If it were intellect, I should see nothing" (105). "I see" only indirectly and by means of the eye as instrument, which instrument serves me because of a corresponding soul power linked to it, but far removed from matter (104); "subtract the mind, and the eye is open to no purpose" (288). My eye sees flat, but I see in relief; this relief is not necessarily a fact, but an idea of relation, which would have validity for me even supposing a total unreality of the external world. The inwardly known aspect (*antarjñeya-rūpa*), relatively immaterial, is the means by which I recognize what the eye sees, the only means by which I can pretend to understand what the eye reports, or with which I can speak of it to others. "I do not see the hand, the stone, itself; I see the image of the stone, but I do not see this image in a second image or by any other means; I see it without means and without image. This image is itself the means: image without image like motion without motion although causing motion and size which has no size though the principle of size" (114). "The soul knows only in effigy" (243), not anything in itself, but more nearly as things are in God, ideally. I can never see what my eye sees (sensibly) nor hear what my ear hears as vibration, I can only know rationally, by means of an image. "We can see the sunlight where it falls upon a tree or any other object, but we fail to apprehend the sun itself" (72) except as an idea. There is nothing exotic in this point of view; it is an axiom of modern science, which knows matter only in mathematical formulae, not in sensation.

From all this it will be understood how from the Scholastic point of view a naturalistic or visual art, made only according to the eyes (this means, made to yield sensations as nearly as possible identical with those evoked by the model itself), and only for the eyes, must be regarded not merely as irreligious or idolatrous (idolatry is the love of creatures as they are in themselves), but also irrational and indeterminate. For the only thing which can be truly likened to the natural species is its reflection in the mirror of the eye, which is a sensation, not an understanding (the eye, having no understanding of its own, remains incomprehensible to intellect, a case of unlike to unlike). Again, the material image, the work of art, is commensurable with natural species only as to substance (both are essence, but essence cannot be measured): fundamentally incommensurable, in difference of material and life. Nature and art are alike (sādṛśya) only in idea, otherwise irreconcilable.

Recognizability, whether of natural species or material image, has nothing to do with any fancied likeness between these two, but is by means of the incorporeal form or image (nāma) which is in the object, in the artist, in the work of art, and finally in the spectator, having been brought into visibility as far as possible in the material image (*rūpa*) in another nature, but still not made of that nature. Just in so far as anything could be made like natural species, that is self-moving which is inconceivable, or as Muḥammadans would say forbidden, it would not be art but Nature, or necromancy at the best; or could the artist, which is conceivable potentially, though it may be temporally impossible, attain perfection, becoming one with God, he would share in God's creation from time everlasting, natural species would be his image in time as they are God's, nothing would remain but the ever-present world-picture as God sees it. There would be no occasion for works of art, the end of art having been accomplished. In the meantime, where we find ourselves, an art made as far as possible according to the eye's intrinsic faculty (253) and merely for the eye can be thought of only as a superposition of illusion upon illusion, a willing substitution of the snake for the rope, Eckhart's own metaphor of double illusion being that of a straight shaft seen in the water as if bent (II, 77).

In what sense art is necessarily conventional or rational he expresses thus: "What the eye sees has to be conveyed to it (the soul) by means, in images" (111, cf. 82). The skilful painter can "do Conrad to the life" (128), but what is doing Conrad to the life? Not making something that could be mistaken for the man himself, but making "the very image of him" (*ibid.*), that is, as far as lies in the painter's power, his "express image" (253) as it exists reflected in the mirror of God's essence, "the exemplary element in him (Conrad) which is on a par with God," "a matter of likeness of form" (157). "Will enjoys things as they are in themselves, whereas intellect enjoys them as they are in it. . . . The eye in itself is a better thing than the eye as painted on the wall. Nevertheless, I still maintain that intellect is higher than the will" (213). He means in that it sees things somewhat as God sees them, *sub specie aeternitatis* (47), at their source, impartially; for "Creatures all come into my mind and are rational in me. I alone prepare all creatures to return to God"; "I alone take all creatures out of their sense into my mind and make them one in me" (143); "Intellect (*manas, prajñā*) raises all things up into God" (86). "Creatures never rest till they have gotten into human nature; therein do they attain to their original form, God namely" (380), human nature having "nothing to do with time" (206). "The most trivial thing perceived in God, a flower for example as espied in God (that is, in its and His true and single aspect, *svarūpa*), would be a thing more perfect than the universe" (206) as it is in itself. It is as artist, seeing rationally or formally, that man sees things in their perfection and eternal youth, as far as his idiosyncrasy permits, "as far as the recipient will allow" (212).

Naturalism in art has nothing to do with subject-matter in itself. An image of God may be made repulsive in its suggestion of actuality; a painting of a flower may be like nothing on earth. Eckhart holds no brief for any one for-

mula, as for hieratic art or art profane with respect to theme.
"He who seeks God under settled forms lays hold of the
form while missing the God concealed in it" (49), is really
an idolater. Sacred subjects are no more valid images of
God than are the forms of natural species: "Eight heavens
are spoken of and nine choirs of angels . . . you must know
that expressions of that sort, which conjure up pictures in
the mind, merely serve as allurements to God" (328), and
as "Augustine says, 'All scripture is vain'" (69). Again
and again Eckhart insists that all content (not all intent) is
God, one should learn to see him anywhere and everywhere:
"to whom God is dearer in one thing than another, that
man is a barbarian, still in the wilds, a child" (419), "finding God in one way rather than another . . . is not the
best," "we should be able to enjoy him in any guise and in
any thing" (482, 483), "what e'er it be" (419), "I am come
like the fragrance of a flower" (284), "any flea as it is in
God is nobler than the highest of the angels in himself"
(240). This is the perfected impartiality of art; the angelic
(*adhidaivata*) point of view, wherein all things are loved
alike, "in itself everything is lovable, and nothing hateful,"
Dante, *Convivio*, IV, 1, 25.

So much for the artist's mode of understanding, intellectual or rational. The work of art, man's "creature," is by
the same token, even more than by its substantial distinction from the object, conventional; to be interpreted and
understood not as a direct reflection of the world as the
world is in itself, but as a symbol or group of symbols hav-

ing an ascertained rational significance and an even deeper
content, not functioning only as means to recognition but
as means to communication and to vision. Thus with reference to the interpretation of scripture and myths in general, and the same holds good for any other kind of art,
"the material things in them, they say, must be translated
to a higher plane. . . . All the stories taken from them
have another, esoteric meaning. Our understanding of them
is as totally unlike the thing as it is in itself and as it is in
God as though it did not exist" (257), but there is more in
the work of art than can be understood, "none so wise but
when he tries to fathom them will find they are beyond his
depth and discover more therein" (*ibid.*). Art is simultaneously denotation, connotation, and suggestion; statement,
implication, and content; literal, allegorical, and anagogic.

If art is thus by nature rational, why is not every work
of art immediately intelligible? Just because the artist sees
only just so much and what of the express image his powers
permit; man's images are a specific selection from an inex-
haustible sum of possibilities. "Words *derive* their power
from the original Word" (99), such selections being differently made in different ages, by different races, and to a
less marked degree by different individuals. As constantly
asserted by Scholastic philosophy, the thing known is in
the knower according to the mode of the knower: therefore
"All souls have not the same aptitude . . . vision . . . is
not enjoyed the same by all" (301). "Art amounts, in
temporal things, to singling out the best" (461),[62] that is,

the most essential from any given point of view, which may be yours or mine, or may have been that of the first or thirteenth century, or that of any other given environment and heritage. That is why in art, even when the same subject has been dealt with, or the same natural species "imitated," we find an unending variety of treatment, constituting what we call styles. Differences of spoken language are the most obvious example of this; but he greatly deludes himself who thinks that any of the arts is a universal language, or that the language of any art is by nature onomatopoetic. The variety of styles, and what has often been called progress and decadence in art but is really the historical procession of the styles, have nothing to do with man's varying and always very limited ability to mimic nature. Styles are idioms of knowledge and communication. They suffice for communication in so far and for so long as they are understood by convention (*saṁketa*); elsewhere or at another time, they must be learnt before the art can be deciphered, which requires "industry and patience," "just as one learns to write" (10, 9), or as "calling requires the uses of discrimination" (II, 93).

We have divined that style or idiom represents a particular modality or partiality of vision; the lineaments (*lakṣaṇas*) of which modality are determined by the relation between the artist individually and his theme (cf. *Śukranītisāra*, IV, 4, 159–160); and as this relation is unique and reflects the powers and limitations of the individual, the mode of pattern in his mind may be called his own. The

accidents of being by which an individuality is recognized
may indeed be called a man's own, man as he is in himself;
"my looks are not my nature, they are accidents of nature"
(94), "accidents are various" (253). In this sense every
artist leaves in all his work something of himself, and "Supposing God had called in any angel to help in the making
of the soul he must have put into the soul something of the
angel, for never did an artist paint, carve an image or write
the letters of the alphabet, but he must have copied the
pattern in *his* mind" (II, 203), and not the pattern in the
universal mind, individual intellect having "in no wise the
perfection nor plenitude for it" (17). Style is not convention as principle, though all styles and all art are conventional, or as Eckhart says "rational": style is a particular
body of convention as distinguished from other bodies. If
then style is the man, as has been said with some measure
of truth, this does not mean that style is in itself a virtue,
or an occasion for pride. Touch and style are the accidents
of art. As Chuang Tzŭ expresses it, the limits of things are
their own limits in so far as they are things. In so far as art
transcends style, we call it universal: Bach surpasses Beethoven. God has no style, *his* "idiosyncrasy is being"
(206).

In intellect, which, as Eckhart so often insists, is the sum-
mit, head, or highest power of the soul, whereby it touches
the consciousness of God, man and God are like, but in
abiding intention (*kratu*) and in working (*karma*) most
unlike, for here enter in the elements of will and time.

Man's ideas live in his mind only for so long, even though it be all his life (238); but creatures have been alive in God for ever, and ever shall be, though in themselves alive only by birth at a given time (352, cf. *Pañcaviṁśa Brāhmaṇa*, VI, 9, 18). And in the case of causes of becoming other than the first cause, such causes "can with safety quit the things they cause when these have gotten being of their own. When the house is in being its builder can depart and for the reason that it is not the builder alone that makes the house: the materials thereof he draws from Nature. But God provides creature with the whole of what it is, so he is bound to stay with it or it will promptly drop out of existence" (427), "as a picture is painted upon canvas, and it fades" (237); similarly "Augustine observes that the architect who builds a house therein displays his art; though it may fall to ruin the art within his soul neither ages nor decays" (129).

With respect to his "staying with creatures to keep them in being" (427, cf. 261) Eckhart thinks of God as a mother (the creations both of God and man are in the nature of children begotten and conceived), and it will not be overlooked that in so far as man takes care of things that have been made and preserves them from decay, he is working temporally in the analogy of God's maternal maintenance. All man's working in creation, preservation, and destruction is a temporal analogy of God's simultaneous expression, maintenance, and resolution, *sṛṣṭi, sthiti, laya*. But "yonder no work is done at all" (238); "if the carpenter were perfect at his work he would not need materials; he would no sooner think a house than, lo, it would be made," as is the case "with works in God; he thinks them and behold they are" (238); or again, "a carpenter building a house will first erect it in his mind and, were the house enough subject to his will, then, materials apart, the only difference between them would be that of begetter and suddenly begotten . . . (as) it is in God . . . one God, there being no distinction of outpouring (*abhisṛṣṭi*) and outpoured (*abhisarga*)" (72).[63]

Alike in man and God, the "art" (intuition-expression) is and remains wholly in the artist; but "think not it is with God as with a human carpenter, who works or works not as he chooses, who can do or leave undone at his good pleasure. It is not thus with God; but finding thee ready, he is obliged to act, to overflow into thee; just as the sun must needs burst forth when the air is bright, and is unable to contain itself" (23). The "being ready" is otherwise expressed as matter's being "insatiable for form" (18); so God "must do, willy-nilly" (162), according to his nature, without a why. In man this becomes what has been called the gratuitousness of art: "man ought not to work for any why, not for God nor for his glory nor for anything at all that is outside him, but only for that which is his being, his very life within him" (163, cf. *Bṛhadāranyaka Upaniṣad*, IV, 5, 6); "have no ulterior purpose in thy work" (149), "work as though no one existed, no one lived, no one had ever come upon the earth" (308); "All happiness to those who have listened to this sermon. Had there been no one here I must have preached it to the poor-box" (143). "God and God's will are one, for if I am a man and if I mean to do real work entirely without or free from will . . . I should do my works in such a way that they entered not into my will. . . . I should do them simply at the will of God" (308), "Above all lay no claim to anything. Let go thyself, and let God act for thee" (308). The artist has some "inkling" (47) of God's manner of working "willingly but not by will, naturally and not by nature" (225) when he has acquired mastery and the habit (*habitus, śliṣṭatva*) of his work and does not hesitate but "can go ahead without a qualm, not wondering, am I right or am I doing wrong? If the painter had to plan out every brush mark before he made his first he would not paint at all" (141). Still, "Heaven does more than the carpenter who builds a house" (II, 209).

"Inspired by his art" (II, 211), "as much like his ideal as he can" (252), and "working for work's sake," sound to modern ears like art for art's sake. But "art" and "his ideal" have not here their modern sentimental connotations, they represent nothing but the artist's understanding of his theme, the work to be done (*kṛtârtha*); working for "the real intention of the work's first cause" (252) is not working for the sake of the workmanship, as the modern doctrine implies; "working for work's sake" means in freedom, without ulterior motive, easily (cf. *Bhagavad Gītā, passim*). To work according to the "dearest conception of his art" (97), that is with all the skill and care he can command, is merely honest, and "By honest I mean doing one's best at the moment" (II, 95), having "good grounds for thinking no one else could do the work as well" (II, 90), and standing for "perfection in temporal works" (II, 92), the "careful" being "those who let nothing hinder them in their work" (II, 90).

The first cause of the work and the good of the work to be done are one and the same, "the ultimate end (*prayojana*) of the work is ever the real intention (*artha*) of the work's first cause" (252), "when the carpenter builds a house his first intention is a roof (that is, the idea of shelter), and that is (actually) the finish of the house" (196). No man being a rational being works for no end: "The builder hewing wood and stone because he wants to build a house 'gainst summer's heat and winter's chill is thinking first and last about the house, excepting for the house he would never hew a single stone or do a hand's turn of the work" (II, 72).

The good of the work is its immediate physical good, not its edifying purpose. Actual work requires a worldly wisdom, industry, and cunning, not to be confused with vision, but matter of fact, and with due regard to the material (II, 93): for instance, "A celebrant (of the mass) over-much intent on recollection is liable to make mistakes. The best way is to try and concentrate the mind before and afterwards, but when actually saying it to do so quite straightforwardly" (II, 175). A work may be undertaken *ad majorem gloriam Dei* or to any more immediate end, but the end can only be enjoyed in the prospect or in completion of the work. In action the workman is nothing but a tool, and should use himself accordingly, concerned with the work and not with its results; he can and should be totally absorbed in the work, like the "heathen philosopher who studied mathematics . . . in pursuance of his art . . . too much absorbed to see or hear his enemy" (12). Working thus is not for the sake of or to display skill, but to serve and praise the first cause of the work, that is, the subject imaged in the artist's mind "without idea of ownership" (35). It is immaterial what the work may be, but it is essential that the artist should be wholly given to it, "it is all the same to him what he is loving" (II, 66), it is working for the love of God in any case, because the perfection of the work is "to prepare all creatures to return to God" (143) as "in their natural mode (they) are exemplified in divine essence" (253), and this will hold good even if the painter paints his own portrait, God's image in himself.[64] He is no true workman but a vainglorious showman who would astonish by his skill; "any proper man ought to be ashamed for good people to know of this in him" (II, 51); having his art which he is expected to practice, he should take his artfulness and cunning for granted. If by reason of his skill he gets a good report in the world, that is to be taken as the "gift of God" (143), not as his due who should work "as though no one existed" (308). Similarly as to wages, the workman is indeed worthy of his hire, but if he is "careful" for anything but the good of the work to be done, he is no workman but a "thrall and hireling" (149).

Working in the world "at some useful occupation" (22) is by no means any hindrance to the perfecting of the man, and though "praying is a better act than spinning" (II, 8) a man should relinquish "rapture" to engage in any activity that may be required of him by way of service (II, 14, etc.), and even that "without which I cannot get into God, is work, vocation or calling in time, which interferes not one whit with eternal salvation" (II, 93). "To be in the right state one of two things has to happen: either he must find God and learn to have him in his works, or else things and works must be abandoned altogether. But no one in this life can be without activities, human ones, and not a few at that, so man has to learn to find his God in everything" (II, 11; cf. *Bhagavad Gītā* III, 33); even for the religious "active life bridges the gaps in the life of contemplation," and, "Those who lead the contemplative life and do no outward works, are most mistaken and all on the wrong tack"; "No person can in this life reach the point at which he is excused from outward works" (425 cf. *Bhagavad Gītā*, III, 16 and 25); therefore "'work in all things' and 'fulfil thy destiny'" (165). Still more in the case of one "who knows nothing of the truth from within, if he woo it without (he) shall find it too within" (440). In any case "God's purpose in the union (*yoga*) of contemplation is fruitfulness in works" (16).

The workman is naturally happy in his work, seeing the image in his mind becoming, in the analogy of God, whose vision of all creatures is the vision of himself in himself; this pleasure taken in the sight of matter in the act of receiving form is, in the workman still at work, a form of aesthetic experience. But in what this experience essentially consists, it will be more convenient to consider from the point of view of the spectator who sees the work completed in intention or in actuality, not in the process of becoming but as it were apart from duration, for "No activity is so perfect but it hinders recollection. The hearing of the mass permits of recollection more than the saying of it does" (II, 174).

So what is aesthetic experience, or, as Eckhart calls it, recollection, contemplation, illumination (*avabhāsa*), the culminating point of vision, rapture, rest? In so far as it is accessible to man as a rumor (95) or foretaste (479), passing like a flash of lightning (255), it is the vision of the world-picture as God sees it, loving all creatures alike, not as of use, but as the image of himself in himself (360), each in its divine nature and in unity, as a conscious eye situated in a mirror (253, 384) might see all things in all their dimensions apart from time and space as the single object of its vision, not turning from one thing to another (12) but seeing without light, in a timeless image-bearing light, where "over all sensible things hangs the motionless haze of unity." That is a seeing of things in their perfection, ever verdant, unaged and unaging (36): "To have all that has being and is lustily to be desired and brings delight; to have it all at once and whole in the undivided soul and that in God, revealed in its perfection, in its flower, where it first burgeons forth in the ground of its existence . . . that is happiness" (82), a "peculiar wonder" (47), "neither in intellect nor will, . . . as happiness and not as intellection" (200), not dialectically but as if one had the knowledge and the power to gather up all time in one eternal now (81), as God enjoys himself (142, 240).

Again, it is compared to the seeing of a play, a play (*līlā*) played eternally before all creatures, where player and audience, sport and players, are the same, their nature proceeding in itself, in clear conception and delight (147, 148), or to an operation in which God and I are one, works wrought there being all living. This sharing of God's vision of himself in his "work," which in so far as we can have an "inkling" of it is what we mean by aesthetic experience, is likewise what we mean by Beauty as distinct from loveliness or liking, which have their drawbacks in their opposites. "The supremely pure splendor of the impartible essence illumines all things at once." According to Dionysius, Beauty is order, symmetry with supreme lucidity. In this sense "the Godhead is the beauty of the three Persons" (366), "beauty with which the sun is nothing to compare" (399), "each Person radiant to the rest as to itself. This illumination is the perfection of beauty." "All things tend toward their ultimate perfection" (72).

So much of pure aesthetic experience as is possible to

anyone is his guarantee of ultimate perfection and of perfect happiness. It is as artist-scholar that man prepares all things to return to God, in so far as he sees them intellectually (*parokṣāt*) and not merely sensibly (*pratyakṣeṇa*). This is from Eckhart's point of view the "meaning" of art. "That is as far as I can understand it" (282).

Chapter III

REACTIONS TO ART IN INDIA

Chapter III

REACTIONS TO ART IN INDIA

When music is too archaic or inaccessible to give us aesthetic data, more may be learned from the disposition of those who were pleased by it than from its recorded technical data.

D. F. Tovey, in Encyclopædia Britannica, s.v. *Music.*

THE purpose of the following notes is to bring together, mainly from the general, non-technical literature, a few passages in which the reaction of the public to works of art is reported, partly as a contribution to the vocabulary of criticism, but more with a view to showing how the art was actually regarded by those for whom it was made. The artist himself (*śilpin, kāraka, kavi*) is commonly described as "knowing his craft" (*śilpa-viśārada*, etc.) and as "skilful" (*kuśala*); nothing like a special sensibility or natural talent is mentioned, but we find that the moral virtues of ordinary men are expected in the artist, and for the rest he has his art which he is expected to practice. His attitude with respect to his commission is naturally expressed in *Jātaka*, II, 254, as follows, "We musicians, O king, live by the practice of our art (*sippaṁ nissāya*); for remuneration, I will play," but as numerous texts and inscriptions prove, the workman when moved by piety was ready to work gratuitously as an act of merit. In the latter case, artist and patron are one, the work being commanded by the artist's own devotional feeling. As to fame, and the purpose of the work, an illuminating couplet attributed to one of the successors of the Aṣṭacchāp of Hindī literature tells us:

Ours is true poetry, if so be it please great poets yet to come,
Otherwise, its pretext is that it is a reminder of Rādhā and Kṛṣṇa.

The workman being a rational being, it is taken for granted that every work has a theme or subject (*vastu, kārya, kṛtārtha, anukārya, ālikhitavya,* etc.) and a corresponding utility or meaning (*artha, arthatā, prayojana*).

The general word for understanding or apprehension is *grahaṇa,* "grasping," for example, *Viṣṇudharmottara,* III, 41, 12; cf. the senses as "apprehenders" (*grahāḥ*) and ideas as "over-apprehenders," *Bṛhadāraṇyaka Upaniṣad,* III, 2, and Pali *gahaṇa* used with *sippa* to denote "learning a craft." An audience is praised as "appreciative of the merits (*guṇa-grāhiṇī*)" of a play, *Priyadarśikā,* I, 3. According to the *Abhinaya Darpaṇa,* "The audience shines like a wishing-tree, when the Vedas are its branches, *śāstras* its flowers, and learned men the bees. . . . The Seven Limbs of the audience are men of learning, poets, elders, singers, buffoons, and those versed in history and mythology," and the chief of the audience, the patron, must be a connoisseur.[65] Applause is *ukkuṭṭhi* in *Jātaka,* II, 253 and 367, more often the still current exclamation, *sādhu,* "well-done."

In the *Dūtavākya* of Bhāsa, 7, the picture (*paṭa*) of the Gambling Scene is called "admirable" (*darśanīya*, cf. modern colloquial "easy to look at"); and, after a detailed description of the subject-matter represented, Duryodhana concludes, *ibid.*, 13, "O what richness of color (*varṇâḍhyatā*)! What a presentation of the moods (*bhāvôpapannatā*)! What a skilful laying on of colors (*yuktalekhatā*)! How explicit the painting (*suvyaktam ālikhito*)! I am pleased."

As to these comments, *varṇâḍhya* is stated to be what most interests "others" (*itare janāḥ*),[66] that is, people in general, not masters (*ācārya*) or connoisseurs (*vicakṣaṇa*, *Viṣṇudharmottara*, III, 41, 11; see *JAOS.*, LII, 11, confirmed by the *Triṣaṣṭiśalākāpuruṣacaritra* passage cited below); for the expression of *bhāva* and *rasa* in painting, see *JAOS.*, LII, 15, n. 5, and Basava Raja, *Śiva-Tattva-Ratnākara*, VI, 2, 19; the exact significance of *yuktalekhatā* is less certain. Cf. the word as cited below.

Darśanīya, "worth seeing," occurs regularly in connection with pictures, sculpture, and architecture. Cf. *Cūlavaṁsa*, C, 251, *manoharaṁ dassanīyaṁ toraṇaṁ*; *ibid.*, 258, an image of the Buddha is *dassanīyaṁ* . . . *cārudassanaṁ*; and *ibid.*, 262, pictures are *dassaniyyâpare cārū cittakamme*; analogous is the use of *savanīya* (*śravanīya*), "worth hearing," and *savanīyataraṁ*, "very well worth hearing," *ibid.*, LXXXIX, 33, while the two terms are used together, *ibid.*, 35, with reference to songs and dances, which are *dassanassavaṇa-ppiyaṁ*, "pleasing to see and hear." Cf. *śrotraṁ sukhayati*, "pleases the ear," and *dṛṣṭiprītiṁ vidhatte*, "pleases the eye," with reference to natural beauties, *Priyadarśikā*, II, 4. A word very commonly applied to pictures is *manorama*, "pleasing the heart." In the *Divyâvadāna*, 361–362, Māra, at Upagupta's request, manifests himself in the form of the Buddha, with all his specific lineaments (*lakṣaṇâḍhyam*). Upagupta bows down to this representation, that is, as he explains, to him whose image it is. The aspect (*rūpa*) assumed by Māra, as an actor assumes a part, is *nayanakāntim ākṛtim*, "a representation delighting the eyes," and *nayanaśāntikaraṁ narāṇām*, "giving peace to the eye of man"; Upagupta is *abhipramudita, pramuditamana*, "overjoyed," *prāmodyam utpannam*, "delight overflows," and he exclaims *A ho, rūpa-śobhā, kiṁ bahunā*, "In short, what beauty of aspect!"

From a monastic point of view, usually but not exclusively Buddhist or Jaina, the arts are rejected altogether as merely a source of pleasant sensations; cf. *vāsanā* in Mahāyāna psychology as "nostalgia," but in art an indispensable innate sensibility. As a single example of the monastic attitude *Triṣaṣṭiśalākāpuruṣacaritra*, I, 1, 361, may be cited, where it is asserted that music (*saṁgīta*) in no way serves for welfare (*kuśala*), but only infatuates by giving a momentary pleasure (*muhurta-sukha*). The fact is that what Hindus mean by the "pleasure of the eyes" may or may not be a disinterested pleasure, and this has always to be determined from the context; cf. the Scholastic *id quod visum placet.*

In the *Śakuntalā* (VI, 13–14, in Kale's edition (K), *ibid.*,

VI, 15–16, in Pischel's (P), the variants in both versions being here utilized), the King, looking at his own memory picture of Śakuntalā, exclaims with reference to the subject rather than the workmanship, "O, the beauty of the painting" (*aho rūpam ālekhyasya*), and later makes a distinction between what is "right" (*sādhu*) in the work, and what is "off" or "out" (*anyathā*, not to be confused with *ardhalikhita*, "unfinished," which occurs below); still, "something of Śakuntalā's charm (*lāvaṇya*) is caught (*kiṁcid-anvita*) in the line (*rekhā*)." The Vidūṣaka finds the line (*rekhā*) full of tender sentiment (*bhāva-madhurā*, P), and the "imitation of mood in the tender passages is noteworthy" (*madhurâvasthāna-darśanīyo bhāvānupraveśaḥ*, K), alternatively "it seems to be the very rendering of reality" (*sattvânupraveśa-śa˙ khaya*, P); he exclaims, "In short" (*kiṁ bahunā*, P), "she makes me want to speak to her" (*ālapana-kautūhalam me janayati*); he pretends that his eye actually stumbles (*skhalati*) over the hills and vales (*nimnônnata-pradeśeṣu*).[67] Miśrakeśī remarks on the King's skill with the "brush and in outline" (*vartikā-rekhā-nipuṇatā*), alternatively "in color and line" (*varṇa-rekhā*).

In the *Pratijñāyaugandharâyaṇa* of Bhāsa, III, 1, the court jester speaks of the skilful laying on of color (*yukta-lekhatā*) in a fresco, shown by the fact that when he rubs the painting it only grows the brighter (*ujjvalatara*).

In the *Mālavikâgnimitra*, II, 2, a lack of correspondence between the beauty of the model and that represented in the painting [68] is spoken of as *kānti-visaṁvāda*, and ascribed to imperfect concentration (*śithila-samādhi*) on the part of the painter. In the *Priyadarśikā*, III, and *Vikramôrvāśī*, II (introductory stanza), imperfections of acting are similarly ascribed to the actor's absent-mindedness (*śūnya-hṛdayatā*).

In the *Pratimānāṭaka* of Bhāsa, III, 5, Bharata, seeing the statues of his parents, whom he does not recognize, exclaims, "Ah, what sweetness in the workmanship of these stones (*aho kriyā-mādhuryaṁ pāṣāṇānām*)! Ah, what feeling (*bhāva*) is embodied in these images (*aho bhāvagatir ākṛtīnām*)!" He wonders what the figures represent, but "Anyhow, there is a great delight (*praharṣa*) in my heart," which delight is perhaps thought of not so much as aesthetic as due to a subconscious recognition of the statues as those of his parents. But *pramudaṁ prayāti*, said of the Self with respect to the pleasure felt at the spectacle of its own manifestation as the world picture (*jagaccitra*, Śaṅkarâcārya, *Svâtmanirūpaṇa*, 95), implies a delight unquestionably disinterested.

In Bhavabhūti's *Uttara-Rāma-Carita*, I, 39, the sight of the paintings leaves a latent or persisting emotional impression (*bhāvanā*), not a mere memory, but a lingering sentiment, in Sītā's mind; this may be compared with "I still seem to hear the music as I walk," cited below, and *Śakuntalā*, V, 8 f. (Pischel), where Duhṣanta, overhearing the singing of his Queen Haṁsavatī, soliloquizes, "What a passion-laden (*rāga-parivāhiṇī*) song! . . . Why then am I so filled with yearning by hearing such a song, as though I were divided from a loved one? Howbeit, if after seeing lovely things, or hearing sweet words, a man is saddened as well as charmed, it may be because unconsciously he remembers loves heart-felt ere birth, survivals of a former disposition (*pūrvaṁ-bhāva-sthirāṇi*)"; the stage direction follows, "He registers (*rūpayati*) perplexity occasioned by a thing forgotten."

In the case of portraits, the excellence of the likeness is naturally commented upon, for example, *Svapnavāsavadattā*, VI, 13, and *Mṛcchakaṭika*, IV, 1, the words *sadṛśī* and *susadṛśī* (not *sādṛśya*) being employed. In the *Svapnavāsavadattā*, *loc. cit.*, the Queen, looking at the picture of Vāsavadattā, is "delighted and perplexed" (*prahṛṣṭôdvignām iva*), but this is because she thinks she recognizes the person represented; it is not an aesthetic effect. In the *Mālatīmādhava*, I, 33 (9–10), the purpose of the portrait (*ālekhya-prayojana*) is said to be consolation in longing (*utkaṇṭhā-vinodana*).

The different ways in which a painting may be regarded by spectators of various classes are stated in some detail in Hemacandra's *Triṣaṣṭiśalākāpuruṣacaritra*, I, 1, 648 ff., where a painting on canvas (*paṭa*) is spread out (*vistārya*) with a practical purpose, viz. in the hope that some spectator will recognize it as a representation of the events of his own former life. Those versed in scripture (*āgamavit*) praise the representation of the Nandīśvara heavens, because "it accords with the purport of the scripture" (*āgamârthâvisaṁvādi*); the very pious (*mahāśraddha*) nod their heads and describe to one another the figures (*bimbāni*) of the saints (*jina*); those expert in the practice of the arts (*kalā-kauśala-śālin*) praise the purity of the outlines (*rekhā-śuddhi*), as they examine them again and again with sideling glances; others talk of the colors, white, black, yellow, blue, and red, that make the painting look like a brilliant sunset.

An appreciation of architectural beauty is frequently expressed in general terms; there is, for instance, a moving description of the ruined city of Poḷonnāruvā, of which the buildings "through decay and old age are like greybeards and unable to stand erect, becoming more and more bowed down from day to day," *Cūlavaṁsa*, LXXXVIII. In the same text, LXXVIII, 39, we find the phrase "creating out of brick and stone an elixir for the eyes" (*rasâyana*); cf. *netrâmṛta*, of a picture, *Avadāna Kalpalatā*, p. vii.

In the *Guttila Jātaka* (No. 243) there is a competition between two *vīṇā* players, who show their art (*sippaṁ dassesanti*) which the people see (*passanti*). At first, when both play equally well, the public is delighted (*tuṭṭho* = *tuṣṭha*).[69] The competition then becomes one not so much in musical talent as in the performance of a stunt, the victor playing on a reduced number of strings, and finally only on the body of his instrument. The public cries out against the defeated competitor, saying, "You do not know the measure (*pamāṇa* = *pramāṇa*) of your capacity."

In the *Vikramacaritra*, III, 2 (*HOS.*, 26, 18 and 27, 15),[70] where there is a dancing competition between two apsarases, Vikramâditya, who knows all the arts (*sakala-kalâbhijña*) and is especially a connoisseur (*vicakṣaṇa*) of the science of the ensemble of musical arts (*saṁgīta-vidyā*), acts as judge.[71] He decides in favor of Urvaśī because she fulfils the requirements of the *Nāṭya Śāstra*, both as to her person and as to her ability; the latter is shown specifically in registering (*sūcanā*) the full meaning by means of language conveyed in bodily movements, in the accurate rhythms of the feet, in the sensitive gestures (*abhinaya*) of the hands and their agreement with the permitted variations (*tadvi-kalpânuvṛttau*), in the constant displacement of one mood by another in the field of representation, and in her skilful blending of the passions (*rāgabandha*). In short, "I preferred Urvaśī because I found her a danseuse of such a sort as is described in the *Nāṭya Śāstra*."

In the *Priyadarśikā*, III, where there is a play within a play, the former raises the spectator's interest to the highest degree, *adhikataraṁ kautūhalaṁ vardhayati*, which is modestly explained by the author as due to the merit of the subject. In the same act of the same work, the verb *avaḥṛ*, "to transport," "enrapture," is used with reference to the effects of a performance on the harp (*vīṇā*); the King, too, evokes admiration or astonishment (*vismaya*) by his performance.

In the *Mṛcchakaṭika*, III, 2–5, Cārudatta has attended a musical performance (*gāndharva*); he is reminiscent, and exclaims, "Ah, ah, well done (*sādhu*)! Master Rebhila's song was excellent (*suṣṭhu*)." Then, more technically,[72] speaking both as expert in the art and as *rasika*, "The sound was informed by the moods (*bhāva*), now passionate (*rakta*),

now sweet (*madhura*), now calm (*sama*), languishing (*lalita*)
and ravishing too; it seemed like the lovely voice of my
own hidden love. The low progressions (*svara-saṁkrama*)
seated in the vibrating strings, the crescendo (*tāra*) of the
scales (*varṇa*) and modes (*mūrcchana*), and their diminuendo
(*mṛdu*) in the pauses — when passion is restrained, desire
repeats its languishing (*lalita*) — and though the reality
was ended with the song itself, I seem to hear it as I walk."
There is a similarly technical appreciation of a *vīṇā* performance in *Priyadarśikā*, III, 10.

To sum up, it will be seen that everyone is thought of as
making use of the work of art in his own way, the work of
visual art, no less than a word, being a *kāma-dhenu*, yielding
to the spectator just what he seeks from it or is capable of
understanding. Everyone is interested in the subject-matter
or application of the work, as a matter of course. More
specifically, we find that learned men, pundits, are concerned about the correctness of the iconography; the pious
are interested in the representation of the holy themes as
such; connoisseurs (*vicakṣaṇa* in the cited passages, elsewhere
rasika, pramātṛ, sahṛdaya) are moved by the expression of
bhāva and *rasa*, and like to express their appreciation in the
technical terminology of rhetoric; masters of the art, fellow artists, regard chiefly the drawing, and technical skill
in general; ordinary laymen like the bright colors, or marvel at the artist's dexterity.[72] Those who are in love are
chiefly interested in portraiture reflecting all the charms
(*kānti, lāvaṇya*) of the original. Rarely do we meet with

any mention of originality or novelty.[74] We ought then, to appreciate Indian art from every point of view, to be equipped with learning, piety, sensibility, knowledge of technique, and simplicity: combining the qualities of the *paṇḍita*, the *bhakta*, the *rasika*, the *ācārya*, and the *alpa-buddki-jana*.

Chapter IV

AESTHETIC OF THE SUKRANĪTISĀRA

Chapter IV

AESTHETIC OF THE ŚUKRANĪTISĀRA

THE *Śukranītisāra* of Śukrâcārya is a mediaeval Indian treatise on statecraft and an encyclopaedic work on social organization considered from every point of view. In the passages dealing with the making of images are embodied some very definite statements of aesthetic principles; and as these passages have been misunderstood and mistranslated, or at least inadequately translated, it seems desirable to present a fresh and complete version. The verses translated begin with Ch. IV, Sec. 4, verse 70, the numbering being that of Vidyāsāgara's text, with those of Sarkar's translation in parentheses: [75]

"One should make use of (*yojayet*) the visual-formulae (*dhyāna*) proper to the angels (*devatā*) whose images are to be made (*ārambhya*). It is for the successful accomplishment of this practice (*yoga*) of visual-formulation (*dhyāna*) that the lineaments (*lakṣaṇa*) of images are prescribed. The human-imager (*pratimākāra*) should be expert in this visual-contemplation, since thus, and in no other way, and verily not by direct observation (*pratyakṣa*), (can the end be achieved)." 70, 71 (147-150).

"Images made of sand (*saikata*), dough (*paiṣṭa*), or painted (*lekhya*), or of stucco (*lepya*), or terracotta (*mṛṇ-*

maya), or wood (*vṛkṣa*), or stone (*pāṣāṇa*), or metal (*dhātu*) are of relative durability in the same order." 72 (151).

"Images made as directed, with all their members complete, are attractive and merit-yielding; those otherwise are destructive of life and wealth, and ever increase sorrow; one should make images of angels (*deva*), for these are productive of good, and heavenward-leading (*svargya*), but those of men or other (creatures) lead not to heaven nor are they auspicious. That image is said to be lovely (*ramya*) which is of neither more nor less than the prescribed proportions (*māna*). Images of the angels, even with lineaments (*lakṣaṇa*) imperfectly depicted, work weal to men, but never those of mortals, even though their lineaments (be accurately represented)." 73–76 (152–158).

"Images of the angels are of three sorts, pure (*sāttvika*, that is, as they are in themselves naturally), active (*rājasika*, expansive, manifesting in 'work'), and dark (*tāmasika*, effectively as if limited by the inertia of matter and engaged in actual work). Those of Viṣṇu and other angels should be employed and worshipped (*yogya pūjya*) according to the necessities of the case. A *sāttvika* image is one in a *yoga*-posture, self-supported, with hands exhibiting bounty and encouragement (*varâbhaya*), and worshipped by the premier angels and such like beings (*devendrâdi*). A *rājasika* image is one supported by a vehicle (*vāhana*), adorned with a variety of ornaments, with hands holding weapons and implements, and exhibiting bounty and encouragement. A *tāmasika* image is one of dread (*ugra*) aspect, engaged in slaying demons by means of weapons and implements, and as if eager for combat." 77–80 (159–166).

"It is prescribed that the veins of the hands and feet should not be shown, nor should the ankle-bones be seen. Those parts of images are said to be really lovely (*suśobhana*) which are neither more nor less in proportion (*māna*) than the limbs of such images as have been made by experts, and every member that is neither too thick nor too thin will be altogether pleasing (*sarvamanorama*). Although hardly one in a hundred thousand is produced that is altogether pleasing in every member, still that which accords with canonical prescription (*śāstramāna*) is alone truly lovely (*ramya*), none other, to be sure! There are some to whom that which captivates their heart (*tat lagnaṁ hṛd*) is lovely; but for those who know, that which falls short of canonical proportion (*śāstramāna*) is not beautiful." 101–106 (209–215).

"One should contrive for every member such grace (*pāṭava*) as is appropriate." 121 (256).

"In the case of painted images, or those made of stucco, sand, terracotta, or dough, an omission of lineaments (*lakṣaṇa*) will do no harm; one should beware of defects of proportion (*māna*) only in the case of images of stone or metal." 152, 153 (306, 309).

"The lineaments (*lakṣaṇa*) of images are known (*smṛta*) from the natures (*bhāva*) of the worshipped and the worshipper (*sevyasevaka*). By the power of the intension (*tapas*) of the officiant (*arcaka*) whose heart is ever set upon the Lord, the faults of an image immediately pass away." 159, 160 (320–322).

"There is no rule (*niyama*) for the thickness of the limbs of a child, they should be devised as may seem lovely." 185 (375).

"The artist (*śilpi*) should ever conceive the beauty (*vapu*) of the images (of the angels) as youthful (*taruṇa*), rarely as childlike (*bāla-sadṛśa*), never as aged (*vṛddha-sadṛśa*)." 201 (403, 404).

"The King should not set up or keep in a temple a disproportioned or broken image; worn out images of the angels, and ruined temples, are to be carefully restored." 203 (407, 408).

The following, from Section 7, refers only to figures of horses: "When a figure (*rūpa*) of a horse is to be made, the model (*bimba*) should always be in view (*vīkṣya*), and if one cannot be looked at (*adṛṣṭvā*) the figure should not be made. The artist (*śilpi*) having first (*agre*) made his visual contemplation (*dhyātvā*) on the horse and attentive to its forms (*avayavânataḥ*) should do his work, embodying all the proportions (*māna*) of horses meet for splendor and divorced from ill-omen." 73, 74 (145–147). It will be seen here, that in spite of the apparent demand for likeness to the horse in view, there is insistence on visualization and on adherence to ideal proportions.

The portions of the text omitted above provide the detailed measurements proper to the various types of beings. It will be quite evident that Śukrâcārya is propounding a purely scholastic and hieratic conception of what is lovely or beautiful, and nowhere admits the validity of individual taste. Just as Professor Masson-Oursel has pointed out,[76] "Indian art is aiming at something quite other than the copying of Nature. What we assume, quite superficially, to be the inspiration of an art for art's sake, really proceeds from a religious scholasticism that implies a traditional classification of types established by convention. If here or there a relief or painting exhibits some feature drawn from life, it is only accidentally that the artist has, in spite of himself, transcribed something from actual Nature: and this is certainly, from the indigenous point of view, the least meritorious part of his work." Those who wish to study the "development" of Indian art must emancipate themselves entirely from the innate European tendency to use a supposedly greater or less degree of the observation of Nature as a measuring rod by which to trace stylistic sequences or recognize aesthetic merit. Indian art can only be studied as showing at different times a greater or less degree of consciousness, a greater or less energy; the criteria are degrees of vitality, unity, grace, and the like, never of illusion. In India, an art of primarily representative interest, that of portraiture, was practiced mainly by amateurs, and even so required a mental visualization only less formal than that of the hieratic work; in itself the portraiture had usually an erotic purpose or content, and in any case a merely personal and temporary value, not an ultimate spiritual significance.[77]

Chapter V

PAROKṢA

Chapter V

PAROKṢA

Which things also we speak, not in the words which man's wisdom teacheth, but which the Holy Ghost teacheth.
Corinthians, I, 2, 13.

THE terms *parokṣa* and *pratyakṣa* are used in contrasted senses. The purely grammatical distinction of *parokṣa* and *pratyakṣa* need not detain us: a stanza referring to an Angel (*deva*), if voiced in the third person, is said to be *parokṣa*, "indirect," or if addressed immediately in the second person, *pratyakṣa*, "direct," *Nirukta*, VII, 1. What concerns us more is the distinction of the *parokṣa* as proper to the Angels (*adhidaivata*), who are accordingly described as *parokṣa-priya*, "fond of" the symbolic, from the *pratyakṣa* as proper to man (*mānuṣa*) as individual (*adhyātma*), who is evidently *pratyakṣa-priya*, "fond of" the obvious, though this is not explicitly stated.

In *Jaim. Up. Br.*, I, 20, *Ait. Br.*, III, 33 and VIII, 30, *Ś. Br.*, VI, 1, 1, 2 and 11 and XIV, 1, 1, 13, *Bṛ. Up.*, IV, 2, 2, and *Ait. Up.*, III, 14, examples are given as follows (the *parokṣa* designations being followed in each case by the *pratyakṣa* designations printed in italics): antarikṣa, *antaryakṣa*; mānuṣa, *māduṣa*; nyagrodha, *nyagroha*; Indra, *indha, idandra*; Agni, *agri*; aśva, *aśru*. To these may be added from passages cited below: Ahi Budhnya, *Agni*

Gārhapatya; Soma, *nyagrodha*; and viśvajit, *vrata*. The *pratyakṣa* term stands for the *parokṣa* referent; for example, "the lotus means the Waters, this Earth is a leaf thereof," *Ś. Br.*, VII, 4, 1, 8, where lotus and leaf have physical, Waters (= Possibility) and Earth (= Ground) metaphysical, referents. Evidently it is not necessary that the *parokṣa* and *pratyakṣa* terms should be sensibly distinct; the *puṣkara* which is spoken of as the birthplace of Agni or Vasiṣṭha, and which represents the Ground of all existence, is not the *puṣkara* of the botanist, though the words are the same. The actual lotus-leaf laid down upon the Fire Altar has no necessary meaning of its own, quâ lotus-leaf; it is merely a datum with respect to which we can have only estimative or affective knowledge; it *is* the referent of *puṣkara-parṇa*, but *impersonates* the referent of the *parokṣa* term *pṛthivī*. The distinction is one of reference, which the student, guided by the context, or if necessary by the Commentator, is expected to understand;[78] and if he takes the reference literally, we say that his understanding is superficial. For the *parokṣa* and *pratyakṣa* references are not coincident: the former are names of assumed or otherwise known but not perceptible referents (cf. Śaṅkarâcārya on *Ait. Up.*, III, 14); and the latter, names of sensibly experienced referents which are, or are regarded as, merely symbols of or suitable substitutes for the aforesaid unseen referents. It follows that the reference of the *parokṣa* term is much wider than that of the *pratyakṣa* term; viz., in that of the many conceivable signs of or substitutes for the operating but unseen referent the *pratyakṣa* term specifies only one. It follows at the same time that the *parokṣa* vocabulary will be much less numerous than the *pratyakṣa*; the Angels have fewer ideas, and use less means than men.

The passage, *Ait. Up.*, III, 14, already cited, may be quoted in full. In the previous verse it is said that the Self, individually conscious in the plurality of beings, beheld the Brahman immediately, that is, recognized its manifestation in the world (cf. *Kena Up.*, 24–28), and "I have seen It (*idaṁ dadarśa*), he said." Then follows, "Therefore his name is Idaṁ-dra ('It-seeing'), Idandra indeed is his name. Him that is Idandra, the Angels speak of (lit. 'regard,' *ācakṣate*) metaphysically (*parokṣeṇa*) as Indra, for the metaphysical, indeed, is proper to the Angels." Śaṅkarâcārya comments as follows: "Because the Supreme Self saw 'This,' the immanent Brahman, face to face directly (*sākṣād aparokṣāt*), immediately (*aparokṣeṇa*) as 'This,' therefore He (the Supreme Self) is called Idandra; God (*Īśvara*) is in the world (*loke*) explicitly (*prasiddha*) by name Idandra. 'Him that is Idandra, Indra metaphysically': that is, the knowers of Brahman speak of Him thus, with metaphysical-reference (*parokṣâbhidhānena*), for practical purposes (*saṁvyavahārikârtha*) in fear of taking (*grahaṇa*) (in vain) His name who is worthy of all worship. 'The metaphysical is proper to the Angels': that is, they are wonted (*priyā*) to metaphysical (*parokṣa*) names, and it is thereby indeed that they are 'Angels.' [79] Much more so in the case of God (*Īśvara*), who is the Angel of all Angels."

Adhidaivata and *adhyātma* are contrasted in the same way as *parokṣa* and *pratyakṣa*: for example, *Kena Up.*, 29–30, with reference to the vision of Brahman. Here "with respect to the Angels" (*adhidaivata*) the vision is compared to a flash of lightning; but "with respect to the incarnate Self" (*adhyātma*) the vision is a thing which, when the Intellect (*manas*) is directed to and ponders intently on Brahman, becomes a concept (*saṁkalpa*). The *Kauṣītaki Upaniṣad*, IV, 2, gives a fuller list of correspondences, beginning with "In the Supernal Sun the Great Principle" (that is, universally, *adhidaivata*) and "In the Mirror the Counter-image" (that is, individually, *adhyātma*).

The problem presents itself both in connection with the literature, and in connection with the ritual and plastic art, the performance of the ritual, or the iconographic representation, securing "indirectly" (*parokṣeṇa, parokṣāt*) practical effects by setting in motion the corresponding forces. Thus the officiant "indirectly by means of Ahi Budhnya" (that is, by incantation of the verse *Ṛg Veda*, VI, 50, 14) though "directly by means of Agni Gārhapatya" (the household fire actually kindled) endows the sacrificer with fiery-energy (*tejas*), *Ait. Br.*, III, 36; the Kṣatriya who eats the shoots and fruits of the *nyagrodha* "indirectly" (*parokṣeṇa*) obtains the drinking of Soma — "he does not partake of Soma directly (*pratyakṣam*)," *ibid.*, VII, 31. Again, in the *Pañcaviṁśa Brāhmaṇa*, XXII, 9, 4 and 3, "The Viśvajit (-rite) is, indirectly, the (Mahā-)vrata; he by means thereof directly obtains food," for "What presents itself directly to men presents itself indirectly (or metaphysically) to the Angels, and what presents itself indirectly to men presents itself directly to the Angels." In this sense all the Vedic rituals are Mysterium und Mimus, Mysteries and Imitations: what anthropologists describe empirically (*pratyakṣeṇa*) as "sympathetic magic" is a metaphysical operation, an enchantment and a conjuration, not a religious, devotional service or "prayer."

In iconography, where again the terms are not of individual choice, but *śāstramāna, smṛta*, etc., we have to do with a visual language of the same kind as the verbal. The lotus of iconography is not the lotus of sensible experience; it is *parokṣa*, "not recognizable" to those who do not "understand art"; most of the accidents proper to the lotus of the botanist are omitted from the symbol, which is, moreover, of indefinite dimensions (again, "out of proportion" for those who do not "understand art," the same who say with regard to Italian primitives, "That was before they knew anything about anatomy"), *amātra*, like the *pṛthivī* that is symbolized, not like the specifically dimensioned objects (*mātrāḥ*) seen by the eye's intrinsic faculty (*cakṣuṣā*), *Maitri Up.*, VI, 6.[80] In other words, the reference of the lotus of iconography is "angelic," *adhidaivata*, that of the "lotus" of the botanist, "sensible," *pratyakṣa*.

In saying "iconography," we do not mean to distinguish iconography from art: [81] all art is "imagination," that is, a presentation of images which correspond to references originally in the mind of the artist, and not (even with the "best," or rather "worst" intentions) to any "natural," *pratyakṣa* model. For example, *Ait. Br.*, VI, 27, "It is in imitation (*anukṛti*) of the angelic (*deva*) works of art (*śilpa*) that any work of art (*śilpa*) is arrived at (*adhigam*) here; [82] for example, a clay elephant, a brazen object, a garment, a golden object, and a mule-chariot are 'works of art'; a (true) work of art is accomplished (*adhigam*) in him who comprehends this"; [83] and *Śukranītisāra*, IV, 4, 70–71, where "the imager must be expert in vision (*dhyāna*), and in no other way, certainly not in the presence of a model (*pratyakṣeṇa*) can the work be accomplished." In distinguishing thus a language of symbols from a language of signs I have in mind the distinctions of symbol and sign as drawn by Jung. [84] A symbolic expression is one that is held to be the best possible formula by which allusion may be made to a relatively unknown "thing," which referent, however, is nevertheless recognized or postulated as "existing." The use of any symbol, such as the figure "*vajra*" or the word "Brahman," implies a conviction, and generally a conventional agreement resting on authority, that the relatively unknown, or it may be unknowable, referent cannot be any more clearly represented. A sign, on the other hand, is an analogous or abbreviated expression for a definitely known thing; every man knows or can be informed, by indication of an object, as to what the sign "means." Thus wings are symbols when they "mean" angelic independence of local motion, but "signs" when they designate an aviator; the cross is a symbol when used (metaphysically) to represent the structure of the Universe with respect to hierarchy and extension, but a sign when used (practically) to warn the motorist of a near-by crossroad. The use of the *words* wings or cross to designate relatively unknown, "occult," or abstract referents is symbolic, *parokṣeṇa*; their use to designate known, visible or potentially visible, concrete referents is semiotic, *pratyakṣeṇa*. Or if we use blue pigment to "represent" blue eyes or blue sky, it is as a sign; but if we make the Virgin's robe blue, then "blue" becomes the symbol of an idea, and the reference is no longer to the thing "sky" but to certain abstract qualities such as "infinity" which we have imputed to the "thing" we see overhead. In this particular case the sign and symbol are the same, viz. blue pigment, and, just as in the case of the sign or symbol *puṣkara*, lotus, the "meaning" must be understood in connection with the context. An understanding of this kind is all-important; for if we take the sign for a symbol, we shall be sentimentalizing our notion of blue eyes, and if we take the symbol for a sign, we are reducing "thought" to "recognition." In the latter case, our tacit assumption can be only that the Virgin wears the sky just as we wear our bodies, which is tantamount to speaking of the Virgin as a "personification of the sky," and to an identification of Mariolatry with the "worship of Nature." [85] The reader may suppose that such a crude mistake is impossible, as it may be impossible for him who as an inheritor of the Christian tradition knows better; nevertheless, it is this very mistake that he makes when, from a point of view supposedly "scientific" but in fact merely "profane," he speaks of Ionian philosophy as "naturalistic," or of the religion of the Vedas as a "worship of natural forces."

We are now, in the first place, led to understand how it is that in certain cases ideas, especially metaphysical or theological ideas (perhaps there are no others, "scientific" ideas being strictly speaking theological in kind) can be better communicated by visual than by verbal symbols (visual symbols will include, of course, the gestures or tones employed in ritual, as well as the surfaces of *factibilia*). The *words* "lotus," "*puṣkara*," for example, are the same however employed, *parokṣāt* or *pratyakṣeṇa*, but the lotus of iconography can scarcely be confused with the lotus of the botanist; an art in which such a confusion becomes possible is no longer art, no longer iconography, but semiotic. It is true that in the decadence of art what should be symbols are replaced by what are merely signs, a formal by an informal referendum; and in such times of decadence it is even believed that the impulses of the "Primitives" were also descriptive; it is believed, as aforesaid, that the Vedic enchantments (*mantra*) are descriptions of natural phenomena. It is just in this connection, in the second place, that we are led to understand how and why it is that "realistic" art must be regarded as "decadent," that is to say, falling short of what is proper to the dignity of man as man, to whom not merely sensible, but also intelligible worlds are accessible. Granted that by restoring to the lotus all, or all we can, of those accidents that are proper to the lotus of the botanist, we produce an object apt to deceive an animal: what we have thus done is to make it clear that our reference is, and is only, to a natural species and not to an idea; our "work of art" is no longer creative, "imitating" an exemplary form,[86] but merely a succedaneum, more or less apt to titillate the senses. If bees have been deceived by painted flowers, why was not honey also provided? The more an image is "true to nature," the more it lies. It lies in both senses, *parokṣa* and *pratyakṣa*: the portrait of the artist's wife posing as the Mother of God is untrue in its implication of likeness (the being of the Mother of God is not in the human mode), and on the other hand, the portrait of the artist's wife as such is untrue with respect to human affectibility, in that it cannot take the place of living flesh ("The eye in itself is a better thing than the eye as painted on the wall," Eckhart). Hence the *Śukranītisāra*, IV, 4, 76, speaks of portraiture as "unheavenly," *asvargya*, and the doctors of Islam disparage representative art because it simulates the work of the Supreme Artist, and is yet devoid of life.

Innumerable examples of the correspondence between what is known to the Angels in one way, to man in another could, of course, be accumulated from the Vedic literature. That these correspondences are thought of as real and necessary implies the notion of the analogical relationship of macrocosm and microcosm, such as is most explicitly asserted in *Ait. Br.*, VIII, 2, where each of the two worlds "this" and "that" is *anurūpam*, "in the image of" the other. And if in fact the word *parokṣa* is not found in the

Ṛg Veda, the notion of an angelic language distinct from that of man is there very clearly expressed in other ways. It will suffice to cite I, 164, 10, 37 and 45: "There on the pitch of heaven (*dyu*) they chant (*mantṛ*) a Wisdom (*vāc*) that is all-knowing (*viśvā-vid*) but not-all-animating (*aviś-vaminva*, perhaps 'all-disposing')"; that is, in accord with Sāyaṇa, the Angels communicate with each other in a hidden (*gupta*) language, which embraces all things but does not extend to, or is not understood by, all (*na sarva-vyāpakam*). Again, "When the First-born of the Law (sc. Agni, or the Sun) approached me, then got I a share of that Wisdom." What is meant by "a" share appears in the verse 45, "Wisdom (*vāc*) has been measured out in four degrees (*pada*), the comprehending Brahmaṇa knows them: three kept close hid (*guhā nihitā*) cause no motion (*na iṅgayanti* glossed by Sāyaṇa *na ceṣṭante*, 'do not strive,' or 'make no gesture'); men speak only the fourth degree of Wisdom." The *mantra* is quoted in *Jaim. Up. Br.*, I, 7, where the three degrees are said to be the (three) Worlds; the notion being evidently the same as that of *Maitri Up.*, VI, 6, where *Prajāpati* "utters" the Three Worlds which are his cosmic (*lokavat*) manifestation (*tanū = rūpa*), these "utterances" (*vyāhṛtiḥ*, viz. *Bhūr, Bhuvas, Svar* = Dante's *infima parta, mezza,* and *cima del mondo*) being the "names" or "forms" (*nāma*) of the Worlds. The triplicity of the utterance corresponds to the triunity of the speaker, these Worlds being the spheres of Śiva, Brahmā, and Viṣṇu, or Agni, Vāyu (or Indra) and Āditya.[87] The three utterances are simple, but

exemplary; they confess all things, but do not specify them.
These three parts of Wisdom (or "Speech") are said to be
"hidden" and to "make no gesture," because, although the
Worlds are moved *by* them, *they* do not move, but are only
"thought" and immanent: "He thinks them, and behold
they are" (Eckhart).[88] It is Man who by giving names to
things (*nāma-dheya*, *Ṛg Veda*, X, 71, 1) contracts and identifies (*vi-dhā, vyākṛ, vi-kalp*) things into variety in time and
space, and so completes the creation in its kinds, as is also
to be understood in Genesis, II, 19–20. By "Man," not you
and I individually, but Universal Man as Seer (*ṛṣi*) or
Poetic Genius (*kavi*) is to be understood. No doctrine of
solipsism is involved.

That "men speak only the fourth degree of Wisdom" corresponds to *Ṛg Veda*, X, 90, 4, "Only one fourth of Him is
born here," that is to say, in time and space. *Maitri Up.*,
VII, 11 (8), and *Māṇḍūkya Up.* make it clear that this one
fourth corresponds to the three states (*āvasatha*) or levels
(*sthāna*) of being, known as "Waking," "Dreaming," and
"Deep Sleep," while the aforesaid three fourths correspond
to that inscrutable (*anirukta, avācya*, etc.) level of "Non-
duality" (of manifestation and non-manifestation, Apara-
and Para-Brahman) which is spoken of as "Fourth" with
respect to the three states of "Waking," "Dreaming" and
"Deep Sleep."

How then can we determine the *parokṣa* level of reference
more exactly? The "three quarters of Him," the Fourth
state, Parabrahman, Eckhart's "Godhead," is excluded

from the problem in that understanding there is neither thought nor spoken; on the other hand, the *parokṣa* language is certainly not inaccessible to human beings, since the Vedic mantras and other traditional scriptures spoken in this language are accessible to any student. Our enquiry must start from the indications given that the level of reference is *adhidaivata*, "angelic," as distinguished from *adhyātma* or *mānuṣa*, "having reference to oneself," and "human" or "mortal." What is "angelic," and what "human"? In terms of Scholastic philosophy, "purely intelligible," and "rational," respectively, nor could any better answers be given in as brief a form. Angels, however, are of many hierarchies and orders: God himself is Mahādeva, the Supreme Angel, or Devadevānām-Devâtideva, Angel of the Angels (cf. "Rex angelorum"), and on the other hand, even the powers of the individual soul may be spoken of as *devāḥ*. In any case, "The kingdom of heaven is within you," "All deities reside in the human breast" (Blake), where "within you" is *antarbhūtasya khe*, and "breast" is *hṛdaya*; cf. *Jaim. Up. Br.*, I, 14, *mayy etāḥ sarvā devatā . . . bhavanti*, "all these Angels are in me." "Human," on the other hand, as is proved by the equivalence *adhyātma = mānuṣa*, and by the correlation of "Human" understanding with the three states of "Waking," "Dreaming," and "Deep Sleep" (and not merely with the first of these), has by no means merely a "corporeal" connotation but one involving all extensions and transpositions of individuality. The state of Deep Sleep, in particular, though super-individual, is still "human" in that a return from this condition to that of corporeality is always possible, by way of *avataraṇa*, "special incarnation," or in the return from *samādhi* to worldly consciousness. It is perfectly clear therefore that the *parokṣa* and *pratyakṣa* understandings are not divided by an impassable wall (we have already seen that "this" and "that" are in the image of one another), but in their degrees represent a hierarchy of types of consciousness extending from animal to deity, and according to which one and the same individual may function upon different occasions. We can only determine the "level of reference" absolutely if we confine our attention to the limiting conditions.

If we ask in this sense at what level of awareness the metaphysical understanding (*parokṣa jñāna*) is all-sufficient, and specific reference superfluous, the answer can be found in *Ṛg Veda* I, 164, 10, *divo pṛṣṭhe*, "on the back (that is, top) of heaven," for it is there that the Angels communicate with one another in a purely *parokṣa* fashion, such speaking being called a chanting (*mantrayante*, "they incant"), and there that the "utterance" of the "Angel of all the Angels" is primordially "heard." That is in the Paradise of Brahmā as described in *Kauṣītaki Up.*, I, 3 ff., beyond the Solar "gateway of the worlds," kept by Agni, the Angel of the Flaming Sword. That is in human (*mānuṣa*) language called "Deep Sleep," but angelically speaking, "Pure Intelligence (*prajñā*)"; "it is a unified and mere understanding (*ekībhūtaḥ prajñāna-ghana*)," [89] *Māṇḍūkya Up.*, 5, and characterized by "the cessation of the consciousness of particulars," *Sar-*

vopaniṣatsāra, 7. The Buddhist equivalents are Sukhāvatī, Sambhogakāya; Christian, the Empyrean or Motionless Heaven, there is the "peace that passeth understanding," "Come unto Me, and I will give you rest," that rest being precisely our "Deep Sleep." Needless to say that rest and sleep which can only be represented to the "Waking" level of reference as an idling and unconsciousness are on the level of "Deep Sleep" a preëminent and creative activity. "Dreaming" and "Deep Sleep" are not places, but conditions of being, "close kept in the empty chamber of the heart," *guhā nihitam, antarbhūtasya khe, antarhṛdayâkāśe.* There within us are the angelic "levels of purely intelligible reference."

The text of *Māṇḍūkya Up.*, 5, continues, *ānanda-mayo hy ānanda-bhuk*, "in the modality of Ecstasy, enjoying Love." Here *ānanda* represents the transformation (*parāvṛtti*)[90] of carnal love, just as *prajñā* the transformation of carnal understanding; the Love is in Eckhart's sense, "We desire a thing while as yet we do not possess it. When we have it, we love it, desire then falling away." Heavenly being is thus at once intellectual and ecstatic. With this conception, and in connection with what has already been said with respect to levels of reference in art, may be cited the definition of aesthetic experience (*rasâsvādana*, "tasting of the tincture") in the *Sāhitya Darpaṇa*, III, 2–4, as *ānanda-cin-maya*, "in the mode of ecstasy and intellect," *lokôttara-camatkāra-prāṇaḥ*, "whereof the life is a supersensual flash," *vedyântara-sparśa-śūnyaḥ*, "without contact of aught else known," *brahmâsvāda-sahôdaraḥ*, "very twin of the tasting of Brahman," and *sacetasām anubhavaḥ pramāṇaṁ tatra kevalam*, "whereof the only evidence is that of intellectual men."

We have not thus far taken into consideration that *pratyakṣa* (= *aparokṣa, sâkṣāt*) is of two very different kinds, with respect to which *parokṣa* occupies a middle place. The *pratyakṣa* so far considered is *saṁvyavahārika*, "worldly," or "practical," proper to the human mode of being. But there is also a *paramârthika-pratyakṣa* (= *aparokṣa-sâkṣāt*) which transcends even angelic modes of understanding and communication. In one way or another, universally or specifically, "the Self (*ātman*) knows everything. But where understanding (*vijñāna*) is without duality (*advaita*), footloose of cause, effect, and operation, wordless, incomparable, and inexplicable . . . what is that? That does not belong to speech (*tad avācyam*)," *Maitri Up.*, VI, 7. As it is said elsewhere, "This Brahman is silence." Knowledge in this sense, neither of the senses nor the intellect, is spoken of as evident (*pratyakṣa, sâkṣāt*) only analogically, with respect to its immediacy. It is *aparokṣa* in both senses, as "self-evident," and "non-symbolic." That which is alien to all speech (*avācya*), and transmundane (*avyavahārika*), is alien equally to *saṁvyavahārika-pratyakṣa* and to *parokṣa* understanding, both of which are in the domain of *avidyā*, where things are spoken of in likenesses. There, there are neither signs nor symbols, reference nor referent; "it" can only be realized immediately, beyond all levels of reference.

It may be observed that with respect to all three kinds of reference, human, angelic, and transcendental, the eye (*akṣa, cakṣu*) is used as the symbol of perception by the senses (actually or analogically), the ear with respect to intellectual reference, thought of as "audition" rather than as hearing, "by the ear" (*śrotreṇa*) in this sense being equivalent to *parokṣa*, "not by the eye," where "eye" stands for the external senses. In the terminology under discussion, three different "eyes" are in question, viz. the carnal eye or eye's intrinsic faculty (*māṁsa-cakṣu*), the angelic eye (*divya-cakṣu*), and the eye of wisdom (*jñāna-cakṣu*, etc.). "Knowledge" accessible to the first two of these is a merely relative or false knowledge (*avidyā*); only that of the last is a true knowledge (*vidyā*) in undifferentiated sameness. Angelic understanding, in that it embodies elements of multiplicity, remains "relative" (*avidyā*), though at its highest level, being in unity, it is virtually absolute (*vidyā*).

How then should the terms *parokṣa* and *pratyakṣa* be translated? Translators of the passages cited above have rendered *parokṣa* as follows:[91] "mystic" or "esoteric" (Eggeling), "cryptic" (Hume and Caland), "mysterious" (Max Müller and Keith), "incognito" (S. Sitaram Sastri), "not recognizable," "occult" (Oertel), "indirect" (Sarup). Le P. Dandoy renders "médiat," in contrast to (*paramârthika-*)*pratyakṣa*, "immédiat."[92]   For the paired terms, *parokṣa* and (*vyavahārika-*)*pratyakṣa* we have already employed or now suggest: angelic, *human*; indirect, *direct*; symbolic, *semiotic*; noumenal, *phenomenal*; universal, *par-*

ticular; theoretical, *practical*; abstract, *concrete*; intelligible, *sensible*; metaphorical, *literal.*

Amongst these terms, "indirect" and "direct" are obviously satisfactory with respect to the purely grammatical definitions, and in the other connection "direct" has the further advantage of corresponding to both senses of *pratyakṣa.* "Immediate" is evidently satisfactory for *paramârthika-pratyakṣa*, but "mediate" evidently unsatisfactory for *parokṣa*, inasmuch as the Angels use less and not more means than men; *saṁvyavahārika-pratyakṣa* is not "immediate" in the technical sense of this word, but merely *"sensibly perceptible,"* or rather *"having a perceptible referent."* For *parokṣa*, terms implying incomprehensibility are certainly to be avoided,[93] inasmuch as *parokṣa* is precisely the "intelligible" as contrasted with the "sensible"; "obscure" and "mysterious" are thus excluded, but "secret" or "hidden" (Sāyaṇa's *"gupta"*) are not incorrect.[94] "Mystic" is unfortunate as having a connotation distinct from, and "inferior" to, that of "metaphysical," and also because "mystic" is often confused with "mysterious." "Esoteric," in relation to "exoteric," represents a kind of distinction hardly proper to metaphysics. "Occult" is excellent, if it can be made evident that the meanings now associated with "occultism" are excluded. "Angelic" in relation to "human" is correct in reference, but not a translation. We suggest as the most desirable renderings, for (*vyavahārika-*) *pratyakṣa*, either "direct," "evident," "obvious," or "semiotic"; for *parokṣa*, either "indirect," "metaphysical," "occult," "universal," "abstract," or "symbolic"; for *para-mârthika-pratyakṣa* (= *aparokṣa, sâkṣāt*), "immediate."

One further point: in the often recurring expression *parokṣa-priyā iva devāḥ*, "*priyā*" must not be rendered "are fond of," because the *parokṣa* understanding is an angelic property, depending not on choice but on nature; it is no doubt true that the Angels "love what is their own" (that is, would not be other than they are), but we cannot imply that this "love" is an "affection" — it is their being, not an accident of being; [95] cf. *Maitri Up.*, VI, 34, "What is one's thought, that he becomes," and similarly *Dhammapada*, I, 1, 2. The last consideration reminds us that in so far as man employs and understands angelic means of communication, the "language of birds," he is of the angelic kind ("Intellect is the swiftest of birds," *mano javiṣṭham patayatsu antaḥ*, *Ṛg Veda*, VI, 9, 5); in so far as his communications and understanding are limited to "matters of fact," he is not merely "a little" but a great deal "lower than the Angels."

Chapter VI

ĀBHĀSA

Chapter VI

ĀBHĀSA

ĀBHĀSA, literally "shining back," "reflection,"
"semblance," is predicated of the individual self
(*jīva*) with respect to Brahman (*Vedânta Sūtra*, II, 3, 50, Śaṅkarâcārya explaining *ābhāsa* as "counter-image," or "reflection," *pratibimba*). In theistic texts, such as those of northern Śaivism, *ābhāsa* implies the world conceived as a theophany. The true Self "counter-sees itself" reflected in the
possibilities of being (*Pañcaviṁśa Brāhmaṇa*, VII, 8, 1), as
the world-picture (*jagac-citra*) painted by the Self on the
canvas of the Self (Śaṅkarâcārya).[96] "He illumines (*bhāsa-
yati*) these worlds. . . . He gladdens (*rañjayati*, 'colors')
these worlds" (*Maitri Upaniṣad*, VI, 7); that is, "God
made man in His own image"; *bhāsa* is Eckhart's "image-
bearing light"; cf. *citra-bhāsa*, *Ṛg Veda*, VI, 10, 3, *sarūpa
jyoti*, ibid., X, 55, 3, *bhā-rūpa*, *Maitri Upaniṣad*, VI, 4.
Ābhāsa, then, and *citra*, "art," are fundamentally "image,"
owing such reality as may be theirs to That whose image
they reflect.

In Śilpa usage, as I have shown in *JAOS*., XLVIII, 251,
ābhāsa means "painting," and not some mysterious and
otherwise unknown material, as suggested by Acharya,

Dictionary of Hindu Architecture, p. 63, and *Mānasāra*, p. 71. I now offer in support of the same view the translation of a text not cited by Acharya, viz. the *Kāśyapaśilpa*, Ch. L, *Pratimā-lakṣaṇa*, vv. 1–7 (Ānandâśrāma Series, No. 95, p. 167):

1. Hearken with singly-directed mind to the exposition of the characteristics of images, the immovable, the movable, and those both movable and immovable, which form a class of three.[97]

2. Those made of terracotta (*mṛnmaya*) or laterite (*śārkara*), of stucco (*sauyaja*), or painted (read *ālekhyaṁ*, cf. *lekhyaṁ* in *Śukranītisāra*, IV, 4, 70), are the immovable; those made of stone, wood, mineral (*dhātu*, possibly jade), or gem,

3. Are both immovable and movable; those of metal (*loha*) are the immovable. (Further) *ardha-citra*, *citra*, and *citrâbhāsa* form a class of three,

4. (of which) *ardha-citra* ('half-representation,' high relief) is an image in which half the body is not seen (read *ardhâṅgadarśaṇam*), *citra* (full round representation) is when the image is visible all round (*sarvâyavasaṁdṛṣṭaṁ*),[98]

5. (And) *ābhāsa* (painting) is said with respect to an image on a canvas or wall (made to appear as if) in relief (*nimnônnate paṭe bhittau*). (Further), *ardha-citra* is done in plaster (*sudhā*), being half in the power of the other full-round representation (*citra*),

6. (And) *ābhāsa* (painting) is to be done with mineral colors (*dhātu*),[99] and so also *citrârdha* (= *ardha-citra*). But

paintings (*citrâbhāsa*) of the Angels are (also) of three kinds, best, middling, and good,

7. (For example), a base (*pīṭha*) of (plain) brick is good, a painted one (*ābhāsaka*) is better, and one of painted terracotta relief (*ābhāsârdham mṛnmayaṁ*) is best.

Another source not cited by Acharya is the *Śilparatna*, XLVI, 1–11; here *citra*, *ardha-citra*, and *citrâbhāsa* are similarly distinguished, the first being *sarvânga-dṛśyakaraṇaṁ*, "having all its parts visible," the second *bhittyādau lagna-bhāvenâpy-ardhaṁ*, "when half of its being is attached to a wall or the like surface," and the third is referred to as a *vilekhanaṁ*, "painting," and further, as *lekhyaṁ . . . nānā-varṇânvitaṁ*, "painted with the use of many colors." It is also stated that *citra* and *citrârdha* may be done in clay or plaster, wood, stone, or metal.

Ābhāsa is used in Śilpa texts also in another sense,[100] with reference to the unit of measurement proper to be employed in various kinds of buildings, the four different units specified being *jāti*, the full cubit (*hasta*), *chanda*, three-quarter cubit, *vikalpa* (not defined), and *ābhāsa*, half cubit. These units are employed respectively in building for Gods and Brahmans, Kṣatriyas, Vaiśyas, and Śūdras. It is therefore clear that *ābhāsa* represents here the least in a series of modifications or transformations of a whole unit. This meaning is quite consistent with that of *ābhāsa*, "painting," regarded as a modification of *citra*, "full-round representation," that of *rasâbhāsa*, "semblance of flavor" in Alaṁkāra terminology, *vastrâbhāsa*, "semblance of clothes" in a painting (*Pañcadaśī*, VI, 6), *cid-ābhāsa*, "reflection of absolute intelligence," *ibid.*, 7, and that of *ābhāsa* as "theophany."

Ābhāsa-gata occurs in Vasubandhu, *Abhidharmakośa*, V, 34 (Poussin, p. 72), with the related meaning "in the field of objective experience," *ābhāsa* being equivalent to *viṣaya-rūpatā*, "sensible objectivity," and *ābhāsa-gata* to *dṛśya*, "empirically perceptible." Dignāga uses *ava-bhāsate* with reference to the seemingly objective character of an intellectual image (*antarjñeya-rūpa*); *ava-bhāsa* can also be used for "illumination" as a spiritual experience. *Bhāvâbhāsa* is "semblance of existence." The opposite of *ābhāsa* is *nir-ābhāsa* or *an-ābhāsa*, "imageless."[101]

The word *ābhāsa* as "painting" involves some interesting considerations bearing on the psychological conception of the relation of painting to sculpture and relief, and on the idea of the third dimension in painting. Verse 5b, literally translated above, implies, as does also the very word *citrâbhāsa*, literally "the shining forth or semblance of *citra*," that painting is thought of as a constricted *mode* of sculpture; relief, which may also be colored, logically occupying an intermediate place. The view that painting, although actually applied to plane surfaces, was nevertheless conventionally regarded as a kind of solid representation can be supported by additional literary evidences. For example, in Vinaya, IV, 61, a monk "raises" (*vuṭṭhāpeti*) a picture (*cittam*) on a cloth; and in *Saṁyutta Nikāya*, Comm., II, 5, a painter "raises up" (*samuṭṭhāpeti*) a shape (*rūpam*) on a wall surface by means of his brushes and colors. In the *Mahāyāna Sūtrâlamkāra* of Asaṅga, XIII, 17, we have *citre* . . . *natônnatam nâsti ca, dṛśyate atha ca,* "there is no actual relief in a painting, and yet we see it there," and similarly in the *Laṅkâvatāra Sūtra*, Nanjio's ed., p. 91, a painted surface (*citrakṛta-pradeśa*) is said to be seen in relief (*nimnônnata*) though actually flat (*animnônnata*). In more than one place we have the metaphor of the eyes stumbling (*skhalati*) over the elevations and depressions (*nimnônnata*) represented in a picture, these hills and vales being either those of the luxuriant forms of women, or those of the landscape background (*Śakuntalā*, VI, 13–14, and perhaps *Triṣaṣṭiśalākāpuruṣacaritra*, I, 1, 360). And in verse 5a, translated above, *nimnônnate* in agreement with *paṭe* and *bhittau* is especially noteworthy, the canvas or wall being spoken of as "in relief," though it is quite certain that a plane painted surface is all that is referred to.

Natônnata and *nimnônnata* thus provide us with exact terms for the relievo, plastic modelling, or modelling in abstract light [102] which is actually seen in the paintings of Ajaṇṭā, while for the process of "shading" by which the relief effect was created and sense of volume conveyed, we have the term *vartanā*, and corresponding Pali *vaṭṭana* and *ujjotana*, "shading" and "adding high lights," in a passage of the *Aṭṭhasālinī*.[103] Such relievo must not, of course, be confused with anything of the nature of "effect of light," chiaroscuro, *chāyâtapa*,[104] "shade and shine." Relievo and chiaroscuro are indeed not merely independent, but actually

contradictory notions, as was realized in Europe even as
late as the time of Leonardo, who, though as a naturalist
he had long studied the effects produced by direct sunlight
and cast shadows, rightly maintained that these effects destroyed the representation of true relief or volume.

The question of relief involves to some degree that of perspective. Recent discussions of the problems of spatial
representation in Far Eastern and Indian art [105] convey the
impression that the authors are devoting much labor to
what is really a rather artificial problem, posed for them
by the unfamiliarity of the arts in question, this unfamiliarity persisting despite their good knowledge of the arts themselves as they exist in countless extant and accessible
examples. It is difficult to believe that problems of spatial
representation were ever in Asia attacked as such, in the
sense that they were wrestled with in Quattrocento Italy,
that is to say from a scientific and visualistic rather than an
aesthetic point of view. It is surely impossible to believe
that there was ever a time when art was unintelligible to
those for whom it was made, for in this case it must have
been unintelligible also to those who made it — the "artist"
not being, as at the present day he is, an isolated and peculiar person. To suppose that art was unintelligible, and
that artists, in the goodness of their hearts, were trying to
make it comprehensible either to themselves or others,
is as if to suppose that speakers made sounds with a view
to the subsequent formation of a valid means of communication, or that carpenters began to build houses with a view

to the appearance of architecture, whereas in fact speech is always adequate to the thing to be expressed, and there can no more be a progress in art than in metaphysics, but only a varying development of different aspects.

All men, and even animals, are aware that objects stand apart from each other in space, up and down, sideways, and backwards; and if animals have not a word for "three dimensions," they still know how to move in different directions, and have a sense of far and near. Space, then, has to be taken for granted as a primary datum of intelligence, and it is obvious that as soon as it became possible to make intelligible representations of objects, it must have been taken for granted by those who understood them that these were representations of objects existing in space. The question of perspective thus becomes a purely historical and descriptive problem; the definition of perspective reduces itself to "means employed to indicate the existence or distribution of objects in space." From the aesthetic point of view, no one variety of perspective can be regarded as superior to any other, and though we naturally prefer that kind of perspective which best corresponds to our own habits of vision and therefore requires least effort of comprehension, all that is really required is intelligibility. It is in fact perfectly possible to learn to read the perspective of an unfamiliar art as fluently as we read that of our own times, and in the same way without being actively conscious of the use of any particular mode of perspective. The question of optical plausibility therefore does not arise, since it always inheres in the kind of perspective to which we are or have become accustomed; if by optical plausibility we mean anything more than this, it can only be in connection with a naïvely illusionistic view of art, as if we wished to paint a picture of the master that should be recognized by the dog.

A discussion of the history of perspective in India, and of the related problem of continuous representation, would take us too far afield; but it may be remarked that while the necessities of iconography, so far as *sāttvika* representations are involved, determine the predominance of frontality at all times, there is a representation of free movement from the earliest times, at Mohenjodaro, in Maurya terracottas, and even at Bhārhut. [106] If we consider literary sources from the Gupta period onward we find a tabulated scheme of positions (*sthāna*) ranging from the frontal (*ṛju*) through stages of *profil perdu* to strict profile (*bhitti-gata*, "gone into the wall") and mixed views, as well as a series of terms denoting various degrees of bending and torsion of the body.[107] The various positions are defined by reference to actually or ideally suspended threads, in terms of the distance between given points on the body and the threads themselves, and also in terms of *kṣaya-vṛddhi*, "loss and gain," that is effectively foreshortening, the parts which in a given position are not seen being described as *chāyā-gata*, "gone into shadow." All these are matters belonging to the history of technique rather than that of principle.

As to the development, it may be added that while the

early sculpture in the round exhibits the strongest possible
feeling for plastic volume, the early reliefs (*ardha-citra*) approximate rather to painting (*citrâbhāsa*) than to solid
sculpture (*citra*), being, for example at Bhārhut, closely
compressed between the two planes of the wrought surface,
though there are already exceptions to this at Bhājā.[108]
Then at Sāñcī the relief is heightened, and the effect moves
in the opposite direction from that of painting to that of
round sculpture; this tendency continues throughout the
Kuṣāna and later Āndhra periods, and reaches its fullest
development in the Gupta period, and subsequently persists, notwithstanding that the intrinsic quality of the volume represented is no longer the same. Needless to say,
early Chinese "relief" is still more like painting than is
early Indian, being in fact only an engraving on stone, employing perspective methods rather difficult to grasp, but in
any case not in the nature of foreshortening as in sculpture; later, the raising of the relief in Chinese stone sculpture is a reflection of Indian methods.

But the earliest Indian relief, notwithstanding its com-
pression, has always the intention of solidity, and the earliest Indian painting by its emphatic modelling demonstrates
its close relation to the contemporary sculpture in the
round, with its impressive volume and mass. A like volume
found expression in the reliefs only gradually, which might
perhaps be thought of as indicating a later origin of relief
technique, and the historical precedence of full-round sculpture and painting. However this may be, in mediaeval

times the two tendencies crossed as it were in opposite directions, the one maintaining in fact a high relief, the other
representing a flattening of the mental image. When sculpture gradually lost its sense of plastic volume, painting was
also actually flattened out; for example, the phrase *nimnôn-
nata-paṭa* could hardly be applied to any painting of the
Gujarātī or Rajput schools, where only vestiges of the old
plastic shading survive. The flattening of the visual concept
must be related to a corresponding psychological modification, and certainly not to any change in technical procedure
undertaken for its own sake; for thought precedes stylistic
expression in the work, and to seek for the causes of changes
in the changes themselves would be a *reductio ad absurdum*
of history.[109]

Psychological changes, manifested in attenuation of form,
can only be thought of as representing a slackening of
energy, a looser concentration, *śithila-samādhi*. When one
considers the impressive volumes of the earlier art, in which
the form is as it were pressed outward from within by an
indomitable will, one thinks also of those numerous passages in literature where the hero is said to swell with anger,
or of women's bodies that expand in adolescence or in passion, or of those pregnant trees whose pent-up flowering
must be released by the touch of a lovely foot. With the
passing of time all these energies were and must have been
brought under greater control, softened and refined in expression, the will no longer asserting, but now rather realizing itself in an active quiescence. We feel this already in the

relative serenity of Gupta sculpture and the sophisticated poesy of the classical drama; we could not imagine in the twelfth century such heroic forms as those of the figures of donors at Kārlī, or that of Friar Bala's "Bodhisattva" at Sārnāth. The impulsive and ruthless heroism of the past survives only in the tradition of Rajput chivalry. In general, the tendency is toward a more purely intellectual conception of experience. It is perhaps worth noting that a like development was also taking place in contemporary mediaeval Europe, as will be apparent if for example we compare St Thomas with Śaṅkarâcārya; in neither case can it be said that any outward disorder could interfere with the supremacy of intellect.

It would be too easy to exaggerate the nature of the change, and very much mistaken to evaluate it only in terms of decadence. Stylistic sequences in thought and art are not in themselves pure loss or pure gain, decadence or progress, but necessary and therefore acceptable developments of special aspects. When the will has been in some measure appeased, the intellect can the better exercise its power. If this change of direction at first involves a loss of animal perfection (immediacy of action), it is nevertheless a becoming toward a higher spontaneity, in which the unity of the inner and outer life is to be restored, and there are even moments at the height of a development and in the lives of individuals when the balance seems to be restored and art transcends style. Apart from these questions of perfection, it might well be argued that the flattening out of art, implying as it does a more conventional symbolism than even that of modelling in abstract light, reflects a more intellectual mode of understanding, which does not require even a suggestion of modelling as an aid to reproduction; as in the case of the angels who have fewer ideas and use less means than men.

In any case, one could not, if one would wish to, turn back the movement of time. To be other than we are would be for us the same as not to be; to wish that the art of any period had been other than it was is the same as to wish that it had never been. Every style is complete in itself, and to be justified accordingly, not to be judged by the standards of a former or any other age.

> With one voice which is wondrous
> He giveth utterance to thoughts innumerable,
> That are received by audiences of all sorts,
> Each understanding them in his own way. [110]

Chapter VII

THE ORIGIN AND USE OF IMAGES IN INDIA

Chapter VII

THE ORIGIN AND USE OF IMAGES IN INDIA

*It may be said that images are to the Hindu worshipper what diagrams
are to the geometrician.*

Rao, *Elements of Hindu Iconography*, II, 28.

FEW of those who condemn idolatry, or make its suppression a purpose of missionary activity, have ever
seriously envisaged the actual use of images, in historical
or psychological perspective, or surmised a possible significance in the fact that the vast majority of men of all races,
and in all ages, including the present, Protestants, Hebrews,
and Musalmans being the chief exceptions, have made use
of more or less anthropomorphic images as aids to devotion.
For these reasons it may be not without value to offer an
account of the use of images in India, as far as possible in
terms of thought natural to those who actually make use
of such images. This may at least conduce to a realization
of the truth enunciated by an incarnate Indian deity,
Kṛṣṇa, that "the path men take from every side is Mine."

In explaining the use of images in India, where the
method is regarded as edifying, it should not be inferred
that Hindus or Buddhists are to be represented *en masse* as
less superstitious than other peoples. We meet with all
kinds of stories about images that speak, or bow, or weep;

images receive material offerings and services, which they are said to "enjoy"; we know that the real presence of the deity is invited in them for the purpose of receiving worship; on the completion of an image, its eyes are "opened" by a special and elaborate ceremony.[111] Thus, it is clearly indicated that the image is to be regarded as if animated by the deity.[112]

Obviously, however, there is nothing peculiarly Indian here. Similar miracles have been reported of Christian images; even the Christian church, like an Indian temple, is a house dwelt in by God in a special sense, yet it is not regarded as his prison, nor do its walls confine his omnipresence, whether in India or in Europe.

Further, superstition, or realism, is inseparable from human nature, and it would be easy to show that this is always and everywhere the case. The mere existence of science does not defend us from it; the majority will always conceive of atoms and electrons as real things, which would be tangible if they were not so small, and will always believe that tangibility is a proof of existence; and are fully convinced that a being, originating at a given moment of time, may yet, as that same being, survive eternally in time. He who believes that phenomena of necessity stand for solid existing actualities, or that there can exist any empirical consciousness or individuality without a material (substantial) basis, or that anything that has come into being can endure as such forever, is an idolater, a fetishist. Even if we should accept the popular Western view of Hinduism as a polytheistic system, it could not be maintained that the Indian icon is an any sense a fetish. As pointed out by Guénon, "Dans l'Inde, en particulier, une image symbolique representant l'un ou l'autre des 'attributs divins,' et qui est appelée *pratīka*, n'est point une 'idole,' car elle n'a jamais été prise pour autre chose que ce qu'elle est réellement, un support de méditation et un moyen auxiliaire de realization" (*Introduction à l'étude des doctrines hindoues*, p. 209). A good illustration of this is to be found in the *Divyâvadāna*, Ch. XXVI, where Upagupta compels Māra, who as a *yakṣa* has the power of assuming shapes at will, to exhibit himself in the shape of the Buddha. Upagupta bows down, and Māra, shocked at this apparent worship of himself, protests. Upagupta explains that he is not worshipping Māra, but the person represented—"just as people venerating earthen images of the undying angels, do not revere the clay as such, but the immortals represented therein."[113] Here we have the case of an individual who has passed beyond individuality, but is yet represented according to human needs by an image. The principle is even clearer in the case of the images of the angels; the image *per se* is neither God nor any angel, but merely an aspect or hypostasis (*avasthā*) of God, who is in the last analysis without likeness (*amūrta*), not determined by form (*arūpa*), trans-form (*para-rūpa*). His various forms or emanations are conceived by a process of symbolic filiation. To conceive of Hinduism as a polytheistic system is in itself a naïveté of which only a Western student, inheriting Graeco-Roman

concepts of "paganism" could be capable; the Muḥammadan view of Christianity as polytheism could be better
justified than this.

In fact, if we consider Indian religious philosophy as a
whole, and regard the extent to which its highest conceptions have passed as dogmas into the currency of daily life,
we shall have to define Hindu civilization as one of the
least supe. stitious the world has known. *Māyā* is not properly *de*lusion, but strictly speaking creative power, *śakti*,
the principle of manifestation; *de*lusion, *moha*, is to conceive
of appearances as things in themselves, and to be attached
to them as such without regard to their procession.

In the *Bhagavad Gītā*, better known in India than the
New Testament in Europe, we are taught of the Real, that
"This neither dies nor is it born; he who regardeth This
as a slayer, he who thinketh This is slain, are equally un-
knowing." Again and again, from the Upaniṣads to the
most devotional theistic hymns the Godhead, ultimate
reality, is spoken of as unlimited by any form, not to be described by any predicate, unknowable. Thus, in the Upaniṣads, "He is, by that alone is He to be apprehended" (cf.
"I am that I am"); in the words of the Śaiva hymnist
Māṇikka Vāçagar, "He is passing the description of words,
not comprehensible by the mind, not visible to the eye or
other senses." Similarly in later Buddhism, in the Vajrayāna (Śūnyavāda) system, we find it categorically stated
that the divinities, that is, the personal God or premier
angel in all His forms, "are manifestations of the essential

nature of non-being"; the doctrine of the only reality of the Void (Behmen's "Abyss") is pushed to the point of an explicit denial of the existence of any Buddha or any Buddhist doctrine.

Again, whereas we are apt to suppose that the religious significance of Christianity stands or falls with the actual historicity of Jesus, we find an Indian commentator (Nīla-kaṇṭha) saying of the Kṛṣṇa Līlā, believed historical by most Hindus, that the narration is not the real point, that this is not an historical event, but is based upon eternal truths, on the actual relation of the soul to God, and that the events take place, not in the outer world, but in the heart of man. Here we are in a world inaccessible to higher criticism, neither of superstition on the one hand, nor of cynicism on the other. It has been more than once pointed out that the position of Christianity could well be strengthened by a similar emancipation from the historical point of view, as was to a large extent actually the case with the Schoolmen.

As for India, it is precisely in a world dominated by an idealistic concept of reality, and yet with the approval of the most profound thinkers, that there flourished what we are pleased to call idolatry. Māṇikka Vāçagar, quoted above, constantly speaks of the attributes of God, refers to the legendary accounts of His actions, and takes for granted the use and service of images. In Vajrayāna Buddhism, often though not quite correctly designated as nihilistic, the development of an elaborate pantheon, fully realized in material imagery, reaches its zenith. Śaṅkâracārya himself, one of the most brilliant intellects the world has known, interpreter of the Upaniṣads and creator of the Vedânta system of pure monism accepted by a majority of all Hindus and analogous to the idealism of Kant, was a devout worshipper of images, a visitor to shrines, a singer of devotional hymns.

True, in a famous prayer, he apologizes for visualizing in contemplation One who is not limited by any form, for praising in hymns One who is beyond the reach of words, and for visiting Him in sacred shrines, who is omnipresent. Actually, too, there exist some groups in Hinduism (the Sikhs, for example) who do not make use of images. But if even he who knew could not resist the impulse to love,—and love requires an object of adoration, and an object must be conceived in word or form,—how much greater must be the necessity of that majority for whom it is so much easier to worship than to know. Thus the philosopher perceives the inevitability of the use of imagery, verbal and visual, and sanctions the service of images. God Himself makes like concession to our mortal nature, "taking the forms imagined by His worshipers," making Himself as we are that we may be as He is.

The Hindu Īśvara (Supreme God) is not a jealous God, because all gods are aspects of Him, imagined by His worshippers; in the words of Kṛṣṇa: "When any devotee seeks to worship any aspect with faith, it is none other than Myself that bestows that steadfast faith, and when by worshipping any aspect he wins what he desires, it is none other than Myself that grants his prayers. Howsoever men approach Me, so do I welcome them, for the path men take from every side is Mine." Those whose ideal is less high attain, indeed, of necessity to lesser heights; but no man can safely aspire to higher ideals than are pertinent to his spiritual age. In any case, his spiritual growth cannot be aided by a desecration of his ideals; he can be aided only by the fullest recognition of these ideals as retaining their validity in any scheme, however profound. This was the Hindu method; Indian religion adapts herself with infinite grace to every human need. The collective genius that made of Hinduism a continuity ranging from the contemplation of the Absolute to the physical service of an image made of clay did not shrink from an ultimate acceptance of every aspect of God conceived by man, and of every ritual devised by his devotion.

We have already suggested that the multiplicity of the forms of images, coinciding with the development of monotheistic Hinduism, arises from various causes, all ultimately referable to the diversity of need of individuals and groups. In particular, this multiplicity is due historically to the inclusion of all pre-existing forms, all local forms, in a greater theological synthesis, where they are interpreted as modes or emanations (*vyūha*) of the supreme Iśvara; and subsequently, to the further growth of theological speculation. In the words of Yāska, "We see actually that because of the greatness of God, the one principle of life is praised in various ways. Other angels are the individual members of a unique Self" (*Nirukta*, VII, 4): cf. Ruysbroeck, *Adornment* . . . , Ch. XXV, "because of His incomprehensible nobility and sublimity, which we cannot rightly name nor wholly express, we give Him all these names."

Iconolatry, however, was not left to be regarded as an ignorant or useless practice fit only for spiritual children; even the greatest, as we have seen, visited temples, and worshipped images, and certainly these greatest thinkers did not do so blindly or unconsciously. A human necessity was recognized, the nature of the necessity was understood, its psychology systematically analyzed, the various phases of image worship, mental and material, were defined, and the variety of forms explained by the doctrines of emanation and of gracious condescension.

In the first place, then, the forms of images are not arbitrary. Their ultimate elements may be of popular origin rather than priestly invention, but the method is adopted and further developed within the sphere of intellectual orthodoxy. Each conception is of human origin, notwithstanding that the natural tendency of man to realism leads to a belief in actually existent heavens where the Angel appears as he is represented. In the words of Śukrâcārya, "the characteristics of images are determined by the relation that subsists between the adorer and the adored"; in those cited by Gopālabhatta from an unknown source, the present spiritual activity of the worshiper, and the actual existence of a traditional iconography, are reconciled as follows —

"Though it is the devotion (*bhakti*) of the devotee that causes the manifestation of the image of the Blessed One (Bhagavata), in this matter (of iconography) the procedure of the ancient sages should be followed." [114]

The whole problem of symbolism (*pratīka*, "symbol") is discussed by Śaṅkarâcārya, Commentary on the Vedânta Sūtras, I, 1, 20. Endorsing the statement that "all who sing here to the harp, sing Him," he points out that this "Him" refers to the highest Lord only, who is the ultimate theme even of worldly songs. And as to anthropomorphic expressions in scripture, "we reply that the highest Lord may, when he pleases, assume a bodily shape formed of Māyā, in order to gratify his devout worshipers"; but all this is merely analogical, as when we say that the Brahman abides here or there, which in reality abides only in its own glory (cf. *ibid.*, I, 2, 29). The representation of the invisible by the visible is also discussed by Deussen, *Philosophy of the Upanishads*, pp. 99–101. Cf. also the discussion of *parokṣa* in Ch. V.

Parenthetically, we may remark that stylistic sequences (change of aesthetic form without change of basic shape) are a revealing record of changes in the nature of religious experience; in Europe, for example, the difference between a thirteenth-century and a modern Madonna betrays the passage from passionate conviction to facile sentimentality. Of this, however, the worshiper is altogether unaware; from the standpoint of edification, the value of an image does not depend on its aesthetic qualities. A recognition of the significance of stylistic changes, in successive periods, important as it may be for us as students of art, is actually apparent only in disinterested retrospect; the theologian, proposing means of edification, has been concerned only with the forms of images. Stylistic changes correspond to linguistic changes: we all speak the language of our own time without question or analysis.

Let us consider now the processes actually involved in the making of images. Long anterior to the oldest surviving images of the supreme deities we meet with descriptions of the gods as having limbs, garments, weapons or other attributes; such descriptions are to be found even in the Vedic lauds and myths. Now in theistic Hinduism, where the method of Yoga is employed, that is, focused attention leading to the realization of identity of consciousness with the object considered, whether or not this object be God, these descriptions, now called *dhyāna mantrams* or trance formulae, or alternatively, *sādhanās*, means, provide the germ from which the form of the deity is to be visualized. For example, "I worship our gentle lady Bhuvaneśvarī, like the risen sun, lovely, victorious, destroying defects in prayer, with a shining crown on her head, three-eyed and with swinging earrings adorned with diverse gems, as a lotus-lady, abounding in treasure, making the gestures of charity and giving assurance. Such is the *dhyānam* of Bhuvaneśvarī" (a form of Devī). To the form thus conceived imagined flowers and other offerings are to be made. Such interior worship of a mantra-body or correspondingly imagined form is called subtle (*sūkṣma*), in contradistinction to the exterior worship of a material image, which is termed gross (*sthūla*), though merely in a descriptive, not a deprecatory, sense.

Further contrasted with both these modes of worship is that called *para-rūpa*, "trans-form," in which the worship is paid directly to the deity as he is in himself. This last mode no doubt corresponds to the ambition of the iconoclast, but such gnosis is in fact only possible, and therefore only permissible, to the perfected Yogin and veritable *jīvan-mukta*, who is so far as he himself is concerned set free from all name and aspect, whatever may be the outward appearance he presents. Had the iconoclast in fact attained to such perfection as this, he could not have been an iconoclast.

In any case it must be realized, in connection with the gross or subtle modes of worship, that the end is only to be attained by an identification of the worshiper's consciousness with the form under which the deity is conceived: *nādevo devaṁ yajet*, "only as the angel can one worship the angel," and so *devo bhūtvā devaṁ yajet*, "to worship the Angel become the Angel." Only when the *dhyānam* is thus realized in full *samādhi* (the consummation of Yoga, which commences with focused attention) is the worship achieved. Thus, for example, with regard to the form of Naṭarāja, representing Śiva's cosmic dance, in the words of Tirumūlar,

The dancing foot, the sound of the tinkling bells,
The songs that are sung, and the various steps,

The forms assumed by our Master as He dances,
Discover these in your own heart, so shall your bonds be broken.

When, on the other hand, a material image is to be produced for purposes of worship in a temple or elsewhere, this as a technical procedure must be undertaken by a professional craftsman, who may be variously designated *śilpin*, "craftsman," *yogin*, "yogi," *sādhaka*, "adept," or simply *rūpakāra* or *pratimākāra*, "imager." Such a craftsman goes through the whole process of self-purification and worship, mental visualization and identification of consciousness with the form evoked, and then only translates the form into stone or metal. Thus the trance formulae become the prescriptions by which the craftsman works, and as such they are commonly included in the *Śilpa Śāstras*, the technical literature of craftsmanship. These books in turn provide invaluable data for the modern student of iconography.

Technical production is thus bound up with the psychological method known as *yoga*. In other words the artist does not resort to models but uses a mental construction, and this condition sufficiently explains the cerebral character of the art, which everyone will have remarked for himself. In the words of the encyclopaedist Śukrâcārya, "One should set up in temples the images of angels who are the objects of his devotion, by mental vision of their attributes; it is for the full achievement of this yoga-vision that the proper lineaments of images are prescribed; therefore the mortal imager should resort to trance-vision, for thus and no otherwise, and surely not by direct perception, is the end to be attained" (translated also above, p.114, in slightly different words).

The proper characteristics of images are further elucidated in the *Śilpa Śāstras* by a series of canons known as *tālamāna* or *pramāṇa*, in which are prescribed the ideal proportions proper to the various deities, whether conceived as Kings of the World, or otherwise. These proportions are expressed in terms of a basic unit, just as we speak of a figure having so many "heads"; but the corresponding Indian measure is that of the "face," from the hair on the forehead to the chin, and the different canons are therefore designated Ten-face, Nine-face, and so on down to the Five-face canon suitable for minor deities of dwarfish character. These ideal proportions correspond to the character of the aspect of the angel to be represented, and complete the exposition of this character otherwise set forth by means of facial expression, attributes, costume, or gesture. And as Śukrâcārya says further (see also more literal versions above, Ch. IV), "Only an image made in accordance with the canon can be called beautiful; some may think that beautiful which corresponds to their own fancy, but that not in accordance with the canon is unlovely to the discerning eye." And again, "Even the misshapen image of an angel is to be preferred to that of a man, however attractive the latter may be"; because the representations of the angels are means to spiritual ends, not so those which are only likenesses of human individuals. "When the consciousness is brought to rest in the form (*nāma*, "name," "idea"), and sees only the form, then, inasmuch as it rests in the form, aspectual perception is dispensed with and only the reference remains; one reaches then the world-without-aspectual-perception, and with further practice attains to liberation from all hindrances, becoming adept." [115] Here, in another language than our own, are contrasted ideal and realistic art: the one a means to the attainment of fuller consciousness, the other merely a means to pleasure. So too might the anatomical limitations of Giotto be defended as against the human charm of Raphael.

It should be further understood that images differ greatly in the degree of their anthropomorphism. Some are merely symbols, as when the Bodhi tree is used to represent the Buddha at the time of the Enlightenment, or when only the feet of the Lord are represented as objects of worship. A very important iconographic type is that of the *yantra*, used especially in the Śākta systems; here we have to do with a purely geometrical form, often for instance composed of interlocking triangles, representing the male and female, static and kinetic aspects of the Two-in-One. Further, images in the round may be *avyakta*, non-manifest, like a *lingam*; or *vyaktâvyakta*, partially manifest, as in the case of a *mukha-lingam*; or *vyakta*, fully manifest in "anthromorphic" or partly theriomorphic types. [116] In the last analysis all these are equally ideal, symbolic forms.

In the actual use of a material image, it should always be remembered that it must be prepared for worship by a ceremony of invocation (*āvahana*); and if intended only for temporary use, subsequently desecrated by a formula of dismissal (*visarjana*). When not in *pūjā*, that is before consecration or after desecration, the image has no more sacrosanct character than any other material object. It should not be supposed that the deity, by invocation and dismissal, is made to come or go, for omnipresence does not move; these ceremonies are really projections of the worshipper's own mental attitude toward the image. By invocation he announces to himself his intention of using the image as a means of communion with the Angel; by dismissal he announces that his service has been completed, and that he no longer regards the image as a link between himself and the deity.

It is only by a change of viewpoint, psychologically equivalent to such a formal desecration, that the worshipper, who naturally regards the icon as a devotional utility, comes to regard it as a mere work of art to be sensationally regarded as such. Conversely, the modern aesthetician and Kunsthistoriker, who is interested only in aesthetic surfaces and sensations, fails to conceive of the work as the necessary product of a given determination, that is, as having purpose and utility. Of these two, the worshipper, for whom the object was made, is nearer to the root of the matter than the aesthetician who endeavors to isolate beauty from function.[117]

Notes

Notes

1 (*page 5*). "A mental concept (*citta-saññā*) arises in the mind of the painter, that such and such a shape (*rūpa*) must be made in such and such a way. . . . All the various arts (*sippa*) in the world are produced by the mind," *Atthasālinī*, PTS. ed., p. 64; see "An Early Passage on Indian Painting," *Eastern Art*, III (1931), and cf. note 43.

2 (*page 6*). "Attracting form" is discussed in *JAOS.*, LII, 16, n. 8. Skr. *kṛṣ* (the root in *ā-karṣati*) has the same dual significance which is found in English "draw," as (1) to drag, drag toward or together, attract, and (2) delineate, draw up, compose, put in due form. English draw corresponds to G. *tragen*, to bear, and Skr. *dhṛ* (*dhar*) to bear, bear in mind, support, conceive, hold fast or firm, etc. While *kṛṣ* is to "draw" in either sense, *ā-kṛṣ* can be accurately rendered to "draw up" or "pro-duce." Cf. "fetch" (of the imagination), and "fetch" as an apparition. A remarkable use of English "draw" in our sense is to be found in Böhme's *Mysterium Pansophicum*, IV, 2 (which I can only cite in Earle's version), in connection with the formative aspect of the creative will (of God), as follows: "the desire is a stern attraction. . . . And it draws magically, viz. its own desiring into a substance" (cf. Skr. *dhar-ma*, as "substance").

3 (*page 6*). Upaniṣads, *passim*. Rabindranath Tagore retains the same phraseology in his song *Ami chini go chini*, where it is "in the immanent space of the heart" that he hears "now and again" the song of Bideśinī, the stranger lady who is ideal beauty — *hṛdi mājhe ākāśe sunecchi tomārī gān*. Where and what is this space in the heart? In the *Chāndogya Upaniṣad*, VIII, 14 (also VIII, 1, 1) *ākāśa* is called "the revealer of name and aspect," and identified with Brahman, the Imperishable, the Self. This

is "that mysterious nothing out of which the soul is made . . . which nothing is *at large* in the almighty power of the Father" (Eckhart). This ideal space is the principle wherein all the possibilities of being can be realized (*Chāndogya Upaniṣad*, VIII, 1, 1–3). The *antarhṛdaya-ākāśa*, "space in the heart," is the totality of this ideal space at the innermost core of our being, where only the full content of life can be experienced in the immediately experienced; that consent, from the point of view of aesthetics, is "Beauty," from the point of view of epistemology "Truth" (cf. "Nirvāṇa is the transcendental knowledge of the sameness of all principles," *Saddharma Puṇḍarīka*, Kern's text, p. 133), and from the standpoint of ethics "Perfection." Thus while Beauty may be equated with Perfection and Truth absolutely (*rasa . . . brahmâsvāda-sahôdara*, *Sāhitya Darpaṇa*, III, 1–2), loveliness is merely a good, ugliness merely an evil. Beauty is invisible and indivisible, only to be known as Deity is known, in the heart; art is an utterance of Beauty, science an utterance of Truth, ethics an utterance of Perfection in terms of light *and* shade, thesis *and* antithesis, good *and* evil. Error consists primarily in the attachment of absolute values to either of these relative factors, which are only means of apprehension, and not ends in themselves.

4 (*page 6*). *Bṛhadāraṇyaka Upaniṣad*, IV, 2, 3, with respect to the consent of essence and nature.

5 (*page 6*). "Contained in the Lotus of the Heart are Heaven and Earth . . . both what is ours here and now, and what is not yet ours," *Chāndogya Upaniṣad*, VIII, 1, 1–3; "the Heart is the same as Prajāpati, it is Brahman, it is all," *Bṛhadāraṇyaka Upaniṣad*, V, 3; cf. *Ṛg Veda*, IV, 58, 11 and VI, 9, 6.

6 (*page 6*). The foregoing summary is based on a Sanskrit text cited by A. Foucher, *L'Iconographie bouddhique de l'Inde*, II (1905), 8–11; B. Bhattacharya, *The Indian Buddhist Iconography* (1924), 169 ff., and *Buddhist Esoterism*, 1932, Ch. XI;

and the *Bṛhadāraṇyaka Upaniṣad*, I, 4, 10. Cf. also the *Śukra-nītisāra*, IV, 4, 70–71, *above*, p. 113.

It will be observed that imagination (the power of having mental images) is here deliberately exercised. The vaguer implications of inspiration, enthusiasm, intoxication, are lacking. Needless to say, imagination may take form either as vision or as audition; what has been said above with reference to visual art applies equally to the case of literature, whether scripture or *belles lettres*. The Vedas, and all their accessory literatures and sciences, for example, are contained in the Word (*vāc, dharma, oṁ*), which having been uttered (*niḥśvasita, vyāhṛti*) is then heard (*śruti*) by the Prophets (*ṛṣi*), that audition depending not on "inspiration," but upon attention. Vālmīki, before he begins dictation, first visualizes in Yoga the entire *Rāmâyaṇa*, the characters "presenting themselves to his vision living and moving as though in real life"; and the work being thus completed before the practical activity is begun, the dictation is then so rapid that none but the four-handed Gaṇeśa, using all his hands, can take it down. Similarly, when the Bodhisattva attains Enlightenment, becoming Buddha, the Dharma presents itself to him in its entirety, ready to be taught, not merely as an idea to be subsequently developed. Similar conceptions of the operation of imagination are to be found already in the *Ṛg Veda*, where for example wisdom (*vāc*) is spoken of as "seen" or "heard" (X, 71, 4), ideas are "hewn out" $\sqrt{takṣ}$) "in the heart" (*hṛd*) (X, 71, 8), and thought is formulated ($\sqrt{dhī}$, cf. $\sqrt{dhyai}$, e.g. in *dhyāna*) as a carpenter shapes wood (III, 38, 1; cf. X, 51, 9–10, and Sāyaṇa on these passages).

The Indian formulation is idiomatic, but the process described is universal. The Scholastic parallels are very close; cf. Eckhart, "What I say springs up in me, then I pause in the idea, and thirdly I speak it out," again when he speaks of the carpenter who "first erects the house in his mind," or explains in what manner the Angels may be visualized (see *above*, p. 78). Cf. also Dante, when he says "I am one that when Love inspires me, pay heed; and in what way He dictates within me, that I speak out to you" (*Purgatorio*, XXIII, 53–54) and requires of his hearer to "hold the image like a firm rock" (*Paradiso*, XIII, 2–3, and it needs not to say that the author in the first place must have "held the image" thus); above all when he says "He who would paint a figure, if he cannot be it, cannot draw it" (*Convivio*, Canzone III, 53–54), glossed "No painter can portray any figure, if he have not first of all made himself such as the figure ought to be" (*Convivio*, IV, 10, 106, p. 309 of the Oxford text); again when he speaks of "figures as I have them in conception" (*Paradiso*, XVIII, 85); until finally the "high fantasy falls short of power" to depict the Deity as he is in himself (*Paradiso*, XXXIII, 142), as also in India *dhyāna* falls short of *samādhi*, failing to visualize the Brahman in any likeness, who is without likeness (*amūrta, nirābhāsa*) — *te contemplans totum deficit.*

Chuang Tzŭ (Giles, p. 240) gives an excellent account of the working of Yoga (though not so-called) in connection with the carpenter making a wooden stand for musical instruments, who, when asked, "What mystery is there in your art?" replies, "No mystery, your Highness, and yet there is something. When I am about to make such a stand . . . I first reduce my mind to absolute quiescence. . . . I become oblivious of any reward to be gained . . . of any fame to be acquired . . . unconscious of my physical frame. Then, with no thought of the Court present to my mind, my skill becomes concentrated, and all disturbing elements from without are gone. I enter some mountain forest. I search for a suitable tree. It contains the form required, which is afterwards elaborated. I see the stand in my mind's eye, and then set to work."

And as to habit (habitus, *tao* as "way"): "Let me take an illustration," said the wheelwright, "from my own trade. In making a wheel, if you work too slowly, you can't make it firm; if you work too fast, the spokes won't fit in. You must go neither too slowly nor too fast. There must be coördination of mind and hand. Words cannot explain what it is, but there is some mysterious art herein. I cannot teach it to my son; nor can he learn it from me. Consequently, though seventy years of age, I am still making wheels in my old age" (*ibid.*, p. 271). Similarly with the sword maker: "Is it your skill, Sir, or have you a way?" "It is concentration. . . . If a thing was not a sword, I did not notice it. I availed myself of whatever energy I did not use in other directions in order to secure greater efficiency in the direction required" (*ibid.*, p. 290).

7 (*page 7*). Dante's theory of art is discussed by Julius Schlosser, *Die Kunstliteratur* (Vienna, 1924), pp. 66–77. Dante's conception derives from Aristotle, St Thomas, and the troubadours, and is still essentially scholastic. In the *De Monarchia* he speaks of art as threefold, (1) as idea in the mind, (2) as technique in the tool (means), and (3) as potentiality in the material. In *Paradiso*, I, 127, he speaks of the *sorda* (*tāmasika*) quality in the material, which seems to resist the intention of the artist, recalling Eckhart's carpenter, who building a house "will first erect it in his mind and, were the house enough subject to his will, then, materials apart, the only difference between them would be that of begetter and suddenly begotten." Needless to say, Dante's *artista* includes those whom we now call artisans; see, for example, *Paradiso*, XVI, 49.

Dante in asserting the necessary identification of the artist with his theme (*chi pinge figura* . . ., as cited above) is still at one with the East and with Eckhart, as when the latter says, "On giving my whole mind to the subject of the angels . . . it seemed to me that I was all the angels," and "the painter who has painted a good portrait therein shows his art; it is not himself that it reveals to us." But Leonardo is already far removed from this point of view when he declares more than once, *il pittore pinge se stesso*, "the painter paints himself," "himself" not being the painter's essence, but the accidents of his being, his physiognomy, which come out in the painting just as a man is somewhat revealed in his handwriting. This inevitable reflection of the physical man in his handiwork is indeed also recognized in India, for example, *Lekhakasya ca yad rūpaṁ citre bhavati tād(rūp)yam*, "the painter's own shape comes out in the picture" (cited from a *Purāṇa*, *Rūpam* 27/28, p. 99); but this is precisely why the painter himself must be a normal man, since otherwise his peculiarity might be reflected in his art. From the Scholastic and Indian point of view, any such reflection of the person of the artist in his work must be regarded as a defect; whereas in later European art, the trace of the artist's individual peculiarities coming to be regarded as a virtue in the art, and flattering the artist's pride, the way to aesthetic exhibitionism and the substitution of the player ("star") for the play were prepared. In the same way the history of artists has replaced the history of art.

8 (*page 9*). See my *History of Indian and Indonesian Art*, p. 125; also, *Mahāvaṁsa*, XVIII, 24, XXVII, 10–20, and XXX, 11, and *Jātaka*, No. 489. For example, "vehicles" or "thrones," Skr. *vāhana*, *āsana*, which are living principles alike from the Christian and Hindu points of view (St Thomas, *Sum. Theol.*, I, Q. 108, A. 5–7; Garuḍa, Haṁsa and Nandi as the seats or vehicles of Viṣṇu, Brahmā, and Śiva); weapons or powers, Angels from the Christian, Devatās from the Hindu point of view (St Thomas, *ibid.*, *Bṛhad Devatā*, I, 74 and LV, 143); or the palaces and chariots (*vimāna*, *ratha*) of the Angels, imitated in their earthly shrines.

In *Mhb.*, XII, 285, 148, Śiva is called *sarva-śilpa-pravartaka*, "instigator of all arts," and *ibid.*, XIII, 18, 2 f., he imparts *kalā-jñāna*, "the understanding of accomplishments," to Garga. Observe that "Sanskrit" (*saṁskṛta*) is *deva-nāgarī*, "the language of the heavenly city," analogous to *deva-śilpāni*, the "angelic works of art" for which see *above*, pp. 8, 126.

With *Aitareya Brāhmaṇa*, VI, 27, cited in the text, cf. *Aitareya Āraṇyaka*, III, 2, 6, where "Prajāpati, the Year, after emanating offspring, was disintegrated (*viyasraṁsata*); he reintegrated himself (*ātmānaṁ samadadhāyat*) by means of the metres (*chan-*

dobhir)," and *Jaiminīya Upaniṣad Brāhmaṇa*, III, 11, where initiation is called a metrical transformation (*dīkṣate* . . . *chandānsy eva abhisambhavati*). In these passages the spiritual significance of rhythm in art is plainly asserted. Conversely they are also of interest in connection with the problem of the origins of art, all rhythm corresponding in the last analysis to cosmic rhythms; cf. *Jaiminīya Upaniṣad Brāhmaṇa*, I, 35, 7, "the Year is endless: its two ends are Winter and Spring. After (*anu*) this it is that the two ends of a village are united; after this that the two ends of a necklet meet"; *ibid.* I, 2, the *Gāyatra-sāman* "should be sung according to the course (*vartman*) of the Spirit and the Waters," and Jeremias, *Der Kosmos von Sumer*, 1932, p. 4, "Eine grosse Leistung Herman Wirths beruht darin, dass er in der Lehre vom Wege Gottes nach dem äonischen Lauf nicht nur die Wurzel der Symbolik gesehen hat — das war nicht neu — sondern auch die Wurzel der Sprache und Schrift."

9 (*page 9*). The Indian words *kalā*, *śilpa* both have the same broad significance that the word "art" once enjoyed in Europe; cf. New Oxford Dictionary, s.v. Art. I, "Skill in doing anything as the result of knowledge and practice," and II, "Anything wherein skill may be attained or displayed." A distinction is, however, to be made between the *śilpas*, or vocational arts, and the *kalās*, or avocational arts (accomplishments). It is not conceived that a *śilpa* can be acquired without training under a master (*ācārya*), or be practiced otherwise than as an hereditary profession. There are various lists of *śilpas*, generally eighteen in number, and always including architecture and painting. In the *Triṣaṣṭiśalākāpuruṣacaritra*, I, 2, 950 ff. (Gaekwar's Oriental Series, LI, 152), there is a list of "Five Arts (*śilpa*)," viz. those of the potter, architect, painter, weaver, and barber, each with its human *raison d'être* (*hetu*). For the sixty-four *kalās* see A. Venkatasubbiah, *The Kalās* (Inaug. Diss., Bern, Madras, 1911) (add to Bibliography L. D. Barnett, *Antagaḍa Dasāo*, p. 30); and A. Venkatasubbiah, and E. Müller, "The Kalās," *JRAS.* (1914).

There is a classification of the vocational arts (*sippa*) as elevated or respectable (*ukkaṭṭha*) and lesser or vulgar (*hīna*) in the *Vinaya*, IV, 6 f. There is also a distinction generally made in the dramatic *śāstras* between a high or cultivated (*mārga*) and a popular or folk (*deśī*) style of dancing, the former embodying *rasa, bhāva, vyañjanā*, etc., the latter consisting only of rhythmic movement, and being regarded (whether rightly or wrongly) as devoid of aesthetic content.

Thus it is hardly possible, except with the connotation "more or less expressive or significant," to speak of a distinction of arts according to their psychological quality or more or less honorable application; the distinctions that are made are rather with reference to the social status of the artist than with reference to the art itself, no professional artist having a high social status as such. Thus music and calligraphy are the highest arts in China because every gentleman and official is supposed to be proficient in them, while the painter, at least until the Sung period, was always regarded *qua* artisan, not *qua* gentleman. The sculptor, though his work served the highest ends of worship, was thought of only as an expert mason; and if in India he sometimes claimed a higher respect, this was not as artist in the modern sense, but because in setting up images he also exercised priestly functions, cf. *Mīmāṁsā Nyāya Prakāśa*, paragraphs 98, 229 (in Edgerton's edition, New Haven, 1929, pp. 78, 130). Although the drama and dancing belong to the most highly developed and sophisticated arts of Asia, the status of the professional actor has been generally no higher in Asia than it was in Europe in the time of Shakespeare.

It is generally true that a concept of vocation has always and everywhere prevailed in Asia, and that the practice of any art is foreordained by birth. There are, nevertheless, exceptions to all these generalizations, even to the extent that any art may be practiced gratuitously by an amateur as an avocation; for example, at the present day in Java some of the most expert actors are members of royal families, and the daughters of princes are accomplished dancers, and this was at one time also permissible in India. Standards in such cases are as high for the amateur as for the professional, but only the latter receives his social designation from his work. Here again it appears clearly that no kind of art is thought of as high or low, noble or ignoble in itself, only *persons* being considered of high or low rank according to their natal status in an established social hierarchy.

10 (*page 10*). *Nāṭya Śāstra*, I, 113 and 112 (Gaekwar's Oriental Series).

11 (*page 10*). *Sāhitya Darpaṇa*, VI, 2, and *Daśarūpa*, I, 7, IV, 47.

12 (*page 10*). For Hsieh Ho see note 19.

13 (*page 10*). For Seami's writings see A. Waley, *The Nō Plays of Japan* (1921), Introduction. Seami says, *Yūgaku no michi wa issai monomane ari*, "The arts of music and dancing consist entirely in imitation." That this does not mean imitation or naturalism of such sort as might, in the case of painting, be based on photographs of galloping horses is well shown in the following story about a particular performance:

In the Nō play *Tahusa*, the action of a player in the part of a reaper from Shinano was criticized by a spectator from Shinano as not corresponding to the actual usage of reapers in that district, that is, as not true to Nature. In the next performance the action was "corrected"; but the performance was a failure, for "it startled the eyes."

14 (*page 12*). The "Six Limbs" are given in Yaśodhara's twelfth- or thirteenth-century commentary on the *Kāma Sūtra*, Benares ed. (1929), p. 30, as follows:

"*Rūpa-bhedaḥ, pramāṇāni, bhāva-lāvaṇya-yojanaṁ
Sādṛśyaṁ, varṇikā-bhaṅga, iti citraṁ ṣaḍaṅgakaṁ,*"

"Differentiation of types, canons of proportion, embodiment of sentiment and charm, correspondence of formal and pictorial elements, preparation (lit. "breaking," "analysis") of pigments, these are the six limbs of painting." For a more subjective interpretation see A. N. Tagore, *Sadanga, ou les Six Canons de la Peinture hindoue* (Paris, 1922).

The "Eight Limbs" of the *Samarânganasûtradhāra* (see *JAOS.*, LII, 16, n. 8) are apparently *vartikā* (the crayon), *bhūmibandhana*, (? preparation of the ground), *rekhā-karmāṇi* (outline work), *lakṣaṇa* (characteristic lineaments of the types), *karṣa-karma* (production, perhaps = *varṇa-karma*, coloring), *vartanā-karma* (shading, that is, indication of plastic modelling, relievo), *lekha-karaṇa* (? corrections), and *dvika-karma* (? final outlines).

15 (*page 14*). See De, *Sanskrit Poetics*, II, 46–47. Sound and meaning (*rutârtha*) as "letter and spirit" are discussed from another point of view, that of the inadequacy of words, in the *Laṅkâvatāra Sūtra* (Suzuki, *Studies in the Laṅkâvatāra Sūtra* (1930), pp. 108, 113, 434, and see note 43). Sound is the physical fact, words are merely an indication, a hint, a pointing out the way — "do not fall into the error of thinking that the full meaning is contained in the letter"; meaning is a manner of inner perception, only to be divined by an activity of the intellect (*prajñā, buddhi*) in distinction from all associated ideas (*vāsanā*). The relation of this view to the *dhvani* theory of suggestion discussed below will be evident. But although words or other images are necessarily incomplete means of statement and communication, the given symbol may be perfect in the sense that it could not have been better found, just as the reflection of the moon in still water may be called perfect, though the moon is not in it otherwise than as an image. Just as the reflection is not substantially a doublet of the moon, so the work of art cannot be a doublet (*savarṇa*) of its subject, though it may be according to the workman's skill a perfect embodiment of the mental image present to his consciousness. The image whether in the mind or in the work is only a means to knowledge, not in itself knowledge.

Art in the artist is the indivisible identity of form and concept, formal and pictorial elements in his mind; art in the work is the embodiment of this identity in a given material. What is meant in either case by the "concomitance" (*sāhitya, sādṛśya*) of sound and sense, pictorial and formal elements, may be inferred from *Raghuvaṁśa*, I, 1, where Pārvatī and Śiva are spoken of as two-in-one, "commingled like a sound and its meaning," *vāgarthāv iva saṁpṛktau*; cf. Bhāmaha, I, 16, *śabdârthau sahitau kāvyaṁ*, "literature is the unity of sound and sense." Sound and sense, pictorial and formal elements, are the body of art, but these intelligible elements are not the soul (*ātman*) or ultimate content of art, as will appear later according to the theories of *rasa* and *dhvani*; and that is why according to Zen doctrine (and St Augustine) all scripture, in its finite sense, is vain.

The similar term *sārūpya*, "co-aspectuality," is used in connection with the theory of empirical (*pratyakṣa*) perception, where it is asserted (see Dasgupta, *History of Indian Philosophy*, I, 151 f., and Stcherbatsky, *Buddhist Logic*, II, 12 f. — my views agreeing with Stcherbatsky's rather than with those of de la Vallée Poussin in *Mélanges chinois et bouddhiques*, p. 415) that knowledge of an object presented to the senses consists in a co-ordination (*sārūpya* = *sādṛśya*) between the form assumed by the perceiving consciousness and the aspect presented by the object. The definition of *sārūpya* cited by Stcherbatsky, *loc. cit.*, I, 213, 552, and 555, viz. *atyanta-vilakṣaṇānām sālakṣaṇyam*, "similarity of things extremely dissimilar," corresponds exactly to the Nyāya-Vaiśeṣika definition of *sādṛśya* cited in our text, implying likeness by analogy. In any case, the terms (*sādṛśya, sārūpya, sāhitya, tadākāratā, anukṛti, anurūpa*, etc.) refer, not to likeness between things (symbol and referent, picture and model, to wit), but to a correspondence between ideas and things. This correspondence tends toward identity at higher levels of reference, but attains this identity only in the Absolute, experienced "like a flash of lightning" as *sādhāraṇya* and *sāyujya* in the consummation (*samādhi*) of contemplation (*dhyāna*).

That *sādṛśya* does not mean "visual resemblance" is further seen in the fact that *sādṛśya* is precisely that kind of "likeness" or "analogy" which is involved in metaphor (*upacāra*); cf. *Sāhitya Darpaṇa*, II, 10, "Metaphor (*upacāra*) consists in the suppression of what implies a difference of sense between two terms which are quite distinct from one another, viz. by means of an overplus of correspondence (*sādṛśya*) which brings them together." Classical examples of metaphor are *gaur bāhīkaḥ*, "a *bāhīka* (peasant) is an ox," and *agnir mānavakaḥ*, "the pupil is a fire."

Corresponding to *sādṛśya*, *sārūpya*, *tadākāratā*, *tadātmya*, etc., are *sādhāraṇya* (see note 47) and *sāyujya*, the consummation of Yoga in Identity. It will be seen that these terms are at the same time exact equivalents of the Scholastic *adaequatio*, and knowledge being an *adaequatio rei et intellectus*; "The knower," in the words of Eckhart (I, 394) "being that which is known."

Hsüan Tsang translates *sādṛśya* by *ch'ou* (2508), implying the notion of reciprocity. But it cannot be said that any Chinese terms actually used in aesthetics represent an exact equivalent of *sādṛśya*; and if one wished to coin such a technical term, *ying* (13294) *ch'ou* might be suggested.

16 (*page 14*). *Sāhitya Darpaṇa*, III, 19 and 20*a*, and *Daśarūpa*, IV, 52; cf. Regnaud, *La Rhétorique sanskrite*, p. 296. The actor may enjoy aesthetic experience (*āsvāda*) as the spectator of his own performance, not *qua* performer; cf. Śaṅkarâcārya, *Śataślokī*, 7, "Or does the actor, playing a woman's part (*strīveṣadhārī*) pant for a husband, imagining himself a woman?"

17 (*page 15*). *Pramāṇa*, from root *mā*, present also in English "measure," "mete," "metre," etc. On *pramāṇa* as principle see Masson-Oursel, *Une Connexion*, etc., and *Esquisse*, etc., pp. 256, 288. Thought of not as principle, but as ascertained standard,

pramāṇa can also be used in the plural, as "canon of proportion"; see note 14. It is essential to understand that even as "authority" *pramāṇa* must not be thought of as a measure possibly contradictory to experience; on the contrary, "correct" knowledge requires a coincidence, *consonantia*, of "theory" and "fact"; cf. note 15 as to *sādṛsya* and *sāhitya*, and Woodroffe, *Garland of Letters*, p. 266. Only *pramāṇa* conceived as an attribute or name of "God" or "Buddha" as "witness" (*sākṣin*) can be called absolute; cf. Vasubandhu, *Abhidharmakośa*, VIII, 40 (Poussin, 222–225).

For Siam, cf. "The form (outline) of an object is judged by the standard of *drong* (proper forms in proper proportions) in accordance with *bāab* or example — referring to teachings of *āchāriya paramparā*" (pupillary succession), P. C. Jinavaravamsa, "Notes on Siamese Arts and Crafts," *Ceylon National Review* (July, 1907). An interesting analogy is presented by Zend *afsman*, generally "metre," but used in *Yasna*, XIX, as criterion or norm, with reference to right thought, right word, and right deed (*humatem, hukhtem, huarestem*).

18 (*page 18*). For Ching Hao see Waley, *Introduction*, etc., p. 169, and Sirén, *A History of Early Chinese Painting* (Index, *s.v.*). I may say that the text of the present work was completed and sent to press long before the appearance of Professor Sirén's admirable work in 1933; Sirén's book is probably the best account of Chinese aesthetics so far made available in a European language.

The two classes of painting here mentioned, viz. *shên* and *miao*, are the first two in the traditional threefold classification, *San p'ing*; see p. 18. Ching Hao has also two other classes, the Amazing (*ch'i*, 991) and the Clever or Skilful (*ch'iao*, 1411); the latter of these corresponds to the Accomplished (*nêng*, 8184) in the *San p'ing*. Cf. "This picture is clever (*ch'iao*) in composition and technique, but deficient in idea-movement (*i ch'ü*, 5367, 3120)."

19 (*page 19*). With Chinese *shên*, divine or spontaneous, compare also the remarks in notes 21 and 64, and Chuang Tzŭ on the Divine Man, Giles, *Chuang Tzŭ*, p. 151. *Shên-daiva*, "angelic."

Pratibhā, "illumination," is the usual designation of the poetic faculty. As to the nature of this faculty there is some difference of view. Some regard it as natural (*naisargikī*) or spontaneous (*sahajā*), or even supersensual (*lokôttarā*), making it one with the principle of form (*prajñā*) or with genius (*śakti*), and thus equivalent to Chinese *i* (5536), except that the Indian "genius" is not thought of in the European and Chinese way as functioning in rebellion against or apart from tradition. To sum up the views which are here and there expressed with varying degrees of emphasis in one direction or the other, one may say that the true artist is both born and made, both theoretically and practically equipped, by genius (*śakti*), imagination or vision (*pratibhā*), scholarship (*vyutpatti*), concentration (*samādhi*), and practice (*abhyāsa*). This is practically the view of the *Kāvyamīmāṁsā*. For the whole problem see De, *Sanskrit Poetics*, pp. 53, 369.

20 (*page 19*). The most elaborate discussion is by Petrucci. *Enclycopédie*, etc., pp. 7 ff., where the versions of Giles, Hirth, and Taki are also cited. Petrucci introduces into his interpretation a number of metaphysical ideas which are significant in themselves, but hardly justified by the text. My versions are based on Far Eastern sources kindly communicated by my friend and colleague Kojiro Tomita. The problems are also fully discussed in Sirén, *A History of Early Chinese Painting* (1933).

A connection of Hsieh Ho's Six Canons with Yaśodhara's Six Limbs (see note 14) has often been suggested. The difference of eight centuries in date does not exclude the possibility of derivation, for the Six Limbs represents nothing but a late list of ideas which were already current in India in the time of Hsieh Ho, and even as it stands may be a direct citation from older sources. However, it seems to me unnecessary to postulate any direct connection, and better to note simply the extent to which the Chinese and Indian ideas actually *correspond*.

In the first canon, the word *ch'i*, spirit, means from the Taoist point of view *life* as it proceeds from Heaven and Earth, the two modalities of the Tao, and even when understood as by Mencius in the sense of "passion-nature" or "fiery nature" represents the principle of life, as desire, the will to life. The word *ch'i* is also to be used with literal accuracy as the proper Chinese rendering of the third member of the Christian Trinity. The Indian equivalent is *prâṇa*, spiration, life, identified either directly with Brahman, or manifested as the Wind by which the Waters are stirred, so that his reflection which is the world-picture appears in them. *Ch'i* is accordingly "form" in the sense that "the soul is the form of the body"; or in the sense of desire or will to life, *ch'i* is represented by Indian *kāma* (Eros). Again, the idea *yün*, of operation or reverberation, is strictly comparable to what is meant by the *dhvani* of Indian rhetoricians (see note 49), it being only as it were by an echoing in the heart of the hearer that the full meaning of a word (or any other symbol) can be realized. The canon asserts that the ultimate theme of all art is the universal energy of the spirit, and for this point of view also many Indian parallels can be found, for example in the words of Kabīr (Bolpur, ed., I, 68) by "He is the true master (*sadguru*, or from the present point of view, true artist) who makes you perceive the Supreme Self (*paramâtman*) wherever the mind attaches itself." More theologically expressed, "Whatever may be apprehended by the mind, whatever may be perceived by the senses, whatever may be discerned by the intellect, all is but a form of Thee" (*Viṣṇu Purāṇa*, I. 4). Śaṅkarâcārya likewise asserts that art is a theophany (*ābhāsa*) when he says that Brahman is the theme equally of sacred and secular songs (Commentary on the *Brahma Sūtra*, I, I, 20). Less metaphysically, in the *Viṣṇudharmottara*, XLIII, 39, it is asserted that he is a true painter who can represent the sleeping as possessed of life or sentience (*cetanā*), the dead as devoid of it.

The second canon asserts that the vehicle of expression (as defined in the first canon) is the brush stroke or line, and it is self-evident that the brush stroke or line is in itself the most abstract and intelligible part of the work, since an outline, boundary, or limiting plane does not correspond to anything *seen* in Nature but represents an interpretation of what we see; in other words, line is not representative, but symbolic. The same is implied by Indian authorities when they remind us that it is the line (*rekhā*) that interests the master, while the public cares most about color (see p. 101 and note 73). The third and fourth canons, taken by themselves, point out that the pictorial or representative elements in a work of art are those of shape (mass or area), and color, and this too becomes self-evident if we reflect that what the eye sees in Nature is nothing but a patchwork of colors, as was recognized early in the development of Indian psychology (see note 54); colored areas, being thus the primary data of sense impression, become in the work of art the primary means of recognition; and because the attempt at recognition is the first, animal, reaction of the naïve spectator, it has been observed that color is what interests the public (see p. 101 and notes 66 and 73).

Further, if we take the first and second pairs of canons together (as we are bound to do, because we must assume the consistency of the series) and assume the general Chinese and Indian principle of the conformity of a thing to its inner nature (for example, *Mṛcchakaṭika*, IX, 16, *na hy ākṛtiḥ susadṛśam vijahāti vṛttam*, "Outer-form by no means contradicts a like inward-disposition"; *Kumārasambhava*, v. 36, *pāpavṛttaye na rūpam*, "beauty goes not with evil nature" — Mallinātha cites *yatrā kṛtis tatra guṇāḥ*, "as are the forms, so are the virtues," and *na surūpāḥ pāpasamācārā bhavanti*, "the fair do not act sinfully"; *Daśakumāracarita*, Mitragupta's adventure, *seyam ākṛtir na vyabhicarati śīlam*, "Such is her person; the character must correspond"), what we have is tantamount to an assertion that the natural unity of a painting inheres in the conformity of its significance and its presentation, and this consent is precisely what we have already recognized (p. 13 and note 15) as *consonantia*, *sādṛśya*, etc. We have seen also that the same necessity is frequently enunciated in Chinese dicta on painting, and have suggested (note 15) that if a term should have to be coined, *ying* (13294) *ch'ou* (2508) might be suitable.

The fifth canon perhaps asserts only the necessity of placing the parts of a painting in their natural logical relation, or may be taken in connection with what has been said about composition, *above*, p. 20.

The last canon is not immediately equivalent to any one of the Six Limbs, but does correspond to what is met with throughout the theory and practice of art in India, *ch'uan* being equivalent to *śāstramāna*, *nāyāt*, *vidhivat*, *sippânurūpena*, etc. For example, it is "because of traditional authority (*nāyāt*) regarding them, displayed in treatises (*śāstrarūpatā*) compiled by learned men of modern times, that the arts (*kalā*), etc., are even today current (*vartate*)," *Triṣaṣṭiśalākāpuruṣacaritra*, I, 2, 972, the reference being to the preservation of the Five Arts and their subdivisions, alluded to in note 9.

21 (*page 22*). The visible (*dṛśya*, *viṣaya*) universe may be regarded as a real theophany, shining forth, *ābhāsa*, of God (cf. Chatterji, *Kashmir Shaivism* (1914), pp. 53–61, and Eckhart's "image-bearing light"), real to the extent that we perceive its ultimate significance, *paramârtha*. More empirically expressed, God is the creator, *nirmāṇa-kāraka*, of the world-picture, *jagaccitra*, of which the beauty, *ramaṇīyatā*, is the same as that which in art is the source of disinterested pleasure, *id quod visum placet*, *dṛṣṭi-prītiṁ vidhatte*. Śankarâcārya himself uses the same simile, as follows: "On the vast canvas of the Self, the picture of the manifold worlds is painted by the Self itself, and that Supreme Self itself seeing but itself, enjoys great delight (*pramudaṁ prayāti*)" (*Svâtmanirūpaṇa*, 95). The world-picture is not here considered from the point of view of the practical activity as made up of lovely and unlovely parts, but as seen in contemplation, as an

aesthetic experience. For God is without motive or ends to be attained (*Bhagavad Gītā*, III, 22); his art is without means and not really a making or becoming, but rather a self-illumined (*svaprakāśa*), reflected modality (*ābhāsa*), or play (*līlā*), in which the gratuitous character of art attains its ultimate perfection. God is not visible in essence, but only as it were in regard, in the sensual world, according to the manner of our vision, which vision when perfected returns all creatures to their source, seeing them as He does.

This conception of God as the supreme artist, as representing the perfection toward which human art tends, has played an important part in both European and Asiatic aesthetics and theology. In Europe the idea has been current from the neo-Platonists onward, and was expressed with particular clarity by St Thomas and by Eckhart. These ideas are expressed in Chinese thought not merely by the term *shên* applied to art conceived as an unwilled manifestation, but also in the Taoist myths of the disappearance of the artist, and the coming to life of works of art, referred to in the text. These are in fact the inevitable consequences of perfection, that the artist becoming as God is no longer seen, and at the same time shares in the everlasting Now of God's timeless productivity. In Chinese Taoist tradition the attainment of perfection through art, as it were by *śilpa-yoga*, has received a specific mythical expression; but the idea of the necessary disappearance (*nivṛtta*, "involution," *abhisambhava*, "re-becoming") of the perfected being, however perfection may have been realized, naturally finds its place in all metaphysical systems. For example, *dhūtvā śarīram akṛtaṁ kṛtātmā brahma-lokam abhisambhavāmi*, "Having shaken off the body (substance), as a self made (-perfect) I am conformed to the unmade world of Brahma," *Chāndogya Upaniṣad*, VIII, 13, where total realization is implied, involving a transformation even with respect to the intelligible plane. The notion recurs, of course, in the *Vedânta Sūtras*; cf. René Guénon, *L'homme et son Devenir selon le Vedanta*, pp. 194, 195. The disappearance or merging of the poet-saint Māṇikka Vāçagar in the image of Śiva (*Tiruvā-tavūrar Purāṇa*, VII, 28–29) affords a case in point. Cf. in the Hebrew tradition, Moses, Enoch, and Elias, the last of these appearing also in the Muhammadan tradition as having drunk of the Water of Life.

The equivalent in Christianity is the Ascension; cf. Eckhart: "We may reasonably suppose that when the time came for John to go, God caused to befall him what was due to happen on the day of judgment. . . . We may take it that his body, which was destined to perish here on earth, was disintegrated in the air, so that there entered into God only the being of his body, which would have accompanied the soul at the last day." The rationale of the disappearance proceeds immediately from the distinction of the sensible from the intelligible spheres of manifestation, Kāmadhātu or Kāmaloka, and Rūpadhātu or Rūpaloka (see note 74). The *śilpa-sthāna-kauśala*, or operative facility of the practical intellect, functions only on the sensible plane, where "work" is to be done; intellectual creation (*nirmāṇa*), functioning on both planes, (1) on the sensible plane is embodied by human will in a *work* of art, which "lives" and has "movement" only metaphorically, and (2) on the intelligible plane is immediately manifested as formal life. In any case, that art may be thought of as a "way" is most of all apparent in the fact that aesthetic perception is essentially disinterested.

22 (*page 24*). Recognition is not dependent on verisimilitude, but is by convention; the realistic spectator reverses the "imitative" procedure of the artist who has given form to natural shape, by interpreting the manufactured image (*rūpa*) as though it were the thing itself present to the eye (*pratyakṣa*) (Bhartṛhari, *Vākyapadīya*, III, 7, 5).

23 (*page 30*). In the *Laṅkâvatāra Sūtra*, *loc. cit.*, the unreality of appearances is illustrated by various similes, among them that of painted surfaces (*citrakṛta-pradeśā*) which are seen as if in relief (*nimnônnatā*), although really flat (*animnônnatā*).

24 (*page 32*). *Svapnavāsavadattā*, VI, 13, and *Mṛcchakaṭika*, IV, 0, 3. So also in *Mṛcchakaṭika*, IX, 16, *susadṛśa* is "true resemblance." Cf. *vṛddhisadṛśa*, "old-looking," in *Śukranītisāra*, IV, 4, 201, and *sadṛśa*, "the like" (= "etc."), in Vasubandhu's *Abhidharmakośa*, IX (Poussin, p. 275). For "exact likeness" we have also *tadānurūvaṁ* (*-rūpam*) in Haribhadra's *Āvaśyaka Ṭīkā*, II, 8, 2 and 3, and *pratyakṣam* in the *Karpūramañjarī*, I, 30.

In the *Viṣṇudharmottara*, III, 41, 2, *sādṛśya* is a noun, and *kiñcilloka-sādṛśya* must be taken to mean "in which there is a similitude only partially connected with the material world"; in any case nothing like an injunction to realism could be thought of, for the *satya* painting in question has clearly to do with the angelic sphere, and *pramāṇa* as well as *sādṛśya* are required in it. My version in *JAOS.*, LII, 13, needs correction accordingly; cf. my "Painter's Art in Ancient India; Ajaṇṭā," in *Journ. Indian Society of Oriental Art*, I, 26, n. 2.

25 (*page 38*). "Imagist" might perhaps be suitably rendered by *adhyavāsana*, "introsusceptive," *Sāhitya Darpaṇa*, II, 8-9.

Indian parallels to Zen are naturally not lacking; for example, in Jātaka, no. 460, the evanescence of the morning dew suffices to enlightenment, and analogous to the story of Tan Hsia is that of the Tamil poetess and devotee, Auvvai, who when she was rebuked for sitting with her feet outstretched towards the image in a temple, an act of formal disrespect, admitted her fault, but added, "If you will point out to me in what direction God is not to be found, I will there stretch out my feet." There are likewise abundant parallels in European tradition, for example in the Gospels, and in Eckhart and Blake.

26 (*page 39*). Chinese *ch'an* (348), Japanese *zen* = Sanskrit *dhyāna*, Pali *jhāna*.

27 (*page 41*). Version by Waley, italics mine.

28 (*page 43*). A Japanese *hokku*; in poems of this kind the hearer is expected to complete the thought in his own mind; cf. the Chinese phrase "to give spiritual form (*shên*) to the very part left undelineated," and what has been said above as to the literal inadequacy but practical efficiency of words (note 15), and below on the spectator's own effort (note 43).

29 (*page 44*). *Ukiyoye* means "pictures of the fleeting world"; the Japanese print is its typical product, but there are also paintings of the same kind.

30 (*page 45*). An allusion to the Persian Ṣūfī story of Lailā and Majñūn. When it was objected to Majñūn that Lailā was not so beautiful as he pretended, he answered, "To see the beauty of Lailā requires the eyes of Majñūn."

31 (*page 45*). Tiruveṅkaṭa's admirable preface to the Telugu edition (1887) of the *Abhinaya Darpaṇa* (see Coomáraswamy and Duggirala, *The Mirror of Gesture*, Cambridge, Massachusetts, 1917) may well be quoted here. Tiruveṅkaṭa first alludes to the neglect of the art and science of the mimetic dance (nautch) in modern times, which neglect had been mainly the result of European and puritanical influences, though he does not say as much, and then proceeds to a reassertion of the normal Hindu point of view:

"It is known to everyone that in these days our people not merely neglect this lore as though it were of a common sort, but go so far as to declare it to be an art that is only suited for the entertainment of the vulgar, unworthy of cultivated men, and fit to be practiced only by play-actors. But it is like the Union-Science (*yoga-śāstra*) which is the means of attaining spiritual freedom (*mokṣa*); and the reason why it has come to be regarded in such a fashion is that it is by movements of the body (*aṅgikābhinaya*) that the lineaments and interplay of the hero and heroine, etc., are clearly exhibited, so as to direct men in the way of righteousness, and to reveal an esoteric meaning, obtaining the appreciation of connoisseurs and those who are learned in the lore of gesture. But if we understand this science with finer insight, it will be evident that it has come into being to set forth the sport and pastime of Śrī Krishna, who is the progenitor of every world, and the patron deity of the flavor of love (*śṛṅgāra-rasa*); so that by clearly expressing the flavor, and enabling men to taste thereof, it gives them the wisdom of Brahmā, whereby they may understand how every business is unstable; from which understanding arises aversion to such business, and therefrom arise the highest virtues of peace and patience, and thence again may be won the Bliss of Brahmā.

"It has been declared by Brahmā and others that the mutual relations of hero and heroine, in their esoteric meaning, partake of the nature of the relation of master and disciple, mutual service and mutual understanding; and therefore the Bharata Śāstra, which is a means to the achievement of the Four Ends of Human Life, Virtue, Wealth, Pleasure, and Spiritual Freedom, — and is a most exalted science, practiced even by the gods, — should also be practiced by ourselves."

32 (*page 45*). *Sāhitya Darpaṇa*, III, 9. *Vāsanā*, as "affect-ion," "perfuming," is the latent memory of past experience, and consequent present sensibility. Alike from the aesthetic and generally human point of view, *vāsanā* may be considered a necessary evil. Regarded as an affective aptitude, a liability to direct sympathy for, or prejudice on behalf of, ourselves or others, it represents a hindrance equally to enlightenment in general and to aesthetic experience in particular; but as the necessary basis for such ideal and disinterested sympathy as we feel at the spectacle of joy and sorrow represented in art, it is prerequisite to aesthetic experience. Cf. note 47.

The ideal character of poetic sensibility, that is to say the disinterested nature of aesthetic contemplation, is constantly insisted upon in the Alaṁkāra literature. It is pointed out, for example, in the *Sāhitya Darpaṇa*, III, 5 and 6, that even in the case of works of art of which the themes are in themselves distressing, no pain is felt by the spectator, but only delight, to which those who take intelligent delight in art bear unanimous witness.

33 (*page 46*). For *rasa*, etc., theories applied to painting or sculpture, see *JAOS.*, LII, 15, n. 5, and Basava Raja, *Śiva Tattva Ratnākara* (ed. Madras, 1927), VI, 2, 19.

34 (*page 46*). *Kāvya*, specifically poetry (prose or verse), also embraces the general idea of "art"; essential meanings present in the root *kū* include "wisdom" and "skill." One may compare Blake's use of "Poetic Genius" as equivalent to "Imagination" in the broadest sense of the word, and to the analogy of Greek ποίησις, denoting to the making of anything, for example, "creatures" or a ship.

35 (*page 46*). For example in the *Mālatīmādhava*, I, 33, 9–10, where the purpose of a portrait (*ālekhya-prayojana*) is consolation in longing (*utkaṇṭhāvinodana*), or *Priyadarśikā*, I, 3, where the play has "desired fruit," *vāñchita-phala*.

36 (*page 46*). *Sāhitya Darpaṇa*, I, 3. Cf. "As to the fact that the soul of poetry is flavor, and the like, there exists no difference of opinion" — *Vyaktiviveka*; and "All poetry lives by *rasa*" — Abhinavagupta.

37 (*page 47*). Meaning or utility is the indispensable motive of all art, but from the Indian point of view that is not art which does not also subserve the ultimate end of aesthetic experience, which is not so, or is so only to the most limited degree, in cases of bare efficacy, bare descriptive statement, or even "illustrative poetry," *citrakāvya*. For example, a piece of corrugated iron may keep out the rain, and may be called art inasmuch as it is a product of knowledge and technical skill, but it is scarcely a roof, architecturally speaking; in science, mere illustration and classification are scarcely art, but an elegant mathematical equation,

or any well-designed tool such as a telescope, is art. Any use of words or application of intelligence is art of a sort, but bare statement and efficacy are the crudest kind of art, not "primitive," but elementary, inasmuch as they are not far removed from functional exclamation. It is here if anywhere that a distinction of degree can be drawn between "fine" and "servile" art. But it is beneath the dignity of man to maintain his existence on a level of bare utility and functional necessity, and, as has been well said by Ruskin, "industry without art is brutality."

38 (*page 47*). To call a work of art *rasavat*, or ideally beautiful, is not strictly legitimate, but simply a manner of speaking and by projection, imputation, or inference (*anumāna*) or figuratively (*upacāra*); for it is constantly insisted that *rasa* is not an objective quality present in the work of art or any of its parts. Cf. Mukherjee, *Essai*, etc., p. 66; De, *Sanskrit Poetics*, II, 205, and note 43, below.

39 (*page 48*). *Sāhitya Darpaṇa*, III, 20*b*, ff.

40 (*page 48*). *Mālavikâgnimitra*, I, 4, *bhinna-rucer janasya*, "people of divers tastes."
    "What Aesthetic, which implies thought and concept of art, can have to do with pure taste without concept is difficult to say," Croce, "The Breviary of Aesthetic," in *Rice Institute Pamphlet*, II (1915), 305.

41 (*page 48*). *Daśarūpa*, IV, 90. The opposite view, that art (especially drama, music, painting, and sumptuary arts) is nothing but a luxury, a tickling of the senses, is maintained only from a monastic, puritanical, and really naïvely materialistic view, mainly in early Buddhist and Jaina works, to a more limited extent in the *Dharma Śāstras*, and in modern times as a result of European influence; cf. note 31. Amongst Buddhist and Jaina texts might be cited *Brahma-Jāla Sutta*, I, 1, 13; *Visuddhi Magga*, 38; and *Āyārāṁga Sutta*, II, lect. 13.

42 (*page 50*). Cf. Maritain, *Introduction to Philosophy*, p. 263,
n. 1: "the word *aesthetics* is derived etymologically from (the
Greek word for) sensibility ($\alpha\iota\sigma\nu\theta\acute{a}\nu o\mu a\iota$ = feel), whereas art,
and beauty also, are matters of the intellect, quite as much as of
feeling." Were this more generally realized, much sentimentality
in current thinking about art might be avoided.

43 (*page 50*). *Daśarūpa*, IV, 47, 50. Cf. *Laṅkâvatāra Sūtra*, II,
117, 118. *Raṅge na vidhyate citraṁ na bhūmau na ca bhājane* . . .
tattvaṁ hy akṣaravarjitam, "the (real) picture is not in the color,
nor in the surface, nor in the surroundings (but in the mind) . . .
the principle transcends the letter." In this passage *bhājana*
may be the painter's saucer of color, as means or material cause
of the work, but more abstractly considered as "receptacle"
means the environment of the work of art, or even the physical
world; cf. the cosmos as *bhājana*, "receptacle," Vasubandhu,
Abhidharmakośa, III, 44 (Poussin, p. 182 f.).

Cf. Confucius, *Analects*, XVII, xi, "Are bells and drums all
that is meant by music?"; and Walt Whitman,

> All music is what wakes in you when you are reminded of it
> by the instruments,
> It is not in the violins and the cornets . . . nor the score of
> the baritone singer,
> It is nearer and further than they.

44 (*page 50*). Dharmadatta, cited in *Sāhitya Darpaṇa*, III, 9a,
commentary.

45 (*page 51*). *Sāhitya Darpaṇa*, III, 2 and 3, and commentary;
Dhvanyālocana, Nirṇaya Sāgara ed., p. 11.

46 (*page 51*). *Daśarūpa*, IV, 51; *Sāhitya Darpaṇa*, III, 19–20.

47 (*page 52*). *Sādhāraṇya* is analogous to empathy, *Einfühlung*;
vāsanā ("perfuming") is innate or acquired sensibility, an emotional tendency which, though it may be developed as sentimentality, is nevertheless essential to the possibility of *sādhāraṇya* as ideal sympathy. *Sādhāraṇya* is another aspect of that

"consent" which we have already recognized as *sādṛsya, sāhitya, sārūpya, tadākāratā.*

To continue what has been said in note 32: aesthetic sympathy is ideal, without any ethical element; that is to say, it is felt equally with respect to good and evil, pleasure or pain, as represented. An ethical sympathy may indeed be legitimately felt with regard to such a hero as Rāma represented as a model of conduct in a poem, play, or painting, but such sympathy belongs to the proximate value of art in relation to *dharma,* not to aesthetic appreciation (*āsvāda*), wherein the spectator sees as if with the eye of God, who "regards neither the good nor the evil works of anyone" (*Bhagavad Gītā,* V, 15), but "makes his sun to shine alike upon the just and the unjust," for "the vision of God transcends virtues," Eckhart, I, 273. The impartiality of aesthetic reproduction, the fact that art as such is related rather to law than to equity, is well brought out in the *Nāṭya Śāstra,* I, 112 ff.; see translation in the *Mirror of Gesture,* p. 2.

48 (*page 52*). *Daśarūpa,* IV, 45.

49 (*page 53*). *Dhvani* is literally "sound," especially sound like that of thunder or a drum, hence "resonance" or "overtone" of meaning. A striking analogy can be found in the first canon of Hsieh Ho as written with the character *yün* (13843), that the essential in art is "the reverberation (*yün*) of the spirit in the forms of life," the idea of sound*ing* rather than of mere sound being present both in *dhvani* and in *yün* (13843). Significant synonyms of *vyañjanā,* lit. "revealing," are *dhvanana,* "echoing," and *gamana,* "motion." As to the latter, it may be observed that when anything is spoken of as represented in an image, it is said to be *citragata,* "gone into representation"; cf. Eckhart, "to be properly expressed, a thing must proceed from within, moved by its form," and Leonardo, "That drawing is best which best expresses the passion that animates the figure." *Vyañjanā,* however, viz. in Buddhist usage, means only the "letter" as opposed to the "spirit" or "meaning" (*attha* = *artha*). The later

sense endows the "letter" with a suggestive significance beyond the literal.

50 (*page 53*). See Dhvanikāra, *Dhvanyālokalocana* ("The Eye of Perception of Content"), cited by Mukherjee, *Essai*, etc., pp. 85–90.

51 (*page 54*). From the point of view of the *Laṅkâvatāra Sūtra*, the two chief hindrances are *kleśâvaraṇa* (sensual attachment) and *jñeyâvaraṇa* (mental or systematic hindrances), one might say affections and prejudices. Cf. Blake, "man has closed himself up. . . . If the doors of perception were cleansed, all things would appear as they are, Infinite." It must be borne in mind that from the Indian point of view enlightenment and perfection are always virtually present, that is, not to be *acquired* by any means but only to be *revealed* when the mirror of the soul is cleansed from dust. This is a metaphor particularly applicable in the aesthetic field; aesthetic contemplation cannot be taught; all that can be done is to break down the barriers that stand in the way of realization.

52 (*page 56*). A clear distinction is here drawn between the functional means of perception as they are in themselves (for example, the eye's intrinsic faculty), and their use determined by intelligence; voice (*vāc* = *viṣaya śabda*) in this passage is to be distinguished from speech (*vāc*) in the *Bṛhadāraṇyaka Upaniṣad*, IV, 1, where speech is identified with discrimination or pure intellect (*prajñā*), and in *Chāndogya Upaniṣad*, VII, 2, where speech "makes known" name.

"Name and aspect" (*nāma-rūpa*) are the fundamental conventions (respectively intelligible and sensible) by which phenomena are knowable (discriminated). Thus in the *Śatapatha Brāhmaṇa*, XI, 2, 3, name and aspect are treated as the two manifestations of the Brahman, whereby He is known in the contingent universe, "aspect being intellect, inasmuch as it is by intellect that one seizes aspect," and "name being speech, inasmuch as it is by speech that one seizes name," and these two are not distinguishable in nature, for "whatever is name is indeed aspect." The last passage really asserts the identity in principle of all arts; cf. Eckhart, "form is a revelation of essence" (380) and "the soul knows only in effigy." Further, "As far as there are name and aspect, so far indeed extends this world" (*Ś. Br., ibid.*). Cf. *Kauṣītaki Upaniṣad*, I, 3, where Mānasī and Cākṣuṣī, "Intelligence" and "Perception," are personified as the consorts of Brahma and immediate causes of the phenomenal universe. But in Brahman, called Spectator or Overseer (*paridraṣṭṛ*), name and aspect as human modes of perception and representation are transcended (*Praśna Upaniṣad*, VI, 5). There are in fact three modes of vision, that of the functional fleshly eye (*māṁsa-cakṣu*), the angelic eye (*divya-cakṣu*, the intellect), and the eye of transcendent wisdom (*prajñā-cakṣu*, gnosis), respectively functional, all-seeing, and seeing in simultaneity. The last is the third eye of Śiva, which destroys, or rather trans-forms, appearance by its non-perception of duality. So, in the last analysis, "It is not aspects that one should seek to understand, but the Seer (*draṣṭṛ*) of aspects" (*Kauṣītaki Upaniṣad*, III, 8): "seeing Whom, nought else remains to be seen, *yad dṛṣṭvā nāparaṁ dṛśyam*" (Śaṅkarâcārya, *Ātmabodha*, 55). He who thus attains the world of Brahman becomes a "Seer without duality (*draṣṭā advaitaḥ*), this is man's highest path, his highest bliss, etc." (*Bṛhadāraṇyaka Upaniṣad*, IV, 3, 32).

It should be noticed once for all that, just as in English, so in Sanskrit very many words, for example *vāc*, *rūpa*, are necessarily used in two senses, empirical and ideal, or even in three senses, literal, ideal, and transcendental. *Rūpa*, however, when correlated with *nāma*, has always to be rendered by "aspect" rather than by "form"; it is really *nāma*, "name," or "idea," that is the determining principle or "form" of the species. Thus with respect to man, *nāma-rūpa* is "soul and body"; the soul being the "form" of the body. To render *nāma-rūpa* by "name and form" is tautological.

For the distinction of speech from sound cf. Chuang Tzŭ:
"Speech is not mere breath. It is differentiated by meaning"
(Giles, *Chuang Tzŭ*, 1889, p. 16).

53 (*page 56*). *Ibid.*, IV, 1, 7, the heart (*hṛdaya*) is said to be the
support of all things, the highest Brahman; cf. note 3. The heart
is thus a synonym for the centre and entirety of being. This has
to be borne in mind in connection also with the term *sahṛdaya*,
"having heart," equivalent to *rasika* and *pramātṛ*.

54 (*page 56*). *Atthasālinī*, p. 317; Woodward, *Gradual Sayings*, I,
159, n. 2; Keith, *Buddhist Philosophy*, p. 169.

55 (*page 61*). Maritain, *Art and Scholasticism*, p. 1.

56 (*page 61*). Meister Eckhart was born in Saxony or Thuringia
about 1260. He became a professor in Paris, and later held
very high clerical positions in Bohemia and Germany. He was
suspected of heresy, and condemned in 1329, two years after
his death. He taught not in Latin but in the vernacular,
and has been called the father of the German language. St
Thomas had died (1274) while he was still a youth; Tauler and
Ruysbroeck were his contemporaries, and had probably heard
him preach. The materials cited in the present essay are derived
from *Meister Eckhart*, translated by C. de B. Evans from Franz
Pfeiffer's collected German edition of 1857, in two volumes, London, 1924 and 1931; the page references are to the first volume
unless otherwise stated.

Eckhart presents an astonishingly close parallel to Indian
modes of thought; some whole passages and many single sentences read like a direct translation from Sanskrit. See from this
point of view R. Otto, *Mysticism East and West* (New York,
1931), and my *New Approach to the Vedas* (London, 1934).

It is not of course suggested that any Indian elements whatever are actually present in Eckhart's writing, though there are
some Oriental factors in the European tradition, derived from
neo-Platonic and Arabic sources. But what is proved by the

analogies is not the influence of one system of thought upon another, but the coherence of the metaphysical tradition in the world and at all times.

57 (*page 62*). In this respect, Eckhart's nearest and natural descendant is Blake; for example, Jesus and his Disciples were all Artists; Praise is the Practice of Art; Israel delivered from Egypt is Art delivered from Nature and Imitation; The Eternal Body of Man is the Imagination; The gods of Greece and Egypt were Mathematical Diagrams; Eternity is in love with the productions of time; Man has no Body distinct from his Soul; If the doors of perception were cleansed, all things would appear to man as they are, infinite; In Eternity All is Vision.

58 (*page 62*). Cf. *tridhā*, *saṁhitā* in the Upaniṣads, for example *Bṛhadāraṇyaka Up.*, I, 2, 3 and *Taittirīya Up.*, I, 3, 1–3.

59 (*page 64*). All ritual, offices, and sacraments (*pūjā*, *yajña*, *saṁskāra*) are art. For transubstantiation see Eckhart, 87, 477: "the sacrament nourishes like any other food. But it has none of the nature of bread" (477), just as with other works of art, which may please any sense, but are to be taken in another sense, allegorical or anagogic. The Catholic view is that though a man may be drawn to any work of art (such as scripture) *causa voluptatis*, he may well proceed *rationem artis intelligere*. Cf. *Laṅkāvatāra Sūtra*, II, 118, 119, where a painting is said to be produced in colors "for the sake of attracting (*karṣaṇa*) spectators," though the very picture is not in the colors (*range na citram*), but subsists as the art in the artist, and by the spectator's own effort again as art in him.

60 (*page 72*). Leonardo's *il pittore pinge se stesso*, perhaps the first enunciation of the principle on which depends the validity of the modern game of attribution.

61 (*page 78*). This point of view still survives in Dante's *Chi pinge figura, si non può esser lei, non la può porre.*

62 (*page 84*). Deliberate conventionalizing, calculated search for the abstract or so-called ideal, as in the modern practice of designing, and in archaism, is a different activity, not a "singling out the best" I *can*, but what I *like* best.

63 (*page 88*). "The heathen philosopher Aristotle says, 'Were there no house nor place and no materials it would be all one being, one matter, which being divided is like another soul'" (II, 290).

St Thomas (*Sum. Theol.*, III, Q. 23, A. 3): "the form of a house already built is like the mental word of the builder in its specific form, but not in intelligibility, because the material form of a house is not intelligible, as it was in the mind of the builder."

64 (*page 91*). Human nature as it is in God "does not appear in the looking-glass image . . . only just the features are seen in the mirror" (51), the features being the accidents of being, not the man as he *is*. Cf. the Chinese phrase for portraiture, *fu shên*, "portraying the divine image in a man."

The history of portraiture in Europe provides an interesting and rather unhappy contrast to the Chinese and Indian notions of *fu shên*, "portraying soul," and *sva-rūpa*, "intrinsic aspect." In what follows, quotations are from Jitta-Zadoks, *Ancestral Portraiture in Rome* (Amsterdam, 1932), pp. 87, 92 f. The tendency to realism and the use of death masks are "two coördinate consequences of one and the same mentality. . . . This mentality will bring about as well portraits of extreme realism (so-called verism) as the practice of making moulds on the actual features" of the living model. Now, tomb effigies came into use about 1200: "These statues first represented the deceased not as he actually appeared after death but as he hoped and trusted to be on the day of Judgment. This . . . is apparent in the pure and happy expression of all the equally youthful and equally beautiful faces which have lost every trace of individuality. But towards the end of the XIIIth century . . . interest turned from the heavenly Future to the worldly Present. Not how the dead would perhaps appear one day but how they had actually been in life was considered important. More or less likeness was now wanted. . . . As the last consequence of this demand for exact likeness the death mask, taken from the actual features, made its appearance . . . rationalism and realism appearing at the same time. . . . The death mask . . . really did help the artist to draw near to Nature and this it achieved by teaching him the construction of the face . . . (at last) . . . the head is constructed from within and is created by the artist as by Nature herself." The history of post-Renaissance European art thus takes on the aspect of a reanimation of the corpses in a charnel house (cf. *Speculum*, April, 1933, Pl. XI), rather than that of a Resurrection of the Dead in a more glorious form. One begins to see why Śukrâcārya could speak of portraiture as *asvargya*. "Portraiture belongs to civilisations that fear death" (Kramrisch, *Indian Sculpture*, p. 134).

With respect to the representation of the deceased, not as they may have looked in real life but as they "hoped and trusted to be on the day of Judgment," compare (1) the Indian, and more typically Cambodian and Javanese, practice of representing deceased ancestors in the form of the deity to whom they had been devoted, and (2) in the *Saddharma Puṇḍarīka* the resurrection of past Buddhas and Bodhisattvas in glorified bodies — iconographic representations always reproducing the "exemplary elements" or lineaments (*lakṣaṇa*) of these glorified bodies, rather than any of those individual accidents by which the man might have been recognized at the time of his earthly ministry.

65 (*page 100*). For the full context see Coomaraswamy and Duggirala, *The Mirror of Gesture*, pp. 14, 15.

66 (*page 101*). It is possible, therefore, that in making *varṇâḍhya* Duryodhana's first exclamation some sarcasm is intended.

67 (*page 103*). Cf. *Triṣaṣṭiśalākāpuruṣacaritra*, I, 1, 360, where a man whose eyes are fastened to the (? painted) forms of beautiful women, etc., is said to stumble (*skhalati*), as if the border of his

garment had been caught on a hedge. Cf. "there is no actual relief in a painting, and yet we see it there," *citre* . . . *natônnataṁ nâsti ca, dṛśyate atha ca, Mahāyāna Sūtrâlaṁkāra*, XIII, 17; cf. *Laṅkâvatāra Sūtra* and see note 23.

In the *Śakuntalā*, the "hills and vales" may be either those of the bodies of beautiful women represented in the picture, *nimnônnata* having this application in *Mālatīmādhava*, IV, 10, or those of the landscape background, *pradeśa* having this sense in the *Śakuntalā* itself, *infra*, VI, 19, and perhaps also in *Laṅkâvatāra Sūtra*, p. 91.

68 (*page 104*). Viz. *rūpa-śobhā*, as in *Divyâvadāna*, p. 361.

69 (*page 106*). Similarly in the case of the dancing competition, *Vikramacaritra, HOS.*, XXVII, 15, the two apsarases first dance together and the assembly of the gods is delighted, *nṛtyaṁ dṛṣṭvā saṁtoṣam agamat*.

70 (*page 106*). The text here, vv. 4, 5, and 6, is almost identical with *Mālavikâgnimitra*, II, 3, 6, and 8.

71 (*page 107*). "Judgment" is *vivādanirṇaya*. In the *Mālavikâgnimitra*, the King as connoisseur is *viśeṣajña*, as judge, *praśnika*.

72 (*page 107*). Ryder, in *HOS.*, IX, 44, renders admirably the substance of Cārudatta's remarks, but with a European nuance and avoiding all the technicalities. The *Mṛcchakaṭika* passage is anticipated in a briefer form in Bhāsa's *Daridra-Cārudatta*, II, 2.

73 (*page 108*). It is constantly brought out that craftsman and critic attach principal importance to the drawing, by which the moods are expressed, but that what the public cares about is color. As Binyon has observed, "The painting of Asia is throughout its main tradition an art of line."

74 (*page 109*). The nearest to anything of this kind in connection with the formative arts occurs in *Jātaka*, VI, 332, where the Bodhisattva employs a master-architect (*mahā-vaḍḍhaki*) to build a hall such as he requires.

The master-architect does not grasp the Great Being's idea (*mahāsatta-cittaṁ na gaṇhati*), and when corrected explains that he can work only according to the tradition of the craft (*sippânurūpena*), and knows no other way (*aññatha na jānāmǐti*). The Bodhisattva himself then lays out the plan "as if Viśvakarma himself had done it." Even so, the form of the hall is determined entirely by the use to which it is to be put; the Bodhisattva's plan is not a personal whim or a piece of self-expression, it is simply that he knows better than the architect all that is present to the mind of the divine craftsman, the "All-maker."

This supernatural virtuosity (*kauśala*) of the Bodhisattva is described in the *Lalita Vistara*, Ch. XII: it is a command of the arts not acquired by study, *na ca . . . yogyā kṛtā . . . śilpakauśalam* (Lefmann's ed., p. 156, l. 1). Cf. the *Mahāyāna Sūtrâlaṁkāra* of Asaṅga, VII, 6, where the sage (*dhīragata*, "who has become a seer") is said to exhibit a threefold *nirmāṇa*, "manifestation" or "facility," the first of these being displayed in the field of art (*śilpakarma-sthāna*).

More fully in Vasubandhu's *Abhidharmakośa*, II, 71–72 (Poussin, p. 320), virtuosity (*kauśala*) in art (*śilpa-sthāna*) and the power of mental creation are two of the four mental activities exhibited by a perfected being on the sensible plane of manifestation (*Kāmadhātu, Kāmaloka*). Of these two, the *śilpa-sthāna-kauśala*, or facility of the practical or operable intellect, is naturally absent on the intelligible plane of manifestation (*Rūpadhātu, Rūpaloka*), while both, of course, are absent on the supersensual super-rational plane of non-manifestation (*Dharmadhātu, Arūpyaloka*). . . . The same idea is expressed in another way by the attribution of an absolute *pramāṇa* to the perfected being, all other *pramāṇas* being merely as to what is correct under certain circumstances; see note 17.

There are some minor references to originality in poetry. Thus, Rājaśekhara, *Kāvyamīmāṁsā*, XI (see De, *Sanskrit Poetics*, II, 373), discussing plagiarism (*haraṇa*, "theft") at some length, says that the great poet (*mahākavi*) depicts something new (*nūtana*) in meaning and expression as well as what is old; and flagrant stealing (*pariharaṇa*) is called unpoetical or inartistic, *akavitvadāyi*. An example occurs in the *Karpūramañjarī*, III, 31, where the King compliments the heroine on her verses, remarking on her seizure (*daṁsaṇa*) of new motifs (*nava-vastu*), varied vocabulary (*ukti-vicitratva*), and sense of beauty (*ramaṇīyatā*) and on the flow of *rasa*.

75 (*page 113*). The printed text is that cited by Paṇḍit Jībânanda Vidyāsāgara (Calcutta, 2nd ed., 1890). The only complete translation is that of Benoy Kumar Sarkar, *The Sukranīti* (Allahābād, 1914, *Sacred Books of the Hindus*, Vol. XII). An introduction to this translation, by Dr. (Sir) Brajendranath Seal, entitled *The Positive Background of Hindu Sociology*, forms vols. XVI and XXV in the same series.

76 (*page 117*). Masson-Oursel, "Une Connexion dans l'Esthétique et la Philosophie de l'Inde," *Rev. des Arts Asiatiques*, II, (1923), and H. Zimmer, *Kunstform und Yoga im indischen Kultbild* (Berlin, 1926).

77 (*page 117*). A. K. Coomaraswamy, "Nāgara Painting," *Rūpam* 37, 40 (1929), and *Viṣṇudharmottara*, III, 41, *JAOS.*, LII (1932).

78 (*page 122*). In English, we often distinguish *parokṣa* terms by capitals; for example, in distinguishing Self from self, both represented in Skr. *ātman*, or when we distinguish Cross as symbol from such crosses as are represented in the letter x.

79 (*page 123*). *yasmād devāh*, Śaṅkarâcārya on *Ait. Up.*, III, 14; more freely translated, "for, indeed, just what the Angels are is Pure Intelligences."

80 (*page 125*). Cf. *Bṛhadār. Up.*, I, 4, 17, "Verily by perception (*cakṣuṣā*) He comes into possession of his human (*mānuṣa*) possessions (*vitta*)."

81 (*page 125*). Iconography (*pratimākaraṇa*) as art in being is to be distinguished from iconography (*rūpa-bheda*) as a science, useful or necessary to the artist or student.

82 (*page 126*). *Anukṛti* is "imitation" in the sense *Ars imitatur naturam in sua operatione*, which does *not* mean *imitatur entem naturatam*, our environment.

The same notion is implicit in many passages of the *Ṛg Veda*; for example, V, 2, 11, where the artistry of the incantation (*mantra*, cf. *mantrayanti* with reference to angelic intercommunication, *ibid.*, I, 164, 10) is compared to that of a carpenter or weaver.

83 (*page 126*). A point of view equating "criticism" and "reproduction" may be represented here, as it is certainly in later Indian aesthetic.

84 (*page 126*). *Psychological Types*, p. 601.

85 (*page 127*). "Nature" here in the popular sense of *ens naturata*, phenomenal environment. The "worship of Nature" in this sense implies "pantheism." Needless to say that "Nature," interpreted at a higher level of reference, viz. as *natura naturans* (= *prakṛti*, *māyā*, etc.), and "Nature" as the "Mother of the Son of God" have both the same reference (it is by Her that He takes on human nature). "To find nature herself" (in this sense) "all her likenesses must be shattered" (Eckhart). That iconoclasm may be accomplished in two different ways, respectively *parokṣāt* and *pratyakṣeṇa*: in the first case, intellectually, by making the proper references, in the second case, brutally, by a literal "destruction of idols."

86 (*page 129*). His intrinsic manifestation (*svarūpa*) is the manifestation of very different things (*viśvarūpa*).

87 (*page 130*). When the Lord (*īśvara*) is spoken of in His unitary aspect, the Spoken Word is single.

88 (*page 131*). Inasmuch as Wisdom is measured out into parts, it cannot be argued that "close hidden" means only *in potentia*, in the Godhead, Para-Brahman, *solus ante principium*, *pūrṇa apravartin*, where things are not even "thought" under the con-

tingent aspect of distinction. "Hidden," etc., is tantamount to *in principio*.

89 (*page 133*). *Ghana*, from *ghan*, to strike, hinder, etc., has a primary sense of "dense mass," implying a condensation of multiple factors without extension in space. Hence "mere" or "essential": or *prajñāna-ghana* might be more freely rendered as "exemplary understanding."

90 (*page 134*). Cf. my "Parāvṛtti = Transformation, regeneration, Anagogy," in *Festschrift Ernst Winternitz*, 1933.

91 (*page 136*). In what follows, the *pratyakṣa* notions are again distinguished by italics.

92 (*page 136*). G. Dandoy, S. J., *L'Ontologie du Vedânta* (Paris, 1932), p. 125.

In *Bṛhadār. Up.*, III, 4, 2, Hume renders *sâkṣāt aparokṣa* (equivalent to *paramârthika pratyakṣa*) by "present and not beyond our ken." But the meaning is "immediately," not as thus implied, "objectively." "Not beyond our ken" belies the sense; the Brahman, who is the Self in us and all things (as is emphasized in the text itself) cannot be an object of knowledge.

Suzuki, *Laṅkâvatāra Sūtra*, p. xxvi, renders (*paramârthika-*) *pratyakṣa* by "intuitive penetration."

Stcherbatsky, *Buddhist Logic*, II, 284, translating a passage from Vācaspatimitra in which the presumed identity of an object known in the past and in the present is under discussion, renders *parokṣa*, qualifying the previous cognition, as "transcends the ken," and *aparokṣa*, qualifying the present cognition as "does not transcend the ken," and this in the given context seems to be quite legitimate. Again, *ibid.*, p. 333, n. 1, "objects are divided into (1) evident facts (*pratyakṣa*), (2) inferred facts (*parokṣa*) of whom (*sic*) we have formerly had some experience, (3) very much concealed facts (*atyanta-parokṣa* = *šin-tu-lkog-pa*) which are either transcendental, unimaginable entities, or else facts never experienced, but nevertheless not unimaginable."

Mānasa-pratyakṣa is "attention" (Stcherbatsky, loc. cit., II, 328, n. 2).

Muir, Sanskrit Texts, IV, 22, renders *parokṣa* "esoterically." "Paradoxical," "enigmatic," or "mysterious" would be satisfactory renderings only if taken in their strictly technical senses.

93 (*page 137*). We do not think of the technical language of a special science as "obscure," or even as "cryptic" or "esoteric," merely because as laymen we may not understand it. Though metaphysics is not a special science, the analogy holds good.

94 (*page 137*). *Guhya* ("hidden") is often the equivalent of *parokṣa*: e.g. in *Ṛg Veda*, V, 5, 10, "Where-e'er it be, O Vanaspati (Agni), that thou knowest the hidden (*guhya*) names of the Angels, there transmit our offerings."

95 (*page 138*). See note 79; and cf. *padmapriyā*, characterising Śrī-Lakṣmī, *Śrīsūkta*, 25, where again-*priyā* implies not "choice" but "nature."

96 (*page 141*). A very beautiful description of the creation as reflection is found in *Pañcaviṁśa Brāhmaṇa*, VII, 8, 1, as follows: "The Waters (representing the principle of substance) being ripe unto conception (lit. 'in their season'), Vāyu (that is, the Wind, as physical symbol of spiration, *prâṇa*) moved over their surface. Wherefrom came into being a lovely (*vāma*) thing (that is, the world-picture), there in the Waters Mitra-Varuṇa beheld-themselves-reflected (*paryapaśyat*)." So Genesis, I, 2, The Spirit of God moved over the waters, and St Thomas, *Summ. Theol.*, I, 74, "the Spirit of the Lord signifies the Holy Ghost, Who is said to *move over the water* — that is to say, over what Augustine holds to mean formless matter . . . it is fittingly implied that the Spirit moved over that which was incomplete and unfinished, since that movement is not one of place, but of preëminent power."

The "waters" here and elsewhere in tradition represent the totality of the *possibilities* of being, which from the standpoint of *existence* are in themselves *nothing* (chaos); this "nothing" being "at large" in the First Cause, as explained in note 3. Hence "ex nihilo fit." For the waters in symbolic representation see my *Yakṣas*, II, and in significance, Guénon, *Symbolisme de la Croix*, Ch. XXIV.

97 (*page 142*). With reference, of course, to the three kinds of icons, (1) *dhruva* or *yoga bera* or *mūla vigraha*, permanently established in a shrine, (2) *bhoga mūrti* or *utsava vigraha*, carried in processions, and (3) *dhyāna bera*, mental images used in private devotions.

98 (*page 142*). The *Suprabhedâgama* describes *citra* as *sarvâvayava-saṁpūrṇa-dṛśyaṁ*, and *ardha-citra* as *ardhavâyava-saṁdṛśyaṁ*, respectively "fully visible in all its parts" and "visible as to a half of its parts."

99 (*page 142*). Here evidently *dhātu-rāga*, mineral color, as in *Meghadūta*, p. 102, where the Commentary has *sindūrâdi*, "vermilion, etc.," not *dhātu*, in verse 2 above, as a mineral or some metal other than *loha*, nor *dhātu*, metal, in *Śukranītisāra*, IV, 4, 72 and 153.

100 (*page 143*). Acharya, *Dictionary of Hindu Architecture*, pp. 63, 65, item 5 (out of place); *Mānasāra*, pp. 48, 49.

101 (*page 144*). We find also *pramāṇâbhāsa*, "fallacious proof," *hetvâbhāsa*, "logical fallacy," *pratyakṣâbhāsa*, "misleading appearance," *parokṣâbhāsa*, "pseudo-symbolism"; and *pratibhāsa*, "mental reflex" (Stcherbatsky, *Buddhist Logic*, II, 6, n. 2, identifies *pratibhāsa* with *nirbhāsa*, *ābhāsa*, and *pratibimbana*).

102 (*page 145*). See notes 23, 67.

103 (*page 145*). See *Eastern Art*, III (1931), 218, 219.

104 (*page 145*). "Shade and shine," *chāyâtapa*, is taken from *Kaṭha Upaniṣad*, III, 1, and VI, 5, where there is no reference to

any work of art; it occurs also in the *Atthasālinī*, p. 317, in connection with the discussion of *rūpâyatana*, "locus of form" defined as "colored appearance"; "it shines (*nibbhāti*), hence appearance."

Chāyâtapa occurs also in Vasubandhu, *Abhidharmakośa*, III, 39. In all these passages the term bears rather the general meaning "pairs of opposites" than the literal meaning "light and shade"; it is nevertheless actually the immediate equivalent of "chiaroscuro."

105 (*page 146*). B. March, "Linear Perspective in Chinese Painting," *Eastern Art*, III (1931); L. Bachhofer, "Der Raumdarstellung in der chinesischen Malerei, etc." *Münchner Jahrbuch für Bildenden Kunst*, VIII (1931); L. Bachhofer, "Frühindische Historienreliefs," *Ostasiatische Zeitscher*. N. F., VIII (1932), 18; A. Ippel, *Indische Kunst und Triumphalbild* (Leipzig, 1929). The most valuable discussion of this kind is H. Zimmer's "Some Aspects of Time in Indian Art," *Journ. Indian Society of Oriental Art*, I (1933), 30–51.

106 (*page 148*). Sir J. H. Marshall, *Mohenjodaro* (London, 1931), pl. XI; *ASI. AR.* (1917–18), pt. 1, pl. XVI; and *Illustrated London News* (March 24, 1928); Cunningham, *The Stūpa of Bharhut*, 1879, and *M.F.A. Bulletin* 175. Cf. G. Gombaz, "La Loi de Frontalité dans la Sculpture Indienne," *Revue des Arts Asiatiques*, VII, 105.

107 (*page 148*) *Sthānas* are defined in the *Viṣṇudharmottara*, III, 39; *Śilparatna*, Ch. LXIV; Basava Raja, *Śiva Tattva Ratnākara*, VI, 2, 55 ff. See also the general literature on Indian iconography, for example, T. A. C. Rao, *Elements of Hindu Iconography* (Madras, 1914–15). The first five *sthānas* range from (1) frontal or full face to (5) exact profile, intermediate positions being represented by 2, 3, 4. A table of the terms as given in the three sources cited follows:

Viṣṇudharmottara	Śilparatna	Śiva-Tattva-Ratnākara
1. Ṛju, Ṛjvāgata	Ṛju	Ṛju, Sammukha
2. Anṛju, Tiryak	Ardharju	Ardharju
3. Sācikṛta	Sācika, Sācigata	Sāci
4. Ardhavilocana, Adhyardhâkṣa	Dvyardhâkṣi	Nyardharju
5. Pārśvagata, Chāyāgata, Bhittika	Pārśvagata, Bhittika, Bhittigata	Bhittika
6. Parâvṛtta, Gaṇḍaparâvṛtta		
7. Pṛṣṭāgata		
8. Parivṛtta		
9. Samânata		

108 (*page 149*). See my *History of Indian and Indonesian Art* (1927), pp. 25–27 and fig. 27.

109 (*page 150*). Style is here the datum, appearance, or authority to be investigated. "Those that attempt by means of a (given) authority (that is, from internal evidence) to understand the consciousness (*bodham*) which (itself) produced the authority (*prabodhayantaṁ mānaṁ*) are such great beings as would burn fire itself by means of fuel," Śaṅkarâcārya, *Svâtmanirūpaṇa*, 46.

110 (*page 152*). From the *Sarvadharma-pravṛtti-nirdeśa Sūtra*, cited by Suzuki, *Outlines of Mahayana Buddhism*, p. 381.

111 (*page 156*). See my *Mediaeval Sinhalese Art* (1908), pp. 70–75.

112 (*page 156*). Cf. Pope, G. U., *The Tiruvâçagam* (Oxford, 1900), p. xxxv.

113 (*page 157*). Cf. the *Hermeneia* of Athos, § 445, cited by Fichtner, *Wandmalereien der Athosklöster* (1931), p. 15: "All honor that we pay the image, we refer to the Archetype, namely Him whose image it is. . . . In no wise honor we the colors or

the art, but the archetype in Christ, who is in Heaven. For as Basilius says, the honoring of an image passes over to its proto-type." Cf. note 43.

114 (*page 163*). "It is for the advantage (*artha*) of the worship-pers (*upāsaka*) (and not by any intrinsic necessity) that the Brahman — whose nature is intelligence (*cin-maya*), beside whom there is no other, who is impartite and incorporeal — is aspectually conceived (*rūpa-kalpanā*)," *Rāmôpaniṣad*, text cited by Bhattacharya, *Indian Images*, p. xvii. That is to say the image, as in the case of any other "arrangement of God," has a merely logical, not an absolute validity. "Worship" (*upāsana*) has been defined as an "intellectual operation (*mānasa-vyāpara*) with respect to the Brahman with attributed-qualities (*saguṇa*)."

115 (*page 168*). Verses cited in the *Triṁśikā* of Vasubandhu; see *Bibliothèque de l'École des Hautes Études*, fasc. 245, 1925, and Lévi, "Matériaux pour l'Étude du Système Vijñaptimātra," *ibid.*, fasc. 260 (Paris, 1932), p. 119.

116 (*page 168*). The stage of partial manifestation is compared to that of the "blooming" of a painting. The term "bloom" or "blossom" (*unmīl*) is used to describe the "coming out" of a painting as the colors are gradually applied (Maheśvarânanda, *Mahârthamañjarī*, p. 44, and my "Further References to Indian Painting," *Artibus Asiae*, p. 127, 1930–1932, item 102).

117 (*page 169*). Cf. my "Hindu Sculpture," in *the league*, vol. V, no. 3 (New York, 1933).

Sanskrit Glossary

Sanskrit Glossary

ābhāsa, "back shining," semblance, reflection; modality (anything regarded as a mode or part of a whole, as painting of sculpture); objectivity; theophany.

abhidhā, denotation; reference.

abhinaya, aesthetic apparatus, means of "registering" (*sūcanā*); especially conventional gestures employed in the dramatic dance (*nṛtya*).

abhi-sambhava, re-becoming, transformation.

abhyāsa, practice, training.

ācārya, a master, one expert in his art.

adhidaivata, from the angelic point of view; *parokṣa*.

adhyātma, from the individual point of view; *pratyakṣa*.

adhyavasāna, introsusceptive, imagist.

āgama, scripture (*śruti*).

āgama-artha-avisaṁvādi, not contradicting the sense of scripture, orthodox, canonical.

āhārya, gotten, acquired, added, adventitious, not innate. *Āhārya-abhinaya*, costume as part of the apparatus of art; -*śobha*, loveliness resulting from adornment.

ākarṣaṇa, attracting, producing; intuition; from *ākṛṣ*.

ākāśa, ether, firmament; immanent space, indefinitely dimensioned, subjective space.

ā-kṛti, image, likeness, outward appearance.

alaṁkāra, ornaments, figures, tropes, associated ideas or images; rhetoric.

a-laukika, not belonging to contingent worlds, supersensuous. Same as *lokôttara*.

ālekhya, painting.

a-mātra, of indefinite measure, undetermined.

ānanda-cin-maya, compounded of delight and reason (characterising *rasâsvādana*, aesthetic experience).

antar-jñeya, known subjectively.

anu-bhāva, means of registration (*sūcanā*) in a work of art; parts or elements of the actual work of art; the physical stimuli to aesthetic reproduction. Cf. *abhinaya*.

anu-kāra, same as *anu-karaṇa*.

anu-karaṇa, "making after," "making in accordance with," imitation; *anukṛti, anukāra.*

anu-kārya, the theme "imitated," the model.

anu-kṛti, made in accordance with, "imitation."

anu-māna, inference, deduction, supposition, imputation.

anu-rūpa, like the model, true to nature; analogous.

anu-śīla, devoted application, obedience.

anvita, "caught," conveyed, rendered in a work of art; contrasted with *anyathā*, "off," or "missed."

anyathā, "out," "off," false (in a work of art).

a-parokṣa, not indirect, not symbolic; immediate.

ardha-citra, "half-art," relief (as distinguished from full round sculpture on the one hand and painting on the other).

ardha-likhita, "half-painted," unfinished (distinct from *anyathā*, imperfect, unsuccessful).

artha, meaning, end, interest, use, advantage, motive, purpose, value, determination; just cause or *raison d'être* of a work; "intenzion dell'arte." Cf. *puruṣârtha.*

arthatva, condition of possessing meaning, etc.

āsvāda, tasting (of *rasa*); aesthetic experience.

ātman, self, Self; Universal Man, Brahman.

aupadeśika, acquired by instruction; one who has acquired the appearance of imagination by instruction.

ava-sthāna, condition, emotional situation.

avayava, the separate parts of an organism.

avayava-ānata, attentive to the actual shapes of an object; realistic, "true to Nature."

a-vidyā, non-knowing, relative, empirical, sensible and rational knowledge of plurality.

bāhya, external, objective, empirical.

bhā, to shine forth, appear; in *prati-bhā*.

bhakti, devotion, self-abandonment in love; also used as equivalent to *lakṣaṇā*, connotation; and as a synonym of *dhvani*, content.

bhās, to shine forth; in *ābhāsa*, etc.

bhāva, nature; emotion, sentiment, or mood, as represented in a work of art; the vehicle of *rasa*.

bhavana, "what has come to be," shape, appearance, Nature.

bhāvanā, origination, production, imagination; persistent image, emotional impression surviving in conscious or unconscious memory.

bhoga, fruition, aesthetic appreciation; *āsvāda*.

bhū, to be, become; in *bhāva*, *bhūta*, etc.

bhūta-mātrā, elements of phenomenal being, shape; pictorial (*citra*) factor in art.

bimba, model, subject (presentation, semblance, as contrasted with *prati-bimba*, re-presentation, re-semblance).

buddhi, pure intellect, "the habit of first principles," *prajñā*.

camat-kāra, amazement.

cāru, lovely.

cetanā, sentience, life.

chandas, rhythm.

chāyâtapa, shadow and sunlight, chiaroscuro; pairs of opposites.

cit (*cid-*, *cin-*), mind, intelligence, reason.

citra, representative art (sculpture, relief, painting); picture, pictorial.

citrâbhāsa, "semblance of art," "reflex of sculpture," painting; *ābhāsa*, *ālekhya*.

citra-gata, represented (in a work of art).

citra-kāvya, pictorial or illustrative poetry, the lowest sort, or not poetry at all; cf. "verses for pictures."

citrârdha, same as *ardha-citra*.

citta-vṛtti, fluctuations of the mind, "fugitive emotions and creature images."

daṁsana, grasp (the artist's apprehension of the theme).

darśanīya, worth looking at, good; *quod visum placet*; that which *dṛṣṭi-prītiṁ vidhatte*.

darśita, shown, exhibited, displayed.

deśī, popular, folk (style); contrasted with *mārga*, "high."

deva, *devatā*, angel.

dharaṇa, exclusive attention to a presented idea.

dharma, conduct, morality, law, virtue, function, character, principle, habit, thing.

dhātu, ore; color.

dhvanana, echoing, synonym of *vyañjanā*; cf. *dhvani*.

dhvani, sound, sound*ing*; overtone of meaning, resonance of sense, content (as distinguished from intent); Chinese *yün* (13843).

dhyai, to meditate upon, be intent upon, practice abstract contemplation, visualize. Corresponds to Vedic *dhī*.

dhyāna, undistracted attention, first stage in Yoga praxis; visualization, contemplation of a mental image; Chinese *ch'an*, Japanese *zen*.

dhyāna-yoga, visual contemplative union, realization of formal identity with an inwardly known image.

divya, *daivata*, angelic.

doṣa, any specific fault in a work of art.

dṛś, to see, look, consider, see intuitively; in *dṛśya*, *sādṛśya*, *sadṛśī*, *draṣṭṛ*, etc.

dṛṣṭādvaita, one who sees without duality, who sees in identity.

dṛṣṭi-prīti, delight of the eyes.

dṛśya, visible, the phenomenal universe.

gamana, motion, movement.

graha, seizer, apprehender, sense-instrument.

grahaṇa, "seizing," comprehension, understanding of anything.

grāhya, seizable, able to be comprehended.

guha, *gupta*, *guhya*, hidden, occult, unseen; transcendental.

guṇa, any specific merit in a work of art. Also factor, quality or qualification in the phenomenal universe, viz. *sattva-guṇa*, purity, *rajo-guṇa*, action, expansion, continuation, and *tamo-guṇa*, inertia, resistance.

haraṇa, plagiarism.

harṣa, delight.

hṛd, *hṛdaya*, heart, the entire being (sensible and intelligent); soul; Self, Brahman.

itihāsa, narrative, history.

jagac-citra, world picture, vision of the Universe apart from time.

jīva, *jīvâtman*, individual, self, soul.

jīvan-mukta, one who has attained spiritual freedom, but is still manifest in human form.

kailāsa-bhāvanā, made after the heavenly pattern.

kalā, art, any art or accomplishment depending on skill. Art as avocation. The *bāhya-kalās* (external arts, or practical arts) are usually listed as sixty-four in number, some being identical with the vocational *śilpas*; there are also sixty-four *kāma-* or *abhyantara*, "arts of love," or "intimate arts."

kāma, pleasure of any kind, specific or natural pleasure, especially in love.

kānti, loveliness (of the subject, esp. in a portrait).

kāraka, maker, creator.

kāraṇa, act, action, cause; formal gesture or position in dancing.

karma, making (with reference to man's handiwork, *factibile*); also conduct (with reference to man's deeds, *agibile*); office, celebration, ritual.

kārya, to be made, *factibile*.

kārayitṛ, creative.

kauśala, skill, expertness, virtuosity, facility; when as in Buddhist usage there is a moral coloring, the idea of "convenience" is also present.

kautūhala, interest in, appreciation of, a work of art.

kavi, in the Vedas, Poetic Genius (personified) a designation of the Sun, as "revealer"; later, "poet," artist.

kavitva, artistry; *-dāyin*, artistic.

kāvya, poetry (prose or verse); "literature" as distinct from *śruti* and *itihāsa*, *śāstras*, etc. By extension, "art" as an abstract concept. *Kavitva-dāyin*, "artistic."

kāvya-śarīra, the body of poetry (consisting of sound, sense and ornaments); the work of art as a physical entity, as distinguished from its soul, or content, *ātman*.

kṛ, to do, make; in *karma*, *karaṇa*, *kārya*, etc.

kṛṣ, to attract, draw, delineate, display; in *ākarṣaṇa*, etc.

kṛta, made, well and truly made.

kṛtârtha, purpose or end of the work to be done.

kha, space; *ākāśa*.

kratv-artha, the good of the work to be done.

lakṣaṇa, characteristic lineament, iconographic requirement, sign, symbol, attribute.

lakṣaṇā, connotation.

lāvaṇya, "salt," charm, "it" (in a feminine subject).

laya, rest, cessation, resolution.

likh, to draw, paint; in *ālekhya*, etc.

līlā, play, unmotivated manifestation.

loka, world, sphere, universe; the conditioned world, including heaven, in part.

loka-vṛtta, "local motions," phenomena; "Nature" (*ens naturata*).

lokôttara, supersensual (rather than "supernatural").

mā, to measure; in *māna*(1), *pramāṇa*, *nirmāṇa*, *pratimā*, *nirmā*, *mātrā*.

mādhurya, sweetness, equanimity, grace, facility.

māna (1), (from root *mā*), measure, canon of proportion.

māna (2), (from root *man*), pride, egoism, ideology. Cf. "mental" (rational) as used by Blake.

manas, intellect, mind, reason; *divyacakṣu* (*Chāndogya Up.*, VIII, 12, 5).

manohara, delighting the mind or heart; affective, seductive.

mantra, incantation, enchantment (e.g., verses of the *Ṛg Veda*, and canonical prescriptions of the *Śilpa Śāstras*, known as *dhyāna mantras*).

mānuṣa, human.

mārga, high (style): same as *rīti*. Contrasted or "stylistic" or "sophisticated" with *deśī*, "folk," "naïve."

mātrā, measure, dimension, principle.

māyā, creative power; magic; *natura naturans*.

mokṣa, liberation, spiritual freedom, realization (not "attainment") of perfection.

mūrta, formal, in a likeness; contrasted with *a-mūrta*, imageleso, transcending form.

mūrti, form, image, likeness.

naisargika, innate, natural; *sahaja*.

nāma, name, idea, form; means of conventional discrimination.

nāma-rūpa, name and aspect, words and images, the means of conventional discrimination, that by which the contingent universe is known.

natônnata, relief, relievo, in a painting.

nāya, traditional authority, prescription.

netrâmṛta, elixir of the eyes, that which delights the eye.

nimnônnata, same as *natônnata*.

nirmā, with *citram*, to paint; with *kośam*, to compose, write.

nirmāṇa, making, creating, manifestation.

nirmāṇa-kāraka, maker, creator; God.

nirvāha, bare statement of fact, narration.

niyama, ascertained rule.

nṛtya, dramatic dance, art-dance, nautch; dance giving expression to *rasa* and *bhāva*.

padminī, "lotus lady," one of the four types of women.

paramârtha, ultimate significance; essence, Brahman, *ātman*.

pāramârthika, with respect to ultimate significance, transcendental, absolute.

parāvṛtti, transformation, transubstantiation, anagogy.

pari-, prefix = *per*.

pari-draṣṭṛ, over-seer, witness, God.

pari-haraṇa, flagrant plagiarism.

paṭa, canvas, painting.

pradeśa, landscape, area.

pra-harṣa, great delight.

pra-hṛṣṭa, delighted (by a work of art).

prajñā, discrimination, wisdom, pure intellect, First Principle, Brahman.

prajñā-mātrā, elements of intelligence or discrimination; formal elements in art.

prajñāna-ghana, exemplary understanding.

pramāṇa, as principle, ideal symmetry, aesthetic conscience, "correction du savoir faire"; as canon, same as *māna*.

pramātṛ, judge, critic, one possessed of a subjective criterion, or aesthetic standard (*pramāṇa*).

pra-muda, delight, great delight; same as *praharṣa*.

prâṇa, spiration, life-breath, *pneuma*; Chinese *ch'i*; life as procession, emanation. In the plural, the distinct life breaths in the individual species.

prati-, a prefix: toward, against, counter-.

prati-bhā, vision, imagination, poetic faculty.

prati-bimba, representation; *-vat*, *quā* representation.

pratīka, symbol.

prati-kṛti, portrait; *ākṛti*, *ākara*.

pratimā, image, likeness; *-kāraka*, imager.

pratīti, self-intelligibility, clear intuition or manifestation (of *rasa*).

prati-vihita, determined (√*dhā*).

pratyakṣa, "before the eye," evident, objective, perceptible; empirical observation; like the model, true to Nature; semiotic. Cf. *parokṣa*.

prayojana, use, application, purpose, intent, theme; cf. *artha*.

pūjā, office, ritual; *pūjya*, to be worshipped.

puruṣa, person, personality. Distinguished from *jīva*, individual.

puruṣârtha, value, the meaning or purpose of life; the Four Ends of Life, viz. *dharma, artha, kāma, mokṣa*. The advantage to be derived from the accomplished work, as distinguished from *kratvartha*, the good of the work to be done.

ramaṇīyatā, beauty in a work of art, especially as seen in disinterested contemplation.

ramya, lovely, truly lovely, beautiful.

raṅga, color.

rasa, flavor, savor, quintessence; the substance of aesthetic experience, knowable only in the activity of tasting, *rasâsvādana*.

rasâsvādana, tasting of *rasa*, aesthetic experience.

rasâtmaka, having *rasa* as its soul.

rasavat, possessing *rasa*, said of a work of art, by imputation or projection.

rasâyana, elixir for the eyes, said of a work of art as good to see.

rasika, one competent to the tasting of *rasa*, true critic.

rekhā, line, outline, drawing.

rekhā-śuddhi, purity of line.

rīti, style, diction, composition, manner.

ruci, taste, preference (not to be confused with *rasa*).

rūpa, shape, natural shape, semblance, color, loveliness; image, effigy, likeness; symbol, ideal form; means of conventional discrimination (see *nāma-rūpa*). (Cf. *vi-rūpa*, having two forms, various, altered, deformed, ugly; and *a-rūpa*, not formed, transcendental.)

rūpa-kāra, imager (maker of images).

rūpa-sobhā, represented beauty.

rūpya, beautiful, shapely; formal.

rutârtha, sound and sense.

śabda, sound, word: Logos.

śabdârtha, same as *rutârtha*.

sādhana, any means employed in worship; a canonical prescription, *dhyāna mantra*.

sā-dhāraṇya, "having a common support"; ideal sympathy, disinterested *Ein-* or *Mitfühlung*.

sādhu, what is good or right in a work of art (opposite of *anyathā*); as an exclamation, "Well done."

sa-dṛśa, sa-dṛśī, like in appearance, sensibly resembling.

sā-dṛśya, concomitance of formal and pictorial elements, conformity, *consonantia*: Chinese *ch'ou* (2508), "answering to," "in response."

sahaja, innate, connatural; spontaneous, spontaneity; "willingly but not from will, naturally but not from nature." Contrasted with *aupadeśika*, and *āhārya*.

sā-hitya, concomitance of sound and sense, word and meaning: *consonantia*.

sa-hṛdaya, "having a heart," imaginatively or spiritually gifted; *rasika*.

sâkṣāt, present to the eye, *pratyakṣa*.

śakti, power, genius.

sālakṣya, having like features, similarity, common denotation.

saṁkalpa, concept, conception, imagining, mental formulation.

saṁketa, convention.

saṁketita, conventional.

saṁskṛ, to con-struct, integrate; *saṁskṛta*, the arti-ficial, constructed, integrated language, Sanskrit.

saṁtoṣa, satisfaction (derived from a work of art).

saṁvādi, agreeing with, conformable to the model or prescription.

saṁvyavahārika, worldly, practical.

sārasvata, inspired by or worthy of Sarasvatī.

śarīra, body, substance: the material body of a work of art, as composed of sounds, tangible forms, etc.; the tangible embodiment of intuition-expression.

sārūpya, co-aspectuality, con-formation, coördination, corre-spondence; cf. *sādṛśya.*

śāstra, a scripture or treatise written by a sage; traditional authority (*smṛti*) as distinguished from revelation (*śruti*).

śāstra-māna, canonical, according to traditional authority.

sat (*sad-*), true, real.

sattva, purity, simplicity; quality of essence, being in itself; the first of the three *guṇas.*

sattva-bhāva, any natural expression of emotion, as represented in art.

satya, true, real, essential; sacred, hieratic (painting).

sa-varṇa, double, substitute.

śilpa (Pali *sippa*) art, any art or work of art, the practice of art, skill of art, art as vocation, taught by a master (*ācārya*).
Śilpa-jīvin, one who lives by his art, a professional. Cf. *kalā.*

śithila, slack, not intense; with *-samādhi,* imperfect concentration of the artist (in medicine, post coitum lassitude).

śliṣṭatva, habitus, wont, facility, knack.

smṛti, "remembered"; tradition, authority, cf. *śāstra.* Also "memory," but in a bad sense, as nostalgia, or sentimentality, not "recollection."

śravaṇīya, worth listening to, good (of music, etc.).

śṛṅgāra, the erotic, most important of the separate *rasas.*

śruti, heard, audition, "revelation," immediate authority, scripture; the Vedas.

sthāna, station, field; pose.

sthāyi, established, stable, permanent. With *-bhāva,* permanent mood, constant motif of a work of art.

sthūla, gross (material, as opposed to mental).

sūcanā, registering (as in cinema parlance).

sūkṣma, subtle (mental, as opposed to physical).

su-kṛta, well and truly made (of the world, as God's art); perfect. See list, n. 107.

suṣṭhu, excellent (in praise of a work of art).

sva, self, own.

sva-bhāva, own-being, essential nature, inwardness.

sva-dharma, vocation, calling, specific function.

sva-prakāśa, self-illuminated, self-manifesting (*rasa*, or Brahman), limpid.

sva-rūpa, own form, very form; intrinsic aspect; *svâkāra*.

tad-ākāratā, con-formation, coordination.

tad-anurūpa, according to the model, like, true to nature.

tad-ātmya, having the same self as.

tat lagnaṁ hṛd, the seductive, intriguing.

tād-rūpya, of like form, like.

takṣ, to hew (wood; or, metaphorically, thought).

tāla, tāla-māna, measure, canon of proportion.

tātparya-artha, meaning or significance of the whole phrase or work of art, as distinct from that of its separate parts or elements.

unmīl, to bloom (said of a painting while being colored).

upacāra, metaphor, analogy.

upāsaka, worshipper.

upāsana, worship.

utsāha, "effort"; the spiritual energy exerted in aesthetic reproduction.

vāc (*vāk-, vāg-*), voice (as function); speech (as discrimination, exterior word); interior word, Logos; wisdom.

vaidagdhya, skill.

vākya, word, phrase; expression.

vāraṇa, wall, barrier, enclosure; hindrance (e. g. prejudice, interest, appetite).

varṇa, color, sound; scale, palette.

varṇanīya, to be depicted or expressed; praiseworthy (theme).

varṇikā-bhaṅga, distribution of color.

vartanā, Pali *vattana*, shading, that is, plastic modelling, in painting.

vartikā, brush.

vāsanā, latent memory of past experience, hence the potentiality of impartial sensibility, fancy, *Einfühlung*. In the bad sense, emotional associations and attachments; power of habit.

vastu, theme, subject.

vi-bhāva, physical stimulant to aesthetic reproduction; the parts of the work of art, aesthetic surfaces.

vicitra, variegated, romantic.

vidyā, gnosis, un-knowing, the immediate knowledge (realization) of unity, absolute truth; = *prajñā, jñāna*.

vikalpa, rational knowledge.

vilekhana, same as *ālekhya*, painting.

visaṁvādi, not agreeing (with the model or prescription).

viśeṣa-jña, of varied knowledge, connoisseur.

vivāda-nirṇaya, judgment, discrimination.

vyabhicāri, fugitive, transient (with *-bhāva*, transient mood or emotion, as contrasted with *sthāyi-bhāva*).

vyāhṛti, utterance, Spoken Word.

vyaṅgyārtha, suggested meaning, content, significance (as distinguished from denotation and connotation).

vyañjanā, suggestive power of an expression.

vyavahārika, worldly, empirical, sensational.

vyutpatti, explicit meaning, conceptual part of art; scholarship.

yajña, sacrificial office.

yantra, "device," "machine"; geometrical representation of a deity.

yoga, lit. "union," "yoking"; skill in action (*Bhagavad Gītā*, II, 50).

yogyā, application, study, practice.

yuj (in *yoga, prayojana*, etc.), to yoke, apply, exert, control.

yukta, yoked, joined to, embodying, united, at-oned.

yukti, skill, accomplishment, acquired facility.

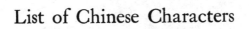

List of Chinese Characters

List of Chinese Characters *

ch'an (Giles, 348), Sanskrit *dhyāna*, Japanese *zen*.

chêng (Giles, 720), used by Hsüan Tsang to render *pramāṇa*.

ch'i (Giles, 991), extraordinary, marvellous, surprising.

ch'i (Giles, 1064), spirit, spiration, breath, life. Sanskrit *prâṇa*, Greek *pneuma*, Arabic *rūḥ*. The procession of *ch'i* is from Heaven and Earth, the primary modalities of the First Principle (Tao), hence *ch'i* is rightly used to render "Holy Ghost."

ch'iao (Giles, 1411), clever, skilful, artful.

chih (Giles, 1783), to know, knowledge; conscience.

ch'ou (Giles, 2508), reciprocity; used by Hsüan Tsang to render *sādṛśya*.

ch'uan (Giles, 2740), handed down, transmitted; tradition. "What he gets by his mind (*shin*) he transmits by his hand" (said of the painter).

fu (Giles, 3632), to lay on color.

hsin (Giles, 4562), heart, mind, spirit. Cf. Sanskrit *hṛdaya*.

hsing (Giles, 4617), natural shape; objective; represented shape. Skr. *rūpa*.

i (Giles, 5536), supersensual perfection of the sage; genius; spontaneity. Cf. *shên* and Skr. *śakti sahaja*.

i (Giles, 5367), idea, mind, intuition, meaning, end. Contrasted with *hsing*. Cf. Sanskrit *artha*, *nāma*, and *pramāṇa*.

i ch'ü (Giles, 5367, 3120) operation of the mind; movement of the idea; significance, thought. Dante's "intenzion dell' arte," *Paradiso*, I, 127.

liang (Giles, 7015), measure, standard. (Sanskrit *pramāṇa?*)

---

* The numbers of the characters are those of Giles's *Chinese-English Dictionary*, where they can easily be found, and the shades of meaning considered.

miao (Giles, 7857), profound, mysterious, wonderful.

nêng (Giles, 8184), ability, skill, accomplishment, virtuosity. Same as *ch'iao.*

san p'in (Giles, 9552, 9273), The three kinds of painting, *shên, miao, nêng.*

shên (Giles, 9819), angel, angelic, divine spirit, soul, God; Skr. *deva.* "The inscrutable operation of Yin and Yang is called *shên*": "to paint a portrait (*fu shên*)": "to give expression (*shên*) to the very part left undelineated." *Ching* (2133) *shên,* "very soul," "true self."

ssŭ (Giles, 10289), likeness, resemblance, imitation.

wu (Giles, 12777), object, Nature; *viṣaya-rūpatā.*

yün (Giles, 13817), operation, revolution; Pacioli's *movimenti.*

yün (Giles, 13843), resonance, reverberation, content. Cf. Sanskrit *dhvani.*

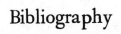

Bibliography

Bibliography

I. European Languages

ACHARYA, P. K. *Dictionary of Hindu Architecture.* Oxford, n.d.[1]
—— *A Summary of the Mānasāra.* Leiden, 1918.[1]
—— *Indian Architecture according to the Mānasāra-Śilpaśāstra.* Oxford, n.d.[1]
ANAND, M. R. *The Hindu View of Art.* London, 1933.
ANESAKI, M. *Buddhist Art in Its Relation to Buddhist Ideals.* Boston, 1911; 2nd ed., 1915.
ARAVAMUTHAN, T. G. *Portrait Sculpture in South India.* London, 1931.
ASANGA. *Mahāyāna Sūtrâlaṁkāra.* Translated by Sylvain Lévi. Paris, 1911.
BACHHOFER, L. "Die Raumdarstellung in der chinesischen Malerei," *Münchner Jahrbuch für bildenden Kunst,* VIII, 1931.
—— "Frühindische Historienreliefs," *Ostas. Zeitschrift,* N. F., VIII, 1932.
BANERJEA, J. N. *Pratimālakṣaṇam.* Edited and translated, Calcutta, 1932.[1]
BARNETT, L. D. *The Lord's Song (Bhagavad Gītā),* Temple Classics.
—— *Antagaḍa Dasāo.* London, 1907.
BHATTACHARYA, B. C. *Indian Images.* Calcutta, 1921.
BHATTACHARYYA, B. *Buddhist Iconography.* Oxford, 1924.
—— *Buddhist Esoterism.* Oxford, 1932. (Ch. XI.)
BINYON, L. *Painting in the Far East,* 3rd ed. London, 1923.
—— *The Flight of the Dragon* (various editions).
BOAS, F. *Primitive Art.* Oslo, 1927.

---

[1] *Śilpa Śāstras.*

238   BIBLIOGRAPHY

BÖHME, J. *Mysterium Pansophicum.* Translated by J. R. Earle. New York, 1920.

BOSE, N. K. *Canons of Orissan Architecture.* Calcutta, 1933.[1]

BOSE, P. N. *Principles of Indian Śilpaśāstra.* Punjab Oriental Series, XI. Lahore, 1926.

—— *Pratimā-Māna-Lakṣaṇam.* Punjab Oriental Series, XVIII. Lahore, 1929.

CHATTERJI, J. C. *Kashmir Shaivism.* 1914.

COOMARASWAMY, A. K. "Teaching of Drawing in Ceylon," *Ceylon National Review,* December, 1906 (also in *Mediaeval Sinhalese Art,* Broad Campden, 1908).

—— *Mediaeval Sinhalese Art.* Broad Campden, 1908.

—— *The Indian Craftsman.* London, 1909.

—— "That Beauty is a State," *Burlington Magazine,* April, 1915.

—— *Rajput Painting.* Oxford, 1916.

—— *The Dance of Śiva.* New York, 1918.

—— *Citra-lakṣaṇa (Śilparatna,* Ch. 64). Sir Ashutosh Mukerjee Memorial Volume. Patnā, 1926–28.

—— "Nāgara Painting," *Rūpam,* Nos. 37, 40, 1929.

—— "An Early Passage on Indian Painting," *Eastern Art,* III, 1931.

—— "One Hundred References to Indian Painting," *Artibus Asiae,* 1930–32, pp. 41–57, and "Further References," pp. 126–129.

—— "Introduction to the Art of Eastern Asia," *Open Court,* March, 1932 (partly identical with the present text).

—— Viṣṇudharmottara (III), 41, *JAOS.,* LII, 1932.[1]

—— "The Technique and Theory of Indian Painting," *Technical Studies in the Field of the Fine Arts,* III, 1934.

—— "Hindu Sculpture," *the league,* V. New York, 1933.

—— *Elements of Buddhist Symbolism.* Cambridge, 1934.[2]

—— *A New Approach to the Vedas.* London, 1934.[2]

[1] *Śilpa Śāstras.*   [2] In Press.

COOMARASWAMY, A. K. "Mediaeval Aesthetic. I. Dionysius the Pseudo-Areopagite, and Ulrich Engelberti of Strasburg," *Art Bulletin*, March, 1935.

COOMARASWAMY, A. K., and DUGGIRALA, G. K. *The Mirror of Gesture*. Cambridge, 1917.

CROCE, B. "The Breviary of Aesthetic," *Rice Institute Pamphlet*, 11, 1915.

DANDOY, J., *L'Ontologie du Vedānta*. Paris, 1932.

DAS GUPTA. *History of Indian Philosophy*. Cambridge, Eng., 1922, 1932.

DE, SUSHIL K. *Sanskrit Poetics*, 2 vols. London, 1923, 1925.

DEUSSEN, P. *Philosophy of the Upanishads*. Edinburgh, 1906.

DUTT, M. N. *Dissertation on Painting*. Calcutta, 1922.[1]

DVOŘAK, M. *Kunstgeschichte als Geistesgeschichte, Studien zur abendländischen Kunstentwicklung*. München, 1924.

EDGERTON, F. *Vikrama's Adventures*. Translation of the *Vikramacarita*. Harvard Oriental Series, XXXVI. Cambridge, 1926.

EVANS, C. de B. *Meister Eckhart*. London, 1924.

FONSEKA, L. DE. *On the Truth of Decorative Art*. London, 1913.

FOX-STRANGWAYS. *The Music of Hindustan*. Oxford, 1914.

FOUCHER, A. *L'Iconographie bouddhique de l'Inde*. Paris, 1900, 1905.

GILES, H. A. *Chuang Tzŭ*. London, 1889.

GILL, E. *Art-Nonsense*. London, 1929.

GOMBAZ, G. "La Loi de Frontalité dans le Sculpture indienne," *Revue des Arts asiatiques*, VII, 1931–32.

GROSLIER, G. "Notes sur la Psychologie de l'Artisan cambodgien," *Arts et Archéologie khmèrs*, I.

—— "Le Fin d'un Art," *Revue des Arts asiatiques*, V.

GUÉNON, R. *L'Homme et son Devenir selon le Vedanta*. Paris, 1925.

—— *Introduction générale à l'Étude des Doctrines hindoues*. Paris, 1932.

[1] Not seen by the author.

240   BIBLIOGRAPHY

GUÉNON, R. La Symbolisme de la Croix. Paris, 1931.

HAVELL, E. B. Ideals of Indian Art. London, 1911.

HEARN, L. Japan, an Interpretation. New York, 1905.

HEMACANDRA. Triṣaṣṭiśalākāpuruṣacaritra. Translated by H. M. Johnson, I. Baroda, 1931.

HIRN, YRJÖ. The Origins of Art. London, 1900.

HUME, R. E. The Thirteen Principal Upanishads, 2nd ed. Oxford, 1931.

IPPEL, A. Indische Kunst und Triumphalbild. Leipzig, 1929.

JACOVLEFF, A., and TCHOU-KIA-KIEN. The Chinese Theatre. London, 1922.

JINAVARAVAMSA, P. C. "Notes on Siamese Arts and Crafts," Ceylon National Review, No. 4, July, 1907.

JITTA-ZADOKS. Ancestral Portraiture in Rome. Amsterdam, 1932.

JUNG, C. G. Psychological Types. London, 1926.

KAKUZO, O. The Ideals of the East. New York, 1904.

—— The Book of Tea. New York, 1906.

KEITH, A.B. History of Sanskrit Literature. Oxford, 1928.

—— Aitareya and Kauṣītaki Brāhmaṇas. Harvard Oriental Series, XXV, 1920.

—— Buddhist Philosophy. Oxford, 1923.

KRAMRISCH, S. The Vishṇudharmottara, 2nd ed. Calcutta, 1928.[1]

—— "Landschaft, Tier, und geometrisches Muster in der indischen Kunst." Josef Strzygowski Festschrift. Klagenfurt, 1932.

—— Indian Sculpture. Calcutta, 1933.

LALOU, M. L'Iconographie des Étoffes peints (paṭa) dans le Mañ-juśrīmulakalpa. Buddhica, VI. Paris, 1930.

LAUFER, B. Dokumente der indischen Kunst: I, Das Citralakṣaṇa. Leipzig, 1913.[1]

LELYVELD, TH. B VAN. La Danse dans le Théâtre javanais. Paris, 1931.

LÉVI, S. Matériaux pour l'Étude du Système Vijñaptimātra. Paris, 1932.

[1] Silpa-Sāstra.

MARCH, B. "Linear Perspective in Chinese Painting," *Eastern Art*, III, 1931.

MARITAIN, J. *Art and Scholasticism*. London, 1930.

—— *Introduction to Philosophy*. London, 1932.

MARSHALL, SIR J. H. *Mohenjodaro*. London, 1931.

MASSON-OURSEL. *Esquisse d'une Histoire de la Philosophie indienne*, esp. pp. 156, 288. Paris, 1923.

—— "Une Connexion dans l'Ésthétique et la Philosophie de l'Inde," *Rev. des Arts asiatiques*, II, 1925 (transl. in *Rūpam*, 27/28, 1926).

——, WILMAN-GRABOWSKA, H. de, and Stern, P., *L'Inde antique et la Civilisation indienne*. Paris, 1933. (Pt. IV, La vie esthétique.)

MEERWARTH, A. "Les Kathakalis du Malabar." *Journal Asiatique*, Paris, CCIX, Oct.–Dec., 1926.

MUKERJI, S. C. *Le Rasa, Essai sur l'Esthétique indienne*. Paris, 1928.

OLDENBERG, H. "Vedic Words for 'Beautiful' and 'Beauty' and the Vedic Sense of the Beautiful," *Rūpam*, No. 32, 1928.

PETRUCCI, R. *Encyclopédie de la Peinture chinoise*. Paris, 1918.

—— *La Philosophie de la Nature dans l'Art d'Extrême-Orient*. Paris, n.d.

PODUVAL, R. V. *The Art of Kathākali*. Trivandrum, 1933.

POPE, G. U. *The Tiruvāçagam*. Oxford, 1900.

RAM RAZ. *Essay on the Architecture of the Hindus*. London, 1834.

RAO, T. A. G. *Elements of Hindu Iconography*. Madras, 1914, 1916.[1]

—— *Tālamāna or Iconometry*. Memoirs of the Archaeological Survey of India, III. Calcutta, 1920.

REGNAUD, P. *La Rhétorique sanskrite*. Paris, 1884.

SARKAR, B. K. *The Śukranīti*. Sacred Books of the Hindus, XII. Allahābād, 1914.

ŚAUNAKA. *Bṛhad Devatā*. Translated by A. A. Macdonell. Harvard Oriental Series, VI. Cambridge, 1904.

[1] *Śilpa-Śāstra*.

SCHLOSSER, J. *Die Kunstliteratur.* Vienna, 1924.

SIRÉN, O. *A History of Early Chinese Painting.* London, 1933.

STCHERBATSKY, TH. *Buddhist Logic.* Leningrad, 1930, 1932.

STRZYGOWSKI, J. *Asiatische Miniaturmalerei, im Anschluss an Wesen und Werden der Mogulmalerei.* Klagenfurt, 1933.

SUZUKI, D. T. *Essays in Zen Buddhism.* London, 1927–

—— *Outlines of Mahayana Buddhism.* London, 1907.

—— *The Laṅkâvatāra Sūtra.* London, 1932.

TAGORE, A., *L'Alpona.* Paris, 1921.

—— *Art et Anatomie hindoue.* Paris, 1921.

—— *Sadanga.* Paris, 1922.

TAGORE, R. *Poems of Kabir* (various editions).

TAKI, S. *Three Essays in Oriental Painting.* London, 1910.

—— *Japanese Fine Arts.* Tokio, 1931.

THOMAS AQUINAS, St. *Summa Theologica.*

VASUBANDHU. *Abhidharmakośa.* Translated by L. de la Vallée Poussin. Louvain, 1923–1931.

VENKATA, RAO, M. A. "Aesthetics in India," *Aryan Path,* IV, 715–720, 1933.

VENKATASSUBBIAH, A. *The Kalās.* Madras, 1911.

VENKATASUBBIAH, A., and MÜLLER, E. The Kalās, *JRAS.,* 1914.

VIŚVANATHA. *Sāhitya Darpaṇa.* Translated as *The Mirror of Composition,* by Premadasa Mitra. Calcutta, 1875.

WALEY, A. *The Nō Plays of Japan.* London, 1921.

—— *Zen Buddhism in its Relation to Art.* London, 1922.

—— *An Introduction to the Study of Chinese Painting.* London, 1923.

—— *The Tale of Genji,* 6 vols. London, 1925–33.

WOODROFFE, SIR J. *The Garland of Letters.* London, 1922.

—— "Psychology of Hindu Religious Ritual," *Indian Art and Letters,* I, 1925.

—— "The Indian Magna Mater," *ibid.,* II, 1926.

WULF, M. DE. *Études historiques sur l'Ésthetique de St. Thomas d'Aquin.* Löwen, 1896.[1]

---

[1] Not seen by the author.

ZIMMER, H. *Kunstform und Yoga im indischen Kultbild.* Berlin, 1926.

—— "Some Aspects of Time in Indian Art," *Journ. Indian Society of Oriental Art,* I, 1933, pp. 30–51.

2. SANSKRIT WORKS

Aitareya Brāhmaṇa. Ed. Sāmaśramī, Bibliotheca Indica, Calcutta, 1895, 1896.

Asaṅga, *Mahāyāna Sūtrâlaṁkāra.* Ed. Sylvain Lévi, Paris, 1925.

Basava Rāja, *Śiva Tattva Ratnākara.* Ed. B. R. Rao and P. S. Sastriar, Madras, 1927. (See *Kalolla* VI, *Taraṅga* 2.)

Bhagavad Gītā. Various editions.

Bharata, *Nāṭya Śāstra.* Ed. M. Ramakrishna Kavi, Gaekwar's Oriental Series, XXXVI (Vol. I), Baroda, 1926.

Bhāsa, *Dūtavākya.* Gaṇapati Śāstri's ed., Trivandrum, 1925.

—— *Pratimānāṭaka.* Paranjape's ed., Poona, 1927.

—— *Pratijñāyaugandhārāyaṇa.* Gaṇapati Śāstri's ed., Trivandrum, 1920.

—— *Svapnavāsavadatta.* Gaṇapati Śāstri's ed., Trivandrum, 1926.

Bhavabhūti, *Uttara-Rāma-carita.* Belvalkar's ed., Poona, 1921.

Bhojadeva, *Samarânganasūtradhāra.* Ed. T. Gaṇapati Śāstri, Gaekwar's Oriental Series, XXV, Baroda, 1924.[1]

—— *Yukti-Kalpataru.* Candra Śāstri's ed., Calcutta, 1917.[1]

Bṛhad Devatā. Ed. Macdonell, Harvard Oriental Series, V, Cambridge, 1904.

Citralakṣaṇa. (1) See Laufer, in Bibliography 1, above. (2) Ch. 64 of the *Śilparatna, q.v.*[1]

Daṇḍin, *Daśakumāracarita.* Ed. Wilson, London, 1846.

Dhanaṁjaya, *Daśarūpa.* Text and translation, ed. Haas, New York, 1912.

Divyâvadāna. Ed. Cowell, E. B., and Neil, R. A., Cambridge, Eng., 1888.

[1] *Śilpa Śāstras.*

244 BIBLIOGRAPHY

Harṣa, *Priyadarśikā.* Ed. and tr. by Nariman and Ogden, Columbia University Indo-Iranian Series, X, New York, 1923.

Hemacandra, *Triṣaṣṭiśalākāpuruṣacaritra (Ādīśvaracaritra).* Bhavnagar, 1905.

Jaiminīya Upaniṣad Brāhmaṇa. Ed. and tr. Oertel, *JAOS.,* XVI, New Haven, 1894.

Kālidāsa, *Śakuntalā.* (1) Pischel's ed., Harvard Oriental Series, XVI, Cambridge, 1922, (2) Kale's ed. (*Abhijñāna-śakuntalam*), Bombay, 1913.

—— *Vikramôrvaśī.* Kale's 6th ed., Bombay, 1922.

—— *Kumārasambhava.* Kale's 5th ed., Bombay, 1923.

—— *Mālavikâgnimitra.* Paranjape's ed., Poona, 1918.

—— *Raghuvaṁśa.* Nandargikar's 3rd ed., Bombay, 1897.

Kāma Sūtra. Kāshī Sanskrit Series, XXIX, Benares, 1929 (with Yaśodhara's commentary).

Kāśyapaśilpam. Anandâśrama Skr. Series, XCV, 1926.[1]

Lalita Vistara. Ed. Lefmann, Halle, 1902.

Laṅkâvatāra Sūtra. Nanjō's ed. Tokyō, 1923.

Mayamuni, *Mayamata.* Ed. T. Gaṇapati Śāstri, Trivandrum Skr. Series, LXV, Trivandrum, 1919.[1]

Pañcaviṁśa Brāhmaṇa. Vedântavāgīśa's ed., Bibliotheca Indica, Calcutta, 1870, 1874.

Prakāśânanda, *Siddhântamuktāvalī.* Reprint from *The Pandit.* Benares, 1898.

Pratimā-Māna-Lakṣaṇam. Ed. P. N. Bose, Punjab Oriental Series, XVIII, Lahore, 1929.[1]

Rājaśekhara, *Karpūramañjarī.* Ed. and tr. by Konow and Lanman, Harvard Oriental Series, IV, Cambridge, 1901.

—— *Kāvyamīmāṁsā.* Gaekwar's Oriental Series, Baroda, 1924.

Ṛg Veda Saṁhitā. Ed. Max Müller. London, 1849–1874.

Saddharma Puṇḍarīka. Kern and Nanjio's ed., Bibliotheca Buddhica, St. Petersburg, 1912.

Sādhanamālā. Ed. B. Bhattacharyya, Gaekwar's Oriental Series, XXVI, XLI, Baroda, 1925, 1928.[1]

---

[1] *Śilpa Śāstras.*

Śaṅkarâcārya: *Svâtmanirūpaṇa*; *Sataślokī*. Minor Works of Shankaracharya. Ed. H. R. Bhagavat, Poona, 1925.

—— *Brahmasūtra-bhāṣya*. Ed. Pañśikar, 2nd ed., Bombay, 1927.

Śatapatha Brāhmaṇa. Ed. Sāmaśramī, Bibliotheca Indica, Calcutta, 1907–1911.

Śrī Kumāra, *Śilparatna*. Ed. T. Gaṇapati Śāstri, Trivandrum Skr. Series, LXXV, XCVIII, Trivandrum, 1922, 1929.[1]

Śūdraka, *Mṛcchakaṭika*. Parab's 5th ed., Bombay, 1922.

Śukrâcārya, *Śukranītisāra*. Vidyāsagara's ed., Calcutta, 1890.

Upaniṣads. Various editions.

Vasubandhu, *Trimśikā*. Ed. Sylvain Lévi, Paris, 1925.

—— *Vimśatikā*. Ed. Sylvain Lévi, Paris, 1925.

Viṣṇudharmottara. Ed. Pandit Mādhavaprasād, Bombay, 1911.

Viśvanātha, *Sāhitya Darpaṇa*. Kane's ed., Bombay, 1923.

Yāska, *Nighaṇṭu and Nirukta*. Ed. Sarup, Lahore, 1927.

3. PALI AND PRAKRIT

Āyāraṁga Sutta. Ed. Jacobi, Pali Text Soc., London, 1882.

Buddhaghoṣa, *Atthasālinī*. Ed. E. Müller, Pali Text Soc., London, 1897.

Cūḷavaṁsa. Ed. Geiger, Pali Text Soc., London, 1925, 1927.

Jātaka. Ed. Fausböll, London, 1877–1896.

Mahāvaṁsa. Ed. Geiger, Pali Text Soc., London, 1908.

Vibhanga. Ed. Mrs. Rhys Davids, Pali Text Soc., London, 1904.

4. CHINESE

Yü Shao-Tsung (ed.). *Hua Fa Yao Lu* (an anthology of Chinese criticism). Shanghai, *ca.* 1930.[2]

---

[1] *Śilpa Śāstras.*
[2] Not seen by the author.

A CATALOGUE OF SELECTED DOVER BOOKS
IN ALL FIELDS OF INTEREST

WHAT IS SCIENCE?, *N. Campbell*
The role of experiment and measurement, the function of mathematics, the nature of scientific laws, the difference between laws and theories, the limitations of science, and many similarly provocative topics are treated clearly and without technicalities by an eminent scientist. "Still an excellent introduction to scientific philosophy," H. Margenau in *Physics Today*. "A first-rate primer . . . deserves a wide audience," *Scientific American*. 192pp. 5⅜ x 8.
60043-2 Paperbound $1.25

THE NATURE OF LIGHT AND COLOUR IN THE OPEN AIR, *M. Minnaert*
Why are shadows sometimes blue, sometimes green, or other colors depending on the light and surroundings? What causes mirages? Why do multiple suns and moons appear in the sky? Professor Minnaert explains these unusual phenomena and hundreds of others in simple, easy-to-understand terms based on optical laws and the properties of light and color. No mathematics is required but artists, scientists, students, and everyone fascinated by these "tricks" of nature will find thousands of useful and amazing pieces of information. Hundreds of observational experiments are suggested which require no special equipment. 200 illustrations; 42 photos. xvi + 362pp. 5⅜ x 8.
20196-1 Paperbound $2.75

THE STRANGE STORY OF THE QUANTUM, AN ACCOUNT FOR THE GENERAL READER OF THE GROWTH OF IDEAS UNDERLYING OUR PRESENT ATOMIC KNOWLEDGE, *B. Hoffmann*
Presents lucidly and expertly, with barest amount of mathematics, the problems and theories which led to modern quantum physics. Dr. Hoffmann begins with the closing years of the 19th century, when certain trifling discrepancies were noticed, and with illuminating analogies and examples takes you through the brilliant concepts of Planck, Einstein, Pauli, Broglie, Bohr, Schroedinger, Heisenberg, Dirac, Sommerfeld, Feynman, etc. This edition includes a new, long postscript carrying the story through 1958. "Of the books attempting an account of the history and contents of our modern atomic physics which have come to my attention, this is the best," H. Margenau, Yale University, in *American Journal of Physics*. 32 tables and line illustrations. Index. 275pp. 5⅜ x 8.
20518-5 Paperbound $2.00

GREAT IDEAS OF MODERN MATHEMATICS: THEIR NATURE AND USE, *Jagjit Singh*
Reader with only high school math will understand main mathematical ideas of modern physics, astronomy, genetics, psychology, evolution, etc. better than many who use them as tools, but comprehend little of their basic structure. Author uses his wide knowledge of non-mathematical fields in brilliant exposition of differential equations, matrices, group theory, logic, statistics, problems of mathematical foundations, imaginary numbers, vectors, etc. Original publication. 2 appendixes. 2 indexes. 65 ills. 322pp. 5⅜ x 8.
20587-8 Paperbound $2.50

A CATALOGUE OF SELECTED DOVER BOOKS
IN ALL FIELDS OF INTEREST

THE MUSIC OF THE SPHERES: THE MATERIAL UNIVERSE — FROM ATOM TO QUASAR, SIMPLY EXPLAINED, *Guy Murchie*
Vast compendium of fact, modern concept and theory, observed and calculated data, historical background guides intelligent layman through the material universe. Brilliant exposition of earth's construction, explanations for moon's craters, atmospheric components of Venus and Mars (with data from recent fly-by's), sun spots, sequences of star birth and death, neighboring galaxies, contributions of Galileo, Tycho Brahe, Kepler, etc.; and (Vol. 2) construction of the atom (describing newly discovered sigma and xi subatomic particles), theories of sound, color and light, space and time, including relativity theory, quantum theory, wave theory, probability theory, work of Newton, Maxwell, Faraday, Einstein, de Broglie, etc. "Best presentation yet offered to the intelligent general reader," *Saturday Review*. Revised (1967). Index. 319 illustrations by the author. Total of xx + 644pp. 5⅜ x 8½.
21809-0, 21810-4 Two volume set, paperbound $5.00

FOUR LECTURES ON RELATIVITY AND SPACE, *Charles Proteus Steinmetz*
Lecture series, given by great mathematician and electrical engineer, generally considered one of the best popular-level expositions of special and general relativity theories and related questions. Steinmetz translates complex mathematical reasoning into language accessible to laymen through analogy, example and comparison. Among topics covered are relativity of motion, location, time; of mass; acceleration; 4-dimensional time-space; geometry of the gravitational field; curvature and bending of space; non-Euclidean geometry. Index. 40 illustrations. x + 142pp. 5⅜ x 8½.
61771-8 Paperbound $1.50

HOW TO KNOW THE WILD FLOWERS, *Mrs. William Starr Dana*
Classic nature book that has introduced thousands to wonders of American wild flowers. Color-season principle of organization is easy to use, even by those with no botanical training, and the genial, refreshing discussions of history, folklore, uses of over 1,000 native and escape flowers, foliage plants are informative as well as fun to read. Over 170 full-page plates, collected from several editions, may be colored in to make permanent records of finds. Revised to conform with 1950 edition of Gray's Manual of Botany. xlii + 438pp. 5⅜ x 8½.
20332-8 Paperbound $2.50

MANUAL OF THE TREES OF NORTH AMERICA, *Charles Sprague Sargent*
Still unsurpassed as most comprehensive, reliable study of North American tree characteristics, precise locations and distribution. By dean of American dendrologists. Every tree native to U.S., Canada, Alaska; 185 genera, 717 species, described in detail—leaves, flowers, fruit, winterbuds, bark, wood, growth habits, etc. plus discussion of varieties and local variants, immaturity variations. Over 100 keys, including unusual 11-page analytical key to genera, aid in identification. 783 clear illustrations of flowers, fruit, leaves. An unmatched permanent reference work for all nature lovers. Second enlarged (1926) edition. Synopsis of families. Analytical key to genera. Glossary of technical terms. Index. 783 illustrations, 1 map. Total of 982pp. 5⅜ x 8.
20277-1, 20278-X Two volume set, paperbound $6.00

IT'S FUN TO MAKE THINGS FROM SCRAP MATERIALS,
Evelyn Glantz Hershoff
What use are empty spools, tin cans, bottle tops? What can be made from rubber bands, clothes pins, paper clips, and buttons? This book provides simply worded instructions and large diagrams showing you how to make cookie cutters, toy trucks, paper turkeys, Halloween masks, telephone sets, aprons, linoleum block- and spatter prints — in all 399 projects! Many are easy enough for young children to figure out for themselves; some challenging enough to entertain adults; all are remarkably ingenious ways to make things from materials that cost pennies or less! Formerly "Scrap Fun for Everyone." Index. 214 illustrations. 373pp. 5⅜ x 8½. 21251-3 Paperbound $2.00

SYMBOLIC LOGIC and THE GAME OF LOGIC, *Lewis Carroll*
"Symbolic Logic" is not concerned with modern symbolic logic, but is instead a collection of over 380 problems posed with charm and imagination, using the syllogism and a fascinating diagrammatic method of drawing conclusions. In "The Game of Logic" Carroll's whimsical imagination devises a logical game played with 2 diagrams and counters (included) to manipulate hundreds of tricky syllogisms. The final section, "Hit or Miss" is a lagniappe of 101 additional puzzles in the delightful Carroll manner. Until this reprint edition, both of these books were rarities costing up to $15 each. Symbolic Logic: Index. xxxi + 199pp. The Game of Logic: 96pp. 2 vols. bound as one. 5⅜ x 8. 20492-8 Paperbound $2.50

MATHEMATICAL PUZZLES OF SAM LOYD, PART I
selected and edited by M. Gardner
Choice puzzles by the greatest American puzzle creator and innovator. Selected from his famous collection, "Cyclopedia of Puzzles," they retain the unique style and historical flavor of the originals. There are posers based on arithmetic, algebra, probability, game theory, route tracing, topology, counter and sliding block, operations research, geometrical dissection. Includes the famous "14-15" puzzle which was a national craze, and his "Horse of a Different Color" which sold millions of copies. 117 of his most ingenious puzzles in all. 120 line drawings and diagrams. Solutions. Selected references. xx + 167pp. 5⅜ x 8. 20498-7 Paperbound $1.35

STRING FIGURES AND HOW TO MAKE THEM, *Caroline Furness Jayne*
107 string figures plus variations selected from the best primitive and modern examples developed by Navajo, Apache, pygmies of Africa, Eskimo, in Europe, Australia, China, etc. The most readily understandable, easy-to-follow book in English on perennially popular recreation. Crystal-clear exposition; step-by-step diagrams. Everyone from kindergarten children to adults looking for unusual diversion will be endlessly amused. Index. Bibliography. Introduction by A. C. Haddon. 17 full-page plates, 960 illustrations. xxiii + 401pp. 5⅜ x 8½. 20152-X Paperbound $2.50

PAPER FOLDING FOR BEGINNERS, *W. D. Murray and F. J. Rigney*
A delightful introduction to the varied and entertaining Japanese art of origami (paper folding), with a full, crystal-clear text that anticipates every difficulty; over 275 clearly labeled diagrams of all important stages in creation. You get results at each stage, since complex figures are logically developed from simpler ones. 43 different pieces are explained: sailboats, frogs, roosters, etc. 6 photographic plates. 279 diagrams. 95pp. 5⅜ x 8⅜. 20713-7 Paperbound $1.00

PRINCIPLES OF ART HISTORY,
H. Wölfflin
Analyzing such terms as "baroque," "classic," "neoclassic," "primitive," "picturesque," and 164 different works by artists like Botticelli, van Cleve, Dürer, Hobbema, Holbein, Hals, Rembrandt, Titian, Brueghel, Vermeer, and many others, the author establishes the classifications of art history and style on a firm, concrete basis. This classic of art criticism shows what really occurred between the 14th-century primitives and the sophistication of the 18th century in terms of basic attitudes and philosophies. "A remarkable lesson in the art of seeing," *Sat. Rev. of Literature.* Translated from the 7th German edition. 150 illustrations. 254pp. 6⅛ x 9¼. 20276-3 Paperbound $2.50

PRIMITIVE ART,
Franz Boas
This authoritative and exhaustive work by a great American anthropologist covers the entire gamut of primitive art. Pottery, leatherwork, metal work, stone work, wood, basketry, are treated in detail. Theories of primitive art, historical depth in art history, technical virtuosity, unconscious levels of patterning, symbolism, styles, literature, music, dance, etc. A must book for the interested layman, the anthropologist, artist, handicrafter (hundreds of unusual motifs), and the historian. Over 900 illustrations (50 ceramic vessels, 12 totem poles, etc.). 376pp. 5⅜ x 8. 20025-6 Paperbound $2.50

THE GENTLEMAN AND CABINET MAKER'S DIRECTOR,
Thomas Chippendale
A reprint of the 1762 catalogue of furniture designs that went on to influence generations of English and Colonial and Early Republic American furniture makers. The 200 plates, most of them full-page sized, show Chippendale's designs for French (Louis XV), Gothic, and Chinese-manner chairs, sofas, canopy and dome beds, cornices, chamber organs, cabinets, shaving tables, commodes, picture frames, frets, candle stands, chimney pieces, decorations, etc. The drawings are all elegant and highly detailed; many include construction diagrams and elevations. A supplement of 24 photographs shows surviving pieces of original and Chippendale-style pieces of furniture. Brief biography of Chippendale by N. I. Bienenstock, editor of *Furniture World.* Reproduced from the 1762 edition. 200 plates, plus 19 photographic plates. vi + 249pp. 9⅛ x 12¼. 21601-2 Paperbound $4.00

AMERICAN ANTIQUE FURNITURE: A BOOK FOR AMATEURS,
Edgar G. Miller, Jr.
Standard introduction and practical guide to identification of valuable American antique furniture. 2115 illustrations, mostly photographs taken by the author in 148 private homes, are arranged in chronological order in extensive chapters on chairs, sofas, chests, desks, bedsteads, mirrors, tables, clocks, and other articles. Focus is on furniture accessible to the collector, including simpler pieces and a larger than usual coverage of Empire style. Introductory chapters identify structural elements, characteristics of various styles, how to avoid fakes, etc. "We are frequently asked to name some book on American furniture that will meet the requirements of the novice collector, the beginning dealer, and . . . the general public. . . . We believe Mr. Miller's two volumes more completely satisfy this specification than any other work," *Antiques.* Appendix. Index. Total of vi + 1106pp. 7⅞ x 10¾. 21599-7, 21600-4 Two volume set, paperbound $10.00

THE BAD CHILD'S BOOK OF BEASTS, MORE BEASTS FOR WORSE CHILDREN, and A MORAL ALPHABET, *H. Belloc*
Hardly and anthology of humorous verse has appeared in the last 50 years without at least a couple of these famous nonsense verses. But one must see the entire volumes — with all the delightful original illustrations by Sir Basil Blackwood — to appreciate fully Belloc's charming and witty verses that play so subacidly on the platitudes of life and morals that beset his day — and ours. A great humor classic. Three books in one. Total of 157pp. 5⅜ x 8.
20749-8 Paperbound $1.25

THE DEVIL'S DICTIONARY, *Ambrose Bierce*
Sardonic and irreverent barbs puncturing the pomposities and absurdities of American politics, business, religion, literature, and arts, by the country's greatest satirist in the classic tradition. Epigrammatic as Shaw, piercing as Swift, American as Mark Twain, Will Rogers, and Fred Allen, Bierce will always remain the favorite of a small coterie of enthusiasts, and of writers and speakers whom he supplies with "some of the most gorgeous witticisms of the English language" (H. L. Mencken). Over 1000 entries in alphabetical order. 144pp. 5⅜ x 8.
20487-1 Paperbound $1.25

THE COMPLETE NONSENSE OF EDWARD LEAR.
This is the only complete edition of this master of gentle madness available at a popular price. *A Book of Nonsense, Nonsense Songs, More Nonsense Songs and Stories* in their entirety with all the old favorites that have delighted children and adults for years. The Dong With A Luminous Nose, The Jumblies, The Owl and the Pussycat, and hundreds of other bits of wonderful nonsense. 214 limericks, 3 sets of Nonsense Botany, 5 Nonsense Alphabets, 546 drawings by Lear himself, and much more. 320pp. 5⅜ x 8. 20167-8 Paperbound $1.75

THE WIT AND HUMOR OF OSCAR WILDE, *ed. by Alvin Redman*
Wilde at his most brilliant, in 1000 epigrams exposing weaknesses and hypocrisies of "civilized" society. Divided into 49 categories—sin, wealth, women, America, etc.—to aid writers, speakers. Includes excerpts from his trials, books, plays, criticism. Formerly "The Epigrams of Oscar Wilde." Introduction by Vyvyan Holland, Wilde's only living son. Introductory essay by editor. 260pp. 5⅜ x 8.
20602-5 Paperbound $1.50

A CHILD'S PRIMER OF NATURAL HISTORY, *Oliver Herford*
Scarcely an anthology of whimsy and humor has appeared in the last 50 years without a contribution from Oliver Herford. Yet the works from which these examples are drawn have been almost impossible to obtain! Here at last are Herford's improbable definitions of a menagerie of familiar and weird animals, each verse illustrated by the author's own drawings. 24 drawings in 2 colors; 24 additional drawings. vii + 95pp. 6½ x 6. 21647-0 Paperbound $1.00

THE BROWNIES: THEIR BOOK, *Palmer Cox*
The book that made the Brownies a household word. Generations of readers have enjoyed the antics, predicaments and adventures of these jovial sprites, who emerge from the forest at night to play or to come to the aid of a deserving human. Delightful illustrations by the author decorate nearly every page. 24 short verse tales with 266 illustrations. 155pp. 6⅝ x 9¼.
21265-3 Paperbound $1.50

THE PRINCIPLES OF PSYCHOLOGY,
William James
The full long-course, unabridged, of one of the great classics of Western literature and science. Wonderfully lucid descriptions of human mental activity, the stream of thought, consciousness, time perception, memory, imagination, emotions, reason, abnormal phenomena, and similar topics. Original contributions are integrated with the work of such men as Berkeley, Binet, Mills, Darwin, Hume, Kant, Royce, Schopenhauer, Spinoza, Locke, Descartes, Galton, Wundt, Lotze, Herbart, Fechner, and scores of others. All contrasting interpretations of mental phenomena are examined in detail—introspective analysis, philosophical interpretation, and experimental research. "A classic," *Journal of Consulting Psychology*. "The main lines are as valid as ever," *Psychoanalytical Quarterly*. "Standard reading . . . a classic of interpretation," *Psychiatric Quarterly*. 94 illustrations. 1408pp. 5⅜ x 8.
20381-6, 20382-4 Two volume set, paperbound $6.00

VISUAL ILLUSIONS: THEIR CAUSES, CHARACTERISTICS AND APPLICATIONS,
M. Luckiesh
"Seeing is deceiving," asserts the author of this introduction to virtually every type of optical illusion known. The text both describes and explains the principles involved in color illusions, figure-ground, distance illusions, etc. 100 photographs, drawings and diagrams prove how easy it is to fool the sense: circles that aren't round, parallel lines that seem to bend, stationary figures that seem to move as you stare at them — illustration after illustration strains our credulity at what we see. Fascinating book from many points of view, from applications for artists, in camouflage, etc. to the psychology of vision. New introduction by William Ittleson, Dept. of Psychology, Queens College. Index. Bibliography. xxi + 252pp. 5⅜ x 8½. 21530-X Paperbound $1.75

FADS AND FALLACIES IN THE NAME OF SCIENCE,
Martin Gardner
This is the standard account of various cults, quack systems, and delusions which have masqueraded as science: hollow earth fanatics. Reich and orgone sex energy, dianetics, Atlantis, multiple moons, Forteanism, flying saucers, medical fallacies like iridiagnosis, zone therapy, etc. A new chapter has been added on Bridey Murphy, psionics, and other recent manifestations in this field. This is a fair, reasoned appraisal of eccentric theory which provides excellent inoculation against cleverly masked nonsense. "Should be read by everyone, scientist and non-scientist alike," R. T. Birge, Prof. Emeritus of Physics, Univ. of California; Former President, American Physical Society. Index. x + 365pp. 5⅜ x 8. 20394-8 Paperbound $2.00

ILLUSIONS AND DELUSIONS OF THE SUPERNATURAL AND THE OCCULT,
D. H. Rawcliffe
Holds up to rational examination hundreds of persistent delusions including crystal gazing, automatic writing, table turning, mediumistic trances, mental healing, stigmata, lycanthropy, live burial, the Indian Rope Trick, spiritualism, dowsing, telepathy, clairvoyance, ghosts, ESP, etc. The author explains and exposes the mental and physical deceptions involved, making this not only an exposé of supernatural phenomena, but a valuable exposition of characteristic types of abnormal psychology. Originally titled "The Psychology of the Occult." 14 illustrations. Index. 551pp. 5⅜ x 8. 20503-7 Paperbound $3.50

FAIRY TALE COLLECTIONS, *edited by Andrew Lang*
Andrew Lang's fairy tale collections make up the richest shelf-full of traditional children's stories anywhere available. Lang supervised the translation of stories from all over the world—familiar European tales collected by Grimm, animal stories from Negro Africa, myths of primitive Australia, stories from Russia, Hungary, Iceland, Japan, and many other countries. Lang's selection of translations are unusually high; many authorities consider that the most familiar tales find their best versions in these volumes. All collections are richly decorated and illustrated by H. J. Ford and other artists.

THE BLUE FAIRY BOOK. 37 stories. 138 illustrations. ix + 390pp. 5⅜ x 8½.
21437-0 Paperbound $1.95

THE GREEN FAIRY BOOK. 42 stories. 100 illustrations. xiii + 366pp. 5⅜ x 8½.
21439-7 Paperbound $2.00

THE BROWN FAIRY BOOK. 32 stories. 50 illustrations, 8 in color. xii + 350pp. 5⅜ x 8½.
21438-9 Paperbound $1.95

THE BEST TALES OF HOFFMANN, *edited by E. F. Bleiler*
10 stories by E. T. A. Hoffmann, one of the greatest of all writers of fantasy. The tales include "The Golden Flower Pot," "Automata," "A New Year's Eve Adventure," "Nutcracker and the King of Mice," "Sand-Man," and others. Vigorous characterizations of highly eccentric personalities, remarkably imaginative situations, and intensely fast pacing has made these tales popular all over the world for 150 years. Editor's introduction. 7 drawings by Hoffmann. xxxiii + 419pp. 5⅜ x 8½.
21793-0 Paperbound $2.25

GHOST AND HORROR STORIES OF AMBROSE BIERCE,
edited by E. F. Bleiler
Morbid, eerie, horrifying tales of possessed poets, shabby aristocrats, revived corpses, and haunted malefactors. Widely acknowledged as the best of their kind between Poe and the moderns, reflecting their author's inner torment and bitter view of life. Includes "Damned Thing," "The Middle Toe of the Right Foot," "The Eyes of the Panther," "Visions of the Night," "Moxon's Master," and over a dozen others. Editor's introduction. xxii + 199pp. 5⅜ x 8½.
20767-6 Paperbound $1.50

THREE GOTHIC NOVELS, *edited by E. F. Bleiler*
Originators of the still popular Gothic novel form, influential in ushering in early 19th-century Romanticism. Horace Walpole's *Castle of Otranto*, William Beckford's *Vathek*, John Polidori's *The Vampyre*, and a *Fragment* by Lord Byron are enjoyable as exciting reading or as documents in the history of English literature. Editor's introduction. xi + 291pp. 5⅜ x 8½.
21232-7 Paperbound $2.00

BEST GHOST STORIES OF LEFANU, *edited by E. F. Bleiler*
Though admired by such critics as V. S. Pritchett, Charles Dickens and Henry James, ghost stories by the Irish novelist Joseph Sheridan LeFanu have never become as widely known as his detective fiction. About half of the 16 stories in this collection have never before been available in America. Collection includes "Carmilla" (perhaps the best vampire story ever written), "The Haunted Baronet," "The Fortunes of Sir Robert Ardagh," and the classic "Green Tea." Editor's introduction. 7 contemporary illustrations. Portrait of LeFanu. xii + 467pp. 5⅜ x 8.
20415-4 Paperbound $2.50

EASY-TO-DO ENTERTAINMENTS AND DIVERSIONS WITH COINS, CARDS, STRING, PAPER AND MATCHES, *R. M. Abraham*
Over 300 tricks, games and puzzles will provide young readers with absorbing fun. Sections on card games; paper-folding; tricks with coins, matches and pieces of string; games for the agile; toy-making from common household objects; mathematical recreations; and 50 miscellaneous pastimes. Anyone in charge of groups of youngsters, including hard-pressed parents, and in need of suggestions on how to keep children sensibly amused and quietly content will find this book indispensable. Clear, simple text, copious number of delightful line drawings and illustrative diagrams. Originally titled "Winter Nights' Entertainments." Introduction by Lord Baden Powell. 329 illustrations. v + 186pp. 5⅜ x 8½.   20921-0 Paperbound $1.25

AN INTRODUCTION TO CHESS MOVES AND TACTICS SIMPLY EXPLAINED, *Leonard Barden*
Beginner's introduction to the royal game. Names, possible moves of the pieces, definitions of essential terms, how games are won, etc. explained in 30-odd pages. With this background you'll be able to sit right down and play. Balance of book teaches strategy — openings, middle game, typical endgame play, and suggestions for improving your game. A sample game is fully analyzed. True middle-level introduction, teaching you all the essentials without oversimplifying or losing you in a maze of detail. 58 figures. 102pp. 5⅜ x 8½.   21210-6 Paperbound $1.25

LASKER'S MANUAL OF CHESS, *Dr. Emanuel Lasker*
Probably the greatest chess player of modern times, Dr. Emanuel Lasker held the world championship 28 years, independent of passing schools or fashions. This unmatched study of the game, chiefly for intermediate to skilled players, analyzes basic methods, combinations, position play, the aesthetics of chess, dozens of different openings, etc., with constant reference to great modern games. Contains a brilliant exposition of Steinitz's important theories. Introduction by Fred Reinfeld. Tables of Lasker's tournament record. 3 indices. 308 diagrams. 1 photograph. xxx + 349pp. 5⅜ x 8.20640-8 Paperbound $2.50

COMBINATIONS: THE HEART OF CHESS, *Irving Chernev*
Step-by-step from simple combinations to complex, this book, by a well-known chess writer, shows you the intricacies of pins, counter-pins, knight forks, and smothered mates. Other chapters show alternate lines of play to those taken in actual championship games; boomerang combinations; classic examples of brilliant combination play by Nimzovich, Rubinstein, Tarrasch, Botvinnik, Alekhine and Capablanca. Index. 356 diagrams. ix + 245pp. 5⅜ x 8½.   21744-2 Paperbound $2.00

HOW TO SOLVE CHESS PROBLEMS, *K. S. Howard*
Full of practical suggestions for the fan or the beginner — who knows only the moves of the chessmen. Contains preliminary section and 58 two-move, 46 three-move, and 8 four-move problems composed by 27 outstanding American problem creators in the last 30 years. Explanation of all terms and exhaustive index. "Just what is wanted for the student," Brian Harley. 112 problems, solutions. vi + 171pp. 5⅜ x 8.   20748-X Paperbound $1.50

SOCIAL THOUGHT FROM LORE TO SCIENCE,
H. E. Barnes and H. Becker
An immense survey of sociological thought and ways of viewing, studying, planning, and reforming society from earliest times to the present. Includes thought on society of preliterate peoples, ancient non-Western cultures, and every great movement in Europe, America, and modern Japan. Analyzes hundreds of great thinkers: Plato, Augustine, Bodin, Vico, Montesquieu, Herder, Comte, Marx, etc. Weighs the contributions of utopians, sophists, fascists and communists; economists, jurists, philosophers, ecclesiastics, and every 19th and 20th century school of scientific sociology, anthropology, and social psychology throughout the world. Combines topical, chronological, and regional approaches, treating the evolution of social thought as a process rather than as a series of mere topics. "Impressive accuracy, competence, and discrimination . . . easily the best single survey," *Nation*. Thoroughly revised, with new material up to 1960. 2 indexes. Over 2200 bibliographical notes. Three volume set. Total of 1586pp. 5⅜ x 8.
20901-6, 20902-4, 20903-2 Three volume set, paperbound $10.50

A HISTORY OF HISTORICAL WRITING, *Harry Elmer Barnes*
Virtually the only adequate survey of the whole course of historical writing in a single volume. Surveys developments from the beginnings of historiography in the ancient Near East and the Classical World, up through the Cold War. Covers major historians in detail, shows interrelationship with cultural background, makes clear individual contributions, evaluates and estimates importance; also enormously rich upon minor authors and thinkers who are usually passed over. Packed with scholarship and learning, clear, easily written. Indispensable to every student of history. Revised and enlarged up to 1961. Index and bibliography. xv + 442pp. 5⅜ x 8½.
20104-X Paperbound $3.00

JOHANN SEBASTIAN BACH, *Philipp Spitta*
The complete and unabridged text of the definitive study of Bach. Written some 70 years ago, it is still unsurpassed for its coverage of nearly all aspects of Bach's life and work. There could hardly be a finer non-technical introduction to Bach's music than the detailed, lucid analyses which Spitta provides for hundreds of individual pieces. 26 solid pages are devoted to the B minor mass, for example, and 30 pages to the glorious St. Matthew Passion. This monumental set also includes a major analysis of the music of the 18th century: Buxtehude, Pachelbel, etc. "Unchallenged as the last word on one of the supreme geniuses of music," John Barkham, *Saturday Review Syndicate*. Total of 1819pp. Heavy cloth binding. 5⅜ x 8.
22278-0, 22279-9 Two volume set, clothbound $15.00

BEETHOVEN AND HIS NINE SYMPHONIES, *George Grove*
In this modern middle-level classic of musicology Grove not only analyzes all nine of Beethoven's symphonies very thoroughly in terms of their musical structure, but also discusses the circumstances under which they were written, Beethoven's stylistic development, and much other background material. This is an extremely rich book, yet very easily followed; it is highly recommended to anyone seriously interested in music. Over 250 musical passages. Index. viii + 407pp. 5⅜ x 8.
20334-4 Paperbound $2.50

THE TIME STREAM
John Taine
Acknowledged by many as the best SF writer of the 1920's, Taine (under the name Eric Temple Bell) was also a Professor of Mathematics of considerable renown. Reprinted here are *The Time Stream*, generally considered Taine's best, *The Greatest Game*, a biological-fiction novel, and *The Purple Sapphire*, involving a supercivilization of the past. Taine's stories tie fantastic narratives to frameworks of original and logical scientific concepts. Speculation is often profound on such questions as the nature of time, concept of entropy, cyclical universes, etc. 4 contemporary illustrations. v + 532pp. 5⅜ x 8⅜.
21180-0 Paperbound $3.00

SEVEN SCIENCE FICTION NOVELS,
H. G. Wells
Full unabridged texts of 7 science-fiction novels of the master. Ranging from biology, physics, chemistry, astronomy, to sociology and other studies, Mr. Wells extrapolates whole worlds of strange and intriguing character. "One will have to go far to match this for entertainment, excitement, and sheer pleasure . . ."*New York Times*. Contents: The Time Machine, The Island of Dr. Moreau, The First Men in the Moon, The Invisible Man, The War of the Worlds, The Food of the Gods, In The Days of the Comet. 1015pp. 5⅜ x 8.
20264-X Clothbound $5.00

28 SCIENCE FICTION STORIES OF H. G. WELLS.
Two full, unabridged novels, *Men Like Gods* and *Star Begotten*, plus 26 short stories by the master science-fiction writer of all time! Stories of space, time, invention, exploration, futuristic adventure. Partial contents: *The Country of the Blind, In the Abyss, The Crystal Egg, The Man Who Could Work Miracles, A Story of Days to Come, The Empire of the Ants, The Magic Shop, The Valley of the Spiders, A Story of the Stone Age, Under the Knife, Sea Raiders,* etc. An indispensable collection for the library of anyone interested in science fiction adventure. 928pp. 5⅜ x 8.
20265-8 Clothbound $5.00

THREE MARTIAN NOVELS,
Edgar Rice Burroughs
Complete, unabridged reprinting, in one volume, of Thuvia, Maid of Mars; Chessmen of Mars; The Master Mind of Mars. Hours of science-fiction adventure by a modern master storyteller. Reset in large clear type for easy reading. 16 illustrations by J. Allen St. John. vi + 490pp. 5⅜ x 8½.
20039-6 Paperbound $2.50

AN INTELLECTUAL AND CULTURAL HISTORY OF THE WESTERN WORLD,
Harry Elmer Barnes
Monumental 3-volume survey of intellectual development of Europe from primitive cultures to the present day. Every significant product of human intellect traced through history: art, literature, mathematics, physical sciences, medicine, music, technology, social sciences, religions, jurisprudence, education, etc. Presentation is lucid and specific, analyzing in detail specific discoveries, theories, literary works, and so on. Revised (1965) by recognized scholars in specialized fields under the direction of Prof. Barnes. Revised bibliography. Indexes. 24 illustrations. Total of xxix + 1318pp.
21275-0, 21276-9, 21277-7 Three volume set, paperbound $7.75

HEAR ME TALKIN' TO YA, *edited by Nat Shapiro and Nat Hentoff*
In their own words, Louis Armstrong, King Oliver, Fletcher Henderson, Bunk Johnson, Bix Beiderbecke, Billy Holiday, Fats Waller, Jelly Roll Morton, Duke Ellington, and many others comment on the origins of jazz in New Orleans and its growth in Chicago's South Side, Kansas City's jam sessions, Depression Harlem, and the modernism of the West Coast schools. Taken from taped conversations, letters, magazine articles, other first-hand sources. Editors' introduction. xvi + 429pp. 5⅜ x 8½.   21726-4 Paperbound $2.50

THE JOURNAL OF HENRY D. THOREAU
A 25-year record by the great American observer and critic, as complete a record of a great man's inner life as is anywhere available. Thoreau's Journals served him as raw material for his formal pieces, as a place where he could develop his ideas, as an outlet for his interests in wild life and plants, in writing as an art, in classics of literature, Walt Whitman and other contemporaries, in politics, slavery, individual's relation to the State, etc. The Journals present a portrait of a remarkable man, and are an observant social history. Unabridged republication of 1906 edition, Bradford Torrey and Francis H. Allen, editors. Illustrations. Total of 1888pp. 8⅜ x 12¼.
20312-3, 20313-1 Two volume set, clothbound $30.00

A SHAKESPEARIAN GRAMMAR, *E. A. Abbott*
Basic reference to Shakespeare and his contemporaries, explaining through thousands of quotations from Shakespeare, Jonson, Beaumont and Fletcher, North's *Plutarch* and other sources the grammatical usage differing from the modern. First published in 1870 and written by a scholar who spent much of his life isolating principles of Elizabethan language, the book is unlikely ever to be superseded. Indexes. xxiv + 511pp. 5⅜ x 8½. 21582-2 Paperbound $3.00

FOLK-LORE OF SHAKESPEARE, *T. F. Thistelton Dyer*
Classic study, drawing from Shakespeare a large body of references to supernatural beliefs, terminology of falconry and hunting, games and sports, good luck charms, marriage customs, folk medicines, superstitions about plants, animals, birds, argot of the underworld, sexual slang of London, proverbs, drinking customs, weather lore, and much else. From full compilation comes a mirror of the 17th-century popular mind. Index. ix + 526pp. 5⅜ x 8½.
21614-4 Paperbound $3.25

THE NEW VARIORUM SHAKESPEARE, *edited by H. H. Furness*
By far the richest editions of the plays ever produced in any country or language. Each volume contains complete text (usually First Folio) of the play, all variants in Quarto and other Folio texts, editorial changes by every major editor to Furness's own time (1900), footnotes to obscure references or language, extensive quotes from literature of Shakespearian criticism, essays on plot sources (often reprinting sources in full), and much more.

HAMLET, *edited by H. H. Furness*
Total of xxvi + 905pp. 5⅜ x 8½.
21004-9, 21005-7 Two volume set, paperbound $5.50

TWELFTH NIGHT, *edited by H. H. Furness*
Index. xxii + 434pp. 5⅜ x 8½.   21189-4 Paperbound $2.75

LA BOHEME BY GIACOMO PUCCINI,
translated and introduced by Ellen H. Bleiler
Complete handbook for the operagoer, with everything needed for full enjoyment except the musical score itself. Complete Italian libretto, with new, modern English line-by-line translation—the only libretto printing all repeats; biography of Puccini; the librettists; background to the opera, Murger's La Boheme, etc.; circumstances of composition and performances; plot summary; and pictorial section of 73 illustrations showing Puccini, famous singers and performances, etc. Large clear type for easy reading. 124pp. 5⅜ x 8½.
20404-9 Paperbound $1.50

ANTONIO STRADIVARI: HIS LIFE AND WORK (1644-1737),
W. Henry Hill, Arthur F. Hill, and Alfred E. Hill
Still the only book that really delves into life and art of the incomparable Italian craftsman, maker of the finest musical instruments in the world today. The authors, expert violin-makers themselves, discuss Stradivari's ancestry, his construction and finishing techniques, distinguished characteristics of many of his instruments and their locations. Included, too, is story of introduction of his instruments into France, England, first revelation of their supreme merit, and information on his labels, number of instruments made, prices, mystery of ingredients of his varnish, tone of pre-1684 Stradivari violin and changes between 1684 and 1690. An extremely interesting, informative account for all music lovers, from craftsman to concert-goer. Republication of original (1902) edition. New introduction by Sydney Beck, Head of Rare Book and Manuscript Collections, Music Division, New York Public Library. Analytical index by Rembert Wurlitzer. Appendixes. 68 illustrations. 30 full-page plates. 4 in color. xxvi + 315pp. 5⅜ x 8½.
20425-1 Paperbound $3.00

MUSICAL AUTOGRAPHS FROM MONTEVERDI TO HINDEMITH,
Emanuel Winternitz
For beauty, for intrinsic interest, for perspective on the composer's personality, for subtleties of phrasing, shading, emphasis indicated in the autograph but suppressed in the printed score, the mss. of musical composition are fascinating documents which repay close study in many different ways. This 2-volume work reprints facsimiles of mss. by virtually every major composer, and many minor figures—196 examples in all. A full text points out what can be learned from mss., analyzes each sample. Index. Bibliography. 18 figures. 196 plates. Total of 170pp. of text. 7⅞ x 10¾.
21312-9, 21313-7 Two volume set, paperbound $5.00

J. S. BACH,
Albert Schweitzer
One of the few great full-length studies of Bach's life and work, and the study upon which Schweitzer's renown as a musicologist rests. On first appearance (1911), revolutionized Bach performance. The only writer on Bach to be musicologist, performing musician, and student of history, theology and philosophy, Schweitzer contributes particularly full sections on history of German Protestant church music, theories on motivic pictorial representations in vocal music, and practical suggestions for performance. Translated by Ernest Newman. Indexes. 5 illustrations. 650 musical examples. Total of xix + 928pp. 5⅜ x 8½.
21631-4, 21632-2 Two volume set, paperbound $5.00

THE METHODS OF ETHICS, *Henry Sidgwick*
Propounding no organized system of its own, study subjects every major methodological approach to ethics to rigorous, objective analysis. Study discusses and relates ethical thought of Plato, Aristotle, Bentham, Clarke, Butler, Hobbes, Hume, Mill, Spencer, Kant, and dozens of others. Sidgwick retains conclusions from each system which follow from ethical premises, rejecting the faulty. Considered by many in the field to be among the most important treatises on ethical philosophy. Appendix. Index. xlvii + 528pp. 5⅜ x 8½.
21608-X Paperbound $3.00

TEUTONIC MYTHOLOGY, *Jakob Grimm*
A milestone in Western culture; the work which established on a modern basis the study of history of religions and comparative religions. 4-volume work assembles and interprets everything available on religious and folkloristic beliefs of Germanic people (including Scandinavians, Anglo-Saxons, etc.). Assembling material from such sources as Tacitus, surviving Old Norse and Icelandic texts, archeological remains, folktales, surviving superstitions, comparative traditions, linguistic analysis, etc. Grimm explores pagan deities, heroes, folklore of nature, religious practices, and every other area of pagan German belief. To this day, the unrivaled, definitive, exhaustive study. Translated by J. S. Stallybrass from 4th (1883) German edition. Indexes. Total of lxxvii + 1887pp. 5⅜ x 8½.
21602-0, 21603-9, 21604-7, 21605-5 Four volume set, paperbound $12.00

THE I CHING, *translated by James Legge*
Called "The Book of Changes" in English, this is one of the Five Classics edited by Confucius, basic and central to Chinese thought. Explains perhaps the most complex system of divination known, founded on the theory that all things happening at any one time have characteristic features which can be isolated and related. Significant in Oriental studies, in history of religions and philosophy, and also to Jungian psychoanalysis and other areas of modern European thought. Index. Appendixes. 6 plates. xxi + 448pp. 5⅜ x 8½.
21062-6 Paperbound $2.75

HISTORY OF ANCIENT PHILOSOPHY, *W. Windelband*
One of the clearest, most accurate comprehensive surveys of Greek and Roman philosophy. Discusses ancient philosophy in general, intellectual life in Greece in the 7th and 6th centuries B.C., Thales, Anaximander, Anaximenes, Heraclitus, the Eleatics, Empedocles, Anaxagoras, Leucippus, the Pythagoreans, the Sophists, Socrates, Democritus (20 pages), Plato (50 pages), Aristotle (70 pages), the Peripatetics, Stoics, Epicureans, Sceptics, Neo-platonists, Christian Apologists, etc. 2nd German edition translated by H. E. Cushman. xv + 393pp. 5⅜ x 8.
20357-3 Paperbound $3.00

THE PALACE OF PLEASURE, *William Painter*
Elizabethan versions of Italian and French novels from *The Decameron*, Cinthio, Straparola, Queen Margaret of Navarre, and other continental sources — the very work that provided Shakespeare and dozens of his contemporaries with many of their plots and sub-plots and, therefore, justly considered one of the most influential books in all English literature. It is also a book that any reader will still enjoy. Total of cviii + 1,224pp.
21691-8, 21692-6, 21693-4 Three volume set, paperbound $8.25

THE WONDERFUL WIZARD OF OZ, *L. F. Baum*
All the original W. W. Denslow illustrations in full color—as much a part of "The Wizard" as Tenniel's drawings are of "Alice in Wonderland." "The Wizard" is still America's best-loved fairy tale, in which, as the author expresses it, "The wonderment and joy are retained and the heartaches and nightmares left out." Now today's young readers can enjoy every word and wonderful picture of the original book. New introduction by Martin Gardner. A Baum bibliography. 23 full-page color plates. viii + 268pp. 5⅜ x 8.
20691-2 Paperbound $1.95

THE MARVELOUS LAND OF OZ, *L. F. Baum*
This is the equally enchanting sequel to the "Wizard," continuing the adventures of the Scarecrow and the Tin Woodman. The hero this time is a little boy named Tip, and all the delightful Oz magic is still present. This is the Oz book with the Animated Saw-Horse, the Woggle-Bug, and Jack Pumpkinhead. All the original John R. Neill illustrations, 10 in full color. 287pp. 5⅜ x 8.
20692-0 Paperbound $1.75

ALICE'S ADVENTURES UNDER GROUND, *Lewis Carroll*
The original *Alice in Wonderland*, hand-lettered and illustrated by Carroll himself, and originally presented as a Christmas gift to a child-friend. Adults as well as children will enjoy this charming volume, reproduced faithfully in this Dover edition. While the story is essentially the same, there are slight changes, and Carroll's spritely drawings present an intriguing alternative to the famous Tenniel illustrations. One of the most popular books in Dover's catalogue. Introduction by Martin Gardner. 38 illustrations. 128pp. 5⅜ x 8½.
21482-6 Paperbound $1.00

THE NURSERY "ALICE," *Lewis Carroll*
While most of us consider *Alice in Wonderland* a story for children of all ages, Carroll himself felt it was beyond younger children. He therefore provided this simplified version, illustrated with the famous Tenniel drawings enlarged and colored in delicate tints, for children aged "from Nought to Five." Dover's edition of this now rare classic is a faithful copy of the 1889 printing, including 20 illustrations by Tenniel, and front and back covers reproduced in full color. Introduction by Martin Gardner. xxiii + 67pp. 6⅛ x 9¼.
21610-1 Paperbound $1.75

THE STORY OF KING ARTHUR AND HIS KNIGHTS, *Howard Pyle*
A fast-paced, exciting retelling of the best known Arthurian legends for young readers by one of America's best story tellers and illustrators. The sword Excalibur, wooing of Guinevere, Merlin and his downfall, adventures of Sir Pellias and Gawaine, and others. The pen and ink illustrations are vividly imagined and wonderfully drawn. 41 illustrations. xviii + 313pp. 6⅛ x 9¼.
21445-1 Paperbound $2.00

Prices subject to change without notice.

Available at your book dealer or write for free catalogue to Dept. Adsci, Dover Publications, Inc., 180 Varick St., N.Y., N.Y. 10014. Dover publishes more than 150 books each year on science, elementary and advanced mathematics, biology, music, art, literary history, social sciences and other areas.